Legal Environment:

Owens Community College 2013-14 Edition

Beatty | Samuelson

CENGAGE
Learning·

Australia • Brazil • Japan • Korea • Mexico • Singapore • Spain • United Kingdom • United States

CENGAGE
Learning·

**Legal Environment: Owens Community
College 2013-14 Edition**

Legal Environment; 5e
Jeffrey F. Beatty | Susan S. Samuelson | Dean A. Bredeson

© 2014 2011 Cengage Learning. All rights reserved.

Senior Project Development Manager:
 Linda deStefano

Market Development Manager:
 Heather Kramer

Senior Production/Manufacturing Manager:
 Donna M. Brown

Production Editorial Manager:
 Kim Fry

Sr. Rights Acquisition Account Manager:
 Todd Osborne

For product information and technology assistance, contact us at
Cengage Learning Customer & Sales Support, 1-800-354-9706

For permission to use material from this text or product,
submit all requests online at **cengage.com/permissions**
Further permissions questions can be emailed to
permissionrequest@cengage.com

This book contains select works from existing Cengage Learning resources and
was produced by Cengage Learning Custom Solutions for collegiate use. As such,
those adopting and/or contributing to this work are responsible for editorial
content accuracy, continuity and completeness.

Compilation © 2013 Cengage Learning
ISBN-13: 978-1-285-91835-8

ISBN-10: 1-285-91835-5

Cengage Learning
5191 Natorp Boulevard
Mason, Ohio 45040
USA

Cengage Learning is a leading provider of customized learning solutions with
office locations around the globe, including Singapore, the United Kingdom,
Australia, Mexico, Brazil, and Japan. Locate your local office at:
international.cengage.com/region.
Cengage Learning products are represented in Canada by Nelson Education, Ltd.
For your lifelong learning solutions, visit **www.cengage.com/custom.**
Visit our corporate website at **www.cengage.com.**

Printed in the United States of America

Students: Accessing a CourseMate Website and Enrolling in an Instructor-Led Course

Prepared by the Cengage Learning CourseMate Team

Introduction

The purpose of this document is to give step-by-step instructions on accessing a CourseMate website and enrolling in a course led by your instructor.

This document includes three sections, only one of which will be appropriate for you.

- If You Purchased CourseMate Access in Your School Bookstore and Don't Have an Account at http://login.cengagebrain.com

Or

- If You Purchased CourseMate Access in Your School Bookstore and Already Have an Account at http://login.cengagebrain.com

Or

- If You Want to Purchase CourseMate Access via http://www.cengagebrain.com

Finally, note that there are hundreds of different CourseMate sites, and many of them have different visual designs. So, if what you are seeing as you travel the registration and enrollment path does not exactly *look like* the screen captures shown in this document, note that the *functionality* described in this document is common to all CourseMate sites.

If You Purchased CourseMate Access in Your School Bookstore and Don't Have an Account at http://login.cengagebrain.com

What is http://login.cengagebrain.com? Imagine that you are using multiple applications from Cengage Learning (CourseMate and other applications). Rather than having credentials to sign into each of these applications, Cengage Learning offers a single location. With one set of Sign On credentials, then, at http://login.cengagebrain.com you can access all of your Cengage Learning tools.

When you access http://login.cengagebrain.com, you will see the following.

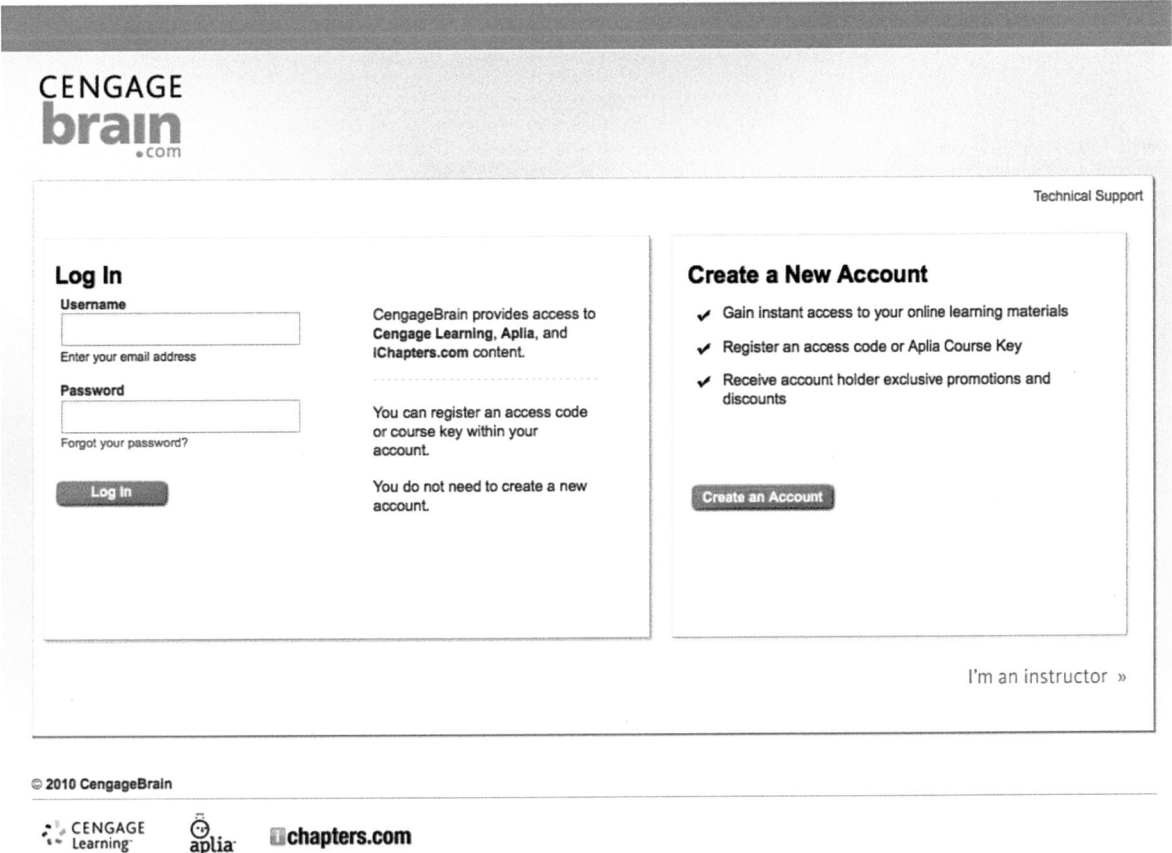

This section you are currently reading assumes that you do not already have an account at this location.

1. Click the "Create a New Account" button.

2. The following will load.

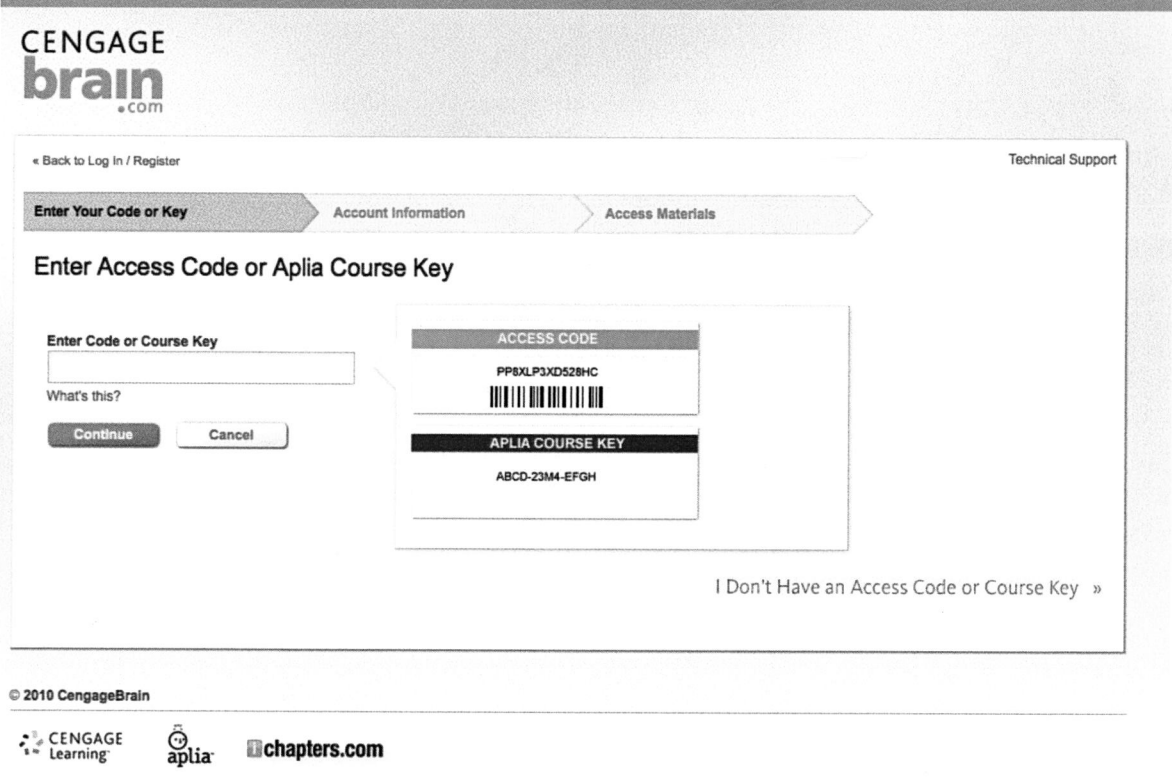

3. Provide the *access code* you find on the printed access card you received with your bookstore purchase, and click "Continue." A page like the following will appear (where not all of the page is shown in the following).

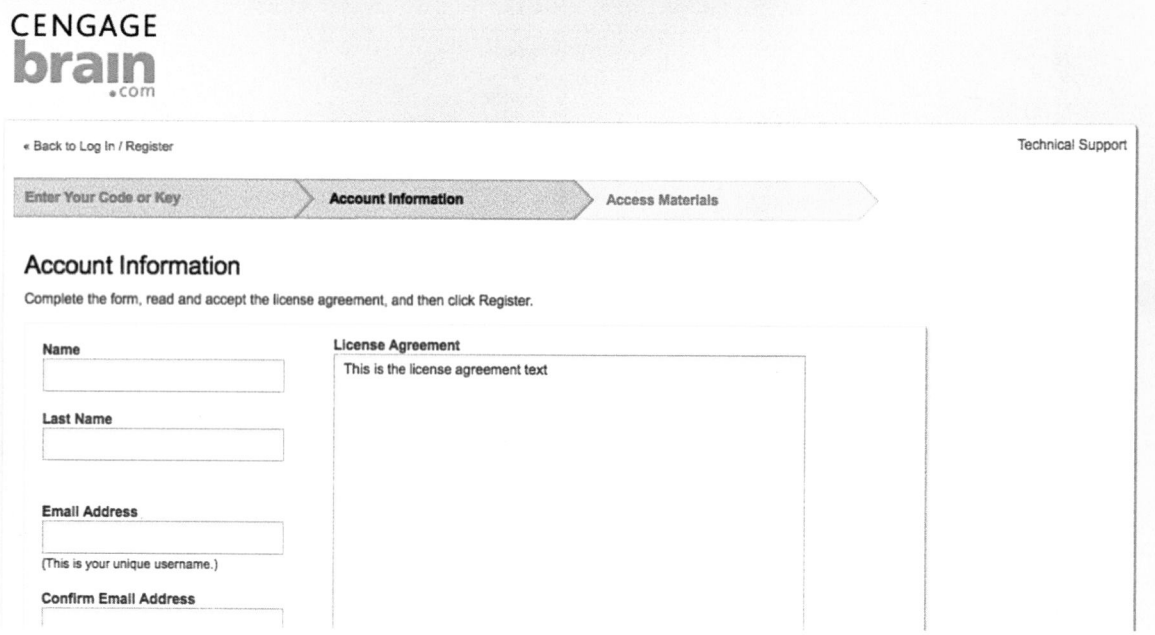

4. Provide First Name, Last Name, Email Address, etc., confirm that you are at least 13 years of age, and click "Register." You will be taken to a page that prompts you to identify the school where you are studying.

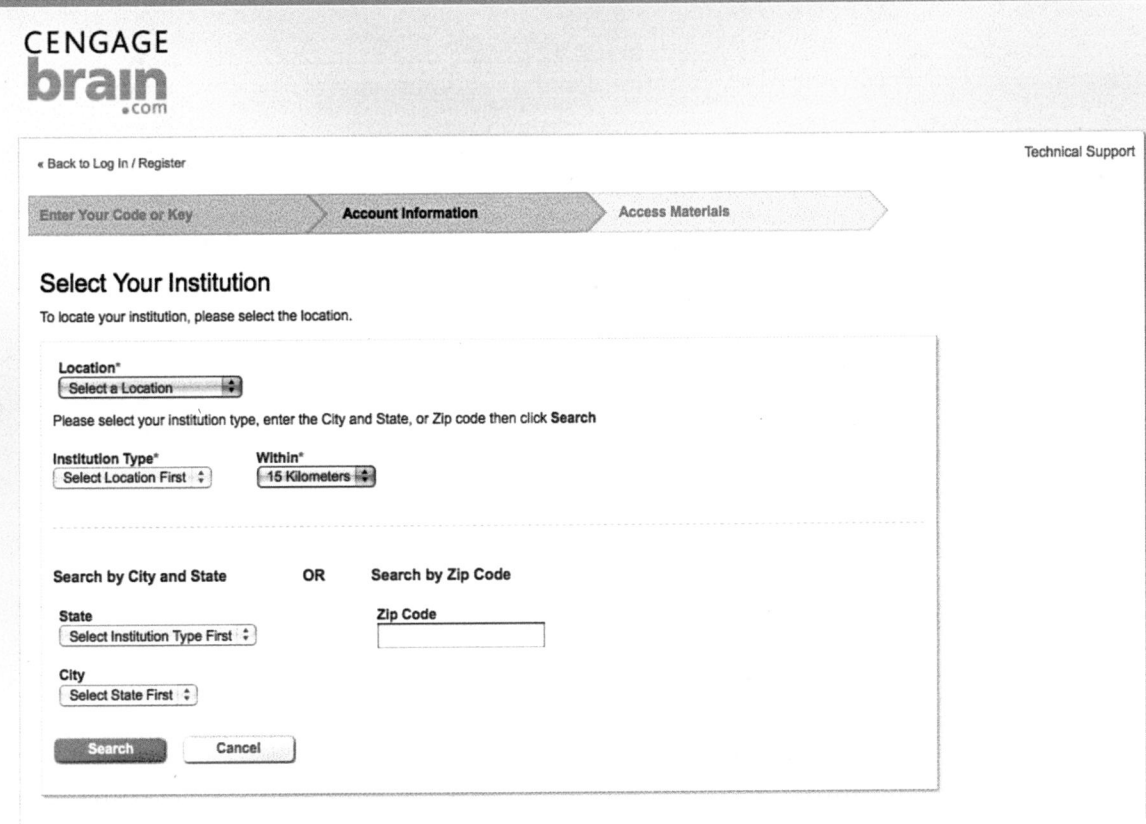

5. Complete the fields on this page, providing the information unique to you, and then click the "Search" button. Something like the following will appear.

Enter Your Code or Key	Account Information	Access Materials

Select Your Institution

54 institutions were found in your search of 4-Year College within **25 miles of San Francisco, CA.** Select your institution from the list below, then click **Register**.

Select	Institution Name	City	State/Province	Country
○	University of California San Francisco	San Francisco	CA	US
○	Academy of Art University	San Francisco	CA	US
○	Art Institute of California, San Francisco	San Francisco	CA	US
○	California Culinary Academy	San Francisco	CA	US
○	San Francisco State Univeristy	San Francisco	CA	US
○	Golden Gate University	San Francisco	CA	US
○	San Francisco Art Institute	San Francisco	CA	US
○	School for Self Healing	San Francisco	CA	US
○	University of California Hastings	San Francisco	CA	US
○	University of San Francisco	San Francisco	CA	US

Register   Cancel

6. Select the proper institution and click the "Register" button. Something like the following will appear.

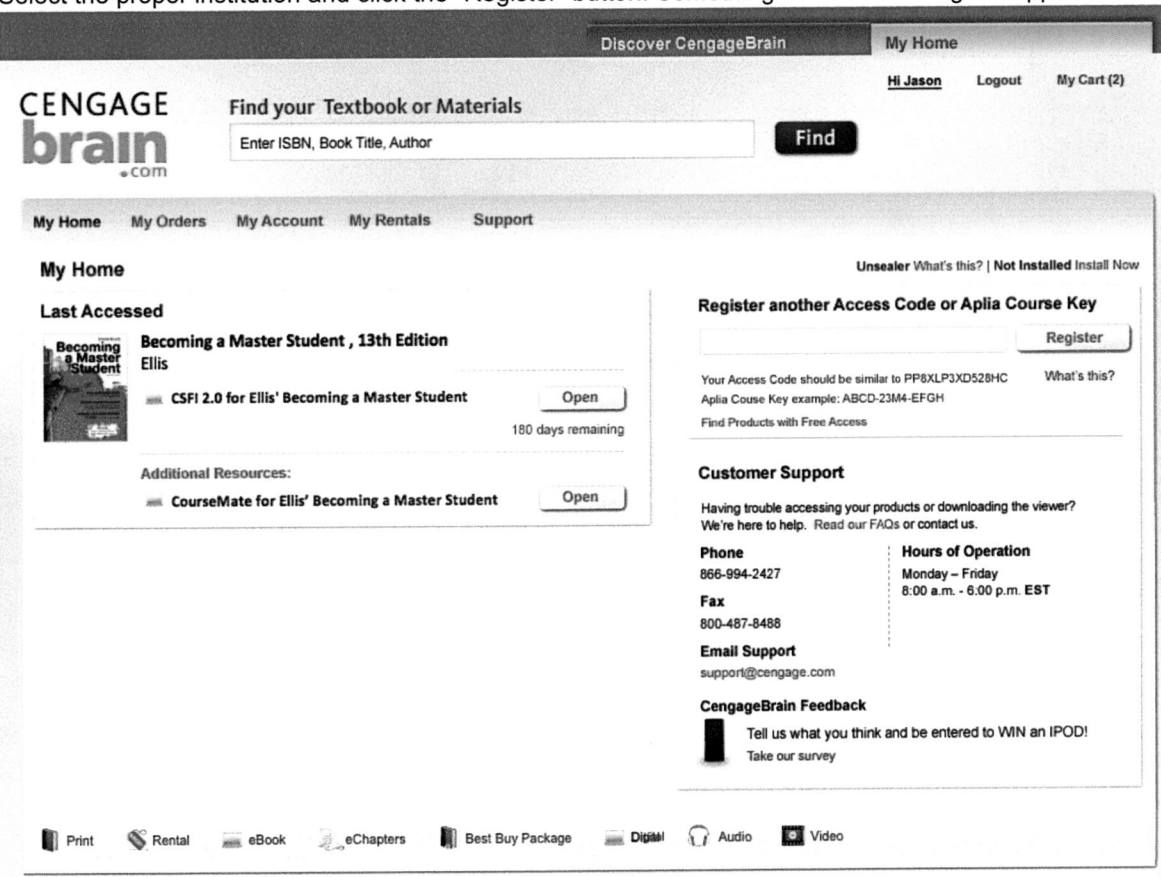

7. There are hundreds of CourseMate sites, and which one you access when you click the "Open" link for the CourseMate resource depends on the textbook you are using. For example, the "Open" link in the example above would take you to the landing page in a College Success CourseMate site, whereas the example below is the landing page on an Art Study CourseMate website.

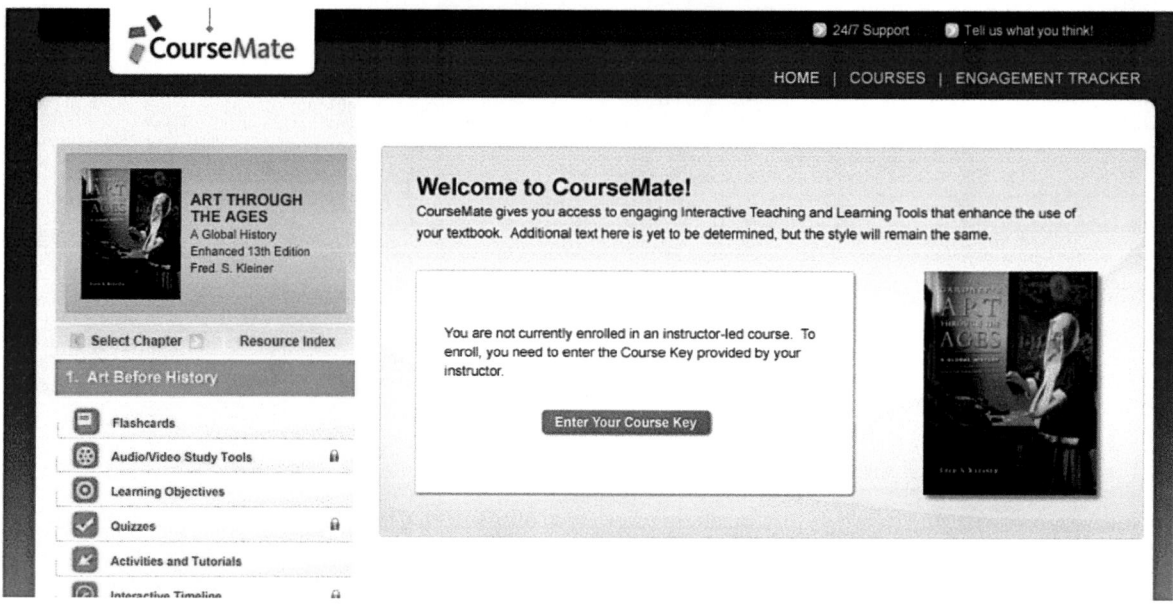

8. You are free to use this website without enrollment in an instructor-led course. If you do so and then later enroll in an instructor-led course, all activity before enrollment will appear to the instructor once enrolled (as will all activity after enrollment).

At the point you wish to enroll in an instructor-led course, you will need to have from the instructor a "Course Key." With this Course Key in hand, click the **Enter Your Course Key** button. An overlay will appear, on top of the current screen.

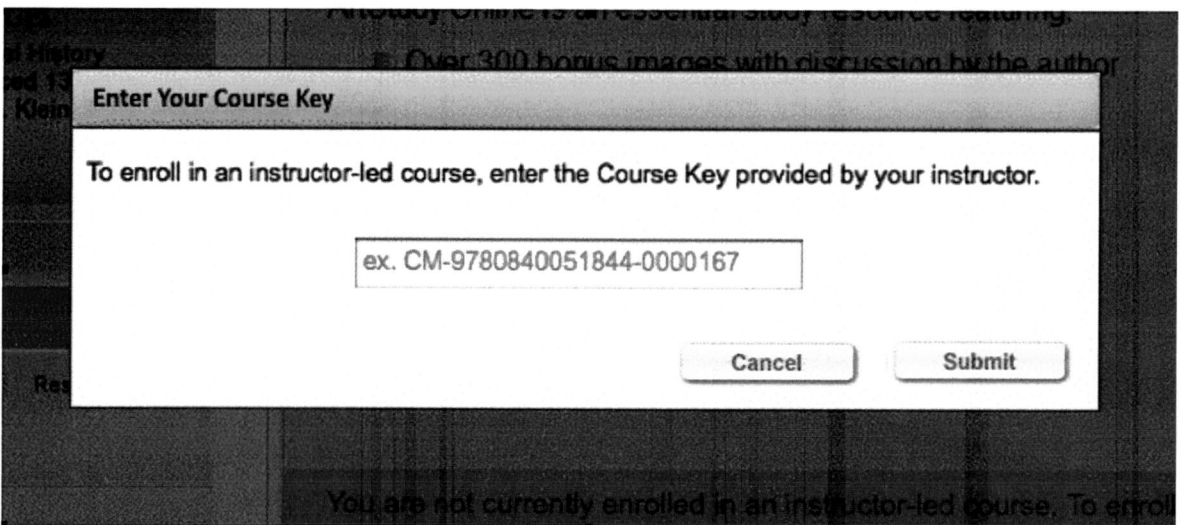

9. Provide the Course Key your instructor gave to you, and click the Submit button. The overlay will disappear, and the Home page of the site will have changed as follows.

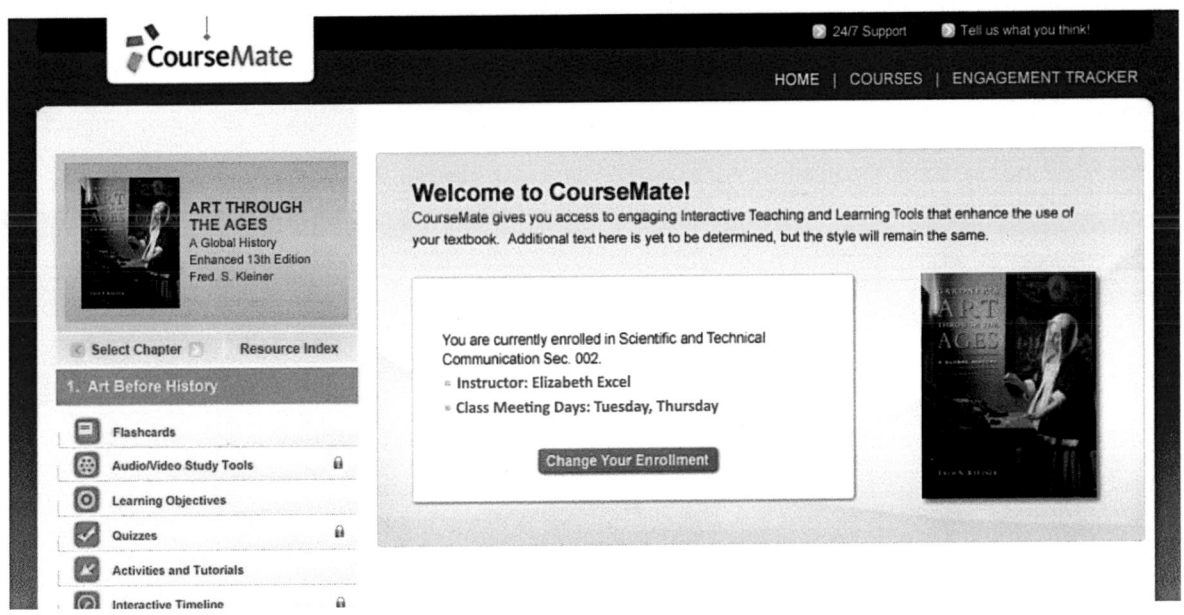

Now that you are enrolled in the instructor-led course, the instructor will be able to see the time you spend on all resources in the CourseMate site, and will also be able to see your scores for the graded quizzes in the site.

Else If You Purchased CourseMate Access in Your School Bookstore and Already Have an Account at http://login.cengagebrain.com

This section assumes you have an existing account at login.cengage.com, a web address that will bring you to the following page.

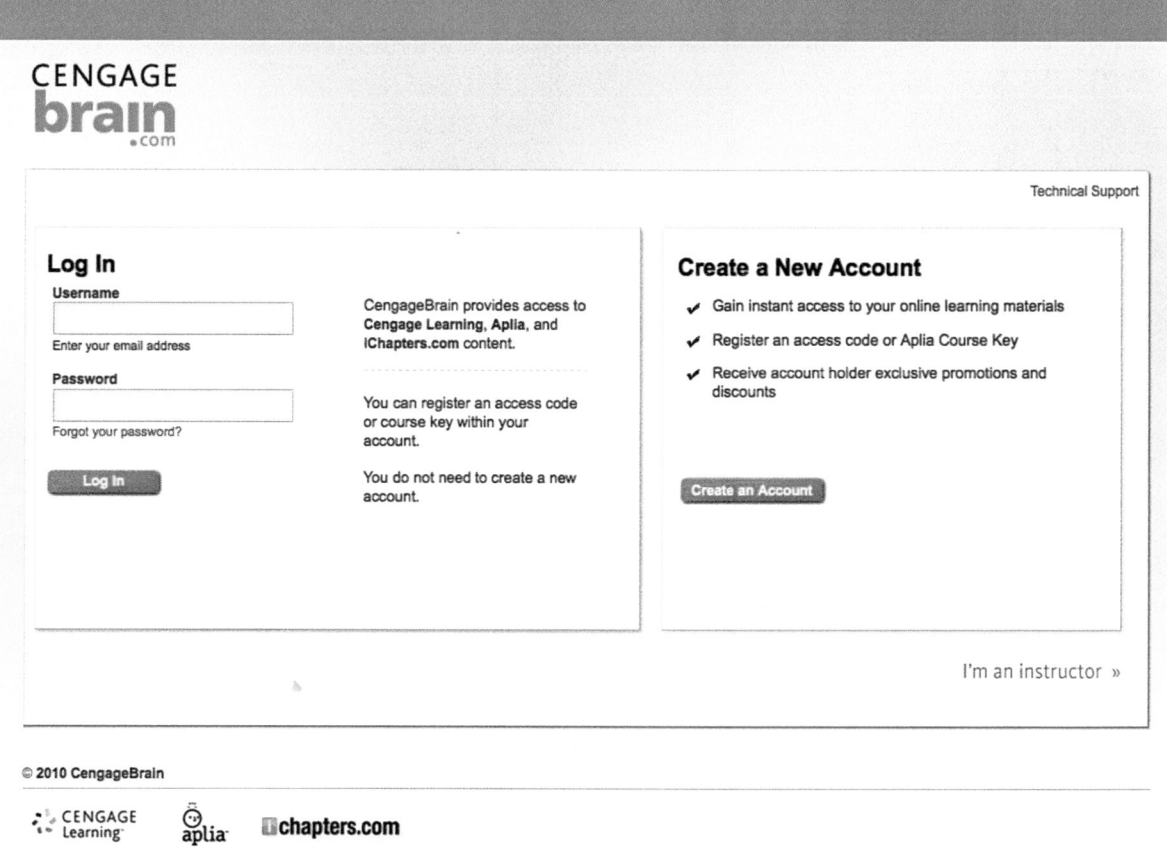

1. Provide the credentials to your existing account, and click the **Log In** button. Your Dashboard will appear, similar to the following.

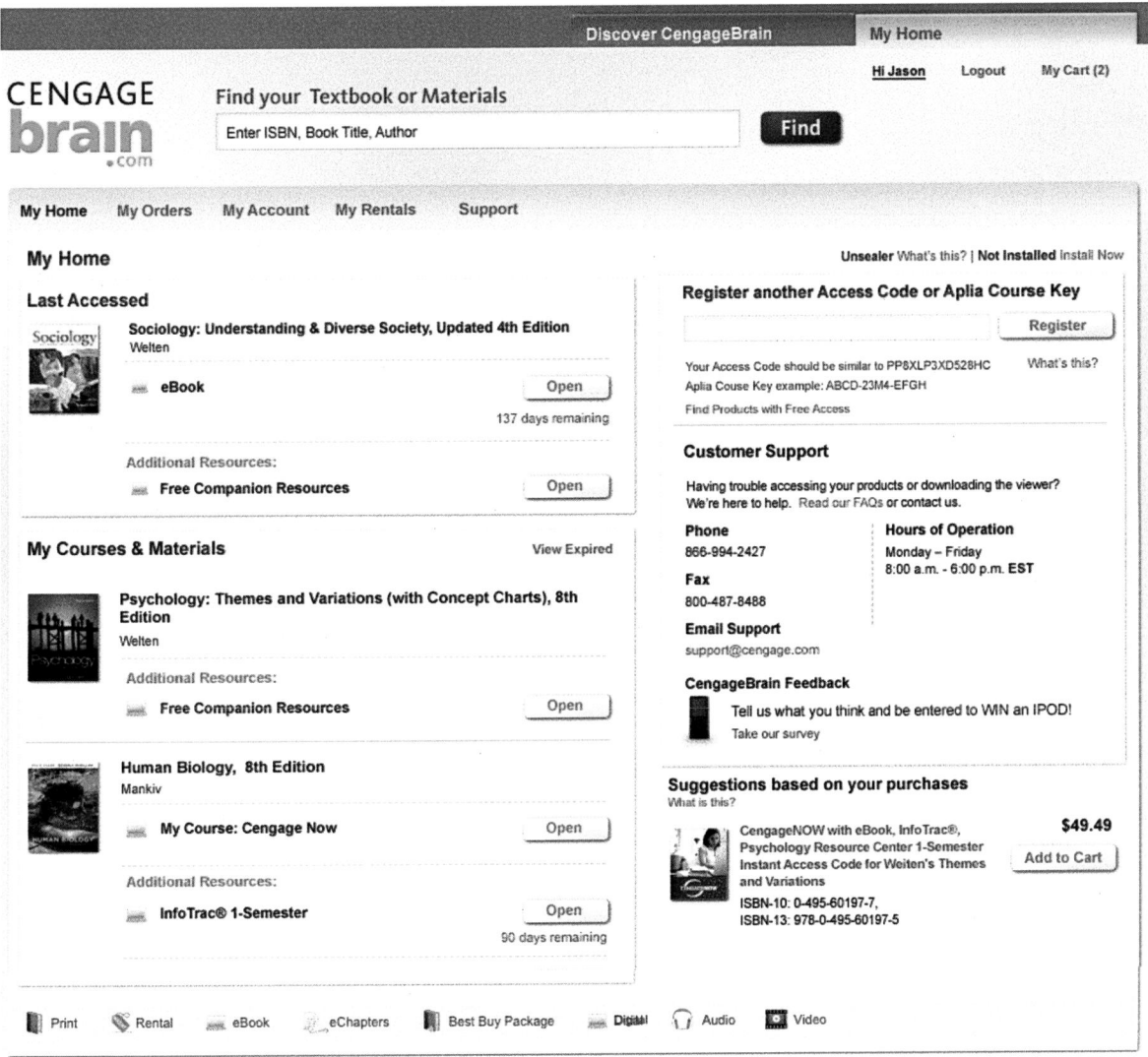

2. Locate the **Register another Access Code or Aplia Course Key** field.

Register another Access Code or Aplia Course Key

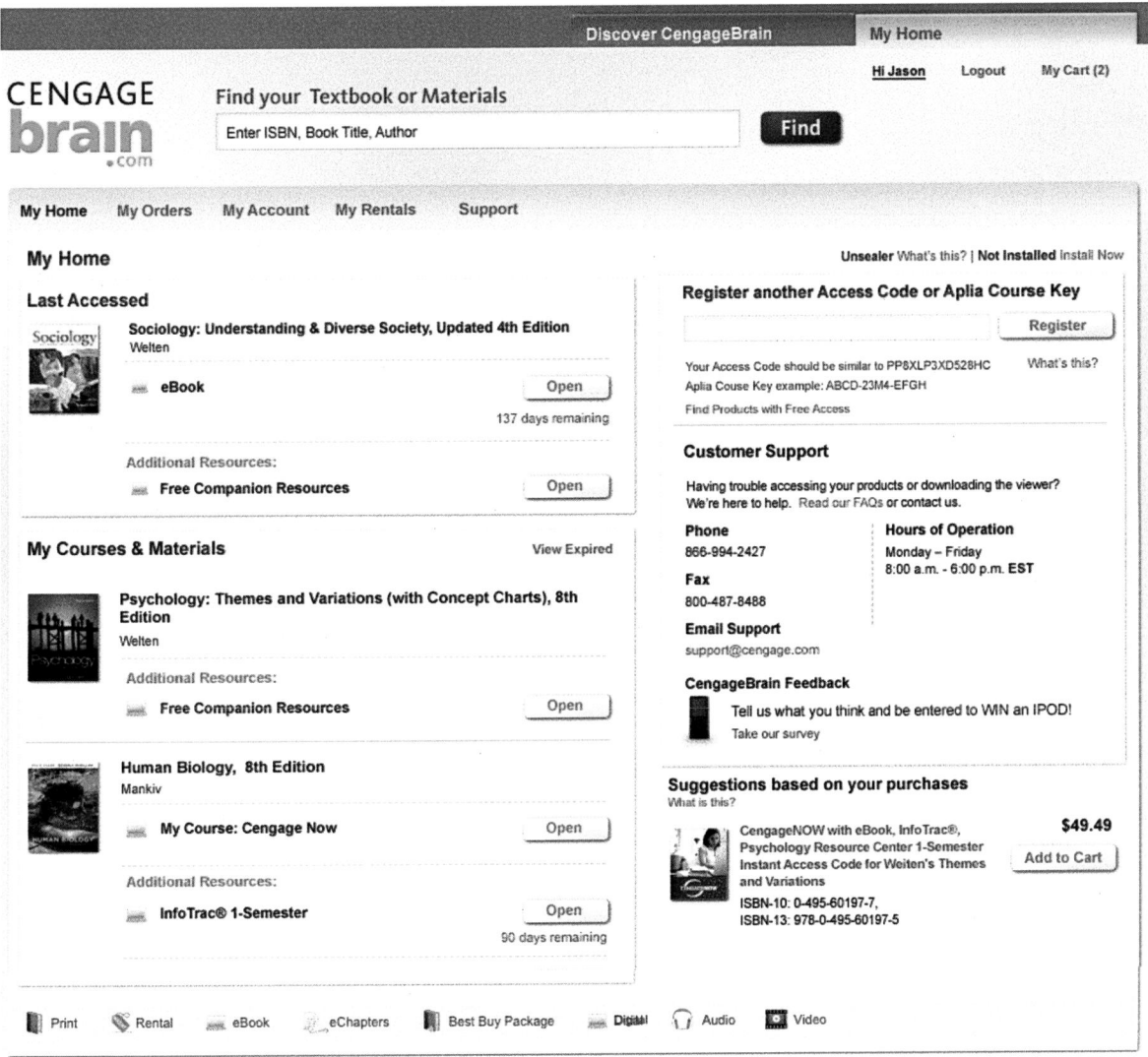

Register

3. Provide the *access code* you find on the printed access card you received with your bookstore purchase, and click "Continue." The Dashboard's **Last Accessed** area will update with your new

product.

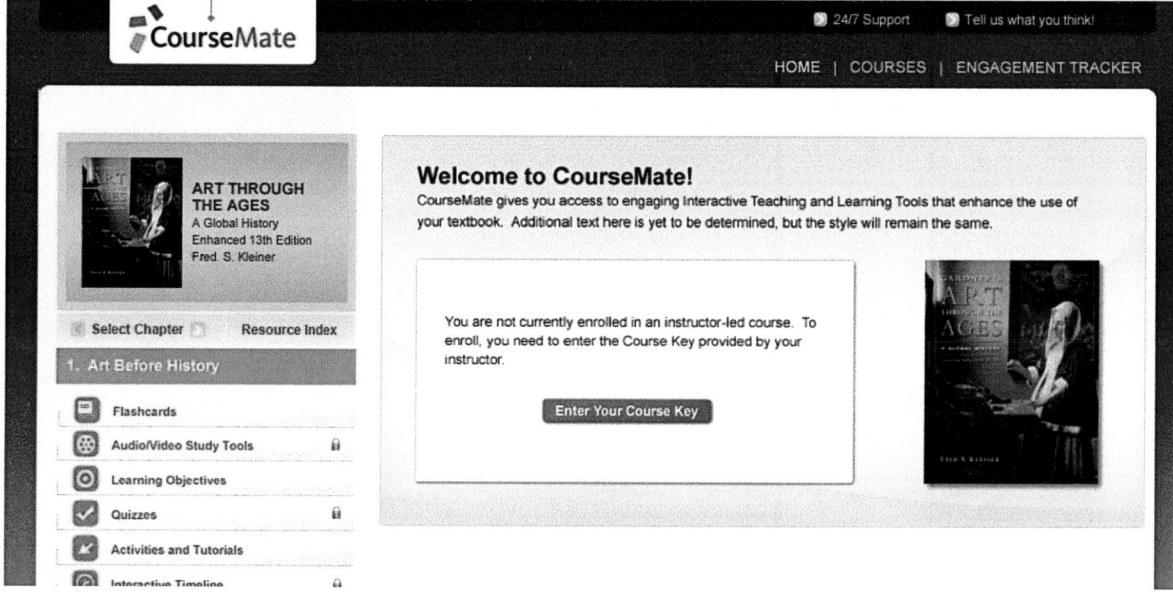

4. There are hundreds of CourseMate sites, and which one you access when you click the "Open" link for the CourseMate resource depends on the textbook you are using. For example, the "Open" link in the example above would take you to the landing page in a College Success CourseMate site, whereas the example below is the landing page on an Art Study CourseMate website.

5. You are free to use this website without enrollment in an instructor's course. If you do so and then later enroll in an instructor-led course, all activity before enrollment will appear to the instructor once enrolled (as will all activity after enrollment).

At the point you wish to enroll in an instructor-led course, you will need to have from the instructor a "Course Key." With this Course Key in hand, click the **Enter Your Course Key** button. An overlay will appear, on top of the current screen.

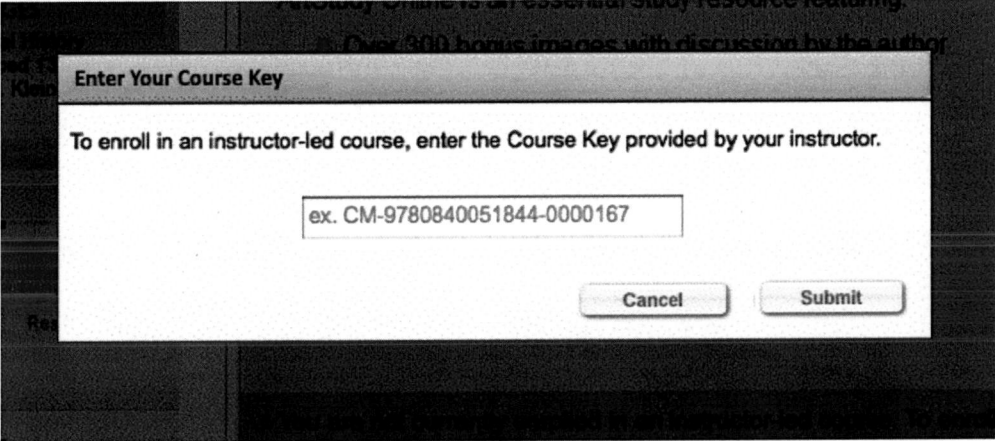

6. Provide the Course Key your instructor gave to you, and click the Submit button. The overlay will disappear, and the Home page of the site will have changed as follows.

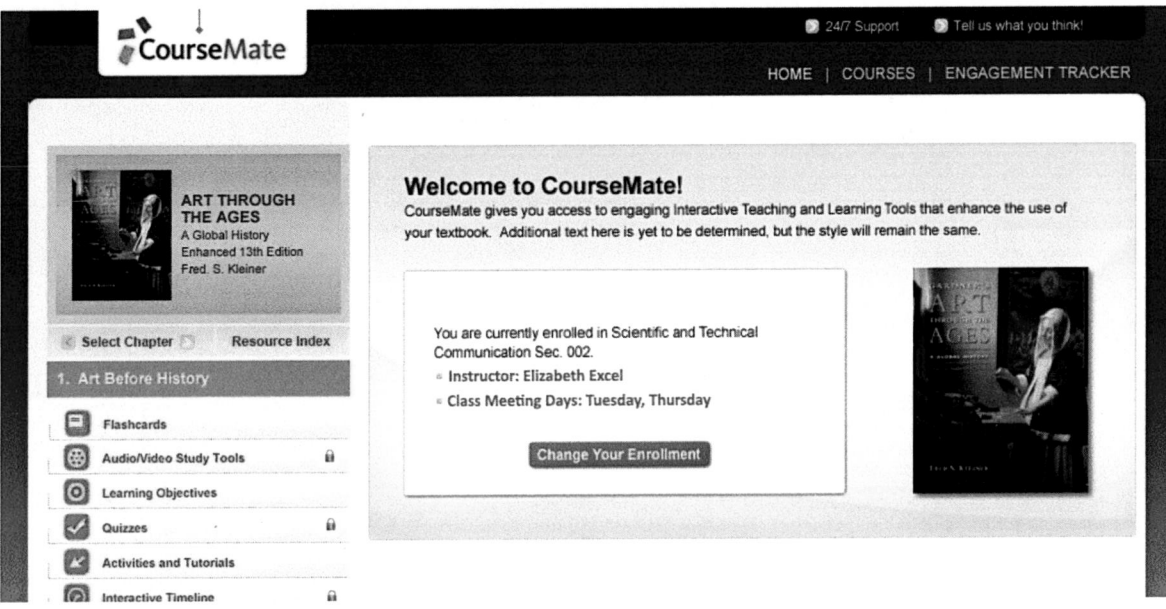

Now that you are enrolled in the instructor-led course, the instructor will be able to see the time you spend on all resources in the CourseMate site, and will also be able to see your scores for the graded quizzes in the site.

Else If You Want to Purchase CourseMate Access via the http://www.cengagebrain.com Website

At http://www.cengagebrain.com, you can use a credit card to purchase Cengage Learning products, such as CourseMate websites. If you are interested in this route, the following steps will guide you.

1. Point your browser to http://www.cengagebrain.com.

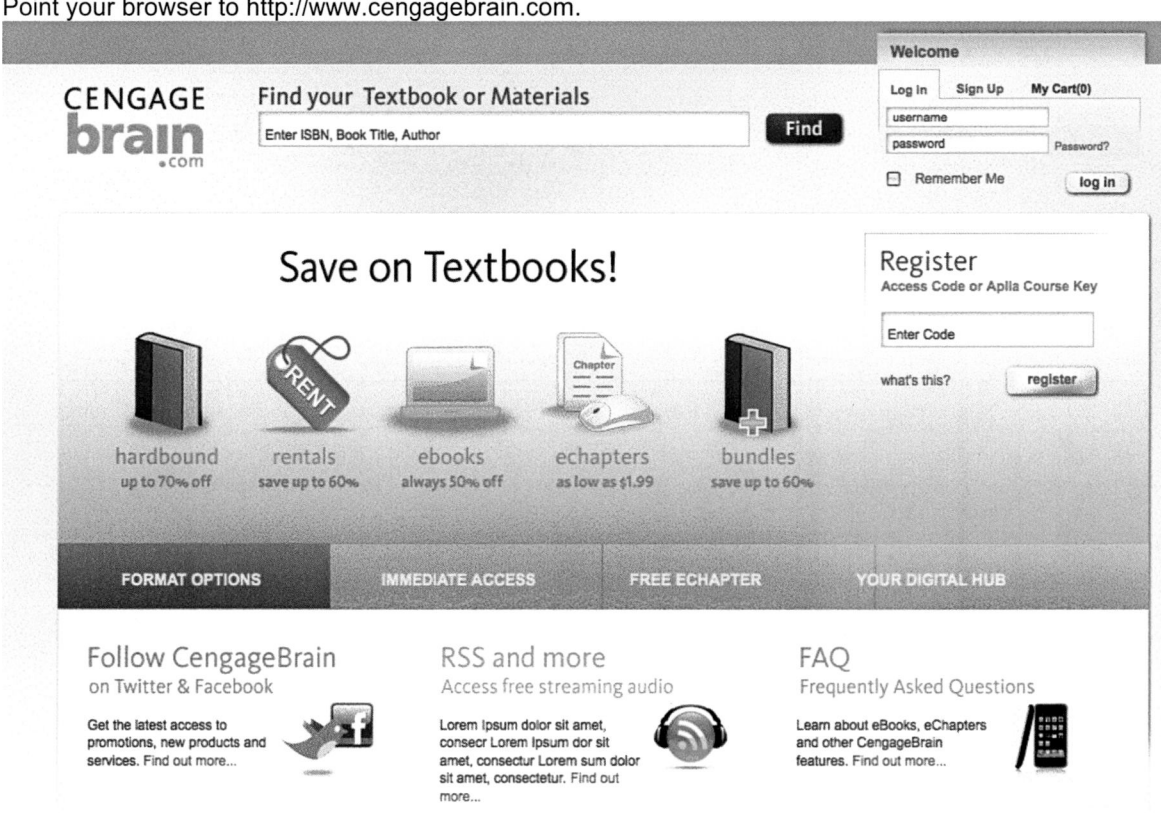

2. In the **Search** box, search for the product you seek. If you want to use the name or ISBN of your textbook, that will work, or you can just search for *CourseMate*.

3. Upon click of "Find," something like the following will appear.

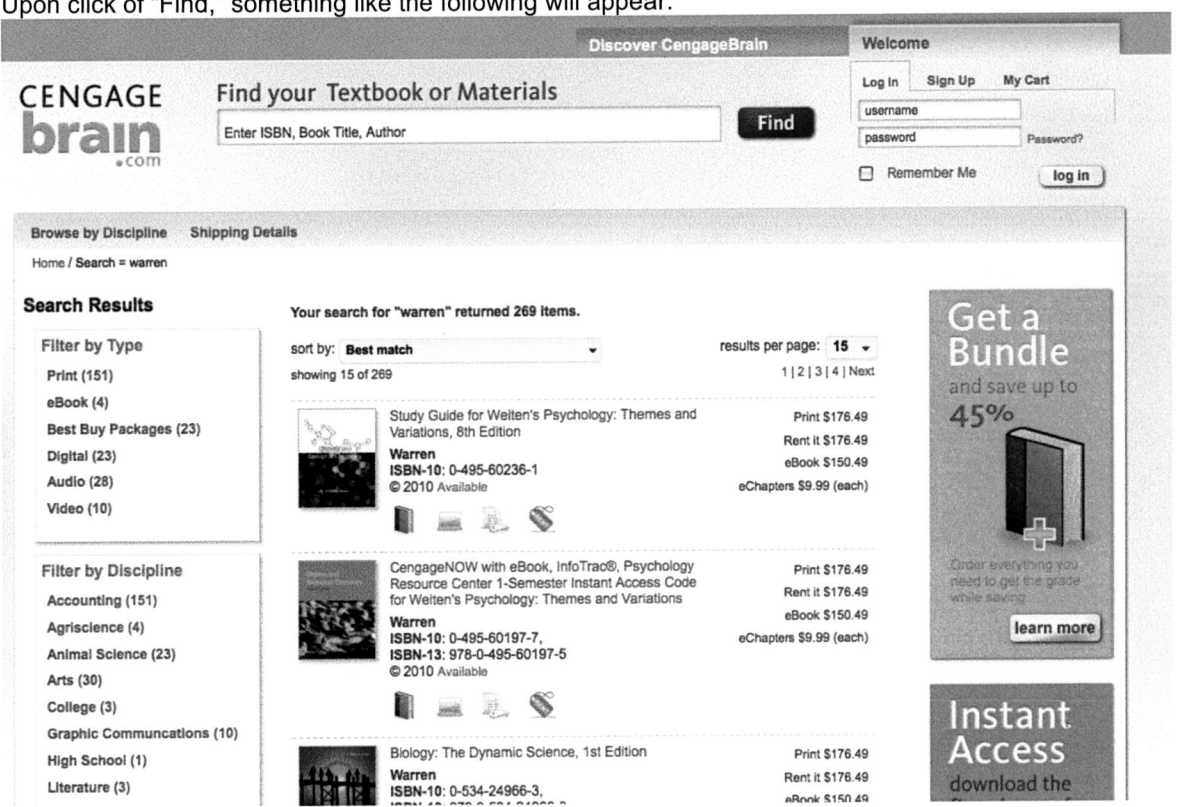

4. Find the product you are interested in, and click on it. Something like the following will appear.

Find your Textbook or Materials

Enter ISBN, Book Title, Author   **Find**

« Back

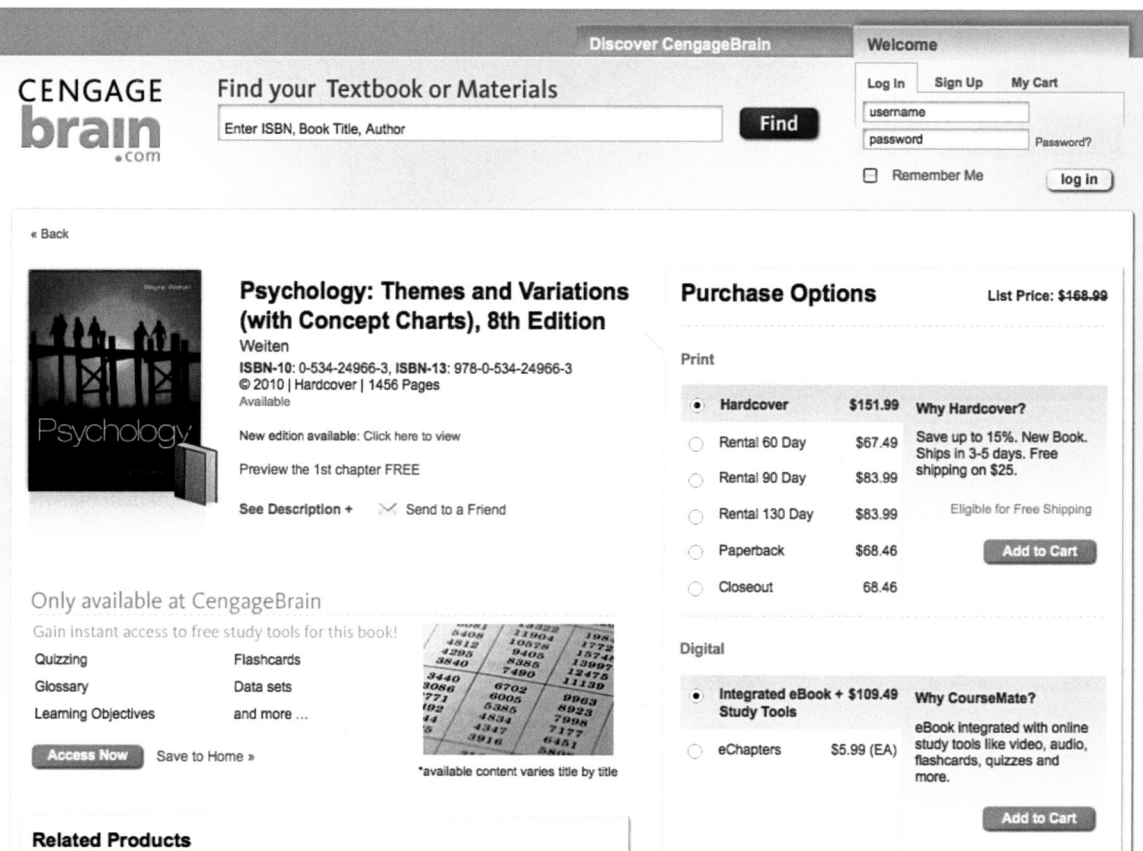

Psychology: Themes and Variations (with Concept Charts), 8th Edition

Weiten

ISBN-10: 0-534-24966-3, **ISBN-13**: 978-0-534-24966-3
© 2010 | Hardcover | 1456 Pages
Available

New edition available: Click here to view

Preview the 1st chapter FREE

See Description +   ✉ Send to a Friend

Purchase Options   List Price: $~~168.99~~

Print

⦿ **Hardcover**	**$151.99**	**Why Hardcover?**
○ Rental 60 Day	$67.49	Save up to 15%. New Book. Ships in 3-5 days. Free shipping on $25.
○ Rental 90 Day	$83.99	
○ Rental 130 Day	$83.99	Eligible for Free Shipping
○ Paperback	$68.46	**Add to Cart**
○ Closeout	68.46	

Only available at CengageBrain

Gain instant access to free study tools for this book!

Quizzing   Flashcards
Glossary   Data sets
Learning Objectives   and more ...

Access Now   Save to Home »

*available content varies title by title

Digital

⦿ **Integrated eBook + $109.49 Study Tools**		**Why CourseMate?**
○ eChapters	$5.99 (EA)	eBook integrated with online study tools like video, audio, flashcards, quizzes and more.
		Add to Cart

Related Products

5. If you want to buy the product, click on the "Add to Cart" button.

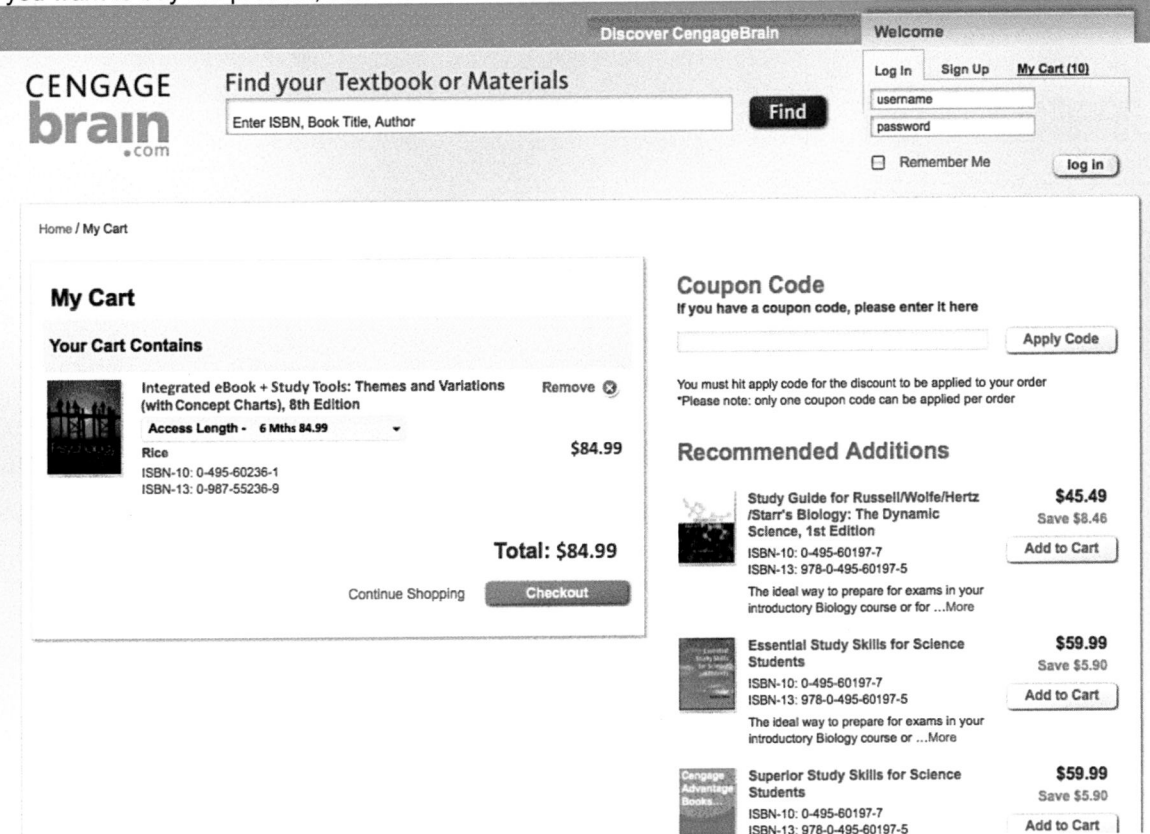

6. Click the "Checkout" button.

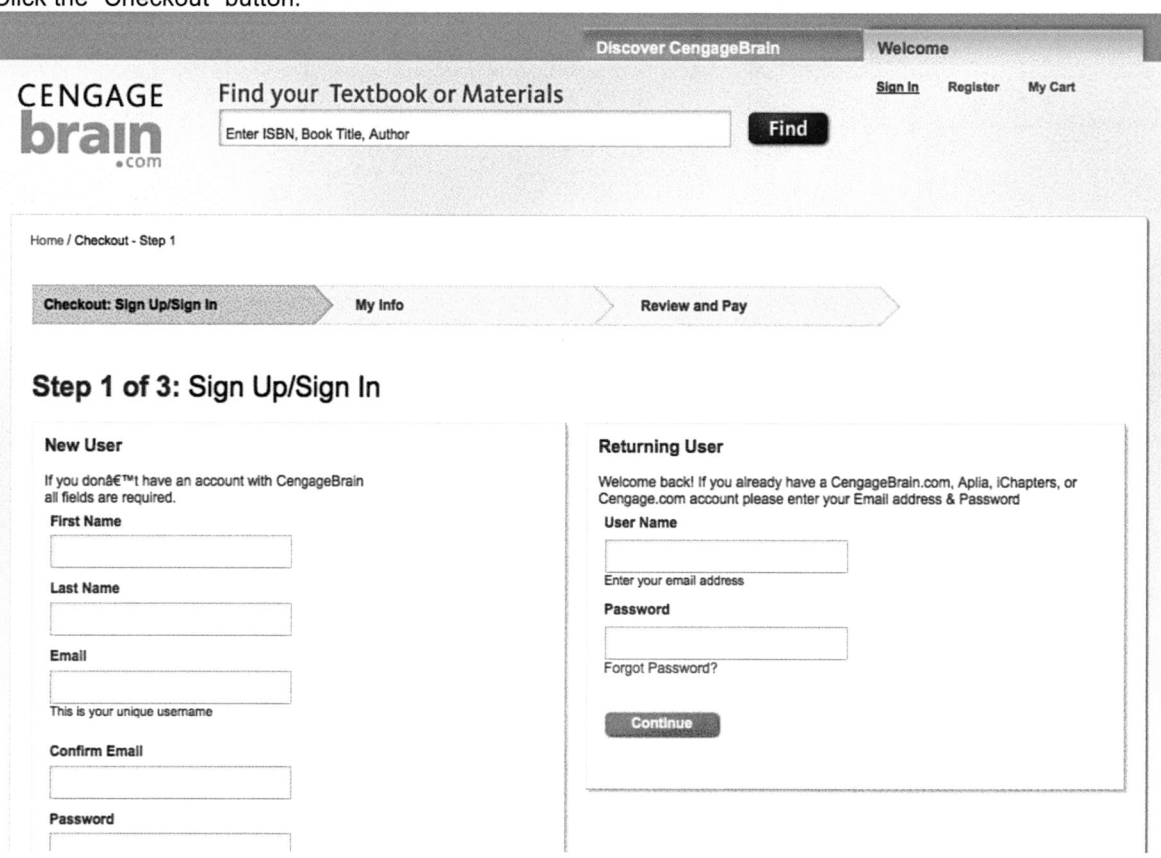

If you have an existing account with Cengage Learning, travel that path. This document, though, focuses on the other path: "New User."

7. Provide all the requested information and click "Continue."

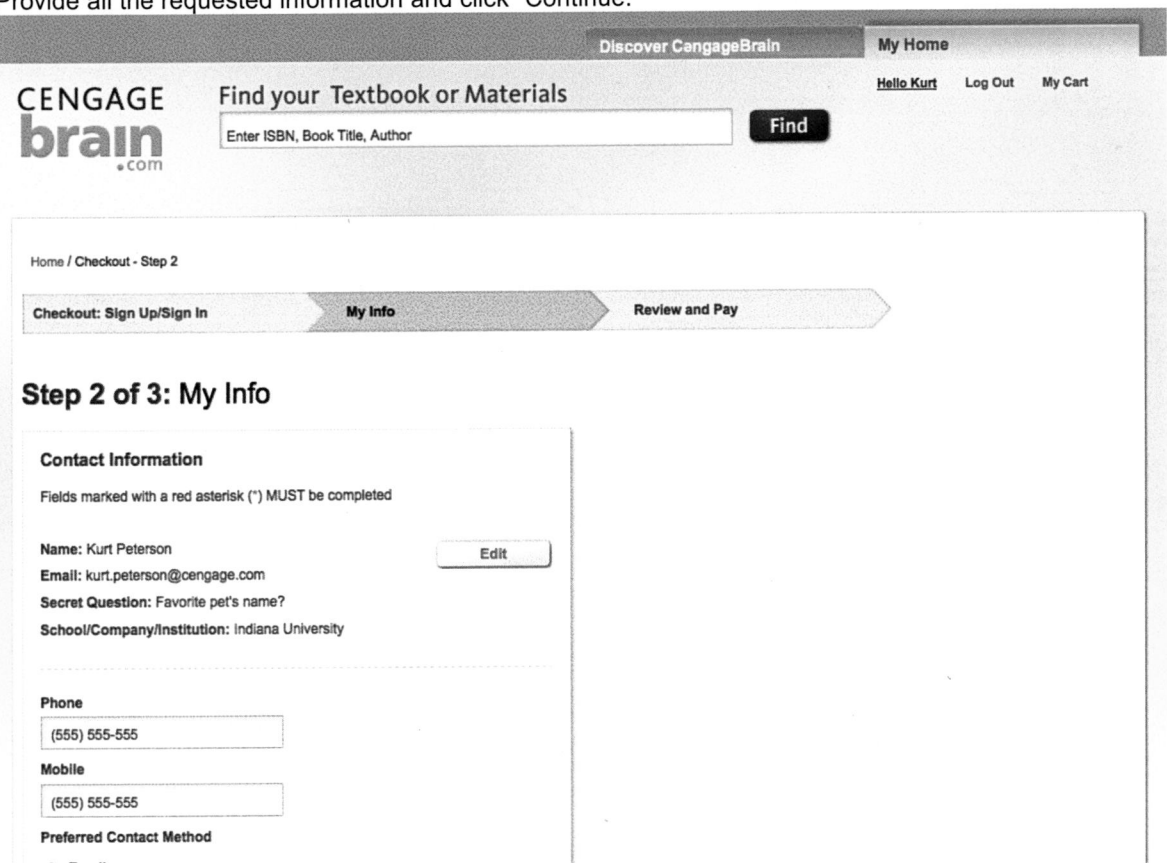

8. Provide the requested information and click "Continue."

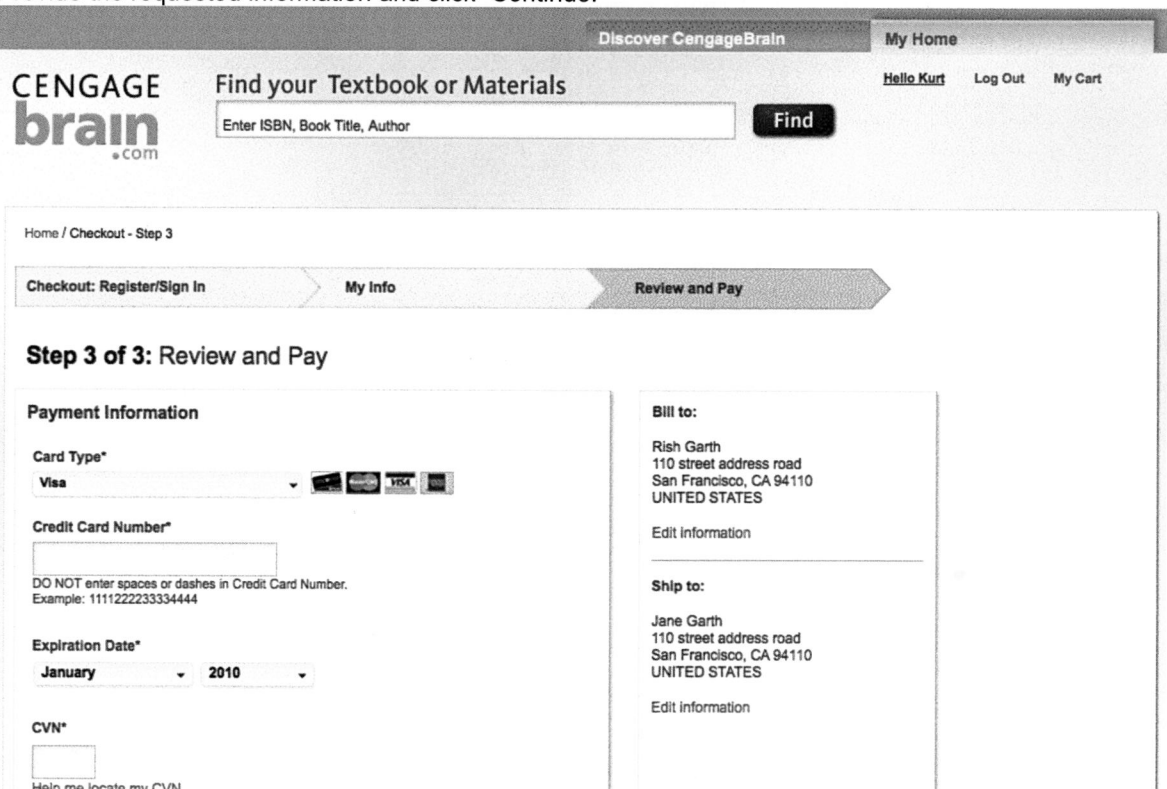

9. Provide payment information, review your order (not seen in the screen capture snippet above), OK the user agreement, and click the "Finish Purchase" button.

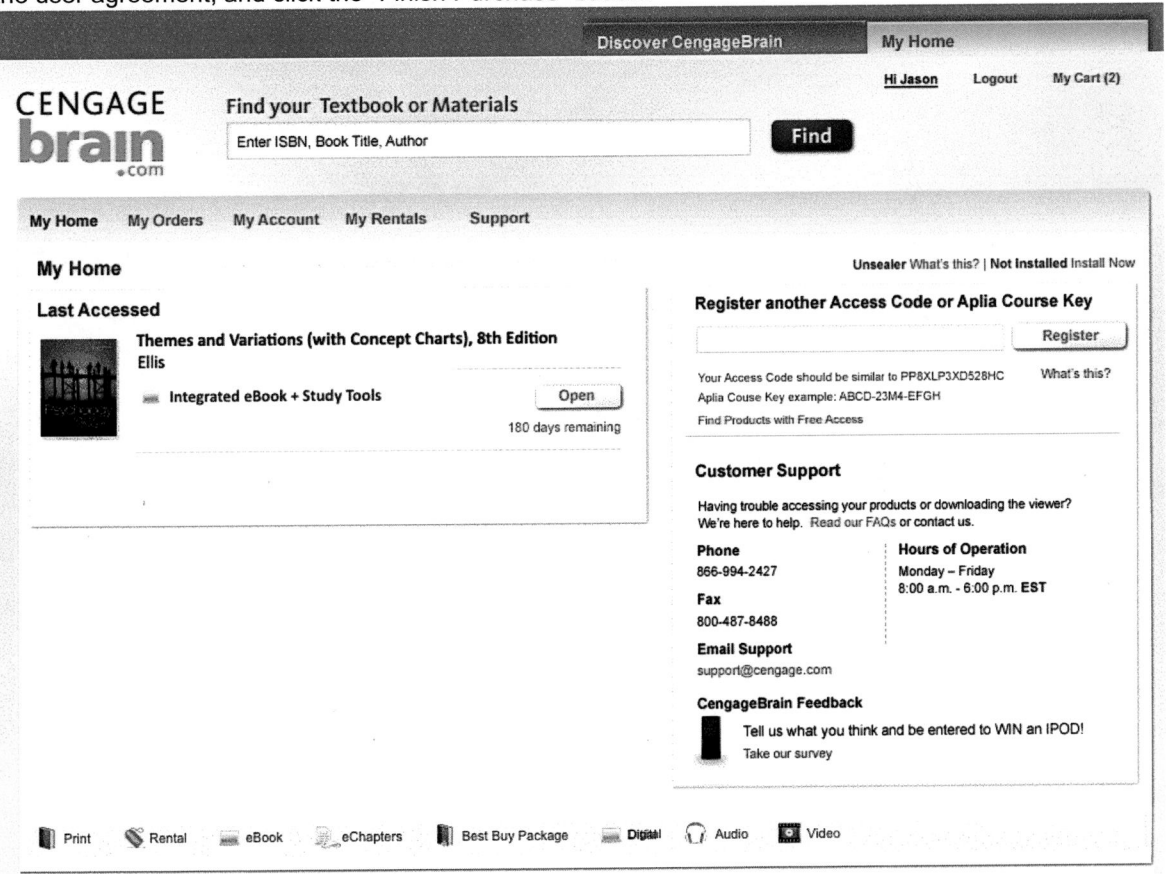

10. There are hundreds of CourseMate sites, and which one you access when you click the "Open" link for the CourseMate resource depends on the textbook you are using. For example, the "Open" link in the example above would take you to the landing page in a Psychology CourseMate site, whereas the example below is the landing page on an Art Study CourseMate website.

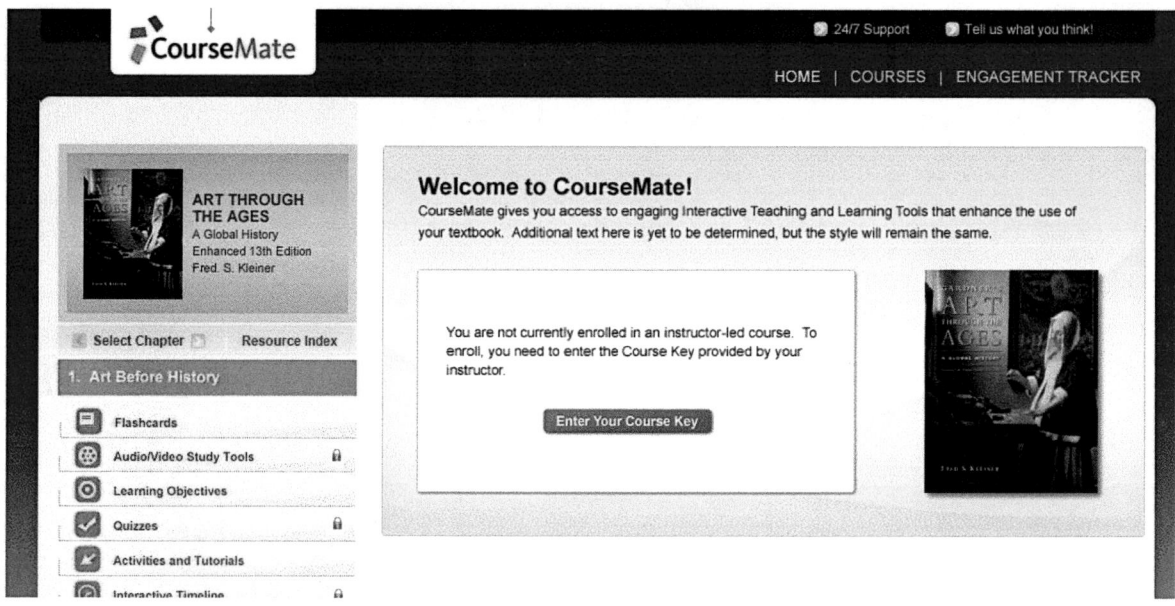

11. You are free to use this website without enrollment in an instructor's course. If you do so and then later enroll in an instructor-led course, all activity before enrollment will appear to the instructor once enrolled (as will all activity after enrollment).

At the point you wish to enroll in an instructor-led course, you will need to have from the instructor a "Course Key." With this Course Key in hand, click the **Enter Your Course Key** button. An overlay will appear, on top of the current screen.

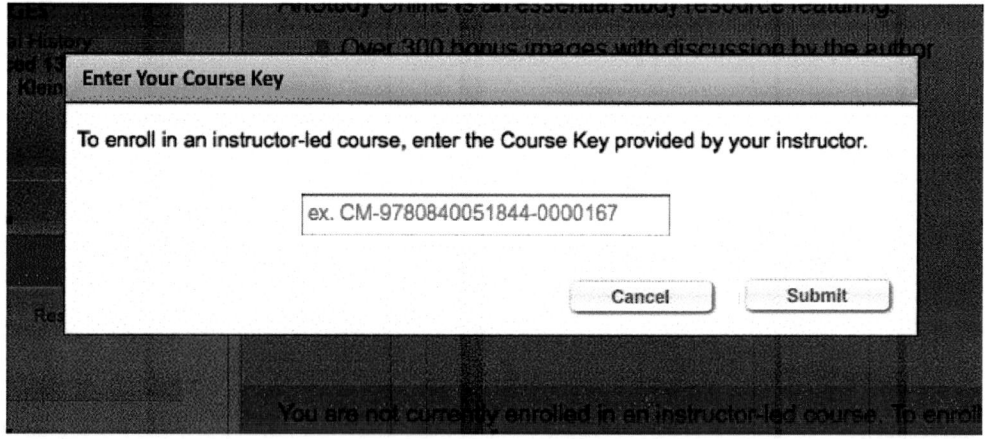

12. Provide the Course Key your instructor gave to you, and click the Submit button. The overlay will disappear, and the Home page of the site will have changed as follows.

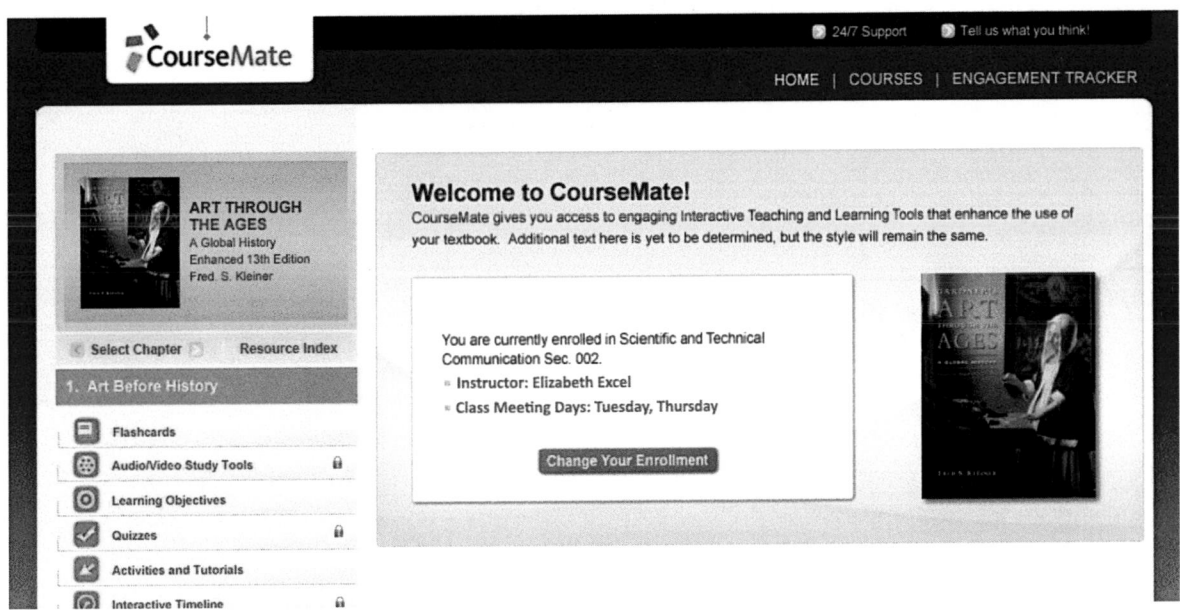

CourseMate

ART THROUGH
THE AGES
A Global History
Enhanced 13th Edition
Fred. S. Kleiner

Select Chapter   Resource Index

1. Art Before History

Flashcards

AudioVideo Study Tools

Learning Objectives

Quizzes

Activities and Tutorials

Interactive Timeline

Welcome to CourseMate!

CourseMate gives you access to engaging Interactive Teaching and Learning Tools that enhance the use of your textbook. Additional text here is yet to be determined, but the style will remain the same.

You are currently enrolled in Scientific and Technical Communication Sec. 002.

- Instructor: Elizabeth Excel
- Class Meeting Days: Tuesday, Thursday

Change Your Enrollment

Now that you are enrolled in the instructor-led course, the instructor will be able to see the time you spend on all resources in the CourseMate site, and will also be able to see your scores for the graded quizzes in the site.

CONTENTS: OVERVIEW

CONTENTS

UNIT 3
Agency & Employment 395

Looking for more examples for class? Do you want the latest developments? Visit our blog at **Bizlawupdate.com**. To be notified when we post updates, just "like" our Facebook page at Beatty Business Law or follow us on Twitter @bizlawupdate.

NOTE FROM THE AUTHORS

New to This Edition

A New Chapter: Practical Contracts

In this textbook, as well as other business law texts, contracts chapters focus on the *theory* of contract law. And that theory is important. But our students tell us that theory, by itself, is not enough. They need to know how these abstract rules operate in *practice*. They want to understand the structure and content of a standard agreement. They have questions such as:

- Do I need a written agreement?
- What do these legal terms *really* mean?
- Are any important provisions missing?
- What happens if a provision is unclear?
- Do I need to hire a lawyer? How can I use a lawyer most effectively?

We answer all these questions in Chapter 12, "Practical Contracts," which is new to this edition. As an illustration throughout the chapter, we use a real-life contract between a movie studio and an actor.

A New Chapter: Employment Discrimination

We have heard from faculty and students alike that employment law plays an increasingly important role in the life of a businessperson. At the same time, fewer and fewer workers belong to labor unions. Therefore, we have rewritten the labor law and employment law chapters from the previous edition. Instead of one chapter on labor law and one on employment law, we now have a new Chapter 17, "Employment and Labor Law," which covers both common law employment issues and labor law. In addition, Chapter 18, "Employment Discrimination," focuses solely on employment discrimination and includes, among other things, an expanded discussion of disparate impact cases, which have become increasingly common and important.

Landmark Cases

As a general rule, we want our cases to be as current as possible, reporting on the world as it is now. However, sometimes students can benefit from reading vintage cases that are still good law and provide a deep understanding of how and why the law has developed as it has. Thus, for example, we have added a discussion about the famous Supreme Court case *Miranda v. Arizona*. Reading this case provides students with a much better understanding of why the Supreme Court created Miranda rights, and this context helps students follow the recent Supreme Court rulings on *Miranda*. Other landmark cases include *Hawkins v. McGee* (the case of the hairy hand), *Griggs v. Duke Power Co.*, and *International Shoe Co. v. State of Washington*.

Reorganized and Revised Material

To reflect requests from faculty, the product liability material is now covered in Chapter 6, "Torts and Product Liability," because most people like to teach these two subjects together. The topics of sales and secured transactions are now in the same chapter, Chapter 13, "Secured Transactions and Sales," while bankruptcy has its own stand-alone chapter devoted to it, Chapter 15.

The new CPA exam no longer includes questions about banks and their customers, and much of that material (such as how long it takes checks to clear) is not very relevant to our students. Therefore, in Chapter 14, "Negotiable Instruments," we have replaced the banking material with information on liability for negotiable instruments.

The New Patent Law

This statute represents the most major change in patent law in our lifetime.

The JOBS Act

The Jumpstart Our Business Startups (JOBS) Act rewrote significant portions of the securities laws. These changes are included in this edition.

End of Chapter Material

To facilitate class discussion and student learning, we have overhauled the study questions at the end of the chapters. They are now divided into three parts:

1. **Multiple-choice questions.** Because many instructors use this format in their tests, it seemed appropriate to provide practice questions. The answers to these multiple-choice questions are available to students online at **www.cengagebrain.com**.

2. **Essay questions.** Students can use these as study questions, and professors can also assign them as written homework problems.

3. **Discussion questions.** Instructors can use these questions to enhance class discussion. If assigned in advance, students will have a chance to think about the answers before class. This format follows one that students are used to from business cases, which often pose discussion questions in advance.

Other New Material

We have, of course, added substantial new material, with a particular focus on the Internet and social media. Chapter 17, "Employment and Labor Law," includes a section on social media. Chapter 20, "Corporations," uses Facebook as an example of how to organize a corporation. There are also new cases involving eBay and craigslist. In addition, Chapter 19, "Starting a Business: LLCs and Other Options," includes a new section about socially conscious organizations.

Staying Current: Our Blog, Facebook, and Twitter

To find out about new developments in business law, visit our blog at Bizlawupdate.com. If you "like" our Facebook page at Beatty Business Law or follow us on Twitter @bizlawupdate, you will receive a notification automatically whenever we post to the blog.

The Beatty/Samuelson Difference

When we began work on the first edition of this textbook, our publisher warned us that our undertaking was risky because there were already so many Legal Environment texts. Despite these warnings, we were convinced that there was a market for a Legal Environment book that was different from all the others. Our goal was to capture the passion and excitement—the sheer enjoyment—of the law. Business law is notoriously complex, and as authors we are obsessed with accuracy. Yet this intriguing subject also abounds with human conflict and hard-earned wisdom, forces that can make a law book sparkle.

Now, as this fifth edition goes to press, we look back over the intervening years and are touched by the many unsolicited comments from students, such as these posted on Amazon:

- "Glad I purchased this. It really helps put the law into perspective and allows me as a leader to make intelligent decisions. Thanks."

- "I enjoyed learning business law and was happy my college wanted this book. THUMBS UP!"

We think of the students who have emailed us to say, "In terms of clarity, comprehensiveness, and vividness of style, I think it's probably the best textbook I've ever used in any subject," and "I had no idea business law could be so interesting." Or the faculty who have told us, "Until I read your book, I never really understood UCC 2-207" and "With your book, we have great class discussions." Comments such as these never cease to thrill us and to make us grateful that we persisted in writing a Legal Environment text like no other—a book that is precise and authoritative, yet a pleasure to read.

Comprehensive.   Staying comprehensive means staying current. This fifth edition contains over 50 new cases. Almost all were reported within the last two or three years. We never include a new court opinion merely because it is recent, but the law evolves continually, and our willingness to toss out old cases and add important new ones ensures that this book—and its readers—remain on the frontier of legal developments.

Look, for example, at the important field of corporate governance. All texts cover par value, and so do we. Yet a future executive is far likelier to face conflicts over Sarbanes-Oxley (SOX), executive compensation, and shareholder proposals. We present a clear path through this thicket of new issues. In Chapter 20, for example, read the section about the election and removal of directors. Typically, students (even those who are high-level executives) have a basic misconception about the process of removing a director from office. They think that it is easy. Once they understand the complexity of this process, their whole view of corporate governance—and compensation—changes. We want tomorrow's business leaders to anticipate the challenges that await them and then use their knowledge to avert problems.

Strong Narrative.   The law is full of great stories, and we use them. Your students and ours should come to class excited. Look at Chapter 3, "Dispute Resolution." No tedious list of next steps in litigation, this chapter teaches the subject by tracking a double-indemnity lawsuit. An executive is dead. Did he drown accidentally, obligating the insurance company to pay? Or did the businessman commit suicide, voiding the policy? The student follows the action from the discovery of the body, through each step of the lawsuit, to the final appeal.

Students read stories and remember them. Strong narratives provide a rich context for the remarkable quantity of legal material presented. When students care about the material they are reading, they persevere. We have been delighted to find that they also arrive in class eager to question, discuss, and learn more about issues.

Precise.   The great joy of using English accurately is the power it gives us to attack and dissect difficult issues, rendering them comprehensible to any lay reader. This text takes on the most complex legal topics of the day, yet it is appropriate for *all college and graduate-level students*. Accessible prose goes hand in hand with legal precision. We take great pride in walking our readers through the most serpentine mazes this tough subject can offer.

As we explore this extraordinary discipline, we lure readers along with quirky anecdotes and colorful diagrams. (Notice that the color display on page 525 clarifies the complex rules of the duty of care in the business judgment rule.) However, before the trip is over, we insist that students:

- Gauge policy and political considerations,

- Grapple with legal and social history,

- Spot the nexus between disparate doctrines, and

- Confront tough moral choices.

Authoritative.   We insist, as you do, on a lawbook that is indisputably accurate. A professor must teach with assurance, confident that every paragraph is the result of exhaustive research and meticulous presentation. Dozens of tough-minded people spent thousands of hours reviewing this book, and we are delighted with the stamp of approval we have received from trial and appellate judges, working attorneys, scholars, and teachers.

We reject the cloudy definitions and fuzzy explanations that can invade judicial opinions and legal scholarship. To highlight the most important rules, we use bold print, and then follow with vivacious examples written in clear, forceful English. (See, for example, the discussion of factual cause on page 149.) We cheerfully venture into contentious areas, relying on very recent appellate decisions. Can a creditor pierce the veil of an LLC? What are the rights of an LLC member in the absence of an operating agreement? (See pages 491–494.) Where there is doubt about the current (or future) status of a doctrine, we say so. In areas of particularly heated debate, we footnote our work: we want you to have absolute trust in this book.

A Book for Students.   We have written this book as if we were speaking directly to our students. We provide black letter law, but we also explain concepts in terms that hook students. Over the years, we have learned how much more successfully we can teach when our students are intrigued. No matter what kind of a show we put on in class, *they are only learning when they want to learn.*

Every chapter begins with a story, either fictional or real, to illustrate the issues in the chapter and provide context. Chapter 23, "Cyberlaw," begins with the true story of a college student who discovers nude pictures of himself online. These photos had been taken in the locker room without his knowledge. What privacy rights do any of us have? Does the Internet jeopardize them? Students want to know—right away.

Many of our students were not yet born when Bill Clinton was elected president. They come to college with varying levels of preparation; many now arrive from other countries. We have found that to teach business law most effectively, we must provide its context. Chapter 21, "Securities Regulation," begins with a brief but graphic description of the 1929 stock market crash and the Great Depression (page 544). Only with this background do students grasp the importance and impact of our securities laws.

At the same time, we enjoy offering "nuts-and-bolts" information that grabs students. For example, in Chapter 26, "Consumer Law," we offer advice about how students can obtain a free credit report (page 700).

Students respond enthusiastically to this approach. One professor asked a student to compare our book with the one that the class was then using. This was the student's reaction: "I really enjoy reading the [Beatty & Samuelson] textbook and I have decided that I will give you this memo ASAP, but I am keeping the book until Wednesday so that I may continue reading. Thanks! :-)"

Along with other professors, we have used this text in courses for undergraduates, MBAs, and Executive MBAs, with the students ranging in age from 18 to 55. The book works, as some unsolicited comments indicate:

- An undergraduate wrote, "This is the best textbook I have had in college, on any subject."

- A business law professor stated that the "clarity of presentation is superlative. I have never seen the complexity of contract law made this readable."

- An MBA student commented, "I think the textbook is great. The book is relevant, easy to understand, and interesting."

- A state supreme court justice wrote that the book is "a valuable blend of rich scholarship and easy readability. Students and professors should rejoice with this publication."

- A Fortune 500 vice president, enrolled in an Executive MBA program, commented, "I really liked the chapters. They were crisp, organized and current. The information was easy to understand and enjoyable."

- An undergraduate wrote, "The textbook is awesome. A lot of the time I read more than what is assigned—I just don't want to stop."

Humor   Throughout the text, we use humor—judiciously—to lighten and enlighten. Not surprisingly, students have applauded—but is wit appropriate? How dare we employ levity in this venerable discipline? We offer humor because we take the law seriously. We revere the law for its ancient traditions; its dazzling intricacy; its relentless, though imperfect, attempt to give order and decency to our world. Because we are confident of our respect for the law, we are not afraid to employ some levity. Leaden prose masquerading as legal scholarship does no honor to the field.

Humor also helps retention. Research shows that the funnier or more bizarre the example, the longer students will remember it. Students are more likely to remember a contract problem described in a fanciful setting, and from that setting recall the underlying principle. By contrast, one widget is hard to distinguish from another.

Features

We chose the features for our book with great care. Each one supports an essential pedagogical goal. Here are some of those goals and the matching feature.

Exam Strategy

GOAL: To help students learn more effectively and to prepare for exams. In preparing this fifth edition, we asked ourselves: What do students want? The short answer is—a good grade in the course. How many times a semester does a student ask you, "What can I do to study for the exam?" We are happy to help them study and earn a good grade because that means they should also be learning.

About six times per chapter, we stop the action and give students a two-minute quiz. In the body of the text, again in the end-of-chapter review, and also in the Instructor's Manual, we present a typical exam question. Here lies the innovation: We guide the student in analyzing the issue. We teach the reader—over and over—how to approach a question: to start with the overarching principle, examine the fine point raised in the question, apply the analysis that courts use, and deduce the right answer. This skill is second nature to lawyers, but not to students. Without practice, too many students panic, jumping at a convenient answer and leaving aside the tools that they have spent the course acquiring. Let's change that. Students who have tried the Exam Strategy feature love it.

You Be the Judge

GOAL: Get students to think independently. When reading case opinions, students tend to accept the court's "answer." Judges, of course, try to reach decisions that appear indisputable, when in reality they may be controversial—or wrong. From time to time we want students to think through the problem and reach their own answer. Virtually every chapter contains a You Be the Judge feature, providing the facts of the case and conflicting appellate arguments. The court's decision, however, appears only in the Instructor's Manual. Because students do not know the result, discussions are more complex and lively.

Ethics

GOAL: Make ethics real. We ask ethical questions about cases, legal issues, and commercial practices. Is it fair for one party to void a contract by arguing, months after the fact, that there was no consideration? What is a manager's ethical obligation when asked to provide a reference for a former employee? What is wrong with bribery? What is the ethical obligation of developed nations to dispose of toxic waste from computers? We believe that asking the questions and encouraging discussion reminds students that ethics is an essential element of justice and of a satisfying life.

Cases

GOAL: Let the judges speak. Each case begins with a summary of the facts and a statement of the issue. Next comes a tightly edited version of the decision, in the court's own language, so that students "hear" the law developing in the diverse voices of our many judges. We cite cases using a modified bluebook form. In the principal cases in each chapter, we provide the state or federal citation, the regional citation, and the LEXIS or Westlaw citation. We also give students a brief description of the court. Because many of our cases are so recent, some will have only a regional reporter and a LEXIS or Westlaw citation.

Exam Review

GOAL: Help students to remember and practice! At the end of every chapter, we provide a list of review points and several additional Exam Strategy exercises in a Question/Strategy/Result format. We also challenge the students with 15 or more problems—Multiple-Choice, Essay Questions, and Discussion Questions. The questions include the following:

- *You Be the Judge Writing Problem.* The students are given appellate arguments on both sides of the question and must prepare a written opinion.

- *Ethics.* This question highlights the ethical issues of a dispute and calls upon the student to formulate a specific, reasoned response.

- *CPA Questions.* Where relevant, practice tests include questions from previous CPA exams administered by the American Institute of Certified Public Accountants.

Answers to all the Multiple-Choice questions are available to students online through **www.cengagebrain.com.**

Author Transition

Jeffrey Beatty fought an unremitting 10-year battle against a particularly aggressive form of leukemia which, despite his great courage and determination, he ultimately lost. Jeffrey, a gentleman to the core, was an immensely kind, funny and thoughtful human being, some-one who sang and danced, and who earned the respect and affection of colleagues and students alike. In writing these books, he wanted students to see and understand the impact of law in their everyday lives, as well as its role in supporting human dignity, and what's more, he wanted students to laugh.

Because of the length of Jeffrey's illness, we had ample time to develop a transition plan. Through a combination of new and old methods (social media and personal connections), we were able to identify a wonderfully talented group of applicants—graduates of top law schools who had earned myriad teaching and writing prizes. We read two rounds of blind submissions and met with finalists. In the end, we are thrilled to report that Dean Bredeson has joined the Beatty/Samuelson team. A member of the faculty of the McCombs School of Business at the University of Texas, Dean is a devoted teacher who has received the school's highest teaching award for the last five years. He is also the author of the textbook, *Applied Business Ethics* (Cengage, 2011). Dean has a number of qualities that are essential to a textbook writer—keen insight into explaining complex material in an engaging manner, meticulous attention to detail, an ability to meet deadlines, and a wry sense of humor.

TEACHING MATERIALS

For more information about any of these ancillaries, contact your Cengage Learning/South-Western Legal Studies Sales Representative for more details, or visit the Beatty & Samuelson *Legal Environment, 5th edition* web page, accessed through **www.cengagebrain.com.**

Instructor's Resource CD.   The Instructor's Resource CD (IRCD) contains the ExamView testing software files, the test bank in Microsoft Word files, the Instructor's Manual in Word files, and Microsoft PowerPoint Lecture Review Slides.

Instructor's Manual.   Available both online at and on the IRCD, this manual includes special features to enhance class discussion and student progress:

- *Exam Strategy problems.* If your students would like more Exam Strategy problems, there is an additional section of these problems in the Instructor's Manual.

- *Dialogues.* These are a series of questions and answers on pivotal cases and topics. The questions provide enough material to teach a full session. In a pinch, you could walk into class with nothing but the manual and use the Dialogues to conduct an exciting class.

- *Action Learning ideas.* Interviews, quick research projects, drafting exercises, classroom activities, commercial analyses, and other suggested assignments get students out of their chairs and into the diverse settings of business law.

- *Skits.* Various chapters have lively skits that students can perform in class, with no rehearsal, to put legal doctrine in a real-life context.

- *Succinct introductions.* Each chapter has a theme and a quote of the day.

- *Current focus.* This feature offers updates of text material.

- *Additional cases and examples.* For those topics that need more attention or coverage, use the additional cases and examples provided in the Instructor's Manual.

- *Solutions.* Answers to You Be the Judge cases from the text and to the Exam Review questions found at the end of each chapter.

Test Bank.   The test bank offers hundreds of essay, short-answer, and multiple-choice problems and may be obtained online or on the IRCD.

ExamView Testing Software–Computerized Testing Software. This testing software contains all of the questions in the test bank. This program is an easy-to-use test creation software compatible with Microsoft Windows. Instructors can add or edit questions, instructions, and answers; and select questions by previewing them on the screen, selecting them randomly, or selecting them by number. Instructors can also create and administer quizzes online. The ExamView testing software is available only on the IRCD.

PowerPoint Lecture Review Slides. PowerPoint slides are available for instructors to use with their lectures. Download these slides online or from the IRCD.

CengageNOW. This robust, online course management system gives you more control in less time and delivers better student outcomes—NOW. CengageNOW for *Legal Environment* 5e has been expanded to include six homework types that align with the six levels of Bloom's taxonomy: Knowledge: Chapter Review, Comprehension: Business Law Scenarios, Application: Legal Reasoning, Analysis: IRAC, Synthesis: Exam Strategy, and Evaluation: Business Wisdom. With all these elements used together, CengageNOW will ensure that students develop the higher-level thinking skills they need to reach an advanced understanding of the material.

Aplia. Engage, prepare, and educate your students with this ideal online learning solution. Aplia's™ business law solution ensures that students stay on top of their coursework with regularly scheduled homework assignments and automatic grading with detailed, immediate feedback on every question. Interactive teaching tools and content further increase engagement and understanding. Aplia™ assignments match the language, style, and structure of *Legal Environment* 5e, allowing your students to apply what they learn in the text directly to their homework.

Business Law CourseMate. Cengage Learning's Business Law CourseMate brings course concepts to life with interactive learning, study, and exam preparation tools—including an e-book—that supports the printed textbook. Designed to address a variety of learning styles, students will have access to flashcards, Learning Objectives, and the Key Terms for quick reviews. A set of auto-gradable, interactive quizzes will allow students to instantly gauge their comprehension of the material. For instructors, all quiz scores and student activity are mapped within Engagement Tracker, a set of intuitive student performance analytical tools that help identify at-risk students. An interactive blog helps connect book concepts to real-world situations happening now.

Business Law Digital Video Library. This dynamic online video library features over 90 video clips that spark class discussion and clarify core legal principles. The library is organized into four series:

- *Legal Conflicts in Business* includes specific modern business and e-commerce scenarios.

- *Ask the Instructor* contains straightforward explanations of concepts for student review.

- *Drama of the Law* features classic business scenarios that spark classroom participation.

- *LawFlix* contains clips related to the law from many popular films, including *Field of Dreams, Midnight Run,* and *Jaws.*

- *Real World Legal* takes students out of the classroom and into real-life situations, encouraging them to consider the legal aspects of decision making in the business world.

- *Business Ethics in Action* challenges students to examine ethical dilemmas in the world of business.

Access to the Business Law Digital Video Library is available as an optional package with each new student text at no additional charge. Students with used books can purchase access to the video clips online. For more information about the Business Law Digital Video Library, visit **www.cengagebrain.com**.

A Handbook of Basic Law Terms, Blacks Law Dictionary Series.   This paperback dictionary, prepared by the editor of the popular Black's Law Dictionary, can be packaged for a small additional cost with any new South-Western Legal Studies in Business text.

Student Guide to the SOX.   This brief overview for business students explains SOX, what is required of whom, and how it might affect students in their business lives. Available as an optional package with the text.

Interaction with the Authors.   This is our standard: Every professor who adopts this book must have a superior experience. We are available to help in any way we can. Adopters of this text often call us or e-mail us to ask questions, obtain a syllabus, offer suggestions, share pedagogical concerns, or inquire about ancillaries. One of the pleasures of working on this project has been this link to so many colleagues around the country. We value those connections, are eager to respond, and would be happy to hear from you.

Susan S. Samuelson
Phone: (617) 353-2033
Email: ssamuels@bu.edu

Dean A. Bredeson
Phone: (512) 471-5248
Email: bredeson@mail.utexas.edu

ACKNOWLEDGMENTS

We appreciate the thoughtful insights of the reviewers for this fifth edition:

Martha Broderick
University of Maine

Burke Christensen
Eastern Kentucky University

Michael Costello
University of Missouri, St. Louis

Suzanne M. Gradisher
University of Akron

Wendy Hind
Doane College

Ronald B. Kowalczyk
Elgin Community College

Colleen Arnott Less
Johnson & Wales University

Carol Nielsen
Bemidji State University

Margaret A. Parker
Owens Community College

Cheryl Staley
Lake Land College

Paulette L. Stenzel
Michigan State University

Kenneth Ray Taurman, Jr.
Indiana University Southeast

Deborah Walsh
Middlesex Community College

And we are continually grateful to the following reviewers who gave such helpful comments on the first four editions of this book:

Manzoor Ahmad
Compton Educational Center, El Camino College

Steven J. Arsenault
College of Charleston

Lois Beier
Kent State University

Amy Chataginer
Mississippi Gulf Coast Community College

Linda Christiansen
Indiana University Southeast

Michael J. Costello
University of Missouri—St. Louis

G. Howard Doty
Nashville State Technical Community College

Teri Elkins
University of Houston

Lizbeth G. Ellis
New Mexico State University

Paul Fiorelli
Xavier University

Gary Greene
Manatee Community College

Elizabeth Grimm-Howell
University of Missouri—St. Louis

Richard Guarino
California State University, Sacramento

Stephen Hearn
Louisiana Tech University

Timothy Jackson
School of Business, California Baptist University

William C. Kostner
Doane College

Maurice J. McCann
Southern Illinois University Carbondale

Russ Meade
Gardner-Webb University

Michael Monhollon
Hardin-Simmons University

Barbara Redman
Gainesville State College

Bruce L. Rockwood
Bloomsburg University

Rebecca Rutz
Mississippi Gulf Coast Community College—Jackson County Campus

Rachel Spooner
Boston University School of Management

Daphyne Saunders Thomas
James Madison University

Glen M. Vogel
Hofstra University

ABOUT THE AUTHORS

Jeffrey F. Beatty was an associate professor of business law at the Boston University School of Management. After receiving his B.A. from Sarah Lawrence and his J.D. from Boston University, he practiced with the Greater Boston Legal Services representing indigent clients. At Boston University, he won the Metcalf Cup and Prize, the university's highest teaching award. Professor Beatty also wrote plays and television scripts that were performed in Boston, London, and Amsterdam.

Susan S. Samuelson is a professor of business law at Boston University's School of Management. After earning her undergraduate and law degrees at Harvard University, Professor Samuelson practiced with the firm of Choate, Hall, and Stewart. She has written many articles on legal issues for scholarly and popular journals, including the *American Business Law Journal, Ohio State Law Journal, Boston University Law Review, Harvard Journal on Legislation, National Law Journal, Sloan Management Review, Better Homes and*

Gardens, and *Boston Magazine.* At Boston University, she won the Broderick Prize for excellence in teaching. For 12 years, Professor Samuelson was the faculty director of the Boston University Executive MBA program.

Dean A. Bredeson is a senior lecturer at the McCombs School of Business at the University of Texas (UT), where he has been on the faculty for 16 years. He holds a J.D. from UT. He has previously published *Student Guide to the Sarbanes-Oxley Act* and two textbooks that explore the intersection of law and ethics: *Applied Business Ethics* (Cengage, 2012) and *Ethics in the Workplace* (Cengage, 2012). He is a five-time winner of the Lockheed-Martin Award, which is awarded each year to the member of the faculty at McCombs with the highest student evaluations in undergraduate courses. He is also among the youngest-ever recipients of the Board of Regents Teaching Award, the UT system's highest teaching honor.

For Jeffrey, best of
colleagues and dearest of
friends.

s.s.s.

The Legal Environment

CHAPTER 1

INTRODUCTION TO LAW

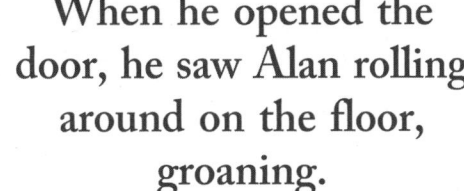

Near Campus

Alan Dawson dumped his Calculus II textbook into his backpack. Outside, a light snow began to fall. With a sigh, he left his apartment and headed out into the early December evening.

Halfway to the library, he encountered a group of his friends. "Hey, Alan, we're done with finals," said Gary with a flourish. "You should come to Thirsty's with us."

"I can't. I have my calculus final tomorrow."

"Carrie's going to be there." Gary raised his eyebrows.

"Come on, Dawson! Be a man! Come on!" said the others. Without a word, Alan reversed direction and headed away from the library. His friends cheered loudly.

At Thirsty's Bar

Anna stood behind the bar and watched four bikers enter. They wore jackets with gang insignia, and purple headscarves. One of them approached the bar. "Four Budweisers," he said to Anna.

> When he opened the door, he saw Alan rolling around on the floor, groaning.

After gathering her courage, Anna said, "Look, you guys know you can't wear your colors in here."

"What are you gonna do about it, missy?" the biker asked. When she didn't reply, he leaned closer to her. "Four beers."

Anna thought about it for a moment, then gathered four Budweiser longnecks and placed them on the bar. The biker tossed down a $10 bill, took the beers, and joined his three associates at a table.

Anna eyed the telephone on the counter behind her. The owner of Thirsty's had told her to call the cops immediately if she saw any gang colors in there. But the bikers were watching her, and she decided not to make a call right away.

At a back table

"I'm not going home for a few more days," Alan said to Carrie.

"I'm not either. We should do something," Carrie said.

"Yeah," Alan said, trying hard to not seem too excited. "Have you, ah, seen the new DiCaprio movie? We could go see that."

"That would be great."

Alan blissfully made small talk with Carrie, unaware of the bikers or anyone else in the bar.

Eventually, he excused himself and made his way to the restroom.

As he washed his hands, he saw two bikers in the mirror. "Howdy, college boy," one of them said. It was the last thing Alan remembered for awhile.

Twenty minutes later

"Hey, where's Alan?" Gary asked.

Carrie said, "I think he went to the restroom."

Frowning, Gary headed back to the men's room. When he opened the door, he saw Alan rolling around on the floor, groaning. His shirt was torn, his face bloody.

"Oh, man, what happened? Are you OK?" Gary asked.

"No," Alan replied.

Gary thumbed 911 on his cell phone.

"Wait a moment," you may be thinking. "Are we reading a chapter on business law or one about biker crimes in a roadside tavern?" Both. Later in the chapter, we examine a real case that mirrors the opening scenario. The crime committed against Alan will enable us to explore one of the law's basic principles, negligence. Should a pub owner pay money damages to the victim of gang violence? The owner herself did nothing aggressive. Should she have prevented the harm? Does her failure to stop the assault make her responsible? What begins as a gang incident ends up an issue of commercial liability.

Law is powerful, essential, and fascinating. We hope this book will persuade you of all three ideas. We place great demands on our courts, asking them to make our large, complex, and sometimes violent society into a safer, fairer, more orderly place. Judges must reason their way through countless complex issues.

THE ROLE OF LAW IN SOCIETY

Power

The strong reach of the law touches nearly everything we do, especially at work. Consider a mid-level manager at Sublime Corp., which manufactures and distributes video games.

During the course of a day's work, she might negotiate a deal with a game developer (contract law). Before signing any deals, she might research whether similar games already exist, which might diminish her ability to market the proposed new game (intellectual property law). One of her subordinates might complain about being harassed by a coworker (employment law). Another worker may complain about being required to work long hours (administrative law). And she may consider investing her own money in her company's stock, but she may wonder whether she will get into trouble if she invests based on inside information (securities law).

It is not only as a corporate manager that you will confront the law. As a voter, investor, juror, entrepreneur, and community member, you will influence and be affected by the law. Whenever you take a stance about a legal issue, whether in the corporate office, in the voting booth, or as part of local community groups, you help to create the fabric of our nation. Your views are vital. This book will offer you knowledge and ideas from which to form and continually reassess your legal opinions and values.

Importance

Law is also essential. *Every* society of which we have any historical record has had some system of laws. For example, consider the Visigoths, a nomadic European people who overran much of present-day France and Spain during the fifth and sixth centuries A.D. Their code admirably required judges to be "quick of perception, clear in judgment, and lenient in the infliction of penalties." It detailed dozens of crimes.

Our legal system is largely based upon the English model, but many societies contributed ideas. The Iroquois Native Americans, for example, played a role in the creation of our own government. Five major nations made up the Iroquois group: the Mohawk, Cayuga, Oneida, Onondaga, and Seneca. Each nation governed its own domestic issues. But each nation also elected "sachems" to a League of the Iroquois. The league had authority over any matters that were common to all, such as relations with outsiders. Thus, by the fifteenth century, the Iroquois had solved the problem of *federalism:* how to have two levels of government, each with specified powers. Their system impressed Benjamin Franklin and others and influenced the drafting of our Constitution, with its powers divided between state and federal governments.[1]

Fascination

In 1835, the young French aristocrat Alexis de Tocqueville traveled through the United States, observing the newly democratic people and the qualities that made them unique. One of the things that struck de Tocqueville most forcefully was the American tendency to file suit: "Scarcely any political question arises in the United States that is not resolved, sooner or later, into a judicial question."[2] De Tocqueville got it right: For better or worse, we do expect courts to solve many problems.

Not only do Americans litigate—they watch each other do it. Every television season offers at least one new courtroom drama to a national audience breathless for more cross-examination. Almost all of the states permit live television coverage of real trials. The most heavily viewed event in the history of the medium was the O. J. Simpson murder trial. In most nations, coverage of judicial proceedings is not allowed.[3]

The law is a big part of our lives, and it is wise to know something about it. Within a few weeks, you will probably find yourself following legal events in the news with keener interest and deeper understanding. In this chapter, we develop the background for our study. We look at where law comes from: its history and its present-day institutions. In the section on jurisprudence, we examine different theories about what "law" really means. And finally we see how courts—and students—analyze a case.

---

[1]Jack Weatherford, *Indian Givers* (New York: Fawcett Columbine, 1988), pp. 133–150.

[2]Alexis de Tocqueville, *Democracy in America* (1835), Vol. 1, Ch. 16.

[3]Regardless of whether we allow cameras, it is an undeniable benefit of the electronic age that we can obtain information quickly. From time to time, we will mention websites of interest. Some of these are for nonprofit groups, while others are commercial sites. We do not endorse or advocate on behalf of any group or company; we simply wish to alert you to what is available.

ORIGINS OF OUR LAW

It would be nice if we could look up "the law" in one book, memorize it, and then apply it. But the law is not that simple, and *cannot* be that simple, because it reflects the complexity of contemporary life. In truth, there is no such thing as "the law." Principles and rules of law actually come from *many different* sources. Why is this so? In part because we inherited a complex structure of laws from England.

Additionally, ours is a nation born in revolution and created, in large part, to protect the rights of its people from the government. The Founding Fathers created a national government but insisted that the individual states maintain control in many areas. As a result, each state has its own government with exclusive power over many important areas of our lives. To top it off, the Founders guaranteed many rights to the people alone, ordering national *and* state governments to keep clear. This has worked, but it has caused a multilayered system, with 50 state governments and one federal government all creating and enforcing law.

English Roots

England in the tenth century was a rustic agricultural community with a tiny population and very little law or order. Vikings invaded repeatedly, terrorizing the Anglo-Saxon peoples. Criminals were hard to catch in the heavily forested, sparsely settled nation. The king used a primitive legal system to maintain a tenuous control over his people.

England was divided into shires, and daily administration was carried out by a "shire reeve," later called a sheriff. The shire reeve collected taxes and did what he could to keep peace, apprehending criminals and acting as mediator between feuding families. Two or three times a year, a shire court met; lower courts met more frequently. Today, this method of resolving disputes lives on as mediation, which we will discuss in Chapter 3.

Because there were so few officers to keep the peace, Anglo-Saxon society created an interesting method of ensuring public order. Every freeman belonged to a group of 10 freemen known as a "tithing," headed by a "tithingman." If anyone injured a person outside his tithing or interfered with the king's property, all 10 men of the tithing could be forced to pay. Today, we still use this idea of collective responsibility in business partnerships. All partners are personally responsible for the debts of the partnership. They could potentially lose their homes and all assets because of the irresponsible conduct of one partner. That liability has helped create new forms of business organization, including limited liability companies.

When cases did come before an Anglo-Saxon court, the parties would often be represented by a clergyman, by a nobleman, or by themselves. There were few professional lawyers. Each party produced "oath helpers," usually 12, who would swear that one version of events was correct. The Anglo-Saxon oath helpers were forerunners of our modern jury of 12 persons.

In 1066, the Normans conquered England. William the Conqueror made a claim never before made in England: that he owned all of the land. The king then granted sections of his lands to his favorite noblemen, as his tenants in chief, creating the system of feudalism. These tenants in chief then granted parts of their land to *tenants in demesne*, who actually occupied a particular estate. Each tenant in demesne owed fidelity to his lord (hence, "landlord"). So what? Just this: land became the most valuable commodity in all of England, and our law still reflects that. One thousand years later, American law still regards land as special. The statute of frauds, which we study in the section on contracts, demands that contracts for the sale or lease of property be in writing. And landlord-tenant law, vital to students and many others, still reflects its ancient roots. Some of a landlord's rights are based on the 1,000-year-old tradition that land is uniquely valuable.

In 1250, Henry de Bracton (d. 1268) wrote a legal treatise that still influences us. *De Legibus et Consuetudinibus Angliae* (*On the Laws and Customs of England*), written in Latin,

Precedent
The tendency to decide current cases based on previous rulings.

summarized many of the legal rulings in cases since the Norman Conquest. De Bracton was teaching judges to rule based on previous cases. He was helping to establish the idea of **precedent**. The doctrine of precedent, which developed gradually over centuries, requires that judges decide current cases based on previous rulings. This vital principle is the heart of American common law. Precedent ensures predictability. Suppose a 17-year-old student promises to lease an apartment from a landlord, but then changes her mind. The landlord sues to enforce the lease. The student claims that she cannot be held to the agreement because she is a minor. The judge will look for precedent, that is, older cases dealing with the same issue, and he will find many holding that a contract generally may not be enforced against a minor. That precedent is binding on this case, and the student wins. The accumulation of precedent, based on case after case, makes up the **common law**.

Common law
Judge-made law.

In the end, today's society is dramatically different from that of medieval English society. But interestingly, legal disputes from hundreds of years ago are often quite recognizable today. Some things have changed but others never do.

Here is an actual case from more than six centuries ago, in the court's own language. The plaintiff claims that he asked the defendant to heal his eye with "herbs and other medicines." He says the defendant did it so badly that he blinded the plaintiff in that eye.

THE OCULIST'S CASE (1329)

LI MS. Hale 137 (1), fo. 150, Nottingham[4]

Attorney Launde [for defendant]: Sir, you plainly see how [the plaintiff claims] that he had submitted himself to [the defendant's] medicines and his care; and after that he can assign no trespass in his person, inasmuch as he submitted himself to his care: but this action, if he has any, sounds naturally in breach of covenant. We demand [that the case be dismissed].

Excerpts from Judge Denum's Decision: I saw a Newcastle man arraigned before my fellow justice and me for the death of a man. I asked the reason for the indictment, and it was said that he had slain a man under his care, who died within four days afterwards. And because I saw that he was a [doctor] and that he had not done the thing feloniously but [accidentally] I ordered him to be discharged. And suppose a blacksmith, who is a man of skill, injures your horse with a nail, whereby you lose your horse: you shall never have recovery against him. No more shall you here.

Afterwards the plaintiff did not wish to pursue his case any more.

This case from 1329 is an ancient medical malpractice action. Attorney Launde does not deny that his client blinded the plaintiff. He claims that the plaintiff has brought the wrong kind of lawsuit. Launde argues that the plaintiff should have brought a case of "covenant"; that is, a lawsuit about a contract.

Judge Denum decides the case on a different principle. He gives judgment to the defendant because the plaintiff voluntarily sought medical care. He implies that the defendant would lose only if he had attacked the plaintiff. As we will see when we study negligence law, this case might have a different outcome today. Note also the informality of the judge's ruling. He rather casually mentions that he came across a related case once before and that he would stand by that outcome. The idea of precedent is just beginning to take hold.

---

[4]J. Baker and S. Milsom, *Sources of English Legal History* (London: Butterworth & Co., 1986).

Law in the United States

The colonists brought with them a basic knowledge of English law, some of which they were content to adopt as their own. Other parts, such as religious restrictions, were abhorrent to them. Many had made the dangerous trip to America precisely to escape persecution, and they were not interested in recreating their difficulties in a new land. Finally, some laws were simply irrelevant or unworkable in a world that was socially and geographically so different. American law ever since has been a blend of the ancient principles of English common law and a zeal and determination for change.

During the nineteenth century, the United States changed from a weak, rural nation into one of vast size and potential power. Cities grew, factories appeared, and sweeping movements of social migration changed the population. Changing conditions raised new legal questions. Did workers have a right to form industrial unions? To what extent should a manufacturer be liable if its product injured someone? Could a state government invalidate an employment contract that required 16-hour workdays? Should one company be permitted to dominate an entire industry?

In the twentieth century, the rate of social and technological change increased, creating new legal puzzles. Were some products, such as automobiles, so inherently dangerous that the seller should be responsible for injuries even if no mistakes were made in manufacturing? Who should clean up toxic waste if the company that had caused the pollution no longer existed? If a consumer signed a contract with a billion-dollar corporation, should the agreement be enforced even if the consumer never understood it? New and startling questions arise with great regularity. Before we can begin to examine the answers, we need to understand the sources of contemporary law.

SOURCES OF CONTEMPORARY LAW

Throughout the text, we will examine countless legal ideas. But binding rules come from many different places. This section describes the significant *categories* of laws in the United States.

United States Constitution

America's greatest legal achievement was the writing of the United States Constitution in 1787. It is the supreme law of the land.[5] Any law that conflicts with it is void. This federal Constitution does three basic things. First, it establishes the national government of the United States, with its three branches. Second, it creates a system of checks and balances among the branches. And third, the Constitution guarantees many basic rights to the American people.

Branches of Government

The Founding Fathers sought a division of government power. They did not want all power centralized in a king or in anyone else. And so, the Constitution divides legal authority into three pieces: legislative, executive, and judicial power.

---

[5]The Constitution took effect in 1788, when 9 of 13 colonies ratified it. Two more colonies ratified it that year, and the last of the 13 did so in 1789, after the government was already in operation. The complete text of the Constitution appears in Appendix A.

Legislative power gives the ability to create new laws. In Article I, the Constitution gives this power to the Congress, which is comprised of two chambers—a Senate and a House of Representatives. Voters in all 50 states elect representatives who go to Washington, D.C., to serve in the Congress and debate new legal ideas.

The House of Representatives has 435 voting members. A state's voting power is based on its population. Large states (Texas, California, and Florida) send dozens of representatives to the House. Some small states (Wyoming, North Dakota, and Delaware) send only one. The Senate has 100 voting members—two from each state.

Executive power is the authority to enforce laws. Article II of the Constitution establishes the President as commander in chief of the armed forces and the head of the executive branch of the federal government.

Judicial power gives the right to interpret laws and determine their validity. Article III places the Supreme Court at the head of the judicial branch of the federal government. Interpretive power is often underrated, but it is often every bit as important as the ability to create laws in the first place. For instance, the Supreme Court ruled that privacy provisions of the Constitution protect a woman's right to abortion, although neither the word "privacy" nor "abortion" appears in the text of the Constitution.[6]

At times, courts void laws altogether. For example, in 1995, the Supreme Court ruled that the Gun-Free School Zones Act of 1990 was unconstitutional because Congress did not have the authority to pass such a law.[7]

Checks and Balances

Sidney Crosby might score 300 goals per season if checking were not allowed in the National Hockey League. But because opponents are allowed to hit Crosby and the rest of his teammates on the Penguins, he is held to a much more reasonable 50 goals per year.

Political checks work in much the same way. They allow one branch of the government to trip up another.

The authors of the Constitution were not content merely to divide government power three ways. They also wanted to give each part of the government some power over the other two branches. Many people complain about "gridlock" in Washington, but the government is slow and sluggish by design. The Founding Fathers wanted to create a system that, without broad agreement, would tend towards inaction.

The President can veto Congressional legislation. Congress can impeach the President. The Supreme Court can void laws passed by Congress. The President appoints judges to the federal courts, including the Supreme Court, but these nominees do not serve unless approved by the Senate. Congress (with help from the 50 states) can override the Supreme Court by amending the Constitution. The President and the Congress influence the Supreme Court by controlling who is placed on the court in the first place.

Many of these checks and balances will be examined in more detail later in this book, starting in Chapter 4.

Fundamental Rights

The Constitution also grants many of our most basic liberties. For the most part, they are found in the amendments to the Constitution. The First Amendment guarantees the rights of free speech, free press, and the free exercise of religion. The Fourth, Fifth, and Sixth Amendments protect the rights of any person accused of a crime. Other amendments ensure that the government treats all people equally and that it pays for any property it takes from a citizen.

---

[6]*Roe v. Wade*, 410 U.S. 113 (1973).
[7]*United States v. Alfonso Lopez, Jr.*, 514 U.S. 549 (1995).

By creating a limited government of three branches and guaranteeing basic liberties to all citizens, the Constitution became one of the most important documents ever written.

Statutes

The second important source of law is statutory law. The Constitution gave to the United States Congress the power to pass laws on various subjects. These laws are called **statutes,** and they can cover absolutely any topic, so long as they do not violate the Constitution.

Statute
A law created by a legislative body.

Almost all statutes are created by the same method. An idea for a new law—on taxes, health care, texting while driving, or any other topic, big or small—is first proposed in the Congress. This idea is called a *bill*. The House and Senate then independently vote on the bill. To pass Congress, the bill must win a simple majority vote in each of these chambers.

If Congress passes a bill, it goes to the White House for the President's approval. If the President signs it, a new statute is created. It is no longer a mere idea; it is the law of the land. If the President refuses to approve, or *vetoes* a bill, it does not become a statute unless Congress overrides the veto. To do that, both the House and the Senate must approve the bill by a two-thirds majority. If this happens, it becomes a statute without the President's signature.

Common Law

Binding legal ideas often come from the courts. Judges generally follow *precedent*. When courts decide a case, they tend to apply the legal rules that other courts have used in similar cases.

The principle that precedent is binding on later cases is called *stare decisis*, which means "let the decision stand." *Stare decisis* makes the law predictable, and this in turn enables businesses and private citizens to plan intelligently.

It is important to note that precedent is binding only on *lower* courts. For example, if the Supreme Court decided a case in one way in 1965, it is under no obligation to follow precedent if the same issue arises in 2015.

Sometimes, this is quite beneficial. In 1896, the Supreme Court decided (unbelievably) that segregation—separating people by race in schools, hotels, public transportation, and other public services—was legal under certain conditions.[8] In 1954, on the exact same issue, the court changed its mind.[9]

In other circumstances, it is more difficult to see the value in breaking with an established rule.

Court Orders

Judges have the authority to issue court orders that place binding obligations on specific people or companies. An injunction, for example, is a court order to stop doing something. A judge might order a stalker to stay more than 500 yards away from an ex-boyfriend or -girlfriend. Lindsey Lohan might be ordered to stop drinking and enter rehab. Courts have the authority to imprison or fine those who violate their orders.

---

[8]*Plessy v. Ferguson*, 163 U.S. 537 (1896).
[9]*Brown v. Board of Education of Topeka*, 347 U.S. 483 (1954).

> **United States senators do not stand around air traffic towers, serving coffee to keep everyone awake.**

Administrative Law

In a society as large and diverse as ours, the executive and legislative branches of government cannot oversee all aspects of commerce. Congress passes statutes about air safety, but United States senators do not stand around air traffic towers, serving coffee to keep everyone awake. The executive branch establishes rules concerning how foreign nationals enter the United States, but Presidents are reluctant to sit on the dock of the bay, watching the ships come in. Administrative agencies do this day-to-day work.

Most government agencies are created by Congress. Familiar examples are the Environmental Protection Agency (EPA), the Securities and Exchange Commission (SEC), and the Internal Revenue Service (IRS), whose feelings are hurt if it does not hear from you every April 15. Agencies have the power to create laws called *regulations*.

Treaties

The Constitution authorizes the President to make treaties with foreign nations. These must then be ratified by the United States Senate by a two-thirds vote. When they are ratified, they are as binding upon all citizens as any federal statute. In 1994, the Senate ratified the North American Free Trade Agreement (NAFTA) with Mexico and Canada. NAFTA was controversial then and remains so today—but it is the law of the land.

CLASSIFICATIONS

We have seen where law comes from. Now we need to classify the various types of laws. First, we will distinguish between criminal and civil law. Then, we will take a look at the intersection between law and morality.

Criminal and Civil Law

Criminal law

Criminal law prohibits certain behavior.

It is a crime to embezzle money from a bank, to steal a car, to sell cocaine. **Criminal law** concerns behavior so threatening that society outlaws it altogether. Most criminal laws are statutes, passed by Congress or a state legislature. The government itself prosecutes the wrongdoer, regardless of what the bank President or car owner wants. A district attorney, paid by the government, brings the case to court. The injured party, for example the owner of the stolen car, is not in charge of the case, although she may appear as a witness. The government will seek to punish the defendant with a prison sentence, a fine, or both. If there is a fine, the money goes to the state, not to the injured party.

Civil law

Civil law regulates the rights and duties between parties.

Civil law is different, and most of this book is about civil law. **The civil law regulates the rights and duties between parties.** Tracy agrees in writing to lease you a 30,000-square-foot store in her shopping mall. She now has a *legal duty* to make the space available. But then another tenant offers her more money, and she refuses to let you move in. Tracy has violated her duty, but she has not committed a crime. The government will not prosecute the case. It is up to you to file a civil lawsuit. Your case will be based on the common law of contract. You will also seek equitable relief, namely, an injunction ordering Tracy not to lease to anyone else. You should win the suit, and you will get your injunction and some money damages. But Tracy will not go to jail.

Some conduct involves both civil and criminal law. Suppose Tracy is so upset over losing the court case that she becomes drunk and causes a serious car accident. She has committed the crime of driving while intoxicated, and the state will prosecute. Tracy may be fined or imprisoned. She has also committed negligence, and the injured party will file a lawsuit against her, seeking money. We will again see civil and criminal law joined together in the *Pub Zone* case, later in the chapter.

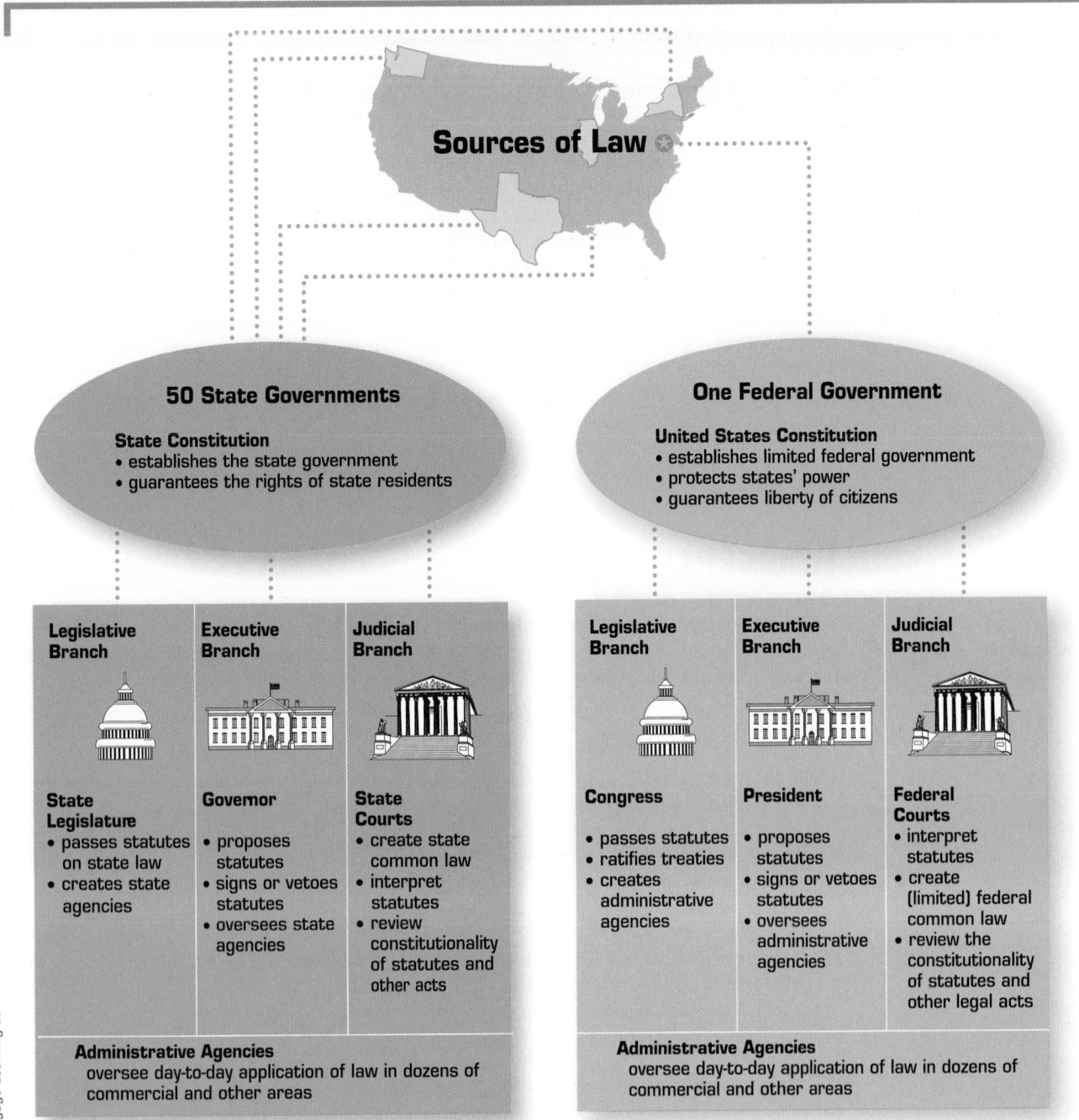

Federal Form of Government. Principles and rules of law come from many sources. The government in Washington creates and enforces law throughout the nation. But 50 state governments exercise great power in local affairs. And citizens enjoy constitutional protection from both state and federal government. The Founding Fathers wanted this balance of power and rights, but the overlapping authority creates legal complexity.

Law and Morality

Law is different from morality, yet the two are obviously linked. There are many instances when the law duplicates what all of us would regard as a moral position. It is negligent to drive too fast in a school zone, and few would dispute the moral value of seeking to limit harm to students. And the same holds with contract law: if the owner of land agrees in writing to sell property to a buyer at a stated price, both the buyer and the seller must go through with the deal, and the legal outcome matches our moral expectations.

On the other hand, we have had laws that we now clearly regard as immoral. At the turn of the century, a factory owner could typically fire a worker for any reason at all—including, for example, his religious or political views. It is immoral to fire a worker because she is Jewish—and today the law prohibits it.

Finally, there are legal issues where the morality is less clear. You are walking down a country lane and notice a three-year-old child playing with matches near a barn filled with hay. Are you obligated to intervene? No, says the law, though many think that is preposterous. (See Chapter 4, on common law, for more about this topic.) A company buys property and then discovers, buried under the ground, toxic waste that will cost $300,000 to clean up. The original owner has gone bankrupt. Should the new owner be forced to pay for the cleanup? If the new owner fails to pay for the job, who will? (See Chapter 27, on environmental law, for more discussion on this issue.)

Chapter 2 will further examine the bond between law and morality.

JURISPRUDENCE

Jurisprudence
The philosophy of law.

We have had a glimpse of legal history and a summary of the present-day sources of American law. But what *is* law? That question is the basis of a field known as **jurisprudence.** What is the real nature of law? Can there be such a thing as an "illegal" law?

Legal Positivism

Sovereign
The recognized political power, whom citizens obey.

This philosophy can be simply stated: law is what the sovereign says it is. The **sovereign** is the recognized political power whom citizens obey, so in the United States, both state and federal governments are sovereign. A legal positivist holds that whatever the sovereign declares to be the law *is* the law, whether it is right or wrong.

The primary criticism of legal positivism is that it seems to leave no room for questions of morality. A law permitting a factory owner to fire a worker because she is Catholic is surely different from a law prohibiting arson. Do citizens in a democracy have a duty to consider such differences? Consider the following example.

Most states allow citizens to pass laws directly at the ballot box, a process called voter referendum. California voters often do this, and during the 1990s, they passed one of the state's most controversial laws. Proposition 187 was designed to curb illegal immigration into the state by eliminating social spending for undocumented aliens. Citizens debated the measure fiercely but passed it by a large margin. One section of the new law forbade public schools from educating illegal immigrants. The law obligated a principal to inquire into the immigration status of all children enrolled in the school and to report undocumented students to immigration authorities. Several San Diego school principals rejected the new rules, stating that they would neither inquire into immigration status nor report undocumented aliens. Their statements produced a heated response. Some San Diego residents castigated the school officials as lawbreakers, claiming that:

- A school officer who knowingly disobeyed a law was setting a terrible example for students, who would assume they were free to do the same;

- The principals were advocating permanent residence and a free education for anyone able to evade our immigration laws; and

- The officials were scorning grass-roots democracy by disregarding a law passed by popular referendum.

Others applauded the principals' position, asserting that:

- The referendum's rules would transform school officials from educators into border police, forcing them to cross-examine young children and their parents;

- The new law was foolish because it punished innocent children for violations committed by their parents; and

- Our nation has long respected civil disobedience based on humanitarian ideals, and these officials were providing moral leadership to the whole community.

Ultimately, no one had to decide whether to obey Proposition 187. A federal court ruled that only Congress had the power to regulate immigration and that California's attempt was unconstitutional and void. The debate over immigration reform—and ethics—did not end, however. It continues to be a thorny issue.

Natural Law

St. Thomas Aquinas (1225–1274) answered the legal positivists even before they had spoken. In his *Summa Theologica*, he argued that an unjust law is no law at all and need not be obeyed. It is not enough that a sovereign makes a command. The law must have a moral basis.

Where do we find the moral basis that would justify a law? Aquinas says that "good is that which all things seek after." Therefore, the fundamental rule of all laws is that "good is to be done and promoted, and evil is to be avoided." This sounds appealing, but also vague. Exactly which laws promote good and which do not? Is it better to have a huge corporation dominate a market or many smaller companies competing? Did the huge company get that way by being better than its competitors? If Wal-Mart moves into a rural area, establishes a mammoth store, and sells inexpensive products, is that "good"? Yes, if you are a consumer who cares only about prices. No, if you are the owner of a Main Street store driven into bankruptcy. Maybe, if you are a resident who values small-town life but wants lower prices.

Legal Realism

Legal realists take a very different tack. They claim it does not matter what is written as law. What counts is who enforces that law and by what process. All of us are biased by issues such as income, education, family background, race, religion, and many other factors. These personal characteristics, they say, determine which contracts will be enforced and which ignored, why some criminals receive harsh sentences while others get off lightly, and so on.

Judge Jones hears a multimillion dollar lawsuit involving an airplane crash. Was the airline negligent? The law is the same everywhere, but legal realists say that Jones's background will determine the outcome. If she spent 20 years representing insurance companies, she will tend to favor the airline. If her law practice consisted of helping the "little guy," she will favor the plaintiff.

Other legal realists argue, more aggressively, that those in power use the machinery of the law to perpetuate their control. The outcome of a given case will be determined by the needs of those with money and political clout. A court puts "window dressing" on a decision, they say, so that society thinks there are principles behind the law. A problem with legal realism, however, is its denial that any lawmaker can overcome personal bias. Yet clearly some do act unselfishly.

SUMMARY OF JURISPRUDENCE

Legal Positivism	Law is what the sovereign says.
Natural Law	An unjust law is no law at all.
Legal Realism	Who enforces the law counts more than what is in writing.

© Cengage Learning 2014

No one school of jurisprudence is likely to seem perfect. We urge you to keep the different theories in mind as you read cases in the book. Ask yourself which school of thought is the best fit for you.

WORKING WITH THE BOOK'S FEATURES

In this section, we introduce a few of the book's features and discuss how you can use them effectively. We will start with *cases*.

Analyzing a Case

A law case is the decision a court has made in a civil lawsuit or criminal prosecution. Cases are the heart of the law and an important part of this book. Reading them effectively takes practice. This chapter's opening scenario is fictional, but the following real case involves a similar situation. Who can be held liable for the assault? Let's see.

KUEHN V. PUB ZONE

364 N. J. Super. 301, 835 A. 2d 692
Superior Court of New Jersey, Appellate Division, 2003

Facts: Maria Kerkoulas owned the Pub Zone bar. She knew that several motorcycle gangs frequented the tavern. From her own experience tending bar, and conversations with city police, she knew that some of the gangs, including the Pagans, were dangerous and prone to attack customers for no reason. Kerkoulas posted a sign prohibiting any motorcycle gangs from entering the bar while wearing "colors"; that is, insignia of their gangs. She believed that gangs without their colors were less prone to violence, and experience proved her right.

Rhino, Backdraft, and several other Pagans, all wearing colors, pushed their way past the tavern's bouncer and approached the bar. Although Kerkoulas saw their colors, she allowed them to stay for one drink. They later moved towards the back of the pub, and Kerkoulas believed they were departing. In fact, they followed a customer named Karl Kuehn to the men's room, where, without any provocation, they savagely beat him. Kuehn was knocked unconscious and suffered brain hemorrhaging, disc herniation, and numerous fractures of facial bones. He was forced to undergo various surgeries, including eye reconstruction.

Although the government prosecuted Rhino and Backdraft for their vicious assault, our case does not concern that prosecution. Kuehn sued the Pub Zone, and that is the case we will read. The jury awarded him $300,000 in damages. However, the trial court judge overruled the jury's verdict. He granted a judgment for the Pub Zone, meaning that the tavern owed nothing. The judge ruled that the pub's owner could not have foreseen the attack on Kuehn, and had no duty to protect him from an outlaw motorcycle gang. Kuehn appealed, and the appeals court's decision follows:

Issue: *Did the Pub Zone have a duty to protect Kuehn from the Pagans' attack?*

Excerpts from Judge Payne's Decision: Whether a duty exists depends upon an evaluation of a number of factors including the nature of the underlying risk of harm, that is, its foreseeability and severity, the opportunity and ability to exercise care to prevent the harm, the comparative interests of and the relationships between or among the parties, and, ultimately, based on considerations of public policy and fairness, the societal interest in the proposed solution.

Since the possessor [of a business] is not an insurer of the visitor's safety, he is ordinarily under no duty to exercise any care until he knows or has reason to know that the acts of the third person are occurring, or are about to occur. He may, however, know or have reason to know, from past experience, that there is a likelihood of conduct on the part of third persons in general which is likely to endanger the safety of the visitor, even though he has no reason to expect it on the part of any particular individual.

We find the totality of the circumstances presented in this case give rise to a duty on the part of the Pub Zone to have taken reasonable precautions against the danger posed by the Pagans as a group. In this case, there was no reason to suspect any particular Pagan of violent conduct. However, the gang was collectively known to Kerkoulas to engage in random violence. Thus, Kerkoulas had knowledge as the result of past experience and from other sources that there was a likelihood of conduct on the part of third persons in general that was likely to endanger the safety of a patron at some unspecified future time. A duty to take precautions against the endangering conduct thus arose.

We do not regard our recognition of a duty in this case to give rise to either strict or absolute liability on the part of the Pub Zone. To fulfill its duty in this context, the Pub Zone was merely required to employ "reasonable" safety precautions. It already had in place a prohibition against bikers who were wearing their colors, and that prohibition, together with the practice of calling the police when a breach occurred, had been effective in greatly diminishing the occurrence of biker incidents on the premises. The evidence establishes that the prohibition was not enforced on the night at issue, that three Pagans were permitted entry while wearing their colors, and the police were not called. Once entry was achieved, the Pub Zone remained under a duty to exercise reasonable precautions against an attack.

The jury's verdict must therefore be reinstated.

Analysis

Let's take it from the top. The case is called *Kuehn v. Pub Zone*. Karl Kuehn is the **plaintiff**, the person who is suing. The Pub Zone is being sued, and is called the **defendant**. In this example, the plaintiff's name happens to appear first, but that is not always true. When a defendant loses a trial and files an appeal, *some* courts reverse the names of the parties.

The next line gives the legal citation, which indicates where to find the case in a law library. We explain in the footnote how to locate a book if you plan to do research. [10]

Plaintiff
The party who is suing.

Defendant
The party being sued.

---

[10]If you want to do legal research, you need to know where to find particular legal decisions. A case citation guides you to the correct volume(s). The full citation of our case is *Kuehn v. Pub Zone*, 364 N. J. Super. 301, 835 A. 2d 692. The string of numbers identifies two different books in which you can find the full text of this decision. The first citation is to "N. J. Super," which means the official court reporter of the state of New Jersey. New Jersey, like most states, reports its law cases in a series of numbered volumes. This case appears in volume 364 of the New Jersey Superior Court reporters. If you go to a law library and find that book, you can then turn to page 301 and—*voila!*—you have the case. The decision is also reported in another set of volumes, called the regional reporters. This series of law reports is grouped by geographic region. New Jersey is included in the Atlantic region, so our case appears in reporters dedicated to that region. The "A" stands for Atlantic. After a series of reporters reaches volume 999, a second set begins. Our case appears in volume 835 of the second set of the Atlantic reporters ("A. 2d"), at page 692. In addition, most cases are now available online, and your professor or librarian can show you how to find them electronically.

The *Facts* section provides a background to the lawsuit, written by the authors of this text. The court's own explanation of the facts is often many pages long, and may involve complex matters irrelevant to the subject covered in this book, so we relate only what is necessary. This section will usually include some mention of what happened at the trial court. Lawsuits always begin in a trial court. The losing party often appeals to a court of appeals, and it is usually an appeals court decision that we are reading. The trial judge ruled in favor of Pub Zone, but later, in the decision we are reading, Kuehn wins.

The *Issue* section is very important. It tells you what the court had to decide—and also why you are reading the case. In giving its decision, a court may digress. If you keep in mind the issue and relate the court's discussion to it, you will not get lost.

Excerpts from Judge Payne's Decision begins the court's discussion. This is called the *holding*, meaning a statement of who wins and who loses. The holding also includes the court's *rationale*, which is the reasoning behind the decision.

The holding that we provide is an edited version of the court's own language. Some judges write clear, forceful prose; others do not. Either way, their words give you an authentic feel for how judges think and rule, so we bring it to you in the original. Occasionally we use brackets [ ] to substitute our language for that of the court, either to condense or to clarify. Notice the brackets in the second paragraph of the Pub Zone decision. Judge Payne explains the point at much greater length, so we have condensed some of his writing into the phrase "of a business."

We omit a great deal. A court's opinion may be 3 pages, or it may be 75. We do not use ellipses (…) to indicate these deletions, because there is more taken out than kept in, and we want the text to be clean. When a court quotes an earlier decision verbatim but clearly adopts those words as its own, we generally delete the quotation marks, as well as the citation to the earlier case. If you are curious about the full holding, you can always look it up.

Let us look at a few of Judge Payne's points. The holding begins with a discussion of *duty*. The court explains that whether one person (or bar) owes a duty to protect another depends upon several factors, including whether the harm could be foreseen, how serious the injury could be, and whether there was an opportunity to prevent it.

Judge Payne then points out that the owner of a business is not an insurer of a visitor's safety. Typically, the owner has a duty to a visitor *only* if he has a reason to know that some harm is likely to occur. How would a merchant know that? Based on the character of the business, suggests the judge, or the owner's experience with particular people.

The judge then applies this general rule to the facts of this case. He concludes that the Pub Zone did in fact have a duty to protect Kuehn from the Pagans' attack. Based on Kerkoulas's experience, and warnings received from the police, she knew that the gang was dangerous and should have foreseen that admitting them in their "colors" greatly increased the chance of an attack.

Next, the court points out that it is not requiring the Pub Zone to *guarantee* everyone's safety. The bar was merely obligated to do a *reasonable* job. The prohibition on colors was a good idea, and calling the police had also proven effective. The problem of course was that in this case, Kerkoulas ignored her own rule about gang insignia and failed to call the police.

Based on all the evidence, the jury's finding of liability was reasonable, and its verdict must be reinstated. In other words, Kuehn, who lost at the trial, wins on appeal. What the court has done is to *reverse* the lower court's decision, meaning to turn the loser into the winner. In other cases, we will see an appellate court *remand* the case, meaning to send it back down to the lower court for additional steps. Or the appellate judges could *affirm* the lower court's decision, meaning to leave it unchanged.

Devil's Advocate

Each chapter has several cases. After some of them, a "Devil's Advocate" feature offers you a contrasting view of the legal issue. This is not part of the case but is instead a suggestion of another perspective on the problem discussed. The authors take no position for or against the court's decision, but merely want you to consider an alternate view, and decide which analysis of the law makes more sense to you—that of the court or the Devil's Advocate. Is the following view persuasive?

Devil's Advocate A court should not force small businesses to guarantee their customers' safety. Two or three violent men, whether motorcycle gang members or frustrated professors, could enter a grocery store or clothing retailer at any time and mindlessly attack innocent visitors. Random attacks are just that—random, unforeseeable. No merchant should be required to anticipate them. Send the criminals to jail, but do not place the burden on honest businesspeople.

Exam Strategy

This feature gives you practice analyzing cases the way lawyers do—and the way *you* must on tests. Law exams are different from most others because you must determine the issue from the facts provided. Too frequently, students faced with a law exam forget that the questions relate to the issues in the text and those discussed in class. Understandably, students new to law may focus on the wrong information in the problem or rely on material learned elsewhere. Exam Strategies teach you to figure out exactly what issue is at stake, and then analyze it in a logical, consistent manner. Here is an example, relating to the element of "duty," which the court discussed in the Pub Zone case.

EXAM Strategy

The Big Red Traveling (BRT) Carnival is in town. Tony arrives at 8:00 p.m., parks in the lot—and is robbed at gunpoint by a man who beats him and escapes with his money. There are several police officers on the carnival grounds, but no officer is in the parking lot at the time of the robbery. Tony sues, claiming that brighter lighting and more police in the lot would have prevented the robbery. There has never before been any violent crime—robbery, beating, or otherwise—at any BRT carnival. BRT claims it had no duty to protect Tony from this harm. Who is likely to win?

Strategy: Begin by isolating the legal issue. What are the parties disputing? They are debating whether BRT had a duty to protect Tony from an armed robbery, committed by a stranger. Now ask yourself: How do courts decide whether a business has a duty to prevent this kind of harm? The Pub Zone case provides our answer. A business owner is not an ensurer of the visitor's safety. The owner generally has no duty to protect a customer from the criminal act of a third party, unless the owner knows the harm is occurring or could foresee it is about to happen. (In the Pub Zone case, the business owner knew of the gang's violent history, and could have foreseen the assault.) Now apply that rule to the facts of this case.

Result: There has never been a violent attack of any kind at a BRT carnival. BRT cannot foresee this robbery, and has no duty to protect against it. The carnival wins.

You Be the Judge

Many cases involve difficult decisions for juries and judges. Often both parties have legitimate, opposing arguments. Most chapters in this book will have a feature called "You Be the Judge," in which we present the facts of a case but not the court's holding.

We offer you two opposing arguments based on the kinds of claims the lawyers made in court. We leave it up to you to debate and decide which position is stronger or to add your own arguments to those given.

The following case is another negligence lawsuit, with issues that overlap those of the Pub Zone case. This time the court confronts a fight that resulted in a death. The victim's distraught family sued the owner of a bar, claiming that one of his employees was partly responsible for the death. Once again, the defendant asked the court to dismiss the case, claiming that he owed no duty to protect the victim—the same argument made by the Pub Zone.

But there is a difference here—this time the defendant owned the bar across the street, not the one where the fight took place. Could he be held legally responsible for the death? You be the judge.

You be the Judge

SOLDANO V. O'DANIELS

141 Cal. App. 3d 443
Court of Appeal of California,
5th Appellate District, 1983

Facts: In the days before cell phones, a fight broke out at Happy Jack's Saloon. A good Samaritan ran across the street to the Circle Inn. He asked the bartender at the Circle Inn to let him use the telephone to call the police, but he refused.

Back at Happy Jack's Saloon, the fight escalated, and a man shot and killed Soldano's father. Soldano sued the owner of the Circle Inn for negligence. He argued that the bartender violated a legal duty when he refused to hand over the inn's telephone and that, as the employer of the bartender, O'Daniels was partially liable for Soldano's father's death.

The lower court dismissed the case, citing the principle that generally a person does not have a legal responsibility to help another unless he created the dangerous situation in the first place. Soldano appealed.

You Be the Judge: *Did the bartender have a duty to allow the use of the Circle Inn's telephone?*

Argument for the Defendant: Your honors, my client did not act wrongfully. He did nothing to create the danger. The fight was not even on his property. We sympathize with the plaintiff, but it is the shooter, and perhaps the bar where the fight took place, that are responsible for his father's death. Our client was not involved. Liability can be stretched only so far.

The court would place a great burden on the citizens of California by going against precedent. The Circle Inn is Mr. O'Daniel's private property. If the court imposes potential liability on him in this case, would citizens be forced to open the doors of their homes whenever a

stranger claims that there is an emergency? Criminals would delight in their newfound ability to gain access to businesses and residences by simply demanding to use a phone to "call the police."

The law has developed sensibly. People are left to decide for themselves whether to help in a dangerous situation. They are not legally required to place themselves in harm's way.

Argument for the Plaintiff: Your honors, the Circle Inn's bartender had both a moral and a legal duty to allow the use of his establishment's telephone. The Circle Inn may be privately owned, but it is a business and is open to the public. Anyone in the world is invited to stop by and order a drink or a meal. The good Samaritan had every right to be there.

We do not argue that the bartender had an obligation to break up the fight or endanger himself in any way. We simply argue he had a responsibility to stand aside and allow a free call on his restaurant's telephone. Any "burden" on him or on the Circle Inn was incredibly slight. The potential benefits were enormous. The trial court made a mistake in concluding that a person *never* has a duty to help another. Such an interpretation makes for poor public policy.

There is no need to radically change the common law. Residences can be excluded from this ruling. People need not be required to allow telephone-seeking strangers into their homes. This court can simply determine that businesses have a legal duty to allow the placement of emergency calls during normal business hours.

Chapter Conclusion

We depend upon the law to give us a stable nation and economy, a fair society, a safe place to live and work. These worthy goals have occupied ancient kings and twenty-first-century lawmakers alike. But while law is a vital tool for crafting the society we want, there are no easy answers about how to create it. In a democracy, we all participate in the crafting. Legal rules control us, yet *we* create *them*. A working knowledge of the law can help build a successful career—and a solid democracy.

EXAM REVIEW

1. **THE FEDERAL SYSTEM** Our federal system of government means that law comes from a national government in Washington, D.C., and from 50 state governments. (p. 11)

2. **LEGAL HISTORY** The history of law foreshadows many current legal issues, including mediation, partnership liability, the jury system, the role of witnesses, the special value placed on land, and the idea of precedent. (pp. 5–7)

3. **PRIMARY SOURCES OF LAW** The primary sources of contemporary law are:

   - United States Constitution and state constitutions;
   - Statutes, which are drafted by legislatures;
   - Common law, which is the body of cases decided by judges, as they follow earlier cases, known as precedent;
   - Court orders, which place obligations on specific people or companies;
   - Administrative law, the rules and decisions made by federal and state administrative agencies; and
   - Treaties, agreements between the United States and foreign nations. (pp. 7–10)

EXAM Strategy

Question: The stock market crash of 1929 and the Great Depression that followed were caused in part because so many investors blindly put their money into stocks they knew nothing about. During the 1920s, it was often impossible for an investor to find out what a corporation was planning to do with its money, who was running the corporation, and many other vital things. Congress responded by passing the Securities Act of 1933, which required a corporation to divulge more information about itself before it could seek money for a new stock issue. What kind of law did Congress create?

Strategy: What is the question seeking? The question asks you which *type* of law Congress created when it passed the 1933 Securities Act. What are the primary kinds of law? Administrative law consists of rules passed by agencies. Congress is not a federal agency. Common law is the body of cases decided by judges. Congress is not a judge. Statutes are laws passed by legislatures. Congress is a legislature. (See the "Result" at the end of this section.)

4. **CRIMINAL LAW** Criminal law concerns behavior so threatening to society that it is outlawed altogether. Civil law deals with duties and disputes between parties, not with outlawed behavior. (p. 10)

EXAM Strategy

Question: Bill and Diane are hiking in the woods. Diane walks down a hill to fetch fresh water. Bill meets a stranger, who introduces herself as Katrina. Bill sells a kilo of cocaine to Katrina, who then flashes a badge and mentions how much she enjoys her job at the Drug Enforcement Agency. Diane, heading back to camp with the water, meets Freddy, a motorist whose car has overheated. Freddy is late for a meeting where he expects to make a $30 million profit; he's desperate for water for his car. He promises to pay Diane $500 tomorrow if she will give him the pail of water, which she does. The next day, Bill is in jail and Freddy refuses to pay for Diane's water. Explain the criminal law/civil law distinction and what it means to Bill and Diane. Who will do what to whom, with what results?

Strategy: You are asked to distinguish between criminal and civil law. What is the difference? The criminal law concerns behavior that threatens society and is therefore outlawed. The government prosecutes the defendant. Civil law deals with the rights and duties between parties. One party files a suit against the other. Apply those different standards to these facts. (See the "Result" at the end of this section.)

5. **JURISPRUDENCE** Jurisprudence is concerned with the basic nature of law. Three theories of jurisprudence are

- Legal positivism: The law is what the sovereign says it is.

- Natural law: An unjust law is no law at all.

- Legal realism: Who enforces the law is more important than what the law says. (pp. 12–14)

3. Result: The Securities Act of 1933 is a statute.

4. Result: The government will prosecute Bill for dealing in drugs. If convicted, he will go to prison. The government will take no interest in Diane's dispute. However, if she chooses, she may sue Freddy for $500, the amount he promised her for the water. In that civil lawsuit, a court will decide whether Freddy must pay what he promised; however, even if Freddy loses, he will not go to jail.

MULTIPLE-CHOICE QUESTIONS

1. The United States Constitution is among the finest legal accomplishments in the history of the world. Which of the following influenced Ben Franklin, Thomas Jefferson, and the rest of the Founding Fathers?
   (a) English common-law principles
   (b) The Iroquois's system of federalism
   (c) Both A and B
   (d) None of the above

2. Which of the following parts of the modern legal system are "borrowed" from medieval England?
   (a) Jury trials
   (b) Special rules for selling land
   (c) Following precedent
   (d) All of the above

3. Union organizers at a hospital wanted to distribute leaflets to potential union members, but hospital rules prohibited leafleting in areas of patient care, hallways, cafeterias, and any areas open to the public. The National Labor Relations Board, a government agency, ruled that these restrictions violated the law and ordered the hospital to permit the activities in the cafeteria and coffee shop. What kind of law was it creating?
   (a) A statute
   (b) Common law
   (c) A constitutional amendment
   (d) Administrative regulation

4. If the Congress creates a new statute with the President's support, it must pass the idea by a _____ majority vote in the House and the Senate. If the President vetoes a proposed statute and the Congress wishes to pass it without his support, the idea must pass by a _____ majority vote in the House and Senate.
   (a) simple; simple
   (b) simple; two-thirds
   (c) simple; three-fourths
   (d) two-thirds; three-fourths

5. What part of the Constitution addresses the most basic liberties?
   (a) Article I
   (b) Article II
   (c) Article III
   (d) Amendments

ESSAY QUESTIONS

1. Burglar Bob breaks into Vince Victim's house. Bob steals a flat-screen television and laptop and does a significant amount of damage to the property before he leaves. Fortunately, Vince has a state-of-the-art security system. It captures excellent images of Bob, who is soon caught by police.

   Assume that two legal actions follow, one civil and one criminal. Who will be responsible for bringing the civil case? What will be the outcome if the jury believes that Bob burgled Vince's house? Who will be responsible for bringing the criminal case? What will be the outcome if the jury believes that Bob burgled Vince's house?

2. As "The Oculist's Case" indicates, the medical profession has faced a large number of lawsuits for centuries. In Texas, a law provides that, so long as a doctor was not reckless and did not intentionally harm a patient, recovery for "pain and suffering" is limited to $750,000. In many other states, no such limit exists. If a patient will suffer a lifetime of pain after a botched operation, for example, he might recover millions in compensation. Which rule seems more sensible to you – the "Texas" rule or the alternative?

3. **YOU BE THE JUDGE WRITING PROBLEM** Should trials be televised? Here are a few arguments on both sides of the issue. You be the judge. **Arguments against live television coverage:** We have tried this experiment and it has failed. Trials fall into two categories: those that create great public interest and those that do not. No one watches dull trials, so we do not need to broadcast them. The few that are interesting have all become circuses. Judges and lawyers have shown that they cannot resist the temptation to play to the camera. Trials are supposed to be about justice, not entertainment. If a citizen seriously wants to follow a case, she can do it by reading the daily newspaper. **Arguments for live television coverage:** It is true that some televised trials have been unseemly affairs, but that is the fault of the presiding judges, not the media. Indeed, one of the virtues of television coverage is that millions of people now understand that we have a lot of incompetent people running our courtrooms. The proper response is to train judges to run a tight trial by prohibiting grandstanding by lawyers. Access to accurate information is the foundation on which a democracy is built, and we must not eliminate a source of valuable data just because some judges are ill-trained or otherwise incompetent.

4. Leslie Bergh and his two brothers, Milton and Raymond, formed a partnership to help build a fancy saloon and dance hall in Evanston, Wyoming. Later, Leslie met with his friend and drinking buddy, John Mills, and tricked Mills into investing in the saloon. Leslie did not tell Mills that no one else was investing cash or that the entire enterprise was already bankrupt. Mills mortgaged his home, invested $150,000 in the saloon—and lost every penny of it. Mills sued all three partners for fraud. Milton and Raymond defended on the grounds that they did not commit the fraud; only Leslie did. The defendants lost. Was that fair? By holding them liable, what general idea did the court rely on? What Anglo-Saxon legal custom did the ruling resemble?

5. *Kuehn v. Pub Zone* and *Soldano v. O'Daniels* both involve attacks in a bar. Should they have the same result? If so, in which way—in favor of the injured plaintiffs or owner-defendants? If not, why should they have different outcomes? What are the key facts that lead you to believe as you do?

DISCUSSION QUESTIONS

1. Do you believe that there are too many lawsuits in the United States? If so, do you place more blame for the problem on lawyers or on individuals who go to court? Is there anything that would help the problem, or will we always have large numbers of lawsuits?

2. In the 1980s, the Supreme Court ruled that it is legal for protesters to burn the American flag. This activity counts as free speech under the Constitution. If the Court hears a new flag-burning case in this decade, should it consider changing its ruling, or should it follow precedent? Is following past precedent something that seems sensible to you: always, usually, sometimes, rarely, or never?

3. When should a business be held legally responsible for customer safety? Consider the following statements, and consider the degree to which you agree or disagree:

   - A business should keep customers safe from its own employees.

   - A business should keep customers safe from other customers.

   - A business should keep customers safe from themselves. (Example: an intoxicated customer who can no longer walk straight.)

   - A business should keep people outside its own establishment safe if it is reasonable to do so.

4. In his most famous novel, *The Red and the Black*, the French author Stendhal (1783–1842) wrote: "There is no such thing as 'natural law': this expression is nothing but old nonsense. Prior to laws, what is natural is only the strength of the lion, or the need of the creature suffering from hunger or cold, in short, need." What do you think? Does legal positivism or legal realism seem more sensible to you?

5. At the time of this writing, voters are particularly disgruntled. A good many people seem to be disgusted with government. For this question, we intentionally avoid distinguishing between Democrats and Republicans, and we intentionally do not name any particular President. Consider the following statements, and consider the degree to which you agree or disagree:

   - I believe that members of Congress usually try to do the right thing for America.

   - I believe that Presidents usually try to do the right thing for America.

   - I believe that Supreme Court justices usually try to do the right thing for America.

BUSINESS ETHICS AND SOCIAL RESPONSIBILITY

Three people talk about their temptation to lie:

1. During college, I used drugs—some cocaine, but mostly prescription painkillers. Things got pretty bad. At one point, I would wait outside emergency rooms hoping to buy drugs from people who were leaving. But that was three years ago. I went into rehab and have been clean ever since. I don't even drink. I've applied for a job, but the application asks if I have ever used drugs illegally. I am afraid that if I tell the truth, I will never get a job. What should I say on the application?

> **I am afraid that if I tell the truth, I will never get a job. What should I say on the application?**

2. I process payroll at my company, so I know how much everyone earns, including the top executives. This could make for some good gossip, but I have kept everything completely secret. I just found out, however, that my boss knew that it is against company policy for me to do payroll for C-level employees. Yesterday, the CEO went to my boss to confirm that *she*, my boss, was personally doing the processing for the top management. My boss lied to the CEO and said that she was. Then she begged me not to tell the truth if the CEO checked with me. I just got a message that he wants to see me. What do I say if he asks about the payroll?

3. I am in charge of a project to redesign a software program that is one of our company's top products. Most of our engineers are French, and I studied the language in college. It is fun for me to go out with the team in the evenings, and I have become pretty good friends with them. Recently, my boss told me that once the project is finished, all the engineers will be laid off. He joked about how "the French will be fried when they find out." Since they are not U.S. citizens, they will have to leave the country

unless they get jobs right away. If I tell them the boss's plan, they will start looking for other jobs and my project could be in the tank. That would be really bad for the company, not to mention a disaster for me. One of the engineers wants to make an offer on a house, so he asked me about his future at the company. What do I say?

INTRODUCTION

This text, for the most part, covers legal ideas. The law dictates how a person *must* behave. This chapter examines **ethics,** or how people *should* behave. It will examine ethical dilemmas that commonly arise in workplaces, and present tools for making decisions when the law does not require or prohibit any particular choice.

Ethics
How people ought to act.

If a person is intent on lying, cheating, and stealing his way through a career, then he is unlikely to be dissuaded by anything in this or any other course. But for the large majority of people who want to do the right thing, it will be useful to study new ways of approaching difficult problems.

Ethics lies largely beyond the realm of law, so we present a unique feature in this chapter. You will notice that it contains "Ethics Cases" and discussion questions in place of legal cases. It is our hope that these scenarios will generate lively classroom debates on right and wrong. It is important for future leaders to hear a variety of points of view. In your career, you will work with and manage diverse groups of people, so it is good to have insight into how different people perceive ethical issues.

We also hope that hearing these different points of view will help you develop your own Life Principles. These principles are the rules by which you live your life. For example, the opening scenario dealt with lying. It is easy to say, "I will always tell the truth," but many people believe that it is ethically acceptable to lie in certain situations. For example, a large man holding a big knife demands, "Where's Jamie?" You know where Jamie is, but you might be tempted to send the murderer off in the opposite direction and then call the police. At the other end of the spectrum, you could decide that you will lie whenever it seems to be in your best interest. The problem with this approach is that you will soon find that no one trusts you. Where in between these two extremes do your Life Principles fit? Something to think about throughout this chapter (and throughout your life as well). If you develop these Life Principles now, you will be prepared when facing ethical dilemmas in the future.

In this chapter, we will present six basic issues:

1. Why bother to act ethically at all?[1]

2. What are the most important considerations when making an ethical decision? What standards should you use?

3. What traps might interfere with your ability to make the right decision?

4. Should you apply your personal ethics in the workplace, or should you have different ethical values at home and at work?

5. Is the primary role of corporations to make money, or do they have responsibilities to workers, communities, customers, and other "stakeholders"?

6. When, if ever, is lying acceptable?

---

[1]Some of the ethics cases and discussion questions featured in this chapter are adapted from *Applied Business Ethics* by Dean A. Bredeson, Cengage Learning, 2011.

WHY BOTHER TO ACT ETHICALLY AT ALL?

Ethical decision making generates a range of benefits for employees, companies, and society. Although ethical business practices are not required by law, the remainder of this chapter makes the case that they are sound.

Society as a Whole Benefits from Ethical Behavior

John Akers, the former chairman of IBM, argues that without ethical behavior, a society cannot be economically competitive. He puts it this way:

> Ethics and competitiveness are inseparable. We compete as a society. No society anywhere will compete very long or successfully with people stabbing each other in the back; with people trying to steal from each other; with everything requiring notarized confirmation because you can't trust the other fellow; with every little squabble ending in litigation; and with government writing reams of regulatory legislation, tying business hand and foot to keep it honest. That is a recipe not only for headaches in running a company, but for a nation to become wasteful, inefficient, and noncompetitive. There is no escaping this fact: the greater the measure of mutual trust and confidence in the ethics of a society, the greater its economic strength.[2]

People Feel Better When They Behave Ethically

Every businessperson has many opportunities to be dishonest. Consider how one person felt when he resisted temptation:

> Occasionally a customer forgot to send a bill for materials shipped to us for processing.... It would have been so easy to rationalize remaining silent. After all, didn't they deserve to lose because of their inefficiency? However, upon instructing our staff to inform the parties of their errors, I found them eager to do so. They were actually bursting with pride....Our honesty was beneficial in subtle ways. The "inefficient" customer remained loyal for years....[O]ur highly moral policy had a marvelously beneficial effect on our employees. Through the years, many an employee visited my office to let me know that they liked working for a "straight" company.[3]

Profitability is generally not what motivates managers to care about ethics. Managers want to feel good about themselves and the decisions they have made; they want to sleep at night. Their decisions—to lay off employees, install safety devices in cars, burn a cleaner fuel—affect people's lives. When two researchers asked businesspeople why they cared about ethics, the answers had little to do with profitability:

> The businesspeople we interviewed set great store on the regard of their family, friends, and the community at large. They valued their reputations, not for some nebulous financial gain but because they took pride in their good names.[4]

---

[2]David Grier, "Confronting Ethical Dilemmas," unpublished manuscript of remarks at the Royal Bank of Canada, Sept. 19, 1989.

[3]Hugh Aaron, "Doing the Right Thing in Business," June 21, 1993, *The Wall Street Journal by News Corporation; Dow Jones & Co.* Copyright 1993. Reproduced with permission of DOW JONES & COMPANY, INC. in the format Republish in a textbook via Copyright Clearance Center.

[4]Amar Bhide and Howard H. Stevenson, "Why Be Honest If Honesty Doesn't Pay?" *Harvard Business Review*, Sept.–Oct. 1990, pp. 121–29, at 127.

Unethical Behavior Can Be Very Costly

Unethical behavior is a risky business strategy—it may lead to disaster. An engaged couple made a reservation, and put down a $1,500 deposit, to hold their wedding reception at a New Hampshire restaurant. Tragically, the bride died four months before the wedding. Invoking the terms of the contract, the restaurant owner refused to return the couple's deposit. In a letter to the groom, he admitted, "Morally, I would of course agree that the deposit should be returned." When newspapers reported this story, customers deserted the restaurant and it was forced into bankruptcy—over a $1,500 disagreement.[5] Unethical behavior does not always damage a business, but it certainly has the potential of destroying a company overnight. So why take the risk?

Even if unethical behavior does not devastate a business, it can cause other, subtler damage. In one survey, a majority of those questioned said that they had witnessed unethical behavior in their workplace and that this behavior had reduced productivity, job stability, and profits. Unethical behavior in an organization creates a cynical, resentful, and unproductive workforce.

Although there is no *guarantee* that ethical behavior pays in the short or long run, there is evidence that the ethical company is more *likely* to win financially. Ethical companies tend to have a better reputation, more creative employees, and higher returns than those that engage in wrongdoing.[6]

But if we decide that we want to behave ethically, how do we know what ethical behavior is?

THEORIES OF ETHICS

When making ethical decisions, people sometimes focus on the reason for the decision—they want to do what is right. Thus, if they think it is wrong to lie, then they will tell the truth no matter what the consequence. Other times, people think about the outcome of their actions. They will do whatever it takes to achieve the right result, no matter what. This choice—between doing right and getting the right result—has been the subject of much philosophical debate.

Utilitarian Ethics

In 1863, Englishman John Stuart Mill wrote *Utilitarianism*. He was not the first person to write on utilitarian ethics, but his book has best stood the test of time. To Mill, a correct decision was one that tended to maximize overall happiness and minimize overall pain, thereby producing the greatest net benefit. As he put it, his goal was to produce the greatest good for the greatest number of people. Risk management and cost-benefit analyses are examples of utilitarian business practices.

Suppose that an automobile manufacturer could add a device to its cars that would reduce air pollution. As a result, the incidence of strokes and lung cancer would decline dramatically, saving society hundreds of millions of dollars over the life of the cars. But by charging a higher price to cover the cost of the device, the company would sell fewer cars and shareholders will earn lower returns, at a total cost of tens of millions of dollars. A utilitarian likely would argue that, despite the decline in profits, the company should install the device.

Or, to take the example at the beginning of the chapter about the recovered drug addict, what harm will be caused if he tells the truth? He will be less likely to get that job, or

---

[5]John Milne, "N.H. Restaurant Goes Bankrupt in Wake of Wedding Refund Flap," *Boston Globe*, Sept. 9, 1994, p. 25.

[6]For sources, see "Ethics: A Basic Framework," Harvard Business School case 9-307-059.

maybe any job—a large and immediate harm. What if he lies? He might argue that no harm would result because he is now clean, and his past drug addiction will not have an adverse impact on his new employer.

The best Hollywood line that reflects utilitarian thinking comes from *Star Trek II: The Wrath of Khan*. Toward the end, Mr. Spock saves the *Enterprise*, but in so doing, he takes a lethal dose of radiation. Captain Kirk cradles the dying Spock and says, "Spock! WHY?" Spock replies, "Because Captain, the needs of the many outweigh the needs of the few…or one."

There are many critics of utilitarian thought. Some argue that it is very difficult to *measure* utility accurately, at least not in the way that one would measure distance or the passage of time. The car company does not really know how many lives will be saved or how much its profits might decline if the device is installed. It is also difficult to *predict* benefit and harm accurately. The recovered drug addict may relapse, or his employer may find out about his lie.

Other critics argue that because utilitarians let the ends justify the means, they can justify bad behavior so long as it generates good in the end. Suppose that wealthy old Ebenezer has several chronic illnesses that cause him great suffering and prevent him from doing any of the activities that once gave meaning to his life. Also, he is such a nasty piece of work that everyone who knows him hates him. If he were to die, all his heirs would benefit tremendously from the money that they inherited from him, including a disabled grandchild who then could afford medical care that would improve his life dramatically. Would it be ethical to kill Ebenezer?

Others argue that utilitarians err in equating pleasure with ethical behavior and pain with wrongful behavior. Caring for an elderly relative with Alzheimer's disease, for example, might generate little pleasure and much pain, but it still would be a noble endeavor.

Deontological Ethics

Deontological

From the Greek word for *obligatory*. The duty to do the right thing, regardless of the result.

Kant's categorical imperative

An act is only ethical if it would be acceptable for everyone to do the same thing.

The word **deontological** comes from the Greek word for *obligatory*. Proponents of deontological ethics believe that utilitarians have it all wrong and that the *results* of a decision are not as important as the *reason* for which it is made. To a deontological thinker, the ends do not justify the means. Rather, it is important to do the right thing, no matter the result.

The best-known proponent of the deontological model was the eighteenth-century German philosopher Immanuel Kant. He believed in what he called the **categorical imperative**. He argued that you should not do something unless you would be willing to have everyone else do it, too. Applying this idea, he concluded that one should always tell the truth because if *everyone* lied, the world would become an irrational and awful place. In all three of the lying examples at the beginning of the chapter, Kant would argue that the truth should be told, no matter the outcome.

Kant also believed that human beings possess a unique dignity and that no decision that treats people as commodities can be considered just, even if the decision tends to maximize overall happiness, or profit, or any other quantifiable measure. Thus, Kant would argue against killing Ebenezer, no matter how unpleasant the man was.

Although not all followers of deontological ethics agree with Kant's specific ideas, most agree that utilitarianism is lacking, and that winning in the end does not automatically make a decision right. Ethical decisions, they argue, are those made for good and moral reasons in the first place, regardless of the outcome.

Rawlsian Justice

How did you manage to get into college or graduate school? Presumably due to some combination of talent, hard work, and support from family and friends. Imagine that you had been born into different circumstances—say, a country where the literacy rate is only 25 percent and almost all of the population lives in desperate poverty. Would you be reading this book now? Most likely not. People are born with wildly different talents into very different circumstances, all of which dramatically affect their outcomes.

John Rawls (1921–2002) was an American philosopher who suggested that we consider what rules for society we would propose if there were a **"veil of ignorance."** In other words, suppose that there is going to be a new lottery tomorrow that would determine all our attributes. We could be a winner, ending up a hugely talented, healthy person in a loving family, or we could be the most miserable person on the face of the earth. What type of society would we set up now, if we did not know whether we would be one of life's winners or losers? First, we would design a society that provided basic freedoms to everyone—of speech and religion, for example. Second, we would apply the **difference principle.** We would *not* plan a system in which everyone received an equal income because society is better off if people have an incentive to work hard. But we would reward the type of work that provides the most benefit to the community as a whole. We might decide, for example, to pay doctors more than baseball players. But maybe not *all* doctors—perhaps just the ones who research cancer cures or provide care for the poor, and not cosmetic surgeons operating on the affluent. Rawls argues that everyone should have the opportunity to earn great wealth so long as the tax system provides enough revenue to provide decent health, education, and welfare for all. In thinking about ethical decisions, it is worth remembering that most of us have been winners in life's lottery and that the unlucky are deserving of our compassion.

In the following example, both sides end up better off, but is the proposed agreement ethically sound?

Veil of ignorance

We set up a societal system without knowing whether we would personally be one of its winners or losers.

Difference principle

Rawls' suggestion that society should reward behavior that provides the most benefit to the community as a whole.

ETHICS CASE: HIV TREATMENT

Alpha Company has developed a new drug that is an effective treatment for HIV, the virus that causes AIDS. It is not a cure, but it postpones the onset of AIDS indefinitely.

Before this breakthrough, HIV-positive patients were treated with a "cocktail" of medications. Although effective, the combination of drugs required patients to take several pills at a time several times per day. Alpha Company's drug is a single pill that must be taken only twice per day. Because it is more convenient, patients would be less likely to miss doses.

Alpha spent tens of millions of dollars developing the drug, but now that is has been developed, each pill only costs a few dollars to manufacture. Alpha charges $4,150 for a 30-day supply, or about $50,000 per year. The pills generally are not covered by insurance plans. The older "cocktail" of drugs is still available from other drug companies at a much lower cost.

Alpha has a program that makes its drug available at no cost in extreme circumstances, and about 1 percent of the patients taking the drug receive it directly from Alpha at no charge. Alpha has several successful drugs and had earnings of nearly $3 billion last year.

Some activists have called on Alpha to do the following:

- Reduce the price of its drugs for all patients to $35,000 per year. This would be $10,000 above the cost of the older treatment.

- Expand its free drug program to cover 10 percent of the drug's current users.

Questions

1. Should Alpha meet the first demand and reduce its prices across the board? What is a fair price?

2. Should Alpha meet the second demand and expand its free drug program? What guidelines should it use?

3. Justify your answers to Questions 1 and 2 using the ideas presented in this section. Utilitarians might respond to this scenario by saying, "A profitable drug company will stay in business longer, develop more useful medications, and benefit more people in the long run. Alpha is under no ethical obligation to make either policy change." A Kantian thinker might argue, "Alpha has a duty to help people when it is able to do so. It should reduce the price to all patients and provide free drugs to those who need it." And John Rawls might say, "Remember that you could have been born an HIV-positive child. But, also, it is important that pharmaceutical companies have an incentive to produce life-saving drugs."

ETHICAL TRAPS

Once you have determined the right thing to do, actually doing it can be very difficult. Ethical traps create great temptation to do what you know to be wrong or fail to do what you know to be right.

Money[7]

Money is a powerful lure because most people believe that they would be happier if only they had more. But that is not necessarily true. Good health, companionship, and enjoyable leisure activities all contribute more to happiness than money does. And, regardless of income, 85 percent of Americans feel happy on a day-to-day basis.

Money *can*, of course, provide some protection against the inevitable bumps in the road of life. If you lose your winter coat, you will be happier if you can replace it. It is easier to maintain friendships if you can afford to go out together occasionally. So money can contribute to happiness, but research indicates that this impact disappears when household income exceeds $75,000. Above that level, income seems to have no impact on day-to-day happiness. Indeed, there is some evidence that higher income levels actually *reduce* the ability to appreciate small pleasures.

Money is also a way of keeping score. If my company pays me more, that must mean I am a better employee. So although an increase in income above $75,000 does not affect *day-to-day* happiness, increases in income can make people feel more satisfied with their lives. They consider themselves more successful and feel that their life is going better.

In short, the relationship between money and happiness is complicated. Above a certain level, more money does not make for more happiness. And, when people work so hard to earn money that their health, friendships, and leisure activities suffer, it has the reverse effect.

Rationalization

A recent study found that more creative people tend to be less ethical. The reason? They are better at rationalizing their bad behavior. Virtually any foul deed can be rationalized. Some common rationalizations:

- If I don't do it, someone else will.

- I deserve this because…

- They had it coming.

- I am not harming a *person*—it is just a big company.

- This is someone else's responsibility.

In the examples at the beginning of the chapter, what rationalizations could justify lying?

Conformity

Warren Buffett has been quoted as saying, "The five most dangerous words in business may be: 'Everybody else is doing it.'" Humans are social animals who are often willing to follow the leader, even to a place where they do not really want to go. If all the salespeople in a

---

[7]This section is based on the article, "High Income Improves Evaluation of Life but not Emotional Well-Being," by Daniel Kahneman and Angus Deaton.

company cheat on their expense accounts, a new hire is much more likely to view this behavior as acceptable.

Following Orders

When someone in authority issues orders, even to do something clearly wrong, it is very tempting to comply. Fear of punishment, the belief in authority figures, and the ability to rationalize all play a role. In a true story (with the facts disguised), Amanda worked at a private school that was struggling to pay its bills. As a result, it kept the lights turned off in the hallways. On a particularly cloudy day, a visitor tripped and fell in one of these darkened passages. When he sued, the principal told Amanda to lie on the witness stand and say that the lights had been on. The school's lawyer reinforced this advice. Amanda did as she was told. When asked why, she said, "I figured it must be the right thing to do if the lawyer said so. Also, if I hadn't lied, the principal would have fired me, and I might not have been able to get another job in teaching."

Euphemisms

To "smooth earnings" sounds a lot better than to "cook the books" or plain old "commit fraud." And "file sharing" sounds friendly and helpful—it has a very different ring than "stealing intellectual property," which is what it really is. In making ethical decisions, it is important to use accurate terminology. Anything else is just a variation on rationalization.

> "File sharing" sounds friendly and helpful—it has a very different ring than "stealing intellectual property," which is what it really is.

Lost in a Crowd

After being struck by a car, a two-year old child lies at the side of the road as people walk and ride by. No one stops to help, and the child dies. On a busy street, a man picks up a seven-year-old girl and carries her away while she screams, "You're not my dad—someone help me!" No one responds. The first incident was real; the second one was a test staged by a news station. It took hours and many repetitions before anyone tried to prevent the abduction.

When in a group, people are less likely to take responsibility, assuming that someone else will. They tend to check the reactions of others, and if everyone else seems calm, they assume that all is right. Bystanders are much more likely to react if they are alone and have to form an independent judgment.

Thus, in a business, if everyone is cheating on their expense accounts, smoothing earnings, or sexually harassing the staff, it is tempting to go with the flow rather than protest the wrongdoing.

APPLYING PERSONAL ETHICS IN THE WORKPLACE

Should you behave in the workplace the way you do at home, or do you have a separate set of ethics for each part of your life? What if your employees behave badly outside of work—should that affect their employment? Consider the following case.

ETHICS CASE: NO SHEEN ON SHEEN

Charlie Sheen, the star of the hit CBS television show *Two and a Half Men*, has admitted to using large quantities of cocaine. He has been hospitalized with drug overdoses and has been charged with both misdemeanor and felony drug offenses, which have led to probation several times. When asked about entering rehab, he said that only losers go to recovery programs and he could cure himself with his mind. He openly spent tens of thousands of dollars on prostitutes. His second wife filed a restraining order against him, alleging that he had pushed her down the stairs and threatened to kill her. He was also charged with a felony for threatening his third wife. She claims that he held a knife to her throat and said, "You better be in fear. If you tell anybody, I'll kill you." Then there was the widely reported incident in the Plaza Hotel in New York City in which the police escorted him to the hospital after he trashed his room and threatened the prostitute whom he had hired—all while his ex-wife and children slept in a room across the hall. Five months later, the police removed his twin sons from his house after their mother obtained a restraining order. On a radio show, Sheen made anti-Semitic comments about his boss, called him a clown and a charlatan, and said that he "violently hated him."

This boss was the most successful producer of comedy shows in the business.

Questions

1. If CBS fired Sheen from his television show, the network would lose tens of millions of dollars. At what point, if any, should CBS have fired him? If not for this, then for what?

2. Would you fire a warehouse worker who behaved this way? How much revenue does an employee have to bring in to be able to buy his way out of bad behavior?

3. What would you say to someone who argues that the goal at work is to make as much money as possible, but at home it is to be a kind and honorable human being?

4. What would Kant and Mill say is the right thing to do in this case?

5. What ethical traps do you face in this situation?

6. What is your Life Principle? What behavior are you willing to tolerate in the interest of profitability?

STAKEHOLDER ETHICS

A fundamental question in business ethics is: *What is the purpose of a corporation?* The answer to this question has changed over time. To begin at the beginning...

In a famous 1919 lawsuit[8], Henry Ford was sued by the Dodge brothers and other major shareholders of Ford Motor Company. The shareholders were upset because Ford paid essentially no dividends, despite fabulous profits. The shareholders complained, especially about Ford's use of corporate profits to support humanitarian and charitable works. The Michigan Supreme Court found in favor of the shareholders because corporation laws at the time required corporate boards to put shareholders first. The Dodge brothers won enough money to start their own car company, which still exists as part of Chrysler.

Companies were legally required to follow the "shareholder model" until the decade after the close of World War II. In the late 1940s and early 1950s, the attitude of many powerful politicians toward corporations changed. Many believed that American companies had contributed mightily to stopping the Nazis, and that without the massive volume of armaments and supplies that American corporations produced, Hitler might well have been victorious. There was a feeling that corporations were an essential part of society.

---

[8]*Dodge v. Ford*, 170 N.W. 668 (Mich. 1919).

Many politicians wanted corporations to be able to participate more fully in American life. They softened restrictive language in corporation laws so that companies could "do good deeds." Such action was not and is still not required, but it is *allowed*.

Definitions

The Shareholder Model

Noted economist Milton Friedman argued that corporations have two primary responsibilities. First, they must comply with the law. Second, they must make as much money as possible for shareholders. In his view, if shareholder and stakeholder interests conflict, the company should act in the best interests of the shareholders. After all, only shareholders have put their own money on the line. To do otherwise is, according to Friedman, "imposing a tax" on the shareholders.

The Stakeholder Model

The alternative point of view is that corporations should take care of more than shareholders alone. It is not that the owners of a corporation should be ignored—shareholders are included as one of several groups of stakeholders in a firm. But, a company must also look out for (among others) its employees, its customers, and the communities in which it operates. It may even be that companies have an obligation to broader interests such as "society" or "the environment."

The basic notion of stakeholder ethics is that even if a company will make a smaller profit for shareholders, it should nonetheless pay decent wages, support charitable causes, and so forth. A great many Fortune 500 companies put the stakeholder model into practice.

The Debate

Every executive will treat employees well if she believes that doing so will lead to increased profits. Every executive is in favor of donating money to charity if the donation improves the company's image and thereby pays for itself. But such win-win cases are not ethical dilemmas.

In a true dilemma, a company considers an action that would not increase the shareholders' return in any certain or measureable way. In such cases, the shareholder model advises, "Don't spend the shareholders' money." The stakeholder model counsels, "It is often OK to consider the interests of stakeholders other than the owners."

As with most all ethics questions, neither side is "right" in the sense that everyone agrees or that the law requires following either set of ideas. Countless companies follow each of the models.

The remainder of this section examines a company's ethical obligation to three specific stakeholders: employees, customers, and international contractors.

The Organization's Responsibility to Its Employees

Organizations cannot be successful without good workers. In many circumstances, the shareholder and stakeholder models agree that employees should be treated well. Disgruntled workers are likely to be unmotivated and unproductive. But sometimes looking out for employees may not lead to higher profits. In these cases, does an organization have a duty to "take care" of its workers? The shareholder model says no; the stakeholder model takes the opposite view.

Corporate leaders are often faced with difficult decisions when the issue of layoffs arises. Choices can be particularly difficult to navigate when outsourcing is an option. *Outsourcing* refers to cutting jobs at home and relocating operations to another country.

Read the following scenario and critique the CEO's decision making.

ETHICS CASE: THE STORM AFTER THE STORM

Yanni is the CEO of Cloud Farm, a company that provides online data centers for Internet companies. Because these data centers are enormous, they are located in rural areas where they are often the main employer. A series of tornados has just destroyed a data center near Farmfield, Arkansas, a town with a population of roughly 5,000 people. Farmfield is a three-hour drive from the nearest city, Little Rock.

Here is the good news: the insurance payout will cover the full cost of rebuilding. Indeed, the payout will be so generous that Cloud Farm could build a bigger and better facility than the one destroyed. The bad news? Data centers are much more expensive to build and operate in the United States than in Africa, Asia, or Latin America. Yanni could take the money from the insurance company and build three data centers overseas. He has asked Adam and Zoe to present the pros and cons of relocating.

Adam says: "If we rebuild overseas, our employees will never find equivalent jobs. We pay $20 an hour, and the other jobs in town are mostly minimum-wage. And remember how some of the guys worked right through Christmas to set up for that new client. They have been loyal to us—we owe them something in return. And it's not just bad for Farmfield or Arkansas, it's bad for the country. We can't continue to ship jobs overseas."

Zoe responds: "That is the government's problem, not ours. We'll pay to retrain the workers, which, frankly, is a generous offer. Our investors get a return of 4 percent; the industry average is closer to 8 percent. If we act like a charity to support Farmfield, we could all lose our jobs. It is our obligation to do what's best for our shareholders—which, in this case, happens to be what's right for us, too."

Questions

1. If you were in Yanni's position, would you rebuild the plant in Arkansas or relocate overseas?

2. Do you agree with Zoe's argument that it is the government's responsibility to create and protect American jobs, and that it is a CEO's job to increase shareholder wealth?

3. Imagine that you personally own $10,000 worth of shares in Cloud Farm. Would you be upset with a decision to rebuild the data center in the United States?

4. If Cloud Farm decides to rebuild in Arkansas, should it pay the workers while the center is being rebuilt? If yes, should it apply to all the workers, or just the high-level ones who might leave if they were not paid?

5. What ethical traps do you face in this situation?

6. What is your Life Principle on this issue? Would you be willing to risk your job to protect your employees?

An Organization's Responsibility to Its Customers

Customers are another group of essential stakeholders. A corporation must gain and retain loyal buyers if it is to stay in business for long. Treating customers well usually increases profits and helps shareholders.

But when, if ever, does an organization go too far? If a leader "puts customers first" in a way that significantly diminishes the bottom line, has she acted inappropriately? The shareholder model says yes.

After reading the following scenario, assess which option is best.

ETHICS CASE: FANNING CUSTOMER WRATH

Mark is the plant manager at Cooper Fan Company. For six months, he has been angling to ink a deal with Rooms-to-Go, a housewares company. With this contract, company profits would soar and he could hire 75 new workers. It would not hurt his bonus or job security either. But now the shift foreman at the factory is reporting bad news—an engineer says there may be a problem with the CPRF-300 model, one of Cooper's most popular offerings. With a sinking heart, Mark goes to investigate.

Ann, the engineer, shows Mark the standard remote control. "Notice," she says, "four buttons—Lo, Hi, Off, and Reverse." Mark hits the Lo button, and a ceiling fan just above his head starts to rotate lazily. He pushes Off, and the blades slow to a stop.

"So what's the problem?" Mark asks.

"It's the Reverse button. Most of our models have a switch on top of the fan itself that allows for the fan to spin clockwise or counterclockwise. This way, fans can blow air downward in the summer to cool the room and then draw air upward in the winter to make the same room feel warmer. But that means twice a year, homeowners have to drag out a ladder to change the switch.

"The CPRF-300 solves this problem by putting the Reverse button on the remote control. No ladders, no changing of switches. The problem is that the remote allows the reverse feature to be engaged while the fan is running. Watch."

Ann presses Hi on the remote and waits for the blades to cycle up to speed. When the blades are a blur, she pushes Reverse. There are several rapid clicks and a soft grinding sound as the blades lose speed. The noises stop after a few seconds, the blades slow, come to a stop, change direction, and begin to speed up again.

"If someone does that once or twice, no problem," Ann says. But eventually, the fans all fail. We tested 50 of them—switching back and forth between Hi and Reverse over and over. At somewhere between 75 and 150 reversals, they break. For most of them, it isn't a big problem—they just stop working. Three of them emitted sparks but did nothing else. One of them started a fire. And the last one threw out a half-inch piece of metal from the inner casing. Probably wouldn't kill someone, but it could certainly have put out an eye."

"So who's going to switch back and forth like that 75 times?" Mark asks.

"A kid might want to make a game of it. And, although there have been no reports of any problems, it may be that we are just lucky. So far. The engineers have designed a new fan that solves this problem. But what do we do in the meantime about the 50,000 CPRF-300s that have already been sold?"

Here are Mark's options:

- Recall all the CPRF-300s. Fixing or replacing the fans would probably cost several million dollars. A recall would also jeopardize the Rooms-to-Go contract.

- Never issue a recall. If a fan fails and someone sues, it would probably cost $20,000 to $200,000 per incident. But if someone dies in a fire or is disabled by flying debris, then all bets are off. There is no upper limit on a worst-case scenario like that.

- Delay the recall for a month or two, until the Rooms-to-Go contract is resolved one way or the other.

Questions

1. If you were in Mark's position, would you recommend a recall today? How about in two months, after the Rooms-to-Go deal has been completed?

2. What would Kant and Mill advise?

3. Ann's testing showed 6 percent "bad" results (sparks) and 4 percent "really bad" results (fire and thrown metal). Would your answers to Question 1 change if Ann's testing had shown 18 percent "bad" and 12 percent "really bad" results? What if it had shown the same number of "bad" results but zero "really bad" results?

4. What ethical traps does Mark face in this situation?

5. What Life Principle would you apply?

6. Assume that no recall is made, that a fan started a fire and burned a home in your town to the ground, and that a local newspaper identified the ceiling fan as the cause. The newspaper later reports that the Cooper Fan Company knew about the potential problem and did nothing about it. As a consumer, would you consider buying Cooper fans, or would you pass them by even if they were competitive in pricing, appearance, and features?

Organization's Responsibility to Overseas Contract Workers

Do an American company's ethical obligations end at the border? What ethical duties does an American manager owe to stakeholders in countries where the culture and economic circumstances are very different? Should American companies (and consumers) buy goods that are produced in sweatshop factories?

Industrialization has always been the first stepping stone out of dire poverty—it was in England in centuries past, and it is now in the developing world. Eventually, higher productivity leads to higher wages. In China, factory managers have complained that their employees want to work even longer hours to earn more money. The results in China have been nothing short of remarkable. During the Industrial Revolution in England, per-capita output doubled in 58 years; in China, it took only 10 years.

During the past 50 years, Taiwan and South Korea welcomed sweatshops. During the same period, India resisted what it perceived to be foreign exploitation. Although all three countries started at the same economic level, Taiwan and South Korea today have much lower levels of infant mortality and much higher levels of education than India.[9]

When governments or customers try to force factories in the developing world to pay higher wages, the factory owners typically either relocate to lower-wage countries or mechanize, thereby reducing the need for workers. In either case, the local economy suffers. Companies argue that higher wages lead to increased prices, which in turn drive away customers.

ETHICS CASE: THE DRAGON'S DEN

Ellen is the CEO of a large electronics manufacturer that makes cell phones, among other items. She is reviewing a consultant's report on Quality Dragon Limited, which operates the factory in China where the cell phones are made. She is considering whether to renew the firm's contract for a new three-year term.

The consultant "infiltrated" the Quality Dragon factory by getting a job and working there for a month. Portions of the consultant's report follow.

We were awakened at 5 a.m. every day. They always shouted at us and ordered us to hurry. We were fed a poor meal, and were always at our stations by 5:30, although work did not begin until 6. We worked from 6 until 1 p.m. with one 10-minute restroom break at 9 a.m. We were not permitted to talk to coworkers. If we did, even quietly, we were docked pay and the supervisors screamed at us. If we made an assembly error, we lost pay and the supervisors screamed at us. If we yawned, we lost pay and the supervisors screamed at us. If we failed to meet an hourly quota, we lost pay and the supervisors screamed at us.

I drilled holes into the outer casing of your phones at the place where a charger can be plugged in. My quota was to process 120 per hour. The holes had to be perfectly located and perfectly straight. Every 30 seconds, a new one. It was difficult to keep focus. I tried to make fewer than 10 errors per day. One day I made only 4 errors. Another day I made 18. On that day, my supervisor slapped me and docked my entire day's pay.

We had 30 minutes for lunch. The company provides a poor meal. We were permitted to pay for better food at the cafeteria, but it was very expensive. We could speak quietly at lunch.

At 1:30, we went back to work until 8:30. We had another 10-minute break at 4:30. Work was more difficult in the afternoon. The sun warmed the factory. Water was not allowed on the assembly floor. Sometimes, water was available at the restroom break. The supervisors were angrier and less patient after lunch. They called us names that no one should be called. If we missed our quota, we had to work late. This happened several times over the month.

[9]The data in this and the preceding paragraph are from Nicholas D. Kristof and Sheryl Wu Dunn, "Two Cheers for Sweatshops," *New York Times Magazine*, Sept. 24, 2000, p. 70.

Eventually, we were fed and returned to our dorm. We had 12 men to a room, and we slept in bunk beds that were three bunks high. The room smelled bad, and there were ants.

We worked six days a week. Sometimes, if a rush order came in, the supervisors would wake us up in the middle of the night and make us work until we finished. On Sundays, most workers spent much of their day sleeping. The company did provide televisions and chess sets in the recreation building.

I was supposed to earn $150 for the month. But the supervisors always looked for reasons to dock my pay. No one gets full pay. I ended up with $110 at the end of the month. For long-term workers, "take-home pay" is actually lower because there are things they must buy from the factory store. Workers are required to shave, but they have to buy their own razor blades. They also have to buy soap. The company provides a jumpsuit once a year, but workers have to buy socks and underwear.

Life in the factory could be worse, but it is very difficult.

Questions

1. Is the CEO morally required to use her negotiating power to insist upon better treatment of the people who make her company's products? What is your Life Principle?

2. In your opinion, does the treatment described seem reasonable? If not, what parts of the consultant's story indicate to you that workers are being treated wrongfully?

3. Assume that correcting the problems listed below would each result in a 1 percent cost increase for this company. Assume that you are in Ellen's position as CEO. Which of the following items would you insist upon, keeping in mind that each one increases your labor costs?

   - Reducing employees' workdays to a maximum of 12 hours

   - Improving the quality of food served to employees

   - Eliminating the practice of reducing pay for employees who exceed their quota for errors

   - Building additional dorms so that workers sleep with no more than four to a room

   - Prohibiting unpaid or forced overtime and night work

4. What would Kant, Mill, and Rawls say?

5. What ethical traps do you face in this situation?

6. As a consumer, are you keenly aware of how much things cost? Would you notice if food prices rose by 5 percent? What about smart phones, computers, and televisions—would a 5 percent increase in the price of these items be noticeable? What if the increase was 2 percent? How much extra would you be willing to pay for your cell phone so that workers could be treated better than the ones in this factory?

WHEN, IF EVER, IS LYING ACCEPTABLE?

We are taught from an early age that we must tell the truth. And usually, honesty is the best policy. The consequences of lying can be severe: students are suspended, employees are fired, and witnesses are convicted of perjury. Sometimes the problems are more subtle but still significant: a loss of trust, a loss of opportunities.

But in some specific circumstances, intentional deception is tolerated, even admired. In sports, for example, athletes spend countless hours perfecting techniques designed to trick opponents. If Eli Manning looks one way and throws the other, no one is upset even though his intention is to deceive the defensive backs. In other settings, lying is equally acceptable. When poker players bluff their way through lousy hands, we call them "skilled."

But what about in business? Does the presence of *competition* make a difference? Can the ends ever justify the means when it is not a life-and -death situation? Consider the following scenario.

ETHICS CASE: TRUTH (?) IN BORROWING

"Yes," Harold insisted indignantly. "I *am* going to walk in there and give them a file of fake documents. And hope to heaven that I can walk out of there with a $100,000 loan, even if it is fraudulent. What of it? Ethics are all very well when business is good, but now I'm desperate. Without that loan, no payroll and then no business."

"And what happens when you get caught?" his brother demanded. "Don't expect me to come visit you in jail every Sunday."

"Don't worry, they'll never figure it out. I'm only exaggerating the numbers a little, and I've never fudged a single thing in 20 years of banking with them. They won't look too closely. And it's not like the bank is going to lose its money. Orders are already picking up, and they'll come all the way back, just like they did in the last two recessions. I'll pay the bank every penny back—with interest—this time next year. Who gets hurt?"

Questions

1. Rate Harold's plan to lie to his bank to secure the $100,000 loan so that he is able to pay his employees. Is it completely wrongful? Completely justified? Somewhere in between? How does it fit with your Life Principles?

2. Now assume that a year passes, and that business does in fact pick up for Harold's company. He is able to repay the loan in full, with interest. No one is laid off from his company, no one misses a paycheck, and his lie is never caught. Is your assessment of his actions the same? Do the ends at least partially justify the means?

3. What is your Life Principle about telling lies? When is making a misrepresentation acceptable? To protect someone's life or physical safety? To protect a job? To protect another person's feelings? To gain an advantage? When others are doing the same?

4. Do you have the same rule when lying to protect yourself, as opposed to others?

Chapter Conclusion

Managers wonder what they can do to create an ethical environment in their companies. In the end, the surest way to infuse ethics throughout an organization is for top executives to behave ethically themselves. Few will bother to "do the right thing" unless they observe that their bosses value and support such behavior. Even employees who are ethical in their personal lives may find it difficult to uphold their standards at work if those around them behave differently. To ensure a more ethical world, managers must be an example for others, both within and outside their organizations.

EXAM REVIEW

1. **ETHICS** The law dictates how a person *must* behave. Ethics governs how people *should* behave. (p. 25)

2. **LIFE PRINCIPLES** Life Principles are the rules by which you live your life. If you develop these Life Principles now, you will be prepared when facing ethical dilemmas in the future. (p. 25)

3. WHY BOTHER TO ACT ETHICALLY AT ALL?

- Society as a whole benefits from ethical behavior.

- People feel better when they behave ethically.

- Unethical behavior can be very costly.

- Ethical behavior is more likely to pay off. (pp. 26–27)

4. THEORIES OF ETHICS

- Utilitarian thinkers believe that moral actions produce the greatest good for the greatest number.

- Deontological thinkers such as Immanuel Kant argue that, when assessing whether a decision is the most ethical choice, the end result is immaterial. Kantian thinkers believe that moral choices must be made for sound reasons, and that decisions motivated by a sense of duty or a respect for human dignity are particularly ethical. With his categorical imperative, Kant argued that you should not do something unless you would be willing to have everyone else do it too.

- John Rawls asked us to consider what type of society we would set up if we did not know whether we would be one of life's winners or losers. He called this situation "the veil of ignorance." (pp. 27–29)

5. ETHICAL TRAPS

- Money

- Rationalization

- Conformity

- Following orders

- Euphemisms

- Lost in a crowd (pp. 30–31)

6. PERSONAL VS. WORK ETHICS Should you apply your personal ethics in the workplace, or should you have different ethical values at home and at work? (pp. 31–32)

7. PURPOSE OF CORPORATIONS Is the primary role of corporations to make money, or do companies have responsibilities to workers, communities, customers, and other stakeholders? (pp. 32–37)

8. ETHICS OVERSEAS What ethical duties does an American manager owe to stakeholders in countries where the culture and economic circumstances are very different? Should American companies (and consumers) buy goods that are produced in sweatshop factories? (pp. 36–37)

9. LYING When, if ever, is lying acceptable? (pp. 37–38)

MULTIPLE-CHOICE QUESTIONS

1. Milton Friedman was a strong believer in the _____ model. He _____ argue that a corporate leader's sole obligation is to make money for the company's owners.

   (a) Shareholder; did

   (b) Shareholder; did not

   (c) Stakeholder; did

   (d) Stakeholder; did not

2. In the 1919 lawsuit *Dodge v. Ford*, the Dodge brothers and other major shareholders sued Henry Ford and his board of directors over nonpayment of dividends. The Michigan Supreme Court sided with _____. Incorporation laws at the time _____ companies to follow the shareholder model.

   (a) Ford; required

   (b) Ford; permitted

   (c) The Dodge brothers; required

   (d) The Dodge brothers; permitted

3. Which of the following historic events led to a significant change in corporation laws, permitting companies to follow the stakeholder model?

   (a) The Great Depression

   (b) World War II

   (c) The election of John F. Kennedy

   (d) The moon landing

   (e) The Supreme Court's decision in *Brown v. Board of Education*

4. Which of the following wrote the book *Utilitarianism* and believed that moral actions should "generate the greatest good for the greatest number"?

   (a) Milton Friedman

   (b) John Stuart Mill

   (c) Immanuel Kant

   (d) None of the above

5. Which of the following believed that the dignity of human beings must be respected, and that the most ethical decisions are made out of a sense of duty or obligation?

   (a) Milton Friedman

   (b) John Stuart Mill

   (c) Immanuel Kant

   (d) None of the above

ESSAY QUESTIONS

1. Executives were considering the possibility of moving their company to a different state. They wanted to determine if employees would be willing to relocate, but they did not want the employees to know the company was contemplating a move because the final decision had not yet been made. Instead of asking the employees directly, the company hired a firm to carry out a telephone survey. When calling the employees, these "pollsters" pretended to be conducting a public opinion poll and identified themselves as working for the new state's Chamber of Commerce.

   Has this company behaved in an ethical manner? Would there have been a better way to obtain this information?

2. When a fire destroyed the Malden Mills factory in Lawrence, Massachusetts, its 70-year-old owner, Aaron Feuerstein, could have shut down the business, collected the insurance money, and sailed off into retirement. But a layoff of the factory's 3,000 employees would have been a major economic blow to the region. So instead, Feuerstein kept the workers on the payroll while he rebuilt the factory. These actions gained him a national reputation as a business hero. Many consumers promised to buy more of the company's Polartec fabric. In the end, however, the story did not have a fairy-tale ending: five years after the fire, Malden Mills filed bankruptcy papers. The company was not able to pay off the loans it had incurred to keep the business going.

   Did Feuerstein do the right thing?

3. Many socially responsible funds are now available to investors who want to make ethical choices. The Amana Fund buys stocks that comply with Islamic laws. For example, it will not invest in holdings that earn interest, which is prohibited under Islamic law. The Ava Maria Fund is designed for Catholic investors, the Timothy Funds for evangelicals. The Sierra Fund focuses on environmentally friendly investments, while the Women's Equity Fund chooses companies that promote women's interests in the workplace. On average, however, these socially responsible investments earn a lower return than standard index funds that mirror the performance of a stock index, such as the Standard & Poor's 500.

   Are socially responsible funds attractive to you? Do you now, or will you in the future, use them in saving for your own retirement?

4. When James Kilts became CEO of Gillette Co., the consumer products giant had been a mainstay of the Boston community for a hundred years. But the organization was going through hard times: its stock was trading at less than half its peak price, and some of its storied brands of razors were wilting under intense competitive pressure. In four short years, Kilts turned Gillette around—strengthening its core brands, cutting jobs, and paying off debt. With the company's stock up 61 percent, Kilts had added $20 billion in shareholder value.

   Then Kilts suddenly sold Gillette to Procter & Gamble (P&G) for $57 billion. So short was Kilts's stay in Boston that he never moved his family from their home in Rye, New York. The deal was sweet for Gillette shareholders—the company's stock price went up 13 percent in one day. And tasty also for Kilts—his payoff was $153 million, including a $23.9 million reward from P&G for having made the deal and for a "change in control" clause in his employment contract that was worth $12.6 million. In addition, P&G agreed to pay him $8 million a year to serve as vice chairman after the merger. When he retired, his pension would be $1.2 million per year. Moreover, two of his top lieutenants were offered payments totaling $57 million.

Any downside to this deal? Four percent of the Gillette workforce—6,000 employees—were fired. If the payouts to the top three Gillette executives were divided among these 6,000, each unemployed worker would receive $35,000. The loss of this many employees (4,000 of whom lived in New England) had a ripple effect throughout the area's economy. Although Gillette shareholders certainly benefited in the short run from the sale, their profit would have been even greater without this $210 million payout to the executives. Moreover, about half the increase in Gillette revenues during the time that Kilts was running the show were attributable to currency fluctuations. A cheaper dollar increased revenue overseas. If the dollar had moved in the opposite direction, there might not have been any increase in revenue. Indeed, for the first two years after Kilts joined Gillette, the stock price declined. It was not until the dollar turned down that the stock price improved.

Do CEOs who receive sweeteners have too strong an incentive to sell their companies? Is it unseemly for them to be paid so much when many employees will lose their jobs?

5. Many of America's largest consumer product companies, such as Wal-Mart, Nike, and Land's End, buy fabric produced in China by Fountain Set Holdings Ltd. Chinese government investigators recently discovered that Fountain Set has contaminated a local river by dumping dye waste into it. What responsibility do U.S. companies have to ensure safe environmental practices by overseas suppliers?

DISCUSSION QUESTIONS

1. Darby has been working for 14 months at Holden Associates, a large management consulting firm. She is earning $75,000 a year, which *sounds* good but does not go very far in New York City. It turns out that her peers at competing firms are typically paid 20 percent more and receive larger annual bonuses. Darby works about 60 hours a week—more if she is traveling. A number of times, she has had to reschedule her vacation or cancel personal plans to meet client deadlines. She hopes to go to business school in a year and has already begun the application process.

Holden has a policy that permits any employee who works as late as 8:00 p.m. to eat dinner at company expense. The employee can also take a taxi home. Darby is in the habit of staying until 8:00 p.m. every night, whether or not her workload requires it. Then she orders enough food for dinner, with leftovers for lunch the next day. She has managed to cut her grocery bill to virtually nothing. Sometimes she invites her boyfriend to join her for dinner. As a student, he is always hungry and broke. Darby often uses the Holden taxi to take them back to his apartment, although the cab fare is twice as high as to her own place.

Sometimes Darby stays late to work on her business school applications. Naturally, she uses Holden equipment to print out and photocopy the finished applications. Darby has also been known to return online purchases through the Holden mailroom on the company dime. Many employees do that, and the mailroom workers do not seem to mind.

Is Darby doing anything wrong? What ethical traps is she facing? What would your Life Principle be in this situation?

2. H. B. Fuller Co. of St. Paul is a leading manufacturer of industrial glues. Its mission statement says the company "will conduct business legally and ethically." It has endowed a university chair in business ethics and donates 5 percent of its profits to charity. But now it is under attack for selling its shoemakers' glue, Resistol, in Central America. Many homeless children in these countries have become addicted to Resistol's fumes. So widespread is the problem that glue-sniffers in Central America are called *resistoleros*. Glue manufacturers in Europe have added a foul-smelling oil to their glue that discourages abusers. Fuller fears that the smell may also discourage legitimate users.

   What should Fuller do? What obligations does it have to stakeholders overseas, as opposed to its shareholders? What would Rawls say?

3. Steve supervises a team of account managers. One night at a company outing, Lawrence, a visiting account manager, made some wildly inappropriate sexual remarks to Maddie, who was on Steve's team. When she told Steve, he was uncertain what to do, so he asked his boss. She was concerned that if Steve took the matter further and Lawrence was fired or even disciplined, her whole area would suffer. Lawrence was one of the best account managers in the region, and everyone was overworked as it was. She told Steve to get Maddie to drop the matter. Just tell her that these things happen, and Lawrence did not mean anything by it.

   What should Steve do? What ethical traps does he face? What would be your Life Principle in this situation?

4. David has just spoken with a member of his sales team who has not met her sales goals for some months. She has also missed 30 days of work in the past six months. It turns out that she is in the process of getting a divorce, and her teenage children are reacting very badly. Some of the missed days have been for court, others because the children have refused to go to school. If David's team does not meet its sales goals, no one will get a bonus and his job may be at risk. What should he do?

5. Rapper Ice-T's song "Cop Killer" generated significant controversy when it was released. Among other things, its lyrics anticipate slitting a policeman's throat.

   When "Cop Killer" was recorded, Time Warner, Inc., was struggling with a $15 billion debt and a depressed stock price. Had Time Warner renounced rap albums with harsh themes, its reputation in the music business—and future profits—might have suffered. This damage might even have spilled over into the multimedia market, which was crucial to Time Warner's future.

   Did Time Warner do anything wrong when it decided to release "Cop Killer"?

6. You are negotiating a new labor contract with union officials. The contract covers a plant that has experienced operating losses over the past several years. You want to negotiate concessions from labor to reduce the losses. However, labor is refusing any compromises. You could tell them that, without concessions, the plant will be closed, although that is not true.

   Is bluffing ethical? Under what circumstances? What would Kant and Mill say? What is your Life Principle?

CHAPTER 3

DISPUTE RESOLUTION

© Steve Allen/Jupiterimages.

Tony Caruso had not returned for dinner, and his wife, Karen, was nervous. She put on some sandals and hurried across the dunes, a half mile to the ocean shore. She soon came upon Tony's dog, Blue, tied to an old picket fence. Tony's shoes and clothing were piled neatly nearby. Karen and friends searched frantically throughout the evening.

A little past midnight, Tony's body washed ashore, his lungs filled with water. A local doctor concluded he had accidentally drowned.

Karen and her friends were not the only ones who were distraught. Tony had been partners with Beth Smiles in an environmental consulting business, Enviro-Vision. They were good friends, and Beth was emotionally devastated. When she was able to focus on business issues, Beth filed an insurance claim with the Coastal Insurance Group. Beth hated to think about Tony's death in financial terms, but she was relieved that the struggling business would receive $2 million on the life insurance policy.

> A little past midnight, Tony's body washed ashore, his lungs filled with water.

Several months after filing the claim, Beth received this reply from Coastal: "Under the policy issued to Enviro-Vision, we are conditionally liable in the amount of $1 million in the event of Mr. Caruso's death. If his death is accidental, we are conditionally liable to pay double indemnity of $2 million. But pursuant to section H(5), death by suicide is not covered.

"After a thorough investigation, we have concluded that Anthony Caruso's death was an act of suicide, as defined in section B(11) of the policy. Your claim is denied in its entirety." Beth was furious. She was convinced Tony was incapable of suicide. And her company could not afford the $2 million loss. She decided to consult her lawyer, Chris Pruitt.

THREE FUNDAMENTAL AREAS OF LAW

This case is a fictionalized version of several real cases based on double indemnity insurance policies. In this chapter, we follow Beth's dispute with Coastal from initial interview through appeal, using it to examine three fundamental areas of law: the structure of our court systems, civil lawsuits, and alternative dispute resolution.

When Beth Smiles meets with her lawyer, Chris Pruitt brings a second attorney from his firm, Janet Booker, who is an experienced **litigator;** that is, a lawyer who handles court cases. If they file a lawsuit, Janet will be in charge, so Chris wants her there for the first meeting. Janet probes about Tony's home life, the status of the business, his personal finances, everything. Beth becomes upset that Janet doesn't seem sympathetic, but Chris explains that Janet is doing her job: she needs all the information, good and bad.

Litigation versus Alternative Dispute Resolution

Janet starts thinking about the two methods of dispute resolution: litigation and alternative dispute resolution. **Litigation** refers to lawsuits, the process of filing claims in court, and ultimately going to trial. **Alternative dispute resolution** is any other formal or informal process used to settle disputes without resorting to a trial. It is increasingly popular with corporations and individuals alike because it is generally cheaper and faster than litigation, and we will focus on this topic in the last part of this chapter.

Litigation
The process of filing claims in court and ultimately going to trial.

Alternative dispute resolution
Any other formal or informal process used to settle disputes without resorting to a trial.

COURT SYSTEMS

The United States has over 50 *systems* of courts. One nationwide system of *federal* courts serves the entire country. In addition, each individual *state*—such as Texas, California, and Florida—has its court system. The state and federal courts are in different buildings, have different judges, and hear different kinds of cases. Each has special powers and certain limitations.

State Courts

The typical state court system forms a pyramid, as Exhibit 3.1 shows. Some states have minor variations on the exhibit. For example, Texas has two top courts: a Supreme Court for civil cases and a Court of Criminal Appeals for criminal cases.

Trial Courts

Almost all cases start in trial courts, which are endlessly portrayed on television and in film. There is one judge, and there will often (but not always) be a jury. This is the only court to hear testimony from witnesses and receive evidence. **Trial courts** determine the facts of a particular dispute and apply to those facts the law given by earlier appellate court decisions.

In the Enviro-Vision dispute, the trial court will decide all important facts that are in dispute. How did Tony Caruso die? Did he drown? Assuming he drowned, was his death accidental or suicide? Once the jury has decided the facts, it will apply the law to those facts. If Tony Caruso died accidentally, contract law provides that Beth Smiles is entitled to double indemnity benefits. If the jury decides he killed himself, Beth gets nothing.

Facts are critical. That may sound obvious, but in a course devoted to legal principles, it is easy to lose track of the key role that factual determinations play in the resolution of any dispute. In the Enviro-Vision case, we will see that one bit of factual evidence goes undetected, with costly consequences.

Trial courts
Determine the facts of a particular dispute and apply to those facts the law given by earlier appellate court decisions.

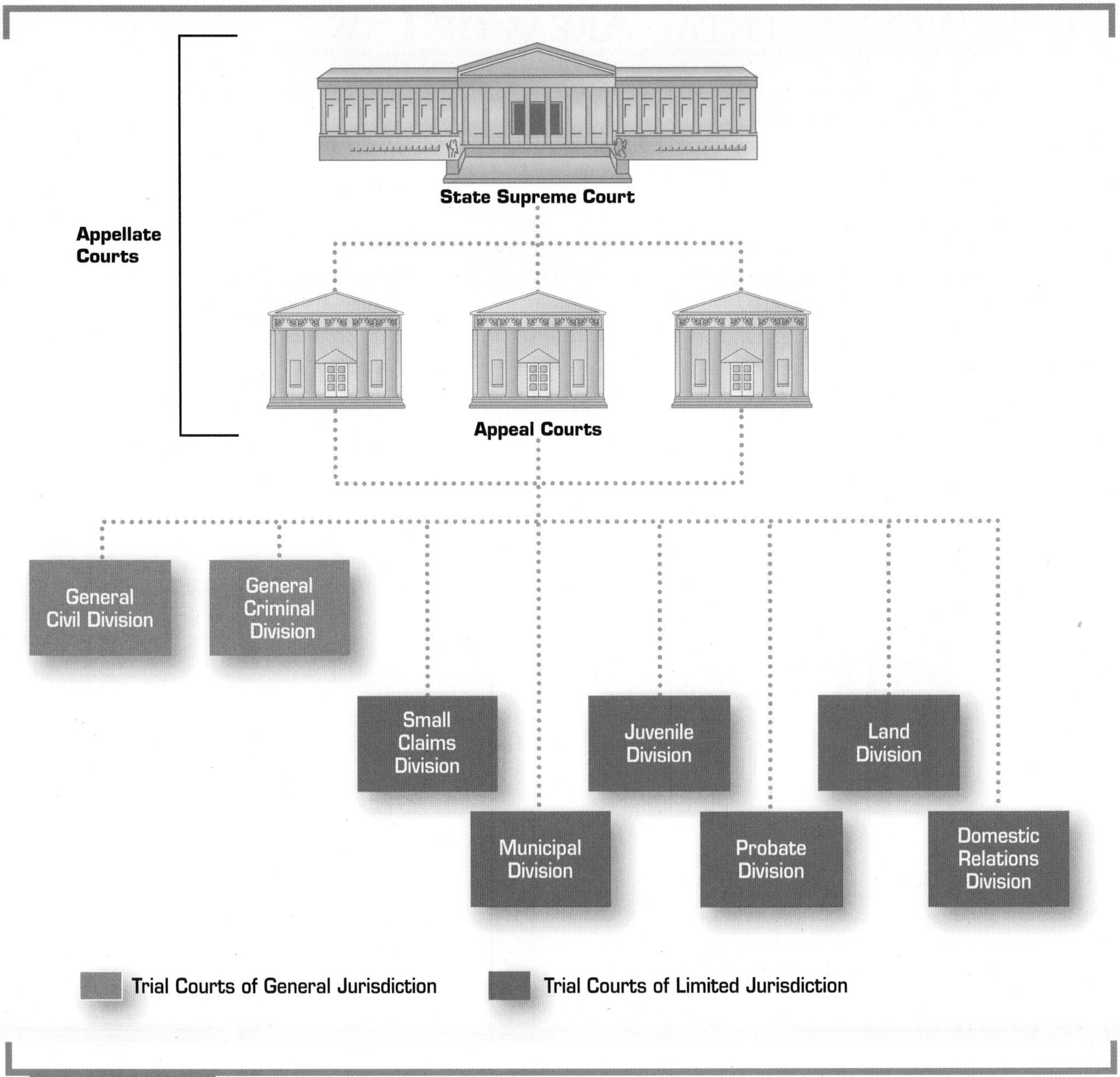

State Supreme Court

Appellate
Courts

Appeal Courts

General
Civil Division

General
Criminal
Division

Small
Claims
Division

Juvenile
Division

Land
Division

Municipal
Division

Probate
Division

Domestic
Relations
Division

◼ Trial Courts of General Jurisdiction   ◼ Trial Courts of Limited Jurisdiction

EXHIBIT 3.1   A trial court determines facts, while an appeals court ensures that the lower court correctly applied the law to those facts.

Jurisdiction
A court's power to hear a case.

Jurisdiction refers to a court's power to hear a case. In state or federal court, a plaintiff may start a lawsuit only in a court that has jurisdiction over that kind of case. Some courts have very limited jurisdiction, while others have the power to hear almost any case.

Subject matter jurisdiction
A court has the authority to hear a particular type of case.

Subject Matter Jurisdiction

Subject matter jurisdiction means that a court has the authority to hear a particular type of case.

Trial Courts of Limited Jurisdiction   These courts may hear only certain types of cases. Small claims court has jurisdiction only over civil lawsuits involving a maximum of, say, $5,000 (the amount varies from state to state). A juvenile court hears only cases involving minors. Probate court is devoted to settling the estates of deceased persons, though in some states it will hear certain other cases as well.

Trial Courts of General Jurisdiction   Trial courts of general jurisdiction, however, can hear a very broad range of cases. The most important court, for our purposes, is the general civil division. This court may hear virtually any civil lawsuit. In one day it might hear a $450 million shareholders' derivative lawsuit, an employment issue involving freedom of religion, and a foreclosure on a mortgage. Most of the cases we study start in this court.[1] If Enviro-Vision's case against Coastal goes to trial in a state court, it will begin in the trial court of general jurisdiction.

Personal Jurisdiction

In addition to subject matter jurisdiction, courts must also have **personal jurisdiction** over the defendant. Personal jurisdiction is the legal authority to require the defendant to stand trial, pay judgments, and the like. When plaintiffs file lawsuits, defendants sometimes make a *special appearance* to challenge a court's personal jurisdiction. If the court agrees with the defendant's argument, the lawsuit will be dismissed.

> **Personal jurisdiction**
> The legal authority to require the defendant to stand trial, pay judgments, and the like.

Personal jurisdiction generally exists, if:

1. For individuals, the defendant is a resident of the state in which a lawsuit is filed. For companies, the defendant is doing business in that state.

2. The defendant takes a formal step to defend a lawsuit. Most papers filed with a court count as formal steps, but special appearances do not.

3. A **summons** is *served* on a defendant. A summons is the court's written notice that a lawsuit has been filed against the defendant. The summons must be delivered to the defendant when she is physically within the state in which the lawsuit is filed.

> **Summons**
> The court's written notice that a lawsuit has been filed against the defendant.

For example, Texarkana straddles the Texas/Arkansas border. If a lawsuit is filed in a Texas court, a defendant who lives in Arkansas can be served if, when walking down the street in Texarkana, she steps across the state line into Texas. Corporations are required to hire a registered agent in any state in which they do business. If a registered agent receives a summons, then the corporation is served.

4. A **long-arm statute** applies. If all else fails—the defendant does not reside in the state, does not defend the lawsuit, and has not been served with a summons while in the state—a court still can obtain jurisdiction under long-arm statutes. These statutes typically claim jurisdiction over someone who commits a tort, signs a contract, or conducts "regular business activities" in the state.

> **Long-arm statute**
> A statute that gives a court jurisdiction over someone who commits a tort, signs a contract, or conducts "regular business activities" in the state.

---

[1] Note that the actual name of the court will vary from state to state. In many states, it is called *superior court* because it has power superior to the courts of limited jurisdiction. In New York, it is called *supreme court* (anything to confuse the layperson); in some states, it is called *court of common pleas;* in Oregon and other states, it is a *circuit court.* They are all civil trial courts of general jurisdiction. Within this branch, some states are beginning to establish specialized business courts to hear complex commercial disputes. At least one state has created a cybercourt for high-tech cases. Lawyers will argue their cases by teleconference and present evidence via streaming video.

As a general rule, courts tend to apply long-arm statutes aggressively, hauling defendants into their courtrooms. However, the due process guarantees in the United States Constitution require fundamental fairness in the application of long-arm statutes. Therefore, courts can claim personal jurisdiction only if a defendant has had *minimum contacts* with a state. In other words, it is unfair to require a defendant to stand trial in another state if he has had no meaningful interaction with that state.

In the following Landmark Case, the Supreme Court explains its views on this important constitutional issue.

Landmark Case

INTERNATIONAL SHOE CO. v. STATE OF WASHINGTON

326 U.S. 310
Supreme Court of the United States, 1945

Facts: Although International Shoe manufactured footwear only in St. Louis, Missouri, it sold its products nationwide. It did not have offices or warehouses in Washington State, but it did send about a dozen salespeople there. The salespeople rented space in hotels and businesses, displayed sample products, and took orders. They were not authorized to collect payments from customers.

When Washington State sought contributions to the state's unemployment fund, International Shoe refused to pay. Washington sued. The company argued that it was not engaged in business in the state, and, therefore, that Washington courts had no jurisdiction over it.

The Supreme Court of Washington ruled that International Shoe did have sufficient contacts with the state to justify a lawsuit there. International Shoe appealed to the United States Supreme Court.

Issue: *Did International Shoe have sufficient minimum contacts in Washington State to permit jurisdiction there?*

Excerpts from Chief Justice Stone's Decision: Appellant insists that its activities within the state were not sufficient to manifest its "presence" there and that in its absence, the state courts were without jurisdiction, that consequently, it was a denial of due process for the state to subject appellant to suit. Appellant [International Shoe] refers to those cases in which it was said that the mere solicitation of orders for the purchase of goods within a state, to be accepted without the state and filled by shipment of the purchased goods interstate, does not render the corporation seller amenable to suit within the state.

Historically the jurisdiction of courts to render judgment is grounded on their power over the defendant's person. Hence his presence within the territorial jurisdiction of a court was prerequisite to a judgment personally binding him. But now

due process requires that [a defendant] have certain minimum contacts with it such that the maintenance of the suit does not offend "traditional notions of fair play and substantial justice."

Since the corporate personality is a fiction, its "presence" without can be manifested only by those activities of the corporation's agent within the state which courts will deem to be sufficient to satisfy the demands of due process.

"Presence" in the state in this sense has never been doubted when the activities of the corporation there have not only been continuous and systematic, but also give rise to the liabilities sued on, even though no consent to be sued or authorization to an agent to accept service of process has been given. Conversely, it has been generally recognized that the casual presence of the corporate agent or even his conduct of single or isolated items of activities in a state in the corporation's behalf are not enough to subject it to suit on causes of action unconnected with the activities there. To require the corporation in such circumstances to defend the suit away from its home or other jurisdiction where it carries on more substantial activities has been thought to lay too great and unreasonable a burden on the corporation to comport with due process.

But to the extent that a corporation exercises the privilege of conducting activities within a state, it enjoys the benefits and protection of the laws of that state. The exercise of that privilege may give rise to obligations.

Applying these standards, the activities carried on in behalf of appellant in the State of Washington were neither irregular nor casual. They were systematic and continuous throughout the years in question. They resulted in a large volume of interstate business, in the course of which appellant received the benefits and protection of the laws of the state, including the right to resort to the courts for the enforcement of its rights. The obligation which is here sued upon arose out of those very activities. It is evident that these operations establish sufficient contacts or ties with the state of the forum to make it reasonable and just, according to our traditional conception of fair play and substantial justice, to permit the state to enforce the obligations which appellant has incurred there.

The state may maintain the present suit to collect the tax.

Affirmed.

Appellate Courts

Appellate courts are entirely different from trial courts. Three or more judges hear the case. There are no juries, ever. These courts do not hear witnesses or take new evidence. They hear appeals of cases already tried below. **Appeals courts** generally accept the facts given to them by trial courts and review the trial record to see if the court made errors of law.

> **Appeals courts**
> Generally accept the facts given to them by trial courts and review the trial record to see if the court made errors of law.

Higher courts generally defer to lower courts on factual findings. Juries and trial court judges see all evidence as it is presented, and they are in the best position to evaluate it. An appeals court will accept a factual finding unless there was *no evidence at all* to support it. If the jury decides that Tony Caruso committed suicide, the appeals court will normally accept that fact, even if the appeals judges consider the jury's conclusion dubious. On the other hand, if a jury concluded that Tony had been murdered, an appeals court would overturn that finding if neither side had introduced any evidence of murder during the trial.

An appeals court reviews the trial record to make sure that the lower court correctly applied the law to the facts. If the trial court made an **error of law**, the appeals court may require a new trial. Suppose the jury concludes that Tony Caruso committed suicide but votes to award Enviro-Vision $1 million because it feels sorry for Beth Smiles. That is an error of law: if Tony committed suicide, Beth is entitled to nothing. An appellate court will reverse the decision. Or suppose that the trial judge permitted a friend of Tony's to state that he was certain Tony would never commit suicide. Normally, such opinions are not permissible in trial, and it was a legal error for the judge to allow the jury to hear it.

> **Error of law**
> Because of this, the appeals court may require a new trial.

Court of Appeals   The party that loses at the trial court may appeal to the intermediate court of appeals. The party filing the appeal is the **appellant**. The party opposing the appeal (because it won at trial) is the **appellee**.

This court allows both sides to submit written arguments on the case, called **briefs**. Each side then appears for oral argument, usually before a panel of three judges. The appellant's lawyer has about 15 minutes to convince the judges that the trial court made serious errors of law, and that the decision should be **reversed;** that is, nullified. The appellee's lawyer has the same time to persuade the court that the trial court acted correctly, and that the result should be **affirmed;** that is, permitted to stand.

> **Appellant**
> The party filing the appeal.
>
> **Appellee**
> The party opposing the appeal.
>
> **Briefs**
> Written arguments on the case.
>
> **Reversed**
> Nullified.
>
> **Affirmed**
> Permitted to stand.

State Supreme Court   This is the highest court in the state, and it accepts some appeals from the court of appeals. In most states, there is no absolute right to appeal to the Supreme Court. If the high court regards a legal issue as important, it accepts the case. It then takes briefs and hears oral argument just as the appeals court did. If it considers the matter unimportant, it refuses to hear the case, meaning that the court of appeals' ruling is the final word on the case.[2]

In most states, seven judges, often called *justices*, sit on the Supreme Court. They have the final word on state law.

Federal Courts

As discussed in Chapter 1, federal courts are established by the United States Constitution, which limits what kinds of cases can be brought in any federal court. See Exhibit 3.2. For our purposes, two kinds of civil lawsuits are permitted in federal court: federal question cases and diversity cases.

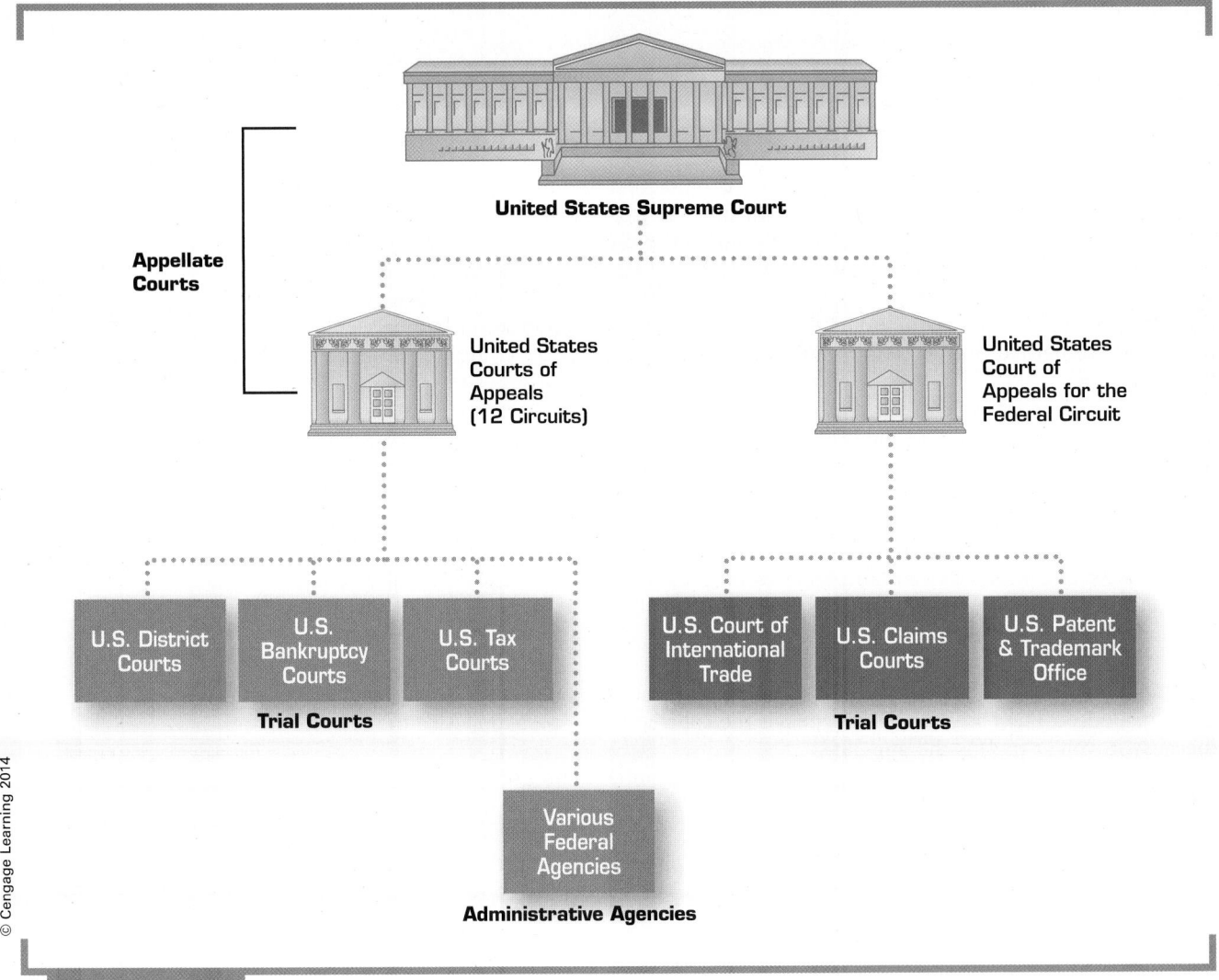

© Cengage Learning 2014

EXHIBIT 3.2

Federal Question Cases

A claim based on the United States Constitution, a federal statute, or a federal treaty is called a **federal question** case.[3] Federal courts have jurisdiction over these cases. If the Environmental Protection Agency (a part of the federal government) orders Logging Company not to cut in a particular forest, and Logging Company claims that the agency has wrongly deprived it of its property, that suit is based on a federal statute and is thus a federal question. If Little Retailer sues Mega Retailer, claiming that Mega has established a monopoly, that claim is also based on a statute—the Sherman Antitrust Act—and creates federal question jurisdiction. Enviro-Vision's potential suit merely concerns an insurance contract. The federal district court has no federal question jurisdiction over the case.

Federal question
A case in which the claim is based on the United States Constitution, a federal statute, or a federal treaty.

Diversity Cases

Even if no federal law is at issue, federal courts have **diversity jurisdiction** when (1) the plaintiff and defendant are citizens of different states *and* (2) the amount in dispute exceeds $75,000. The theory behind diversity jurisdiction is that courts of one state might be biased against citizens of another state. To ensure fairness, the parties have the option to use a federal court as a neutral playing field.

Enviro-Vision is located in Oregon and Coastal Insurance is incorporated in Georgia.[4] They are citizens of different states and the amount in dispute far exceeds $75,000. Janet could file this case in United States District Court based on diversity jurisdiction.

Diversity jurisdiction
(1) When the plaintiff and defendant are citizens of different states and (2) When the amount in dispute exceeds $75,000.

Trial Courts

United States District Court   This is the primary trial court in the federal system. The nation is divided into about 94 districts, and each has a district court. States with smaller populations have one district. States with larger populations have several; Texas is divided geographically into four districts.

Other Trial Courts   There are other, specialized trial courts in the federal system. Bankruptcy Court, Tax Court, and the United States Court of International Trade all handle name-appropriate cases. The United States Claims Court hears cases brought against the United States, typically on contract disputes. The Foreign Intelligence Surveillance Court is a very specialized, secret court, which oversees requests for surveillance warrants against suspected foreign agents.

Judges   The President of the United States nominates all federal court judges, from district court to Supreme Court. The nominees must be confirmed by the Senate. Once confirmed, federal judges serve for "life in good behavior." Many federal judges literally stay on the job for life. Recently, still-active Judge Wesley Brown of Kansas tied a record as the oldest federal judge in history when he turned 103.

Appellate Courts

United States Courts of Appeals   These are the intermediate courts of appeals. As the map below shows, they are divided into "circuits," which are geographical areas. There are 11 numbered circuits, hearing appeals from district courts. For example, an appeal from the Northern District of Illinois would go to the Court of Appeals for the Seventh Circuit.

---

[3]28 U.S.C. §1331 governs federal question jurisdiction and 28 U.S.C. §1332 covers diversity jurisdiction.
[4]For diversity purposes, a corporation is a citizen of the state in which it is incorporated and the state in which it has its principal place of business.

A twelfth court, the Court of Appeals for the District of Columbia, hears appeals only from the district court of Washington, D.C. This is a particularly powerful court because so many suits about federal statutes begin in the district court for the District of Columbia. Also in Washington is the Thirteenth Court of Appeals, known as the Federal Circuit. It hears appeals from specialized trial courts, as shown in Exhibit 3.2.

Within one circuit there are many circuit judges, up to about 50 judges in the largest circuit, the Ninth. When a case is appealed, three judges hear the appeal, taking briefs and hearing oral arguments.

United States Supreme Court   This is the highest court in the country. There are nine justices on the Court. One justice is the chief justice and the other eight are associate justices. When they decide a case, each justice casts an equal vote. The chief justice's special power comes from his authority to assign opinions to a given justice. The justice assigned to write an opinion has an opportunity to control the precise language and thus to influence the voting by other justices.

The Supreme Court has the power to hear appeals in any federal case, and in certain cases that began in state courts. Generally, it is up to the Court whether or not it will accept a case. A party that wants the Supreme Court to review a lower court ruling must file a petition for a **writ of *certiorari***, asking the Court to hear the case. Four of the nine justices must vote in favor of hearing a case before a writ will be granted. The Court receives several thousand requests every year but usually accepts fewer than 100. Most cases accepted involve either an important issue of constitutional law or an interpretation of a major federal statute.

Writ of *certiorari*
A petition asking the Supreme Court to hear a case.

EXAM Strategy

Question: Mark has sued Janelle, based on the state common law of negligence. He is testifying in court, explaining how Janelle backed a rented truck out of her driveway and slammed into his Lamborghini, causing $82,000 in damages. Where would this take place?

(a) State appeals court

(b) United States Court of Appeals

(c) State trial court

(d) Federal District Court

(e) Either state trial court or Federal District Court

Strategy: The question asks about trial and appellate courts, and also about state versus federal courts. One issue at a time, please. What are the different functions of trial and appellate courts? *Trial* courts use witnesses, and often juries, to resolve factual disputes. *Appellate* courts never hear witnesses and never have juries. Applying that distinction to these facts tells us whether we are in a trial or appeals court.

Next Issue: *State* trial courts may hear lawsuits on virtually any issue. *Federal District Courts* may only hear two kinds of cases: federal question (those involving a statute or constitutional provision); or diversity (where the parties are from different states *and* the amount at issue is $75,000 or higher). Apply what we know to the facts here.

Result: We are in a trial court because Mark is testifying. Could we be in Federal District Court? No. The suit is based on state common law. This is not a diversity case because the parties live in the same state. We are in a state trial court.

LITIGATION

Janet Booker decides to file the Enviro-Vision suit in the Oregon trial court. She thinks that a state court judge may take the issue more seriously than a federal district court judge.

Pleadings

The documents that begin a lawsuit are called the **pleadings**. These consist of the complaint, the answer, and sometimes a reply.

Pleadings
The documents that begin a lawsuit, consisting of the complaint, the answer, and sometimes a reply.

Complaint

Complaint

A short, plain statement of the facts alleged and the legal claims made.

The plaintiff files in court a **complaint**, which is a short, plain statement of the facts she is alleging and the legal claims she is making. The purpose of the complaint is to inform the defendant of the general nature of the claims and the need to come into court and protect his interests.

Janet Booker files the complaint, as shown below. Since Enviro-Vision is a partnership, she files the suit on behalf of Beth personally.

STATE OF OREGON
CIRCUIT COURT

Multnomah County   Civil Action No. _____

_____
Elizabeth Smiles,
Plaintiff   JURY TRIAL DEMANDED

v.
Coastal Insurance Company, Inc.,
Defendant
_____

COMPLAINT

Plaintiff Elizabeth Smiles states that:

1. She is a citizen of Multnomah County, Oregon.
2. Defendant Coastal Insurance Company, Inc., is incorporated under the laws of Georgia and has as its usual place of business 148 Thrift Street, Savannah, Georgia.
3. On or about July 5, 2012, plaintiff Smiles ("Smiles"), Defendant Coastal Insurance Co, Inc. ("Coastal") and Anthony Caruso entered into an insurance contract ("the contract"), a copy of which is annexed hereto as Exhibit "A." This contract was signed by all parties or their authorized agents, in Multnomah County, Oregon.
4. The contract obligates Coastal to pay to Smiles the sum of two million dollars ($2 million) if Anthony Caruso should die accidentally.
5. On or about September 20, 2012, Anthony Caruso accidentally drowned and died while swimming.
6. Coastal has refused to pay any sum pursuant to the contract.
7. Coastal has knowingly, willingly and unreasonably refused to honor its obligations under the contract.

WHEREFORE, plaintiff Elizabeth Smiles demands judgment against defendant Coastal for all monies due under the contract; demands triple damages for Coastal's knowing, willing, and unreasonable refusal to honor its obligations; and demands all costs and attorney's fees, with interest.
ELIZABETH SMILES,
By her attorney,
[Signed]
Janet Booker
Pruitt, Booker & Bother
983 Joy Avenue
Portland, OR
October 18, 2012

Service

When she files the complaint in court, Janet gets a summons, which is a paper ordering the defendant to answer the complaint within 20 days. A sheriff or constable then *serves* the two papers by delivering them to the defendant. Coastal's headquarters are in Georgia, so the state of Oregon has required Coastal to specify someone as its agent for receipt of service in Oregon.

Answer

Once the complaint and summons are served, Coastal has 20 days in which to file an answer. Coastal's answer, shown below, is a brief reply to each of the allegations in the complaint. The answer tells the court and the plaintiff exactly what issues are in dispute. Since Coastal admits that the parties entered into the contract that Beth claims they did, there is no need for her to prove that in court. The court can focus its attention on the disputed issue: whether Tony Caruso died accidentally.

STATE OF OREGON
CIRCUIT COURT

Multnomah County   Civil Action No. 09-5626

_____
Elizabeth Smiles,
Plaintiff
v.
Coastal Insurance Company, Inc.,
Defendant
_____

ANSWER

Defendant Coastal Insurance Company, Inc., answers the complaint as follows:

1. Admit.
2. Admit.
3. Admit.
4. Admit.
5. Deny.
6. Admit.
7. Deny.

COASTAL INSURANCE COMPANY, INC.,
By its attorney,
[Signed]
Richard B. Stewart
Kiley, Robbins, Stewart & Glote
333 Victory Boulevard
Portland, OR
October 30, 2012

If the defendant fails to answer in time, the plaintiff will ask for a **default judgment**. In granting a default judgment, the judge accepts every allegation in the complaint as true and renders a decision that the plaintiff wins without a trial.

Recently, two men sued PepsiCo, claiming that the company stole the idea for Aquafina water from them. They argued that they should receive a portion of the profits for every bottle of Aquafina ever sold.

PepsiCo failed to file a timely answer, and the judge entered a default judgment in the amount of $1.26 billion. On appeal, the default judgment was overturned and PepsiCo was able to escape paying the massive sum, but other defendants are sometimes not so lucky.

It is important to respond to courts on time.

Default judgment
A decision that the plaintiff wins without trial because the defendant failed to answer in time.

Counter-Claim

Sometimes a defendant does more than merely answer a complaint and files a **counter-claim**, meaning a second lawsuit by the defendant against the plaintiff. Suppose that after her complaint was filed in court, Beth had written a letter to the newspaper, calling Coastal a bunch of "thieves and scoundrels who spend their days mired in fraud and larceny." Coastal

Counter-claim
A second lawsuit by the defendant against the plaintiff.

would not have found that amusing. The company's answer would have included a counter-claim against Beth for libel, claiming that she falsely accused the insurer of serious criminal acts. Coastal would have demanded money damages.

Reply
An answer to a counter-claim.

If Coastal counter-claimed, Beth would have to file a **reply**, which is simply an answer to a counter-claim. Beth's reply would be similar to Coastal's answer, admitting or denying the various allegations.

Class Actions

Class action
One plaintiff represents the entire group of plaintiffs, including those who are unaware of the lawsuit or even unaware they were harmed.

Suppose Janet uncovers evidence that Coastal denies 80 percent of all life insurance claims, calling them suicide. She could ask the court to permit a **class action**. If the court granted her request, she would represent the entire group of plaintiffs, including those who are unaware of the lawsuit or even unaware they were harmed. Class actions can give the plaintiffs much greater leverage, since the defendant's potential liability is vastly increased. In the back of her mind, Janet has thoughts of a class action, *if* she can uncover evidence that Coastal has used a claim of suicide to deny coverage to a large number of claimants.

Notice how potent a class action can be. From his small town in Maine, Ernie decides to get rich quickly. On the Internet, he advertises "Energy Breakthrough! Cut your heating costs 15 percent for only $25." In response, 100,000 people send him their money, and they receive a photocopied graph, illustrating that if you wear two sweaters instead of one, you will feel 15 percent warmer. Ernie has deceitfully earned $2,500,000 in pure profit. What can the angry homeowners do? Under the laws of fraud and consumer protection, they have a legitimate claim to their $25, and perhaps even to treble damages ($75). But few will sue, because the time and effort required would be greater than the money recovered.

Economists analyze such legal issues in terms of *efficiency*. The laws against Ernie's fraud are clear and well intended, but they will not help in this case because it is too expensive for 100,000 people to litigate such a small claim. The effort would be hugely *inefficient*, both for the homeowners and for society generally. The economic reality may permit Ernie to evade the law's grasp.

That is one reason we have class actions. A dozen or so "heating plan" buyers can all hire the same lawyer. This attorney will file court papers in Maine on behalf of *everyone*, nationwide, who has been swindled by Ernie—including the 99,988 people who have yet to be notified that they are part of the case. Now the con artist, instead of facing a few harmless suits for $25, must respond to a multimillion-dollar claim being handled by an experienced lawyer. Treble damages become menacing: three times $25 times 100,000 is no joke, even to a cynic like Ernie. He may also be forced to pay for the plaintiffs' attorney, as well as all costs of notifying class members and disbursing money to them. With one lawyer representing an entire class, the legal system has become fiercely efficient.

Congress recently passed a statute designed to force large, multi-state class actions out of state courts, into federal. Proponents of the new law complained that state courts often gave excessive verdicts, even for frivolous lawsuits. They said the cases hurt businesses while enriching lawyers. Opponents argued that the new law was designed to shield large corporations from paying for the harm they caused by sending the cases into a federal system that is often hostile to such suits.

Judgment on the Pleadings

Motion
A formal request to the court that the court take some step or issue some order.

Motion to dismiss
A request that the court terminate a case without permitting it to go further.

A party can ask the court for a judgment based simply on the pleadings themselves, by filing a motion to dismiss. A **motion** is a formal request to the court that the court take some step or issue some order. During a lawsuit, the parties file many motions. A **motion to dismiss** is a request that the court terminate a case without permitting it to go further. Suppose that a state law requires claims on life insurance contracts to be filed within three years, and Beth files her claim four years after Tony's death. Coastal would move to dismiss based on this late filing. The court might well agree, and Beth would never get into court.

Discovery

Few cases are dismissed on the pleadings. Most proceed quickly to the next step. **Discovery** is the critical, pre-trial opportunity for both parties to learn the strengths and weaknesses of the opponent's case.

The theory behind civil litigation is that the best outcome is a negotiated settlement and that parties will move toward agreement if they understand the opponent's case. That is likeliest to occur if both sides have an opportunity to examine most of the evidence the other side will bring to trial. Further, if a case does go all the way to trial, efficient and fair litigation cannot take place in a courtroom filled with surprises. On television dramas, witnesses say astonishing things that amaze the courtroom (and keep viewers hooked through the next commercial). In real trials, the lawyers know in advance the answers to practically all questions asked because discovery has allowed them to see the opponent's documents and question its witnesses. The following are the most important forms of discovery.

Interrogatories   These are written questions that the opposing party must answer, in writing, under oath.

Depositions   These provide a chance for one party's lawyer to question the other party, or a potential witness, under oath. The person being questioned is the **deponent**. Lawyers for both parties are present. During depositions, and in trial, good lawyers choose words carefully and ask questions calculated to advance their cause. A fine line separates ethical, probing questions from those that are tricky, and a similar line divides answers that are merely unhelpful from perjury.

Production of Documents and Things   Each side may ask the other side to produce relevant documents for inspection and copying; to produce physical objects, such as part of a car alleged to be defective; and for permission to enter on land to make an inspection, for example, at the scene of an accident.

Physical and Mental Examination   A party may ask the court to order an examination of the other party, if his physical or mental condition is relevant, for example, in a case of medical malpractice.

Janet Booker begins her discovery with interrogatories. Her goal is to learn Coastal's basic position and factual evidence and then follow up with more detailed questioning during depositions. Her interrogatories ask for every fact Coastal relied on in denying the claim. She asks for the names of all witnesses, the identity of all documents, including electronic records, the description of all things or objects that they considered. She requests the names of all corporate officers who played any role in the decision and of any expert witnesses Coastal plans to call. Interrogatory No. 18 demands extensive information on all *other* claims in the past three years that Coastal has denied based on alleged suicide. Janet is looking for evidence that would support a class action.

Beth remarks on how thorough the interrogatories are. "This will tell us what their case is." Janet frowns and looks less optimistic: she's done this before.

Coastal has 30 days to answer Janet's interrogatories. Before it responds, Coastal mails to Janet a notice of deposition, stating its intention to depose Beth Smiles. Beth and Janet will go to the office of Coastal's lawyer, and Beth will answer questions under oath. But at the same time Coastal sends this notice, it sends *25 other notices of deposition*. The company will depose Karen Caruso as soon as Beth's deposition is over. Coastal also plans to depose all seven employees of Enviro-Vision; three neighbors who lived near Tony and Karen's beach house; two policemen who participated in the search; the doctor and two nurses involved in the case; Tony's physician; Jerry Johnson, Tony's tennis partner; Craig Bergson,

Discovery
The pre-trial opportunity for both parties to learn the strengths and weaknesses of the opponent's case.

Deponent
The person being questioned.

> But there may be another reason that Coastal is doing this: the company wants to make this litigation hurt.

Motion for a protective order
Request that the court limit discovery.

a college roommate; a couple who had dinner with Tony and Karen a week before his death; and several other people.

Beth is appalled. Janet explains that some of these people might have relevant information. But there may be another reason that Coastal is doing this: the company wants to make this litigation hurt. Janet will have to attend every one of these depositions. Costs will skyrocket.

Janet files a **motion for a protective order**. This is a request that the court limit Coastal's discovery by decreasing the number of depositions. Janet also calls Rich Stewart and suggests that they discuss what depositions are really necessary. Rich insists that all of the depositions are important. This is a $2 million case, and Coastal is entitled to protect itself. As both lawyers know, **the parties are entitled to discover anything that could reasonably lead to valid evidence.**

Before Beth's deposition date arrives, Rich sends Coastal's answers to Enviro-Vision's interrogatories. The answers contain no useful information whatsoever. For example, Interrogatory No. 10 asked, "If you claim that Anthony Caruso committed suicide, describe every fact upon which you rely in reaching that conclusion." Coastal's answer simply says, "His state of mind, his poor business affairs, and the circumstances of his death all indicate suicide."

Janet calls Rich and complains that the interrogatory answers are a bad joke. Rich disagrees, saying that it is the best information they have so early in the case. After they debate it for 20 minutes, Rich offers to settle the case for $100,000. Janet refuses and makes no counteroffer.

Janet files a **motion to compel answers to interrogatories**, in other words, a formal request that the court order Coastal to supply more complete answers. Janet submits a **memorandum** with the motion, which is a supporting argument. Although it is only a few pages long, the memorandum takes several hours of online research and writing to prepare—more costs. Janet also informs Rich Stewart that Beth will not appear for the deposition, since Coastal's interrogatory answers are inadequate.

Rich now files *his* motion to compel, asking the court to order Beth Smiles to appear for her deposition. The court hears all of the motions together. Janet argues that Coastal's interrogatory answers are hopelessly uninformative and defeat the whole purpose of discovery. She claims that Coastal's large number of depositions creates a huge and unfair expense for a small firm.

Rich claims that the interrogatory answers are the best that Coastal can do thus far and that Coastal will supplement the answers when more information becomes available. He argues against Interrogatory No. 18, the one in which Janet asked for the names of other policyholders whom Coastal considered suicides. He claims that Janet is engaging in a fishing expedition that would violate the privacy of Coastal's insurance customers and provide no information relevant to this case. He demands that Janet make Beth available for a deposition.

These discovery rulings are critical because they will color the entire lawsuit. A trial judge has to make many discovery decisions before a case reaches trial. At times, the judge must weigh the need of one party to see documents against the other side's need for privacy. One device a judge can use in reaching a discovery ruling is an **in camera inspection**, meaning that the judge views the requested documents alone, with no lawyers present, and decides whether the other side is entitled to view them.

E-Discovery   The biggest change in litigation in the last decade is the explosive rise of electronic discovery. Companies send hundreds, or thousands, or millions of emails—every day. Many have attachments, sometimes hundreds of pages long. In addition, businesses large and small have vast amounts of data stored electronically. All of this information is potentially subject to discovery.

It is enormously time-consuming and expensive for companies to locate all of the relevant material, separate it from irrelevant or confidential matter, and furnish it. A firm may be obligated to furnish *millions* of emails to the opposing party. In one recent case, a defendant had to pay 31 lawyers full time, for six months, just to wade through the e-ocean of documents and figure out which had to be supplied and how to produce it. Not surprisingly, this data eruption has created a new industry: high-tech companies that assist law firms in finding, sorting, and delivering electronic data.

Who is to say what must be supplied? What if an email string contains individual emails that are clearly privileged (meaning a party need not divulge them), but others that are not privileged? May a company refuse to furnish the entire string? Many will try. However, some courts have ruled that companies seeking to protect email strings must create a log describing every individual email and allow the court to determine which are privileged.[5]

When the cost of furnishing the data becomes burdensome, who should pay, the party seeking the information or the one supplying it? In a recent $4 million corporate lawsuit, the defendant turned over 3,000 emails and 211,000 other documents. But the trial judge noted that many of the email attachments—sometimes 12 to an email—had gone missing, and required the company to produce them. The defendant protested that finding the attachments would cost an additional $206,000. The judge ordered the company to do it, and bear the full cost.

Both sides in litigation sometimes use gamesmanship during discovery. Thus, if an individual sues a large corporation, for example, the company may deliberately make discovery so expensive that the plaintiff cannot afford the legal fees. And if a plaintiff has a poor case, he might intentionally try to make the discovery process more expensive for the defendant than his settlement offer. Even if a defendant expects to win at trial, an offer to settle a case for $50,000 can look like a bargain if discovery alone will cost $100,000. Some defendants refuse, but others are more pragmatic.

The following case illustrates another common discovery problem: refusal by one side to appear for deposition. Did the defendant cynically believe that long delay would win the day, given that the plaintiff was 78 years old? What can a court do in such a case?

STINTON V. ROBIN'S WOOD, INC.

45 A.D. 3d 203, 842 NYS2d 477
New York App. Div., 2007

Facts: Ethel Flanzraich, 78 years old, slipped and fell on the steps of property owned by Robin's Wood. She broke her left leg and left arm. Flanzraich sued, claiming that Robin's Wood caused her fall because its employee, Anthony Monforte, had negligently painted the stairs. In its answer to the complaint, Robin's Wood denied all of the significant allegations.

During a preliminary conference with the trial judge, the parties agreed to hold depositions of both parties on August 4. Flanzraich appeared for deposition but Robin's Wood did not furnish its employee, Monforte, nor did it offer any other company representative. The court then ordered the deposition of the defendant to take place the following April 2. Again, Robin's Wood produced neither Monforte nor anyone else. On July 16, the court ordered the defendant to produce its representative within 30 days. Once more, no one showed up for deposition.

---

[5] *Universal Service Fund Telephone Billing Practices Litigation*, 232 F.R.D. 669 (D. Kan. 2005).

On August 18—over *one year* after the original deposition date—Flanzraich moved to strike the defendant's answer, meaning that the plaintiff would win by default. The company argued that it had made diligent efforts to locate Monforte and force him to appear. However, all of the letters sent to Monforte were addressed care of Robin's Wood. Finally, the company stated that it no longer employed Monforte.

The trial judge granted the motion to strike the answer. That meant that Robin's Wood was liable for Flanraich's fall. The only remaining issue was damages. The court determined that Robin's Wood owed $22,631 for medical expenses, $150,000 for past pain and suffering, and $300,000 for future pain and suffering. One day later, Flanraich died, of other causes. Robin's Wood appealed.

Issue: *Did the trial court abuse its discretion by striking the defendant's answer?*

Excerpts from Judge McCarthy's Decision: We find no merit to the defendant's claim that the [trial court] improvidently exercised its discretion in striking its answer. An action should be determined on the merits whenever possible. However, a court, in its discretion, may invoke the drastic remedy of striking an answer if it determines that the defendant's failure to comply with discovery demands is willful and contumacious.

The willful and contumacious character of [defendant's] conduct may be inferred from the defendant's noncompliance with [three] court orders directing such a deposition. Although the defendant may not have been able to produce Monforte after he left its employ, the defendant failed to explain why it produced neither another representative for the deposition nor timely disclosed to the decedent that it no longer employed Monforte. Either of these actions would have afforded the decedent the opportunity to subpoena Monforte for a nonparty deposition, had she so desired. For instance, by producing its representative for a deposition, the decedent would have had the ability to explore the whereabouts of Monforte and, in all likelihood, would have obtained information regarding how to contact him since the record indicates that the defendant had such information. This is especially important here where the decedent was elderly at the time of the accident and delays in discovery could only serve to prejudice her and unjustly benefit the defendant. Moreover, the defendant failed to explain why it did not produce Monforte for a deposition during the time he was under its employ.

Affirmed.

In the Enviro-Vision case, the judge rules that Coastal must furnish more complete answers to the interrogatories, especially as to why the company denied the claim. However, he rules against Interrogatory No. 18, the one concerning other claims Coastal has denied. This simple ruling kills Janet's hope of making a class action of the case. He orders Beth to appear for the deposition. As to future depositions, Coastal may take any 10 but then may take additional depositions only by demonstrating to the court that the deponents have useful information.

Rich proceeds to take Beth's deposition. It takes two full days. He asks about Enviro-Vision's past and present. He learns that Tony appeared to have won their biggest contract ever from Rapid City, Oregon, but that he then lost it when he had a fight with Rapid City's mayor. He inquires into Tony's mood, learns that he was depressed, and probes in every direction he can to find evidence of suicidal motivation. Janet and Rich argue frequently over questions and whether Beth should have to answer them. At times, Janet is persuaded and permits Beth to answer; other times, she instructs Beth not to answer. For example, toward the end of the second day, Rich asks Beth whether she and Tony had been sexually involved. Janet instructs Beth not to answer. This fight necessitates another trip into court to determine whether Beth must answer. The judge rules that Beth must discuss Tony's romantic life only if Coastal has some evidence that he was involved with someone outside his marriage. The company lacks any such evidence.

Now limited to 10 depositions, Rich selects his nine other deponents carefully. For example, he decides to depose only one of the two nurses; he chooses to question Jerry Johnson, the tennis partner, but not Craig Bergson, the former roommate; and so forth. When we look at the many legal issues this case raises, his choices seem minor. In fact, unbeknownst to Rich or anyone else, his choices may determine the outcome of the case. As we will see later, Craig Bergson has evidence that is possibly crucial to the lawsuit. If Rich decides not to depose him, neither side will ever learn the evidence and the jury will never hear it. A jury can decide a case only based on the evidence presented to it. *Facts are elusive—and often controlling.*

In each deposition, Rich carefully probes with his questions, sometimes trying to learn what he actually does not know, sometimes trying to pin down the witness to a specific version of facts so that Rich knows how the witness will testify at trial. Neighbors at the beach testify that Tony seemed tense; one testifies about seeing Tony, unhappy, on the beach with his dog. Another testifies he had never before seen Blue tied up on the beach. Karen Caruso admits that Tony had been somewhat tense and unhappy the last couple of months. She reluctantly discusses their marriage, admitting there were problems.

Other Discovery Rich sends Requests to Produce Documents, seeking medical records about Tony. Once again, the parties fight over which records are relevant, but Rich gets most of what he wants. Janet does less discovery than Rich because most of the witnesses she will call are friendly witnesses. She can interview them privately without giving any information to Coastal. With the help of Beth and Karen, Janet builds her case just as carefully as Rich, choosing the witnesses who will bolster the view that Tony was in good spirits and died accidentally.

She deposes all the officers of Coastal who participated in the decision to deny insurance coverage. She is particularly aggressive in pinning them down as to the limited information they had when they denied Beth's claim.

Summary Judgment

When discovery is completed, both sides may consider seeking summary judgment. **Summary judgment** is a ruling by the court that no trial is necessary because some essential facts are not in dispute. The purpose of a trial is to determine the facts of the case; that is, to decide who did what to whom, why, when, and with what consequences. If there are no relevant facts in dispute, then there is no need for a trial.

In the following case, the defendant won summary judgment, meaning that the case never went to trial. And yet, this was only the beginning of trouble for that defendant, Bill Clinton.

Summary judgment
A ruling by the court that no trial is necessary because some essential facts are not in dispute.

JONES V. CLINTON

990 F. Supp. 657, 1998 U.S. Dist. LEXIS 3902
United States District Court for the Eastern District of Arkansas, 1998

Facts: In 1991, Bill Clinton was governor of Arkansas. Paula Jones worked for a state agency, the Arkansas Industrial Development Commission (AIDC). When Clinton became President, Jones sued him, claiming that he had sexually harassed her. She alleged that, in May 1991, the governor arranged for her to meet him in a hotel room in Little Rock, Arkansas. When they were alone, he put his hand on her leg and slid it toward her pelvis. She escaped from his grasp, exclaimed, "What are you doing?" and said she was "not that kind of girl." She was upset and confused, and sat on a sofa near the door. She claimed that Clinton approached her, "lowered his trousers and underwear, exposed his penis and told her to kiss it."

Jones was horrified, jumped up and said she had to leave. Clinton responded by saying, "Well, I don't want to make you do anything you don't want to do," and pulled his pants up. He added that if she got in trouble for leaving work, Jones should "have Dave call me immediately and I'll take care of it." He also said, "You are smart. Let's keep this between ourselves." Jones remained at AIDC until February 1993, when she moved to California because of her husband's job transfer.

President Clinton denied all of the allegations. He also filed for summary judgment, claiming that Jones had not alleged facts that justified a trial. Jones opposed the motion for summary judgment.

Issue: *Was Clinton entitled to summary judgment, or was Jones entitled to a trial?*

Excerpts from Judge Wright's Decision: [To establish this type of a sexual harassment case, a plaintiff must show that her refusal to submit to unwelcome sexual advances resulted in a tangible job detriment, meaning that she suffered a specific loss. Jones claims that she was denied promotions, given a job with fewer responsibilities, isolated physically, required to sit at a workstation with no work to do, and singled out as the only female employee not to be given flowers on Secretary's Day.]

There is no record of plaintiff ever applying for another job within AIDC, however, and the record shows that not only was plaintiff never downgraded, her position was reclassified upward from a Grade 9 classification to a Grade 11 classification, thereby increasing her annual salary. Indeed, it is undisputed that plaintiff received every merit increase and cost-of-living allowance for which she was eligible during her nearly two-year tenure with the AIDC and consistently received satisfactory job evaluations.

Although plaintiff states that her job title upon returning from maternity leave was no longer that of purchasing assistant, her job duties prior to taking maternity leave and her job duties upon returning to work both involved data input. That being so, plaintiff cannot establish a tangible job detriment. A transfer that does not involve a demotion in form or substance and involves only minor changes in working conditions, with no reduction in pay or benefits, will not constitute an adverse employment action, otherwise every trivial personnel action that an irritable employee did not like would form the basis of a discrimination suit.

Finally, the Court rejects plaintiff's claim that she was subjected to hostile treatment having tangible effects when she was isolated physically, made to sit in a location from which she was constantly watched, made to sit at her workstation with no work to do, and singled out as the only female employee not to be given flowers on Secretary's Day. Plaintiff may well have perceived hostility and animus on the part of her supervisors, but these perceptions are merely conclusory in nature and do not, without more, constitute a tangible job detriment. Although it is not clear why plaintiff failed to receive flowers on Secretary's Day in 1992, such an omission does not give rise to a federal cause of action.

In sum, the Court finds that a showing of a tangible job detriment or adverse employment action is an essential element of plaintiff's sexual harassment claim and that plaintiff has not demonstrated any tangible job detriment or adverse employment action for her refusal to submit to the Governor's alleged advances. The President is therefore entitled to summary judgment [on this claim].

In other words, the court acknowledged that there were factual disputes, but concluded that even if Jones proved each of her allegations, she would *still* lose the case, because her allegations fell short of a legitimate case of sexual harassment. Jones appealed the case. Later the same year, as the appeal was pending and the House of Representatives was considering whether to impeach President Clinton, the parties settled the dispute. Clinton, without acknowledging any of the allegations, agreed to pay Jones $850,000 to drop the suit.

Janet and Rich each consider moving for summary judgment, but both correctly decide that they would lose. There is one major fact in dispute: did Tony Caruso commit suicide? Only a jury may decide that issue. As long as there is *some evidence* supporting each side of a key factual dispute, the court may not grant summary judgment.

EXAM Strategy

Question: You are a judge. Mel has sued Kevin, claiming that while Kevin was drunk, he negligently drove his car down Mel's street, and destroyed rare trees on a lot that Mel owns, next to his house. Mel's complaint stated that three witnesses at a bar saw Kevin take at least eight drinks less than an hour before the damage was done. In Kevin's answer, he denied causing the damage and denied being in the bar that night.

Kevin's lawyer has moved for summary judgment. He proves that three weeks before the alleged accident, Mel sold the lot to Tatiana.

Mel's lawyer opposes summary judgment. He produces a security camera tape proving that Kevin was in the bar, drinking beer, 34 minutes before the damage was done. He produces a signed statement from Sandy, a landscape gardener who lives across the street from the scene. Sandy states that she heard a crash, hurried to the windows, and saw Kevin's car weaving away from the damaged trees. She is a landscape gardener and estimates the tree damage at $30,000 to $40,000. How should you rule on the motion?

Strategy: Do not be fooled by red herrings about Kevin's drinking or the value of the trees. Stick to the question: should you grant summary judgment? Trials are necessary to resolve disputes about essential factual issues. Summary judgment is appropriate when there are no essential facts in dispute. Is there an essential fact not in dispute? Find it. Apply the rule. Being a judge is easy!

Result: It makes no difference whether Kevin was drunk or sober, whether he caused the harm or was at home in bed. Because Mel does not own the property, he cannot recover for the damage to it. He cannot win. You should grant Kevin's summary judgment motion.

Final Preparation

Well over 90 percent of all lawsuits are settled before trial. But the parties in the Enviro-Vision dispute are unable to compromise, so each side gears up for trial. The attorneys make lists of all witnesses they will call. They then prepare each witness very carefully, rehearsing the questions they will ask. It is considered ethical and proper to rehearse the questions, provided the answers are honest and come from the witness. It is unethical and illegal for a lawyer to tell a witness what to say. It also makes for a weaker presentation of evidence—witnesses giving scripted answers are often easy to spot. The lawyers also have colleagues cross-examine each witness, so that the witnesses are ready for the questions the other side's lawyer will ask.

This preparation takes hours and hours, for many days. Beth is frustrated that she cannot do the work she needs to for Enviro-Vision because she is spending so much time preparing the case. Other employees have to prepare as well, especially for cross-examination by Rich Stewart, and it is a terrible drain on the small firm. More than a year after Janet filed her complaint, they are ready to begin trial.

TRIAL

Adversary System

Our system of justice assumes that the best way to bring out the truth is for the two contesting sides to present the strongest case possible to a neutral factfinder. Each side presents its witnesses and then the opponent has a chance to cross-examine. The adversary system presumes that by putting a witness on the stand and letting both lawyers question her, the truth will emerge.

The judge runs the trial. Each lawyer sits at a large table near the front. Beth, looking tense and unhappy, sits with Janet. Rich Stewart sits with a Coastal executive. In the back of the courtroom are benches for the public. On one bench sits Craig Bergson. He will watch the entire proceeding with intense interest and a strange feeling of unease. He is convinced he knows what really happened.

Janet has demanded a jury trial for Beth's case, and Judge Rowland announces that they will now impanel the jury.

Right to Jury Trial

Not all cases are tried to a jury. As a general rule, both plaintiff and defendant have a right to demand a jury trial when the lawsuit is one for money damages. For example, in a typical contract lawsuit, such as Beth's insurance claim, both plaintiff and defendant have a jury trial right whether they are in state or federal court. Even in such a case, though, the parties may *waive* the jury right, meaning they agree to try the case to a judge. Also, if the plaintiff is seeking an equitable remedy such as an injunction, there is no jury right for either party.

Voir Dire

Voir dire
The process of selecting a jury.

The process of selecting a jury is called **voir dire**, which means "to speak the truth."[6] The court's goal is to select an impartial jury; the lawyers will each try to get a jury as favorable to their side as possible. A court sends letters to potential jurors who live in its county. Those who do not report for jury duty face significant consequences.

Challenges for cause
A claim that a juror has demonstrated probably bias.

When voir dire begins, potential jurors are questioned individually, sometimes by the judge and sometimes by the two lawyers, as each side tries to ferret out potential bias. Each lawyer may make any number of **challenges for cause**, claiming that a juror has demonstrated probable bias. For example, if a prospective juror in the Enviro-Vision case works for an insurance company, the judge will excuse her on the assumption that she would be biased in favor of Coastal. If the judge perceives no bias, the lawyer may still make a limited number of **peremptory challenges**, entitling him to excuse that juror for virtually any reason, which need not be stated in court. For example, if Rich Stewart believes that a juror seems hostile to him personally, he will use a peremptory challenge to excuse that juror, even if the judge sensed no animosity. The process continues until 14 jurors are seated. Twelve will comprise the jury; the other two are alternates who hear the case and remain available in the event one of the impaneled jurors becomes ill or otherwise cannot continue.

Peremptory challenges
The right to excuse a juror for virtually any reason.

Although jury selection for a case can sometimes take many days, in the Enviro-Vision case, the first day of the hearing ends with the jury selected. In the hallway outside the court, Rich offers Janet $200,000 to settle. Janet reports the offer to Beth and they agree to reject it. Craig Bergson drives home, emotionally confused. Only three weeks before his death, Tony had accidentally met his old roommate and they had had several drinks. Craig believes that what Tony told him answers the riddle of this case.

PEREDA V. PARAJON

957 So.2d 1194
Florida Court of Appeals, 2007

Facts: Maria Parajon sued Diana Pereda for injuring her in a car accident. During voir dire, Parajon's lawyer asked the panel of prospective jurors these questions: "Is there anybody sitting on this panel now that has ever been under the care of a physician for personal injuries, whether you had a lawsuit or not? In other words, you may not have had any sort of lawsuit, but you slipped and fell—you had any accidents?"

Several of the prospective jurors raised their hands, allowing the lawyers to question more deeply into possible

---

[6]Students of French note that *voir* means "to see" and assume that *voir dire* should translate as "to see, to speak." However, the legal term is centuries old and derives not from modern French but from Old French, in which *voir* meant "truth."

bias. However, Lisa Berg, a prospective juror who happened to be a lawyer, did not respond. Berg and others were seated as jurors, and ultimately awarded Parajon $450,000 for medical damages and pain and suffering.

After the trial, questioned in court by the judge, Berg admitted that three years earlier she had been injured in a car accident, hired a lawyer to sue, and settled out of court for $4,000. Asked about the settlement, Berg replied, "I think everyone always wants more money."

Parajon moved for a new trial but the judge denied the motion. Parajon appealed.

Issue: *Is Parajon entitled to a new trial based on Berg's failure to disclose her own personal injury lawsuit?*

Excerpts from Judge Rothenberg's Decision: To determine whether a juror's nondisclosure warrants a new trial, the complaining party must show that: (1) the information is relevant and material to jury service in the case; (2) the juror concealed the information during questioning; and (3) the failure to disclose the information was not attributable to the complaining party's lack of diligence.

Both Parajon's and Pereda's respective counsels may indeed have been influenced to challenge Berg peremptorily had the facts of her personal injury litigation history been known. Berg's personal injury claim was not remote in time. Berg settled out of court at the urging of her parents in order to put the matter behind her. Her involvement in this matter may have affected her point of view in [this case]. Her nondisclosure, which precluded counsel's ability to question Berg about the experience and to fairly evaluate her as a prospective juror, was material.

It is clear from the record that Berg concealed her personal injury litigation history. She is a lawyer and an officer of the court. It is, therefore, difficult to imagine that she did not think the questions posed by Parajon's counsel applied to her.

The record evidence demonstrates that other prospective jurors, none of whom were lawyers, clearly understood what type of information Parajon's counsel was asking them to disclose. We find that Parajon's counsel made a diligent inquiry.

Reversed and remanded for a new trial.

Opening Statements

The next day, each attorney makes an opening statement to the jury, summarizing the proof he or she expects to offer, with the plaintiff going first. Janet focuses on Tony's successful life, his business and strong marriage, and the tragedy of his accidental death.[7]

Rich works hard to establish a friendly rapport with the jury. If members of the jury like him, they will tend to pay more attention to his presentation of evidence. He expresses regret about the death. Nonetheless, suicide is a clear exclusion from the policy. If insurance companies are forced to pay claims never bargained for, everyone's insurance rates will go up.

Burden of Proof

In civil cases, the plaintiff has the burden of proof. That means that the plaintiff must convince the jury that its version of the case is correct; the defendant is not obligated to disprove the allegations.

The plaintiff's burden in a civil lawsuit is to prove its case by a **preponderance of the evidence**. It must convince the jury that its version of the facts is at least *slightly more likely* than the defendant's version. Some courts describe this as a "51–49" persuasion; that is, that plaintiff's proof must "just tip" credibility in its favor. By contrast, in a criminal case, the prosecution must demonstrate **beyond a reasonable doubt** that the defendant is guilty. The burden of proof in a criminal case is much tougher because the likely consequences are, too. See Exhibit 3.3.

Preponderance of the evidence

The plaintiff's burden in a civil lawsuit.

Beyond a reasonable doubt

The government's burden in a criminal prosecution.

---

[7]Janet Booker has dropped her claim for triple damages against Coastal. To have any hope of such a verdict, she would have to show that Coastal had no legitimate reason at all for denying the claim. Discovery has convinced her that Coastal will demonstrate some rational reasons for what it did.

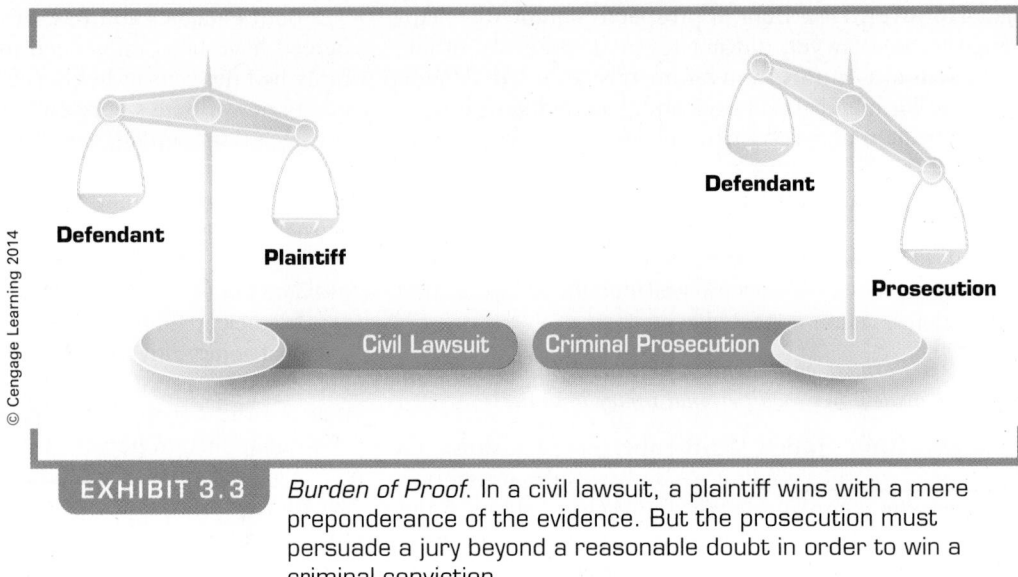

EXHIBIT 3.3   *Burden of Proof.* In a civil lawsuit, a plaintiff wins with a mere preponderance of the evidence. But the prosecution must persuade a jury beyond a reasonable doubt in order to win a criminal conviction.

Plaintiff's Case

Because the plaintiff has the burden of proof, Janet puts in her case first. She wants to prove two things. First, that Tony died. That is easy because the death certificate clearly demonstrates it and Coastal does not seriously contest it. Second, in order to win double indemnity damages, she must show that the death was accidental. She will do this with the testimony of the witnesses she calls, one after the other. Her first witness is Beth. When a lawyer asks questions of her own witness, it is **direct examination**. Janet brings out all the evidence she wants the jury to hear: that the business was basically sound, though temporarily troubled, that Tony was a hard worker, why the company took out life insurance policies, and so forth.

Direct examination
When a lawyer asks questions of her own witness.

Then Rich has a chance to **cross-examine** Beth, which means to ask questions of an opposing witness. He will try to create doubt in the jury's mind. He asks Beth only questions for which he is certain of the answers, based on discovery. Rich gets Beth to admit that the firm was not doing well the year of Tony's death; that Tony had lost the best client the firm ever had; that Beth had reduced salaries; and that Tony had been depressed about business.

Cross-examine
To ask questions of an opposing witness.

Rules of Evidence

The lawyers are not free simply to ask any question they want. The **law of evidence** determines what questions a lawyer may ask and how the questions are to be phrased, what answers a witness may give, and what documents may be introduced. The goal is to get the best evidence possible before the jurors so they can decide what really happened. In general, witnesses may only testify about things they saw or heard.

These rules are complex, and a thorough look at them is beyond the scope of this chapter. However, they can be just as important in resolving a dispute as the underlying substantive law. Suppose that a plaintiff's case depends upon the jury hearing about a certain conversation, but the rules of evidence prevent the lawyer from asking about it. That conversation might just as well never have occurred.

Janet calls an expert witness, a marine geologist, who testifies about the tides and currents in the area where Tony's body was found. The expert testifies that even experienced swimmers can be overwhelmed by a sudden shift in currents. Rich objects strenuously that this is irrelevant, because there is no testimony that there *was* such a current at the time of Tony's death. The judge permits the testimony.

Karen Caruso testifies that Tony was in "reasonably good" spirits the day of his death, and that he often took Blue for walks along the beach. Karen testifies that Blue was part Newfoundland. Rich objects that testimony about Blue's pedigree is irrelevant, but Janet insists it will show why Blue was tied up. The judge allows the testimony. Karen says that whenever Blue saw them swim, he would instinctively go into the water and pull them to shore. Does that explain why Blue was tied up? Only the jury can answer.

Cross-examination is grim for Karen. Rich slowly but methodically questions her about Tony's state of mind and brings out the problems with the company, his depression, and tension within the marriage. Janet's other witnesses testify essentially as they did during their depositions.

Motion for Directed Verdict

At the close of the plaintiff's case, Rich moves for a directed verdict; that is, a ruling that the plaintiff has entirely failed to prove some aspect of her case. Rich is seeking to win without even putting in his own case. He argues that it was Beth's burden to prove that Tony died accidentally and that she has entirely failed to do that.

A **directed verdict is permissible only if the evidence so clearly favors the defendant that reasonable minds could not disagree on it**. If reasonable minds could disagree, the motion must be denied. Here, Judge Rowland rules that the plaintiff has put in enough evidence of accidental death that a reasonable person could find in Beth's favor. The motion is denied.

There is no downside for Rich to ask for a directed verdict. The trial continues as if he had never made such a motion.

Directed verdict
A ruling that the plaintiff has entirely failed to prove some aspect of her case.

Defendant's Case

Rich now puts in his case, exactly as Janet did, except that he happens to have fewer witnesses. He calls the examining doctor, who admits that Tony could have committed suicide by swimming out too far. On cross-examination, Janet gets the doctor to acknowledge that he has no idea whether Tony intentionally drowned. Rich also questions several neighbors as to how depressed Tony had seemed and how unusual it was that Blue was tied up. Some of the witnesses Rich deposed, such as the tennis partner Jerry Johnson, have nothing that will help Coastal's case, so he does not call them.

Craig Bergson, sitting in the back of the courtroom, thinks how different the trial would have been had he been called as a witness. When he and Tony had the fateful drink, Tony had been distraught: business was terrible, he was involved in an extramarital affair that he could not end, and he saw no way out of his problems. He had no one to talk to and had been hugely relieved to speak with Craig. Several times Tony had said, "I just can't go on like this. I don't want to, anymore." Craig thought Tony seemed suicidal and urged him to see a therapist Craig knew and trusted. Tony had said that it was good advice, but Craig is unsure whether Tony sought any help.

This evidence would have affected the case. Had Rich Stewart known of the conversation, he would have deposed Craig and the therapist. Coastal's case would have been far stronger, perhaps overwhelming. But Craig's evidence will never be heard. Facts are critical. Rich's decision to depose other witnesses and omit Craig may influence the verdict more than any rule of law.

Closing Arguments

Both lawyers sum up their case to the jury, explaining how they hope the jury will interpret what they have heard. Janet summarizes the plaintiff's version of the facts, claiming that Blue was tied up so that Tony could swim without worrying about him. Rich claims that business and personal pressures had overwhelmed Tony. He tied up his dog, neatly folded his clothes, and took his own life.

Jury Instructions

Judge Rowland instructs the jury as to its duty. He tells them that they are to evaluate the case based only on the evidence they heard at trial, relying on their own experience and common sense.

He explains the law and the burden of proof, telling the jury that it is Beth's obligation to prove that Tony died. If Beth has proven that Tony died, she is entitled to $1 million; if she has proven that his death was accidental, she is entitled to $2 million. However, if Coastal has proven suicide, Beth receives nothing. Finally, he states that if they are unable to decide between accidental death and suicide, there is a legal presumption that it was accidental. Rich asks Judge Rowland to rephrase the "legal presumption" part, but the judge declines.

Verdict

The jury deliberates informally, with all jurors entitled to voice their opinion. Some deliberations take two hours; some take two weeks. Many states require a unanimous verdict; others require only, for example, a 10–2 vote in civil cases.

This case presents a close call. No one saw Tony die. Yet even though they cannot know with certainty, the jury's decision will probably be the final word on whether he took his own life. After a day and a half of deliberating, the jury notifies the judge that it has reached a verdict. Rich Stewart quickly makes a new offer: $350,000. (The two sides have the right to settle a case until the moment when the last appeal is decided.) Beth hesitates but turns it down.

The judge summons the lawyers to court, and Beth goes as well. The judge asks the foreman if the jury has reached a decision. He states that it has: the jury finds that Tony Caruso drowned accidentally, and awards Beth Smiles $2 million.

Motions after the Verdict

Judgment *non obstante veredicto*

A judgment notwithstanding the jury's verdict.

Rich immediately moves for a **judgment *non obstante veredicto*** (JNOV), meaning a judgment notwithstanding the jury's verdict. He is asking the judge to overturn the jury's verdict. Rich argues that the jury's decision went against all of the evidence. He also claims that the judge's instructions were wrong and misled the jury.

Judge Rowland denies the JNOV. Rich immediately moves for a new trial, making the same claim, and the judge denies the motion. Beth is elated that the case is finally over—until Janet says she expects an appeal. Craig Bergson, leaving the courtroom, wonders if he did the right thing. He felt sympathy for Beth and none for Coastal. Yet now he is neither happy nor proud.

APPEALS

Two days later, Rich files an appeal to the court of appeals. The same day, he phones Janet and increases his settlement offer to $425,000. Beth is tempted but wants Janet's advice. Janet says the risks of an appeal are that the court will order a new trial, and they would start all over. But to accept this offer is to forfeit over $1.5 million. Beth is unsure what to do. The firm desperately needs cash now, and appeals may take years. Janet suggests they wait until oral argument, another eight months.

Rich files a brief arguing that there were two basic errors at the trial: first, that the jury's verdict is clearly contrary to the evidence; and second, that the judge gave the wrong instructions to the jury. Janet files a reply brief, opposing Rich on both issues. In her brief,

Janet cites many cases that she claims are **precedent**: earlier decisions by the state appellate courts on similar or identical issues.

Eight months later, the lawyers representing Coastal and Enviro-Vision appear in the court of appeals to argue their case. Rich, the appellant, goes first. The judges frequently interrupt his argument with questions. They show little sympathy for his claim that the verdict was against the facts. They seem more sympathetic with his second point, that the instructions were wrong.

When Janet argues, all of their questions concern the judge's instructions. It appears they believe the instructions were in error. The judges take the case under advisement, meaning they will decide some time in the future—maybe in two weeks, maybe in five months.

Appeals Court Options

The court of appeals can **affirm** the trial court, allowing the decision to stand. The court may **modify** the decision, for example, by affirming that the plaintiff wins but decreasing the size of the award. (That is unlikely here; Beth is entitled to $2 million or nothing.) The court might **reverse and remand**, nullifying the lower court's decision and returning the case to the lower court for a new trial. Or it could simply **reverse**, turning the loser (Coastal) into the winner, with no new trial.

What will it do here? On the factual issue, it will probably rule in Beth's favor. There *was* evidence from which a jury could conclude that Tony died accidentally. It is true that there was also considerable evidence to support Coastal's position, but that is probably not enough to overturn the verdict. If reasonable people could disagree on what the evidence proves, an appellate court generally refuses to change the jury's factual findings. The court of appeals is likely to rule that a reasonable jury *could* have found accidental death, even if the appellate judges personally suspect that Tony may have killed himself.

The judge's instructions raise a more difficult problem. Some states would require a more complex statement about "presumptions."[8]

What does a court of appeals do if it decides the trial court's instructions were wrong? If it believes the error rendered the trial and verdict unfair, it will remand the case; that is, send it back to the lower court for a new trial. However, the court may conclude that the mistake was **harmless error**. A trial judge cannot do a perfect job, and not every error is fatal. The court may decide the verdict was fair in spite of the mistake.

Janet and Beth talk. Beth is very anxious and wants to settle. She does not want to wait four or five months, only to learn that they must start all over. Janet urges that they wait a few weeks to hear from Rich: they don't want to seem too eager.

A week later, Rich telephones and offers $500,000. Janet turns it down, but says she will ask Beth if she wants to make a counter-offer. She and Beth talk. They agree that they will settle for $1 million. Janet then calls Rich and offers to settle for $1.7 million. Rich and Janet debate the merits of the case. Rich later calls back and offers $750,000, saying he doubts that he can go any higher. Janet counters with $1.4 million, saying she doubts she can go any lower. They argue, both predicting that they will win on appeal.

Rich calls, offers $900,000 and says, "That's it. No more." Janet argues for $1.2 million, expecting to nudge Rich up to $1 million. He doesn't nudge, instead saying, "Take it or leave it." Janet and Beth talk it over. Janet telephones Rich and accepts $900,000 to settle the case.

---

[8]Judge Rowland probably should have said, "The law presumes that death is accidental, not suicide. So if there were no evidence either way, the plaintiff would win because we presume accident. But if there is competing evidence, the presumption becomes irrelevant. If you think that Coastal Insurance has introduced some evidence of suicide, then forget the legal presumption. You must then decide what happened based on what you have seen and heard in court, and on any inferences you choose to draw." Note that the judge's instructions were different, though similar.

Precedent

Earlier decisions by the state appellate courts on similar or identical issues.

Affirm

To allow the decision to stand.

Modify

To affirm the outcome but with changes.

Reverse and remand

To nullify the lower decision and return the case for reconsideration or retrial.

Harmless error

A mistake by the trial judge that was too minor to affect the outcome.

If they had waited for the court of appeals decision, would Beth have won? It is impossible to know. It is certain, though, that whoever lost would have appealed. Months would have passed waiting to learn if the state supreme court would accept the case. If that court had agreed to hear the appeal, Beth would have endured another year of waiting, brief writing, oral argument, and tense hoping. The high court has all of the options discussed: to affirm, modify, reverse and remand, or simply reverse.

ALTERNATIVE DISPUTE RESOLUTION

As we have seen in the previous section, trials can be trying. Lawsuits can cause prolonged periods of stress, significant legal bills, and general unpleasantness. Many people and companies prefer to settle cases out of court. Alternative dispute resolution (ADR) provides several semi-formal methods of resolving conflicts. We will look at different types of ADR and analyze their strengths and weaknesses.

Negotiation

In most cases, the parties negotiate, whether personally or through lawyers. Fortunately, the great majority of disputes are resolved this way. Negotiation often begins as soon as a dispute arises and may last a few days or several years.

Mediation

Mediation is the fastest growing method of dispute resolution in the United States. Here, a neutral person, called a *mediator*, attempts to guide the two disputing parties toward a voluntary settlement. (In some cases, there may be two or more mediators, but we will use the singular.) Generally, the two disputants voluntarily enter mediation, although some judges order the parties to try this form of ADR before allowing a case to go to trial.

A mediator does not render a decision in the dispute, but uses a variety of skills to move the parties toward agreement. Often a mediator will shuttle between the antagonists, hearing their arguments, sorting out the serious issues from the less important, prompting the parties and lawyers alike to consider new perspectives, and looking for areas of agreement. Mediators must earn the trust of both parties, listen closely, try to diffuse anger and fear, and build the will to settle. Good mediators do not need a law degree, but they must have a sense of humor and low blood pressure.

Mediation has several major advantages. Because the parties maintain control of the process, the two antagonists can speak freely. They need not fear conceding too much, because no settlement takes effect until both parties sign. All discussions are confidential, further encouraging candid talk. This is particularly helpful in cases involving proprietary information that might be revealed during a trial.

Of all forms of dispute resolution, mediation probably offers the strongest "win–win" potential. Since the goal is voluntary settlement, neither party needs to fear that it will end up the loser. This is in sharp contrast to litigation, where one party is very likely to lose. Removing the fear of defeat often encourages thinking and talking that are more open and realistic than negotiations held in the midst of a lawsuit. Studies show that over 75 percent of mediated cases do reach a voluntary settlement. Such an agreement is particularly valuable to parties that wish to preserve a long-term relationship. Consider two companies that have done business successfully for 10 years but now are in the midst of a million-dollar trade dispute. A lawsuit could last three or more years and destroy any chance of future trade. However, if the parties mediate the disagreement, they might reach an amicable settlement within a month or two and could quickly resume their mutually profitable business.

This form of ADR works for disputes both big and small. Two college roommates who cannot get along may find that a three-hour mediation session restores tranquility in the apartment. On a larger scale, consider the work of former U.S. Senator George Mitchell, who mediated the Anglo-Irish peace agreement, setting Northern Ireland on the path to peace for the first time in three centuries. Like most good mediators, Mitchell was remarkably patient. In an early session, Mitchell permitted the head of one militant party to speak without interruption—for seven straight hours. The diatribe yielded no quick results, but Mitchell believed that after Northern Ireland's tortured history, any nonviolent discussions represented progress.

Arbitration

In this form of ADR, the parties agree to bring in a neutral third party, but with a major difference: the arbitrator has the power to impose an award. The arbitrator allows each side equal time to present its case and, after deliberation, issues a binding decision, generally without giving reasons. Unlike mediation, arbitration ensures that there will be a final result, although the parties lose control of the outcome.

Judge Judy and similar TV court shows are examples of arbitration. Before the shows are taped, people involved in a real dispute sign a contract in which they give up the right to go to court over the incident and agree to be bound by the judge's decision.

Parties in arbitration give up many additional rights that litigants retain, including discovery and class action. In arbitration, as already discussed as applied to trials, *discovery* allows the two sides in a lawsuit to obtain documentary and other evidence from the opponent before the dispute is decided. Arbitration permits both sides to keep secret many files that would have to be divulged in a court case, potentially depriving the opposing side of valuable evidence. A party may have a stronger case than it realizes, and the absence of discovery may permanently deny it that knowledge. As discussed earlier in this chapter, a *class action* is a suit in which one injured party represents a large group of people who have suffered similar harm. Arbitration eliminates this possibility, since injured employees face the employer one at a time. Finally, the fact that an arbitrator may not provide a written, public decision bars other plaintiffs, and society generally, from learning what happened.

Traditionally, parties sign arbitration agreements *after* some incident took place. A car accident would happen first, and the drivers would agree to arbitration second. But today, many parties agree *in advance* to arbitrate any disputes that may arise in the future. For example, a new employee may sign an agreement requiring arbitration of any future disputes with his employer; a customer opening an account with a stockbroker or bank—or health plan—may sign a similar form, often without realizing it. The good news is fewer lawsuits; the bad news is you might be the person kept out of court.

Assume that you live in Miami. Using the Internet, you order a $1,000 ThinkLite laptop computer, which arrives in a carton loaded with six fat instructional manuals and many small leaflets. You read some of the documents and ignore others. For four weeks, you struggle to make your computer work, to no avail. Finally, you call ThinkLite and demand a refund, but the company refuses. You file suit in your local court, at which time the company points out that buried among the hundreds of pages it mailed you was a *mandatory arbitration form*. This document prohibits you from filing suit against the company and states that if you have any complaint with the company, you must fly to Chicago, pay a $2,000 arbitrator's fee, plead your case before an arbitrator selected by the Laptop Trade Association of America, and, should you lose, pay ThinkLite's attorneys' fees, which could be several thousand dollars. Is that mandatory arbitration provision valid? It is too early to say with finality, but thus far, the courts that have faced such clauses have enforced them.[9]

---

[9]See, e.g., *Hill v. Gateway* 2000, 105 F.3d 1147, 1997 U.S. App. LEXIS 1877 (7th Cir. 1997), upholding a similar clause.

Chapter Conclusion

No one will ever know for sure whether Tony Caruso took his own life. Craig Bergson's evidence might have tipped the scales in favor of Coastal. But even that is uncertain, since the jury could have found him unpersuasive. After two years, the case ends with a settlement and uncertainty—both typical lawsuit results. The missing witness is less common but not extraordinary. The vaguely unsatisfying feeling about it all is only too common and indicates why most parties settle out of court.

EXAM REVIEW

1. **COURT SYSTEMS** There are many *systems* of courts, one federal and one in each state. A federal court will hear a case only if it involves a federal question or diversity jurisdiction. (pp. 45–51)

2. **TRIAL AND APPELLATE COURTS** Trial courts determine facts and apply the law to the facts; appeals courts generally accept the facts found by the trial court and review the trial record for errors of law. (pp. 45–49)

EXAM Strategy

Question: Jade sued Kim, claiming that Kim promised to hire her as an in-store model for $1,000 per week for eight weeks. Kim denied making the promise, and the jury was persuaded: Kim won. Jade has appealed, and now she offers Steve as a witness. Steve will testify to the appeals court that he saw Kim hire Jade as a model, exactly as Jade claimed. Will Jade win on appeal?

Strategy: Before you answer, make sure you know the difference between trial and appellate courts. What is the difference? Apply that distinction here. (See the "Result" at the end of this section.)

3. **PLEADINGS** A complaint and an answer are the two most important pleadings; that is, documents that start a lawsuit. (p. 54)

4. **DISCOVERY** Discovery is the critical pre-trial opportunity for both parties to learn the strengths and weaknesses of the opponent's case. Important forms of discovery include interrogatories, depositions, production of documents and objects, physical and mental examinations, and requests for admission. (pp. 57–61)

5. **MOTIONS** A motion is a formal request to the court. (p. 56)

6. **SUMMARY JUDGMENT** Summary judgment is a ruling by the court that no trial is necessary because there are no essential facts in dispute. (pp. 61–63)

7. **JURY TRIALS** Generally, both plaintiff and defendant may demand a jury in any lawsuit for money damages. (p. 64)

8. **VOIR DIRE** Voir dire is the process of selecting jurors in order to obtain an impartial panel. (p. 64)

EXAM Strategy

Question: You are a lawyer, representing the plaintiff in a case of alleged employment discrimination. The court is selecting a jury. Based on questions you have asked, you believe that juror number 3 is biased against your client. You explain this to the judge, but she disagrees. Is there anything you can do?

Strategy: The question focuses on your rights during voir dire. If you believe that a juror will not be fair, you may make two different types of challenge. What are they? (See the "Result" at the end of this section.)

9. **BURDEN OF PROOF** The plaintiff's burden of proof in a civil lawsuit is preponderance of the evidence, meaning that its version of the facts must be at least slightly more persuasive than the defendant's. In a criminal prosecution, the government must offer proof beyond a reasonable doubt in order to win a conviction. (pp. 65–66)

10. **RULES OF EVIDENCE** The rules of evidence determine what questions may be asked during trial, what testimony may be given, and what documents may be introduced. (pp. 66–67)

11. **VERDICTS** The verdict is the jury's decision in a case. The losing party may ask the trial judge to overturn the verdict, seeking a JNOV or a new trial. Judges seldom grant either. (p. 68)

12. **APPEALS** An appeals court has many options. The court may affirm, upholding the lower court's decision; modify, changing the verdict but leaving the same party victorious; reverse, transforming the loser into the winner; and/or remand, sending the case back to the lower court. (pp. 69–70)

13. **ADR** Alternative dispute resolution is any formal or informal process to settle disputes without a trial. Mediation, arbitration, and other forms of ADR are growing in popularity. (pp. 70–71)

2. Result: Trial courts use witnesses to help resolve fact disputes. Appellate courts review the record to see if there have been errors of law. Appellate courts never hear witnesses, and they will not hear Steve. Jade will lose her appeal.

8. Result: You have already made a *challenge for cause*, claiming bias, but the judge has rejected your challenge. If you have not used up all of your *peremptory challenges*, you may use one to excuse this juror, without giving any reason.

Multiple-Choice Questions

1. The burden of proof in a civil trial is to prove a case _____. The burden of proof rests with the _____.
   (a) beyond a reasonable doubt; plaintiff
   (b) by a preponderance of the evidence; plaintiff
   (c) beyond a reasonable doubt; defendant
   (d) by a preponderance of the evidence; defendant

2. Alice is suing Betty. After the discovery process, Alice believes that no relevant facts are in dispute, and that there is no need for a trial. She should move for:
   (a) a judgment on the pleadings
   (b) a directed verdict
   (c) a summary judgment
   (d) a JNOV

3. Glen lives in Illinois. He applies for a job with a Missouri company, and he is told, amazingly, that the job is open only to white applicants. He will now sue the Missouri company under the Civil Rights Act, a federal statute. Can Glen sue in federal court?
   (a) Yes, absolutely.
   (b) Yes, but only if he seeks damages of at least $75,000. Otherwise, he must sue in a state court.
   (c) Yes, but only if the Missouri company agrees. Otherwise, he must sue in a state court.
   (d) No, absolutely not. He must sue in a state court.

4. A default judgment can be entered if which of the following is true?
   (a) A plaintiff presents her evidence at trial and clearly fails to meet her burden of proof.
   (b) A defendant loses a lawsuit and does not pay a judgment within 180 days.
   (c) A defendant fails to file an answer to a plaintiff's complaint on time.
   (d) A citizen fails to obey an order to appear for jury duty.

5. Barry and Carl are next-door neighbors. Barry's dog digs under Carl's fence and does $500 worth of damage to Carl's garden. Barry refuses to pay for the damage, claiming that Carl's cats "have been digging up my yard for years."

   The two argue repeatedly, and the relationship turns frosty. Of the following choices, which has no outside decision maker and is most likely to allow the neighbors to peacefully coexist after working out the dispute?
   (a) Trial
   (b) Arbitration
   (c) Mediation

Essay Questions

1. You plan to open a store in Chicago, specializing in rugs imported from Turkey. You will work with a native Turk who will purchase and ship the rugs to your store. You are wise enough to insist on a contract establishing the rights and obligations of both parties and would prefer an ADR clause. But you do not want a clause that will alienate your overseas partner. What kind of ADR clause should you include, and why?

2. Which court(s) have jurisdiction over each of these lawsuits—state or federal? Explain your reasoning for each answer.

   - Pat wants to sue his next-door neighbor, Dorothy, claiming that Dorothy promised to sell him the house next door.

   - Paula, who lives in New York City, wants to sue Dizzy Movie Theatres, whose principal place of business is Dallas. She claims that while she was in Texas on holiday, she was injured by their negligent maintenance of a stairway. She claims damages of $30,000.

   - Phil lives in Tennessee. He wants to sue Dick, who lives in Ohio. Phil claims that Dick agreed to sell him 3,000 acres of farmland in Ohio, worth over $2 million.

   - Pete, incarcerated in a federal prison in Kansas, wants to sue the United States government. He claims that his treatment by prison authorities violates three federal statutes.

3. British discovery practice differs from that in the United States. Most discovery in Britain concerns documents. The lawyers for the two sides, called *solicitors*, must deliver to the opposing side a list of all relevant documents in their possession. Each side may then request to look at and copy those it wishes. Depositions are rare. What advantages and disadvantages are there to the British practice?

4. Trial practice also is dramatically different in Britain. The parties' solicitors do not go into court. Courtroom work is done by different lawyers, called barristers. The barristers have very limited rights to interview witnesses before trial. They know the substance of what each witness intends to say but do not rehearse questions and answers, as in the United States. Which approach do you consider more effective? More ethical? What is the purpose of a trial? Of pre-trial preparation?

5. Claus Scherer worked for Rockwell International and was paid over $300,000 per year. Rockwell fired Scherer for alleged sexual harassment of several workers, including his secretary, Terry Pendy. Scherer sued in United States District Court, alleging that Rockwell's real motive in firing him was his high salary.

   Rockwell moved for summary judgment, offering deposition transcripts of various employees. Pendy's deposition detailed instances of harassment, including comments about her body, instances of unwelcome touching, and discussions of extramarital affairs. Another deposition, from a Rockwell employee who investigated the allegations, included complaints by other employees as to Scherer's harassment. In his own deposition, which he offered to oppose summary judgment, Scherer testified that he could not recall the incidents alleged by Pendy and others. He denied generally that he had sexually harassed anyone. The district court granted summary judgment for Rockwell. Was its ruling correct?

DISCUSSION QUESTIONS

1. In the Tony Caruso case described throughout this chapter, the defendant offers to settle the case at several stages. Knowing what you do now about litigation, would you have accepted any of the offers? If so, which one(s)? If not, why not?

2. The burden of proof in civil cases is fairly low. A plaintiff wins a lawsuit if he is 51 percent convincing, and then he collects 100 percent of his damages. Is this result reasonable? Should a plaintiff in a civil case be required to prove his case beyond a reasonable doubt? Or, if a plaintiff is only 51 percent convincing, should he get only 51 percent of his damages?

3. Large numbers of employees have signed mandatory arbitration agreements in employment contracts. Courts usually uphold these clauses. Imagine that you signed a contract with an arbitration agreement, that the company later mistreated you, and that you could not sue in court. Would you be upset? Or would you be relieved to go through the faster and cheaper process of arbitration?

4. Imagine a state law that allows for residents to sue "spammers"—those who send uninvited commercial messages through email—for $30. One particularly prolific spammer sends messages to hundreds of thousands of people.

   John Smith, a lawyer, signs up 100,000 people to participate in a class-action lawsuit. According to the agreements with his many clients, Smith will keep one-third of any winnings. In the end, Smith wins a $3 million verdict and pockets $1 million. Each individual plaintiff receives a check for $20.

   Is this lawsuit a reasonable use of the court's resources? Why or why not?

5. Higher courts are reluctant to review a lower court's *factual* findings. Should this be so? Would appeals be fairer if appellate courts reviewed *everything*?

CHAPTER 4

© Steve Allen/Jupiterimages

COMMON LAW, STATUTORY LAW, AND ADMINISTRATIVE LAW

> **"Just hit the big red STOP button on the wall next to you, and I'll untie myself."**
> **The hiker looks at the button, then back at Gary.**
> **"I really need to go,"**
> **he says.**
> **"WHAT?!"**
> **"If I don't get home soon, I'm going to miss *Oprah*."**

Harry Homicide captures Gary and hauls him to the Old Abandoned Mill. Inside the mill, Harry sets a plank of wood atop a conveyor belt and ties Gary securely to the board.

"And now, Gary… my arch-enemy… I will have my REVENGE," Harry shouts. With a flourish, he presses a large green button marked START. The conveyor belt starts to move. A very large circular blade at the end of the belt begins to turn and cut into the plank. "Bwah hah hah hah!" Harry laughs in triumph.

Gary moves slowly toward the blade. Very, very slowly. Harry Homicide taps his foot. He sighs, frowns, and checks his watch. "Well," he says, "I think it is safe to assume that it's all over for you, Gary. You should never have crossed me. And so, farewell!" Harry makes a dramatic exit.

Gary works at his bonds frantically. He begins to weep. But then—a hiker appears in the doorway! "Hey! Help! Untie me!" Gary shouts. He can't believe his good fortune.

The hiker mumbles something. "What's that?" Gary shouts. "I can't hear you. Help me—hurry!"

The hiker speaks up. "I said I'm not any good untying knots. Never have been."

Gary's mouth drops open. "Fine, that's fine," he says. "Just hit the big red STOP button on the wall next to you, and I'll untie myself."

The hiker looks at the button, then back at Gary. "I really need to go," he says.

"WHAT?!"

"If I don't get home soon, I'm going to miss *Oprah*."

"You can't be serious!"

"I am serious. I find her empathy and common sense refreshing."

"Oh, boy," Gary mutters to himself. Then, louder, "That's fine, just fine. Just punch the button and you can be on your way in two seconds. Please!"

The hiker takes one last look at the STOP button. "I have to go," he says. Without another word, he leaves.

In his last moments, Gary cannot decide whether he is more irritated with the hiker or Harry Homicide.

COMMON LAW

Gary and the hiker present a classic legal puzzle: what, if anything, must a bystander do when he sees someone in danger? We will examine this issue to see how the common law works.

The **common law** is judge-made law. It is the sum total of all the cases decided by appellate courts. The common law of Pennsylvania consists of all cases decided by appellate courts in that state. The Illinois common law is made up of all of the cases decided by Illinois appellate courts. Two hundred years ago, almost all of the law was common law. Today, common law still predominates in tort, contract, and agency law, and it is very important in property, employment, and some other areas.

Stare Decisis

Nothing perks up a course like Latin. ***Stare decisis*** means "let the decision stand." It is the essence of the common law. Once a court has decided a particular issue, it will generally apply the same rule in similar cases in the future. Suppose the highest court of Arizona must decide whether a contract signed by a 16-year-old can be enforced against him. The court will look to see if there is **precedent;** that is, whether the high court of Arizona has already decided a similar case. The Arizona court looks and finds several earlier cases, all holding that such contracts may not be enforced against a minor. The court will probably apply that precedent and refuse to enforce the contract in this case. Courts do not always follow precedent, but they generally do: *stare decisis.*

A desire for predictability created the doctrine of *stare decisis.* The value of predictability is apparent: people must know what the law is. If contract law changed daily, an entrepreneur who leased factory space and then started buying machinery would be uncertain if the factory would actually be available when she was ready to move in. Will the landlord slip out of the lease? Will the machinery be ready on time? The law must be knowable. Yet there must also be flexibility in the law, some means to respond to new problems and a changing social climate. Sometimes, we are better off if we are not encumbered by ironclad rules established before electricity was discovered. These two ideas are in conflict: the more flexibility we permit, the less predictability we enjoy. We will watch the conflict play out in the bystander cases.

Common law
Judge-made law.

Stare decisis
"Let the decision stand," that is, the ruling from a previous case.

Precedent
An earlier case that decided the issue.

Bystander Cases

This country inherited from England a simple rule about a **bystander's obligations: you have no duty to assist someone in peril unless you created the danger.** In *Union Pacific Railway Co. v. Cappier,*[1] through no fault of the railroad, a train struck a man. Railroad employees saw the incident happen but did nothing to assist him. By the time help arrived, the victim had died. The court held that the railroad had no duty to help the injured man:

> With the humane side of the question courts are not concerned. It is the omission or negligent discharge of legal duties only which come within the sphere of judicial cognizance. For withholding relief from the suffering, for failure to respond to the calls of worthy charity, or for faltering in the bestowment of brotherly love on the unfortunate, penalties are found not in the laws of men but in [the laws of God].

As harsh as this judgment might seem, it was an accurate statement of the law at that time in both England and the United States: bystanders need do nothing. Contemporary writers found the rule inhumane and cruel, and even judges criticized it. But—*stare decisis*—they followed it. With a rule this old and well established, no court was willing to scuttle it. What courts did do was seek openings for small changes.

Eighteen years after the Kansas case of *Cappier,* a court in nearby Iowa found the basis for one exception. Ed Carey was a farm laborer, working for Frank Davis. While in the fields, Carey fainted from sunstroke and remained unconscious. Davis simply hauled him to a nearby wagon and left him in the sun for an additional four hours, causing serious permanent injury. The court's response:

> It is unquestionably the well-settled rule that the master is under no legal duty to care for a sick or injured servant for whose illness or injury he is not at fault. Though not unjust in principle, this rule, if carried unflinchingly and without exception to its logical extreme, is sometimes productive of shocking results. To avoid this criticism [we hold that where] a servant suffers serious injury, or is suddenly stricken down in a manner indicating the immediate and emergent need of aid to save him from death or serious harm, the master, if present is in duty bound to take such reasonable measures as may be practicable to relieve him, even though such master be not chargeable with fault in bringing about the emergency.[2]

And this is how the common law often changes: bit by tiny bit. In Iowa, a bystander could now be liable *if* he was the employer and *if* the worker was suddenly stricken and *if* it was an emergency and *if* the employer was present. That is a small change but an important one.

For the next 50 years, changes in bystander law came very slowly. Consider *Osterlind v. Hill,* a case from 1928.[3] Osterlind rented a canoe from Hill's boatyard, paddled into the lake, and promptly fell into the water. For *30 minutes,* he clung to the side of the canoe and shouted for help. Hill heard the cries but did nothing; Osterlind drowned. Was Hill liable? No, said the court: a bystander has no liability. Not until half a century later did the same court reverse its position and begin to require assistance in extreme cases. Fifty years is a long time for the unfortunate Osterlind to hold on.[4]

In the 1970s, changes came more quickly.

---

[1]66 Kan. 649, 72 P. 281 (1903).

[2]*Carey v. Davis,* 190 Iowa 720, 180 N.W. 889 (1921).

[3]263 Mass. 73, 160 N.E. 301 (1928).

[4]*Pridgen v. Boston Housing Authority,* 364 Mass. 696, 308 N.E.2d 467 (Mass. 1974).

TARASOFF V. REGENTS OF THE UNIVERSITY OF CALIFORNIA

17 Cal. 3d 425, 551 P.2d 334, 131 Cal. Rptr. 14
Supreme Court of California, 1976

Facts: On October 27, 1969, Prosenjit Poddar killed Tatiana Tarasoff. Tatiana's parents claimed that two months earlier, Poddar had confided his intention to kill Tatiana to Dr. Lawrence Moore, a psychologist employed by the University of California at Berkeley. They sued the university, claiming that Dr. Moore should have warned Tatiana and/or should have arranged for Poddar's confinement.

Issue: *Did Dr. Moore have a duty to Tatiana Tarasoff, and did he breach that duty?*

Excerpts from Justice Tobriner's Decision: Although under the common law, as a general rule, one person owed no duty to control the conduct of another, nor to warn those endangered by such conduct, the courts have carved out an exception to this rule in cases in which the defendant stands in some special relationship to either the person whose conduct needs to be controlled or in a relationship to the foreseeable victim of that conduct. Applying this exception to the present case, we note that a relationship of defendant therapists to either Tatiana or Poddar will suffice to establish a duty of care.

We recognize the difficulty that a therapist encounters in attempting to forecast whether a patient presents a serious danger of violence. Obviously we do not require that the therapist, in making that determination, render a perfect performance; the therapist need only exercise that reasonable degree of skill, knowledge, and care ordinarily possessed and exercised by members of [the field] under similar circumstances.

In the instant case, however, the pleadings do not raise any question as to failure of defendant therapists to predict that Poddar presented a serious danger of violence. On the contrary, the present complaints allege that defendant therapists did in fact predict that Poddar would kill, but were negligent in failing to warn.

In our view, once a therapist does in fact determine, or under applicable professional standards reasonably should have determined, that a patient poses a serious danger of violence to others, he bears a duty to exercise reasonable care to protect the foreseeable victim of that danger.

[The Tarasoffs have stated a legitimate claim against Dr. Moore.]

The *Tarasoff* exception applies when there is some special relationship, such as therapist–patient. What if there is no such relationship? Remember the *Soldano v. O'Daniels* case from Chapter 1, in which the bartender refused to call the police.

As in the earlier cases we have seen, this lawsuit presented an emergency. But the exception created in *Carey v. Davis* applied only if the bystander was an employer, and that in *Tarasoff* only for a doctor. In *Soldano*, the bystander was neither. Should the law require him to act, that is, should it carve a new exception? Here is what the California court decided:

> Many citizens simply "don't want to get involved." No rule should be adopted [requiring] a citizen to open up his or her house to a stranger so that the latter may use the telephone to call for emergency assistance. As Mrs. Alexander in Anthony Burgess' *A Clockwork Orange* learned to her horror, such an action may be fraught with danger. It does not follow, however, that use of a telephone in a public portion of a business should be refused for a legitimate emergency call.
>
> We conclude that the bartender owed a duty to [Soldano] to permit the patron from Happy Jack's to place a call to the police or to place the call himself. It bears emphasizing that the duty in this case does not require that one must go to the aid of another. That is not the issue here. The employee was not the good samaritan intent on aiding another. The patron was.

And so, courts have made several subtle changes to the common law rule. Let's apply them to the opening scenario. If Gary's family sues the hiker, will they be successful? Probably not.

The hiker did not employ Gary, nor did the two men have any special relationship. The hiker did not stand in the way of someone else trying to call the police. He may be morally culpable for refusing to press a button and save a life, but he will not be legally liable unless an entirely new change to the common law occurs.

The bystander rule, that hardy oak, is alive and well. Various initials have been carved into its bark—the exceptions we have seen and a variety of others—but the trunk is strong and the leaves green. Perhaps someday the proliferating exceptions will topple it, but the process of the common law is slow and that day is nowhere in sight.

EXAM Strategy

Question: When Rachel is walking her dog, Bozo, she watches a skydiver float to earth. He lands in an enormous tree, suspended 45 feet above ground. "Help!" the man shouts. Rachel hurries to the tree and sees the skydiver bleeding profusely. She takes out her cell phone to call 911 for help, but just then Bozo runs away. Rachel darts after the dog, afraid that he will jump in a nearby pond and emerge smelling of mud. She forgets about the skydiver and takes Bozo home. Three hours later, the skydiver expires.

The victim's family sues Rachel. She defends by saying she feared that Bozo would have an allergic reaction to mud, and that in any case she could not have climbed 45 feet up a tree to save the man. The family argues that the dog is not allergic to mud, that even if he is, a pet's inconvenience pales compared to human life, and that Rachel could have phoned for emergency help without climbing an inch. Please rule.

Strategy: The family's arguments might seem compelling, but are they relevant? Rachel is a bystander, someone who perceives another in danger. What is the rule concerning a bystander's obligation to act? Apply the rule to the facts of this case.

Result: A bystander has no duty to assist someone in peril unless she created the danger. Rachel did not create the skydiver's predicament. She had no obligation to do anything. Rachel wins.

STATUTORY LAW

More law is created by statute than by the courts. Statutes affect each of us every day, in our business, professional, and personal lives. When the system works correctly, this is the one part of the law over which "we the people" have control. We elect the legislators who pass state statutes; we vote for the senators and representatives who create federal statutes.

Every other November, voters in all 50 states cast ballots for members of Congress. The winners of congressional elections convene in Washington, D.C. and create statutes. In this section, we look at how Congress does its work creating statutes.[5] Using the Civil Rights Act as a backdrop, we will follow a bill as it makes its way through Congress and beyond.

---

[5]State legislatures operate similarly in creating state laws.

Bills

Bill

A proposed statute, submitted to Congress or a state legislature.

Veto

The power of the President to reject legislation passed by Congress.

Congress is organized into two houses, the House of Representatives and the Senate. Either house may originate a proposed statute, which is called a **bill**. To become law, the bill must be voted on and approved by both houses. Once both houses pass it, they will send it to the President. If the President signs the bill, it becomes law and is then a statute. If the President opposes the bill, he will **veto** it, in which case it is not law.[6]

If you visit either house of Congress, you will probably find half a dozen legislators on the floor, with one person talking and no one listening. This is because most of the work is done in committees. Both houses are organized into dozens of committees, each with special functions. The House currently has about 25 committees (further divided into about 150 subcommittees), and the Senate has approximately 20 committees (with about 86 subcommittees). For example, the armed services committee of each house oversees the huge defense budget and the workings of the armed forces. Labor committees handle legislation concerning organized labor and working conditions. Banking committees develop expertise on financial institutions. Judiciary committees review nominees to the federal courts. There are dozens of other committees, some very powerful, because they control vast amounts of money, and some relatively weak. Few of us ever think about the House Agricultural Subcommittee on Specialty Crops. But if we owned a family peanut farm, we would pay close attention to the subcommittee's agenda, because those members of Congress would pay close attention to us.

When a bill is proposed in either house, it is referred to the committee that specializes in that subject. Why are bills proposed in the first place? For any of several reasons:

- **New Issue, New Worry**. If society begins to focus on a new issue, Congress may respond with legislation. We consider below, for example, the congressional response in the 1960s to employment discrimination.

- **Unpopular Judicial Ruling**. If Congress disagrees with a judicial interpretation of a statute, the legislators may pass a new statute to modify or "undo" the court decision. For example, if the Supreme Court misinterprets a statute about musical copyrights, Congress may pass a new law correcting the Court's error. However, the legislators have no such power to modify a court decision based on the Constitution. When the Supreme Court ruled that lawyers had a right *under the First Amendment* to advertise their services, Congress lacked the power to change the decision.

- **Criminal Law**. Statutory law, unlike common law, is prospective. Legislators are hoping to control the future. And that is why almost all criminal law is statutory. A court cannot retroactively announce that it *has been* a crime for a retailer to accept kickbacks from a wholesaler. Everyone must know the rules in advance because the consequences—prison, a felony record—are so harsh.

Discrimination: Congress and the Courts

The civil rights movement of the 1950s and 1960s convinced most citizens that African Americans suffered significant and unacceptable discrimination in jobs, housing, voting, schools, and other basic areas of life. Demonstrations and boycotts, marches and countermarches, church bombings and killings persuaded the nation that the problem was vast and urgent.

---

[6]Congress may, however, attempt to override the veto. See the discussion following.

In 1963, President Kennedy proposed legislation to guarantee equal rights in these areas. The bill went to the House Judiciary Committee, which heard testimony for weeks. Witnesses testified that blacks were often unable to vote because of their race, that landlords and home sellers adamantly refused to sell or rent to African Americans, that education was grossly unequal, and that blacks were routinely denied good jobs in many industries. Eventually, the Judiciary Committee approved the bill and sent it to the full House.

The bill was dozens of pages long and divided into "titles," with each title covering a major issue. Title VII concerned employment. We will consider the progress of Title VII in Congress and in the courts. Here is one section of Title VII, as reported to the House floor:[7]

Sec. 703(a). It shall be an unlawful employment practice for an employer—

(1) to fail or refuse to hire or to discharge any individual, or otherwise to discriminate against any individual with respect to his compensation, terms, conditions, or privileges of employment, because of such individual's race, color, religion, or national origin; or

(2) to limit, segregate, or classify his employees in any way which would deprive or tend to deprive any individual of employment opportunities or otherwise adversely affect his status as an employee, because of such individual's race, color, religion, or national origin.

Debate

The proposed bill was intensely controversial and sparked argument throughout Congress. Here are some excerpts from one day's debate on the House floor, on February 8, 1964:[8]

MR. WAGGONNER. I speak to you in all sincerity and ask for the right to discriminate if I so choose because I think it is my right. I think it is my right to choose my social companions. I think it is my right if I am a businessman to run it as I please, to do with my own as I will. I think that is a right the Constitution gives to every man. I want the continued right to discriminate and I want the other man to have the right to continue to discriminate against me, because I am discriminated against every day. I do not feel inferior about it.

I ask you to forget about politics, forget about everything except the integrity of the individual, leaving to the people of this country the right to live their lives in the manner they choose to live. Do not destroy this democracy for a Socialist government. A vote for this bill is no less.

MR. CONTE. If the serious cleavage which pitted brother against brother and citizen against citizen during the tragedy of the Civil War is ever to be justified, it can be justified in this House and then in the other body with the passage of this legislation which can and must reaffirm the rights to all individuals which are inherent in our Constitution.

The distinguished poet Mark Van Doren has said that "equality is absolute or no, nothing between can stand," and nothing should now stand between us and the passage of strong and effective civil rights legislation. It is to this that we are united in a strong bipartisan coalition today, and when the laws of the land proclaim that the 88th Congress acted effectively, judiciously, and wisely, we can take pride in our accomplishments as free men.

---

[7]The section number in the House bill was actually 704(a); we use 703 here because that is the number of the section when the bill became law and the number to which the Supreme Court refers in later litigation.

[8]The order of speakers is rearranged, and the remarks are edited.

Other debate was less rhetorical and aimed more at getting information. The following exchange anticipates a 30-year controversy on quotas:

Mr. Johansen. I have asked for this time to raise a question and I would ask particularly for the attention of the gentleman from New York [Mr. Goodell] because of a remark he made—and I am not quarreling with it. I understood him to say there is no plan for balanced employment or for quotas in this legislation....I am raising a question as to whether in the effort to eliminate discrimination—and incidentally that is an undefined term in the bill—we may get to a situation in which employers and conceivably union leaders, will insist on legislation providing for a quota system as a matter of self-protection.

Now let us suppose this hypothetical situation exists with 100 jobs to be filled. Let us say 150 persons apply and suppose 75 of them are Negro and 75 of them are white. Supposing the employer...hires 75 white men. [Does anyone] have a right to claim they have been discriminated against on the basis of color?

Mr. Goodell. It is the intention of the legislation that if applicants are equal in all other respects there will be no restriction. One may choose from among equals. So long as there is no distinction on the basis of race, creed, or color it will not violate the act.

The debate on racial issues carried on. Later in the day, Congressman Smith of Virginia offered an amendment that could scarcely have been smaller—or more important:

Amendment offered by Mr. Smith of Virginia: On page 68, line 23, after the word "religion," insert the word "sex."

In other words, Smith was asking that discrimination on the basis of sex also be outlawed, along with the existing grounds of race, color, national origin, and religion. Congressman Smith's proposal produced the following comments:

Mr. Celler. You know, the French have a phrase for it when they speak of women and men. They say "vive la difference." I think the French are right. Imagine the upheaval that would result from adoption of blanket language requiring total equality. Would male citizens be justified in insisting that women share with them the burdens of compulsory military service? What would become of traditional family relationships? What about alimony? What would become of the crimes of rape and statutory rape? I think the amendment seems illogical, ill timed, ill placed, and improper.

Mrs. St. George. Mr. Chairman, I was somewhat amazed when I came on the floor this afternoon to hear the very distinguished chairman of the Committee on the Judiciary [Mr. Celler] make the remark that he considered the amendment at this point illogical. I can think of nothing more logical than this amendment at this point.

There are still many States where women cannot serve on juries. There are still many States where women do not have equal educational opportunities. In most States and, in fact, I figure it would be safe to say, in all States—women do not get equal pay for equal work. That is a very well known fact. And to say that this is illogical. What is illogical about it? All you are doing is simply correcting something that goes back, frankly to the Dark Ages.

The debate continued. Some supported the "sex" amendment because they were determined to end sexual bias. But politics are complex. Some *opponents* of civil rights supported the amendment because they believed that it would make the legislation less popular and cause Congress to defeat the entire Civil Rights bill.

That strategy did not work. The amendment passed, and sex was added as a protected trait. And, after more debate and several votes, the entire bill passed the House. It went to the Senate, where it followed a similar route from Judiciary Committee to full Senate. Much of the Senate debate was similar to what we have seen. But some senators raised a new issue, concerning §703(2), which prohibited *segregating or classifying* employees based on any of the protected categories (race, color, national origin, religion, or sex). Senator Tower was concerned that §703(2) meant that an employee in a protected category could never be given any sort of job test. So the Senate amended §703 to include a new subsection:

> Sec. 703(h). Notwithstanding any other provision of this title, it shall not be an unlawful employment practice for an employer…to give and to act upon the results of any professionally developed ability test provided that such test…is not designed, intended or used to discriminate because of race, color, religion, sex or national origin.

With that amendment, and many others, the bill passed the Senate.

Conference Committee

Civil rights legislation had now passed both houses, but the bills were no longer the same due to the many amendments. This is true with most legislation. The next step is for the two houses to send representatives to a House–Senate Conference Committee. This committee examines all of the differences between the two bills and tries to reach a compromise. With the Civil Rights bill, Senator Tower's amendment was left in; other Senate amendments were taken out. When the Conference Committee had settled every difference between the two versions, the new, modified bill was sent back to each house for a new vote.

The House of Representatives and the Senate again angrily debated the compromise language reported from the Conference Committee. Finally, after years of violent public demonstrations and months of debate, each house passed the same bill. President Johnson promptly signed it. The Civil Rights Act of 1964 was law. See Exhibit 4.1.

But the passing of a statute is not always the end of the story. Sometimes courts must interpret congressional language and intent.

Statutory Interpretation

Title VII of the Civil Rights Act obviously prohibited an employer from saying to a job applicant, "We don't hire minorities." In some parts of the country, that had been common practice; after the Civil Rights Act passed, it became rare. Employers who routinely hired whites only, or promoted only whites, found themselves losing lawsuits. A new group of cases arose, those in which some job standard was set that appeared to be racially neutral, yet had a discriminatory effect. In North Carolina, the Duke Power Co. required that applicants for higher paying, promotional positions meet two requirements: they must have a high school diploma, and they must pass a standardized written test. There was no evidence that either requirement related to successful job performance. Blacks met the requirements in lower percentages than whites, and consequently whites obtained a disproportionate share of the good jobs.

Title VII did not precisely address this kind of case. It clearly outlawed overt discrimination. Was Duke Power's policy overt discrimination, or was it protected by Senator Tower's amendment, §703(h)? The case went all the way to the Supreme Court, where the Court had to interpret the new law.

Courts are often called upon to interpret a statute, that is, to explain precisely what the language means and how it applies in a given case. There are three primary steps in a court's statutory interpretation:

- **Plain Meaning Rule.** When a statute's words have ordinary, everyday significance, the court will simply apply those words. Section 703(a)(1) of the Civil Rights Act prohibits firing someone because of her religion. Could an employer who had fired a Catholic because of her religion argue that Catholicism is not really a religion, but more of a social group? No. The word "religion" has a plain meaning and courts apply its commonsense definition.

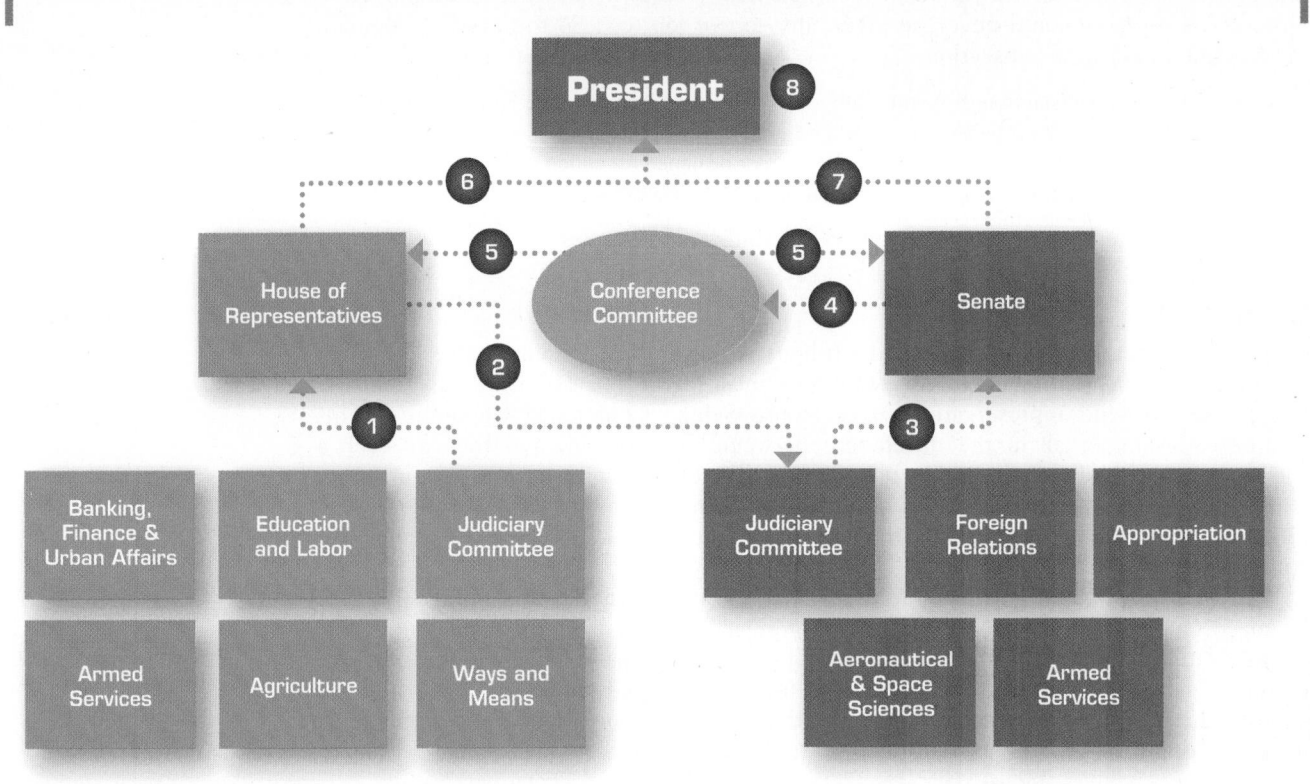

| EXHIBIT 4.1 | The two houses of Congress are organized into dozens of committees, a few of which are shown here. The path of the 1964 Civil Rights Act (somewhat simplified) was as follows: (1) The House Judiciary Committee approved the bill and sent it to the full House; (2) the full House passed the bill and sent it to the Senate, where it was assigned to the Senate Judiciary Committee; (3) the Senate Judiciary Committee passed an amended version of the bill and sent it to the full Senate; (4) the full Senate passed the bill with additional amendments. Since the Senate version was now different from the bill the House passed, the bill went to a Conference Committee. The Conference Committee (5) reached a compromise and sent the new version of the bill back to both houses. Each house passed the compromise bill (6 and 7) and sent it to the President, who signed it into law (8). |

- **Legislative History and Intent.** If the language is unclear, the court must look deeper. Section 703(a)(2) prohibits classifying employees in ways that are discriminatory. Does that section prevent an employer from requiring high school diplomas, as Duke Power did? The explicit language of the statute does not answer the question. The court will look at the law's history to determine the intent of the legislature. The court will examine committee hearings, reports, and the floor debates that we have seen.

- **Public Policy.** If the legislative history is unclear, courts will rely on general public policies, such as reducing crime, creating equal opportunity, and so forth. They may include in this examination some of their own prior decisions. Courts assume that the legislature is aware of prior judicial decisions, and if the legislature did not change those decisions, the statute will be interpreted to incorporate them.

Here is how the Supreme Court interpreted the 1964 Civil Rights Act.

Landmark Case

GRIGGS V. DUKE POWER CO.

401 U.S. 424, 91 S. Ct. 849, 1971 U.S. LEXIS 134
United States Supreme Court, 1971

Facts: See the discussion of the Duke Power Company's job requirements in the "Statutory Interpretation" section above.

Issue: *Did Title VII of the 1964 Civil Rights Act require that employment tests be job-related?*

Excerpts from Chief Justice Burger's Decision: The objective of Congress in the enactment of Title VII is plain from the language of the statute. It was to achieve equality of employment opportunities and remove barriers that have operated in the past to favor an identifiable group of white employees over other employees. Under the Act, practices, procedures, or tests neutral on their face, and even neutral in terms of intent, cannot be maintained if they operate to "freeze" the status quo of prior discriminatory employment practices.

The Act proscribes not only overt discrimination but also practices that are fair in form, but discriminatory in operation. The touchstone is business necessity. If an employment practice which operates to exclude Negroes cannot be shown to be related to job performance, the practice is prohibited.

On the record before us, neither the high school completion requirement nor the general intelligence test is shown to bear a demonstrable relationship to successful performance of the jobs for which it was used.

Senator Tower offered an amendment which was adopted verbatim and is now the testing provision of section 703(h). Speaking for the supporters of Title VII, Senator Humphrey endorsed the amendment, stating: "Senators on both sides of the aisle who were deeply interested in Title VII have examined the text of this amendment and have found it to be in accord with the intent and purpose of that title." The amendment was then adopted. From the sum of the legislative history relevant in this case, the conclusion is inescapable that the…requirement that employment tests be job related comports with congressional intent.

And so the highest Court ruled that if a job requirement had a discriminatory impact, the employer could use that requirement only if it was related to job performance. Many more cases arose. For almost two decades courts held that, once workers showed that a job requirement had a discriminatory effect, the employer had the burden to prove that the requirement was necessary for the business. The requirement had to be essential to achieve an important goal. If there was any way to achieve that goal without discriminatory impact, the employer had to use it.

Changing Times

But things changed. In 1989, a more conservative Supreme Court decided *Wards Cove Packing Co. v. Atonio.*[9] The plaintiffs were nonwhite workers in salmon canneries in Alaska. The canneries had two types of jobs, skilled and unskilled. Nonwhites (Filipinos and native Alaskans) invariably worked as low-paid, unskilled workers, canning the fish. The higher paid, skilled positions were filled almost entirely with white workers, who were hired during the off-season in Washington and Oregon.

There was no overt discrimination. But plaintiffs claimed that various practices led to the racial imbalances. The practices included failing to promote from within the company, hiring through separate channels (cannery jobs were done through a union hall, skilled positions were

---

[9]490 U.S. 642, 109 S. Ct. 2115, 1989 U.S. LEXIS 2794 (1989).

filled out of state), nepotism, and an English language requirement. Once again the case reached the Supreme Court, where Justice White wrote the Court's opinion.

If the plaintiffs succeeded in showing that the job requirements led to racial imbalance, said the Court, the employer now only had to demonstrate that the requirement or practice "serves, in a significant way, the legitimate employment goals of the employer…. [T]here is no requirement that the challenged practice be 'essential' or 'indispensable' to the employer's business." In other words, the Court removed the "business necessity" requirement of *Griggs* and replaced it with "legitimate employment goals."

Voters' Role

The response to *Wards Cove* was quick. Liberals decried it; conservatives hailed it. Everyone agreed that it was a major change that would make it substantially harder for plaintiffs to bring successful discrimination cases. Democrats introduced bills to reverse the interpretation of *Wards Cove*. President George H. W. Bush strongly opposed any new bill. He said it would lead to "quotas," that is, that employers would feel obligated to hire a certain percentage of workers from all racial categories to protect themselves from suits. This was the issue that Congressman Johansen had raised in the original House debate in 1964.

Both houses passed bills restoring the "business necessity" holding of *Griggs*. Again there were differences, and a Conference Committee resolved them. After acrimonious debate, both houses passed the compromise bill in October 1990. Was it therefore law? No. President Bush immediately vetoed the bill. He said it would compel employers to adopt quotas.

Congressional Override

When the President vetoes a bill, Congress has one last chance to make it law: an override. If both houses repass the bill, each by a two-thirds margin, it becomes law over the President's veto. Congress attempted to pass the 1990 Civil Rights bill over the Bush veto, but it fell short in the Senate by one vote.

Civil rights advocates tried again, in January 1991, introducing a new bill to reverse the *Wards Cove* rule. Again both houses debated and bargained. The new bill stated that, once an employee proves that a particular employment practice causes a discriminatory impact, the employer must "demonstrate that the challenged practice is job related for the position in question and consistent with business necessity."

Now the two sides fought over the exact meanings of two terms: "job related" and "business necessity." Each side offered definitions, but they could not reach agreement. It appeared that the entire bill would founder over those terms. So Congress did what it often does when faced with a problem of definition: it dropped the issue. Liberals and conservatives agreed not to define the troublesome terms. They would leave that task to courts to perform through statutory interpretation.

With the definitions left out, the new bill passed both houses. In November 1991, President Bush signed the bill into law. The President stated that the new bill had been improved and no longer threatened to create racial quotas. His opponents charged he had reversed course for political reasons, anticipating the 1992 presidential election.

And so, the Congress restored the "business necessity" interpretation to its own 1964 Civil Rights Act. No one would say, however, that it had been a simple process.

EXAM Strategy

Question: Kelly Hackworth took a leave of absence from her job at Progressive Insurance to care for her ailing mother. When she offered to return, Progressive refused to give her the same job or one like it. She sued based on the Family Medical

Leave Act, a federal statute that requires firms to give workers returning from family leave their original job or an equivalent one. However, the statute excludes from its coverage workers whose company employs "fewer than 50 people within 75 miles" of the worker's jobsite. Between Ms. Hackworth's jobsite in Norman, Oklahoma, and the company's Oklahoma City workplace (less than 75 miles away), Progressive employed 47 people. At its Lawton, Oklahoma facility, Progressive employed three more people—but Lawton was 75.6 miles (wouldn't you know it) away from Norman. Progressive argued that the job was not covered by the statute. Hackworth claimed that this distance should be considered "within 75 miles," thereby rendering her eligible for FMLA leave. Even if it were not, she urged, it would be absurd to disqualify her from important rights based on a disparity of six-tenths of a mile. Please rule.

Strategy: The question asks you to interpret a statute. How do courts do that? There are three steps: the plain meaning rule; legislative history; and public policy. Apply those steps to these facts.

Result: In this real case, the court ruled that the plain meaning of "within 75 miles" was *75 miles or less*. Lawton was not 75 miles or less from Norman. The statute did not apply and Ms. Hackworth lost.[10]

ADMINISTRATIVE LAW

Before beginning this section, please return your seat to its upright position. Stow the tray firmly in the seatback in front of you. Turn off any laptops, cell phones, or other electronic devices. Sound familiar? Administrative agencies affect each of us every day in hundreds of ways. They have become the fourth branch of government. Supporters believe that they provide unique expertise in complex areas; detractors regard them as unelected government run amok.

Many administrative agencies are familiar. The Federal Aviation Administration, which requires all airlines to ensure that your seats are upright before takeoff and landing, is an administrative agency. The Internal Revenue Service expects to hear from us every April 15. The Environmental Protection Agency regulates the water quality of the river in your town. The Federal Trade Commission oversees the commercials that shout at you from your television set.

Other agencies are less familiar. You may never have heard of the Bureau of Land Management, but if you go into the oil and gas industry, you will learn that this powerful agency has more control over your land than you do. If you develop real estate in Palos Hills, Illinois, you will tremble every time the Appearance Commission of the City of Palos Hills speaks, since you cannot construct a new building without its approval. If your software corporation wants to hire an Argentine expert on databases, you will get to know the complex workings of Immigration and Customs Enforcement: no one lawfully enters this country without its nod of approval.

> **Before beginning this section, please return your seat to its upright position. Stow the tray firmly in the seatback in front of you.**

---

[10]*Hackworth v. Progressive Casualty Ins. Co.*, 468 F.3d 722, 10th Cir. 2006 (10th Cir. 2006).

Background

By the 1880s, trains crisscrossed America. But this technological miracle became an economic headache. Congress worried that the railroads' economic muscle enabled a few powerful corporations to reap unfair profits. The railroad industry needed closer regulation. Who would do it? Courts decide individual cases; they do not regulate industries. Congress itself passes statutes, but it has no personnel to oversee the day-to-day working of a huge industry. For example, Congress lacks the expertise to establish rates for freight passing from Kansas City to Chicago, and it has no personnel to enforce rates once they are set.

A new entity was needed. Congress passed the Interstate Commerce Act, creating the Interstate Commerce Commission (ICC), the first administrative agency. The ICC began regulating freight and passenger transportation over the growing rail system and continued to do so for over 100 years. Congress gave the ICC power to regulate rates and investigate harmful practices, to hold hearings, issue orders, and punish railroads that did not comply.

The ICC was able to hire and develop a staff that was expert in the issues that Congress wanted controlled. The agency had enough flexibility to deal with the problems in a variety of ways: by regulating, investigating, and punishing. And that is what has made administrative agencies an attractive solution for Congress: one entity, focusing on one industry, can combine expertise and flexibility. However, the ICC also developed great power, which voters could not reach, and thereby started the great and lasting conflict over the role of agencies.

During the Great Depression of the 1930s, the Roosevelt administration and Congress created dozens of new agencies. Many were based on social demands, such as the need of the elderly population for a secure income. Political and social conditions dominated again in the 1960s, as Congress created agencies, such as the Equal Employment Opportunity Commission, to combat discrimination.

Then during the 1980s, the Reagan administration made an effort to decrease the number and strength of the agencies. For several years some agencies declined in influence, though others did not. Today, there is still controversy about how much power agencies should have.

Classification of Agencies

Agencies exist at the federal, state, and local level. We will focus on federal agencies because they have national impact and great power. Most of the principles discussed apply to state and local agencies as well. Virtually any business or profession you choose to work in will be regulated by at least one administrative agency, and it may be regulated by several.

Executive-Independent

Some federal agencies are part of the executive branch, while others are independent agencies. This is a major distinction. The President has much greater control of executive agencies for the simple reason that he can fire the agency head at any time. An executive agency will seldom diverge far from the President's preferred policies. Some familiar executive agencies are the Internal Revenue Service (part of the Treasury Department); the Federal Bureau of Investigation (Department of Justice); the Food and Drug Administration (Department of Health and Human Services); and the Nuclear Regulatory Commission (Department of Energy).

The President has no such removal power over independent agencies. The Federal Communications Commission (FCC) is an independent agency. For many corporations involved in broadcasting, the FCC has more day-to-day influence on their business than

Congress, the courts, and the President combined. Other powerful independent agencies are the Federal Trade Commission, the Securities and Exchange Commission, the National Labor Relations Board, and the Environmental Protection Agency.

Enabling Legislation

Congress creates a federal agency by passing **enabling legislation**. The Interstate Commerce Act was the enabling legislation that established the ICC. Typically, the enabling legislation describes the problems that Congress believes need regulation, establishes an agency to do it, and defines the agency's powers.

Critics argue that Congress is delegating to another body powers that only the legislature or courts are supposed to exercise. This puts administrative agencies above the voters. But legal attacks on administrative agencies have consistently failed for several decades. Courts acknowledge that agencies have become an integral part of a complex economy, and so long as there are some limits on an agency's discretion, courts will generally uphold its powers.

POWER OF AGENCIES

Administrative agencies use three kinds of power to do the work assigned to them: they make rules, they investigate, and they adjudicate.

Rulemaking

One of the most important functions of an administrative agency is to make rules. In doing this, the agency attempts, prospectively, to establish fair and uniform behavior for all businesses in the affected area. **To create a new rule is to promulgate it**. Agencies promulgate two types of rules: legislative and interpretive.

Types of Rules: Legislative and Interpretive

Legislative rules are the most important agency rules, and they are much like statutes. Here, an agency creates law by requiring businesses or private citizens to act in a certain way. Suppose you operate a website for young shoppers, aged 10 to 18. Like most online merchants, you consider yourself free to collect as much data as possible about consumers. Wrong. The Federal Trade Commission, a federal agency, has promulgated detailed rules governing any site directed to young children. Before obtaining private data from these immature consumers, you must let them know exactly who you are, how to contact site operators, precisely what you are seeking, and how it will be used. You must also obtain verifiable parental consent before collecting, using, or disclosing any personal information. Failure to follow the rules can result in a substantial civil penalty. This modest legislative rule, in short, will be more important to your business than most statutes passed by Congress.

Interpretive rules do not change the law. They are the agency's interpretation of what the law already requires. But they can still affect all of us. For example, in 1977, Congress amended the Clean Air Act in an attempt to reduce pollution from factories. The act required the Environmental Protection Agency (EPA) to impose emission standards on "stationary sources" of pollution. But what did "stationary source" mean? It was the EPA's job to define that term. Obscure work, to be sure, yet the results could be seen and even smelled, because the EPA's definition would determine the quality of air entering our lungs every time we breathe. Environmentalists wanted the term defined to include every smokestack in a factory so that the EPA could regulate each one. The EPA, however, developed the "bubble concept," ruling that "stationary source" meant an entire factory, but not the individual smokestacks. As a result, polluters could shift emission among smokestacks in a single factory to avoid EPA regulation. Environmentalists howled that this gutted the purpose of the statute, but to no avail. The agency had spoken, merely by interpreting a statute.[11]

How Rules Are Made

Corporations fight many a court battle over whether an agency has the right to issue a particular rule and whether it was promulgated properly. The critical issue is this: how much participation is the public entitled to before an agency issues a rule? There are two basic methods of rulemaking.[12]

Informal Rulemaking   On many issues, agencies may use a simple "notice and comment" method of rulemaking. The agency must publish a proposed rule in advance and permit the public a comment period. During this period, the public may submit any objections and arguments, with supporting data. The agency will make its decision and publish the final rule.

For example, the Department of Transportation may use the informal rulemaking procedure to require safety features for all new automobiles. The agency must listen to objections from interested parties, notably car manufacturers, and it must give a written response to the objections. The agency is required to have rational reasons for the final choices it makes. However, it is not obligated to satisfy all parties or do their bidding.

Formal Rulemaking   In the enabling legislation, Congress may require that an agency hold a hearing before promulgating rules. Congress does this to make the agency more accountable to the public. After the agency publishes its proposed rule, it must hold a public hearing. Opponents of the rule, typically affected businesses, may cross-examine the agency experts about the need for the rule and may testify against it. When the agency makes its final decision about the rule, it must prepare a formal, written response to everything that occurred at the hearing.

When used responsibly, these hearings give the public access to the agency and can help formulate sound policy. When used irresponsibly, hearings can be manipulated to stymie needed regulation. The most famous example concerns peanut butter. The Food and Drug Administration (FDA) began investigating peanut butter content in 1958. It found, for example, that Jif peanut butter, made by Procter & Gamble, had only 75 percent peanuts and 20 percent of a Crisco-type base. P&G fought the investigation, and any changes, for years. Finally, in 1965, the FDA proposed a minimum of 90 percent peanuts in peanut butter; P&G wanted 87 percent. The FDA wanted no more than 3 percent hydrogenated vegetable oil; P&G wanted no limit.

The hearings dragged on for months. One day, the P&G lawyer objected to the hearing going forward because he needed to vote that day. Another time, when an FDA official testified that consumer letters indicated the public wanted to know what was really in peanut butter, the P&G attorney demanded that the official bring in and identify

---

[11]An agency's interpretation can be challenged in court, and this one was.

[12]Certain rules may be made with no public participation at all. For example, an agency's internal business affairs and procedures can be regulated without public comment, as can its general policy statements. None of these directly affect the public, and the public has no right to participate.

the letters—all 20,000 of them. Finally, in 1968, a decade after beginning its investigation, the FDA promulgated final rules requiring 90 percent peanuts but eliminating the 3 percent cap on vegetable oil.[13]

Investigation

Agencies do a wide variety of work, but they all need broad factual knowledge of the field they govern. Some companies cooperate with an agency, furnishing information and even voluntarily accepting agency recommendations. For example, the U.S. Consumer Product Safety Commission investigates hundreds of consumer products every year and frequently urges companies to recall goods that the agency considers defective. Many firms comply.

Other companies, however, jealously guard information, often because corporate officers believe that disclosure would lead to adverse rules. To force disclosure, agencies use *subpoenas* and *searches*.

Subpoenas

A **subpoena** is an order to appear at a particular time and place to provide evidence. A **subpoena duces tecum** requires the person to appear and bring specified documents. Businesses and other organizations intensely dislike subpoenas and resent government agents plowing through records and questioning employees. What are the limits on an agency's investigation? The information sought:

- Must be *relevant* to a lawful agency investigation. The FCC is clearly empowered to investigate the safety of broadcasting towers, and any documents about tower construction are obviously relevant. Documents about employee racial statistics might indicate discrimination, but the FCC lacks jurisdiction on that issue and thus may not demand such documents.

- Must not be *unreasonably burdensome*. A court will compare the agency's need for the information with the intrusion on the corporation.

- Must not be *privileged*. The Fifth Amendment privilege against self-incrimination means that a corporate officer accused of criminal securities violations may not be compelled to testify about his behavior.

Subpoena
An order to appear at a particular place and time. A subpoena *duces tecum* requires the person to produce certain documents or things.

Search and Seizure   At times an agency will want to conduct a surprise **search** of an enterprise and **seize** any evidence of wrongdoing. May an agency do that? Yes, although there are limitations. When a particular industry is *comprehensively regulated*, courts will assume that companies know they are subject to periodic, unannounced inspections. In those industries, an administrative agency may conduct a search without a warrant and seize evidence of violations. For example, the mining industry is minutely regulated, with strict rules covering equipment, mining depths, and air quality. Mining executives understand that they are closely watched. Accordingly, the Bureau of Mines may make unannounced, warrantless searches to ensure safety.[14]

The following case established many of the principles just described.

---

[13]For an excellent account of this high-fat hearing, see Mark J. Green, *The Other Government* (New York: W. W. Norton & Co., 1978), pp. 136–150.
[14]*Donovan v. Dewey*, 452 U.S. 594, 101 S. Ct. 2534, 1980 U.S. LEXIS 58 (1981).

Landmark Case

UNITED STATES V. BISWELL
406 U.S. 311
United States Supreme Court, 1972

Facts: Biswell operated a pawnshop and had a license to sell "sporting weapons." Treasury agents demanded to inspect Biswell's locked storeroom. The officials claimed that the Gun Control Act of 1968 gave them the right to search without a warrant.

That law says, in part, "the Secretary [of the Treasury] may enter during business hours the premises of any firearms dealer for the purpose of inspecting or examining (1) any records or documents required to be kept by such dealer, and (2) any firearms or ammunition kept or stored by such dealer."

Biswell voluntarily opened the storeroom, and the agent found two sawed-off rifles inside. The guns did not remotely meet the definition of "sporting weapons," and Biswell was convicted on firearms charges.

The appellate court found that because the search violated the Fourth Amendment, the rifles could not be admitted as evidence. It reversed the conviction, and the government appealed to the Supreme Court.

Issue: *Did the agent's warrantless search violate the Constitution?*

Excerpts from Justice White's Decision: When the officers asked to inspect respondent's locked storeroom, they were merely asserting their statutory right, and respondent was on notice as to their identity and the legal basis for their action. Respondent's submission to lawful authority and his decision to step aside and permit the inspection rather than face a criminal prosecution is analogous to a householder's acquiescence in a search pursuant to a warrant when the alternative is a possible criminal prosecution for refusing entry or a forcible entry. In neither case does the lawfulness of the search depend on consent; in both, there is lawful authority independent of the will of the householder who might, other things being equal, prefer no search at all.

In the context of a regulatory inspection system of business premises that is carefully limited in time, place, and scope, the legality of the search depends not on consent but on the authority of a valid statute.

Federal regulation of the interstate traffic in firearms is undeniably of central importance to federal efforts to prevent violent crime. Large interests are at stake, and inspection is a crucial part of the regulatory scheme.

Here, if inspection is to be effective and serve as a credible deterrent, unannounced, even frequent, inspections are essential. In this context, the prerequisite of a warrant could easily frustrate inspection; and if the necessary flexibility as to time, scope, and frequency is to be preserved, the protections afforded by a warrant would be negligible.

It is also plain that inspections for compliance with the Gun Control Act pose only limited threats to the dealer's justifiable expectations of privacy. When a dealer chooses to engage in this pervasively regulated business and to accept a federal license, he does so with the knowledge that his business records, firearms, and ammunition will be subject to effective inspection. Each licensee is annually furnished with a revised compilation of ordinances that describe his obligations. The dealer is not left to wonder about the purposes of the inspector or the limits of his task.

We have little difficulty in concluding that where, as here, regulatory inspections further urgent federal interest, and the possibilities of abuse and the threat to privacy are not of impressive dimensions, the inspection may proceed without a warrant where specifically authorized by statute. The seizure of respondent's sawed-off rifles was not unreasonable under the *Fourth Amendment*, the judgment of the Court of Appeals is reversed, and the case is remanded to that court.

Adjudication

Adjudicate
To hold a formal hearing about an issue and then decide it.

To **adjudicate** a case is to hold a hearing about an issue and then decide it. Agencies adjudicate countless cases. The FCC adjudicates which applicant for a new television license is best qualified. The Occupational Safety and Health Administration (OSHA) holds adversarial hearings to determine whether a manufacturing plant is dangerous.

Most adjudications begin with a hearing before an **administrative law judge** (ALJ). There is no jury. An ALJ is an employee of the agency but is expected to be impartial in her rulings. All parties are represented by counsel. The rules of evidence are informal, and an ALJ may receive any testimony or documents that will help resolve the dispute.

After all evidence is taken, the ALJ makes a decision. The losing party has a right to appeal to an appellate board within the agency. The appellate board may ignore the ALJ's decision. If it does not, an unhappy party may appeal to federal court.

Administrative law judge (ALJ)

An agency employee who acts as an impartial decision maker.

LIMITS ON AGENCY POWER

There are four primary methods of reining in these powerful creatures: statutory, political, judicial, and informational.

Statutory Control

As discussed, the enabling legislation of an agency provides some limits. It may require that the agency use formal rulemaking or investigate only certain issues. The Administrative Procedure Act imposes additional controls by requiring basic fairness in areas not regulated by the enabling legislation.

Political Control

The President's influence is greatest with executive agencies. Congress, though, "controls the purse." No agency, executive or independent, can spend money it does not have. An agency that angers Congress risks having a particular program defunded or its entire budget cut. Further, Congress may decide to defund an agency as a cost-cutting measure. In its effort to balance the budget, Congress abolished the Interstate Commerce Commission, transferring its functions to the Transportation Department.

Congress has additional control because it must approve presidential nominees to head agencies. Before approving a nominee, Congress will attempt to determine her intentions. And, finally, Congress may amend an agency's enabling legislation, limiting its power.

Judicial Review

An individual or corporation directly harmed by an administrative rule, investigation, or adjudication may generally have that action reviewed in federal court.[15] The party seeking review, for example, a corporation, must have suffered direct harm; the courts will not listen to theoretical complaints about an agency action.[16] And that party must first have taken all possible appeals within the agency itself.[17]

---

[15]In two narrow groups of cases, a court may not review an agency action. In a few cases, courts hold that a decision is "committed to agency discretion," a formal way of saying that courts will keep hands off. This happens only with politically sensitive issues, such as international air routes. In some cases, the enabling legislation makes it absolutely clear that Congress wanted no court to review certain decisions. Courts will honor that.

[16]The law describes this requirement by saying that a party must have standing to bring a case. A college student who has a theoretical belief that the EPA should not interfere with the timber industry has no standing to challenge an EPA rule that prohibits logging in a national forest. A lumber company that was ready to log that area has suffered a direct economic injury: it has standing to sue.

[17]This is the doctrine of exhaustion of remedies. A lumber company may not go into court the day after the EPA publishes a proposed ban on logging. It must first exhaust its administrative remedies by participating in the administrative hearing and then pursuing appeals within the agency before venturing into court.

Standard on Review

Suppose OSHA promulgates a new rule limiting the noise level within steel mills. Certain mill operators are furious because they will have to retool their mills in order to comply. After exhausting their administrative appeals, they file suit seeking to force OSHA to withdraw the new rule. How does a court decide the case? Or, in legal terms, what standard does a court use in reviewing the case? Does it simply substitute its own opinion for that of the agency? No, it does not. The standard a court uses must take into account:

Facts　Courts generally defer to an agency's fact finding. If OSHA finds that human hearing starts to suffer when decibels reach a particular level, a court will probably accept that as final. The agency is presumed to have expertise on such subjects. As long as there is *substantial evidence* to support the fact decision, it will be respected.

Law　Courts often—but not always—defer to an agency's interpretation of the law. This is due in part to the enormous range of subjects that administrative agencies monitor. Consider the following example. "Chicken catchers" work in large poultry operations, entering coops, manually capturing broilers, loading them into cages, and driving them to a processing plant where they…well, never mind. On one farm, the catchers wanted to organize a union, but the company objected, pointing out that *agricultural* workers had no right to do so. Were chicken catchers agricultural workers? The National Labor Relations Board, an administrative agency, declared that chicken catchers were in fact *ordinary* workers, entitled to organize. The Supreme Court ruled that courts were obligated to give deference to the agency's decision about chicken catchers. If the agency's interpretation was *reasonable*, it was binding, even if the court itself might not have made the same analysis. The workers were permitted to form a union—though the chickens were not.

In the following case, however, the Supreme Court disagreed with the FCC's standards about profanity on TV. The high court ruled that these standards were too vague to be enforceable. The case contains vulgar language, so *please do not read it.*

FEDERAL COMMUNICATIONS COMMISSION *v.* FOX TELEVISION STATIONS

567 U. S. _____ , 2012 U.S. LEXIS 4661
United States Supreme Court, 2012

Facts: "People have been telling me I'm on the way out every year, right? So f**** 'em," said Cher, on a televised Billboard Music Awards ceremony. A year later, on the same program, Nicole Richie asked, "Have you ever tried to get cow s*** out of a Prada purse? It's not so f****** simple." In a third incident, Bono won a Golden Globe. In his acceptance speech, he said that the award was "really, really, f****** brilliant." The FCC, which regulates the broadcast industry, received complaints about this and other profanity on the airwaves.

The FCC declared that these words were *invariably* indecent, explicit, and shocking. Their utterance violated the Commission's decency standards, and the Commis-

sion had the right to fine the networks for broadcasting them. The networks protested, arguing that the utterances were fleeting and isolated. They claimed that the Commission had traditionally permitted such sporadic usage, that this new ruling was an arbitrary change of policy, and that it violated the networks' First Amendment free speech rights. The Commission disagreed, declaring that it had the right to prohibit even the *occasional* use of the words.

The networks appealed to federal court. The Second Circuit held that the FCC's policy was unconstitutionally vague, and that it had a chilling effect on free speech. The FCC appealed to the Supreme Court.

Issue: *Did the FCC abuse its discretion and violate the Constitution by prohibiting even the occasional use of profanity on the air?*

Excerpts from Justice Kennedy's Decision: In 2001, the Commission issued a policy statement describing the framework of what it considered patently offensive:

> (1) The explicitness or graphic nature of the description or depiction of sexual or excretory organs or activities; (2) whether the material dwells on or repeats at length descriptions of sexual or excretory organs or activities; (3) whether the material appears to pander or is used to titillate, or whether the material appears to have been presented for its shock value.

It was against this regulatory background that the three incidents of alleged indecency at issue here took place. Reversing a decision by its enforcement bureau, the Commission found the use of the F-word actionably indecent. The Commission held that the word was "one of the most vulgar, graphic and explicit descriptions of sexual activity in the English language". Turning to the isolated nature of the expletive, the Commission reversed prior rulings that had found fleeting expletives not indecent.

The Court of Appeals determined that the Commission's presumptive prohibition on the F-word was plagued by vagueness because the Commission had on occasion found the fleeting use of those words notindecent provided they occurred during a bona fide news interview or were demonstrably essential to the nature of an artistic or educational work. The Commission's application of these exceptions, according to the Court of Appeals, left broadcasters guessing whether an expletive would be deemed artistically integral to a program or whether a particular broadcast would be considered a bona fide news interview.

A fundamental principle in our legal system is that laws which regulate persons or entities must give fair notice of conduct that is forbidden or required. A punishment fails to comply with due process if the regulation under which it is obtained fails to provide a person of ordinary intelligence fair notice of what is prohibited.

Under the Guidelines in force when the broadcasts occurred, a key consideration was whether the material dwelled on or repeated at length the offending description or depiction. The Commission's lack of notice to Fox and ABC that its interpretation had changed so the fleeting moments of indecency contained in their broadcasts were a violation failed to provide a person of ordinary intelligence fair notice of what is prohibited. Therefore, the Commission's standards as applied to these broadcasts were vague, and the Commission's orders must be set aside.

Because the Court resolves these cases on fair notice grounds under the Due Process Clause, it need not address the First Amendment implications of the Commission's indecency policy. [T]his opinion leaves the courts free to review the current policy or anymodified policy in light of its content and application.

Informational Control and the Public

We started this section describing the pervasiveness of administrative agencies. We should end it by noting one way in which all of us have some direct control over these ubiquitous authorities: information.

> A popular government, without popular information, or the means of acquiring it, is but a Prologue to a Farce or a Tragedy—or perhaps both. Knowledge will forever govern ignorance, and a people who mean to be their own Governors must arm themselves with the power which knowledge gives.

James Madison, President, 1809–17

Two federal statutes arm us with the power of knowledge.

Freedom of Information Act

Congress passed the landmark Freedom of Information Act (known as "FOIA") in 1966. It is designed to give all of us, citizens, businesses, and organizations alike, access to the information that federal agencies are using. The idea is to avoid government by secrecy.

Any citizen or executive may make a "FOIA request" to any federal government agency. It is simply a written request that the agency furnish whatever information it has on the subject specified. Two types of data are available under FOIA. Anyone is entitled to information about how the agency operates, how it spends its money, and what statistics and other information it has collected on a given subject. People routinely obtain records about agency policies, environmental hazards, consumer product safety, taxes and spending, purchasing decisions, and agency forays into foreign affairs. A corporation that believes that OSHA is making more inspections of its textile mills than it makes of the competition could demand all relevant information, including OSHA's documents on the mill itself, comparative statistics on different inspections, OSHA's policies on choosing inspection sites, and so forth.

Second, all citizens are entitled to any records the government has *about them*. You are entitled to information that the Internal Revenue Service, or the Federal Bureau of Investigation, has collected about you.

FOIA does not apply to Congress, the federal courts, or the executive staff at the White House. Note also that, since FOIA applies to federal government agencies, you may not use it to obtain information from state or local governments or private businesses.

Exemptions   An agency officially has 10 days to respond to the request. In reality, most agencies are unable to meet the deadline but are obligated to make good faith efforts. FOIA exempts altogether nine categories from disclosure. The most important exemptions permit an agency to keep confidential information that relates to national security, criminal investigations, internal agency matters such as personnel or policy discussions, trade secrets or financial institutions, or an individual's private life.

Privacy Act

This 1974 statute prohibits federal agencies from giving information about an individual to other agencies or organizations without written consent. There are exceptions, but overall this act has reduced the government's exchange of information about us "behind our back."

EXAM Strategy

Question: Builder wants to develop 1,000 acres in rural Montana, land that is home to the Kite Owl. The EPA rules that the Kite Owl is an endangered species, and prohibits development of the property. The developer appeals to court. The EPA based its decision on five statistical studies, and the opinions of three out of seven experts. The court looks at the same evidence and acknowledges that the EPA decision is carefully reasoned and fair. However, the judges believe that the other four experts were right: the owl is *not* endangered. Should the court permit development?

Strategy: What is the legal standard for deciding whether a court should affirm or reverse an agency decision? As long as there is *substantial evidence* to support the factual conclusions, and a *reasonable basis* for the legal conclusion, the court should not impose its judgment. Agencies are presumed to have special expertise in their areas. As the *Fox Television* case tells us, an agency ruling should generally be affirmed unless it is arbitrary and capricious. Apply that standard here.

Result: The EPA made a careful, reasoned decision. The court may disagree, but it should not impose its views. The court must affirm the agency's ruling and prohibit development.

Chapter Conclusion

"Why can't they just fix the law?" They can, and sometimes they do—but it is a difficult and complex task. "They" includes a great many people and forces, from common law courts to members of Congress to campaign donors to administrative agencies. The courts have made the bystander rule slightly more humane, but it has been a long and bumpy road. Congress managed to restore the legal interpretation of its own 1964 Civil Rights Act, but it took months of debate and compromising. The FDA squeezed more peanuts into a jar of Jif, but it took nearly a decade to get the lid on.

A study of law is certain to create some frustrations. This chapter cannot prevent them all. However, an understanding of how law is made is the first step toward controlling that law.

EXAM REVIEW

1. **COMMON LAW** The common law evolves in awkward fits and starts because courts attempt to achieve two contradictory purposes: predictability and flexibility. (p. 78)

2. **STARE DECISIS** *Stare decisis* means "let the decision stand" and indicates that once a court has decided a particular issue, it will generally apply the same rule in future cases. (p. 78)

3. **BYSTANDER RULE** The common law bystander rule holds that, generally, no one has a duty to assist someone in peril unless the bystander himself created the danger. Courts have carved some exceptions during the last 100 years, but the basic rule still stands. (pp. 79–81)

4. **LEGISLATION** Bills originate in congressional committees and go from there to the full House of Representatives or Senate. If both houses pass the bill, the legislation normally must go to a Conference Committee to resolve differences between the two versions. The compromise version then goes from the Conference Committee back to both houses, and if passed by both, to the President. If the President signs the bill, it becomes a statute; if he vetoes it, Congress can pass it over his veto with a two-thirds majority in each house. (pp. 81–89)

5. **STATUTORY INTERPRETATION** Courts interpret a statute by using the plain meaning rule; then, if necessary, legislative history and intent; and finally, if necessary, public policy. (pp. 84–87)

EXAM Strategy

Question: Whitfield, who was black, worked for Ohio Edison. Edison fired him, but then later offered to rehire him. Another employee argued that Edison's original termination of Whitfield had been race discrimination. Edison rescinded its offer to rehire Whitfield. Whitfield sued Edison, claiming that the company was retaliating for the other employee's opposition to discrimination. Edison pointed out that Title VII of the 1964 Civil Rights Act did not explicitly apply in such cases. Among other things, Title VII prohibits an employer from retaliating against *an employee* who has opposed illegal discrimination. But it does not say anything about retaliation based on *another employee's* opposition to discrimination. Edison argued that the statute did not protect Whitfield.

Strategy: What three steps does a court use to interpret a statute? First, the plain meaning rule. Does that rule help us here? The statute neither allows nor prohibits Edison's conduct. The law does not mention this situation, and the plain meaning rule is of no help. Second step: Legislative history and intent. What did Congress intend with Title VII generally? With the provision that bars retaliation against a protesting employee? Resolving those issues should give you the answer to this question. (See the "Result" at the end of this section.)

6. **ADMINISTRATIVE AGENCIES** Congress creates federal administrative agencies with enabling legislation. The Administrative Procedure Act controls how agencies do their work. (pp. 89–91)

7. **RULEMAKING** Agencies may promulgate legislative rules, which generally have the effect of statutes, or interpretive rules, which merely interpret existing statutes. (pp. 91–93)

8. **INVESTIGATION** Agencies have broad investigatory powers and may use subpoenas and, in some cases, warrantless searches to obtain information. (pp. 93–94)

EXAM Strategy

Question: When Hiller Systems, Inc., was performing a safety inspection on board the M/V *Cape Diamond*, an ocean-going vessel, an accident killed two men. The Occupational Safety and Health Administration (OSHA), a federal agency, attempted to investigate, but Hiller refused to permit any of its employees to speak to OSHA investigators. What could OSHA do to pursue the investigation? What limits would there have been on OSHA's actions?

Strategy: Agencies make rules, investigate, and adjudicate. Which is involved here? Investigation. During an investigation, what power has an agency to force a company to produce data? What are the limits on that power? (See the "Result" at the end of this section.)

9. **ADJUDICATION** Agencies adjudicate cases, meaning that they hold hearings and decide issues. Adjudication generally begins with a hearing before an administrative law judge and may involve an appeal to the full agency or ultimately to federal court. (pp. 94–95)

10. **AGENCY LIMITATIONS** The four most important limitations on the power of federal agencies are statutory control in the enabling legislation and the APA; political control by Congress and the President; judicial review; and the informational control created by the FOIA and the Privacy Act. (pp. 95–99)

> **5. Result:** Congress passed Title VII as a bold, aggressive move to end race discrimination in employment. Further, by specifically prohibiting retaliation against an employee, Congress indicated it was aware that companies might punish those who spoke in favor of the very goals of Title VII. Protecting an employee from anti-discrimination statements made by a *coworker* is a very slight step beyond that, and appears consistent with the goals of Title VII and the anti-retaliation provision. Whitfield should win, and in the real case, he did.[18]
>
> **8. Result:** OSHA can issue a subpoena *duces tecum*, demanding that those on board the ship, and their supervisors, appear for questioning, and bring with them all relevant documents. OSHA may ask for anything that is (1) relevant to the investigation, (2) not unduly burdensome, and (3) not privileged. Conversations between one of the ship inspectors and his supervisor is clearly relevant; a discussion between the supervisor and the company's lawyer is privileged.

MULTIPLE-CHOICE QUESTIONS

1. A bill is vetoed by _____.
  (a) the Speaker of the House
  (b) a majority of the voting members of the Senate
  (c) the President
  (d) the Supreme Court

2. If a bill is vetoed, it may still become law if it is approved by _____.
  (a) two-thirds of the Supreme Court
  (b) two-thirds of registered voters
  (c) two-thirds of the Congress
  (d) the President
  (e) an independent government agency

3. Which of the following Presidents was most influential in the passing of the Civil Rights Act?
  (a) Franklin D. Roosevelt
  (b) Ronald Reagan
  (c) Abraham Lincoln
  (d) John F. Kennedy
  (e) George W. Bush

4. Under FOIA, any citizen may demand information about _____.
  (a) how an agency operates
  (b) how an agency spends its money
  (c) files that an agency has collected on the citizen herself
  (d) all of the above

---

[18]*EEOC v. Ohio Edison*, 7 F.3d 541 (6th Cir. 1993).

5. If information requested under FOIA is not exempt, an agency has _____ to comply with the request.

   (a) 10 days

   (b) 30 days

   (c) 3 months

   (d) 6 months

ESSAY QUESTIONS

1. Until recently, every state had a statute outlawing the burning of American flags. But in *Texas v. Johnson*,[19] the Supreme Court declared such statutes unconstitutional, saying that flag burning is symbolic speech protected by the First Amendment. Does Congress have the power to overrule the Court's decision?

2. In 1988, terrorists bombed Pan Am Flight 103 over Lockerbie, Scotland, killing all passengers on board. Congress sought to remedy security shortcomings by passing the Aviation Security Improvement Act of 1990, which, among other things, ordered the Federal Aviation Authority (FAA) to prescribe minimum training requirements and staffing levels for airport security. The FAA promulgated rules according to the informal rulemaking process. However, the FAA refused to disclose certain rules concerning training at specific airports. A public interest group called Public Citizen, Inc., along with family members of those who had died at Lockerbie, wanted to know the details of airport security. What steps should they take to obtain the information? Are they entitled to obtain it?

3. The Aviation Security Improvement Act (ASIA) states that the FAA can refuse to divulge information about airport security. The FAA interprets this to mean that it can withhold data in spite of the FOIA. Public Citizen and the Lockerbie family members interpret FOIA as being the controlling statute, requiring disclosure. Is the FAA interpretation binding?

4. An off-duty, out-of-uniform police officer and his son purchased some food from a 7-Eleven store and were still in the parking lot when a carload of teenagers became rowdy. The officer went to speak to them, and the teenagers assaulted him. The officer shouted to his son to get the 7-Eleven clerk to call for help. The son entered the store, told the clerk that a police officer needed help, and instructed the clerk to call the police. He returned 30 seconds later and repeated the request, urging the clerk to say it was a Code 13. The son claimed that the clerk laughed at him and refused to do it. The policeman sued the store. **Argument for the Store:** We sympathize with the policeman and his family, but the store has no liability. A bystander is not obligated to come to the aid of anyone in distress unless the bystander created the peril, and obviously the store did not do so. The policeman should sue those who attacked him. **Argument for the Police Officer:** We agree that in general a bystander has no obligation to come to the aid of one in distress. However, when a business that is open to the public receives an urgent request to call the police, the business should either make the call or permit someone else to do it

---

[19]491 U.S. 397, 109 S. Ct. 2533, 1989 U.S. LEXIS 3115 (1989).

5. Federal antitrust statutes are complex, but the basic goal is straightforward: to prevent a major industry from being so dominated by a small group of corporations that they destroy competition and injure consumers. Does Major League Baseball violate the antitrust laws? Many observers say that it does. A small group of owners not only dominate the industry, but actually *own* it, controlling the entry of new owners into the game. This issue went to the United States Supreme Court in 1922. Justice Holmes ruled, perhaps surprisingly, that baseball is exempt from the antitrust laws, holding that baseball is not "trade or commerce." Suppose that members of Congress dislike this ruling and the current condition of baseball. What can they do?

DISCUSSION QUESTIONS

1. Courts generally follow precedent, but in the *Tarasoff* and *Soldano* cases discussed earlier in this chapter, they did not. Consider the opening scenario at the Old Abandoned Mill. *Should* the hiker bear any *legal* responsibility for Gary's untimely end; or should a court follow precedent and hold the lazy hiker blameless?

2. Revisit the *Fox Television Stations* case. Do you agree with the opinion? What would a sensible broadcast obscenity policy contain? When (if ever) should a network face fines for airing bad language?

3. Revisit *United States v. Biswell*. Do you agree with the Court's decision? Is it reasonable that government agencies can conduct searches more freely if a business is in an industry that is comprehensively regulated? Should a pawnshop face more searches than other kinds of enterprises, or should the rules be the same for all companies?

4. FOIA applies to government agencies, but it exempts Congress. Should top lawmakers be obligated to comply with FOIA requests, or would that create more problems than it would solve?

5. Suppose you were on a state supreme court and faced with a restaurant-choking case. Should you require restaurant employees to know and employ the Heimlich maneuver to assist a choking victim? If they do a bad job, they could cause additional injury. Should you permit them to do nothing at all? Is there a compromise position? What social policies are most important?

CHAPTER 5

CONSTITUTIONAL LAW

© Steve Allen/Jupiterimages

The consultant started his presentation to the energy company's board of directors. "So I don't have to tell you that if the Smith-Jones bill ever passes Congress, it will be an utter disaster for your company. The House has already passed it. The President wants it. The only thing that kept it from becoming law this summer is that the Senate was too chicken to bring it up for a vote in an election year.

"Here's the bottom line: to be comfortable, you need three candidates who see things your way to beat current senators who support the bill."

The next slide showed a large map of the United States with three states highlighted in red. "These are your best bets. Attempting wins here would cost $60 million total—not so much for a billion-dollar-a-year operation like yours.

> "In state #3, we go negative. Really negative."

"The money would go to saturation advertising from Labor Day to Election Day. I want to buy TV ads during local news programs all day, and during most prime time shows. I want the viewers to see your ads at least a dozen times before they go to the polls.

"In state #1, the challenger—your candidate—is a squeaky-clean state representative, but no one knows much about her outside her own district. She carries herself well, has a nice family. People will like her if they see her. Your money makes sure people will see her.

"In state #2, your guy hasn't really done much. But his grandfather was a hero at Normandy, and his dad was a coal miner. Great-grandparents were immigrants who came through New York with nothing in their pockets—I can see the ad with the Statue of Liberty already. A lot of voters will appreciate his family's story. This strategy will work if we have the funds to tell the story often enough.

"In state #3, we go negative. Really negative. Our opponent has been in the Senate a long time, and he's taken maybe 100,000 photos. We have three of them showing him with world leaders who have become unpopular of late. We're going to use them to tell a story about the senator putting foreign interests above American jobs and national security. People are angry—they think America is losing its place in the world. Our polling shows that this kind of campaign will be highly effective.

"You need to get into this election. All of your stakeholders benefit if the Smith-Jones bill dies—your workers stay on the job, your shareholders make more money, and your customers pay lower prices. Corporations are nothing more or less than the people who work for them, and they have the right to express their political opinions. These ads would simply give your workers the chance to exercise their right to free speech."

The CFO interrupted, "Look, we're all against the Smith-Jones bill. But is this plan *legal?*"

GOVERNMENT POWER

One in a Million

The Constitution of the United States is the greatest legal document ever written. No other written constitution has lasted so long, governed so many, or withstood such challenge. This amazing work was drafted in 1787, when two weeks were needed to make the horseback ride from Boston to Philadelphia, a pair of young cities in a weak and disorganized nation. Yet today, when that trip requires less than two hours by jet, the same Constitution successfully governs the most powerful country on earth. This longevity is a tribute to the wisdom and idealism of the Founding Fathers. The Constitution is not perfect, but overall, it has worked astonishingly well and has become the model for many constitutions around the world.

The Constitution sits above everything else in our legal system. No law can conflict with it. The chapter opener raises a constitutional issue: does Congress have the right to prohibit corporations from spending money to affect elections, or are these actions protected as free speech under the First Amendment? We will explore this later in the chapter when we discuss the *Citizens United* case.

The Constitution is short and relatively easy to read. This brevity is potent. The Founding Fathers, or **Framers**, wanted it to last for centuries, and they understood that would happen only if the document permitted interpretation and "fleshing out" by later generations. The Constitution's versatility is striking. In this chapter, the first part provides an overview of the Constitution, discussing how it came to be and how it is organized. The second part describes the power given to the three branches of government. The third part explains the individual rights the Constitution guarantees to citizens.

OVERVIEW

Thirteen American colonies declared independence from Great Britain in 1776 and gained it in 1783. The new status was exhilarating. Ours was the first nation in modern history founded on the idea that the people could govern themselves, democratically. The idea was daring, brilliant, and fraught with difficulties. The states were governing themselves under the Articles of Confederation, but these articles gave the central government no real power. The government could not tax any state or its citizens and had no way to raise money. The national government also lacked the power to regulate commerce between the states or between foreign nations and any state. This was disastrous. States began to impose taxes on goods entering from other states. The young "nation" was a collection of poor relations, threatening to squabble themselves to death.

In 1787, the states sent a group of 55 delegates to Philadelphia. Rather than amend the old articles, the Framers set out to draft a new document and to create a government that had never existed before. It was hard going. What structure should the government have? How much power? Representatives like Alexander Hamilton, a *federalist*, urged a strong central government. The new government must be able to tax and spend, regulate commerce, control the borders, and do all things that national governments routinely do. But Patrick Henry and other *antifederalists* feared a powerful central government. They had fought a bitter war precisely to get rid of autocratic rulers; they had seen the evil that a distant government could inflict. The antifederalists insisted that the states retain maximum authority, keeping political control closer to home.

The debate continues to this day, and periodically it plays a key role in elections. The "tea party" movement, for example, is a modern group of antifederalists with a growing political influence.

Another critical question was how much power the *people* should have. Many of the delegates had little love for the common people and feared that extending this idea of democracy too far would lead to mob rule. Antifederalists again disagreed. The British had been thrown out, they insisted, to guarantee individual liberty and a chance to participate in the government. Power corrupted. It must be dispersed among the people to avoid its abuse.

How to settle these basic differences? By compromise, of course. **The Constitution is a series of compromises about power**. We will see many provisions granting power to one branch of the government while at the same time restraining the authority given.

Separation of Powers

The Framers did not want to place too much power in any single place. One method of limiting power was to create a national government divided into three branches, each independent and equal. Each branch would act as a check on the power of the other two. Article I of the Constitution created a Congress, which was to have legislative, or lawmaking, power. Article II created the office of President, defining the scope of executive, or enforcement, power. Article III established judicial, or interpretive, power by creating the Supreme Court and permitting additional federal courts.

Consider how the three separate powers balance one another: Congress was given the power to pass statutes, a major grant of power. But the President was permitted to veto, or block, proposed statutes, a nearly equal grant. Congress, in turn, had the right to override the veto, ensuring that the President would not become a dictator. The President was allowed to appoint federal judges and members of his cabinet, but only with a consenting vote from the Senate.

Individual Rights

The original Constitution was silent about the rights of citizens. This alarmed many who feared that the new federal government would have unlimited power over their lives. So in 1791, the first 10 amendments, known as the **Bill of Rights**, were added to the Constitution, guaranteeing many liberties directly to individual citizens.

In the next two sections, we look in more detail at the two sides of the great series of compromises: power granted and rights protected.

POWER GRANTED

Congressional Power

To recap two key ideas from Chapter 1:

1. Voters in all 50 states elect representatives who go to Washington, D.C., to serve in Congress.

2. The Congress is comprised of the House of Representatives and the Senate. The House has 435 voting members, and states with large populations send more representatives. The Senate has 100 members—two from each state.

Congress wields tremendous power. Its members create statutes that influence our jobs, money, health care, military, communications, and virtually everything else. But can Congress create *any* kind of law that it wishes? No.

Article I, section 8 is a critically important part of the Constitution. It lists the 18 types of statutes that Congress is allowed to pass, such as imposing taxes, declaring war, and coining money. Thus, only the national government may create currency. The state of Texas cannot print $20 bills with George W. Bush's profile.

States like Texas *are* supposed to create all other kinds of laws for themselves because the Tenth Amendment says, "All powers not delegated to the United States by the Constitution … are reserved to the States."

The **Commerce Clause** is the specific item in Article I, section 8, most important to your future as a businessperson. It calls upon Congress "to regulate commerce … among the several States," and its impact is described in the next section.

Commerce Clause
The part of Article I, Section 8, that gives Congress the power to regulate commerce with foreign nations and among states.

Interstate Commerce

With the Commerce Clause, the Framers sought to accomplish several things in response to the commercial chaos that existed under the Articles of Confederation. They wanted the federal government to speak with one voice when regulating commercial relations with foreign governments.[1] The Framers also wanted to give Congress the power to bring coordination and fairness to trade among the states, and to stop the states from imposing the taxes and regulations that were wrecking the nation's domestic trade.

Virtually all of the numerous statutes that affect businesses are passed under the Commerce Clause. But what does it mean to regulate interstate commerce? Are all business transactions "interstate commerce," or are there exceptions? In the end, the courts must interpret what the Constitution means.

Substantial Effect Rule

An important test of the Commerce Clause came in the Depression years of the 1930s, in *Wickard v. Filburn*.[2] The price of wheat and other grains had fluctuated wildly, severely harming farmers and the national food market. Congress sought to stabilize prices by limiting the bushels per acre that a farmer could grow. Filburn grew more wheat than federal law allowed and was fined. In defense, he claimed that Congress had no right to regulate him because none of his wheat went into *interstate* commerce. He sold some locally and used the rest on his own farm as food for livestock and as seed. The Commerce Clause, Filburn claimed, gave Congress no authority to limit what he could do.

---

[1] *Michelin Tire Corp. v. Wages, Tax Commissioner*, 423 U.S. 276, 96 S. Ct. 535, 1976 U.S. LEXIS 120 (1976).
[2] 317 U.S. 111, 63 S. Ct. 82, 1942 U.S. LEXIS 1046 (1942).

The Supreme Court disagreed and held that **Congress may regulate any activity that has a substantial economic effect on interstate commerce.** Filburn's wheat *affected* interstate commerce because the more he grew for use on his own farm, the less he would need to buy in the open market of interstate commerce. In the end, "interstate commerce" does not require that things travel from one state to another.

In *United States v. Lopez*,[3] however, the Supreme Court ruled that Congress *had* exceeded its power under the Commerce Clause. Congress had passed a criminal statute called the "Gun-Free School Zones Act," which forbade any individual from possessing a firearm in a school zone. The goal of the statute was obvious: to keep schools safe. Lopez was convicted of violating the act and appealed his conviction all the way to the high Court, claiming that Congress had no power to pass such a law. The government argued that the Commerce Clause gave it the power to pass the law, but the Supreme Court was unpersuaded.

> The possession of a gun in a local school zone is in no sense an economic activity that might, through repetition elsewhere, substantially affect any sort of interstate commerce. [Lopez] was a local student at a local school; there is no indication that he had recently moved in interstate commerce, and there is no requirement that his possession of the firearm have any concrete tie to interstate commerce. To uphold the Government's contentions here, we would have to pile inference upon inference in a manner that would bid fair to convert congressional authority under the Commerce Clause to a general police power of the sort retained by the States. [The statute was unconstitutional and void.]

Congress's power is great—but still limited.

Current Application: The Affordable Healthcare Act   In 2010, Congress passed the Affordable Healthcare Act and President Barack Obama signed it into law. The wide-ranging legislation may result in as many as 30 million uninsured Americans gaining health care coverage. Almost immediately after it passed, many states sued and argued that the law violated the Constitution by exceeding Congress's power to regulate interstate commerce.

The challenge centers on a provision (which the press refers to as the "individual mandate") in the Act that requires many people to purchase health insurance or face fines. The states argue that requiring people to buy something is fundamentally different from regulating people who *voluntarily* decide to participate in commerce.

At this writing, the lower courts are divided on whether the healthcare statute is constitutional. The Supreme Court will have the final word. In the end, the fate of this law hinges upon how the justices define "commerce."

State Legislative Power

The "dormant" or "negative" aspect of the Commerce Clause governs state efforts to regulate interstate commerce. **The dormant aspect holds that a state statute which discriminates against interstate commerce is almost always unconstitutional.** Here is an example, but please do not read it if you plan to drive later today. Michigan and New York permitted in-state wineries to sell directly to consumers. They both denied this privilege to out-of-state producers, who were forced to sell to wholesalers, who offered the wine to retailers, who sold to consumers. This created an impossible barrier for many small vineyards, which did not produce enough wine to attract wholesalers. Even if they did, the multiple resales drove their prices prohibitively high.

Local residents and out-of-state wineries sued, claiming that the state regulations violated the dormant Commerce Clause. The Supreme Court ruled that these statutes

---

[3]514 U.S. 549, 115 S. Ct. 1624, 1995 U.S. LEXIS 3039 (1995).

obviously discriminated against out-of-state vineyards; the schemes were illegal unless Michigan and New York could demonstrate an important goal that could not be met any other way. The states' alleged motive was to prevent minors from purchasing wine over the Internet. However, Michigan and New York offered no evidence that such purchases were really a problem. The Court said that minors seldom drink wine, and when they do, they seek instant gratification, not a package in the mail. States that allowed direct shipment to consumers reported no increase in purchases by minors. This discrimination against interstate commerce, like most, was unconstitutional.[4]

Devil's Advocate   Underage drinking is a serious problem. The Court should allow states wide leeway in their efforts to limit the harm. Even if the regulations are imperfect, they may help reduce the damage.

Supremacy Clause

What happens when both the federal and state governments pass regulations that are permissible, but conflicting? For example, Congress passed the federal Occupational Safety and Health Act (OSHA) establishing many job safety standards, including those for training workers who handle hazardous waste. Congress had the power to do so under the Commerce Clause. Later, Illinois passed its own hazardous waste statutes, seeking to protect both the general public and workers. The state statute did not violate the Commerce Clause because it imposed no restriction on interstate commerce.

Each statute specified worker training and employer licensing. But the requirements differed. Which statute did Illinois corporations have to obey? Article VI of the Constitution contains the answer. **The Supremacy Clause** states that the Constitution, and federal statutes and treaties, shall be the supreme law of the land.

The Supremacy Clause
Makes the Constitution, and federal statutes and treaties, the supreme law of the land.

- If there is a conflict between federal and state statutes, the federal law **preempts** the field, meaning it controls the issue. The state law is void.

- Even in cases where there is no conflict, if Congress demonstrates that it intends to exercise exclusive control over an issue, federal law preempts.

Thus state law controls only when there is no conflicting federal law *and* Congress has not intended to dominate the issue. In the Illinois case, the Supreme Court concluded that Congress intended to regulate the issue exclusively. Federal law therefore preempted the field, and local employers were obligated to obey only the federal regulations.

EXAM Strategy

Question: Dairy farming was more expensive in Massachusetts than in other states. To help its farmers, Massachusetts taxed all milk sales, regardless of where the milk was produced. The revenues went into a fund that was then distributed to in-state dairy farmers. Discuss.

[4]*Granholm v. Heald*, 544 U.S. 460, 1255 S.Ct. 1885 (2005).

Strategy: By giving a subsidy to local farmers, the state is treating them differently than out-of-state dairies. This raises Commerce Clause issues. The dormant aspect applies. What does it state? Apply that standard to theses facts.

Result: The dormant aspect holds that a state statute that discriminates against interstate commerce is almost always invalid. Massachusetts was subsidizing its farmers at the expense of those from other states. The tax violates the Commerce Clause and is void.

Executive Power

Article II of the Constitution defines executive power. The President's most basic job function is to enforce the nation's laws. Three of his key powers concern appointment, legislation, and foreign policy.

Appointment

Administrative agencies play a powerful role in business regulation, and the President nominates the heads of most of them. These choices dramatically influence what issues the agencies choose to pursue and how aggressively they do it. For example, a President who seeks to expand the scope of regulations on air quality may appoint a forceful environmentalist to run the Environmental Protection Agency (EPA), whereas a President who dislikes federal regulations will choose a more passive agency head.[5]

Legislation

The President and his advisers propose bills to Congress. During the last 50 years, a vast number of newly proposed bills have come from the executive branch. Some argue that *too many* proposals come from the President and that Congress has become overly passive. When a President proposes controversial legislation on a major issue, such as Social Security reform, the bill can dominate the news—and Congress—for months or even years. The President, of course, also has the power to veto bills.[6]

Foreign Policy

The President conducts the nation's foreign affairs, coordinating international efforts, negotiating treaties, and so forth. The President is also the commander in chief of the armed forces, meaning that he heads the military. But Article II does not give him the right to declare war—only the Senate may do that. A continuing tension between the President and Congress has resulted from the President's use of troops overseas *without* a formal declaration of war.

Judicial Power

Article III of the Constitution creates the Supreme Court and permits Congress to establish lower courts within the federal court system.[7] Federal courts have two key functions: adjudication and judicial review.

---

[5]For a discussion of administrative agency power, see Chapter 4, on administrative law.

[6]For a discussion of the President's veto power and Congress's power to override a veto, see Chapter 4, on statutory law.

[7]For a discussion of the federal court system, see Chapter 3, on dispute resolution.

Adjudicating Cases

The federal court system hears criminal and civil cases. Generally, prosecutions of federal crimes begin in United States District Court. That same court has limited jurisdiction to hear civil lawsuits, a subject discussed in Chapter 3, on dispute resolution.

Judicial Review

One of the greatest "constitutional" powers appears nowhere in the Constitution. In 1803, the Supreme Court decided *Marbury v. Madison*.[8] Congress had passed a relatively minor statute that gave certain powers to the Supreme Court, and Marbury wanted the Court to use those powers. The Court refused. In an opinion written by Chief Justice John Marshall, the Court held that the statute violated the Constitution because Article III of the Constitution did not grant the Court those powers. The details of the case were insignificant, but the ruling was profound: because the statute violated the Constitution, said the Court, it was void. **Judicial review refers to the power of federal courts to declare a statute or governmental action unconstitutional and void.**

This formidable grab of power has produced two centuries of controversy. The Court was declaring that it alone had the right to evaluate acts of the other two branches of government—the Congress and the executive—and to decide which were valid and which void. The Constitution nowhere grants this power. Undaunted, Marshall declared that "[I]t is emphatically the province and duty of the judicial department to say what the law is." In later cases, the Supreme Court expanded on the idea, holding that it could also nullify state statutes, rulings by state courts, and actions by federal and state officials. In this chapter, we have already encountered an example of judicial review in the *Lopez* case, where the justices declared that Congress lacked the power to pass local gun regulations.

Is judicial review good for the nation? Those who oppose it argue that federal court judges are all appointed, not elected, and that we should not permit judges to nullify a statute passed by elected officials because that diminishes the people's role in their government. Those who favor judicial review insist that there must be one cohesive interpretation of the Constitution and the judicial branch is the logical one to provide it. The following example of judicial review shows how immediate and emotional the issue can be. This is a criminal prosecution for a brutal crime. Cases like this force us to examine two questions about judicial review. What is the proper punishment for such a horrible crime? Just as important, *who should make that decision*—appointed judges, or elected legislators?

KENNEDY V. LOUISIANA

128 S.Ct. 2641
United States Supreme Court, 2008

Facts: Patrick Kennedy raped his eight-year-old step-daughter. Her injuries were the most severe that the forensic expert had ever seen. Kennedy was convicted of aggravated rape because the victim was under 12 years of age.

The jury voted to sentence Kennedy to death, which was permitted by the Louisiana statute. The state supreme court affirmed the death sentence, and Kennedy appealed to the United States Supreme Court. He argued that the Louisiana statute was unconstitutional. The Eighth Amendment prohibits cruel and unusual punishment, which includes penalties that are out of proportion to the crime. Kennedy claimed that capital punishment was out of proportion to rape and violated the Eighth Amendment.

Issues: *Did the Louisiana statute violate the Constitution by permitting the death penalty in a case of child rape? Is it proper for the Supreme Court to decide this issue?*

---

[8]5 U.S. 137, 1 Cranch 137 (1803).

Excerpts from Justice Kennedy's Decision: The constitutional prohibition against excessive or cruel and unusual punishments mandates that the State's power to punish be exercised within the limits of civilized standards. Evolving standards of decency that mark the progress of a maturing society counsel us to be most hesitant before interpreting the Eighth Amendment to allow the extension of the death penalty, a hesitation that has special force where no life was taken in the commission of the crime.

Consistent with evolving standards of decency and the teachings of our precedents we conclude that, in determining whether the death penalty is excessive, there is a distinction between intentional first-degree murder on the one hand and nonhomicide crimes against individual persons, even including child rape, on the other. The latter crimes may be devastating in their harm, as here, but in terms of moral depravity and of the injury to the person and to the public, they cannot be compared to murder in their severity and irrevocability.

Louisiana reintroduced the death penalty for rape of a child in 1995. Five States have since followed Louisiana's lead: Georgia, Montana, Oklahoma, South Carolina, and Texas. By contrast, 44 States have not made child rape a capital offense. As for federal law, Congress in the Federal Death Penalty Act of 1994 expanded the number of federal crimes for which the death penalty is a permissible sentence, including certain nonhomicide offenses; but it did not do the same for child rape or abuse. [The court concludes that there is a national consensus against imposing the death penalty for rape, and strikes down the Louisiana statute.]

Justice Alito, dissenting: If anything can be inferred from state legislative developments, the message is very different from the one that the Court perceives. In just the past few years, five States have enacted targeted capital child-rape laws. Such a development would not be out of step with changes in our society's thinking. During that time, reported instances of child abuse have increased dramatically; and there are many indications of growing alarm about the sexual abuse of children.

Judicial Activism/Judicial Restraint   The power of judicial review is potentially dictatorial. The Supreme Court nullifies statutes passed by Congress (*Marbury v. Madison, United States v. Lopez*) and executive actions. May it strike down any law it dislikes? In theory, no—the Court should nullify only laws that violate the Constitution. But in practice, yes—the Constitution means whatever the majority of the current justices says that it means, since it is the Court that tells us which laws are violative.

Judicial activism refers to a court's willingness, or even eagerness, to become involved in major issues and to decide cases on constitutional grounds. Activists are sometimes willing to "stretch" laws beyond their most obvious meaning. **Judicial restraint** is the opposite, an attitude that courts should leave lawmaking to legislators and nullify a law only when it unquestionably violates the Constitution. Some justices believe that the Founding Fathers never intended the judicial branch to take a prominent role in sculpting the nation's laws and its social vision.

From the 1950s through the 1970s, the Supreme Court took an activist role, deciding many major social issues on constitutional grounds. The landmark 1954 decision in *Brown v. Board of Education* ordered an end to racial segregation in public schools, not only changing the nation's educational systems, but altering forever its expectations about race.[9] The Court also struck down many state laws that denied minorities the right to vote. Beginning with *Miranda v. Arizona*, the Court began a sweeping reappraisal of the police power of the state and the rights of criminal suspects during searches, interrogations, trials, and appeals.[10] And in *Roe v. Wade*, the Supreme Court established certain rights to abortion, most of which remain after nearly 40 years of continuous litigation.[11]

Judicial activism

A court's willingness to decide issues on constitutional grounds.

Judicial restraint

A court's attitude that it should leave lawmaking to legislators.

---

[9]347 U.S. 483, 74 S. Ct. 686, 1954 U.S. LEXIS 2094 (1954).
[10]384 U.S. 436, 86 S. Ct. 1602, 1966 U.S. LEXIS 2817 (1966).
[11]410 U.S. 113, 93 S. Ct. 705, 1973 U.S. LEXIS 159 (1973).

Beginning in the late 1970s, and lasting to the present, the Court has pulled back from its social activism. Exhibit 5.1 illustrates the balance among Congress, the President, and the Court.

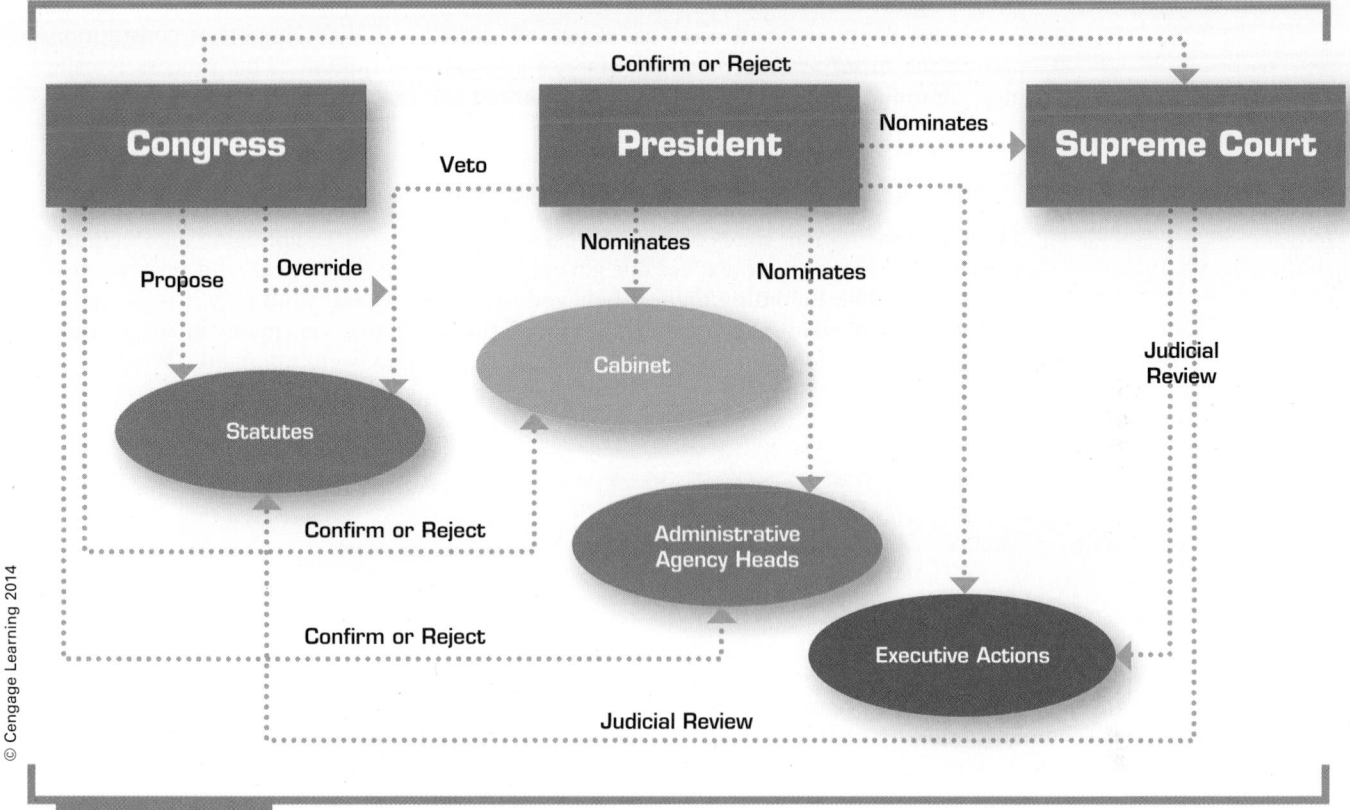

EXHIBIT 5.1   The Constitution established a federal government of checks and balances. Congress may propose statutes; the President may veto them; and Congress may override the veto. The President nominates cabinet officers, administrative heads, and Supreme Court justices, but the Senate must confirm his nominees. Finally, the Supreme Court (and lower federal courts) exercise judicial review over statutes and executive actions. Unlike the other checks and balances, judicial review is not provided for in the Constitution, but is a creation of the Court itself in *Marbury v. Madison*.

PROTECTED RIGHTS

The amendments to the Constitution protect the people of this nation from the power of state and federal government. The First Amendment guarantees rights of free speech, free press, and religion; the Fourth Amendment protects against illegal searches; the Fifth Amendment ensures due process; the Sixth Amendment demands fair treatment for defendants in criminal prosecutions; and the Fourteenth Amendment guarantees equal protection of the law. We consider the First, Fifth, and Fourteenth Amendments in this chapter and the Fourth, Fifth, and Sixth Amendments in Chapter 7, on crime.

The "people" who are protected include citizens and, for most purposes, corporations. Corporations are considered persons and receive most of the same protections. The great majority of these rights also extends to citizens of other countries who are in the United States.

Constitutional rights generally protect only against governmental acts. The Constitution generally does not protect us from the conduct of private parties, such as corporations or other citizens.

Incorporation

A series of Supreme Court cases has extended virtually all of the important constitutional protections to *all levels* of national, state, and local government. This process is called **incorporation** because rights explicitly guaranteed at one level are incorporated into rights that apply at other levels.

First Amendment: Free Speech

The First Amendment states that "Congress shall make no law ... abridging the freedom of speech..." In general, we expect our government to let people speak and hear whatever they choose. The Founding Fathers believed democracy would work only if the members of the electorate were free to talk, argue, listen, and exchange viewpoints in any way they wanted. The people could only cast informed ballots if they were informed. "Speech" also includes symbolic conduct, as the following case flamingly illustrates.

TEXAS V. JOHNSON

491 U.S. 397, 109 S. Ct. 2533, 1989 U.S. LEXIS 3115
United States Supreme Court, 1989

Facts: Outside the Republican National Convention in Dallas, Gregory Johnson participated in a protest against policies of the Reagan administration. Participants gave speeches and handed out leaflets. Johnson burned an American flag. He was arrested and convicted under a Texas statute that prohibited desecrating the flag, but the Texas Court of Criminal Appeals reversed on the grounds that the conviction violated the First Amendment. Texas appealed to the United States Supreme Court.

Issue: *Does the First Amendment protect flag burning?*

Excerpts from Justice Brennan's Decision: The First Amendment literally forbids the abridgment only of "speech," but we have long recognized that its protection does not end at the spoken or written word. While we have rejected the view that an apparently limitless variety of conduct can be labeled "speech," we have acknowledged that conduct may be sufficiently imbued with elements of communication to fall within the scope of the First and Fourteenth Amendments.

In deciding whether particular conduct possesses sufficient communicative elements to bring the First Amendment into play, we have asked whether an intent to convey a particularized message was present, and [whether] the likelihood was great that the message would be understood by those who viewed it. Hence, we have recognized the expressive nature of students' wearing of black armbands to protest American military involvement in Vietnam; of a sit-in by blacks in a "whites only" area to protest segregation; of the wearing of American military uniforms in a dramatic presentation criticizing American involvement in Vietnam; and of picketing about a wide variety of causes.

[The Court concluded that burning the flag was in fact symbolic speech.]

It remains to consider whether the State's interest in reserving the flag as a symbol of nationhood and national unity justifies Johnson's conviction. Johnson was prosecuted because he knew that his politically charged expression would cause "serious offense."

If there is a bedrock principle underlying the First Amendment, it is that the Government may not prohibit the expression of an idea simply because society finds the idea itself offensive or disagreeable. Nothing in our precedents suggests that a State may foster its own view of the flag by prohibiting expressive conduct relating to it.

Could the Government, on this theory, prohibit the burning of state flags? Of copies of the presidential seal? Of the Constitution? In evaluating these choices under the First Amendment, how would we decide which symbols were sufficiently special to warrant this unique status? To do so, we would be forced to consult our own political preferences, and impose them on the citizenry, in the very way that the First Amendment forbids us to do.

The way to preserve the flag's special role is not to punish those who feel differently about these matters. It is to persuade them that they are wrong. We can imagine no more appropriate response to burning a flag than waving one's own, no better way to counter a flag-burner's message than by saluting the flag that burns, no surer means of preserving the dignity even of the flag that burned than by—as one witness here did—according its remains a respectful burial. We do not consecrate the flag by punishing its desecration, for in doing so we dilute the freedom that this cherished emblem represents.

The judgment of the Texas Court of Criminal Appeals is therefore *affirmed.*

Political Speech

Because the Framers were primarily concerned with enabling democracy to function, political speech has been given an especially high degree of protection. Such speech may not be barred even when it is offensive or outrageous. A speaker, for example, could accuse a U.S. senator of being insane and could use crude, violent language to describe him. The speech is still protected. **Political speech is protected unless it is intended and likely to create imminent lawless action.**[12] For example, suppose the speaker said, "The senator is inside that restaurant. Let's get some matches and burn the place down." Speech of this sort is not protected. The speaker could be arrested for attempted arson or attempted murder.

One of the most important recent developments in constitutional law concerns the ability of *organizations* to engage in political speech. In the case that follows, a sharply divided Supreme Court weighed in on the issue raised in this chapter's opening scenario.

CITIZENS UNITED V. FEDERAL ELECTION COMMISSION

130 S. Ct. 876
United States Supreme Court, 2010

Facts: Citizens United, a nonprofit organization, produced a documentary on presidential candidate Hillary Clinton. The group wanted to run television ads promoting *Hillary: The Movie.* The Bipartisan Campaign Reform Act of 2002 banned "electioneering communication" by corporations and unions for the 30 days before a presidential primary. Citizens United challenged the Act, arguing that it violated the First Amendment.

Issue: *Did the Bipartisan Campaign Reform Act violate the First Amendment?*

Excerpts from Justice Kennedy's Decision: The First Amendment provides that "Congress shall make no law... abridging the freedom of speech." The law before us makes it a felony for all corporations—including nonprofit advocacy corporations—either to expressly advocate the election or defeat of candidates or to broadcast electioneering communications within 30 days of a primary election and 60 days of a general election. These prohibitions are classic examples of censorship.

As a restriction on the amount of money a person or group can spend on political communication during a campaign, that statute necessarily reduces the quantity of expression by restricting the number of issues discussed, the depth of their exploration, and the size of the audience reached.

Speech is an essential mechanism of democracy, for it is the means to hold officials accountable to the people. The right of citizens to inquire, to hear, to speak, and to use information to reach consensus is a precondition to enlightened self-government and a necessary means to protect it. For these reasons, political speech must prevail against laws that would suppress it, whether by design or inadvertence.

The Government may not deprive the public of the right and privilege to determine for itself what speech and

---

[12]*Brandenburg v. Ohio*, 395 U.S. 444, 89 S. Ct. 1827, 1969 U.S. LEXIS 1367 (1969).

speakers are worthy of consideration. The First Amendment protects speech and speaker, and the ideas that flow from each.

The Court has recognized that First Amendment protection extends to corporations. This protection has been extended by explicit holdings to the context of political speech. Corporations and other associations, like individuals, contribute to the discussion, debate, and the dissemination of information and ideas that the First Amendment seeks to foster. The Court has thus rejected the argument that political speech of corporations or other associations should be treated differently under the First Amendment simply because such associations are not "natural persons."

The Government falls back on the argument that corporate political speech can be banned in order to prevent corruption or its appearance. We must give weight to attempts by Congress to seek to dispel either the appearance or the reality of these influences. The remedies enacted by law, however, must comply with the First Amendment; and, it is our law and our tradition that more speech, not less, is the governing rule. An outright ban on corporate political speech during the critical preelection period is not a permissible remedy.

Modern-day movies, television comedies, or skits on YouTube might portray public officials or public policies in unflattering ways. Yet if a covered transmission during the blackout period creates the background for candidate endorsement or opposition, a felony occurs solely because a corporation has made the purchase in order to engage in political speech. Speech would be suppressed in the realm where its necessity is most evident: in the public dialogue preceding a real election. Governments are often hostile to speech, but under our law and our tradition it seems stranger than fiction for our Government to make this political speech a crime. Yet this is the statute's purpose and design.

Some members of the public might consider Hillary to be insightful and instructive; some might find it to be neither high art nor a fair discussion on how to set the Nation's course; still others simply might suspend judgment on these points but decide to think more about issues and candidates. Those choices and assessments, however, are not for the Government to make.

The judgment of the District Court is reversed.

It is so ordered.

Time, Place, and Manner

Even when speech is protected, the government may regulate the *time, place*, and *manner* of such speech. A town may require a group to apply for a permit before using a public park for a political demonstration. The town may insist that the demonstration take place during daylight hours and that there be adequate police supervision and sanitation provided. However, the town may not prohibit such demonstrations outright.

Many public universities have designated "free speech zones" located in high-traffic areas of campus that are not immediately adjacent to a large number of classrooms. The zones allow for debates to proceed and reach many students, but they minimize the chances that noisy demonstrations will interfere with lectures.

Morality and Obscenity

The regulation of morality and obscenity presents additional problems. Obscenity has never received constitutional protection. The Supreme Court has consistently held that it does not play a valued role in our society and has refused to give protection to obscene works. That is well and good, but it merely forces the question: what is obscene?

In *Miller v. California*,[13] the Court created a three-part test to determine if a creative work is obscene. The basic guidelines for the factfinder are:

- Whether the average person, applying contemporary community standards, would find that the work, taken as a whole, appeals to the prurient interest;

---

[13]413 U.S. 15, 93 S. Ct. 2607, 1973 U.S. LEXIS 149 (1973).

- Whether the work depicts or describes, in a patently offensive way, sexual conduct specifically defined by the applicable state law; and

- Whether the work, taken as a whole, lacks serious literary, artistic, political, or scientific value.

If the trial court finds that the answer to all three of those questions is "yes," it may judge the material obscene; the state may then prohibit the work. If the state fails to prove any one of the three criteria, though, the work is not obscene.[14] A United States District Court ruled that "As Nasty As They Wanna Be," recorded by 2 Live Crew, was obscene. The appeals court, however, reversed, finding that the state had failed to prove lack of artistic merit.[15]

Commercial Speech

This refers to speech that has a dominant theme to propose a commercial transaction. For example, most advertisements on television and in the newspapers are **commercial speech**. This sort of speech is protected by the First Amendment, but the government is permitted to regulate it more closely than other forms of speech. Commercial speech that is false or misleading may be outlawed altogether. **The government may regulate other commercial speech, provided that the rules are reasonable and directed to a legitimate goal.** The following case demonstrates the very different treatment given to this type of speech.

Commercial speech
Communication, such as advertisements, that has the dominant theme of proposing a business transaction.

SALIB V. CITY OF MESA

133 P.3d 756, 212 Ariz. 446
Arizona Court of Appeals, 2006.

Facts: Edward Salib owned a Winchell's Donut House in Mesa, Arizona. To attract customers, he displayed large signs in his store window. The city ordered him to remove the signs, because they violated its Sign Code, which prohibited covering more than 30% of a store's windows with signs. Salib sued, claiming that the Sign Code violated his First Amendment free speech rights. The trial court gave summary judgment for Mesa, and the store owner appealed.

Issue: *Did Mesa's Sign Code violate the First Amendment?*

Excerpts from Judge Irvine's Decision: Under [a Supreme Court case called] *Central Hudson*, commercial speech that concerns unlawful activity or is misleading is not protected by the First Amendment. Commercial speech that falls into neither of these categories may be regulated if the government satisfies a three-prong test. First, the government must assert a substantial interest in support of the regulation. Mesa argues, and Salib concedes, that the governmental regulation of aesthetics constitutes

a substantial interest, so the first prong of *Central Hudson* is not at issue.

Under the second prong of *Central Hudson*, the government must demonstrate that the challenged regulation advances its interest in a direct and material way. Salib argues that this prong has not been met because no studies were conducted to determine what aesthetic or safety problems existed and how the Sign Code could solve such problems.

Mesa responds that the Sign Code was enacted because of legitimate concerns among business owners that many businesses in the area had 100% coverage of their storefront windows and that this total coverage was unattractive and detracted from the aesthetics of the city. The First Amendment does not require a formal study before a regulation may be enacted. The record shows that the city council received considerable input on the subject of window coverage and aesthetics before enacting the Sign Code. Although its final adoption of the Sign Code may have rested on anecdote, history, consensus or

---

[14]*Penthouse Intern Ltd. v. McAuliffe*, 610 F.2d 1353 (5th Cir. 1980).

simple common sense, rather than a formal study or survey addressed specifically to the window coverage provision, the constitution requires no greater proof.

Salib argues the restriction is not narrow enough and therefore violates the third prong of *Central Hudson*. It is clear from the First Amendment cases that narrowly tailored or narrowly drawn does not mean that the least restrictive means must be used. Rather, a "reasonable fit" between the intent and purpose of the regulation and the means chosen to accomplish those goals is required. The regulation does not have to be perfect, but its scope must be in proportion to the interest served.

Mesa argues that 30% is a reasonable compromise between 100% coverage and a total ban of signage. Further, Mesa argues, the Sign Code is narrow because it only addresses signs that are inside the pane, and the Code allows alternative methods of communication, including signs hanging outside of the window sill area. Additionally, Mesa conducted comparisons with other communities and found that the 30% restriction on window coverage was comparable to other cities' restrictions.

We are not in a position to determine what percentage of window coverage is optimal. Rather, we only decide if the 30% figure that was adopted by the Sign Code is a reasonable fit to further the goal of improving aesthetics. We conclude that it is. Reasonable minds can differ as to whether Mesa's interest would best be served by a 15%, 25%, 30%, or 40% limitation on window coverage, but under the facts of this case we cannot conclude that these differences of degree are of a constitutional dimension. The exact balance between the size of the signs and the aesthetic benefits attained is ultimately a subjective decision best left to the city council.

We conclude the Sign Code directly advances a substantial governmental interest and is narrowly tailored to directly advance the goal of improved aesthetics. We therefore affirm the trial court's granting of Mesa's Motion for Summary Judgment.

EXAM Strategy

Question: Maria owns a lot next to a freeway that passes through Tidyville. She has rented a billboard to Huge Mart, a nearby retailer, and a second billboard to Green, a political party. However, Tidyville prohibits off-premises signs (those not on the advertiser's property) that are visible from the freeway. Tidyville's rule is designed to make the city more attractive, to increase property values, and to eliminate distractions that may cause freeway accidents. Huge Mart and Green sue, claiming that Tidyville's law violates their First Amendment rights.

    A.   Huge Mart is likely to win; Green is likely to lose.

    B.   Green is likely to win; Huge Mart is likely to lose.

    C.   Huge Mart and Green are both likely to win.

    D.   Huge Mart and Green are both likely to lose.

Strategy: What is the difference between the two cases? Huge Mart wants the billboard for commercial speech; Green wants it for a political message. What are the legal standards for commercial and political free speech? Apply those standards.

Result: The government may regulate commercial speech, provided that the rules are reasonable and directed to a legitimate goal. Political speech is given much stronger protection, and can be prohibited only if it is intended and likely to create imminent lawless action. The regulation outlawing *advertising* will be upheld, but Tidyville will not be allowed to block political messages.

Fifth Amendment: Due Process and the Takings Clause

> **Four years of work and your entire career are suddenly on the line.**

You are a senior at a major state university. You feel great about a difficult exam you took in Professor Watson's class. The Dean's Office sends for you, and you enter curiously, wondering if your exam was so good that the dean is awarding you a prize. Not quite. The exam proctor has accused you of cheating. Based on the accusation, Watson has flunked you. You protest that you are innocent and demand to know what the accusation is. The dean says that you will learn the details at a hearing, if you wish to have one. She reminds you that if you lose the hearing, you will be expelled from the university. Four years of work and your entire career are suddenly on the line.

The hearing is run by Professor Holmes, who will make the final decision. Holmes is a junior faculty member in Watson's department. (Next year, Watson will decide Holmes's tenure application.) At the hearing, the proctor accuses you of copying from a student sitting in front of you. Both Watson and Holmes have already compared the two papers and concluded that they are strongly similar. Holmes tells you that you must convince him the charge is wrong. You examine the papers, acknowledge that there are similarities, but plead as best you can that you never copied. Holmes doesn't buy it. The university expels you, placing on your transcript a notation of cheating.

Have you received fair treatment? To answer that, we must look to the Fifth Amendment, which provides several vital protections. We will consider two related provisions, the Due Process Clause and the Takings Clause. Together, they state: "No person shall be . . . deprived of life, liberty, or property without due process of law; nor shall private property be taken for public use, without just compensation." These clauses prevent the government from arbitrarily taking the most valuable possessions of a citizen or corporation. The government has the right to take a person's liberty or property. But there are three important limitations:

- **Procedural Due Process**. Before depriving anyone of liberty or property, the government must go through certain steps, or procedures, to ensure that the result is fair.

- **The Takings Clause**. When the government takes property for public use, such as to build a new highway, it has to pay a fair price.

- **Substantive Due Process**. Some rights are so fundamental that the government may not take them from us at all. The substance of any law or government action may be challenged on fundamental fairness grounds.

Procedural Due Process

The government deprives citizens or corporations of their property in a variety of ways. The Internal Revenue Service may fine a corporation for late payment of taxes. The Customs Service may seize goods at the border. As to liberty, the government may take it by confining someone in a mental institution or by taking a child out of the home because of parental neglect. The purpose of **procedural due process** is to ensure that before the government takes liberty or property, the affected person has a fair chance to oppose the action.

There are two steps in analyzing a procedural due process case:

- Is the government attempting to take liberty or property?

- If so, how much process is due? (If the government is *not* attempting to take liberty or property, there is no due process issue.)

Takings Clause
A clause in the Fifth Amendment that ensures that when any governmental unit takes private property for public use, it must compensate the owner.

Procedural due process
The doctrine that ensures that before the government takes liberty or property, the affected person has a fair chance to oppose the action.

Is the Government Attempting to Take Liberty or Property?   Liberty interests are generally easy to spot: confining someone in a mental institution and taking a child from her home are both deprivations of liberty. A property interest may be obvious. Suppose that, during a civil lawsuit, the court **attaches** a defendant's house, meaning it bars the defendant from selling the property at least until the case is decided. This way, if the plaintiff wins, the defendant will have assets to pay the judgment. The court has clearly deprived the defendant of an important interest in his house, and the defendant is entitled to due process. However, a property interest may be subtler than that. A woman holding a job with a government agency has a "property interest" in that job, because her employer has agreed not to fire her without cause, and she can rely on it for income. If the government does fire her, it is taking away that property interest, and she is entitled to due process. A student attending any public school has a property interest in her education. If a public university suspends a student as described above, it is taking her property, and she, too, should receive due process.

How Much Process Is Due?   Assuming that a liberty or property interest is affected, a court must decide how much process is due. Does the person get a formal trial, or an informal hearing, or merely a chance to reply in writing to the charges against her? If she gets a hearing, must it be held before the government deprives her of her property, or is it enough that she can be heard shortly thereafter? **What sort of hearing the government must offer depends upon how important the property or liberty interest is and on whether the government has a competing need for efficiency.** The more important the interest, the more formal the procedures must be.

Neutral Factfinder   Regardless of how formal the hearing, one requirement is constant: the factfinder must be neutral. Whether it is a superior court judge deciding a multimillion-dollar contract suit or an employment supervisor deciding the fate of a government employee, the factfinder must have no personal interest in the outcome. In *Ward v. Monroeville*,[16] the plaintiff was a motorist who had been stopped for traffic offenses in a small town. He protested his innocence and received a judicial hearing. But the "judge" at the hearing was the town mayor. Traffic fines were a significant part of the town's budget. The motorist argued that the town was depriving him of procedural due process because the mayor had a financial interest in the outcome of the case. The United States Supreme Court agreed and reversed his conviction.

Attachment of Property   As described earlier, a plaintiff in a civil lawsuit often seeks to *attach* the defendant's property. This protects the plaintiff, but it may also harm the defendant if, for example, he is about to close a profitable real estate deal. Attachments used to be routine. In *Connecticut v. Doehr*, the Supreme Court required more caution.[17] Based on *Doehr*, when a plaintiff seeks to attach at the beginning of the trial, a court must look at the plaintiff's likelihood of winning. Generally, the court must grant the defendant a hearing *before* attaching the property. The defendant, represented by a lawyer, may offer evidence as to how attachment would harm him and why it should be denied.

Government Employment   A government employee must receive due process before being fired. Generally, this means some kind of hearing, but not necessarily a formal court hearing. The employee is entitled to know the charges against him, to hear the employer's evidence, and to have an opportunity to tell his side of the story. He is not entitled to have a lawyer present. The hearing "officer" need only be a neutral employee. Further, in an emergency, where the employee is a danger to the public or the organization, the

---

[16]409 U.S. 57, 93 S. Ct. 80, 1972 U.S. LEXIS 11 (1972).
[17]501 U.S. 1, 111 S. Ct. 2105, 1991 U.S. LEXIS 3317 (1991).

government may suspend with pay, before holding a hearing. It then must provide a hearing before the decision becomes final.

Academic Suspension   There is still a property interest here, but it is the least important of those discussed. When a public school concludes that a student has failed to meet its normal academic standards, such as by failing too many courses, it may dismiss him without a hearing. Due process is served if the student receives notice of the reason and has some opportunity to respond, such as by writing a letter contradicting the school's claims.

In cases of disciplinary suspension or expulsion, courts generally require schools to provide a higher level of due process. In the hypothetical at the beginning of this section, the university has failed to provide adequate due process.[18] The school has accused the student of a serious infraction. The school must promptly provide details of the charge and cannot wait until the hearing to do so. The student should see the two papers and have a chance to rebut the charge. Moreover, Professor Holmes has demonstrated bias. He appears to have made up his mind in advance. He has placed the burden on the student to disprove the charges. And he probably feels obligated to support Watson's original conclusion, since Watson will be deciding his tenure case next year.

The Takings Clause

Florence Dolan ran a plumbing store in Tigard, Oregon. She and her husband wanted to enlarge it on land they already owned. But the city government said that they could expand only if they dedicated some of their own land for use as a public bicycle path and for other public use. Does the city have the right to make them do that? For an answer, we must look to a different part of the Fifth Amendment.

The Takings Clause prohibits a state from taking private property for public use without just compensation. A town wishing to build a new football field may boot you out of your house. But the town must compensate you. The government takes your land through the power of **eminent domain**. Officials must notify you of their intentions and give you an opportunity to oppose the project and to challenge the amount the town offers to pay. But when the hearings are done, the town may write you a check and level your house, whether you like it or not.

Eminent domain

The power of the government to take private property for public use.

More controversial issues arise when a local government does not physically take the property but passes regulations that restrict its use. Tigard is a city of 30,000 in Oregon. The city developed a comprehensive land use plan for its downtown area in order to preserve green space, to encourage transportation other than autos, and to reduce its flooding problems. Under the plan, when a property owner sought permission to build in the downtown section, the city could require some of her land to be used for public purposes. This has become a standard method of land use planning throughout the nation. States have used it to preserve coastline, urban green belts, and many environmental features.

When Florence Dolan applied for permission to expand, the city required that she dedicate a 15-foot strip of her property to the city as a bicycle pathway and that she preserve, as greenway, a portion of her land within a floodplain. She sued, and though she lost in the Oregon courts, she won in the United States Supreme Court. The Court held that Tigard City's method of routinely forcing all owners to dedicate land to public use violated the Takings Clause. The city was taking the land, even though title never changed hands.[19]

The Court did not outlaw all such requirements. What it required was that, **before a government may require an owner to dedicate land to a public use, it must show that this owner's proposed building requires this dedication of land.** In other words, it is not enough for Tigard to have a general plan, such as a bicycle pathway, and to make all owners

---

[18]See, e.g., *University of Texas Medical School at Houston v. Than*, 901 S.W.2d 926, 1995 Tex. LEXIS 105 (Tex. 1995).

[19]*Dolan v. City of Tigard*, 512 U.S. 374, 114 S. Ct. 2309, 1994 U.S. LEXIS 4826 (1994).

participate in it. Tigard must show that it needs *Dolan's* land *specifically for a bike path and greenway.* This will be much harder for local governments to demonstrate than merely showing a city-wide plan. A related issue arose in the following controversial case. A city used eminent domain to take property on behalf of *private developers.* Was this a valid public use?

The *Kelo* decision was controversial, and in response, some states passed statutes prohibiting eminent domain for private development.

KELO V. CITY OF NEW LONDON, CONNECTICUT

545 U.S. 469, 125 S.Ct. 2655
United States Supreme Court, 2005

Facts: New London, Connecticut, was declining economically. The city's unemployment rate was double that of the state generally, and the population at its lowest point in 75 years. In response, state and local officials targeted a section of the city, called Fort Trumbull, for revitalization. Located on the Thames River, Fort Trumbull comprised 115 privately owned properties and 32 additional acres of an abandoned naval facility. The development plan included one section for a waterfront conference hotel and stores; a second one for 80 private residences; and one for research facilities.

The state bought most of the properties from willing sellers. However, nine owners of 15 properties refused to sell and filed suit. The owners claimed that the city was trying to take land for *private* use, not public, in violation of the Takings Clause. The case reached the United States Supreme Court.

Issue: *Did the city's plan violate the Takings Clause?*

Excerpts from Justice Stevens's Decision: It has long been accepted that the sovereign may not take the property of A for the sole purpose of transferring it to another private party B, even though A is paid just compensation. On the other hand, it is equally clear that a State may transfer property from one private party to another if future "use by the public" is the purpose of the taking; the condemnation of land for a railroad with common-carrier duties is a familiar example.

This is not a case in which the City is planning to open the condemned land—at least not in its entirety—to use by the general public. Nor will the private lessees of the land in any sense be required to operate like common carriers, making their services available to all comers. But this Court long ago rejected any literal requirement that condemned property be put into use for the general public, [embracing] the broader and more natural interpretation of public use as "public purpose." Thus, in a case upholding a mining company's use of an aerial bucket line to transport ore over property it did not

own, Justice Holmes' opinion for the Court stressed "the inadequacy of use by the general public as a universal test."

The City has carefully formulated an economic development plan that it believes will provide appreciable benefits to the community, including—but by no means limited to—new jobs and increased tax revenue. As with other exercises in urban planning and development, the City is endeavoring to coordinate a variety of commercial, residential, and recreational uses of land, with the hope that they will form a whole greater than the sum of its parts. Because that plan unquestionably serves a public purpose, the takings challenged here satisfy the public use requirement of the Fifth Amendment.

To avoid this result, petitioners urge us to adopt a new bright-line rule that economic development does not qualify as a public use. [However, promoting] economic development is a traditional and long accepted function of government. There is, moreover, no principled way of distinguishing economic development from the other public purposes that we have recognized. In our cases upholding takings that facilitated agriculture and mining, for example, we emphasized the importance of those industries to the welfare of the States in question. Clearly, there is no basis for exempting economic development from our traditionally broad understanding of public purpose.

The judgment of the Supreme Court of Connecticut is affirmed.

Justice O'Connor, dissenting: The Court today significantly expands the meaning of public use. It holds that the sovereign may take private property currently put to ordinary private use, and give it over for new, ordinary private use, so long as the new use is predicted to generate some secondary benefit for the public—such as increased tax revenue, more jobs, maybe even esthetic pleasure. But nearly any lawful use of real private property can be said to generate some incidental benefit to the public. Thus, if predicted (or even guaranteed) positive side-effects are enough to render transfer from one private party to another constitutional, then the words "for public use" do not realistically exclude *any* takings, and thus do not exert any constraint on the eminent domain power.

Any property may now be taken for the benefit of another private party, but the fallout from this decision will not be random. The beneficiaries are likely to be those citizens with disproportionate influence and power in the political process, including large corporations and development firms. As for the victims, the government now has license to transfer property from those with fewer resources to those with more.

Substantive Due Process

This doctrine is part of the Due Process Clause, but it is entirely different from procedural due process and from government taking. During the first third of the twentieth century, the Supreme Court frequently nullified state and federal laws, asserting that they interfered with basic rights. For example, in a famous 1905 case, *Lochner v. New York*,[20] the Supreme Court invalidated a New York statute that had limited the number of hours that bakers could work in a week. New York had passed the law to protect employee health. But the Court declared that private parties had a basic constitutional right to contract. In this case, the statute interfered with the rights of the employer and the baker to make any bargain they wished. Over the next three decades, the Court struck down dozens of state and federal laws that were aimed at working conditions, union rights, and social welfare generally. This was called **substantive due process**[21] because the Court was looking at the underlying rights being affected, such as the right to contract, not at any procedures.

> **Substantive due process**
> A form of due process that holds that certain rights are so fundamental that the government may not eliminate them.

Critics complained that the Court was interfering with the desires of the voting public by nullifying laws that the justices personally disliked (judicial activism). During the Great Depression, however, things changed. Beginning in 1934, the Court completely reversed itself and began to uphold the types of laws it earlier had struck down.

The Supreme Court made an important substantive due process ruling in the case of *BMW v. Gore*.[22] A BMW dealership sold Gore a car that had sustained water damage. Instead of telling him of the damage, they simply repainted the car and sold it as new.

In Chapter 6, we will examine two different types of cash awards that juries may make in tort cases. For now, let's call them "ordinary" and "punitive" damages. When plaintiffs win tort cases, juries may always award ordinary damages to offset real, measureable losses. In addition, juries are sometimes allowed to add to an award to further punish a defendant for bad behavior.

In the BMW case, the jury awarded Gore $4,000 in ordinary damages as the difference in value between a flawless new car and a water-damaged car. The jury then awarded a delighted Gore $4 *million* in punitive damages. In the end, the Supreme Court decided that the punitive award was so disproportionate to the harm actually caused that it violated substantive due process rights.

Fourteenth Amendment: Equal Protection Clause

Shannon Faulkner wanted to attend The Citadel, a state-supported military college in South Carolina. She was a fine student who met every admission requirement that The Citadel set except one: she was not a man. The Citadel argued that its long and distinguished history demanded that it remain all male. Faulkner responded that she was a citizen

---

[20]198 U.S. 45, 25 S. Ct. 539, 1905 U.S. LEXIS 1153 (1905).

[21]Be the first on your block to pronounce this word correctly. The accent goes on the first syllable: *sub*stantive.

[22]517 U.S. 559 (1996).

of the state and ought to receive the benefits that others got, including the right to a military education. Could the school exclude her on the basis of gender?

The Fourteenth Amendment provides that "No State shall … deny to any person within its jurisdiction the equal protection of the laws." This is the **Equal Protection Clause**, and it means that, generally speaking, **governments must treat people equally**. Unfair classifications among people or corporations will not be permitted. A notorious example of unfair classification would be race discrimination: permitting only white children to attend a public school violates the Equal Protection Clause.

Yet clearly, governments do make classifications every day. People with high incomes pay a higher tax rate than those with low incomes; some corporations are permitted to deal in securities, while others are not. To determine which classifications are constitutionally permissible, we need to know what is being classified. There are three major groups of classifications. The outcome of a case can generally be predicted by knowing which group it is in.

- **Minimal Scrutiny: Economic and Social Relations**. Government actions that classify people or corporations on these bases are almost always upheld.

- **Intermediate Scrutiny: Gender**. Government classifications are sometimes upheld.

- **Strict Scrutiny: Race, Ethnicity, and Fundamental Rights**. Classifications based on any of these are almost never upheld.

Minimal Scrutiny: Economic and Social Regulation

Just as with the Due Process Clause, laws that regulate economic or social issues are presumed valid. They will be upheld if they are *rationally related to a legitimate goal*. This means a statute may classify corporations and/or people, and the classifications will be upheld if they make any sense at all. The New York City Transit Authority excluded all methadone users from any employment. The United States District Court concluded that this violated the Equal Protection Clause by unfairly excluding all those who were on methadone. The court noted that even those who tested free of any illegal drugs and were seeking non-safety-sensitive jobs, such as clerks, were turned away. That, said the district court, was irrational.

Not so, said the United States Supreme Court. The Court admitted that the policy might not be the wisest. It would probably make more sense to test individually for illegal drugs rather than automatically exclude methadone users. But, said the Court, it was not up to the justices to choose the best policy. They were only to decide if the policy was rational. Excluding methadone users related rationally to the safety of public transport and therefore did not violate the Equal Protection Clause.[23]

Intermediate Scrutiny: Gender

Classifications based on sex must meet a tougher test than those resulting from economic or social regulation. Such laws must *substantially relate to important government objectives*. Courts have increasingly nullified government sex classifications as societal concern with gender equality has grown.

At about the same time Shannon Faulkner began her campaign to enter The Citadel, another woman sought admission to the Virginia Military Institute (VMI), an all-male state school. The Supreme Court held that Virginia had violated the Equal Protection Clause by excluding women from VMI. The Court ruled that gender-based government discrimina-

---

[23]*New York City Transit Authority v. Beazer*, 440 U.S. 568, 99 S. Ct. 1355, 1979 U.S. LEXIS 77 (1979).

tion requires an "exceedingly persuasive justification," and that Virginia had failed that standard of proof. The Citadel promptly opened its doors to women as well.[24]

Strict Scrutiny: Race, Ethnicity, and Fundamental Rights

Any government action that intentionally discriminates against racial or ethnic minorities, or interferes with a fundamental right, is presumed invalid. In such cases, courts will look at the statute or policy with *strict scrutiny;* that is, courts will examine it very closely to determine whether there is compelling justification for it. The law will be upheld only if it is *necessary to promote a compelling state interest*. Very few meet that test.

- **Racial and Ethnic Minorities**. Any government action that intentionally discriminates on the basis of race, or ethnicity is presumed invalid. For example, in *Palmore v. Sidoti*,[25] the state had refused to give child custody to a mother because her new spouse was racially different from the child. The practice was declared unconstitutional. The state had made a racial classification, it was presumed invalid, and the government had no *compelling need* to make such a ruling.

- **Fundamental Rights**. A government action interfering with a fundamental right also receives strict scrutiny and will likely be declared void. For example, New York State gave an employment preference to any veteran who had been a state resident when he entered the military. Newcomers who were veterans were less likely to get jobs, and therefore this statute interfered with the right to travel, a fundamental right. The Supreme Court declared the law invalid.[26]

Fundamental rights
Rights so basic that any governmental interference with them is suspect and likely to be unconstitutional.

EXAM Strategy

Question: Megan is a freshman at her local public high school; her older sister Jenna attends a nearby private high school. Both girls are angry because their schools prohibit them from joining their respective wrestling teams, where only boys are allowed. The two girls sue based on the U.S. Constitution. Discuss the relevant law and predict the outcomes.

Strategy: One girl goes to private school and one to public school. Why does that matter? Now ask what provision of the Constitution is involved, and what legal standard it establishes.

Result: The Constitution offers protection from the *government*. A private high school is not part of the government, and Jenna has no constitutional case. Megan's suit is based on the Equal Protection Clause. This is gender discrimination, meaning that Megan's school must convince the court that keeping girls off the team *substantially relates to an important government objective*. The school will probably argue that wrestling with stronger boys will be dangerous for girls. However, courts are increasingly suspicious of any gender discrimination and are unlikely to find the school's argument persuasive.

[24]*United States v. Virginia*, 518 U.S. 515, 116 S. Ct. 2264, 1996 U.S. LEXIS 4259 (1996).
[25]466 U.S. 429, 104 S. Ct. 1879, 1984 U.S. LEXIS 69 (1984).
[26]*Attorney General of New York v. Soto-Lopez*, 476 U.S. 898, 106 S. Ct. 2317, 1986 U.S. LEXIS 59 (1986).

Chapter Conclusion

The legal battle over power never stops. The obligation of a state to provide equal educational opportunity for both genders relates to whether Tigard, Oregon, may demand some of Ms. Dolan's store lot for public use. Both issues are governed by one amazing document. That same Constitution determines what tax preferences are permissible and even whether a state may require you to wear clothing. As social mores change in step with broad cultural developments, as the membership of the Supreme Court changes, the balance of power between federal government, state government, and citizens will continue to evolve. There are no easy answers to these constitutional questions because there has never been a democracy so large, so diverse, or so powerful.

EXAM REVIEW

1. **CONSTITUTION** The Constitution is a series of compromises about power. (p. 106)

2. **ARTICLES I, II, AND III** Article I of the Constitution creates the Congress and grants all legislative power to it. Article II establishes the office of President and defines executive powers. Article III creates the Supreme Court and permits lower federal courts; the article also outlines the powers of the federal judiciary. (p. 106)

3. **COMMERCE CLAUSE** Under the Commerce Clause, Congress may regulate any activity that has a substantial effect on interstate commerce. (p. 107)

4. **INTERSTATE COMMERCE** A state may not regulate commerce in any way that will interfere with interstate commerce. (p. 107)

EXAM Strategy

Question: Maine exempted many charitable institutions from real estate taxes but denied this benefit to a charity that primarily benefited out-of-state residents. Camp Newfound was a Christian Science organization, and 95 percent of its summer campers came from other states. Camp Newfound sued Maine. Discuss.

Strategy: The state was treating organizations differently depending on what states their campers come from. This raised Commerce Clause issues. Did the positive aspect or dormant aspect of that clause apply? The dormant aspect applied. What does it state? Apply that standard to these facts. (See the "Result" at the end of this section.)

5. **SUPREMACY CLAUSE** Under the Supremacy Clause, if there is a conflict between federal and state statutes, the federal law preempts the field. Even without a conflict, federal law preempts if Congress intended to exercise exclusive control. (p. 109)

6. **PRESIDENTIAL POWERS** The President's key powers include making agency appointments, proposing legislation, conducting foreign policy, and acting as commander in chief of the armed forces. (p. 110)

7. **FEDERAL COURTS** The federal courts adjudicate cases and also exercise judicial review, which is the right to declare a statute or governmental action unconstitutional and void. (pp. 110–113)

8. **FREEDOM OF SPEECH** Freedom of speech includes symbolic acts. Political speech by both people and organizations is protected unless it is intended and likely to create imminent lawless action. (pp. 114–116)

9. **REGULATION OF SPEECH** The government may regulate the time, place, and manner of speech. (p. 116)

10. **COMMERCIAL SPEECH** Commercial speech that is false or misleading may be outlawed; otherwise, regulations on this speech must be reasonable and directed to a legitimate goal. (pp. 117–118)

EXAM Strategy

Question: A federal statute prohibits the broadcasting of lottery advertisements, except by stations that broadcast in states permitting lotteries. The purpose of the statute is to support efforts of states that outlaw lotteries. Truth Broadcasting operates a radio station in State A (a nonlottery state) but broadcasts primarily in State B (a lottery state). Truth wants to advertise State A's lottery but is barred by the statute. Does the federal statute violate Truth's constitutional rights?

Strategy: This case involves a particular kind of speech. What kind? What is the rule about that kind of speech? (See the "Result" at the end of this section.)

11. **PROCEDURAL DUE PROCESS** Procedural due process is required whenever the government attempts to take liberty or property. The amount of process that is due depends upon the importance of the liberty or property threatened. (pp. 119–121)

EXAM Strategy

Question: Fox's Fine Furs claims that Ermine owes $68,000 for a mink coat on which she has stopped making payments. Fox files a complaint and also asks the court clerk to *garnish* Ermine's wages. A garnishment is a court order to an employer to withhold an employee's wages, or a portion of them, and pay the money into court so that there will be money for the plaintiff, if it wins. What constitutional issue does Fox's request for garnishment raise?

Strategy: Ermine is in danger of losing part of her income, which is property. The Due Process Clause prohibits the government (the court) from taking life, liberty, or property without due process. What process is Ermine entitled to? (See the "Result" at the end of this section.)

12. **TAKINGS CLAUSE** The Takings Clause prohibits a state from taking private property for public use without just compensation. (pp. 121–123)

13. **SUBSTANTIVE DUE PROCESS** A substantive due process analysis presumes that any economic or social regulation is valid, and presumes invalid any law that infringes upon a fundamental right. (pp. 123–124)

14. **EQUAL PROTECTION CLAUSE** The Equal Protection Clause generally requires the government to treat people equally. Courts apply strict scrutiny in any equal protection case involving race, ethnicity, or fundamental rights; intermediate scrutiny to any case involving gender; and minimal scrutiny to an economic or social regulation. (pp. 124–126)

---

4. Result: The dormant aspect holds that a state statute that discriminates against interstate commerce is almost always invalid. Maine was subsidizing charities that served in-state residents and penalizing those that attracted campers from elsewhere. The tax rules violated the Commerce Clause and was void.[27]

10. Result: An advertisement is *commercial* speech. The government may regulate this speech so long as the rules are reasonable and directed to a legitimate goal. The goal of supporting nonlottery states is reasonable, and there is no violation of Truth's free speech rights.[28]

11. Result: Ermine is entitled to notice of Fox's claim and to a hearing *before* the court garnishes her wages.[29]

MULTIPLE-CHOICE QUESTIONS

1. Greenville College, a public community college, has a policy of admitting only male students. If the policy is challenged under the Fourteenth Amendment, _____ scrutiny will be applied.

   (a) strict

   (b) intermediate

   (c) rational

   (d) none of the above

2. You begin work at Everhappy Corp. at the beginning of November. On your second day at work, you wear a political button on your overcoat, supporting your choice for governor in the upcoming election. Your boss glances at it and says, "Get that stupid thing out of this office or you're history, chump." Your boss _____ violated your First Amendment rights. After work, you put the button back on and start

---

[27]*Camps Newfound/Owatonna, Inc. v. Town of Harrison, Maine*, 520 U.S. 564, 117 S.Ct. 1590 (1997).
[28]*United States v. Edge Broadcasting*, 509 U.S. 418, 113 S.Ct. 2696 (1993).
[29]*Sniadach v. Family Finance Corp.*, 395 U.S. 337 (1969).

walking home. You pass a police officer who blocks your path and says, "Take off that stupid button or you're going to jail, chump." The officer _____ violated your First Amendment rights.

(a) has; has

(b) has; has not

(c) has not; has

(d) has not; has not

3. Which of the following statements accurately describes statutes that Congress and the President may create?

(a) Statutes must be related to a power listed in Article I, section 8, of the Constitution.

(b) Statutes must not infringe on the liberties in the Bill of Rights.

(c) Both A and B

(d) None of the above

4. Which of the following is true of the origin of judicial review?

(a) It was created by Article II of the Constitution.

(b) It was created by Article III of the Constitution.

(c) It was created in the *Marbury v. Madison* case.

(d) It was created by the Fifth Amendment.

(e) It was created by the Fourteenth Amendment.

5. Consider *Kelo v. City of New London*, in which a city with a revitalization plan squared off against property owners who did not wish to sell their property. The key constitutional provision was the Takings Clause in the _____ Amendment. The Supreme Court decided the city _____ use eminent domain and take the property from the landowners.

(a) Fifth; could

(b) Fifth; could not

(c) Fourteenth; could

(d) Fourteenth; could not

Essay Questions

1. **YOU BE THE JUDGE WRITING PROBLEM** Scott Fane was a CPA licensed to practice in New Jersey and Florida. He built his New Jersey practice by making unsolicited phone calls to executives. When he moved to Florida, the Board of Accountancy there prohibited him (and all CPAs) from personally soliciting new business. Fane sued. Does the First Amendment force Florida to forgo foreclosing Fane's phoning? **Argument for Fane:** The Florida regulation violates the First Amendment, which protects commercial speech. Fane was not saying anything false or misleading, but was just trying to secure business. This is an unreasonable regulation, designed to keep newcomers out of the marketplace and maintain steady business and high prices for established CPAs. **Argument for the Florida Board of Accountancy:** Commercial speech deserves—and gets—a lower level of protection

than other speech. This regulation is a reasonable method of ensuring that the level of CPA work in our state remains high. CPAs who personally solicit clients are obviously in need of business. They are more likely to bend legal and ethical rules to obtain clients and keep them happy, and will lower the standards throughout the state.

2. President George H. W. Bush insisted that he had the power to send American troops into combat in the Middle East, without congressional assent. Yet before authorizing force in Operation Desert Storm, he secured congressional authorization. President Bill Clinton stated that he was prepared to invade Haiti without a congressional vote. Yet he bargained hard to avoid an invasion, and ultimately American troops entered without the use of force. Why the seeming doubletalk by both Presidents?

3. In the landmark 1965 case of *Griswold v. Connecticut*, the Supreme Court examined a Connecticut statute that made it a crime for any person to use contraception. The majority declared the law an unconstitutional violation of the right of privacy. Justice Black dissented, saying, "I do not to any extent whatever base my view that this Connecticut law is constitutional on a belief that the law is wise or that its policy is a good one. [It] is every bit as offensive to me as it is to the majority. [There is no criticism by the majority of this law] to which I cannot subscribe—except their conclusion that the evil qualities they see in the law make it unconstitutional." What legal doctrines are involved here? Why did Justice Black distinguish between his personal views on the statute and the power of the Court to overturn it?

4. Gilleo opposed American participation in the war in the Persian Gulf. She displayed a large sign on her front lawn that read, "Say No to War in the Persian Gulf, Call Congress Now." The city of Ladue prohibited signs on front lawns and Gilleo sued. The city claimed that it was regulating "time, place, and manner." Explain that statement, and decide who should win.

5. David Lucas paid $975,000 for two residential lots on the Isle of Palms near Charleston, South Carolina. He intended to build houses on them. Two years later, the South Carolina legislature passed a statute that prohibited building seaward of a certain line, and Lucas's property fell in the prohibited zone. Lucas claimed that his land was now useless and that South Carolina owed him its value. Explain his claim. Should he win?

DISCUSSION QUESTIONS

1. Return to the opening scenario and the *Citizens United* case. Is political advertising purchased by corporations appropriate? Do you agree with the five members of the Supreme Court who voted to allow it, or with the four who dissented and would have drawn distinctions between free speech by individuals and organizations? Why?

2. **Ethics** Is political advertising by a nonprofit political organization like Citizens United any more or less appropriate than advertising by for-profit corporations like the one described in the opening scenario? If you were a board member in the opening scenario, which (if any) of the three ads would you vote to authorize?

3. Consider the "tea party" movement. Do you believe that the federal government should be able to create whatever laws it deems to be in the country's best interests, or do you believe that individual states, like Florida and California, should have more control over the laws within their own borders?

4. This chapter is filled with examples of statutes that have been struck down by the courts. A Texas law banning flag burning was rejected by the Supreme Court, as was a Louisiana death penalty statute. The Affordable Healthcare Act was voided by multiple lower court judges before the Supreme Court ultimately upheld the law.

   Do you like the fact that courts can void laws which they determine to be in violation of the Constitution? Or is it wrong for appointed judges to overrule "the will of the majority," as expressed by elected members of Congress and state legislatures?

5. Gender discrimination currently receives "intermediate" Fourteenth Amendment scrutiny. Is this right? Should gender receive "strict" scrutiny as does race? Why or why not?

CHAPTER 6

TORTS

© Steve Allen/Jupiterimages

In a small Louisiana town, Don Mashburn ran a restaurant called Maison de Mashburn. The *New Orleans States-Item* newspaper reviewed his eatery, and here is what the article said:

> "'Tain't Creole, 'tain't Cajun, 'tain't French, 'tain't country American, 'tain't good. I don't know how much real talent in cooking is hidden under the mélange of hideous sauces which make this food and the menu a travesty of pretentious amateurism, but I find it all quite depressing. Put a yellow flour sauce on top of the duck, flame it for drama, and serve it with some horrible multiflavored rice in hollowed-out fruit and what have you got? A well-cooked duck with an ugly sauce that tastes too sweet and thick and makes you want to scrape off the glop to eat the plain duck. [The stuffed eggplant was prepared by emptying] a shaker full (more or less) of paprika on top of it. [One sauce created] trout à la green plague [while another should have been called] yellow death on duck."

Mashburn sued, claiming that the newspaper had committed libel, damaging his reputation and hurting his business.[1] Trout à la green plague will be the first course on our menu of tort law. Mashburn learned, as you will, why filing such a lawsuit is easier than winning it.

> 'Tain't Creole, 'tain't Cajun, 'tain't French, 'tain't country American, 'tain't good.

---

[1]*Mashburn v. Collin*, 355 So.2d 879 (La. 1977).

The odd word "tort" is borrowed from the French, meaning "wrong." And that is what it means in law: a wrong. More precisely, a **tort** is a violation of a duty imposed by the civil law. When a person breaks one of those duties and injures another, it is a tort. The injury could be to a person or her property. Libel, which the restaurant owner in the opening scenario alleged, is one example of a tort. A surgeon who removes the wrong kidney from a patient commits a different kind of tort, called negligence. A business executive who deliberately steals a client away from a competitor, interfering with a valid contract, commits a tort called interference with a contract. A con artist who tricks you out of your money with a phony offer to sell you a boat commits fraud, yet another tort.

Because tort law is so broad, it takes a while to understand its boundaries. To start with, we must distinguish torts from two other areas of law: criminal law and contract law.

It is a *crime* to steal a car, to embezzle money from a bank, to sell cocaine. As discussed in Chapter 1, society considers such behavior so threatening that the government itself will prosecute the wrongdoer, whether or not the car owner or bank president wants the case to go forward. A district attorney, who is paid by the government, will bring the case to court, seeking to send the defendant to prison, fine him, or both. If there is a fine, the money goes to the state, not to the victim.

In a tort case, it is up to the injured party to seek compensation. She must hire her own lawyer, who will file a lawsuit. Her lawyer must convince the court that the defendant breached some legal duty and ought to pay money damages to the plaintiff. The plaintiff has no power to send the defendant to jail. Bear in mind that a defendant's action might be both a crime and a tort. A man who punches you in the face for no reason commits the tort of battery. You may file a civil suit against him and will collect money damages if you can prove your case. He has also committed a crime, and the state may prosecute, seeking to imprison and fine him.

Tort

A violation of a duty imposed by the civil law.

Differences between Contract, Tort, and Criminal Law

Type of Obligation	Contract	Tort	Criminal Law
How the obligation is created	The parties agree on a contract, which creates duties for both.	The civil law imposes duties of conduct on all persons.	The criminal law prohibits certain conduct.
How the obligation is enforced	Suit by plaintiff.	Suit by plaintiff.	Prosecution by government.
Possible result	Money damages for plaintiff.	Money damages for plaintiff.	Punishment for defendant, including prison and/or fine.
Example	Raul contracts to sell Deirdre 5,000 pairs of sneakers at $50 per pair, but fails to deliver them. Deirdre buys the sneakers elsewhere for $60 per pair and receives $50,000, her extra expense.	A newspaper falsely accuses a private citizen of being an alcoholic. The plaintiff sues and wins money damages to compensate for her injured reputation.	Leo steals Kelly's car. The government prosecutes Leo for grand theft, and the judge sentences him to two years in prison. Kelly gets nothing.

© Cengage Learning 2014

A tort is also different from a contract dispute. A contract case is based on an agreement two people have already made. For example, Deirdre claims that Raul promised to sell her 10,000 pairs of sneakers at a good price but has failed to deliver them. She files a contract lawsuit. In a tort case, there is usually no "deal" between the parties. Don Mashburn had never met the restaurant critic who attacked his restaurant and obviously had never made any kind of contract. The plaintiff in a tort case claims that the law itself creates a duty that the defendant has breached.

Intentional torts

Harm caused by a deliberate action.

Tort law is divided into categories. In the first part of this chapter, we consider **intentional torts**; that is, harm caused by a deliberate action. The newspaper columnist who wrongly accuses someone of being a drunk has committed the intentional tort of libel. In the last sections, we examine negligence and strict liability, which involve injuries and losses caused by neglect and oversight rather than by deliberate conduct.

A final introductory point: when we speak of intentional torts, we do not necessarily mean that the defendant intended to harm the plaintiff. If the defendant does something deliberately and it ends up injuring somebody, she is probably liable even if she meant no harm. For example, intentionally throwing a snowball at a friend is a deliberate act. If the snowball permanently damages his eye, the *harm* is unintended, but the defendant is liable for the intentional tort of battery because the *act* was intentional.

We look first at the most common intentional torts and then at the most important intentional torts that are related to business.

INTENTIONAL TORTS

Defamation

The First Amendment guarantees the right to free speech, a vital freedom that enables us to protect other rights. But that freedom is not absolute.

Libel

Written defamation.

Slander

Oral defamation.

The law of defamation concerns false statements that harm someone's reputation. Defamatory statements can be written or spoken. Written defamation is called **libel**. Suppose a newspaper accuses a local retail store of programming its cash registers to overcharge customers when the store has never done so. That is libel. Oral defamation is **slander**. If Professor Wisdom, in class, refers to Sally Student as a drug dealer when she has never sold drugs, he has slandered her.

There are four elements to a defamation case. An element is something that a plaintiff must prove to win a lawsuit. The plaintiff in any kind of lawsuit must prove *all* of the elements to prevail. The elements in a defamation case are

- **Defamatory statement.** This is a statement likely to harm another person's reputation. Professor Wisdom's accusation will clearly harm Sally's reputation.

- **Falseness.** The statement must be false. If Sally Student actually sold marijuana to a classmate, then Professor Wisdom has a defense to slander.

- **Communicated.** The statement must be communicated to at least one person *other than the plaintiff*. If Wisdom speaks privately to Sally and accuses her of dealing drugs, there is no slander.

Slander per se

Slander involving false statements about sexual behavior, crimes, contagious diseases, and professional abilities.

- **Injury.** In many slander cases, the plaintiff generally must show some injury. Sally's injury would be lower reputation in the school, embarrassment, and humiliation. But in slander cases that involve false statements about sexual behavior, crimes, contagious diseases, and professional abilities, the law is willing to assume injury without requiring the plaintiff to prove it. Lies in these four categories amount to **slander per se**.

Libel cases are treated like cases of slander per se, and courts award damages without proof of injury.[2]

Opinion

Thus far, what we have seen is uncontroversial. If a television commentator refers to Frank Landlord as a "vicious slumlord who rents uninhabitable units," and Frank actually maintains his buildings perfectly, Frank will be compensated for the harm. But what if the television commentator states a harsh *opinion* about Frank? Remember that the plaintiff must demonstrate a "false" statement. Opinions generally cannot be proven true or false, and so they do not usually amount to defamation.

Suppose that the television commentator says, "Frank Landlord certainly does less than many rich people do for our community." Is that defamation? Probably not. Who are the "rich people"? How much do they do? How do we define "does less"? These vague assertions indicate the statement is one of opinion. Even if Frank works hard feeding homeless families, he will probably lose a defamation case.

A related defense involves cases where a supposed statement of fact clearly should not be taken literally. Mr. Mashburn, who opened the chapter suing over his restaurant review, lost his case. The court held that a reasonable reader would have understood the statements to be opinion only. "A shaker full of paprika" and "yellow death on duck" were not to be taken literally but were merely the author's expression of his personal dislike.

Public Personalities

The rules of the game change for those who play in the open. Government officials and other types of public figures such as actors and athletes receive less protection from defamation. In the landmark case *New York Times Co. v. Sullivan*,[3] the Supreme Court ruled that the free exchange of information is vital in a democracy and is protected by the First Amendment to the Constitution.

The rule from the *New York Times* case is that a public official or public figure can win a defamation case only by proving **actual malice** by the defendant. Actual malice means that the defendant knew the statement was false or acted with reckless disregard of the truth. If the plaintiff merely shows that the defendant newspaper printed incorrect statements, even

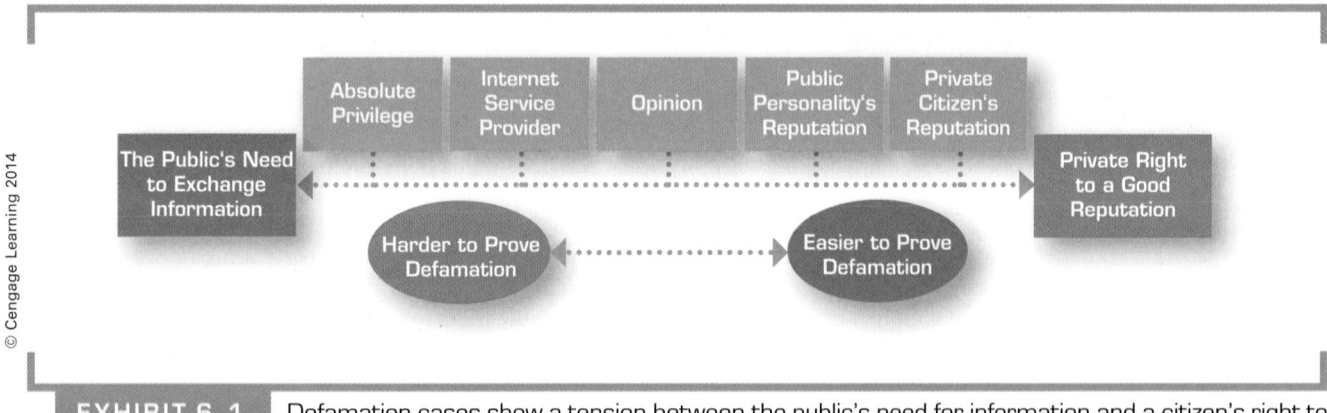

EXHIBIT 6.1 Defamation cases show a tension between the public's need for information and a citizen's right to protect his reputation.

---

[2]When defamation by radio and television became possible, the courts chose to consider it libel, analogizing it to newspapers because of the vast audience. This means that in broadcasting cases, a plaintiff generally does not have to prove damages.
[3]376 U.S. 254, 84 S.Ct. 710, 1964 U.S. LEXIS 1655 (1964).

very damaging ones, that will not suffice to win the suit. In the *New York Times* case, the police chief of Birmingham, Alabama, claimed that the *Times* falsely accused him of racial violence in his job. He lost because he could not prove that the *Times* had acted with actual malice. If he had shown that the *Times* knew the accusation was false, he would have won.

Online Defamation

Kenneth Zeran awoke one day to learn he had become notorious. An unidentified person had posted a message on an AOL bulletin board advertising "Naughty Oklahoma T-Shirts." The shirts featured deeply offensive slogans relating to the 1995 bombing of a federal building in Oklahoma City, in which hundreds of innocent people died. Those interested in purchasing such a T-shirt were instructed to call "Ken" at Zeran's home telephone number. In fact, Zeran had nothing to do with the posting or the T-shirts. He was quickly inundated with phone messages from furious callers, some of whom made death threats.

Zeran could not conveniently change his number because he ran his business from his home. A radio talk show host in Oklahoma City angrily urged its listeners to call Zeran, which they did. Before long, Zeran was receiving an abusive call every two minutes. He sued AOL for defamation—and lost.

The court held that AOL was immune from a defamation suit based on a third-party posting, based on the Communications Decency Act (CDA). Section 230 of the CDA creates this immunity for any Internet service provider, the court declared, adding:

> It would be impossible for service providers to screen each of their millions of postings for possible problems. Faced with potential liability for each message republished by their services, interactive computer service providers might choose to severely restrict the number and type of messages posted. Congress considered the weight of the speech interests implicated and chose to immunize service providers to avoid any such restrictive effect.[4]

Privilege

Absolute privilege
A witness testifying in a court or legislature may never be sued for defamation.

Defendants receive additional protection from defamation cases when it is important for them to speak freely. **Absolute privilege** exists in courtrooms and legislative hearings. Anyone speaking there, such as a witness in court, can say anything at all and never be sued for defamation. (Deliberately false testimony would be *perjury*, but still not *slander*.)

False Imprisonment

False imprisonment
Is the intentional restraint of another person without reasonable cause and without consent.

False imprisonment is the intentional restraint of another person without reasonable cause and without consent. Suppose that a bank teller becomes seriously ill and wants to go to the doctor, but the bank will not permit her to leave until she makes a final tally of her accounts. Against her wishes, company officials physically bar her from leaving the bank. That is false imprisonment. The restraint was unreasonable because her accounts could have been verified later.[5]

False imprisonment cases most commonly arise in retail stores, which sometimes detain employees or customers for suspected theft. Most states now have statutes governing the detention of suspected shoplifters. **Generally, a store may detain a customer or worker for alleged shoplifting provided there is a reasonable basis for the suspicion and the detention is done reasonably**. To detain a customer in the manager's office for 20 minutes and question him about where he got an item is lawful. To chain that customer to a display counter for three hours and humiliate him in front of other customers is unreasonable and constitutes false imprisonment.

---

[4]*Zeran v. America Online, Inc.*, 129 F.3d 327, 1997 U.S. App. LEXIS 31791 (4th Cir. 1997).
[5]*Kanner v. First National Bank of South Miami*, 287 So.2d 715, 1974 Fla. App. LEXIS 8989 (Fla. Dist. Ct. App. 1974).

Intentional Infliction of Emotional Distress

What should happen when a defendant's conduct hurts a plaintiff emotionally but not physically? Historically, not much did happen. Courts once refused to allow recovery, assuming that if they awarded damages for mere emotional injury, they would be inviting a floodgate of dubious claims. But gradually judges reexamined their thinking and reversed this tendency. Today, most courts allow a plaintiff to recover for emotional injury that a defendant intentionally caused. As we see in the next chapter, some courts will also permit recovery when a defendant's negligent conduct caused the emotional injury.

The **intentional infliction of emotional distress** results from extreme and outrageous conduct that causes serious emotional harm. A credit officer was struggling vainly to locate Sheehan, who owed money on his car. The officer phoned Sheehan's mother, falsely identified herself as a hospital employee, and said she needed to find Sheehan because his children had been in a serious auto accident. The mother provided Sheehan's whereabouts, which enabled the company to seize his car. But Sheehan spent seven hours frantically trying to locate his supposedly injured children, who in fact were fine. The credit company was liable for the intentional infliction of emotional distress.[6]

By contrast, a muffler shop, trying to collect a debt from a customer, made six phone calls over three months, using abusive language. The customer testified that this caused her to be upset, to cry, and to have difficulty sleeping. The court ruled that the muffler shop's conduct was neither extreme nor outrageous.[7]

The following case arose in a setting that guarantees controversy—an abortion clinic.

> **Intentional infliction of emotional distress**
> An intentional tort in which the harm results from extreme and outrageous conduct that causes serious emotional harm.

JANE DOE AND NANCY ROE v. LYNN MILLS

212 Mich. App. 73, 536 N.W.2d 824, 1995 Mich. App. LEXIS 313
Michigan Court of Appeals, 1995

Facts: Late one night, an anti-abortion protestor named Robert Thomas climbed into a dumpster located behind the Women's Advisory Center, an abortion clinic. He found documents indicating that the plaintiffs were soon to have abortions at the clinic. Thomas gave the information to Lynn Mills. The next day, Mills and Sister Lois Mitoraj created signs, using the women's names, indicating that they were about to undergo abortions, and urging them not to "kill their babies."

Doe and Roe (not their real names) sued, claiming intentional infliction of emotional distress (as well as breach of privacy, discussed later in this chapter). The trial court dismissed the lawsuit, ruling that the defendants' conduct was not extreme and outrageous. The plaintiffs appealed.

Issue: *Have the plaintiffs made a valid claim of intentional infliction of emotional distress?*

Excerpts from the Court's *Per Curiam* Decision: Liability for the intentional infliction of emotional distress has been found only where the conduct complained of has been so outrageous in character, and so extreme in degree, as to go beyond all possible bounds of decency, and to be regarded as atrocious and utterly intolerable in a civilized community. Liability does not extend to mere insults, indignities, threats, annoyances, petty oppressions, or other trivialities. It has been said that the case is generally one in which the recitation of the facts to an average member of the community would arouse his resentment against the actor, and lead him to exclaim, "Outrageous!"

[6]*Ford Motor Credit Co. v. Sheehan*, 373 So.2d 956, 1979 Fla. App. LEXIS 15416 (Fla. Dist. Ct. App. 1979).
[7]*Midas Muffler Shop v. Ellison*, 133 Ariz. 194, 650 P.2d 496, 1982 Ariz. App. LEXIS 488 (Ariz. Ct. App. 1982).

The conduct in this case involved defendants identifying plaintiffs by name and publicizing the fact of their abortions by displaying such information on large signs that were held up for public view. In ruling that defendants' conduct was not sufficiently extreme and outrageous so as to permit recovery, the trial court was influenced in part by its conclusion that the information disclosed did not concern a private matter, inasmuch as it was obtained from a document that had been discarded into the trash. [But the plaintiffs themselves never placed their names on the discarded papers, and even if they had, such an act would not have indicated consent to such publicity.] The trial court also observed that defendants have a constitutional right to "protest peaceably against abortion." However, the objectionable aspect of defendants' conduct does not relate to their views on abortion or their right to express those views, but, rather, to the fact that defendants gave unreasonable or unnecessary publicity to purely private matters involving plaintiffs. Finally, the trial court observed that

there is no statute prohibiting the kind of activity engaged in by defendants. It is not necessary, however, that a defendant's conduct constitute a statutory violation in order for it to be found extreme and outrageous.

We are of the opinion that the trial court erred in granting the defendants' motion for summary disposition of plaintiffs' claim of intentional infliction of emotional distress. Defendants' conduct involved more than mere insults, indignities, threats, annoyances, or petty oppressions. We believe this is the type of case that might cause an average member of the community, upon learning of defendants' conduct, to exclaim, "Outrageous!" Because reasonable men may differ with regard to whether defendants' conduct may be considered sufficiently outrageous and extreme so as to subject them to liability for intentional infliction of emotional distress, this matter should be determined by the trier of fact.

[Summary judgment for the defendants is reversed, and the case is remanded for trial.]

Additional Intentional Torts

Battery
An intentional touching of another person in a way that is harmful or offensive.

Battery is an intentional touching of another person in a way that is unwanted or offensive. There need be no intention to *hurt* the plaintiff. If the defendant intended to do the physical act, and a reasonable plaintiff would be offended by it, battery has occurred.

Suppose an irate parent throws a chair at a referee during his daughter's basketball game, breaking the man's jaw. It is irrelevant that the father did not intend to injure the referee. But a parent who cheerfully slaps the winning coach on the back has not committed battery because a reasonable coach would not be offended.

Assault
An act that makes a person reasonably fear an imminent battery.

Assault occurs when a defendant does some act that makes a plaintiff fear an imminent battery. It is assault even though the battery never occurs. Suppose Ms. Wilson shouts "Think fast!" at her husband and hurls a toaster at him. He turns and sees it flying at him. His fear of being struck is enough to win a case of assault, even if the toaster misses.

Fraud
Injuring another person by deliberate deception.

Fraud is injuring another person by deliberate deception. It is fraud to sell real estate knowing that there is a large toxic waste deposit underground of which the buyer is ignorant. Fraud is a tort that typically occurs during contract negotiation, and it is discussed in more detail in Unit 2, on contracts.

DAMAGES

Compensatory Damages

Mitchel Bien, who is deaf and mute, enters the George Grubbs Nissan dealership, where folks sell cars aggressively. Very aggressively. Maturelli, a salesman, and Bien communicate by writing messages back and forth. Maturelli takes Bien's own car keys, and the two then test drive a 300ZX. Bien says he does not want the car, but Maturelli escorts him back inside and fills out a sales sheet. Bien repeatedly asks for his keys, but Maturelli only laughs, pressuring him to buy the new car. Minutes pass. Hours pass. Bien becomes frantic, writing a dozen notes, begging to leave, threatening to call the police. Maturelli mocks Bien and his physical disabilities. Finally, after four hours, the customer escapes.

Bien sues for the intentional infliction of emotional distress. Two former salesmen from Grubbs testify they have witnessed customers cry, yell, and curse as a result of the aggressive tactics. Doctors state that the incident has traumatized Bien, dramatically reducing his confidence and self-esteem and preventing his return to work even three years later.

The jury awards Bien damages. But how does a jury calculate the money? For that matter, why should a jury even try? Money can never erase pain or undo a permanent injury. The answer is simple: money, however inexact, is often the only thing a court has to give.

A successful plaintiff generally receives **compensatory damages**, meaning an amount of money that the court believes will restore him to the position he was in before the defendant's conduct caused injury. Here is how damages are calculated.

First, a plaintiff receives money for medical expenses that he has proven by producing bills from doctors, hospitals, physical therapists, and psychotherapists. Bien receives all the money he has paid. If a doctor testifies that he needs future treatment, Bien will offer evidence of how much that will cost. The **single recovery principle** requires a court to settle the matter once and for all, by awarding a lump sum for past *and future* expenses, if there will be any. A plaintiff may not return in a year and say, "Oh, by the way, there are some new bills."

Second, the defendants are liable for lost wages. The court takes the number of days or months that Bien missed work and multiplies that times his salary. If Bien is currently unable to work, a doctor estimates how many more months he will miss work, and the court adds that to his damages.

Third, a plaintiff is paid for pain and suffering. Bien testifies about how traumatic the four hours were and how the experience has affected his life. He may state that he now fears shopping, suffers nightmares, and seldom socializes. To bolster the case, a plaintiff uses expert testimony, such as the psychiatrists who testified for Bien. Awards for pain and suffering vary enormously, from a few dollars to many millions, depending on the injury and depending on the jury. In some lawsuits, physical and psychological pain are momentary and insignificant; in other cases, the pain is the biggest part of the verdict. In this case, the jury awarded Bien $573,815, calculated as in the following table.[8]

> **Bien becomes frantic, writing a dozen notes, begging to leave, threatening to call the police.**

Compensatory damages
Money intended to restore a plaintiff to the position he was in before the injury.

Single recovery principle
Requires a court to settle the matter once and for all, by awarding a lump sum for past and future expenses.

[8]The compensatory damages are described in *George Grubbs Enterprises v. Bien*, 881 S.W.2d 843, 1994 Tex. App. LEXIS 1870 (Tex. Ct. App. 1994). In addition to the compensatory damages described, the jury awarded $5 million in punitive damages. The Texas Supreme Court reversed the award of punitive damages, but not the compensatory. *Id.*, 900 S.W.2d 337, 1995 Tex. LEXIS 91 (Tex. 1995). The high court did not dispute the appropriateness of punitive damages, but reversed because the trial court failed to instruct the jury properly as to how it should determine the assets actually under the defendants' control, an issue essential to punitive damages but not compensatory.

Past medical	$ 70.00
Future medical	6,000.00
Past rehabilitation	3,205.00
Past lost earning capacity	112,910.00
Future lost earning capacity	34,650.00
Past physical symptoms and discomfort	50,000.00
Future physical symptoms and discomfort	50,000.00
Past emotional injury and mental anguish	101,980.00
Future emotional injury and mental anguish	200,000.00
Past loss of society and reduced ability to socially interact with family, former fiancée, and friends, and hearing (i.e., nondeaf) people in general	10,000.00
Future loss of society and reduced ability to socially interact with family, former fiancee, and friends, and hearing people	5,000.00
TOTAL	**$573,815.00**

© Cengage Learning 2014

Awards for future harm (such as future pain and suffering) involve the court making its best estimate of the plaintiff's hardship in the years to come. This is not an exact science. If the judgment is reasonable, it will rarely be overturned. Ethel Flanzraich, aged 78, fell on stairs that had been badly maintained. In addition to her medical expense, the court awarded her $150,000 for future pain and suffering. The day after the court gave its award, Ms. Flanzraich died of other causes. Did that mean her family must forfeit that money? No. The award was reasonable when made and had to be paid.[9]

Punitive Damages

Punitive damages

Damages that are intended to punish the defendant for conduct that is extreme and outrageous.

Here we look at a different kind of award, one that is more controversial and potentially more powerful: punitive damages. The purpose is not to compensate the plaintiff for harm, because compensatory damages will have done that. **Punitive damages** are intended to punish the defendant for conduct that is extreme and outrageous. Courts award these damages in relatively few cases. The idea behind punitive damages is that certain behavior is so unacceptable that society must make an example of it. A large award of money should deter the defendant from repeating the mistake and others from ever making it. Some believe punitive damages represent the law at its most avaricious, while others attribute to them great social benefit.

Although a jury has wide discretion in awarding punitive damages, the Supreme Court has ruled that a verdict must be reasonable. Ira Gore purchased a new BMW automobile from an Alabama dealer and then discovered that the car had been repainted. He sued. At trial, BMW acknowledged a nationwide policy of not informing customers of predelivery

---

[9]We looked at discovery issues from this case in Chapter 3. *Stinton v. Robin's Wood*, 45 A.D.3d 203, 842 N.Y.S.2d 477 (N.Y.App.Div., 2007).

repairs when the cost was less than 3% of the retail price. The company had sold about 1,000 repainted cars nationwide. The jury concluded that BMW had engaged in gross, malicious fraud and awarded Gore $4,000 in compensatory damages and $4 million in punitive damages. The Alabama Supreme Court reduced the award to $2 million, but the United States Supreme Court ruled that even that amount was grossly excessive. The Court held that in awarding punitive damages, a court must consider three "guideposts":

- The reprehensibility of the defendant's conduct;

- The ratio between the harm suffered and the award; and

- The difference between the punitive award and any civil penalties used in similar cases.

The Court concluded that BMW had shown no evil intent and that Gore's harm had been purely economic (as opposed to physical). Further, the Court found the ratio of 500 to 1, between punitive and compensatory damages, to be excessive, although it offered no definitive rule about a proper ratio. On remand, the Alabama Supreme Court reduced the punitive damages award to $50,000.[10]

The U.S. Supreme Court gave additional guidance on punitive damages in the following landmark case.

---

[10]*BMW of North America, Inc. v. Gore*, 517 U.S. 559, 116 S.Ct. 1589, 1996 U.S. LEXIS 3390 (1996).

Landmark Case

STATE FARM V. CAMPBELL
538 U.S. 408
Supreme Court of the United States (2003)

Facts: While attempting to pass several cars on a two-lane road, Campbell drove into oncoming traffic. An innocent driver swerved to avoid Campbell and died in a collision with a third driver. The family of the deceased driver and the surviving third driver both sued Campbell.

As Campbell's insurer, State Farm represented him in the lawsuit. It turned down an offer to settle the case for $50,000, the limit of Campbell's policy. The company had nothing to gain by settling because even if Campbell lost big at trial, State Farm's liability was capped at $50,000.

A jury returned a judgment against Campbell for $185,000. He was responsible for the $135,000 that exceeded his policy limit. He argued with State Farm, claiming that it should have settled the case. Eventually, State Farm paid the entire $185,000, but Campbell still sued the company, alleging fraud and intentional infliction of emotional distress.

His lawyers presented evidence that State Farm had deliberately acted in its own best interests rather than his. The jury was convinced, and in the end, Campbell won an award of $1 million in compensatory damages and $145 million in punitive damages. State Farm appealed.

Issue: *What is the limit on punitive damages?*

Excerpts from Justice Kennedy's Opinion: We address whether an award of $145 million in punitive damages, where full compensatory damages are $1 million, is excessive and in violation of the Due Process Clause. The Utah Supreme Court relied upon testimony indicating that State Farm's actions, because of their clandestine nature, will be punished at most in 1 out of every 50,000 cases as a matter of statistical probability, and concluded that the ratio between punitive and compensatory damages was not unwarranted.

Compensatory damages are intended to redress the concrete loss that the plaintiff has suffered by reason of the defendant's wrongful conduct. By contrast, punitive damages serve a broader function; they are aimed at deterrence and retribution.

The Due Process Clause prohibits the imposition of grossly excessive or arbitrary punishments. The reason is that elementary notions of fairness dictate that a person receive fair notice not only of the conduct that will subject him to punishment, but also of the severity of the penalty that a State may impose. To the extent an award is grossly excessive, it furthers no legitimate purpose and constitutes an arbitrary deprivation of property. A defendant should be punished for the conduct that harmed the plaintiff, not for being an unsavory.

We decline to impose a bright-line ratio which a punitive damages award cannot exceed. Our jurisprudence and the principles it has now established demonstrate, however, that, in practice, few awards exceeding a single-digit ratio between punitive and compensatory damages, to a significant degree, will satisfy due process. Single-digit multipliers are more likely to comport with due process, while still achieving the State's goals of deterrence and retribution, than awards with ratios in the range of 145 to 1.

Nonetheless, because there are no rigid benchmarks that a punitive damages award may not surpass, ratios greater than those we have previously upheld may comport with due process where a particularly egregious act has resulted in only a small amount of economic damages. The precise award in any case must be based upon the facts and circumstances of the defendant's conduct and the harm to the plaintiff.

In sum, courts must ensure that the measure of punishment is both reasonable and proportionate to the amount of harm to the plaintiff and to the general damages recovered. In the context of this case, we have no doubt that there is a presumption against an award that has a 145-to-1 ratio. The compensatory award in this case was substantial; the Campbells were awarded $1 million for a year and a half of emotional distress. This was complete compensation. The harm arose from a transaction in the economic realm, not from some physical assault or trauma; there were no physical injuries; and State Farm paid the excess verdict before the complaint was filed, so the Campbells suffered only minor economic injuries.

The judgment of the Utah Supreme Court is reversed, and the case is remanded for proceedings not inconsistent with this opinion.

And so, the Supreme Court seeks to limit, but not completely prohibit, enormous punitive damages.

BUSINESS TORTS

In this section, we look at several intentional torts that occur almost exclusively in a commercial setting: interference with a contract, interference with a prospective advantage, and the rights to privacy and publicity. Note that several business torts are discussed elsewhere in the book:

- Patents, copyrights, and trademarks are discussed in Chapter 24, on intellectual property.

- False advertising, discussed in part under the Lanham Act section (later in this chapter), is considered more broadly in Chapter 26, on consumer law.

- Consumer issues are also covered in Chapter 26. The material in the present chapter focuses not on consumer claims but on disputes between businesses.

Tortious Interference with Business Relations

Competition is the essence of business. Successful corporations compete aggressively, and the law permits and expects them to. But there are times when healthy competition becomes illegal interference. This is called tortious interference with business relations. It can take one of two closely related forms—interference with a contract or interference with a prospective advantage.

Tortious Interference with a Contract

Tortious interference with a contract exists if the plaintiff can establish the following four elements:

Tortious interference with a contract
An intentional tort in which the defendant improperly induced a third party to breach a contract with the plaintiff.

- There was a contract between the plaintiff and a third party;

- The defendant knew of the contract;

- The defendant improperly *induced* the third party to breach the contract or made performance of the contract impossible; and

- There was injury to the plaintiff.

Because businesses routinely compete for customers, employees, and market share, it is not always easy to identify tortious interference. There is nothing wrong with two companies bidding against each other to buy a parcel of land, and nothing wrong with one corporation doing everything possible to convince the seller to ignore all competitors. But once a company has signed a contract to buy the land, it is improper to induce the seller to break the deal. The most commonly disputed issues in these cases concern elements one and three: was there a contract between the plaintiff and another party? Did the defendant improperly induce a party to breach it? Defendants will try to show that the plaintiff had no contract.

A defendant may also rely on the defense of **justification;** that is, a claim that special circumstances made its conduct fair. To establish justification, a defendant must show that:

- It was acting to protect an existing economic interest, such as its own contract with the third party;

- It was acting in the public interest, for example, by reporting to a government agency that a corporation was overbilling for government services; or

- The existing contract could be terminated at will by either party, meaning that although the plaintiff had a contract, the plaintiff had no long-term assurances because the other side could end it at any time.

Texaco v. Pennzoil   One of the largest verdicts in the history of American law came in a case of contract interference. Pennzoil made an unsolicited bid to buy 20 percent of Getty Oil at $112.50 per share, and the Getty board approved the agreement. Before the lawyers for both sides could complete the paperwork, Texaco appeared and offered Getty stockholders $128 per share for the entire company. Getty officers turned their attention to Texaco, but Pennzoil sued, claiming tortious interference. Texaco replied that it had not interfered because there was no binding contract.

The jury bought Pennzoil's argument, and they bought it big: $7.53 billion in actual damages, and $3 billion more in punitive damages. After appeals and frantic negotiations, the two parties reached a settlement. Texaco agreed to pay Pennzoil $3 billion as settlement for having wrongfully interfered with Pennzoil's agreement to buy Getty.

Tortious Interference with a Prospective Advantage

Interference with a prospective advantage is an awkward name for a tort that is simply a variation on interference with a contract. The difference is that, for this tort, there need be no contract; the plaintiff is claiming outside interference with an expected economic relationship. Obviously, the plaintiff must show more than just the hope of a profit.

Tortious interference with a prospective advantage
Malicious interference with a developing economic relationship.

A plaintiff who has a definite and reasonable expectation of obtaining an economic advantage may sue a corporation that maliciously interferes and prevents the relationship from developing.

Suppose that Jump Co. and Block Co. both hope to purchase a professional basketball team. The team's owners reject the offer from Block. They informally agree to a price with Jump but refuse to make a binding deal until Jump leases a stadium. Block owns the only stadium in town and refuses to lease to Jump, meaning that Jump cannot buy the team. Block has interfered with Jump's prospective advantage.

Privacy and Publicity

We live in a world of dazzling technology, and it is easier than ever—and more profitable—to spy on someone. Does the law protect us? What power do we have to limit the intrusion of others into our lives and to prohibit them from commercially exploiting information about us?

Intrusion

Intrusion

A tort in which a reasonable person would find the invasion of her private life offensive.

Intrusion into someone's private life is a tort if a reasonable person would find it offensive. Peeping through someone's windows or wiretapping his telephone are obvious examples of intrusion. In a famous case involving a "paparazzo" photographer and Jacqueline Kennedy Onassis, the court found that the photographer had invaded her privacy by making a career out of photographing her. He had bribed doormen to gain access to hotels and restaurants she visited, had jumped out of bushes to photograph her young children, and had driven power boats dangerously close to her. The court ordered him to stop.[11] Nine years later, the paparazzo was found in contempt of court for again taking photographs too close to Ms. Onassis. He agreed to stop once and for all—in exchange for a suspended contempt sentence.

Commercial Exploitation

The right to commercial exploitation prohibits the use of someone's likeness or voice for commercial purposes without permission. This business tort is the flip side of privacy and covers the right to make money from publicity. For example, it would be illegal to run a magazine ad showing Keira Knightley holding a can of soda without her permission. The ad would imply that she endorses the product. Someone's identity is her own, and it cannot be used for commercial gain unless she permits it.

Ford Motor Co. hired a singer to imitate Bette Midler's version of a popular song. The imitation was so good that most listeners were fooled into believing that Ms. Midler was endorsing the product. That, ruled a court, violated her right to commercial exploitation.

NEGLIGENCE

Party time! A fraternity at the University of Arizona welcomed new members, and the alcohol flowed freely. Several hundred people danced and shrieked and drank, and no one checked for proof of age. A common occurrence—but one that ended tragically. A minor

---

[11]*Exxon Shipping Co. v. Baker*, 128 S.Ct. 2605 (2008).

student drove away, intoxicated, and slammed into another car. The other driver, utterly innocent of wrongdoing, was gravely injured.

The drunken student was obviously liable, but his insurance did not cover the huge medical bills. The injured man also sued the fraternity. Should that organization be legally responsible? The question leads to other similar issues. Should a restaurant that serves an intoxicated adult be liable for resulting harm? If *you* give a party, should you be responsible for any damage caused by your guests?

These are moral questions—but very practical ones, as well. They are typical issues of negligence law. In this contentious area, courts continually face one question: *When someone is injured, how far should responsibility extend?*

We might call negligence the "unintentional" tort because it concerns harm that arises by accident. A person, or perhaps an organization, does some act, neither intending nor expecting to hurt anyone, yet someone is harmed. Should a court impose liability? The fraternity members who gave the party never wanted—or thought—that an innocent man would suffer terrible damage. But he did. Is it in society's interest to hold the fraternity responsible?

Before we can answer this question, we need some background knowledge. Things go wrong all the time, and society needs a means of analyzing negligence cases consistently and fairly.

To win a negligence case, a plaintiff must prove five elements. Much of the remainder of this chapter will examine them in detail. They are:

- **Duty of Due Care.** The defendant had a legal responsibility *to the plaintiff*.

- **Breach.** The defendant breached her duty of care or failed to meet her legal obligations.

- **Factual Cause.** The defendant's conduct actually caused the injury.

- **Proximate Cause.** It was *foreseeable* that conduct like the defendant's might cause *this type of harm*.

- **Damages.** The plaintiff has actually been hurt or has actually suffered a measureable loss.

To win a case, a plaintiff must prove all the elements listed above. If a defendant eliminates only one item on the list, there is no liability.

Duty of Due Care

Each of us has a duty to behave as a reasonable person would under the circumstances. If you are driving a car, you have a duty to all the other people near you to drive like a reasonable person. If you drive while drunk, or send text messages while behind the wheel, then you fail to live up to your duty of care.

But how *far* does your duty extend? Judges draw an imaginary line around the defendant and say that she owes a duty to the people within the circle, but not to those outside it. The test is generally "foreseeability." If the defendant could have foreseen injury to a particular person, she has a duty to him. Suppose that one of your friends posts a YouTube video of you texting behind the wheel and her father is so upset from watching it that he falls down the stairs. You would not be liable for the father's downfall because it was not foreseeable that he would be harmed by your texting.

Let us apply these principles to the case described in the scenario that opened this section.

HERNANDEZ V. ARIZONA BOARD OF REGENTS

177 Ariz. 244, 866 P.2d 1330, 1994 Ariz. LEXIS 6
Arizona Supreme Court, 1994

Facts: At the University of Arizona, the Epsilon Epsilon chapter of Delta Tau Delta fraternity gave a welcoming party for new members. The fraternity's officers knew that the majority of its members were under the legal drinking age, but they permitted everyone to consume alcohol. John Rayner, who was under 21 years of age, left the party. He drove negligently and caused a collision with an auto driven by Ruben Hernandez. At the time of the accident, Rayner's blood alcohol level was .15, exceeding the legal limit. The crash left Hernandez blind and paralyzed.

Hernandez sued Rayner, who settled the case based on the amount of his insurance coverage. The victim also sued the fraternity, its officers and national organization, all fraternity members who contributed money to buy alcohol, the university, and others. The trial court granted summary judgment for all defendants, and the court of appeals affirmed. Hernandez appealed to the Arizona Supreme Court.

Issue: *Did the fraternity and the other defendants have a duty of due care to Hernandez?*

Excerpts from Justice Feldman's Decision: Before 1983, this court arguably recognized the common-law rule of non-liability for tavern owners and, presumably, for social hosts. Traditional authority held that when "an able-bodied man" caused harm because of his intoxication, the act from which liability arose was the consuming not the furnishing of alcohol.

However, the common law also provides that:

One who supplies [a thing] for the use of another whom the supplier knows or has reason to know to be likely because of his youth, inexperience, or otherwise to use it in a manner involving unreasonable risk of physical harm to himself and others is subject to liability for physical harm resulting to them.

We perceive little difference in principle between liability for giving a car to an intoxicated youth and liability for giving drinks to a youth with a car. A growing number of cases have recognized that one of the very hazards that makes it negligent to furnish liquor to a minor is the foreseeable prospect that the [youthful] patron will become drunk and injure himself or others. Accordingly, modern authority has increasingly recognized that one who furnishes liquor to a minor breaches a common-law duty owed to innocent third parties who may be injured.

Furnishing alcohol to underaged drinkers violates numerous statutes. The conduct in question violates well-established common-law principles that recognize a duty to avoid furnishing dangerous items to those known to have diminished capacity to use them safely. We join the majority of other states and conclude that as to Plaintiffs and the public in general, Defendants had a duty of care to avoid furnishing alcohol to underage consumers.

Arizona courts, therefore, will entertain an action for damages against [one] who negligently furnishes alcohol to those under the legal drinking age when that act is a cause of injury to a third person. [Reversed and remanded.]

In several circumstances, people have special duties to others. Three of them are outlined below.

Special Duty: Landowners

The common law applies special rules to a landowner for injuries occurring on her property. In most states, the owner's duty depends on the type of person injured.

Trespasser

A person on another's property without consent.

Lowest Liability: Trespassing Adults   A **trespasser** is anyone on another's property without consent. A landowner is liable to a trespasser only for intentionally injuring him or for some other gross misconduct. The landowner has no liability to a trespasser for mere negligence. Jake is not liable if a vagrant wanders onto his land and is burned by defective electrical wires.

Mid-level Liability: Trespassing Children   The law makes exceptions when the trespassers are **children**. If there is some manmade thing on the land *that may be reasonably expected to attract children*, the landowner is probably liable for any harm. Daphne lives next door to a day-care center and builds a treehouse on her property. Unless she has fenced off the dangerous area, she is probably liable if a small child wanders onto her property and injures himself when he falls from the rope ladder to the treehouse.

Higher Liability: Licensee   A **licensee** is anyone on the land for her own purposes but with the owner's permission. A social guest is a typical licensee. A licensee is entitled to a warning of hidden dangers that the owner knows about. If Juliet invites Romeo for a late supper on the balcony and fails to mention that the wooden railing is rotted, she is liable when her hero plunges to the courtyard.

But Juliet is liable only for injuries caused by *hidden* dangers—she has no duty to warn guests of obvious dangers. She need not say, "Romeo, oh Romeo, don't place thy hand in the toaster, Romeo."

Licensee
A person on another's land for her own purposes but with the owner's permission.

Highest Liability: Invitee   An **invitee** is someone who has a right to be on the property because it is a public place or a business open to the public. The owner has a duty of reasonable care to an invitee. Perry is an invitee when he goes to the town beach. If riptides have existed for years and the town fails to post a warning, it is liable if Perry drowns. Perry is also an invitee when he goes to Dana's coffee shop. Dana is liable if she ignores spilled coffee that causes Perry to slip.

With social guests, you must have *actual knowledge* of some specific hidden danger to be liable. Not so with invitees. You are liable even if you had *no idea* that something on your property posed a hidden danger. Therefore, if you own a business, you must conduct inspections of your property on a regular basis to make sure that nothing is becoming dangerous.

The courts of some states have modified these distinctions, and a few have eliminated them altogether. California, for example, requires "reasonable care" as to all people on the owner's property, regardless of how or why they got there. But most states still use the classifications outlined above.

Invitee
A person who has a right to enter another's property because it is a public place or a business open to the public.

Special Duty: Professionals

A person at work has a heightened duty of care. While on the job, she must act as a reasonable person *in her profession*. A taxi driver must drive as a reasonable taxi driver would. A heart surgeon must perform bypass surgery with the care of a trained specialist in that field.

Two medical cases illustrate the reasonable person standard. A doctor prescribes a powerful drug without asking his patient about other medicines she is currently taking. The patient suffers a serious drug reaction from the combined medications. The physician is liable for the harm. A reasonable doctor *always* checks current medicines before prescribing new ones.

On the other hand, assume that a patient dies on the operating table in an emergency room. The physician followed normal medical procedures at every step of the procedure and acted with reasonable speed. In fact, the man had a fatal stroke. The surgeon is not liable. A doctor must do a reasonable professional job, but she cannot guarantee a happy outcome.

Special Duty: Hiring and Retention

Employers also have special responsibilities.

In a recent one-year period, more than 1,000 homicides and 2 million attacks occurred in the workplace. Companies must beware because they can be liable for hiring or retaining violent employees. A mailroom clerk with a previous rape and robbery conviction followed a secretary home after work and killed her. Even though the murder took place off the company premises, the court held that the defendant would be liable if it knew or should have known of the mail clerk's criminal history.[12] In other cases, companies have been found liable for failing to check an applicant's driving record, contact personal references, or search criminal records.

Courts have also found companies negligent for *retaining* dangerous workers. If an employee threatens a coworker, the organization is not free to ignore the menacing conduct. If the employee acts on his threats, the company may be liable.[13]

Breach of Duty

The second element of a plaintiff's negligence case is **breach of duty**. If a legal duty of care exists, then a plaintiff must show that the defendant did not meet it. Did the defendant act as a reasonable person, or as a reasonable professional? Did she warn social guests of hidden dangers she knew to exist in her apartment?

Normally, a plaintiff proves this part of a negligence case by convincing a jury that they would not have behaved as the defendant did—indeed, that no reasonable person would.

Negligence Per Se

In certain areas of life, courts are not free to decide what a "reasonable" person would have done because the state legislature has made the decision for them. **When a legislature sets a minimum standard of care for a particular activity, in order to protect a certain group of people, and a violation of the statute injures a member of that group, the defendant has committed negligence per se.** A plaintiff who can show negligence per se need not prove breach of duty.

In Minnesota, the state legislature became alarmed about children sniffing glue, which they could easily purchase in stores. The legislature passed a statute prohibiting the sale to a minor of any glue containing toluene or benzene. About one month later, 14-year-old Steven Zerby purchased Weldwood Contact Cement from the Coast-to-Coast Store in his hometown. The glue contained toluene. Steven inhaled the glue and died from injury to his central nervous system.

The store clerk had not realized that the glue was dangerous. Irrelevant: he was negligent per se because he violated the statute. Perhaps a reasonable person would have made the same error. Irrelevant. The legislature had passed the statute to protect children, the sale of the glue violated the law, and a child was injured. The store was automatically liable.

Causation

We have seen that a plaintiff must show that the defendant owed him a duty of care and that the defendant breached the duty. To win, the plaintiff must also show that the defendant's breach of duty *caused* the plaintiff's harm. Courts look at two separate causation issues: Was the defendant's behavior the *factual cause* of the harm? Was it the *proximate cause?*

Factual Cause

If the defendant's breach led to the ultimate harm, it is the factual cause. Suppose that Dom's Brake Shop tells a customer his brakes are now working fine, even though Dom knows that is false. The customer drives out of the shop, cannot stop at a red light, and hits a bicyclist crossing the intersection. Dom is liable to the cyclist. Dom's unreasonable behavior

---

[12]*Gaines v. Monsanto*, 655 S.W.2d 568, 1983 Mo. LEXIS 3439 (Mo. Ct. App. 1983).
[13]*Yunker v. Honeywell*, 496 N.W.2d 419, 1993 Minn. App. LEXIS 230 (Minn. Ct. App. 1993).

was the factual cause of the harm. Think of it as a row of dominoes. The first domino (Dom's behavior) knocked over the next one (failing brakes), which toppled the last one (the cyclist's injury).

Suppose, alternatively, that just as the customer is exiting the repair shop, the cyclist hits a pothole and tumbles off her cycle. Dom has breached his duty to his customer, but he is not liable to the cyclist—she would have been hurt anyway. This is a row of dominoes that veers off to the side, leaving the last domino (the cyclist's injury) untouched. No factual causation.

Proximate Cause

For the defendant to be liable, the *type of harm* must have been reasonably *foreseeable*. In the first example just discussed, Dom could easily foresee that bad brakes would cause an automobile accident. He need not have foreseen *exactly* what happened. He did not know there would be a cyclist nearby. What he could foresee was this *general type* of harm involving defective brakes. Because the accident that occurred was of the type he could foresee, he is liable.

By contrast, assume the collision of car and bicycle produces a loud crash. Two blocks away, a pet pig, asleep on the window ledge of a twelfth-story apartment, is startled by the noise, awakens with a start, and plunges to the sidewalk, killing a veterinarian who was making a house call. If the vet's family sues Dom, should it win? Dom's negligence was the factual cause: it led to the collision, which startled the pig, which flattened the vet. Most courts would rule, though, that Dom is not liable. The type of harm is too bizarre. Dom could not reasonably foresee such an extraordinary chain of events, and it would be unfair to make him pay for it. See Exhibit 6.2. Another way of stating that Dom is not liable to the vet's family is by calling the falling pig a *superseding cause*. When one of the "dominoes" in the row is entirely unforeseeable, courts will call that event a superseding cause, letting the defendant off the hook.

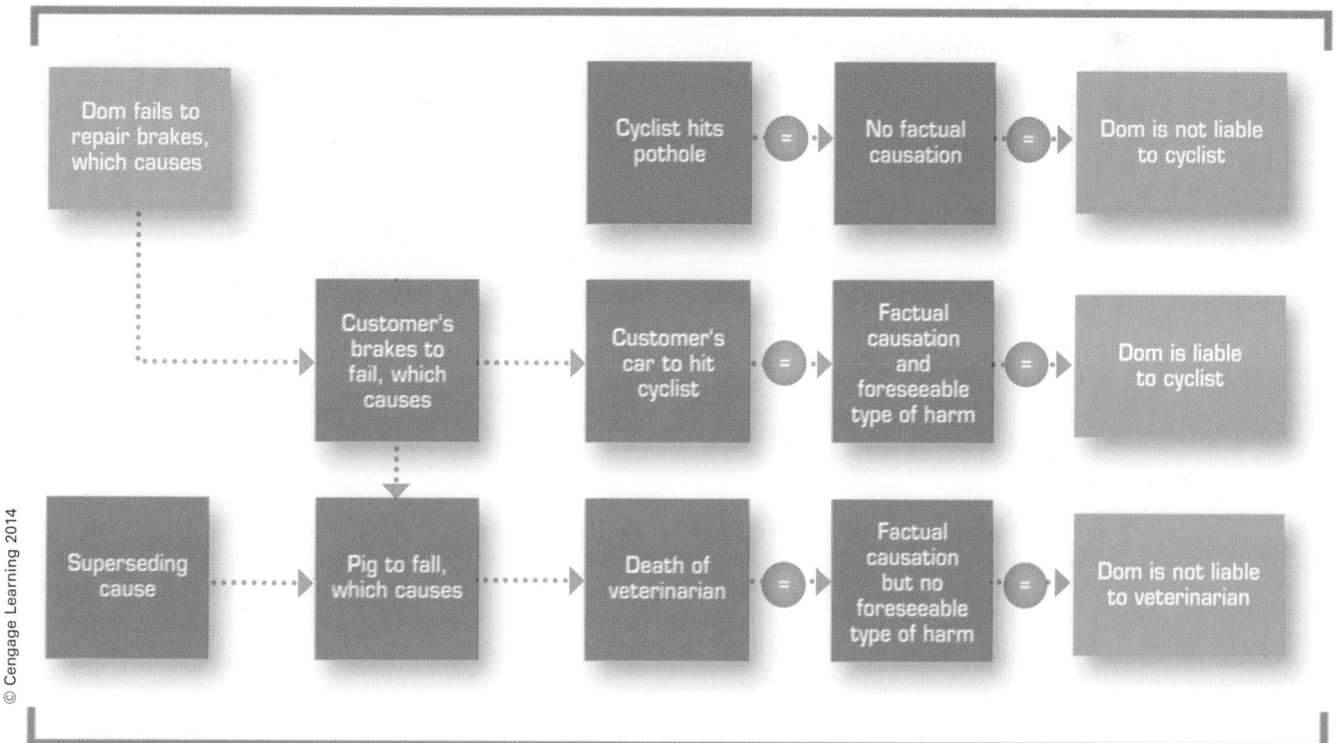

EXHIBIT 6.2

EXAM Strategy

Question: Jenny asked a neighbor, Tom, to water her flowers while she was on vacation. For three days, Tom did this without incident, but on the fourth day, when he touched the outside faucet, he received a violent electric shock that shot him through the air, melted his sneakers and glasses, set his clothes on fire, and seriously burned him. Tom sued, claiming that Jenny had caused his injuries by negligently repairing a second-floor toilet. Water from the steady leak had flooded through the walls, soaking wires and eventually causing the faucet to become electrified. You are Jenny's lawyer. Use one (and only one) element of negligence law to move for summary judgment.

Strategy: The four elements of negligence we have examined thus far are duty to this plaintiff, breach, factual cause, and proximate cause. Which element seems to be most helpful to Jenny's defense? Why?

Result: Jenny is entitled to summary judgment because this was not a foreseeable type of injury. Even if she did a bad job of fixing the toilet, she could not reasonably have anticipated that her poor workmanship could cause *electrical* injuries to anyone.[14]

Res Ipsa Loquitur

Res ipsa loquitur
The facts *imply* that the defendant's negligence caused the accident.

Normally, a plaintiff must prove factual cause and a foreseeable type of harm in order to establish negligence. But in a few cases, a court may be willing to *infer* that the defendant caused the harm under the doctrine of **res ipsa loquitur** ("the thing speaks for itself"). Suppose a pedestrian is walking along a sidewalk when an air conditioning unit falls on his head from a third-story window. The defendant, who owns the third-story apartment, denies any wrongdoing, and it may be difficult or impossible for the plaintiff to prove why the air conditioner fell. In such cases, many courts will apply *res ipsa loquitur* and declare that **the facts imply that the defendant's negligence caused the accident**. If a court uses this doctrine, then the defendant must come forward with evidence establishing that it did *not* cause the harm.

Because res ipsa loquitur dramatically shifts the burden of proof from plaintiff to defendant, it applies only when (1) the defendant had exclusive control of the thing that caused the harm, (2) the harm normally would not have occurred without negligence, and (3) the plaintiff had no role in causing the harm. In the air conditioner example, most states would apply the doctrine and force the defendant to prove that she did nothing wrong.

Damages

Finally, a plaintiff must prove that he has been injured or that he has had some kind of measureable losses. In some cases, injury is obvious. For example, Ruben Hernandez suffered grievous harm when struck by the drunk driver. But in other cases, injury is unclear. **The plaintiff must persuade the court that he has suffered harm that is genuine, not speculative.**

---

[14]Based on *Hebert v. Enos*, 60 Mass. App. Ct. 817, 806 N.E.2d 452 (Mass. Ct. App. 2004).

Some cases raise tough questions. Among the most vexing are suits involving *future* harm. Exposure to toxins or trauma may lead to serious medical problems down the road—or it may not. A woman's knee is damaged in an auto accident, causing severe pain for two years. She is clearly entitled to compensation for her suffering. After two years, all pain may cease for a decade—or forever. Yet there is also a chance that in 15 or 20 years, the trauma will lead to painful arthritis. A court must decide today the full extent of present *and future* damages; a plaintiff cannot return to court years later and demand compensation for newly arisen ailments. The challenge to our courts is to weigh the possibilities and percentages of future suffering and decide whether to compensate a plaintiff for something that might never happen.

DEFENSES

Contributory and Comparative Negligence

Sixteen-year-old Michelle Wightman was out driving at night, with her friend Karrie Wieber in the passenger seat. They came to a railroad crossing, where the mechanical arm had descended and warning bells were sounding. They had been sounding for a long time. A Conrail train had suffered mechanical problems and was stopped 200 feet from the crossing, where it had stalled for roughly an hour. Michelle and Karrie saw several cars ahead of them go around the barrier and cross the tracks. Michelle had to decide whether she would do the same.

Long before Michelle made her decision, the train's engineer had seen the heavy Saturday night traffic crossing the tracks and realized the danger. The conductor and brakeman also understood the peril, but rather than posting a flagman, who could have stopped traffic when a train approached, they walked to the far end of their train to repair the mechanical problem. A police officer had come upon the scene, told his dispatcher to notify the train's parent company Conrail of the danger, and left.

Michelle decided to cross the tracks. She slowly followed the cars ahead of her. Seconds later, both girls were dead. A freight train traveling at 60 miles per hour struck the car broadside, killing both girls instantly.

Michelle's mother sued Conrail for negligence. The company claimed that it was Michelle's foolish risk that led to her death. Who wins when both parties are partly responsible? It depends on whether the state uses a legal theory called contributory negligence. **Under contributory negligence, if the plaintiff is even slightly negligent, she recovers nothing.** If Michelle's death occurred in a contributory negligence state, and the jury considered her even minimally responsible, her estate would receive no money.

Critics attacked this rule as unreasonable. A plaintiff who was 1 percent negligent could not recover from a defendant who was 99 percent responsible. So most states threw out the contributory negligence rule, replacing it with comparative negligence. **In a comparative negligence state, a plaintiff may generally recover even if she is partially responsible.** The jury will be asked to assess the relative negligence of the two parties.

Michelle died in Ohio, which is a comparative negligence state. The jury concluded that reasonable compensatory damages were $1 million. It also concluded that Conrail was 60 percent responsible for the tragedy and Michelle 40 percent. See Exhibit 6.3. The girl's mother received $600,000 in compensatory damages.

Today, most but not all states have adopted some form of comparative negligence. Critics claim that this principle rewards a careless plaintiff. If Michelle had obeyed the law, she would still be alive. In response to this complaint, many comparative negligence states do *not* permit a plaintiff to recover anything if he was more than 50 percent responsible for his own injury.

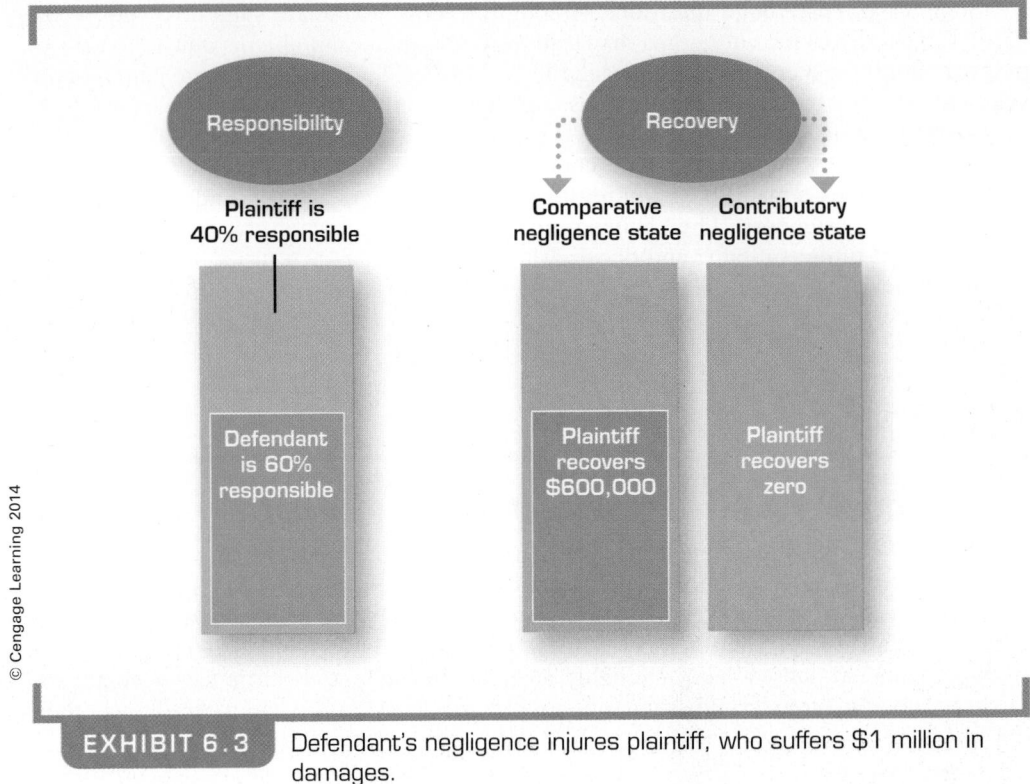

© Cengage Learning 2014

| EXHIBIT 6.3 | Defendant's negligence injures plaintiff, who suffers $1 million in damages. |

In the Conrail case, the jury decided that the rail company was extraordinarily negligent. Expert witnesses testified that similar tragedies occurred every year around the nation and the company knew it. Conrail could easily have prevented the loss of life by posting a flagman on the road. The jury awarded the estate $25 million in punitive damages. The trial judge reduced the verdict by 40 percent to $15 million. The state supreme court affirmed the award.[15]

Assumption of the Risk

Good Guys, a restaurant, holds an ice-fishing contest on a frozen lake to raise money for accident victims. Margie grabs a can full of worms and strolls to the middle of the lake to try her luck, but slips on the ice and suffers a concussion. If she sues Good Guys, how will she fare? She will fall a second time. Wherever there is an obvious hazard, a special rule applies. **Assumption of the risk: a person who voluntarily enters a situation that has an obvious danger cannot complain if she is injured.** Ice is slippery, and we all know it. If you venture onto a frozen lake, any falls are your own tough luck.

However, the doctrine does not apply if someone is injured in a way that is not an inherent part of the dangerous activity. NFL players assume substantial risks each time they take the field, but some injuries fall outside the rule. In a game between the Jets and

---

[15]*Wightman v. Consolidated Rail Corporation*, 86 Ohio St. 3d 431, 715 N.E.2d 546, 1999 Ohio LEXIS 2924 (Ohio 1999).

the Dolphins, Jets assistant coach Sal Alosi, standing on the sideline, tripped Dolphins player Nolan Carroll during a punt return. The trip was not a "normal" part of a football game, and the "assumption of the risk" doctrine would not prevent Carroll from recovering damages.

The following case involves a lake, jet skis—and a great tragedy.

TRUONG V. NGUYEN

67 Cal. Rptr.3d 675, 156 Cal.App.4th 865
California Court of Appeals, 2007

Facts: On a warm California day, there were about 30 personal watercraft (jet skis) operating on Coyote Lake. The weather was fair and visibility good. Anthony Nguyen and Rachael Truong went for a ride on Anthony's Polaris watercraft. Cu Van Nguyen and Chuong Nguyen (neither of whom were related to Anthony) were both riding a Yamaha Waverunner. Both jet skis permitted a driver and passenger, each seated. The two watercraft collided near the middle of the lake. Rachael was killed, and the others all injured.

Rachael's parents sued Anthony, Cu Van, and Chuong, alleging that negligent operation of their watercraft caused their daughter's death. The defendants moved for summary judgment, claiming that assumption of the risk applies to jet skiing. The parents appealed, arguing that jet skiing was not a sport and Rachael never assumed any risk.

Issue: *Does assumption of the risk apply to jet skiing?*

Excerpts from Judge McAdams's Decision: In a sports context, [assumption of the risk] bars liability because the plaintiff is said to have assumed the particular risks inherent in a sport by choosing to participate. Thus, a court need not ask what risks a particular plaintiff subjectively knew of and chose to encounter, but instead must evaluate the fundamental nature of the sport and the defendant's role in or relationship to that sport.

In baseball, a batter is not supposed to carelessly throw the bat after getting a hit and starting to run to first base. However, assumption of risk recognizes that vigorous bat deployment is an integral part of the sport and a risk players assume when they choose to participate. A batter does not have a duty to another player to avoid carelessly throwing the bat after getting a hit.

Even when a participant's conduct violates a rule of the game and may subject the violator to internal sanctions prescribed by the sport itself, imposition of legal liability for such conduct might well alter fundamentally the nature of the sport by deterring participants from vigorously engaging in activity. Coparticipants' limited duty of care is to refrain from intentionally injuring one another or engaging in conduct that is so reckless as to be totally outside the range of the ordinary activity involved in the sport.

It appears that an activity falls within the meaning of "sport" if the activity is done for enjoyment or thrill, requires physical exertion as well as elements of skill, and involves a challenge containing a potential risk of injury.

As a matter of common knowledge, jet skiing is an active sport involving physical skill and challenges that pose a significant risk of injury, particularly when it is done—as it often is—together with other jet skiers in order to add to the exhilaration of the sport by racing, jumping the wakes of the other jet skis or nearby boats, or in other respects making the sporting activity more challenging and entertaining. In response to the plaintiff's complaint that the trial court erroneously assumed that the litigants were contestants in some sort of consensual competition event and/or spectator sport, [we conclude] that the doctrine applies equally to competitive and non-competitive but active sports.

Plaintiffs urge [that] Rachael was merely a passenger on the Polaris and was not actively involved in the sport. The record supports the conclusion that riding as a passenger on a personal watercraft [is participating in a sport], because it is done for enjoyment or thrill, requires physical exertion as well as elements of skill, and involves a challenge containing a potential risk of injury. The vessel is open to the elements, with no hull or cabin. It is designed for high performance, speed, and quick turning maneuvers. The thrill of riding the vessel is shared by both the operator and the passenger. Obstacles in the environment such as spraying water, wakes to be crossed, and other watercraft are part of the thrill of the sport, both for the operator and the passenger.

The summary judgment is affirmed.

STRICT LIABILITY

Some activities are so naturally dangerous that the law places an especially high burden on anyone who engages in them. A corporation that produces toxic waste can foresee dire consequences from its business that a stationery store cannot. This higher burden is **strict liability**. There are two main areas of business that incur strict liability: *ultrahazardous activity* and *defective products*.

Strict liability
A branch of tort law that imposes a much higher level of liability when harm results from ultrahazardous acts or defective products.

Ultrahazardous Activity

Ultrahazardous activities include using harmful chemicals, operating explosives, keeping wild animals, bringing dangerous substances onto property, and a few similar activities where the danger to the general public is especially great. **A defendant engaging in an ultrahazardous activity is almost always liable for any harm that results.** Plaintiffs do not have to prove duty or breach or foreseeable harm. Recall the deliberately bizarre case we posed earlier of the pig falling from a window ledge and killing a veterinarian. Dom, the mechanic whose negligence caused the car crash, could not be liable for the veterinarian's death because the plunging pig was a superseding cause.

But now imagine that the pig is jolted off the window ledge by a company engaged in an ultrahazardous activity. Sam's Blasting Co. sets off a perfectly lawful blast to clear ground for a new building down the street. When the pig is startled and falls, the blasting company is liable. Even if Sam took extraordinary care, it will do him no good at trial. The "reasonable person" rule is irrelevant in a strict liability case.

Because "strict liability" translates into "defendant is liable," parties in tort cases often fight over whether the defendant was engaged in an ultrahazardous activity. If the court rules that the activity was ultrahazardous, the plaintiff is assured of winning. If the court rules that it was not ultrahazardous, the plaintiff must prove all elements of negligence.

The line is often hazy. A lawful fireworks display does not incur strict liability, but crop dusting does. Cutting timber is generally not abnormally dangerous, but hauling logs might be. The enormous diversity of business activities in our nation ensures continual disputes over this important principle.

Product Liability

Defective products can also create strict liability. Most states have adopted the following model:

1. One who sells any product in a defective condition unreasonably dangerous to the user or consumer or to his property is subject to liability for physical harm thereby caused to the ultimate user or consumer, or to his property, if

   a. the seller is engaged in the business of selling such a product, and

   b. it is expected to and does reach the user or consumer without substantial change in the condition in which it is sold.

2. The rule stated in Subsection (1) applies although

   a. the seller has exercised all possible care in the preparation and sale of his product, and

   b. the user or consumer has not bought the product from or entered into any contractual relation with the seller.[16]

---

[16]Restatement (Second) of Torts Section 402A

These are the key terms in subsection (1):

- **Defective condition unreasonably dangerous to the user.** The defendant is liable only if the product is defective when it leaves his hands. There must be something wrong with the goods. If they are reasonably safe and the buyer's mishandling of the goods causes the harm, there is no strict liability. If you attempt to open a soda bottle by knocking the cap against a counter, and the glass shatters and cuts you, the manufacturer owes nothing. A carving knife can produce a lethal wound, but everyone knows that, and a sharp knife is not unreasonably dangerous. On the other hand, prescription drugs may harm in ways that neither a layperson nor a doctor would anticipate. The manufacturer *must provide adequate warnings* of any dangers that are not apparent.

- **In the business of selling.** The seller is liable only if she normally sells this kind of product. Suppose your roommate makes you a peanut butter sandwich and, while eating it, you cut your mouth on a sliver of glass that was in the jar. The peanut butter manufacturer faces strict liability, as does the grocery store where your roommate bought the goods. But your roommate is not strictly liable because he is not in the food business.

- **Reaches the user without substantial change.** Obviously, if your roommate put the glass in the peanut butter thinking it was funny, neither the manufacturer nor the store is liable.

And here are the important phrases in subsection (2).

- **Has exercised all possible care.** This is the heart of strict liability, which makes it a potent claim for consumers. *It is no defense that the seller used reasonable care.* If the product is dangerously defective and injures the user, the seller is liable even if it took every precaution to design and manufacture the product safely. Suppose the peanut butter jar did in fact contain a glass sliver when it left the factory. The manufacturer proves that it uses extraordinary care in keeping foreign particles out of the jars and thoroughly inspects each container before it is shipped. The evidence is irrelevant. The manufacturer has shown that it was not *negligent* in packaging the food, but reasonable care is irrelevant in strict liability cases.

- **No contractual relation.** When two parties contract, they are in privity. Privity only exists between the user and the person from whom she actually bought the goods, but in strict liability cases, *privity is not required*. Suppose the manufacturer that made the peanut butter sold it to a distributor, which sold it to a wholesaler, which sold it to a grocery store, which sold it to your roommate. You may sue the manufacturer, distributor, wholesaler, and store, even though you had no privity with any of them.

Contemporary Trends

If the steering wheel on a brand new car falls off, and the driver is injured, that is a clear case of defective manufacturing, and the company will be strictly liable. Those are the easy cases. But defective design cases have been more contentious. Suppose a vaccine that prevents serious childhood illnesses inevitably causes brain damage in a very small number of children because of the nature of the drug. Is the manufacturer liable? What if a racing sailboat, designed only for speed, is dangerously unstable in the hands of a less-experienced sailor? Is the boat's maker responsible for fatalities? Suppose an automobile made of lightweight metal uses less fuel but exposes its occupants to more serious injuries in an accident. How is a court to decide whether the design was defective? Often, these design cases also involve issues of warnings: did the drug designer diligently detail dangers to doctors? Should a sailboat seller sell speedy sailboats solely to seasoned sailors?

Over the years, most courts have adopted one of two tests for design and warning cases. The first is *consumer expectation*. Here, a court finds the manufacturer liable for defective design if the product is less safe than a reasonable consumer would expect. If a smoke detector has a 3 percent failure rate and the average consumer has no way of anticipating that danger, effective cautions must be included, though the design may be defective anyway.

Many other states use a *risk-utility test*. Here, a court must weigh the benefits for society against the dangers that the product poses. Principal factors in the risk-utility test include:

- The *value* of the product,
- The *gravity*, or seriousness, of the danger,
- The *likelihood* that such danger will occur,
- The mechanical feasibility of a *safer alternative* design, and
- The *adverse consequences* of an alternative design.

Chapter Conclusion

This chapter has been a potpourri of misdeeds, a bubbling cauldron of conduct best avoided. Although tortious acts and their consequences are diverse, two generalities apply. First, the boundaries are imprecise, the outcome of a particular case depending to a considerable extent upon the factfinder who analyzes it. Second, the thoughtful executive and the careful citizen, aware of the shifting standards and potentially vast liability, will strive to ensure that his or her conduct never provides that factfinder an opportunity to give judgment.

EXAM REVIEW

1. TORT A tort is a violation of a duty imposed by the civil law. (pp. 133)

EXAM Strategy

Question: Keith is driving while intoxicated. He swerves into the wrong lane and causes an accident, seriously injuring Caroline. Which statement is true?

a. Caroline could sue Keith, who might be found guilty in her suit.

b. Caroline and the state could start separate criminal cases against Keith.

c. Caroline could sue Keith, and the state could prosecute Keith for drunk driving.

d. The state could sue Keith but only with Caroline's consent.

e. The state could prosecute Keith and sue him at the same time, for drunk driving.

Strategy: What party prosecutes a criminal case? The government does, not the injured party. What is the result in a criminal case? Guilt or innocence. What about a tort lawsuit? The injured party brings a tort suit. The defendant may be found liable but never guilty. (See the "Result" at the end of this section.)

2. **DEFAMATION** Defamation involves a defamatory statement that is false, uttered to a third person, and causes an injury. Opinion and privilege are valid defenses. (pp. 134–135)

Question: Benzaquin had a radio talk show. On the program, he complained about an incident in which state trooper Fleming had stopped his car, apparently for lack of a proper license plate and safety sticker. Benzaquin explained that the license plate had been stolen and the sticker fallen onto the dashboard, but Fleming refused to let him drive away. Benzaquin and two young grandsons had to find other transportation. On the show, Benzaquin angrily recounted the incident, then described Fleming and troopers generally: "we're not paying them to be dictators and Nazis"; "this man is an absolute barbarian, a lunkhead, a meathead." Fleming sued Benzaquin for defamation. Comment.

Strategy: Review the elements of defamation. Can these statements be proven true or false? If not, what is the result? Look at the defenses. Does one apply? (See the "Result" at the end of this section.)

3. **MALICE** Public personalities can win a defamation suit only by proving actual malice. (pp. 135–136)

4. **FALSE IMPRISONMENT** False imprisonment is the intentional restraint of another person without reasonable cause and without consent. (p. 136)

5. **EMOTIONAL DISTRESS** The intentional infliction of emotional distress involves extreme and outrageous conduct that causes serious emotional harm. (pp. 137–138)

6. **ADDITIONAL INTENTIONAL TORTS** Battery is an intentional touching of another person in a way that is unwanted or offensive. Assault involves an act that makes the plaintiff fear an imminent battery. Fraud is injuring another person by intentional deception. (p. 138)

7. **DAMAGES** Compensatory damages are the normal remedy in a tort case. In unusual cases, the court may award punitive damages, not to compensate the plaintiff but to punish the defendant. (pp. 138–142)

8. **TORTIOUS INTERFERENCE** Tortious interference with business relations involves the defendant harming an existing contract or a prospective relationship that has a definite expectation of success. (pp. 142–144)

9. **PRIVACY AND PUBLICITY** The related torts of privacy and publicity involve unreasonable intrusion into someone's private life and unfair commercial exploitation by using someone's name, likeness, or voice without permission. (p. 144)

10. **NEGLIGENCE ELEMENTS** The five elements of negligence are duty of due care, breach, factual causation, proximate causation, and damage. (p. 145)

11. **DUTY OF DUE CARE** If the defendant could foresee that misconduct would injure a particular person, he probably has a duty to her. Special duties exist for people on the job, landowners, and employers. (pp. 145–148)

EXAM Strategy

Question: A supervisor reprimanded an employee for eating in a restaurant when he should have been at work. Later, the employee showed up at the supervisor's office and shot him. Although the employee previously had been violent, management withheld this information from supervisory personnel. Is the company liable for the supervisor's injury?

Strategy: An employer must do a *reasonable* job of hiring and retaining employees. (See the "Result" at the end of this section.)

12. **BREACH OF DUTY** A defendant breaches his duty of due care by failing to meet his duty of care. (p. 148)

13. **NEGLIGENCE PER SE** If a legislature sets a minimum standard of care for a particular activity in order to protect a certain group of people, and a violation of the statute injures a member of that group, the defendant has committed negligence per se. (p. 148)

14. **FACTUAL CAUSE** If one event directly led to the ultimate harm, it is the factual cause. (pp. 148–149)

15. **PROXIMATE CAUSE** For the defendant to be liable, the type of harm must have been reasonably foreseeable. (p. 149)

16. **DAMAGES** The plaintiff must persuade the court that he has suffered a harm that is genuine, not speculative. Damages for emotional distress, without a physical injury, are awarded only in select cases. (pp. 150–151)

17. **STRICT LIABILITY** A defendant is strictly liable for harm caused by an ultrahazardous activity or a defective product. Ultrahazardous activities include using harmful chemicals, blasting, and keeping wild animals. Strict liability means that if the defendant's conduct led to the harm, the defendant is liable, even if she exercises extraordinary care. (pp. 154–155)

EXAM Strategy

Question: Marko owned a cat and allowed it to roam freely outside. In the three years he had owned the pet, the animal had never bitten anyone. The cat entered Romi's garage. When Romi attempted to move it outside, the cat bit her. Romi underwent four surgeries, was fitted with a plastic finger joint, and spent more than $39,000 in medical bills. She sued Marko, claiming both strict liability and ordinary negligence. Assume that state law allows a domestic cat to roam freely. Evaluate both of Romi's claims.

Strategy: Negligence requires proof that the defendant breached a duty to the plaintiff by behaving unreasonably, and that the resulting harm was foreseeable. Was it? When would harm by a domestic cat be foreseeable? A defendant can be strictly liable for keeping a wild animal. Apply that rule as well. (See the "Result" at the end of this section.)

> **1. Result:** (a) is wrong because a defendant cannot be found guilty in a civil suit. (b) is wrong because a private party has no power to prosecute a criminal case. (c) is correct. (d) is wrong because the state will prosecute Keith, not sue him. (e) is wrong for the same reason.
>
> **2. Result:** The court ruled in favor of Benzaquin because a reasonable person would understand the words to be opinion and ridicule. They are not statements of fact because most of them could not be proven true or false. A statement like "dictators and Nazis" is not taken literally by anyone.[17]
>
> **11. Result:** This employer *may* have been liable for negligently hiring a previously violent employee, and it *certainly* did an unreasonable job in retaining him without advising his supervisor of the earlier violence. The assault was easily foreseeable, and the employer is liable.[18]
>
> **17. Result:** If Marko's cat had bitten or attacked people in the past, this harm was foreseeable and Marko is liable. If the cat had never done so, and state law allows domestic animals to roam, Romi probably loses her suit for negligence. Her strict liability case definitely fails: a housecat is not a wild animal.

MULTIPLE-CHOICE QUESTIONS

1. Jane writes an article for a newspaper reporting that Ann was arrested for stealing a car. The story is entirely false. Ann is not a public figure. Which of the following torts has Jane committed?

    (a) Ordinary slander

    (b) Slander per se

    (c) Libel

    (d) None of the above

2. Refer back to Question 1. If Ann decides to sue, she _____ have to show evidence that she suffered an injury. If she ultimately wins her case, a jury _____ have the option to award punitive damages.

    (a) will; will

    (b) will; will not

    (c) will not; will

    (d) will not; will not

[17]*Fleming v. Benzaquin*, 390 Mass. 175, 454 N.E.2d 95 (1983).
[18]*Caudle v. Betts*, 512 So.2d 389 (La. 1987).

3. Sam sneaks up on Tom, hits him with a baseball bat, and knocks him unconscious. Tom never saw Sam coming. He wakes up with a horrible headache. Which of the following torts has Sam committed?

   (a) Assault

   (b) Battery

   (c) Both A and B

   (d) None of the above

4. Al runs a red light and hits Carol's car. She later sues, claiming the following losses:

   $10,000—car repairs

   $10,000—medical expenses

   $10,000—lost wages (she could not work for two months after the accident)

   $10,000—pain and suffering

   If the jury believes all of Carol's evidence and she wins her case, how much will she receive in *compensatory* damages?

   (a) $40,000

   (b) $30,000

   (c) $20,000

   (d) $10,000

   (e) $0

5. Zack lives in a state that prohibits factory laborers from working more than 12 hours in any 24-hour period. The state legislature passed the law to cut down on accidents caused by fatigued workers.

   Ignoring the law, Zack makes his factory employees put in 14-hour days. Eventually, a worker at the end of a long shift makes a mistake and severely injures a coworker. The injured worker sues Zack.

   Which of the following terms will be most relevant to the case?

   (a) Res ipsa loquitur

   (b) Assumption of the risk

   (c) Negligence per se

   (d) Strict liability

ESSAY QUESTIONS

1. Caldwell was shopping in a K-Mart store, carrying a large purse. A security guard observed her looking at various small items such as stain, hinges, and antenna wire. On occasion, she bent down out of sight of the guard. The guard thought he saw Caldwell put something in her purse. Caldwell removed her glasses from her purse and returned them a few times. After she left, the guard approached her in the parking lot and said that he believed she had store merchandise in her pocketbook, but he could not say what he thought was put there. Caldwell opened the purse, and the guard testified that he saw no K-Mart merchandise in it. The guard then told Caldwell to return to the store with him. They walked around the store for

approximately 15 minutes, while the guard said six or seven times that he saw her put something in her purse. Caldwell left the store after another store employee indicated she could go. Caldwell sued. What kind of suit did she file, and what should the outcome be?

2. Tata Consultancy of Bombay, India, is an international computer consulting firm. It spends considerable time and effort recruiting the best personnel from India's leading technical schools. Tata employees sign an initial three-year employment commitment, often work overseas, and agree to work for a specified additional time when they return to India. Desai worked for Tata, but then he quit and formed a competing company, which he called Syntel. His new company contacted Tata employees by phone, offering higher salaries, bonuses, and assistance in obtaining permanent resident visas in the United States if they would come work for Syntel. At least 16 former Tata employees left their jobs without completing their contractual obligations and went to work for Syntel. Tata sued. What did it claim, and what should be the result?

3. **YOU BE THE JUDGE WRITING PROBLEM** Johnny Carson was for many years the star of a well-known television show, *The Tonight Show*. For about 20 years, he was introduced nightly on the show with the phrase, "Here's Johnny!" A large segment of the television watching public associated the phrase with Carson. A Michigan corporation was in the business of renting and selling portable toilets. The company chose the name "Here's Johnny Portable Toilets," and coupled the company name with the marketing phrase, "The World's Foremost Commodian." Carson sued, claiming that the company's name and slogan violated his right to commercial exploitation.

Argument for Carson: The toilet company is deliberately taking advantage of Johnny Carson's good name. He worked hard for decades to build a brilliant career and earn a reputation as a creative, funny, likable performer. No company has the right to use his name, his picture, or anything else closely identified with him, such as the phrase "Here's Johnny." The pun is personally offensive and commercially unfair.

Argument for Here's Johnny Portable Toilets: Johnny Carson doesn't own his first name. It is available for anyone to use for any purpose. Further, the popular term "john," meaning toilet, has been around much longer than Carson or even television. We are entitled to make any use of it we want. Our corporate name is amusing to customers who have never heard of Carson, and we are entitled to profit from our brand recognition.

4. At approximately 7:50 p.m, bells at the train station rang and red lights flashed, signaling an express train's approach. David Harris walked onto the tracks, ignoring a yellow line painted on the platform instructing people to stand back. Two men shouted to Harris, warning him to get off the tracks. The train's engineer saw him too late to stop the train, which was traveling at approximately 55 mph. The train struck and killed Harris as it passed through the station. Harris's widow sued the railroad, arguing that the railroad's negligence caused her husband's death. Evaluate her argument.

5. A new truck, manufactured by General Motors Corp. (GMC), stalled in rush hour traffic on a busy interstate highway because of a defective alternator, which caused a complete failure of the truck's electrical system. The driver stood nearby and waved traffic around his stalled truck. A panel truck approached the GMC truck, and immediately behind the panel truck, Davis was driving a Volkswagen fastback.

Because of the panel truck, Davis was unable to see the stalled GMC truck. The panel truck swerved out of the way of the GMC truck, and Davis drove straight into it. The accident killed him. Davis's widow sued GMC. GMC moved for summary judgment, alleging (1) no duty to Davis, (2) no factual causation, and (3) no foreseeable harm. Comment.

DISCUSSION QUESTIONS

1. You have most likely heard of the *Liebeck v. McDonalds* case. Liebeck spilled hot McDonald's coffee in her lap and suffered third-degree burns. At trial, evidence showed that her cup of coffee was brewed at 190 degrees, and that, more typically, a restaurant's "hot coffee" is in the range of 140 to 160 degrees. A jury awarded Liebeck $160,000 in compensatory damages and $2.7 million in punitive damages. The judge reduced the punitive award to $480,000, or three times the compensatory award. Comment on the case and whether the result was reasonable.

2. Celebrities often have problems with tabloids and the paparazzi. It is difficult for public figures to win libel lawsuits because they must show actual malice. Intrusion lawsuits are also tricky, and flocks of photographers often stalk celebrities at all hours. Is this right? Should the law change to offer more privacy to famous people? Or is a loss of privacy just the price of success?

3. Many retailers have policies that instruct employees *not* to attempt to stop shoplifters. Some store owners fear false imprisonment lawsuits and possible injuries to workers more than losses related to stolen merchandise. Are these "don't be a hero" policies reasonable? Would you put one in place if you owned a retail store?

4. Imagine an undefeated high school football team on which the average lineman weighs 300 pounds. Also, imagine an 0–10 team on which the average lineman weighs 170 pounds. The undefeated team sets out to hit as hard as they can on every play and to run up the score as much as possible. Before the game is over, 11 players from the lesser team have been carried off the field with significant injuries. All injuries were the result of "clean hits"—none of the plays resulted in a penalty. Even late in the game, when the score is 70–0, the undefeated team continues to deliver devastating hits that are far beyond what would be required to tackle and block. The assumption of the risk doctrine exempts the undefeated team from liability. Is this reasonable?

5. People who serve alcohol to others take a risk. In some circumstances, they can be held legally responsible for the actions of the people they serve. Is this fair? Should an intoxicated person be the only one liable if harm results? If not, in what specific circumstances is it fair to stretch liablility to other people?

CHAPTER 7

CRIME

© Steve Allen/Jupiterimages

Crime can take us by surprise. Stacey tucks her nine-year-old daughter, Beth, into bed. Promising her husband, Mark, that she will be home by 11:00 P.M., she jumps into her car and heads back to Be Patient, Inc. She plugs her iPhone into the player of her $85,000 sedan and tries to relax by listening to music. Be Patient is a healthcare organization that owns five geriatric hospitals. Most of its patients use Medicare, and Stacey supervises all billing to their largest client, the federal government.

She parks in a well-lighted spot on the street and walks to her building, failing to notice two men, collars turned up, watching from a parked truck. Once in her office, she goes straight to her computer and works on billing issues. Tonight's work goes more quickly than she expected, thanks to new software she helped develop. At 10:30 she emerges from the building with a quick step and a light heart, walks to her car—and finds it missing.

A major crime has occurred during the 90 minutes Stacey was at her desk, but she will never report it to the police. It is a crime that costs Americans countless dollars each year, yet Stacey will not even mention it to friends or family. Stacey is the criminal.

> **A major crime has occurred during the 90 minutes Stacey was at her desk, but she will never report it to the police.**

When we think of crime, we imagine the drug dealers and bank robbers endlessly portrayed on television. We do not picture corporate executives sitting at polished desks. "Street crimes" are indeed serious threats to our security and happiness. They deservedly receive the attention of the public and the law. But when measured only in dollars, street crime takes second place to white-collar crime, which costs society *tens of billions* of dollars annually.

The hypothetical about Stacey is based on many real cases and is used to illustrate that crime does not always dress the way we expect. Her car was never stolen; it was simply towed. Two parking bureau employees, watching from their truck, saw Stacey park illegally and did their job. It is Stacey who committed a crime—Medicare fraud. Every month, she has billed the government about $10 million for work that her company has not performed. Stacey's scheme was quick and profitable—and a distressingly common crime.

Crime, whether violent or white-collar, is detrimental to all society. It imposes a huge cost on everyone. Just the *fear* of crime is expensive—homeowners buy alarm systems and businesses hire security guards. But the anger and fear that crime engenders sometimes tempt us to forget that not all accused people are guilty. Everyone suspected of a crime should have the protections that you yourself would want in that situation. As the English jurist William Blackstone said, "Better that ten guilty persons escape than that one innocent suffer."

Thus, criminal law is a balancing act—between making society safe and protecting us all from false accusations and unfair punishment.

This chapter has four parts:

Criminal procedure
The process by which criminals are accused, tried, and sentenced.

- The differences between a civil and criminal case;

- **Criminal procedure**—the *process* by which criminals are accused, tried, and sentenced;

- Crimes that *harm* businesses;

- Crimes committed *by* businesses.

THE DIFFERENCES BETWEEN A CIVIL AND CRIMINAL CASE

Most of this book focuses on civil law, so we begin with a discussion of the differences between a civil and criminal case.

Civil law involves the rights and liabilities that exist between private parties. As we have seen, if one person claims that another has caused her a civil injury, she must file a lawsuit and convince a court of her damages.

Criminal law
Prohibits and punishes conduct that threatens public safety and welfare.

Criminal law is different. Conduct is criminal when society outlaws it. When a state legislature or Congress concludes that certain behavior threatens public safety and welfare, it passes a statute forbidding that behavior; in other words, declaring it criminal. Medicare fraud, which Stacey committed, is a crime because Congress has outlawed it. Money laundering is a crime because Congress concluded that it was a fundamental part of the drug trade and prohibited it.

Prosecution

Suppose the police arrest Roger and accuse him of breaking into a store and stealing 50 computers. The owner of the store is the one harmed, and he has the right to sue the thief in civil court to recover money damages. **But only the government can prosecute a crime and punish Roger by sending him to prison.** The government may also impose a fine on Roger, but it keeps the fine and does not share it with the victim. (However, the court will sometimes order **restitution**, meaning that the defendant must reimburse the victim for harm suffered.) The local prosecutor has total discretion in deciding whether to bring Roger to trial on criminal charges.

Burden of Proof

In a civil case, the plaintiff must prove her case only by a preponderance of the evidence.[1] But because the penalties for conviction in a criminal case are so serious, the government must prove its case **beyond a reasonable doubt**. Also, the stigma of a criminal conviction would stay with Roger forever, making it more difficult to obtain work and housing. Therefore, in all criminal cases, if the jury has any significant doubt at all that Roger stole the computers, it *must* acquit him.

Right to a Jury

The facts of a case are decided by a judge or jury. A criminal defendant has a right to a trial by jury for any charge that could result in a sentence of six months or longer. The defendant may demand a jury trial or may waive that right, in which case the judge will be the factfinder.

Felony/Misdemeanor

A **felony** is a serious crime, for which a defendant can be sentenced to one year or more in prison. Murder, robbery, rape, drug dealing, money laundering, wire fraud, and embezzlement are felonies. A **misdemeanor** is a less serious crime, often punishable by a year or less in a county jail. Public drunkenness, driving without a license, and simple possession of a single marijuana cigarette are considered misdemeanors in most states.

CRIMINAL PROCEDURE

The title of a criminal case is usually the government versus someone: *The United States of America v. Simpson* or *The State of Texas v. Simpson*, for example. This name illustrates a daunting thought—if you are Simpson, the vast power of the government is against you. Because of the government's great power and the severe penalties it can impose, criminal procedure is designed to protect the accused and ensure that the trial is fair. Moreover, a criminal defendant is often engaged in an uphill climb from the beginning because people often assume that anyone accused of a crime must be guilty. Many of the protections for those accused of a crime are found in the first 10 amendments to the United States Constitution, known as the Bill of Rights.

Conduct Outlawed

Crimes are created by statute. The prosecution must demonstrate to the court that the defendant's conduct is indeed outlawed by a statute. Returning to Roger, the alleged computer thief, the state charges that he stole computer equipment from a store, a crime clearly defined by statute as larceny.

The Fifth and Fourteenth Amendments to the Constitution require that the language of criminal statutes be clear and definite enough that (1) ordinary people can understand what conduct is prohibited and (2) the police are discouraged from arbitrary and discriminatory enforcement. Thus, for example, the Supreme Court ruled that a statute that prohibited

Restitution
A court order that a guilty defendant reimburse the victim for the harm suffered.

Beyond a reasonable doubt
The very high burden of proof in a criminal trial, demanding much more certainty than required in a civil trial.

Felony
A serious crime, for which a defendant can be sentenced to one year or more in prison.

Misdemeanor
A less serious crime, often punishable by less than a year in a county jail.

---

[1]See the earlier discussion in Chapter 3, on dispute resolution.

loitering was unconstitutionally vague because it did not clarify exactly what behavior was prohibited and it tended to be enforced arbitrarily.[2]

State of Mind
Voluntary Act

Guilty
A judge or jury's finding that a defendant has committed a crime.

A defendant is not guilty of a crime if she was forced to commit it. In other words, she is not guilty if she acted under duress. However, the defendant bears the burden of proving by a preponderance of the evidence that she did act under duress. In 1974, a terrorist group kidnapped heiress Patricia Hearst from her apartment near the University of California at Berkeley. After being tortured for two months, she participated in a bank robbery with the group. Despite opportunities to escape, she stayed with the criminals until her capture by the police a year later. The State of California put on her on trial for bank robbery. One question for the jury was whether she had voluntarily participated in the crime. This was an issue on which many people had strong opinions. Ultimately Hearst was convicted, sent to prison, and then later pardoned.

Entrapment

When the government induces the defendant to break the law, the prosecution must prove beyond a reasonable doubt that the defendant was predisposed to commit the crime. The goal is to separate the cases where the defendant was innocent before the government tempted him from those where the defendant was only too eager to break the law.

Kalchinian and Sherman met in the waiting room of a doctor's office where they were both being treated for drug addiction. After several more meetings, Kalchinian told Sherman that the treatment was not working for him and he was desperate to buy drugs. Could Sherman help him? Sherman repeatedly refused, but ultimately agreed to help end Kalchinian's suffering by providing him with drugs. Little did Sherman know that Kalchinian was a police informant. Sherman sold drugs to Kalchinian a number of times. Kalchinian rewarded this act of friendship by getting Sherman hooked again and then turning him in to the police. A jury convicted Sherman of drug dealing, but the Supreme Court overturned the conviction on the grounds that Sherman had been entrapped.[3] The court felt there was no evidence that Sherman was predisposed to commit the crime.

Gathering Evidence: The Fourth Amendment

If the police suspect that a crime has been committed, they will need to obtain evidence. **The Fourth Amendment to the Constitution prohibits the government from making illegal searches and seizures of individuals, corporations, partnerships, and other organizations.** The goal of the Fourth Amendment is to protect the individual from the powerful state.

Warrant

As a general rule, the police must obtain a warrant before conducting a search. A warrant is written permission from a neutral official, such as a judge or magistrate, to conduct a search.[4] **The warrant must specify with reasonable certainty the place to be searched and the items to be seized.** Thus, if the police say they have reason to believe that they will find bloody clothes in the suspect's car in his garage, they cannot also look through his house and confiscate file folders.

---

[2]*Kolender v. Lawson*, 461 U.S. 352 (S. Ct., 1983).

[3]*Sherman v. United States*, 356 U.S. 369 (S. Ct., 1958).

[4]A magistrate is a judge who tries minor criminal cases or undertakes primarily administrative responsibilities.

If the police search without a warrant, they have, in most cases, violated the Fourth Amendment. **But even a search conducted with a warrant violates the Fourth Amendment if:**

- There was no probable cause to issue the warrant;
- The warrant does not specify the place to be searched and the things sought; or
- The search extends beyond what is specified in the warrant.

Probable Cause

The magistrate will issue a warrant only if there is probable cause. **Probable cause** means that based on all the information presented, **it is likely that evidence of a crime will be found in the place to be searched**. Often, the police base their applications for a warrant on data provided by an informant. The magistrate will want evidence to support the informant's reliability. If it turns out that this informant has been wrong the last three times he gave evidence to the police, the magistrate will probably refuse the request for a warrant.

Probable cause
It is likely that evidence of crime will be found in the place to be searched.

Searches Without a Warrant

There are seven circumstances under which police may **search without a warrant**:

- **Plain View.** Police may search if they see a machine gun, for example, sticking out from under the front seat of a parked car.
- **Stop and Frisk.** None of us wants to live in a world in which police can randomly stop and frisk us on the street anytime they feel like it. The police do have the right to stop and frisk, but *only if* they have a clear and specific reason to suspect that criminal activity may be afoot and that the person may be armed and dangerous.[5]
- **Emergencies.** If, for example, the police believe that evidence is about to be destroyed, they can search.
- **Automobiles.** If police have lawfully stopped a car and observe evidence of other crimes in the car, such as burglary tools, they may search.
- **Lawful Arrest.** Police may always search a suspect they have arrested. The goal is to protect the officers and preserve evidence.
- **Consent.** Anyone lawfully living in a dwelling can allow the police in to search without a warrant. If your roommate gives the police permission to search your house, that search is legal.
- **No Expectation of Privacy.** The police have a right to search any area in which the defendant does not have a reasonable expectation of privacy. For example, Rolando Crowder was staying at his friend Bobo's apartment. Hearing the police in the hallway, he ran down to the basement. The police found Crowder in the basement with drugs nearby. Crowder argued that the police should have obtained a warrant, but the court ruled that Crowder had no expectation of privacy in Bobo's basement.[6]

Apart from these seven exceptions, a warrant is required.

Exclusionary Rule

Under the exclusionary rule, evidence obtained illegally may not be used at trial. The Supreme Court created the exclusionary rule to ensure that police conduct legal searches. The theory is simple: if police know in advance that illegally obtained evidence cannot be

Exclusionary Rule
Evidence obtained illegally may not be used at trial.

---

[5]*Terry v. Ohio*, 392 U.S. 1 (S. Ct., 1968).
[6]*Ohio v. Crowder*, 2010 Ohio 3766; 2010 Ohio App. LEXIS 3210 (2010).

used in court, they will not be tempted to make improper searches. Is the exclusionary rule a good idea?

Opponents of the rule argue that a guilty person may go free because one police officer bungled. They are outraged by cases like *Coolidge v. New Hampshire.*[7] Pamela Mason, a 14-year-old babysitter, was brutally murdered. Citizens of New Hampshire were furious, and the state's attorney general personally led the investigation. Police found strong evidence that Edward Coolidge had done it. They took the evidence to the attorney general, who personally issued a search warrant. A search of Coolidge's car uncovered incriminating evidence, and he was found guilty of murder and sentenced to life in prison. But the United States Supreme Court reversed the conviction. The warrant had not been issued by a neutral magistrate. A law officer may not lead an investigation and simultaneously decide what searches are permissible.

After the Supreme Court reversed Coolidge's conviction, New Hampshire scheduled a new trial, attempting to convict him with evidence lawfully obtained. Before the trial began, Coolidge pleaded guilty to second degree murder. He was sentenced and remained in prison until his release years later.

In fact, very few people do go free because of the exclusionary rule. One study showed that evidence is actually excluded in only 1.3 percent of all prosecutions; and in about one-half of *those* cases, the court convicted the defendant on other evidence. Only in 0.7 percent of all prosecutions did the defendant go free after the evidence was suppressed.[8]

There are two exceptions to the exclusionary rule:

- **Inevitable Discovery.** The inevitable discovery exception permits the use of evidence that would inevitably have been discovered even without the illegal search. If an informant was about to tell the police about Coolidge's car, then the evidence found there would have been admissible, so long as the court believed the testimony was true.

- **Good Faith Exception.** Suppose the police use a search warrant believing it to be proper, but it later proves to have been defective. Is the search therefore illegal? No, so long as the police reasonably believed the warrant was valid, the search is legal.[9]

Should the exclusionary rule apply in the following case? You be the judge.

---

[7]403 U.S. 443, 91 S. Ct. 2022, 1971 U.S. LEXIS 25 (S. Ct., 1971).
[8]See the discussion in *United States v. Leon* (Justice Brennan, dissenting), 468 U.S. 897, 1985 U.S. LEXIS 153 (S. Ct., 1984).
[9]Ibid.

You be the Judge

Ohio v. Smith
2009 Ohio 6426; 920 N.E.2d 949;
2009 Ohio Lexis 3496
Supreme Court of Ohio, 2009

Facts: Wendy Northern was hospitalized for a drug overdose. When police questioned her in the hospital, she identified her drug dealer as Antwaun Smith. She then called him to arrange for the purchase of crack cocaine at her house that evening. When Smith arrived at her house, the police arrested him, searched him, and confiscated his cell phone. When the police looked at the phone some time later, they discovered call records and phone numbers confirming that this phone had been used to speak with Northern.

The police had neither a warrant nor Smith's consent to search the phone. Smith filed a motion requesting that the evidence from his cell phone be excluded because it had been obtained without a warrant. After the judge denied this motion, Smith was found guilty and sentenced to 12 years in prison. The appeals court upheld his conviction. He appealed to the Ohio Supreme Court.

You Be the Judge: *Was the search of Smith's cell phone legal? Should the evidence found on the phone be excluded?*

Argument for the Police: The police have the right to search anyone they arrest. During a perfectly legal search, they discovered Smith's cell phone. Prior courts have ruled that defendants have a low expectation of privacy in address books and that police can search them without a warrant. A cell phone is an electronic address book. Therefore, the search of Smith and the subsequent search of the contents of the phone were both legal. The evidence was properly admitted in court.

Argument for Smith: Police have the right to search someone they have arrested so that they can protect themselves and prevent evidence from being destroyed.

A search of the cell phone's contents was not necessary to ensure officer safety, and there was no evidence that the call records and phone numbers were in danger of being destroyed. Once the police had the phone, they had plenty of time to ensure that the data were preserved. In addition, they might have been able to obtain Smith's phone records from his service provider.

The police were entitled to search Smith and discover his cell phone. But they did not have the right to search the phone without a warrant. Modern cell phones are much more similar to a laptop than to an old-fashioned address book—they have the ability to transmit large amounts of personal data in various forms. Courts have ruled that defendants have a high expectation of privacy in laptop computers and that the police must obtain a warrant before searching one. It would be a terrible precedent to declare that the police could search cell phones without a warrant.

The Patriot Act

In response to the devastating attacks of September 11, 2001, Congress passed a sweeping antiterrorist law known as the Patriot Act. The statute was designed to give law enforcement officials greater power to investigate and prevent potential terrorist assaults. The bill raced through Congress nearly unopposed. Proponents hailed it as a vital weapon for use against continuing lethal threats. Opponents argued that the hastily passed law would not provide serious benefits but did threaten the liberties of the very people it purported to shield.

In an early legal test, a federal judge permitted the government to use secret evidence in its effort to freeze the assets of Global Relief Foundation, a religious organization suspected of terrorist activity. The group, which claimed to be purely humanitarian, asserted that it could hardly defend itself against unseen evidence. Finding "acute national security concerns," the judge allowed the government to introduce the evidence in private, without the foundation ever seeing it.[10]

The law also permitted the FBI to issue a **national security letter** (NSL) to communications firms such as Internet service providers (ISPs) and telephone companies. An NSL typically demanded that the recipient furnish to the government its customer records, *without ever divulging* to anyone what it had done. NSLs could be used to obtain access to subscriber billing records, phone, financial, credit, and other information—even records of books taken from libraries. However, an appeals court ruled that a secret NSL could be issued only if the government first demonstrated to a court's satisfaction that disclosure of the NSL would risk serious harm.[11]

---

[10]*Global Relief Found., Inc. v. O'Neill*, 315 F.3d 748, 2002 U.S. App. LEXIS 27172 (7th Cir., 2002).

[11]*Doe v. Mukasey*, 549 F.3d 861; 2008 U.S. App. LEXIS 25193, (2d Cir., 2008).

EXAM Strategy

Question: Police bang down the door of Mary Beth's apartment, enter without her permission, and search the apartment. They had no warrant. When the officers discover that she is smoking marijuana, they arrest her. What motion will the defense lawyer make before trial? Please rule on the defendant's motion. Are there any facts that would make you change your ruling?

Strategy: The defendant's motion is based on the police conduct. What was wrong with that conduct, and what are the consequences?

Result: The defense lawyer will argue that the police violated the Fourth Amendment because they lacked a warrant for the search. He will ask that the court suppress the drug evidence. Ordinarily, the court would grant that motion unless there was other evidence—for example, the police smelled marijuana from the hallway and Mary Beth would have smoked it all if the police had taken the time to obtain a warrant.

The Case Begins

The trial is now ready to begin. But, the government may not be able to use all the evidence it has gathered.

The Fifth Amendment

The Fifth Amendment to the Constitution protects criminal defendants—both the innocent and the guilty—in several ways.

Due process

Requires fundamental fairness at all stages of the case.

Due Process **Due process** requires fundamental fairness at all stages of the case. The basic elements of due process are discussed in Chapter 5, on constitutional law. In the context of criminal law, due process sets additional limits. The requirement that the prosecution disclose evidence favorable to the defendant is a due process rule. Similarly, if a witness says that a tall white male robbed the liquor store, it would violate due process for the police to place the male suspect in a lineup with four short women.

Self-Incrimination The Fifth Amendment bars the government from forcing any person to provide evidence against himself. In other words, the police may not use mental or physical coercion to force a confession or any other information out of someone. Society does not want a government that engages in torture. Such abuse might occasionally catch a criminal, but it would grievously injure innocent people and make all citizens fearful of the government that is supposed to represent them. Also, coerced confessions are inherently unreliable. The defendant may confess simply to end the torture. (The protection against self-incrimination applies only to people; corporations and other organizations are not protected and may be required to provide incriminating information.)

Exclusionary Rule (Again) If the police do force a confession, the exclusionary rule prohibits the prosecution from using it or any information they obtain as a result of what the defendant has said. (This secondary information is referred to as "the fruit of the poisonous tree.") For example, when the police illegally arrest Alice, she tells them that she has bought drugs from Beau. The police go to Beau's house, where they find drugs.

He tells them that Caitlyn is his dealer and, indeed, the police find drugs in Caitlyn's bedroom. None of this evidence—neither the confessions nor the drugs—is admissible in court because it all stemmed from Alice's illegal arrest.

The rationale is the same as for Fourth Amendment searches: suppressing the evidence means that police will not attempt to get it illegally. But remember that the confession is void only if it results from custodial questioning. Suppose a policeman, investigating a bank robbery, asks a pedestrian if he noticed anything peculiar. The pedestrian says, "You mean after I robbed the bank?" Result? There was no custodial questioning, and the confession *may* be used against him.

Miranda Rights   The police cannot legally force a suspect to provide evidence against himself. But sometimes, under forceful interrogation, he might forget his constitutional rights. In the following landmark case, the Supreme Court established the requirement that police remind suspects of their rights—with the very same warning that we have all heard so many times on television shows.

Landmark Case

MIRANDA V. ARIZONA

**384 U.S. 436; 1966 U.S. Lexis 2817
Supreme Court of the United States, 1966**

Facts: Ernesto Miranda was a mentally ill, indigent citizen of Mexico. The Phoenix police arrested him at his home and brought him to a police station, where a rape victim identified him as her assailant. Two police officers took him to an interrogation room but did not tell him that he had a right to have a lawyer present during the questioning. Two hours later, the officers emerged with a written confession signed by Miranda. At the top of the statement was a typed paragraph stating that the confession was made voluntarily "with full knowledge of my legal rights, understanding any statement I make may be used against me."

At Miranda's trial, the judge admitted this written confession into evidence over the objection of defense counsel. The officers testified that Miranda had also made an oral confession during the interrogation. The jury found Miranda guilty of kidnapping and rape. He was sentenced to 20 to 30 years imprisonment. On appeal, the Supreme Court of Arizona affirmed the conviction. In reaching its decision, the court relied heavily on the fact that Miranda did not specifically request a lawyer. The Supreme Court of the United States granted *certiorari*.

Issues: *Was Miranda's confession admissible at trial? Should his conviction be upheld?*

Excerpts from Chief Justice Warren's Decision: Our holding briefly stated is this: the prosecution may not use statements, whether exculpatory or inculpatory, stemming from custodial interrogation of the defendant unless it demonstrates the use of procedural safeguards effective to secure the privilege against self-incrimination. By custodial interrogation, we mean questioning initiated by law enforcement officers after a person has been taken into custody or otherwise deprived of his freedom of action in any significant way. As for the procedural safeguards to be employed, the following measures are required. Prior to any questioning, the person must be warned that he has a right to remain silent, that any statement he does make may be used as evidence against him, and that he has a right to the presence of an attorney, either retained or appointed.

The defendant may waive these rights, provided the waiver is made voluntarily, knowingly, and intelligently. If, however, he indicates in any manner and at any stage of the process that he wishes to consult with an attorney before speaking, there can be no questioning. Likewise, if the individual is alone and indicates in any manner that he does not wish to be interrogated, the police may not question him. The mere fact that he may have answered some questions or volunteered some statements on his own does not deprive him of the right to refrain from answering any further inquiries until he has consulted with an attorney and thereafter consents to be questioned.

In a series of cases decided by this Court, the police resorted to physical brutality—beating, hanging, whipping—and to sustained and protracted questioning incommunicado in order to extort confessions. Only recently in Kings County, New York, the police brutally beat, kicked, and placed lighted cigarette butts on the back of a potential witness under interrogation for the purpose of securing a statement incriminating a third party.

Unless a proper limitation upon custodial interrogation is achieved, there can be no assurance that practices of this nature will be eradicated in the foreseeable future. Not only does the use of the third degree involve a flagrant violation of law by the officers of the law, but it involves also the dangers of false confessions, and it tends to make police and prosecutors less zealous in the search for objective evidence. As [an official] remarked: "If you use your fists, you are not so likely to use your wits."

[C]oercion can be mental as well as physical, and the blood of the accused is not the only hallmark of an unconstitutional inquisition. In a serious case, the interrogation may continue for days, with the required intervals for food and sleep, but with no respite from the atmosphere of domination. It is possible in this way to induce the subject to talk without resorting to duress or coercion.

Even without employing brutality, the very fact of custodial interrogation exacts a heavy toll on individual liberty and trades on the weakness of individuals. In [this case before the Court], the defendant was thrust into an unfamiliar atmosphere and run through menacing police interrogation procedures. It is obvious that such an interrogation environment is created for no purpose other than to subjugate the individual to the will of his examiner. This atmosphere carries its own badge of intimidation. To be sure, this is not physical intimidation, but it is equally destructive of human dignity. The current practice of incommunicado interrogation is at odds with one of our Nation's most cherished principles—that the individual may not be compelled to incriminate himself.

All these policies point to one overriding thought: the constitutional foundation underlying the privilege is the respect a government—state or federal—must accord to the dignity and integrity of its citizens. To maintain a fair state-individual balance, to respect the inviolability of the human personality, our accusatory system of criminal justice demands that the government seeking to punish an individual produce the evidence against him by its own independent labors, rather than by the cruel, simple expedient of compelling it from his own mouth.

From the testimony of the officers and by the admission of [the defendant], it is clear that Miranda was not in any way apprised of his right to consult with an attorney and to have one present during the interrogation, nor was his right not to be compelled to incriminate himself effectively protected in any other manner. Without these warnings, the statements were inadmissible. The mere fact that he signed a statement which contained a typed-in clause stating that he had "full knowledge" of his "legal rights" does not approach the knowing and intelligent waiver required to relinquish constitutional rights.

Right to a Lawyer

As *Miranda* made clear, a criminal defendant has the right to a lawyer before being interrogated by the police. The Sixth Amendment guarantees the **right to a lawyer** at all important stages of the criminal process. Because of this right, the government must **appoint a lawyer** to represent, free of charge, any defendant who cannot afford one.

After Arrest
Indictment

Grand jury
A group of ordinary citizens who decides whether there is probable cause the defendant committed the crime with which she is charged.

Once the police provide the local prosecutor with evidence, he presents this evidence to a **grand jury** and asks its members to indict the defendant. The grand jury is a group of ordinary citizens, like a trial jury, but the grand jury holds hearings for several weeks at a time, on many different cases. It is the grand jury's job to determine whether there is probable cause that this defendant committed the crime with which she is charged. At the hearing in front of the grand jury, only the prosecutor presents evidence, not the defense attorney because it is better for the defendant to save her evidence for the trial jury. After all, the defense attorney may want to see what evidence the prosecution has before deciding how to present the case.

If the grand jury determines that there is probable cause, an **indictment** is issued. An indictment is the government's formal charge that the defendant has committed a crime and must stand trial.

Indictment
The government's formal charge that the defendant has committed a crime and must stand trial.

Arraignment

At an arraignment, a clerk reads the formal charges of the indictment. The judge asks whether the defendant has a lawyer. If she does not, the judge urges her to get one quickly. If a defendant cannot afford a lawyer, the court will appoint one to represent her free of charge. The judge now asks the lawyer how the defendant pleads to the charges. At this stage, most defendants plead not guilty.

Discovery

During the months before trial, both prosecution and defense will prepare the most effective case possible. There is less formal discovery than in civil trials. The prosecution is obligated to hand over any evidence favorable to the defense that the defense attorney requests. The defense has a more limited obligation to inform the prosecution of its evidence. In most states, for example, if the defense will be based on an alibi, counsel must reveal the alibi to the government before trial.

Plea Bargaining

Sometime before trial, the two attorneys will meet to try to negotiate a plea bargain. A **plea bargain** is an agreement between prosecution and defense that the defendant will plead guilty to a reduced charge, and the prosecution will recommend to the judge a relatively lenient sentence. In the federal court system, about 75 percent of all prosecutions end in a plea bargain. In state court systems, the number is often higher. A judge need not accept the bargain but usually does.

For example, astronaut Lisa Nowak drove across country dressed in a wig and trenchcoat to attack fellow astronaut Colleen Shipman, whom she viewed as a romantic rival. After Nowak's arrest, police found in her car a BB gun, a knife, and surgical tubing, which was thought to be evidence of her violent intent. Nowak was charged with attempted murder and attempted kidnapping, but much of the evidence was thrown out of court under the exclusionary rule because of police misconduct. Nowak ultimately pleaded guilty to battery and burglary of a car. At that point, she had served two days in jail. She did not receive further jail time, but she was required to complete 50 hours of community service and to attend anger-management classes.

Plea bargain
An agreement in which the defendant pleads guilty to a reduced charge, and the prosecution recommends to the judge a relatively lenient sentence.

Trial and Appeal

When there is no plea bargain, the case must go to trial. The mechanics of a criminal trial are similar to those for a civil trial, described in Chapter 3, on dispute resolution. It is the prosecution's job to convince the jury beyond a reasonable doubt that the defendant committed every element of the crime charged. The defense counsel will do everything possible to win an acquittal. In federal courts, prosecutors obtain a conviction in about 80 percent of cases; in state courts, the percentage is slightly lower. Convicted defendants have a right to appeal, and again, the appellate process is similar to that described in Chapter 3.

Double Jeopardy

The prohibition against **double jeopardy** means that a defendant may be prosecuted only once for a particular criminal offense. The purpose is to prevent the government from destroying the lives of innocent citizens with repetitive prosecutions. Imagine that Rod and Lucy are accused of murdering a taxi driver. Rod is tried first and wins an acquittal. At Lucy's trial, Rod testifies that he is, indeed, the murderer. The jury acquits Lucy. The Double Jeopardy Clause prohibits the state from retrying Rod again for the same offense, even though he has now confessed to it.

Double jeopardy
A criminal defendant may be prosecuted only once for a particular criminal offense.

Punishment

The Eighth Amendment prohibits cruel and unusual punishment. The most dramatic issue litigated under this clause is the death penalty. The Supreme Court has ruled that capital punishment is not inherently unconstitutional. Most state statutes divide a capital case into two parts, so that the jury first considers only guilt or innocence, and then, if the defendant is found guilty, deliberates on the death penalty. As part of that final decision, the jury must consider aggravating and mitigating circumstances that may make the ultimate penalty more or less appropriate.[12]

As you might expect from the term "cruel and unusual," courts are generally unsympathetic to such claims unless the punishment is truly outrageous. For example, Mickle pleaded guilty to rape. The judge sentenced him to prison for five years and also ordered that he undergo a vasectomy. The appeals court ruled that this sentence was cruel and unusual. Although the operation in itself is not cruel (indeed, many men voluntarily undergo it), when imposed as punishment, it is degrading and in that sense cruel. It is also an unusual punishment.[13]

In the following case, the Supreme Court was not moved to overturn a harsh punishment.

EWING V. CALIFORNIA

538 U.S. 11, 123 S. Ct. 1179, 155 L. Ed. 2d 108
United States Supreme Court, 2003

Facts: California passed a "three strikes" law, dramatically increasing sentences for repeat offenders. A defendant with two or more serious convictions, who was convicted of a third felony, had to receive a sentence of life imprisonment. Such a sentence required the defendant to serve a minimum of 25 years, and in some cases much more.

Gary Ewing, on parole from a nine-year prison term, stole three golf clubs worth $399 each, and was prosecuted. Because he had prior convictions, the crime, normally a misdemeanor, was treated as a felony. Ewing was convicted and sentenced to 25 years to life. He appealed, claiming that the sentence violated the Eighth Amendment.

Issue: *Did Ewing's sentence violate the Eighth Amendment?*

Excerpts from Justice O'Connor's Decision: When the California Legislature enacted the three strikes law, it made a judgment that protecting the public safety requires incapacitating criminals who have already been convicted of at least one serious or violent crime. Nothing in the Eighth Amendment prohibits California from making that choice. To the contrary, our cases establish that States have a valid interest in deterring and segregating habitual criminals.

California's justification is no pretext. Recidivism is a serious public safety concern in California and throughout the Nation. According to a recent report, approximately 67 percent of former inmates released from state prisons were charged with at least one "serious" new crime within three years of their release. In particular, released property offenders like Ewing had higher recidivism rates than those released after committing violent, drug, or public-order offenses.

To be sure, California's three strikes law has sparked controversy. Critics have doubted the law's wisdom, cost-efficiency, and effectiveness in reaching its goals. This criticism is appropriately directed at the legislature, which has primary responsibility for making the difficult policy choices that underlie any criminal sentencing scheme. We do not sit as a "superlegislature" to second-guess these policy choices.

Ewing's sentence is justified by the State's public-safety interest in incapacitating and deterring recidivist felons, and amply supported by his own long, serious criminal record. Ewing has been convicted of numerous misdemeanor and felony offenses, served nine separate terms of incarceration, and committed most of his crimes while on probation or parole. His prior "strikes" were serious felonies, including robbery and three residential burglaries. To be sure, Ewing's sentence is a long one. But it reflects a rational legislative judgment, entitled to deference, that offenders

[12]*Gregg v. Georgia*, 428 U.S. 153, 96 S. Ct. 2909, 1976 U.S. LEXIS 82 (S. Ct., 1976).
[13]*Mickle v. Henrichs*, 262 F. 687 (1918).

who have committed serious or violent felonies and who continue to commit felonies must be incapacitated. The State of California was entitled to place upon Ewing the onus of one who is simply unable to bring his conduct within the social norms prescribed by the criminal law of the State.

We hold that Ewing's sentence of 25 years to life in prison, imposed for the offense of felony grand theft under the three strikes law, is not grossly disproportionate and therefore does not violate the Eighth Amendment's prohibition on cruel and unusual punishments.

Devil's Advocate Are we really going to send Ewing to prison for a minimum of 25 years—for *shoplifting?* It is true that Ewing is a recidivist, and undoubtedly a state is entitled to punish chronic troublemakers more harshly than first-time offenders. However, this still seems excessive. In California, a first-time offense of "arson causing *great bodily injury*" incurs a maximum nine-year sentence. A first-time offender convicted of voluntary manslaughter receives a sentence of no more than 11 years. Only a first-time murderer receives a penalty equal to Ewing's—25 years to life. It is unfair to Ewing to equate his property crimes with a homicide, and foolish for society to spend this much money locking him up.

The Eighth Amendment also outlaws excessive fines. Forfeiture is the most controversial topic under this clause. **Forfeiture** is a *civil* law proceeding that is permitted by many different *criminal* statutes. Once a court has convicted a defendant under certain criminal statutes—such as a controlled substance law—the government may seek forfeiture of property associated with the criminal act. *How much* property can the government take? To determine if forfeiture is fair, courts generally look at three factors: whether the property was used in committing the crime, whether it was purchased with proceeds from illegal acts, and whether the punishment is disproportionate to the defendant's wrongdoing. Neal Brunk pleaded guilty to selling 2.5 ounces of marijuana, and the government promptly sought forfeiture of his house on 90 acres, worth about $99,000. The court found that forfeiture was legitimate because Brunk had used drug money to buy the land and then sold narcotics from the property.[14] By contrast, Hosep Bajakajian attempted to leave the United States without reporting $375,000 cash to customs officials as the law requires. The government demanded forfeiture of the full sum, but the Supreme Court ruled that seizure of the entire amount was grossly disproportionate to the minor crime of failing to report cash movement.[15]

CRIMES THAT HARM BUSINESS

Businesses must deal with four major crimes: larceny, fraud, arson, and embezzlement.

Larceny

It is holiday season at the mall, the period of greatest profits—and the most crime. At the Foot Forum, a teenager limps in wearing ragged sneakers and sneaks out wearing Super Sneakers, valued at $145. Down the aisle at a home furnishing store, a man is so taken by a $375 power saw that he takes it. Sweethearts swipe sweaters, pensioners pocket produce. All are committing larceny.

[14]*U.S. v. Brunk*, 2001 U.S. App. LEXIS 7566 (4th Cir., 2001).
[15]*U.S. v. Bajakajian*, 524 U.S. 321, 118 S. Ct. 2028, 1998 U.S. LEXIS 4172 (S. Ct., 1998).

Larceny
The trespassory taking of personal property with the intent to steal it.

Larceny is the trespassory taking of personal property with the intent to steal it. "Trespassory taking" means that someone else originally has the property. The Super Sneakers are personal property (not real estate), they were in the possession of the Foot Forum, and the teenager deliberately left without paying, intending never to return the goods. That is larceny. By contrast, suppose Fast Eddie leaves Bloomingdale's in New York, descends to the subway system, and jumps over a turnstile without paying. Larceny? No. He has "taken" a service—the train ride—but not personal property.

Each year, about $10 billion in merchandise is stolen from retail stores in the United States. Economists estimate that *12 cents out of every dollar* spent in retail stores covers the cost of shoplifting. Some criminal experts believe that drug addicts commit over half of all shoplifting to support their habits. Stores have added electronic surveillance, security patrols, and magnetic antitheft devices, but the problem will not disappear.

> **Economists estimate that *12 cents out of every dollar* spent in retail stores covers the cost of shoplifting.**

Fraud

Robert Dorsey owned Bob's Chrysler in Highland, Illinois. When he bought cars, the First National Bank of Highland paid Chrysler, and Dorsey—supposedly—repaid the bank as he sold the autos. Dorsey, though, began to suffer financial problems, and the bank suspected he was selling cars without repaying his loans. A state investigator notified Dorsey that he planned to review all dealership records. One week later, a fire engulfed the dealership. An arson investigator discovered that an electric iron, connected to a timer, had been placed on a pile of financial papers doused with accelerant.

The saddest part of this true story is that it is only too common. Some experts suggest that 1 percent of corporate revenues are wasted on fraud alone. Dorsey was convicted and imprisoned for committing two crimes that cost business billions of dollars annually—fraud (for failing to repay the loans) and arson (for burning down the dealership).[16]

Fraud
Deception for the purpose of obtaining money or property.

Fraud refers to various crimes, all of which have a common element: **the deception of another person for the purpose of obtaining money or property from him**. Robert Dorsey's precise violation was bank fraud, a federal crime.[17] It is bank fraud to use deceit to obtain money, assets, securities, or other property under the control of any financial institution.

Wire Fraud and Mail Fraud

Wire and mail fraud are additional federal crimes, involving the use of interstate mail, telegram, telephone, radio, or television to obtain property by deceit.[18] For example, if Marsha makes an interstate phone call to sell land that she does not own, that is wire fraud.

Theft of Honest Services

Under traditional standards, a culprit could only be convicted of fraud if he had deceived the victim to get something of value from *her*. But what if a CEO manipulates the financial results of his company and otherwise misleads investors to keep the stock price high? He

---

[16]*United States v. Dorsey*, 27 F.3d 285, 1994 U.S. App. LEXIS 15010 (7th Cir., 1994).
[17]18 U.S.C. §1344.
[18]18 U.S.C. §§1341–1346.

has not committed fraud under this traditional definition because he did not personally obtain money from the investors—they bought their stock either from other shareholders or from the company.

To find a way to punish these wrongdoers, prosecutors looked to a statute that prohibits the **theft of honest services.**[19] Originally, this law was used to prosecute public officials who took bribes or kickbacks. But then prosecutors began to apply it to employees in the private sector as well. Prosecutors took the view that an employee violated this law if she did not fully perform the job for which she was paid. Thus, the CEO could be charged for not having done his job properly. But under this standard, the scope of the statute became enormous. In theory, an employee who called in sick so that he could watch his son's play has violated this statute. The scope of the statute permitted enormous discretion on the part of prosecutors.

The Supreme Court has stepped in to limit its scope. As the following case reveals, **the theft of honest services statute prohibits public and private employees from taking bribes or kickbacks**.

SKILLING V. UNITED STATES

130 S. Ct. 2896, 2010 U.S. LEXIS 5259
Supreme Court of the United States, 2010

Facts: The Enron Corporation was founded as an energy company in Houston, Texas. Five years later, it hired Jeffrey Skilling, a young Harvard Business School graduate, to run one of its subsidiaries. He was promoted to president and chief operating officer 11 years later. At that time, only six companies in the United States had higher revenues than Enron. Six months after Skilling's promotion, he resigned. Four months after that, Enron filed for bankruptcy protection.

The company's stock, which had been trading at $90 per share, became virtually worthless. A government investigation uncovered an elaborate conspiracy to prop up Enron's stock prices by overstating the company's financial well-being. The government prosecuted dozens of Enron employees who participated in the scheme. Skilling's indictment charged that he had violated the honest services statute. He was convicted and sentenced to 292 months imprisonment, 3 years supervised release, and $45 million in restitution. Skilling appealed, arguing that he had not violated the honest services statute because it only applied to bribery and kickback schemes. The Fifth Circuit affirmed his conviction. The Supreme Court granted *certiorari*.

Issue: *Did Skilling violate the honest services statute?*

Excerpts from Justice Ginsburg's Opinion: Unlike fraud, in which the victim's loss of money or property

supplied the defendant's gain, with one the mirror image of the other, the honest-services theory targeted corruption that lacked similar symmetry. While the offender profited, the betrayed party suffered no deprivation of money or property; instead, a third party, who had not been deceived, provided the enrichment. For example, if a city mayor (the offender) accepted a bribe from a third party in exchange for awarding that party a city contract, yet the contract terms were the same as any that could have been negotiated at arm's length, the city (the betrayed party) would suffer no tangible loss. Even if the scheme occasioned a money or property *gain* for the betrayed party, courts reasoned, actionable harm lay in the denial of that party's right to the offender's "honest services." Over time, an increasing number of courts recognized that a recreant employee—public or private—could be prosecuted under this statute if he breached his allegiance to his employer by accepting bribes or kickbacks in the course of his employment.

Skilling asserts that [the honest services statute] is unconstitutionally vague. To satisfy due process, a penal statute must define the criminal offense [1] with sufficient definiteness that ordinary people can understand what conduct is prohibited and [2] in a manner that does not encourage arbitrary and discriminatory enforcement. According to Skilling, [the honest services statute] meets neither of the two due process essentials. First, the phrase "the right of honest services," he contends, does not adequately

[19]18 U.S.C. § 1346.

define what behavior it bars. Second, he alleges, [the honest services statute's] standardless sweep allows policemen, prosecutors, and juries to pursue their personal predilections, thereby facilitating opportunistic and arbitrary prosecutions.

In the main, prosecutions under this statute involved fraudulent schemes to deprive another of honest services through bribes or kickbacks supplied by a third party who had not been deceived. Confined to these paramount applications, [the honest services statute] presents no vagueness problem. Reading the statute to proscribe a wider range of offensive conduct, we acknowledge, would raise the due process concerns underlying the vagueness doctrine. To preserve the statute without transgressing constitutional limitations, we now hold that [the honest services statute] criminalizes only the bribe-and-kickback core.

The Government did not, at any time, allege that Skilling solicited or accepted side payments from a third party in exchange for making these misrepresentations. It is therefore clear that Skilling did not commit honest-services fraud.

Skilling had been found guilty of three crimes: honest services fraud, wire fraud, and securities fraud. Although the Supreme Court ruled that Skilling had not violated the honest services statute, they remanded the case to the appeals court to determine if the other two convictions were independent enough to stand on their own without the honest services element. If not, he would have to be retried. The appeals court did uphold Skilling's two other convictions.

Insurance Fraud

Insurance fraud is another common crime. A Ford suddenly swerves in front of a Toyota, causing it to brake hard. A Mercedes, unable to stop, slams into the Toyota, as the Ford races away. Regrettable accident? No: a "swoop and squat" fraud scheme. The Ford and Toyota drivers were working together, hoping to cause an accident with someone else. The "injured" Toyota driver now goes to a third member of the fraud team—a dishonest doctor—who diagnoses serious back and neck injuries and predicts long-term pain and disability. The driver files a claim against the Mercedes's driver, whose insurer may be forced to pay tens or even hundreds of thousands of dollars for an accident that was no accident. Insurance companies investigate countless cases like this each year, trying to distinguish the honest victim from the criminal.

EXAM Strategy

Question: Eric mails glossy brochures to 25,000 people, offering to sell them a one-month time-share in a stylish apartment in Las Vegas. The brochure depicts an imposing building, an opulent apartment, and spectacular pools. To reserve a space, customers need only send in a $2,000 deposit. Three hundred people respond, sending in the money. In fact, there is no such building. Eric, planning to flee with the cash, is arrested and prosecuted. His sentence could be as long as 20 years. (1) With what crime is he charged? (2) Is this a felony or misdemeanor prosecution? (3) Does Eric have a right to a jury trial? (4) What is the government's burden of proof?

Strategy: (1) Eric is deceiving people, and that should tell you the *type* of crime. (2, 3) The potential 20-year sentence determines whether Eric's crime is a misdemeanor or felony, and whether or not he is entitled to a jury trial. (4) We know that the government has the burden of proof in criminal prosecutions—but *how much* evidence must it offer?

Result: Eric has committed fraud. A felony is one in which the sentence could be a year or more. The potential penalty here is 20 years, so the crime is a felony. Eric has a right to a jury, as does any defendant whose sentence could be six months or longer. The prosecution must prove its case beyond a reasonable doubt, a much higher burden than that in a civil case.

Arson

Robert Dorsey, the Chrysler dealer, committed a second serious crime. **Arson** is the malicious use of fire or explosives to damage or destroy any real estate or personal property. It is both a federal and a state crime. Dorsey used arson to conceal his bank fraud. Most arsonists hope to collect on insurance policies. Every year thousands of buildings burn, particularly in economically depressed neighborhoods, as owners try to make a quick kill or extricate themselves from financial difficulties. Everyone who purchases insurance ends up paying higher premiums because of this immorality.

Arson
The malicious use of fire or explosives to damage or destroy real estate or personal property.

Embezzlement

This crime also involves illegally obtaining property, but with one big difference: the culprit begins with legal possession. **Embezzlement** is the fraudulent conversion of property already in the defendant's possession.

This is a story without romance: for 15 years, Kristy Watts worked part-time as a bookkeeper for romance writer Danielle Steele, handling payroll and accounting. During that time, Watts stole $768,000 despite earning a salary of $200,000 a year. Watts said that she had been motivated by envy and jealousy. She was sentenced to three years in prison and agreed to pay her former boss almost $1 million.

Embezzlement
The fraudulent conversion of property already in the defendant's possession.

CRIMES COMMITTED BY BUSINESS

A corporation can be found guilty of a crime based on the conduct of any of its **agents**, who include anyone undertaking work on behalf of the corporation. An agent can be a corporate officer, an accountant hired to audit financial statements, a sales clerk, or almost any other person performing a job at the company's request.

If an agent commits a criminal act within the scope of his employment and with the intent to benefit the corporation, the company is liable.[20] This means that the agent himself must first be guilty. If the agent is guilty, the corporation is, too.

Critics believe that the criminal law has gone too far. It is unfair, they argue, to impose *criminal* liability on a corporation, and thus penalize the shareholders, unless high-ranking officers were directly involved in the illegal conduct. The following case concerns a corporation's responsibility for a death caused by its employee.

---

[20]*New York Central & Hudson River R.R. Co. v. United States,* 212 U.S. 481, 29 S. Ct. 304, 1909 U.S. LEXIS 1832 (S. Ct., 1909). Note that what counts is the intention to benefit, not actual benefit. A corporation will not escape liability by showing that the scheme failed.

COMMONWEALTH V. ANGELO TODESCA CORP.

446 Mass. 128, 842 N.E. 2d 930
Supreme Judicial Court of Massachusetts, 2006

Facts: Brian Gauthier, an experienced truck driver, worked for Todesca, a paving company. After about a year driving a particular 10-wheel tri-axle dump truck, Gauthier noticed that the back-up alarm had stopped working. When he reported this, the company mechanic realized that the old alarm needed replacement. The mechanic had none in stock, so the company instructed Gauthier to drive the truck without the alarm.

About a month later, Gauthier and other Todesca drivers were delivering asphalt to the work site on a highway at the entrance to a shopping mall. A police officer directed the construction vehicles and the routine mall traffic. A different driver asked the officer to "watch our backs" as the trucks backed through the intersection. All of the other trucks were equipped with back-up alarms. When it was Gauthier's turn to back up, he struck the police officer, killing him.

The state charged the Todesca corporation with motor vehicle homicide, and the jury found the company guilty. The trial judge imposed a fine—of $2,500. The court of appeals reversed the conviction, and the prosecution appealed to the state's highest court.

Issue: *Could the company be found guilty of motor vehicle homicide?*

Excerpts from Justice Spina's Decision: Before criminal liability may be imposed on a corporate defendant, the Commonwealth must prove that the individual for whose conduct it seeks to charge the corporation criminally was placed in a position by the corporation where he had enough responsibility to act for the corporation, and that he was acting in behalf of the corporation [when] he committed a criminal act.

The defendant maintains that a corporation never can be criminally liable for motor vehicle homicide because the language of a criminal statute must be construed strictly, and a "corporation" cannot "operate" a vehicle. We agree with the Commonwealth. Because a corporation is not a living person, it can act only through its agents. By the defendant's reasoning, a corporation never could be liable for any crime. A "corporation" can no more serve alcohol to minors, or bribe government officials, or falsify data on loan applications, than operate a vehicle negligently: only human agents, acting for the corporation, are capable of these actions. Nevertheless, we consistently have held that a corporation may be criminally liable for such acts when performed by corporate employees, acting within the scope of their employment and on behalf of the corporation.

It was undisputed that Gauthier's truck was not equipped with a functioning back-up alarm at the time of the collision, and that he knew the alarm was missing. Although a back-up alarm was not required by statute, the defendant had a written safety policy mandating that all its trucks be equipped with such alarms. An employee's violation of his employer's rules, intended to protect the safety of third persons, is evidence of the employee's negligence, for which the employer may be held liable.

Other drivers at the work site had functioning back-up alarms, and although they spoke moments before the collision, Gauthier never informed the victim that his truck did not have an alarm. The jury could have inferred that the victim, a veteran police officer, was aware that the defendant's custom was to equip its trucks with back-up alarms, and that the victim expected to hear a back-up alarm when a driver operated a truck in reverse.

The jury also could have inferred that an alarm on Gauthier's truck would have sounded practically in the victim's ear, alerting him to the truck's movement in time to get out of its way. The back-up alarm makes a distinctive beeping sound, intended to warn people behind the vehicle that it is operating in reverse, and the victim did not realize Gauthier's truck was backing up because he did not hear that sound.

Affirmed.

Selected Crimes Committed by Business
Workplace Crimes

The workplace can be dangerous. Working on an assembly line exposes factory employees to fast-moving machinery. For a roofer, the first slip may be the last. The invisible radiation in a nuclear power plant can be deadlier than a bullet. The most important statute regulating the workplace is the federal **Occupational Safety and Health Act of 1970 (OSHA)**,[21] which sets safety standards for many industries.[22] May a state government go beyond standards set by OSHA and use the criminal law to punish dangerous conditions? In *People v. O'Neill*,[23] the courts of Illinois answered that question with a potent "yes," permitting a *murder prosecution* against corporate executives themselves.

Film Recovery Systems was an Illinois corporation in business to extract silver from used X-ray film and then resell it. Steven O'Neill was president of Film Recovery, Charles Kirschbaum was its plant manager, and Daniel Rodriguez the foreman. To extract the silver, workers at Film Recovery soaked the X-ray film in large, open, bubbling vats that contained sodium cyanide.

A worker named Stefan Golab became faint. He left the production area and walked to the lunchroom, where workers found him trembling and foaming at the mouth. He lost consciousness. Rushed to a hospital, he was pronounced dead on arrival. The medical examiner determined that Golab died from acute cyanide poisoning caused by inhalation of cyanide fumes in the plant.

Illinois indicted Film Recovery and several of its managers for murder. The indictment charged that O'Neill and Kirschbaum committed murder by failing to disclose to Golab that he was working with cyanide and other potentially lethal substances and by failing to provide him with appropriate and necessary safety equipment.

The case was tried to a judge without a jury. Workers testified that O'Neill, Kirschbaum, and other managers never told them they were using cyanide or that the fumes they inhaled could be harmful; that management made no effort to ventilate the factory; that Film Recovery gave the workers no goggles or protective clothing; that the chemicals they worked with burned their skin; that breathing was difficult in the plant because of strong, foul orders; and that workers suffered frequent dizziness, nausea, and vomiting.

The trial judge found O'Neill, Kirschbaum, and others guilty of murder. Illinois defines murder as performing an act that the defendant *knows will create a strong probability of death* in the victim, and the judge found they had done that. He found Film Recovery guilty of involuntary manslaughter. Involuntary manslaughter is *recklessly* performing an act that causes death. He sentenced O'Neill, Kirschbaum, and Rodriguez to 25 years in prison.

The defendants appealed, contending that the verdicts were inconsistent. They argued, and the Illinois Court of Appeals agreed, that the judge had made contradictory findings. Murder required the specific intent of *knowing there was a strong probability of death*, whereas the manslaughter conviction required *reckless* conduct. The appeals court reversed the convictions and remanded for a new trial.

Moments before the new trial was to start, O'Neill, Kirschbaum, and Rodriguez all pleaded guilty to involuntary manslaughter. They received sentences of three years, two years, and four months, respectively.

Hiring Illegal Workers

Employers are required to verify their workers' eligibility for employment in the United States. It is illegal to knowingly employ unauthorized workers. Within three days of hiring a worker, the employer must complete an I-9 form, which lists the items that can be used as documentation of eligibility. The government has the right to arrest illegal employees, and it can also bring charges against the business that hired them.

---

[21] 29 U.S.C. §§651 et seq. (1982).
[22] See Chapter 17 on employment law.
[23] 194 Ill. App. 3d 79, 550 N.E.2d 1090, 1990 Ill. App. LEXIS 65 (Ill. App. Ct. 1990).

RICO

**Racketeer Influenced and
Corrupt Organizations Act
(RICO)**

A powerful federal statute,
originally aimed at organized
crime, now used in many
criminal prosecutions and civil
lawsuits.

The **Racketeer Influenced and Corrupt Organizations Act** (RICO) is one of the most powerful and controversial statutes ever written.[24] Congress passed the law primarily to prevent gangsters from taking money they earned illegally and investing it in legitimate businesses. But RICO has expanded far beyond the original intentions of Congress and is now used more often against ordinary businesses than against organized criminals. Some regard this wide application as a tremendous advance in law enforcement, but others view it as an oppressive weapon used to club ethical companies into settlements they should never have to make.

What is a violation of this law? **RICO prohibits using two or more racketeering acts to accomplish any of these goals: (1) investing in or acquiring legitimate businesses with criminal money; (2) maintaining or acquiring businesses through criminal activity; or (3) operating businesses through criminal activity.**

What does that mean in English? It is a two-step process to prove that a person or an organization has violated RICO.

Racketeering acts

Any of a long list of specified
crimes, such as
embezzlement, arson, mail
fraud, wire fraud, and so forth.

- The prosecutor must show that the defendant committed two or more **racketeering acts**, which are any of a long list of specified crimes: embezzlement, arson, mail fraud, wire fraud, and so forth. Thus, if a gangster ordered a building torched in January and then burned a second building in October, that would be two racketeering acts. If a stockbroker told two customers that Bronx Gold Mines was a promising stock, when she knew that it was worthless, that would be two racketeering acts.

- The prosecutor must then show that the defendant used these racketeering acts to accomplish one of the three *purposes* listed above. If the gangster committed two arsons and then used the insurance payments to buy a dry cleaning business, that would violate RICO. If the stockbroker gave fraudulent advice and used the commissions to buy advertising for her firm, that would also violate RICO.

The government may prosecute both individuals and organizations for violating RICO. For example, the government prosecuted financier Michael Milken for manipulating stock prices. It also threatened to prosecute his employer, Drexel Burnham Lambert. If the government proves its case, the defendant can be hit with large fines and a prison sentence of up to 20 years. RICO also permits the government to seek forfeiture of the defendant's property. A court may order a convicted defendant to hand over any property or money used in the criminal acts or derived from them. Courts often freeze a defendant's assets once charges are brought to ensure that he will not hide the assets. If all his assets are frozen, he will have a hard time paying his defense lawyer, so a freeze often encourages a defendant to plea bargain on a lesser charge. Both Milken and Drexel entered into plea agreements with the government, rather than face a freeze on their assets, or in Milken's case, a long prison sentence.

In addition to criminal penalties, RICO also creates civil law liabilities. The government, organizations, and individuals all have the right to file civil lawsuits, seeking damages and, if necessary, injunctions. For example, a physician sued State Farm Insurance, alleging that the company had hired doctors to produce false medical reports that the company used to cut off claims by injured policy holders. As a result of these fake reports, the company refused to pay the plaintiff for legitimate services he performed on the policy holders. RICO is powerful (and for defendants, frightening) in part because a civil plaintiff can recover **treble damages;** that is, a judgment for three times the harm actually suffered, as well as attorney's fees.

---

[24]18 U.S.C. §§1961–1968.

Money Laundering

Money laundering consists of taking the proceeds of certain criminal acts and either (1) using the money to promote crime, or (2) attempting to conceal the source of the money.[25]

Money laundering is an important part of major criminal enterprises. Successful criminals earn enormous sums, which they must filter back into the flow of commerce so that their crimes go undetected. Laundering is an essential part of the corrosive traffic in drugs. Profits, all in cash, may mount so swiftly that dealers struggle to use the money without attracting the government's attention. For example, Colombian drug cartels set up a sophisticated system in which they shipped money to countries such as Dubai that do not keep records on cash transactions. This money was then transferred to the U.S. disguised as offshore loans. Prosecution by the U.S. government led to the demise of some of the banks involved.

But drug money is not the only or even major component of so-called flight capital. Criminals also try to hide the vast sums they earn from arms dealing and tax evasion. Some of this money is used to support terrorist organizations.

Money laundering
Using the proceeds of criminal acts either to promote crime or conceal the source of the money.

EXAM Strategy

Question: Explain the difference between embezzlement and money laundering. Give an example of each.

Strategy: Both crimes involve money illegally obtained, but they are very different. As to embezzlement, how did the criminal obtain the funds? In a laundering case, to what use is the criminal trying to put the cash?

Result: Embezzlement refers to fraudulently taking money that is already in the defendant's possession. For example, if a financial advisor, *lawfully entrusted* with his client's funds for investing, uses some of the cash to buy himself a luxurious yacht, he has embezzled the client's money. Money laundering consists of taking *illegally obtained* money and either using the funds to promote additional crimes or attempting to *conceal* the source of the cash. Thus, an arms dealer might launder money so that he can use it to finance a terrorist organization.

Other Crimes

Additional crimes that affect business appear elsewhere in the text. An increasing number of federal and state statutes are designed to punish those who harm the environment. (See Chapter 27, on environmental law.) Antitrust violations, in which a corporation fixes prices, can lead to criminal prosecutions. (See Chapter 22, on antitrust law.) Finally, securities fraud is a crime and can lead to severe prison sentences. (See Chapter 21, on securities regulation.)

Punishing a Corporation

Fines

The most common punishment for a corporation is a fine, as demonstrated in the Todesca case. This makes sense in that the purpose of a business is to earn a profit, and a fine, theoretically, hurts. But most fines are modest by the present standards of corporate wealth.

---

[25]18 U.S.C. §§1956 et seq.

In the Todesca prosecution, does a $2,500 fine force corporate leaders to be more cautious, or does it teach them that cutting corners makes economic sense, because the penalties will be a tolerable cost of doing business?

Sometimes the fines are stiffer. British Petroleum (BP) was found guilty of two serious environmental violations. In Alaska, the company's failure to inspect and clean pipelines caused 200,000 gallons of crude oil to spill onto the tundra. In Texas, the company's failure to follow standard procedures for ensuring safe refineries caused a catastrophic explosion that killed 15 people and injured 170 more. The total fine for both criminal violations was $62 million.[26] Is that enough to change BP's practices? Evidently not. In the spring of 2010, a BP well called Deepwater Horizon exploded, killing 11 workers and releasing into the Gulf of Mexico the largest marine oil spill ever. The Deepwater rig had violated many safety requirements.

Compliance Programs

Federal Sentencing Guidelines

The detailed rules that judges must follow when sentencing defendants convicted of crimes in federal court.

Compliance program

A plan to prevent and detect criminal conduct at all levels of the company.

The **Federal Sentencing Guidelines** are the detailed rules that judges must follow when sentencing defendants convicted of crimes in federal court. The guidelines instruct judges to determine whether, at the time of the crime, the corporation had in place a serious **compliance program**; that is, a plan to prevent and detect criminal conduct at all levels of the company. A company that can point to a detailed, functioning compliance program may benefit from a dramatic reduction in the fine or other punishment meted out. Indeed, a tough compliance program may even convince federal investigators to curtail an investigation and to limit any prosecution to those directly involved, rather than attempting to get a conviction against high-ranking officers or the company itself.

For a compliance plan to be deemed effective:

- The program must be reasonably capable of reducing the prospect of criminal conduct.
- Specific, high-level officers must be responsible for overseeing the program.
- The company must not place in charge any officers it knows or should have known, from past experience, are likely to engage in illegal conduct.
- The company must effectively communicate the program to all employees and agents.
- The company must ensure compliance by monitoring employees in a position to cheat and by promptly disciplining any who break the law.

Chapter Conclusion

Crime has an enormous impact on business. Companies are victims of crimes, and sometimes they also commit criminal actions. Successful business leaders are ever-vigilant to protect their company from those who wish to harm it, whether from the inside or the outside.

---

[26]Source: *http://epa.gov/*.

EXAM REVIEW

1. **BURDEN OF PROOF** In all prosecutions, the government must prove its case beyond a reasonable doubt. (p. 165)

> **Question:** Arnie owns a two-family house in a poor section of the city. A fire breaks out, destroying the building and causing $150,000 damage to an adjacent store. The state charges Arnie with arson. Simultaneously, Vickie, the store owner, sues Arnie for the damage to her property. Both cases are tried to juries, and the two juries hear identical evidence of Arnie's actions. But the criminal jury acquits Arnie, while the civil jury awards Vickie $150,000. How did that happen?
>
> **Strategy:** The opposite outcomes are probably due to the different burdens of proof in a civil and criminal case. Make sure you know that distinction. (See the "Result" at the end of this section.)

2. **RIGHT TO A JURY**. A criminal defendant has a right to a trial by jury for any charge that could result in a sentence of six months or longer. (p. 165)

3. **DURESS** A defendant is not guilty of a crime if she committed it under duress. However, the defendant bears the burden of proving by a preponderance of the evidence that she acted under duress. (p. 166)

4. **ENTRAPMENT**. When the government induces the defendant to break the law, the prosecution must prove beyond a reasonable doubt that the defendant was predisposed to commit the crime. (p. 166)

5. **FOURTH AMENDMENT**. The Fourth Amendment to the Constitution prohibits the government from making illegal searches and seizures of individuals, corporations, partnerships, and other organizations. (p. 166)

6. **WARRANT**. As a general rule, the police must obtain a warrant before conducting a search, but there are seven circumstances under which the police may search without a warrant. (pp. 166–167)

7. **THE EXCLUSIONARY RULE**. Under the exclusionary rule, a prosecutor may not use evidence obtained illegally. (pp. 167–169)

8. **FIFTH AMENDMENT** The Fifth Amendment requires due process in all criminal procedures and prohibits double jeopardy and self-incrimination. (pp. 170–172)

9. **SIXTH AMENDMENT** The Sixth Amendment guarantees criminal defendants the right to a lawyer. (p. 172)

10. **EIGHTH AMENDMENT** The Eighth Amendment prohibits excessive fines and cruel and unusual punishments. (pp. 174–175)

11. **LARCENY** Larceny is the trespassory taking of personal property with the intent to steal. (pp. 175–176)

12. **FRAUD** Fraud refers to a variety of crimes, all of which involve the deception of another person for the purpose of obtaining money or property. (p. 176)

EXAM Strategy

Question: Chuck is a DJ on a radio station. A music company offers to pay him every time he plays one of its songs. Soon enough, Chuck is earning $10,000 a week in these extra payments, and his listeners love the music. In Chuck's view, this is a win-win situation. Is Chuck right?

Strategy: This is not traditional fraud because Chuck is not getting money from the people he is cheating—his listeners. Indeed, they are happy. Is there another type of fraud that applies in this situation? (See the "Result" at the end of this section.)

13. **ARSON** Arson is the malicious use of fire or explosives to damage or destroy real estate or personal property. (p. 179)

14. **EMBEZZLEMENT** Embezzlement is the fraudulent conversion of property already in the defendant's possession. (p.179)

15. **CORPORATE LIABILITY** If a company's agent commits a criminal act within the scope of her employment and with the intent to benefit the corporation, the company is liable. (pp. 179–181)

16. **RICO** RICO prohibits using two or more racketeering acts to invest in legitimate business or carry on certain other criminal acts. RICO permits civil lawsuits as well as criminal prosecutions. (pp. 182–183)

EXAM Strategy

Question: Cheryl is a bank teller. She figures out a way to steal $99.99 per day in cash without getting caught. She takes the money daily for eight months and invests it in a catering business she is starting with Floyd, another teller. When Floyd learns what she is doing, he tries it, but is caught in his first attempt. He and Cheryl are both prosecuted.

(a) Both are guilty only of larceny.

(b) Both are guilty of larceny and violating RICO.

(c) Both are guilty of embezzlement; Cheryl is also guilty of violating RICO.

(d) Both are guilty of embezzlement and violating RICO.

Strategy: You need to know the difference between larceny and embezzlement. What is it? Once you have that figured out, focus on RICO. The government must prove two things: First, that the defendant committed crimes more than once— how many times? Second, that the defendant used the criminal proceeds for a specific purpose—what? (See the "Result" at the end of this section.)

17. **MONEY LAUNDERING** Money laundering consists of taking profits from a criminal act and either using them to promote crime or attempting to conceal their source. (p. 183)

> **1. Result:** The plaintiff offered enough proof to convince a jury by a preponderance of the evidence that Arnie had damaged her store. However that same evidence, offered in a criminal prosecution, was not enough to persuade the jury beyond a reasonable doubt that Arnie had lit the fire.
>
> **12. Result:** Chuck has committed a theft of honest services because he has taken a bribe.
>
> **16. Result:** Cheryl and Floyd both committed embezzlement, which refers to fraudulently taking money that was properly in their possession. Floyd did it once, but a RICO conviction requires two or more racketeering acts—Floyd has not violated RICO. Cheryl embezzled dozens of times and invested the money in a legitimate business. She is guilty of embezzlement and RICO; the correct answer is C.

MULTIPLE-CHOICE QUESTIONS

1. In a criminal case, which statement is true?
   (a) The prosecution must prove the government's case by a preponderance of the evidence.
   (b) The criminal defendant is entitled to a lawyer even if she cannot afford to pay for it herself.
   (c) The police are never allowed to question the accused without a lawyer present.
   (d) All federal crimes are felonies.

2. The police are not required to obtain a warrant before conducting a search if:
   (a) a reliable informant has told them they will find evidence of a crime in a particular location.
   (b) they have a warrant for part of a property and another section of the property is in plain view.
   (c) they see someone on the street who could possibly have committed a criminal act.
   (d) someone living on the property has consented to the search.

3. Under the exclusionary rule, which statement is true?
   (a) Evidence must be excluded from trial if the search warrant is defective, even if the police believed at the time of the search that it was valid.
   (b) The prosecution cannot use any evidence the police found at the site of the illegal search, but it can use any evidence the police discover elsewhere as a result of the illegal search.
   (c) Any statements a defendant makes after arrest are inadmissible if the police do not read him his Miranda rights.
   (d) If a conviction is overturned because of the exclusionary rule, the prosecution is not allowed to retry the defendant.

4. Benry asks his girlfriend, Alina, to drive his car to the repair shop. She drives his car all right—to Las Vegas, where she hits the slots. Alina has committed:

   (a) fraud.

   (b) embezzlement.

   (c) larceny.

   (d) a RICO violation.

5. Which of the following elements is *required* for a RICO conviction?

   (a) Investment in a legitimate business

   (b) Two or more criminal acts

   (c) Maintaining or acquiring businesses through criminal activity

   (d) Operating a business through criminal activity

Essay Questions

1. **YOU BE THE JUDGE WRITING PROBLEM** An undercover drug informant learned from a mutual friend that Philip Friedman "knew where to get marijuana." The informant asked Friedman three times to get him some marijuana, and Friedman agreed after the third request. Shortly thereafter, Friedman sold the informant a small amount of the drug. The informant later offered to sell Friedman three pounds of marijuana. They negotiated the price and then made the sale. Friedman was tried for trafficking in drugs. He argued entrapment. Was Friedman entrapped? **Argument for Friedman**: The undercover agent had to ask three times before Friedman sold him a small amount of drugs. A real drug dealer, predisposed to commit the crime, leaps at an opportunity to sell. If the government spends time and money luring innocent people into the commission of crimes, all of us are the losers. **Argument for the Government**: Government officials suspected Friedman of being a sophisticated drug dealer, and they were right. When he had a chance to buy three pounds, a quantity only a dealer would purchase, he not only did so, but he bargained with skill, showing a working knowledge of the business. Friedman was not entrapped—he was caught.

2. Conley owned video poker machines. Although they are outlawed in Pennsylvania, he placed them in bars and clubs. He used profits from the machines to buy more machines. Is he guilty of money laundering?

3. Karin made illegal firearm purchases at a gun show. At her trial, she alleged that she had committed this crime because her boyfriend had threatened to harm her and her two daughters if she did not. Her lawyer asked the judge to instruct the jury that the prosecution had an obligation to prove beyond a reasonable doubt that Karin had acted freely. Instead, the judge told the jury that Karin had the burden of proving duress by a preponderance of the evidence. Who is correct?

4. An informant bought drugs from Dorian. The police obtained a search warrant to search Dorian's house. But before they acted on the warrant, they sent the informant back to try again. This time, Dorian said he did not have any drugs. The police then acted on the warrant and searched his house. Did the police have probable cause?

5. Shawn was caught stealing letters from mailboxes. After pleading guilty, he was sentenced to two months in prison and three years supervised release. One of the supervised release conditions required him to stand outside a post office for eight hours wearing a signboard stating, "I stole mail. This is my punishment." He appealed this requirement on the grounds that it constituted cruel and unusual punishment. Do you agree?

DISCUSSION QUESTIONS

1. Under British law, a police officer must now say the following to a suspect placed under arrest: "You do not have to say anything. But if you do not mention now something which you later use in your defense, the court may decide that your failure to mention it now strengthens the case against you. A record will be made of anything you say and it may be given in evidence if you are brought to trial." What is the goal of this British law? What does a police officer in the United States have to say, and what difference does it make at the time of an arrest? Which approach is better?

2. **Ethics** You are a prosecutor who thinks it is possible that Naonka, in her role as CEO of a brokerage firm, has stolen money from her customers, many of whom are not well off. If you charge her and her company with RICO violations, you know that she is likely to plea bargain because otherwise her assets and those of the company may be frozen by the court. As part of the plea bargain, you might be able to get her to disclose evidence about other people who might have taken part in this criminal activity. But you do not have any hard evidence at this point. Would such an indictment be ethical? Do the ends justify the means? Is it worth it to harm Naonka for the chance of protecting thousands of innocent investors?

3. Van is brought to the police station for questioning about a shooting at a mall. The police read him his Miranda rights. For the rest of the three-hour interrogation, he remains silent except for a few one-word responses. Has he waived his right to remain silent? Can those few words be used against him in court?

4. Police arrested Hank on a warrant issued in a neighboring county. When they searched him, the police found drugs and a gun. Only later did the police discover that when they had used the warrant, it was not valid because it had been recalled months earlier. The notice of recall had not been entered into the database. Should the evidence of drugs and a gun be suppressed under the exclusionary rule?

5. Andy was arrested for driving under the influence of alcohol (DUI). He had already been convicted of another driving offense. The court in the *first* offense was notified of this later DUI charge and took that information into consideration when determining Andy's sentence. Did the state violate Andy's protection against double jeopardy when it subsequently tried and convicted him for the DUI offense?

CHAPTER 8

INTERNATIONAL LAW

The month after Anfernee graduates from business school, he opens a clothing store. Sales are brisk, but Anfernee is making little profit because his American-made clothes are expensive. Then an Asian company offers to sell him identical merchandise for 45 percent less than the American suppliers charge. Anfernee is elated, but quickly begins to wonder: Why is the new price so low? The sales representative expects Anfernee to sell no clothes except his. Is that legal? He also requests a $50,000 cash "commission" to smooth the export process in his country. That sounds suspicious, too. The questions multiply. Will the contract be written in English or a foreign language? Must Anfernee pay in dollars or some other currency? The foreign company wants a letter of credit. What does that mean? What law will govern the agreement? If the clothes are defective, how will disputes be resolved—and where?

© Steve Allen/Jupiterimages

Transnational business grows with breathtaking speed. The United States now exports more than $1 trillion worth of goods and services. Leading exports include industrial machinery, computers, aircraft, agricultural products, electronic equipment, and chemicals. Anfernee should put this lesson under his cap: the world is now one vast economy, and deals can cross borders quickly.

> The world is now one vast economy, and deals can cross borders quickly.

TRADE REGULATION: THE BIG PICTURE

Nations regulate international trade in many ways. In this section, we look at export and import controls that affect trade out of and into the United States. **Exporting** is shipping goods or services out of a country. The United States, with its huge farms, is the world's largest exporter of agricultural products. **Importing** is shipping goods and services into a country. The United States suffers trade deficits every year because the value of its imports exceeds that of its exports, as the following table demonstrates.

Exporting
Shipping goods or services out of a country.

Importing
Shipping goods or services into a country.

Rank	Country	Exports (in billions of U.S. dollars)	Imports (in billions of U.S. dollars)
	Total, All Countries	1,278	1,912
1	Canada	249	277
2	China	92	365
3	Mexico	163	230

© Cengage Learning 2014

Export Controls

You and a friend open an electronics business, intending to purchase goods in this country for sale abroad. A representative of Interlex stops in to see you. Interlex is a Latin American electronics company, and the firm wants you to help it acquire a certain kind of infrared dome, that helps helicopters identify nearby aircraft. You find a Pennsylvania company that manufactures the domes, and you realize that you can buy and sell them to Interlex for a handsome profit. Any reason not to? As a matter of fact, there is.

All nations limit what may be exported. In the United States, several statutes do this. The **Export Administration Act of 1985**[1] is one. This statute balances the need for free trade, which is essential in a capitalist society, with important requirements of national security. The statute permits the federal government to restrict exports if they endanger national security, harm foreign policy goals, or drain scarce materials.

The Secretary of Commerce makes a **Controlled Commodities List** of those items that meet any of these criteria. No one may export any commodity on the list without a license.

A second major limitation comes from the **Arms Export Control Act.**[2] This statute permits the President to create a second list of controlled goods, all related to military weaponry. Again, no person may export any listed item without a license.

The AECA will prohibit you from exporting the infrared domes. They are used in the guidance system of one of the most sophisticated weapons in the American defense arsenal. Foreign governments have attempted to obtain the equipment through official channels, but the federal government has placed the domes on the list of restricted military items. When a U.S. citizen did send such goods overseas, he was convicted and imprisoned.[3]

---

[1] 50 U.S.C. §2402 (1994).
[2] 22 U.S.C. §2778 (1994).
[3] *United States v. Tsai*, 954 F.2d 155, 1992 U.S. App. LEXIS 601 (3d Cir. 1992).

Import Controls

Tariffs

Tariffs are the most widespread method of limiting what may be imported into a nation. **A tariff is a tax imposed on goods when they enter a country.** Tariffs are also called *duties*. Nations use tariffs primarily to protect their domestic industries. Because the company importing the goods must pay this duty, the importer's costs increase, making the merchandise more expensive for consumers. This renders domestic products more attractive. High tariffs unquestionably help local industry, but they may harm local buyers. Consumers often benefit from zero tariffs because the unfettered competition drives down prices.

Tariffs change frequently and vary widely from one country to another. For manufactured goods, the United States imposes an average tariff of less than 4 percent, about the same as that in the European Union. However, some major trading partners around the world set tariffs of 10 to 30 percent for identical items, with those duties generally being highest in developing countries. Foodstuffs show even greater diversity. For agricultural products, average tariffs are about 25 percent in North America, but over 100 percent in South Asia. As we will see later in the chapter, regional trade treaties have changed the tariff landscape. The majority of all U.S. products entering Mexico are duty free. Almost all trade between Canada and the United States is done with zero tariffs, which is partly why the two nations do more bilateral commerce than any others in the world.

Classification   The U.S. Customs Service[4] imposes tariffs at the point of entry into the United States. A customs official inspects the merchandise as it arrives and classifies it, in other words, decides precisely what the goods are. This decision is critical because tariffs can vary greatly depending on the classification. Disputes at this stage typically involve an importer claiming that the Customs Service has imposed the wrong classification. Companies will often go to great lengths to convince a court to lower tariffs on their products.

In the following case, Isotoner claimed that a tariff violated the Constitution. Did the company make a sensible argument? You be the judge.

---

[4]The Customs Service is part of the United States Customs and Border Protection, which is itself a division of the Department of Homeland Security.

You be the Judge

TOTES-ISOTONER CO. V. UNITED STATES
594 F.3d 1346
United States Court of Appeals for the Federal Circuit, 2010

Facts: Isotoner imports gloves for sale in the United States. The U.S. imposes a higher tariff on "men's" leather gloves than it does on gloves manufactured "for other persons." Isotoner argued that this difference violated the Constitution's Equal Protection Clause and amounted to illegal gender discrimination. The lower court dismissed the complaint, and Isotoner appealed.

Issue: *Do differing tariff rates for men's and women's gloves amount to illegal gender discrimination?*

Argument for Isotoner: Because the Constitution requires equal protection under the law, the government must treat people the same. In this instance, the government treats men worse than women—with the result that men will have to pay more for gloves. This is unacceptable. Surely this court would not allow a special tax on yarmulkes, or higher tariffs linked to race. Distinctions that disfavor an entire group of people cannot stand.

Argument for the United States: To be in violation of the Equal Protection Clause, the government must intend to discriminate. That is not the case here. Tariff rates are set for a variety of reasons. Men's and women's gloves may be made by different companies, in different countries, with different impacts on American industry. Surely the government has the discretion to set different tariff rates for gloves or any other kind of imported goods.

Valuation   After classifying the imported goods, customs officials impose the appropriate duty **ad valorem**, meaning "according to the value of the goods." In other words, the service must determine the value of the merchandise before it can tax a percentage of that value. This step can be equally contentious, since goods will have different prices at each stage of manufacturing and delivery. The question is supposed to be settled by the **transaction value** of the goods, meaning the price actually paid for the merchandise when sold for export to the United States (plus shipping and other minor costs). But there is often room for debate, so importers use customs agents to help negotiate the most favorable valuation.

Ad valorem
Customs officials impose duties "according to the value of the goods."

Duties for Dumping and Subsidizing

Dumping means selling merchandise at one price in the domestic market and at a cheaper, unfair price in an international market. Suppose a Singapore company, CelMaker, makes cellular telephones for $20 per unit and sells them in the United States for $12 each, vastly undercutting domestic American competitors. CelMaker may be willing to suffer short-term losses in order to bankrupt competitors. Once it has gained control of that market, it will raise its prices, more than compensating for its initial losses. And CelMaker may get help from its home government. Suppose the Singapore government prohibits foreign cellular phones from entering Singapore. CelMaker may sell its phones for $75 at home, earning such high profits that it can afford the temporary losses in America.

Dumping
Selling merchandise at one price in the domestic market and at a cheaper, unfair price in an international market.

In the United States, the Commerce Department investigates suspected dumping. If the department concludes that the foreign company is selling items at **less than fair value**, and that this harms an American industry, it will impose a **dumping duty** that is sufficiently high to put the foreign goods back on fair footing with domestic products.

Subsidized goods are also unfair. Suppose the Singapore government permits CelMaker to pay no taxes for 10 years. This enormous benefit will enable the company to produce cheap phones and undersell competitors. Again, the United States imposes a tariff on subsidized goods, called **countervailing duties**. If CelMaker sells phones for $15 that would cost an unsubsidized competitor $21 to make, it will pay a $6 countervailing duty on every phone entering the United States.

Treaties

Recall from Chapter 1 that the President makes treaties with foreign nations. To take effect, treaties must then be approved by at least two-thirds of the United States Senate. This section will examine three significant trade agreements.

General Agreement on Tariffs and Trade (GATT)

What is GATT? The greatest boon to American commerce in a century—or perhaps it is the worst assault on the American economy in 200 years. It depends on whom you ask. Let's start where everyone agrees.

GATT is the General Agreement on Tariffs and Trade. This massive international treaty has been negotiated on and off since the 1940s as nations have sought to eliminate trade barriers and bolster commerce. GATT has already had a considerable effect. In 1947,

GATT
The General Agreement on Tariffs and Trade.

the worldwide average tariff on industrial goods was about 40 percent. Now it is about 4 percent. The world's economies have exploded over the past six decades. Leading supporters of GATT suggest that its lower tariffs vastly increase world trade. The United States is one of the biggest beneficiaries because for decades this country has imposed lower duties than most other nations. A typical American family's annual income has increased due to the more vigorous domestic economy, and at the same time, many goods are less expensive because they enter with low duties.

But opponents claim that the United States now competes against nations with unlimited pools of exploited labor. These countries dominate labor-intensive industries such as textiles, clothing, and manufacturing, and are steadily taking jobs from millions of American workers. Because domestic job losses come in low-end employment, those put out of work are precisely those least able to find a new job.

World Trade Organization (WTO)

Organization created by GATT to stimulate international commerce and resolve trade disputes.

GATT created the **World Trade Organization** (WTO) to stimulate international commerce and resolve trade disputes. The WTO is empowered to hear arguments from any signatory nation about tariff violations or nontariff barriers. This international "court" may order compliance from any nation violating GATT and may penalize countries by imposing trade sanctions.

Here is how the WTO decides a trade dispute. Suppose that the United States believes that Brazil is unfairly restricting trade. The United States uses the WTO offices to request a consultation with Brazil's trade representative. In the majority of cases, these discussions lead to a satisfactory settlement. If the consultation does not resolve the problem, the United States asks the WTO's Dispute Settlement Body (DSB) to form a panel, which consists of three nations uninvolved in the dispute. After the panel hears testimony and arguments from both countries, it releases its report. The DSB generally approves the report, unless either nation appeals. If there is an appeal, the WTO Appellate Body hears the dispute and generally makes the final decision, subject to approval by the entire WTO. No single nation has the power to block final decisions. If a country refuses to comply with the WTO's ruling, affected nations may retaliate by imposing punitive tariffs. The following case forced the WTO to weigh the merits of two important, competing goals: environmental protection and trade growth.

UNITED STATES—IMPORT PROHIBITION OF CERTAIN SHRIMP AND SHRIMP PRODUCTS

AB-1998-4
WTO Appellate Body, 1998

Facts: Sea turtles are migratory animals that live throughout the world. The United States recognizes the animals as an endangered species. Studies showed that the greatest threat to the turtles, around the world, came from shrimp fishermen inadvertently catching the animals in their nets. The federal government responded by requiring any importers to certify that shrimp had been caught using Turtle Excluder Devices (TEDs), which keep the animals out of the nets.

India, Pakistan, Malaysia, and Thailand filed complaints with the WTO, claiming that the United States had no right to impose its environmental concerns on world trade. The United States argued that Article XX of the WTO Agreement permitted trade restrictions based on environmental concerns. Article XX states in part:

Nothing in this Agreement shall be construed to prevent the adoption or enforcement by any Member of measures:

(b) necessary to protect human, animal or plant life or health;

(g) relating to the conservation of exhaustible natural resources if such measures are made effective in conjunction with restrictions on domestic production or consumption;

The Dispute Settlement Body declared that the United States had no right to impose its policies on shrimp importers, and the United States appealed.

Issue: *Did Article XX permit the United States to impose environmental restrictions on shrimp importers?*

Excerpts from the Appellate Body's Report: The [shrimp policy] requires other WTO Members to adopt a regulatory program that is not merely comparable, but rather essentially the same, as that applied to the United States shrimp trawl vessels. The effect is to establish a rigid and unbending standard by which United States officials determine whether or not countries will be certified, thus granting or refusing other countries the right to export shrimp to the United States.

The United States requires the use of approved TEDs at all times by domestic, commercial shrimp trawl vessels. It may be quite acceptable for a government to adopt a single standard applicable to all its citizens throughout that country. However, it is not acceptable, in international trade relations, for one WTO Member to use an economic embargo to require other Members to adopt essentially the same comprehensive regulatory program, without taking into consideration different conditions which may occur in the territories of those other Members.

The United States [failed] to engage other Members exporting shrimp to the United States, in serious, across-the-board negotiations with the objective of concluding bilateral or multilateral agreements for the protection and conservation of sea turtles.

We have not decided that the protection and preservation of the environment is of no significance to the Members of the WTO. Clearly, it is. We have not decided that the sovereign nations that are Members of the WTO cannot adopt effective measures to protect endangered species, such as sea turtles. Clearly, they can and should.

What we have decided in this appeal is simply this: although the measure of the United States in dispute in this appeal serves an environmental objective that is recognized as legitimate, this measure has been applied by the United States in a manner which constitutes arbitrary and unjustifiable discrimination between Members of the WTO.

Environmental groups attacked the ruling, declaring that the WTO paid lip service to the environment but ensured further killing of an important endangered species. Trade supporters applauded it. In addition to the trade versus environment tension, there is a second conflict: rich versus poor. Critics of the shrimp regulations claim that it is unseemly for a wealthy nation to punish subsistence fishermen because of environmental concerns. Their opponents argue that we all share this planet, and long-term growth for each of us depends upon living in harmony with limited resources and fragile ecosystems. Which of the competing goals is more important to you?

Ethics **Child labor** is a wrenching issue. The practice exists to some degree in all countries and is common throughout the developing world. The International Labor Organization estimates that more than 250 million children under the age of 14 work full or part time. As the world generally becomes more prosperous, this ugly problem has actually increased. Children in developing countries typically work in agriculture and domestic work, but many toil in mines and factories.

The rug industry illustrates the international nature of this tragedy. In the 1970s, the Shah of Iran banned child labor in rug factories, but many manufacturers simply packed up and moved to southern Asia. Today, tens of millions of children, some as young as four, toil in rug workrooms, seven days a week, 12 hours a day. Child labor raises compelling moral questions—and economic ones as well. In 1997, Congress passed a statute prohibiting the import of goods created by forced or indentured child labor. The first suit under the new law targeted the carpet factories of southern Asia and sought an outright ban on most rugs from that area. Is this statute humane legislation or cultural imperialism dressed as a nontariff barrier? Should the voters of this country or the WTO decide the issue? In answering such difficult questions, we must bear in mind that child labor is truly universal. The United Farm Workers union estimates that 800,000 underage children help their migrant parents harvest U.S. crops.

> Our response to such a troubling moral issue need not take the form of a statute or lawsuit. Duke University is one of the most popular names in sports apparel, and the school sells millions worth of T-shirts, sweatshirts, jackets, caps, and other sportswear bearing its logo. In response to the troubling issue of child labor, Duke adopted a code of conduct that prohibits its manufacturers from using forced or child labor and requires all of the firms to pay a minimum wage, permit union organizing, and maintain a safe workplace. The university plans to monitor the companies producing its apparel and terminate the contract for any firm that violates its rules.

Regional Agreements: NAFTA and the European Union

North American Free Trade Agreement (NAFTA)

A treaty eliminating almost all trade barriers, tariff and nontariff, between the United States, Canada, and Mexico.

In 1993, the United States, Canada, and Mexico signed the **North American Free Trade Agreement (NAFTA)**. The principal goal was to eliminate almost all trade barriers between the three nations. Like GATT, this treaty has been controversial. Unquestionably, trade between the three nations has increased enormously. Mexico now exports more goods to the United States than do Germany, Britain, and Korea combined. Opponents of the treaty argue that NAFTA costs the United States jobs and lowers the living standards of American workers by forcing them to compete with low-paid labor. For example, Swingline Staplers closed a factory in Queens, New York, after 75 years of operation and moved to Mexico. Instead of paying its American workers $11.58 per hour, Swingline decided to pay Mexican workers 50 cents an hour to do the same job.

Proponents contend that although some jobs are lost, many others are gained, especially in fields with a bright future, such as high technology. They claim that as new jobs invigorate the Mexican economy, consumers there will be able to afford American goods for the first time, providing an enormous new market.

EXAM Strategy

Question: California producers of sea salt protest to the American government that they cannot compete with the same product imported from China. How do the California producers want the United States government to respond? May the U.S. government legally oblige?

Strategy: Domestic producers who cannot compete with foreign competition typically ask their government to impose higher tariffs on the imported goods. However, the whole point of GATT, and the WTO, is to avoid trade wars. There are two instances in which the U.S. government is free to levy increased duties on the Chinese goods. What are they?

Result: When a company *dumps* goods, it sells them overseas at an artificially low price, generally to destroy competition and gain a foothold. That is illegal, and the domestic (U.S.) government may impose dumping duties to protect local producers. Subsidized goods—those supported by the foreign company's government—are also illegal. If the United States government can demonstrate illegal subsidies, it will impose countervailing duties designed to give all producers an equal chance.

Twenty-seven countries belong to the **European Union (EU),** including Great Britain, Germany, France, Italy, and Spain, as well as Latvia and Slovakia.

The EU is one of the world's most powerful associations, with a population of nearly half a billion people. Its sophisticated legal system sets EU-wide standards for tariffs, dumping, subsidies, antitrust, transportation, and many other issues. The first goals of the EU were to eliminate trade barriers between member nations, establish common tariffs with respect to external countries, permit the free movement of citizens across its borders, and coordinate its agricultural and fishing policies for the collective good. The EU has largely achieved these goals. Most, but not all, of the EU countries have adopted a common currency, the euro. During the next decade the union will focus on further economic integration and effective coordination of foreign policy.

INTERNATIONAL SALES AGREEMENTS

Overseas markets offer tremendous growth potential. Foreign customers have an astonishing desire for some kinds of American goods and services.

Cowboy boots are hot in France. Imagine that you own and operate Big Heel, Inc., a small Texas company that makes superb boots. You realize that France could be a bonanza. What should you consider as you proceed? Several things.

The Sales Contract

Le Pied D'Or, a new, fast-growing French chain of shoe stores, is interested in buying 10,000 pairs of your boots at about $300 per pair. You are wise enough to know that you must have a written contract—$3 million is a lot of money for Big Heel.

What Law Governs?

The EU (European Union) Countries)

© Cengage Learning 2014

Potentially, three conflicting laws could govern your boot contract: Texas law, French law, and an international treaty. Each is different, and it is therefore essential to negotiate which law will control.

Texas lawyers are familiar with the Texas law and will generally prefer that it govern. French law is obviously different, and French lawyers and business executives are naturally partial to it. How to compromise? Perhaps by using a neutral law.

The **United Nations Convention on Contracts for the International Sale of Goods (CISG)** is the result of 50 years of work by various international groups, all seeking to create a uniform, international law on this important subject. The United States and most of its principal trading partners have adopted this important treaty.

The CISG applies automatically to any contract for the sale of goods between two parties from different countries if each operates in a country that is a signatory. (Goods are moveable objects like boots.) France and the United States have both signed. Thus, the CISG automatically applies to the Big Heel–Pied D'Or deal unless the parties *specifically opt out.* If the parties want to be governed by other law, their contract must state very clearly that they exclude the CISG and elect, for example, French law.

Signatory
A nation that signs a treaty.

Choice of Forum

The parties must decide not only what law governs, but also where disagreements will be resolved. This can be a significant part of a contract, because the French and American legal systems are dramatically different. In a French civil lawsuit, generally neither side is entitled to depose the other or to obtain interrogatories or even documents. This is in sharp contrast to the American system, where such discovery methods dominate litigation. American lawyers, accustomed to discovery to prepare a case and advance settlement talks, are sometimes frankly unnerved by the French system. Similarly, French lawyers are dismayed at the idea of spending two years taking depositions, exchanging paper, and arguing motions, all at great expense. At trial, the contrasts grow. In a French civil trial, there is generally no right to a jury. The rules of evidence are more flexible (and unpredictable), neither side employs its own expert witnesses, and the parties themselves never appear as witnesses.

Choice of Language and Currency

The parties must select a language for the contract and a currency for payment. Language counts because legal terms seldom translate literally. Currency is vital because the exchange rate may alter between the signing and payment. Suppose the Argentine peso falls 30 percent against the dollar in one week. An Argentine company that contracted on Monday to pay $1 million for U.S. aircraft engines will suddenly have to pay 30 percent more in pesos to meet its contractual obligations. To avoid such calamities, companies engaged in international commerce often purchase from currency dealers a guarantee to obtain the needed currency at a future date for a guaranteed price. Assuming that Big Heel insists on being paid in U.S. dollars, Pied D'Or could obtain a quote from a currency dealer as to the present cost of obtaining $3 million at the time the boots are to be delivered. Pied D'Or might pay a 5 percent premium for this guarantee, but it will have insured itself against disastrous currency swings.

Choices Made   The parties agree that the contract price will be paid in U.S. dollars. Pied D'Or is unfamiliar with U.S. law and absolutely refuses to make a deal unless either French law or the CISG governs. Your lawyer, Susan Fisher, recommends accepting the CISG, provided that the contract is written in English and that any disputes will be resolved in Texas courts. Pied D'Or balks at this, but Fisher presses hard, and ultimately those are the terms agreed upon. Fisher is delighted with the arrangement, pointing out that the CISG provisions can all be taken into account as the contract is written, and that by using Texas courts to settle any dispute, Big Heel has an advantage in terms of familiarity and location.

Letter of Credit

Because Pied D'Or is new and fast growing, you are not sure it will be able to foot the bill. Pied D'Or provides a letter of reference from its bank, La Banque Bouffon, but this is a small bank and it is unfamiliar to you. You need greater assurance of payment, and your lawyer recommends that payment be made by **letter of credit**. Here is how the letter will work.

Letter of credit
A commercial device used to guarantee payment in international trade.

Big Heel demands that the contract include a provision requiring payment by confirmed, irrevocable letter of credit. Le Pied D'Or agrees. The French company now contacts its bank, La Banque Bouffon, and instructs Bouffon to issue a letter of credit to Big Heel. The letter of credit is a promise *by the bank itself* to pay Big Heel if Big Heel presents certain documents. Banque Bouffon, of course, expects to be repaid by Pied D'Or. The bank is in a good position to assess Pied D'Or's creditworthiness since it is local and can do any investigating it wants before issuing the credit. It may also insist that Pied D'Or give Bouffon a mortgage on property, or that Pied D'Or deposit money in a separate Bouffon account. Pied D'Or is the **account party** on the letter of credit, and Big Heel is the **beneficiary**.

But at Big Heel, you are still not entirely satisfied. You feel that a bank is unlikely to default on its promises, but still, you don't know anything about Bouffon. That is why you have required a *confirmed* letter of credit. Bouffon will forward its letter of credit to Big Heel's own bank, Wells Fargo. Wells Fargo examines the letter and then *confirms* the letter. This is *Wells Fargo's own legal guarantee* that it will pay Big Heel. Wells Fargo will do this only if it knows, through international banking contacts, that Bouffon is a sound and trustworthy bank. The risk has now been spread to two banks, and at Big Heel, you are finally confident of payment.

You get busy, make excellent boots, and pack them. When they are ready, you truck them to Galveston, where they are taken alongside a ship, *Le Fond de la Mer.* Your agent presents the goods to the ship's officials, along with customs documents that describe the goods. *Le Fond de la Mer*'s officer in turn issues your agent a **negotiable bill of lading**. This document describes *exactly* the goods received—their quantity, color, quality, and anything else important.

You now take the negotiable bill of lading to Wells Fargo. You also present to Wells Fargo a **draft**, which is simply a formal order to Wells Fargo to pay, based on the letter of credit. Wells Fargo will look closely at the bill of lading, which must specify *precisely* the goods described in the letter of credit. Why so cautious? Because the bank is dealing only in paper. It never sees the boots. Wells Fargo is exchanging $3 million of its own money based on instructions in the letter of credit. The bank should pay only if the bill of lading indicates that *Le Fond de la Mer* received exactly what is described in the letter of credit. Wells Fargo will decide whether the bill of lading is *conforming* or *nonconforming*. If the terms of both documents are identical, the bill of lading is conforming and Wells Fargo must pay. If the terms vary, the bill of lading is nonconforming and Wells Fargo will deny payment. Thus, if the bill of lading indicated 9,000 pairs of boots and 1,000 pairs of sneakers, it is nonconforming and Big Heel would get no money.

Wells Fargo concludes that the documents are conforming, so it issues a check to Big Heel for $3 million. In return, you endorse the bill of lading and other documents over to Wells Fargo, which endorses the same documents and sends them to Banque Bouffon. Bouffon makes the same minute inspection and then writes a check to Wells Fargo. Bouffon then demands payment from Le Pied D'Or. Pied D'Or pays its bank, receiving in exchange the bill of lading and customs documents. Note that payment in all stages is now complete, though the boots are still rolling on the high seas. Finally, when the boots arrive in Le Havre, Pied D'Or trucks roll up to the wharf and, using the bill of lading and customs documents, collect the boots. See Exhibit 8.1.

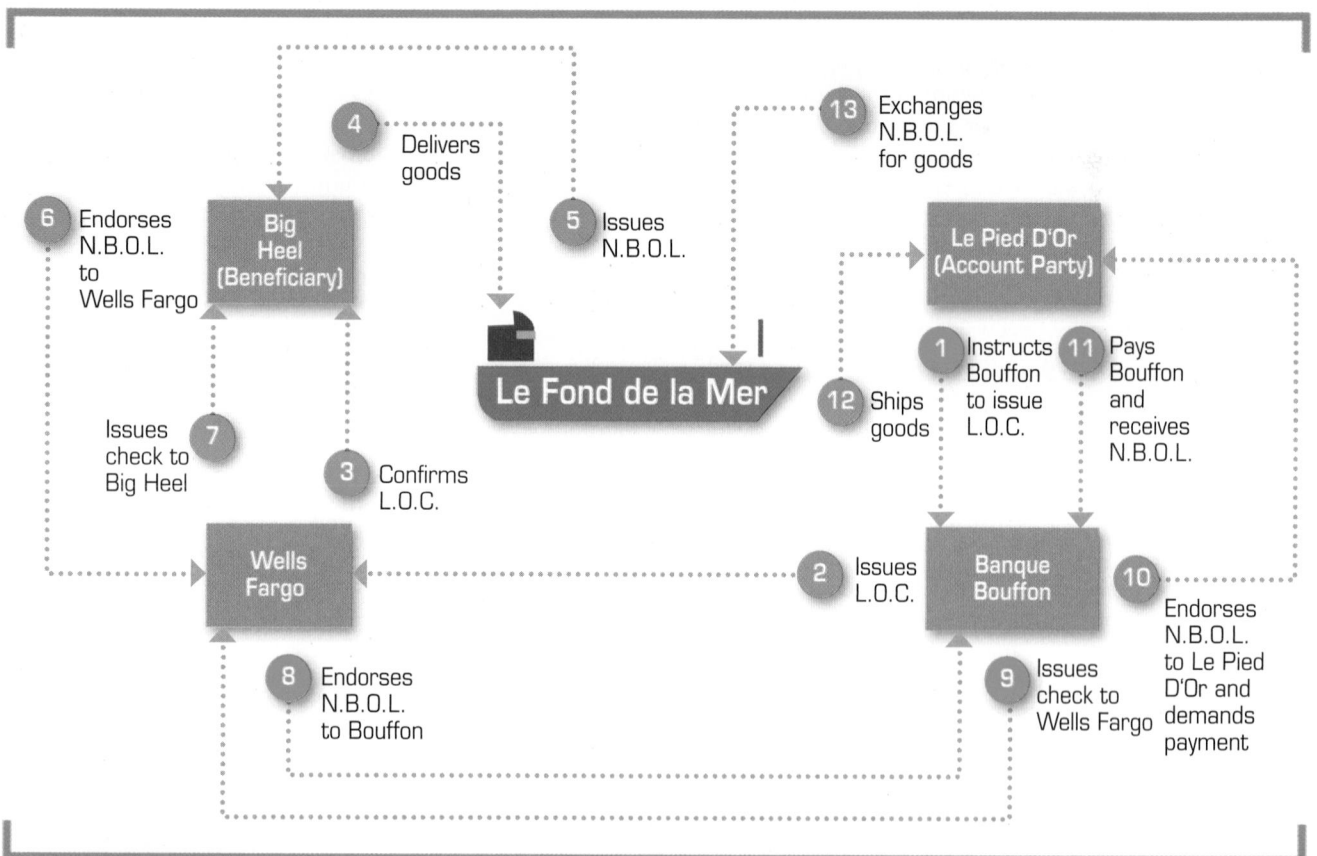

© Cengage Learning 2014

EXHIBIT 8.1

Good news: They fit! Not all customers walk away in such comfort, as the following case indicates.

CENTRIFUGAL CASTING MACHINE CO., INC. v. AMERICAN BANK & TRUST CO.

966 F.2d 1348, 1992 U.S. App. LEXIS 13089
Tenth Circuit Court of Appeals, 1992

Facts: Centrifugal Casting Machine Co. (CCM) entered into a contract with the State Machinery Trading Co. (SMTC), an agency of the Iraqi government. CCM agreed to manufacture cast iron pipe plant equipment for a total price of $27 million. The contract specified payment of the full amount by confirmed irrevocable letter of credit. The Central Bank of Iraq then issued the letter, on behalf of SMTC (the "account party") to be paid to CCM (the "beneficiary"). The Banca Nazionale del Lavorov (BNL) confirmed the letter.

Following Iraq's invasion of Kuwait on August 2, 1990, President George H. W. Bush issued two executive orders blocking the transfer of property in the United States in which Iraq held any interest. In other words, no one could use, buy, or sell any Iraqi property or cash. When CCM attempted to draw upon the letter of credit, the United States government intervened. The government claimed that like all Iraqi money in the United States, this money was frozen by the executive order. The United States District Court rejected the government's claim, and the government appealed.

Issue: *Is CCM entitled to be paid pursuant to the letter of credit?*

Excerpts from Judge Sentelle's Decision: The United States contends on appeal that the freeze of Iraq's assets furthers national policy to punish Iraq by preventing it from obtaining economic benefits from transactions with American citizens, and by preserving such assets both for use as a bargaining chip in resolving this country's differences with Iraq and as a source of compensation for claims Americans may have against Iraq. We agree that these policy considerations are compelling and that we are therefore required to construe Iraqi property interests broadly. However, we are not persuaded these policies would be furthered by [creating] a property interest on behalf of Iraq that would not otherwise be cognizable under governing legal principles.

Two interrelated features of the letter of credit provide it with its unique value in the marketplace and are of critical importance in our consideration of the United States' claim here. First, the simple result [of a letter of credit] is that the issuer [i.e., the bank] substitutes its credit, preferred by the beneficiary, for that of the account party. Second, the issuer's obligation to pay on a letter of credit is completely independent from the underlying commercial transaction between the beneficiary and the account party. Significantly, the issuer must honor a proper demand even though the beneficiary has breached the underlying contract; even though the insolvency of the account party renders reimbursement impossible; and notwithstanding supervening illegality, impossibility, war or insurrection. This principle of independence is universally viewed as essential to the proper functioning of a letter of credit and to its particular value, i.e., its certainty of payment.

This assurance of payment gives letters of credit a central role in commercial dealings, and gives them a particular value in international transactions, in which sophisticated investors knowingly undertake such risks as political upheaval or contractual breach in return for the benefits to be reaped from international trade. Law affecting such an essential instrument of the economy must be shaped with sensitivity to its special characteristics. Accordingly, courts have concluded that the whole purpose of a letter of credit would be defeated by examining the merits of the underlying contract dispute to determine whether the letter should be paid.

Because of the nature of a letter of credit, we conclude that Iraq does not have a property interest in the money CCM received under the letter. The United States contends in essence that Iraq has a property interest in this money because it was allegedly a contract payment made by Iraq, which Iraq should recover because CCM breached the contract. In so arguing, the United States makes a breach of contract claim on behalf of Iraq that Iraq has never made, creates a remedy for the contracting parties in derogation of the remedy they themselves provided and, most importantly, disregards the controlling legal principles with respect to letters of credit.

Affirmed.

EXAM Strategy

Question: In an international contract for the sale of goods, Seller is to be paid by a confirmed irrevocable letter of credit. Buyer claims that the goods are defective and threatens to sue. If the parties are going to end up in court anyway, why bother with a letter of credit?

Strategy: A confirmed letter of credit is unique because the seller is assured of payment as soon as it presents a proper bill of lading to the appropriate local bank—regardless of the quality of the goods. Seller would much rather defend this lawsuit against Buyer than sue for its money in foreign courts.

Result: There *may* be a lawsuit, but Seller is not worried. It is Buyer who must sue, probably in Seller's home country. Buyer now risks substantial time and cash for an uncertain outcome. When the parties discuss a settlement, as surely they will, Seller is holding a big advantage—the cash.

INTERNATIONAL TRADE ISSUES

Assume that Ambux is an American communications corporation that decides to invest in a growing overseas market. The president of Ambux is particularly interested in building telephone systems in the former republics of the Soviet Union, reasoning that these economies offer great opportunity for growth. She hires a consultant to advise her on the most important issues concerning possible investment in Uzbekistan and other former Soviet republics. The consultant presents several related issues:

- Repatriation of profits
- Expropriation
- Sovereign immunity
- Act of State doctrine
- The Foreign Corrupt Practices Act (FCPA)
- Extraterritoriality

Repatriation of Profits

Repatriation of profits occurs when an investing company pulls its earnings out of a foreign country and takes them back home. If Ambux builds a telephone system in Uzbekistan, it will plan to make money and then repatriate the profit to its headquarters in the United States. But Ambux must not assume an automatic right to do so. Many countries impose a much higher tax on repatriated profits than on normal income in order to keep the money in domestic commerce. Others bar repatriation altogether. Developing countries in particular want the money to "stay home." Thus, before Ambux invests anywhere, it must ensure that it can repatriate profits or live with any limitations the foreign country might impose.

> Many countries impose a much higher tax on repatriated profits than on normal income in order to keep the money in domestic commerce.

Fortunately, investing in Uzbekistan is relatively secure. Uzbekistan and the United States have signed a trade treaty guaranteeing unlimited repatriation for American investors. This treaty should suffice. But Ambux might still feel cautious. Uzbekistan is a relatively new nation, and the mechanisms for actually getting the money out of Uzbekistan banks may be slow or faulty. The solution is to get a written agreement from the Minister of Commerce explicitly permitting Ambux to repatriate all profits and providing a clear mechanism to do it through the local banks.

Expropriation

Nationalize

Action in which a government assumes ownership of property.

Many nations, both developed and developing, **nationalize** property, meaning that they declare the national government to be the new owner. For example, during the 1940s and 1950s, Great Britain nationalized its coal, steel, and other heavy industries. The state assumed ownership and paid compensation to the previous owners. In the United States, nationalization is rare, but local governments often take land by eminent domain, to be used for roads or other public works. As we have seen, the United States Constitution requires that the owners be fairly compensated.

Expropriation

The government's seizure of property owned by foreign investors.

When a government takes property owned by *foreign* investors, it is called **expropriation**. The U.S. government historically has acknowledged that the expropriation of American interests is legal, provided the host government pays the owners *promptly and fully, in dollars*. But if compensation is inadequate or long delayed, or made in a local currency that is hard to exchange, the taking is a **confiscation**.

Confiscation

The government takes property without fair payment.

The courts of almost all nations agree that confiscation is illegal. But it can be difficult or impossible to prevent because courts of a host country may be partial to their own government.

Sovereign Immunity

Sovereign immunity holds that the courts of one nation lack the jurisdiction (power) to hear suits against foreign governments. Most nations respect this principle. In the United States, the **Foreign Sovereign Immunities Act** (FSIA) states that American courts generally cannot entertain suits against foreign governments. This is a difficult hurdle for a company to overcome when seeking compensation for foreign expropriation, but there are three possible exceptions.

Foreign Sovereign Immunities Act (FSIA)

A statute which states that American courts generally cannot entertain suits against foreign governments.

Waiver   A lawsuit is permitted against a foreign country that waives its immunity, that is, voluntarily gives up this protection. Suppose the Czech government wishes to buy fighter planes from an American manufacturer. The manufacturer might insist on a waiver in the sales contract, and the Czech Republic might be willing to grant one to get the weapons it desires. If the planes land safely but the checks bounce, the manufacturer may sue.

Commercial Activity   A plaintiff in the United States can sue a foreign country engaged in commercial, but not political, activity. Suppose the government of Iceland hires an American ecology-consulting firm to help its fishermen replenish depleted fishing grounds. Since fishing is a for-profit activity, the contract is commercial, and if Iceland refuses to pay, the company may sue in American courts.

Violation of International Law   A plaintiff in this country may sue a foreign government that has confiscated property in violation of international law, provided that the property either ends up in the United States or is involved in commercial activity that affects someone in the United States. Suppose a foreign government confiscates a visiting American ship, with no claim of right, and begins to use it for shipping goods for profit. Later, the ship carries some American produce. The taking was illegal, and it now affects American commerce. The original owner may sue.

Investment Insurance

Companies eager to do business abroad but anxious about expropriation should consider publicly funded insurance. In 1971, Congress established the **Overseas Private Investment Corporation (OPIC)** to insure U.S. investors against overseas losses due to political violence and expropriation. OPIC insurance is available to investors at relatively low rates for investment in almost any country.

Should Ambux investigate OPIC insurance before investing in Uzbekistan? Absolutely. While the Uzbekistan government has the best of intentions with respect to foreign investment, the nation is young and the government has no track record. A government can change course quickly. Why take unnecessary risks?

Foreign Corrupt Practices Act

The Foreign Corrupt Practices Act (FCPA)[5] makes it illegal for an American businessperson to give "anything of value" to any foreign official in order to influence an official decision. It is sad but true that in many countries, bribery is routine and widely accepted. When Congress investigated foreign bribes to see how common they were, more than 450 U.S. companies admitted paying hundreds of millions of dollars in bribes to foreign officials. Legislators concluded that such massive payments distorted competition among American companies for foreign contracts, interfered with the free market system, and undermined confidence everywhere in our way of doing business. In response, Congress passed the FCPA.

American executives have long complained that the FCPA puts their companies at a competitive disadvantage. Of the more than 200 nations in the world, very few aggressively prevent their nationals from bribing foreign officials. (In some countries, a bribe paid to a foreign official may even be treated as a tax deduction!) Others argue that the United States should not try to affect the way other countries do business by creating laws that apply outside its own borders.

The FCPA has two principal requirements:

- **Bribes.** The statute makes it illegal for U.S. companies and citizens to bribe foreign officials to influence a governmental decision. The statute prohibits giving anything of value and also bars using third parties as a conduit for such payments. Interestingly, the bribe need not be actually paid. A *promise* to pay bribes violates the Act. Also, the bribe need not be successful. If an American company makes an unauthorized payment but never gains any benefit, the company has still violated the law.

- **Recordkeeping.** All publicly traded companies—whether they engage in international trade or not—must keep detailed records that prevent hiding or disguising bribes. These records must be available for inspection by U.S. officials.

Not all payments violate the FCPA. A **grease or facilitating payment is legal.** Grease payments are common in many foreign countries to obtain a permit, process governmental papers, or obtain utility service. For example, the cost of a permit to occupy an office building might be $100, but the government clerk suggests that you will receive the permit faster (within this lifetime) if you pay $150, one-third of which he will pocket. Such small payments are legal. You cannot bribe the high-level decision makers who award contracts in the first place. But, once a contract has been secured, you may often bribe lower-level government workers to encourage them to speed things along.

Further, a payment **does not violate the FCPA if it was legal under the written laws of the country in which it was made.** Since few countries establish written codes *permitting* officials to receive bribes, this defense is unlikely to help many Americans who hand out gifts.

[5] 15 U.S.C. §§78 et seq.

Punishments can be severe. A company may face large fines and the loss of profits earned as a result of illegal bribes. In 2011, Johnson & Johnson agreed to pay $77 million to settle an FCPA action. In addition to financial penalties, individuals who violate the FCPA can face up to five years in prison.

The following case is a classic example of bribery. Not much loyalty within Owl Securities. Why is that? What does it teach us?

UNITED STATES V. KING

351 F.3d 859
Eighth Circuit Court of Appeals, 2004

Facts: Owl Securities and Investments, Ltd., hoped to develop a large port in Limon, Costa Rica. The project included docks, housing, recreational facilities, an airport, and more. Richard King was one of Owl's largest investors, and Stephen Kingsley its CEO. The government charged King with attempting to bribe Costa Rican officials to obtain land and other concessions needed for their project. At trial, several of Owl's officers, including Kingsley, Richard Halford, and Albert Reitz, testified against King. A jury convicted King of violating the FCPA. He received a 30-month sentence and a fine of $60,000. He appealed.

Issue: *Was there sufficient evidence that King had violated the FCPA?*

Excerpts from Judge Beam's Decision: Viewing the evidence in the light most favorable to the verdict, there was ample evidence in the record to support the jury's convictions. The tape recordings, alone, support the jury's verdict. There was sufficient evidence to prove King's knowledge of the proposed payment long before Kingsley became an informant for the government.

For example, the following exchanges are just a small sample of what the jury heard:

Kingsley: Well you've always known about the closing cost fees and that.
King: I've known what?
Kingsley: You've known about the closing costs.
King: The one million dollars?
Kingsley: Yeah.
King: I've known about that for five years, yeah, . . .[A later tape recording:]
Kingsley: Yeah, what, um, what Pablo had said, was why just pay, pay off the current politicians. Pay off the future ones.
King: That's right. Because we're gonna have to work with them anyway.

Kingsley: And so what he was saying was double, you know, give them more money. Buy the opposition. If you buy the current party and the opposition, then it doesn't matter who's in because there's only two parties.
King: The thing that really worries me is that, uh, if the Justice Department gets a hold of. Finds out how many people we've been paying off down there. Uh, or even if they don't. Are we gonna have to spend the rest of our lives paying off these petty politicians to keep them out of our hair? I can just see us, every, every day some politician on our doorstep down there wanting a hand out for this or that . . . . Think we could pay the top people enough, that the rest of the people won't bother us any. That's what I'm hoping this million and a half dollars does. I'm hoping it pays enough top people . . .[A later recording:]
Kingsley: Now Pablo's continued to talk to the politicians. They know about the toll, closing costs call it what you will.
King: Does everybody agree to what we talked about recently?
Kingsley: Yeah, a million into escrow for the toll.
King: And then we get the property and then we do the (unintelligible)?
Kingsley: Um hum. Yeah now let me I'll, I'll, I'll come on to that because I'll explain how we work through that. Uh, essentially once the politicians see the money in escrow, they'll move. That's what it comes down to [clears throat]. Pablo's gonna send a list, an e-mail with a list of politicians already paid off and the ones he's gonna pay off.
King: Isn't that awfully dangerous?
Kingsley: No, e-mail's probably the most secure form of communication.
King: From what I read it's not, number one and number two, there's got to be a better way.

We affirm the judgment of the district court.

Ethics   What's wrong with bribery, anyway? Many businesspeople think it is relatively harmless—just a cost of doing business, like New York City's high taxes or Germany's high labor costs. Corruption is not a victimless crime. Poor people in poor countries are the losers when officials are on the take; corruption means that good projects are squeezed out by bad ones. And corruption can reduce a country's entire administration to a state of decay. Honest officials give up. Bribes grow ever bigger and more ubiquitous. The trough becomes less well stocked; the snouts plunge deeper. Worldwide about $400 billion is lost each year to corruption in government procurement. The anticorruption czar in Mexico estimated that bribes reduce Mexico's gross domestic product annually by 9.5 percent. This sum is twice the country's education budget.[6]

EXAM Strategy

Question: Splash is a California corporation that develops resorts. Lawrence, a Splash executive, is hoping to land a $700 million contract with a developing country in Southeast Asia. He seeks your advice. "I own a beach house in Australia, worth about $2 million. If I give it to a certain government official in the Asian country, I know that will close the resort deal. If I don't, someone else will, and my company loses out. Do you think that's wrong? Should I do it?" Please advise him.

Strategy: Lawrence has phrased his question in terms of ethics, but there is more involved. What law governs his proposed conduct? Is Lawrence legally safe, given that the land is foreign and the contract will be signed overseas?

Result: If Lawrence gives anything of value (such as a house) to secure a government contract, he has violated the FCPA. It makes no difference where the property is located or the deal signed. He could go to jail, and his company could be harshly penalized. Ethically, his gift would exacerbate corruption in a developing nation and mean that the agreement was determined by a bribe, not the merits of Splash. Other companies might do a superior job employing local workers, constructing an enduring resort, and protecting the environment, all for less money.

Extraterritoriality

The United States has many statutes designed to protect employees, such as those that prohibit discrimination on race, religion, gender, and so forth. Do these laws apply overseas? This is an issue of **extraterritoriality—the power of one nation to impose its laws in other countries**.[7] Many American companies do business through international **subsidiaries**— foreign companies that they control. The subsidiary may be incorporated in a nation that denies workers the protection they would receive in the United States. What should happen when an employee of a foreign subsidiary argues that his rights under an American statute have been violated? You make the call.

[6]"Who Will Listen to Mr. Clean?" *The Economist*, August 2, 1997, p. 52.
[7]Extraterritoriality can also refer to exemption from local laws. For example, ambassadors are generally exempt from the law of the nation in which they serve.

You be the Judge

CARNERO V. BOSTON SCIENTIFIC CORPORATION

433 F.3d 1
First Circuit Court of Appeals, 2006

Facts: Boston Scientific (BSC) was an American company that manufactured medical equipment. The company had its headquarters in Massachusetts but did business around the world through foreign subsidiaries. One of the company's subsidiaries was Boston Scientific Argentina (BSA), and it was there that Ruben Carnero began working. His employment contract stated he would work at BSA's headquarters in Buenos Aires and be paid in pesos. Argentine law was to govern the contract. Four years later, Carnero took an assignment to work as country manager for a different BSC subsidiary, Boston Scientific Do Brasil (BSB). Carnero frequently traveled to Massachusetts to meet with company executives, but he did most of his work in South America.

About a year later, BSB fired Carnero, and BSA soon did the same. Carnero claimed that the companies terminated him in retaliation for his reporting to BSC executives that the Argentine and Brazilian subsidiaries inflated sales figures and engaged in other accounting fraud. Carnero filed suit in Massachusetts, alleging that his firing violated an American statute, the Sarbanes-Oxley Act of 2002 (SOX).

Congress passed that law in response to the massive fraud cases involving Enron, Arthur Andersen, and others. The law was passed primarily to protect investors, but included a "whistleblower" provision. That section was designed to guard employees who informed superiors or investigating officials of fraud within the company. The law allows injured employees reinstatement and back pay.

BSC argued that SOX did not apply overseas and the District Court agreed, dismissing the case. Carnero appealed.

Issue: *Does SOX protect a whistleblower employed overseas by a subsidiary of an American company?*

Argument for Carnero: Congress passed SOX because the American people were appalled by the massive fraud in major corporations, and the resulting harm to employees, investors, the community, and the economy. The whistleblower protection is designed to encourage honest employees to come forward and report wrongdoing—an act that no employee wants to do, and one which has historically led to termination. Mr. Carnero knew his report would be poorly received, but believed he had an ethical obligation to protect his company. For that effort, he was fired, and now Boston Scientific attempts to avoid liability using the technicality of corporate hierarchy.

Yes, Mr. Carnero was employed by BSB and BSA. But both of those companies are owned and operated by Boston Scientific. It is the larger company, with headquarters in the United States, which calls the shots. That is why executives in Massachusetts frequently asked Mr. Carnero to report to them—and why he brought them his unhappy news.

A whistleblower deserves gratitude and a pay raise. Mr. Carnero may well have saved his employer from massive losses and public disgrace. Would Boston Scientific like to wind up as Enron did—the company in bankruptcy court, its executives in prison? If Boston Scientific is too petty to acknowledge Mr. Carnero's contribution, the company should at least honor the purpose and intent of SOX by protecting his job.

Argument for Boston Scientific: First, we do not know whether there have been any accounting irregularities or not. Second, the fact that Mr. Carnero is employed by companies incorporated in Argentina and Brazil is more than a technicality. He is asking an American court to go into two foreign countries—sovereign nations with good ties to the United States—and investigate accounting and employment practices of companies incorporated and operating there. The very idea is offensive. No nation can afford to treat its allies and trading partners with such contempt.

If the United States can impose its whistleblowing law in foreign countries, may those nations impose their rules and values here? Suppose that a country forbids women to do certain work. May companies in those nations direct American subsidiaries to reject all female job applicants? Neither the citizens nor courts of this country would tolerate such interference for a moment.

Mr. Carnero's idea is also impractical. How would an American court determine why he was fired? Must the trial judge here subpoena Brazilian witnesses and demand documentary evidence from that country?

Finally, the SOX law does not apply overseas because Congress never said it did. The legislators—well aware that American corporations operate subsidiaries abroad—made no mention of those companies when they passed this statute.

Chapter Conclusion

Overseas investment, like sales abroad, offers potentially great rewards but significant pitfalls. A working knowledge of international law is essential to any entrepreneur or executive seriously considering foreign commerce. Issues such as choice of law, repatriation of profits, and expropriation can mean the difference between profit and loss. As the WTO lowers barriers, international trade will only increase, and your awareness of these principles will grow still more valuable.

EXAM REVIEW

1. **EXPORT RESTRICTIONS** Several statutes restrict exports from the United States that would harm national security, foreign policy, or certain other goals. (p. 191)

2. **TARIFFS** A tariff is a tax imposed on goods entering a country. The Customs Service classifies goods when they enter the United States and imposes appropriate tariffs. (pp. 192–193)

EXAM Strategy

Question: Sports Graphics, Inc. imports "Chill" brand coolers from Taiwan. Chill coolers have an outer shell of vinyl, with handles and pockets, and an inner layer of insulation. In a recent lawsuit, the issue was whether "Chill" coolers were "luggage" or "articles used for preparing, serving, or storing food or beverages," as Sports Graphics claimed. Who was the other party to the dispute, why did the two sides care about this, and what arguments did they make?

Strategy: The Customs Service (the other party) classifies goods and then imposes an appropriate *ad valorem* tax. What is at stake, of course, is money. (See the "Result" at the end of this section.)

3. **DUMPED AND SUBSIDIZED IMPORTS** Most countries, including the United States, impose duties for goods that have been dumped (sold at an unfairly low price in the international market) and for subsidized goods (those benefiting from government financial assistance in the country of origin). (p. 193)

4. **GATT** The General Agreement on Tariffs and Trade (GATT) is lowering the average duties worldwide. Proponents see it as a boon to trade; opponents see it as a threat to workers. (pp. 193–194)

5. **WTO** GATT created the WTO, which resolves disputes between signatories to the treaty. (pp. 194–195)

EXAM Strategy

Question: In a recent WTO case, several nations claimed that American laws concerning shrimp fishing were unfair and illegal. The case demonstrated a conflict between two important values. What were the values? In your view, which is more important? Who won and why?

Strategy: Make sure you understand the *Shrimp Products* case in the text. (See the "Result" at the end of this section.)

6. **CISG** A sales agreement between an American company and a foreign company may be governed by American law, by the law of the foreign country, or by the CISG. (p. 197)

7. **LETTERS OF CREDIT** A confirmed, irrevocable letter of credit is an important means of facilitating international sales contracts, because the seller is assured of payment by a local bank so long as it delivers the specified goods. (pp. 198–201)

EXAM Strategy

Question: Flyby Knight (FK) contracts to sell 12 helicopters to Air Nigeria for $8 million each. Payment is to be made by letter of credit, issued by the Bank of Nigeria, confirmed by Citibank in New York, and due when the confirming bank receives a bill of lading indicating all helicopters are on board ship, ready for sailing to Nigeria. FK loads the aircraft on board ship, and the next day delivers the bill of lading to Citibank. The same day, Air Nigeria informs FK that its inspectors onboard ship have discovered serious flaws in the rotator blades and the fuel lines. Air Nigeria states it will neither accept nor pay for the helicopters. Is FK entitled to its $96 million?

a. FK is entitled to no money.

b. FK is entitled to no money *provided* Air Nigeria can prove the helicopters are defective.

c. Air Nigeria is obligated to pay FK the full price.

d. Bank of Nigeria is obligated to pay FK the full price.

e. Citibank is obligated to pay FK the full price.

Strategy: Payment is to be made by confirmed letter of credit. Ask yourself what that means. In such a case, the confirming bank is obligated to pay the seller when the bank receives a bill of lading indicating that conforming goods have been delivered. What about the fact that the goods seem defective? That is irrelevant. It is precisely to avoid long-distance arguments over such problems that sellers insist on these letters. (See the "Result" at the end of this section.)

8. **REPATRIATION** A foreign government may restrict repatriation of profits. (pp. 201–202)

9. **EXPROPRIATION** Expropriation refers to a government taking property owned by foreign investors. U.S. courts regard this as lawful, provided the country pays the American owner promptly and fully in dollars. (p. 202)

10. **SOVEREIGN IMMUNITY** Sovereign immunity means that, in general, American courts lack jurisdiction to hear suits against foreign governments unless the foreign nation has waived immunity, is engaging in commercial activity, or has violated international law. (p. 202)

11. **FOREIGN CORRUPT PRACTICES ACT (FCPA)** The FCPA makes it illegal for an American businessperson to bribe foreign officials. (pp. 203–205)

12. **EXTRATERRITORIALITY** The principle that refers to the power of one nation to impose its laws in other countries. (pp. 205–206)

2. Result: Customs evidently claimed the goods were luggage, with a higher tariff than food storage articles. Customs argued that the handles and portability made the articles luggage. But Sports Graphics prevailed, convincing the court that the primary purpose of the containers was the storage of food. The lawsuit reduced the company's tariff from 20 percent to 3.4 percent.

5. Result: Small nations sued, claiming that American regulations made it difficult or impossible for them to fish, devastating their economic growth. The United States argued that vital environmental concerns mandated such rules. The WTO found in favor of the small nations, ruling that before the United States imposed its environmental standards on other countries, it must engage in multinational negotiations, seeking an acceptable compromise. Environmentalists argued that the decision was short-sighted, and contributed to the destruction of an endangered species. Supporters of the decision responded that long-term environmental concerns sound patronizing and hollow to people with empty stomachs.

7. Result: When Citibank receives the bill of lading, indicating delivery of the helicopters, it is obligated to pay. The correct answer is (E).

MULTIPLE-CHOICE QUESTIONS

1. A letter of credit is issued by a _____.

   (a) buyer

   (b) seller

   (c) shipping company

   (d) bank

2. Tariffs are a tax on _____. Treaties like NAFTA seek to _____ tariffs.

   (a) imports; increase

   (b) imports; decrease

   (c) exports; increase

   (d) exports; decrease

3. The President negotiates a defense agreement with a foreign government. To take effect, the agreement must be ratified by which of the following?

   (a) Two-thirds of the House of Representatives

   (b) Two-thirds of the Senate

   (c) The Supreme Court

   (d) A and B

   (e) A, B, and C

4. Lynn owns a small printing company in Nevada. She makes a contract with a company in France to print custom children's books and ship them to France. The contract does not say anything about which body of law will be used to resolve any disputes that arise. If there is a conflict, which body of law will actually be applied to the case?

   (a) Nevada law

   (b) French law

   (c) The CISG

   (d) None of the above

5. Countervailing duties are imposed when _____.

   (a) dumping occurs

   (b) goods are unreasonably subsidized

   (c) Both A and B

   (d) None of the above

ESSAY QUESTIONS

1. Arnold Mandel exported certain high-technology electronic equipment. Later, he was in court arguing that the equipment he shipped should not have been on the Department of Commerce's Commodity Control List. What items may be on that list, and why does Mandel care?

2. **YOU BE THE JUDGE WRITING PROBLEM** Continental Illinois National Bank issued an irrevocable letter of credit on behalf of Bill's Coal Co. for $805,000, with the Allied Fidelity Insurance Co. as beneficiary. Bill's Coal Co. then went bankrupt. Allied then presented to Continental documents that were complete and conformed to the letter of credit. Continental refused to pay. Since Bill's Coal was bankrupt, there was no way Continental would collect once it had paid on the letter. Allied filed suit. Who should win? **Argument for Allied Fidelity:** An irrevocable letter of credit serves one purpose: to assure the seller that it will be paid if it performs the contract. Allied has met its obligation. The company furnished documents demonstrating compliance with the agreement. Continental *must* pay. Continental's duty to pay is an independent obligation, unrelated to the status of Bill's Coal. The bank issued this letter knowing the rules of the game and expecting to make a profit. It is time for Continental to honor its word. **Argument for Continental Bank:** In this transaction, the bank was merely a middleman, helping to facilitate payment of a contract. Allied has fulfilled its obligations under the contract, and we understand the company's desire to be paid. Regrettably, Bill's Coal is bankrupt. No one is going to be paid on this deal. Allied should have researched Bill's financial status more thoroughly before entering into the agreement. While we sympathize with Allied's dilemma, it has only itself to blame and cannot expect the bank to act as some sort of insurance company for a deal gone awry.

3. Jean-François, a French wine exporter, sues Bobby Joe, a Texas importer, claiming that Bobby Joe owes him $2 million for wine. Jean-François takes the witness stand to describe how the contract was created. Where is the trial taking place?

4. The Kyrgyz Republic is one of the new nations that broke away from the old Soviet Union. In September 1994, the government of Kyrgyzstan made two independent announcements: (1) it was abolishing all taxes on repatriation; and (2) the government was resigning and would shortly be replaced. Explain the significance of these announcements for an American company considering a major investment in Kyrgyzstan.

5. The Instituto de Auxilios y Viviendas is a government agency of the Dominican Republic. Dr. Marion Fernandez, the general administrator of the Instituto and Secretary of the Republic, sought a loan for the Instituto. She requested that Charles Meadows, an American citizen, secure the Instituto a bank loan of $12 million. If he obtained a loan on favorable terms, he would receive a fee of $240,000. Meadows secured a loan on satisfactory terms, which the Instituto accepted. He then sought his fee, but the Instituto and the Dominican government refused to pay. He sued the government in United States District Court. The Dominican government claimed immunity. Comment.

DISCUSSION QUESTIONS

1. The United States consistently imports much more than it exports. The annual gap is consistently several hundred billion dollars. Does this concern you? If so, what should be done about it? If not, why not?

2. Does the FCPA seem sensible? Is fighting corruption the right thing to do, or does the statute place American companies at an unacceptable competitive disadvantage?

3. Generally speaking, should the United States pass laws that seek to control behavior outside its borders? Or, when in Rome, should our companies and subsidiaries be allowed to do as the Romans do?

4. Do you favor free trade agreements like NAFTA? Do you believe that free trade benefits everyone in the long run, or are you more concerned that American jobs may be lost?

5. Imagine that you read an article that reports the maker of your favorite brand of clothing uses child labor in its overseas factories. Being realistic, would you avoid buying that kind of clothing in the future? Why or why not?

Contracts &
the UCC

CHAPTER 9

Introduction to Contracts

Austin Electronics had a terrible year. John, the store's owner, decided to get out of the electronics business. Before closing his doors, he hung a sign reading "Everything Must Go!" and held a going-out-of-business sale.

© neelsky/Shutterstock.com

Customer #1—Fran

"Nice TV," Fran commented. "Price says $400. I'll give you $250 for it."

"Sorry, but I need at least $400," John replied.

"Hmm. Nope, that's just too much."

"OK, OK, I'll let it go for $250."

"Well … no. No, I've changed my mind. No deal."

Customer #2—Ricky

"How much for that iPod, mister?" said Ricky, a 10-year-old boy.

"Twenty bucks, kid," John said.

"Wow! I'll take it! Keep it for me while I ride home to get my money."

"Sure thing, kid."

Customer #3—Carla

"That's a good-looking home theater projector," Carla said. "I don't see a price tag. How much?"

"Well," John replied, "how much are you offering?"

"Hmm … I could give you $700 for it."

John was pleasantly surprised. "You've got yourself a deal." The two shook hands.

"I'll be back with my checkbook later today," Carla said.

"I'll give you $50 for these speakers," Dave said in a raspy voice. "Sorry, man, but I can't let them go for less than $100," John replied. "Well," Dave said, leaning closer, "how's about you sell them to me for $50 or I'll beat your face in for you." "O … kay."

Customer #4—Dave

As the sun set and the shadows lengthened, John waited patiently for his last customer to finish looking around. Truth be told, the guy looked kind of creepy.

"I'll give you $50 for these speakers," Dave said in a raspy voice.

"Sorry, man, but I can't let them go for less than $100," John replied.

"Well," Dave said, leaning closer, "how's about you sell them to me for $50 or I'll beat your face in for you."

"O … kay," John said, startled. "$50 it is, then."

Dave smiled. He slid a fifty-dollar bill across the counter, picked up the speakers, and left without a word.

John has made four agreements, but are they contracts? Can he require Fran to buy the TV for $250? If Ricky and Carla never return to buy the iPod and the projector, can John take them to court and force them to follow through on the deals? Can John undo his transaction with the disreputable Dave?

Throughout this unit on contracts, we will consider issues like these. It is vital for a businessperson to understand the difference between an ordinary promise and a legally enforceable contract.

Most contracts work out precisely as intended because the parties fulfill their obligations. Most—but not all. In this unit, we will study contracts that have gone wrong. We look at these errant deals so that you can learn how to avoid problems.

CONTRACTS

Elements of a Contract

A contract is merely a legally enforceable agreement. People regularly make promises, but only some of them are enforceable. For a contract to be enforceable, seven key characteristics *must* be present. We will study this "checklist" at length in the next several chapters.

- **Offer**. All contracts begin when a person or a company proposes a deal. It might involve buying something, selling something, doing a job, or anything else. But only proposals made in certain ways amount to a legally recognized offer.

- **Acceptance**. Once a party receives an offer, he must respond to it in a certain way.

- **Consideration**. There has to be bargaining that leads to an *exchange* between the parties. Contracts cannot be a one-way street; both sides must receive some measureable benefit.

- **Legality**. The contract must be for a lawful purpose. Courts will not enforce agreements to sell cocaine, for example.

- **Capacity**. The parties must be adults of sound mind.

- **Consent**. Certain kinds of trickery and force can prevent the formation of a contract.

- **Writing**. While verbal agreements often amount to contracts, some types of contracts must be in writing to be enforceable.

Other Important Issues

Once we have examined the essential parts of contracts, the unit will turn to other important issues:

- **Performance and Discharge.** If a party fully accomplishes what the contract requires, his duties are discharged. But what if his obligations are performed poorly, or not at all?

- **Remedies.** A court will award money or other relief to a party injured by a breach of contract.

Let's apply these principles to the opening scenario.

Fran is not obligated to buy the TV for $250 because John did not accept her offer. Ricky does not have to buy the iPod because he is under 18. If he changes his mind, there is nothing John can do about it. Nor is Carla required to buy the projector. Agreements concerning a sale of goods valued at more than $500 must be in writing. John can successfully sue Dave. He accepted Dave's offer to buy the speakers for $50, but he did so under duress. Agreements made under threats of violence are not enforceable contracts.

TYPES OF CONTRACTS

Before undertaking a study of contracts, you need to familiarize yourself with some important vocabulary. This section will present five sets of terms.

Bilateral and Unilateral Contracts

Bilateral contract
A promise made in exchange for another promise.

In a **bilateral contract**, both parties make a promise. A producer says to Gloria, "I'll pay you $2 million to star in my new romantic comedy, which we are shooting three months from now in Santa Fe." Gloria says, "It's a deal." That is a bilateral contract. Each party has made a promise to do something. The producer is now bound to pay Gloria $2 million, and Gloria is obligated to show up on time and act in the movie. The vast majority of contracts are bilateral contracts. They can be for services, such as this acting contract; they can be for the sale of goods, such as 1,000 tons of steel, or for almost any other purpose. When the bargain is a promise for a promise, it is a bilateral agreement.

Unilateral contract
A binding agreement in which one party has made an offer that the other party can accept only by action, not words.

In a unilateral contract, one party makes a promise that the other party can accept only by *actually doing* something. These contracts are less common. Suppose the movie producer tacks a sign to a community bulletin board. It has a picture of a dog with a phone number, and it reads, "I'll pay $100 to anyone who returns my lost dog." If Leo sees the sign, finds the producer, and merely promises to find the dog, he has not created a contract. Because of the terms on the sign, Leo must actually find and return the dog to stake a claim to the $100.

Executory and Executed Contracts

Executory contract
An agreement in which one or more parties have not yet fulfilled their obligations.

A contract is **executory** when it has been made, but one or more parties have not yet fulfilled their obligations. Recall Gloria, who agrees to act in the producer's film beginning in three months. The moment Gloria and the producer strike their bargain, they have an executory bilateral express contract.

Executed contract
An agreement in which all parties have fulfilled their obligations.

A contract is **executed** when all parties have fulfilled their obligations. When Gloria finishes acting in the movie and the producer pays her final fee, their contract will be fully executed.

EXAM Strategy

Question: Abby has long coveted Nicola's designer handbag because she saw one of them in a movie. Finally, Nicola offers to sell her friend the bag for $350 in cash. "I don't have the money right now," Abby replies, "but I'll have it a week from Friday. Is it a deal?" Nicola agrees to sell the bag. Use two terms to describe the contract.

Strategy: In a bilateral contract, both parties make a promise, but in a unilateral agreement, only one side does so. An executory contract is one with unfulfilled obligations, while an executed agreement is one with nothing left to be done.

Result: Nicola promised to sell the bag for $350 cash, and Abby agreed to pay. Because both parties made a promise, this a bilateral agreement. The deal is not yet completed, meaning that they have an executory contract.

Valid, Unenforceable, Voidable, and Void Agreements

A **valid contract** is one that satisfies all of the law's requirements. It has no problems in any of the seven areas listed at the beginning of this chapter, and a court will enforce it. The contract between Gloria and the producer is a valid contract, and if the producer fails to pay Gloria, she will win a lawsuit to collect the unpaid fee.

An **unenforceable agreement** occurs when the parties intend to form a valid bargain, but a court declares that some rule of law prevents enforcing it. Suppose Gloria and the producer orally agree that she will star in his movie, which he will start filming in 18 months. The law, as we will see in Chapter 11, requires that this contract be in writing because it cannot be completed within one year. If the producer signs up another actress two months later, Gloria has no claim against him.

A **voidable contract** occurs when the law permits one party to terminate the agreement. This happens, for example, when the other party has committed fraud, or when an agreement has been signed under duress. In the opening scenario, Dave threatened John when he would not sell the speakers for $50. The agreement is voidable at John's option. If John later decides that the $50 is acceptable, he may keep it. But if he decides that he wants to cancel the agreement and sue for the return of his speakers, he can do that as well.

> **Voidable contract**
> An agreement that may be terminated by one of the parties.

A **void agreement** is one that neither party can enforce, usually because the purpose of the deal is illegal or because one of the parties had no legal authority to make a contract.

The following case illustrates the difference between voidable and void agreements.

> **Void agreement**
> A contract that neither party can enforce, because the bargain is illegal or one of the parties had no legal authority to make it.

MR. W FIREWORKS, INC. v. OZUNA

2009 Tex. App. LEXIS 8237
Court of Appeals of Texas, Fourth District, San Antonio, 2009

Facts: Mr. W sells fireworks. Under Texas law, retailers may sell fireworks to the public only during the two weeks immediately before the Fourth of July and during two weeks immediately before New Year's Day. And so, fireworks sellers like Mr. W tend to lease property.

Mr. W leased a portion of Ozuna's land. The lease contract contained two key terms:

"In the event the sale of fireworks on the aforementioned property is or shall become unlawful during the period of this lease and the term granted, this lease shall become void.

"Lessor(s) agree not to sell or lease any part of said property, including any adjoining, adjacent, or contiguous property, to any person(s) or corporation for the purpose of selling fireworks in competition to the Lessee during the term of this lease, *and for a period of ten years after lease is terminated*." (Emphasis added.)

A longstanding San Antonio city ordinance bans the sale of fireworks inside city limits, and also within 5,000 feet of city limits. Like all growing cities, San Antonio sometimes annexes new land, and its city limits change. One annexation caused the Ozuna property to fall within 5,000 feet of the new city limits, and it became illegal to sell fireworks from the property. Mr. W stopped selling fireworks and paying rent on Ozuna's land.

Two years later, San Antonio's border shifted again. This time, the city *disannexed* some property and *shrank*. The new city limits placed Ozuna's property just beyond the 5,000-foot no-fireworks zone. Ozuna then leased a part of his land to Alamo Fireworks, a competitor of Mr. W.

Mr. W sued for breach of contract, arguing that Ozuna had no right to lease to a competitor for a period of 10 years. The trial court granted Ozuna's motion for summary judgment. Mr. W appealed.

Issue: *Did Ozuna breach his contract with Mr. W by leasing his land to a competitor?*

Excerpts from Judge Angelini's Decision: The property owners [argue] that when the city ordinance made the sale of fireworks illegal on the subject properties, the leases became void, resulting in the property owners and Mr. W no longer having an enforceable agreement. Mr. W's argues that the provision restricting the property owners from leasing to competitors survived the agreement. This is inconsistent with the meaning of "voidable" contracts. For example, when a minor enters into a contract, that contract is not void, but is voidable at the election of the minor. This means that the minor may set aside the entire contract at his option, but he *is not entitled to enforce portions that are favorable to him and at the same time disaffirm other provisions that he finds burdensome.* He is not permitted to retain the benefits of a contract while repudiating its obligations.

Here, while Mr. W is arguing that the illegalization of the sale of fireworks made the contract "voidable," it is still seeking to enforce the provision of the contract prohibiting the property owners from leasing to competitors. We decline to adopt such an interpretation.

Further, contracts requiring an illegal act are void. We therefore hold that the illegalization of the sale of the fireworks on the respective properties did not trigger the provision in the leases prohibiting the property owners from leasing to competitors of Mr. W.

We affirm the judgment of the trial court.

Express and Implied Contracts

Express contract
An agreement with all the important terms explicitly stated.

In an **express contract**, the two parties explicitly state all the important terms of their agreement. The vast majority of contracts are express contracts. The contract between the producer and Gloria is an express contract because the parties explicitly state what Gloria will do, where and when she will do it, and how much she will be paid. Some express contracts are oral, as that one was, and some are written. They might be bilateral express contracts, as Gloria's was, or unilateral express contracts, as Leo's was. Obviously, it is wise to make express contracts, and to put them in writing. We emphasize, however, that many oral contracts are fully enforceable.

Implied contract
The words and conduct of the parties indicate they intended an agreement.

In an implied contract, the words and conduct of the parties indicate that they intended an agreement. Suppose every Friday, for two months, the producer asks Lance to mow his lawn, and loyal Lance does so each weekend. Then, for three more weekends, Lance simply shows up without the producer asking, and the producer continues to pay for the work done. But on the 12th weekend, when Lance rings the doorbell to collect, the producer suddenly says, "I never asked you to mow it. Scram." The producer is correct that there was no express contract because the parties had not spoken for several weeks. But a court will probably rule that the conduct of the parties has *implied* a contract. Not only did Lance mow the lawn every weekend, but the producer even paid on three weekends when they had not spoken. It was reasonable for Lance to assume that he had a weekly deal to mow and be paid.

Today, the hottest disputes about implied contracts continue to arise in the employment setting. Many corporate employees have at-will relationships with their companies. This means that the employees are free to quit at any time and the company has the right to fire them for virtually any reason. But often a company provides its workers with personnel manuals that lay out certain rights. Does a handbook create a contract guaranteeing those rights? What is your opinion?

You be the Judge

DEMASSE V. ITT CORPORATION
194 Ariz. 500, 984 P.2d 1138
Supreme Court of Arizona, 1999

Facts: Roger DeMasse and five others were employees-at-will at ITT Corporation, where they started working at various times between 1960 and 1979. Each was paid an hourly wage.

ITT issued an employee handbook, which it revised four times over two decades.

The first four editions of the handbook stated that within each job classification, any layoffs would be made in reverse order of seniority. The fifth handbook made two important changes. First, the document stated that "nothing contained herein shall be construed as a guarantee of continued employment. ITT does not guarantee continued employment to employees and retains the right to terminate or lay off employees."

Second, the handbook stated that "ITT reserves the right to amend, modify, or cancel this handbook, as well as any or all of the various policies [or rules] outlined in it." Four years later, ITT notified its hourly employees that layoff guidelines for hourly employees would be based not on seniority, but on ability and performance. About 10 days later, the six employees were laid off, though less-senior employees kept their jobs. The six employees sued.

You Be The Judge: *Did ITT have the right to unilaterally change the layoff policy?*

Argument for the workers: It is true that all of the plaintiffs were originally employees-at-will, subject to termination at the company's whim. However, things changed when the company issued the first handbook. ITT chose to include a promise that layoffs would be based on seniority. Long-term workers and new employees all understood the promise and relied on it. The company put it there to attract and retain good workers. The policy worked. Responsible employees understood that the longer they remained at ITT, the safer their job was. Company and employees worked together for many years with a common

understanding, and that is a textbook definition of an implied contract.

Once a contract is formed, whether express or implied, it is binding on both sides. That is the whole point of a contract. If one side could simply change the terms of an agreement on its own, what value would any contract have? The company's legal argument is a perfect symbol of its arrogance: it believes that because these workers are mere hourly workers, they have no rights, even under contract law. The company is mistaken. Implied contracts are binding, and ITT should not make promises it does not intend to keep.

Argument for ITT: Once an at-will employee, always one. ITT had the right to fire any of its employees at any time—just as the workers had the right to quit whenever they wished. That never changed, and in case any workers forgot it, the company reiterated the point in its most recent handbook. If the plaintiffs thought layoffs would happen in any particular order, that is their error, not ours.

All workers were bound by the terms of whichever handbook was then in place. For many years, the company had made a seniority-layoff promise. Had we fired a senior worker during that period, he or she would have had a legitimate complaint—and that is why we did not do it. Instead, we gave everyone four years' notice that things would change. Any workers unhappy with the new policies should have left to find more congenial work.

Why should an employee be allowed to say, "I prefer to rely on the old, outdated handbooks, not the new one"? The plaintiffs' position would mean that no company is ever free to change its general work policies and rules. Since when does an at-will employee have the right to dictate company policy? That would be disastrous for the whole economy—but fortunately it is not the law.

Promissory Estoppel and Quasi-Contracts

Now we turn away from "true" contracts and consider two unusual circumstances. Sometimes, courts will enforce agreements even if they fail to meet the usual requirement of a contract. We emphasize that these remedies are uncommon exceptions to the general rules. Most of the agreements that courts enforce are the express contracts that we have already studied. Nonetheless, the next two remedies are still pivotal in some lawsuits. In each case, a sympathetic plaintiff can demonstrate an injury but *there is no contract*. The plaintiff cannot claim that the defendant breached a contract, because none ever existed. The plaintiff must hope for more "creative" relief.

The two remedies can be confusingly similar. The best way to distinguish them is this:

- In promissory estoppel cases, the defendant made a promise that the plaintiff relied on.

- In quasi-contract cases, the defendant received a *benefit* from the plaintiff.

Promissory Estoppel

Promissory estoppels

A *possible* remedy for an injured plaintiff in a case with no valid contract, where the plaintiff can show a promise, reasonable reliance, and injustice.

A fierce fire swept through Dana and Derek Andreason's house in Utah, seriously damaging it. The good news was that agents for Aetna Casualty promptly visited the Andreasons and helped them through the crisis. The agents reassured the couple that all of the damage was covered by their insurance, instructed them on which things to throw out and replace, and helped them choose materials for repairing other items. The bad news was that the agents were wrong: the Andreasons' policy had expired six weeks before the fire. When Derek Andreason presented a bill for $41,957 worth of meticulously itemized work that he had done under the agents' supervision, Aetna refused to pay.

The Andreasons sued—but not for breach of contract. There *was* no contract—they allowed their policy to expire. They sued Aetna under the legal theory of promissory estoppel: even when there is no contract, a plaintiff may use **promissory estoppel** to enforce the defendant's promise if he can show that:

- The defendant made a promise knowing that the plaintiff would likely rely on it;

- The plaintiff did rely on the promise; and

- The only way to avoid injustice is to enforce the promise.

Aetna made a promise to the Andreasons—namely, its assurance that all of the damage was covered by insurance. The company knew that the Andreasons would rely on that promise, which they did by ripping up a floor that might have been salvaged, throwing out some furniture, and buying materials to repair the house. Is enforcing the promise the only way to avoid injustice? Yes, ruled the Utah Court of Appeals.[1] The Andreasons' conduct was reasonable and based entirely on what the Aetna agents told them. Under promissory estoppel, the Andreasons received virtually the same amount they would have obtained had the insurance contract been valid.

Quasi-Contract

Don Easterwood leased over 5,000 acres of farmland in Jackson County, Texas, from PIC Realty for one year. The next year, he obtained a second one-year lease. During each year, Easterwood farmed the land, harvested the crops, and prepared the land for the following year's planting. Toward the end of the second lease, after Easterwood had harvested his crop, he and PIC began discussing the terms of another lease. While they negotiated,

---

[1]*Andreason v. Aetna Casualty & Surety Co.*, 848 P.2d 171, 1993 Utah App. LEXIS 26 (Utah App. 1993).

Easterwood prepared the land for the following year, cutting and plowing the soil. But the negotiations for a new lease failed, and Easterwood moved off the land. He sued PIC Realty for the value of his work preparing the soil.

Easterwood had neither an express nor an implied contract for the value of his work. How could he make any legal claim? By relying on the legal theory of a quasi-contract: Even when there is no contract, a court may use **quasi-contract** to compensate a plaintiff who can show that:

- The plaintiff gave some benefit to the defendant;
- The plaintiff reasonably expected to be paid for the benefit and the defendant knew this; and
- The defendant would be unjustly enriched if he did not pay.

If a court finds all of these elements present, it will generally award the value of the goods or services that the plaintiff has conferred. The damages awarded are called *quantum meruit*, meaning that the plaintiff gets "as much as he deserves." The court is awarding money that it believes the plaintiff *morally ought to have*, even though there was no valid contract entitling her to it. This again is judicial activism, with the courts inventing a "quasi" contract where no true contract exists. The purpose is justice, the term is contradictory.

Don Easterwood testified that in Jackson County, it was quite common for a tenant farmer to prepare the soil for the following year but then be unable to farm the land. In those cases, he claimed, the landowner compensated the farmer for the work done. Other witnesses agreed that this was the local custom. The court ruled that indeed there was no contract, but that all elements of quasi-contract had been satisfied. Easterwood gave a benefit to PIC because the land was ready for planting. Jackson County custom caused Easterwood to assume he would be paid, and PIC Realty knew it. Finally, said the court, it would be unjust to let PIC benefit without paying anything. The court ordered PIC to pay the fair market value of Easterwood's labors.

Quasi-contract
A *possible* remedy for an injured plaintiff in a case with no valid contract, where the plaintiff can show benefit to the defendant, reasonable expectation of payment, and unjust enrichment.

Quantum meruit
"As much as he deserves"—the damages awarded in a quasi-contract case.

SOURCES OF CONTRACT LAW

Common Law

Express and implied contracts, promissory estoppel, and quasi-contract were all crafted, over centuries, by courts deciding one contract lawsuit at a time. Many contract lawsuits continue to be decided using common-law principles developed by courts.

Uniform Commercial Code

Business methods changed quickly during the first half of the last century. Transportation speeded up. Corporations routinely conducted business across state borders and around the world. These developments presented a problem. Common-law principles, whether related to contracts, torts, or anything else, sometimes vary from one state to another. New York and California courts often reach similar conclusions when presented with similar cases, but they are under no obligation to do so. Business leaders became frustrated that, to do business across the country, their companies had to deal with many different sets of common law rules.

Executives, lawyers, and judges wanted a body of law for business transactions that reflected modern commercial methods and provided uniformity throughout the United States. It would be much easier, they thought, if some parts of contract law were the same in every state. That desire gave birth to the Uniform Commercial Code (UCC), created in 1952. The drafters intended the UCC to facilitate the easy formation and enforcement of contracts in a fast-paced world. The Code governs many aspects of commerce, including the sale and leasing of goods, negotiable instruments, bank deposits, letters of credit, investment securities, secured transactions, and other commercial matters. Every state has adopted at least part of the UCC to govern commercial transactions within that state. For our purposes in studying contracts, the most important part of the Code is Article 2, which governs the sale of goods. **"Goods" means anything movable, except for money, securities, and certain legal rights.** Goods include pencils, commercial aircraft, books, and Christmas trees. Goods do not include land or a house because neither is movable, nor do they include a stock certificate. A contract for the sale of 10,000 sneakers is governed by the UCC; a contract for the sale of a condominium in Marina del Rey is governed by the California common law.

When analyzing any contract problem as a student or businessperson, you must note whether the agreement concerns the sale of goods. For many issues, the common law and the UCC are reasonably similar. But sometimes, the law is quite different under the two sets of rules.

And so, the UCC governs contracts for a sale of goods, while common law principles govern contracts for sales of services and everything else. Most of the time, it will be clear whether the UCC or the common law applies. But what if a contract involves both goods and services? When you get your oil changed, you are paying in part for the new oil and oil filter (goods) and in part for the labor required to do the job (services). In a mixed contract, Article 2 governs only if the *primary purpose* was the sale of goods.

EXAM **Strategy**

Question: Leila agrees to pay Kendrick $35,000 to repair windmills. Confident of this cash, Kendrick contracts to buy Derrick's used Porsche for $33,000. Then Leila informs Kendrick she does not need his help and will not pay him. Kendrick tells Derrick that he no longer wants the Porsche. Derrick sues Kendrick, and Kendrick files suit against Leila. What law or laws govern these lawsuits?

Strategy: Always be conscious of whether a contract is for services or the sale of goods. Different laws govern. To make that distinction, you must understand the term "goods." If you are clear about that, the question is answered easily.

Result: *Goods* means anything movable, and a Porsche is movable—one might say "super-movable." The UCC will control Derrick's suit. Repairing windmills is primarily a service. Kendrick's lawsuit is governed by the common law of contracts.

Contracts Checklist

- ☑ Offer
- ☑ Acceptance
- ☐ Consideration
- ☐ Legality
- ☐ Capacity
- ☐ Consent
- ☐ Writing

Offer

An act or statement that proposes definite terms and permits the other party to create a contract by accepting those terms.

THE AGREEMENT

Meeting of the Minds

Remember that contracts have seven key characteristics. Agreements that have a problem in any of the areas do not amount to valid contracts. In this section, we examine the first two items on the checklist.

Parties form a contract only if they have a meeting of the minds. For this to happen, one side must make an **offer** and the other must make an **acceptance**. An offer proposes definite terms, and an acceptance unconditionally agrees to them.

Throughout the chapter, keep in mind that courts make *objective* assessments when evaluating offers and acceptances. A court will not try to get inside anyone's head and decide what she was thinking as she made an agreement. Instead, it will decide how a reasonable person would interpret her words and conduct.

Offer

Bargaining begins with an offer. The person who makes an offer is the **offeror**. The person to whom he makes that offer is the **offeree**. The terms are annoying but inescapable because, like handcuffs, all courts use them.

Two questions determine whether a statement is an offer:

- Do the offeror's words and actions indicate an *intention* to make a bargain?

- Are the terms of the offer reasonably definite?

Zachary says to Sharon, "Come work in my English-language center as a teacher. I'll pay you $800 per week for a 35-hour week, for six months starting Monday." This is a valid offer. Zachary's words seem to indicate that he intends to make a bargain and his offer is definite. If Sharon accepts, the parties have a contract that either one can enforce.

In the following section, we present categories of statements that are generally *not* valid offers.

Offeror
The person who makes an offer.

Offeree
The person to whom an offer is made.

Statements That Usually Do Not Amount to Offers

Invitations to Bargain   **An invitation to bargain is not an offer.** Suppose Martha telephones Joe and leaves a message on his answering machine, asking if Joe would consider selling his vacation condo on Lake Michigan. Joe faxes a signed letter to Martha saying, "There is no way I could sell the condo for less than $150,000." Martha promptly sends Joe a cashier's check for that amount. Does she own the condo? No. Joe's fax was not an offer. It is merely an invitation to negotiate. Joe is indicating that he might well be happy to receive an offer from Martha, but he is not promising to sell the condo for $150,000 or for any amount.

Letters of Intent   In complex business negotiations, the parties may spend months bargaining over dozens of interrelated issues. Because each party wants to protect itself during the discussions, ensuring that the other side is serious without binding itself to premature commitments, it may be tempting during the negotiations to draft a **letter of intent**. The letter *might* help distinguish a serious party from one with a casual interest, summarize the progress made thus far, and assist the parties in securing necessary financing. Usually, letters of intent do not create any legal obligation. They merely state what the parties are considering, not what they have actually agreed to. But note that is possible for a letter of intent to bind the parties if its language indicates that the parties *intended* to be bound.

Letter of intent
A letter that summarizes negotiating progress.

Advertisements   Mary Mesaros received a notice from the United States Bureau of the Mint, announcing a new $5 gold coin to commemorate the Statue of Liberty. The notice contained an order form stating:

VERY IMPORTANT—PLEASE READ: YES, Please accept my order for the U.S. Liberty Coins I have indicated. I understand that all sales are final and not subject to refund. Verification of my order will be made by the Department of the Treasury, U.S. Mint. If my order is received by December 31, I will be entitled to purchase the coins at the Pre-Issue Discount price shown.

Mesaros ordered almost $2,000 worth of the coins. But the Mint was inundated with so many requests for the coin that the supply was soon exhausted. Mesaros and thousands of others never got their coins. This was particularly disappointing because the market value of the coins doubled shortly after their issue. Mesaros sued on behalf of the entire class of disappointed purchasers. Like most who sue based on an advertisement, she lost.[2] **An advertisement is generally not an offer.** An advertisement is merely a request for offers. The consumer makes the offer, whether by mail, as above, or by arriving at a merchant's store ready to buy. The seller is free to reject the offer.

---

[2]*Mesaros v. United States*, 845 F.2d 1576, 1988 U.S. App. LEXIS 6055 (Fed. Cir. 1988).

Advertisers should be careful, however, not to be too specific in their ads. Some ads do count as offers, as the following case illustrates.

Landmark Case

CARLILL V. CARBOLIC SMOKE BALL COMPANY
1 QB 256
Court of Appeal, 1892

Facts: In the early 1890s, English citizens greatly feared the Russian flu. The Carbolic Smoke Ball Company ran a newspaper ad that contained two key passages:

> "£100 reward will be paid by the Carbolic Smoke Ball Company to any person who contracts the influenza after having used the ball three times daily for two weeks according to the printed directions supplied with each ball.
>
> "£1000 is deposited with the Alliance Bank, shewing our sincerity in the matter."

The product was a ball that contained carbolic acid. Users would inhale vapors from the ball through a long tube.

Carlill purchased a smoke ball and used it as directed for two months. She then caught the flu. She sued, arguing that because her response to the ad had created a contract with the company, she was entitled to £100.

The trial court agreed, awarding Carlill the money. The company appealed.

Issues: *Did the advertisement amount to an offer? If so, was the offer accepted?*

Excerpts from Lord Justice Lindley's Decision: The first observation I will make is that we are dealing with an express promise to pay £100 in certain events. Read the advertisement how you will, and twist it about as you will, here is a distinct promise expressed in language which is perfectly unmistakable.

We must first consider whether this was intended to be a promise at all. The deposit is called by the advertiser as proof of his sincerity in the matter—that is, the sincerity of his promise to pay this £100 in the event which he has specified. I say there is the promise, as plain as words can make it.

Then it is contended that it is not binding. In the first place, the performance of the conditions is the acceptance of the offer. Unquestionably, as a general proposition, when an offer is made, it is necessary that the acceptance should be notified. But is that so in cases of this kind? I think that in a case of this kind that the person who makes the [offer] shews by his language and from the nature of the transaction that he does not expect and does not require notice of the acceptance apart from notice of the performance.

We, therefore, find here all the elements which are necessary to form a binding contract enforceable in point of law.

It appears to me, therefore, that the defendants must perform their promise, and, if they have been so unwary as to expose themselves to a great many actions, so much the worse for them. Appeal dismissed.

Carlill lived 50 years more, dying at the age of 96—of the flu.

This case serves as a cautionary tale. Running a "normal" ad that describes a product, its features, and its price does not amount to an offer. But, if a company proposes to take an action—like pay $100 to customers who take certain, specific actions—then it may find itself contractually obligated to follow through on its promises. The acceptance of the offer makes a unilateral contract.

Problems with Definiteness

It is not enough that the offeror indicates that she intends to enter into an agreement. **The terms of the offer must also be definite.** If they are vague, then even if the offeree agrees to the deal, a court does not have enough information to enforce it, and there is no contract.

You want a friend to work in your store for the holiday season. This is a definite offer: "I offer you a job as a sales clerk in the store from November 1 through December 29, 40 hours per week at $10 per hour." But suppose, by contrast, you say: "I offer you a job as a sales clerk in the store during the holiday season. We will work out a fair wage once we see how busy things get." Your friend replies, "That's fine with me." This offer is indefinite, and there is no contract. What is a fair wage? $15 per hour? Or $20 per hour? What is the "holiday season"? How will the determinations be made? There is no binding agreement.

EXAM Strategy

Question: Niels owned three adjoining parcels of land in Arizona ranging from 60 to 120 acres. Hannah wanted to buy one. The two had dinner in Chicago and then sketched this agreement: "Binding Contract: Niels agrees to sell one of his three Arizona lots to Hannah. Within 14 days, the parties will meet on the land, decide which lot Hannah is buying, and settle on a price. If they cannot agree on a price, they will decide a fair method of doing so. Both parties agree to be bound by this contract." Each signed. When they meet in Arizona, Niels refuses to sell any land, and Hannah sues. What will happen?

Strategy: Do not be fooled by wording such as "Binding Contract." Focus on the legal issues: Was there a meeting of the minds? Niels and Hannah *thought* they had a contract—but courts make an objective assessment, not subjective. Did Niels make an offer? Were the terms definite?

Result: Both parties believed they had a binding deal, and both parties were wrong. There are two primary issues—which lot is being sold and how much will it cost—and neither is specified. How are they to select a lot? What is a "fair method" of determining price? Other issues are not touched upon: When will the deal close, how will payment be made, what happens if Hannah cannot finance the purchase? The terms are too vague. The parties never reached a meeting of the minds, and Hannah will lose her suit.

Termination of Offers

Once an offer has been made, it faces only two possible fates—it can be terminated or accepted. If an offer is terminated, it can never be accepted. If it is accepted, and if there are no problems with any of the five remaining elements on the Contracts Checklist, then a valid contract is created. Offers can be terminated in four ways: by revocation, rejection, expiration, and operation of law.

Termination by Revocation

An offer is **revoked** when the offeror "takes it back" before the offeree accepts. In general, the offeror may revoke the offer any time before it has been accepted. Imagine that I call you and say, "I'm going out of town this weekend. I'll sell you my ticket to this weekend's football game for $75." You tell me that you'll think it over and call me back. An hour later, my plans change. I call you a second time and say, "Sorry, but the deal's off—I'm going to the game after all." I have revoked my offer, and you can no longer accept it.

In the next case, this rule was worth $100,000 to one of the parties.

NADEL V. TOM CAT BAKERY

2009 N.Y. Misc. Lexis 5105
Supreme Court of New York, New York County, 2009

Facts: A Tom Cat Bakery delivery van struck Elizabeth Nadel as she crossed a street. Having suffered significant injuries, Nadel filed suit. Before the trial began, the attorney representing the bakery's owner offered a $100,000 settlement, which Nadel refused.

While the jury was deliberating, the bakery's lawyer again offered Nadel the $100,000 settlement. She decided to think about it during lunch. Later that day, the jury sent a note to the judge. The bakery owner told her lawyer that if the note indicated the jury had reached a verdict, that he should revoke the settlement offer.

Back in the courtroom, the bakery's lawyer said, "My understanding is that there's a note…. I was given an instruction that if the note is a verdict, my client wants to take the verdict."

Nadel's lawyer then said, "My client will take the settlement. My client will take the settlement."

The trial court judge allowed the forewoman to read the verdict, which awarded Nadel—nothing. She appealed, claiming that a $100,000 settlement had been reached.

Issue: *Did Nadel's lawyer accept the settlement offer in time?*

Excerpts from Judge Figueroa's Decision: Plaintiff's motion to enforce "the settlement" has generated considerable debate between the parties. Plaintiff asserts that the defendant is bound to a settlement. Plaintiff's problem is that there was no "agreement" to speak of. To be sure, there was an offer from defendant. During the above-quoted colloquy, clearly there were also words of acceptance from plaintiff. But when the words, "my client will take the settlement" were uttered, it was too late for them to be effective. By that time, defense counsel had made it clear that if the jury had already come to a verdict, the offer was off the table. That condition could not be ignored, as the verdict that would mean all bets were off had already been reached. For the foregoing reasons, plaintiff's motion is denied.

Termination by Rejection

If an offeree clearly indicates that he does not want to take the offer, then he has rejected it. If an offeree rejects an offer, the rejection immediately terminates the offer. Suppose a major accounting firm telephones you and offers a job, starting at $80,000. You respond, "Nah. I'm gonna work on my surfing for a year or two." The next day, you come to your senses and write the firm, accepting its offer. No contract. Your rejection terminated the offer and ended your power to accept it.

Counteroffer   A party makes a **counteroffer** when it responds to an offer with a new and different proposal. Frederick faxes Kim, offering to sell a 50 percent interest in the Fab Hotel in New York for only $135 million. Kim faxes back and says, "That's too much, but I'll pay $115 million." Moments later, Kim's business partner convinces her that Frederick's offer was a bargain, and she faxes an acceptance of his $135 million offer. Does Kim have a binding deal? No. **A counteroffer is a rejection.** When Kim offered $115 million, she rejected Frederick's offer. Her original fax created a new offer, for $115 million, which Frederick never accepted. The parties have no contract at any price.

Termination by Expiration

An offeror may set a time limit. Quentin calls you and offers you a job in his next motion picture. He tells you, "I've got to know by tomorrow night." If you call him in three days to accept, you are out of the picture. **When an offer specifies a time limit for acceptance, that period is binding.**

If the offer specifies no time limit, the offeree has a reasonable period in which to accept. A reasonable period varies, depending upon the type of offer, previous dealings between the parties, and any normal trade usage or customary practices in a particular industry.

Termination by Operation of Law

In some circumstances, the law itself terminates an offer. **If an offeror dies or becomes mentally incapacitated, the offer terminates automatically and immediately.** Arnie offers you a job as an assistant in his hot-air balloon business. Before you can even accept, Arnie tumbles out of a balloon at 3,000 feet. The offer terminates along with Arnie.

Destruction of the subject matter terminates the offer. A car dealer offers to sell you a rare 1938 Bugatti for $7,500,000 if you bring cash the next day. You arrive, suitcase stuffed with cash, just in time to see Arnie drop 3,000 feet through the air and crush the Bugatti. The dealer's offer is terminated.

> Arnie offers you a job as an assistant in his hot-air balloon business. Before you can even accept, Arnie tumbles out of a balloon at 3,000 feet. The offer terminates along with Arnie.

Acceptance

As we have seen, when there is a valid offer outstanding, it remains effective until it is terminated or accepted. An offeree accepts by saying or doing something that a reasonable person would understand to mean that he definitely wants to take the offer. Assume that Ellie offers to sell Gene her old iPod for $50. If Gene says, "I accept your offer," then he has indeed accepted, but there is no need to be so formal. He can accept the offer by saying, "It's a deal," or, "I'll take it," or any number of things. He need not even speak. If he hands her a $50 bill, he also accepts the offer.

It is worth noting that **the offeree must say or do *something* to accept.** Marge telephones Vick and leaves a message on his answering machine: "I'll pay $75 for your business law textbook from last semester. I'm desperate to get a copy, so I will assume you agree unless I hear from you by 6:00 tonight." Marge hears nothing by the deadline and assumes she has a deal. She is mistaken. Vick neither said nor did anything to indicate that he accepted.

Mirror Image Rule

If only he had known! A splendid university, an excellent position as department chair—gone. And all because of the mirror image rule.

Ohio State University wrote to Philip Foster offering him an appointment as a professor and chair of the art history department. His position was to begin July 1, and he had until June 2 to accept the job. On June 2, Foster telephoned the dean and left a message accepting the position, *effective July 15*. Later, Foster thought better of it and wrote the university, accepting the school's starting date of July 1. Too late! Professor Foster never did occupy that chair at Ohio State. The court held that since his acceptance varied the starting date, it was a counteroffer. And a counteroffer, as we know, is a rejection.[3]

Was it sensible to deny the professor a job over a mere 14-day difference? Sensible or not, that is the law. The common-law **mirror image rule** requires that acceptance be on *precisely* the same terms as the offer. If the acceptance contains terms that add or contradict the offer, even in minor ways, courts generally consider it a counteroffer. The rule worked reasonably well in the nineteenth century, when parties would write an original contract and

Mirror image rule
Requires that acceptance be on precisely the same terms as the offer.

---

[3]*Foster v. Ohio State University*, 41 Ohio App. 3d 86, 534 N.E.2d 1220, 1987 Ohio App. LEXIS 10761 (Ohio Ct. App. 1987).

exchange it, penciling in any changes. But now that businesses use standardized forms to purchase most goods and services, the rule creates enormous difficulties. Sellers use forms they have prepared, with all conditions stated to their advantage, and buyers employ their own forms, with terms they prefer. The forms are exchanged in the mail or electronically, with neither side clearly agreeing to the other party's terms.

The problem is known as the "battle of forms." Once again, the UCC has entered the fray, attempting to provide flexibility and common sense for those contracts involving the sale of goods. But for contracts governed by the common law, such as Professor Foster's, the mirror image rule is still the law.

UCC and the Battle of Forms

Earlier in this chapter, we introduced the UCC. Article 2 of the UCC governs contracts when the primary purpose is a sale of goods. Remember that goods are moveable, tangible objects. Usually, UCC provisions are not significantly different from common law rules. But on occasion, the UCC modifies the common law rule in some major way. In such cases, we will present a separate description of the key UCC provision.

UCC §2-207 dramatically modifies the mirror image rule for the sale of goods. Under this provision, an acceptance that adds additional or different terms will often create a contract. The rule is intricate, but it may be summarized this way:

- For the sale of goods, the most important factor is whether the parties believe they have a binding agreement. If their conduct indicates that they have a deal, they probably do.

- If the offeree *adds new* terms to the offer, acceptance by the offeror generally creates a binding agreement.

- If the offeree *changes* the terms of the offer, a court will probably rely on general principles of the UCC to create a fair contract.

- If a party wants a contract on its terms only, with no changes, it must clearly indicate that.

Suppose Wholesaler writes to Manufacturer, offering to buy "10,000 wheelbarrows at $50 per unit. Payable on delivery, 30 days from today's date." Manufacturer writes back, "We accept your offer of 10,000 wheelbarrows at $50 per unit, payable on delivery. Interest at normal trade rates for unpaid balances." Manufacturer clearly intends to form a contract. The company has added a new term, but there is still a valid agreement.

Clickwraps and Shrinkwraps

You want to purchase Attila brand software and download it to your computer. You type in your credit card number and other information, agreeing to pay $99. Attila also requires that you "read and agree to" all of the company's terms. You click "I agree," without having read one word of the terms. Three frustrating weeks later, tired of trying to operate defective Attilaware, you demand a refund and threaten to sue. The company replies that you are barred from suing because the terms you agreed to included an arbitration clause. To resolve any disputes, you must travel to Attila's hometown, halfway across the nation, use an arbitrator that the company chooses, pay one-half the arbitrator's fee, and also pay Attila's legal bills if you should lose. The agreement makes it financially impossible for you to get your money back. Is that contract enforceable?

You have entered into a "clickwrap" agreement. Similar agreements, called "shrink-wraps," are packaged inside many electronic products. A shrinkwrap notice might require that before inserting a purchased CD into your computer, you must read and agree to all terms in the brochure. Clickwraps and shrinkwraps often include arbitration clauses. They frequently limit the seller's liability if anything goes wrong, saying that the manufacturer's maximum responsibility is to refund the purchase price (even if the software destroys your hard drive).

Many courts that have analyzed these issues have ruled that clickwrap and shrinkwrap agreements are indeed binding, even against consumers. The courts have emphasized that sellers are entitled to offer a product on any terms they wish, and that shrinkwrap and clickwrap are the most efficient methods of including complicated terms in a small space. Think before you click![4]

Consideration

The central idea of consideration is simple: contracts must be a two-way street. If one side gets all the benefit and the other side gets nothing, then an agreement lacks consideration and is not an enforceable contract.

There are three rules of consideration:

Contracts Checklist
- ☐ Offer
- ☐ Acceptance
- ☑ Consideration
- ☐ Legality
- ☐ Capacity
- ☐ Consent
- ☐ Writing

1. Both parties must get something of *measureable value* from the contract. That thing can be money, boots, an agreement not to sue, or anything else that has real value.

2. A *promise* to give something of value counts as consideration. A *promise* to mow someone's lawn next week is the equivalent of actually *doing* the yardwork when evaluating whether consideration exists.

3. The two parties must have *bargained for* whatever was exchanged and struck a deal: "If you do this, I'll do that." If you just decide to deliver a cake to your neighbor's house without her knowing, that may be something of value, but since you two did not bargain for it, there is no contract, and she does not owe you the price of the cake.

Let's take an example: Sally's Shoe Store and Baker Boots agree that she will pay $20,000 for 100 pairs of boots. They both get something of value—Sally gets the boots, Baker gets the money. A contract is formed when the promises are made because a promise to give something of value counts. The two have bargained for this deal, so there is valid consideration.

Now for an example where there is no consideration. Marvin works at Sally's. At 9 a.m., he is in a good mood and promises to buy his coworker a Starbucks during the lunch hour. The delighted coworker agrees. Later that morning, the coworker is rude to Marvin, who then changes his mind about buying the coffee. He is free to do so. His promise created a one-way street: the coworker stood to receive all the benefit of the agreement, while Marvin got nothing. Because Marvin received no value, there is no contract.

What Is Value?

As we have seen, an essential part of consideration is that both parties must get something of value. That item of value can be either an "act" or a "forbearance."

Act   A party commits an **act** when she does something she was not legally required to do in the first place. She might do a job, deliver an item, or pay money, for example. An act does not count if the party was simply complying with the law or fulfilling her obligations under an existing contract. Thus, for example, suppose that your professor tells the university that she will not post final grades unless she is paid an extra $5,000. Even if the university agrees to this outrageous demand, that agreement is not a valid contract because the professor is already under an obligation to post final grades.

---

[4]*ProCD, Inc. v. Zeidenberg*, 86 F.3d 1447 (7th Cir. 1996), is the leading case to enforce shrinkwrap agreements (and, by extension, clickwraps). *Klocek v. Gateway*, 104 F. Supp. 1332 (D. Kan. 2000), is one of the few cases to reject such contracts. *Klocek*, however, was dismissed for failure to reach the federal court $75,000 jurisdictional level.

Forbearance

Refraining from doing something that one has a legal right to do.

Forbearance   A **forbearance** is, in essence, the opposite of an act. A plaintiff forbears if he agrees *not* to do something he had a legal right to do. An entrepreneur might promise a competitor not to open a competing business, or an elderly driver (with a valid driver's license) might promise concerned family members that he will not drive at night.

Let's apply these ideas to the most famous of all consideration lawsuits. Our story begins in 1869, when a well-meaning uncle makes a promise to his nephew. Ever since *Hamer v. Sidway* appeared, generations of American law students have dutifully inhaled the facts and sworn by its wisdom; now you, too, may drink it in.

Landmark Case

HAMER V. SIDWAY
124 N.Y. 538, 27 N.E. 256, 1891 N.Y. LEXIS 1396
New York Court of Appeals, 1891

Facts: This is a story with two Stories. William Story wanted his nephew to grow up healthy and prosperous. In 1869, he promised the fifteen-year-old boy (who was also named William Story) $5,000 if the lad would refrain from drinking liquor, using tobacco, swearing, and playing cards or billiards for money until his twenty-first birthday. (In that wild era—can you believe it?—the nephew had a legal right to do all those things.) The nephew agreed and, what is more, he kept his word. When he reached his twenty-first birthday, the nephew notified his uncle that he had honored the agreement. The uncle congratulated the young man and promised to give him the money, but said he would wait a few more years before handing over the cash, until the nephew was mature enough to handle such a large sum. The uncle died in 1887 without having paid, and his estate refused to honor the promise. Because the nephew had transferred his rights in the money, it was a man named Hamer who eventually sought to collect from the uncle's estate. The estate argued that since the nephew had given no consideration for the uncle's promise, there was no enforceable contract. The trial court found for the plaintiff, and the uncle's estate appealed.

Issue: *Did the nephew give consideration for the uncle's promise?*

Excerpts from Justice Parker's Decision: The defendant contends that the contract was without consideration to support it, and therefore invalid. He asserts that the promisee, by refraining from the use of liquor and tobacco, was not harmed, but benefited; that

that which he did was best for him to do, independently of his uncle's promise, and insists that it follows that, unless the promisor was benefited, the contract was without consideration, a contention which, if well founded, would seem to leave open for controversy in many cases whether that which the promisee did or omitted to do was in fact of such benefit to him as to leave no consideration to support the enforcement of the promisor's agreement. Such a rule could not be tolerated, and is without foundation in the law. Courts will not ask whether the thing which forms the consideration does in fact benefit the promisee or a third party, or is of any substantial value to anyone. It is enough that something is promised, done, forborne, or suffered by the party to whom the promise is made as consideration for the promise made to him.

Now applying this rule to the facts before us, the promisee used tobacco, occasionally drank liquor, and he had a legal right to do so. That right he abandoned for a period of years upon the strength of the promise of the testator [that is, the uncle] that for such forbearance he would give him $5,000. We need not speculate on the effort which may have been required to give up the use of those stimulants. It is sufficient that he restricted his lawful freedom of action within certain prescribed limits upon the faith of his uncle's agreement, and now, having fully performed the conditions imposed, it is of no moment whether such performance actually proved a benefit to the promisor, and the court will not inquire into it.

Chapter Conclusion

Contracts govern countless areas of our lives, from intimate family issues to multibillion-dollar corporate deals. Understanding contract principles is essential for a successful business or professional career and is invaluable in private life. This knowledge is especially important because courts no longer rubber-stamp any agreement that two parties have made. If we know the issues that courts scrutinize, the agreement we draft is likelier to be enforced. We thus achieve greater control over our affairs—the very purpose of a contract.

EXAM REVIEW

1. **CONTRACTS: DEFINITION AND ELEMENTS** A contract is a legally enforceable promise. Analyzing whether a contract exists involves inquiring into these issues: offer, acceptance, consideration, capacity, legal purpose, consent, and sometimes, whether the deal is in writing. (p. 215)

2. **UNILATERAL AND BILATERAL CONTRACTS** In bilateral contracts, the parties exchange promises. In a unilateral contract, only one party makes a promise, and the other must take some action—his return promise is insufficient to form a contract. (p. 216)

3. **EXECUTORY AND EXECUTED CONTRACTS** In an executory contract, one or both of the parties have not yet done everything that they promised to do. In an executed contract, all parties have fully performed. (pp. 216–217)

4. **ENFORCEABILITY: VALID, VOID, AND VOIDABLE AGREEMENTS**

   - Valid contracts are fully enforceable.
   - An unenforceable agreement is one with a legal defect.
   - A voidable contract occurs when one party has an option to cancel the agreement.
   - A void agreement means that the law will ignore the deal regardless of what the parties want. (pp. 217–218)

EXAM Strategy

Question: Yasmine is negotiating to buy Stewart's house. She asks him what condition the roof is in. "Excellent," he replies. "It is only 2 years old, and should last 25 more." In fact, Stewart knows that the roof is 26 years old and has had a series of leaks. The parties sign a sales contract for $600,000. A week before Yasmine is to pay for the house and take possession, she discovers the leaks and learns that the mandatory new roof will cost $35,000. At the same time, she learns that the house has increased in value by $60,000 since she signed the agreement. What options does Yasmine have?

Strategy: You know intuitively that Stewart's conduct is as shabby as his roof. What is the legal térm for his deception? Fraud. Does fraud make an agreement void or voidable? Does it matter? (See the "Result" at the end of this section.)

5. **EXPRESS AND IMPLIED CONTRACTS** If the parties formally agreed and stated explicit terms, there is probably an express contract. If the parties did not formally agree but their conduct, words, or past dealings indicate they intended a binding agreement, there may be an implied contract. (pp. 218–219)

6. **OTHER REMEDIES** If there is no contract, are there other reasons to give the plaintiff damages?

   • A claim of promissory estoppel requires that the defendant made a promise knowing that the plaintiff would likely *rely*, and the plaintiff did so. It would be wrong to deny recovery.

   • A claim of quasi-contract requires that the defendant received a benefit, knowing that the plaintiff would expect compensation, and it would be unjust not to grant it. (pp. 220–221)

EXAM Strategy

Question: The Hoffmans owned and operated a successful small bakery and grocery store. They spoke with Lukowitz, an agent of Red Owl Stores, who told them that for $18,000, Red Owl would build a store and fully stock it for them. The Hoffmans sold their bakery and grocery store and purchased a lot on which Red Owl was to build the store. Lukowitz then told Hoffman that the price had gone up to $26,000. The Hoffmans borrowed the extra money from relatives, but then Lukowitz informed them that the cost would be $34,000. Negotiations broke off, and the Hoffmans sued. The court determined that there was no contract because too many details had not been worked out—the size of the store, its design, and the cost of constructing it. Can the Hoffmans recover any money?

Strategy: Because there is no contract, the Hoffmans must rely on either promissory estoppel or quasi-contract. Promissory estoppel focuses on the defendant's promise and the plaintiff's reliance. Those suing in quasi-contract must show that the defendant received a benefit for which it should reasonably expect to pay. Does either fit here? (See the "Result" at the end of this section.)

7. **SOURCES OF CONTRACT LAW** If a contract is for the sale of goods, the UCC is the relevant body of law. For anything else, the common law governs. If a contract involves both goods and services, a court will determine the agreement's primary purpose. (pp. 221–222)

8. **MEETING OF THE MINDS** The parties can form a contract only if they have a meeting of the minds, which requires that they understand each other and show that they intend to reach an agreement. (p. 222)

9. **OFFER** An offer is an act or statement that proposes definite terms and permits the other party to create a contract by accepting those terms. (p. 223)

10. **OTHER STATEMENTS** Invitations to bargain, price quotes, and advertisements are generally not offers. However, an ad in which a company proposes to take a specific action when a customer takes a specific action can amount to an offer. (pp. 223–224)

EXAM Strategy

Question: "**Huge** selection of Guernsey sweaters," reads a newspaper ad from Stuffed Shirt, a clothing retailer. "Regularly $135, today only $65." Waldo arrives at Stuffed Shirt at 4:00 that afternoon, but the shop clerk says there are no more sweaters. He shows Waldo a newly arrived Shetland sweater that sells for $145. Waldo sues, claiming breach of contract and violation of a consumer protection statute. Who will prevail?

(a) Waldo will win the breach of contract suit and the consumer protection suit.

(b) Waldo will lose the breach of contract suit but might win the consumer protection suit.

(c) Waldo will lose the consumer protection suit but should win the breach of contract suit.

(d) Waldo will win the consumer protection suit only if he wins the contract case.

(e) Waldo will lose both the breach of contract suit and the consumer protection suit.

Strategy: Waldo assumes that he is accepting the store's offer. But did Stuffed Shirt make an offer? If not, there cannot be a contract. Does the consumer protection statute help him? (See the "Result" at the end of this section.)

11. **DEFINITENESS** The terms of the offer must be definite, although under the UCC, the parties may create a contract that has open terms. (pp. 224–225)

12. **TERMINATION** An offer may be terminated by revocation, rejection, expiration, or operation of law. (pp. 225–227)

EXAM Strategy

Question: Rick is selling his espresso coffeemaker. He sends Tamara an email, offering to sell the machine for $350. Tamara promptly emails back, offering to buy the item for $300. She hears nothing from Rick, so an hour later, Tamara stops by his apartment, where she learns that he just sold the machine to his roommate for $250. She sues Rick. Outcome?

(a) Tamara will win because her offer was higher than the roommate's.

(b) Tamara will win because Rick never responded to her offer.

(c) Tamara will win because both parties made clear offers, in writing.

(d) Tamara will lose because she rejected Rick's offer.

(e) Tamara will lose because her offer was not definite.

Strategy: A valid contract requires a definite offer and acceptance. Rick made a valid offer. When Tamara said she would buy the machine for a lower amount, was that acceptance? If not, what was it? (See the "Result" at the end of this section.)

13. **MIRROR IMAGE RULE AND UCC §2-207** The common law mirror image rule requires acceptance on precisely the same terms as the offer. Under the UCC, an offeree may often create a contract even when the acceptance includes terms that are additional to or different from those in the offer. (pp. 227–228)

14. **CLICKWRAPS** Clickwrap and shrinkwrap agreements are generally enforceable. (pp. 228–229)

15. **CONSIDERATION** There are three rules of consideration:

   • Both parties must get something of *measureable value* from the contract.

   • A *promise* to give something of value counts as consideration.

   • The two parties must have *bargained for* whatever was exchanged. (p. 229)

---

4. Result: Indeed, it does matter. Stewart's fraud makes the contract voidable by Yasmine. She has the right to terminate the agreement and pay nothing. However, she may go through with the contract if she prefers. The choice is hers—but not Stewart's.

6. Result: Red Owl received no benefit from the Hoffmans' sale of their store or purchase of the lot. However, Red Owl did make a promise and expected the Hoffmans to rely on it, which they did. The Hoffmans won their claim of promissory estoppel.

10. Result: An advertisement is usually not an offer, but merely a solicitation of one. It is Waldo who is making the offer, which the store may reject. Waldo loses his contract case, but he may win under the consumer protection statute. The correct answer is (b). If Stuffed Shirt proclaimed "huge selection" when there were only five sweaters, the store was deliberately misleading consumers, and Waldo wins. However, if there was indeed a large selection, and Waldo arrived too late, he is out of luck.

12. Result: Tamara made a counteroffer of $300. A counteroffer is a rejection. Tamara rejected Rick's offer and simultaneously offered to buy the coffeemaker at a lower price. Rick was under no obligation to sell to Tamara at any price. He will win Tamara's suit.

MULTIPLE-CHOICE QUESTIONS

1. A sitcom actor, exhausted after his 10-hour workweek, agrees to buy a briefcase full of cocaine from Lewis for $12,000. Lewis and the actor have a _____ contract.
   (a) valid
   (b) unenforceable
   (c) voidable
   (d) void

2. Linda goes to an electronics store and buys a high-definition television. Lauren hires a company to clean her swimming pool once a week. The _____ governs Linda's contract with the store, and the _____ governs Lauren's contract with the cleaning company.
   (a) common law; common law
   (b) common law; UCC
   (c) UCC; common law
   (d) UCC; UCC

3. Consider the following scenarios:
   I. Madison says to a group of students, "I'll pay $35 to the first one of you who shows up at my house and mows my lawn."
   II. Lea posts a flyer around town that reads, "Reward: $500 for information about the person who keyed my truck last Saturday night in the Wag-a-Bag parking lot. Call Lea at 555-5309."
   Which of these proposes a *unilateral* contract?
   (a) I only
   (b) II only
   (c) Both I and II
   (d) None of the above

4. Which of the following amounts to an offer?
   (a) Ed says to Carmen, "I offer to sell you my pen for $1."
   (b) Ed says to Carmen, "I'll sell you my pen for $1."
   (c) Ed writes, "I'll sell you my pen for $1," and gives the note to Carmen.
   (d) All of the above.
   (e) A and C only.

5. Rebecca, in Honolulu, faxes a job offer to Spike, in Pittsburgh, saying, "We can pay you $55,000 per year, starting June 1." Spike faxes a reply, saying, "Thank you! I accept your generous offer, though I will also need $3,000 in relocation money. See you June 1. Can't wait!" On June 1, Spike arrives, to find that his position is filled by Gus. He sues Rebecca.
   (a) Spike wins $55,000.
   (b) Spike wins $58,000.
   (c) Spike wins $3,000.
   (d) Spike wins restitution.

ESSAY QUESTIONS

1. In the bleachers …

   "You're a prince, George!" Mike exclaimed. "Who else would give me a ticket to the big game?"

   "No one, Mike, no one."

   "Let me offer my thanks. I'll buy you a beer!"

   "Ah," George said. "A large beer would hit the spot right now."

   "Small. Let me buy you a small beer."

   "Ah, well, good enough."

   Mike stood and took his wallet from his pocket. He was distressed to find a very small number of bills inside. "There's bad news, George!" he said.

   "What's that?"

   "I can't buy you the beer, George."

   George considered that for a moment. "I'll tell you what, Mike," he said. "If you march to the concession stand right this minute and get me my beer, I won't punch you in the face."

   "It's a deal!" Mike said.

   Discuss the consideration issues raised by this exchange.

2. Interactive Data Corp. hired Daniel Foley as an assistant product manager at a starting salary of $18,500. Over the next six years, Interactive steadily promoted Foley until he became Los Angeles branch manager at a salary of $56,116. Interactive's officers repeatedly told Foley that he would have his job so long as his performance was adequate. In addition, Interactive distributed an employee handbook that specified "termination guidelines," including a mandatory seven-step pre-termination procedure. Two years later, Foley learned that his recently hired supervisor, Robert Kuhne, was under investigation by the FBI for embezzlement at his previous job. Foley reported this to Interactive officers. Shortly thereafter, Interactive fired Foley. He sued, claiming that Interactive could fire him only for good cause, after the seven-step procedure. What kind of a claim is he making? Should he succeed?

3. **YOU BE THE JUDGE WRITING PROBLEM** John Stevens owned a dilapidated apartment that he rented to James and Cora Chesney for a low rent. The Chesneys began to remodel and rehabilitate the unit. Over a four-year period, they installed two new bathrooms, carpeted the floors, installed new septic and heating systems, and rewired, replumbed, and painted. Stevens periodically stopped by and saw the work in progress. The Chesneys transformed the unit into a respectable apartment. Three years after their work was done, Stevens served the Chesneys with an eviction notice. The Chesneys counterclaimed, seeking the value of the work they had done. Are they entitled to it? **Argument for Stevens:** Mr. Stevens is willing to pay the Chesneys exactly the amount he agreed to pay: nothing. The parties never contracted for the Chesneys to fix up the apartment. In fact, they never even discussed such an agreement. The Chesneys are making the absurd argument that anyone who chooses to perform certain work, without ever discussing it with another party, can finish the job and then charge it to the other person. If the Chesneys expected to get paid, obviously they should have said so. If the court were to allow this claim, it would be inviting other tenants to make improvements and then bill the landlord. The law has never been so foolish. **Argument for the Chesneys:** The law of

quasi-contract was crafted for cases exactly like this. The Chesneys have given an enormous benefit to Stevens by transforming the apartment and enabling him to rent it at greater profit for many years to come. Stevens saw the work being done and understood that the Chesneys expected some compensation for these major renovations. If Stevens never intended to pay the fair value of the work, he should have stopped the couple from doing the work or notified them that there would be no compensation. It would be unjust to allow the landlord to seize the value of the work, evict the tenants who did it, and pay nothing.

4. The town of Sanford, Maine, decided to auction off a lot it owned. The town advertised that it would accept bids through the mail, up to a specified date. Arthur and Arline Chevalier mailed in a bid that turned out to be the highest. When the town refused to sell them the lot, they sued. Result?

5. The Dukes leased land from Lillian Whatley. Toward the end of their lease, they sent Ms. Whatley a new contract, renewing the lease for three years and giving themselves the option to buy the land at any time during the lease for $50,000. Ms. Whatley crossed out the clause giving them an option to buy. She added a sentence at the bottom, saying, "Should I, Lillian Whatley, decide to sell at end [sic] of three years, I will give the Dukes the first chance to buy." Then she signed the lease, which the Dukes accepted in the changed form. They continued to pay the rent until Ms. Whatley sold the land to another couple for $35,000. The Dukes sued. Are the Dukes entitled to the land at $50,000? At $35,000?

DISCUSSION QUESTIONS

1. Have you ever made an agreement that mattered to you, only to have the other person refuse to follow through on the deal? Looking at the list of elements in the chapter, did your agreement amount to a contract? If not, which element did it lack?

2. Consider promissory estoppel and quasi-contracts. Do you like the fact that these doctrines exist? Should courts have "wiggle room" to enforce deals that fail to meet formal contract requirements? Or, should the rule be "If it's not an actual contract, too bad. No deal."

3. Is it sensible to have two different sets of contract rules—one for sales of goods and another for everything else? Would it be better to have a single set of rules for all contracts?

4. Return to the opening scenario. Fran, Ricky, Carla, and Dave each made an agreement with John. None is valid under contract law. For the sake of fairness, *should* any of them be legally enforceable? If so, which?

5. Someone offers to sell you a concert ticket for $50, and you reply, "I'll give you $40." The seller refuses to sell at the lower price, and you say, "OK, OK, I'll pay you $50." Clearly, no contract has been formed because you made a counteroffer. If the seller has changed her mind and no longer wants to sell for $50, she doesn't have to. But is this fair? If it is all part of the same conversation, should you be able to accept the $50 offer and get the ticket?

CHAPTER 10

LEGALITY, CONSENT, AND WRITING

Soheil Sadri, a California resident, did some serious gambling at Caesar's Tahoe casino in Nevada. And lost. To keep gambling, he wrote checks to Caesar's and then signed two memoranda pledging to repay all money advanced. After two days, with his losses totaling more than $22,000, he went home. Back in California, Sadri stopped payment on the checks and refused to pay any of the money he owed Caesar's. The casino sued. In defense, Sadri claimed that California law considered his agreements illegal and unenforceable. He was unquestionably correct about one thing: a contract that is illegal is void and unenforceable.

© neelsky/Shutterstock.com

A contract that is illegal is void and unenforceable.

Gambling is big business. Almost all states now permit some form of wagering, from casinos to racetracks to lotteries, and they eagerly collect the billions of dollars in revenue generated. Supporters urge that casinos create jobs and steady income, boost state coffers, and take business away from organized crime. Critics argue that naive citizens inevitably lose money they can ill afford to forfeit, and that addicted gamblers destroy their families and weaken the fabric of communities. With citizens and states divided over the ethics of gambling, it is inevitable that we have conflicts such as the dispute between Sadri and Caesar's. The basic rule, however, is clear: **a gambling contract is illegal unless it is a type of wagering *specifically authorized* by state statute**.

In California, as in many states, gambling on credit is not allowed. In other words, it is illegal to lend money to help someone wager. But in Nevada, gambling on credit is legal, and debt memoranda such as Sadri's are enforceable contracts. Caesar's sued Sadri in California (where he lived). The result? The court admitted that California's attitude toward gambling had changed, and that bingo, poker clubs, and lotteries were common. Nonetheless, the court denied that the new tolerance extended to wagering on credit:

> There is a special reason for treating gambling on credit differently from gambling itself. Having lost his or her cash, the pathological gambler will continue to play on credit, if extended, in an attempt to win back the losses. This is why enforcement of gambling debts has always been against public policy in California and should remain so, regardless of shifting public attitudes about gambling itself. If Californians want to play, so be it. But the law should not invite them to play themselves into debt. The judiciary cannot protect pathological gamblers from themselves, but we can refuse to participate in their financial ruin.[1]

Caesar's lost and Sadri kept his money. However, do not become too excited at the prospect of risk-free wagering. Casinos responded to cases like *Sadri* by changing their practices. Most now extend credit only to a gambler who agrees that disputes about repayment will be settled in *Nevada* courts. Because such contracts are legal in that state, the casino is able to obtain a judgment against a defaulting debtor and—yes—enforce that judgment in the gambler's home state.

Despite these more restrictive casino practices, Sadri's dispute is a useful starting place from which to examine contract legality because it illustrates two important themes.

First, morality is a significant part of contract legality. In refusing to enforce an obligation that Sadri undeniably had made, the California court relied on the human and social consequences of gambling and on the ethics of judicial enforcement of gambling debts. Second, "void" really means just that: a court will not intercede to assist either party to an illegal agreement, even if its refusal leaves one party shortchanged.

LEGALITY

Noncompete Agreements

In a **noncompete agreement** (sometimes called a *covenant not to compete*), an employee promises not to work for a competitor for some time after leaving his company. For example, an anchorwoman for an NBC news affiliate in Miami might agree that she will not anchor any other Miami station's news show for one year after she leaves her present employer. Noncompetes are often valid, but the common law places some restrictions on them.

Contracts Checklist
- [ ] Offer
- [ ] Acceptance
- [ ] Consideration
- [x] Legality
- [ ] Capacity
- [ ] Consent
- [ ] Writing

---

[1] *Metropolitan Creditors Service of Sacramento v. Sadri*, 15 Cal. App. 4th 1821, 1993 Cal App. LEXIS 559, 19 Cal. Rptr. 2d 646 (Cal. Ct. App. 1993).

It was once true that these covenants were rare and reserved for top corporate officers, but they have now become commonplace in many organizations at virtually all levels. Employers have legitimate concerns that employees might go to work for a competitor and take with them valuable information about doing business in that industry. Some employers, though, attempt to place harsh restrictions on their employees simply to discourage them from leaving.

Employees often view noncompetes as unfair and unduly burdensome. Nonetheless, noncompete agreements are enforceable, so long as they are reasonable in time, activity, and territory. In other words, a noncompete providing that you cannot work in the same industry in the same city for one year is likely to be valid, but not an agreement that essentially prevents you from working at all, such as one that prohibits you from doing any job, anywhere, for ten years.

Was the noncompete in the following case styled fairly, or was the employee clipped?

KING V. HEAD START FAMILY HAIR SALONS, INC.

886 So.2d 769
Supreme Court of Alabama, 2004

Facts: Kathy King was a single mother supporting a college-age daughter. For 25 years, she had worked as a hairstylist. For the most recent 16 years, she had worked at Head Start, which provided haircuts, coloring, and styling for men and women. King was primarily a stylist, though she had also managed one of the Head Start facilities.

King quit Head Start and began working as manager of a Sport Clips shop, located in the same mall as the store she just left. Sport Clips offered only haircuts and primarily served men and boys. Head Start filed suit, claiming that King was violating the noncompetition agreement that she had signed. The agreement prohibited King from working at a competing business within a two-mile radius of any Head Start facility for 12 months after leaving the company. The trial court issued an injunction enforcing the noncompete. King appealed.

Issue: *Was the noncompetition agreement valid?*

Excerpts from Justice Lyons's Decision: King's most persuasive argument is that the geographic restriction contained in the noncompetition agreement imposes an undue hardship on her. King has been in the hair-care industry for 25 years, and it is the only industry in which she is skilled and the only industry in which she can find employment. Head Start has 30 locations throughout the Jefferson County and Shelby County area, making it virtually impossible for her to find employment in the hair-care industry at a facility that does not violate the terms of the noncompetition agreement. According to King, the geographic restriction constitutes a blanket prohibition on practicing her trade.

It cannot reasonably be argued that King, at the age of 40 and having spent more than half of her life as a hair stylist, can learn a new job skill that would allow her to be gainfully employed and meet her needs and the needs of her daughter. Under the circumstances presented here, enforcement of the noncompetition agreement works an undue hardship upon King. The noncompetition agreement cannot so burden King that it would result in her impoverishment.

Head Start is nevertheless entitled to some of the protection it sought in the noncompetition agreement. Head Start has a valid concern that King would be able to attract many of her former Head Start customers if she is allowed to provide hair-care services unencumbered by any limitations. To prevent an undue burden on King and to afford some protection to Head Start, the trial court should enforce a more reasonable geographic restriction—such as one prohibiting King from providing hair-care services within a two-mile radius of the location of the Head Start facility at which she was formerly employed or imposing some other limitation that does not unreasonably interfere with King's right to gainful employment while, at the same time, protecting Head Start's interest in preventing King from unreasonably competing with it during the one-year period following her resignation.

Reversed and remanded.

Sale of a Business

Kory has operated a real estate office, Hearth Attack, in a small city for 35 years, building an excellent reputation and many ties with the community. She offers to sell you the business and its goodwill for $300,000. But you need assurance that Kory will not take your money and promptly open a competing office across the street. With her reputation and connections, she would ruin your chances of success. Also, you have paid her a significant sum, so even if she does not work, she is unlikely to go hungry any time soon. You insist on a noncompete clause in the sale contract. In this clause, Kory promises that for one year, she will not open a new real estate office or go to work for a competing company within a 10-mile radius of Hearth Attack. Suppose, six months after selling you the business, Kory goes to work for a competing real estate agency two blocks away. You seek an injunction to prevent her from working. Who wins?

Noncompete agreements related to the sale of a business are also enforceable if reasonable in time, activity, and territory. Courts are generally stricter in enforcing agreements related to the sale of a business than they are ones that are based simply on employment. Kory is almost certainly bound by her agreement. One year is a reasonable time to allow you to get your new business started. A 10-mile radius is probably about the area that Hearth Attack covers, and realty is obviously a fair business from which to prohibit Kory. A court will probably grant the injunction, barring Kory from her new job.

EXAM Strategy

Question: Caf-Fiend is an expanding chain of coffeehouses. The company offers to buy Bessie's Coffee Shop, in St. Louis, on these terms: Bessie will manage the store, as Caf-Fiend's employee, for one year after the sale. For four years after the sale, Bessie will not open a competing restaurant anywhere within 12 miles. For the same four years, she will not work anywhere in the United States for a competing coffee retailer. Are the last two terms enforceable against Bessie?

Strategy: This contract includes two noncompete clauses. In the first, Bessie agrees not to open a competing business. Courts generally enforce such clauses if they are reasonable in time, geography, and scope of activity. Is this clause reasonable? The second clause involves employment. Courts take a dimmer view of these agreements. Is this clause essential to protect the company's business? Is it unduly harsh for Bessie?

Result: The first restriction is reasonable. Caf-Fiend is entitled to prevent Bessie from opening her own coffeehouse around the corner and drawing her old customers. The second clause is unfair to Bessie. If she wants to move from St. Louis to San Diego and work as a store manager, she is prohibited. It is impossible to see how such employment would harm Caf-Fiend—but it certainly takes away Bessie's career options. The first restriction is valid, the second one unenforceable.

The California Exception

In California, the law on noncompetes is different from the rest of the country. **In this important state, noncompete agreements are *not* enforceable in employment contracts.** In other words, a noncompete is valid only if (1) the employee signs it at the same time she is selling her share of a company and (2) it is reasonable in time, activity, and territory.[2]

---

[2]California Business and Professions Code §16600.

Exculpatory Clauses

You decide to capitalize on your expert ability as a skier and open a ski school in Colorado, "Pike's Pique." But you realize that skiing sometimes causes injuries, so you require anyone signing up for lessons to sign this form:

> I agree to hold Pike's Pique and its employees entirely harmless in the event that I am injured in any way or for any reason or cause, including but not limited to any acts, whether negligent or otherwise, of Pike's Pique or any employee or agent thereof.

The day your school opens, Sara Beth, an instructor, deliberately pushes Toby over a cliff because Toby criticized her clothes. Eddie, a beginning student, "blows out" his knee attempting an advanced racing turn. And Maureen, another student, reaches the bottom of a steep run and slams into a snowmobile that Sara Beth parked there. Maureen, Eddie, and Toby's family all sue Pike's Pique. You defend based on the form you had the three students sign. Does it save the day?

Exculpatory clause

A contract provision that attempts to release one party from liability in the event the other is injured.

The form on which you are relying is an **exculpatory clause**; that is, one that attempts to release you from liability in the event of injury to another party. Exculpatory clauses are common. Ski schools use them, and so do parking lots, landlords, warehouses, sports franchises, and day-care centers. All manner of businesses hope to avoid large tort judgments by requiring their customers to give up any right to recover. Is such a clause valid? Sometimes. Courts frequently—but do not always—ignore exculpatory clauses, finding that one party was forcing the other party to give up legal rights that no one should be forced to surrender.

An exculpatory clause is generally unenforceable when it attempts to exclude an intentional tort or gross negligence. When Sara Beth pushes Toby over a cliff, that is the intentional tort of battery. A court will not enforce the exculpatory clause. Sara Beth is clearly liable.[3] As to the snowmobile at the bottom of the run, if a court determines that was gross negligence (carelessness far greater than ordinary negligence), then the exculpatory clause will again be ignored. If, however, it was ordinary negligence, then we must continue the analysis.

An exculpatory clause is usually unenforceable when the affected activity is in the public interest, such as medical care, public transportation, or some essential service. Suppose Eddie goes to a doctor for surgery on his damaged knee, and the doctor requires him to sign an exculpatory clause. The doctor negligently performs the surgery, accidentally leaving his cuff links in Eddie's left knee. The exculpatory clause will not protect the doctor. Medical care is an essential service, and the public cannot give up its right to demand reasonable work.

But what about Eddie's suit against Pike's Pique? Eddie claims that he should never have been allowed to attempt an advanced maneuver. His suit is for ordinary negligence, and the exculpatory clause probably *does* bar him from recovery. Skiing is a recreational activity. No one is obligated to do it, and there is no strong public interest in ensuring that we have access to ski slopes.

An exculpatory clause is generally unenforceable when the parties have greatly unequal bargaining power. When Maureen flies to Colorado, suppose that the airline requires her to sign a form contract with an exculpatory clause. Because the airline almost certainly has much greater bargaining power, it can afford to offer a "take it or leave it" contract. The bargaining power is so unequal, though, that the clause is probably unenforceable. Does Pike's Pique have a similar advantage? Probably not. Ski schools are not essential and are much smaller enterprises. A dissatisfied customer might refuse to sign such an agreement and take her business elsewhere. A court probably will not see the parties as *grossly* unequal.

An exculpatory clause is generally unenforceable unless the clause is clearly written and readily visible. If Pike's Pique gave all ski students an eight-page contract, and the exculpatory

---

[3]Note that Pike's Pique is probably not liable under agency law principles that preclude an employer's liability for an employee's intentional tort.

clause was at the bottom of page 7 in small print, the average customer would never notice it. The clause would be void.

In the following case, the court focused on the public policy concerns of exculpatory clauses used in a very common setting. Should the exculpatory clause stop the tenant from suing the landlord? You be the judge.

You be the Judge

RANSBURG V. RICHARDS
770 N.E.2d 393
Indiana Court of Appeals, 2002

Facts: Barbara Richards leased an apartment at Twin Lakes, a complex owned by Lenna Ransburg. The written lease declared that:

- Twin Lakes would "gratuitously" maintain the common areas.

- Richards's use of the facilities would be "at her own risk."

- Twin Lakes was not responsible for any harm to the tenant or her guests, anywhere on the property (including the parking lot), even if the damage was caused by Twin Lakes' negligence.

It snowed. As Richards walked across the parking lot to her car, she slipped and fell on snow-covered ice. Richards sued Ransburg, who moved for summary judgment based on the exculpatory clause. The trial court denied Ransburg's motion, and she appealed.

You Be the Judge: *Was the exculpatory clause valid?*

Argument for Tenant: An exculpatory clause in a contract for an essential service violates public policy. When an ill person seeks medical care, his doctor cannot require him to sign an exculpatory clause. In the same way, a person has to live somewhere. Her landlord cannot force her to sign a waiver.

Landlords tend to be wealthy and powerful. There is generally no equality of bargaining power between them. The tenants are not freely agreeing to the exculpatory language.

Moreover, if a landlord fails to maintain property, not just the tenant is at risk. Visitors, the mail carrier, and the general public could all walk through the Twin Lakes parking lot. The public's interest is served when landlords maintain their properties. They must be held liable when they negligently fail to maintain common areas and injuries result.

Argument for Landlord: Ms. Richards does indeed have to live somewhere, but she does not have to live on the plaintiff's property. Surely there are many dozens of properties nearby. If Richards had been dissatisfied with any part of the proposed lease—excessive rent, strict rules, or an exculpatory clause—she was free to take her business to another landlord.

Landlords may generally be wealthier than their tenants, but that fact alone does not mean that a landlord is so powerful that leases are offered on a "take it or leave it" basis. Here, the landlord stated the exculpatory clause plainly. This is a clear contract between adults, and it should stand in its entirety.

Unconscionable Contracts

Gail Waters was young, naive, and insecure. A serious injury when she was 12 years old left her with an annuity; that is, a guaranteed annual payment for many years. When Gail was 21, she became involved with Thomas Beauchemin, an ex-convict, who introduced her to drugs. Beauchemin suggested that Gail sell her annuity to some friends of his, and she agreed. Beauchemin arranged for a lawyer to draw up a contract, and Gail signed it. She received $50,000 for her annuity, which at that time had a cash value of $189,000 and was worth, over its remaining 25 years, $694,000. Gail later decided this was not a wise bargain. Was the contract enforceable? That depends on the law of unconscionability.

An unconscionable contract is one that a court refuses to enforce because of fundamental unfairness. Even if a contract does not violate any specific statute or public policy, it may still be void if it "shocks the conscience" of the court.

Historically, a contract was considered unconscionable if it was "such as no man in his senses and not under delusion would make on the one hand, and as no honest and fair man would accept on the other."[4] The two factors that most often led a court to find unconscionability were (1) **oppression**, meaning that one party used its superior power to force a contract on the weaker party, and (2) **surprise**, meaning that the weaker party did not fully understand the consequences of its agreement.

Oppression
One party uses its superior power to force a contract on the weaker party.

These cases have always been controversial because it is not easy to define oppression and unfair surprise. Further, anytime a court rejects a contract as unconscionable, it diminishes freedom of contract. If one party can escape a deal based on something as hard to define as unconscionability, then no one can rely as confidently on any agreement. As an English jurist said in 1824, "public policy is a very unruly horse, and when once you get astride it, you never know where it will carry you."[5]

Gail Waters won her case. The Massachusetts high court ruled:

> Beauchemin introduced the plaintiff to drugs, exhausted her credit card accounts to the sum of $6,000, unduly influenced her, suggested that the plaintiff sell her annuity contract, initiated the contract negotiations, was the agent of the defendants, and benefited from the contract between the plaintiff and the defendants. The defendants were represented by legal counsel; the plaintiff was not. The cash value of the annuity policy at the time the contract was executed was approximately four times greater than the price to be paid by the defendants. For payment of not more than $50,000, the defendants were to receive an asset that could be immediately exchanged for $189,000, or they could elect to hold it for its guaranteed term and receive $694,000.
>
> The defendants assumed no risk and the plaintiff gained no advantage. We are satisfied that the disparity of interests in this contract is so gross that the court cannot resist the inference that it was improperly obtained and is unconscionable.[6]

VOIDABLE CONTRACTS: CAPACITY AND CONSENT

Katie, age 17, visits her local electronics store to buy a new laptop. At the register, she pays $400 in cash for the machine. No one is with her, and the cashier does not ask her to show her ID.

Out in the parking lot, Katie's cell phone rings. As she fumbles for it, she loses her grip on the new laptop. It falls to the pavement—crack!—bounces once, and comes to rest a few feet away from her.

Just then, an H2 Hummer rounds the corner. It runs over Katie's new laptop. "Ugg…" she says, feeling nauseous. The SUV stops, and the reverse lights come on. It backs slowly over the laptop again. The driver, oblivious, rolls down his window and asks Katie, "Say, is there a gas station around here?"

"Ah … that way," a shocked Katie says, pointing to a sign in the distance. "But you just …"

"Oh, I see it! Thanks a million!" The driver puts the Hummer in gear and drives over the laptop a third time. The small jolt loosens the one lug nut securing the spare tire to the back of the SUV. The heavy spare falls directly on top of what remains of Katie's new laptop.

[4]*Hume v. United States*, 132 U.S. 406, 411, 10 S. Ct. 134, 1889 U.S. LEXIS 1888 (1889), quoting *Earl of Chesterfield v. Janssen*, 38 Eng. Rep. 82, 100 (Ch. 1750).
[5]*Richardson v. Mellish*, 2 Bing. 229, 103 Eng. Rep. 294, 303 (1824).
[6]*Waters v. Min Ltd.*, 412 Mass. 64, 587 N.E.2d 231, 1992 Mass. LEXIS 66 (1992).

Scooping up wires, bits of plastic, and pieces of metal, she goes back inside the store. Dumping the pieces on the customer service desk, she says, "I've changed my mind about this computer."

The clerk looks at the collection of laptop parts, shakes his head, and points to a sign behind him. "Look, I can't take merchandise back if it's damaged. And this laptop is, ah, damaged."

"Too bad," Katie says. "I want my money back. Now."

Is Katie entitled to a full refund? In most states, *yes*.

This section examines **voidable contracts**. When a contract is voidable, one party has the option either to enforce or terminate the agreement. Two specific issues are presented.

Capacity concerns the legal ability of a party to enter a contract in the first place. Someone may lack capacity because of his young age or mental infirmity. **Consent** refers to whether a contracting party truly understood what she was getting into and whether she made the agreement voluntarily. Consent issues arise in cases of fraud, mistake, duress, and undue influence.

Capacity

Capacity is the legal ability to enter into a contract. An adult of sound mind has capacity. Generally, any deal she enters into will be enforced if all elements on the Contracts Checklist—agreement, consideration, and so forth—are present. But two groups of people usually lack legal capacity: minors and those with a mental impairment. We discuss only minors, but similar rules protect mentally impaired people.

Minors

In contract law, a minor is someone under the age of 18. Because a minor lacks legal capacity, she normally can create only a voidable contract. **A voidable contract may be canceled by the party who lacks capacity.** Notice that *only the party lacking capacity* may cancel the agreement. So a minor who enters into a contract generally may choose between enforcing the agreement or negating it. The other party—an adult, or perhaps a store—has no such right. Voidable contracts are very different from those that are void. A *void* contract is illegal from the beginning and may not be enforced by either party. A *voidable* contract is legal but permits one party to escape, if she so wishes.

Disaffirmance   A minor who wishes to escape from a contract generally may **disaffirm** it; that is, he may notify the other party that he refuses to be bound by the agreement. There are several ways a minor may disaffirm a contract. He may simply tell the other party, orally or in writing, that he will not honor the deal. Or he may disaffirm a contract by refusing to perform his obligations under it. A minor may go further—he can undo a contract that has already been completed by filing a suit to **rescind** the contract; that is, to have a court formally cancel it.

Kevin Green was 16 when he signed a contract with Star Chevrolet to buy a used Camaro. Because he was a minor, the deal was voidable. When the Camaro blew a gasket and Kevin informed Star Chevrolet that he wanted his money back, he was disaffirming the contract. He happened to do it because the car suddenly seemed a poor buy, but he could have disaffirmed for any reason at all, such as deciding that he no longer liked Camaros. When Kevin disaffirmed, he was entitled to his money back.

Restitution   **A minor who disaffirms a contract must return the consideration he has received, to the extent he is able.** Restoring the other party to its original position is called **restitution**. The consideration that Kevin Green received in the contract was, of course, the Camaro.

Contracts Checklist
- [ ] Offer
- [ ] Acceptance
- [ ] Consideration
- [ ] Legality
- [x] Capacity
- [ ] Consent
- [ ] Writing

Disaffirm

To give notice of refusal to be bound by an agreement.

Rescind

To cancel a contract.

Restitution

Restoring an injured party to its original position.

What happens if the minor is not able to return the consideration because he no longer has it or it has been destroyed? Most states hold that the minor is *still* entitled to his money back. A minority of states follow the **status quo rule**, which provides that, if a minor cannot return the consideration, the adult or store is only required to return its *profit margin* to the minor.

In the opening scenario, Katie attempted to return a destroyed laptop for the full purchase price of $400. Assume that the store paid a computer manufacturer $350 for the laptop and then marked it up $50.

In most states, Katie would be entitled to the full $400 purchase price, even though the laptop is now worthless. The sign at the customer service desk would have no effect, and the store would have to absorb the loss. But if Katie lives in a state with the status quo rule, then the store will have to refund only $50 to Katie. It is permitted to keep the other $350 so that it breaks even on the transaction, or is "returned to the status quo."

Reality of Consent

Contracts Checklist
- ☐ Offer
- ☐ Acceptance
- ☐ Consideration
- ☐ Legality
- ☐ Capacity
- ☑ Consent
- ☐ Writing

Smiley offers to sell you his house for $300,000, and you agree in writing to buy it. After you move in, you discover that the house is sinking into the earth at the rate of six inches per week. In twelve months, your only access to the house may be through the chimney. You sue, seeking to rescind. You argue that when you signed the contract, you did not truly consent because you lacked essential information. In this section, we look at three claims that parties make in an effort to rescind a contract based on lack of valid consent: (1) fraud, (2) mistake, and (3) duress.

Fraud

Fraud begins when a party to a contract says something that is factually wrong. "This house has no termites," says a homeowner to a prospective buyer. If the house is swarming with the nasty pests, the statement is a misrepresentation. But does it amount to fraud? An injured person must show the following:

1. The defendant knew that his statement was false, or that he made the statement recklessly and without knowledge of whether it was false.

2. The false statement was material.

3. The injured party justifiably relied on the statement.

Element One: Intentional or Reckless Misrepresentation of Fact The injured party must show a false statement of fact. Notice that this does not mean the statement was a necessarily a "lie." If a homeowner says that the famous architect Stanford White designed her house, but Bozo Loco actually did the work, it is a false statement.

Now, if the owner knows that Loco designed the house, she has committed the first element of fraud. And, if she has no idea who designed the house, her assertion that it was "Stanford White" also meets the first element.

But the owner might have a good reason for the error. Perhaps a local history book identifies the house as a Stanford White. If she makes the statement with a reasonable belief that she is telling the truth, she has made an innocent misrepresentation (discussed in the next section) and not fraud.

Opinions and "puffery" do not amount to fraud. An opinion is not a statement of fact. A seller says, "I think land values around here will be going up 20 or 30 percent

> If a homeowner says that the famous architect Stanford White designed her house, but Bozo Loco actually did the work, it is a false statement.

for the foreseeable future." That statement is pretty enticing to a buyer, but it is not a false statement of fact. The maker is clearly stating her own opinion, and the buyer who relies on it does so at his peril. A close relative of opinion is something called "puffery."

Get ready for one of the most astonishing experiences you've ever had! This section on puffery is going to be the finest section of any textbook you have ever read! You're going to find the issue intriguing, the writing dazzling, and the legal summary unforgettable!

"But what happens," you might wonder, "if this section fails to astonish? What if I find the issue dull, the writing mediocre, and the legal summary incomprehensible? Can I sue for fraud?" No. The promises we made were mere puffery. A statement is puffery when a reasonable person would realize that it is a sales pitch, representing the exaggerated opinion of the seller. Puffery is not a statement of fact. Because puffery is not factual, it is never a basis for rescission.

Consumers filed a class action against Intel Corporation, claiming fraud. They asserted that Intel advertised its "Pentium 4" computer chip as the "best" in the market, when in fact, it was no faster than the Pentium III chip. The Illinois Supreme Court dismissed the claims, asserting that no reasonable consumer would make a purchase relying solely on the name "Pentium 4." Even if the consumers could show that Intel plotted to persuade the market that the Pentium 4 was the finest processor, they are demonstrating nothing but puffery.

Saying that the Pentium 4 is "better" or "best" could mean that the Pentium 4 is cheaper, smaller, more reliable, of higher quality, better for resale, more durable, creates less heat, uses less electricity, is more compatible with some versions of software, or is simply the latest in a temporal line of processors. Because the term "better," as a mere suggestion, is not capable of precise measuring, it is mere puffery and therefore not actionable. That is true even if Intel specifically set out to show the market that the Pentium 4 was the best processor to date.[7]

Courts have found many similar phrases to be puffery, including "high-quality" and "expert workmanship."

Element Two: Materiality

The injured party must demonstrate that the statement was material, or important. A minor misstatement does not meet this second element of fraud. Was the misstatement likely to influence the decision of the misled party significantly? If so, it was material.

Imagine a farmer selling a piece of his land. He measures the acres himself, and calculates a total of 200. If the actual acreage is 199, he has almost certainly not made a *material* misstatement. But if the actual acreage is 150, he has.

Element Three: Justifiable Reliance

The injured party also must show that she actually did rely on the false statement and that her reliance was reasonable. Suppose the seller of a gas station lies through his teeth about the structural soundness of the building. The buyer believes what he hears but does not much care because he plans to demolish the building and construct a day-care center. There was a material misstatement, but no reliance, and the buyer may not rescind.

The reliance must be justifiable—that is, reasonable. If the seller of wilderness land tells Lewis that the area is untouched by pollution, but Lewis can see a large lake on the property covered with six inches of oily red scum, Lewis is not justified in relying on the seller's statements. If he goes forward with the purchase, he may not rescind.

---

[7]*Barbara's Sales, Inc. v. Intel Corp.*, 879 N.E.2d 910 (Ill 2007).

Plaintiff's Remedies for Fraud

In the case of fraud, the injured party generally has a choice of rescinding the contract or suing for damages or, in some cases, doing both. The contract is voidable, which meant that the injured party is not *forced* to rescind the deal but may if he wants. Fraud *permits* the injured party to cancel. Alternatively, the injured party can sue for damages—the difference between what the contract promised and what it delivered.

Nancy learns that the building she bought has a terrible heating system. A new one will cost $12,000. If the seller told her the system was "like new," Nancy may rescind the deal. But it may be economically harmful for her to do so. She might have sold her old house, hired a mover, taken a new job, and so forth. What are her other remedies? She could move into the new house and sue for the difference between what she got and what was promised, which is $12,000, the cost of replacing the heating system.

In some states, a party injured by fraud may both rescind *and* sue for damages. In these states, Nancy could rescind her contract, get her deposit back, and then sue the seller for any damages she has suffered. Her damages might be, for example, a lost opportunity to buy another house or wasted moving expenses.

Mistake

Contract law principles come from many sources, and in the area of "legal mistake," a cow significantly influenced the law. The cow was named Rose. She was a gentle animal that lived in Michigan in 1886. Rose's owner, Hiram Walker & Sons, bought her for $850. After a few years, the company concluded that Rose could have no calves. As a barren cow, she was worth much less than $850, so Walker contracted to sell her to T. C. Sherwood for a mere $80. But when Sherwood came to collect Rose, the parties realized that (surprise!) she was pregnant. Walker refused to part with the happy mother, and Sherwood sued. Walker defended, claiming that both parties had made a *mistake* and that the contract was voidable.

A mistake can take many forms. It may be a basic error about an essential characteristic of the thing being sold, as in Rose's case. It could be an erroneous prediction about future prices, such as an expectation that oil prices will rise. It might be a mechanical error, such as a builder offering to build a new home for $300 when he clearly meant to bid $300,000. Some mistakes lead to voidable contracts, others create enforceable deals. The first distinction is between bilateral and unilateral mistakes.

Bilateral Mistake

Bilateral mistake
Occurs when both parties negotiate based on the same factual error.

A **bilateral mistake** occurs when both parties negotiate based on the same factual error. Sherwood and Walker both thought Rose was barren, both negotiated accordingly, and both were wrong. The Michigan Supreme Court gave judgment for Walker, the seller, permitting him to rescind the contract because the parties were *both* wrong about the essence of what they were bargaining for.

If the parties contract based on an important factual error, the contract is voidable by the injured party. Sherwood and Walker were both wrong about Rose's reproductive ability, and the error was basic enough to cause a tenfold difference in price. Walker, the injured party, was entitled to rescind the contract. Note that the error must be *factual*. Suppose Walker sold Rose thinking that the price of beef was going to drop, when in fact, the price rose 60 percent in five months. That would be simply a *prediction* that proved wrong, and Walker would have no right to rescind.

Conscious Uncertainty   No rescission is permitted where one of the parties knows he is taking on a risk; that is, he realizes there is uncertainty about the quality of the thing being exchanged. Rufus offers 10 acres of mountainous land to Priscilla. "I can't promise you anything about this land," he says, "but they've found gold on every adjoining parcel."

Priscilla, eager for gold, buys the land, digs long and hard, and discovers—mud. She may not rescind the contract. She understood the risk she was assuming, and there was no mutual mistake.

Unilateral Mistake

Sometimes only one party enters a contract under a mistaken assumption, a situation called **unilateral mistake.** In these cases, it is more difficult for the injured party to rescind a contract. This makes sense since in a bilateral error, neither side really knew what it was getting into, and rescission seems a natural remedy. But with unilateral mistakes, one side may simply have made a better bargain than the other. As we have seen throughout this unit on contracts, courts are unwilling to undo an agreement merely because someone made a foolish deal. Nonetheless, if her proof is strong, the injured party in a case of unilateral mistakes still may sometimes rescind a contract. **To rescind for unilateral mistake, a party must demonstrate that she entered the contract because of a basic factual error and that *either* (1) enforcing the contract would be *unconscionable* or (2) the nonmistaken party *knew* of the error.**[8]

Unilateral mistake
Occurs when only one party enters a contract under a mistaken assumption.

Duress

True consent is also lacking when one party agrees to a contract under **duress**. If kindly Uncle Hugo signs over the deed to the ranch because Niece Nelly is holding a gun to his head, Hugo has not consented in any real sense, and he will have the right to rescind the contract. **If one party makes an improper threat that causes the victim to enter into a contract, and the victim had no reasonable alternative, the contract is voidable.**[9]

Duress
An improper threat made to force another party to enter into a contract.

On a Sunday morning, Bancroft Hall drove to pick up his daughter Sandra, who had slept at a friend's house. The Halls are black and the neighborhood was white. A suspicious neighbor called the police, who arrived, aggressively prevented the Halls from getting into their own car, and arrested the father. The Halls had not violated any law or done anything wrong whatsoever. Later, an officer told Hall that he could leave immediately if he signed a full release (stating that he had no claims of any kind against the police), but that if he refused to sign it, he would be detained for a bail hearing. Hall signed the release but later filed suit. The police defended based on the release.

The court held that the release was voidable because Hall had signed it under duress. The threat to detain Hall for a bail hearing was clearly improper because he had committed no crime. He also had no reasonable alternative to signing. A jury awarded the Halls over half a million dollars.[10]

Can "improper threats" take other forms? Does *economic* intimidation count? Many plaintiffs have posed that question over the last half century, and courts have grudgingly yielded.

Today, in most states, economic duress *can* also be used to void a contract. But economic duress sounds perilously close to hard bargaining—in other words, business. The free market system is expected to produce tough competition. A smart, aggressive executive may bargain fiercely. How do we distinguish economic duress from legal, successful business tactics? Courts have created no single rule to answer the question, but they do focus on certain issues.

In analyzing a claim of economic duress, courts look at these factors:

- Acts that have no legitimate business purpose

- Greatly unequal bargaining power

- An unnaturally large gain for one party

- Financial distress to one party

---

[8]Restatement (Second) of Contracts §153.
[9]Restatement (Second) of Contracts §175(1).
[10]*Halls v. Ochs*, 817 F.2d 920, U. S. App. LEXIS 5822 (1st Cir. 1987).

WRITTEN CONTRACTS

Contracts Checklist
- ☐ Offer
- ☐ Acceptance
- ☐ Consideration
- ☐ Legality
- ☐ Capacity
- ☐ Consent
- ✓ Writing

Oliver and Perry were college roommates, two sophomores with contrasting personalities. They were sitting in the cafeteria with some friends, Oliver chatting away, Perry slumped on a plastic bench. Oliver suggested that they buy a lottery ticket, as the prize for that week's drawing was $13 million. Perry muttered, "Nah. You never win if you buy just one ticket." Oliver bubbled up, "O.K., we'll buy a ticket every week. We'll keep buying them from now until we graduate. Come on, it'll be fun. This month, I'll buy the tickets. Next month, you will, and so on." Other students urged Perry to do it, and finally, he agreed.

The two friends carefully reviewed their deal. Each party was providing consideration—namely, the responsibility for purchasing tickets during his month. The amount of each purchase was clearly defined at $1. They would start that week and continue until graduation day, two and a half years down the road. Finally, they would share equally any money won. As three witnesses looked on, they shook hands on the bargain. That month, Oliver bought a ticket every week, randomly choosing numbers, and won nothing. The next month, Perry bought a ticket with equally random numbers—and won $52 million. Perry moved out of their dorm room into a suite at the Ritz and refused to give Oliver one red cent. Oliver sued, seeking $26 million and the return of an Eric Clapton CD. If the former friends had understood the Statute of Frauds, they would never have gotten into this mess.[11]

The rule we examine in this chapter is not exactly new. Originally passed by the British Parliament in 1677, the Statute of Frauds has changed little over the centuries. The purpose was to prevent lying (fraud) in civil lawsuits. It required that in several types of cases, a contract would be enforced only if it were in writing. Contracts involving interests in land were first on the list. Almost all states in this country have passed their own version of the Statute of Frauds. It is important to remember, as we examine the rules and exceptions, that Parliament and the state legislatures all had a commendable, straightforward purpose in passing their respective statutes of fraud: *to provide a court with the best possible evidence of whether the parties intended to make a contract.*

The Statute of Frauds: A plaintiff may not enforce any of the following agreements unless the agreement, or some memorandum of it, is in writing and signed by the defendant.

- For any interest in **land**
- That **cannot be performed within one year**
- To pay the **debt of another**
- Made by an **executor of an estate**
- Made **in consideration of marriage**; and
- For the sale of goods worth $500 or more.

In other words, when two parties make an agreement covered by any one of these six topics, it must be in writing to be enforceable. Oliver and Perry made a definite agreement to purchase lottery tickets during alternate months and share the proceeds of any winning ticket. But their agreement was to last two and a half years. As the second item on the list indicates, a contract must be in writing if it cannot be performed within one year. The good news is that Oliver gets back his Eric Clapton CD. The bad news is that he gets none of the lottery money. Even though three witnesses saw the deal made, it is unlikely to be enforced in any state. Perry will walk away with all $52 million.

---

[11]Based loosely on *Lydon v. Beauregard* (Middlesex Sup. Ct., Mass., Dec. 22, 1989), reported in Paul Langher, "Couple Lose Suit to Share $2.8M Prize," *Boston Globe*, December 23, 1989, p. 21.

Note that although the Oliver-Perry agreement is unenforceable, it is not void. Suppose that Perry does the right thing, agreeing to share the winnings with Oliver. Over the next 20 years, as he receives the winnings, Perry gives one-half to his friend. But then, having squandered his own fortune, Perry demands the money back from Oliver, claiming that the original contract violated the Statute of Frauds. Perry loses. **Once a contract is fully executed, it makes no difference that it was unwritten.** The Statute of Frauds prevents the enforcement of an executory contract; that is, one in which the parties have not fulfilled their obligations. But the contract is not *illegal*. Once both parties have fully performed, neither party may demand rescission. The Statute of Frauds allows a party to cancel future obligations but not undo past actions.

Ethics The *law* permits Perry to keep all of the lottery money. But does Perry have a *moral* right to deny Oliver his half-share? Is the Statute of Frauds serving a useful purpose here? Remember that Parliament passed the original Statute of Frauds believing that a written document would be more reliable than the testimony of alleged witnesses. If we permitted Oliver to enforce the oral contract, based on his testimony and that of the witnesses, would we simply be inviting other plaintiffs to invent lottery "contracts" that had never been made?

Common Law Statute of Frauds: Contracts That Must Be in Writing

Agreements for an Interest in Land

A contract for the sale of any interest in land must be in writing to be enforceable. Notice the phrase "interest in land." This means *any legal right* regarding land. A house on a lot is an interest in land. A mortgage, an easement, and a leased apartment are all interests in land. As a general rule, leases must therefore be in writing, although most states have created an exception for short-term leases. A short-term lease is often one for a year or less, although the length varies from state to state.

Exception: Full Performance by the Seller If the seller completely performs her side of a contract for an interest in land, a court is likely to enforce the agreement, even if it was oral. Adam orally agrees to sell his condominium to Maggie for $150,000. Adam delivers the deed to Maggie and expects his money a week later, but Maggie fails to pay. Most courts will allow Adam to enforce the oral contract and collect the full purchase price from Maggie.

Exception: Part Performance by the Buyer **The buyer of land may be able to enforce an oral contract if she paid part of the purchase price *and either* entered upon the land *or* made improvements to it.** Suppose that Eloise sues Grover to enforce an alleged oral contract to sell a lot in Happydale. She claims they struck a bargain in January. Grover defends based on the Statute of Frauds, saying that even if the two did reach an oral agreement, it is unenforceable. Eloise proves that she paid 10 percent of the purchase price, that she began excavating on the lot in February to build a house, and that Grover knew of the work. Eloise has established part performance and will be allowed to enforce her contract.

Agreements That Cannot Be Performed within One Year

Contracts that cannot be performed within one year are unenforceable unless they are in writing. This one-year period begins on the date the parties make the agreement. The critical word here is "cannot." If a contract *could possibly* be completed within one year, it need not be in writing. Betty gets a job at Burger Brain, throwing fries in oil. Her boss tells her she can have Fridays off for as long as she works there. That oral contract is enforceable whether Betty stays one week or twenty years. "As long as she works there" *could* last for less than one year. Betty might quit the job after six months. Therefore, it does not need to be in writing.[12]

If an agreement will *necessarily* take longer than one year to finish, it must be in writing to be enforceable. If Betty is hired for a term of three years as manager of Burger Brain, the agreement is unenforceable unless put in writing. She cannot perform three years of work in one year.

Or, if you hire a band to play at your wedding 15 months from today, the agreement must be in writing. The gig may take only a single day, but that day will definitely not fall in the next 12 months.

Promise to Pay the Debt of Another

When one person agrees to pay the debt of another as a favor to that debtor, it is called a *collateral promise,* and it must be in writing to be enforceable. D. R. Kemp was a young entrepreneur who wanted to build housing in Tuscaloosa, Alabama. He needed $25,000 to complete a project he was working on, so he went to his old college professor, Jim Hanks, for help. The professor said he would see what he could do about getting Kemp a loan. Professor Hanks spoke with his good friend Travis Chandler, telling him that Kemp was highly responsible and would be certain to repay any money loaned. Chandler trusted Professor Hanks but wanted to be sure of his money. Professor Hanks assured Chandler that if for any reason Kemp did not repay the loan, he, Hanks, would pay Chandler in full. With that assurance, Chandler wrote out a check for $25,000, payable to Kemp, never having met the young man.

Kemp, of course, never repaid the loan. (Thank goodness he did not; this textbook has no use for people who do what they are supposed to.) Kemp exhausted the cash trying to sustain his business, which failed anyway, so he had nothing to give his creditor. Chandler approached Professor Hanks, who refused to pay, and Chandler sued. The outcome was easy to predict. Professor Hanks had agreed to repay Kemp's debt *as a favor to Kemp,* making it a collateral promise. Chandler had nothing in writing, and that is exactly what he got from his lawsuit—nothing.

Promise Made by an Executor of an Estate

This rule is merely a special application of the previous one, concerning the debt of another person. An *executor* is the person who is in charge of an estate after someone dies. The executor's job is to pay debts of the deceased, obtain money owed to him, and disburse the assets according to the will. In most cases, the executor will use only the estate's assets to pay those debts. The Statute of Frauds comes into play when an executor promises to pay an estate's debts with her own funds. An executor's promise to use her own funds to pay a debt of the deceased must be in writing to be enforceable.

Promise Made in Consideration of Marriage

Barney is a multimillionaire with the integrity of a gangster and the charm of a tax collector. He proposes to Li-Tsing, who promptly rejects him. Barney then pleads that if Li-Tsing will be his bride, he will give her an island he owns off the coast of California. Li-Tsing

---

[12]This is the majority rule. In most states, if a company hires an employee "for life," the contract need not be in writing because the employee could die within one year. "Contracts of uncertain duration are simply excluded [from the statute of frauds]; the provision covers only those contracts whose performance cannot possibly be completed within a year." Restatement (Second) of Contracts §130, Comment a, at 328 (1981). However, a few states disagree. The Illinois Supreme Court ruled that a contract for lifetime employment is enforceable only if written. *McInerney v. Charter Golf, Inc.,* 176 Ill. 2d 482, 680 N.E.2d 1347, 1997 Ill. LEXIS 56 (Ill. 1997).

begins to see his good qualities and accepts. After they are married, Barney refuses to deliver the deed. Li-Tsing will get nothing from a court, either, because **a promise made in consideration of marriage must be in writing to be enforceable**.

The Common Law Statute of Frauds: What the Writing Must Contain

Each of the types of contract described above must be in writing in order to be enforceable. What must the writing contain? It may be a carefully typed contract, using precise legal terminology, or an informal memo scrawled on the back of a paper napkin at a business lunch. The writing may consist of more than one document, written at different times, with each document making a piece of the puzzle. But there are some general requirements: the writing

- Must be signed by the defendant, and

- Must state with reasonable certainty the name of each party, the subject matter of the agreement, and all of the essential terms and promises.[13]

Signature

A state's Statute of Frauds typically requires that the writing be "signed by the party to be charged therewith"; that is, the party who is resisting enforcement of the contract. Throughout this chapter, we refer to that person as the "defendant" because when these cases go to court, it is the defendant who is disputing the existence of a contract.

Judges define "signature" very broadly. Using a pen to write one's name certainly counts, but it is not required. A secretary who stamps an executive's signature on a letter fulfills this requirement. In fact, any mark or logo placed on a document to indicate acceptance, even an "X," will generally satisfy the Statute of Frauds. And electronic commerce, as we discuss below, creates new methods of signing.

Reasonable Certainty

Suppose Garfield and Hayes are having lunch, discussing the sale of Garfield's vacation condominium. They agree on a price and want to make some notation of the agreement even before their lawyers work out a detailed purchase and sales agreement. A perfectly adequate memorandum might say, "Garfield agrees to sell Hayes his condominium at 234 Baron Boulevard, Apartment 18, for $350,000 cash, payable on June 18, 2015, and Hayes promises to pay the sum on that day." They should make two copies of their agreement and sign both. Notice that although Garfield's memo is short, it is *certain* and *complete*. This is critical because problems of vagueness and incompleteness often doom informal memoranda.

Electronic Contracts and Signatures

E-commerce has grown at a dazzling rate—each year, U.S. enterprises buy and sell tens of billions of dollars worth of goods and services over the Internet. What happens to the writing requirement, though, when there is no paper? The present Statute of Frauds requires some sort of "signature" to ensure that the defendant committed to the deal. Today, an "electronic signature" could mean a name typed (or automatically included) at the bottom of an email message, a retinal or vocal scan, or a name signed by electronic pen on a writing tablet, among others.

E-signatures are valid in all 50 states. Almost all states have adopted the Uniform Electronic Transactions Act (UETA).[14] UETA declares that *electronic* contracts and signatures

---

[13]Restatement (Second) of Contracts §131.

[14]The states that have not adopted the UETA, at the time of this writing, are Illinois, New York, and Washington.

are as enforceable as those on paper. In other words, the normal rules of contract law apply, and neither party can avoid such a deal merely because it originated in cyberspace. A federal statute, the **Electronic Signatures in Global and National Commerce Act** (E-SIGN), also declares that contracts cannot be denied enforcement simply because they are in electronic form, or signed electronically. It applies in states that have not adopted UETA.

Note that, in many states, certain documents still require a traditional (non-electronic) signature. Wills, adoptions, court orders, and notice of foreclosure are common exceptions. If in doubt, get a hard copy, signed in ink.

The UCC's Statute of Frauds

We have reached another section dedicated to the Uniform Commercial Code (UCC). Remember that UCC rules govern only contracts involving a sale of goods. Because some merchants make dozens or even hundreds of oral contracts every year, the drafters of the UCC wanted to make the writing requirement less onerous for the sale of goods.

The UCC requires a writing for the sale of goods worth $500 or more. The Code's requirements are easier to meet than those of the common law.

UCC §2-201(1)—The Basic Rule

A contract for the sale of goods worth $500 or more is not enforceable unless there is some writing, signed by the defendant, indicating that the parties reached an agreement. The key difference between the common law rule and the UCC rule is that the Code does *not* require *all* of the terms of the agreement to be in writing. The Code looks for something simpler: *an indication that the parties reached an agreement.* Only two things are required: the signature of the defendant and the quantity of goods being sold. Suppose a short memorandum between textile dealers indicates that Seller will sell to Buyer "grade AA 100 percent cotton, white athletic socks." If the writing does not state the price, the parties can testify at court about what the market price was at the time of the deal. If the writing says nothing about the delivery date, the court will assume a reasonable delivery date—say, 60 days. But how many socks were to be delivered? 100 pairs or 100,000? The court will have no objective evidence, so the quantity must be written.

Parol Evidence

Tyrone agrees to buy Martha's house for $800,000. The contract obligates Tyrone to make a 10 percent down payment immediately and pay the remaining $720,000 in 45 days. As the two parties sign the deal, Tyrone discusses his need for financing. Unfortunately, at the end of 45 days, he has been unable to get a mortgage for the full amount. He claims that the parties orally agreed that he would get his deposit back if he could not obtain financing. But the written agreement says no such thing, and Martha disputes the claim. Who will win? Probably Martha, because of the parol evidence rule.

Parol evidence refers to anything (apart from the written contract itself) that was said, done, or written *before* the parties signed the agreement or *as they signed it.* Martha's conversation with Tyrone about financing the house was parol evidence because it occurred as they were signing the contract. Another important term is **integrated contract**, which means a writing that the parties intend as the final, complete expression of their agreement. Now for the rule.

The parol evidence rule: when two parties make an integrated contract, neither one may use parol evidence to contradict, vary, or add to its terms. Negotiations may last for hours, weeks, or even months. Almost no contract includes everything that the parties said. When parties consider their agreement integrated, any statements they made before or while signing are irrelevant. If a court determines that Martha and Tyrone intended their agreement

Integrated contract

A writing that the parties intend as the final, complete expression of their agreement.

to be integrated, it will prohibit testimony about Martha's oral promises. One way to avoid parol evidence disputes is to include an *integration clause.* That is a statement clearly proclaiming that this writing is the "full and final expression" of the parties' agreement, and that anything said before signing or while signing is irrelevant. In the following case, learned people learned about parol evidence the hard way.

MAYO v. NORTH CAROLINA STATE UNIVERSITY

2005 WL 350567
North Carolina Court of Appeals, 2005

Facts: Dr. Robert Mayo was a tenured faculty member of the engineering department at North Carolina State University (NCSU), and director of the school's nuclear engineering program. In July, he informed his department chair, Dr. Paul Turinsky, that he was leaving NCSU effective September 1. Turinsky accepted the resignation.

In October, after Mayo had departed, Phyllis Jennette, the university's payroll coordinator, informed him that he had been overpaid. She explained that for employees who worked 9 months but were paid over 12 months, the salary checks for July and August were in fact prepayments for the period beginning that September. Because Mayo had not worked after September 1, the checks for July and August were overpayment. When he refused to refund the money, NCSU sought to claim it in legal proceedings. The first step was a hearing before an administrative agency.

At the hearing, Turinsky and Brian Simet, the university's payroll director, explained that the "prepayment" rule was a basic part of every employee's contract. However, both acknowledged that the prepayment rule was not included in any of the documents that formed Mayo's contract, including his appointment letter, annual salary letter, and policies adopted by the university's trustees. The university officials used other evidence, outside the written documents, to establish the prepayment policy.

Based on the additional evidence, the agency ruled that NCSU was entitled to its money. However, Mayo appealed to court, and the trial judge declared that he owed nothing, ruling that the university was not permitted to rely on parol evidence to establish its policy. NCSU appealed.

Issue: *May NCSU rely on parol evidence to establish its prepayment rule?*

Excerpts from Judge Bryant's Decision: Here, the language of the employment agreement is clear and unambiguous—petitioner is to be paid in twelve monthly installments for his service as a nine-month, academic year, tenured faculty member.

The terms relied upon by NCSU were not expressly included in the employment agreement. Dr. Turinsky testified that petitioner's written employment agreement is comprised of terms found in petitioner's appointment letter, annual salary letter, and written policies adopted and amended by the UNC Board of Governors and the NCSU Board of Trustees. However, none of these documents forming the employment agreement set forth the compensation policies upon which NCSU bases its claim. Simet, Director of NCSU's Payroll Department, admitted at the agency hearing that the policies were "not stated anywhere specifically." Further, Dr. Turinsky testified he did not know of the existence of the terms until September, after petitioner left his employment with NCSU. NCSU, however, attempts to offer parol evidence to explain that payments made in July and August were prepayments for the following academic year.

The parol evidence rule prohibits the admission of parol evidence to vary, add to, or contradict a written instrument intended to be the final integration of the transaction. The rule is otherwise where it is shown that the writing is not a full integration of the terms of the contract, or when a contract is ambiguous, parol evidence is admissible to show and make certain the intention behind the contract.

Here Dr. Turinsky testified that petitioner's employment agreement consisted only of petitioner's appointment letter, his annual salary letter, and the policies adopted and amended by the UNC Board of Governors and by the NCSU Board of Trustees. It therefore appears the parties intended the above documents to be the final integration of the employment agreement. Additionally, we have already noted the language contained in the documents are unambiguous; thus, parol evidence may not be introduced to explain the terms of the agreement.

We hold petitioner does not owe a debt to NCSU as result of an alleged overpayment of salary.

[Affirmed.]

Chapter Conclusion

It is not enough to bargain effectively and obtain a contract that gives you exactly what you want. You must also be sure that the contract is legal. Both parties must be of sound mind and must give genuine consent. Finally, some contracts must be in writing to be enforceable, and the writing must be clear and unambiguous.

EXAM REVIEW

1. **NONCOMPETE** Noncompete clauses often arise in employment contracts and when businesses are sold. They must be limited to a reasonable time, activity, and territory. (pp. 239–240)

EXAM Strategy

Question: The purchaser of a business insisted on putting this clause in the sales contract: The seller would not compete, for five years, "anywhere in the United States, the continent of North America, or anywhere else on earth." What danger does that contract represent *to the purchaser?*

Strategy: This is a noncompete clause based on the sale of a business. Such clauses are valid if reasonable. Is this clause reasonable? If it is unreasonable, what might a court do? (See the "Result" at the end of this section.)

2. **EXCULPATORY CLAUSES** These clauses are generally void if the activity involved is in the public interest, the parties are greatly unequal in bargaining power, or the clause is unclear. In other cases, they are generally enforced. (pp. 242–243)

3. **UNCONSCIONABILITY** Oppression and surprise may create an unconscionable bargain. An adhesion contract is especially suspect when it is imposed by a corporation on a consumer or small company. Under the UCC, a limitation of liability is less likely to be unconscionable when both parties are sophisticated corporations. (pp. 243–244)

4. **VOIDABLE CONTRACT** Capacity and consent are different contract issues that can lead to the same result: a voidable contract. A voidable agreement is one that can be canceled by a party who lacks legal capacity or who did not give true consent. (p. 245)

5. **MINORS** A minor (someone under the age of 18) generally may disaffirm any contract while she is still a minor or within a reasonable time after reaching age 18. (p. 245)

6. **FRAUD** Fraud is grounds for rescinding a contract. The injured party must prove all of the following:

   a. A false statement of fact made intentionally or recklessly

   b. Materiality

   c. Justifiable reliance (pp. 246–247)

7. **MISTAKE** In a case of bilateral mistake, either party may rescind the contract. In a case of unilateral mistake, the injured party may rescind only upon a showing that enforcement would be unconscionable or that the other party knew of her mistake. (pp. 248–249)

8. **DURESS** If one party makes an improper threat that causes the victim to enter into a contract, and the victim had no reasonable alternative, the contract is voidable. (p. 249)

Question: Andreini's nerve problem diminished the use of his hands. Dr. Beck operated, but the problem grew worse. A nurse told the patient that Beck might have committed a serious error that exacerbated the problem. Andreini returned for a second operation, which Beck assured him would correct the problem. But after Andreini had been placed in a surgical gown, shaved, and prepared for surgery, the doctor insisted that he sign a release relieving Beck of liability for the first operation. Andreini did not want to sign it, but Beck refused to operate until he did. Later, Andreini sued Beck for malpractice. A trial court dismissed Andreini's suit based on the release. You are on the appeals court. Will you affirm the dismissal or reverse?

Strategy: Adreini is claiming physical duress. Did Beck act *improperly* in demanding a release? Did Adreini have a *realistic alternative?* (See the "Result" at the end of this section.)

9. **THE STATUTE OF FRAUDS** Several types of contract are enforceable only if they fall into the following categories:

   • **LAND** The sale of any interest in land (p. 251)

   • **ONE YEAR** An agreement that *cannot* be performed within one year (pp. 251–252)

CPA Question: Able hired Carr to restore Able's antique car for $800. The terms of their oral agreement provided that Carr had 18 months to complete the work. Actually, the work could be completed within one year. The agreement is:

(a) Unenforceable, because it covers services with a value in excess of $500

(b) Unenforceable, because it covers a time period in excess of one year

(c) Enforceable, because personal service contracts are exempt from the Statute of Frauds

(d) Enforceable, because the work could be completed within one year

Strategy: This is a subtle question. Notice that the contract is for a sum greater than $500. But that is a red herring. Why? The contract also might take 18 months to perform. But it *could* be finished in less than a year. (See the "Result" at the end of this section.)

- **DEBT OF ANOTHER** A promise to pay the debt of another person or entity. (p. 252)

Question: Donald Waide had a contracting business. He bought most of his supplies from Paul Bingham's supply center. Waide fell behind on his bills, and Bingham told Waide that he would extend no more credit to him. That same day, Donald's father, Elmer Waide, came to Bingham's store and said to Bingham that he would "stand good" for any sales to Donald made on credit. Based on Elmer's statement, Bingham again gave Donald credit, and Donald ran up $10,000 in goods before Bingham sued Donald and Elmer. What defense did Elmer make, and what was the outcome?

Strategy: This was an oral agreement, so the issue is whether the promise had to be in writing to be enforceable. Review the list of six contracts that must be in writing. Is this agreement there? (See the "Result" at the end of this section.)

- **EXECUTORS** A promise made by an executor of an estate (p. 252);
- **MARRIAGE** A promise made in consideration of marriage (pp. 252–253); and
- **GOODS** The sale of goods worth $500 or more (p. 250).

Question: James River-Norwalk, Inc., was a paper and textile company that needed a constant supply of wood. James River orally contracted with Gary Futch to supply wood for the company, and Futch did so for several years. The deal was worth many thousands of dollars, but nothing was put in writing. Futch actually purchased the wood for his own account and then resold it to James River. After a few years, James River refused to do more business with Futch. Did the parties have a binding contract?

Strategy: If this is a contract for services, it is enforceable without anything in writing. However, if it is one for the sale of goods, it must be in writing. Clearly what James River wanted was the wood, and it did not care where Futch found it. (See the "Result" at the end of this section.)

10. **CONTENTS** The writing must be signed by the defendant and must state the name of all parties, the subject matter of the agreement, and all essential terms and promises. Electronic signatures usually are valid. (pp. 253–254)

EXAM Strategy

11. **UNIFORM COMMERCIAL CODE (UCC)** A contract or memorandum for the sale of goods may be less complete than those required by the common law.

   - The basic UCC rule requires only a memorandum signed by the defendant, indicating that the parties reached an agreement and specifying the quantity of goods.

12. **PAROL EVIDENCE** When an integrated contract exists, neither party may generally use parol evidence to contradict, vary, or add to its terms. Parol evidence refers to anything (apart from the written contract itself) that was said, done, or written before the parties signed the agreement or as they signed it. (pp. 254–256)

---

1. Result: "Anywhere else on earth"? This is almost certainly unreasonable. It is hard to imagine a purchaser who would legitimately need such wide-ranging protection. In some states, a court might rewrite the clause, limiting the effect to the seller's state, or some reasonable area. However, in other states, a court finding a clause unreasonable will declare it void in its entirety—enabling the seller to open a competing business next door.

8. Result: The Utah Supreme Court reversed the trial court, so you probably should as well. Beck forced Adreini to sign under duress. The threat to withhold surgery was improper, and Adreini had no reasonable alternative.

9. "One Year" Result: (d) A contract for the sale of goods worth $500 or more must be in writing—but this is a contract for *services*, not the sale of goods, so the $800 price is irrelevant. The contract *can* be completed within one year, and thus it falls outside the Statute of Frauds. This is an enforceable agreement.

9. "Debt of Another" Result: Elmer made a promise to pay the debt of another. He did so as a favor to his son. This is a collateral promise. Elmer never signed any such promise, and the agreement cannot be enforced against him.

9. "Goods" Result: James River was buying wood, and this is a contract for the sale of goods. With nothing in writing, signed by James River, Futch has no enforceable agreement.

MULTIPLE-CHOICE QUESTIONS

1. Ricki goes to a baseball game. The back of her ticket clearly reads: "Fan agrees to hold team blameless for all injuries—pay attention to the game at all times for your own safety!" In the first inning, a foul ball hits Ricki in the elbow. She _____ sue the team over the foul ball. Ricki spends the next several innings riding the opposing team's first baseman. The *nicest* thing she says to him is, "You suck, Franklin!" In the eighth inning, Franklin has had enough. He grabs the ballboy's chair and throws it into the stands, injuring Ricki's other elbow. Ricki _____ sue the team over the thrown chair.

   (a) can; can

   (b) can; cannot

   (c) cannot; can

   (d) cannot; cannot

2. Kerry finds a big green ring in the street. She shows it to Leroy, who says, "Wow. That could be valuable." Neither Kerry nor Leroy knows what the ring is made of or whether it is valuable. Kerry sells the ring to Leroy for $100, saying, "Don't come griping if it turns out to be worth two dollars." Leroy takes the ring to a jeweler, who tells him it is an unusually perfect emerald, worth at least $75,000. Kerry sues to rescind.

   (a) Kerry will win based on fraud.

   (b) Kerry will win based on mutual mistake.

   (c) Kerry will win based on unilateral mistake.

   (d) Kerry will lose.

3. **CPA QUESTION** Two individuals signed a contract that was intended to be their entire agreement. The parol evidence rule will prevent the admission of evidence offered to:

   (a) explain the meaning of an ambiguity in the written contract.

   (b) establish that fraud had been committed in the formation of the contract.

   (c) prove the existence of a contemporaneous oral agreement modifying the contract.

   (d) prove the existence of a subsequent oral agreement modifying the contract.

4. Raul wants to plant a garden, and he agrees to buy a small piece of land for $300. Later, he agrees to buy a table for $300. Neither agreement is put in writing. The agreement to buy the land _____ enforceable, and the agreement to buy the table _____ enforceable.

   (a) is; is

   (b) is; is not

   (c) is not; is

   (d) is not; is not

5. In December 2012, Eric hires a band to play at a huge graduation party he is planning to hold in May 2014. The deal is never put into writing. In January 2014, if he wanted to cancel the job, Eric _____ be able to do so. If he does not cancel, and if the band shows up and plays at the party in May 2014, Eric _____ have to pay them.

   (a) will; will

   (b) will; will not

   (c) will not; will

   (d) will not; will not

ESSAY QUESTIONS

1. For 20 years, Art's Flower Shop relied almost exclusively on advertising in the yellow pages to bring business to its shop in a small West Virginia town. One year, the yellow pages printer accidentally did not print Art's ad, and Art's suffered an enormous drop in business. Art's sued for negligence and won a judgment of $50,000 from the jury, but the printing company appealed, claiming that under an exculpatory clause in the

contract, the company could not be liable to Art's for more than the cost of the ad, about $910. Art's claimed that the exculpatory clause was unconscionable. Please rule.

2. Guyan Machinery, a West Virginia manufacturing corporation, hired Albert Voorhees as a salesman and required him to sign a contract stating that if he left Guyan, he would not work for a competing corporation anywhere within 250 miles of West Virginia for a two-year period. Later, Voorhees left Guyan and began working at Polydeck Corp., another West Virginia manufacturer. The only product Polydeck made was urethane screens, which comprised half of 1 percent of Guyan's business. Is Guyan entitled to enforce its noncompete clause?

3. Morell bought a security guard business from Conley, including the property on which the business was located. Neither party knew that underground storage tanks were leaking and contaminating the property. After the sale, Morell discovered the tanks and sought to rescind the contract. Should he be allowed to do so?

4. Richard Griffin and three other men owned a grain company called Bearhouse, Inc., which needed to borrow money. First National Bank was willing to loan $490,000, but it insisted that the four men sign personal guaranties on the loan, committing themselves to repaying up to 25 percent of the loan each if Bearhouse defaulted. Bearhouse went bankrupt. The bank was able to collect some of its money from Bearhouse's assets, but it sued Griffin for the balance. At trial, Griffin wanted to testify that before he signed his guaranty, a bank officer assured him that he would only owe 25 percent of *whatever balance was unpaid*, not 25 percent of the total loan. How will the court decide whether Griffin is entitled to testify about the conversation?

5. When Deana Byers married Steven Byers, she was pregnant with another man's child. Shortly after the marriage, Deana gave birth. The marriage lasted only two months, and the couple separated. In divorce proceedings, Deana sought child support. She claimed that Steven had orally promised to support the child if Deana would marry him. Steven claims he never made the promise. Comment on the outcome.

DISCUSSION QUESTIONS

1. ***ETHICS:*** Richard and Michelle Kommit traveled to New Jersey to have fun in the casinos. While in Atlantic City, they used their MasterCard to withdraw cash from an ATM conveniently located in the "pit"—the gambling area of a casino. They ran up debts of $5,500 on the credit card and did not pay. The Connecticut National Bank sued for the money. Law aside, who has the moral high ground? Is it acceptable for the *casino* to offer ATM services in the gambling pit? If a *credit card* company allows customers to withdraw cash in a casino, is it encouraging them to lose money? Do *the Kommits* have any ethical right to use the ATM, attempt to win money by gambling, and then seek to avoid liability?

2. Should noncompete agreements in employment contracts be illegal altogether? Is there equality of bargaining power between the company and the employee? Should noncompetes be limited to top officers of a company? Would you be upset if a prospective employer asked *you* to agree to a one year covenant not to compete?

3. Sixteen-year-old Travis Mitchell brought his Pontiac GTO into M&M Precision Body and Paint for body work and a paint job. M&M did the work and charged $1,900,

which Travis paid. When Travis later complained about the quality of the work, M&M did some touching up, but Travis was still dissatisfied. He demanded his $1,900 back, but M&M refused to refund it because all of the work was "in" the car and Travis could not return it to the shop. The state of Nebraska, where this occurred, follows the majority rule on this issue. Does Travis get his money? Is this a *fair* result?

4. Contract law gives minors substantial legal protection. But does a modern high school student *need* so much protection? Older teens may have been naive in the 1700s, but today, they are quite savvy. Should the law change so that only younger children—perhaps those aged 14 and under—have the ability to undo agreements? Or is the law reasonable the way it currently exists?

5. Is the Statute of Frauds reasonable, or does it unacceptably allow people to escape their obligations on a mere technicality? Would it be better to expand the law and require that all contracts be in writing? Or should the law be done away with altogether?

© neelsky/Shutterstock.com

PERFORMANCE, DISCHARGE, AND REMEDIES

When it comes to contracts, must we be our brother's keeper? Suppose two parties have reached an agreement. As they perform the contract, is each side obligated to protect the *other* party's interest, or are both free to get away with whatever they can under the agreement's terms?

Brunswick Hills owned a tennis club on property that it leased from Route 18 Associates. The lease ran for 25 years, and when it expired, Brunswick had the option to buy the property or purchase a 99-year lease, both on very favorable terms. To exercise the option, Brunswick had to notify Route 18 by a specified date and to pay the option price of $150,000. If Brunswick failed to exercise its option, the existing lease automatically renewed for 25 more years, but at triple the current rent.

> **When it comes to contracts, must we be our brother's keeper?**

Nineteen months before the original lease expired, Brunswick's lawyer wrote to Route 18 management, stating that Brunswick intended to exercise the option for a 99-year lease. He requested that the lease be sent well in advance so he could review it, but he failed to make the required payment of $150,000.

Route 18 never replied. For over a year and a half, Brunswick's lawyer repeatedly asked for a copy of the new lease or information about it, but he got no response. Finally, after nineteen months, the deadline passed and Route 18 notified Brunswick that it could not exercise its option because it had failed to pay the $150,000 on time.

Brunswick sued, claiming that Route 18 had deliberately stalled to obtain the higher rent.

Who should win? Did Route 18 have a duty to act more quickly? Was there a moral or legal obligation to remind Brunswick about the $150,000 payment? Route 18 claimed that the terms of the lease were clear and Brunswick had failed to follow them. Brunswick replied that Route 18 had an obligation to act in good faith but instead had tricked Brunswick into paying treble rent.

The case raises issues of contract performance and discharge. We will keep you in breathless anticipation just long enough to make some introductory remarks, and then we shall learn who won.

PERFORMANCE AND DISCHARGE

Discharge

A party is discharged when she no longer has duties under the contract.

A party is **discharged** when she has no more duties under a contract. Most contracts are discharged by full performance. In other words, the parties generally do what they promise. Sally agrees to sell Arthur 300 tulip-shaped wine glasses for his new restaurant. Right on schedule, Sally delivers the correct glasses, and Arthur pays in full. Contract, full performance, discharge, end of case.

Rescind

To terminate a contract.

Sometimes the parties discharge a contract by agreement. For example, the parties may agree to **rescind** their contract, meaning that they terminate it by mutual agreement. At times, a court may discharge a party who has not performed. When things have gone amiss, a judge must interpret the contract and issues of public policy to determine who in fairness should suffer the loss. We will analyze the most common issues of performance and discharge.

Performance

Caitlin has an architect draw up plans for a monumental new house, and Daniel agrees to build it by September 1. Caitlin promises to pay $900,000 on that date. The house is ready on time, but Caitlin has some complaints. The living room ceiling was supposed to be 18 feet high, but it is only 17 feet; the pool was to be azure, yet it is aquamarine; the maid's room was not supposed to be wired for cable television, but it is. Caitlin refuses to pay anything for the house. Is she justified? Of course not, it would be absurd to give her a magnificent house for free when it has only tiny defects. But in this easy answer lurks a danger. Technically, Daniel did breach the contract, and yet the law allows him to recover the full contract price, or virtually all of it. Once that principle is established, how far will a court stretch it? Suppose the living room ceiling is only 14 feet high, or 12 feet, or 5 feet? What if the foundation has a small crack? A vast and dangerous split? What if Daniel finishes the house a month late? Six months late? Three years late? At some point, a court will conclude that Daniel has so thoroughly botched the job that he deserves little or no money. But where, exactly, is that point? This is a question that businesses—and judges—face often.

Strict Performance and Substantial Performance

Strict Performance   When Daniel built Caitlin's house with three minor defects, she refused to pay, arguing that he had not *strictly performed* his obligations. Her assertion was correct, yet she lost anyway. Courts dislike strict performance because it enables one party to benefit without paying and sends the other one home empty-handed. A party is generally not required to render **strict performance** unless the contract expressly demands it *and* such a demand is reasonable. Caitlin's contract never suggested that Daniel would forfeit all payment if there were minor problems. Even if Caitlin had insisted on such a clause, few courts would have enforced it because the requirement would be unreasonable for a project as complicated as the construction of a $900,000 home.

Strict performance

Requires one party to perform its obligations precisely, with no deviation from the contract terms.

Substantial Performance   Daniel, the house builder, won his case against Caitlin because he fulfilled *most* of his obligations, even though he did an imperfect job. Courts often rely on the substantial performance doctrine, especially in cases involving services as opposed to those concerning the sale of goods or land. In a contract for services, a party that **substantially performs** its obligations will generally receive the full contract price, minus the value of any defects. Daniel receives $900,000, the contract price, minus the value of a ceiling that is 1 foot too low, a pool the wrong color, and so forth. It will be for the trial court to decide how much those defects are worth. If the court decides the low ceiling is a $10,000 defect, the pool color is worth $5,000, and the cable television wiring error is worth $500, then Daniel receives $884,500

On the other hand, **a party that fails to perform substantially receives nothing on the contract itself and will recover only the value of the work, if any.** If the foundation cracks in Caitlin's house and the walls collapse, Daniel will not receive his $900,000. In such a case, he collects only the market value of the work he has done, which, since the house is a pile of rubble, is probably zero.

When is performance substantial? There is no perfect test, but courts look at these issues:

- How much benefit has the promisee received?

- If it is a construction contract, can the owner use the thing for its intended purpose?

- Can the promisee be compensated with money damages for any defects?

- Did the promisor act in good faith?

Substantial performance
Occurs when one party fulfills enough of its contract obligations to warrant payment.

EXAM Strategy

Question: Jade owns a straight track used for drag racing. She hires Trevor to resurface it, for $180,000, paying $90,000 down. When the project is completed, Jade refuses to pay the balance and sues Trevor for her down payment. He counterclaims for the $90,000 still due. At trial, Trevor proves that all of the required materials were applied by trained workers in an expert fashion, the dimensions were perfect, and his profit margin very modest. The head of the national drag racing association testifies that his group considers the strip unsafe. He noticed puddles in both asphalt lanes, found the concrete starting pads unsafe, and believed the racing surface needed to be ground off and reapplied. His organization refuses to sanction races at the track until repairs are made. Who wins the suit?

Strategy: When one party has performed imperfectly, we have an issue of substantial performance. To decide whether Trevor is entitled to his money, we apply four factors: (1) How much benefit did Jade receive? (2) Can she use the racing strip for its intended purpose? (3) Can Jade be compensated for defects? (4) Did Trevor act in good faith?

Result: Jade has received no benefit whatsoever. She cannot use her drag strip for racing. Compensation will not help Jade—she needs a new strip. Trevor's work must be ripped up and replaced. Trevor may have acted in good faith, but he failed to deliver what Jade bargained for. Jade wins all of the money she paid. (As we will see in the next section, she may also win additional sums for her lost profits.)

Good Faith

The parties to a contract must carry out their obligations in good faith. The difficulty, of course, is applying this general rule to the wide variety of problems that may arise when people or companies do business. How far must one side go to meet its good faith burden? Marvin Shuster was a physician in Florida. Three patients sued him for alleged malpractice. Shuster denied any wrongdoing and asked his insurer to defend the claims. But the insurance company settled all three claims without defending and with a minimum of investigation. Shuster paid nothing out of his own pocket, but he sued the insurance company, claiming that it acted in bad faith. The doctor argued that the company's failure to defend him caused emotional suffering and meant that it would be impossible for him to obtain new malpractice insurance. The Florida Supreme Court found that the insurer acted in good faith. The contract clearly gave all control of malpractice cases to the company. It could settle or defend as it saw fit. Here, the company considered it more economical to settle quickly, and Shuster should have known, from the contract language, that the insurer might choose to do so.[1]

The following case answers the questions we asked in the opening scenario.

BRUNSWICK HILLS RACQUET CLUB INC. v. ROUTE 18 SHOPPING CENTER ASSOCIATES

182 N.J. 210, 864 A.2d 387
Supreme Court of New Jersey, 2005

Facts: Brunswick Hills Racquet Club (Brunswick) owned a tennis club on property that it leased from Route 18 Shopping Center Associates (Route 18). The lease ran for 25 years, and Brunswick had spent about $1 million in capital improvements. The lease expired, and Brunswick had the option of either buying the property or purchasing a 99-year lease, both on very favorable terms. To exercise its option, Brunswick had to notify Route 18 no later than September 30 and had to pay the option price of $150,000. If Brunswick failed to exercise its options, the existing lease automatically renewed as of September 30, for 25 more years, but at more than triple the current rent.

Brunswick's lawyer wrote to Rosen Associates, the company that managed Route 18, nineteen months before the option deadline, stating that Brunswick intended to exercise the option for a 99-year lease. He requested that the lease be sent well in advance so that he could review it. He did not make the required payment of $150,000. Rosen replied that it had forwarded Spector's letter to its attorney, who would be in touch. In April, Spector again wrote, asking for a reply from Rosen or its lawyer.

Over the next six months, the lawyer continually asked for a copy of the lease or further information, but neither Route 18's lawyer nor anyone else provided any data. Eventually, the September deadline passed.

Route 18's lawyer notified Brunswick that it could not exercise its option to lease because it had failed to pay the $150,000 by September 30.

Brunswick sued, claiming that Route 18 had breached its duty of good faith and fair dealing. The trial court found that Route 18 had no duty to notify Brunswick of impending deadlines, and it gave summary judgment for Route 18. The appellate court affirmed, and Brunswick appealed to the state supreme court.

Issue: *Did Route 18 breach its duty of good faith and fair dealing?*

Excerpts from Justice Albin's Decision: Courts generally should not tinker with a finely drawn and precise contract entered into by experienced business people that regulates their financial affairs. [However,] every party to a contract is bound by a duty of good faith and fair dealing in both the performance and enforcement of the contract. Good faith is a concept that defies precise definition. Good faith conduct is conduct that does not violate community standards of decency, fairness, or reasonableness. The covenant of good

---

[1]*Shuster v. South Broward Hospital Dist. Physicians' Prof. Liability Ins. Trust,* 591 So. 2d 174, 1992 Fla. LEXIS 20 (Fla. 1992).

faith and fair dealing calls for parties to a contract to refrain from doing anything which will have the effect of destroying or injuring the right of the other party to receive the benefits of the contract.

Our review of the undisputed facts of this case leads us to the inescapable conclusion that defendant breached the covenant of good faith and fair dealing. Nineteen months in advance of the option deadline, plaintiff notified defendant in writing of its intent to exercise the option to purchase the 99-year lease. Plaintiff mistakenly believed that the purchase price was not due until the time of closing.

During a 19-month period, defendant, through its agents, engaged in a pattern of evasion, sidestepping every request by plaintiff to discuss the option and ignoring plaintiff's repeated written and verbal entreaties to move forward on closing the 99-year lease despite the impending option deadline and obvious potential harm to plaintiff.

Defendant never requested the purchase price of the lease. Indeed, as defendant's attorney candidly admitted at oral argument, defendant did not want the purchase price because the successful exercise of the option was not in defendant's economic interest.

Ordinarily, we are content to let experienced commercial parties fend for themselves and do not seek to introduce intolerable uncertainty into a carefully structured contractual relationship by balancing equities. But there are ethical norms that apply even to the harsh and sometimes cutthroat world of commercial transactions. We do not expect a landlord or even an attorney to act as his brother's keeper in a commercial transaction. We do expect, however, that they will act in good faith and deal fairly with an opposing party. Plaintiff's repeated letters and telephone calls to defendant concerning the exercise of the option and the closing of the 99-year lease obliged defendant to respond, and to respond truthfully.

[Plaintiff is entitled to exercise the 99-year lease.]

EXAM Strategy

Question: Sun operates an upscale sandwich shop in New Jersey, in a storefront that she leases from Ricky for $18,000 per month. The lease, which expires soon, allows Sun to renew for five years at $22,000 per month. Ricky knows, but Sun does not, that in a year, Prada will open a store on the same block. The dramatic increase in pedestrian traffic will render Sun's space more valuable. Ricky says nothing about Prada, Sun declines to renew, and Ricky leases the space for $40,000 a month. Sun sues Ricky, claiming he breached his duty of good faith and fair dealing. Based on the *Brunswick Hills* case, how would the New Jersey Supreme Court rule?

Strategy: In the *Brunswick Hills* case, the court, on the one hand, criticized the defendant for cynically evading the plaintiff's efforts to renew. However, the court also said, "We do not expect a landlord or even an attorney to act as his brother's keeper in a commercial transaction." Using those opposing themes as guidelines, examine the court's decision and predict the ruling in Sun's suit.

Result: *Brunswick Hills* begins: "Courts generally should not tinker with a finely drawn and precise contract entered into by experienced business people." Sun's lease imposes no responsibility on Ricky to report on neighborhood changes or forecast profitability. Further, Sun made no requests to Ricky about the area's future. Sun is asking Ricky to be "her brother's keeper," and neither this court nor any other will do that. She loses.

Time of the Essence Clauses

Go, sir, gallop, and don't forget that the world was made in six days. You can ask me for anything you like, except time.

Napoleon, to an aide, 1803

Generals are not the only ones who place a premium on time. Ask Gene LaSalle. The Seabreeze Restaurant agreed to sell him all of its assets. The parties signed a contract stating the price and closing date. Seabreeze insisted on a clause saying, "Seabreeze considers that time is of the essence in consummating the proposed transaction." Such clauses are common in real estate transactions and in any other agreement where a delay would cause serious damage to one party. LaSalle was unable to close on the date specified and asked for an extension. Seabreeze refused and sold its assets elsewhere. A Florida court affirmed that Seabreeze acted legally. A **time of the essence clause** will generally make contract deadlines strictly enforceable. Seabreeze regarded a timely sale as important, and LaSalle agreed to the provision. There was nothing unreasonable about the clause, and LaSalle suffered the consequences of his delay.[2]

Time of the essence clauses

Generally make contract dates strictly enforceable.

Suppose the contract had named a closing date but included no time of the essence clause. If LaSalle offered to close three days late, could Seabreeze sell elsewhere? No. **Merely including a date for performance does not make time of the essence.** Courts dislike time of the essence arguments because even a short delay may mean that one party forfeits everything it expected to gain from the bargain. If the parties do not *clearly* state that prompt performance is essential, then both are entitled to reasonable delays.

Breach

When one party breaches a contract, the other party is discharged. The discharged party has no obligation to perform and may sue for damages. Edwin promises that on July 1, he will deliver 20 tuxedos, tailored to fit male chimpanzees, to Bubba's circus for $300 per suit. After weeks of delay, Edwin concedes he hasn't a cummerbund to his name. Bubba is discharged and owes nothing. In addition, he may sue Edwin for damages.

Material Breach

As we know, parties frequently perform their contract duties imperfectly, which is why courts accept substantial performance rather than strict performance, particularly in contracts involving services. In a more general sense, **courts will discharge a contract only if a party committed a *material* breach.** A material breach is one that substantially harms the innocent party and for which it would be hard to compensate without discharging the contract. Suppose Edwin fails to show up with the tuxedos on July 1 but calls to say they will arrive under the big top the next day. He has breached the agreement. Is his breach material? No. This is a trivial breach, and Bubba is not discharged. When the tuxedos arrive, he must pay.

The following case raises the issue in the context of a major college sports program.

O'BRIEN V. OHIO STATE UNIVERSITY

2007 WL 2729077
Ohio Court of Appeals, 2007

Facts: The Ohio State University (OSU), experiencing a drought in its men's basketball program, brought in Coach Jim O'Brien to turn things around. The plan was success- ful. In only his second year, he guided the team to its best record ever. The team advanced to the Final Four, and O'Brien was named national coach of the year. OSU's

---

[2]*Seabreeze Restaurant, Inc. v. Paumgardhen,* 639 So.2d 69, 1994 Fla. App. LEXIS 4546 (Fla. Dist. Ct. App. 1994).

athletic director promptly offered the coach a new, multiyear contract worth about $800,000 per year.

Section 5.1 of the contract included termination provisions. The university could fire O'Brien *for cause* if (a) there was a material breach of the contract by the coach or (b) O'Brien's conduct subjected the school to NCAA sanctions. OSU could also terminate O'Brien *without cause*, but in that case, it had to pay him the full salary owed.

O'Brien began recruiting a talented 21-year-old Serbian player named Alex Radojevic. While getting to know the young man, O'Brien discovered two things. First, it appeared that Radojevic had been paid to play briefly for a Yugoslavian team, meaning that he was ineligible to play college basketball. Second, it was clear that Radojevic's family had suffered terribly during the strife in his homeland.

O'Brien concluded that Radojevic would never play for OSU or any major college. He also decided to loan Radojevic's mother some money. Any such loan would violate an NCAA rule if done to recruit a player, but O'Brien believed the loan was legal since Radojevic could not play in the NCAA anyway. Several years later, the university learned of the loan and realized that O'Brien had never reported it. Hoping to avoid trouble with the NCAA, OSU imposed sanctions on itself. The university also fired the coach, claiming he had lied, destroyed the possibility of postseason play, and harmed the school's reputation.

O'Brien sued, claiming he had not materially breached the contract. The trial court awarded the coach $2.5 million, and the university appealed.

Issue: *Did O'Brien materially breach the contract?*

Excerpts from Judge Tyack's Decision: OSU argued that it was substantially injured by the self-imposed sanctions, which included a ban from post-season and NCAA tournament play [during the current season], and relinquishing two basketball scholarships from the [next] recruiting class. Contrary to OSU's argument, however, the trial court found these sanctions to be insubstantial. [Athletic Director] Geiger announced the one-year post-season ban in December, and it appears from the timing of that announcement that Geiger made the decision based on the fact that the team was unlikely to be invited to a post-season tournament in the first place.

The second alleged harm was harm to OSU's reputation. The trial court found that any reputational harm was similarly exaggerated, at least as it specifically related to the Radojevic matter. Radojevic never enrolled at OSU, and never played a single second for OSU's basketball team.

NCAA violations happen all the time. It's the nature of the beast. Also relevant to the issue of OSU's allegedly damaged reputation is the fact that almost immediately after firing O'Brien, OSU was able to lure one of the nation's top coaching prospects, [Thad Matta], to assume O'Brien's former position. Shortly thereafter, Matta successfully recruited possibly the best recruiting class ever. Based on this evidence, the trial court could reasonably find the Radojevic loan did not cause serious harm to OSU.

OSU argues that O'Brien acted in bad faith by covering up his misconduct for several years. In the words of OSU's counsel at oral argument: *"If lying to your employer for four years is not a material breach, it's hard to imagine what would be!"* Although the premise for counsel's argument is sound, it is unsound in application because it assumes facts not in evidence. Counsel for OSU assumes for the purposes of the argument that O'Brien systematically either denied allegations about the Radojevic loan, or took affirmative steps to conceal it from OSU. The evidence does not support such a conclusion. After Radojevic was drafted by the NBA, there is not a single inference that can be drawn from the record to suggest that O'Brien even thought about the loan. In O'Brien's own mind, he did not believe he had done anything wrong; thus, he would not have had a motive to conceal what he had done.

[There was no material breach.]

Affirmed.

Statute of Limitations

A party injured by a breach of contract should act promptly. A **statute of limitations** begins to run at the time of injury and will limit the time within which the injured party may file suit. These laws set time limits for filing lawsuits. Statutes of limitation vary from state to state and from issue to issue within a state. Failure to file suit within the time limits discharges the party who breached the contract. Always consult a lawyer promptly in the case of a legal injury.

Statute of limitations

A statutory time limit within which an injured party must file suit.

> "Your honor, my client wanted to honor the contract. He just couldn't. *Honest.*"

Impossibility

"Your honor, my client wanted to honor the contract. He just couldn't. *Honest.*" This plea often echoes around courtrooms as one party seeks discharge without fulfilling his contract obligations. Does the argument work? It depends. If performing a contract was truly impossible, a court will discharge the agreement. But if honoring the deal merely imposed a financial burden, the law will generally enforce the contract.

True Impossibility

These cases are easy—and rare. **True impossibility means that something has happened making it literally impossible to do what the promisor said he would do.** Francoise owns a vineyard that produces Beaujolais Nouveau wine. She agrees to ship 1,000 cases of her wine to Tyrone, a New York importer, as soon as this year's vintage is ready. Tyrone will pay $50 per case. But a fungus wipes out her entire vineyard. Francoise is discharged. It is theoretically impossible for Francoise to deliver wine from her vineyard, and she owes Tyrone nothing.

Meanwhile, though, Tyrone has a contract with Jackson, a retailer, to sell 1,000 cases of Beaujolais Nouveau wine at $70 per case. Tyrone has no wine from Francoise, and the only other Beaujolais Nouveau available will cost him $85 per case. Instead of earning $20 per case, Tyrone will lose $15. Does this discharge Tyrone's contract with Jackson? No. It is possible for him to perform—it's just more expensive. He must fulfill his agreement.

True impossibility is generally limited to these three causes:

- **Destruction of the Subject Matter,** as happened with Francoise's vineyard.

- **Death of the Promisor in a Personal Services Contract.** When the promisor agrees personally to render a service that cannot be transferred to someone else, her death discharges the contract. Producer hires Josephine to write the lyrics for a new Broadway musical, but Josephine dies after writing only two words: "Act One." The contract was personal to Josephine and is now discharged. Neither Josephine's estate nor Producer has any obligation to the other. But notice that most contracts are not for personal services. Suppose that Tyrone, the wine importer, dies. His contract to sell wine to Jackson is not discharged because anyone can deliver the required wine. Tyrone's estate remains liable on the deal with Jackson.

- **Illegality.** Chet, a Silicon Valley entrepreneur, wants to capitalize on his computer expertise. He contracts with Construction Co. to build a factory in Iran that will manufacture computers for sale in that country. Construction Co. fails to build the factory on time, and Chet sues. Construction Co. defends by pointing out that the President of the United States has issued an executive order barring trade between the United States and Iran. Construction Co. wins; the executive order discharged the contract.

Commercial Impracticability and Frustration of Purpose

It is rare for contract performance to be truly impossible but very common for it to become a financial burden to one party. Suppose Bradshaw Steel in Pittsburgh agrees to deliver 1,000 tons of steel beams to Rice Construction in Saudi Arabia at a given price, but a week later, the cost of raw ore increases 30 percent. A contract once lucrative to the manufacturer is suddenly a major liability. Does that change discharge Bradshaw? Absolutely not. Rice signed the deal *precisely to protect itself against price increases.* As we have seen, the primary purpose of contracts is to enable the parties to control their future.

Yet there may be times when a change in circumstances is so extreme that it would be unfair to enforce a deal. What if a strike made it impossible for Bradshaw to ship the steel to Saudi Arabia, and the only way to deliver would be by air, at *five times* the sea cost? Must Bradshaw fulfill its deal? What if a new war meant that any ships or planes delivering the goods might be fired upon? Other changes could make the contract undesirable for *Rice*. Suppose the builder wanted steel for a major public building in Riyadh, but the Saudi government decided not to go forward with the construction. The steel would then be worthless to Rice. Must the company still accept it?

None of these hypotheticals involves true impossibility. It is physically possible for Bradshaw to deliver the goods and for Rice to receive. But in some cases, it may be so dangerous, costly, or pointless to enforce a bargain that a court will discharge it instead. Courts use the related doctrines of commercial impracticability and frustration of purpose to decide when a change in circumstances should permit one side to escape its duties.

Commercial impracticability means some event has occurred that neither party anticipated and *fulfilling the contract would now be extraordinarily difficult and unfair to one party.* If a shipping strike forces Bradshaw to ship by air, the company will argue that neither side expected the strike and that Bradshaw should not suffer a fivefold increase in shipping costs. Bradshaw will probably win the argument.

Frustration of purpose means some event has occurred that neither party anticipated and *the contract now has no value for one party.* If Rice's building project is canceled, Rice will argue that the steel now is useless to the company. Frustration cases are hard to predict. Some states would agree with Rice, but others would hold that it was Rice's obligation to protect itself with a government guarantee that the project would be completed. Courts consider the following factors in deciding impracticability and frustration claims:

- *Mere financial difficulties will never suffice to discharge a contract. The event must have been truly unexpected. If the promisor must use a different means to accomplish her task, at a greatly increased cost, she probably does have a valid claim of impracticability.*

- *The UCC, like the common law, permits discharge only for major, unforeseen disruptions.*

REMEDIES

A remedy is the method a court uses to compensate an injured party. The most common remedy, used in the great majority of lawsuits, is money damages.

The first step that a court takes in choosing a specific remedy is to decide what interest it is trying to protect. An **interest** is a legal right in something. Someone can have an interest in property, for example, by owning it, or renting it to a tenant, or lending money so someone else may buy it. He can have an interest in a *contract* if the agreement gives him some benefit. There are four principal contract interests that a court may seek to protect:

Interest
A legal right in something.

- **Expectation interest.** This refers to what the injured party reasonably thought she would get from the contract. The goal is to put her in the position she would have been in if both parties had fully performed their obligations.

- **Reliance interest.** The injured party may be unable to demonstrate expectation damages, perhaps because it is unclear he would have profited. But he may still prove that he *spent money* in reliance on the agreement and that in fairness, he should receive compensation.

- **Restitution interest.** The injured party may be unable to show an expectation interest or reliance. But perhaps she has conferred a benefit *on the other party.* Here, the objective is to restore to the injured party the benefit she has provided.

- **Equitable interest.** In some cases, money damages will not suffice to help the injured party. Something more is needed, such as an order to transfer property to the injured party (specific performance) or an order forcing one party to stop doing something (an injunction).

In this section, we look at all four interests.

Expectation Interest

This is the most common remedy that the law provides for a party injured by a breach of contract. **The expectation interest is designed to put the injured party in the position she would have been in had both sides fully performed their obligations.** A court tries to give the injured party the money she would have made from the contract. If accurately calculated, this should take into account all the gains she reasonably expected and all the expenses and losses she would have incurred. The injured party should not end up better off than she would have been under the agreement, nor should she suffer a loss.

If you ever go to law school, you will almost certainly encounter the following case during your first week of classes. It has been used to introduce the concept of damages in contract lawsuits for generations. Enjoy the famous "case of the hairy hand."

Expectation interest
Is designed to put the injured party in the position she would have been had both sides fully performed their obligations.

Landmark Case

HAWKINS v. McGEE

84 N.H. 114, 146 A. 641
Supreme Court of New Hampshire, 1929

Facts: Hawkins suffered a severe electrical burn on the palm of his right hand. After years of living with disfiguring scars, he went to visit Dr. McGee, who was well known for his early attempts at skin-grafting surgery. The doctor told Hawkins "I will guarantee to make the hand a hundred percent perfect." Hawkins hired him to perform the operation.

McGee cut a patch of healthy skin from Hawkins's chest and grafted it over the scar tissue on Hawkins' palm. Unfortunately, the chest hair on the skin graft was very thick, and it continued to grow after the surgery. The operation resulted in a hairy palm for Hawkins. Feeling rather … embarrassed … Hawkins sued Dr. McGee.

The trial court judge instructed the jury to calculate damages in this way: "If you find the plaintiff entitled to anything, he is entitled to recover for what pain and suffering he has been made to endure and what injury he has sustained over and above the injury that he had before."

The jury awarded Hawkins $3,000, but the court reduced the award to $500. Dissatisfied, Hawkins appealed.

Issue: *How should Hawkins's damages be calculated?*

Excerpts from Justice Branch's Decision: The jury was permitted to consider two elements of damage, (1) pain and suffering due to the operation, and (2) positive ill effects of the operation upon the plaintiff's hand. [T]he foregoing instruction was erroneous.

By damages as that term is used in the law of contracts, is intended compensation to put the plaintiff in as good a position as he would have been in had the defendant kept his contract. The measure of recovery is what the defendant should have given the plaintiff, not what the plaintiff has given the defendant or otherwise expended.

We conclude that the true measure of the plaintiff's damage in the present case is the difference between the value to him of a perfect hand and the value of his hand in its present condition, including any incidental consequences fairly within the contemplation of the parties when they made their contract.

The extent of the plaintiff's suffering does not measure this difference in value. The pain necessarily incident to a serious surgical operation was a part of the contribution which the plaintiff was willing to make to his joint undertaking with the defendant to produce a good hand. It furnished no test of the difference between the value of the hand which the defendant promised and the one which resulted from the operation.

[Remanded for a] new trial.

Now let's consider a more modern example.

William Colby was a former director of the CIA. He wanted to write a book about his 15 years in Vietnam. He paid James McCarger $5,000 for help in writing an early draft and promised McCarger another $5,000 if the book was published. Then he hired Alexander Burnham to cowrite the book. Colby's agent secured a contract with Contemporary Books, which included a $100,000 advance. But Burnham was hopelessly late with the manuscript and Colby missed his publication date. Colby fired Burnham and finished the book without him. Contemporary published *Lost Victory* several years late, and the book flopped, earning no significant revenue. Because the book was so late, Contemporary paid Colby a total of only $17,000. Colby sued Burnham for his lost expectation interest. The court awarded him $23,000, calculated as follows:

	$100,000	advance, the only money Colby was promised
	− 10,000	agent's fee
	= 90,000	Fee for the two authors, combined
divided by 2	= 45,000	Colby's fee (the other half went to the coauthor)
	− 5,000	owed to McCarger under the earlier agreement
	= 40,000	Colby's expectation interest
	− 17,000	Fee Colby eventually received from Contemporary
	= 23,000	Colby's expectation damages; that is, the additional amount he would have received had Burnham finished on time

The *Colby* case[3] presented a relatively easy calculation of damages. Other contracts are complex. Courts typically divide the expectation damages into three parts: (1) direct (or "compensatory") damages, which represent harm that flowed directly from the contract's breach; (2) consequential (or "special") damages, which represent harm caused by the injured party's unique situation; and (3) incidental damages, which are minor costs such as storing or returning defective goods, advertising for alternative goods, and so forth. The first two, direct and consequential, are the important ones.

Note that punitive damages are absent from our list. The golden rule in contracts cases is to give successful plaintiffs "the benefit of the bargain" and not to punish defendants. Punitive damages are occasionally awarded in lawsuits that involve both a contract *and* either an intentional tort (such as fraud) or a breach of fiduciary duty, but they are not available in "simple" cases involving only a breach of contract.

Direct Damages

Direct damages are those that flow directly from the contract. They are the most common monetary award for the expectation interest. These are the damages that inevitably result from the breach. Suppose Ace Productions hires Reina to star in its new movie, *Inside Straight*. Ace promises Reina $3 million, providing she shows up June 1 and works until the film is finished. But in late May, Joker Entertainment offers Reina $6 million to star in its new feature, and on June 1, Reina informs Ace that she will not appear. Reina has breached her contract, and Ace should recover direct damages.

What are the damages that flow directly from the contract? Ace has to replace Reina. If Ace hires Kayla as its star and pays her a fee of $4 million, Ace is entitled to the difference between what it expected to pay ($3 million) and what the breach forced it to pay ($4 million), or $1 million in direct damages.

Direct damages
Are those that flow directly from the contract.

[3]*Colby v. Burnham*, 31 Conn. App. 707, 627 A.2d 457, 1993 Conn. App LEXIS 299 (Conn. App. Ct. 1993).

Consequential Damages

In addition to direct damages, the injured party may seek consequential damages or, as they are also known, "special damages." **Consequential damages** reimburse for harm that results from the *particular* circumstances of the plaintiff. These damages are only available if they are a *foreseeable consequence* of the breach. Suppose, for example, Raould breaches two contracts—he is late picking both Sharon and Paul up for a taxi ride. His breach is the same for both parties, but the consequences are very different. Sharon misses her flight to San Francisco and incurs a substantial fee to rebook the flight. Paul is simply late for the barber, who manages to fit him in anyway. Thus, Raould's damages would be different for these two contracts.

Let us return briefly to *Inside Straight*. Suppose that, long before shooting began, Ace had sold the film's soundtrack rights to Spinem Sound for $2 million. Spinem believed it would make a profit only if Reina appeared in the film, so it demanded the right to discharge the agreement if Reina dropped out. When Reina quit, Spinem terminated the contract. Now, when Ace sues Reina, it will also seek $2 million in consequential damages for the lost music revenue.

The $2 million is not a direct damage. The contract between Reina and Ace has nothing directly to do with selling soundtrack rights. But the loss is nonetheless a consequence of Reina bailing out on the project. And so, if Reina knew about Ace's contract with Spinem when she signed to do the film, the loss would be foreseeable to her, and she would be liable for $2 million. If she never realized she was an essential part of the music contract, and if a jury determines that she had no reason to expect the $2 million loss, she owes nothing for the lost soundtrack profits. Injured plaintiffs often try to recover lost profits. Courts will generally award these damages if (1) the lost profits were foreseeable and (2) plaintiff provides enough information so that the factfinder can reasonably estimate a fair amount. The calculation need not be done with mathematical precision. In the following case, the plaintiffs lost not only profits—but their entire business. Can they recover for harm that is so extensive? You decide.

You be the Judge

BI-ECONOMY MARKET, INC. v. HARLEYSVILLE INS. CO. OF NEW YORK
2008 WL 423451
New York Court of Appeals, 2008

Facts: Bi-Economy Market was a family-owned meat market in Rochester, New York. The company was insured by Harleysville Insurance. The "Deluxe Business Owner's" policy provided replacement cost for damage to buildings and inventory. Coverage also included "business interruption insurance" for one year, meaning the loss of pretax profit plus normal operating expenses, including payroll.

The company suffered a disastrous fire, which destroyed its building and all inventory. Bi-Economy immediately filed a claim with Harleysville, but the insurer responded slowly. Harleysville eventually offered a settlement of $163,000. A year later, an arbitrator awarded the Market $407,000. During that year, Harleysville paid for seven months of lost income but declined to pay more. The company never recovered or reopened.

Bi-Economy sued, claiming that Harleysville's slow, inadequate payments destroyed the company. The company also sought consequential damages for the permanent destruction of its business. Harleysville claimed that it was only responsible for damages specified in the contract: the building, inventory, and lost income. The trial court granted summary judgment for Harleysville. The appellate court affirmed, claiming that when they entered into the contract, the parties did not contemplate damages for termination of the business. Bi-Economy appealed to the state's highest court.

You Be the Judge: *Is Bi-Economy entitled to consequential damages for the destruction of its business?*

Argument for Bi-Economy: Bi-Economy is a small, family business. We paid for business interruption insurance for an obvious reason: in the event of a disaster, we lacked the resources to keep going while buildings were constructed and inventory purchased. We knew that in such a calamity, we would need prompt reimbursement—compensation covering the immediate damage and our ongoing lost income. Why else would we pay the premiums?

At the time we entered into the contract, Harleysville could easily foresee that if it responded slowly, with insufficient payments, we could not survive. They knew that is what we wanted to avoid—and it is just what happened. The insurer's bad faith offer of a low figure, and its payment of only seven months' lost income, ruined a fine family business. When the insurance company agreed to business interruption coverage, it was declaring that it would act fast and fairly to sustain a small firm in crisis. The insurer should now pay for the full harm it has wrought.

Argument for Harleysville: We contracted to insure the Market for three losses: its building, inventory, and lost income. After the fire, we performed a reasonable, careful evaluation and made an offer we considered fair. An arbitrator later awarded Bi-Market additional money, which we paid. However it is absurd to suggest that in addition to that, we are liable for an open-ended commitment for permanent destruction of the business.

Consequential damages are appropriate in cases where a plaintiff suffers a loss that was not covered in the contract. In this case, though, the parties bargained over exactly what Harleysville would pay in the event of a major fire. If the insurer has underpaid for lost income, let the court award a fair sum. However, the parties never contemplated an additional, enormous payment for cessation of the business. There is almost no limit as to what that obligation could be. If Bi-Market was concerned that a fire might put the company permanently out of business, it should have said so at the time of negotiating for insurance. The premium would have been dramatically higher.

Neither Bi-Market nor Harleysville ever imagined such an open-ended insurance obligation, and the insurer should not pay an extra cent.

Incidental Damages

Incidental damages are the relatively minor costs that the injured party suffers when *responding to* the breach. When Reina, the actress, breaches the film contract, the producers may have to leave the set and fly back to Los Angeles to hire a new actress. The travel cost is an incidental damage. In another setting, suppose Maud, a manufacturer, has produced 5,000 pairs of running shoes for Foot The Bill, a retail chain, but Foot The Bill breaches the agreement and refuses to accept the goods. Maud will have to store the shoes and advertise for alternate buyers. The storage and advertising costs are incidental expenses, and Maud will recover them.

We turn now to cases where the injured party cannot prove expectation damages.

> **Incidental damages**
> Relatively minor costs that the injured party suffers when responding to the breach.

Reliance Interest

To win expectation damages, the injured party must prove the breach of contract caused damages that can be *quantified with reasonable certainty*. This rule sometimes presents plaintiffs with a problem.

George plans to manufacture and sell silk scarves during the holiday season. In the summer, he contracts with Cecily, the owner of a shopping mall, to rent a high-visibility stall for $100 per day. George then buys hundreds of yards of costly silk and gets to work cutting and sewing. But in September, Cecily refuses to honor the contract. George sues and proves Cecily breached a valid contract. But what is his remedy?

George cannot establish an expectation interest in his scarf business. He *hoped* to sell each scarf for a $40 gross profit. He *planned* on making $2,000 per day. But how much would he *actually* have earned? Enough to retire on? Enough to buy a salami sandwich for lunch? He has no way of proving his profits, and a court cannot give him his expectation interest.

Instead, George will ask for *reliance damages*. The **reliance interest** is designed to put an injured party in the position he would have been in had the parties never entered into a

> **Reliance interest**
> Puts the injured party in the position he would have been in had the parties never entered into a contract.

contract. This remedy focuses on the time and money that the injured party spent performing his part of the agreement.

George should be able to recover reliance damages from Cecily. Assuming he is unable to sell the scarves to a retail store, which is probable since retailers will have made purchases long ago, George should be able to recover the cost of the silk fabric he bought and perhaps something for the hours of labor he spent cutting and sewing. But reliance damages can be difficult to win because *they are harder to quantify*. Courts prefer to compute damages using the numbers provided in a contract. If a contract states a price of $25 per Christmas tree and one party breaches, the arithmetic is easy. Judges can become uncomfortable when asked to base damages on vague calculations. How much was George's time worth in making the scarves? How good was his work? How likely were the scarves to sell? If George has a track record in the industry, he will be able to show a market price for his services. Without such a record, his reliance claim becomes a tough battle.

Restitution Interest

Lillian and Harold Toews signed a contract to sell 1,500 acres of Idaho farmland to Elmer Funk. (No, not him—the Bugs Bunny character you are thinking of is Elmer Fudd.) He was to take possession immediately, but he would not receive the deed until he finished paying for the property, in 10 years. This arrangement enabled him to enroll in a government program that would pay him "set-asides" for *not* farming. Funk kept most aspects of his agreement. He did move onto the land and did receive $76,000 from the government for a year's worth of inactivity. (Nice work if you can get it.) The only part of the bargain Funk did not keep was his promise to pay. Lillian and Harold sued. Funk had clearly breached the deal. But what remedy?

The couple still owned the land, so they did not need it reconveyed. Funk had no money to pay for the farm, so they would never get their expectation interest. And they had expended almost no money based on the deal, so they had no reliance interest. What they had done, though, was to *confer a benefit* on Funk. They had enabled him to obtain $76,000 in government money. Harold and Lillian wanted a return of the benefit they had conferred on Funk, a remedy called *restitution*. The **restitution interest** is designed to return to the injured party a benefit that he has conferred on the other party, which it would be unjust to leave with that person. The couple argued that they had bestowed a $76,000 benefit on Funk and that it made absolutely no sense for him to keep it. The Idaho Court of Appeals agreed. It ruled that the couple had a restitutionary interest in the government set-aside money and ordered Funk to pay them the money.[4]

Restitution interest
Is designed to return to the injured party a benefit he has conferred on the other party.

Reformation
The process by which a court rewrites a contract to ensure its accuracy or viability.

Other Remedies

In contract lawsuits, plaintiffs are occasionally awarded the remedies of specific performance, injunction, and **reformation**.

Specific Performance

Leona Claussen owned Iowa farmland. She sold some of it to her sister-in-law, Evelyn Claussen, and, along with the land, granted Evelyn an option to buy additional property at $800 per acre. Evelyn could exercise her option anytime during Leona's lifetime or within six months of Leona's death. When Leona died, Evelyn informed the estate's executor that she was exercising her option. But other relatives wanted the property, and the executor refused to sell. Evelyn sued and asked for *specific performance*. She did not want an award of damages; she wanted *the land itself*. The remedy of specific performance forces the two parties to perform their contract.

[4]*Toews v. Funk*, 129 Idaho 316, 924 P.2d 217, 1994 Idaho App. LEXIS 75 (Idaho Ct. App. 1994).

A court will award specific performance ordering the parties to perform the contract, only in cases involving the sale of land or some other asset that is considered "unique." Courts use this remedy when money damages would be inadequate to compensate an injured party. If the subject is unique and irreplaceable, money damages will not put the injured party in the same position she would have been in had the agreement been kept. So a court will order the seller to convey the rare object and the buyer to pay for it.

> **Specific performance**
> Forces both parties to complete the deal.

Historically, every parcel of land has been regarded as unique, and therefore specific performance is always available in real estate contracts. Family heirlooms and works of art are also often considered unique. Evelyn Claussen won specific performance. The Iowa Supreme Court ordered Leona's estate to convey the land to Evelyn for $800 per acre.[5] Generally speaking, either the seller or the buyer may be granted specific performance. One limitation in land sales is that a buyer may obtain specific performance only if she was ready, willing, and able to purchase the property on time. If Evelyn had lacked the money to buy Leona's property for $800 per acre within the six-month time limit, the court would have declined to order the sale.

EXAM Strategy

Question: The Monroes, a retired couple who live in Illinois, want to move to Arizona to escape the northern winter. In May, the Monroes contract in writing to sell their house to the Temples for $450,000. Closing is to take place June 30. The Temples pay a deposit of $90,000. However, in early June, the Monroes travel through Arizona and discover it is too hot for them. They promptly notify the Temples they are no longer willing to sell, and return the $90,000, with interest. The Temples sue, seeking the house. In response, the Monroes offer evidence that the value of the house has dropped from about $450,000 to about $400,000. They claim that the Temples have suffered no loss. Who will win?

Strategy: Most contract lawsuits are for money damages, but not this one. The Temples want the house. Because they want the house itself, and not money damages, the drop in value is irrelevant. What legal remedy are the Temples seeking? They are suing for specific performance. When will a court grant specific performance? Should it do so here?

Result: In cases involving the sale of land or some other unique asset, a court will grant specific performance, ordering the parties to perform the agreement,. All houses are regarded as unique. The court will force the Monroes to sell their house, provided the Temples have sufficient money to pay for it.

Other unique items, for which a court will order specific performance, include such things as secret formulas, patents, and shares in a closely held corporation. Money damages would be inadequate for all these things since the injured party, even if she got the cash, could not go out and buy a substitute item. By contrast, a contract for a new Cadillac Escalade is not enforceable by specific performance. If the seller breaches, the buyer is entitled to the difference between the contract price and the market value of the car. The buyer can take his money elsewhere and purchase a virtually identical SUV.

---

[5]*In re Estate of Claussen*, 482 N.W.2d 381, 1992 Iowa Sup. LEXIS 52 (Iowa 1992).

Injunction

injunction

A court order that requires someone to do something or to refrain from doing something.

An **injunction** is a court order that requires someone to refrain from doing something.

In the increasingly litigious world of professional sports, injunctions are commonplace. In the following basketball case, the trial court issued a **preliminary injunction;** that is, an order issued early in a lawsuit prohibiting a party from doing something *during the course of the lawsuit*. The court attempts to protect the interests of the plaintiff immediately. If, after trial, it appears that the plaintiff has been injured and is entitled to an injunction, the trial court will make its order a **permanent injunction**. If it appears that the preliminary injunction should never have been issued, the court will terminate the order.

MILICIC v. BASKETBALL MARKETING COMPANY, INC.

2004 Pa.A Super. 333, 857 A.2d 689
Superior Court of Pennsylvania, 2004

Facts: The Basketball Marketing Company (BMC) markets, distributes, and sells basketball apparel and related products. BMC signed a long-term endorsement contract with a 16-year-old Serbian player, Darko Milicic, who was virtually unknown in the United States. Two years later, Milicic became the second pick in the National Basketball Association (NBA) draft, making him an immensely marketable young man.

Four days after his 18th birthday, Milicic made a buyout offer to BMC, seeking release from his contract so that he could arrange a more lucrative one elsewhere. BMC refused to release him. A week later, Milicic notified BMC in writing that he was disaffirming the contract, and he returned all money and goods he had received from the company. BMC again refused to release Milicic.

Believing that Milicic was negotiating an endorsement deal with either Reebok or Adidas, BMC sent both companies letters informing them it had an enforceable endorsement deal with Milicic that was valid for several more years. Because of BMC's letter, Adidas ceased negotiating with Milicic just short of signing a contract. Milicic sued BMC, seeking a preliminary injunction that would prohibit BMC from sending such letters to competitors. The trial court granted the preliminary injunction, and BMC appealed.

Issue: *Is Milicic entitled to a preliminary injunction?*

Excerpts from Judge McCaffery's Decision:[6] BMC argues that the trial court erred by concluding that Milicic had proven the four essential prerequisites necessary for injunctive relief. However, Milicic did meet these four requirements.

1. Milicic had a strong likelihood of success on the merits.

   Pennsylvania law recognizes, except as to necessities, the contract of a minor is voidable if the minor disaffirms it at any reasonable time after the minor attains majority. Just 11 days after his 18th birthday, Milicic sent BMC a letter withdrawing from the agreement. This letter was sent within a reasonable time after Milicic's reaching the age of majority and stated his unequivocal revocation and voidance of the agreement. There exists more than a reasonable probability that Milicic will succeed in [nullifying the contract with BMC].

2. Injunctive relief was necessary to prevent immediate and irreparable harm that could not be adequately compensated by the awarding of monetary damages.

   Top N.B.A. draft picks generally solicit, negotiate, and secure endorsement contracts within a short time after the draft to take advantage of the publicity, excitement, and attendant marketability associated with the promotion. BMC blocked Milicic's efforts to enter into such an endorsement agreement. After being contacted by BMC, advanced negotiations between Milicic and Adidas were suspended. These business opportunity and market advantage losses may aptly be characterized as irreparable injury for purposes of equitable relief.

3. Greater injury would have occurred from denying the injunction than from granting the injunction.

---

[6]Because we are unwilling to assume, as the court apparently does, that this decision will be read only by robots, the authors have substituted "BMC" for "appellant" and "Milicic" for "appellee."

BMC's refusal to acknowledge Milicic's ability to disaffirm the contract is at odds with public policy. Because infants are not competent to contract, the ability to disaffirm protects them from their own immaturity and lack of discretion. It is established practice in Pennsylvania to petition the court to appoint a guardian for the child, to protect the interests of both parties. It confounds the Court that BMC, a corporation of great magnitude, whose business may be said to be based in contract law, failed to have a guardian appointed for Milicic. Harm to the public is an additional consideration. The public policy consideration underlying the rule which allows a child to disaffirm a contract within a reasonable time after reaching the age of majority is that minors should not be bound by mistakes resulting from their immaturity or the overbearance of unscrupulous adults.

4. The preliminary injunction restored the parties to the status quo that existed prior to the wrongful conduct:

Enjoining BMC from further interfering with Milicic's ability to contract will place the parties where they were prior to BMC's wrongful conduct. As all four of the essential prerequisites have been satisfied in this case, the Court properly granted injunctive relief.

Order affirmed.

Special Issues

Finally, we consider some special issues of damages, beginning with a party's obligation to minimize its losses.

Mitigation of Damages

A party injured by a breach of contract may not recover for damages that he could have avoided with reasonable efforts. In other words, when one party perceives that the other has breached or will breach the contract, the injured party must try to prevent unnecessary loss. A party is expected to **mitigate** his damages; that is, to keep damages as low as he reasonably can.

> **Mitigate**
> To keep damages as low as is reasonable.

Malcolm agrees to rent space in his mall to Zena, for a major department store. As part of the lease, Malcolm agrees to redesign the interior to meet her specifications. After Malcolm has spent $20,000 in architect and design fees, Zena informs Malcolm that she is renting other space and will not occupy his mall. Malcolm nonetheless continues the renovation work, spending an additional $50,000 on materials and labor. Malcolm will recover the lost rental payments and the $20,000 expended in reliance on the deal. He will *not* recover the extra $50,000. He should have stopped work when he learned of Zena's breach.

Liquidated Damages

It can be difficult or even impossible to prove how much damage the injured party has suffered. So lawyers and executives negotiating a deal may include in the contract a **liquidated damages** clause, a provision stating in advance how much a party must pay if it breaches. Assume that Laurie has hired Bruce to build a five-unit apartment building for $800,000. Bruce promises to complete construction by May 15. Laurie insists on a liquidated damages clause providing that if Bruce finishes late, Laurie's final price is reduced by $3,000 for each week of delay. Bruce finishes the apartment building June 30, and Laurie reduces her payment by $18,000. Is that fair? The answer depends on two factors: **A court will generally enforce a liquidated damages clause if (1) at the time of creating the contract, it was very difficult to estimate actual damages, and (2) the liquidated amount is reasonable.** In any other case, the liquidated damage will be considered a mere penalty and will prove unenforceable.

> **Liquidated damages**
> A clause stating in advance how much a party must pay if it breaches.

We will apply the two factors to Laurie's case. When the parties made their agreement, would it have been difficult to estimate actual damages caused by delay? Yes. Laurie could not prove that all five units would have been occupied or how much rent the tenants would have agreed to pay. Was the $3,000 per week reasonable? Probably. To finance an $800,000 building, Laurie will have to pay at least $6,000 interest per month. She must also pay taxes on the land and may have other expenses. Laurie does not have to prove that every penny of the liquidated damages clause is justified, but only that the figure is reasonable. A court will probably enforce her liquidated damages clause.

On the other hand, suppose Laurie's clause demanded $3,000 per day. There is no basis for such a figure, and a court will declare it a penalty clause and refuse to enforce it. Laurie will be back to square one, forced to prove in court any damages she claims to have suffered from Bruce's delay.

Chapter Conclusion

A moment's caution! Often that is the only thing needed to avoid years of litigation. Yes, the broad powers of a court may enable it to compensate an injured party, but problems of proof and the uncertainty of remedies demonstrate that the best solution is a carefully crafted contract and socially responsible behavior.

EXAM REVIEW

1. **SUBSTANTIAL PERFORMANCE** Strict performance, which requires one party to fulfill its duties perfectly, is unusual. In construction and service contracts, substantial performance is generally sufficient to entitle the promisor to the contract price, minus the cost of defects in the work. (pp. 264–265)

2. **GOOD FAITH** Good faith performance is required in all contracts. (pp. 266–267)

3. **TIME OF THE ESSENCE** Time of the essence clauses result in strict enforcement of contract deadlines. (pp. 267–268)

EXAM Strategy

Question: Colony Park Associates signed a contract to buy 44 acres of residential land from John Gall. The contract stated that closing would take place exactly one year later. The delay was to enable Colony Park to obtain building permits to develop condominiums. Colony Park worked diligently to obtain all permits, but delays in sewer permits forced Colony Park to notify Gall it could not close on the agreed date. Colony Park suggested a date exactly one month later. Gall refused the new date and declined to sell. Colony Park sued. Gall argued that since the parties specified a date, time was of the essence and Colony Park's failure to buy on time discharged Gall. Please rule.

Strategy: A time of the essence clause generally makes a contract date strictly enforceable. Was there one in this agreement? (See the "Result" at the end of this section.)

4. **MATERIAL BREACH** A material breach is the only kind that will discharge a contract; a trivial breach will not. (pp. 268–269)

5. **IMPOSSIBILITY** True impossibility means that some event has made it impossible to perform an agreement. It is typically caused by destruction of the subject matter, the death of an essential promisor, or intervening illegality. (pp. 270–271)

EXAM Strategy

Question: Omega Concrete had a gravel pit and factory. Access was difficult, so Omega contracted with Union Pacific Railroad (UP) for the right to use a private road that crossed UP property and tracks. The contract stated that use of the road was solely for Omega employees and that Omega would be responsible for closing a gate that UP planned to build where the private road joined a public highway. In fact, UP never constructed the gate; Omega had no authority to construct the gate. Mathew Rogers, an Omega employee, was killed by a train while using the private road. Rogers's family sued Omega, claiming that Omega failed to keep the gate closed as the contract required. Is Omega liable?

Strategy: True impossibility means that the promisor cannot do what he promised to do. Is this such a case? (See the "Result" at the end of this section.)

6. **COMMERCIAL IMPRACTICABILITY** Commercial impracticability means that some unexpected event has made it extraordinarily difficult and unfair for one party to perform its obligations. (pp. 270–271)

7. **FRUSTRATION OF PURPOSE** Frustration of purpose may occur when an unexpected event renders a contract completely useless to one party. (pp. 270–271)

8. **REMEDY** A remedy is the method a court uses to compensate an injured party. (p. 271)

9. **INTERESTS** An interest is a legal right in something, such as a contract. The first step that a court takes in choosing a remedy is to decide what interest it is protecting. (p. 271)

10. **EXPECTATION** The expectation interest puts the injured party in the position she would have been in had both sides fully performed. It has three components:

(a) Direct damages, which flow directly from the contract.

(b) Consequential damages, which result from the unique circumstances of the particular injured party. The injured party may recover consequential damages only if the breaching party should have foreseen them.

(c) Incidental damages, which are the minor costs an injured party incurs responding to a breach. (pp. 272–275)

Question: Mr. and Ms. Beard contracted for Builder to construct a house on property he owned and sell it to the Beards for $785,000. The house was to be completed by a certain date, and Builder knew that the Beards were selling their own home in reliance on the completion date. Builder was late with construction, forcing the Beards to spend $32,000 in rent. Ultimately, Builder never finished the house, and the Beards moved elsewhere. They sued. At trial, expert testimony indicated the market value of the house as promised would have been $885,000. How much money are the Beards entitled to, and why?

Strategy: Normally, in cases of property, an injured plaintiff may use specific performance to obtain the land or house. However, there *is* no house, so there will be no specific performance. The Beards will seek their expectation interest. Under the contract, what did they reasonably expect? They anticipated a finished house, on a particular date, worth $885,000. They did not expect to pay rent while waiting. Calculate their losses. (See the "Result" at the end of this section.)

11. **RELIANCE** The reliance interest puts the injured party in the position he would have been in had the parties never entered into a contract. It focuses on the time and money that the injured party spent performing his part of the agreement. If there was no valid contract, a court might still award reliance damages under a theory of promissory estoppel. (pp. 275–276)

Question: Bingo is emerging as a rock star. His last five concerts have all sold out. Lucia signs a deal with Bingo to perform two concerts in one evening in Big City for a fee of $50,000 for both shows. Lucia then rents the Auditorium for that evening, guaranteeing to pay $50,000. Bingo promptly breaks the deal before any tickets are sold. Lucia sues, pointing out that the Auditorium seats 3,000 and she anticipated selling all tickets for an average of $40 each, for a total gross of $120,000. How much will Lucia recover, if anything?

Strategy: The parties created a valid contract, and Lucia relied on it. She claims two losses: the payment to rent the hall and her lost profits. A court may award reliance damages if the plaintiff can quantify them, provided that the damages are not speculative. Can Lucia quantify either of those losses? Both of them? Were they speculative? (See the "Result" at the end of this section.)

12. **RESTITUTION** The restitution interest returns to the injured party a benefit that she has conferred on the other party which would be unjust to leave with that person. Restitution can be awarded in the case of a contract created, for example, by fraud, or in a case of quasi-contract, where the parties never created a binding agreement. (p. 276)

13. **SPECIFIC PERFORMANCE** Specific performance, ordered only in cases of land or a unique asset, requires both parties to perform the contract. (pp. 276–277)

14. **INJUNCTION** An injunction is a court order that requires someone to do something or refrain from doing something. (pp. 278–279)

15. **MITIGATION**   The duty to mitigate means that a party injured by a breach of contract may not recover for damages that he could have avoided with reasonable efforts. (p. 279)

16. **LIQUIDATED DAMAGES**   A liquidated damages clause will be enforced if and only if, at the time of creating the contract, it was very difficult to estimate actual damages and the liquidated amount is reasonable. (pp. 279–280)

---

3. Result: Merely including a date for performance does not make time of the essence. A party that considers a date critical must make that clear. This contract did not indicate that the closing date was vital to either party, so a short delay was reasonable. Gail was ordered to convey the land to Colony Park.

5. Result: There was no gate, and Omega had no right to build one. This is a case of true impossibility. Omega was not liable.

10. Result: The Beards' direct damages represent the difference between the market value of the house and the contract price. They expected a house worth $100,000 more than their contract price, and they are entitled to that sum. They also suffered consequential damages. The Builder knew they needed the house as of the contract date, and he could foresee that his breach would force them to pay rent. He is liable for a total of $132,000.

11. Result: Lucia can easily demonstrate that Bingo's breach cost her $50,000—the cost of the hall. However, it is uncertain how many tickets she would have sold. Unless Lucia has a strong track record selling tickets to concerts featuring Bingo, a court is likely to conclude that her anticipated profits were speculative. She will probably receive nothing for that claim.

MULTIPLE-CHOICE QUESTIONS

1. Most contracts are discharged by:
   (a) Agreement of the parties.
   (b) Full performance.
   (c) Failure of conditions.
   (d) Commercial impracticability.
   (e) A material breach.

2. Big Co., a construction company, builds a grocery store. The contract calls for a final price of $5 million. Big Co. incurred $4.5 million in costs and stands to make a profit of $500,000. On a final inspection, the grocery store owner is upset. His blueprints called for 24 skylights, but the finished building has only 12. Installing the additional skylights would cost $100,000. Big Co. made no other errors. How much must the grocery store owner pay Big Co.?
   (a) $5,000,000
   (b) $4,900,000
   (c) $4,500,000
   (d) $0

3. Lenny makes K2, a synthetic form of marijuana, in his basement. He signs an agreement with the Super Smoke Shop to deliver 1,000 cans of K2 for $10,000. After the contract is signed, but before the delivery, Super Smoke Shop's state legislature makes the sale of K2 illegal. Lenny's contract will be discharged because of _____.

   (a) true impossibility

   (b) commercial impracticability

   (c) frustration of purpose

   (d) None of the above

4. A manufacturer delivers a new tractor to Farmer Ted on the first day of the harvest season—but the tractor will not start. It takes two weeks for the right parts to be delivered and installed. The repair bill comes to $1,000. During the two weeks, some acres of Farmer Ted's crops die. He argues in court that his lost profit on those acres is $60,000. If a jury awards $1,000 for tractor repairs, it will be in the form of _____ damages. If it awards $60,000 for the lost crops, it will be in the form of _____ damages.

   (a) direct; direct

   (b) direct; consequential

   (c) consequential; direct

   (d) consequential; consequential

   (e) direct; incidental

5. Julie signs a contract to buy Nick's 2002 Mustang GT for $5,000. Later, Nick changes his mind and refuses to sell his car. Julie soon buys a similar 2002 Mustang GT for $5,500. She then sues Nick and wins $500. The $500 represents her _____.

   (a) expectation interest

   (b) reliance interest

   (c) restitution interest

   (d) None of the above

ESSAY QUESTIONS

1. Loehmann's clothing stores, a nationwide chain with headquarters in New York, was the anchor tenant in the Lincoln View Plaza Shopping Center in Phoenix, Arizona, with a 20-year lease from the landlord, Foundation Development, beginning in 1978. Loehmann's was obligated to pay rent the first of every month and to pay common-area charges four times a year. The lease stated that if Loehmann's failed to pay on time, Foundation could send a notice of default, and that if the store failed to pay all money due within 10 days, Foundation could evict. On February 23, 1987, Foundation sent to Loehmann's the common-area charges for the quarter ending January 31, 1987. The balance due was $3,500. Loehmann's believed the bill was in error and sent an inquiry on March 18, 1987. On April 10, 1987, Foundation insisted on payment of the full amount within 10 days. Foundation sent the letter to the Loehmann's store in Phoenix. On April 13, 1987, the Loehmann's store received the

bill and, since it was not responsible for payments, forwarded it to the New York office. Because the company had moved offices in New York, a Loehmann's officer did not see the bill until April 20. Loehmann's issued a check for the full amount on April 24 and mailed it the following day. On April 28, Foundation sued to evict; on April 29, the company received Loehmann's check. Please rule.

2. **YOU BE THE JUDGE WRITING PROBLEM** Kuhn Farm Machinery, a European company, signed an agreement with Scottsdale Plaza Resort, of Arizona, to use the resort for its North American dealers' convention during March 1991. Kuhn agreed to rent 190 guest rooms and spend several thousand dollars on food and beverages. Kuhn invited its top 200 independent dealers from the United States and Canada and about 25 of its own employees from the United States, Europe, and Australia, although it never mentioned those plans to Scottsdale.

   On August 2, 1990, Iraq invaded Kuwait, and on January 16, 1991, the United States and allied forces were at war with Iraq. Saddam Hussein and other Iraqi leaders threatened terrorist acts against the United States and its allies. Kuhn became concerned about the safety of those traveling to Arizona, especially its European employees. By mid-February, 11 of the top 50 dealers with expense-paid trips had either canceled their plans to attend or failed to sign up. Kuhn postponed the convention. The resort sued. The trial court discharged the contract under the doctrines of commercial impracticability and frustration of purpose. The resort appealed. Did commercial impracticability or frustration of purpose discharge the contract? **Argument for Scottsdale Plaza Resort:** The resort had no way of knowing that Kuhn anticipated bringing executives from Europe, and even less reason to expect that if anything interfered with their travel, the entire convention would become pointless. Most of the dealers could have attended the convention, and the resort stood ready to serve them. **Argument for Kuhn:** The parties never anticipated the threat of terrorism. Kuhn wanted this convention so that its European executives, among others, could meet top North American dealers. That is now impossible. No company would risk employee lives for a meeting. As a result, the contract has no value at all to Kuhn, and its obligations should be discharged by law.

3. Lewis signed a contract for the rights to all timber located on Nine-Mile Mine. He agreed to pay $70 per thousand board feet ($70/mbf). As he began work, Nine-Mile became convinced that Lewis lacked sufficient equipment to do the job well and forbade him to enter the land. Lewis sued. Nine-Mile moved for summary judgment. The mine offered proof that the market value of the timber was exactly $70/mbf, and Lewis had no evidence to contradict Nine-Mile. The evidence about market value proved decisive. Why? Please rule on the summary judgment motion.

4. Racicky was in the process of buying 320 acres of ranchland. While that sale was being negotiated, Racicky signed a contract to sell the land to Simon. Simon paid $144,000, the full price of the land. But Racicky went bankrupt before he could complete the *purchase* of the land, let alone its sale. Which of these remedies should Simon seek: expectation, restitution, specific performance, or reformation?

5. Evans built a house for Sandra Dyer, but the house had some problems. The garage ceiling was too low. Load-bearing beams in the "great room" cracked and appeared to be steadily weakening. The patio did not drain properly. Pipes froze. Evans wanted the money promised for the job, but Dyer refused to pay. Comment.

DISCUSSION QUESTIONS

1. Krug International, an Ohio corporation, had a contract with Iraqi Airways to build aeromedical equipment for training pilots. Krug then contracted for Power Engineering, an Iowa corporation, to build the specialized gearbox to be used in the training equipment for $150,000. Power did not know that Krug planned to resell the gearbox to Iraqi Airways. When Power had almost completed the gearbox, the Gulf War broke out and the United Nations declared an embargo on all shipments to Iraq. Krug notified Power that it no longer wanted the gearbox. Power sued. Please rule.

2. **Ethics** The National Football League (NFL) owns the copyright to the broadcasts of its games. It licenses local television stations to telecast certain games and maintains a "blackout rule," which prohibits stations from broadcasting home games that are not sold out 72 hours before the game starts. Certain home games of the Cleveland Browns team were not sold out, and the NFL blocked local broadcast. But several bars in the Cleveland area were able to pick up the game's signal by using special antennas. The NFL wanted the bars to stop showing the games. What did it do? Was it unethical of the bars to broadcast the games that they were able to pick up? Apart from the NFL's legal rights, do you think it had the moral right to stop the bars from broadcasting the games?

3. Consequential damages can be many times higher than direct damages. Consider the "Farmer Ted" scenario raised in the multiple-choice section of this review, which is based on a real case.[7] Is it fair for consequential damages to be 60 times higher than direct damages? The Supreme Court is skeptical that *punitive* damages should be more than 9 times compensatory damages in a tort case. Should a similar "soft limit" apply to consequential damages in contract cases?

4. If someone breaks a contract, the other party can generally sue and win some form of damages. But for centuries, the law has considered land to be unique. And so, a lawsuit that involves a broken agreement for a sale of land will usually result in an order of specific performance. Is this ancient rule still reasonable? If someone backs out of an agreement to sell an acre of land, should he be ordered to turn over the land itself? Why not just require him to pay an appropriate number of dollars in damages?

5. Is it reasonable to require the mitigation of damages? If a person is wronged because the other side breached a contract, should she have any obligations at all? For example, suppose that a tenant breaches a lease by leaving early. Should the landlord have an obligation to try to find another tenant before the end of the lease?

---

[7] *Prutch v. Ford*, 574 P.2d 102 (Colo. 1977)

CHAPTER 12

PRACTICAL CONTRACTS

© neelsky/Shutterstock.com

> I don't know what the *contract* says—that's just the legal stuff.

Two true stories:

One

Holly (on the phone to her client, Judd): Harry's lawyer just emailed me a letter that Harry says he got from you last year. I'm reading from the letter now: "Each year that you meet your revenue goals, you'll get a 1 percent equity interest." Is it possible you sent that letter?

Judd: I don't remember the exact wording, but probably something like that.

Holly: You told me, absolutely, positively, you had never promised Harry any stock. That he was making the whole thing up.

Judd: He was threatening to leave unless I gave him some equity, so I said what he wanted to hear. But that letter didn't *mean* anything. This is a family business, and no one but my children will ever get stock.

Two

Grace (on the phone with her lawyer): Providential has raised its price to $12 a pound. I can't afford to pay that! We had a deal that the price would never go higher than 10 bucks. I've talked to Buddy over there, but he is refusing to back down. We need to do something!

Lawyer: Let me look at the contract.

Grace (her voice rising): I don't know what the *contract* says—that's just the legal stuff. Our *business* deal was no more than $10 a pound!

You have been studying the theory of contract law. This chapter is different—its purpose is to demonstrate how that theory operates in practice. We will look at the structure and content of a standard agreement and answer questions such as: Do you need a written agreement? What do all these legal terms mean? Are any important provisions missing? By the end of the chapter, you will have a road map for understanding a written contract.[1] (Note that we do not repeat here what you have learned in prior chapters about the *substantive* law of contracts.) This chapter has another goal, too: we will look at the relationship between lawyers and their clients and their different roles in creating a contract.

Businesspeople, not surprisingly, tend to focus more on business than on the technicalities of contract law. However, *ignoring* the role of a written agreement can lead to serious trouble. Both of the clients in the opening scenario ended up being bound by a contract they did not want.

To illustrate our discussion of specific contract provisions, we will use a real contract between an actor and a producer to make a movie. For reasons of confidentiality, however, we have changed the names.

Before we begin our discussion of written contracts, let's ask: **do you need a written agreement at all?** Some years ago, this author was with a group of lawyers, all of whom had done a major home renovation and *none of whom* had signed a contract with the builder. All of the projects had turned out well. The lawyers had not prepared a written contract because they trusted their builders. They all had good recommendations from prior clients. Also, a building project by its very nature requires regular negotiations because it is impossible to predict all the potential changes: How much would it cost to move that door? How much do we save if we use Caesarstone instead of granite?

These cases worked out well without a written contract, but there are times when you should *definitely* sign an agreement:

1. The Statute of Frauds requires it.

2. The deal is crucial to your life or the life of your business.

3. The terms are complex.

4. You do not have an ongoing relationship of trust with the other party.

Once you decide you need a written contract, then what?

THE LAWYER

The American Bar Association commissioned a study to find out what people think of lawyers. Survey participants responded with these words: greedy, corrupt, manipulative, snakes, and sharks.[2] Businesspeople refer to their lawyers with terms like *business prevention department*. They are reluctant to ask an attorney to draft a contract for fear of the time and expense that lawyers can inject into the process. And they worry that the lawyers will interfere in the business deal itself, at best causing unnecessary hindrance, at worst killing the deal. Part of the problem is that lawyers and clients have different views of the future.

---

[1]For further reading on practical contracts, see Scott Burnham, *Drafting and Analyzing Contracts*, Lexis/Nexis, 2003; Charles M. Fox, *Working with Contracts*, Practical Law Institute, 2008; George W. Kuney, *The Elements of Contract Drafting*, Thomson/West, 2006.

[2]Robert Clifford, *Opening Statement: Now More than Ever*, Litigation, 28 Litigation 1, Spring 2002.

Lawyers and Clients

Businesspeople are optimists—they believe that they have negotiated a great deal and everything is going to go well—sales will boom, the company will prosper. **Lawyers have a different perspective—their primary goal is to protect their clients by avoiding litigation, now and in the future.** For this reason, lawyers are trained to be pessimists—they try to foresee and protect against everything that can possibly go wrong. Businesspeople sometimes view this lawyering as a waste of time and a potential deal-killer. What if the two parties cannot agree about what to do in the event of a very unlikely circumstance? The deal might just collapse.

To take one example of this lawyerly perspective, a couple happily married nigh on 40 years went to see a lawyer about changes in their will. The husband wanted to transfer some assets to his wife. The lawyer advised against it—after all, the couple might divorce. They became angry and indignant because *they would never get divorced*. And they may very well be right. However, just that week, the lawyer had seen another couple who did divorce after 41 years of marriage. He thought it better to be on the safe side and consider the possibility that such events might happen.

Lawyers also prefer to negotiate touchy subjects at the beginning of a relationship, when everyone is on friendly terms and eager to make a deal, rather than waiting until trouble strikes. In the long run, nothing harms a relationship more than unpleasant surprises. For example, the Artist in the movie contract we will refer to throughout this chapter did not know in advance what conditions on the set would be, how grueling the shooting schedule, or how many friends and family would visit him. So his lawyer negotiated a deal in which the Producer agreed to provide a driver, a "first-class star trailer (which shall be a double pop-out)," a luxury hotel suite, and an adjacent room for visitors. In the end, because the role called for the Artist to live in the wilderness, he ultimately slept in a tent on the set to experience his part more fully, so he did not need the double pop-out trailer or the luxury suite. He also dispensed with the driver. But, under different circumstances, he might have wanted those luxuries, and his lawyer's goal was to protect his interests. It is a lot easier to forgo an expense than to add one to a movie budget.

Another advantage of using lawyers to conduct these negotiations is that they can serve as the bad guys. Instead of the client raising tough issues, the lawyers do. Many a client has said, "but my lawyer insists …" If the lawyer takes the blame, the client is able to maintain a better relationship with the other party. And hiring a lawyer communicates to the other parties that you are taking the deal seriously, and they will not be able to take advantage of you.

Of course, this lawyerly protection comes at a cost—legal fees, time spent bargaining, the hours used to read complex provisions, and the potential for good will to erode during negotiations.

Do you need a lawyer? The answer largely depends on the complexity of the deal. Most people do not hire a lawyer to review an apartment lease—the language is standard, and the prospective tenant has little power to change the terms of the deal. On the other hand, you should not undertake a significant acquisition or purchase agreement on your own.

Hiring a Lawyer

If you do hire a lawyer, be aware of certain warning signs. Although the lawyer's goal is to protect you, a good attorney should be a dealmaker, not a deal-breaker. She should help you do what you want and, therefore, should never (or, at least, hardly ever) say, "You cannot do this." Instead, she should say, "Here are the risks to this approach" or "Here is another way to achieve your goal."

Moreover, your lawyer's goal should not be to annihilate the other side. In the end, the contract will be more beneficial to everyone if the parties' relationship is harmonious. Trying to exact every last ounce of flesh, using whatever power you have to an abusive extreme, is not a sound long-term strategy. In the end, the best deals are those in which all the parties' incentives are aligned. Success for one means success for all—or at least, success for one party does not *prohibit* a positive outcome for the other side. If either side in the movie contract behaved unreasonably, word would quickly spread in the insular Hollywood world, damaging the troublemaker's ability to make other deals.

Now either you have a lawyer or you do not. The next step is to think about developing the contract.

THE CONTRACT

In this section, we discuss how a contract is prepared and what provisions it should include.

Who Drafts It?

Once businesspeople have agreed to the terms of the deal, it is time to prepare a draft of the contract. Generally, both sides would prefer to *control the pen* (that is, to prepare the first draft of the contract) because the drafter has the right to choose a structure and wording that best represents his interests. Typically, the party with the most bargaining power prepares the drafts. In the movie contract, Producer's lawyer prepared the first draft. The contract then went to Artist's lawyer, who added the provisions that mattered to his client.

How to Read a Contract

Reading a contract is not like cracking open a novel. Instead, it should be a focused, multi-step process:

- **Pre-reading**. Before you begin reading the first draft of a contract, spend some time thinking about the provisions that are important to you. If you skip this step, you may find that as you read, your attention is so focused on the specific language of the contract that you lose sight of the larger picture.

- **The first read.** Read through once, just to get the basic idea of the contract—its structure and major provisions.

- **What-ifs.** This is the time to think about various outcomes, good and bad. Under the terms of the contract, what happens if all goes according to your plan? Also consider worst-case scenarios. In both situations, does the contract produce the result that you want? What happens if sales are higher than you expect, or if the product causes unexpected harm?

- **The second read.** Now read the contract to make sure that it handles the what-ifs in a manner that is satisfactory to you. Think about the relationship between various provisions—does it make sense?

Following this approach will help you avoid mistakes.

Mistakes

This author once worked with a lawyer who made a mistake in a contract. "No problem," he said. "I can win that one in court." Not a helpful attitude, given that one purpose of a contract is to *avoid* litigation. In this section, we look at the most common types of mistakes and how to avoid them.

Vagueness

Businesspeople sometimes *deliberately* choose vagueness. They do not want the terms of the contract to be clear. It may be that they are not sure what they can get from the other side, or in some cases, even what they really want. So they try to create a contract that leaves their options open. However, as the following case illustrates: **vagueness is your enemy.**

QUAKE CONSTRUCTION V. AMERICAN AIRLINES

141 Ill. 2d 281, 565 N.E.2d 990, 1990 Ill. LEXIS 151
Supreme Court of Illinois, 1990

Facts: Jones Brothers Construction was the general contractor on a job to expand American Airlines' facilities at O'Hare International Airport. Jones Brothers invited Quake Construction to bid on the employee facilities and automotive maintenance shop ("the project"). After Quake bid, Jones Brothers orally informed Quake that it was awarding Quake the project and would forward a contract soon. Jones Brothers wanted the license numbers of the subcontractors that Quake would be using, but Quake could not furnish those numbers until it had assured its subcontractors that they had the job. Quake did not want to give that assurance until *it* was certain of its own work. So Jones Brothers sent a letter of intent that stated, among other things:

> We have elected to award the contract for the subject project to your firm as we discussed on April 15. A contract agreement outlining the detailed terms and conditions is being prepared and will be available for your signature shortly.
>
> Your scope of work includes the complete installation of expanded lunchroom, restaurant, and locker facilities for American Airlines employees, as well as an expansion of American Airlines' existing Automotive Maintenance Shop. A sixty (60) calendar day period shall be allowed for the construction of the locker room, lunchroom, and restaurant area beginning the week of April 22. The entire project shall be completed by August 15.
>
> Subject to negotiated modifications for exterior hollow metal doors and interior ceramic floor tile material as discussed, this notice of award authorizes the work set forth in the [attached] documents at a lump sum price of $1,060,568.00.
>
> Jones Brothers Construction Corporation reserves the right to cancel this letter of intent if the parties cannot agree on a fully executed subcontract agreement.

The parties never signed a more detailed written contract, and ultimately Jones Brothers hired another company. Quake sued, seeking to recover the money it spent in preparation and its loss of anticipated profit.

Issue: *Was the letter of intent a valid contract?*

Excerpts from Justice Calvo's Decision: [A]lthough letters of intent may be enforceable, such letters are not necessarily enforceable unless the parties intend them to be.

In determining whether the parties intended to reduce their agreement to writing, the following factors may be considered: whether the type of agreement involved is one usually put into writing, whether the agreement contains many or few details, whether the agreement involves a large or small amount of money, whether the agreement requires a formal writing for the full expression of the covenants, and whether the negotiations indicated that a formal written document was contemplated at the completion of the negotiations.

[We conclude that] the letter was ambiguous. The letter of intent included detailed terms of the parties' agreement. The letter stated that Jones awarded the contract for the project to Quake. The letter stated further, "this notice of award authorizes the work." Moreover the letter indicated that the work was to commence approximately 4 to 11 days after the letter was written. This short period of time reveals the parties intent to be bound by the letter so that work could begin on schedule. We also agree that the cancellation clause exhibited the parties' intent to be bound by the letter because no need would exist to provide for the cancellation of the letter unless the letter had some binding effect. The cancellation clause also implies the parties' intention to be bound by the letter, at least until they entered into the formal contract. These factors evinced the parties' intent to be bound by the letter.

On the other hand, the letter referred several times to the execution of a formal contract by the parties, thus indicating the parties' intent not to be bound by the letter. The cancellation clause could be interpreted to mean that the parties did not intend to be bound until they entered into a formal agreement.

Thus, we hold that the letter of intent in the case at bar is ambiguous regarding the parties' intent to be bound by it. Therefore, on remand, the circuit court shall allow the parties to present parol evidence regarding their intent. The trier of fact must then determine, based on the parties' intent, whether the letter of intent is a binding contract.

So after years of litigation, Jones Brothers and Quake had to go *back* to court to try to prove whether they intended the letter to be binding. The problem is that both sides permitted vagueness to enter their negotiations. Sometimes parties adopt vagueness as a *strategy*. One party may be trying to get a commitment from the other side without obligating itself. A party may feel *almost* ready to commit and yet still have reservations. It wants the *other* party to make a commitment so that planning can go forward. This is understandable but dangerous.

If you were negotiating for Jones Brothers and wanted to clarify negotiations without committing your company, how could you do it? State in the letter that it is *not a contract*, and that *neither side is bound by it*. State that it is a memorandum summarizing negotiations thus far, but that neither party will be bound until a full written contract is signed.

But what if Quake cannot get a commitment from its subcontractors until they are certain that it has the job? Quake should take the initiative and present Jones Brothers with its own letter of intent, stating that the parties *do* have a binding agreement for $1 million worth of work. Insist that Jones Brothers sign it. Jones Brothers would then be forced to decide whether it is willing to make a binding commitment. If Jones Brothers is not willing to commit, let it openly say so. At least both parties will know where they stand.

The movie contract provides another example of deliberate vagueness. In these contracts, nudity is always a contentious issue. Producers believe that nudity sells movie tickets; actors are afraid that it may tarnish their reputation. In the first draft of our contract, Artist's lawyer specified:

> Artist may not be photographed and shall not be required to render any services nude below the waist or in simulated sex scenes without Artist's prior written consent.

(This clause also applied to any double depicting Artist.) However, the script called for a scene in which Artist was swimming nude and the director wanted the option of showing him below the waist from the back. Ultimately, the nudity clause read as follows:

> Producer has informed Artist that Artist's role in the Picture might require Artist to appear and be photographed (a) nude, which nudity may include only above-the-waist nudity and rear below-the-waist nudity, but shall exclude frontal below-the-waist nudity; and (b) in simulated sex scenes. Artist acknowledges and agrees that Artist has accepted such employment in the Picture with full knowledge of Artist's required participation in nude scenes and/or in simulated sex scenes and Artist's execution of the Agreement constitutes written consent by Artist to appear in the nude scenes and simulated sex scenes and to perform therein as reasonably required by Producer. A copy of the scenes from the screenplay requiring Artist's nudity and/or simulated sex are attached hereto. Artist shall have a right of meaningful prior consultation with the director of the Picture regarding the manner of photography of any scenes in which Artist appears nude or engaged in simulated sex acts.
>
> Artist may wear pants or other covering that does not interfere with the shooting of the nude scenes or simulated sex scenes. Artist's buttocks and/or genitalia shall not be shown, depicted, or otherwise visible without Artist's prior written consent. Artist shall have the absolute right to change his mind and not perform in any nude scene or simulated sex scene, notwithstanding that Artist had prior thereto agreed to perform in such scene.

What does this provision mean? Has Artist agreed to perform in nude scenes or not? He has acknowledged that the script calls for nude scenes and he has agreed, in principle, that he will appear in them. However, he did not want to agree categorically, before shooting had even started and he had experience working with this director. Actor has a number of options—he can refuse to shoot nude scenes altogether, or he can shoot them and then, after viewing them, decide not to allow them in the movie. With a clause such as this one, the director shot different versions of the scene—some with nudity and some without—so that if Artist rejected the nude scene, the director still had options.

The true test of whether a vague clause belongs in a contract is this: would you sign the contract if you knew that the other side's interpretation would prevail in litigation? In this example, each side was staking out its position, and deferring a final negotiation until there was an actual disagreement about a nude scene. If you would be happy enough with the other side's position in the end, the vague clause simply defers a fight that you can afford to lose. But if the point is really important to you, it may be wiser to resolve the issue before you sign the contract by writing the clause in a way that clearly reflects your desired outcome.

EXAM Strategy

Question: The nudity provision in the movie contract is vague. Rewrite it so that it accurately expresses the agreement between the parties.

Strategy: This is easy! Just say what the parties intended the deal to be.

Result: "The script for the Picture includes scenes showing Artist (a) with frontal nudity from the waist up and with rear below-the-waist nudity (but no frontal below-the-waist nudity); and (b) in simulated sex scenes. However, no scenes shall be shot in which Artist's buttocks and/or genitalia are shown, depicted, or otherwise visible without Artist's prior written consent. Artist shall have the absolute right not to perform in any nude scene or simulated sex scene. If shot, no nude or sex scenes may appear in the Picture without Artist's prior written consent."

Ambiguity

Vagueness occurs when the parties do not want the contract to be clear. Ambiguity is different—it means that the provision is *accidentally* unclear. It occurs in contracts when the parties think only about what *they* want a provision to mean, without considering the literal meaning or the other side's perspective. When reading a contract, try to imagine all the different ways a clause can be interpreted. Because you think it means one thing does not mean that the other side will share your view. For example, suppose that an employment contract says, "Employee agrees not to work for a competitor for a period of three years from employment." Does that mean three years from the date of hiring or the date of termination? Unclear, so who knows?

To take another example, the dictionary defines vandalism as *deliberately mischievous or malicious destruction or damage of property*. Arson is *the malicious burning of a house or property*. Seems clear enough—but does arson count as vandalism? In the following case, no one thought about this question until a house burned down.

CIPRIANO V. PATRONS MUTUAL INSURANCE COMPANY OF CONNECTICUT

2005 Conn. Super. LEXIS 3577
Superior Court of Connecticut, 2005

Facts: Juacikino Cipriano purchased an insurance policy on his house from Patrons Mutual Insurance Company. The policy stated that the company would not pay for any damage to the *residence* caused by vandalism or burglary if the residence was vacant for more than 30 days in a row just before the loss. Furthermore, the company would not pay for damage to *personal property* caused by fire, lightning, or vandalism.

After Cipriano's house had been vacant for more than 30 days, an arsonist burned it down. Patrons denied his claim on the grounds that arson is vandalism, which his policy did not cover. Cipriano filed suit against Patrons. The insurance company filed a motion for summary judgment.

Issues: *Does arson count as vandalism? Must Patrons pay Cipriano's claim?*

Excerpts from Judge Devine's Decision: [T]here are no genuine issues of fact that the fire was the result of arson and that the dwelling house was vacant for more than 30 days prior to the fire. The defendant contends that the term "vandalism" includes the act of arson. The plaintiff argues that, in reviewing the insurance policy as a whole, an insured may not be able to discern what "vandalism" means, as that term is used in the separate sections of the insurance policy.

Under our law, the terms of an insurance policy are to be construed according to the general rules of contract construction. It is a basic principle of insurance law that policy language will be construed as laymen would understand it and not according to the interpretation of sophisticated underwriters, and that ambiguities in contract documents are resolved against the party responsible for its drafting;

the policyholder's expectations should be protected, as long as they are objectively reasonable from the layman's point of view. However, a court will not torture words to import ambiguity where the ordinary meaning leaves no room for ambiguity, and words do not become ambiguous simply because lawyers or laymen contend for different meanings.

In the present case, the defendant has drafted an insurance policy where "vandalism" and "fire" are undefined terms. Reading the insurance policy as whole, the terms "vandalism" and "fire" are found to be included as separate perils covered under the personal property coverage. In the exclusionary provision for the coverage of the residence, "vandalism" is listed as an excluded loss. "Fire" is not mentioned.

Because the terms "vandalism" and "fire" are undefined, and are listed as two distinct perils, it is ambiguous as to which peril, "vandalism" or "fire," covers arson. Therefore, "vandalism" is susceptible of two reasonable interpretations. As such, the insurance policy must be construed against the party responsible for its drafting.

The defendant's motion for summary judgment is hereby denied.

This case illustrates an important rule of contract drafting: **any ambiguity is interpreted against the drafter of the contract**. (The *Cipriano* policy is a good example of how incomprehensible insurance policies can be. This complexity tends to erode judicial sympathy for the perpetrator.) Although both sides need to be careful in reading a contract—litigation benefits no one—the side that prepares the documents bears a special burden. This rule is meant to:

1. Protect laypeople from the dangers of form contracts that they have little power to change. Even if the insured in this case had read the contract carefully, it is unlikely that an insurance company would change its form contract for him.

2. Protect people who are unlikely to be represented by a lawyer. Most people do not hire a lawyer to read insurance contracts (or any form contract). And without an experienced lawyer, it is highly unlikely that an insured would ask, "So is arson included in the vandalism clause?"

3. Encourage those who prepare contracts to do so carefully.

Typos

The bane of a lawyer's existence! This author worked on a securities offering in which the sales document almost went out with part of the company's name spelled *Pertoleum* instead of *Petroleum*. (And legend has it that a United Airlines securities offering once featured "Untied Airlines.") Although clients tend not to have a sense of humor about such errors, at least there would be no adverse legal result. That is not always the case with typos.

A group of condominium buyers ended up in litigation over a tiny typo in their purchase agreements: an "8" instead of a "9." What difference could that possibly make? A lot, it turns out. Extell Development Corporation built the Rushmore, a luxury condominium complex in Manhattan. When Extell began selling the units, it agreed to refund any buyer's down payment if the first closing did not occur by September 1, 2009. (The goal was to protect buyers who might not have any place to live if the building was not finished on time.) In the end, the first closing occurred in February 2009. No problem, right? No problem except that, by accident, the purchase contract said September 1, *2008* rather than *2009*. In the meantime, the Manhattan real estate market tumbled, and many purchasers of Rushmore condominiums wanted to back out. After litigation all the way to the Federal Court of Appeals, Extell was required to refund the deposits.

What is the law of typos? First of all, the law has a fancier word than *typo*—it is **scrivener's error.** A scrivener is a clerk who copies documents. **In the case of a scrivener's error, a court will reform a contract if there is clear and convincing evidence that the mistake does not reflect the true intent of the parties.** In the Rushmore case, an arbitrator refused to reform the contract, ruling that there was no clear and convincing evidence that the parties intended something other than the contract term as written.

Scrivener's error
A typo.

In the following case, even more money was at stake. What would you do if you were the judge?

You be the Judge

Facts: Heritage wanted to buy a substance called tribasic copper chloride (TBCC) from Phibro but, because of uncertainty in the industry, the two companies could not agree on a price for future years. It turned out, though, that the price of TBCC tended to rise and fall with that of copper sulfate, so Heritage proposed that the amount it paid for TBCC would increase an additional $15 per ton for each $0.01 increase in the cost of copper sulfate over $0.38 per pound.

Two top officers of Heritage and Phibro met in the Delta Crown Room at LaGuardia Airport to negotiate the purchase contract. At the end of their meeting, the Phibro officer hand wrote a document stating the terms of their deal and agreeing to the Heritage pricing proposal.

Negotiations between the two companies continued, leading to some changes and additions to their Crown Room agreement. In a draft prepared by Phibro, the $.01 number was changed to $0.1—that is, from 1 cent to 10 cents. In other words, in the original draft, Heritage agreed to a first increase if copper sulfate went above 39 cents per pound, an additional price rise at 40 cents, and so on. But in the Phibro draft, Heritage's first increase would not occur until the price of copper sulfate went to 48 cents a pound, with a second rise at 58 cents. In short, the Phibro draft was much

HERITAGE TECHNOLOGIES V. PHIBRO-TECH
2008 U.S. Dist. LEXIS 329
United States District Court for the Southern District of Indiana, 2008

more favorable to Heritage than the Heritage proposal had been.

At some point during the negotiations, the lawyer for Heritage asked his client if the $0.1 figure was accurate. The Heritage officer said that the increase in this amount was meant to be payment for other provisions that favored Phibro. There is no evidence that this statement was true. The contract went through eight drafts and numerous changes, but after the Crown Room meeting, the two sides never again discussed the $0.1 figure.

After the execution of the agreement, Heritage discovered a different mistake. When Heritage brought the error to Phibro's attention, Phibro agreed to make the change even though it was to Phibro's disadvantage to do so.

All was peaceful until the price of copper sulfate went to $0.478 per pound. Phibro believed that because the price was above $0.38 per pound, it was entitled to an increased payment. Heritage responded that the increase would not occur until the price went above $0.48. Phibro then looked at the agreement and noticed the $0.1 term for the first time. Phibro contacted Heritage to say that the $0.1 term was a typo and not what the two parties had originally agreed in the Delta Crown Room. Heritage refused to amend the agreement and Phibro filed suit.

You Be the Judge: *Should the court enforce the contract as written, or as the parties agreed in their Crown Room meeting? Which number is correct—$0.10 or $0.01?*

Argument for Phibro: In the Delta Crown Room, the two negotiators agreed to a $15 per ton increase in the price of TBCC for each 1-cent increase in copper sulfate price. Then by mistake, the contract said 10 cents. The two parties never negotiated the 10-cent provision, and there is no evidence that they had agreed to it. The court should revise this contract to be consistent with the parties' agreement, which was 1 cent.

Also, the 10-cent figure makes no economic sense. The point of the provision was that the price of TBCC would go up at the same rate as copper sulfate, and 1 cent for each ton is a much more accurate reflection of the relationship between these two commodities than 10 cents per ton.

Argument for Heritage: The Delta Crown Room agreement was nothing more than a draft. The contract went through eight rounds of changes. The change in price was in return for other provisions that benefited Phibro.

The parties conducted negotiations by sending drafts back and forth rather than by talking on the phone. Both parties were represented by a team of lawyers, the agreement went through eight drafts, and this pricing term was never altered despite several other changes and additions. There is no clear and convincing evidence that both parties were mistaken about what the document actually said. Ultimately, the parties agreed to 10 cents, and that is what the court should enforce.

Ethics   When Heritage found a different mistake in the contract, Phibro agreed to correct it, even though the correction was unfavorable to Phibro. But when a mistake occurred in Heritage's favor, it refused to honor the intended terms of the agreement. Is Heritage behaving ethically? Does Heritage have an obligation to treat Phibro as well as Phibro behaved towards Heritage? Is it right to take advantage of other people's mistakes? What Life Principle would you apply in this situation?

Preventing Mistakes

Here are ways to prevent mistakes in a contract.

> As a general rule, your lawyer is less likely to make mistakes than you are.

Let your lawyer draft the contract   As a general rule, your lawyer is less likely to make mistakes than you are. Of all the players in the Heritage case, only one person noticed the error—Heritage's lawyer.

Resist overlawyering   Yes, your lawyer should draft the contract, but that does not mean she should have free rein, no matter what. This author once worked with a real estate attorney who had developed his own standard mortgage contract, of which he was immensely proud. Whenever he saw a provision in another contract that was missing from his own, he immediately added it. His standard form contract soon topped 100 pages. That contract was painful to read and did no service to his clients.

Read the important terms carefully   Before signing a contract, check carefully and thoughtfully the names of the parties, the dates, dollar amounts, and interest rates. If all these elements are correct, you are unlikely to go too far wrong. And, of course, having read this chapter, you will never mistake $0.10 for $0.01.

Finally, when your lawyer presents you with a written contract, you should follow these rules:

1. Complain if your lawyer gives you a contract with provisions that are irrelevant to your situation.

2. If you do not know what a provision means, ask. If you still do not know (or if your lawyer does not know), ask her to take it out. Lawyers rarely draft from scratch; they tend to use other contracts as templates. Just because a provision was in another agreement does not mean that it is appropriate for you.

3. Remember that a contract is also a reference document. During the course of your relationship with the other party, you may need to refer to the contract regularly. That will be difficult if you do not understand portions of it, or if the contract is so disorganized you cannot find a provision when you need it.

Which brings us to our next topic—the structure of a contract. Once you understand the standard outline of a contract, it will be much easier for you to find your way through the thicket of provisions.

The Structure of a Contract

Traditional contracts tended to use archaic words—*whereas* and *heretofore* were common. Modern contracts are more straightforward, without as many linguistic flourishes. Our movie contract takes the modern approach.

Title

Contracts have a title, which generally is in capital letters, underlined, and centered at the top of the page. The title should be as descriptive as possible—a generic title such as AGREEMENT does not distinguish one contract from another. Much better to entitle it EMPLOYMENT AGREEMENT or CONFIDENTIALITY AGREEMENT. The title of our movie contract is MEMORANDUM OF AGREEMENT (not a particularly useful name), but in the upper right-hand corner, there is space for the date of the contract and the subject. Let's say the subject is "Dawn Rising/Clay Parker." It would have been even better if the title of the movie had been: Agreement between Clay Parker and Winterfield Productions for Dawn Rising.

Introductory Paragraph

The introductory paragraph includes the date, the names of the parties, and the nature of the contract. The names of the parties and the movie are defined terms, e.g., Clay Parker ("Artist"). By defining the names, the actual names do not have to be repeated throughout the agreement. In this way, a standard form contract can be used in different deals without worrying about whether the names of the parties are correct throughout the document.

The introductory paragraph should also include specific language indicating that the parties entered into an agreement. In our contract, the opening paragraph states:

> This shall confirm the agreement ("Agreement") between WINTERFIELD PRODUCTIONS ("Producer") and CLAY PARKER ("Artist") regarding the acting services of Artist in connection with the theatrical motion picture tentatively entitled "DAWN RISING" (the "Picture")[3], as follows:

This introductory paragraph is not numbered.

---

[3]These are not the parties' real names but are offered to illustrate the concepts.

It is here that traditional contracts included their "Whereas" provisions. Thus, for example, a traditional movie contract might say the following:

> WHEREAS, Producer desires to retain the services of Artist for the purpose of making a theatrical motion picture; and
>
> WHEREAS, Artist desires to work for Producer on the terms and subject to the conditions set forth herein;
>
> NOW, THEREFORE, in consideration of the mutual covenants contained herein, and for other good and valuable consideration, the receipt and adequacy of which are hereby acknowledged, the parties agree as follows:

None of these flourishes are necessary, but some people prefer them.

Definitions

Most contracts have some definitions. As we have seen in the movie contract, *Artist*, *Producer*, and *Movie* were defined in the introductory paragraph. Sometimes, definitions are included in a separate section. Alternatively, they can appear throughout the contract. The movie contract does not have a definitions section, but many terms, such as *fixed compensation* and *teaser*, are defined within it.

Covenants

Now we get to the heart of the contract: what are the parties agreeing to do? Failure to perform these obligations constitutes a breach of the contract and damages will result. **Covenant** is a legal term that means a promise in a contract.

Covenant
A promise in a contract.

At this stage, the relationship between lawyer and client is particularly important. They will obtain the best result if they work well together. And to achieve a successful outcome, both need to contribute. Clients should figure out what they need for the agreement to be successful. It is at this point that they have the most control over the deal, and they should exercise it. *It is a mistake to assume that everything will work itself out.* Instead, clients need to protect themselves now as best they can. Lawyers can help in this process because they have worked on other similar deals and they know what can go wrong. Listen to them—they are on your side.

Imagine you are an actor about to sign a contract to make a movie. What provisions would you want? Begin by asking what your goals are for the project. Certainly, to make a movie that gets good reviews and good box office. So you will ask for as much control over the process and product as you can get—selection of the director and costars, for instance. Maybe influence on the editing process. But you also want to make sure that the movie does not hurt your career. What provisions would you need to achieve that goal? And shooting a movie can be grueling work, so you want to ensure that your physical and emotional needs are met, particularly when you are on location away from home. Try to think of all the different events that could happen and how they would affect you. The contract should make provisions for these occurrences.

Now take the other side and imagine what you would want if you were the producer. The producer's goal is to make money—which means creating a quality movie while spending as little as possible and maintaining control over the process and final product. As you can see, some of the goals conflict—both Artist and Producer want control over the final product. Who will win that battle?

Here are the terms of the movie contract.
The Artist negotiated:

1. A fixed fee of $1,800,000, to be paid in equal installments at the end of each week of filming.

2. Extra payment if the filming takes longer than 10 weeks.

3. 7.5 percent of the gross receipts of the movie.

4. A royalty on any product merchandising, the rate to be negotiated in good faith.

5. Approval over (but approval shall not be unreasonably withheld):

   a. the director, costars, hairdresser, makeup person, costume designer, stand-ins, and the look of his role (although he lists one director and costar whom he has preapproved);

   b. any changes in the script that materially affect his role;

   c. all product placements, but he preapproves the placement of Snickers candy bars;

   d. locations where the filming takes place;

   e. all videos, photos, and interviews of him;

   f. the translation of the script for French subtitles (he is fluent in French).

6. Approval (at his sole discretion) over the release of any blooper videos.

7. His name to be listed first in the movie credits, on a separate card (i.e., alone on the screen).

8. That the producer not give any photographs from the set to a tabloid (such as, the *National Enquirer* or the *Star*).

9. At least 12 hours off duty from the end of each day of filming to the start of the next day.

10. That he fly first class to any locations outside of Los Angeles.

11. That the producer pay for 10 first-class airline tickets for his friends to visit him on location.

12. A luxury hotel suite for himself and a room for his friends.

13. A driver and four-wheel-drive SUV to transport him to the set.

14. The right to keep some wardrobe items.

The Producer negotiated:

1. All intellectual property rights to the movie.

2. The right not to make the movie, although he would still have to pay Artist the fixed fee.

3. Control over the final cut of the movie.

4. That the Artist will show up on a certain date and work in good faith for

   a. 2 weeks in pre-production (wardrobe and rehearsals);

   b. 10 weeks shooting the movie;

   c. 2 free weeks after the shooting ends, in case the director wants to reshoot some scenes. The Artist must in good faith make himself available whenever the director needs him.

5. The right to fire Artist if his appearance or voice materially changes before or during the filming of the movie.

6. That the Artist help promote the movie on dates subject to Artist's approval, which shall not be unreasonably withheld.

Breach

So now we have the covenants in the movie contract. What happens if one of the parties breaches a covenant? Throughout the life of a contract, there could be many small breaches. Say, Artist shows up one day late for filming or he gains five pounds. Maybe Producer deposits Artist's paycheck a few days late. Perhaps a pop-out trailer is not available. Although these events may technically be violations, a court would not impose sanctions

Material breach
A violation of a contract that defeats an essential purpose of the agreement.

over such minor issues. To constitute a violation of the contract, the breach must be material. A **material breach** is important enough to defeat an essential purpose of the contract. Although a court would probably not consider one missed day to be a material breach, if Artist repeatedly failed to show up, that would be material.

Given that the goal of a contract is to avoid litigation, it is can be useful to define what a breach is. The movie contract uses this definition:

Artist fails or refuses to perform in accordance with Producer's instructions or is otherwise in material breach or material default hereof," and "Artist's use of drugs [other than prescribed by a medical doctor]."

The contract goes on, however, to give Artist one free pass:

It being agreed that with regard to one instance of default only, Artist shall have 24 hours after receipt of notice during principal photography, or 48 hours at all other times, to cure any alleged breach or default hereof.

Sometimes, you will recall, contracts state the consequences of a breach, such as the amount of damages. A damages clause can specify a certain amount, a limitation on the total, or other variations. In other words, the contract could say, "If Artist breaches, Producer is entitled to $1 million in damages." (You remember from prior chapters that these are called *liquidated damages*.) Alternatively, a damage clause could say, "Damages will not exceed $1 million." But the vast majority of contracts have neither liquidated damages nor damage caps.

Sole discretion
A party to a contract has the absolute right to make a decision on that issue.

Reasonable
Ordinary or usual under the circumstances.

Good faith
An honest effort to meet both the spirit and letter of a contract.

Good Faith   Note that many of the covenants in the movie contract provide that the right must be exercised reasonably or that a decision must be made in good faith (except for the right to approve blooper videos, over which Artist has sole discretion). A party with **sole discretion** has the absolute right to make any decision on that issue. Sole discretion clauses are not entered into lightly. **Reasonable** means ordinary or usual under the circumstances. **Good faith** means an honest effort to meet both the spirit and letter of the contract. These are the technical definitions. What do material, reasonably, and in good faith mean in practice?

In the following case, a famous athlete felt that the other party had committed a material breach of their contract, behaved unreasonably, and acted in bad faith. Do you agree?

LeMond Cycling, Inc. v. PTI Holding, Inc.

2005 U.S. Dist. LEXIS 742
United States District Court for the District of Minnesota, 2005

Facts: American Greg LeMond won the Tour de France, cycling's most prestigious race. *Sports Illustrated* named him one of the 40 most influential people in sports during the prior 40 years. He formed LeMond Cycling, Inc. (LCI) to handle his business dealings. Protective Technologies International, Inc. (PTI) sold cycling accessories under brand names like Barbie, Playskool, and Tonka to retailers such as Target, Wal-Mart, K-Mart, and Toys R Us.

LeMond and PTI signed a contract (the Deal Memo) providing that PTI would use LeMond's name to sell bicycle accessories. In return, PTI would pay LCI $500,000 a year plus a 6 percent royalty on annual sales exceeding $8.33 million. The Deal Memo required PTI to

- Use commercially reasonable efforts to produce and market LeMond bicycle accessories

- Keep LCI apprised of PTI's efforts, including information about marketing and media plans

PTI tried to sell LeMond products to Target, Wal-Mart, and Toys R Us. Only Target was interested, and then only in a minor way. It agreed to allocate just 6 feet of shelf space to LeMond products. It also rejected PTI's proposal to install a video kiosk that featured LeMond. PTI did not tell LCI about this deal.

LeMond accessories sold poorly at Target. PTI itself did not do any promotional activities or advertising for the products beyond the initial video for the kiosk, which

Target rejected. PTI argued that it was Target's role to advertise the products.

Because of poor sales, Target reduced the amount of shelf space for LeMond items to just 4 feet. Ultimately, Target discontinued these products altogether. In neither instance did PTI inform LCI. PTI did try to sell LeMond accessories to Wal-Mart, Toys R Us, and other stores, but there were no takers.

Shortly thereafter, PTI began to sell Schwinn bicycle accessories to the retailers that had rejected LeMond products. PTI earned over $30 million from Schwinn sales. The company then abandoned all efforts to sell LeMond items.

LCI filed suit against PTI for breach of contract. In response, PTI filed a motion for summary judgment, seeking to have the suit dismissed.

Issue: *Did PTI breach its contract with LCI?*

Excerpts from Judge Magnuson's Decision: To prevail on a breach of contract claim, LCI must prove that PTI breached a material term of the contract. A material breach goes to the root or essence of the contract and is so fundamental to the contract that the failure to perform that obligation defeats an essential purpose of the contract. Even when express conditions of the contract are violated, the breach is not necessarily material.

LCI contends that PTI's alleged failure to provide LCI with annual marketing and media plans was material. LCI submits that these documents serve a critical purpose in licensing agreements because they allow the licensor to monitor sales and corresponding royalty payments.

The Court disagrees. The fact that PTI failed to give reports or other documents to LeMond does not frustrate the essential purpose of the contract. Furthermore, there is no causal connection between PTI's failure to provide LCI with these reports and LCI's lost profit. Therefore, these terms of the Deal Memo, by themselves, are not material as a matter of law.

However, whether or not PTI used commercially reasonable efforts to produce [and] market the Product Line is a material term of the contract, as it is the primary purpose of the contract itself. Thus, the issue is whether PTI breached this duty.

The Deal Memo fails to define commercially reasonable. LCI is convinced that commercially reasonable requires an examination of customary practices within the licensing industry. LCI's broad argument that only industry standards are relevant to the commercial reasonableness determination is unpersuasive. Although an objective component is instructive as to whether or not PTI acted with commercial reasonableness, there must be a subjective evaluation as well. No business would agree to perform to its detriment, and therefore whether or not PTI performed with commercial reasonableness also depends on the financial resources, business expertise, and practices of PTI.

The Complaint also alleges that PTI breached its implied covenant of good faith and fair dealing with LCI. Good faith requires a party to act honestly. Bad faith exists when a party's refusal to fulfill its obligations is based on an ulterior motive. LCI submits that PTI abandoned LCI and its obligations under the Deal Memo when it engaged in its relationship with Schwinn. Indeed, LCI has submitted evidence that PTI narrowly focused on its Schwinn obligations despite its continuing obligation to LCI under the Deal Memo. There is a dispute of fact as to whether PTI exercised good faith in its performance under the terms of the Deal Memo. Thus, PTI's Motion on this point is denied.

IT IS HEREBY ORDERED that:

Defendants' Motion for Summary Judgment is GRANTED in part and DENIED in part as set forth in this Order.

In drafting covenants, there are two issues to keep in mind.

Reciprocal Promises and Conditions Suppose that a contract provides that:

1. Actor shall take part in the principal photography of Movie for 10 weeks, commencing on March 1.

2. Producer shall pay Artist $180,000 per week.

In this case, even if Artist does not show up for shooting, Producer is still required to pay him. These provisions are **reciprocal promises, which means that they are each enforceable independently.** Producer must make payment and then sue Artist, hoping to recover damages in court.

The better approach is for the covenants to be **conditional**—a party agrees to perform them only if the other side has first done what it promised. For example, in the real movie contract, Producer promises to pay Artist "On the condition that Artist fully performs all of Artist's services and obligations and agreements hereunder and is not in material breach or

Reciprocal promises
Promises that are each enforceable independently.

Conditional promises
Promises that a party agrees to perform only if the other side has first done what it promised.

otherwise in material default hereof." And Artist has the right to attend any premieres of the movie and invite three friends, "On the condition that Artist fully performs all services and material obligations hereunder."

In short, if you do not expect to perform under the contract until the other side has met its obligations, be sure to say so.

Language of the Covenants   To clarify who exactly is doing what, covenants in a contract should use the active, not passive voice. In other words, a contract should say "Producer shall pay Artist $1.8 million," not "Artist shall be paid $1.8 million."

For important issues where disputes are likely to arise, the language should be precise, detailed, and complete. The movie contract uses 453 words to define the Artist's services just for shooting the movie, not including promotional efforts once the film is released. These acting services include, "dubbing, retakes, reshoots, and added scenes."

Representations and Warranties

Representations and warranties

Statements of fact about the past or present.

Covenants are the promises the parties make about what they will do in the future. Representations and warranties are statements of fact about the past or present; they are true when the contract is signed (or at some other specific, designated time).[4] Representations and warranties are important—without them, the other party might not have agreed to the contract. For example, in the movie contract, Artist warrants that he is a member of the Screen Actors Guild. This provision is important because, if it were not true, Producer would either have to obtain a waiver or pay a substantial penalty.

In a contract between two companies, each side will generally represent and warrant facts such as: they legally exist, they have the authority to enter into the contract, their financial statements are accurate, they have revealed all material litigation, and they own all relevant assets. In a contract for the sale of goods, the contract will include warranties about the condition of the goods being sold.

EXAM Strategy

Question: Producer does not want Artist to pilot an airplane during the term of the contract. Would that provision be a warranty and representation or a covenant? How would you phrase it?

Strategy: Warranties and representations are about events in the past or present. A covenant is a promise for the future. If, for example, Producer wanted to know that Artist had never used drugs in the past, that provision would be a warranty and representation.

Result: A promise not to pilot an airplane is a covenant. The contract could say, "Until Artist completes all services required hereunder, he shall not pilot an airplane."

Boilerplate

These standard previsions are typically placed in a section entitled *Miscellaneous*. Many people think that *boilerplate* is a synonym for *boring and irrelevant*, but it is worth remembering that the term comes from the iron or steel that protects the hull of a ship—something that

---

[4]Although, technically, there is a slight difference between a representation and a warranty, many lawyers confuse the two terms, and the distinction is not important. We will treat them as synonyms, as many lawyers do.

shipbuilders ignore to the passengers' peril. A contract without boilerplate is valid and enforceable—so it can be tempting to skip these provisions, but they do play an important protective role. In essence, boilerplate creates a private law that governs disputes between the parties. Courts can also play this role and, indeed, in the absence of boilerplate they will. But remember that an important goal of a contract is to avoid court involvement.

Here are some standard, and important, boilerplate provisions.

Choice of Law and Forum

Choice of law provisions determine which state's laws will be used to interpret the contract. **Choice of forum** determines the state in which any litigation would take place. (One state's courts can apply another state's laws.) Lawyers often view these two provisions as the most important boilerplate. Individual states might have dramatically different laws. Even the so-called uniform statutes, such as the Uniform Commercial Code, can vary widely from state to state. Variations are even more pronounced in other areas of the law, in particular in the common law, which is created by state courts. As for forum, it is a lot more convenient and cheaper to litigate a case in one's home courts.

When resolving a dispute, the choice of law and forum can strongly influence the outcome. For this reason, sometimes parties are reluctant to negotiate the provision and instead decide not to designate a forum and just take their chances. Or they may choose a neutral, equally inconvenient forum like Delaware. Without a choice of forum clause, the parties may well end up litigating where to litigate, or they may find themselves even worse off—with parallel cases filed by each in his preferred forum.

The movie contract states: "This Agreement shall be deemed to have been made in the State of California and shall be construed and enforced in accordance with the law of the State of California." The contract did not, but might have, also specified the forum—that any litigation would be tried in California.

> **Choice of law provisions**
> Determine which state's laws will be used to interpret the contract.
>
> **Choice of forum provisions**
> Determine the state in which any litigation would take place.

Modification

Contracts should contain a provision governing modification. The movie contract states: "This Agreement may not be amended or modified except by an instrument in writing signed by the party to be charged with such amendment or modification."

"Charged with such amendment" means the party who is adversely affected by the change. For example, if Producer agrees to pay Artist more, then Producer must sign the amendment. Without this provision, a conversation over beers between Producer and Artist about a change in pay might turn out to be an enforceable amendment.

The original version of the movie contract said that Artist would be photographed nude only above the waist. He ultimately agreed to rear-below-the-waist photography. That amendment (which the parties called a *rider*—another term for amendment or addition) took the form of a letter from Artist agreeing to the change. Producer then signed the letter, acknowledging receipt and acceptance. The amendment would have been valid even without Producer's signature because Artist was "charged with such Amendment."

> **Rider**
> An amendment or addition to a contract.

If a contract has a provision requiring that amendments be in writing, there are three ways to amend it:

1. Signing an amendment (or rider).

2. Crossing out by hand the wrong language and replacing it with the correct terms. It is good practice for both parties to initial each change. This method is typically used before the document is signed—say, at the closing if the parties notice a mistake.

3. Rewriting the entire contract to include the changed provisions. In this case, the contract is typically renamed: The Amended and Restated Agreement. This method is most appropriate if there are many complex alterations.

Note that amending a contract may raise issues of consideration, a topic discussed in Chapter 9.

Assignment of rights
A transfer of benefits under a contract to another person.

Delegation of duties
A transfer of obligations in a contract.

Assignment of Rights and Delegation of Duties   An **assignment of rights** is a transfer of your benefits under a contract to another person, while **delegation of duties** is a transfer of your obligations. In the movie contract, Producer has the right to assign the contract, but he must stay secondarily liable to it. In other words, someone else can take over the contract for him, but if that person fails to live up to his obligations, Producer is liable. Artist might be unhappy if another production company takes over the movie, but he is still required under the contract to perform his acting services. At least he knows that Producer is liable for his paycheck.

Delegation means that someone else performs the duties under the contract. It certainly matters to Producer which actor shows up to do the shooting. Artist cannot say, "I'm too busy—here's my cousin Jack." So the movie contract provides:

> It is expressly understood and agreed that the services to be rendered by Artist hereunder are of the essence of this Agreement and that such services shall not be delegated to any other person or entity, nor shall Artist assign the right to receive compensation hereunder.

In essence, Producer not only cares who shows up for shooting, but he also wants to make sure that no one else cashes the checks. He wants to deal only with Artist. And he worries that if Artist assigns the right to receive payment, he will feel less motivated to do his job well.

Arbitration   Some contracts prohibit the parties from suing in court and require that disputes be settled by an arbitrator. The parties to a contract do not have to arbitrate a dispute unless the contract specifically requires it. Arbitration has its advantages—flexibility and savings in time and money—but it also has disadvantages. For example, most contracts between consumers and brokerage houses require arbitration. Consumer advocates argue that the arbitrators in these disputes are biased in favor of the brokerage houses—who engage in many arbitrations—over consumers who are likely to be one-time customers. And many believe that employees receive a less favorable result when they arbitrate, rather than litigate, disputes with their employer. Also, if a court makes a mistake in applying the law, an appellate court can correct the error. But if an arbitrator makes a mistake, there is generally no appeal. The movie contract does not include an arbitration provision.

Attorney's Fees   As a general rule, parties to a contract must pay their own legal fees, no matter who is in the wrong. But contracts may override this general rule and provide that the losing party in a dispute must pay the attorney's fees for both sides. Such a provision tends to discourage the poorer party from litigating with a rich opponent for fear of having to pay two sets of attorney's fees. The movie contract provides:

> Artist hereby agrees to indemnify Producer from and against any and all losses, costs (including, without limitation, reasonable attorneys' fees), liabilities, damages, and claims of any nature arising from or in connection with any breach by Artist of any agreement, representation, or warranty made by Artist under this Agreement.

There is no equivalent provision for breaches by Producer. What does that omission tell you about the relative bargaining power of the two parties?

Integration   During contract negotiations, the parties may discuss many ideas that are not ultimately included in the final version. The point of an integration clause is to prevent either side from later claiming that the two parties had agreed to additional provisions. The movie contract states:

> This Agreement, along with the exhibits attached hereto, shall constitute a binding contract between the parties hereto and shall supersede any and all prior negotiations and communications, whether written or oral, with respect hereto.

Without this clause, even a detailed written contract can be amended by an undocumented conversation—a dangerous situation since the existence and terms of the amendment will depend on what a court *thinks* was said and intended, which may or may not be what actually happened.

EXAM Strategy

Question: Daniel and Annie signed a contract providing that Daniel would lend $50,000 to Annie's craft beer business at an interest rate of 8 percent. During negotiations, Daniel and Annie agreed that the interest rate would go down to 5 percent once she had sold 25,000 cases. This provision never made it into the contract. After the contract had been signed, Daniel agreed to reduce the interest rate to 6 percent once volume exceeded 25,000 cases. The contract had an integration provision but no modification clause. What interest rate must Annie pay once she has sold 25,000 cases?

Strategy: If a contract has an integration provision, then side agreements made during negotiations are unenforceable unless included in the written contract. Without a modification provision, oral agreements made after the contract was signed may be enforceable.

Result: A court would not enforce the side agreement that reduced the interest rate to 5 percent. However, it is possible that a court would enforce the 6 percent agreement.

Severability   If, for whatever reason, some part of the contract turns out to be unenforceable, a severability provision asks the court simply to delete the offending clause and enforce the rest of the contract. For example, courts will not enforce unreasonable noncompete clauses. (California courts will not enforce any noncompetes, unless made in connection with the sale of a business.) In one case, a consultant signed an employment contract that prohibited him from engaging in his occupation "anyplace in the world." The court struck down this noncompete provision but ruled that the rest of the contract (which contained trade secret clauses) was valid.

The movie contract states:

> In the event that there is any conflict between any provision of this Agreement and any statute, law, or regulation, the latter shall prevail; provided, however, that in such event, the provision of this Agreement so affected shall be curtailed and limited only to the minimum extent necessary to permit compliance with the minimum requirement, and no other provision of this Agreement shall be affected thereby and all other provisions of this Agreement shall continue in full force and effect.

Force Majeure   A **force majeure event** is a disruptive, unexpected occurrence for which neither party is to blame that prevents one or both parties from complying with the contract. Force majeure events typically include war, terrorist attack, fire, flood, or general acts of God. If, for example, a major terrorist event were to halt air travel, Artist might not be able to appear on set as scheduled. The movie contract defines force majeure events thus:

Force majeure event
A disruptive, unexpected occurrence for which neither party is to blame that prevents one or both parties from complying with a contract.

> fire, war, governmental action or proceeding, third-party breach of contract, injunction, or other material interference with the production or distribution of motion pictures by Producer, or any other unexpected or disruptive event sufficient to excuse performance of this Agreement as a matter of law or other similar causes beyond Producer's control or by reason of the death, illness, or incapacity of the producer, director, or a member of the principal cast or other production personnel.

Notices   After a contract is signed, there may be times when the parties want to send each other official notices—of a breach, an objection, or an approval, for example. In this section, the parties list the addresses where these notices may be sent. For Producer, it is company headquarters. For Artist, there are three addresses: his agent, his manager, and his lawyer. The notice provision also typically specifies when the notice is effective: when sent, when it would normally be expected to arrive, or when it actually does arrive.

Closing   To indicate that the parties have agreed to the terms of the contract, they must sign it. A simple signature is sufficient, but contracts often contain flourishes. The movie contract, for example, states:

> IN WITNESS WHEREOF, the parties hereto have executed this Agreement as of the date first written above.

With clauses like this, it is important to make sure that there is an (accurate) date on the first page. If not otherwise provided in the "Notices" section, it is a good idea to include the parties' addresses. The movie contract also listed Artist's social security number.

When a party to the contract is a corporation, the signature lines should read like this:

Winterfield Productions, Inc.
By:_____
Name:
Title:

If an individual signs her own name without indicating that she is doing so in her role as an employee of Winterfield Productions, Inc., she would be personally liable.

In the end, both parties signed the contract and the movie was made. According to Rotten Tomatoes, the online movie site, professional reviewers rated it 7.9 out of 10.

Chapter Conclusion

You will undoubtedly sign many contracts in your life. Their length and complexity can be daunting. (In the movie contract, one of the paragraphs is 1,000 words.) The goal of this chapter is to help you understand the structure and meaning of the most important provisions so that you can read and analyze contracts more effectively.

EXAM REVIEW

1. **AMBIGUITY** Any ambiguity in a contract is interpreted against the party who drafted the agreement. (pp. 293–294)

2. **SCRIVENER'S ERROR** A scrivener's error is a typographical mistake. In the case of a scrivener's error, a court will reform a contract if there is clear and convincing evidence that the mistake does not reflect the true intent of the parties. (p. 295)

EXAM Strategy

Question: Martha intended to transfer a piece of land to Paul. By mistake, she signed a contract transferring two parcels of land. Each piece was accurately described in the contract. Will the court reform this contract and transfer one piece of land back to her?

Strategy: Begin by asking if this was a scrivener's error. Then consider whether the court will correct the mistake.

3. **BEFORE SIGNING A CONTRACT** Before signing a contract, check carefully and thoughtfully the names of the parties, the dates, dollar amounts, and interest rates. (p. 296)

4. **MATERIAL BREACH** A material breach is important enough to defeat an essential purpose of the contract. (p. 300)

EXAM Strategy

Question: Laurie's contract to sell her tortilla chip business to Hudson contained a provision that she must continue to work at the business for five years. One year later, she quit. Hudson refused to pay her the amounts still owing under the contract. Laurie alleged that he is liable for the full amount because her breach was not material. Is Laurie correct?

Strategy: What was the essential purpose of the contract? Was Laurie's breach important enough to defeat it?

5. **SOLE DISCRETION** A party with sole discretion has the absolute right to make any decision on that issue. (p. 300)

EXAM Strategy

Question: A tenant rented space from a landlord for a seafood restaurant. Under the terms of the lease, the tenant could assign the lease only if the landlord gave her consent, which she had the right to withhold "for any reason whatsoever, at her sole discretion." The tenant grew too ill to run the restaurant and asked permission to assign the lease. The landlord refused. In court, the tenant argued that the landlord could not unreasonably withhold her consent. Is the tenant correct?

Strategy: A sole discretion clause grants the absolute right to make a decision. Are there any exceptions?

6. **REASONABLE** Reasonable means ordinary or usual under the circumstances. (p. 300)

7. **GOOD FAITH** Good faith means an honest effort to meet both the spirit and letter of the contract. (p. 300)

8. **STRUCTURE OF A CONTRACT** The structure of a contract looks like this:

   1. Title
   2. Introductory Paragraph
   3. Definitions
   4. Covenants
   5. Breach
   6. Conditions
   7. Representations and Warranties
      i. Covenants are the promises the parties make about what they will do in the future.
      ii. Representations and warranties are statements of fact about the present or past— they are true when the contract is signed (or at some other specific, designated time).

8. Boilerplate
   i. Choice of Law and Forum
   ii. Modification
   iii. Assignment of Rights and Delegation of Duties
   iv. Arbitration
   v. Attorney's Fees
   vi. Integration
   vii. Severability
   viii. Force Majeure
   ix. Notices
   x. Closing (pp. 297–306)

---

2. Result: The court ruled that it was not a scrivener's error because it was not a typo or clerical error. Therefore, the court did not reform the contract and the land was not transferred back to Martha.

4. Result: The purpose of the contract was for Hudson to build up the business and make a profit. Laurie's departure interfered with that goal. The court ruled that the breach was material and Hudson did not have to pay the sums still owing under the contract.

5. Result: The court ruled for the landlord. She had the absolute right to make any decision so long as the decision was not illegal. The moral: sole discretion clauses are serious business. Do not enter into one lightly.

MULTIPLE-CHOICE QUESTIONS

1. In the *Quake* case, the appellate court ruled:
   (a) the letter of intent was a valid contract.
   (b) letters of intent are *never* a valid contract.
   (c) a letter of intent can be a valid contract, but this one was not.
   (d) the trial court had to determine if the letter of intent was a valid contract.

2. In the *Cipriano* case, what happened?
   (a) The jury decided in favor of Cipriano because arson is vandalism.
   (b) The jury decided against Cipriano because arson is not vandalism.
   (c) The judge dismissed the motion for summary judgment because the contract was ambiguous.
   (d) The judge granted the motion for summary judgment because the contract was not ambiguous.

3. In the case of a scrivener's error, what happens?

   (a) A court will not reform the contract. The parties must live with the document they signed.

   (b) A court will reform the contract if there is clear and convincing evidence that the clause in question does not reflect the true intent of the parties.

   (c) A court will reform the contract if a preponderance of the evidence indicates that that the clause in question does not reflect the true intent of the parties.

   (d) A court will invalidate the contract in its entirety.

4. In the *LeMond* case, the court ruled:

   (a) PTI's failure to supply marketing and media plans was a material breach of the contract because without those plans, LCI could not monitor sales.

   (b) PTI's failure to supply marketing and media plans was a material breach of the contract because PTI had agreed to supply the plans.

   (c) The requirement that PTI use commercially reasonable means to promote the product line was not enforceable because the term was ambiguous.

   (d) PTI's failure to supply marketing and media plans was not a material breach of the contract.

5. A contract states (1) that Buzz Co. legally exists and (2) will provide 2,000 pounds of wild salmon each week. Which of the following statements is true?

   (a) Clause 1 is a covenant and Clause 2 is a representation.

   (b) Clause 1 is a representation and Clause 2 is a covenant.

   (c) Both clauses are representations.

   (d) Both clauses are covenants.

ESSAY QUESTIONS

1. List three types of contracts that should definitely be in writing, and one that probably does not need to be.

2. Make a list of provisions that you would expect in an employment contract.

3. List three provisions in a contract that would be material, and three that would not be.

4. Slimline and Distributor signed a contract providing that Distributor would use reasonable efforts to promote and sell Slimline's diet drink. Slimline was already being sold in Warehouse Club. After the contract was signed, Distributor stopped conducting in-store demos of Slimline. It did not repackage the product as Slimline and Warehouse requested. Sales of Slimline continued to increase during the term of the contract. Slimline sued Distributor, alleging a violation of the agreement. Who should win?

5. **YOU BE THE JUDGE WRITING PROBLEM** Chip bought an insurance policy on his house from Insurance Co. The policy covered damage from fire but explicitly excluded coverage for harm caused "by or through an earthquake." When an

earthquake struck, Chip's house suffered no fire damage, but the earthquake caused a building some blocks away to catch on fire. That fire ultimately spread to Chip's house, burning it down. Is Insurance Co. liable to Chip? **Argument for Insurance Co.:** The policy could not have been clearer or more explicit. If there had been no earthquake, Chip's house would still be standing. The policy does not cover his loss. **Argument for Chip:** His house was not damaged by an earthquake; it burned down. The policy covered fire damage. If a contract is ambiguous, it must be interpreted against the drafter of the contract.

DISCUSSION QUESTIONS

1. In the movie contract, which side was the more successful negotiator? Can you think of any terms that either party left out? Are any of the provisions unreasonable?

2. What are the advantages and disadvantages of hiring a lawyer to draft or review a contract?

3. What are the penalties if Artist breaches the movie contract? Are these reasonable? Too heavy? Too light?

4. **ETHICS** In the *Heritage* case, the two companies had agreed to a price change of $0.01. When Heritage's lawyer pointed out to his client the change to $0.10, the Heritage officer did not tell Phibro. The change was subtle in appearance but important in its financial impact. Was Heritage's behavior ethical? When the opposing side makes a mistake in a contract, do you have an ethical obligation to tell them? What Life Principles would you apply in this situation?

5. Blair Co.'s top officers approached an investment bank to find a buyer for the company. The bank sent an engagement letter to Blair with the following language:

   > If, within 24 months after the termination of this agreement, Blair is bought by anyone with whom Bank has had substantial discussions about such a sale, Blair must pay Bank its full fee.

   Is there any problem with the drafting of this provision? What could be done to clarify the language?

© neelsky/Shutterstock.com

The UCC: Sales and Secured Transactions

He Sued, She Sued. Harold and Maude made a great couple because both were compulsive entrepreneurs. One evening they sat on their penthouse roofdeck, overlooking the twinkling Chicago skyline. Harold sipped a decaf coffee while negotiating, over the phone, with a real estate developer in San Antonio. Maude puffed a cigar as she bargained on a different line with a toy manufacturer in Cleveland. They hung up at the same time. "I did it!" shrieked Maude, "I made an incredible deal for the robots—five bucks each!" "No, *I* did it!" trumpeted Harold, "I sold the 50 acres in Texas for $300,000 more than it's worth." They dashed indoors.

> "Confirming our deal— 100,000 Psychopath Robots—you deliver Chicago—end of summer."

Maude quickly scrawled a handwritten memo, which said, "Confirming our deal—100,000 Psychopath Robots—you deliver Chicago—end of summer." She didn't mention a price, or an exact delivery date, or when payment would be made. She signed her memo and faxed it to the toy manufacturer. Harold took more time. He typed a thorough contract, describing precisely the land he was selling, the $2.3 million price, how and when each payment would be made and the deed conveyed. He signed the contract and faxed it, along with a plot plan showing the surveyed land. Then the happy couple grabbed a bottle of champagne, returned to the deck—and placed a side bet on whose contract would prove more profitable. The loser would have to cook and serve dinner for six months.

Neither Harold nor Maude ever heard again from the other parties. The toy manufacturer sold the Psychopath Robots to another retailer at a higher price. Maude was forced to buy comparable toys elsewhere for $9 each. She sued. And the Texas property buyer changed his mind, deciding to develop a Club Med in Greenland and refusing to pay Harold for his land. He sued. Only one of the two plaintiffs succeeded. Which one?

The adventures of Harold and Maude illustrate the Uniform Commercial Code (UCC) in action. The Code is the single most important source of law for people engaged in commerce and controls the vast majority of contracts made every day in every state. The Code is ancient in origin, contemporary in usage, admirable in purpose, and flawed in application. "Yeah, yeah, that's fascinating," snaps Harold, "but who wins the bet?" Relax, Harold, we'll tell you in a minute.

DEVELOPMENT OF THE UCC

In the middle of the twentieth century, contract law required a reinvention. Two problems had become apparent in the United States.

1. Old contract law principles often did not reflect modern business practices.

2. Laws had become different from one state to another.

On many legal topics, contract law included, the national government has had little to say and has allowed the states to act individually. Texas decides what kinds of agreements count as contracts in Texas, and next door in Oklahoma, the rules may be very different. On many issues, states reached essentially similar conclusions, so contract law developed in the same direction. But sometimes, the states disagreed, and contract law took on the aspect of a patchwork quilt.

The UCC was created as an attempt to solve these two problems. It was a proposal written by legal scholars and not a law drafted by members of Congress or state legislatures. The scholars at the American Law Institute and the National Conference of Commissioners on Uniform State Laws had great ideas, but they had no legal authority to make anyone do anything.

Over time, lawmakers in all 50 states were persuaded to adopt many parts of the Uniform Commerical Code. They responded to these persuasive arguments:

1. Businesses will benefit if most commercial transactions are governed by the modern and efficient contract law principles that are outlined in the UCC.

2. Businesses everywhere will be able to operate more efficiently, and transactions will be more convenient, if the law surrounding most of their transactions is the same in all 50 states.

This chapter will first focus on Article 2 of the UCC, which applies to the sale of goods. A **good** is a moveable physical object except for money and securities (like stock certificates). We will then turn our attention to Article 9, which sets out rules for secured transactions.

It is worth noting that the UCC is not a total replacement for older principles in contract law. Contract lawsuits not involving goods are still resolved using the older common law rules.

The entire Code is available online at **http://www.law.cornell.edu/ucc/ucc.table.html**.

Harold and Maude, Revisited

Harold and Maude each negotiated what they believed was an enforceable agreement, and both filed suit: Harold for the sale of his land, Maude for the purchase of toy robots. Only one prevailed. The difference in outcome demonstrates one of the changes that the UCC has wrought in the law of commercial contracts and illustrates why everyone in business needs a working knowledge of the Code. As we revisit the happy couple, Harold is clearing the dinner dishes. Maude sits back in her chair, lights a cigar, and compliments her husband on the apple tart. Harold, scowling and spilling coffee, wonders what went wrong.

Harold's contract was for the sale of land and governed by the common law of contracts. The common law statute of frauds requires any agreement for the sale of land to be in writing and *signed by the defendant*, in this case the buyer in Texas. Harold signed it, but the buyer never did, so Harold's meticulously detailed document was worth less than a five-cent cigar.

Maude's quickly scribbled memorandum concerning psychotic robot toys was for the sale of goods and was governed by Article 2 of the UCC. The Code requires less detail and formality in a writing. Because Maude and the seller were both merchants, the document she scribbled could be enforced *even against the defendant*, who had never signed anything. The fact that Maude left out the price and other significant terms was not fatal to a contract under the UCC, although under the common law, such omissions would have made the bargain unenforceable. We will look in greater detail at these UCC changes. For now, it is enough to see that the Code has carved major changes into the common law of contracts—alterations that Harold is beginning to appreciate.

Scope of Article 2

Because the UCC changes the common law, it is essential to know whether the Code applies in a given case. Negotiations may lead to an enforceable agreement when the UCC applies, even though the same bargaining would create no contract under the common law.

UCC §2-102: Article 2 applies to the sale of goods.[1] **Goods** are things that are moveable, other than money and investment securities. Hats are goods, and so are railroad cars, lumber, books, and bottles of wine. Land is not a good, nor is a house. So an agreement for the delivery of 10,000 board feet of white pine is a contract for the sale of goods, and Article 2 governs it. But the article does not apply to a contract for the sale of an office building. A skyscraper is not moveable (although an entire city *may* be[2]).

Goods
Are things that are moveable, other than money and investment securities.

Article 2 regulates **sales**, which means that one party transfers title to the other in exchange for money. If you sell your motorcycle to a friend, that is a sale of goods. If you lend the bike to your friend for the weekend, that is not a sale and Article 2 does not apply. Article 2 also does not apply to the leasing of goods, for example, when you rent a car. A sale involves a permanent change in ownership, whereas a lease concerns a temporary change in possession.

Mixed Contracts

To determine whether the UCC governs, we need to know what kind of an agreement the parties made. Was it one for the sale of goods (UCC) or one for services (common law)? What if the agreement combined both goods and services and was therefore a *mixed contract?* **In a mixed contract involving sales and services, the UCC will govern if the *predominant purpose* is the sale of goods, but the common law will control if the predominant purpose is providing services.**

For example, assume that you take your car to a mechanic for repairs and that there are problems with the work. If a lawsuit ensues, a court will have to determine whether the predominant purpose of the contract was the parts (goods) that were replaced or the labor (service) involved in the work.

---

[1]Officially, Article 2 tells us that it applies to transactions in goods, which is a slightly broader category than sale of goods. But most sections of Article 2, and most court decisions, focus exclusively on sales, and so shall we.

[2]"If you are lucky enough to have lived in Paris as a young man, then wherever you go for the rest of your life, it stays with you, for Paris is a moveable feast." Ernest Hemingway, 1950.

Merchants

UCC §2-104: A **merchant** is someone who routinely deals in the particular goods involved, *or* who appears to have special knowledge or skill in those goods, *or* who uses agents with special knowledge or skill in those goods. A used car dealer is a "merchant" when it comes to selling autos, because he routinely deals in them. A man selling his own car to someone who responded to his classified ad is not acting as a merchant. **The UCC frequently holds a merchant to a higher standard of conduct than a non-merchant.**

CONTRACT FORMATION

The common law expected the parties to form a contract in a fairly predictable and traditional way: the offeror made a clear offer that included all important terms, and the offeree agreed to all terms. Nothing was left open. The drafters of the UCC recognized that businesspeople frequently do not think or work that way and that the law should reflect business reality.

Formation Basics: Section 2-204

UCC §2-204 provides three important rules that enable parties to make a contract quickly and informally:

1. **Any Manner That Shows Agreement.** The parties may make a contract in any manner sufficient to show that they reached an agreement. They may show the agreement with words, writings, or even their conduct. Lisa negotiates with Ed to buy 300 barbecue grills. The parties agree on a price, but other business prevents them from finishing the deal. Then six months later, Lisa writes, "Remember our deal for 300 grills? I still want to do it if you do." Ed doesn't respond, but a week later, a truck shows up at Lisa's store with the 300 grills and Lisa accepts them. The combination of their original discussion, Lisa's subsequent letter, Ed's delivery, and her acceptance all adds up to show that they reached an agreement. The court will enforce their deal, and Lisa must pay the agreed-upon price.

2. **Moment of Making Is Not Critical.** The UCC will enforce a deal even though it is difficult, in common law terms, to say exactly when it was formed. Was Lisa's deal formed when they orally agreed? When he delivered? She accepted? The Code's answer: it does not matter. The contract is enforceable.

3. **One or More Terms May Be Left Open.** The common law insisted that the parties clearly agree on all important terms. If they did not, there was no meeting of minds and no enforceable deal. The Code changes that. **Under the UCC, a court may enforce a bargain even though one or more terms were left open.** Lisa's letter never said when she required delivery of the barbecues or when she would pay. Under the UCC, the omission is not fatal. So long as there is some certain basis for giving damages to the injured party, the court will do just that. Suppose Lisa refused to pay, claiming that the agreement included no date for her payment. A court would rule that the parties assumed she would pay within a commercially reasonable time, such as 30 days.

Statute of Frauds

UCC §2-201 requires a writing for any sale of goods worth $500 or more. However, under the UCC, the writing need not summarize the agreement completely, and it need not even be entirely accurate. Once again, the Code is modifying the common law rule, permitting parties to enforce deals with less formality. In some cases, the court grants an exception and enforces an agreement with no writing at all. Here are the rules.

Contracts for Goods Worth $500 or More

Section 2-201 demands a writing for any contract of goods over this limit, meaning that virtually every significant sale of goods has some writing requirement. Remember that a contract for goods costing less than $500 is still covered by the UCC, but it may be oral.

Writing Sufficient to Indicate a Contract

The Code only requires a writing *sufficient to indicate* that the parties made a contract. In other words, the writing need not *be* a contract. A simple memo is enough, or a letter or informal note, mentioning that the two sides reached an agreement, is enough. **In general, the writing must be signed by the defendant;** that is, whichever party is claiming there was no deal. Dick signs and sends to Shirley a letter saying, "This is to acknowledge your agreement to buy all 650 books in my rare book collection for $188,000." Shirley signs nothing. A day later, Louis offers Dick $250,000. Is Dick free to sell? No. He signed the memo, it indicates a contract, and Shirley can enforce it against him.

Now reverse the problem. Suppose that after Shirley receives Dick's letter, she decides against rare books in favor of original scripts from the *South Park* television show. Dick sues. Shirley wins because *she* signed nothing.

Enforceable Only to the Quantity Stated

Since the writing only has to indicate that the parties agreed, it need not state every term of their deal. But one term is essential: quantity. **The Code will enforce the contract only up to the quantity of goods stated in the writing.** This is logical, since a court can surmise other terms, such as price, based on market conditions. Buyer agrees to purchase pencils from Seller. The market value of the pencils is easy to determine, but a court would have no way of knowing whether Buyer meant to purchase 1,000 pencils or 100,000; the quantity must be stated.

Exception

In the following three sets of circumstances, the UCC statute of frauds is "turned off".

Merchant Exception This is a major change from the common law. **When two merchants make an oral contract, and one sends a confirming memo to the other within a reasonable time, and the memo is sufficiently definite that it could be enforced against the sender herself, then the memo is also valid against the merchant who receives it, unless he objects within 10 days.** Laura, a tire wholesaler, signs and sends a memo to Scott, a retailer, saying, "Confm yr order today—500 tires cat #886—cat price." Scott realizes he can get the tires cheaper elsewhere and ignores the memo. Big mistake. Both parties are merchants, and Laura's memo is sufficient to bind her. So it also satisfies the statute of frauds against Scott, unless he objects within 10 days.

Specialty Goods Exception If a buyer orders goods that are to be specially manufactured for the buyer and are not suitable for sale to others in the ordinary course of the seller's business, then a verbal agreement is enforceable even if it exceeds $500.

Judicial Admission Exception If a defendant admits in his pleading, testimony, or otherwise in court that a contract for sale was made, then the contract he admitted to is enforceable against him.

The following case examines all three of these exceptions in the context of an agreement to buy carpet and tile. Because many of the cases in this chapter involve more than one Code section, we will outline the relevant provisions at the outset.

When the Supreme Court of Virginia issued its ruling, one company was floored.

CODE PROVISIONS DISCUSSED IN THIS CASE	
Issue	**Relevant Code Section**
1. Is there a confirmatory memo?	UCC 2-201(2)
2. Has the buyer ordered specialty goods?	UCC 2-201(3)(a)
3. Did the buyer admit in its testimony that an agreement existed?	UCC 2-201(3)(b)

DELTA STAR, INC. v.. MICHAEL'S CARPET WORLD

276 Va. 524
Supreme Court of Virginia, 2008

Facts: Ivan Tepper, the CEO of Delta Star, met with the sales manager at Michael's, a flooring company. In a verbal agreement, he hired Michael's to install carpet in the entryway of his office suite, and tile in his personal office and the office of Nash, his assistant.

Michael's faxed Delta Star a purchase order which read, "Carpet for entrance to lobby, $832.22." Michael's installed the carpet and Delta Star paid the $832.22. But Delta Star sought to cancel part of the remaining work installing tile, and Michael's sued.

At trial, Delta Star argued that, because the tiling was priced at more than $500, the UCC statute of frauds made the agreement unenforceable. The trial court disagreed, holding that the tile was specially manufactured, because Michael's had never ordered that type of tile for a customer before. The lower court also determined that Delta Star had admitted the existence of the contract in its testimony, and that the purchase order amounted to a writing in any event. Michael's was awarded $2,565 in damages, and Delta Star appealed.

Issue: *Was the contract enforceable?*

Excerpts from Judge Stephenson's Decision: We first consider the trial court's finding that the flooring materials were specially manufactured goods or products for [Delta Star] and not readily suitable for sale [to] others in the ordinary course of [Michael's] business. The flooring materials chosen by Delta Star were selected from samples displayed, were not altered in any way to suit only Delta Star, and were suitable for sale to others in Michael's ordinary course of business. Therefore, the flooring materials were not "specifically manufactured" for Delta Star.

We next consider the trial court's finding that there exists a confirmatory writing establishing an enforceable contract. We do not agree that such a writing exists. At trial, Michael's contended that its invoice for the purchase and installation of flooring in Delta Star's entryway constituted confirmatory writings. [It] cannot serve as confirmation of a contract for the purchase and installation of flooring in Tepper's office. The invoice confirms only the parties' agreement with regard to the entryway flooring.

Finally, we consider the trial court's ruling that Delta Star admitted in its testimony the existence of a contract for the purchase and installation of flooring in Tepper's office. At trial, Michael's contended that Nash's testimony regarding her attempt to cancel that portion of the alleged contract dealing with Tepper's office constituted an admission that a contract existed because "you can't cancel something unless you're admitting that you got a contract and you want to cancel it." Delta Star contends that Nash did not admit that there existed a contract for the purchase and installation of flooring in Tepper's office.

We agree with Delta Star. A review of Nash's trial testimony reveals that she stated that Delta Star "didn't want to act on the estimate" [and] that Delta Star "hadn't agreed to … order [the flooring for Tepper's office] yet." Therefore, Nash did not admit the existence of a contract for the purchase and installation of flooring in Tepper's office.

For the foregoing reasons, we hold that the trial court erred in overruling Delta Star's Statute of Frauds defense and in finding that an enforceable contract existed between Michael's and Delta Star for the purchase and installation of flooring in Tepper's office.

Reversed.

Added Terms: Section 2-207

Under the common law's mirror image rule, when one party makes an offer, the offeree must accept those exact terms. If the offeree adds or alters any terms, the acceptance is ineffective and the offeree's response becomes a counteroffer. In one of its most significant modifications of contract law, the UCC changes that result. **Under §2-207, an acceptance that adds or alters terms will often create a contract.** The Code has made this change in response to *battles of the form*. Every day, corporations buy and sell millions of dollars of goods using pre-printed forms. The vast majority of all contracts involve such documents. Typically, the buyer places an order using a pre-printed form, and the seller acknowledges with its own pre-printed acceptance form. Because each form contains language favorable to the party sending it, the two documents rarely agree. The Code's drafters concluded that the law must cope with real practices.

Intention

The parties must still *intend* to create a contract. Section 2-207 is full of exceptions, but there is no change in this basic requirement of contract law. If the differing forms indicate that the parties never reached agreement, there is no contract.

Additional or Different Terms

An offeree may include a new term in his acceptance and still create a binding deal. Suppose Breeder writes to Pet Shop, offering to sell 100 guinea pigs at $2 each. Pet Shop faxes a memo saying, "We agree to buy 100 g.p. We get credit for any unhealthy pig." Pet Shop has added a new term, concerning unhealthy pigs, but the parties *have* created a binding contract because the writings show they intended an agreement. Now the court must decide what the terms of the contract are, since there is some discrepancy. The first step is to decide whether the new language is an *additional term* or a *different term*.

Additional Terms   **Additional terms** are those that raise issues not covered in the offer. The "unhealthy pig" issue is an additional term because the offer said nothing about it. **When both parties are *merchants*, additional terms generally become part of the bargain.** Pet Shop's insistence on credit for sick guinea pigs is binding on Breeder. In three circumstances, however, additional terms *do not* bind the parties:

Additional terms
Terms that raise issues not covered in the offer.

- If the original offer *insisted on its own terms*. If Breeder offered the pets for sale "on these and no other terms," Pet Shop's additional language would not become part of their deal.

- If the additional terms *materially alter* the offer. Pet Shop's new language about credit for unhealthy animals is fairly uncontroversial. But suppose Pet Shop wrote back, "Breeder is liable for any illness of any animal in Pet Shop within 90 days of shipment of guinea pigs." Breeder would potentially have to pay for a $500 iguana with pneumonia or a $6,000 parrot with gout. This is a material alteration of the bargain and is not part of the contract.

- If the offeror *promptly objects* to the new terms. If Breeder received Pet Shop's fax and immediately called up to say "No credit for unhealthy pigs," then Pet Shop's additional term is not part of their deal.

In all other circumstances, additional terms do become part of an agreement between merchants.

Different Terms   **Different terms** are terms that *contradict* those in the offer. Suppose Brilliant Corp. orders 1,500 cell phones from Makem Co., for use by Brilliant's sales force. Brilliant places the order using a pre-printed form stating that the product is fully warranted for normal use and that seller is liable for compensatory *and consequential* damages. This means, for example, that Makem could be liable for lost profits if a salesman's phone fails during a lucrative sales pitch. Makem responds with its own memo stating that in the event of defective phones, Makem is liable only to repair or replace, and *is not liable for consequential damages, lost profits, or any other damages.*

Different terms
Terms that contradict those in the offer.

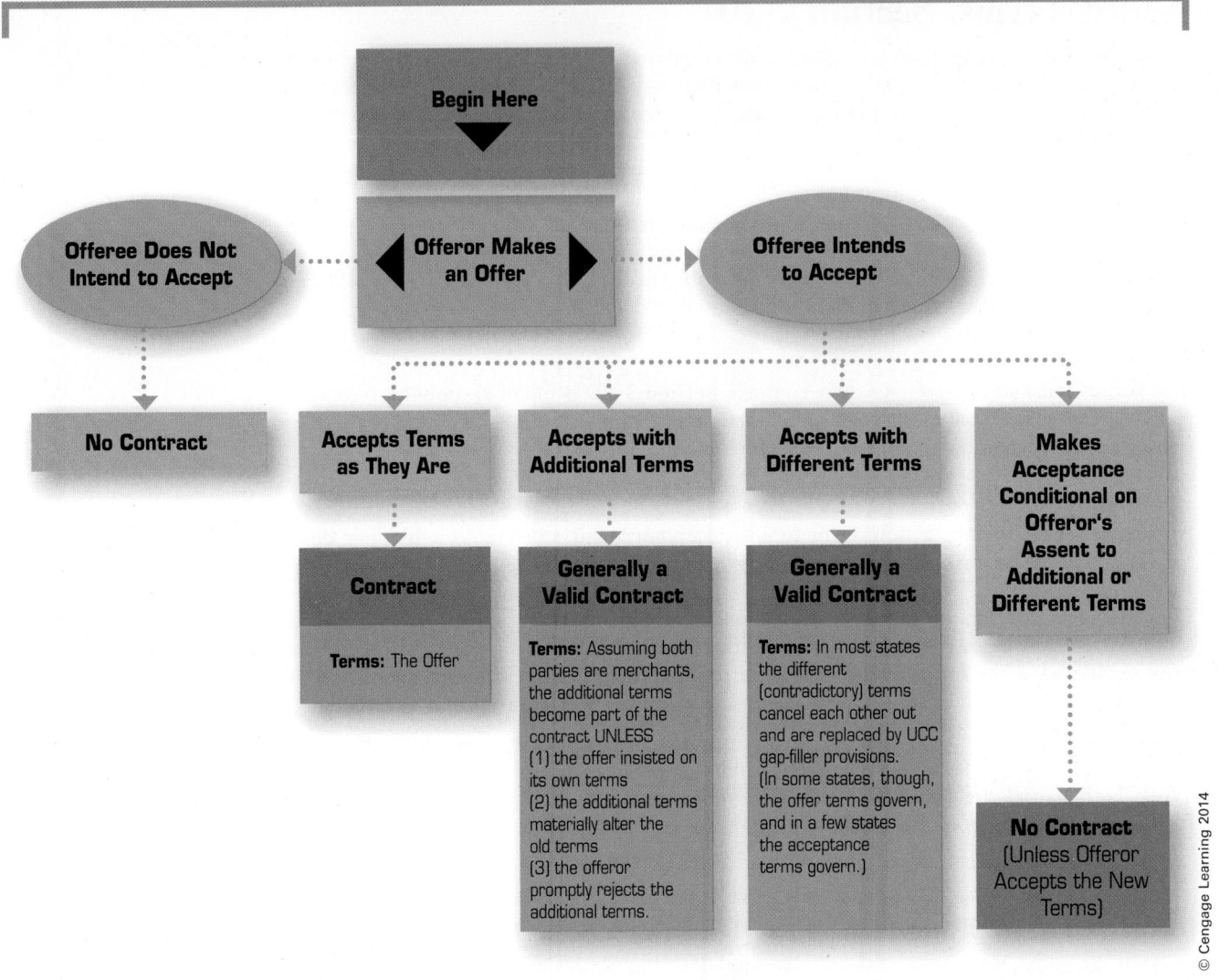

Begin Here ▼

Offeror Makes an Offer ◄ ►

Offeree Does Not Intend to Accept

Offeree Intends to Accept

No Contract

Accepts Terms as They Are

Accepts with Additional Terms

Accepts with Different Terms

Makes Acceptance Conditional on Offeror's Assent to Additional or Different Terms

Contract

Terms: The Offer

Generally a Valid Contract

Terms: Assuming both parties are merchants, the additional terms become part of the contract UNLESS
(1) the offer insisted on its own terms
(2) the additional terms materially alter the old terms
(3) the offeror promptly rejects the additional terms.

Generally a Valid Contract

Terms: In most states the different (contradictory) terms cancel each other out and are replaced by UCC gap-filler provisions. (In some states, though, the offer terms govern, and in a few states the acceptance terms govern.)

No Contract (Unless Offeror Accepts the New Terms)

© Cengage Learning 2014

EXHIBIT 13.1

Makem's acceptance has included a *different* term because its language contradicts the offer. Almost all courts would agree that the parties intended to reach an agreement and therefore the contract is enforceable. The question is, what are its terms? Is the full warranty of the offer included, or the very limited warranty of the acceptance? The majority of states hold that **different terms cancel each other out**. Neither party's language goes into the contract. But what then *are* the terms of the deal?

If the evidence indicates that the parties had orally agreed on the issue disputed in the forms, then the courts will ignore the contradictory writings and enforce the oral contract. **If there is no clear oral agreement, the Code supplies its own terms, called gap-fillers,** which cover prices, delivery dates and places, warranties, and other subjects. In the cell phone case, the contradicting warranty provisions cancel each other out. The parties had not orally agreed on a warranty, so a court would enforce the Code's gap-filler warranty, which does permit recovery of compensatory and consequential damages. Therefore, Makem *would* be liable for lost profits.

EXAM Strategy

Question: Martin, a diamond wholesaler, writes Serge, a jewelry retailer, offering to sell 75 specified diamonds for $2 million. Martin's offer sheet specifies the price, quantity, date of delivery, and other key terms. The sheet also states, "Offer is made on these terms and no other." Serge sends Martin his own purchase order, naming the diamonds, price, and so forth, but adding a clause requiring any disputes to be settled by a diamond-industry arbitrator. In the diamond industry, arbitration by such a person is standard. Martin does not object to the arbitration clause. Martin delivers the gems but Serge refuses to pay the full price, claiming that many of the stones are of inferior quality. Martin sues for the balance due, but Serge insists that any dispute must be settled by arbitration. May Martin litigate, or must he arbitrate the case?

Strategy: Under the common law, there might not be a contract between these parties, because Serge added a new term. However, this agreement concerns the sale of goods, meaning that the UCC governs. Under UCC §2-207, when both parties are merchants (as they are here), additional terms become part of the contract except in three instances. Review those three instances, and apply them here.

Result: Additional terms become part of the agreement unless the original offeror insisted on its own terms, the new term materially alters the offer, or the offeror promptly rejects the new term. Martin's offer insisted on its own terms, and Serge's arbitration clause does not become part of the agreement. Martin may litigate his dispute.

Modification

Another way in which the UCC is pro-contract and pro-business is in its treatment of contract modifications. If two sides have a contract and seek to make changes, are the changes enforceable?

Example 1. Being the best at almost anything pays well, and soccer is no exception. Cristiano Ronaldo's contract with Real Madrid runs through 2015 and averages a whopping $22 million per season. Assume that this year, he leads Real to the fabled treble—a La Liga championship, a victory in the Copa del Rey, and a win in the Champions League. Afterward, the club offers him a raise to $28 million per season through 2015, and Ronaldo accepts. If Spanish law is the same as American law, does the team have a legal obligation to pay the extra millions? No.

This is a services contract, and not a sale of goods. Therefore, common law principles would apply, and they require new consideration for contract modifications to stand. Since Ronaldo did not agree to play any additional seasons or give any other new value to the team, no consideration exists.

We hate to leave out fans of Spain's other big club, so for the next example, we will pay our 65 euros for a ticket on the AVE train and settle in for a three-hour, 500-kilometer trip eastward to Barcelona.

Example 2. FC Barcelona is planning "Lionel Messi Bobblehead Day," and the team orders 10,000 units for the occasion. Unfortunately, the boat carrying the shipment from China is boarded by Somali pirates, who are, it turns out, Barca supporters. The entire shipment is stolen, and the headlines read, "*Trade Hobbled! Pirates Gobble Bobbles!*"

The manufacturer calls the team and asks for a three-week extension on the original delivery deadline. The team is very understanding, agrees to the delay, and reschedules the promotion for a later game. Is this modification, which extends the delivery deadline, now a valid part of the contract? Yes.

In §2-209, the UCC does away with the consideration requirement for changes to contracts, so long as both sides agree to the modification. In this example, no consideration exists to support the extended deadline because the manufacturer gets all the benefit, and the team gets nothing. But that does not create a problem in enforcing the new deal.

PERFORMANCE AND REMEDIES

The Code's practical, flexible approach also shapes its rules about contract performance and remedy. Once again, our goal in this chapter is to highlight doctrines that demonstrate a *change or an evolution in common-law principles.*

Buyer's Remedies

A seller is expected to deliver what the buyer ordered. Conforming goods satisfy the contract terms. Nonconforming goods do not.[3] Frame Shop orders from Wholesaler a large quantity of walnut wood, due on March 15, to be used for picture frames. If Wholesaler delivers, on March 8, high-quality *cherry* wood, it has shipped nonconforming goods.

A buyer has the right to inspect the goods before paying or accepting[4] and may reject nonconforming goods by notifying the seller within a reasonable time.[5] Frame Shop may lawfully open Wholesaler's shipping crates before paying and is entitled to refuse the cherry wood. However, when the buyer rejects nonconforming goods, the seller has the right to cure, by delivering conforming goods before the contract deadline.[6] If Wholesaler delivers walnut wood by March 15, Frame Shop must pay in full. The Code even permits the seller to cure *after* the delivery date if doing so is reasonable. Notice the UCC's eminently pragmatic goal: to make contracts work.

Cover

If the seller breaches, the buyer may *cover* by reasonably obtaining substitute goods; it may then obtain the difference between the contract price and its cover price, plus incidental and consequential damages, minus expenses saved.[7] Retailer orders 10,000 pairs of ballet shoes from Shoemaker, at $55 per pair, to be delivered August 1. When no shoes dance through the door, Shoemaker explains that its workers in Europe are on strike and no delivery date can be guaranteed. Retailer purchases comparable shoes elsewhere for $70 and files suit. Retailer will win $150,000, representing the increased cost of $15 per pair.

HESSLER V. CRYSTAL LAKE CHRYSLER-PLYMOUTH, INC.

338 Ill.App.3d 1010, 788 N.E.2d 405, 273 Ill.Dec. 96
Appellate Court of Illinois, 2003

Facts: Was it a 1930s roadster? A drag racing car from the 1950s? Both. Neither. *Untouchable.* When the Plymouth Prowler first hit the road, with its motorcycle-styled front fenders and low-slung hot rod body, it was nearly impossible to get your hands on one. Dealers were swamped with orders but did not know if they would receive a single car

[3]UCC §2-106(2).
[4]UCC §2-513.
[5]UCC §§2-601, 602.
[6]UCC §2-508.
[7]UCC §2-712.

from the manufacturer. Donald Hessler was one of those who wanted a Prowler—and he was a determined man.

Hessler went to Crystal Lake Chrysler-Plymouth, met with its owner, Gary Rosenberg, and signed an agreement to buy a Prowler anytime during the next year for $5,000 over the manufacturer's list price. Three months later, Rosenberg revealed that the list price would be $39,000. However, the car dealer also entered into a contract to sell a Prowler to another customer for $50,000.

The next time they spoke, Rosenberg told Hessler that Crystal Lake would not be allotted any Prowlers. The eager buyer, though, responded that a Chrysler representative had told him Crystal Lake would receive at least one car. Rosenberg was furious with a customer who had "gone behind his back" to contact Chrysler, and said he would not sell Hessler a car, even if he did receive one.

Hessler telephoned 38 Chrysler dealers, but none would promise him a car. One month later, at a promotional event for the car, he saw a new Prowler—with Crystal Lake's name on it! He located Rosenberg, offered to buy the car on the spot—and was again rebuffed. Frustrated and angry, but still determined, Hessler somehow found a Prowler later the same day from another dealer and bought it—for $77,706.

Hessler drove straight to court, where he sued Crystal Lake. The trial court awarded Hessler $29,853, representing the difference between his contract with Crystal Lake and the sum he ultimately spent purchasing a new Prowler. Crystal Lake appealed, arguing that Hessler covered unreasonably.

Issue: *Did Hessler cover reasonably?*

Excerpts from Judge Callum's Decision: We conclude that the trial court did not err in finding that defendant's foregoing actions reasonably indicated to plaintiff that defendant would not deliver to him a Prowler under the Agreement. As we determined above, defendant contracted to deliver a Prowler to plaintiff as soon as possible. It was not against the manifest weight of the evidence for the trial court to find that defendant [breached] the Agreement when it repeatedly informed plaintiff that it would not deliver to him the first Prowler it received. Such actions

made it sufficiently clear to plaintiff that defendant would not perform under the Agreement.

Defendant's final argument is that the trial court erred in calculating the damages award because plaintiff effected an inappropriate cover. Defendant contends that plaintiff did not recontact the 38 dealers he had called in September to inquire if they would sell him a Prowler. Instead, on the same day that Rosenberg refused to sell him a car, plaintiff visited another dealership and purchased a Prowler for about $40,000 over the list price.

Comment 2 to section 2-712 of the UCC provides, in relevant part:

> The test of proper cover is whether at the time and place the buyer acted in good faith and in a reasonable manner, and it is immaterial that hindsight may later prove that the method of cover used was not the cheapest and most effective.

Plaintiff testified that he called Rosenberg on September 22 to inform him that defendant was on a tentative list to receive a Prowler and that Rosenberg responded that he would not sell to plaintiff a car and that plaintiff was not the first person with whom he had contracted. Rosenberg testified that he informed plaintiff on this date that the Prowler was "already committed." The trial court also heard plaintiff's testimony that, following his September 22 conversation with Rosenberg, he had "serious doubts" that defendant would sell to him a Prowler and he contacted about 38 dealerships to inquire about purchasing a vehicle, but was unable to obtain a car.

Following Rosenberg's refusal to sell a car to plaintiff on October 25, plaintiff visited another dealership on that day and purchased a Prowler for about $30,000 over what he would have paid defendant for the same car. The trial court concluded that the price plaintiff ultimately paid for a Prowler was the "best price" he could receive after defendant refused to sell a car to him. We agree. The trial court heard testimony from both parties about the Prowler's limited supply. It also heard plaintiff's testimony about his efforts to obtain a car one month before his purchase date. We conclude that the court's determination that plaintiff effected a proper cover was not against the manifest weight of the evidence.

For the foregoing reasons, the judgment of the circuit court is affirmed.

Incidental and Consequential Damages

An injured buyer is generally entitled to incidental and consequential damages. Incidental damages cover such costs as advertising for replacements, sending buyers to obtain new goods, and shipping the replacement goods. Consequential damages are those resulting from the unique circumstances of *this injured party*. They can be much more extensive and may include lost profits. A buyer expecting to resell goods may obtain the loss of profit caused by the seller's failure to deliver. In the ballet shoes case, suppose Retailer has contracts to resell the goods to ballet companies at an average profit of $10 per pair. Retailer is also entitled to those lost profits.

Seller's Remedies

Of course, a seller has rights, too. Sometimes a buyer breaches before the seller has delivered the goods, for example, by failing to make a payment due under the contract. If that happens, the seller may refuse to deliver the goods.[8]

If a buyer unjustly refuses to accept or pay for goods, the injured seller may resell them. If the resale is commercially reasonable, the seller may recover the difference between the resale price and contract price, plus incidental damages, minus expenses saved.[9] Incidental damages here are expenses the seller incurs in holding the goods and reselling them, costs such as storage, shipping, and advertising for resale. The seller must deduct expenses saved by the breach. For example, if the contract required the seller to ship heavy machinery from Detroit to San Diego, and the buyer's breach enables the seller to market its goods profitably in Detroit, the seller must deduct from its claimed losses the transportation costs that it saved.

Finally, the seller may simply sue for the contract price if the buyer has accepted the goods *or* if the goods are conforming and resale is impossible.[10] If the goods were manufactured to the buyer's unique specifications, there might be no other market for them, and the seller should receive the contract price.

WARRANTIES

You are sitting in a fast-food restaurant in Washington, D.C. Your friend Harley, who works for a member of Congress, is eating with one hand and gesturing with the other. "We want product liability reform and we want it now," he proclaims, stabbing the air with his free hand. "It's absurd, these multimillion dollar verdicts, just because something has a *slight defect*." He waves angrily at the absurdity, takes a ferocious bite from his burger—and with a loud CRACK breaks a tooth. Harley howls in pain and throws down the bun, revealing a large piece of bone in the meat. As he tips back in misery, his defectively manufactured chair collapses, and Harley slams into the tile, knocking himself unconscious. Hours later, when he revives in the hospital, he refuses to speak to you until he talks with his lawyer. He may have a choice of possible remedies, including negligence and strict liability, which we discussed in Chapter 6. In addition, the fast-food restaurant may have breached a warranty.

> He waves angrily at the absurdity, takes a ferocious bite from his burger—and with a loud CRACK breaks a tooth.

Express Warranties

warranty
A contractual assurance that goods will meet certain standards.

A **warranty** is a contractual assurance that goods will meet certain standards. It is normally a manufacturer or a seller who gives a warranty, and a buyer who relies on it. A warranty might be explicit and written: "The manufacturer warrants that the light bulbs in this package will provide 100 watts of power for 2,000 hours." Or a warranty could be oral: "Don't worry, this machine can harvest any size of wheat crop ever planted in the state."

Express warranty
One that the seller creates with his words or actions.

An **express warranty** is one that the seller creates with his words or actions.[11] Whenever a seller *clearly indicates* to a buyer that the goods being sold will meet certain standards, she has created an express warranty. For example, if the salesclerk for a paint store tells a

---

[8]UCC §2-705.
[9]UCC §2-706.
[10]UCC §2-709.
[11]UCC §2-313.

professional house painter that "this exterior paint will not fade for three years, even in direct sunlight," that is an express warranty and the store is bound by it. The store is also bound by express warranty if the clerk gives the painter a brochure making the same promise or a sample that indicates the same thing.

The seller may disclaim a warranty. A **disclaimer** is a statement that a particular warranty *does not* apply. The seller may disclaim an oral express warranty by including in the sales contract a statement such as "sold as is," or "any oral promises are disclaimed." Written express warranties generally *cannot* be disclaimed.

Disclaimer
A statement that a particular warranty does not apply.

Implied Warranties

Emily sells Sam a new jukebox for his restaurant, but the machine is so defective, it never plays a note. When Sam demands a refund, Emily scoffs that she never made any promises. She is correct that she made no express warranties but is liable nonetheless. Many sales are covered by implied warranties.

Implied warranties are those created by the Code itself, not by any act or statement of the seller.

Implied Warranty of Merchantability

This is the most important warranty in the Code. Unless excluded or modified, a warranty that the goods shall be merchantable is implied in a contract for their sale if the seller is a merchant with respect to goods of that kind. **Merchantable** means that the goods are fit for the ordinary purposes for which they are used.[12] This rule contains several important principles:

Merchantable
Means that the goods are fit for the ordinary purposes for which they are used.

- *Unless excluded or modified* means that the seller does have a chance to escape this warranty. A seller may disclaim this warranty provided he actually mentions the word *merchantability*. A seller also has the option to disclaim *all* warranties by stating that the goods are sold "as is" or "with all faults."

- *Merchantability* requires that goods be fit for their normal purposes. A ladder, to be merchantable, must be able to rest securely against a building and support someone who is climbing it. The ladder need not be serviceable as a boat ramp.

- *Implied* means that the law itself imposes this liability on the seller.

- *A merchant with respect to goods of that kind* means that the seller is someone who routinely deals in these goods or holds himself out as having special knowledge about these goods.

Dacor Corp. manufactured and sold scuba diving equipment. Dacor ordered air hoses from Sierra Precision, specifying the exact size and couplings so that the hose would fit safely into Dacor's oxygen units. Within a year, customers returned a dozen Dacor units, complaining that the hose connections had cracked and were unusable. Dacor recalled 16,000 units and refit them at a cost of $136,000. Dacor sued Sierra and won its full costs. Sierra was a merchant with respect to scuba hoses because it routinely manufactured and sold them. The defects were life-threatening to scuba divers, and the hoses could not be used for normal purposes.[13]

The scuba equipment was not merchantable, because a properly made scuba hose should never crack under normal use. What if the product being sold is food, and the food contains something that is harmful—yet quite normal?

---

[12]UCC §2-314(1).
[13]*Dacor Corp. v. Sierra Precision*, 1993 U.S. Dist. LEXIS 8009 (N.D. Ill. 1993).

GOODMAN v. WENCO FOODS, INC.

333 N.C. 1, 423 S.E.2d 444, 1992 N.C.LEXIS 671
Supreme Court of North Carolina, 1992

Facts: Fred Goodman and a friend stopped for lunch at a Wendy's restaurant in Hillsborough, North Carolina. Goodman had eaten about half of his double hamburger when he bit down and suddenly felt terrible pain in his lower jaw. He took from his mouth a triangular piece of cow bone, about one-sixteenth to one-quarter inch thick and one-half inch long, along with several pieces of his teeth. Goodman's pain was intense, and his dental repairs took months.

The restaurant purchased all its meat from Greensboro Meat Supply Company (GMSC). Wendy's required its meat to be chopped and "free from bone or cartilage in excess of 1/8 inch in any dimension." GMSC beef was inspected continuously by state regulators and was certified by the United States Department of Agriculture (USDA). The USDA considered any bone fragment less than three-quarters of an inch long to be "insignificant."

Goodman sued, claiming a breach of the implied warranty of merchantability. The trial court dismissed the claim, ruling that the bone was natural to the food and that the hamburger was therefore fit for its ordinary purpose. The appeals court reversed this, holding that a hamburger could be unfit even if the bone occurred naturally. Wendy's appealed to the state's highest court.

Issue: *Was the hamburger unfit for its ordinary purpose because it contained a harmful but natural bone?*

Excerpts from Judge Exum's Decision: We hold that when a substance in food causes injury to a consumer of the food, it is not a bar to recovery against the seller that the substance was "natural" to the food, provided the substance is of such a size, quality or quantity that the substance's presence should not reasonably have been anticipated by the consumer.

A triangular, one-half-inch, inflexible bone shaving is indubitably "inherent" in or "natural" to a cut of beef, but whether it is so "natural" to hamburger as to put a consumer on his guard—whether it "is to be reasonably expected by the consumer"—is, in most cases, a question for the jury. We are not requiring that the respondent's hamburgers be perfect, only that they be fit for their intended purpose. It is difficult to conceive of how a consumer might guard against the type of injury present here, short of removing the hamburger from its bun, breaking it apart, and inspecting its small components.

Wendy's argues that the evidence supported its contention that its hamburger complied with [federal and state] standards. Wendy's reasons that [state and federal regulators permit] some bone fragments in meat and that its hamburgers are therefore merchantable as a matter of law. The court of appeals rejected this argument, noting that compliance "with all state and federal regulations is only some evidence which the jury may consider in determining whether the product was merchantable." We agree.

We thus conclude, as did the court of appeals majority, that a jury could reasonably determine the meat to be of such a nature, i.e., hamburger, and the bone in the meat of such a size that a consumer of the meat should not reasonably have anticipated the bone's presence. The court of appeals therefore properly reversed the directed verdict for Wendy's on plaintiff's implied warranty of merchantability claim.

Implied Warranty of Fitness for a Particular Purpose

The other warranty that the law imposes on sellers is the implied warranty of fitness for a particular purpose. This cumbersome name is often shortened to *warranty of fitness.* Where the seller at the time of contracting knows about a particular purpose for which the buyer wants the goods, and knows that the buyer is relying on the seller's skill or judgment, there is (unless excluded or modified) an implied warranty that the goods shall be fit for such purpose.[14]

Notice that the seller must know about some special use the buyer intends and realize that the buyer is relying on the seller's judgment. Suppose a lumber sales clerk knows that a buyer is relying on his advice to choose the best wood for a house being built in a swamp. The Code implies a warranty that the wood sold will withstand those special conditions.

---

[14]UCC §2-315.

Once again, a seller may disclaim this warranty if she clearly states "as is" or "sold with all faults," or some similar language.

Consumer Sales

The Code often provides stronger protection for consumers than for businesses. Many states prohibit a seller from disclaiming implied warranties in the sale of consumer goods. In these states, if a home furnishings store sells a bunk bed to a consumer and the top bunk tips out the window on the first night, the seller is liable. If the sales contract clearly stated "no warranties of merchantability or fitness," the court would reject the clause and find that the seller breached the implied warranty of merchantability.

SECURED TRANSACTIONS

Article 9: Terms and Scope

Article 9 of the UCC governs *secured transactions* in personal property. It is essential to understand the basics of this law because we live and work in a world economy based on credit. Gravity may cause the earth to spin, but it is secured transactions that keep the commercial world going 'round. The quantity of disputes tells us how important this law is: about *one-half* of all UCC lawsuits involve Article 9.

Article 9 applies to any transaction intended to create a security interest in personal property or fixtures. The personal property used as collateral may be goods, such as cars or jewelry, but it may also be a variety of other things, including checks, stocks, bonds, and bills of lading.

This part of the Code employs terms not used elsewhere, so we must lead off with some definitions.

Article 9 Vocabulary

- **Fixtures** are goods that have become attached to real estate. For example, heating ducts are *goods* when a company manufactures them, and also when it sells them to a retailer. But when a contractor installs the ducts in a new house, they become *fixtures*.

- **Security interest** means an interest in personal property or fixtures that secures the performance of some *obligation*. If an automobile dealer sells you a new car on credit and retains a security interest in the car, it means she is keeping legal rights *in your car*, including the right to drive it away if you fall behind in your payments.

- **Secured party** is the person or company that holds the security interest. The automobile dealer who sells you a car on credit is the secured party.

- **Collateral** is the property subject to a security interest. When a dealer sells you a new car and keeps a *security interest*, the vehicle is the collateral.

- **Debtor** and **obligor**. For our purposes, **debtor** refers to a person who has some *original* ownership interest in the collateral. Having a security interest in the collateral does *not* make one a debtor. If Alice borrows money from a bank and uses her Mercedes as collateral, she is the debtor because she owns the car. **Obligor** means a person who must repay money, or perform some other task.

- **Security agreement** is the contract in which the debtor gives a security interest to the secured party. This agreement protects the secured party's rights in the collateral.

- **Default** occurs when the debtor fails to pay money that is due, for example, on a loan or for a purchase made on credit.

Fixtures
Goods that have become attached to real estate.

Security interest
An interest in personal property or fixtures that secures the performance of an obligation.

Secured party
A person or company that holds a security interest.

Collateral
Property that is subject to a security interest.

Debtor
A person who has original ownership interest in the collateral.

Obligor
A person who must repay money or perform some other task to satisfy a debt.

Security agreement
A contract in which the debtor gives a security interest to the secured party.

Default
The failure of a debtor to pay money due on a loan or credit purchase.

Repossession
Occurs when the secured party takes back collateral because the debtor has defaulted.

Perfection
A series of steps that the secured party must take to protect its rights in the collateral against people other than the debtor.

Financing Statement
A document that the secured party files to give the general public notice that it has a secured interest in the collateral.

Record
Information written on paper or stored in an electronic or other medium.

Authenticate
Means to sign a document or to use any symbol or encryption method that identifies the person and clearly indicates she is adopting the record as her own.

- **Repossession** occurs when the secured party takes back collateral because the debtor has defaulted.

- **Perfection** is a series of steps the secured party must take to protect its rights in the collateral against people other than the debtor. This is important because if the debtor cannot pay his debts, several creditors may attempt to seize the collateral, but only one may actually obtain it. To perfect its rights in the collateral, the secured party will typically file specific papers with a state agency.

- **Financing statement** is a document that the secured party files to give the general public notice that it has a secured interest in the collateral.

- **Record** refers to information written on paper or stored in an electronic or other medium.

- **Authenticate** means to sign a document or to use any symbol or encryption method that identifies the person and clearly indicates she is adopting the record as her own. You authenticate a security agreement when you sign papers at an auto dealership, for example.

An Example

Here is an example using the terms just discussed. A medical equipment company manufactures a CAT scan machine and sells it to a clinic for $2 million, taking $500,000 cash and the clinic's promise to pay the rest over five years. The clinic simultaneously authenticates a security agreement, giving the manufacturer a security interest in the CAT scan. If the clinic fails to make its payments, the manufacturer can repossess the machine. The manufacturer then electronically files a financing statement with an appropriate state agency. This *perfects* the manufacturer's rights, meaning that its security interest in the CAT scanner is now valid against all the world. If the clinic goes bankrupt and many creditors try to seize its assets, the manufacturer has first claim to the CAT scan machine.

The clinic's bankruptcy is of great importance. When a debtor has money to pay all of its debts, there are no concerns about security interests. But what if there is not enough money to go around? A creditor insists on a security interest to protect itself in the event the debtor *cannot* pay all of its debts. The secured party intends (1) to give itself a legal interest in specific property of the debtor and (2) to establish a priority claim in that property, ahead of other creditors. In this chapter, we look at a variety of issues that arise in secured transactions.

A Note on Software

Article 9 takes into account the increasingly important role that computer software plays in all business. The Code distinguishes *software* from *goods*, and this becomes important when competing creditors are fighting over both a computer system and the software inside it. A program embedded in a computer counts as goods *if* it is customarily considered part of the computer *or* if, by purchasing the computer, the owner acquires the right to use the program. A program that does *not* meet those criteria is termed *software*, and will be treated differently for some purposes.

ATTACHMENT OF A SECURITY INTEREST

Attachment
A three-step process that creates an enforceable security interest.

Attachment is a vital step in a secured transaction. This means that the secured party has taken all of the following steps to create an enforceable security interest:

- The two parties made a security agreement, and either the debtor has *authenticated a security agreement* describing the collateral *or* the secured party has obtained *possession* or *control;*

- The secured party has given value to obtain the security agreement; and
- The debtor has rights in the collateral.[15]

Agreement

Without an agreement, there can be no security interest. Generally, the agreement will be in writing and signed by the debtor or electronically recorded and authenticated by the debtor. The agreement must reasonably identify the collateral. A description of collateral by *type* is often acceptable. For example, a security agreement may properly describe the collateral as "all equipment in the store at 123 Periwinkle Street."[16] In a security agreement for consumer goods, however, a description by type is *not* sufficient, and more specificity is required.

A security agreement at a minimum might:

- State that Happy Homes, Inc., and Martha agree that Martha is buying an Arctic Co. refrigerator and identify the exact unit by its serial number;
- Give the price, the down payment, the monthly payments, and interest rate;
- State that because Happy Homes is selling Martha the refrigerator on credit, it has a security interest in the refrigerator; and
- Provide that if Martha defaults on her payments, Happy Homes is entitled to repossess the refrigerator.

An actual security agreement will add many details, such as Martha's obligation to keep the refrigerator in good condition and to deliver it to the store if she defaults; a precise definition of "default"; and how Happy Homes may go about repossessing if Martha defaults and fails to return the refrigerator.

Control and Possession

In many cases, the security agreement need not be in writing if the parties have an oral agreement and the secured party has either **control** or **possession**. For many kinds of collateral, it is safer for the secured party actually to take the item than to rely upon a security agreement.

Value

For the security interest to attach, the secured party must give value. Usually, the value will be apparent. If a bank loans $400 million to an airline, that money is the value, and the bank, therefore, may obtain a security interest in the planes that the airline is buying. If a store sells a living room set to a customer for a small down payment and two years of monthly payments, the value given is the furniture.

The parties may also agree that some of the value will be given in the future. For example, a finance company might extend a $5 million line of credit to a retail store, even though the store initially takes only $1 million of the money. The remaining credit is available whenever the store needs it to purchase inventory. The UCC considers the entire $5 million line of credit to be value.[17]

Debtor Rights in the Collateral

The debtor can grant a security interest in goods only if he has some legal right to those goods himself. Typically, the debtor owns the goods. But a debtor may also give a security interest if he is leasing the goods or even if he is a bailee, meaning that he is lawfully holding them for

---

[15]UCC §9-203.

[16]A security agreement may not use a **super-generic** term such as "all of Smith's personal property." We will see later that, by contrast, such a super-generic description is legally adequate in a *financing statement*.

[17]UCC §9-204(c).

someone else. Suppose Importer receives a shipment of scallops on behalf of Seafood Wholesaler. Wholesaler asks Importer to hold the scallops for three days as a favor, and to keep a customer happy, Importer agrees. Importer then arranges a $150,000 loan from a bank, using the scallops as collateral. Although Importer has acted unethically, it does have *some right* in the collateral—the right to hold them for three days. That is enough to satisfy this rule.

PERFECTION

Nothing Less than Perfection

Once the security interest has attached to the collateral, the secured party is protected against *the debtor*, but it may not be protected against *anyone else*. Pesto Bank loaned money to Basil and has a security interest in all of his property. If Basil defaults on his loan, Pesto may insist he deliver the goods to the bank. If he fails to do that, the bank can seize the collateral. But Pesto's security interest is valid only against Basil; if a third person claims some interest in the goods, the bank may never get them. For example, Basil might have taken out *another* loan, from his friend Olive, and used the same property as collateral. Olive knew nothing about the bank's original loan. To protect itself against Olive, and all other parties, the bank must *perfect* its interest.

There are several kinds of perfection:

- Perfection by filing
- Perfection by possession
- Perfection of consumer goods
- Perfection of moveable collateral and fixtures

In some cases, the secured party will have a choice of which method to use; in other cases, only one method works.

Perfection by Filing

Financing statement
A statement that gives the names of all parties, describes the collateral, and outlines the security interest.

The most common way to perfect an interest is by filing a financing statement with one or more state agencies. A **financing statement** gives the names of all parties, describes the collateral, and outlines the security interest, enabling any interested person to learn about it. Suppose the Pesto Bank obtains a security interest in Basil's catering equipment and then perfects by filing with the Secretary of State. When Basil asks his friend Olive for a loan, she has the opportunity to check the records to see if anyone already has a security interest in the catering equipment. If Olive's search uncovers Basil's previous security agreement, she will realize it would be unwise to make the loan. If Basil were to default, the collateral would go straight to Pesto Bank, leaving Olive empty-handed.

Article 9 prescribes one form to be used nationwide for financing statements.[18] The financing form is available online at many websites. Remember that the filing may be done on paper or electronically.

Contents of the Financing Statement

A financing statement is sufficient if it provides the name of the debtor, the name of the secured party, and an indication of the collateral.[19]

---

[18]UCC §9-521.
[19]UCC §9-502(a).

The name of the debtor is critical because that is what an interested person will use to search among the millions of other financing statements on file. Faulty descriptions of the debtor's name have led to thousands of disputes and untold years of litigation, as subsequent creditors have failed to locate any record of an earlier claim on the debtor's property. In response, the UCC is now very precise about what name must be used. If the debtor is a "registered organization," such as a corporation, limited partnership, or limited liability company, the official registered name of the company is the only one acceptable. If the debtor is a person or an unregistered organization (such as a club), then the *correct* name is required. Trade names are not sufficient.

Because misnamed debtors have created so much conflict, the Code now offers a straightforward test: a financing statement is effective if an Internet search run under the debtor's correct name produces it. That is true even if the financing statement used the *incorrect* name. If the search does not reveal the document, then the financing statement is ineffective as a matter of law. The burden is on the secured party to file accurately, not on the searcher to seek out erroneous filings.[20]

The collateral must be described reasonably so that another party contemplating a loan to the debtor will understand which property is already secured. A financing statement could properly state that it applies to "all inventory in the debtor's Houston warehouse." If the debtor has given a security interest in everything he owns, then it is sufficient to state simply that the financing statement covers "all assets" or "all personal property."

The filing must be done by the debtor's last name. But which name is the last? The answer is not always entirely straightforward, as the following case indicates. Did the court get it right?

CORONA FRUITS & VEGGIES, INC. v. FROZSUN FOODS, INC.

143 Cal. App. 4th 319, 48 Cal. Rptr. 3d 868
California Court of Appeals, 2006

Facts: Corona Fruits & Veggies (Corona) leased farmland to a strawberry farmer named Armando Munoz Juarez. He signed the lease, "Armando Munoz." Corona advanced money for payroll and farm production expenses. The company filed a UCC-1 financing statement, claiming a security interest in the strawberry crop. The financing statement listed the debtor's name as "Armando Munoz." Six months later, Armando Munoz Juarez contracted with Frozsun Foods, Inc., to sell processed strawberries. Frozsun advanced money and filed a financing statement listing the debtor's name as "Armando Juarez."

By the next year, the strawberry farmer owed Corona $230,000 and Frozsun $19,600. When he was unable to make payments on Corona's loan, the company repossessed the farmland. And, while it may sound a bit … lame … it also repossessed the strawberries.

Both Corona and Frozsun claimed the proceeds of the crop. The trial court awarded the money to Frozsun, find-

ing that Corona had filed its financing statement under the wrong last name and therefore had failed to perfect its security interest in the strawberry crop. Corona appealed.

Issue: *Did Corona correctly file its financing statement?*

Excerpts from Judge Yegan's Decision: Shakespeare asked, "What's in a name?" We supply an answer only for the Uniform Commercial Code lien priority statutes: Everything when the last name is true and nothing when the last name is false. When a creditor files a UCC-1 financing statement, the debtor's true last name is crucial because the financing statements are indexed by last names. A subsequent creditor who loans money to a debtor with the same name is put on notice that its lien is secondary.

Substantial evidence supports the finding that debtor's true last name was "Juarez" and not "Munoz." The pleadings state that debtor's last name is "Juarez," as do many of appellants' business records. Debtor provided

---

[20]UCC §9-506.

appellants with a photo I.D. and Green Card bearing the name "Armando Munoz Juarez." The name appears on the sublease and other documents including the Farmer Agreement, a Crop Exhibit, a second sublease agreement (identifying debtor as "Juarez Farms, Armando Munoz Juarez"), a crop assignment, appellants' accounting records, receipts for advances, appellants' letters to debtor, and checks issued by appellants.

As a general rule, minor errors in a UCC financing statement do not affect the effectiveness of the financing statement unless the errors render the document seriously misleading to other creditors. If a search of the filing office's records under the debtor's correct name, using the filing office's standard search logic, would nevertheless disclose that financing statement, the name provided does not make the financing statement seriously misleading.

The record indicates that Frozsun's agent conducted a "Juarez" debtor name search and did not discover appellants' UCC-1 financing statement. No evidence was presented that the financing statement would have been discovered under debtor's true legal name, using the filing office's standard search logic. Absent such a showing, the trial court reasonably concluded that the "Armando Munoz" debtor name in appellants' financing statement was seriously misleading. The secured party, not the debtor or uninvolved third parties, has the duty of insuring proper filing and indexing of the notice.

Appellants contend that the debtor name requirement is governed by the naming convention of Latin American countries because debtor is from Mexico. We reject the argument because the strawberries were planted in and the debt obligation arose in Santa Barbara County, not Mexico. In most Latin American countries, the surname is formed by listing first the father's name, then the mother's name. This is exactly opposite Anglo-American tradition. Debtor's last name did not change when he crossed the border into the United States. The "naming convention" is legally irrelevant for UCC-1 purposes and, if accepted, would seriously undermine the concept of lien perfection.

Appellants knew that debtor's legal name was "Armando Juarez" or "Armando Munoz Juarez." Elodia Corona, appellants' account manager, prepared the UCC Financing Statements and testified: "I don't know why I didn't put his last name on the financing statement. I could have made a mistake." Ms. Corona was asked: "So the last name on all the Agreements is Juarez, but on the U.C.C. 1 Forms, you filed them as Munoz?" Ms. Corona answered, "Yes."

Appellants are [defeated by their own] pleadings, the contracts, business records, the checks for the cash advances, debtor's identification papers and tax papers, and the testimony of appellants' account manager. Appellants could have protected themselves by using both names on their financing statements. The trial court did not err in finding that the UCC-1 financing statement filed by Frozsun Foods perfected a security interest superior to appellants' liens.

The judgment is affirmed.

Article 9—2010 Amendments   In 2010, the authors of the UCC—the National Conference of Commissioners on Uniform State Laws (NCCUSL)—created a set of Amendments to Article 9. Remember that the NCCUSL has no power to make law. Once it creates a set of model rules, it is up to the states to decide whether or not to actually enact the proposals.

At the time of this writing, seventeen states have adopted the changes to Article 9 as law, and several others are actively considering doing the same. It appears likely that many states will adopt the changes soon. For all adopting states, the Amendments will take effect on July 1, 2013.

While most of these changes are so technical as to be beyond the scope of this chapter, one of the Amendments addresses the issue of what name must appear on a financing statement. Under the proposed 2010 Amendments, states will require that for individuals, the name on a financing statement be the same as that *on a person's driver's license.* If a state also issues official identification cards from a driver's license office to non-drivers, then the name on such an ID card will be acceptable. If a person has neither kind of state ID card, then her surname and first personal name will be required to perfect by filing.

Place of Filing

The United States is a big country, and potential creditors do not want to stagger from one end of it to the other to learn whether particular collateral is already secured elsewhere. Article 9 specifies *where* a secured party must file. These provisions may vary from state to state, so it is essential to check local law because a misfiled record accomplishes nothing. The general rule is as follows: a secured party must file **in the state of the debtor's location**. An *individual* is located at his principal residence. If Luigi, the debtor, lives in Maryland, works in Virginia, and has a vacation home in Florida, a secured party must file in Maryland. An organization that has only one place of business is located in that state. If the organization has more than one place of business, it is considered to be located at its chief executive office.[21]

Article 9 prescribes central filing within the state for most types of collateral. For *goods*, the central location will typically be the Secretary of State's office, although a state may designate some other office if it wishes. For *fixtures*, the secured party generally has a choice between filing in the same central office that is used for goods (which, again, is usually the Secretary of State's office), or filing in the local *county* office that would be used to file real estate mortgages.[22]

Duration of Filing

Once a financing statement has been filed, it is effective for five years.[23] After five years, the statement will expire and leave the secured party unprotected, unless she files a continuation statement within six months prior to expiration. The continuation statement is valid for an additional five years, and if necessary, a secured party may continue to file one periodically, forever.[24]

Perfection by Possession or Control

For most types of collateral, in addition to filing, a secured party generally may perfect by possession or control (described earlier). So if the collateral is a diamond brooch or 1,000 shares of stock, a bank may perfect its security interest by holding the items until the loan is paid off.

Perfection by possession has some advantages. Notice to other parties is very clear, and if the debtor defaults, a secured party obviously has no difficulties repossessing. However, both possession and control impose one important duty: a secured party must use reasonable care in the custody and preservation of collateral in her possession or control.[25] You lend $30,000 to your friend Joyce, taking as collateral a rare Sèvres serving plate worth $50,000. Keep it safe, please. If you use the platter for indoor Frisbee practice, you are liable for any loss. On the other hand, suppose Joyce gives you $50,000 worth of computer stock as collateral. Several months later, the stock plummets 40 percent. Are you responsible? No. Joyce has chosen to put her money in stock, and as much as she would like, she cannot shift to you the inevitable risk of such an investment.

Perfection of Consumer Goods

The UCC gives special treatment to security interests in most consumer goods. Merchants sell a vast amount of consumer goods on credit. They cannot file a financing statement for every bed, television, and stereo for which a consumer owes money. Yet perfecting by possession is also impossible since the consumer expects to take the goods home. To understand the UCC's treatment of these transactions, we need to know two terms. The first is *consumer goods*, which as we saw earlier means goods used primarily for personal, family, or household purposes. The second term is *Purchase Money Security Interest*.

A **purchase money security interest (PMSI)** is one taken by the person who sells the collateral or by the person who advances money so the debtor can buy the collateral.[26] Assume the Gobroke Home Center sells Marion a $5,000 stereo system. The sales document requires

Purchase money security interest (PMSI)

An interest taken by the person who sells the collateral or advances the money so the debtor can buy it.

---

[21]UCC §9-307.

[22]UCC §9-501.

[23]The exception to this is for a manufactured home, where it lasts 30 years.

[24]UCC §9-515.

[25]UCC §9-207.

[26]UCC §9-103.

a payment of $500 down and $50 per month for the next three centuries, and gives Gobroke a security interest in the system. Because the security interest was "taken by the seller," the document is a PMSI. It would also be a PMSI if a bank had loaned Marion the money to buy the system and the document gave the bank a security interest.

But aren't all security interests PMSIs? No, many are not. Suppose a bank loans a retail company $800,000 and takes a security interest in the store's present inventory. That is not a PMSI since the store did not use the $800,000 to purchase the collateral.

What must Gobroke Home Center do to perfect its security interest? Nothing. **A PMSI in** *consumer goods* **perfects** *automatically*, **without filing.**[27] Marion's new stereo is clearly consumer goods because she will use it only in her home. Gobroke's security interest is a PMSI, so the interest has perfected automatically.

EXAM Strategy

Question: Winona owns a tropical fish store. To buy a spectacular new aquarium, she borrows $25,000 from her sister, Pauline, and signs an agreement giving Pauline a security interest in the tank. Pauline never files the security agreement. Winona's business goes belly up, and both Pauline and other creditors angle to repossess the tank. Does Pauline have a perfected interest in the tank?

Strategy: Generally, a creditor obtains a perfected security interest by filing or possession. However, a PMSI in consumer goods perfects automatically, without filing. Was Pauline's security agreement a PMSI? Was the fish tank a consumer good?

Result: A PMSI is one taken by the person who sells the collateral or advances money for its purchase. Pauline advanced the money for Winona to buy the tank, so Pauline does have a PMSI, but she has a problem, because PMSIs perfect automatically only for *consumer goods*. Consumer goods are those used primarily for personal, family, or household purposes, and so this was not a consumer purchase. Pauline failed to perfect and is unprotected against other creditors.

PROTECTION OF BUYERS

Generally, once a security interest is perfected, it remains effective regardless of whether the collateral is sold, exchanged, or transferred in some other way. Bubba's Bus Co. needs money to meet its payroll, so it borrows $150,000 from Francine's Finance Co., which takes a security interest in Bubba's 180 buses and perfects its interest. Bubba, still short of cash, sells 30 of his buses to Antelope Transit. But even that money is not enough to keep Bubba solvent: he defaults on his loan to Francine and goes into bankruptcy. Francine pounces on Bubba's buses. May she repossess the 30 that Antelope now operates? Yes. The security interest continued in the buses even after Antelope purchased them, and Francine can whisk them away. (Antelope has a valid claim against Bubba for the value of the buses, but the claim may prove fruitless since Bubba is now bankrupt.)

Buyers in ordinary course of business (BIOC)

Someone who buys goods in good faith from a seller who routinely deals in such goods.

There is a key exception to this rule. The Code gives **buyers in the ordinary course of business** special protection. A buyer in ordinary course of business (BIOC) is someone who buys goods in good faith from a seller who routinely deals in such goods.[28] For

---

[27]UCC §9-309(1).
[28]UCC §1-201(9).

example, Plato's Garden Supply purchases 500 hemlocks from Socrates' Farm, a grower. Plato is a BIOC: he is buying in good faith, and Socrates routinely deals in hemlocks. This is an important status because a BIOC is generally *not affected* by security interests in the goods. However, if Plato *actually realized* that the sale violated another party's rights in the goods, there would be no good faith. If Plato knew that Socrates was bankrupt and had agreed with a creditor not to sell any of his inventory, Plato would not achieve BIOC status.

A buyer in ordinary course of business takes the goods free of a security interest created by its seller even though the security interest is perfected.[29] Suppose that, a month before Plato made his purchase, Socrates borrowed $200,000 from the Athenian Bank. Athenian took a security interest in all of Socrates' trees and perfected by filing. Then Plato purchased his 500 hemlocks. If Socrates defaults on the loan, Athenian will have *no right* to repossess the 500 trees that are now at the Garden Supply. Plato took them free and clear. (Of course, Athenian can still attempt to repossess other trees from Socrates.)

The BIOC exception is designed to encourage ordinary commerce. A buyer making routine purchases should not be forced to perform a financing check before buying. But the rule, efficient though it may be, creates its own problems. A creditor may extend a large sum of money to a merchant based on collateral, such as inventory, only to discover that by the time the merchant defaults the collateral has been sold to BIOCs.

Because the BIOC exception undercuts the basic protection given to a secured party, the courts interpret it narrowly. BIOC status is available only if the *seller* created the security interest. Oftentimes, a buyer will purchase goods that have a security interest created by someone other than the seller. If that happens, the buyer is not a BIOC. However, should that rule be strictly enforced even when the results are harsh? You make the call.

---

[29]UCC §9-320(a). In fact, the buyer takes free of the security interest even if the buyer knew of it. Yet a BIOC, by definition, must be acting in good faith. Is this a contradiction? No. Plato might know that a third party has a security interest in Socrates' crops, yet not realize that his purchase violates the third party's rights. Generally, for example, a security interest will permit a retailer to sell consumer goods, the presumption being that part of the proceeds will go to the secured party. A BIOC cannot be expected to determine what a retailer plans to do with the money he is paid.

You be the Judge

CONSECO FINANCE SERVICING CORP. V. LEE
2004 WL 1243417
Court of Appeals of Texas, 2004

Facts: Lila Williams purchased a new Roadtrek 200 motor home from New World R.V., Inc. She paid about $14,000 down and financed $63,000, giving a security interest to New World. The RV company assigned its security interest to Conseco Finance, which perfected. Two years later, Williams returned the vehicle to New World (the record does not indicate why), and New World sold the RV to Robert and Ann Lee for $42,800. A year later, Williams defaulted on her payments to Conseco.

The Lees sued Conseco, claiming to be BIOCs and asking for a court declaration that they had sole title to the Roadtrek. Conseco counterclaimed, seeking title based on its perfected security interest. The trial court ruled that the Lees were BIOCs, with full rights to the vehicle. Conseco appealed.

You Be the Judge: *Were the Lees BIOCs?*

Argument for Conseco: Under UCC §9-319, a buyer in ordinary course takes free of a security interest *created by the buyer's seller*. The buyers were the Lees. The seller was New World. New World did not create the security interest—Lila Williams did. There is no security interest created by New World. The security interest held by Conseco was created by someone else (Williams) and is not affected by the Lees' status as BIOC. The law is clear and Conseco is entitled to the Roadtrek.

Argument for the Lees: Conseco weaves a clever argument, but let's look at what they are really saying. Two honest buyers, acting in perfect good faith, can walk into an RV dealership, spend $42,000 for a used vehicle, and end up with—nothing. Conseco claims it is entitled to an RV that the Lees paid for because someone that the Lees have never dealt with, never even heard of, gave *to this RV seller* a security interest which the seller, years earlier, passed on to a finance company. Conseco's argument defies common sense and the goals of Article 9.

Rebuttal from Conseco: The best part of the Lees' argument is the emotional appeal; the worst part is that it does not reflect the law. Yes, $42,000 is a lot of money. That is why a reasonable buyer is careful to do business with conscientious, ethical sellers. New World, which knew that Williams financed the RV and knew who held the security interest, never bothered to check on the status of the payments. If the Lees have suffered wrongdoing, it is at the hands of an irresponsible seller—the company they chose to work with, the company from whom they must seek relief.

Rebuttal from the Lees: The purpose of the UCC is to make dealing fair and commerce work; one of its methods is to get away from obscure, technical arguments. Conseco's suggestion would demolish the used-car industry. What buyers will ever pay serious money—*any* money—for a used vehicle, knowing that thousands of dollars later, the car might be towed out of their driveway by a finance company they never heard of?

PRIORITIES AMONG CREDITORS

What happens when two creditors have a security interest in the same collateral? The party who has **priority** in the collateral gets it. Typically, the debtor lacks assets to pay everyone, so all creditors struggle to be the first in line. After the first creditor has repossessed the collateral, sold it, and taken enough of the proceeds to pay off his debt, there may be nothing left for anyone else. Who gets priority? There are three principal rules.

The first rule is easy: **a party with a perfected security interest takes priority over a party with an unperfected interest**.[30] This, of course, is the whole point of perfecting: to ensure that your security interest gets priority over everyone else's. The second rule: **if neither secured party has perfected, the first interest to attach gets priority**.[31] Suppose that Suspicion Bank and Happy Bank had both failed to perfect. In that case, Happy Bank would have the first claim to Meredith's inventory since Happy's interest *attached* first.

And the third rule follows logically: **between perfected security interests, the first to file or perfect wins**.[32] Diminishing Perspective, a railroad, borrows $75 million from the First Bank, which takes a security interest in Diminishing's railroad cars and immediately perfects by filing. Two months later, Diminishing borrows $100 million from Second Bank, which takes a security interest in the same collateral and also files. When Diminishing arrives, on schedule, in bankruptcy court, both banks will race to seize the rolling stock. First Bank gets the railcars because it perfected first.

[30] UCC §9-322(a)(2).
[31] UCC §9-322(a)(3).
[32] UCC §9-322(a)(1).

DEFAULT AND TERMINATION

We have reached the end of the line. Either the debtor has defaulted or it has performed its obligations and may terminate the security agreement.

Default

The parties define "default" in their security agreement. **Generally, a debtor defaults when he fails to make payments due or enters bankruptcy proceedings.** The parties can agree that other acts will constitute default, such as the debtor's failure to maintain insurance on the collateral. When a debtor defaults, the secured party has two principal options: (1) it may take possession of the collateral, or (2) it may file suit against the debtor for the money owed. The secured party does not have to choose between these two remedies; it may try one remedy, such as repossession, and if that fails, attempt the other.[33]

Taking Possession of the Collateral

When the debtor defaults, the secured party may take possession of the collateral.[34] How does the secured party accomplish this? In either of two ways: the secured party may act on its own, without any court order, and simply take the collateral, provided this can be done *without a breach of the peace*. Otherwise, the secured party must file suit against the debtor and request that the court *order* the debtor to deliver the collateral.

Disposition of the Collateral

Once the secured party has obtained possession of the collateral, it may **sell, lease, or otherwise dispose of the collateral in any commercially reasonable manner.**[35]

   The debtor is liable for any deficiency. On the other hand, sometimes the sale of the collateral yields a surplus; that is, a sum greater than the debt. In that case, the secured party must pay the surplus to the debtor.[36] A secured party may also simply retain the collateral as full satisfaction of the debt.

Termination

Finally, we need to look at what happens when a debtor *does not* default, but pays the full debt. (You are forgiven if you have lost track of the fact that things sometimes work out smoothly.) Once that happens, the secured party must complete a termination statement, a document indicating that it no longer claims a security interest in the collateral.[37]

Chapter Conclusion

The development of the UCC was an enormous and ambitious undertaking. Its goal was to facilitate the free flow of commerce across this large nation. By any measure, the UCC has been a success. Every day, millions of businesspeople make contracts based on the Code. It is worth remembering, however, that the terms of the UCC are precise and that failure to comply with these exacting provisions can lead to unhappy consequences.

---

[33]UCC §9-601(a)(b)(c).
[34]UCC §9-609.
[35]UCC §9-610.
[36]UCC §9-615(d).
[37]UCC §9-513.

EXAM REVIEW

1. **UNIFORM COMMERCIAL CODE** The Code is designed to modernize commercial law and make it uniform throughout the country. Article 2 applies to the sale of goods, and Article 9 applies to any transaction intended to create a security interest in personal property or fixtures. (pp. 312–313)

EXAM Strategy

Question: While shopping at his local mall, Fred buys an iPad for $499, a barbecue grill for $509, and then pays $25 to have his watchband cleaned. Which of Fred's transactions are governed by Article 2 of the UCC?

Strategy: To answer this question, you must identify the transactions that amount to a sale of goods. Land and buildings are not goods. Neither are money and securities, but other moveable physical objects are. Also, be sure not to confuse the question "Does Article 2 apply?" with the question "Does this agreement need to be in writing?" (See the "Result" at the end of this section)

2. **MIXED CONTRACTS** In a mixed contract involving goods and services, the UCC applies if the predominant purpose is the sale of goods. (p. 313)

3. **MERCHANTS** A merchant is someone who routinely deals in the particular goods involved, or who appears to have special knowledge or skill in those goods, or who uses agents with special knowledge or skill. The UCC frequently holds a merchant to a higher standard of conduct than a non-merchant. (p. 314)

4. **FORMATION** UCC §2-204 permits the parties to form a contract in any manner that shows agreement. (p. 314)

5. **WRITING** For the sale of goods worth $500 or more, UCC §2-201 requires some writing that indicates an agreement. Terms may be omitted or misstated, but the contract will be enforced only to the extent of the quantity stated. (p. 315)

EXAM Strategy

Question: To satisfy the UCC statute of frauds regarding the sale of goods, which of the following must generally be in writing?

a. Designation of the parties as buyer and seller

b. Delivery terms

c. Quantity of the goods

d. Warranties to be made

Strategy: Okay, this may be overkill. But the question illustrates two basic points of UCC law: first, the Code allows a great deal of flexibility in the formation of contracts. Second, there is one term for which no flexibility is allowed. Make sure you know which it is. (See the "Result" at the end of this section.)

6. **ADDITIONAL TERMS** UCC §2-207 governs an acceptance that does not "mirror" the offer. *Additional terms* usually, but not always, become part of the contract. *Different terms* contradict a term in the offer. When that happens, most courts reject both parties' proposals and rely on gap-filler terms. (pp. 317–319)

EXAM Strategy

Question: Cookie Co. offered to sell Distrib Markets 20,000 pounds of cookies at $1.00 per pound, subject to certain specified terms for delivery. Distrib replied in writing as follows: "We accept your offer for 20,000 pounds of cookies at $1.00 per pound, weighing scale to have valid city certificate." Under the UCC:

a. A contract was formed between the parties.

b. A contract will be formed only if Cookie agrees to the weighing scale requirement.

c. No contract was formed because Distrib included the weighing scale requirement in its reply.

d. No contract was formed because Distrib's reply was a counteroffer.

Strategy: Distrib's reply included a new term. That means it is governed by UCC §2-207. Is the new term an additional term or a different term? An additional term goes beyond what the offeror stated. Additional terms become a part of the contract except in three specified instances. A different term contradicts one made by the offeror. Different terms generally cancel each other out. (See the "Result" at the end of this section.)

7. **MODIFICATION** UCC §2-209 permits contracts to be modified even if there is no consideration. The parties may prohibit oral modifications, but such a clause is ineffective against a non-merchant unless she signed it. (pp. 319–320)

8. **REMEDIES** If a seller breaches, the buyer may cover and then obtain the difference between the contract price and the cover price, plus incidental and consequential damages, minus expenses saved. If a buyer breaches, sellers may refuse to deliver the goods. Sellers may resell the goods and seek damages if a buyer unjustly refuses to accept or pay for a delivery. (pp. 320–322)

9. **WARRANTIES** The UCC recognizes express warranties created by sellers, and also creates important implied warranties. Consumers often receive the stronger protection than do businesses. (pp. 322–325)

10. **ARTICLE 9 COVERAGE** Article 9 of the UCC governs secured transactions in personal property. (p. 325)

11. **ATTACHMENT** Attachment means that (1) the two parties made a security agreement *and* either the debtor has *authenticated a security agreement* describing the collateral *or* the secured party has obtained *possession* or *control;* and (2) the secured party gave value in order to get the security agreement; and (3) the debtor has rights in the collateral. (pp. 326–328)

12. **PERFECTION** Attachment protects against the debtor. Perfection of a security interest protects the secured party against parties other than the debtor. Filing is the most common way to perfect. For many forms of collateral, the secured party may also perfect by obtaining either possession or control. (pp. 328–332)

13. **PMSI** A purchase money security interest (PMSI) is one taken by the person who sells the collateral or advances money so the debtor can buy the collateral. A PMSI in consumer goods perfects automatically, without filing. (pp. 331–332)

EXAM Strategy

Question: John and Clara Lockovich bought a 22-foot Chaparrel Villian II boat from Greene County Yacht Club for $32,500. They paid $6,000 cash and borrowed the rest of the purchase price from Gallatin National Bank, which took a security interest in the boat. Gallatin filed a financing statement in Greene County, Pennsylvania, where the bank was located. But Pennsylvania law requires financing statements to be filed in the county of the debtor's residence, and the Lockoviches lived in Allegheny County. The Lockoviches soon washed up in bankruptcy court. Other creditors demanded that the boat be sold, claiming that Gallatin's security interest had been filed in the wrong place. Who wins?

Strategy: Gallatin National Bank obtained a special kind of security interest in the boat. Identify that type of interest. What special rights does this give to the bank? (See the "Result" at the end of this section.)

---

14. **BIOC** A buyer in ordinary course of business (BIOC) takes the goods free of a security interest created by his seller even though the security interest is perfected. (pp. 332–334)

15. **PRIORITY** Priority among secured parties is generally as follows:

    a. A party with a perfected security interest takes priority over a party with an unperfected interest.
    b. If neither secured party has perfected, the first interest to attach gets priority.
    c. Between perfected security interests, the first to file or perfect wins. (p. 334)

EXAM Strategy

Question: Barwell, Inc., sold McMann Golf Ball Co. a "preformer," a machine that makes golf balls, for $55,000. Barwell delivered the machine on February 20. McMann paid $3,000 down, the remainder to be paid over several years, and signed an agreement giving Barwell a security interest in the preformer. Barwell did not perfect its interest. On March 1, McMann borrowed $350,000 from First of America Bank, giving the bank a security interest in McMann's present and after-acquired property. First of America perfected by filing on March 2. McMann, of course, became insolvent, and both Barwell and the bank attempted to repossess the preformer. Who gets it?

Strategy: Two parties have a valid security interest in this machine. When that happens, there is a three-step process to determine which party gets priority. Apply it. (See the "Result" at the end of this section.)

16. **DEFAULT**   When the debtor defaults, the secured party may take possession of the collateral on its own, without a court order, if it can do so without a breach of the peace. A secured party may sell, lease, or otherwise dispose of the collateral in any commercially reasonable way; in many cases, it may accept the collateral in satisfaction of the debt. (p. 335)

17. **TERMINATION**   When the debtor pays the full debt, the secured party must complete a termination statement, notifying the public that it no longer claims a security interest in the collateral. (p. 335)

---

1. Result: The purchases of the iPad and the barbecue grill are covered by Article 2 of the UCC. Both agreements involve goods. $500 is a figure that is relevant to whether the statute of frauds applies to the agreements, but it is not material to the threshold question of whether Article 2 applies in the first place. All sales of goods, from pencils to Ferarris, fall under Article 2. The watch cleaning is a service, and not a sale of goods. It is not governed by Article 2.

5. Result: (c). The contract will be enforced only to the extension of the quantity stated.

6. Result: The "valid city certificate" phrase raises a new issue; it does not contradict anything in Cookie's offer. That means it is an additional term, and becomes part of the deal unless Cookie insisted on its own terms, the additional term materially alters the offer, or Cookie promptly rejects it. Cookie did not insist on its terms, this is a minor addition, and Cookie never rejected it. The new term is part of a valid contract and the answer is "a."

13. Result: Gallatin advanced the money that the Lockoviches used to buy the boat, meaning the bank obtained a PMSI. A PMSI in consumer goods perfects automatically, without filing. The boat was a consumer good. Gallatin's security interest perfected without any filing at all, and so the bank wins.

15. Result: This question is resolved by the first of those three steps. A party with a perfected security interest takes priority over a party with an unperfected interest. The bank wins because its perfected security interest takes priority over Barwell's unperfected interest.

MULTIPLE-CHOICE QUESTIONS

1. Which of the following transactions is *not* governed by Article 2 of the UCC?
   (a) Purchasing an automobile for $35,000
   (b) Leasing an automobile worth $35,000
   (c) Purchasing a stereo worth $501
   (d) Purchasing a stereo worth $499

2. Under the UCC statute of frauds, a contract must be signed by the _____ to count as being "in writing." Also, the _____ of the goods must be written.
   (a) plaintiff; price
   (b) plaintiff; quantity
   (c) defendant; price
   (d) defendant; quantity

3. Assume that a contract is modified. New consideration must be present for the modification to be binding if the deal is governed by which of the following?

   (a) The common law

   (b) The UCC

   (c) Both A and B

   (d) Neither A nor B

4. **CPA QUESTION** Under the UCC Secured Transactions Article, which of the following actions will best perfect a security interest in a negotiable instrument against any other party?

   (a) Filing a security agreement

   (b) Taking possession of the instrument

   (c) Perfecting by attachment

   (d) Obtaining a duly executed financing statement

5. **CPA QUESTION** Under the UCC Secured Transactions Article, perfection of a security interest by a creditor provides added protection against other parties in the event the debtor does not pay its debts. Which of the following parties is not affected by perfection of a security interest?

   (a) Other prospective creditors of the debtor

   (b) The trustee in a bankruptcy case

   (c) A BIOC

   (d) A subsequent personal injury judgment creditor

6. When Michelle buys a laptop, she pays an extra fee so that the computer arrives at her door with the latest version of Microsoft Word pre-installed. Under Article 9, the word processing program is considered:

   (a) "goods"

   (b) "services"

   (c) "software"

   (d) None of the above

7. Alpha perfects its security interest by properly filing a financing statement on January 1, 2010. Alpha files a continuation statement on September 1, 2014. It files another continuation statement on September 1, 2018. When will Alpha's financing statement expire?

   (a) January 1, 2015

   (b) September 1, 2019

   (c) September 1, 2023

   (d) Never

ESSAY QUESTIONS

1. Hasbro used to manufacture a toy called "Wonder World Aquarium." The toy included a powder that, when mixed with water, formed a gel that filled a plastic aquarium. Children could then place plastic fish in the aquarium and create underwater scenes. Cloud Corporation supplied the powder to Hasbro. The toy sold poorly, and Hasbro's need for the powder diminished.

   The two companies discussed changing the powder's formula. Cloud believed the conversation amounted to an indication that Hasbro would continue to buy powder, so it produced large quantities. Although it did not receive an order from Hasbro, Cloud sent an order acknowledgment for 9.5 million packets to Hasbro. Hasbro made no objection to it.

   Did the order acknowledgment create an enforceable agreement? What specific facts determine your answer?

2. Nina owns a used car lot. She signs and sends a fax to Seth, a used car wholesaler who has a huge lot of cars in the same city. The fax says, "Confirming our agrmt—I pick any 15 cars fr yr lot—30% below blue book." Seth reads the fax, laughs, and throws it away. Two weeks later, Nina arrives and demands to purchase 15 of Seth's cars. Is he obligated to sell?

3. Eugene Ables ran an excavation company. He borrowed $500,000 from the Highland Park State Bank. Ables signed a note promising to repay the money and an agreement giving Highland a security interest in all of his equipment, including after-acquired equipment. Several years later, Ables agreed with Patricia Myers to purchase a Bantam Backhoe from her for $16,000, which he would repay at the rate of $100 per month, while he used the machine. Ables later defaulted on his note to Highland, and the bank attempted to take the backhoe. Myers and Ables contended that the bank had no right to take the backhoe. Was the backhoe covered by Highland's security interest? Did Ables have sufficient rights in the backhoe for the bank's security interest to attach?

4. The Copper King Inn, Inc., had money problems. It borrowed $62,500 from two of its officers, Noonan and Patterson, but that did not suffice to keep the inn going. So Noonan, on behalf of Copper King, arranged for the inn to borrow $100,000 from Northwest Capital, an investment company that worked closely with Noonan in other ventures. Copper King signed an agreement giving Patterson, Noonan, and Northwest a security interest in the inn's furniture and equipment. But the financing statement that the parties filed made no mention of Northwest. Copper King went bankrupt. Northwest attempted to seize assets, but other creditors objected. Is Northwest entitled to Copper King's furniture and equipment?

5. The state of Kentucky filed a tax lien against Panbowl Energy, claiming unpaid taxes. Six months later, Panbowl bought a powerful drill from Whayne Supply, making a down payment of $11,500 and signing a security agreement for the remaining debt of $220,000. Whayne perfected the next day. Panbowl defaulted. Whayne sold the drill for $58,000, leaving a deficiency of just over $100,000. The state filed suit, seeking the $58,000 proceeds. The trial court gave summary judgment to the state, and Whayne appealed. Who gets the $58,000?

DISCUSSION QUESTIONS

Apply the following facts to the next two questions.

The publication of the original UCC in 1952 sparked an expansion of the statute of frauds in the United States to cover sales of goods of $500 or more. At about the same time (in 1954), the British Parliament repealed its longstanding statute of frauds as applied to sales of goods. Some have argued that we should scrap UCC §2-201 on the grounds that it encourages misdealing as much as it prevents fraud. Consider the following two hypotheticals:

(In the United States) Johnny is looking at a used Chevy Tahoe. He knows that the $7,000 price is a good one, but he wants to go online and see if he can find an even better deal. In the 20 minutes he has been with the car's current owner, the owner has received three phone calls about the car. Johnny wants to make sure that no one else buys the car while he is thinking the deal over, so he makes a verbal agreement to buy the car and shakes the seller's hand. He knows that because of the statute of frauds and the fact that nothing is in writing, he does not yet have any enforceable obligation to buy the car.

(In the United Kingdom) Nigel sells used Peugeots in Liverpool. When he senses interest from customers, he aggressively badgers them until they verbally commit to buy. If the customers later get cold feet and try to back out of the deal, he holds them to the verbal contracts. Because there is no longer a UCC-style statute of frauds in Britain, the buyers are stuck.

1. Rate the degree to which you believe Johnny and Nigel acted wrongfully. Did one behave more wrongfully than the other? If so, which one, and why?

2. Do you think that the UCC statute of frauds as it currently exists is more likely to prevent fraud, or is it more likely to encourage misunderstandings and deception? Why? Overall, is it sensible to require that purchases of big-ticket items be in writing before they are final?

3. **ETHICS** The Dannemans bought a Kodak copier worth over $40,000. Kodak arranged financing by GECC and assigned its rights to that company. Although the Dannemans thought they had purchased the copier on credit, the papers described the deal as a lease. The Dannemans had constant problems with the machine and stopped making payments. GECC repossessed the machine and, without notifying the Dannemans, sold it back to Kodak for $12,500, leaving a deficiency of $39,927. GECC sued the Dannemans for that amount. The Dannemans argued that the deal was not a lease, but a sale on credit. Why does it matter whether the parties had a sale or a lease? Is GECC entitled to its money? Finally, comment on the ethics. Why did the Dannemans not understand the papers they had signed? Who is responsible for that? Are you satisfied with the ethical conduct of the Dannemans? Kodak? GECC?

4. After reading this chapter, will your behavior as a consumer change? Are there any types of transactions that you might be more inclined to avoid? After reading this chapter, will your future behavior as a businessperson change? What specific steps will you be most careful to take to protect your interests?

5. A perfected security interest is far from perfect. We examined, for example, an exception to normal perfection rules involving BIOCs. Are exceptions reasonable? Should the UCC change to give the holder of a perfected interest absolute rights against *absolutely* everyone else?

© neelsky/Shutterstock.com

NEGOTIABLE INSTRUMENTS

When Calvin was in love with Leann, he kept lending her small amounts of money, which eventually added up to $500. Then Calvin saw a photo on Facebook of Leann and Hugh hooking up. After a huge fight, Calvin demanded that Leann pay him what she owed. She said she had no cash, so she wrote and signed an IOU that said, "I am giving Calvin five hundred dollars." But still Leann did not pay! And more photos appeared on Hugh's wall! Fed up, Calvin took Leann to small claims court, where he discovered that the paper was not enforceable because Leann had not actually *promised* to pay him. He was out of luck.

Calvin tracked Leann down (at Hugh's apartment) and persuaded her to write him a check for five hundred dollars. But he did not notice until he tried to deposit the check that Leann never signed it. The bank refused the check.

Calvin felt that he had learned a costly lesson on negotiable instruments, but his education was about to get a lot more expensive. He answered his phone one day to hear a gruff voice demanding that he pay the $2,000 Leann owed on a car she had bought last year. Calvin had forgotten that he had agreed to do Leann a favor and co-sign the note on the car. Calvin got indignant and shouted, "You have to go after Leann first! I can give you her address." Calvin was wrong. When he signed the note, he became an accommodation party and was every bit as liable as Leann, even though he had never even ridden in the car. "A sadder and wiser man is he."

> **After a huge fight, Calvin demanded that Leann pay him what she owed.**

COMMERCIAL PAPER

The law of commercial paper is important to anyone who borrows money or writes checks (or takes the CPA exam). In early human history, people lived on whatever they could hunt, grow, or make for themselves. Imagine what your life would be like if you had to subsist only on what you could make yourself. Over time, people improved their standard of living by bartering for goods and services they could not make themselves. But traders needed a method for keeping account of who owed how much to whom. That was the role of currency. Many items have been used for currency over the years, including silver, gold, copper, and cowrie shells. These currencies have two disadvantages—they are easy to steal and difficult to carry.

Paper currency weighs less than gold or silver, but it is even easier to steal. As a result, money had to be kept in a safe place, and banks developed to meet that need. However, money in a vault is not very useful unless it can be readily spent. Society needed a system for transferring paper funds easily. Commercial paper is that system.

TYPES OF NEGOTIABLE INSTRUMENTS

There are two kinds of commercial paper: negotiable and non-negotiable instruments. Article 3 of the Uniform Commercial Code (UCC) covers only negotiable instruments; non-negotiable instruments are governed by ordinary contract law. There are also two categories of negotiable instruments: notes and drafts.

A **note** (also called a **promissory note**) is your promise that you will pay money. A promissory note is used in virtually every loan transaction, whether the borrower is buying a multimillion dollar company or a television set. For example, when you borrow money from AutoLoans to buy a car, you will sign a note promising to repay the money. You are the **maker** because you are the one who has made the promise. AutoLoans is the **payee** because it expects to be paid.

A **draft** is an order directing someone else to pay money for you. A **check** is the most common form of a draft—it is an order telling a bank to pay money. In a draft, three people are involved: the **drawer** orders the **drawee** to pay money to the **payee.** Now before you slam the book shut in despair, let us sort out the players. Suppose that Danica Patrick wins the Daytona 500. NASCAR writes her a check for $1,500,000. This check is simply an order by NASCAR (the drawer) to its bank (the drawee) to pay money to Patrick (the payee). The terms make sense if you remember that, when you take money out of your account, you *draw* it out. Therefore, when you write a check, you are the draw*er* and the bank is the draw*ee*. The person to whom you make out the check is being paid, so she is called the pay*ee.*

The following table illustrates the difference between notes and drafts. Even courts sometimes confuse the terms *drawer* (the person who signs a check) and *maker* (someone who signs a promissory note). **Issuer** is an all-purpose term that means both maker and drawer.

Note

A promise that you will pay money. Also called a *promissory note.*

Maker

The issuer of a promissory note.

Payee

Someone who is owed money under the terms of an instrument.

Draft

The drawer of this instrument orders someone else to pay money.

Check

The most common form of a draft, it is an order telling a bank to pay money.

Drawer

The person who issues a draft.

Drawee

The one ordered by the drawer to pay money to the payee.

Issuer

The maker of a promissory note or the drawer of a draft.

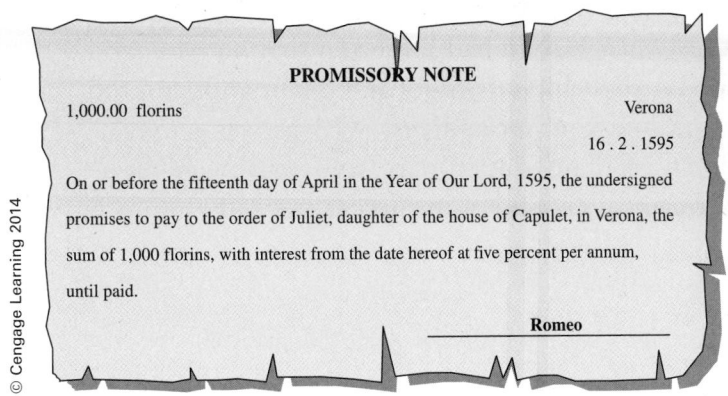

PROMISSORY NOTE

1,000.00 florins   Verona

16 . 2 . 1595

On or before the fifteenth day of April in the Year of Our Lord, 1595, the undersigned promises to pay to the order of Juliet, daughter of the house of Capulet, in Verona, the sum of 1,000 florins, with interest from the date hereof at five percent per annum, until paid.

Romeo

In this note, Romeo is the maker and Juliet is the payee.

	Who Pays	Who Plays
Note	You make a promise that you will pay.	Two people are involved: maker and payee.
Draft	You order someone else to pay.	Three people are involved: drawer, drawee, and payee.

THE FUNDAMENTAL "RULE" OF COMMERCIAL PAPER

The possessor of a piece of commercial paper has an unconditional right to be paid, so long as (1) the paper is *negotiable*; (2) it has been *negotiated* to the possessor; (3) the possessor is a *holder in due course*; and (4) the issuer cannot claim a valid defense.

Negotiable

To work as a substitute for money, commercial paper must be freely transferable in the marketplace, just as money is. In other words, it must be *negotiable*.

The possessor of *non*-negotiable commercial paper has the same rights—no more, no less—as the person who made the original contract. With *non*-negotiable commercial paper, the transferee's rights are *conditional* because they depend upon the rights of the original party to the contract. If, for some reason, the original party loses his right to be paid, so does the transferee. The value of non-negotiable commercial paper is greatly reduced because the transferee cannot be absolutely sure what his rights are or whether he will be paid at all.

Suppose that Krystal buys a used car from the Trustie Car Lot for her business, Krystal Rocks. She cannot afford to pay the full $15,000 right now, but she is willing to sign a note promising to pay later. So long as Trustie keeps the note, Krystal's obligation to pay is contingent upon the validity of the underlying contract. If, for example, the car is defective, then Krystal might not be liable to Trustie for the full amount of the note. Trustie, however, does not want to keep the note. He needs the cash *now* so that he can buy more cars to sell to other customers. Reggie's Finance Co. is happy to buy Krystal's promissory note from Trustie, but the price Reggie is willing to pay depends upon whether her note is negotiable.

If Krystal's promissory note is non-negotiable, Reggie gets exactly the same rights that Trustie had. As the saying goes, he steps into Trustie's shoes. Suppose that Trustie tampered with the odometer and, as a result, Krystal's car is worth only $12,000. If, under contract law, she owes Trustie only $12,000, then that is all she has to pay Reggie, even though the note *says* $15,000.

The possessor of *negotiable* commercial paper has *more* rights than the person who made the original contract. With negotiable commercial paper, the transferee's rights are *unconditional*. He is entitled to be paid the full amount of the note, regardless of the relationship between the original parties. If Krystal's promissory note is a negotiable instrument, she must pay the full amount to whoever has possession of it, no matter what complaints she might have against Trustie.

Exhibit 14.1 illustrates the difference between negotiable and non-negotiable commercial paper.

Checklist
- ☑ Negotiable
- ☐ Negotiated
- ☐ Holder in Due Course
- ☐ No Valid Defenses

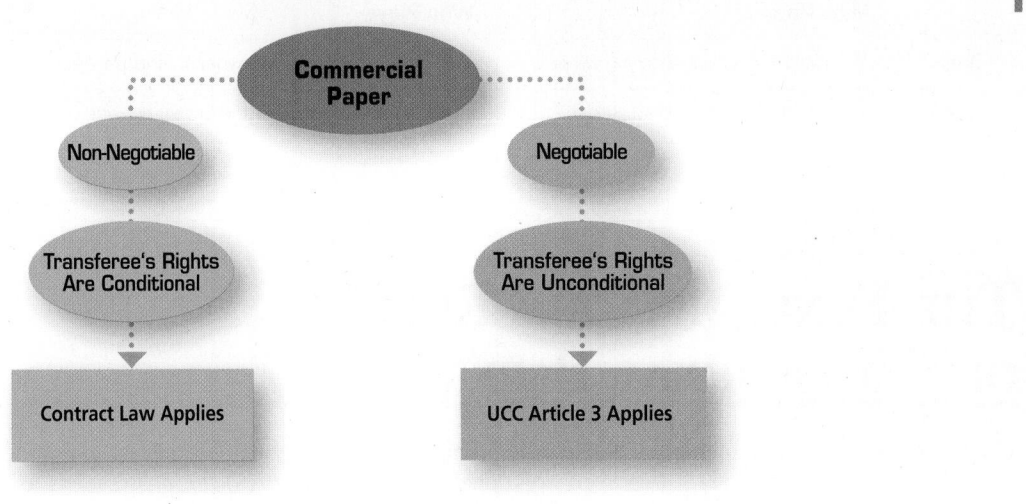

© Cengage Learning 2014

EXHIBIT 14.1

Because negotiable instruments are more valuable than non-negotiable ones, it is important for buyers and sellers to be able to tell, easily and accurately, if an instrument is indeed negotiable. To be negotiable:

1. **The instrument must be in *writing*.**

2. **The instrument must be *signed* by the maker or drawer.**

3. **The instrument must contain an *unconditional promise* or *order to pay*.** If Krystal's promissory note says, "I will pay $15,000 as long as the car is still in working order," it is not negotiable because it is making a conditional promise. The instrument must also contain a promise or order to pay. It is not enough simply to say, "Krystal owes Trustie $15,000." She has to indicate that she owes the money and also that she intends to pay it. "Krystal promises to pay Trustie $15,000" would work.

4. **The instrument must state a *definite amount* of money that is clear "within its four corners."** "I promise to pay Trustie one-third of my profits this year" would not work, because the amount is unclear. If Krystal's note says, "I promise to pay $15,000 worth of diamonds," it is not negotiable because it does not state a definite amount of *money*.

5. **The instrument must be payable on *demand* or at a *definite time*.** A demand instrument is one that must be paid whenever the holder requests payment. If an instrument is undated, it is treated as a demand instrument and is negotiable. An instrument can be negotiable even if it will not be paid until sometime in the future, provided that the payment date can be determined when the document is made. A graduate of a well-known prep school wrote a generous check to his alma mater, but for payment date he put, "The day the headmaster is fired." This check is not negotiable because it is payable neither on demand nor at a definite time.

6. **The instrument must be payable to *order* or to *bearer*.** Order paper must include the words "Pay to the order of" someone. By including the word "order," the maker is indicating that the instrument is not limited to only one person. "Pay to the order of Trustie Car Lot" means that the money will be paid to Trustie *or to anyone Trustie*

designates. If the note is made out "To bearer," it is bearer paper and can be redeemed by *any* holder in due course. "To cash" is the equivalent of "to bearer."

The rules for checks are different from other negotiable instruments. If properly filled out, checks are negotiable. And sometimes they are negotiable even if not completed correctly. Most checks are preprinted with the words "Pay to the order of," but sometimes people inadvertently cross out "order of." Even so, the check is still negotiable. Checks are frequently received by consumers who, sadly, have not completed a course on business law. The drafters of the UCC did not think it fair to penalize them when the drawer of the check was the one who made the mistake.

EXAM Strategy

Question: Sam had a checking account at Piggy Bank. Piggy sent him special checks that he could use to draw down a line of credit. When he used these checks, Piggy did not take money out of his account; instead it treated the checks as loans and charged him interest. Piggy then sold these used checks to Wolfe. Were the checks negotiable instruments?

Strategy: When faced with a question about negotiability, begin by looking at the list of six requirements. In this case, there is no reason to doubt that the checks are in writing, signed by the issuer, with an unconditional promise to pay to order at a definite time. But do the checks state a definite amount of money? Can the holder "look at the four corners of the check" and determine how much Sam owes?

Result: Sam was supposed to pay Piggy the face amount of the check plus interest. Wolfe does not know the amount of the interest unless he reads the loan agreement. Therefore, the checks are not negotiable.

Interpretation of Ambiguities

Perhaps you have noticed that people sometimes make mistakes. Although the UCC establishes simple and precise rules for creating negotiable instruments, people do not always follow these rules to the letter. So the UCC has created rules that help to resolve uncertainty and supply missing terms.

Notice anything odd about the check pictured here? Is it for $1,500 or $15,000? When the terms in a negotiable instrument contradict each other, three rules apply:

- Words take precedence over numbers.

- Handwritten terms prevail over typed and printed terms.

- Typed terms win over printed terms.

According to these rules, Krystal's check is for $15,000 because, in a conflict between words and numbers, words win.

In the following case, the amount of the check was not completely clear. Was it a negotiable instrument?

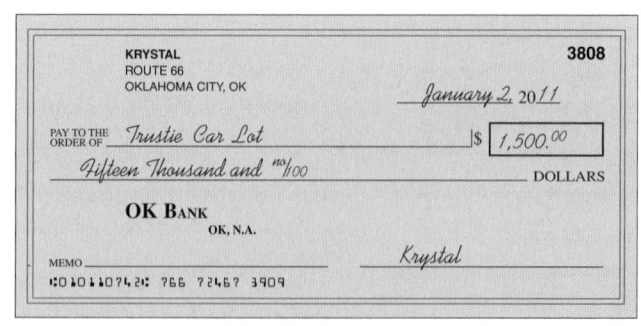

© Cengage Learning 2014

You be the Judge

Facts: Christina Blasco ran out of money. She went to the Money Services Center (MSC) and borrowed $500. To repay the loan, she gave MSC a check for $587.50, which it promised not to cash for two weeks. This kind of transaction is called a "payday loan" because it is made to someone who needs money to tide over until the next paycheck. (Note that in this case, Blasco was paying 17.5 percent interest for a two-week loan, which is an annual compounded interest rate of 6,500 percent. This is the dark side of payday loans – interest rates are often exorbitant.)

Before MSC could cash the check, Blasco filed for bankruptcy protection. Although MSC knew about Blasco's filing, it deposited the check. It is illegal for creditors to collect debts after a bankruptcy filing, except that creditors are entitled to payment on negotiable instruments.

Ordinarily checks are negotiable instruments, but only if they are for a definite amount. This check had a wrinkle: the numerical amount of the check was $587.50 but the amount in words was written as "five eighty-seven and 50/100 dollars." Did the words mean "five hundred eighty-seven" or "five thousand eighty-seven" or perhaps "five million eighty-seven"? Was the check negotiable despite this ambiguity?

You Be the Judge: *Was this check a negotiable instrument? Was it for a definite amount?*

BLASCO V. MONEY SERVICES CENTER

2006 Bankr. Lexis 2899
United States Bankruptcy Court
for the Northern District of Alabama, 2006

Argument for Blasco: For a check to be negotiable, two rules apply:

1. The check must state a definite amount of money, which is clear within its four corners.

2. If there is a contradiction between the words and numbers, words take precedence over numbers.

Words prevail over numbers, which means that the check is for "five eighty-seven and 50/100 dollars." This amount is not definite. A holder cannot be sure of the precise amount of the check. Therefore the check is not a negotiable instrument, and MSC had no right to submit it for payment.

Argument for MSC: Blasco is right about the two rules. However, she is wrong in their interpretation. If there is a contradiction between the words and numbers, words take precedence over numbers. In this case, there was no contradiction. The words were ambiguous but they did not contradict the numbers. If the words had said "five thousand eighty-seven," that would have been a contradiction. Instead, the numbers simply clarified the words. Even someone who was a stranger to this transaction could safely figure out the amount of the check. Therefore, it is negotiable.

Checklist
- ☐ Negotiable
- ☑ Negotiated
- ☐ Holder in Due Course
- ☐ No Valid Defenses

Negotiation
means that an instrument has been transferred to the holder by someone other than the issuer.

Negotiated

Negotiation means that an instrument has been transferred to the holder by someone *other than the issuer*. If the issuer has transferred the instrument to the holder, then it has not been negotiated and the issuer can refuse to pay the holder if there was some flaw in the underlying contract. Thus, if Jake gives Madison a promissory note for $2,000 in payment for a new computer, but the computer crashes and burns the first week, Jake has the right to refuse to pay the note. Jake was the issuer and the note was not negotiated. But if, before the computer self-destructs, Madison indorses and transfers the note to Kayla, then Jake is liable to Kayla for the full amount of the note, regardless of his claims against Madison.

To be negotiated, order paper must first be *indorsed* and then *delivered* to the transferee. Bearer paper must simply be *delivered* to the transferee; no indorsement is required.[1]

An indorsement is the signature of a payee. Tess writes a rent check for $475 to her landlord, Larnell. If Larnell signs the back of the check and delivers it to Patty, he has met the two requirements for negotiating order paper: indorsement and delivery. (Note that, for indorsements, a signature is sufficient. Larnell need not write, "pay to" or "pay to the order of.") If Larnell delivers the check to Patty but forgets to sign it, the check has not been indorsed and therefore cannot be negotiated—it has no value to Patty.

> **Order paper**
> An instrument that includes the words "pay to the order of" or their equivalent.
>
> **Bearer paper**
> A note is bearer paper if it is made out to "bearer" or it is not made out to any specific person. It can be redeemed by any holder in due course.
>
> **Indorsement**
> The signature of a payee.

EXAM Strategy

Question: Antoine makes a check out to cash and delivers it to Barley. He writes on the back, "Pay to the order of Charlotte." She signs her name. Is this check bearer paper or order paper? Has it been negotiated?

Strategy: "To cash" is the equivalent of "to bearer," so a check made out to cash is bearer paper. Whenever a negotiable instrument is transferred, it is important to ask if the instrument has been properly negotiated. To be negotiated, order paper must be indorsed and delivered; bearer paper need only be delivered, but in both cases by someone other than the issuer.

Result: This check changes back and forth between order and bearer paper, depending on what the indorsement says. When Antoine makes out a check to cash, it is bearer paper. When he gives it to Barley, it is not negotiated because he is the issuer. When Barley writes on the back "Pay to the order of Charlotte," it becomes order paper. When he gives it to Charlotte, it is properly negotiated because he is not the issuer and he has both indorsed the check and transferred it to her. When she signs it, the check becomes bearer paper. And so on it could go forever.

Holder in Due Course

A holder in due course has an automatic right to receive payment for a negotiable instrument (unless the issuer can claim a valid defense). If the possessor of an instrument is just a holder, not a holder in due course, then his right to payment is no better than the rights of the person from whom he obtained the instrument. If, for example, the issuer has a valid claim against the payee, then the holder may also lose his right to be paid, because he inherits whatever claims and defenses arise out of that contract. Clearly, then, holder in due course status dramatically increases the value of an instrument because it enhances the probability of being paid.

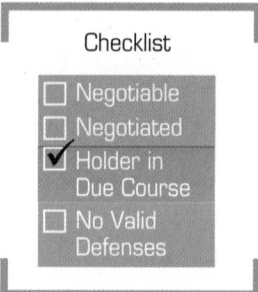

> **Checklist**
> ☐ Negotiable
> ☐ Negotiated
> ☑ Holder in Due Course
> ☐ No Valid Defenses

Requirements for Being a Holder in Due Course

A holder in due course is a *holder* who has given *value* for the instrument, in *good faith*, and *without notice* of outstanding claims or other defects.

> **Holder in due course**
> Someone who has given value for an instrument, in good faith, without notice of outstanding claims or other defenses.

---

[1] §3-201. The UCC spells the word "indorsed." Outside the UCC, the word is more commonly spelled "endorsed."

Holder

For order paper, anyone in possession of the instrument if it is payable to or indorsed to her. For bearer paper, anyone in possession.

Value

The holder has already done something in exchange for the instrument.

Holder   For order paper, a **holder** is anyone in possession of the instrument if it is payable to or indorsed to her. For bearer paper, a **holder** is anyone in possession. Tristesse gives Felix a check payable to him. Because Felix owes his mother money, he indorses the check and delivers it to her. This is a valid negotiation because Felix has both indorsed the check (which is order paper) and delivered it. Therefore, Felix's mother is a holder.

Value   A holder in due course must give value for an instrument. **Value** means that the holder has *already* done something in exchange for the instrument. Felix's mother has already loaned him money, so she has given value.

Good Faith   There are two tests to determine if a holder acquired an instrument in good faith. The holder must meet *both* these tests:

- *Subjective Test.* Did the holder *believe* the transaction was honest in fact?

- *Objective Test.* Did the transaction *appear* to be commercially reasonable?

In the following case, the plaintiff passed the subjective test, but failed the objective one.

BUCKEYE CHECK CASHING, INC. V. CAMP

159 Ohio App. 3d 784; 825 N.E.2d 644; 2005 Ohio App. Lexis 929
Court of Appeals of Ohio, 2005

Facts: On October 12, James Camp agreed to provide services to Shawn Sheth by October 15. In payment, Sheth gave Camp a check for $1,300 that was postdated October 15. On October 13, Camp sold the check to Buckeye Check Cashing for $1,261.31. On October 14, fearing that Camp would violate the contract, Sheth stopped payment on the check. Also, on October 14, Buckeye deposited the check with its bank, believing that the check would reach Sheth's bank on October 15. Buckeye was unaware of the stop payment order. Sheth's bank refused to pay the check. Buckeye filed suit against Sheth.

The trial court ruled that, because Buckeye was a holder in due course, the check was valid and Sheth had to pay Buckeye. Sheth appealed.

Issues: *Was Buckeye a holder in due course? Must Sheth pay Buckeye?*

Excerpts from Justice Donovan's Decision: A holder in due course must satisfy both a subjective and an objective test of good faith.

Check cashing is an unlicensed and unregulated business in Ohio. Thus, there are no concrete commercial standards by which check-cashing businesses must operate. Buckeye argues that its own internal operating policies do not require that it verify the availability of funds, nor does Buckeye apparently have any guidelines with respect to the acceptance of postdated checks.

Under a purely subjective "honesty in fact" analysis, it is clear that Buckeye accepted the check from Camp in good faith and would therefore achieve holder-in-due-course status. When the objective prong of the good faith test is applied, however, we find that Buckeye did not conduct itself in a commercially reasonable manner. [T]he presentation of a postdated check should put the check cashing entity on notice that the check might not be good. Some attempt at verification should be made before a check-cashing business cashes a postdated check. Such a failure to act does not constitute taking an instrument in good faith under the current objective test of "reasonable commercial standards."

This court in no way seeks to curtail the free negotiability of commercial instruments. [However, without] taking any steps to discover whether the postdated check issued by Sheth was valid, Buckeye failed to act in a commercially reasonable manner and therefore was not a holder in due course.

Judgment reversed, and cause remanded.

Notice of Outstanding Claims or Other Defects   In certain circumstances, a holder is on notice that an instrument has an outstanding claim or other defect:

1. **The instrument is overdue**. An instrument is overdue the day after its due date. At that point, the recipient ought to wonder why no one has bothered to collect the money owed. A check is overdue 90 days after its date. Any other demand instrument is overdue (1) the day after a request for payment is made or (2) a reasonable time after the instrument was issued.

2. **The instrument is dishonored**. To dishonor an instrument is to refuse to pay it. For example, once a check has been stamped "Insufficient Funds" by the bank, it has been dishonored, and no one who obtains it afterward can be a holder in due course.

3. **The instrument is altered, forged, or incomplete**. Anyone who knows that an instrument has been altered or forged cannot be a holder in due course. Suppose Joe wrote a check to Tony for $200. While showing the check to Liza, Tony cackles to himself and says, "Can you believe what that goof did? Look, he left the line blank after the words 'two hundred.'" Taking his pen out with a flourish, Tony changes the zeroes to nines and adds the words "ninety-nine." He then indorses the check over to Liza, who is definitely not a holder in due course.

4. **The holder has notice of certain claims or disputes**. No one can qualify as a holder in due course if she is on notice that (1) someone else has a claim to the instrument or (2) there is a dispute between the original parties to the instrument. Matt hires Sheila to put aluminum siding on his house. In payment, he gives her a $15,000 promissory note with the due date left blank. They agree that the note will not be due until 60 days after completion of the work. Despite the agreement, Sheila fills in the date immediately and sells the note to Rupert at American Finance Corp., who has bought many similar notes from Sheila. Rupert knows that the note is not supposed to be due until after the work is finished. Usually, before he buys a note from her, he demands a signed document from the home owner certifying that the work is complete. Also, he lives near Matt and can see that Matt's house is only half finished. Rupert is not a holder in due course because he has reason to suspect there is a dispute between Sheila and Matt.

Defenses against a Holder in Due Course

Negotiable instruments are meant to be a close substitute for money, and, as a general rule, holders expect to be paid. **However, the issuer of a negotiable instrument is not required to pay if:**

- His signature on the instrument was forged.

- After signing the instrument, his debts were discharged in bankruptcy.

- He was a minor (typically under age 18) at the time he signed the instrument.

- The amount of the instrument was altered after he signed it. (If he left the instrument blank, however, he is liable for any amounts later filled in.)

- He signed the instrument under duress, while mentally incapacitated, or as part of an illegal transaction.

- He was tricked into signing the instrument without knowing what it was and without any reasonable way to find out.

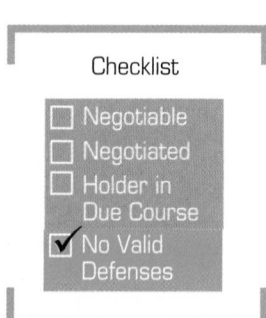

Checklist

☐ Negotiable
☐ Negotiated
☐ Holder in
   Due Course
☑ No Valid
   Defenses

Consumer Exception

The most common use for negotiable instruments is in consumer transactions. A consumer pays for a refrigerator by giving the store a promissory note. The store promptly sells the note to a finance company. Even if the refrigerator is defective, under Article 3 the consumer must pay full value on the note because the finance company is a holder in due course. However, some states require promissory notes given by a consumer to carry the words "consumer paper." Notes with this legend are non-negotiable.

Consumer credit contract

A contract in which a consumer borrows money from a lender to purchase goods and services from a seller who is affiliated with the lender.

Meanwhile, the Federal Trade Commission (FTC) has special rules for consumer credit contracts. A **consumer credit contract** is one in which a consumer borrows money from a lender to purchase goods and services from a seller who is affiliated with the lender. If Sears loans money to Gerald to buy a high definition television at Sears, that is a consumer credit contract. It is not a consumer credit contract if Gerald borrows money from his cousin Vinnie to buy the television from Sears. The FTC requires all promissory notes in consumer credit contracts to contain the following language:

NOTICE

ANY HOLDER OF THIS CONSUMER CREDIT CONTRACT IS SUBJECT TO ALL CLAIMS AND DEFENSES WHICH THE DEBTOR COULD ASSERT AGAINST THE SELLER OF GOODS OR SERVICES OBTAINED WITH THE PROCEEDS HEREOF.

No one can be a holder in due course of an instrument with this language. If the language is omitted from a consumer note, it is possible to be a holder in due course, but the seller is subject to a fine.

In the following case, consumers found that a home improvement contract, far from improving their home, almost caused them to lose it.

ANTUNA V. NESCOR, INC.

2002 Conn. Super. Lexis 1003
Superior Court of Connecticut, 2002

Facts: Steven Vlohotis was a salesman for NESCOR, a home improvement company. He convinced the Antunas to sign a consumer credit contract with NESCOR to install vinyl siding and windows. The contract provided that the Antunas would pay for the improvements in installments. NESCOR assigned the contract to First Consumer Credit, LLC, which reassigned it to The Money Store (TMS). In keeping with FTC requirements, the contract contained the following language: "Any holder of this consumer credit contract is subject to all claims and defenses which the debtor could assert against the Seller of the goods or services pursuant hereto or with the proceeds hereof."

Connecticut law (the Act) provides that, "No home improvement contract shall be valid or enforceable against an owner unless it is entered into by a registered salesman or a registered contractor." The NESCOR salesman, Vlohotis, was not registered.

Unhappy with NESCOR's work, the Antunas stopped making payments under the contract. TMS filed suit, seeking to foreclose on their house. The Antunas moved for summary judgment, arguing that TMS could not enforce the contract because it was not a holder in due course.

Issues: *Does TMS have the right to foreclose on the Antunas' home? Was TMS a holder in due course?*

Excerpts from Judge Shortall's Decision: In employing Vlohotis to call on the plaintiffs as its salesman, NESCOR was performing an illegal act, one explicitly prohibited. Accordingly, the court finds that NESCOR's material noncompliance with [the Act] renders the home improvement contract invalid and unenforceable and precludes it from enforcing the consumer credit contract against the plaintiffs.

The language appearing in the consumer credit contract held by TMS, viz., that the contract is "subject to all claims and defenses which" the plaintiffs could assert against NESCOR is mandated in all such contracts by the FTC to prevent the seller of goods from cutting off the consumer's right to assert claims and defenses against the seller's assignee. So, in this case, where the Act, itself, gives the plaintiffs the right to defend against enforcement of the home improvement contract, the language in the consumer credit contract held by TMS gives them the same right as against TMS.

Accordingly, because the TMS is subject to those same claims and defenses under the very language of its contract with the plaintiffs. TMS may not enforce the consumer credit contract it holds by foreclosing on the plaintiffs' property for nonpayment.

The plaintiffs' motion for summary judgment is granted.

LIABILITY FOR NEGOTIABLE INSTRUMENTS

Thus far in this chapter, you have learned that the possessor of a piece of commercial paper has an unconditional right to be paid, so long as (1) the paper is *negotiable*; (2) it has been *negotiated* to the possessor; (3) the possessor is a *holder in due course;* and (4) the issuer cannot claim a valid defense.

The life of a negotiable instrument, however, is more complicated than this simple statement indicates. Not everyone who signs a negotiable instrument is an issuer, and not everyone who presents an instrument for payment is a holder in due course. This section focuses on the liability of these extra players: non-issuers who sign an instrument and non-holders who receive payment. The liability of someone who has signed an instrument is called **signature liability**. The liability of someone who receives payment on an instrument is called **warranty liability**.

Signature liability
The liability of someone who signs an instrument.

Warranty liability
The liability of someone who receives payment on an instrument.

Primary versus Secondary Liability

A number of different people may be liable on the same negotiable instrument, but some are *primarily* liable, others are only *secondarily* liable. Someone with **primary liability** is unconditionally liable—he must pay unless he has a valid defense. Those with **secondary liability** only pay if the person with primary liability does not. The holder of an instrument must first ask for payment from those who are primarily liable before making demand against anyone who is only secondarily liable.

SIGNATURE LIABILITY

Virtually everyone who signs an instrument is potentially liable for it, but the liability depends upon the capacity in which it was signed. The maker of a note, for example, has different liability from an indorser. Capacity can sometimes be difficult to determine if the signature is not labeled—"maker," "indorser," etc. In the absence of a label, courts generally look at the location of the signature. Someone who signs a check or a note in the lower right-hand corner is presumed to be an issuer. If a drawee bank signs on the face of a check, it is an acceptor. Someone who signs on the back of an instrument is considered to be an indorser.

Maker

The maker of a note is *primarily* liable. He has promised to pay, and pay he must, unless he has a valid defense.[2] If two makers sign a note, they are both **jointly and severally** liable. The holder can demand full payment from either or partial payment from both. Suppose that Shane offers to buy Marilyn's bookstore in return for a $20,000 promissory note. Because Shane has no assets, Marilyn insists that his supplier, Alexis, also sign the note as co-maker. Once Alexis signs the note, Marilyn has the right to demand full payment from either her or Shane.

Drawer

The drawer of a check has *secondary* liability. He is not liable until he has received notice that the bank has dishonored the check. Although the bank pays the check with the drawer's funds, the drawer is secondarily liable in the sense that he does not have to write a new check or give cash to the holder unless the bank dishonors the original check. Suppose that Shane writes a $10,000 check to pay Casey for new inventory. Casey is nervous, and before he can get to the bank to deposit the check, he calls Shane seven times to ask whether the check is good. He even asks Shane for payment in cash instead of by check. Shane finally snarls at Casey, "Just go cash the check and get off my back, will you?" At this point, Casey has no recourse against Shane because Shane is only secondarily liable.

Sadly, however, Casey's fears are realized. When he presents the check to the bank teller, she informs him that Shane's account is overdrawn. Casey snatches the check off the counter and hurries over to Shane's shop. It makes no difference that Casey forgot to let the teller stamp "Insufficient Funds" on the check—notice of dishonor can be made orally. Once the bank has refused to pay, the check has been dishonored. Casey has informed Shane, who must now pay the $10,000.

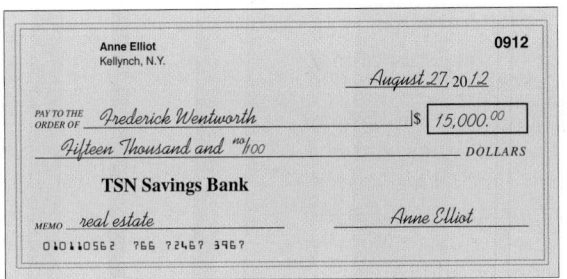

Anne Elliot is only secondarily liable, but no one is primarily liable until the bank accepts the check.

© Cengage Learning 2014

Drawee

The **drawee** is the bank on which a check is drawn. Since the draw*er* of a check is only secondarily liable, logically you might expect the drawee bank to be primarily liable. That is not the case, however. When a drawer signs a check, the instrument enters a kind of limbo. **The bank is not liable to the holder and owes no damages to the holder for refusing to pay the check.** The bank may be liable to the *drawer* for violating their checking account agreement, but this contract does not extend to the holder of the check.

When a holder presents a check, the bank can do one of the following:

- Pay the check. In this case, the holder has no complaints.

- Dishonor the check. In this case, the holder must pursue remedies against the *drawer*.

What if Casey is afraid to take a check from Shane? After all, even if Shane has enough money in his account at the moment, it may be gone by the time Casey deposits the check and his bank presents it for payment. To protect himself, Casey can insist that Shane give him a certified check or a cashier's check. A **certified check** is one that the issuer's bank has signed (typically on the front), indicating its acceptance of the check. The bank is then referred to as an **acceptor** and becomes primarily liable. A **cashier's check** is drawn on the

Certified Check

A check the issuer's bank has signed, indicating its acceptance of the check.

Acceptor

A bank (or other drawee) that accepts a check (or other draft), thereby becoming primarily liable on it.

Cashier's Check

A check drawn on the bank itself. It is a promise that the bank will pay out of its own funds.

---

[2]For example, if the maker goes bankrupt, he does not have to pay the note because bankruptcy is a defense even against a holder in due course.

bank itself and is a promise that the bank will pay out of its own funds. In either case, Casey is sure to be paid so long as the bank stays solvent. To protect itself once it issues either check, Shane's bank will immediately remove that money from his account.

These rules are precise and must be followed to the letter. In the following example, the court pointed out that the real estate lawyer had been "bamboozled." The MacNabs purchased a piece of property from Richard Harrington's client. The couple came to the closing with an uncertified check drawn on their Merrill Lynch cash management account for $150,000. Harrington called Merrill Lynch and spoke with a Ms. Ruark, who told him there were sufficient funds in the MacNabs' account to cover the check and that she would put a hold on the account in the amount of the check. She also sent the following fax to Harrington: "This letter is to verify that the funds are available in the Merrill Lynch account. There is a pend on the funds for the check that was given you." In fact, the MacNabs' account did not contain sufficient *cleared* funds to cover the check, which bounced. After paying off the McNabs, Harrington sought recovery from Merrill Lynch. But Merrill Lynch was not liable because it had not *signed* the check. An oral certification is invalid.[3]

Indorser

An **indorser** is anyone, other than an issuer or acceptor, who signs an instrument. Shane gives Hannah a check to pay her for installing new shelves in his bookstore. On the back of Shane's check, Hannah writes, "Pay to Christian," signs her name, and then gives the check to Christian in payment for back rent. Underneath Hannah's name, Christian signs his own name and gives the check to Trustie Car Lot as a deposit on his new Prius. Hannah and Christian are both indorsers. This is the chain of ownership:

Indorser
Anyone, other than an issuer or acceptor, who signs an instrument.

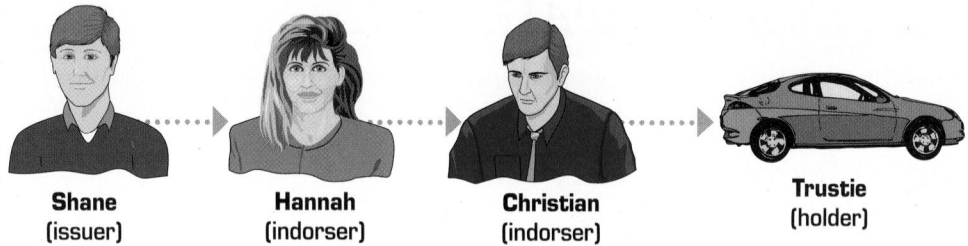

Shane (issuer) → **Hannah** (indorser) → **Christian** (indorser) → **Trustie** (holder)

Indorsers are *secondarily* liable; they must pay if the issuer does not. But indorsers are only liable to those who come *after* them in the chain of ownership, not to those who held the instrument beforehand. If Shane refuses to pay Trustie, the auto dealership can demand payment from Christian or Hannah. If Christian pays Trustie, Christian can then demand payment from Hannah. If, however, Hannah pays Trustie, she has no right to go after Christian because he is not liable to a previous indorser.

There are some exceptions to this rule. **Indorsers are not liable if:**

1. They write the words "without recourse" next to their signature on the instrument,

2. A bank certifies the check,

3. The check is presented for payment more than 30 days after the indorsement, or

4. The check is dishonored and the indorser is not notified within 30 days.

---

[3]*Harrington v. McNab*, 163 F. Supp. 2d 583; (Fed Dt. Ct., MD, 2001).

Accommodation Party

An **accommodation party** is someone—other than an issuer, acceptor, or indorser—who adds her signature to an instrument for the purpose of being liable on it. The accommodation party typically receives no direct benefit from the instrument but is acting for the benefit of the **accommodated party**. Shane wants to buy a truck from the Trustie Car Lot. Trustie, however, will not accept a promissory note from Shane unless his father, Walter, also signs it. Shane has no assets, but Walter is wealthy. When Walter signs, he becomes an accommodation party to Shane, who is the accommodated party. The accommodation party can sign for an issuer, acceptor, or indorser. Anyone who signs an instrument is deemed to be an accommodation party unless it is clear that he is an issuer, acceptor, or indorser.

An accommodation party has the same liability to the holder as the person for whom he signed. The holder can make a claim directly against the accommodation party without first demanding payment from the accommodated party. Walter is liable to Trustie, whether or not Trustie first demands payment from Shane. If forced to pay Trustie, Walter can try to recover from Shane.

In an earlier example, Shane's supplier, Alexis, had signed a note as co-maker. What is the difference between a co-maker and an accommodation party? The co-maker is liable both to the holder and to the other co-maker. The accommodation party is liable only to the holder, not to the other maker. If Shane pays the note on which Alexis is co-maker, then Alexis is liable to him for half the payment. But if Shane pays the note on which Walter is the accommodation party, Walter has no liability to Shane.

WARRANTY LIABILITY

Warranty liability rules apply when someone receives payment on an instrument that has been forged, altered, or stolen.

Basic Rules of Warranty Liability

1. **The wrongdoer is always liable.** If a forger signs someone else's name to an instrument, that signature counts as the forger's, not as that of the person whose name she signed. The forger is liable for the value of the instrument, plus any other expenses or lost interest that subsequent parties may experience because of the forgery. If Hope signs David's name on one of his checks, Hope is liable, but not David. Although this is a sensible rule, the problem is that forgers are difficult to catch and, even when found, often do not have the money to pay what they owe.

2. **The drawee bank is liable if it pays a check on which the *drawer's* name is forged. The bank can recover from the payee only if the payee had reason to suspect the forgery.** If a bank cashes David's forged check, it must reimburse him whether or not it ever recovers from Hope. Suppose that Hope forged the check to pay for a new tattoo. If Gus, the owner of the tattoo parlor, deposits the check and the bank pays it, the bank can only recover from Gus if he had reason to suspect the forgery. Perhaps Gus did suspect because "David" was the name on the check and Hope does not look much like a David.

   Why hold the bank liable for something that is not its fault? In theory, the bank has David's signature on file and can determine that Hope's version does not match. As the saying goes, the drawee bank must know the drawer's signature as a mother knows her own child. Such a rule may have been appropriate in an era when people went to their neighborhood bank to cash checks and a teller would indeed recognize dear Miss Plotkin's signature. In this day and age, most checks—especially those for small amounts—are handled by machine, so perhaps this rule makes less sense. Nonetheless, the rule stands.

3. **In any other case of wrongdoing, a person who first acquires an instrument from a wrongdoer is ultimately liable to anyone else who pays value for it.** These rules are based on the provisions in Article 3 of the UCC that establish transfer and presentment warranties.

Transfer Warranties

When someone transfers an instrument, she warrants that:

- She is a holder of the instrument – in other words, she is a legitimate owner

- All signatures are authentic and authorized

- The instrument has not been altered

- No defense can be asserted against her, and

- As far as she knows, the issuer is solvent.

When someone transfers an instrument, she promises that it is valid. The wrongdoer—the person who created the defective instrument in the first place—is always liable, but if he does not pay what he owes, the person who took it from him is liable in his place. She may not be that much at fault, but she is more at fault than any of the other innocent people who paid good value for the instrument.

Suppose that Annie writes a check for $100 to pay for a fancy dinner at Barbara's Bistro. Cecelia steals the check from Barbara's cash register, indorses Barbara's name, and uses the check to buy a leather jacket from Deirdre. In her turn, Deirdre takes the check home and indorses it over to her condominium association to pay her monthly service fee. Barbara notices the check is gone and asks Annie to stop payment on it. Once payment is stopped, the condominium association cannot cash the check. Who is liable to whom? The chain of ownership looks like this:

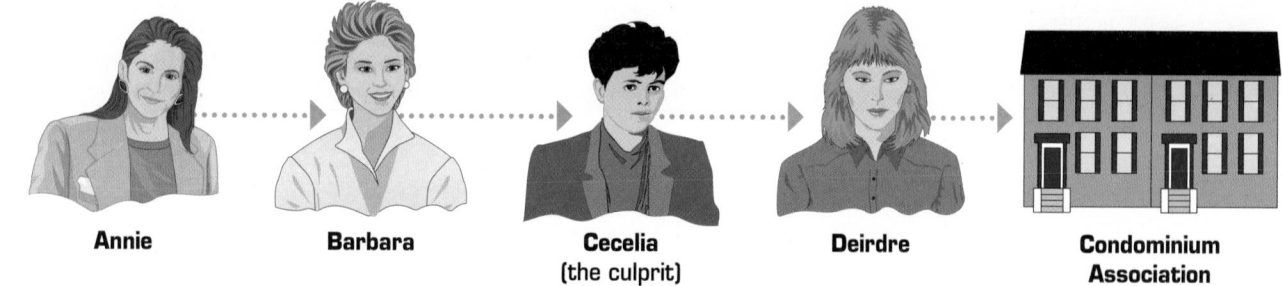

Annie   Barbara   Cecelia (the culprit)   Deirdre   Condominium Association

Cecelia is the wrongdoer and, of course, she is liable. Unfortunately, she is currently studying at the University of the Azores and refuses to return to the United States. The condominium association makes a claim against Deirdre. When she transferred the check, she warranted that all the signatures were authentic and authorized, but that was not true because Barbara's signature was forged. (Deirdre should have asked Cecelia for identification.) Deirdre cannot make a claim against Annie or Barbara because neither of them violated their transfer warranties—all the signatures at that point were authentic and authorized.

There are a few additional wrinkles to the transfer warranty rules:

- Transfer warranties flow to all subsequent holders in good faith who have indorsed the instrument. If the condominium association indorses the check over to its maintenance company, Deirdre is liable to the condo association when the maintenance company makes a claim against it.

- If the instrument is *bearer* paper, the transfer warranties extend only to the first transferee. If Annie had made her check out to cash, it would have been bearer paper, and her transfer warranties would have extended only to Barbara. If Barbara transfers the check to Hannah, Barbara's transfer warranties extend to Hannah; Annie's do not.

- If a warranty claim is not made within 30 days of discovering the breach, damages are reduced by the amount of harm that the delay caused. Suppose that the condominium association waits two months to tell Deirdre the check is invalid. Cecelia has been into Deirdre's store several times to try on matching leather pants. By the time Deirdre finds out the check is bad, Cecelia has again left town. Deirdre may not be liable on the check at all because the delay has prevented her from making a claim against Cecelia.

- Transfer warranties apply only if the instrument has been transferred for consideration. Suppose Deirdre gives the check to an employee, Emily, as a birthday present. When the check turns out to be worthless, Emily has no claim against Deirdre.

The following sad case illustrates how important transfer warranties are and how easy it is, even for a careful person, to be conned. Think about what Quimby could have done to protect himself.

You be the Judge

QUIMBY V. BANK OF AMERICA

2009 U.S. Dist. Lexis 98575
United States District Court
for the District of Oregon, 2009

Facts: Steve Szabo, a Venezuelan resident, had a checking account with the Bank of America in Palm Beach Gardens, Florida. Someone with an internet address in Nigeria hacked into Szabo's accounts online, called customer service to change the telephone number listed on his account, and ordered blank checks.

Someone then wrote a check on Szabo's account for $120,000 to pay for an investment in Freddie Quimby's gold mine. On February 20, Quimby presented the check for payment at the Bank of America's branch in Osburn, Idaho. At Quimby's request, the branch manager verified through Bank of America's records that Szabo's account had sufficient funds to cover the check. The branch manager also called the telephone number in Szabo's account records and spoke to someone claiming to be Szabo who confirmed that the check was valid.

Quimby endorsed the check to the bank and received in return a cashier's check for $120,000, which he deposited to his account at Bank of America in Baker City, Oregon. [You remember that a cashier's check is a check drawn on the bank itself.] "Szabo" then contacted Quimby, stating that he had changed his mind about the gold mine investment and asking Quimby to return the funds. On February 22, Quimby wired $111,000.00 from his account with Bank of America to an account in Hong Kong. Those funds disappeared and Bank of America has been unable to reclaim them.

On March 3, the real Szabo reported to the Bank that his signature on the Quimby check was a forgery. The Bank repaid Szabo and then filed suit against Quimby, seeking repayment on the cashier's check it had issued to him, with interest. The Bank argued that Quimby had violated his transfer warranties when he endorsed the forged check to it.

You Be the Judge: *Did Quimby violate his transfer warranties? Is he liable to the Bank of America for $120,000?*

Argument for the Bank: When Quimby endorsed the check to the Bank, he warranted that all signatures were authentic and authorized. That was not true—the signature was a forgery and the check was invalid. Moreover, he only waited two days before wiring the funds. If he had waited longer, the fraud might have been discovered in time.

The Bank had to refund $120,00 to Szabo. Quimby must repay the Bank.

Argument for Quimby: This whole problem is the Bank's fault. Let us count the ways: the Bank (1) permitted a thief to hack into Szabo's account; (2) issued blank checks to the thief; (3) assured Quimby that there were good funds to pay the check; (4) issued a cashier's check to Quimby; and (5) wired funds to Hong Kong that it cannot trace.

In short, the Bank was repeatedly negligent and now it seeks recovery from Quimby, who did all he could to ensure that the check was valid. That is unfair and preposterous.

Comparison of Signature Liability and Transfer Warranties

Transfer warranties fill in holes left by the signature liability rules:

- A forged signature is invalid and therefore creates no signature liability on the part of the person whose name was signed. However, someone who receives a forged instrument may recover under transfer warranty rules, which provide that anyone who transfers a forged instrument is liable for it.

- The signature liability rules do not apply to the transfer of bearer paper. Bearer paper can be negotiated simply by delivery; no indorsement is required. No signature means no signature liability (for anyone other than the issuer—who is the only person actually signing the instrument). Transfer warranties apply to each transfer of bearer paper (although the transferor of bearer paper is liable only to the person to whom he gives the instrument, not to any transferees further down the line).

Presentment Warranties

Transfer warranties impose liability on anyone who sells a negotiable instrument, such as Deirdre. **Presentment warranties** apply to someone who demands payment for an instrument from the maker, drawee, or anyone else liable on it. Thus, if the condominium association cashes Annie's check, it is subject to presentment warranties because it is demanding payment from her bank, the drawee. In a sense, transfer warranties apply to all transfers *away* from the issuer; presentment warranties apply when the instrument *returns* to the maker or drawee for payment. As a general rule, payment on an instrument is final, and the payer has no right to a refund, unless the presentment warranties are violated.

Anyone who presents a *check* for payment warrants that:

- She is a holder,
- The check has not been altered, and
- She has no reason to believe the drawer's signature is forged.

If any of these promises is untrue, the bank has a right to demand a refund from the presenter. Suppose that Adam writes a $500 check to pay Bruce for repairing his motorcycle. Bruce changes the amount of the check to $1,500 and indorses it over to Chip as payment for an oil bill. When Chip deposits the check, the bank credits his account for $1,500 and deducts the same amount from Adam's account. When Adam discovers the alteration, the bank credits his account for $1,000. Chip violated his *presentment* warranties when he deposited an altered check (even though he did not *know* it was altered). Although Chip was not at fault, he must still reimburse the bank for $1,000. But Chip is not without recourse—Bruce violated his *transfer* warranties to Chip (by transferring an altered check). Bruce must repay the $1,000. Chip loses out only if he cannot make Bruce pay.

The presentment warranty rules for a promissory note are different from those for a check. **Anyone who presents a *promissory note* for payment makes only one warranty—that he is a holder of the instrument.** Someone presenting a note does not need to warrant that the note is unaltered or the maker's signature is authentic because a note is presented for payment to the issuer himself. The issuer presumably remembers the amount of the note and whether he signed it. Suppose Adam gives a promissory note to Bruce to pay for a new motorcycle. If Bruce increases the note from $5,000 to $10,000 before he presents it for payment in six months' time, Adam will almost certainly realize the note has been changed and refuse to pay it.

The presenter of a note warrants that he is a holder, i.e., that the instrument was payable to or indorsed to her. But if the signature was forged, subsequent owners are not holders because the instrument was not, in fact, payable to or indorsed to her. Thus, anyone who presents a note with a forged signature is violating the presentment warranties. Suppose that Bruce is totally honest and does not alter the note, but Chip steals it and forges Bruce's indorsement before passing the note on to Donald, who presents it to Adam for payment. Donald has violated his *presentment* warranties because he is not a holder. Adam can refuse to pay him. For his part, Donald can claim repayment from Chip who violated his *transfer* warranties by passing on a note with a forged signature.

EXAM Strategy

Question: Hillary owed Evan $500. She gave Evan's roommate John a check made out to Evan. John indorsed the check to Mike by signing Evan's name. Mike deposited the check in his account at the Amstel Bank. Amstel removed $500 from Hillary's account. Are John and Mike liable on this check?

Strategy: Whenever an instrument goes astray, begin by asking which warranties have been violated and by whom.

Result: Transfer warranties apply to all transfers *away* from the issuer; presentment warranties apply when the instrument *returns* to the maker or drawee for payment. John violated transfer warranties because Evan's signature is neither authentic nor authorized. When Mike deposited the check, he violated presentment warranties. He is not a holder because this check was not properly indorsed to Mike.

Conversion
Means that (1) someone has stolen an instrument or (2) a bank has paid a check that has a forged indorsement.

... he forged her indorsement and deposited the check in his own account without telling her.

OTHER LIABILITY RULES

This section contains other UCC rules that establish liability for wrongdoing on instruments.

Conversion Liability

Conversion means that (1) someone has stolen an instrument or (2) a bank has paid a check that has a forged indorsement. The rightful owner of the instrument can recover from either the thief or the bank.

For example, Glenn Altman was a lawyer representing Barbara Kirchoff. He settled her case for $12,000, but when he received the check, he forged her indorsement and deposited the check in his own account without telling her. He gave her the money four months later, but by then she had discovered his dishonesty. What claims do the various parties have?

Kirchoff has a claim against the bank because it paid a check with a forged indorsement. If the bank pays Kirchoff, then it can recover from Altman because he violated his presentment warranties. Note, however, that Kirchoff could not sue Altman for violating presentment warranties because he had not presented the check to her for payment. Nor could she sue him for violating transfer warranties because he had not transferred the check *to* her. To the contrary, he had transferred the check *away* from her.

Kirchoff does have a claim against Altman for conversion because he stole the check from her. What about the issuer of the check—can it also sue Altman for conversion? No, an action for conversion cannot be brought by an issuer because the check technically belongs to the payee (Kirchoff). The issuer can bring a claim only against the bank that pays the forged check.

Impostor Rule

If someone issues an instrument to an impostor, then any indorsement in the name of the payee is valid as long as the person (a bank, say) who pays the instrument does not know of the fraud. A teenager knocks on your door one afternoon. He tells you he is selling magazine subscriptions to pay for a school trip to Washington, D.C. After signing up for *Career* and *Popular Accounting*, you make out a check to "Family Magazine Subscriptions." Unfortunately, the boy does not represent Family Magazine at all. He does cash the check, however, by forging an indorsement for the magazine company. Is the bank liable for cashing the fraudulent check?

No. The teenager was an impostor—he said he represented the magazine company, but he did not. If anyone indorses the check in the name of the payee (Family Magazine Subscriptions), you must pay the check and the bank is not liable. Does this rule seem harsh? Maybe, but you were in the best position to determine if the teenager really worked for the magazine company. You were more at fault than the bank, and you must pay. Of course, the teenager would be liable to you, if you could ever find him.

Fictitious Payee Rule

If someone issues an instrument to a person who does not exist, then any indorsement in the name of the payee is valid as long as the person (a bank, say) who pays the instrument does not know of the fraud. The *impostor* rule applies if you give a check with a real name to the wrong person. The *fictitious payee* rule applies if you write a check to someone who does not exist. This type of fraud can be very difficult to prevent. Even a large law firm was stung. Dennis Masellis, the manager of payroll for Baker & McKenzie's New York office stole more than $7 million from the firm by creating fictitious employees and then depositing their salaries in his own account.

Employee Indorsement Rule

If an employee with responsibility for issuing instruments forges a check or other instrument, then any indorsement in the name of the payee, or a similar name, is valid as long as the person (a bank, say) who pays the instrument does not know of the fraud. A dishonest employee, especially one with the authority to issue checks, has the opportunity to steal a great deal of money. The employer cannot shift blame (and liability) onto the bank that unknowingly cashes the forged checks because the employer was more to blame—it not only hired the thief, it failed to supervise him carefully.

Dennis M. Hartotunian had a major gambling problem—he owed nearly $10 million. Unfortunately, he was also the controller and accountant for the Aesar Group. Over the course of three years, he wrote himself 154 checks worth $9.24 million. Any check for more than $500 required the signature of Aesar's general manager, but Hartotunian forged it.

After an internal audit revealed that millions were missing, company officers asked to talk with Hartotunian. When he heard they were coming, he walked out and never came back.

It is always a bad sign when the company controller disappears. If an employee is generally authorized to prepare or sign checks, then the bank is not liable on checks that the employee forges. Hartotunian was clearly covered by this rule because he was the company controller. If he had been a mailroom employee without authority to sign checks, the bank would have been liable.

Negligence

Regardless of the impostor rule, the fictitious payee rule, and the employee indorsement rule (the "three rules"), **anyone who behaves negligently in creating or paying an unauthorized instrument is liable to an innocent third party**. If two people are negligent, they share the loss according to their negligence. Here are two examples:

- **Anyone who is careless in paying an unauthorized instrument is liable, despite the three rules.** Suppose that the boy selling bogus magazine subscriptions goes into the bank and indorses the check: "Family Magazine Subscriptions, by Butch McGraw." The teller peers over her counter and sees a 13-year-old boy standing there with torn jeans and a baseball cap on backwards. She may be negligent if she cashes the check without asking for further identification.

- **Anyone who is careless in allowing a forged or altered instrument to be created is also liable, whether or not he has violated one of the three rules.** The classic case establishing this rule is more than 200 years old. In it, a businessman who was going abroad signed five checks and gave them to his wife with instructions that they were to be used for business expenses. A clerk in the company helpfully showed the missus how to fill out the checks, carefully instructing her to leave a blank space in front of the number. The clerk used this space to add a "3" in front of a "50" and then cashed the £350 check. The court held that the drawee bank was not liable because, "If Young, instead of leaving the check with a female, had left it with a man of business, he would have guarded against fraud in the mode of filling it up."[4] Today, we hiss at the sexist sentiment, but it illustrates the point. Anyone who carelessly creates a situation that facilitates the forgery or alteration of an instrument cannot recover against a party who pays the instrument in good faith.

EXAM Strategy

Question: Jonathan is the head of payroll at Yearbook. He issues checks to his sister, Elizabeth, who happens *not* to work for Yearbook. She does, however, deposit the checks into her bank account. A teller at the bank knows that Elizabeth does not work for Yearbook but he deposits the checks for her without raising any questions. Is the bank liable for the fraudulent checks?

Strategy: Whenever fraudulent checks are signed by an authorized employee, you will naturally think first of the Employee Indorsement Rule. However, it is important to remember that the bank's negligence overrides the Employee Indorsement Rule.

Result: If the bank were not negligent then, under the Employee Indorsement Rule, it would not be liable because Jonathan was authorized to sign checks. However, because the bank was negligent in paying the checks, it must share the loss with Yearbook. The amount each would have to pay depends upon their share of the blame.

---

[4]*Young v. Grote*, 4 Bing. 253 (Common Pleas), quoted in Douglas J. Whaley, *Problems and Materials on Payment Law* (Boston: Little, Brown & Co., 1995), p. 253.

Chapter Conclusion

It is never wise to play an important game without understanding the rules. As you can see from the cases in this chapter, real harm can come to those who do not know the rules of negotiable instruments.

EXAM REVIEW

1. **NEGOTIABILITY** The possessor of non-negotiable commercial paper has the same rights—no more, no less—as the person who made the original contract. The possessor of negotiable commercial paper has more rights than the person who made the original contract. (p. 345)

2. **THE FUNDAMENTAL RULE OF COMMERCIAL PAPER** The possessor of a piece of commercial paper has an unconditional right to be paid, as long as:

   - The paper is negotiable;

   - It has been negotiated to the possessor;

   - The possessor is a holder in due course; and

   - The issuer cannot claim a valid defense. (p. 345)

3. **REQUIREMENTS FOR NEGOTIABILITY** To be negotiable, an instrument must:

   - Be in writing;

   - Be signed by the maker or drawer;

   - Contain an unconditional promise or order to pay;

   - State a definite amount of money which is clear "within its four corners";

   - Be payable on demand or at a definite time; and

   - Be payable to order or to bearer. (pp. 346–347)

4. **AMBIGUITY** When the terms in a negotiable instrument contradict each other, three rules apply:

   - Words take precedence over numbers.

   - Handwritten terms prevail over typed and printed terms.

   - Typed terms win over printed terms. (p. 347)

5. **NEGOTIATION** An instrument has been transferred to the holder by someone other than the issuer. To be negotiated, order paper must first be indorsed and then delivered to the transferee. Bearer paper must simply be delivered to the transferee; no indorsement is required. (pp. 348–349)

6. **HOLDER IN DUE COURSE** A holder in due course has an automatic right to receive payment for a negotiable instrument (unless the issuer can claim a valid defense). A holder in due course is a holder who has given value for the instrument, in good faith, without notice of outstanding claims or other defects. (p. 349)

EXAM Strategy

Question: After Irene fell behind on her mortgage payments, she answered an advertisement from Best Financial Consultants offering attractive refinancing opportunities. During a meeting at a McDonald's restaurant, a Best representative told her that the company would arrange for a complete refinancing of her home, pay off two of her creditors, and give her an additional $5,000 in spending money. Irene would only have to pay Best $4,000. Irene signed a blank promissory note that was filled in later by Best representatives for $14,986.61. Best did not fulfill its promises to Irene, but within two weeks, it sold the note to Robin for just under $14,000. Irene refused to pay the note, alleging that Robin was not a holder in due course. Is Irene liable to Robin?

Strategy: Whenever a question asks if someone is a holder in due course, begin by reviewing the requirements. Is this person a *holder* who has given *value* for the instrument, in *good faith, without notice* of outstanding claims or other defects? (See the "Result" at the end of this section.)

7. **DEFENSES** The issuer of a negotiable instrument is not required to pay if:

- His signature was forged.

- After signing the instrument, his debts were discharged in bankruptcy.

- He was a minor at the time he signed the instrument.

- The amount of the instrument was altered after he signed it.

- He signed the instrument under duress, while mentally incapacitated, or as part of an illegal transaction.

- He was tricked into signing the instrument without knowing what it was and without any reasonable way to find out. (p. 351)

8. **CONSUMER EXCEPTION** The Federal Trade Commission requires all promissory notes in consumer credit contracts to contain language preventing any subsequent holder from being a holder in due course. (p. 352)

EXAM Strategy

Question: Gina purchased a Chrysler car with a 70,000-mile warranty. She signed a loan contract with the dealer to pay for the car in monthly installments. The dealer sold the contract to the Chrysler Credit Corp. Soon, the car developed a tendency to accelerate abruptly and without warning. Two Chrysler dealers were unable to correct the problem. Gina filed suit against Chrysler Credit Corp., but the company refused to rescind the loan contract. The company argued that, as a holder in due course on the note, it was entitled to be paid regardless of any defects in the car. How would you decide this case if you were the judge?

Strategy: Whenever consumers are involved, consider the possibility that there is a consumer credit contract. The plaintiff in this case is a consumer who borrowed money from a lender to purchase goods from a seller who is affiliated with the lender (both seller and lender are owned by Chrysler). Thus the contract is a consumer credit contract. (See the "Result" at the end of this section.)

9. **PRIMARY V. SECONDARY LIABILITY** Someone who is primarily liable on a negotiable instrument must pay unless he has a valid defense. Those with secondary liability only pay if the person with primary liability does not. (p. 353)

10. **PRIMARY SIGNATURE LIABILITY** The maker of a note is primarily liable. (p. 354)

11. **SECONDARY SIGNATURE LIABILITY**

   a. The drawer of a check has secondary liability: he is not liable until he has received notice that the bank has dishonored the check.
   b. Indorsers of a note are secondarily liable; they must pay if the issuer does not. But an indorser is only liable to those who come after him in the chain of ownership, not to those who held the instrument before he did. (p. 355)

12. **SIGNATURE LIABILITY FOR AN ACCOMMODATION PARTY** The accommodation party signs an instrument to benefit the accommodated party. By signing the instrument, an accommodation party agrees to be liable on it, whether or not she directly benefits from it. She has the same liability as the person for whom she signed. (pp. 353–356)

Question: Jean borrowed $6,000 from a bank. As part of the loan process, she executed a note to the bank. Her son's widow, Kathy, signed as an accommodation party. The bank issued a check payable to "Kathy *and* Jean." Somehow this check was altered to read "Kathy *or* Jean." Jean cashed the check and spent the proceeds. The bank sought recovery from Kathy, who refused to pay, arguing (1) the bank had to go after Jean first, and (2) her contract with the bank was unenforceable because she had not received any consideration—all of the proceeds of the loan had gone to Jean.

Strategy: An accommodation party is primarily liable; therefore the bank has no obligation to go after Kathy first. An accommodation party is liable whether or not she received any benefit from the loan. (See the "Result" at the end of this section.)

13. **WARRANTY LIABILITY** The basic rules of warranty liability are as follows:

   • The wrongdoer is always liable.

   • The drawee bank is responsible if it pays a check on which the drawer's name is forged.

   • In any other case of wrongdoing, a person who initially acquires an instrument from a wrongdoer is ultimately liable to anyone else who pays value for it. (pp. 356–357)

14. **TRANSFER WARRANTIES** When someone transfers an instrument, she warrants that:

- She is a holder of the instrument

- All signatures are authentic and authorized

- The instrument has not been altered

- No defense can be asserted against her, and

- As far as she knows, the issuer is solvent. (pp. 357–359)

15. **PRESENTMENT WARRANTIES FOR A CHECK** Anyone who presents a check for payment warrants that:

- She is a holder

- The check has not been altered, and

- She has no reason to believe the drawer's signature is forged. (p. 359)

16. **PRESENTMENT WARRANTIES FOR A NOTE** The presenter of a note only warrants that he is a holder. (p. 360)

17. **CONVERSION** Conversion means that (1) someone has stolen an instrument or (2) a bank has paid a check that has a forged indorsement. (p. 360)

18. **IMPOSTOR RULE** If someone issues an instrument to an impostor, then any indorsement in the name of the payee is valid as long as the person who pays the instrument is ignorant of the fraud. (p. 361)

19. **FICTITIOUS PAYEE RULE** If someone issues an instrument to a person who does not exist, then any indorsement in the name of the payee is valid as long as the person who pays the instrument does not know of the fraud. (p. 361)

20. **EMPLOYEE INDORSEMENT RULE** If an employee with responsibility for issuing instruments forges a check or other instrument, then any indorsement in the name of the payee is valid as long as the person who pays the instrument is ignorant of the fraud. (pp. 361–362)

21. **LIABILITY FOR NEGLIGENCE** Anyone who behaves negligently in creating or paying an unauthorized instrument is liable to an innocent third party. (p. 362)

---

6. Result: In this case, Robin is a holder who has given value. Did she act in good faith? We don't know if she actually *believed* the transaction was honest, but the court held that the transaction did not *appear* to be commercially reasonable because Robin's profit was so high. Thus, Robin was not a holder in due course, and Irene was not liable to her.

8. Result: Chrysler Credit was not a holder in due course. Therefore, it is subject to any defenses Gina might have against the dealer, including that the car was defective.

12. Result: Kathy is liable, even though she received no benefit from the loan.

MULTIPLE-CHOICE QUESTIONS

1. Which of the following statements are true?
   (a) A draft is always a check.
   (b) A check is always a draft.
   (c) A note must involve at least three people.
   (d) All of the above.

2. Which of the following standards are *required* for negotiability?
   (a) The instrument must be signed by the payee.
   (b) The instrument must be payable on demand.
   (c) The instrument must be payable to order.
   (d) None of the above.

3. Marla is not a holder in due course if she takes an instrument:
   (a) believing that the underlying contract was honest, although it turned out to be dishonest.
   (b) that is a consumer credit contract
   (c) that appeared commercially reasonable when made but turned out to be dishonest.
   (d) All of the above.

4. **CPA QUESTION** In order to negotiate bearer paper, one must:
   (a) indorse the paper.
   (b) indorse and deliver the paper with consideration.
   (c) deliver the paper.
   (d) deliver and indorse the paper.

5. What is the difference between a co-maker and an accommodation party?
   (a) A co-maker is liable both to the holder and the other co-maker, while an accommodation party is liable only to the holder.
   (b) A co-maker is liable to subsequent indorsers, while an accommodation party is not.
   (c) A co-maker is liable only to the other co-maker, while the accommodation party is liable to the holder.
   (d) A co-maker is not liable once a bank certifies a check, while an accommodation party is still liable even after certification.

ESSAY QUESTIONS

1. Duncan Properties, Inc. agrees to buy a car from Shifty for $25,000. The company issues a promissory note in payment. The car that Duncan bought is defective. If Shifty still has the note, does Duncan have to pay it?

2. Shifty sells that note to Honest Abe for $22,000. Does Duncan have to pay Abe?

3. Kay signed a promissory note for $220,000 that was payable to Investments, Inc. The company then indorsed the note over to its lawyers to pay past and future legal fees. Were the lawyers holders in due course?

4. Shelby wrote the following check to Dana. When is it payable, and for how much?

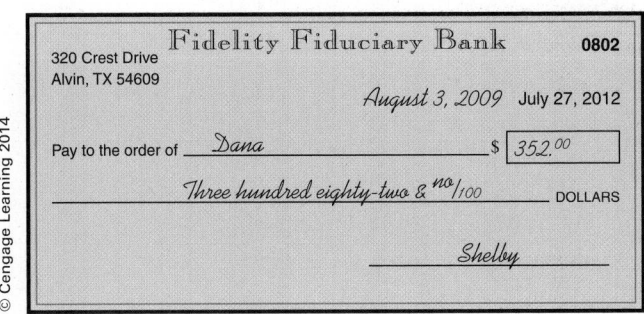

Fidelity Fiduciary Bank

320 Crest Drive
Alvin, TX 54609

0802

August 3, 2009   July 27, 2012

Pay to the order of ___Dana_____ $ 352.00

___Three hundred eighty-two & no/100_____ DOLLARS

Shelby

© Cengage Learning 2014

5. Railroad issued a check to Parris which somehow came to be in Eddy's possession. Eddy indorsed the check "Railroad Eddy" and deposited it in his own account at Bank. Parris sued Bank, alleging that it was liable to him for having paid the check over an unauthorized indorsement. Is Bank liable to Parris? On what theory?

6. Sidney entered into a contract for $35,000 with MacDonald Roofing Co., Inc., to reroof his building. Sidney made his initial payment by writing a check for $17,500 payable to "MacDonald Roofing Company, Inc., and Friendly Supply Company." MacDonald took the check to Friendly and requested an indorsement, which Friendly provided. When MacDonald failed to complete the roofing work, Sidney filed suit for damages against Friendly. Sidney argued that Friendly was liable as an indorser. Do you agree?

7. Using her company's check-signing machine, Doris forged $150,000 of checks on the account of her employer, Winkie, Inc. One of Doris's jobs at the company was to prepare checks for the company president, Zach, to sign. He did not (1) look at the sequence of check numbers; (2) examine the monthly account statements; or (3) reconcile company records with bank statements. Winkie's bank, as a matter of policy, did not check indorsements on checks with a face value of less than $1,000. By accident, it paid a forged check that had not even been indorsed. Is the bank liable to Winkie for the forged checks?

8. **ETHICS** When Steven was killed in an automobile accident, his wife, Debra, received $60,000 in life insurance benefits. She decided she needed a fresh start, so she sold her house in Bunkie and moved to Sulphur, Louisiana. Before she left, though, she signed several blank checks and gave them to her mother-in-law, Helen, with instructions to use them to pay off the remaining debt on Debra's mobile home. Instead, Helen used one of the checks to withdraw $50,000 from the account for her own personal use, not to pay off the debt. When Debra discovered the theft, she sued the bank for having paid an unauthorized check. How would you rule in this case? Debra has suffered a grievous loss—her husband died tragically in an automobile accident. She trusted her mother-in-law and counted on her help. Should the bank show compassion? If the bank made good on the forged checks, how great would be the injury to the bank's shareholders compared with the harm to Debra if she loses this entire sum?

DISCUSSION QUESTIONS

1. In the *Buckeye* case, the court ruled that Buckeye was not a holder in due course and the check was not valid because Buckeye should have checked with Sheth's bank before buying the check. Would this remedy have worked? What could Buckeye have done to protect itself?

2. In the *Antuna* case, the Antunas were foolish to sign an agreement with an unlicensed contractor to install aluminum siding. There is no evidence that TMS was acting in bad faith. Why should it suffer for the Antunas' mistake? What could TMS have done to protect itself?

3. Recall the *Quimby* case. This type of fraud is increasingly common. What could Quimby have done to protect himself?

4. Catherine suffered serious physical injuries in an automobile accident and became acutely depressed as a result. One morning, she received a check for $17,400 in settlement of her claims arising out of the accident. She indorsed the check and placed it on the kitchen table. She then called Robert, her longtime roommate, to tell him the check had arrived. That afternoon, she jumped from the roof of her apartment building, killing herself. The police found the check and a note from her, stating that she was giving it to Robert. Had Catherine negotiated the check to Robert?

5. Banks are liable for forged checks except in the case of the three rules (Imposter Rule, Fictitious Payee Rule, and the Employee Indorsement Rule). Do you think this is the proper allocation of liability? Why should banks be liable for forged checks, in this era of automated check machines? Alternatively, could you argue that the three rules provide too much protection to banks?

CHAPTER 15

BANKRUPTCY

© neelsky/Shutterstock.com

Three bankruptcy stories:

1. Tim's account: "First, there was Christmas. Was I really not going to buy my eight-year-old the Xbox he'd been begging for? Then my daughter's basketball team qualified for the nationals at Disney World. She's a talented player, and if she sticks with it, maybe she'll get a college scholarship. The kids had never been to Disney World. How could we say no? Then my car died. And I didn't get a bonus this year. Next thing you know, we had $27,000 in credit card debt. Then we had some uninsured medical bills. We were seriously underwater. There was just no way we could pay all that money back."

> **We were seriously underwater. There was just no way we could pay all that money back.**

2. Kristen was a talented gardener and had always loved flowers. Sometimes she did the flowers for friends' weddings. When the guy who owned the local flower shop wanted to retire, it seemed a great opportunity to buy the business. She had lots of good ideas for improving it. First, she renovated the space so that people could hold parties there. She hired staff to keep the shop open longer hours. Everything went really well. Then the recession hit, and people cut back on nonessentials like flowers. How could she pay her loans?

3. General Motors (GM), once a symbol of American business, filed for bankruptcy in 2009. At the time, its liabilities were $90 billion more than its assets. It also had 325,000 employees and even more stakeholders: retired employees, car owners, suppliers, investors, and communities in which it operated and its employees lived and paid taxes. GM emerged from bankruptcy 40 days later with fewer brands, factories, and workers, but ready to do business. The next year, the company was profitable.

Bankruptcy law always has been and always will be controversial. Typically, in other countries, the goal of bankruptcy law is to protect creditors and punish debtors, even sending debtors to prison. Indeed, many of America's first settlers fled England to escape debtors' prison. As if to compensate for Europe's harsh regimes, American bankruptcy laws were traditionally more lenient toward debtors.[1]

The General Motors example illustrates the good news about American bankruptcy. It is efficient (40 days!) and effective at reviving ailing companies. Everyone—investors, employees, the country—benefits from GM's survival. And although Kristen's flower shop did not survive, bankruptcy laws will protect her so that she is not afraid to try entrepreneurship again.[2] New businesses fail more often than not, but they are nonetheless important engines of growth for our country. We all benefit from the jobs they create and the taxes they pay.

Tim represents the bad news in bankruptcy laws. Unfortunately, he is often the type of person who first comes to mind when people think about bankrupts. And people do not like Tim very much. They think: why should he be rewarded for his irresponsibility, when I get stuck paying all my bills? But a more difficult bankruptcy process will probably not discourage Tim. He is the kind of guy who cares a lot about current pleasures and little about future pain. No matter what bankruptcy laws we have, he will not say no to Disney World. Should the laws become too onerous, businesses will fail, entrepreneurs will be discouraged, and the Tims of the world will continue to spend more than they should.

But maybe America has too much of a good thing. This nation has the highest bankruptcy rate in the world. In the most recent year, there was one bankruptcy filing for every 200 Americans.[3] Clearly, bankruptcy laws play a vital role in our economy. They have the potential to resuscitate failing companies while encouraging entrepreneurship. At the same time, it is important not to enable irresponsible spendthrifts. Do American bankruptcy laws reach the right balance?

OVERVIEW OF THE BANKRUPTCY CODE

The federal Bankruptcy Code (the Code) is divided into eight chapters. All chapters except one have odd numbers. Chapters 1, 3, and 5 are administrative rules that generally apply to all types of bankruptcy proceedings. These chapters, for example, define terms and establish the rules of the bankruptcy court. Chapters 7, 9, 11, 12, and 13 are substantive rules for different types of bankruptcies. All of these substantive chapters have one of two objectives—rehabilitation or liquidation.

Rehabilitation

The objective of Chapters 11 and 13 is to rehabilitate the debtor. Many debtors can return to financial health provided they have the time and breathing space to work out their problems. These chapters hold creditors at bay while the debtor develops a payment plan. In return for retaining some of their assets, debtors typically promise to pay creditors a portion of their future earnings.

---

[1] Bankruptcy law was so important to the drafters of the Constitution that they specifically listed it as one of the subjects that Congress had the right to regulate (Article 1, section 8).

[2] See, for example, Seung-Hyun Lee, Yasuhiro Yamakawa, Mike W. Peng, and Jay B. Barney, "How do bankruptcy laws affect entrepreneurship development around the world?" in the *Journal of Business Venturing*, JBV-05559, 2010.

[3] Some of these filings are by businesses, although that percentage is small. In the last 15 years, more than 95 percent of all bankruptcy filings have been by consumers.

Liquidation

Straight bankruptcy
Also known as *liquidation*, this form of bankruptcy mandates that the bankrupt's assets be distributed to creditors but the debtor has no obligation to share future earnings.

When debtors are unable to develop a feasible plan for rehabilitation under Chapter 11 or 13, Chapter 7 provides for liquidation (also known as a **straight bankruptcy**). Most of the debtor's assets are distributed to creditors, but the debtor has no obligation to share future earnings.

Chapter Description

The following options are available under the Bankruptcy Code:

Number	Topic	Description
Chapter 7	Liquidation	The bankrupt's assets are sold to pay creditors. If the debtor owns a business, it terminates. The creditors have no right to the debtor's future earnings.
Chapter 11	Reorganization	This chapter is designed for businesses and wealthy individuals. Businesses continue in operation, and creditors receive a portion of the debtor's current assets and future earnings.
Chapter 13	Consumer reorganization	Chapter 13 offers reorganization for the typical consumer. Creditors usually receive a portion of the individual's current assets and future earnings.

© Cengage Learning 2014

Debtors are sometimes eligible to file under more than one chapter. No choice is irrevocable because both debtors and creditors have the right to ask the court to convert a case from one chapter to another at any time during the proceedings. For example, if creditors have asked for liquidation under Chapter 7, a bankrupt consumer may request rehabilitation under Chapter 13.

Goals

The Bankruptcy Code has three primary goals:

- **To preserve as much of the debtor's property as possible.** In keeping with this goal, the Code requires debtors to disclose all of their assets and prohibits them from transferring assets immediately before a bankruptcy filing.

- **To divide the debtor's assets fairly between the debtor and creditors.** On the one hand, creditors are entitled to payment. On the other hand, debtors are often so deeply in debt that full payment is virtually impossible in any reasonable period of time. The Code tries to balance the creditors' right to be paid with the debtors' desire to get on with their lives, unburdened by prior debts.

- **To divide the debtor's assets fairly among creditors.** Creditors rarely receive all they are owed, but at least they are treated fairly, according to established rules. Creditors do not benefit from simply being the first to file or from any other gamesmanship.

CHAPTER 7 LIQUIDATION

All bankruptcy cases proceed in a roughly similar pattern, regardless of chapter. We use Chapter 7 as a template to illustrate common features of all bankruptcy cases. Later on, the discussions of the other chapters will indicate how they differ from Chapter 7.

Filing a Petition

Any individual, partnership, corporation, or other business organization that lives, conducts business, or owns property in the United States can file under the Code. (Chapter 13, however, is available only to individuals.) The traditional term for someone who could not pay his debts was "bankrupt," but the Code uses the term **"debtor"** instead. We use both terms interchangeably.

A case begins with the filing of a bankruptcy petition in federal district court. The district court typically refers bankruptcy cases to a specialized bankruptcy judge. Either party can appeal the decision of the bankruptcy judge back to the district court and, from there, to the federal appeals court.

Debtors may go willingly into the bankruptcy process by filing a **voluntary petition**, or they may be dragged into court by creditors who file an **involuntary petition**. Originally, when the goal of bankruptcy laws was to protect creditors, voluntary petitions did not exist; all petitions were involuntary. Because the bankruptcy process is now viewed as being favorable to debtors, the vast majority of bankruptcy filings in this country are voluntary petitions.

Voluntary Petition

Any debtor (whether a business or an individual) has the right to file for bankruptcy. It is not necessary that the debtor's liabilities exceed assets. Debtors sometimes file a bankruptcy petition because cash flow is so tight they cannot pay their debts, even though they are not technically insolvent. However, *individuals* must meet two requirements before filing:

- Within 180 days before the filing, an individual debtor must undergo credit counseling with an approved agency.

- Individual debtors may only file under Chapter 7 if they earn less than the median income in their state *or* they cannot afford to pay back at least $7,025 over five years.[4] Generally, all other debtors must file under Chapter 11 or Chapter 13. (These Chapters require the bankrupt to repay some debt.)

The voluntary petition must include the following documents:

Document	Description
Petition	Begins the case. Easy to fill out, it requires checking a few boxes and typing in little more than name, address, and Social Security number.
List of Creditors	The names and addresses of all creditors.
Schedule of Assets and Liabilities	A list of the debtor's assets and debts.
Claim of Exemptions	A list of all assets that the debtor is entitled to keep.
Schedule of Income and Expenditures	The debtor's job, income, and expenses.
Statement of Financial Affairs	A summary of the debtor's financial history and current financial condition. In particular, the debtor must list any recent payments to creditors and any other property held by someone else for the debtor.

© Cengage Learning 2014

Debtor
Someone who cannot pay his debts and files for protection under the Bankruptcy Code.

Voluntary petition
Filed by a debtor to initiate a bankruptcy case.

Involuntary petition
Filed by creditors to initiate a bankruptcy case.

---

[4]In some circumstances, debtors with income higher than $7,025 may still be eligible to file under Chapter 7, but the formula is highly complex and more than most readers want to know. The formula is available at 11 USC Section 707(b)(2)(A). Also, you can google "bapcpa means test" and then click on the Department of Justice website. The dollar amounts are updated every three years. You can find them by googling "federal register bankruptcy revision of dollar amounts."

Involuntary Petition

Creditors may force a debtor into bankruptcy by filing an involuntary petition. The creditors' goal is to preserve as much of the debtor's assets as possible and to ensure that all creditors receive a fair share. Naturally, the Code sets strict limits—debtors cannot be forced into bankruptcy every time they miss a credit card payment. **An involuntary petition must meet all of the following requirements:**

- The debtor must owe at least $14,425 in unsecured claims to the creditors who file.[5]

- If the debtor has at least 12 creditors, 3 or more must sign the petition. If the debtor has fewer than 12 creditors, any one of them may file a petition.

- The creditors must allege either that a custodian for the debtor's property has been appointed in the prior 120 days or that the debtor has generally not been paying debts that are due.

What does "a custodian for the debtor's property" mean? *State* laws sometimes permit the appointment of a custodian to protect a debtor's assets. The Code allows creditors to pull a case out from under state law and into federal bankruptcy court by filing an involuntary petition. In the event that a debtor objects to an involuntary petition, the bankruptcy court must hold a trial to determine whether the creditors have met the Code's requirements.

Once a voluntary petition is filed or an involuntary petition approved, the bankruptcy court issues an **order for relief**. This order is an official acknowledgment that the debtor is under the jurisdiction of the court, and it is, in a sense, the start of the whole bankruptcy process. An involuntary debtor must now make all the filings that accompany a voluntary petition.

Order for relief
An official acknowledgment that a debtor is under the jurisdiction of the bankruptcy court.

Trustee

The trustee is responsible for gathering the bankrupt's assets and dividing them among creditors. This is a critical role in a bankruptcy case. Trustees are typically lawyers or CPAs, but any generally competent person can serve. Creditors have the right to elect the trustee, but often they do not bother. If the creditors do not elect a trustee, then the **U.S. Trustee** appoints one. Each region of the country has a U.S. Trustee selected by the U.S. attorney general. Besides appointing trustees as necessary, this U.S. Trustee oversees the administration of bankruptcy law in the region.

U.S. Trustee
Oversees the administration of bankruptcy law in a region.

Creditors

After the court issues an order for relief, the U.S. Trustee calls a meeting of all of the creditors. At the meeting, the bankrupt must answer (under oath) any question the creditors pose about his financial situation. If the creditors want to elect a trustee, they do so at this meeting.

After the meeting of creditors, unsecured creditors must submit a *proof of claim*. This document is a simple form stating the name of the creditor and the amount of the claim. The trustee and the debtor also have the right to file on behalf of a creditor. But if a claim is

Proof of claim
A form stating the name of an unsecured creditor and the amount of the claim against the debtor.

---

[5]In Chapter 13, on secured transactions, we discuss the difference between secured and unsecured claims at some length. A secured claim is one in which the creditor has the right to foreclose on a specific piece of the debtor's property (known as **collateral**) if the debtor fails to pay the debt when due. For example, if Lee borrows money from GMAC Finance to buy a car, the company has the right to repossess the car if Lee fails to repay the loan. GMAC's loan is **secured**. An **unsecured** loan has no collateral. If the debtor fails to repay, the creditor can make a general claim against the debtor but has no right to foreclose on a particular item of the debtor's property.

not filed, the creditor loses any right to be paid. The trustee, debtor, or any creditor can object to a claim on the grounds that the debtor does not really owe that money. The court then holds a hearing to determine the validity of the claim.

Secured creditors do not file proofs of claim unless the claim exceeds the value of their collateral. In this case, they are unsecured creditors for the excess amount and must file a proof of claim for it. Suppose that Deborah borrows $750,000 from Morton in return for a mortgage on her house. If she does not repay the debt, he can foreclose. Unfortunately, property values plummet, and by the time Deborah files a voluntary petition in bankruptcy, the house is worth only $500,000. Morton is a secured creditor for $500,000 and need file no proof of claim for that amount. But he is an unsecured creditor for $250,000 and will lose his right to this excess amount unless he files a proof of claim for it.

Automatic Stay

A fox chased by hounds has no time to make rational long-term decisions. What that fox needs is a safe burrow. Similarly, it is difficult for debtors to make sound financial decisions when hounded night and day by creditors shouting, "Pay me! Pay me!" The Code is designed to give debtors enough breathing space to sort out their affairs sensibly. An automatic stay is a safe burrow for the bankrupt. It goes into effect as soon as the petition is filed. An **automatic stay** prohibits creditors from collecting debts that the bankrupt incurred before the petition was filed. Creditors may not sue a bankrupt to obtain payment, nor may they take other steps, outside of court, to pressure the debtor for payment. The following case illustrates how persistent creditors can be.

Automatic stay
Prohibits creditors from collecting debts that the bankrupt incurred before the petition was filed.

Jackson v. Holiday Furniture

309 B.R. 33, 2004 Bankr. LEXIS 548
United States Bankruptcy Court for the Western District of Missouri, 2004

Facts: In April, Cora and Frank Jackson purchased a recliner chair on credit from Dan Holiday Furniture. They made payments until November. That month, they filed for protection under the Bankruptcy Code. Dan Holiday received a notice of the bankruptcy. This notice stated that the store must stop all efforts to collect on the Jacksons' debt.

Despite this notice, a Dan Holiday collector telephoned the Jacksons' house 10 times between November 15 and December 1 and left a card in their door threatening repossession of the chair. On December 1, Frank (without Cora's knowledge) went to Dan Holiday to pay the $230 owed for November and December. He told the store owner about the bankruptcy filing but allegedly added that he and his wife wanted to continue making payments directly to Dan Holiday.

In early January, employees at Dan Holiday learned that Frank had died the month before. Nevertheless, after Cora failed to make the payment for the month of January, a collector telephoned her house 26 times between January 14 and February 19. The store owner's sister left the following message on Cora's answering machine:

Hello. This is Judy over at Dan Holiday Furniture. And this is the last time I am going to call you. If you do not call me, I will be at your house. And I expect you to call me today. If there is a problem, I need to speak to you about it. You need to call me. We need to get this thing going. You are a January and February payment behind. And if you think you are going to get away with it, you've got another thing coming.

When Cora returned home on February 18, she found seven bright yellow slips of paper in her doorjamb stating that a Dan Holiday truck had stopped by to repossess her furniture. The cards read: "OUR TRUCK was here to **REPOSSESS** Your furniture (sic). 241-6933 Dan Holiday Furn. & Appl. Co."

The threat to send a truck was merely a ruse designed to frighten Cora. In truth, Dan Holiday did not really want the recliner back. The owner just wanted to talk directly with Cora about making payments.

Also on February 18, Dan Holiday sent Cora a letter stating that she had 24 hours to bring her account current or else **"Repossession** Will Be Made and **Legal Action Will Be Taken."** That same day, Cora's bankruptcy attorney contacted Dan Holiday. Thereafter, all collection activity ceased.

Issues: *Did Dan Holiday violate the automatic stay provisions of the Bankruptcy Code? What is the penalty for a violation?*

Excerpts from Judge Venters's Decision:[6] The automatic stay prohibits the commencement or continuation of any action against the debtor that arose before the commencement of the bankruptcy case and forbids any act by a pre-petition creditor to obtain possession of property of the bankruptcy estate. An individual injured by a creditor's violation of the automatic stay shall recover actual damages, including costs and attorneys' fees, and in appropriate circumstances, may recover punitive damages.

In this case, there is no question that Dan Holiday repeatedly violated the automatic stay. [T]he Court finds that the Jacksons suffered financial damages in the amount of $230.00, which represents the coerced payments that Dan Holiday received from Frank Jackson on December 1.

The Court finds that punitive damages are warranted in this case based on Dan Holiday's egregious, intentional violations of the automatic stay. Dan Holiday's conduct was remarkably bad in that, after it had actual knowledge of the Jacksons' bankruptcy, and after coercing payments from the Jacksons covering the months of November and

December, it made no less than twenty-six telephone calls to the Jacksons' household in January and February. Dan Holiday's continued collection efforts were in flagrant violation of the protections Congress afforded to debtors under the automatic stay.

In this matter, the Court is somewhat hampered in assessing punitive damages by the lack of evidence concerning the ability of Dan Holiday to pay. [An owner] testified that Dan Holiday was a family-owned business that has been in existence for 52 years, and the Court assumes that it is a relatively small business. Under the circumstances of this case, the Court believes that an appropriate penalty would be $100.00 for each illegal contact with the Jacksons after December 1, when it is crystal clear that Dan Holiday had actual knowledge of the Jacksons' bankruptcy filing, for a total of $2,800.00. The Court believes that this penalty will be sufficient to sting the pocketbook of Dan Holiday and impress upon Dan Holiday and its owners and employees the importance of debtor protections under the Bankruptcy Code, as well as to deter further transgressions.

The Court also will award the Jacksons their attorneys' fees and costs in the amount of $1,142.42, an amount the Court considers eminently fair and reasonable under the circumstances of this case.

Bankruptcy Estate

Bankruptcy estate
The new legal entity created when a debtor files a bankruptcy petition. The debtor's existing assets pass into the estate.

The filing of the bankruptcy petition creates a new legal entity separate from the debtor—the **bankruptcy estate**. All of the bankrupt's assets pass to the estate except exempt property and new property that the debtor acquires after the petition is filed.

Exempt Property

Unpaid creditors may be angry, but generally they do not want the debtor to starve to death. **The Code permits *individual* debtors (but not organizations) to keep some property for themselves.** This exempt property saves the debtor from destitution during the bankruptcy process and provides the foundation for a new life once the process is over.

In this one area of bankruptcy law, the Code defers to state law. Although the Code lists various types of exempt property, it permits states to opt out of the federal system and define a different set of exemptions. A majority of states have indeed opted out of the Code, and for their residents, the Code exemptions are irrelevant. Alternatively, some states allow the debtor to choose between state or federal exemptions.

Under the *federal* Code, a debtor is allowed to exempt only $21,625 of the value of her home. If the house is worth more than that, the trustee sells it and returns $21,625 of the proceeds to the debtor. Most *states* exempt items such as the debtor's home, household goods, cars, work tools, disability and pension benefits, alimony, and health aids. Indeed, some states set no limit on the value of exempt property. Both Florida and Texas, for example, permit debtors to keep homes of unlimited value and a certain amount of land. (Texas also allows debtors to hang on to two firearms; athletic and sporting equipment; two

---

[6]For readability's sake, we refer to the plaintiffs as "the Jacksons," not "debtors," as the court did.

horses, mules or donkeys and a saddle, blanket, and bridle for each; up to a total value of $60,000 per family.) Not surprisingly, these generous exemptions sometimes lead to abuses. Therefore, the Code provides that debtors can take advantage of state exemptions only if they have lived in that state for two years prior to the bankruptcy. And they can exempt only $146,450 of any house that was acquired during the 40 months before the bankruptcy.

Voidable Preferences

A major goal of the bankruptcy system is to divide the debtor's assets fairly among creditors. It would not be fair, or in keeping with this goal, if debtors were permitted to pay off some of their creditors immediately before filing a bankruptcy petition. These transfers are called **preferences** because they give unfair preferential treatment to some creditors. The trustee has the right to void such preferences.

Preference
When a debtor unfairly pays creditors immediately before filing a bankruptcy petition.

Preferences can take two forms: payments and liens. A *payment* simply means that the debtor gives a creditor cash that would otherwise end up in the bankruptcy estate. A *lien* means a security interest in the debtor's property. In bankruptcy proceedings, secured creditors are more likely to be paid than unsecured creditors. If the debtor grants a security interest in specific property, he vaults that creditor out of the great unwashed mass of unsecured creditors and into the elite company of secured creditors. If it happens immediately before the petition is filed, it is unfair to other unsecured creditors.

The trustee can void any transfer (whether payment or lien) that meets all of the following requirements:

- The transfer was to a creditor of the bankrupt.

- It was to pay an existing debt.

- The creditor received more from the transfer than she would have received during the bankruptcy process.

- The debtor's liabilities exceeded assets at the time of the transfer.

- The transfer took place in the 90-day period before the filing of the petition.

In addition, the trustee can void a transfer to an insider that occurs in the *year* preceding the filing of the petition. **Insiders** are family members of an individual, officers and directors of a corporation, or partners of a partnership.

Insider
Family members of an individual debtor, officers and directors of a corporation, or partners of a partnership.

Fraudulent Transfers

Suppose that a debtor sees bankruptcy approaching across the horizon like a tornado. He knows that, once the storm hits and he files a petition, everything he owns except a few items of exempt property will become part of the bankruptcy estate. Before that happens, he may be tempted to give some of his property to friends or family to shelter it from the tornado. If he succumbs to temptation, however, he is committing a fraudulent transfer.

A transfer is fraudulent if it is made within the year before a petition is filed and its purpose is to hinder, delay, or defraud creditors. The trustee can void any fraudulent transfer. The debtor has committed a crime and may be prosecuted.

> Even the insolvent are allowed to shower with the lights on.

Not all payments by a debtor prior to filing are considered voidable preferences or fraudulent transfers. **A trustee cannot void pre-petition payments made *in the ordinary course*.** In a business context, that means a trustee cannot void payments from, say, a grocery store to its regular cookie supplier. For consumers, the trustee cannot void payments below $600 or other routine payments, say, to the electric or water company. In these situations, the bankrupt is clearly not trying to cheat creditors. Even the insolvent are allowed to shower with the lights on.

EXAM Strategy

Question: Eddie and Lola appeared to be happily married. But then Eddie's business failed, and he owed millions. Suddenly, Lola announced that she wanted a divorce. Eddie immediately agreed to transfer all of the couple's remaining assets to her as part of the divorce settlement. Are you suspicious? Is there a problem?

Strategy: Was this a voidable preference or a fraudulent transfer? What difference does it make?

Result: In a voidable preference, the debtor makes an unfair transfer to a creditor. In a fraudulent transfer, the bankrupt's goal is to hold on to assets himself. In a case similar to this one, the court ruled that the transfer was fraudulent because Eddie intended to shield his assets from all creditors.

Payment of Claims

Imagine a crowded delicatessen on a Saturday evening. People are pushing and shoving because they know there is not enough food for everyone; some customers will go home hungry. The delicatessen could simply serve whoever pushes to the front of the line, or it could establish a number system to ensure that the most deserving customers are served first—longtime patrons or those who called ahead. The Code has, in essence, adopted a number system to prevent a free-for-all fight over the bankrupt's assets. Indeed, one of the Code's primary goals is to ensure that creditors are paid in the proper order, not according to who pushes to the front of the line.

All claims are placed in one of three classes: (1) secured claims, (2) priority claims, and (3) unsecured claims. The second class—priority claims—has seven subcategories; the third class—unsecured claims—has three. **The trustee pays the bankruptcy estate to the various classes of claims in order of rank.** A higher class is paid in full before the next class receives any payment at all. In the case of *priority* claims, each *subcategory* is paid in order, with the higher subcategory receiving full payment before the next subcategory receives anything. If there are not enough funds to pay an entire subcategory, all claimants in that group receive a *pro rata* share. The rule is different for unsecured claims. All categories of *unsecured* claims are treated the same, and if there are not enough funds to pay the *entire* class, everyone in the class shares *pro rata*. If, for example, there is only enough money to pay 10 percent of the claims owing to unsecured creditors, then each creditor receives 10 percent of her claim. In bankruptcy parlance, this is referred to as "getting 10 cents on the dollar." The debtor is entitled to any funds remaining after all claims have been paid. The payment order is shown in Exhibit 15.1.

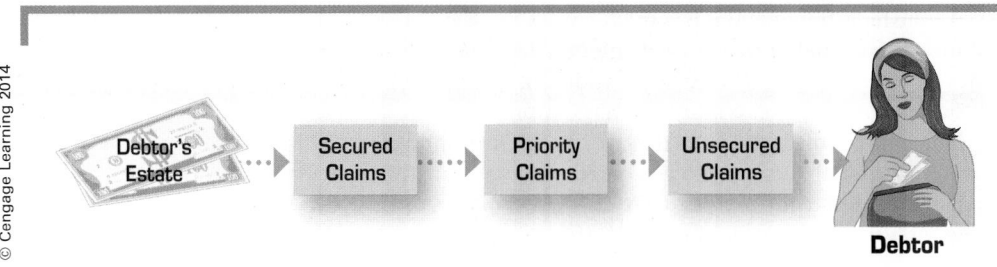

© Cengage Learning 2014

EXHIBIT 15.1

Secured Claims

Creditors whose loans are secured by specific collateral are paid first. Secured claims are fundamentally different from all other claims because they are paid by selling a specific asset, not out of the general funds of the estate. Sometimes, however, collateral is not valuable enough to pay off the entire secured debt. In this case, the creditor must wait in line with the unsecured creditors for the balance. Deborah (whom we met earlier in the section entitled "Creditors") borrowed $750,000 from Morton, secured by a mortgage on her house. By the time she files a voluntary petition, the house is worth only $500,000. Morton is a secured creditor for $500,000 and is paid that amount as soon as the trustee sells the house. But Morton is an unsecured creditor for $250,000 and will only receive this amount if the estate has enough funds to pay the unsecured creditors.

Priority Claims

There are seven subcategories of priority claims. Each category is paid in order, with the first group receiving full payment before the next group receives anything.

- *Alimony and child support.* The trustee must first pay any claims for alimony and child support. However, if the trustee is administering assets that could pay these support claims, then the trustee's fees are paid first.

- *Administrative expenses.* These include fees to the trustee, lawyers, and accountants.

- *Gap expenses.* If creditors file an involuntary petition, the debtor will continue to operate her business until the order for relief. Any expenses she incurs in the ordinary course of her business during this so-called **gap period** are paid now.

- *Payments to employees.* The trustee now pays back wages to the debtor's employees for work performed during the 180 days prior to the date of the petition. The trustee, however, can pay no more than $11,725 to each employee. Any other wages become unsecured claims.

- *Employee benefit plans.* The trustee pays what the debtor owes to employee pension, health, or life insurance plans for work performed during the 180 days prior to the date of the petition. The total payment for wages and benefits under this and the prior paragraph cannot exceed $11,725 times the number of employees.

- *Consumer deposits.* Any individual who has put down a deposit with the bankrupt for consumer goods is entitled to a refund of up to $2,600. If Stewart puts down a $3,000 deposit on a Miata sports car, he is entitled to a refund of $2,600 when the Trustie Car Lot goes bankrupt.

- *Taxes.* The trustee pays the debtor's income taxes for the three years prior to filing and property taxes for one prior year.

- *Intoxication injuries.* The trustee next pays the claims of anyone injured by a bankrupt who was driving a vehicle while drunk or on drugs.

Gap period
The period between the time that a creditor files an involuntary petition and the court issues the order for relief.

Unsecured Claims

Last, and frequently very much least, the trustee pays unsecured claims. All three of these unsecured subcategories have an equal claim and must be paid together.

- *Secured claims that exceed the value of the available collateral.* If funds permit, the trustee pays Morton the $250,000 that his collateral did not cover.

- *Priority claims that exceed the priority limits.* The trustee now pays employees, Stewart, and the tax authorities who were not paid in full the first time around because their claims exceeded the priority limits.

- *All other unsecured claims.* Unsecured creditors have now reached the delicatessen counter. They can only hope that some food remains.

Discharge

Fresh start

After the termination of a bankruptcy case, creditors cannot make a claim against the debtor for money owed before the initial bankruptcy petition was filed.

Discharge

The debtor no longer has an obligation to pay a debt.

Filing a bankruptcy petition is embarrassing, time-consuming, and disruptive. It can affect the debtor's credit rating for years, making the simplest car loan a challenge. To encourage debtors to file for bankruptcy despite the pain involved, the Code offers a powerful incentive: the **fresh start**. Once a bankruptcy estate has been distributed to creditors, they cannot make a claim against the debtor for money owed before the filing, *whether or not they actually received any payment.* These pre-petition debts are **discharged**. All is forgiven, if not forgotten.

Discharge is an essential part of bankruptcy law. Without it, debtors would have little incentive to take part. To avoid abuses, however, the Code limits both the type of debts that can be discharged and the circumstances under which discharge can take place. In addition, a debtor must complete an approved course on financial management before receiving a discharge.

Debts That Cannot Be Discharged

The following debts are *never* discharged, and the debtor remains liable in full until they are paid:

- Income taxes for the three years prior to filing and property taxes for the prior year.

- Money obtained fraudulently. Kenneth Smith ran a home repair business that fleeced senior citizens by making unnecessary repairs. Three months after he was found liable for fraud, he filed a voluntary petition in bankruptcy. The court held that his liability on the fraud claim could not be discharged.[7]

- Any loan of more than $600 that a consumer uses to purchase luxury goods within 90 days before the order for relief is granted.

- Cash advances on a credit card totaling more than $875 that an individual debtor takes out within 70 days before the order for relief.

- Debts omitted from the Schedule of Assets and Liabilities that the debtor filed with the petition, if the creditor did not know about the bankruptcy and therefore did not file a proof of claim.

- Money that the debtor stole or obtained through a violation of fiduciary duty.

- Money owed for alimony or child support.

- Debts stemming from intentional and malicious injury.

- Fines and penalties owed to the government.

- Liability for injuries caused by the debtor while operating a vehicle under the influence of drugs or alcohol. (Yet another reason why friends don't let friends drive drunk.)

- Liability for breach of duty to a bank. During the 1980s, a record number of savings and loans failed because their officers had made too many risky loans (in some cases to friends and family). This provision, added to the Code in 1990, was designed to prevent these officers from declaring bankruptcy to avoid their liability to bank shareholders.

---

[7]*In re Smith*, 848 F.2d 813, 1988 U.S. App. LEXIS 8037 (7th Cir. 1988).

- Debts stemming from a violation of securities laws.

- Student loans can be discharged only if repayment would cause undue hardship. As the following case illustrates, proving undue hardship is difficult.

In Re Stern

288 B.R. 36; 2002 Bankr. LEXIS 1609
United States Bankruptcy Court for the Northern District of New York, 2002

Facts: James Stern took out student loans to attend Bates College and Syracuse College of Law. Afterward, he had difficulty finding a job as a lawyer, so he opened his own practice. Both he and his wife earned less than $20,000 a year.

A client sued Stern for malpractice. Although Stern won, his malpractice premiums increased so much that he could no longer afford the insurance. Believing that his debt and default on his student loans made him unemployable as a lawyer, he moved with his wife to her native country, France. Unfortunately, he did not speak French and, therefore, could not obtain a job, even as a street sweeper. His wife's total income over six months in France was $2,200. Even more unfortunately, their expenses in France were higher than in the United States.

Stern owed $147,000 in student loans: $56,000 in principal and $91,000 in interest. He calculated that paying this debt would cost $1,167 per month over 30 years. He asked the court to discharge these student loans on grounds of undue hardship. As he put it, "I'm never going to be able to get a house, I'm never going to be able to have a car, and I won't—you know, I want to have kids. I want to be responsible, and I can't—I can't possibly pay this amount and have a life, not with what I expect I'll be able to earn."

Issue: *Is Stern entitled to a discharge of his student loans on grounds of undue hardship?*

Excerpts from Judge Gerling's Decision:[8] [E]ducational loans are different from most loans. They are made without business considerations, without security, without cosigners, and rely for repayment solely on the debtor's future increased income resulting from the education. In this sense, the loan is viewed as a mortgage on the debtor's future.

[To obtain a discharge,] Stern must prove more than his present inability to pay his student loan obligations. He must also establish that his current financial hardship is likely to be long-term. In this case, Stern possesses both a bachelor's degree and a Juris Doctorate. Stern

apparently has decided that he no longer wishes to pursue a legal career. He is certainly well within his rights to make such a choice. Nevertheless, [b]orrowers under the various guaranteed student loan programs are obligated to repay their loans even if they are unable to obtain employment in their chosen field of study.

The Court finds disturbing Stern's failure to maximize his income and minimize his expenses. He and his wife have elected to relocate to France, where Stern admitted that the cost of living is higher. Nor is there any evidence that he ever made any effort to obtain employment in the United States in order to enhance his earnings, whether it be in business, government, or in a private law firm in Syracuse or elsewhere. Instead, he opted to move to a country where he acknowledges he cannot even get a job as a street sweeper because of his inability to speak the language.

Obviously, Stern would prefer to be in a position that would allow him to allocate those monies [he owes] to a mortgage on a home or to the raising of children. Those are certainly commendable goals; but the fact that they may not be attainable at this time because of the student loans and Stern's, as well as his wife's, current employment situation, does not meet the fundamental standard from which "undue hardship" is measured and does not provide a basis for granting Stern [even] a partial discharge at this time.

While Stern and his wife have experienced some "bumps in the road," the direction they take in the future appears very much in their control based on their age, health, and education. Indeed, it is the very education that he obtained as a result of the student loans at both the undergraduate and graduate levels, which, arguably, should ultimately allow him to pursue employment opportunities not available to others who were unable to pursue higher education for whatever reason. While Stern testified that he no longer wishes to continue in the legal profession, certainly, there are other career opportunities available to him by virtue of his education, training, and experience.

---

[8]Although the court refers to Stern as "Debtor," we use his surname.

Circumstances That Prevent Debts from Being Discharged

Apart from identifying the *kinds* of debts that cannot be discharged, the Code also prohibits the discharge of debts under the following *circumstances:*

- **Business organizations.** Under Chapter 7 (but *not* the other Chapters), only the debts of individuals can be discharged, not those of business organizations. Once its assets have been distributed, the organization must cease operation. If it continues in business, it is responsible for all pre-petition debts. Shortly after E. G. Sprinkler Corp. entered into an agreement with its union employees, it filed for bankruptcy under Chapter 7. Its debts were discharged, and the company began operation again. A court ordered it to pay its obligations to the employees because, once the company resumed business, it was responsible for all of its pre-filing debts.[9]

- **Revocation.** A court can revoke a discharge within one year if it discovers the debtor engaged in fraud or concealment.

- **Dishonesty or bad faith behavior.** The court may deny discharge altogether if the debtor has, for example, made fraudulent transfers, hidden assets, falsified records, disobeyed court orders, refused to testify, or otherwise acted in bad faith. For instance, a court denied discharge under Chapter 7 to a couple who failed to list 15 pounds of marijuana on their Schedule of Assets and Liabilities. The court was unsympathetic to their arguments that a listing of this asset might have caused larger problems than merely being in debt.[10]

- **Repeated filings for bankruptcy.** Congress feared that some debtors, attracted by the lure of a fresh start, would make a habit of bankruptcy. Therefore, a debtor who has received a discharge under Chapter 7 or 11 cannot receive another discharge under Chapter 7 for at least eight years after the prior filing. And a debtor who received a prior discharge under Chapter 13 cannot in most cases receive one under Chapter 7 for at least six years.

Ethics   Banks and credit card companies lobbied Congress hard for the prohibition against repeated bankruptcy filings. They argued that irresponsible consumers run up debt and then blithely walk away. You might think that, if this were true, lenders would avoid customers with a history of bankruptcy. Research indicates, though, that lenders actually *target* those consumers, repeatedly sending them offers to borrow money. The reason is simple: these consumers are much more likely to take cash advances, which carry very high interest rates. And this is one audience that *must* repay its loans for the simple reason that these borrowers cannot obtain a discharge again anytime soon.[11] Is this strategy ethical?

---

[9]*In re Goodman*, 873 F.2d 598, 1989 U.S. App. LEXIS 5472 (2d Cir. 1989).

[10]*In re Tripp*, 224 B.R. 95, 1998 Bankr. LEXIS 1108 (1998).

[11]See Katherine M. Porter, "Bankrupt Profits: The Credit Industry's Business Model for Postbankruptcy Lending," University of Iowa Legal Studies Research Paper No. 07-26, Iowa Law Review, Vol. 94, 2008. This paper is available by googling "ssrn katherine porter bankrupt profits."

EXAM Strategy

Question: Someone stole a truck full of cigarettes. Zeke found the vehicle abandoned at a truck stop. Not being a thoughtful fellow, he took the truck and sold it with its cargo. Although Tobacco Company never found out who stole the truck originally, it did discover Zeke's role. A court ordered Zeke to pay Tobacco $50,000. He also owed his wife $25,000 in child support. Unfortunately, he only had $20,000 in assets. After he files for bankruptcy, who will get paid what?

Strategy: There are two issues: the order in which the debts are paid and whether they will be discharged.

Result: Child support is a priority claim, so that will be paid first. In a similar case, the court refused to discharge the claim over the theft of the truck, ruling that that was an intentional and malicious injury. Nor will a court discharge the child support claim. So Zeke will be on the hook for both debts, but the child support must be paid first.

Reaffirmation

Sometimes debtors are willing to **reaffirm** a debt, meaning they promise to pay even after discharge. They may want to reaffirm a secured debt to avoid losing the collateral. For example, a debtor who has taken out a loan secured by a car may reaffirm that debt so that the finance company will not repossess it. Sometimes debtors reaffirm because they feel guilty or want to maintain a good relationship with the creditor. They may have borrowed from a family member or an important supplier. Because discharge is a fundamental pillar of the bankruptcy process, creditors are not permitted to unfairly pressure the bankrupt. To be valid, the reaffirmation must:

> **Reaffirm**
> To promise to pay a debt even after it is discharged.

- Not violate common law standards for fraud, duress, or unconscionability. If creditors force a bankrupt into reaffirming a debt, the reaffirmation is invalid.

- Have been filed in court before the discharge is granted.

- Include the detailed disclosure statement required by the statute (Section 524).

- Be approved by the court if the debtor is not represented by an attorney or if, as a result of the reaffirmed debt, the bankrupt's expenses exceed his income.

In the following case, the debtor sought to reaffirm the loan on his truck. He may have been afraid that if he did not, the lender would repossess it, leaving him stranded. It is hard to get around Dallas without a car. Should the court permit the reaffirmation?

In Re Grisham

436 B.R. 896; 2010 Bankr. LEXIS 2907
United States Bankruptcy Court for the Northern District of Texas, 2010

Facts: Two months before filing for bankruptcy, William Grisham bought a Dodge truck (Nitro-V6 Utility 4D SLT 2WD). At the time of his bankruptcy filing, the vehicle was worth $16,000, but he owed $17,500 on it. The annual interest rate was 17.5 percent, the monthly payments were $400, and the payment schedule was almost 6 years. In addition, Grisham owed:

$29,000 to the IRS

$75,000 in alimony

$100,000 in student loans

$70,000 in unsecured debt

$274,000 total in addition to the truck

Grisham sought to reaffirm the truck loan. Should the court allow him to do so?

Issue: *Would reaffirmation of this debt create an undue hardship for the debtor?*

Excerpts from Judge Jernigan's Decision: [F]rom the outset, this court was concerned that the Debtor wished to reaffirm debt on personal property in which there is no equity. [T]he Debtor describes himself as "retired/unemployed." The Debtor's only source of income is $1,928 per month of social security income and $1,698 per month of unemployment benefits—the latter of which will soon expire. The Debtor owns no real property and testified that he currently resides rent-free at a relative's home. The Debtor's monthly net income, after deducting his living expenses, is a negative $1,091.

While the monthly payments on the vehicle are not eye-popping, for this Debtor, in his current situation, it is unduly burdensome. In particular, this Debtor is burdened with several obligations that will likely survive his discharge in bankruptcy (large IRS debt; large alimony; and large student loan debt). Finally, the court heard no compelling testimony to justify why the Debtor purchased his vehicle right before filing bankruptcy (sometimes this may be defensible and sometimes not). In summary, the court will not stamp its seal of approval on the Debtor's reaffirmation of the debt. To do so would create a hardship on this Debtor and does not otherwise seem justified.

Bankruptcy is about "fresh starts" and new beginnings. It is about belt-tightening and shedding past bad habits. Too often, a reaffirmation agreement will reveal that someone just does not comprehend this and wants to go forward in a manner that will impair his fresh start and perpetuate bad habits from the past.

The court realizes that this is sometimes complicated. [T]here are probably situations in which a vehicle-lender will repossess the debtor's vehicle post-discharge, even when the debtor is making regular and timely contractual payments for the car post-discharge—for the simple reason that the debtor did not "reaffirm." Thus, the court can understand why a debtor and his counsel might see the wisdom of entering into a reaffirmation agreement, even if they can envision the court may never approve it because of the negative math. Perhaps they imagine that this will help the debtor with the car lender post-discharge, if they at least tried to get the reaffirmation agreement approved with the court. Moreover, perhaps the debtor genuinely needs a car and worries that, absent an attempt at a reaffirmation agreement, he will surely lose the car post-discharge and may not be able to purchase (*i.e.*, obtain financing) for another vehicle in the near future.

The court realizes that we are in a world where car lenders may not always act like economically rational animals. And, the court appreciates that car lenders may sometimes have their own economic pressures with which to contend. But, again, the fresh start is the overriding purpose of a chapter 7 bankruptcy case. Many reaffirmation agreements presented to the court are the farthest thing from a "fresh start" that one could ever imagine. Many times it is time to say "good riddance" to the car. And many times—maybe, just maybe—a car lender will see the wisdom of renegotiating a car loan if reaffirmation is denied.

Accordingly,

IT IS ORDERED that the Reaffirmation Agreement is disapproved.

CHAPTER 11 REORGANIZATION

For a business, the goal of a Chapter 7 bankruptcy is euthanasia—putting it out of its misery by shutting it down and distributing its assets to creditors. Chapter 11 has a much more complicated and ambitious goal—resuscitating a business so that it can ultimately emerge as a viable economic concern, as General Motors did. Keeping a business in operation benefits virtually all company stakeholders: employees, customers, creditors, shareholders, and the community.

Both individuals and businesses can use Chapter 11. Businesses usually prefer Chapter 11 over Chapter 7 because Chapter 11 does not require them to dissolve at the end, as Chapter 7 does. The threat of death creates a powerful incentive to try rehabilitation under Chapter 11. Individuals, however, tend to prefer Chapter 13 because it is specifically designed for them.

A Chapter 11 proceeding follows many of the same steps as Chapter 7: a petition (either voluntary or involuntary), order for relief, meeting of creditors, proofs of claim, and an automatic stay. There are, however, some significant differences.

Debtor in Possession

Chapter 11 does not require a trustee. The bankrupt is called the **debtor in possession** and, in essence, serves as trustee. The debtor in possession has two jobs: to operate the business and to develop a plan of reorganization. A trustee is chosen only if the debtor is incompetent or uncooperative. In that case, the creditors can elect the trustee, but if they do not choose to do so, the U.S. Trustee appoints one.

Debtor in possession
The debtor acts as trustee in a Chapter 11 bankruptcy.

Creditors' Committee

In a Chapter 11 case, the creditors' committee is important because typically, there is no neutral trustee to watch over their interests. The committee generally protects the interests of its constituency and may play a role in developing the plan of reorganization. Moreover, the Bankruptcy Code requires the committee to communicate diligently with all creditors. The U.S. Trustee typically appoints the seven largest *un*secured creditors to the committee. However, the court may require the U.S. Trustee to appoint some small-business creditors as well. Secured creditors do not serve because their interests require less protection. If the debtor is a corporation, the U.S. Trustee may also appoint a committee of shareholders. The Code refers to the **claims** of creditors and the **interests** of shareholders.

Plan of Reorganization

Once the bankruptcy petition is filed, an automatic stay goes into effect to provide the debtor with temporary relief from creditors. The next stage is to develop a plan of reorganization that provides for the payment of debts and the continuation of the business. For the first 120 days (which the court can extend up to 18 months), the debtor has the exclusive right to propose a plan. If the debtor fails to file a plan, or if the court rejects it, then creditors and shareholders can develop their own plan.

Confirmation of the Plan

Anyone who proposes a plan of reorganization must also prepare a **disclosure statement** to be mailed out with the plan. The purpose of this statement is to provide creditors and shareholders with enough information to make an informed judgment. The statement describes the company's business, explains the plan, calculates the company's liquidation value, and assesses the likelihood that the debtor can be rehabilitated. The court must approve a disclosure statement before it is sent to creditors and shareholders.

All the creditors and shareholders have the right to vote on the plan of reorganization. In preparation for the vote, each creditor and shareholder is assigned to a class. Everyone in a class has similar claims or interests. Chapter 11 classifies claims in the same way as Chapter 7: (1) secured claims, (2) priority claims, and (3) unsecured claims. Each secured claim is usually in its own class because each one is secured by different collateral. Shareholders are also divided into classes depending upon their interests. For example, holders of preferred stock are in a different class from common shareholders.

Creditors and shareholders receive a ballot with their disclosure statement to vote for or against the plan of reorganization. After the vote, the bankruptcy court holds a **confirmation hearing** to determine whether it should accept the plan. **The court will approve a plan if a majority *of each class* votes in favor of it *and* if the "yes" votes hold at least two-thirds of the total debt in that class.**

Even if some classes vote against the plan, the court can still confirm it under what is called a **cramdown** (as in "the plan is crammed down the creditors' throats"). The court will not impose a cramdown unless, in its view, the plan is feasible and fair. If the court rejects the plan of reorganization, the creditors must develop a new one. In the following case, the court did impose a cramdown.

IN RE FOX

2000 Bankr. LEXIS 1713
United States Bankruptcy Court, District of Kansas, 2000

Facts: Donald Fox founded Midland Fumigant, Inc., a company in the business of fumigating stored wheat, corn, and other grain. In a prior case, a competitor, United Phosphorus, Ltd., obtained a verdict of $2 million against Midland and Fox for fraud.

Unable to pay the judgment, Fox filed a voluntary petition under Chapter 11 of the Bankruptcy Code. His plan of reorganization envisioned that he would use revenues from Midland to pay off his creditors in full over five years, with interest. To ensure that the plan of reorganization was feasible, Fox hired CPA Kirk Wiesner to analyze Midland's financial statements and prepare projections of its income and expenses. Wiesner also reviewed Midland's operations, business, products, and the industry. He concluded that the plan's projections were conservative and could be met easily.

Midland had six classes of creditors. All of the classes accepted the plan except the two classes in which United was a member. The bankruptcy judge noted that United had an incentive to oppose Midland's reorganization because this business was highly competitive and, if Midland were to cease operations, United would be able to raise its prices substantially.

Issues: *Was Fox's plan of reorganization feasible and fair? Should the court impose a cramdown?*

Excerpts from Judge Robinson's Decision: Debtor has proposed a plan which pays all creditors in full, with interest. United, the only objecting creditor, will be paid in full [within 16 months]. Debtor has provided a reasonable and orderly repayment of his debts. Debtor's desire and intent to provide a mechanism for him to retain his business interests and assets is consistent with the purposes of the Bankruptcy Code. The plan may satisfy [the Code] even though the plan may not be one which the creditors would themselves design.

United contends that the Plan is not feasible because the projections of Midland's income and expenses are unreliable. The purpose [of the Bankruptcy Code] is to prevent confirmation of visionary schemes that promise creditors and equity security holders more than the debtor can possibly attain after confirmation.

Will the reorganized debtor emerge from bankruptcy solvent and with a reasonable prospect of success? Debtor's expert, Kirk Wiesner, analyzed Midland's financial statements, and determined that Midland would have sufficient income and cash flow during the life of Debtor's Plan, to make the anticipated distributions and loans that will fund Debtor's Plan. Based on Wiesner's Projections, which proved conservative in [the past], when Midland's actual income doubled the projected income, the Court concludes that Midland will have a continuing ability to distribute and loan funds to the Debtor as contemplated.

The Plan has a reasonable assurance of success and is not likely to be followed by liquidation, or the need for further financial reorganization. As such, the Debtor's Plan meets the feasibility requirement. The Court further notes that the United States Trustee has filed a statement in support of confirmation of the Plan.

[T]he Court finds that the Debtor's Plan is fair and equitable and, as a result, the fact that [two] Classes did not accept the Plan does not preclude confirmation.

The Debtor's Plan is confirmed over the objection of United and over the dissenting votes of [two] Classes for the reasons stated.

Discharge

A confirmed plan of reorganization is binding on the debtor, creditors, and shareholders. **The debtor now owns the assets in the bankrupt estate, free of all obligations except those listed in the plan.** Under a typical plan of reorganization, the debtor gives some current assets to creditors and also promises to pay them a portion of future earnings. In contrast, the Chapter 7 debtor typically relinquishes all assets (except exempt property) to creditors but then has no obligation to turn over future income. Exhibit 15.2 illustrates the steps in a Chapter 11 bankruptcy.

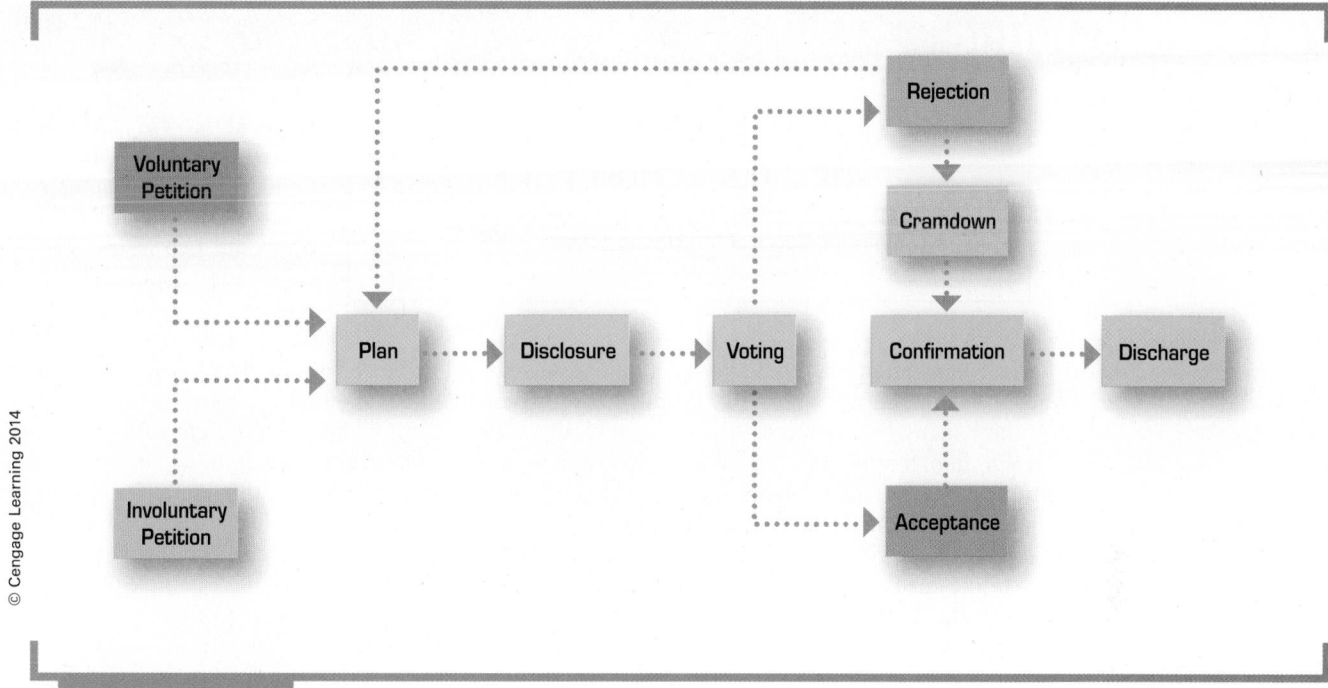

EXHIBIT 15.2

Small-Business Bankruptcy

Out of concern that the lengthy procedure in Chapter 11 was harming the creditors of small businesses, in 2005 Congress included provisions designed to speed up the process for businesses with less than $2 million in debt. After the order for relief, the bankrupt has the exclusive right to file a plan for 180 days. Both a plan and a disclosure statement must be filed within 300 days. The court must confirm or reject the plan within 45 days after its filing. If these deadlines are not met, the case can be converted to Chapter 7 or dismissed.

CHAPTER 13 CONSUMER REORGANIZATIONS

The purpose of Chapter 13 is to rehabilitate an individual debtor. It is not available at all to businesses or to individuals with more than $360,475 in unsecured debts or $1,081,400 in secured debts. Under Chapter 13, the bankrupt consumer typically keeps most of her assets in exchange for a promise to repay some of her debts using future income. Therefore, to be eligible, the debtor must have a regular source of income. Individuals usually choose this chapter because it is easier and cheaper than Chapters 7 and 11. Consequently, more money is retained for both creditors and debtor.

As you read at the beginning of the chapter, debtors can convert from one chapter to another as they wish. In the following case, the trustees objected to a conversion. The case went all the way to the Supreme Court, which split 5-4. How would you have voted?

You be the Judge

MARRAMA V. CITIZENS BANK OF MASSACHUSETTS

127 S. Ct. 1105; 2007 U.S. LEXIS 2651
Supreme Court of the United States, 2007

Facts: When Robert Marrama filed a voluntary petition under Chapter 7, he lied. Although he disclosed that he was the sole beneficiary of a trust that owned a house in Maine, he listed its value as zero. Marrama also denied that he had transferred any property during the prior year. Neither statement was true: the Maine property was valuable (how many houses are worth zero?), and he had given it for free to the trust seven months prior to filing for bankruptcy protection. Marrama also lied when he claimed that he was not entitled to a tax refund. In fact, he knew that a check for $8,700 from the Internal Revenue Service was in the mail.

Once Marrama found out that the bankruptcy trustees were going after the Maine property, he filed a notice to convert his Chapter 7 bankruptcy to Chapter 13. The trustee and creditors objected. They contended that because Marrama had acted in bad faith when he tried to conceal the Maine property from his creditors, he should not be permitted to convert. The bankruptcy court and the appeals court agreed. The Supreme Court granted *certiorari*.

You Be The Judge: *Can a bankruptcy court refuse to allow a debtor to convert from Chapter 7 to Chapter 13?*

Argument for Marrama: Under the Bankruptcy Code, a Chapter 7 debtor may convert a case, with only two restrictions. First, the bankrupt can convert only once. Second, the debtor must meet the conditions that would have been required for him to file under the new chapter in the first place. Nothing in the Code suggests that a bankruptcy judge has the right to prohibit a conversion because of the debtor's bad faith.

If a debtor acts in bad faith, the court has other remedies: it can convert the case back to a Chapter 7 liquidation; it can refuse to approve the plan of payment; or it can charge the debtor with perjury. That is the law, whether the trustee and creditors like it or not.

Argument for the Bankruptcy Trustee: A bankruptcy court has the unquestioned right to dismiss a Chapter 13 petition if the debtor demonstrates bad faith. There seems no logical reason why a court would have the right to dismiss a case for bad faith but not the right to prohibit a filing under Chapter 13 to begin with. In both cases, the court is simply saying that the individual does not qualify as a debtor under Chapter 13. That individual is not a member of the class of honest but unfortunate debtors whom the bankruptcy laws were enacted to protect.

EXAM Strategy

Question: Why did Marrama first file under Chapter 7 and then try to switch to Chapter 13 after he was caught lying?

Strategy: This question is a good test of your understanding of the advantages and disadvantages of the different chapters. For help in answering this question, you might want to look at the chart at the end of the chapter. Remember that Chapter 7 is a liquidation provision—it takes more of the bankrupt's money upfront but then discharges his debts and gives him a fresh start for the future. Chapter 13 does not take as many assets during the bankruptcy process but may attach all the debtor's disposable income for the next five years.

Result: Marrama filed under Chapter 7 in the hope that he could hold on to his house while all his debts were discharged. Once that plan failed, he tried to switch to Chapter 13 in the hope that he could keep the house and give up his disposable income instead. This case illustrates the different emphases of Chapters 7 and 13.

A bankruptcy under Chapter 13 generally follows the same course as Chapter 11: the debtor files a petition, creditors submit proofs of claim, the court imposes an automatic stay, the debtor files a plan, and the court confirms the plan. But there are some differences.

Beginning a Chapter 13 Case

To initiate a Chapter 13 case, the debtor must file a voluntary petition. **Creditors cannot use an involuntary petition to force a debtor into Chapter 13.** In all Chapter 13 cases, the U.S. Trustee appoints a trustee to supervise the debtor, although the debtor remains in possession of the bankruptcy estate. The trustee also serves as a central clearinghouse for the debtor's payments to creditors. The debtor pays the trustee who, in turn, transmits these funds to creditors. For this service, the trustee is allowed up to 10 percent of the payments.

Plan of Payment

The debtor must file a plan of payment within 15 days after filing the voluntary petition. Only the debtor can file a plan; the creditors have no right to file their own version. Under the plan, the debtor must (1) commit some future earnings to pay off debts, (2) promise to pay all secured and priority claims in full, and (3) treat all remaining classes equally. If the plan does not provide for the debtor to pay off creditors in full, then all of the debtor's disposable income for the next five years must go to creditors.

Within 30 days after filing the plan of payment, the debtor must begin making payments to the trustee under the plan. The trustee holds these payments until the plan is confirmed and then transmits them to creditors. The debtor continues to make payments to the trustee until the plan has been fully implemented. If the plan is rejected, the trustee returns the payments to the debtor.

Only the bankruptcy court has the authority to confirm or reject a plan of payment. Creditors have no right to vote on it. However, to confirm a plan, the court must ensure that:

- The creditors have the opportunity to voice their objections at a hearing;

- All of the unsecured creditors receive at least as much as they would have if the bankruptcy estate had been liquidated under Chapter 7;

- The plan is feasible and the bankrupt will be able to make the promised payments;

- The plan does not extend beyond three years without good reason and in no event lasts longer than five years; and

- The debtor is acting in good faith, making a reasonable effort to pay obligations.

Discharge

Once confirmed, a plan is binding on all creditors whether they like it or not. **The debtor is washed clean of all pre-petition debts except those provided for in the plan, but, unlike Chapter 7, the debts are not *permanently* discharged.** If the debtor violates the plan, all of the debts are revived, and the court may either dismiss the case or convert it to a liquidation proceeding under Chapter 7. The debts become permanently discharged only when the bankrupt fully complies with the plan.

Note, however, that any debtor who has received a discharge under Chapter 7 or 11 within the prior four years, or under Chapter 13 within the prior two years, is not eligible under Chapter 13.

If the debtor's circumstances change, the debtor, the trustee, or unsecured creditors can ask the court to modify the plan. Most such requests come from debtors whose income has declined. However, if the debtor's income rises, the creditors or the trustee can ask that payments increase, too.

Chapter Conclusion

Whenever an individual or organization incurs more debts than it can pay in a timely fashion, everyone loses. The debtor loses control of his assets and the creditors lose money. Bankruptcy laws cannot create assets where there are none (or not enough), but they can ensure that the debtor's assets, however limited, are fairly divided between the debtor and creditors. Any bankruptcy system that accomplishes this goal must be deemed a success. Is the U.S. Bankruptcy Code fair?

EXAM REVIEW

This chart sets out the important elements of each bankruptcy chapter.

	Chapter 7	Chapter 11	Chapter 13
Objective	Liquidation	Reorganization	Consumer reorganization
Who May Use It	Individual or organization	Individual or organization	Individual
Type of Petition	Voluntary or involuntary	Voluntary or involuntary	Only voluntary
Administration of Bankruptcy Estate	Trustee	Debtor in possession (trustee selected only if debtor is unable to serve)	Trustee
Selection of Trustee	Creditors have right to elect trustee; otherwise, U.S. Trustee makes appointment	Usually no trustee	Appointed by U.S. Trustee
Participation in Formulation of Plan	No plan is filed	Both creditors and debtor can propose plans	Only debtor can propose a plan
Creditor Approval of Plan	Creditors do not vote	Creditors vote on plan, but court may approve plan without the creditors' support	Creditors do not vote on plan
Impact on Debtor's Post-petition Income	Not affected; debtor keeps all future earnings	Must contribute toward payment of pre-petition debts	Must contribute toward payment of pre-petition debts

EXAM Strategy

1. Question: Mark Milbank's custom furniture business was unsuccessful, so he repeatedly borrowed money from his wife and her father. He promised that the loans would enable him to spend more time with his family. Instead, he spent more time in bed with his next-door neighbor. After the divorce, his ex-wife and her father demanded repayment of the loans. Milbank filed for protection under Chapter 13. What could his ex-wife and her father do to help their chances of being repaid?

Strategy: First ask yourself what kind of creditor they are: secured or unsecured. Then think about what creditors can do to get special treatment. (See the "Result" at the end of this section.)

EXAM Strategy

2. After a jury ordered actor Kim Basinger to pay $8 million for violating a movie contract, she filed for bankruptcy protection, claiming $5 million in assets and $11 million in liabilities. Under which Chapter should she file? Why?

Strategy: Look at the requirements for each Chapter. Was Basinger eligible for Chapter 13? What would be the advantages and disadvantages of Chapters 7 and 11? (See the "Result" at the end of this section.)

1. Result: The father and the ex-wife were unsecured creditors who, as a class, come last on the priority list. The court granted their request not to discharge their loans on the grounds that Milbank had acted in bad faith.

2. Result: Basinger was not eligible to file under Chapter 13 because she had debts of $11 million. She first filed under Chapter 11 in a effort to retain some of her assets, but then her creditors would not approve her plan of reorganization, so she converted to liquidation under Chapter 7.

MULTIPLE-CHOICE QUESTIONS

1. **CPA QUESTION** A voluntary petition filed under the liquidation provisions of Chapter 7 of the federal Bankruptcy Code:

   (a) is not available to a corporation unless it has previously filed a petition under the reorganization provisions of Chapter 11 of the Code.

   (b) automatically stays collection actions against the debtor **except** by secured creditors.

   (c) will be dismissed unless the debtor has 12 or more unsecured creditors whose claims total at least $5,000.

   (d) does **not** require the debtor to show that the debtor's liabilities exceed the fair market value of assets.

2. **CPA QUESTION** Decal Corp. incurred substantial operating losses for the past three years. Unable to meet its current obligations, Decal filed a petition of reorganization under Chapter 11 of the federal Bankruptcy Code. Which of the following statements is correct?

   (a) A creditors' committee, if appointed, will consist of unsecured creditors.

   (b) The court must appoint a trustee to manage Decal's affairs.

   (c) Decal may continue in business only with the approval of a trustee.

   (d) The creditors' committee must select a trustee to manage Decal's affairs.

3. **CPA QUESTION** Unger owes a total of $150,000 to eight unsecured creditors and one fully secured creditor. Quincy is one of the unsecured creditors and is owed $32,000. Quincy has filed a petition against Unger under the liquidation provisions of Chapter 7 of the federal Bankruptcy Code. Unger has been unable to pay debts as they become due. Unger's liabilities exceed Unger's assets. Unger has filed papers opposing the bankruptcy petition. Which of the following statements regarding Quincy's petition is correct?

   (a) It will be dismissed because the secured creditor failed to join in the filing of the petition.

   (b) It will be dismissed because three unsecured creditors must join in the filing of the petition.

   (c) It will be granted because Unger's liabilities exceed Unger's assets.

   (d) It will be granted because Unger is unable to pay Unger's debts as they become due.

4. Dale is in bankruptcy proceedings under Chapter 13. Which of the following statements is true?

   (a) His debtors must have filed an involuntary petition.

   (b) His unsecured creditors will be worse off than if he had filed under Chapter 7.

   (c) All of his debts are discharged as soon as the court approves his plan.

   (d) His creditors have an opportunity to voice objections to his plan.

5. Grass Co. is in bankruptcy proceedings under Chapter 11. _____ serves as trustee. In the case of _____ the court can approve a plan of reorganization over the objections of the creditors.

   (a) The debtor in possession; a cramdown

   (b) A person appointed by the U.S. Trustee; fraud

   (c) The head of the creditors' committee; reaffirmation

   (d) The U.S. Trustee; voidable preference

ESSAY QUESTIONS

1. James, the owner of an auto parts store, told his employee, Rickey, to clean and paint some tires in the basement. Highly flammable gasoline fumes accumulated in the poorly ventilated space. James threw a firecracker into the basement as a joke, intending only to startle Rickey. Sparks from the firecracker caused an explosion and fire that severely burned him. Rickey filed a personal injury suit against James for $1 million. Is this debt dischargeable under Chapter 7?

2. Mary Price went for a consultation about a surgical procedure to remove abdominal fat. When Robert Britton met with her, he wore a name tag that identified him as a doctor, and was addressed as "doctor" by the nurse. Britton then examined Price, touching her stomach and showing her where the incision would be made. But Britton was the office manager, not a doctor. Although a doctor actually performed the surgery on Price, Britton was present. It turned out that the doctor left a tube in Price's body at the site of the incision. The area became infected, requiring corrective surgery. A jury awarded Price $275,000 in damages in a suit against Britton. He subsequently filed a Chapter 7 bankruptcy petition. Is this judgment dischargeable in bankruptcy court?

3. **YOU BE THE JUDGE WRITING PROBLEM** Lydia D'Ettore received a degree in computer programming at the DeVry Institute of Technology, with a grade point average of 2.51. To finance her education, she borrowed $20,516.52 from a federal student loan program. After graduation, she could not find a job in her field, so she went to work as a clerk at an annual salary of $12,500. D'Ettore and her daughter lived with her parents free of charge. After setting aside $50 a month in savings and paying bills that included $233 for a new car (a Suzuki Samurai) and $50 for jewelry from Zales, her disposable income was $125 per month. D'Ettore asked the bankruptcy court to discharge the debts she owed DeVry for her education. Did the debts to the DeVry Institute impose an undue hardship on D'Ettore? **Argument for D'Ettore:** Lydia D'Ettore lives at home with her parents. Even so, her disposable income is a meager $125 a month. She would have to spend every single penny of her disposable income for nearly 15 years to pay back her $20,500 debt to DeVry. That would be an undue hardship. **Argument for the Creditors:** The U.S. government guaranteed D'Ettore's loan. Therefore, if the court discharges it, the American taxpayer will have to pay the bill. Why should taxpayers subsidize an irresponsible student? D'Ettore must also stop buying new cars and jewelry. And why should the government pay her debts while she saves money every month?

4. Dr. Ibrahim Khan caused an automobile accident in which a fellow physician, Dolly Yusufji, became a quadriplegic. Khan signed a contract for the lifetime support of Yusufji. When he refused to make payments under the contract, she sued him and obtained a judgment for $1,205,400. Khan filed a Chapter 11 petition. At the time of the bankruptcy hearing, five years after the accident, Khan had not paid Yusufji anything. She was dependent on a motorized wheelchair; he drove a Rolls-Royce. Is Khan's debt dischargeable under Chapter 11?

5. After filing for bankruptcy, Yvonne Brown sought permission of the court to reaffirm a $6,000 debt to her credit union. The debt was unsecured, and she was under no obligation to pay it. The credit union had published the following notice in its newsletter:

> If you are thinking about filing bankruptcy, THINK about the long-term implications. This action, filing bankruptcy, closes the door on TOMORROW. Having no credit means no ability to purchase cars, houses, credit cards. Look into the future—no loans for the education of your children.

Should the court approve Brown's reaffirmation?

Discussion Questions

1. **ETHICS** On November 5, Hawes, Inc., a small subcontractor, opened an account with Basic Corp., a supplier of construction materials. Hawes promised to pay its bills within 30 days of purchase. Although Hawes purchased a substantial quantity of goods on credit from Basic, it made few payments on the accounts until the following March,

when it paid Basic over $21,000. On May 14, Hawes filed a voluntary petition under Chapter 7. Does the bankruptcy trustee have a right to recover this payment? Is it fair to Hawes's other creditors if Basic is allowed to keep the $21,000 payment?

2. Look on the web for your state's rules on exempt property. Compared with other states and the federal government, is your state generous or stingy with exemptions? In considering a new bankruptcy statute, Congress struggled mightily over whether or not to permit state exemptions at all. Is it fair for exemptions to vary by state? Why should someone in one state fare better than his her neighbor across the state line?

3. Some states permit debtors an unlimited exemption on their homes. Is it fair for bankrupts to be allowed to keep multimillion dollar homes while their creditors remain unpaid? But other states allow as little as $5,000. Should bankrupts be thrown out on the street? What amount is fair?

4. What about the rules regarding repeated bankruptcy filings? Debtors cannot obtain a discharge under Chapter 7 within eight years of a prior filing. Under Chapter 13, no discharge is available within four years of a prior Chapter 7 or 11 filing and within two years of a prior Chapter 13 filing. Are these rules too onerous, too lenient, or just right?

5. A bankrupt who owns a house has the option of either paying the mortgage or losing his home. The only advantage of bankruptcy is that his debt to the bank is discharged. The U.S. House of Representatives passed a bill permitting a bankruptcy judge to adjust the terms of mortgages to aid debtors in holding onto their houses. Proponents argued that this change in the law would reduce foreclosures and stabilize the national housing market. Opponents said that it was not fair to reward homeowners for being irresponsible. How would you vote if you were in the Senate?

6. In the *Grisham* case, the debtor had virtually no income but owed about $200,000 in debts that could not be discharged. What kind of fresh start is that? Should limits be placed on the total debt that cannot be discharged? Is the list of non-dischargeable debts appropriate?

Agency & Employment

CHAPTER 16

AGENCY LAW

The good news is that Mac's parents gave him a car when he went off to college. (An SUV, which he called "the Tank.") The bad news is that his friends were constantly borrowing it. And you know how these things go.

© Stas Volik/Shutterstock.com

One night, James borrowed the Tank to drive a friend to the airport. On the way home, he rear-ended a Mini Cooper at a stoplight. Although there was no damage to the Tank, the Mini was totaled. Then Peter borrowed the Tank to drive to work. While at work, he and Teddy went out to buy pizza for the office. When Peter hit a curb, the airbag deployed and broke Teddy's nose. So Mac had to take the Tank to the repair shop. While the car was there overnight, one of the repair people got drunk, took the SUV out for a joy ride, and banged it up. Who is liable for all this damage?

The Mini Cooper: Mac is liable only if James was acting as his agent. But in this case, James was not doing Mac any favors, so he was not his agent. If, on the other hand, James had agreed to pick up some food for Mac, then Mac would be liable for the accident.

> The good news is that Mac's parents gave him a car when he went off to college. The bad news is that his friends were constantly borrowing it.

Teddy's nose: Mac is clearly not liable because Peter was not his agent. What about Peter's employer? If Peter was acting within the scope of his employment, his employer would be liable. Was buying pizza for the office within this scope? Probably.

The joy ride: The repair shop owner is liable even though the drunk worker was clearly violating company policy. He was on duty at the time, and it is the garage owner's fault for hiring such an unreliable worker.

Thus far, this book has primarily dealt with issues of individual responsibility: what happens if *you* knock someone down or *you* sign an agreement? Agency law, on the other hand, is concerned with your responsibility for the actions of others. What happens if your agent assaults someone or signs a contract in your name? Agency law presents a significant trade-off: if you do everything yourself, you have control over the result. But the size and scope of your business (and your life) will be severely limited. Once you hire other people, you can accomplish a great deal more, but your risks increase immensely. Your agents may violate your instructions, and still you could be liable for what they have done. Although it might be safer to do everything yourself, that is not a practical decision for most business owners (or most people). The alternative is to hire carefully and to limit the risks as much as possible by understanding the law of agency.

CREATING AN AGENCY RELATIONSHIP

Let us begin with two important definitions:

- **Principal:** A person who has someone else acting for him.

- **Agent:** A person who acts for someone else.

Principals have substantial liability for the actions of their agents.[1] Therefore, disputes about whether an agency relationship exists are not mere legal quibbles but important issues with potentially profound financial consequences.

In an agency relationship, someone (the agent) agrees to perform a task for, and under the control of, someone else (the principal). **To create an agency relationship, there must be:**

- A **principal** and

- An **agent**

- Who mutually **consent** that the agent will act on behalf of the principal and

- Be subject to the principal's **control**

- Thereby creating a **fiduciary** relationship.

Principal
In an agency relationship, the person for whom an agent is acting.

Agent
In an agency relationship, the person who is acting on behalf of a principal.

Consent

To establish consent, the principal must ask the agent to do something, and the agent must agree. In the most straightforward example, you ask a neighbor to walk your dog, and she agrees. Matters were more complicated, however, when Steven James met some friends one evening at a restaurant. During the two hours he was there, he drank four to six beers. (It is probably a bad sign that he cannot remember how many.) From then on, one misfortune piled upon another. After leaving the restaurant at about 7:00 p.m., James sped down a highway and crashed into a car that had stalled on the road, thereby killing the driver. James told the police at the scene that he had not seen the parked car (another bad sign). Evidently, James's lawyer was not as perceptive as the police in recognizing drunkenness. In a misguided attempt to help his client, James's lawyer took him to the local hospital for a blood test. Unfortunately, the test confirmed that James had indeed been drunk at the time of the accident.

The attorney knew that if this evidence was admitted at trial, his client would soon be receiving free room and board from the Massachusetts Department of Corrections. So at trial, the lawyer argued that the blood test was protected by the client-attorney privilege

---

[1]The word "principal" is always used when referring to a person. It is not to be confused with the word "principle," which refers to a fundamental idea.

because the hospital had been his agent and therefore a member of the defense team. The court disagreed, however, holding that the hospital employees were not agents for the lawyer because they had not consented to act in that role.

The court upheld James's conviction of murder in the first degree by reason of extreme atrocity or cruelty.[2]

Control

Principals are liable for the acts of their agents because they exercise control over the agents. If principals direct their agents to commit an act, it seems fair to hold the principal liable when that act causes harm. How would you apply that rule to the following situation?

William Stanford was an employee of the Agency for International Development. While on his way home to Pakistan to spend the holidays with his family, his plane was hijacked and taken to Iran, where he was killed. Stanford had originally purchased a ticket on Northwest Airlines but had traded it for a seat on Kuwait Airways (KA). The airlines had an agreement permitting passengers to exchange tickets from one to the other. Stanford's widow sued Northwest on the theory that KA was Northwest's agent. The court found, however, that no agency relationship existed because Northwest had no control over KA.[3] Northwest did not tell KA how to fly planes or handle terrorists; therefore, it should not be liable when KA made fatal errors. Not only must an agent and principal consent to an agency relationship, but the principal also must have control over the agent.

Fiduciary Relationship

In a **fiduciary relationship**, a trustee acts for the benefit of the beneficiary, always putting the interests of the beneficiary before his own. A fiduciary relationship is a special relationship with high standards. The beneficiary places special confidence in the fiduciary who, in turn, is obligated to act in good faith and candor, putting his own needs second. The purpose of a fiduciary relationship is for one person to benefit another. **Agents have a fiduciary duty to their principals.**

All three elements—consent, control, and a fiduciary duty—are necessary to create an agency relationship. In some relationships, for example, there might be a *fiduciary duty* but no *control*. A trustee of a trust must act for the benefit of the beneficiaries, but the beneficiaries have no right to control the trustee. Therefore, a trustee is not an agent of the beneficiaries. *Consent* is present in every contractual relationship, but that does not necessarily mean that the two parties are agent and principal. If Horace sells his car to Lily, they both expect to benefit under the contract, but neither has a *fiduciary duty* to the other and neither *controls* the other, so there is no agency relationship.

Elements Not Required for an Agency Relationship

Consent, control, and a fiduciary relationship are necessary to establish an agency relationship. The following elements are *not* required:

Equal dignities rule

If an agent is empowered to enter into a contract that must be in writing, then the appointment of the agent must also be written.

- **A Written Agreement.** In most cases, an agency agreement does not have to be in writing. An oral understanding is valid, except in one circumstance—the **equal dignities rule**. According to this rule, if an agent is empowered to enter into a contract that must be in writing, then the appointment of the agent must also be written. For example, under the statute of frauds, a contract for the sale of land is unenforceable unless in writing, so the agency agreement to sell land must also be in writing.

- **A Formal Agreement.** The principal and agent need not agree formally that they have an agency relationship. They do not even have to think the word "agent." So long as they act like an agent and a principal, the law will treat them as such.

---

[2]*Commonwealth v. James*, 427 Mass. 312, 693 N.E.2nd 148, 1998 Mass. LEXIS 175. (S.J.C. MA, 1998)
[3]*Stanford v. Kuwait Airways Corp.*, 648 F. Supp. 1158, 1986 U.S. Dist. LEXIS 18880 (S.D.N.Y. 1986).

- *Compensation.* An agency relationship need not meet all the standards of contract law. For example, a contract is not valid without consideration, but an agency agreement is valid *even if the agent is not paid.*

DUTIES OF AGENTS TO PRINCIPALS

Agents owe a fiduciary duty to their principals. There are four elements to this duty.

Duty of Loyalty

An agent has a fiduciary duty to act loyally for the principal's benefit in all matters connected with the agency relationship.[4] The agent has an obligation to put the principal first, to strive to accomplish the principal's goals. As the following case illustrates, this duty applies to all employees, no matter how lowly.

OTSUKA V. POLO RALPH LAUREN CORPORATION

2007 U.S. DIST. LEXIS 86523
United States District Court for the Northern District of California, 2007

Facts: Justin Kiser and Germania worked together at a Ralph Lauren Polo store in San Francisco. After she left the job, he let her buy clothing using merchandise credits made out to nonexistent people. He also let her use his employee discount. Not surprisingly, both of these activities were against store policies. Polo sued Kiser, alleging that he had violated his duty of loyalty.

Kiser filed a motion to dismiss on the grounds that he was such a low-level employee that he did not owe a duty of loyalty to Polo.

Issue: *Do all employees owe a duty of loyalty to their employer?*

Excerpts from Judge Illston's Decision: Kiser moves to dismiss this cause of action, contending that a lower-level employee owes no fiduciary duty to his employer. In response, [Polo] argues that there is a duty of loyalty akin to a fiduciary duty that all employees owe to their employers.

The Court agrees with Kiser that the cases cited by [Polo] address the duty of loyalty with respect to higher-ranking employees than Kiser, who worked as a sales clerk in a retail store. [But t]he Third Restatement provides that all employees are agents, and that "[a]s agents, all employees owe a duty of loyalty to their employers." Restatement (Third) of Agency §1.01. This is true regardless of how ministerial or routinized a work assignment may be.

Accordingly, the Court DENIES Kiser's motion to dismiss the cause of action.

The various components of the duty of loyalty follow.

Outside Benefits

An agent may not receive profits unless the principal knows and approves. Suppose that Hope is an employee of the agency Big Egos and Talents, Inc. (BEAT). She has been representing Will Smith in his latest movie negotiations.[5] Smith often drives her to meetings in his new Maybach. He is so thrilled that she has arranged for him to star in the new movie

---

[4]Restatement (Third) of Agency §8.01.
[5]Do not be confused by the fact that Hope works as an agent for movie stars. As an employee of BEAT, her duty is to the company. She is an agent of BEAT, and BEAT works for the celebrities.

Little Men that he buys her a Maybach. Can Hope keep this generous gift? Only with BEAT's permission. She must tell BEAT about the Maybach; the company may then take the vehicle itself or allow her to keep it.

Confidential Information

The ability to keep secrets is important in any relationship, but especially a fiduciary relationship. Agents can neither disclose nor use for their own benefit any confidential information they acquire during their agency. As the following case shows, this duty continues even after the agency relationship ends.

ABKCO MUSIC, INC. v. HARRISONGS MUSIC, LTD.

722 F.2d 988, 1983 U.S. App. LEXIS 15562
United States Court of Appeals for the Second Circuit, 1983

Facts: Bright Tunes Music Corp. (Bright Tunes) owned the copyright to the song "He's So Fine." The company sued George Harrison, a Beatle, alleging that the Harrison composition "My Sweet Lord" copied "He's So Fine." At the time the suit was filed, Allen B. Klein handled the business affairs of the Beatles.

Klein (representing Harrison) met with the president of Bright Tunes to discuss possible settlement of the copyright lawsuit. Klein suggested that Harrison might be interested in purchasing the copyright to "He's So Fine." Shortly thereafter, Klein's management contract with the Beatles expired. Without telling Harrison, Klein began negotiating with Bright Tunes to purchase the copyright to "He's So Fine" for himself. To advance these negotiations, Klein gave Bright Tunes information about royalty income for "My Sweet Lord"—information that he had gained as Harrison's agent.

The trial judge in the copyright case ultimately found that Harrison had infringed the copyright on "He's So Fine" and assessed damages of $1,599,987. After the trial, Klein purchased the "He's So Fine" copyright from Bright Tunes and with it, the right to recover from Harrison for the breach of copyright.

Issue: *Did Klein violate his fiduciary duty to Harrison by using confidential information after the agency relationship terminated?*

Excerpts from Judge Pierce's Decision: There is no doubt that the relationship between Harrison and [Klein] prior to the termination of the management agreement was that of principal and agent, and that the relationship was fiduciary in nature. [A]n agent has a duty not to use confidential knowledge acquired in his employment in competition with his principal. This duty exists as well after the employment is terminated as during its continuance. On the other hand, use of information based on general business knowledge or gleaned from general business experience is not covered by the rule, and the former agent is permitted to compete with his former principal in reliance on such general publicly available information. The evidence presented herein is not at all convincing that the information imparted to Bright Tunes by Klein was publicly available.

While the initial attempt to purchase [the copyright to "He's So Fine"] was several years removed from the eventual purchase on [Klein]'s own account, we are not of the view that such a fact rendered [Klein] unfettered in the later negotiations. Taking all of these circumstances together, we agree that [Klein's] conduct did not meet the standard required of him as a former fiduciary.

To listen to the two songs involved in this case, google "benedict copyright."

Ethics Klein was angry that the Beatles had failed to renew his management contract. Was it reasonable for him to think that he owed no duty to the principal who had fired him? Why kind of world would it be if everyone acted like Klein? Why would George Harrison prefer to owe money to Bright Tunes rather than to Klein?

Competition with the Principal

Agents are not allowed to compete with their principal in any matter within the scope of the agency business. If Allen Klein had purchased the "He's So Fine" copyright while he was George Harrison's agent, he would have committed an additional sin against the agency relationship. Owning song rights was clearly part of the agency business, so Klein could not make such purchases without Harrison's consent. Once the agency relationship ends, however, so does the rule against competition. Klein was entitled to buy the "He's So Fine" copyright after the agency relationship ended (so long as he did not use confidential information).

Conflict of Interest Between Two Principals

Unless otherwise agreed, an agent may not act for two principals whose interests conflict. Suppose Travis represents both director Steven Spielberg and actor Amy Adams. Spielberg is casting the title role in his new movie, *Nancy Drew: Girl Detective*, a role that Adams covets. Travis cannot represent these two clients when they are negotiating with each other unless they both know about the conflict and agree to ignore it. The following example illustrates the dangers of acting for two principals at once.

EXAM Strategy

Question: The Sisters of Charity was an order of nuns in New Jersey. Faced with growing health care and retirement costs, they decided to sell off a piece of property. The nuns soon found, however, that the world is not always a charitable place. They agreed to sell the land to Linpro for nearly $10 million. But before the deal closed, Linpro signed a contract to resell the property to Sammis for $34 million. So, you say, the sisters made a bad deal. There is no law against that. But it turned out that the nuns' law firm also represented Linpro. Their lawyer at the firm, Peter Berkley, never told the sisters about the deal between Linpro and Sammis. Was that the charitable—or legal—thing to do?

Strategy: Always begin by asking if there is an agency relationship. Was there consent, control, and a fiduciary relationship? *Consent*: Berkley had agreed to work for the nuns. *Control*: they told him what he was to do—sell the land. The purpose of a *fiduciary relationship* is for one person to benefit another. The point of the nuns' relationship with Berkley is for him to help them. Once you know there is an agency relationship, then ask if the agent has violated his duty of loyalty.

Result: You know that an agent is not permitted to act for two principals whose interests conflict. Here, Berkley is working for the nuns, who want the highest possible price for their land, and Linpro, who wants the lowest price. Berkley has violated his duty of loyalty.

Secretly Dealing with the Principal

If a principal hires an agent to arrange a transaction, the agent may not become a party to the transaction without the principal's permission. Matt Damon became an overnight sensation after starring in the movie *Good Will Hunting*. Suppose that he hired Trang to read scripts for him. Unbeknownst to Damon, Trang has written her own script, which she thinks would be ideal for him. She may not sell it to him without revealing that she wrote it herself. Damon may be perfectly happy to buy Trang's script, but he has the right, as her principal, to know that she is the person selling it.

Appropriate Behavior

An agent may not engage in inappropriate behavior that reflects badly on the principal. This rule applies even to *off-duty* conduct. For example, a coed trio of flight attendants went wild at a hotel bar in London. They kissed and caressed each other, showed off their underwear, and poured alcohol down their trousers. The airline fired two of the employees and gave a warning letter to the third.

Other Duties of an Agent

Before Taylor left for a five-week trip to England, he hired Angie to rent his vacation house. Angie never got around to listing his house on the Multiple Listing Service used by all the area brokers, nor did she post it on the Web herself, but when the Fords contacted her looking for rental housing, she did show them Taylor's place. They offered to rent it for $750 per month.

Angie called Taylor in England to tell him. He responded that he would not accept less than $850 a month, which Angie thought the Fords would be willing to pay. He told Angie to call back if there was any problem. The Fords decided that they would go no higher than $800 a month. Although Taylor had told Angie that he could not receive text messages in England, she texted him the Fords' counteroffer. Taylor never received it, so he never responded. When the Fords pressed Angie for an answer, she said she could not get in touch with Taylor. Not until Taylor returned home did he learn that the Fords had rented another house. Did Angie violate any of the duties that agents owe to their principals?

Duty to Obey Instructions

An agent must obey her principal's instructions unless the principal directs her to behave illegally or unethically. Taylor instructed Angie to call him if the Fords rejected the offer. When Angie failed to do so, she violated her duty to obey instructions. If, however, Taylor had asked her to say that the house's basement was dry when in fact it looked like a swamp every spring, Angie would be under no obligation to follow those illegal instructions.

Duty of Care

An agent has a duty to act with reasonable care. In other words, an agent must act as a reasonable person would, under the circumstances. A reasonable person would not have texted Taylor while he was in England.

Under some circumstances, an agent is held to a higher—or lower—standard than usual. **An agent with special skills is held to a higher standard because she is expected to use those skills.** A trained real estate agent should know enough to post all listings on the Web.

But suppose Taylor had asked his neighbor, Jed, to help him sell the house. Jed is not a trained real estate agent, and he is not being paid, which makes him a *gratuitous agent*. A gratuitous agent is held to a lower standard because he is doing his principal a favor and, as the old saying goes, you get what you pay for—up to a point. **Gratuitous agents are liable if they commit *gross* negligence, but not *ordinary* negligence.** If Jed, as a gratuitous agent, texted Taylor an important message because he forgot that Taylor could not receive these messages in England, he would not be liable for that ordinary negligence. But if Taylor had, just that day, sent Jed an email complaining that he could not get any text messages, Jed would be liable for gross negligence and a violation of his duty.

Duty to Provide Information

An agent has a duty to provide the principal with all information in her possession that she has reason to believe the principal wants to know. She also has a duty to provide accurate information. Angie knew that the Fords had counteroffered for $800 a month. She had a duty to pass this information on to Taylor.

EXAM Strategy

Question: Jonah tells his friend Derek that he would like to go parasailing. Derek is very enthusiastic and suggests that they try an outfit called Wind Beneath Your Wings because he has heard good things about them. Derek offers to arrange everything. He makes a reservation, puts the $600 fee on his credit card, and picks Jonah up to drive him to the Wings location. What a friend! But the day does not turn out as Jonah had hoped. While he is soaring up in the air over the Pacific Ocean, his sail springs a leak, he goes plummeting into the sea and breaks both legs. During his recuperation in the hospital, he learns that Wings is unlicensed. He also sees an ad for Wings offering parasailing for only $350. And Derek is listed in the ad as one of the company's owners. Is Derek an agent for Jonah? Has he violated his fiduciary responsibility?

Strategy: There are three issues to consider in answering this question: (1) Was there an agency relationship? This requires consent, control, and a fiduciary relationship. (2) Is anything missing—does it matter if the agent is unpaid or the contract is not in writing? (3) Has the agent fulfilled his duties?

Result: There is an agency relationship: Derek had agreed to help Jonah; it was Jonah who set the goal for the relationship (parasailing); the purpose of this relationship is for one person to benefit another. It does not matter if Derek was not paid or the agreement not written. Derek has violated his duty to exercise due care. He should not have taken Jonah to an unlicensed company. He has also violated his duty to provide information: he should have told Jonah the true cost for the lessons and also revealed that he was a principal of the company. And he violated his duty of loyalty when he worked for two principals whose interests were in conflict.

Principal's Remedies when the Agent Breaches a Duty

A principal has three potential remedies when an agent breaches her duty:

- The principal can recover from the agent any **damages** the breach has caused. Thus, if Taylor can rent his house for only $600 a month instead of the $800 the Fords offered, Angie would be liable for $2,400—$200 a month for one year.

- If an agent breaches the duty of loyalty, he must turn over to the principal any **profits** he has earned as a result of his wrongdoing. Thus, after Klein violated his duty of loyalty to Harrison, he forfeited profits he would have earned from the copyright of "He's So Fine."

- If the agent has violated her duty of loyalty, the principal may **rescind** the transaction. When Trang sold a script to her principal, Matt Damon, without telling him that she was the author, she violated her duty of loyalty. Damon could rescind the contract to buy the script.[6]

---

[6]A principal can rescind his contract with an agent who has violated her duty, but, as we shall see later in the chapter, the principal might not be able to rescind a contract with a third party when the agent misbehaves.

DUTIES OF PRINCIPALS TO AGENTS

In a typical agency relationship, the agent agrees to perform tasks for the principal, and the principal agrees to pay the agent. The range of tasks undertaken by an agent is limited only by the imagination of the principal. Because the agent's job can be so varied, the law needs to define an agent's duties carefully. The role of the principal, on the other hand, is typically less complicated—often little more than paying the agent as required by the agreement. Thus, the law enumerates fewer duties for the principal. Primarily, the principal must reimburse the agent for reasonable expenses and cooperate with the agent in performing agency tasks. The respective duties of agents and principals can be summarized as follows:

Duties of Agents to Principals	Duty of Principals to Agents
Duty of loyalty	Duty to compensate as provided by the agreement
Duty to obey instructions	Duty to reimburse for reasonable expenses
Duty of care	Duty to cooperate
Duty to provide information	

As a general rule, the principal must indemnify (i.e., reimburse) the agent for any expenses she has reasonably incurred. These reimbursable expenses fall into three categories:

- **A principal must indemnify an agent for any expenses or damages reasonably incurred in carrying out his agency responsibilities.** For example, Peace Baptist Church of Birmingham, Alabama, asked its pastor to buy land for a new church. He paid part of the purchase price out of his own pocket, but the church refused to reimburse him. Although the pastor lost in church, he won in court.[7]

- **A principal must indemnify an agent for tort claims brought by a third party if the principal authorized the agent's behavior and the agent did not realize he was committing a tort.** Marisa owns all the apartment buildings on Elm Street, except one. She hires Rajiv to manage the units and tells him that, under the terms of the leases, she has the right to ask guests to leave if a party becomes too rowdy. But she forgets to tell Rajiv that she does not own one of the buildings, which happens to house a college sorority. One night, when the sorority is having a rambunctious party, Rajiv hustles over and starts ejecting the noisy guests. The sorority is furious and sues Rajiv for trespass. If the sorority wins its suit against Rajiv, Marisa would have to pay the judgment, plus Rajiv's attorney's fees, because she had told him to quell noisy parties and he did not realize he was trespassing.

- **The principal must indemnify the agent for any liability she incurs from third parties as a result of entering into a contract on the principal's behalf, including attorney's fees and reasonable settlements.** An agent signed a contract to buy cucumbers for Vlasic Food Products Co. to use in making pickles. When the first shipment of cucumbers arrived, Vlasic inspectors found them unsuitable and directed the agent to refuse the shipment. The agent found himself in a pickle when the cucumber farmer sued. The agent notified Vlasic, but the company refused to defend him. He settled

---

[7]*Lauderdale v. Peace Baptist Church of Birmingham*, 246 Ala. 178, 19 So. 2d 538, 1944 Ala. LEXIS 508 (S. Ct. AL, 1944).

the claim himself and, in turn, sued Vlasic. The court ordered Vlasic to reimburse the agent because he had notified them of the suit and had acted reasonably and in good faith.[8]

Duty to Cooperate

Principals have a duty to cooperate with their agent:

- **The principal must furnish the agent with the opportunity to work.** If Lewis agrees to serve as Ida's real estate agent in selling her house, Ida must allow Lewis access to the house. It is unlikely that Lewis will be able to sell the house without taking anyone inside.

- **The principal cannot unreasonably interfere with the agent's ability to accomplish his task.** Ida allows Lewis to show the house, but she refuses to clean it and then makes disparaging comments to prospective purchasers. "I really get tired of living in such a dark, dreary house," she says. "And the neighborhood children are vicious thugs." This behavior would constitute unreasonable interference with an agent.

- **The principal must perform her part of the contract.** Once the agent has successfully completed the task, the principal must pay him, even if the principal has changed her mind and no longer wants the agent to perform. Ida is a 78-year-old widow who has lived alone for many years in a house that she loves. Her asking price is outrageously high. But lo and behold, Lewis finds a couple happy to pay Ida's price. There is only one problem. Ida does not really want to sell. She put her house on the market because she enjoys showing it to all the folks who move to town. She rejects the offer. Now there is a second problem. The contract provided that Lewis would find a willing buyer at the asking price. Because he has done so, Ida must pay his real estate commission even if she does not want to sell her house.

TERMINATING AN AGENCY RELATIONSHIP

Either the agent or the principal can terminate the agency relationship at any time. In addition, the relationship terminates automatically if the principal or agent no longer can perform their required duties or a change in circumstances renders the agency relationship pointless.

Termination by Agent or Principal

The two parties—principal and agent—have three choices in terminating their relationship:

- **Term Agreement.** If the principal and agent agree in advance how long their relationship will last, they have a term agreement. For example:

  - **Time.** Alexandra hires Boris to help her add to her collection of guitars previously owned by rock stars. If they agree that the relationship will last two years, they have a term agreement.

  - **Achieving a Purpose.** The principal and agent can agree that the agency relationship will terminate when the principal's goals have been achieved.

---

[8]*Long v. Vlasic Food Products Co.*, 439 F.2d 229, 1971 U.S. App. LEXIS 11455 (4th Cir. 1971).

406 UNIT 3 *Agency & Employment*

Alexandra and Boris might agree that their relationship will end when Alexandra has purchased 10 guitars.

- **Mutual Agreement.** No matter what the principal and agent agree at the start, they can always change their minds later on, so long as the change is mutual. If Boris and Alexandra originally agree to a two-year term, but Boris decides he wants to go back to business school and Alexandra runs out of money after only one year, they can decide together to terminate the agency.

- **Agency at Will.** If they make no agreement in advance about the term of the agreement, either principal or agent can terminate at any time.

- **Wrongful Termination.** An agency relationship is a personal relationship. Hiring an agent is not like buying a book. You might not care which copy of the book you buy, but you do care which agent you hire. If an agency relationship is not working out, the courts will not force the agent and principal to stay together. **Either party always has the *power* to walk out. They may not, however, have the *right*.** If one party's departure from the agency relationship violates the agreement and causes harm to the other party, the wrongful party must pay damages. Nonetheless, he will be permitted to leave. If Boris has agreed to work for Alexandra for two years but he wants to leave after one, he can leave, provided he pays Alexandra the cost of hiring and training a replacement.

  If the agent is a **gratuitous** agent (i.e., is not being paid), he has both the power and the right to quit any time he wants, regardless of the agency agreement. If Boris is doing this job for Alexandra as a favor, he will not owe her damages when he stops work.

Principal or Agent Can No Longer Perform Required Duties

If the principal or the agent is unable to perform the duties required under the agency agreement, the agreement terminates.

- **If either the agent or the principal fails to obtain (or keep) a license necessary to perform duties under the agency agreement, the agreement ends.** Caleb hires Allegra to represent him in a lawsuit. If she is disbarred, their agency agreement terminates because the agent is no longer allowed in court. Alternatively, if Emil hires Bess to work in his gun shop, their agency relationship terminates when he loses his license to sell firearms.

- **The bankruptcy of the agent or the principal terminates an agency relationship only if it affects their ability to perform.** Bankruptcy rarely interferes with an agent's responsibilities. After all, there is generally no reason why an agent cannot continue to act for the principal whether the agent is rich or poor. If Lewis, the real estate agent, becomes bankrupt, he can continue to represent Ida or anyone else who wants to sell a house. The bankruptcy of a principal is different, however, because after filing for bankruptcy, the principal loses control of his assets. A bankrupt principal may be unable to pay the agent or honor contracts that the agent enters into on his behalf. Therefore, the bankruptcy of a principal is more likely to terminate an agency relationship.

- **An agency relationship terminates upon the death or incapacity of either the principal or the agent.** Agency is a personal relationship, and when the principal dies, the agent cannot act on behalf of a nonexistent person.[9] Of course, a nonexistent person cannot

---

[9]Restatement (Third) of Agency §§3.05, 3.06, 3.07, 3.08.

act either, so the relationship also terminates when the agent dies. Incapacity has the same legal effect because either the principal or the agent is at least temporarily unable to act.

- **If the agent violates her duty of loyalty, the agency agreement automatically terminates.** Agents are appointed to represent the principal's interest; if they fail to do so, there is no point to the relationship. Louisa is negotiating a military procurement contract on behalf of her employer, Missiles R Us, Inc. In the midst of these negotiations, she becomes very friendly with Sam, the government negotiator. One night over drinks, she tells Sam what Missiles' real costs are on the project and the lowest bid it could possibly make. By passing on this confidential information, Louisa has violated her duty of loyalty, and her agency relationship terminates.

Change in Circumstances

After the agency agreement is negotiated, circumstances may change. If these changes are significant enough to undermine the purpose of the agreement, the relationship ends automatically. Andrew hires Melissa to sell his country farm for $100,000. Shortly thereafter, the largest oil reserve in North America is discovered nearby. The farm is now worth 10 times Andrew's asking price. Melissa's authority terminates automatically.

Other changes in circumstance that affect an agency agreement are:

- **Change of Law.** If the agent's responsibilities become illegal, the agency agreement terminates. Oscar has hired Marta to ship him succulent avocados from California's Imperial Valley. Before she sends the shipment, Mediterranean fruit flies are discovered, and all fruits and vegetables in California are quarantined. The agency agreement terminates because it is now illegal to ship the California avocados.

- **Loss or Destruction of Subject Matter.** Andrew hired Damian to sell his Palm Beach condominium, but before Damian could even measure the living room, Andrew's creditors attached the condo. Damian is no longer authorized to sell the real estate because Andrew has "lost" the subject matter of his agency agreement with Damian.

Effect of Termination

Once an agency relationship ends, the agent no longer has the authority to act for the principal. If she continues to act, she is liable to the principal for any damages he incurs as a result. The Mediterranean fruit fly quarantine ended Marta's agency. If she sends Oscar the avocados anyway and he is fined for possession of a fruit fly, Marta must pay the fine.

The agent loses her authority to act, but some of the duties of both the principal and agent continue even after the relationship ends:

- **Principal's Duty to Indemnify Agent.** Oscar must reimburse Marta for expenses she incurred before the agency ended. If Marta accumulated mileage on her car during her search for the perfect avocado, Oscar must pay her for gasoline and depreciation. But he owes her nothing for her expenses after the agency relationship ends.

- **Confidential Information.** Remember the "He's So Fine" case earlier in the chapter? George Harrison's agent used confidential information to negotiate on his own behalf the purchase of the "He's So Fine" copyright. An agent is not entitled to use confidential information even after the agency relationship terminates.

LIABILITY

Thus far, this chapter has dealt with the relationship between principals and agents. Although an agent can dramatically increase his principal's ability to accomplish her goals, an agency relationship also dramatically increases the risk of legal liability to third parties. A principal may be liable in tort for any harm the agent causes and also liable in contract for agreements that the agent signs. Indeed, once a principal hires an agent, she may be liable to third parties for his acts, even if he disobeys instructions. Agents may also find themselves liable to third parties.

PRINCIPAL'S LIABILITY FOR CONTRACTS

Many agents are hired for the primary purpose of entering into contracts on behalf of their principals. Salespeople, for example, may do little other than sign on the dotted line. Most of the time, the principal wants to be liable on these contracts. But even if the principal is unhappy (because, say, the agent has disobeyed orders), the principal generally cannot rescind contracts entered into by the agent. After all, if someone is going to be penalized, it should be the principal who hired the disobedient agent, not the innocent third party.

The principal is liable for the acts of an agent if (1) the agent had *authority*, or (2) the principal *ratifies* the acts of the agent.

To say that the principal is "liable for the acts" of the agent means that the principal is as responsible as if he had performed the acts himself. It also means that the principal is liable for statements the agent makes to a third party. Thus, when a lawyer lied on an application for malpractice insurance, the insurance company was allowed to void the policy for the entire law firm. It was as if the firm had lied. In addition, the principal is deemed to know any information that the agent knows or should know.

Authority

A principal is bound by the acts of an agent if the agent has authority. There are three types of authority: express, implied, and apparent. Express and implied authority are categories of actual authority because the agent is truly authorized to act for the principal. In apparent authority, the principal is liable for the agent's actions even though the agent was *not* authorized.

Express Authority

The principal grants **express authority** by words or conduct that, reasonably interpreted, cause the agent to believe the principal desires her to act on the principal's account.[10] In other words, the principal asks the agent to do something and the agent does it. Craig calls his stockbroker, Alice, and asks her to buy 100 shares of Banshee Corp. for his account. She has *express authority* to carry out this transaction.

Implied Authority

Unless otherwise agreed, authority to conduct a transaction includes authority to do acts that are reasonably necessary to accomplish it.[11] The principal does not have to micromanage the agent. David has recently inherited a house from his grandmother. He hires Nell to auction off the house and its contents. She hires an auctioneer, advertises the event, rents a tent,

[10]Restatement (Third) of Agency §2.01.
[11]Restatement (Third) of Agency §2.02.

and generally does everything necessary to conduct a successful auction. After withholding her expenses, she sends the tidy balance to David. Totally outraged, he calls her on the phone, "How dare you hire an auctioneer and rent a tent? I never gave you permission! I absolutely *refuse* to pay these expenses!"

David is wrong. A principal almost never gives an agent absolutely complete instructions. Unless some authority is implied, David would have had to say, "Open the car door, get in, put the key in the ignition, drive to the store, buy stickers, mark an auction number on each sticker …" and so forth. To solve this problem, the law assumes that the agent has authority to do anything that is reasonably necessary to accomplish her task.

Apparent Authority

A principal can be liable for the acts of an agent who is not, in fact, acting with authority if the *principal's* conduct causes a third party reasonably to believe that the agent is authorized.[12] In the case of *express* and *implied* authority, the principal has authorized the agent to act. Apparent authority is different: the principal has *not* authorized the agent, but has done something to make an innocent third party *believe* the agent is authorized. As a result, the principal is every bit as liable to the third party as if the agent did have authority.

For example, Zbigniew Lambo and Scott Kennedy were brokers at Paulson Investment Co., a stock brokerage firm in Oregon. The two men violated securities laws by selling unregistered stock, which ultimately proved to be worthless. Kennedy and Lambo were liable, but they were unable to repay the money. Either Paulson or its customers would end up bearing the loss. What is the fair result? The law takes the view that the principal is liable, not the third party, because the principal, by word or deed, allowed the third party to believe that the agent was acting on the principal's behalf. The principal could have prevented the third party from losing money.

Although the two brokers did not have *express* or *implied* authority to sell the stock (Paulson had not authorized them to break the law), the company was nonetheless liable on the grounds that the brokers had *apparent* authority. Paulson had sent letters to its customers notifying them when it hired Kennedy. The two brokers made sales presentations at Paulson's offices. The company had never told customers that the two men were not authorized to sell this worthless stock.[13] Thus the agents *appeared* to have authority, even though they did not. Of course, Paulson had the right to recover from Kennedy and Lambo, if it could ever compel them to pay.

Remember that the issue in apparent authority is always what the *principal* has done to make the *third party* believe that the *agent* has authority. Suppose that Kennedy and Lambo never worked for Paulson but, on their own, printed up Paulson stationery. The company would not be liable for the stock the two men sold because it had never done or said anything that would reasonably make a third party believe that the men were its agents.

Ratification

If a person accepts the benefit of an unauthorized transaction or fails to repudiate it, then he is as bound by the act as if he had originally authorized it. He has *ratified* the act.[14] Many of the cases in agency law involve instances in which one person acts *without* authority for another. To avoid liability, the alleged principal shows that he had not authorized the task at issue. But sometimes after the fact, the principal decides that he approves of what the agent has done even though it was not authorized at the time. The law would be perverse if it did not permit the principal, under those circumstances, to agree to the deal the agent has made.

---

[12]Restatement (Third) of Agency §2.03.
[13]*Badger v. Paulson Investment Co.*, 311 Ore. 14, 803 P.2d 1178, 1991 Ore. LEXIS 7 (S. Ct. OR, 1991).
[14]Restatement (Third) of Agency §4.01.

The law is not perverse, but it is careful. Even if an agent acts without authority, the principal can decide later to be bound by her actions so long as these requirements are met:

- The "agent" indicates to the third party that she is acting for a principal.
- The "principal" knows all the material facts of the transaction.
- The "principal" accepts the benefit of the whole transaction, not just part.
- The third party does not withdraw from the contract before ratification.

A night clerk at the St. Regis Hotel in Detroit, Michigan, was brutally murdered in the course of a robbery. A few days later, the *Detroit News* reported that the St. Regis management had offered a $1,000 reward for any information leading to the arrest and conviction of the killer. Two days after the article appeared, Robert Jackson turned in the man who was subsequently convicted of the crime. But then it was Jackson's turn to be robbed—the hotel refused to pay the reward on the grounds that the manager who had made the offer had no authority. Jackson still had one weapon left: he convinced the court that the hotel had ratified the offer. One of the hotel's owners admitted he read the *Detroit News*. The court concluded that if someone reads a newspaper, he is sure to read any articles about a business he owns; therefore, the owner must have been aware of the offer. He accepted the benefit of the offer by failing to revoke it publicly by, say, announcing to the press that the reward was invalid. This failure to revoke constituted a ratification, and the hotel was liable.[15]

Subagents

Many of the examples in this chapter involve a single agent acting for a principal. Real life is often more complex. Daniel, the owner of a restaurant, hires Michaela to manage it. She in turn hires chefs, waiters, and dishwashers. Daniel has never even met the restaurant help, yet they are also his agents, albeit a special category called **subagent.** Michaela is called an **intermediary agent**—someone who hires subagents for the principal.

As a general rule, an agent has no authority to delegate her tasks to another unless the principal authorizes her to do so. But when an agent is authorized to hire a subagent, the principal is as liable for the acts of the subagent as he is for the acts of a regular agent. Daniel authorizes Michaela to hire a restaurant staff, so she hires Lydia to serve as produce buyer. When Lydia buys food for the restaurant, Daniel must pay the bill.

AGENT'S LIABILITY FOR CONTRACTS

The agent's liability on a contract depends upon how much the third party knows about the principal. Disclosure is the agent's best protection against liability.

Fully Disclosed Principal

An agent is not liable for any contracts she makes on behalf of a *fully* disclosed principal. A principal is fully disclosed if the third party knows of his *existence* and his *identity*. Augusta acts as agent for Parker when he buys Tracey's prize-winning show horse. Augusta and Tracey both grew up in posh Grosse Pointe, Michigan, where they attended the same elite schools. Tracey does not know Parker, but she figures any friend of Augusta's must be OK. She figures wrong—Parker is a charming deadbeat. He injures Tracey's horse, fails to pay the full contract price, and promptly disappears. Tracey angrily demands that Augusta make

---

[15]*Jackson v. Goodman*, 69 Mich. App. 225, 244 N.W.2d 423, 1976 Mich. App., LEXIS 741 (Mich. Ct. App., 1976).

good on Parker's debt. Unfortunately for Tracey, Parker was a fully disclosed principal—Tracey knew of his *existence* and his *identity*. Although Tracey partly relied on Augusta's good character when contracting with Parker, Augusta is not liable because Tracey knew who the principal was and could have (should have) investigated him. Augusta did not promise anything herself, and Tracey's only recourse is against the principal, Parker (wherever he may be).

To avoid liability when signing a contract on behalf of a principal, an agent must clearly state that she is an agent and also must identify the principal. Augusta should sign a contract on behalf of her principal, Parker, as follows: "Augusta, as agent for Parker" or "Parker, by Augusta, Agent."

Unidentified Principal

In the case of an *unidentified* principal, the third party can recover from either the agent or the principal. (An unidentified principal is also sometimes called a "partially disclosed principal.") A principal is unidentified if the third party knew of his *existence* but not his *identity*. Suppose that, when approaching Tracey about the horse, Augusta simply says, "I have a friend who is interested in buying your champion." Any friend of Augusta's is a friend of Tracey's—or so Tracey thinks. Parker is an unidentified principal because Tracey knows only that he exists, not who he is. She cannot investigate his creditworthiness because she does not know his name. Tracey relies solely on what she is able to learn from the agent, Augusta. Both Augusta and Parker are liable to Tracey. (They are jointly and severally liable, which means that Tracey can recover from either or both of them. However, she cannot recover more than the total she is owed: if her damages are $100,000, she can recover that amount from either Augusta or Parker, or partial amounts from both, but in no event more than $100,000.)

Undisclosed Principal

In the case of an *undisclosed* principal, the third party can recover from either the agent or the principal. A principal is undisclosed if the third party did not know of his existence. Suppose that Augusta simply asks to buy the horse herself, without mentioning that she is purchasing it for Parker. In this case, Parker is an undisclosed principal because Tracey does not know that Augusta is acting for someone else. Both Parker and Augusta are jointly and severally liable. As Exhibit 16.1 illustrates, the principal is always liable, but the agent is not unless the principal's identity is a mystery.

In some ways, the concept of an undisclosed principal violates principles of contract law. If Tracey does not even know that Parker exists, how can they have an agreement or a meeting of the minds? Is such an arrangement fair to Tracey? No matter—a contract with an undisclosed principal is binding. The following incident illustrates why.

William Zeckendorf was a man with a plan. For years, he had been eyeing a six-block tract of land along New York's East River. It was a wasteland of slums and slaughterhouses, but he could see its potential. The meat packers had refused to sell to him, however, because they knew they would never be permitted to build slaughterhouses in Manhattan again. Finally, he got the phone call he had been waiting for. The companies were willing to sell—at more than three times the market price of surrounding land. Undeterred, Zeckendorf immediately put down a $1 million deposit. But to make his investment worthwhile, he needed to buy the neighboring property—once the slaughterhouses were gone, the other land would be much more valuable. Zeckendorf was well known as a wealthy developer; he had begun his business career managing the Astor family's real estate holdings. If he personally tried to negotiate the purchase of the surrounding land, word would soon get out that he wanted to put together a large parcel. Prices would skyrocket, and the project would become too costly. So he hired agents to purchase the land for him. To conceal his involvement further, he went to South America for a month. When he returned, his agents had completed 75 different purchases, and he owned 18 acres of land.

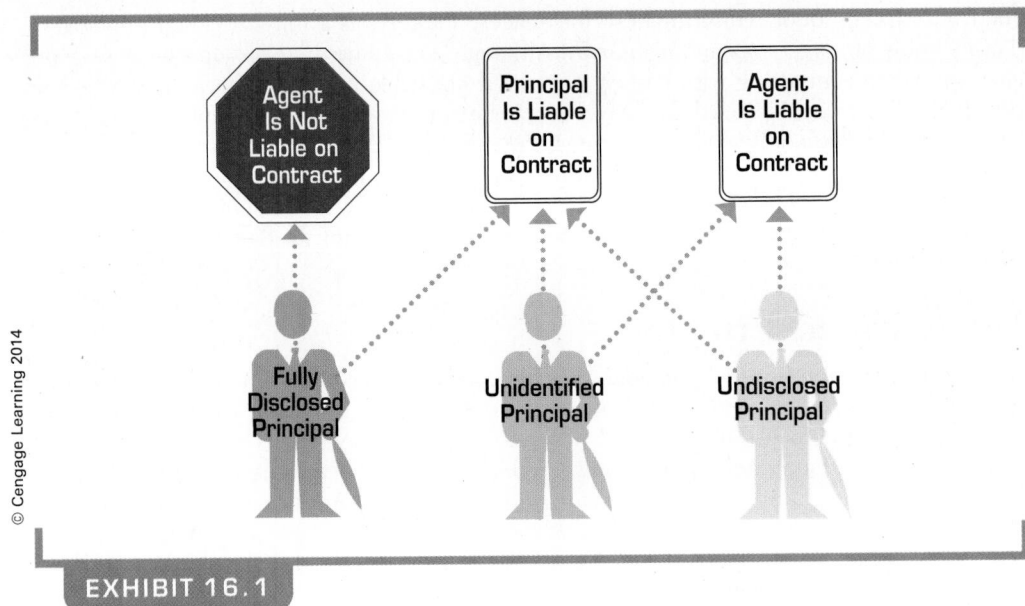

© Cengage Learning 2014

EXHIBIT 16.1

> **Without the cooperation of agency law, the UN headquarters would not be in New York today.**

Shortly afterwards, the United Nations (UN) began seeking a site for its headquarters. President Truman favored Boston, Philadelphia, or a location in the Midwest. The UN committee suggested Greenwich or Stamford, Connecticut. But John D. Rockefeller settled the question once and for all. He purchased Zeckendorf's land and donated it to the UN (netting Zeckendorf a 25 percent profit). Without the cooperation of agency law, the UN headquarters would not be in New York today.

Because of concerns about fair play, there are some exceptions to the rule on undisclosed principals. **A third party is not bound to the contract with an undisclosed principal if (1) the contract specifically provides that the third party is not bound to anyone other than the agent, or (2) the agent lies about the principal because she knows the third party would refuse to contract with him.** Suppose that a large university is buying up land in an impoverished area near its campus. An owner of a house there wants to make sure that if he sells to the university, he gets a higher price than if he sells to an individual with more limited resources. A cagey property owner, when approached by one of the university's agents, could ask for a clause in the contract providing that the agent was not representing someone else. If the agent told the truth, the owner could demand a higher price. If the agent lied, then the owner could rescind the contract when the truth emerged.

Unauthorized Agent

Thus far in this section, we have been discussing an agent's liability to a third party for a transaction that was authorized by the principal. Sometimes, however, agents act without the authority of a principal. **If the agent has no authority (express, implied, or apparent), the principal is not liable to the third party, and the agent is.** Suppose that Augusta agrees to sell Parker's horse to Tracey. Unfortunately, Parker has never met Augusta and has certainly not authorized this transaction. Augusta is hoping that she can persuade him to sell, but Parker refuses. Augusta, but not Parker, is liable to Tracey for breach of contract.

PRINCIPAL'S LIABILITY FOR TORTS

An employer is liable for a tort committed by its employee acting within the scope of employment or acting with authority.[16] This principle of liability is called ***respondeat superior***, which is a Latin phrase that means "let the master answer." Under the theory of *respondeat superior*, the employer (that is, the principal) is liable for misbehavior by the employee (that is, the agent) whether or not the employer was at fault. Indeed, the employer is liable even if he *forbade* or tried to *prevent* the employee from misbehaving. Thus, a company could be liable for the damage a worker causes while driving and talking on her cell phone, even if she is violating company policy at the time. This sounds like a harsh rule. The logic is that because the principal controls the agent, he should be able to *prevent* misbehavior. If he cannot prevent it, at least he can *insure* against the risks. Furthermore, the principal may have deeper pockets than the agent or the injured third party and thus be better able to *afford* the cost of the agent's misbehavior.

To apply the principle of *respondeat superior*, it is important to understand each part of the rule.

Employee

There are two kinds of agents: (1) *employees* and (2) *independent contractors*. **A principal *may be* liable for the torts of an employee but generally is *not* liable for the torts of an independent contractor.** Because of this rule, the distinction between an employee and an independent contractor is important.

Employee or Independent Contractor?

The more control the principal has over an agent, the more likely that the agent will be considered an employee. Therefore, when determining if agents are employees or independent contractors, courts consider whether:

- The principal supervises details of the work.
- The principal supplies the tools and place of work.
- The agents work full time for the principal.
- The agents receive a salary or hourly wages, not a fixed price for the job.
- The work is part of the regular business of the principal.
- The principal and agents believe they have an employer-employee relationship.
- The principal is in business.[17]

Suppose, for example, that Mutt and Jeff work 40 hours a week at Swansong Media preparing food for the company's onsite dining room. They earn a weekly salary. Swansong provides food, utensils, and kitchen. This year, however, Swansong decides to go all out for its holiday party, so it hires FiFi LaBelle to prepare special food. She buys the food, prepares it in her own kitchen, and delivers it to the company in time for the party. She is an independent contractor, while Mutt and Jeff are employees.

---

[16]Restatement (Third) of Agency §7.07.
[17]Ibid.

Negligent Hiring

Principals prefer agents to be considered independent contractors, not employees, because, as a general rule, principals are not liable for the torts of an independent contractor. There is, however, one exception to this rule: **the principal is liable for the torts of an independent contractor *if* the principal has been negligent in hiring or supervising her.** Remember that, under *respondeat superior*, the principal is liable *without fault* for the torts of employees. The case of independent contractors is different: the principal is liable only if he was *at fault* by being careless in his hiring or supervising.

Exhibit 16.2 illustrates the difference in liability between an employee and an independent contractor.

Scope of Employment

Principals are liable only for torts that an employee commits within the *scope of employment.* If an employee leaves a pool of water on the floor of a store and a customer slips and falls, the employer is liable. But if the same employee leaves water on his own kitchen floor and a friend falls, the employer is not liable because the employee is not acting within the scope of employment. An employee is acting within the scope of employment if the act:

- Is one that employees are generally responsible for
- Takes place during hours that the employee is generally employed
- Is part of the principal's business
- Is similar to the one the principal authorized
- Is one for which the principal supplied the tools; and
- Is not seriously criminal.

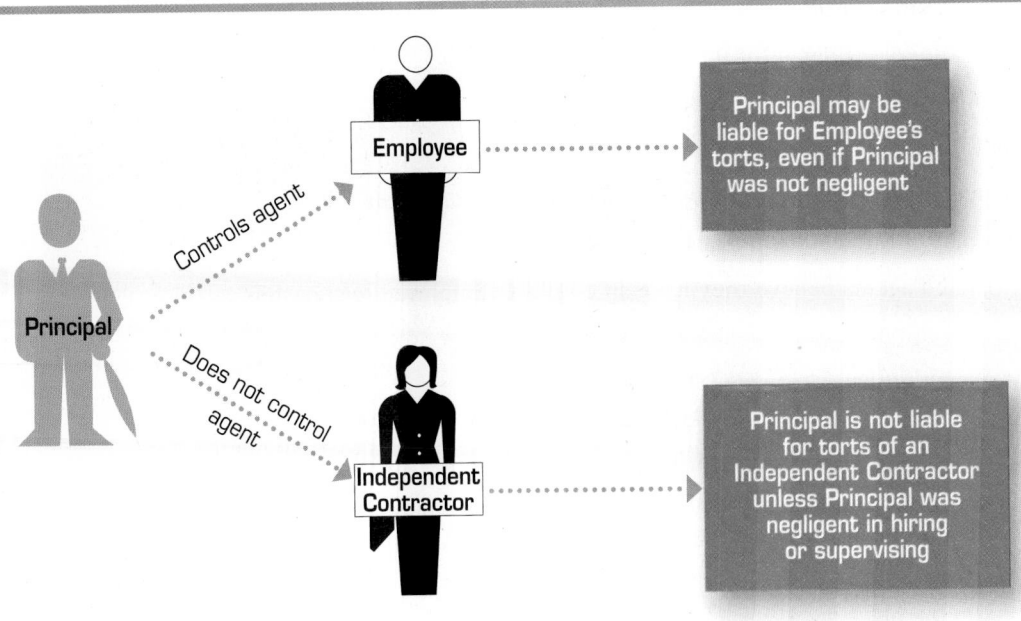

© Cengage Learning 2014

EXHIBIT 16.2

Scope of employment cases raise two major issues: authorization and abandonment.

Authorization

In authorization cases, the agent is clearly working for the principal but commits an act that the principal has not authorized. Although Jane has often told the driver of her delivery van not to speed, Hank ignores her instructions and plows into Bernadette. At the time of the accident, he is working for Jane, delivering flowers for her shop, but his act is not authorized. **An act is within the scope of employment, even if expressly forbidden, if it is of the same general nature as that authorized or if it is incidental to the conduct authorized.** Hank was authorized to drive the van, but not to speed. However, his speeding was of the same general nature as the authorized act, so Jane is liable to Bernadette.

Abandonment

The second major issue in a *scope of employment* case involves abandonment. **The principal is liable for the actions of the employee that occur while the employee is at work, but not for actions that occur after the employee has abandoned the principal's business.** Although the rule sounds straightforward, the difficulty lies in determining whether the employee has in fact abandoned the principal's business. The employer is liable if the employee is simply on a *detour* from company business, but the employer is not liable if the employee is off on a *frolic of his own.* Suppose that Hank, the delivery van driver, speeds during his afternoon commute home. An employee is generally not acting within the scope of his employment when he commutes to and from work, so his principal, Jane, is not liable. Or suppose that, while on the way to a delivery, he stops to view his favorite movie classic, *Dead on Arrival.* Unable to see in the darkened theater, he knocks Anna down, causing grave harm. Jane is not liable because Hank's visit to the movies is outside the scope of his employment. On the other hand, if Hank stops at the Burger Box drive-in window en route to making a delivery, Jane is liable when he crashes into Anna on the way out of the parking lot because this time, he is simply making a detour.

Was the employee in the following case acting within the scope of his employment while driving to work? You be the judge.

You be the Judge

Facts: Staff Sergeant William E. Dreyer was a recruiter for the United States Marine Corps. Driving to work one morning at 6:40 a.m., in a government-owned car, he struck and killed 12-year-old Justin Zankel. The child's parents sued the federal government, claiming that it was liable for Dreyer's actions because he had been acting within the scope of his employment at the time of the accident.

The Marine Corps had provided Dreyer with a car to drive while on government business, but he was not permitted to use this car while commuting to and from home unless he had specific authorization from his boss,

ZANKEL V. UNITED STATES OF AMERICA

2008 U.S. Dist. LEXIS 23655
United States District Court for the Western District of Pennsylvania, 2008

Major Michael Sherman. However, Sherman was flexible in giving authorization and even permitted his soldiers simply to leave a message on his voicemail. Indeed, he had denied only about a dozen such requests over a three-year period.

Each month, Dreyer was expected to meet specific quotas for the number of contracts signed and recruits shipped to basic training. However, despite working 16 to 18 hours every day of the week, Dreyer had not met his recruiting quotas for months. Sherman had formally reprimanded him and increased his target for the following month.

On the day before the accident, Dreyer left home at 6:30 a.m., driving his own car. At the office, he switched to a government car and worked until 10:45 p.m. He then discovered that his personal car would not start. He did not want to call Sherman that late, so he drove his government car home without permission. He believed that, had he called, Sherman would have said it was OK.

Dreyer arrived home at midnight. He was under orders to attend an early-morning training session the next day. So he awoke early and left home at 6:35 a.m. At 6:40 a.m., his car hit Justin Zankel.

You Be the Judge: *Was Dreyer within the scope of employment when he killed Zankel?*

Argument for the Zankels: At the time of the accident, Dreyer was driving a government vehicle. Although he had not requested permission to drive the car, if he had done so, permission certainly would have been granted.

Moreover, even if Dreyer was not authorized to drive the Marine Corps car, the government is still liable because his activity was of the same general nature as that authorized and it was incidental to the conduct authorized. Driving the car was part of Dreyer's work. Indeed, he could not perform his job without it. In addition, Dreyer was on the road early so that he could attend a required training session. He was exhausted from trying to reach impossible goals. The Marine Corps must bear responsibility for this tragic accident.

Argument for United States: The government had a clear policy stating that recruiters were not authorized to drive a government car without first requesting permission. Dreyer had not done so. Therefore, he was not authorized to drive the government car at the time of the accident.

Moreover, it is well established that an employee commuting to and from work is not within the scope of employment. If Dreyer had been driving from one recruiting effort to another, that would be a different story. But in this case, he had not yet started work for the Marine Corps, and therefore the government is not liable.

Intentional Torts

A principal is *not* liable for the *intentional* torts of an employee unless (1) the employee intended to serve some purpose of the employer; or (2) the employer was negligent in hiring or supervising this employee. During an NBA basketball game, Kobe pushes LeBron into some chairs under the basket to prevent him from scoring a breakaway layup. Kobe's team is liable for his actions because he was motivated, at least in part, by a desire to help his team. But if Kobe hits LeBron in the parking lot after the playoffs are over, Kobe's team is *not* liable because he is no longer motivated by a desire to help the team. His motivation now is personal revenge or frustration.

In the following case, a priest did wrong. Was he serving some purpose of the Church? Was the Church liable for his criminal acts?

DOE V. LIBERATORE

478 F. Supp. 2d 742; 2007 U.S. Dist. Lexis 19067
United States District Court for the Middle District of Pennsylvania, 2007

Facts: A number of priests wrote to James Timlin, the Bishop of Scranton, warning him that Father Albert Liberatore was engaging in a sexual relationship with one of his male students. Bishop Timlin transferred Liberatore from the school to a parish church.

Fourteen year-old John Doe was a member of Liberatore's parish. Liberatore befriended Doe, taking him on outings and giving him expensive gifts. Doe routinely slept in Liberatore's bed. A number of priests told Bishop Timlin that they feared Liberatore was sexually abusing Doe. One witness reported that she had seen Doe put his hand down Liberatore's pants. Eventually, Doe himself told a priest that he was being sexually abused. The priest instructed Doe to forgive Liberatore and not to tell other people because it would ruin Doe's life and the lives of others.

Only after Liberatore pleaded guilty to multiple counts of sexual abuse did the Church dismiss him from the priesthood. Doe filed suit against the Church and Bishop Timlin, alleging that they were liable for the torts committed by Liberatore. The defendants filed a motion to dismiss.

Issues: *Was Liberatore acting within the scope of his employment? Was the Church liable for his criminal acts?*

Excerpts from Judge Caputo's Decision: Under Pennsylvania law, an employer is held liable for the negligent acts of his employee which cause injuries to a third party, provided that such acts were committed during the course of and within the scope of the employment.

The conduct of an employee is considered within the scope of employment if: (1) it is of a kind and nature that the employee is employed to perform; (2) it occurs substantially within the authorized time and space limits; (3) it is actuated, at least in part, by a purpose to serve the employer; and (4) if force is intentionally used by the employee against another, the use of force is not unexpected by the employer.

Here, it is clear that Liberatore's sexual molestation of Plaintiff was not within the scope or nature of his employment as a priest. Indeed, the activity of which Plaintiff now complains is wholly inconsistent with the role of one who is received into the Holy Orders as an ordained priest of the Roman Catholic Church. Moreover, the acts of sexual abuse perpetrated by Liberatore were both outrageous and certainly not actuated by any purpose of serving the Diocese, Sacred Heart, or Bishop Timlin. Therefore, the Court will grant summary judgment in favor of the Diocese, Sacred Heart, and Bishop Timlin as to [this issue].

Plaintiff next claims that the Diocese, Sacred Heart, and Bishop Timlin are liable for negligence in their hiring, supervision, and retention of Liberatore as a Diocesan priest. [A]n employer owes a duty to exercise reasonable care in selecting, supervising and controlling employees. The Supreme Court of Pennsylvania has held that, to fasten liability on an employer, it must be shown that the employer knew or, in the exercise of ordinary care, should have known of the necessity for exercising control of his employee.

In the instant case, the Diocese, Sacred Heart, and Bishop Timlin may be liable if they knew or should have known that Liberatore had a propensity for committing sexual abuse and his employment as Pastor at Sacred Heart might create a situation where his propensity would harm a third person, such as Plaintiff. [A] reasonable jury could conclude that the Diocese, Sacred Heart, and Bishop Timlin were negligent or reckless in supervising and retaining Liberatore. However, the Court concludes that a reasonable jury could not find that the Diocese, Sacred Heart, and Bishop Timlin were negligent or reckless in hiring Liberatore because there is no evidence suggesting that Liberatore was or would become a child sex predator when he was hired.

Physical or Nonphysical Harm

In the case of *physical* torts, a principal is liable for the negligent conduct of a employee that occurs within the scope of employment. The rule for *nonphysical* torts (that is, torts that harm only reputation, feelings, or wallet) is different. **Nonphysical torts are treated more like a contract claim, and the principal is liable if the employee acted with express, implied, or apparent authority.**[18] For example, suppose that Dwayne buys a house insurance policy from Andy, who is an agent of the Balls of Fire Insurance Company. Andy throws away Dwayne's policy and pockets his premiums. When Dwayne's house burns down, Balls of Fire is liable because Andy was acting with apparent authority.

EXAM Strategy

Question: Daisy was the founder of an Internet start-up company. Jay was her driver. One day, after he had dropped her at a board meeting, he went to the car wash. There, he told an attractive woman that he worked for a money management firm.

[18]Restatement (Third) Agency §7.08.

She gave him money to invest. On the way out of the car wash, he was so excited that he hit another customer's expensive car. Who is liable for Jay's misdeeds?

Strategy: In determining a principal's liability, begin by figuring out whether the agent has committed a physical or nonphysical tort. Remember that the principal is liable for physical torts within the scope of employment, but for nonphysical torts, she is liable only if the employee acted with authority.

Result: In this case, Daisy is liable for the damage to the car because that was a physical tort within the scope of employment. But she is not liable for the investment money because Mac did not have authority (express, implied, or apparent) to take those funds.

AGENT'S LIABILITY FOR TORTS

The focus of the prior section was on the *principal's* liability for the agent's torts. But it is important to remember that **agents are always liable for their own torts.** Agents who commit torts are personally responsible, whether or not their principal is also liable. Even if the tort was committed to benefit the principal, the agent is still liable. So the sailor who got into a fistfight while rousting a shipmate from bed is liable even though he thought he was acting for the benefit of his principal.

This rule makes obvious sense. If the agent were not liable, he would have little incentive to be careful. Imagine Hank driving his delivery van for Jane. If he were not personally liable for his own torts, he might think, "If I drive fast enough, I can make it through that light even though it just turned red. And if I don't, what the heck, it'll be Jane's problem, not mine." Agents, as a rule, may have fewer assets than their principal, but it is important that their personal assets be at risk in the event of their negligent behavior.

If the agent and principal are *both* liable, which does the injured third party sue? The principal and the agent are *jointly and severally liable*, which means, as we have seen, that the injured third party can sue either one or both, as she chooses. If she recovers from the principal, he can sue the agent.

Chapter Conclusion

When students enroll in a business law course, they fully expect to learn about torts and contracts, corporations and partnerships. They probably do not think much about agency law; many of them have not even heard the term before. Yet it is an area of the law that affects us all because each of us has been and will continue to be both an agent and a principal many times in our lives.

EXAM REVIEW

1. **CREATING AN AGENCY RELATIONSHIP** A principal and an agent mutually consent that the agent will act on behalf of the principal and be subject to the principal's control, thereby creating a fiduciary relationship. (pp. 397–398)

2. **ELEMENTS NOT REQUIRED** An agency relationship can exist without either a written agreement, a formal agreement, or compensation. (pp. 398–399)

3. **AN AGENT'S DUTIES TO THE PRINCIPAL** An agent owes these duties to the principal: duty of loyalty, duty to obey instructions, duty of care, and duty to provide information. (pp. 399–403)

4. **THE PRINCIPAL'S REMEDIES IN THE EVENT OF A BREACH** The principal has three potential remedies when the agent breaches her duty: recovery of damages the breach has caused, recovery of any profits earned by the agent from the breach, and rescission of any transaction with the agent. (p. 403)

5. **THE PRINCIPAL'S DUTIES TO THE AGENT** The principal has three duties to the agent: to compensate as provided by the agreement, to reimburse legitimate expenses, and to cooperate with the agent. (pp. 404–405)

6. **POWER AND RIGHT TO TERMINATE** Both the agent and the principal have the power to terminate an agency relationship, but they may not have the right. If the termination violates the agency agreement and causes harm to the other party, the wrongful party must pay damages. (pp. 405–406)

7. **AUTOMATIC TERMINATION** An agency relationship automatically terminates if the principal or agent no longer can perform the required duties or if a change in circumstances renders the agency relationship pointless. (pp. 406–407)

8. **A PRINCIPAL'S LIABILITY FOR CONTRACTS** A principal is liable for the contracts of the agent if the agent has express, implied, or apparent authority. (pp. 408–409)

9. **EXPRESS AUTHORITY** The principal grants express authority by words or conduct that, reasonably interpreted, cause the agent to believe that the principal desires her to act on the principal's account. (p. 408)

10. **IMPLIED AUTHORITY** Implied authority includes authority to do acts that are incidental to a transaction, usually accompany it, or are reasonably necessary to accomplish it. (pp. 408–409)

11. **APPARENT AUTHORITY** Apparent authority means that a principal is liable for the acts of an agent who is not, in fact, acting with authority if the principal's conduct causes a third party reasonably to believe that the agent is authorized. (p. 409)

EXAM Strategy

Question: Dr. James Leonard wrote Dr. Edward Jacobson to offer him the position of chief of audiology at Jefferson Medical College in Philadelphia. In the letter, Leonard stated that this appointment would have to be approved by the promotion and appointment committee. Jacobson believed that the appointment committee acted only as a "rubber stamp," affirming whatever recommendation Leonard made. Jacobson accepted Leonard's offer and proceeded to sell his house and quit his job in Colorado. You can guess what happened next. Two weeks later, Leonard sent Jacobson another letter, rescinding his offer because of opposition from the appointment committee. Did Leonard have apparent authority?

Strategy: In cases of apparent authority, begin by asking what the principal did to make the third party believe that the agent was authorized. What did the Medical College do? (See the "Result" at the end of this section.)

12. **AN AGENT'S LIABILITY FOR A CONTRACT** An agent is not liable for any contract she makes on behalf of a fully disclosed principal. The principal is liable. In the case of a unidentified or undisclosed principal, both the agent and the principal are liable on the contract. (pp. 410–412)

13. **A PRINCIPAL'S LIABILITY FOR TORTS** An employer is liable for a tort committed by its employee acting within the scope of employment or acting with authority. (pp. 413–418)

EXAM Strategy

Question: While drunk, the driver of a subway car plows into the back of the car ahead of him, killing a passenger. It was against the rules for the driver to be drunk. Is the subway authority liable for the negligence of its employee?

Strategy: With a tort case, always determine first if the agents are employees or independent contractors. This worker was an employee. Then ask if the employee was acting within the scope of employment. Yes, he was driving a subway car, which is what he was hired to do. Does it matter than he had violated subway rules? No, his violation of the rules does not eliminate his principal's liability. (See the "Result" at the end of this section.)

14. **INDEPENDENT CONTRACTOR** The principal is liable for the physical torts of an independent contractor only if the principal has been negligent in hiring or supervising him. (p. 414)

15. **INTENTIONAL TORTS** A principal is not liable for the intentional torts of an employee unless (1) the employee intended to serve some purpose of the employer; or (2) the employer was negligent in hiring or supervising the employee. (pp. 416–417)

Question: What if the subway driver mentioned above had stabbed a passenger?

Strategy: In the case of an intentional tort, the principal is liable only if the agent was intending to serve some purpose of the employer or the employer was negligent in hiring or supervising him. (See the "Result" at the end of this section.)

16. **NONPHYSICAL TORTS** A principal is liable only for the nonphysical torts of an employee who is acting with express, implied or apparent authority. (p. 417)

17. **AGENT'S LIABILITY FOR TORTS** Agents are always liable for their own torts. (p. 418)

---

11. Result: No. Indeed, Leonard had told Jacobson that he did not have authority. If Jacobson chose to believe otherwise, that was his problem.

13. Result: The subway authority is liable.

15. Result: When he stabbed a passenger, the driver was not serving the purpose of the employer, so the subway authority would not be liable. There was no evidence that the subway authority had been negligent in its hiring or supervising of employees.

MULTIPLE-CHOICE QUESTIONS

1. At Business University, semester enrollment begins at midnight on April 1. Jasper asked his roommate, Alonso, to register him for an important required course as a favor. Alonso agreed to do so but then overslept. As a result, Jasper could not enroll in the required course he needed to graduate and had to stay in school for an additional semester. Is Alonso liable to Jasper?

   (a) No, because an agency agreement is invalid unless the agent receives payment.

   (b) No, because Alonso was not grossly negligent.

   (c) No, because the cost of the extra semester is unreasonably high.

   (d) Yes, because Alonso disobeyed his instructions.

2. Finn learns that, despite his stellar record, he is being paid less than other salespeople at Barry Co., so he decides to start his own company. During his last month on the Barry payroll, he tells all of his clients about his new business. He also tells them that Barry is a great company, but his fees will be lower. After he opens the doors of his new business, most of his former clients move with him. Is Finn liable to Barry?

   (a) No, because he has not been disloyal to Barry—he praised the company.

   (b) No, because Barry was underpaying him.

   (c) No, because his clients have the right to hire whichever company they choose.

   (d) Yes, Finn has violated his duty of loyalty to Barry.

3. Kurt asked his car mechanic, Quinn, for help in buying a used car. Quinn recommends a Ford Focus that she has been taking care of its whole life. Quinn was working for the seller. Which of the following statements is true?

   (a) Quinn must pay Kurt the amount of money she received from the Ford's prior owner.

   (b) After buying the car, Kurt finds out that it needs $1,000 in repairs. He can recover that amount from Quinn, but only if Quinn knew about the needed repairs before Kurt bought the car.

   (c) Kurt cannot recover anything because Quinn had no obligation to reveal her relationship with the car's seller.

   (d) Kurt cannot recover anything because he had not paid Quinn for her help.

4. Figgins is the dean of a college. He appointed Sue as acting dean while he was out of the country and posted an announcement on the college website announcing that she was authorized to act in his place. He also told Sue privately that she did not have the right to make admissions decisions. While Figgins was gone, Sue overruled the admissions committee to admit the child of a wealthy alumnus. Does the child have the right to attend this college?

   (a) No, because Sue was not authorized to admit him.

   (b) No, because Figgins did not ratify Sue's decision.

   (c) Yes, because Figgins was a fully disclosed principal.

   (d) Yes, because Sue had apparent authority.

5. **CPA QUESTION** A principal will not be liable to a third party for a tort committed by an agent:

   (a) unless the principal instructed the agent to commit the tort.

   (b) unless the tort was committed within the scope of the agency relationship.

   (c) if the agency agreement limits the principal's liability for the agent's tort.

   (d) if the tort is also regarded as a criminal act.

6. **CPA QUESTION** Cox engaged Datz as her agent. It was mutually agreed that Datz would not disclose that he was acting as Cox's agent. Instead, he was to deal with prospective customers as if he were a principal acting on his own behalf. This he did and made several contracts for Cox. Assuming Cox, Datz, or the customer seeks to avoid liability on one of the contracts involved, which of the following statements is correct?

   (a) Cox must ratify the Datz contracts to be held liable.

   (b) Datz has no liability once he discloses that Cox was the real principal.

   (c) The third party can avoid liability because he believed he was dealing with Datz as a principal.

   (d) The third party may choose to hold either Datz or Cox liable.

ESSAY QUESTIONS

1. An elementary school custodian hit a child who wrote graffiti on the wall. Is the school district liable for this intentional tort by its employee?

2. What if the custodian hit one of the schoolchildren for calling him a name? Is the school district liable?

3. A soldier was drinking at a training seminar. Although he was told to leave his car at the seminar, he disobeyed orders and drove to a military club. On the way to the club, he was involved in an accident. Is the military liable for the damage he caused?

4. One afternoon while visiting friends, tennis star Vitas Gerulaitis fell asleep in their pool house. A mechanic had improperly installed the swimming pool heater, which leaked carbon monoxide fumes into the house where he slept, killing him. His mother filed suit against the owners of the estate. On what theory would they be liable?

5. **YOU BE THE JUDGE WRITING PROBLEM** Sarah went to an auction at Christie's to bid on a tapestry for her employer, Fine Arts Gallery. The good news is that she purchased a Dufy tapestry for $77,000. The bad news is that it was not the one her employer had told her to buy. In the excitement of the auction, she forgot her instructions. Fine Art refused to pay, and Christie's filed suit. Is Fine Arts liable for the unauthorized act of its agent? **Argument for Christie's:** Christie's cannot possibly ascertain in each case the exact nature of a bidder's authority. Whether or not Sarah had actual authority, she certainly had apparent authority, and Fine Arts is liable. **Argument for Fine Arts:** Sarah was not authorized to purchase the Dufy tapestry, and therefore Christie's must recover from her, not Fine Arts.

DISCUSSION QUESTIONS

1. **ETHICS** Mercedes has just begun work at Photobook.com. What a great place to work! Although the salary is not high, the company has fabulous perks. The dining room provides great food from 7 a.m. to midnight, five days a week. There is also a free laundry and dry-cleaning service. Mercedes's social life has never been better. She invites her friends over for Photobook meals and has their laundry done for free. And because her job requires her to be online all the time, she has plenty of opportunity to stay in touch with her friends by g-chatting, tweeting, and checking Facebook updates. She is, however, shocked that one of her colleagues takes paper home from the office for his children to use at home. Are these employees behaving ethically?

2. Kevin was the manager of a radio station, WABC. A competing station lured him away. In his last month on the job at WABC, he notified two key on-air personalities that if they were to leave the station, he would not hold them to their noncompete agreements. What can WABC do?

3. Jesse worked as a buyer for the Vegetable Co. Rachel offered to sell Jesse 10 tons of tomatoes for the account of Vegetable. Jesse accepted the offer. Later, Jesse discovered that Rachel was an agent for Sylvester Co. Who is liable on this contract?

4. The Pharmaceutical Association holds an annual convention. At the convention, Brittany, who was president of the association, told Luke that Research Corp. had a promising new cancer vaccine. Luke was so excited that he chartered a plane to fly to Research's headquarters. On the way, the plane crashed and Luke was killed. Is the Pharmaceutical Association liable for Luke's death?

5. Betsy has a two-year contract as a producer at Jackson Movie Studios. She produces a remake of the movie *Footloose*. Unfortunately, it bombs, and Jackson is so furious that he fires her on the weekend the movie opens. Does he have the power to do this?

CHAPTER 17

EMPLOYMENT AND LABOR LAW

© Stas Volik/Shutterstock.com

> … you would see them plunging their feet and ankles into the steaming hot carcass of the steer.

"On the killing beds you were apt to be covered with blood, and it would freeze solid; if you leaned against a pillar, you would freeze to that, and if you put your hand upon the blade of your knife, you would run a chance of leaving your skin on it. The men would tie up their feet in newspapers and old sacks, and these would be soaked in blood and frozen, and then soaked again, and so on, until by nighttime a man would be walking on great lumps the size of the feet of an elephant. Now and then, when the bosses were not looking, you would see them plunging their feet and ankles into the steaming hot carcass of the steer…. The cruelest thing of all was that nearly all of them—all of those who used knives—were unable to wear gloves, and their arms would be white with frost and their hands would grow numb, and then of course there would be accidents."[1]

---

[1] From Upton Sinclair, *The Jungle* (New York: Bantam Books, 1981), p. 80, a 1906 novel about the meat-packing industry.

INTRODUCTION

For most of history, the concept of career planning was unknown. By and large, people were born into their jobs. Whatever their parents had been—landowner, soldier, farmer, servant, merchant, or beggar—they became, too. People not only knew their place, they also understood the rights and obligations inherent in each position. The landowner had the right to receive labor from his tenants, but he also cared for them if they fell ill. Certainly, there were abuses, but at a time when people held religious convictions about their position in life and workers had few expectations that their lives would be better than their parents', the role of law was limited.

The primary English law of employment simply established that, in the absence of a contract, an employee was hired for a year at a time. This rule was designed to prevent injustice in a farming society. If an employee worked through harvest time, the landowner could not fire him in the unproductive winter. Conversely, a worker could not stay the winter and then leave for greener pastures in the spring.

In the eighteenth and nineteenth centuries, the Industrial Revolution profoundly altered the employment relationship. Many workers left the farms and villages for large factories in the city. Bosses no longer knew their workers personally, so they felt little responsibility toward them. The old laws that had suited an agrarian economy with stable relationships did not fit the new employment conditions. Instead of duties and responsibilities, courts emphasized the freedom to contract. Since employees could quit their factory jobs whenever they wanted, it seemed only fair for employers to have the same freedom to fire a worker. That was indeed the rule adopted by the courts: unless workers had an explicit employment contract, they were employees at will. **An *employee at will* could be fired for a good reason, a bad reason, or no reason at all.** For nearly a century, this was the basic common law rule of employment. A court explained the rule this way:

> Precisely as may the employee cease labor at his whim or pleasure, and, whatever be his reason, good, bad, or indifferent, leave no one a legal right to complain; so, upon the other hand, may the employer discharge, and, whatever be his reason, good, bad, or indifferent, no one has suffered a legal wrong.[2]

However evenhanded this common law rule of employment may have sounded in theory, in practice, it could lead to harsh results. The lives of factory workers were grim. It was not as if they could simply pack up and leave; conditions were no better elsewhere. Courts and legislatures gradually began to recognize that individual workers were generally unable to negotiate fair contracts with powerful employers. Since the beginning of the twentieth century, employment law has changed dramatically. Now, the employment relationship is more strictly regulated by statutes and by the common law.

Note well, though: **in the absence of a specific legal exception, the rule in the United States is *still* that an employee at will can be fired for any reason.** But today there are several important exceptions to this rule. Many of the statutes discussed in this chapter were passed by Congress and therefore apply nationally. The common law, however, comes from state courts and only applies locally. We will look at a sampling of cases that illustrates national trends, even though the law may not be the same in every state.

This chapter covers five topics in employment law: (1) employment security, (2) privacy in the workplace, (3) safety issues, (4) financial protection, and (5) labor law. Chapter 18 covers employment discrimination.

---

[2]*Union Labor Hospital Assn. v. Vance Redwood Lumber Co.*, 112 P.886, 888, 1910 Cal. LEXIS 417 (Cal., 1910).

EMPLOYMENT SECURITY

Family and Medical Leave Act

The Family and Medical Leave Act (FMLA) guarantees both men and women up to 12 weeks of *unpaid* leave each year for childbirth, adoption, or a serious health condition of their own or in their immediate family. This statute defines an immediate family member as a spouse, child, or parent—but not a sibling, grandchild, or in-law. An employee who takes a leave must be allowed to return to the same or an equivalent job with the same pay and benefits. The FMLA applies only to companies with at least 50 workers and to employees who have been with the company full time for at least a year.

Here are some examples of what counts as a "serious health condition" under this statute:

- Any health issue that requires hospitalization.

- A condition that requires more than one visit to a health care provider. The visits may be spread out over as long as a year.

- A condition that requires only one visit to a health care provider, but which also requires a course of treatment such as physical therapy or prescription medication.

Thus, the FMLA would apply in the case of a heart attack, ongoing kidney dialysis, and an ear infection that required antibiotics. It would generally not cover food poisoning that did not require hospitalization, the common cold, or a sprained ankle.

Kevin Knussman was the first person to win a lawsuit under the FMLA. While a Maryland state trooper, he requested eight weeks of leave to care for his pregnant wife, who was suffering severe complications. His boss granted only two weeks. After Knussman's daughter was born, his boss again denied leave, saying that "God made women to have babies." Knussman ultimately recovered $40,000.[3]

In many FMLA lawsuits, a worker claims that he or she was fired in retaliation for taking leave, while the employer argues that the termination was for some other reason. The following case illustrates this dynamic.

PETERSON v. EXIDE TECHNOLOGIES

2012 U.S. App. LEXIS 7139
Tenth Circuit Court of Appeals, 2012

Facts: Exide Technologies issued repeated warnings to Robert Peterson for driving forklifts too fast and violating other safety rules. After he was injured in a forklift crash, Exide granted him FMLA leave for 10 days while he recovered.

Peterson's manager fired him during the leave period for "flagrant violations of safety rules." Peterson sued, claiming that he was terminated in retaliation for exercising his right to take FMLA leave. The lower court granted summary judgment to Exide, and Peterson appealed.

Issue: *Was Peterson fired in retaliation for claiming FMLA leave?*

Excerpts from Judge Baldock's Decision: The FMLA makes it unlawful for any employer to interfere with, restrain, or deny the exercise of the rights provided by the FMLA, or to discriminate against any individual for opposing any practice prohibited by the FMLA.

[I]f Plaintiff makes out a prima facie retaliation case, the burden shifts to Defendant to demonstrate a legitimate, nonretaliatory reason for its termination decision. If Defendant meets this burden, the burden shifts back to Plaintiff to show that there is a genuine dispute of material fact as to whether Defendant's explanations are pretextual.

---

[3]Eyal Press, "Family-Leave Values," *New York Times,* July 29, 2007.

Defendant asserts it dismissed Plaintiff for the legitimate reason that he violated company safety policies. According to Defendant's Plant Manager:

> Based on my own review of the photographs and the damage they depicted, Plaintiff was driving too fast at the time of the crash and was not operating his forklift in a safe manner. Such conduct on Plaintiff's part was a flagrant violation of company health and safety policy and posed a threat to the safety of Plaintiff and other Exide employees.

The Plant Manager also based his decision to fire Plaintiff on the "history of careless and unsafe conduct" reflected in Plaintiff's personnel file. Defendant has adequately demonstrated a nonretaliatory reason for Plaintiff's termination: his repeated safety violations. Thus, the burden shifts back to Plaintiff to show pretext.

Plaintiff argues Defendant's asserted justification is pretextual because the forklift accident was a "minor incident." Whether the accident was "minor" is questionable. But even if it was, we see nothing that prevents Defendant from firing employees for minor safety violations. Particularly where, as here, the employee has a record of unsafe work performance, even a minor infraction could be the last straw.

Plaintiff has produced no evidence to undermine Defendant's nonretaliatory explanation for the termination. Aside from the fact Plaintiff was on FMLA leave when he was fired, no evidence suggests a causal connection between Plaintiff's firing and his exercise of FMLA rights. Therefore, the district court properly granted summary judgment.

AFFIRMED.

Ethics Although the FMLA offers important protections, the United States is the only wealthy country that does not provide mandatory *paid* maternity leave. Should Congress modify the FMLA to require some period of paid leave for new mothers? If so, for how long? A few weeks while they recuperate from childbirth? Or a few months to care for the newborn? What about paternity leave, which many countries require? And how about workers who take FMLA leave to deal with a serious illness? Should they be paid?

Health Insurance

Companies are *not* required to provide their employees with health insurance. However, current legislation specifies that, starting in 2014, employers who have more than 50 full-time employees must pay a penalty if they do not provide basic health insurance. In addition, company insurance policies must cover employees' children up to the age of 26.

Losing your job does not mean that you must also give up your health insurance—at least not right away. Under the Consolidated Omnibus Budget Reconciliation Act (COBRA), **former employees must be allowed to continue their health insurance for 18 months after being terminated from their job.** The catch is that employees must pay for it themselves, up to 102 percent of the cost. (The extra 2 percent covers administrative expenses.) COBRA applies to any company with 20 or more workers.

Common-Law Protections

The employment-at-will doctrine was created by the courts. Because that rule has sometimes led to grossly unfair results, the courts have now created a major exception to the rule—**wrongful discharge**.

Wrongful discharge
An employer may not fire a worker for a reason that violates basic social rights, duties or responsibilities.

Wrongful Discharge: Violating Public Policy

Olga Monge was a schoolteacher in her native Costa Rica. After moving to New Hampshire, she attended college in the evenings to earn U.S. teaching credentials. At night, she worked at the Beebe Rubber Co. During the day, she cared for her husband and three children. When she applied for a better job at her plant, the foreman offered to promote her if she would be "nice" and go out on a date with him. When she refused, he assigned her to a lower-wage job, took away her overtime, made her clean the washrooms, and generally ridiculed her. Finally, she collapsed at work, and he fired her.[4]

Imagine that you are one of the judges who decided this case. Olga Monge has been treated abominably, but she was an employee at will and, as you well know, could be fired for any reason. But how can you let the foreman get away with this despicable behavior? The New Hampshire Supreme Court decided that even an employee at will has some rights:

> We hold that a termination by the employer of a contract of employment at will which is motivated by bad faith or malice or based on retaliation is not in the best interest of the economic system or the public good and constitutes a breach of the employment contract.[5]

The *Monge* case illustrates the concept of wrongful discharge, which prohibits **an employer from firing a worker for certain particularly *bad reasons*.**

How do the courts define a "bad reason"? It is a reason that violates public policy. Unfortunately, this **public policy rule** is easier to name than it is to define because its definition and application vary from state to state. **In essence, the public policy rule prohibits an employer from firing a worker for a reason that violates basic social rights, duties, or responsibilities.** Almost every employee who has ever been fired feels that a horrible injustice has been done. The difficulty, from the courts' perspective, is to distinguish those cases of dismissal that are offensive enough to affront the community at large from those that outrage only the employee. The courts have primarily applied the public policy rule when an employee refuses to violate the law, performs a legal duty, exercises a legal right, or supports basic societal values.

Refusing to Violate the Law

Larry Downs went to Duke Hospital for surgery on his cleft palate. When he came out of the operating room, the doctor instructed a nurse, Marie Sides, to give Downs enough anesthetic to immobilize him. Sides refused because she thought the anesthetic was wrong for this patient. The doctor angrily administered the anesthetic himself. Shortly thereafter, Downs stopped breathing. Before the doctors could resuscitate him, he suffered permanent brain damage. When Downs's family sued the hospital, Sides was called to testify. A number of Duke doctors told her that she would be "in trouble" if she testified. She did testify, and after three months of harassment, she was fired. When she sued Duke University, the court held:

> It would be obnoxious to the interests of the state and contrary to public policy and sound morality to allow an employer to discharge any employee, whether the employment be for a designated or unspecified duration, on the ground that the employee declined to commit perjury, an act specifically enjoined by statute. To hold otherwise would be without reason and contrary to the spirit of the law.[6]

As a general rule, employees may not be discharged for refusing to break the law. For example, courts have protected employees who refused to participate in an illegal price-fixing scheme, falsify pollution control records required by state law, pollute navigable waters in violation of federal law, or assist a supervisor in stealing from customers.[7]

---

[4]*Monge v. Beebe*, 114 N.H. 130, 316 A.2d 549, 1974 N.H. LEXIS 223 (NH S. Ct., 1974).

[5]*Id.* at 133.

[6]*Sides v. Duke University*, 74 N.C. App. 331, 328 S.E.2d 818, 1985 N.C. App. LEXIS 3501 (N.C. Ct. App. 1985).

[7]*Tameny v. Atlantic Richfield Co.*, 27 Cal. 3d 167, 610 P.2d 1330, 1980 Cal. LEXIS 171 (1980); *Trombetta v. Detroit*, T. & I. R., 81 Mich. App. 489, 265 N.W.2d 385, 1978 Mich. App. LEXIS 2153 (Mich. Ct. App. 1978); *Sabine Pilot Service, Inc. v. Hauck*, 28 Tex. Sup. J. 339, 687 S.W.2d 733, 1985 Tex. LEXIS 755 (1985); *Vermillion v. AAA Pro Moving & Storage*, 146 Ariz. 215, 704 P.2d 1360, 1985 Ariz. App. LEXIS 592 (Ariz. Ct. App. 1985).

Performing a Legal Duty   **Courts have consistently held that an employee may not be fired for serving on a jury.** Employers sometimes have difficulty replacing employees who are called up for jury duty and, therefore, prefer that their workers find some excuse for not serving. But jury duty is an important civic obligation that employers are not permitted to undermine.

Exercising a Legal Right   **As a general rule, an employer may not discharge a worker for exercising a legal right if that right supports public policy.** Dorothy Frampton injured her arm while working at the Central Indiana Gas Co. Her employer (and its insurance company) paid her medical expenses and her salary during the four months she was unable to work. When she discovered that she also qualified for benefits under the state's workers' compensation plan, she filed a claim and received payment. One month later, the company fired her without giving a reason. In her suit against the gas company, the court held:

> The [Workers' Compensation] Act creates a duty in the employer to compensate employees for work-related injuries and a right in the employee to receive such compensation. If employers are permitted to penalize employees for filing workmen's compensation claims, a most important public policy will be undermined. Employees will not file claims for justly deserved compensation—opting, instead, to continue their employment without incident. The end result, of course, is that the employer is effectively relieved of his obligation.[8]

Supporting Societal Values   Courts are sometimes willing to protect employees who do the right thing, even if they violate the boss's orders. Kevin Gardner had just parked his armored truck in front of a bank in Spokane, Washington, when he saw a man with a knife chase the manager out of the bank. While running past the truck, the manager looked directly at Gardner and yelled, "Help me, help me." Gardner got out of his truck and locked the door. By then, the suspect had grabbed another woman, put his knife to her throat, and dragged her into the bank. Gardner followed them in, tackled the suspect, and disarmed him. The rescued woman hailed Gardner as a hero, but his employer fired him for violating a "fundamental" company rule that prohibited drivers from leaving their armored trucks unattended. However, the court held for Gardner on the grounds that, although he had no affirmative legal duty to intervene in such a situation, society values and encourages voluntary rescuers when a life is in danger.[9] This issue is, however, one on which the courts are divided. Not all would have made the same decision.

In the following case, two employees objected when their company supplied defective human tissue for transplantation into live patients. Should the court protect them from termination?

Kozloski v. American Tissue Services Foundation

2006 U.S. Dist. LEXIS 95435
United States District Court for the District of Minnesota, 2006

Facts: American Tissue Services Foundation (ATSF) was in the business of supplying human tissue from cadavers for transplantation into live patients. Mike Slack, an employee of ATSF, revealed to his boss that he had falsified a donor medical record and changed the donor's blood type on the form. This falsification was not only dangerous to recipients of the tissue, it also violated Food and Drug Administration (FDA) regulations. Slack was fired and the infractions were reported to the FDA, as required by law.

---

[8]*Frampton v. Central Indiana Gas Co.*, 260 Ind. 249, 297 N.E.2d 425, 1973 Ind. LEXIS 522 (1973).
[9]*Gardner v. Loomis Armored, Inc.*, 913 P.2d 377, 1996 Wash. LEXIS 109 (1996).

It turned out, however, that Slack was the foster child of the company's chairman. And, in this case, (foster) blood was thicker than water. The chairman not only hired Slack at another company as a quality assurance specialist (believe it or not), but he fired Slack's boss and the two men who had reported the problem to the FDA. The men filed suit against ATSF for wrongful discharge, but the company filed a motion to dismiss on the grounds that the public policy doctrine in Minnesota applied only to employees who had refused to violate the law.

Issue: *Does the public policy doctrine in Minnesota apply only if the employee has been fired for refusing to violate the law?*

Excerpts from Judge Graham's Decision: Plaintiffs claim their terminations occurred as a direct result of and in retaliation for their reporting to their employer and the FDA concerns about public safety, violations of federal regulations and federal law, and related concerns regarding

quality control issues that may directly affect public safety. [T]he Court rejects Defendant's contention that the only common law wrongful discharge claim in Minnesota is one based on allegations that termination was in retaliation for refusing to violate the law. Instead the Court concludes the Minnesota Supreme Court has recognized a common law wrongful discharge claim when a discharge is for a reason that clearly violates public policy. In other words, it is the clarity of the violation of public policy that defines the existence of the common law claim.

[T]he FDA regulations concerning the safe transfer of tissues from cadavers for use in live patients emphasize the public safety and protection of citizens, and thus encompass *clear* public policy regarding [the] public's safety. Plaintiffs' allegations that they were required by law to report the violations to the FDA for ATSF to remain in compliance also bolsters this determination. [T]he Court concludes Plaintiffs have sufficiently alleged common law claims for wrongful discharge.

Contract Law

Traditionally, many employers (and employees) thought that only a formal, signed document qualified as an employment contract. Increasingly, however, courts have been willing to enforce an employer's more casual promises, whether written or oral. Sometimes courts have also been willing to *imply* contract terms in the absence of an *express* agreement.

Truth in Hiring   **Oral promises made during the hiring process can be enforceable, even if not approved by the company's top executives.** When the Tanana Valley Medical-Surgical Group, Inc., hired James Eales as a physician's assistant, it promised him that so long as he did his job, he could stay there until retirement age. Six years later, the company fired him without cause. The Alaska Supreme Court held that the clinic's promise was enforceable.[10]

Employee Handbooks   The employee handbook at Blue Cross & Blue Shield stated that employees could be fired only for just cause and then only after warnings, notice, a hearing, and other procedures. Charles Toussaint was fired summarily five years after he joined the company. Although this decision was ultimately reviewed by the personnel department, company president, and chairman of the board of trustees, Toussaint was not given the benefit of all of the procedures in the handbook. The court held that **an employee handbook creates a contract.**[11]

Covenant of Good Faith and Fair Dealing   A covenant of good faith and fair dealing prohibits one party to a contract from interfering with the other's right to benefit under the contract. All parties are expected to behave in a fair, decent, and reasonable manner. **In almost all states, courts will imply a covenant of good faith and fair dealing in an at-will employment relationship.** These cases, however, have all arisen in situations in which an employer fires a worker to avoid paying promised income or benefits.

[10]*Eales v. Tanana Valley Medical-Surgical Group, Inc.*, 663 P.2d 958, 1983 Alas. LEXIS 430 (Alaska 1983).
[11]*Toussaint v. Blue Cross & Blue Shield*, 408 Mich. 579, 292 N.W.2d 880, 1980 Mich. LEXIS 227 (1980).

When Forrest Fleming went to work for Parametric Technology Corp., the company promised him valuable stock options if he met his sales goals. He would not be able to *exercise* the options (that is, purchase the stock), however, until several years after they were granted, and then only if he was still employed by the company. During his four years with Parametric, Fleming received options to purchase about 18,000 shares for a price as low as 25 cents each. The shares ultimately traded in the market for as much as $50. Although Fleming exercised some options, the company fired him three months before he became eligible to purchase an additional 1,000 shares. The jury awarded him $1.6 million in damages. Although Parametric had not violated the explicit terms of the option agreement, the jury believed it had violated the covenant of good faith and fair dealing by firing Fleming to prevent him from exercising his remaining options.[12]

Tort Law

Workers have successfully sued their employers under the following tort theories.

Defamation   **Employers may be liable for defamation when they give false and unfavorable references about a former employee.** In his job as a bartender at the Capitol Grille restaurant, Christopher Kane often flirted with customers. After he was fired from his job, his ex-boss claimed that Kane had been "fired from every job he ever had for sexual misconduct." In fact, Kane had never been fired before. He recovered $300,000 in damages for this defamation.

More than half of the states, however, recognize a qualified privilege for employers who give references about former employees. A **qualified privilege** means that employers are liable only for false statements that they know to be false or that are primarily motivated by ill will. After Becky Chambers left her job at American Trans Air, Inc., she discovered that her former boss was telling anyone who called for a reference that Chambers "does not work good with other people," is a "troublemaker," and "would not be a good person to rehire." Chambers was unable, however, to present compelling evidence that her boss had been primarily motivated by ill will. Neither Trans Air nor the boss was held liable for these statements because they were protected by the qualified privilege.[13]

Even if the employer wins, a trial is an expensive and time-consuming undertaking. Not surprisingly, companies are leery about offering any references for former employees. The company gains little benefit from giving an honest evaluation and may suffer substantial liability. As a matter of policy, many companies instruct their managers to reveal only a person's salary and dates of employment and not to offer an opinion on job performance.

On the flip side, do employers have any obligation to warn about risky workers? **Generally, courts have held that employers do *not* have a legal obligation to disclose information about former employees.** For example, while Jeffrey St. Clair worked at the St. Joseph Nursing Home, he was disciplined 24 times for actions ranging from extreme violence to drug and alcohol use. When he applied for a job with Maintenance Management Corp., St. Joseph refused to give any information other than St. Clair's dates of employment. After he savagely murdered a security guard at his new job, the guard's family sued, but the court dismissed the case.[14]

In some recent cases, however, courts have held that, when a former worker is potentially dangerous, employers do have an obligation to disclose this information. For example, officials from two junior high schools gave Robert Gadams glowing letters of recommendation without mentioning that he had been fired for inappropriate sexual conduct with students. While an assistant principal at a new school, he molested a 13-year-old. Her parents sued the former employers. The court held that the writer of a letter of recommendation owes to

Qualified privilege
Employers who give references are liable only for false statements that they know to be false or that are primarily motivated by ill will.

---

[12]*Fleming v. Parametric Tech. Corp.*, 1999 U.S. App. LEXIS 14864.
[13]*Chambers v. American Trans Air, Inc.*, 577 N.E.2d 612, 1991 Ind. App. LEXIS 1413 (Ind. Ct. App. 1991).
[14]*Moore v. St. Joseph Nursing Home, Inc.*, 184 Mich. App. 766, 459 N.W.2d 100, 1990 Mich. App. LEXIS 285 (Mich. Ct. App. 1990).

third parties (in this case, the student) "a duty not to misrepresent the facts in describing the qualifications and character of a former employee, if making these misrepresentations would present a substantial, foreseeable risk of physical injury to the third persons."[15] As a result of cases such as this, it makes sense to disclose past violent behavior.

To assist employers who are asked for references, Lehigh economist Robert Thornton has written "The Lexicon of Intentional Ambiguous Recommendations" (LIAR). For a candidate with interpersonal problems, he suggests saying, "I am pleased to say that this person is a former colleague of mine." For a candidate with drug or alcohol problems, there are several possibilities: "She was always high in my opinion," "We remember the hours she spent working with us as happy hours," or "I would say that her real talent is getting wasted at her current job."[16]

> **Ethics** All joking aside, what if someone calls you to check references on a former employee who had a drinking problem? The job is driving a van for junior high school sports teams. What is the manager's ethical obligation in this situation? Many managers say that, in the case of a serious problem such as alcoholism, sexual harassment, or drug use, they will find a way to communicate that an employee is unsuitable. What if the ex-employee says she is reformed? Aren't people entitled to a second chance? Is it right to risk a defamation suit against your company to protect others from harm?

Intentional Infliction of Emotional Distress **Employers who condone cruel treatment of their workers may face liability under the tort of intentional infliction of emotional distress.** For example, when a 57-year-old social-work manager at Yale–New Haven Hospital was fired, she was forced to place her personal belongings in a plastic bag and was escorted out the door by security guards in full view of gaping coworkers. A supervisor told her that she would be arrested for trespassing if she returned. A jury awarded her $105,000.

Whistleblowing

No one likes to be accused of wrongdoing even if (or, perhaps, especially if) the accusations are true. **This is exactly what whistleblowers do: they are employees who disclose illegal behavior on the part of their employer.** Not surprisingly, some companies, when faced with such an accusation by an employee, prefer to shoot the messenger. Rather than fixing the reported problem, they retaliate against the informer. Here is one such story.

Although FMC Corp. sold 9,000 Bradley Fighting Vehicles to the U.S. Army, there had been doubts about the Bradley from the beginning. It was designed to ferry soldiers across rivers, but prototypes leaked badly when driven into water. Testing supervisor Henry Boisvert refused to sign a report stating that the Bradley functioned well, and FMC fired him. A jury ultimately agreed with his version of events and awarded him $171 million.

The law on whistleblowers varies across the country. As a general rule, however, whistleblowers are protected in the following situations:

- **The False Claims Act.** Boisvert recovered under the federal False Claims Act, a statute that permits lawsuits against anyone who defrauds the government. The recovery is shared by the government (who receives 75 percent to 85 percent) and the whistleblower (who gets the rest). The Act prohibits employers from firing workers who file suit under the statute.

---

[15]*Randi W. v. Muroc Joint Unified School District*, 14 Cal. 4th 1066, 929 P.2d 582, 1997 Cal. LEXIS 10 (1997), modified, 14 Cal. 4th 1282c, 97 Cal. Daily Op. Service 1439.

[16]Robert J. Thornton, *Lexicon of Intentionally Ambiguous Recommendations*, Barnes and Noble Books, 2005.

- **The Dodd-Frank Wall Street Reform and Consumer Protection Act.** Anyone who provides information to the government about violations of securities or commodities laws is entitled to a payout of from 10 to 30 percent of whatever award the government receives, provided that the award tops $1 million. If a company retaliates against tipsters, they are entitled to reinstatement, double back pay, and attorney's fees. The whistleblowing provision is intended to encourage tips to the government, but companies fear it may also discourage employees from reporting wrongdoing to corporate compliance offices—why report a problem to your own company for free when you could get paid a lot of money to report it to the government?

- **Sarbanes-Oxley Act of 2002.** This act protects employees of publicly traded companies who provide evidence of fraud to investigators (whether in or outside the company). A successful plaintiff is entitled to reinstatement, back pay, and attorney's fees.

- **Constitutional protection for government employees.** Employees of federal, state, and local governments have a right to free speech under the United States Constitution. Therefore, the government cannot retaliate against public employees who blow the whistle if the employee is speaking out on a matter of *public concern*. For example, a New York City social worker complained on TV that the city child welfare agency was not adequately protecting children from horrible abuse. When the city suspended the social worker from her job, she sued. The court ruled that the government has the right to prohibit some employee speech, but if the employee speaks on matters of public concern, the government bears the burden of justifying any retaliation. In this case, the court held for the social worker.[17]

- **Statutory protection for federal employees.** The Civil Service Reform Act and the Whistleblower Protection Act prevent retaliation against federal employees who report wrongdoing. They also permit the award of back pay and attorney's fees to the whistleblower. This statute was used to prevent the National Park Service from disciplining two managers who wrote a report expressing concern over development in Yellowstone National Park.

- **State laws.** The good news is that all 50 states have laws that protect whistleblowers from retaliation by their employers. The bad news is that the scope of this protection varies greatly from state to state. Most courts, however, prohibit the discharge of employees who report illegal activity. For example, a Connecticut court held a company liable when it fired a quality control director who reported to his boss that some products had failed quality tests.[18]

EXAM Strategy

Question: When Shiloh interviewed for a sales job at a medical supply company, the interviewer promised that she could work exclusively selling medical devices and would not have to be involved in the sale of drugs. Once she began work (as an employee at will), Shiloh discovered that the sales force was organized around regions, not products, so she had to sell both devices and drugs. When she complained to her boss over lunch in the employee lunchroom, he said in a loud voice, "You are a big girl now—it's time you learned that you don't always get what you want." That afternoon, she was fired. Does she have a valid claim against the company?

---

[17]*Harman v. City of New York*, 140 F.3d 111, 1998 U.S. App. LEXIS 5567 (2d Cir. 1998).
[18]*Smith v. Calgon Carbon Corp.*, 917 F.2d 1338, 1990 U.S. App. LEXIS 19193 (3rd Cir. 1990).

Strategy: We know that Shiloh is an employee at will. We also know that she is not protected by any statute we have studied. What about the *common law*? Shiloh has had two key interactions with the company—being hired and being fired. What protections does the common law provide during the hiring process? The employer's promises are enforceable. Here, the company is liable because the interviewer clearly made a promise that the company did not keep. What about the way in which Shiloh was fired? Is it intentional infliction of emotional distress? Was this treatment cruel? Probably not cruel enough to constitute intentional infliction of emotional distress.

Result: The company is liable to Shiloh for making false promises to her during the hiring process, but not for the manner in which she was fired.

Privacy in the Workplace

Upon opening the country's first moving assembly line in the early 1900s, Henry Ford issued a booklet, "Helpful Hints and Advice to Employees," that warned against drinking, gambling, borrowing money, taking in boarders, and practicing poor hygiene. Ford also created a department of 100 investigators for door-to-door checks on his employees' drinking habits, sexual practices, and housekeeping skills.

The right to hire, fire, and make an honest profit is enshrined in American tradition. But so is the right to privacy. Justice Louis D. Brandeis called it the "right to be let alone—the most comprehensive of rights and the right most valued by civilized men." Workers are entitled under the common law to a **reasonable expectation of privacy**. Thus, employers no longer have the right to conduct home inspections, even if, say, looking for items that the worker might have stolen from the company

However, in the absence of a specific law to the contrary, employers *do* have the right to fire workers for off-duty conduct. Employees have been fired or disciplined for such extracurricular activities as taking part in dangerous sports (such as sky-diving), dating coworkers, smoking, or even having high cholesterol. But some governments have passed statutes that change this common law rule. These statutes take two forms: (1) general lifestyle statutes and (2) laws that protect specific behavior.

Lifestyle Laws

A few states, such as California, have passed so-called lifestyle laws that protect the right of employees to engage in any *lawful* activity or use any *lawful* product when off duty. Thus, if California residents sky-dive while smoking a cigarette, they may lose their lives, but not their jobs.

About half the states and the federal government have passed laws that protect *particular* off-duty conduct, such as smoking or use of legal drugs.

Smoking

Smokers tend to take more sick days and have higher healthcare expenses than other employees. Indeed, the federal government estimates that it costs an extra $3,400 a year to employ a worker who smokes. As a result, several thousand employers, including Union Pacific and Alaska Airlines, simply refuse to hire those who light up. Such a policy is legal unless state law prohibits it.

Massachusetts is a state that does not specifically protect smokers from employment discrimination. But in the following case, the plaintiff argued that his employer's actions violated his privacy rights. Does his argument have merit? You be the judge.

You be the Judge

RODRIGUES V. SCOTTS LAWNSERVICE

639 F. Supp. 2d 131
United States District Court for the District of
Massachusetts, 2009

Facts: Scotts Lawnservice refused to hire tobacco users. It also tested all employees for both illegal drugs and nicotine.

Scotts offered Rodrigues a job "contingent upon successful completion of a pre-hire screening which includes a nicotine test." Rodrigues voluntarily submitted a urine sample and started work.

Shortly thereafter, a Scotts supervisor saw a pack of cigarettes on Rodrigues's dashboard and issued a warning. Two weeks later, when Rodrigues's test came back positive for nicotine, he was told not to return to work. He sued, claiming a violation of his privacy rights. Massachusetts law states: "A person shall have a right against unreasonable, substantial, or serious interference with his privacy."

You Be The Judge: *Did Scotts' enforcement of its anti-tobacco policy violate Rodrigues's privacy rights?*

Argument for Rodrigues: Under Massachusetts law, a person has a right to be free from unreasonable interference with his privacy. As a result, employers are not allowed to exercise total control over their employees' personal lives. For Scotts to require a test that reveals what Rodrigues has been doing at home or in his car is a clear violation of his privacy rights.

Smoking outside of work has nothing to do with Rodrigues's job performance.

We would have no argument with Scotts if the company prohibited employees from smoking *while on duty*. But a policy that disallows tobacco use at any time goes too far and is an unreasonable invasion of workers' right to privacy. Tobacco is a legal substance, and it is absurd for a private business to ban what the government does not.

Argument for Scotts: There is nothing private about smoking. Smokers typically light up in their cars and in public places. They purchase cigarettes openly. A person does not have a right to privacy when he does not attempt to keep information private. Rodrigues had a pack of cigarettes in his truck while at work. He made no effort to keep his tobacco use secret.

Scotts has a legitimate interest in hiring workers who do not use tobacco. No law, including the Massachusetts privacy statute, prohibits the company's anti-tobacco policy.

Some workers have also claimed that nicotine addiction is a disability under the Americans with Disabilities Act (ADA; see Chapter 18 for more information about that statute), but so far, courts have been skeptical that Congress intended ADA coverage for the roughly 60 million Americans who smoke.[19] Several amendments to the ADA passed in 2008 could provide more protection for smokers, but the courts have not yet decided such a case.

Alcohol and Drug Use

Private Employers Under *federal* law, *private* employers are permitted to test job applicants and workers for alcohol and *illegal* drugs. They may sanction workers who fail the test, even if the drug or alcohol use was off duty. *State* laws on drug testing vary widely.

Although employers were traditionally most concerned about illegal drugs, they now also worry about *legal* use of prescription drugs such as Xanax and Oxycodone because these medications may cause impairment. In one study, workers drug-tested after accidents in the workplace were four times more likely to have opiates in their system than job applicants. However, the Equal Employment Opportunity Commission (EEOC), the federal agency charged with enforcing federal employment laws, prohibits testing for prescription drugs unless a worker seems impaired. The EEOC filed suit against a company that randomly tested for legal use of prescription drugs, and a jury awarded substantial damages to the employees.[20]

---

[19]See *Brashear v. Simms*, 138 F.Supp.2d 693 (D.Md. 2001).
[20]*Bates v. Dura Auto Sys Inc.*, 2011 U.S. Dist. LEXIS 97469 (M.D. Tenn 2011).

Government Employers Governments are sometimes allowed to conduct drug and alcohol tests of their employees. Public safety workers, such as police and firefighters, can be randomly tested for illegal drugs, and they may also be required to report legal drug use that could compromise their ability to perform their jobs. If their drug use (legal or not) is a threat to public safety, they may be suspended or fired from their jobs. Other government employees, whose work does not involve public safety, can be tested only if they show signs of impairment.

Polygraph Tests

A polygraph exam is a type of lie detector test. Under the Employee Polygraph Protection Act of 1988, employers may not require, or even *suggest*, that an employee or job candidate submit to a polygraph test *except in the following cases*:

- An employee who is part of an "ongoing investigation" into crimes that have already occurred,

- An applicant applying for a government job, or

- An applicant for a job in public transport or banking, or at pharmaceutical firms that deal with controlled substances.

If an employer requires a polygraph test, it must give advance written notice of when the test will be given and advise workers that they are entitled to legal counsel. A private employer may not fire or discriminate against an employee who fails a polygraph exam unless it also finds supporting evidence that the worker has done something wrong.

Ethics By law, there are few situations in which private employers may require polygraph tests. What would be the advantages and disadvantages of requiring polygraph tests? Should there be different rules for job applicants, as opposed to employees?

Electronic Monitoring of the Workplace

Technological advances in communications have raised a host of new privacy issues. Many companies monitor employee use of electronic equipment in the workplace: telephone calls, voicemail, email, and Internet usage. **The Electronic Communications Privacy Act of 1986 (ECPA) permits employers to monitor workers' telephone calls and email messages if (1) the employee consents, (2) the monitoring occurs in the ordinary course of business, or (3) in the case of email, the employer provides the email system.** However, bosses may not disclose any private information revealed by the monitoring.

Sending personal emails through a company server is dangerous. In one case, a court permitted an employer to fire two workers who exchanged (they claimed) joking emails threatening violence to sales managers even though the company had an explicit policy stating that emails were confidential and would not be intercepted or used against an employee.[21] Over 75 percent of U.S. firms monitor their employees' computer usage. About one third of companies have fired a worker over inappropriate email or Internet use.

A few courts have carved out narrow rights for employees. For example, a New Jersey court recently held that unless company policy explicitly informs workers otherwise, the company does not have the right to monitor a personal, password-protected, web-based

[21]*Smyth v. Pillsbury*, 914 F. Supp. 97, 1996 U.S. Dist. LEXIS 776, (Fed. Dist. Ct., 1996).

email account.[22] But unless you enjoy the prospect of engaging in years of litigation to clarify this issue, it is still good advice to consider all email you send through a company server to be public.

Social Media

Social media are the newest challenge facing both employers and workers. On the one hand, employers may find themselves liable for statements that their workers make electronically. For example, Cisco Systems Inc., has settled two lawsuits brought against the company for statements made by a company lawyer on his blog. Not surprisingly, employers have fired workers who posted inappropriate information in cyberspace. But companies may find themselves liable for violations of employee privacy if a boss reads workers' Facebook or MySpace pages. A high school teacher in Georgia sued her school district after she was forced to resign because of vacation photos on Facebook that showed her holding a glass of wine.

And privacy rights aside, some workers have discovered a new way to fight back. The National Labor Relations Act (NLRA; discussed later in this chapter) gives employees the right to discuss wages, hours, and working conditions. So when American Medical Response fired an employee for making negative comments about her boss on Facebook, the National Labor Relations Board (NLRB) filed a complaint against the company. American Medical Response settled the complaint by promising it would not fire or discipline workers for discussing wages, hours, and working conditions. But in some similar cases, the NLRB has deemed online rants against employers to be mere venting, not a genuine discussion of their jobs, which means that these employees could be fired for their hostile postings.

In short, the law is evolving, subtle, and varies by state, so employees at will should err on the side of caution and remember that the law often does not protect their electronic lives from employer prying. They should consider anything they publish on the Internet to be public.

As for companies, it makes sense to establish policies providing that:

1. Employees should never reveal their company's name on a blog or social website such as Facebook.

2. In addition, all employees' personal blogs must contain a disclaimer that "All postings on this blog are my opinion and not those of my employer, who has neither vetted nor approved them." The blogger should not reveal the company's name.

3. Blog comments should never be offensive, impolite, or reflect badly on the employer. Nor should they reveal confidential or proprietary information.

4. Supervisors have the right to read and take action based on most kinds of electronic information posted by an employee.

Immigration

Because of discrimination laws, employers should not ask about an applicant's country of origin, but they are permitted to inquire if the person is authorized to work in the United States. If the applicant says, "Yes," the interviewer cannot ask for evidence until the person is hired. At that point, the employer must complete an I-9 form—Employment Eligibility Verification—within three days. This form lists the acceptable documents that can be used for verification. Employees have the right to present whichever documents they want from the list of acceptable items. The employer may not ask for some other document. The I-9 forms must be kept for three years after the worker is hired or one year after termination.

---

[22]*Stengart v. Loving Care Agency, Inc.*, 201 N.J. 300, 2010 N.J. LEXIS 241, (S.Ct. NJ, 2010).

EXAM Strategy

Question: To ensure that its employees did not use illegal drugs in or outside the workplace, Marvel Grocery Store required all employees to take a polygraph exam. Moreover, managers began to screen the company email system for drug references. Jagger was fired for refusing to take the polygraph test. Jonathan was dismissed when a search of his email revealed that he had used marijuana during the prior weekend. Has the company acted legally?

Strategy: First: As employees at will, are Jagger and Jonathan protected by a statute? The Employee Polygraph Protection Act permits employers to require a polygraph test as part of ongoing investigations into crimes that have occurred. Here, Marvel has no reason to believe that a crime occurred, so it cannot require a polygraph test.

Second: What about Jonathan's marijuana use? The ECPA permits Marvel to monitor email messages on its own system. But can the company fire Jonathan for illegal off-duty conduct? Some statutes protect employees for *legal* behavior outside the workplace, but no state protects employees for behavior that violates the law.

Result: The company is liable to Jagger for requiring him to take the polygraph exam, but not to Jonathan for monitoring his email or firing him for illegal drug use.

Workplace Safety

In 1970, Congress passed the Occupational Safety and Health Act (OSHA) to ensure safe working conditions. Under OSHA:

- Employers must comply with specific health and safety standards. For example, health care personnel who work with blood are not permitted to eat or drink in areas where the blood is kept. Protective clothing—gloves, gowns, and laboratory coats—must be impermeable to blood.

- Employers are under a general obligation to keep their workplace "free from recognized hazards that are causing or are likely to cause death or serious physical harm" to employees.

- Employers must keep records of all workplace injuries and accidents.

- The Occupational Safety and Health Administration (which is also known as OSHA) may inspect workplaces to ensure that they are safe. OSHA may assess fines for violations and order employers to correct unsafe conditions.

OSHA has done a lot to make the American workplace safer. In 1900, roughly 35,000 workers died at work. A century later, the workforce had grown five times larger, but the number of annual deaths had fallen to about 5,500.

FINANCIAL PROTECTION

Congress and the states have enacted laws designed to provide employees with a measure of financial security. All of the laws in this section were created by statute, not by the courts.

Fair Labor Standards Act: Minimum Wage, Overtime, and Child Labor

Passed in 1938, the Fair Labor Standards Act (FLSA) regulates wages and limits child labor nationally. It provides that hourly workers must be paid a minimum wage of $7.25 per hour, plus time and a half for any hours over 40 in one week. These wage provisions do not apply to salaried workers, such as managerial, administrative, or professional staff. More than half the states set a higher minimum wage, so it is important to check state guidelines as well.

Today, the biggest issue that employers face under the FLSA is: "What counts as work, and how do you keep track of it?" What if a worker answers email during lunch or takes a phone call on the train ride home? Although these activities count as work, how can the employer keep track of it? Carla Bird, an assistant at Oprah Winfrey's production company, submitted timesheets showing 800 hours of overtime in 17 weeks. She said she had worked 12 or 13 hours a day, seven days a week, for four months. The company paid her $32,000 in overtime.[23] If employees work all the time, or even if they are just on call, they are entitled to be paid for those hours.

The FLSA also prohibits "oppressive child labor," which means that children under 14 may work only in agriculture and entertainment. Fourteen- and fifteen-year-olds are permitted to work *limited* hours after school in nonhazardous jobs. Sixteen- and seventeen-year-olds may work *unlimited* hours in nonhazardous jobs.

Workers' Compensation

Workers' compensation statutes ensure that employees receive payment for injuries incurred at work. Before workers' comp, injured employees could recover damages only if they sued their employer. It is the brave (or carefree) worker who is willing to risk a suit against his own boss. Lawsuits poison the atmosphere at work. Moreover, employers frequently won these suits by claiming that (1) the injured worker was contributorily negligent, (2) a fellow employee had caused the accident, or (3) the injured worker had assumed the risk of injury. As a result, seriously injured workers (or their families) often had no recourse against the employer.

Workers' comp statutes provide a fixed, certain recovery to the injured employee, no matter who was at fault for the accident. In return, employees are not permitted to sue their employers for negligence. The amounts allowed (for medical expenses and lost wages) under workers' comp statutes are often less than a worker might recover in court, but the injured employee trades the certainty of some recovery for the higher risk of rolling the dice at trial. Payments are approved by an administrative board that conducts an informal hearing into each claim.

Social Security

The federal social security system began in 1935, during the depths of the Great Depression, to provide a basic safety net for the elderly, ill, and unemployed. **Currently, the social security system pays benefits to workers who are retired, disabled, or temporarily unemployed and to the spouses and children of disabled or deceased workers.** It also provides medical insurance to the retired and disabled. The social security program is financed through a tax on wages that is paid by employers, employees, and the self-employed.

Although the social security system has done much to reduce poverty among the elderly, many worry that it cannot survive in its current form. The system was designed to be "pay as you go"; that is, when workers pay taxes, the proceeds do not go into a savings account for their retirement, but instead are used to pay benefits to current retirees. In 1940,

---

[23]LisaBelkin,"O.T. Isn't as Simple as Telling Time."*The New York Times*, September 20, 2007.

there were 40 workers for each retiree; currently, there are 3.3. As a result, the system now pays out more in benefits each year than it receives in tax revenues. By 2025, when the last baby boomers retire, there will be only 2 workers to support each retiree—a prohibitive burden. No wonder younger workers are often cautioned not to count on social security when making their retirement plans.

The Federal Unemployment Tax Act (FUTA) is the part of the social security system that provides support to the unemployed. FUTA establishes some national standards, but states are free to set their own benefit levels and payment schedules. A worker who quits voluntarily or is fired for just cause is ineligible for benefits. While receiving payments, she must make a good-faith effort to look for other employment.

Pension Benefits

In 1974, Congress passed the Employee Retirement Income Security Act (ERISA) to protect workers covered by private pension plans. Under ERISA, employers are not required to establish pension plans, but if they do, they must follow these federal rules. The law was aimed, in particular, at protecting benefits of retired workers if their companies subsequently go bankrupt. The statute also prohibits risky investments by pension plans. In addition, the statute sets rules on the vesting of benefits. (An employer cannot cancel *vested* benefits; *nonvested* benefits are forfeited when the employee leaves.) Before ERISA, retirement benefits at some companies did not vest until the employee retired—if he quit or was fired before retirement, even after years of service, he lost his pension. Under current law, employee benefits normally must vest within five years of employment.

LABOR LAW AND COLLECTIVE BARGAINING

The opening scenario of this chapter provdes a graphic example of how painful (literally) working conditions could be. Indeed, during the nineteenth and early twentieth centuries, as industrialization spread across the United States, many workers found their employment environment unbearable. Seeking better pay and improved working conditions, some began to band together into unions. But in this era, American courts regarded any coordinated effort by workers as a criminal conspiracy. Courts convicted workers merely for the *act* of joining together, even if no strike took place. A company could usually obtain an immediate injunction merely by alleging that a strike *might* cause harm. Courts were so quick to issue injunctions that most companies became immune to union efforts. But with the economic collapse of 1929 and the vast suffering of the Great Depression, public sympathy shifted to the workers. Congress responded with two landmark statutes.

Key Pro-Union Statutes

In 1932, Congress passed the **Norris-LaGuardia Act** which prohibited federal court injunctions in nonviolent labor disputes. No longer could management stop a strike merely by mentioning the word "strike." By taking away the injunction remedy, Congress was declaring that workers should be permitted to organize unions and to use their collective power to achieve legitimate economic ends. The statute led to explosive growth in union membership.

In 1935, Congress passed the Wagner Act, generally known as the **National Labor Relations Act (NLRA).** This is the most important of all labor laws. A fundamental aim of the NLRA is the establishment and maintenance of industrial peace, to preserve the flow

Norris-LaGuardia Act
Prohibits federal court injunctions in nonviolent labor disputes.

National Labor Relations Act (NLRA)
Ensures the right of workers to form unions and encourages management and unions to bargain collectively and productively.

of commerce. The NLRA ensures the right of workers to form unions and encourages management and unions to bargain collectively and productively. For our purposes, Sections 7 and 8 of the NLRA are the most important.

Section 7 guarantees employees the right to organize and join unions, bargain collectively through representatives of their own choosing, and engage in other concerted activities. This is the cornerstone of union power. With the enactment of the NLRA, Congress put an end to any notion that unions were inherently illegal by explicitly recognizing that workers could join together, bargain as a group, and use their collective power to seek better conditions.

Section 8 prohibits employers from engaging in the following unfair labor practices (ULPs):

- Interfering with union organizing efforts,

- Dominating or interfering with any union,

- Discriminating against a union member, or

- Refusing to bargain collectively with a union.

The NLRA also established the **National Labor Relations Board (NLRB)** to administer and interpret the statute and to adjudicate labor cases. For example, when a union charges that an employer has committed a ULP—say, by refusing to bargain—the claim goes first to the NLRB.

National Labor Relations Board (NLRB)

Administers and interprets the NLRA and adjudicates labor cases.

Labor Unions Today

Organized labor is in flux in the United States. In the 1950s, about 1 in 4 workers belonged to a union. Today, only about 1 in 8, or 15 million total U.S. workers, are union members. Employers point to this figure with satisfaction and claim that it shows that unions have failed their memberships. In an increasingly high-tech, service-oriented economy, employers argue, there is no place for organized labor. Union supporters respond that although the country has shed many old factories, workers have not benefited. Throughout the last 20 years, they assert, compensation for executives has soared into the stratosphere while wages for the average worker, in real dollars, have fallen.

Unions continue to attract political attention. In 2011, legislators in Wisconsin voted to strip most collective bargaining rights from schoolteachers and other state government workers. Public employees are five times more likely to be union members than private sector workers, but they are generally not protected by the NLRA. Instead, state labor laws apply, which tend to provide less protection than federal statutes.

Crowds of as many as 100,000 gathered in Madison, Wisconsin, to protest the proposed legislation, but it passed nonetheless. Commentators on the left forecast significant political consequences for the Wisconsin lawmakers, while editorialists on the right predicted that many states would soon follow the Wisconsin model.

Although overall membership is down, unions still matter.

Organizing a Union
Exclusivity

Management is generally opposed—sometimes fiercely opposed—to any union organizing effort. The fight can become ugly, and all because of one principle: *exclusivity*.

Under §9 of the NLRA, a validly recognized union is the *exclusive* representative of the employees. This means that the union will represent all of the designated employees, regardless of whether a particular worker *wants* to be represented. The company may not bargain directly with any employee in the group, nor with any other organization representing the designated employees.

However, a union may not exercise power however it likes: along with a union's exclusive bargaining power goes a duty of fair representation, which requires that a union treat all members fairly, impartially, and in good faith. A union may not favor some members over others, nor may a union discriminate against a member based on characteristics such as race or gender.

Organizing: Stages

A union organizing effort generally involves the following pattern.

Campaign   Union organizers talk—or attempt to talk—with employees and interest them in forming a union. The organizers may be employees of the company, who simply chat with fellow workers about unsatisfactory conditions; or a union may send nonemployees of the company to hand out union leaflets to workers as they arrive and depart from work.

Authorization Cards   Union organizers ask workers to sign authorization cards, which state that the particular worker requests the specified union to act as her sole bargaining representative.

If a union obtains authorization cards from a sizable percentage of workers, it seeks **recognition** as the exclusive representative for the bargaining unit. The union may ask the employer to recognize it as the bargaining representative, but most of the time, employers refuse to recognize the union voluntarily.

Petition   Assuming that the employer does not voluntarily recognize a union, the union generally petitions the NLRB for an election. It must submit to the NLRB regional office authorization cards signed by at least 30 percent of the workers. The regional office verifies whether there are enough valid cards to warrant an election and looks closely at the proposed bargaining unit to make sure that it is appropriate. If the regional director determines that the union has identified an appropriate bargaining unit and has enough valid cards, it orders an election.

Election   The NLRB closely supervises the election to ensure fairness. All members of the proposed bargaining unit vote on whether they want the union to represent them. If more than 50 percent of the workers vote for the union, the NLRB designates that union as the exclusive representative of all members of the bargaining unit. When unions hold representation elections in private corporations, they win about half the time.

The "Card-Check" Debate   Before becoming president, then–U.S. senator Barack Obama co-introduced a bill called the Employee Free Choice Act. This bill provides that when more than 50 percent of workers sign an authorization card, the NLRB must immediately designate that union as the exclusive representative of all members in the bargaining unit *without an election*.

Supporters argue that, if a majority of workers return authorization cards, an election is unnecessary and only gives companies an opportunity to intimidate workers. Those who dislike the bill argue that workers may feel bullied into signing an authorization card and should always have the right to a final vote by secret ballot.

The bill has generated much debate but has not passed Congress at the time of this writing.

Organizing: Actions

The NLRA guarantees employees the right to talk among themselves about forming a union, to hand out literature, and ultimately to join a union.[24] Workers may urge other employees to sign authorization cards and may vigorously push their cause. When employees hand out leaflets, the employer generally may not limit the content, so long as it is somewhat related to union activity.

---

[24]NLRA §7.

There are, of course, limits to what union organizers may do. The statute permits an employer to restrict organizing discussions if they interfere with discipline or production. A worker on a moving assembly line has no right to walk away from his task to talk with other employees about organizing a union; these discussions must be left until lunch or some other break time.[25]

May the employer speak out against a union organizing drive? Yes. Management is entitled to communicate to the employees why it believes a union will be harmful to the company. But the employer's efforts must be limited to explanation and advocacy. **The employer may vigorously present anti-union views to its employees but may not use either threats or promises of benefits to defeat a union drive.**[26]

EXAM Strategy

Question: We Haul is a trucking company. The Teamsters Union is attempting to organize the drivers. Workers who favor a union have been using the lunchroom to hand out petitions and urge other drivers to sign authorization cards. The company posts a notice in the lunchroom: "No Union Discussions. Many employees do not want unions discussed in the lunchroom. Out of respect for them, we are prohibiting further union efforts in this lunchroom." Comment.

Strategy: The NLRA guarantees employees the right to talk among themselves about forming a union and to hand out literature. Union workers may vigorously push their cause. Management is entitled to communicate to the employees why it believes a union will be harmful to the company, but the employer's efforts must be limited to explanation and advocacy.

Result: We Haul has violated the NLRA. The company has the right to urge employees not to join the union. However, it is not entitled to block the union from its organizing campaign. Even assuming the company is correct that some employees do not want unions discussed, it has no right to prohibit such advocacy.

Collective Bargaining

Collective bargaining agreement (CBA)

A contract between a union and management.

Once a union is formed, a company must then bargain with it toward the goal of creating a new contract, which is called a **collective bargaining agreement (CBA)**.

The NLRA *permits* the parties to bargain almost any subject they wish, but it only *requires* them to bargain certain issues. **Mandatory subjects include wages, hours, and other terms and conditions of employment.** Courts generally also find these subjects to be mandatory: benefits, order of layoffs and recalls, production quotas, work rules (such as safety practices), retirement benefits, and onsite food service and prices. An employer may not *unilaterally* make changes in conditions of employment without first bargaining with the union.

Both the union and the employer must bargain in good faith. However, they are *not* obligated to reach an agreement. In the end, this means that the two sides must meet with open minds and make a reasonable effort to reach a contract. In the following case, the Supreme Court examined the requirements of bargaining in good faith.

---

[25]*NLRB v. Babcock & Wilcox Co.*, 351 U.S. 105, 76 S. Ct. 679, 1956 U.S. LEXIS 1721 (1956).
[26]*NLRB v. Gissel Packing Co.*, 395 U.S. 575, 89 S. Ct. 1918, 1969 U.S. LEXIS 3172 (1969).

Landmark Case

NLRB v. Truitt Manufacturing Co.

351 U.S. 149
United States Supreme Court, 1956

Facts: A union representing workers at Truitt Manufacturing Company requested a raise of 10 cents per hour for all members. The company offered an additional 2.5 cents per hour and argued that a larger increase would bankrupt the company. The union demanded to examine Truitt's books, and when the company refused, the union complained to the NLRB.

The NLRB determined that the company had failed to bargain in good faith and ordered it to allow union representatives to examine its finances. A court of appeals found no ULP and refused to enforce the Board's order. The Supreme Court granted certiorari.

Issue: *Did the company refuse to bargain in good faith?*

Excerpts from Justice Black's Decision: We think that in determining whether the obligation of good-faith bargaining has been met, the Board has a right to consider an employer's refusal to give information about its financial status. While Congress did not compel agreement between employers and bargaining representatives, it did require collective bargaining in the hope that agreements would result. [T]he Act admonishes both employers and employees to exert every reasonable effort to make and maintain agreements.

In their effort to reach an agreement here, both the union and the company treated the company's ability to pay increased wages as highly relevant. Claims for increased wages have sometimes been abandoned because of an employer's unsatisfactory business condition; employees have even voted to accept wage decreases because of such conditions.

Good-faith bargaining necessarily requires that claims made by either bargainer should be honest claims. This is true about an asserted inability to pay an increase in wages. If such an argument is important enough to present in the give and take of bargaining, it is important enough to require some sort of proof of its accuracy.

The Board concluded that under the facts and circumstances of this case, the respondent was guilty of an unfair labor practice in failing to bargain in good faith. We see no reason to disturb the findings of the Board.

Reversed.

Concerted Action

Concerted action refers to any tactics that union members take in unison to gain some bargaining advantage. It is this power that gives a union strength. **The NLRA guarantees the right of employees to engage in concerted action for mutual aid or protection.**[27] The most common forms of concerted action are strikes and picketing.

Concerted action
Tactics taken by union members to gain bargaining advantage.

Strikes

The NLRA guarantees employees the right to strike, but with some limitations.[28] A union has a guaranteed right to call a strike if the parties are unable to reach a CBA. A union may call a strike to exert economic pressure on management, to protest a ULP, or to preserve work that the employer is considering sending elsewhere. Note that the right to strike can be waived. Management will generally insist that the CBA include a **no-strike clause**, which prohibits the union from striking while the CBA is in force. A strike is illegal in several other situations as well; here, we mention the most important.

No-strike clause
A clause in a CBA that prohibits the union from striking while the CBA is in force.

---

[27]NLRA §7.
[28]NLRA §13.

Cooling Off Period   Before striking to terminate or modify a CBA, a union must give management 60 days' notice. Suppose a union contract expires July 1. The two sides attempt to bargain a new contract, but progress is slow. The union may strike as an economic weapon, but it must notify management of its intention to do so *and then must wait 60 days.* This cooling-off period is designed to give both sides a chance to reassess negotiations and to decide whether some additional compromise would be wiser than enduring a strike.

Statutory Prohibition   Many states have outlawed strikes by public employees. In some states, the prohibition applies to selected employees, such as firefighters or teachers. In other states, all public employees are barred from striking, whether or not they have a contract. The purpose of these statutes is to ensure that unions do not use the public health or welfare as a weapon to secure an unfair bargaining advantage. However, even employees subject to such a rule may find other tactics to press their cause.

Violent Strikes   The NLRA prohibits violent strikes. Violence does sometimes occur on the picket line when union members attempt to prevent other workers from entering the job site. Or a union may stage a **sit-down strike**, in which members stop working but remain at their job posts, physically blocking replacement workers from taking their places. Any such action is illegal.

Partial Strikes   A partial strike occurs when employees stop working temporarily, then resume, then stop again, and so forth. This tactic is particularly disruptive because management cannot bring in replacement workers. A union may either walk off the job or stay on it, but it may not alternate.

Replacement Workers

When employees go on strike, management generally wants to replace them to keep the company operating. When replacement workers begin to cross a union picket line, tempers are certain to explode, and entire communities may feel the repercussions. Are replacement workers legal? Yes. **Management has the right to hire replacement workers during a strike.** May the employer offer the replacement workers *permanent* jobs, or must the company give union members their jobs back when the strike is over? It depends on the type of strike.

After an *economic strike,* **an employer may not discriminate against a striker, but the employer is** *not* **obligated to lay off a replacement worker to give a striker his job back.** An economic strike is one intended to gain wages or benefits. When a union bargains for a pay raise but fails to get it and walks off the job, that is an economic strike. During such a strike, an employer may hire permanent replacement workers. When the strike is over, the company has no obligation to lay off the replacement workers to make room for the strikers. However, if the company does hire more workers, it may not discriminate against the strikers.

After a *unfair labor practices (ULP) strike,* **a union member is entitled to her job back, even if that means the employer must lay off a replacement worker.** Suppose that management refuses to bargain in good faith by claiming poverty, without producing records to substantiate its claim. The union strikes. Management's refusal to bargain was a ULP, and the strike is a ULP strike. When it ends, the striking workers must get their jobs back.

Picketing

Picketing the employer's workplace in support of a strike is generally lawful. Striking workers are permitted to establish picket lines at the employer's job site and to urge all others— employees, replacement workers, and customers—not to cross the line. But the picketers are not permitted to use physical force to *prevent* anyone from crossing the line. The company may terminate violent picketers and permanently replace them, regardless of the nature of the strike.

Lockouts

The workers have bargained with management for weeks, and discussions have turned belligerent. It is 6:00 a.m., the start of another day at the factory. But as 150 employees arrive for work, they are amazed to find the company's gate locked and armed guards standing on the other side. In a so-called lockout, management prohibits workers from entering the premises and earning their paychecks. Most lockouts are legal.

Chapter Conclusion

Since the first time one person hired another, there has been tension in the workplace. The law attempts to balance the right of a boss to run a business with the right of a worker to fair treatment. Other countries balance these rights differently. For instance, Japan, Great Britain, France, Germany, and Canada all require employers to show just cause before terminating workers. Indeed, the United States guarantees its workers fewer rights than virtually any other industrialized nation. On the one hand, being mistreated at work or fired can be a terrible, life-altering experience; but on the other, companies that cannot lay off unproductive employees are less likely to add to their workforce, which may be one reason that Europe tends to have a higher unemployment rate than the United States. Although American bosses are not insulated from minimum standards of fairness, reasonable behavior, and compliance with important policies, they still have great freedom to manage their employees.

> The workers have bargained with management for weeks, and discussions have turned belligerent.... as 150 employees arrive for work, they are amazed to find the company's gate locked and armed guards standing on the other side.

EXAM REVIEW

1. **TRADITIONAL COMMON LAW RULE** The traditional common law rule of employment provided that an employee at will could be fired for a good reason, a bad reason, or no reason at all. (p. 426)

2. **FMLA** The Family and Medical Leave Act guarantees workers up to 12 weeks of unpaid leave each year for childbirth, adoption, a serious health condition of their own or in their immediate family. (p. 427)

3. **HEALTH INSURANCE** Starting in 2014, employers who have more than 50 full-time employees must pay a penalty if they do not provide basic health insurance. Under the Consolidated Omnibus Budget Reconciliation Act, former employees must be allowed to continue their health insurance for 18 months after being terminated from their job, but they must pay for it themselves. (p. 428)

4. **WRONGFUL DISCHARGE AND PUBLIC POLICY** An employer who fires a worker for certain bad reasons may be liable under a theory of wrongful discharge. Generally, an employee may not be fired for refusing to violate the law, performing a legal duty, exercising a legal right, or supporting basic societal values. (pp. 428–431)

Question: When Theodore Staats went to his company's "Council of Honor Convention," he was accompanied by a woman who was not his wife, although he told everyone she was. The company fired him. Staats alleged that his termination violated public policy because it infringed upon his freedom of association. He also alleged that he had been fired because he was too successful—his commissions were so high, he outearned even the highest-paid officer of the company. Has Staat's employer violated public policy?

Strategy: Is Staats protected by a statute? No. Is he being asked to break the law? No. Is he trying to perform a legal duty? No. Is he being denied a legal right? (See the "Result" at the end of this section.)

5. **PROMISES MADE DURING THE HIRING PROCESS** Promises made during the hiring process may be enforceable, even if not approved by the company's top executives. An employee handbook may also create a contract. (p. 431)

Question: When Phil McConkey interviewed for a job as an insurance agent with Alexander & Alexander, the company did not tell him that it was engaged in secret negotiations to merge with Aon. When the merger went through soon thereafter, Aon fired McConkey. Was Alexander liable for not telling McConkey about the possible merger?

Strategy: Was McConkey protected by a statute? No. Did the company make any promises to him during the hiring process? (See the "Result" at the end of this section.)

6. **COVENANT OF GOOD FAITH AND FAIR DEALING** In almost all states, courts will imply this covenant in an at-will employment relationship. (pp. 431–432)

7. **DEFAMATION** Employers may be liable for defamation if they give false and unfavorable references. (pp. 432–433)

8. **WHISTLEBLOWERS** Whistleblowers receive some protection under both federal and state laws. (pp. 433–435)

9. **EMPLOYEE PRIVACY** An employer may not violate a worker's reasonable expectation of privacy. However, unless a state has passed a statute to the contrary, employers may monitor many types of off-duty conduct (even legal activities such as smoking). Most states permit private employers to administer alcohol and drug tests, and employers are generally free to monitor employees' email and Facebook pages. But many employers are restricted by the Employee Polygraph Protection Act if they wish to administer polygraph exams. (pp. 435–439)

10. **OSHA** The goal of the Occupational Safety and Health Act is to ensure safe conditions in the workplace. (p. 439)

11. **WORKERS' COMPENSATION** Workers' compensation statutes ensure that employees receive payment for injuries incurred at work. (p. 440)

12. **SOCIAL SECURITY** The social security system pays benefits to workers who are retired, disabled, or temporarily unemployed and to the spouses and children of disabled or deceased workers. (pp. 440–441)

13. **ERISA** The Employee Retirement Income Security Act regulates private pension plans. (p. 441)

14. **RIGHT TO ORGANIZE** Section 7 of the National Labor Relations Act (NLRA) guarantees employees the right to organize and join unions, bargain collectively, and engage in other concerted activities. Section 8(a) of the NLRA makes it a ULP for an employer to interfere with union organizing, discriminate against a union member, or refuse to bargain collectively. (p. 442)

15. **DISCRIMINATION** Section 8 of the NLRA makes it a ULP for a union to interfere with employees who are exercising their rights under §7, to encourage an employer to discriminate against an employee because of a labor dispute, or to refuse to bargain collectively. (p. 442)

16. **EXCLUSIVITY** Section 9 of the NLRA makes a validly recognized union the *exclusive* representative of the employees. Along with exclusivity comes a duty of fair representation, which requires that a union treat all members fairly, impartially, and in good faith. (pp. 442–443)

17. **EMPLOYER OPPOSITION** During a union organizing campaign, an employer may vigorously present anti-union views to its employees, but it may not use threats or promises of benefits to defeat the union effort. (pp. 443–444)

EXAM Strategy

Question: Power, Inc., which operated a coal mine, suffered financial losses and had to lay off employees. The United Mine Workers of America (UMWA) began an organizing drive. Power's general manager warned miners that if the company was unionized, it would be shut down. An office manager told one of the miners that the company would get rid of union supporters. Shortly before the election was to take place, Power laid off 13 employees, all of whom had signed union cards. A low-seniority employee who had not signed a union card was not laid off. The union claimed that Power had committed ULPs. Comment.

Strategy: Section 7 of the NLRA guarantees employees the right to organize. An employer may vigorously advocate against a union organizing campaign. However, Section 8 (a) makes it a ULP to interfere with union organizing or discriminate against a union member. (See the "Result" at the end of this section.)

18. **BARGAINING** The employer and the union *must* bargain over wages, hours, and other terms and conditions of employment. They *may* bargain other subjects, but neither side may insist on doing so. The union and the employer must bargain in good faith, but they are not obligated to reach an agreement. (p. 444)

19. STRIKES The NLRA guarantees employees the right to strike, with some limitations. After an *economic* strike, an employer is not obligated to lay off replacement workers to give a striker her job back, but it may not discriminate against a striker when filling job openings. After a ULP strike, the striking worker must get her job back. (p. 446)

20. LOCKOUTS Most lockouts are legal. (p. 447)

---

4. Result: The court held that freedom of association is an important social right and should be protected. However, being fired for bringing a lover to an employer's convention is not a threat to public policy. Nor is discharge for being too successful.

5. Result: The court held that when Alexander hired him, it was making an implied promise that he would not be fired immediately. The company was liable for not having revealed the merger negotiations.

17. Result: Each of the acts described was a ULP. Threatening layoffs or company closure are classic examples of ULPs. Laying off those who had signed union cards, but not those who refused, was clear discrimination. In this case, the NLRB found the violations so extreme that it certified the union without an election and issued an order to bargain.

MULTIPLE-CHOICE QUESTIONS

1. Brook moved from Denver to San Francisco to take a job with an advertising agency. His employment contract stated that he was "at will and could be terminated at any time." After 28 months with the company, he was fired without explanation. Which of the following statements is true?

   (a) His contract implied that he could only be fired for cause.

   (b) Because he had a contract, he was not an employee at will.

   (c) He could only be fired for a good reason.

   (d) He could be fired for any reason.

   (e) He could be fired for any reason except a bad reason.

2. **CPA QUESTION** An unemployed CPA generally would receive unemployment compensation benefits if the CPA:

   (a) was fired as a result of the employer's business reversals.

   (b) refused to accept a job as an accountant while receiving extended benefits.

   (c) was fired for embezzling from a client.

   (d) left work voluntarily without good cause.

3. During a job interview with Venetia, Jack reveals that he and his wife are expecting twins. Venetia asks him if he is planning to take a leave once the babies are born. When Jack admits that he would like to take a month off work, he can see her face fall. She ultimately decides not to hire him because of the twins. Which of the following statements are true?

   (a) Venetia has violated the FMLA.

   (b) Venetia has violated COBRA .

   (c) Both (a) and (b)

   (d) None of the above

4. Which of the following statutes defines ULPs and ensures workers' right to form a union?

(a) The Norris-LaGuardia Act

(b) The National Labor Relations Act

(c) Both (a) and (b)

(d) None of the above

5. Alpha Company's workers go on strike. The company hires replacement workers so that it can continue to operate its business. When the strike ends, Alpha must rehire the original workers if the strike was over _____.

(a) wages

(b) a ULP

(c) both (a) and (b)

(d) none of the above

ESSAY QUESTIONS

1. Debra Agis worked as a waitress in a Ground Round restaurant. The manager informed the waitresses that "there was some stealing going on." Until he found out who was doing it, he intended to fire all the waitresses in alphabetical order, starting with the letter "A." Dionne then fired Agis. Does she have a valid claim against her employer?

2. **YOU BE THE JUDGE WRITING PROBLEM** FedEx gave Marcie Dutschmann an employment handbook stating that (1) she was an at-will employee, (2) the handbook did not create any contractual rights, and (3) employees who were fired had the right to a termination hearing. The company fired Dutschmann, claiming that she had falsified delivery records. She said that FedEx was retaliating against her because she had complained of sexual harassment. FedEx refused her request for a termination hearing. Did the employee handbook create an implied contract guaranteeing Dutschmann a hearing? **Argument for FedEx:** The handbook could not have been clearer—it did not create a contract. Dutschmann is an employee at will and is not entitled to a hearing. **Argument for Dutschmann:** FedEx intended that employees would rely on the handbook. The company used promises of a hearing to attract and retain good employees. Dutschmann was entitled to a hearing.

3. Triec, Inc., is a small electrical contracting company in Springfield, Ohio, owned by its executives, Yeazell, Jones, and Heaton. Employees contacted the International Brotherhood of Electrical Workers, which began an organizing drive, and 6 of the 11 employees in the bargaining unit signed authorization cards. The company declined to recognize the union, which petitioned the NLRB to schedule an election. The company then granted several new benefits for all workers, including higher wages, paid vacations, and other measures. When the election was held, only 2 of the 11 bargaining unit members voted for the union. Did the company violate the NLRA?

4. Q-1 Motor Express was an interstate trucking company. When a union attempted to organize Q-1's drivers, it met heavy resistance. A supervisor told one driver that if he knew what was good for him, he would stay away from the union organizer. The company president told another employee that he had the right to fire everybody, close

the company, and then rehire new drivers after 72 hours. He made numerous other threats to workers and their families. Based on the extreme nature of the company's opposition, what exceptional remedy did the union seek before the NLRB?

5. Billy comes down with chicken pox and is sent home from school. His mother takes him to a pediatrician. The doctor tells her, "Well … he should be fine in about a week. Bed rest is all he really needs—and plenty of fluids." Billy's mother calls her employer and requests FMLA leave to take care of Billy for the next few days. Must the employer grant the leave? Why or why not?

DISCUSSION QUESTIONS

1. When Walton Weiner interviewed for a job with McGraw-Hill, Inc., he was assured that the company would not terminate an employee without "just cause." Weiner also signed a contract specifying that his employment would be subject to the provisions of McGraw-Hill's handbook. The handbook said, "[The] company will resort to dismissal for just and sufficient cause only, and only after all practical steps toward rehabilitation or salvage of the employee have been taken and failed. However, if the welfare of the company indicates that dismissal is necessary, then that decision is arrived at and is carried out forthrightly." After eight years, Weiner was fired suddenly for "lack of application." Does Weiner have a valid claim against McGraw-Hill?

2. Some companies now require all job applicants to provide their Facebook login information so that the potential employer can learn more about them. Is this behavior ethical on the part of an employer?

3. Should employers be allowed to fire smokers? Nicotine is highly addictive and many smokers begin as teenagers, when they may not fully understand the consequences of their decisions. As Mark Twain, who began smoking at 12, famously said, "Giving up smoking is the easiest thing in the world. I know because I've done it thousands of times."

4. Union membership has fallen steadily in recent decades, in part because many unionized manufacturing jobs have been shipped overseas. Do you believe that unions will make a comeback in new industries? Would you prefer to be a member of a union if you had a choice? Why or why not?

5. Would you personally be less likely to apply for a job if you were required to first pass a polygraph exam? What if you were required to pass a drug test? For legal or illegal drugs? Would you be less likely to apply because you thought the company was too intrusive or because you want the right to use these substances? What if the company required you to quit smoking or chewing tobacco?

CHAPTER 18

© Stas Volik/Shutterstock.com

EMPLOYMENT DISCRIMINATION

Imagine that you are on the hiring committee of a top San Francisco law firm. You come across a resume from a candidate who grew up on an isolated ranch in Arizona. Raised in a house without electricity or running water, he had worked alongside the ranch hands his entire childhood. At the age of 16, he left home for Stanford University, and from there had gone on to Stanford Law School, where he finished third in his class. You think to yourself, "This sounds like a real American success story. A great combination of grit and intelligence." But without hesitation, you toss the resume into the wastebasket.

> You think, "This sounds like a real American success story." But you toss the resume into the wastebasket.

This is a true story. Indeed, there was a candidate with these credentials who was unable to find a job in any San Francisco law firm. The only jobs on offer were as a secretary, because this candidate was a woman—Sandra Day O'Connor, who went on to become one of the most influential lawyers of her era and the first woman justice on the Supreme Court of the United States. When she graduated from law school, women and minorities had limited job options, and not just in the legal profession. Before 1960, you might never see a female or African American doctor, engineer, police officer, or firefighter. What a terrible waste of resources—so many talented people unable to use their abilities.

INTRODUCTION

This chapter is the story of how the United States has travelled the long and bumpy road toward equality of opportunity in the workplace. This story begins after the Civil War, when a torn and bleeding country sought to protect the rights of freed slaves and undo the terrible harm of a century of slavery. The country began by ratifying three Constitutional amendments: the Thirteenth prohibits slavery, the Fourteenth guarantees due process of law and equal protection under the law, and the Fifteenth prohibits restrictions on the right to vote because of race or color. In addition, Congress passed the Civil Rights Act of 1866, which provided that all people born in the United States (except Native Americans) were citizens of the United States and had the same rights as white citizens.[1]

However, in response to these laws, many states passed (and the Supreme Court upheld) statutes that made these protections worthless. The most notorious case was *Plessy v. Ferguson*, in which the Supreme Court upheld the constitutionality of a Louisiana law that prohibited blacks from riding in railroad cars reserved for whites. Blacks were provided with "separate but equal" cars.[2]

Not until 1954, almost a century after the Civil War, did the Supreme Court reverse its *Plessy* decision. In the landmark case *Brown v. Board of Education*, the high court ruled that "separate but equal" policies were unconstitutional.[3] In particular, it prohibited segregated public schools. However, many school districts were slow to apply the case, and even ten years later, segregated public schools still existed in many parts of the country. Nonetheless, *Brown* inspired a generation of civil rights leaders such as Martin Luther King and Rosa Parks, who led protests, boycotts, and voter registration drives.

These actions inspired Congress to pass the Civil Rights Act of 1964. Title VII of this Act prohibits certain types of employment discrimination and is the focus of this chapter. However, the statute was even more far-reaching because it prohibited a broad range of discrimination: in, for example, education, voting, and public accommodations (such as hotels, restaurants, and movie theaters).

We begin now with a review of constitutional provisions that prohibit discrimination in the workplace and follow with a discussion of the major federal anti-discrimination statutes: the Civil Rights Act of 1866, Title VII of the Civil Rights Act of 1964, the Equal Pay Act, the Pregnancy Discrimination Act, the Age Discrimination in Employment Act, the Rehabilitation Act of 1973, the Americans with Disabilities Act, and the Genetic Information Nondiscrimination Act.

THE UNITED STATES CONSTITUTION

The Fifth Amendment to the Constitution prohibits the *federal government* from depriving individuals of "life, liberty, or property" without due process of law. The Fourteenth Amendment prohibits *state governments* from violating an individual's right to due process

---

[1] 42 USC 21 §1981.
[2] 163 U.S. 537, (S. Ct., 1896).
[3] 347 U.S. 483 (S. Ct. 1954).

and equal protection. The courts have interpreted these provisions to prohibit employment discrimination by federal, state, and local governments.

CIVIL RIGHTS ACT OF 1866

As we have seen, the Civil Rights Act of 1866 was meant to provide freed slaves with the same rights as white citizens. It has been interpreted to prohibit *racial* discrimination in both private and public employment (except it does not apply to the federal government). As we will see later in the Enforcement section of this chapter, it offers plaintiffs some significant advantages over Title VII.

TITLE VII OF THE CIVIL RIGHTS ACT OF 1964

Under Title VII of the Civil Rights Act of 1964, it is illegal for employers with 15 or more employees to discriminate on the basis of race, color, religion, sex, or national origin. Discrimination under Title VII applies to every aspect of the employment process, from job ads to postemployment references, and includes hiring, firing, promoting, placement, wages, benefits, and working conditions of anyone who is in one or more of the so-called protected categories under the statute.

Prohibited Activities

There are four types of illegal activity under this statute: disparate treatment, disparate impact, hostile environment, and retaliation. All of these activities are illegal if used against anyone in a protected category.

Disparate Treatment

To prove a disparate treatment case, the plaintiff must show that she was *treated* less favorably than others because of her sex, race, color, religion, or national origin. Note that the burden of proof is on the plaintiff: she must prove that the employer *intentionally* discriminated, but this motive can be inferred from the mere fact of differences in treatment. The required steps in a disparate treatment case are:

Step 1. The plaintiff presents evidence that:

- He belongs to a protected category under Title VII.

- He was treated differently from other similar people who are not protected under Title VII.

> If the plaintiff can show these facts, he has made a ***prima facie*** case. The plaintiff is not required to prove discrimination; he need only create a *presumption* that discrimination occurred.
>
> Suppose that Louisa applies for a job coaching a boys' high school hockey team. She was an All-American hockey star in college. Although Louisa is obviously qualified for the job, Harry, the school principal, rejects her and continues to interview other people. This is not *proof* of discrimination because Harry may have a perfectly good, nondiscriminatory explanation. However, his behavior *could have been* motivated by discrimination.

Prima facie

From the Latin, meaning "from its first appearance," something that appears to be true upon a first look.

Step 2. The defendant must present evidence that its decision was based on *legitimate, nondiscriminatory* reasons. Harry might say, for example, that he wanted someone with prior coaching experience. Although Louisa is clearly a great player, she has never coached before.

Step 3. To win, the plaintiff must now prove that the employer intentionally discriminated. She may do so either by showing that (1) the reasons offered were simply a *pretext*, or (2) that a discriminatory intent is more likely than not. Louisa might show that Harry had recently hired a male tennis coach who had no prior coaching experience (pretext), or Harry's assistant might testify that Harry said, "No way I'm going to put a woman on the ice with those guys." If she can present evidence such as this, Louisa wins.

In the following case, was the bartender treated differently because of her sex? You be the judge.

---

[4]See for example, Michael Kinsley, "Making Up Is Hard to Do," *The Washington Post*, March 26, 2008.

You be the Judge

JESPERSEN V. HARRAH'S
444 F.3D 1104, 2006 U.S. APP. LEXIS 9307
United States Court of Appeals for the Ninth Circuit, 2006

Facts: Darlene Jespersen was a bartender at the sports bar in Harrah's Casino in Reno, Nevada. She was an outstanding employee, frequently praised by both her supervisors and customers.

After Jespersen had been at Harrah's for almost 20 years, the casino implemented a program that required bartenders to be "well groomed, appealing to the eye." More explicitly, for men:

- Hair must not extend below top of shirt collar. Ponytails are prohibited.

- Hands and fingernails must be clean and nails neatly trimmed at all times.

- No colored polish is permitted.

- Eye and facial makeup is not permitted.

- Shoes will be solid black leather or leather type with rubber (non-skid) soles.

The rules for women were:

- Hair must be teased, curled, or styled. Hair must be worn down at all times, no exceptions.

- Nail polish can be clear, white, pink, or red color only. No exotic nail art or length.

- Shoes will be solid black leather or leather type with rubber (non-skid) soles.

- Makeup (foundation/concealer and/or face powder, as well as blush and mascara) must be worn and applied neatly in complimentary colors, and lip color must be worn at all times.

An expert was brought in to show the employees (both male and female) how to dress. The workers were then photographed and told that they must look like the photographs every day at work.

Jespersen tried wearing makeup for a short period of time but then refused to do so. She did not like the feel of it and also believed that this new appearance interfered with her ability to deal with unruly, intoxicated guests because it "took away [her] credibility as an individual and as a person."

After Harrah's fired Jespersen, she sued under Title VII. The district court granted Harrah's motion for summary judgment. Jespersen appealed.

You Be The Judge: *Did Harrah's requirement that women wear makeup violate Title VII?*

Argument for Jespersen: Jespersen refused to wear makeup to work because the cost—in time, money, and personal dignity—was too high.

Employers are free to adopt different appearance standards for each sex, but these standards may not impose a greater burden on one sex than the other. Men were not required to wear makeup, but women were. That difference meant a savings for men of hundreds of dollars and hours of time.[4] Harrah's did not have the right to fire Jespersen for violating a rule that applies only to women, with no equivalent for men.

Argument for Harrah's: Employers are permitted to impose different appearance rules on women than on men so long as the overall burden on employees is the same. For example, it is not discriminatory to require men to wear their hair short. On balance, Harrah's rules did not impose a heavier burden on women than on men.

Disparate Impact

Disparate impact applies if the employer has a rule that, *on its face*, is not discriminatory, but *in practice* excludes too many people in a protected category. Unlike disparate treatment, in a disparate impact case, the plaintiff does not have to prove *intentional* discrimination. The following landmark case established the principle of disparate impact.

Landmark Case

GRIGGS V. DUKE POWER CO.

401 U.S. 424, 91 S. Ct. 849, 1971 U.S. LEXIS 134
United States Supreme Court, 1971

Facts: Before Title VII, Duke Power hired black employees only in the Labor department, where the highest pay was less than the lowest earnings in the other departments. After Title VII, the company required all new hires for jobs in the desirable departments to have a high school education or satisfactory scores on two tests that measured intelligence and mechanical ability. Neither test gauged the ability to perform a particular job. The pass rate for whites was much higher than for blacks, and whites were also more likely than blacks to have a high school diploma. The new policy did not apply to the (exclusively white) employees who were already working in the preferred departments. These "unqualified" whites all performed their jobs satisfactorily.

Black employees sued Duke Power, alleging that this hiring policy violated Title VII. The trial court dismissed the case. The Court of Appeals ruled that the policy was not in violation of Title VII because Duke Power did not have a discriminatory purpose. The Supreme Court granted *certiorari*.

Issue: *Does a policy violate Title VII if it has a discriminatory impact but no discriminatory purpose?*

Excerpts from Chief Justice Burger's Decision: The Act proscribes not only overt discrimination but also practices that are fair in form, but discriminatory in operation. The touchstone is business necessity. If an employment practice which operates to exclude Negroes cannot be shown to be related to job performance, the practice is prohibited.

On the record before us, neither the high school completion requirement nor the general intelligence test is shown to bear a demonstrable relationship to successful performance of the jobs for which it was used. Both were adopted without meaningful study of their relationship to job-performance ability. Rather, the requirements were instituted on the Company's judgment that they generally would improve the overall quality of the work force. The evidence, however, shows that employees who have not completed high school or taken the tests have continued to perform satisfactorily and make progress in departments for which the high school and test criteria are now used.

[G]ood intent or absence of discriminatory intent does not redeem employment procedures or testing mechanisms that operate as "built-in headwinds" for minority groups and are unrelated to measuring job capability. Congress directed the thrust of the Act to the *consequences* of employment practices, not simply the motivation. More than that, Congress has placed on the employer the burden of showing that any given requirement must have a manifest relationship to the employment in question.

History is filled with examples of men and women who rendered highly effective performance without the conventional badges of accomplishment in terms of certificates, diplomas, or degrees. Diplomas and tests are useful servants, but Congress has mandated the common-sense proposition that they are not to become masters of reality.

Nothing in the Act precludes the use of testing or measuring procedures; obviously they are useful. What Congress has commanded is that any tests used must measure the person for the job and not the person in the abstract.

The judgment of the Court of Appeals is reversed.

The steps in a disparate impact case are:

Step 1. The plaintiff must present a *prima facie* case. The plaintiff is not required to prove discrimination; he need only show a disparate impact—that the employment practice in question excludes a disproportionate number of people in a protected group (women and minorities, for instance). In the *Griggs* case, a far higher percentage of whites than blacks passed the tests required for a job in one of the good departments. The Equal Employment Opportunity Commission (EEOC) defines a disparate impact as one in which the pass rate for a protected category is less than 80 percent of that for others. (As we will see, the EEOC is the federal agency charged with enforcing most discrimination statutes.)

Step 2. The defendant must offer some evidence that the employment practice was a *job-related business necessity*. Duke Power would have to show that the tests predicted job performance.

Step 3. To win, the plaintiff must now prove either that the employer's reason is a *pretext* or that other, *less discriminatory*, rules would achieve the same results. The plaintiffs in *Griggs* showed that the tests were not a job-related business necessity—after all, whites who had not passed any of these tests performed the jobs well. Duke Power could no longer use them as a hiring screen. If the power company wanted to use tests, it would have to find some that measured an employee's ability to perform particular jobs.

Hiring tests remain controversial. For example, New Haven, Connecticut, used an exam to determine which firefighters to promote. When twice as many whites as blacks passed the test, black firefighters threatened to sue on the grounds that the exams were discriminatory. But the city could not win for losing—when it decided to discard the test results, the white firefighters (and one Hispanic) who had done well on the test sued, alleging that the city was now discriminating against them.[5] Ultimately, the Supreme Court ruled against the city, holding that an employer cannot discard test results unless it first clearly shows that it would have lost a disparate impact case. In this case, ruled the court, New Haven could not make this showing because, indeed, the tests *were* valid and the city would have *won* a disparate impact lawsuit. The court reached this decision despite the fact that the test in question consisted of written multiple-choice questions, which are generally thought to be a less useful gauge in employment decisions than actually requiring candidates to perform necessary tasks. In short, the mere existence of a disparate impact does not mean that an employment practice violates the law.

Hostile Work Environment

Employers violate Title VII if they permit a work environment that is so hostile toward people in a protected category that it affects their ability to work. This rule applies whether the hostility is based on race, color, religion, sex, or national origin. (As we shall see, this rule also applies to those treated badly because of pregnancy, age, or disability.) This concept of hostile environment first arose in the context of sexual harassment.

> Everyone has heard of sexual harassment, but few people know exactly what it is.

Sexual Harassment When Professor Anita Hill accused Supreme Court nominee Clarence Thomas of sexually harassing her, people across the country were glued to their televisions, watching the Senate hearings on her charges. Thomas was ultimately confirmed to the Supreme Court, but "sexual harassment" became a household phrase. The number of cases—and the size of the damage awards—skyrocketed.

[5] *Ricci v. DeStefano*, 129 S. Ct. 2658, 2009 U.S. LEXIS 4945 (S. Ct. 2009).

Everyone has heard of sexual harassment, but few people know exactly what it is. Men fear that a casual comment or glance will be met with career-ruining charges; women claim that men "just don't get it." So what is sexual harassment anyway? **Sexual harassment involves unwelcome sexual advances, requests for sexual favors, and other verbal or physical conduct of a sexual nature which are so severe and pervasive that they interfere with an employee's ability to work.** There are two categories: (1) *quid pro quo* and (2) hostile work environment.

Named for a Latin phrase that means "one thing in return for another," **quid pro quo** harassment occurs if any aspect of a job is made contingent upon sexual activity. In other words, when a banker says to an assistant, "You can be promoted to teller if you sleep with me," that is *quid pro quo* sexual harassment. As for hostile environment, courts have found that offensive jokes, intrusive comments about clothes or body parts, and public displays of pornographic pictures can create a hostile environment.

Text messages have become a new frontier in sexual harassment—so-called *textual harassment.* In behavior that can only make you ask, "What were they thinking?" bosses have sent wildly inappropriate text messages to their subordinates—in some cases offering promotions in return for sex—that provide clear evidence of wrongdoing. News flash: text messages can be recovered, and juries can read. "She said, he said" cases are a lot harder to win than "She said, he texted."

In the following case, the Supreme Court defined the standard for a hostile work environment.

Quid pro quo

A Latin phrase that means "one thing in return for another."

TERESA HARRIS V. FORKLIFT SYSTEMS, INC.

510 U.S. 17, 114 S.CT. 367, 1993 U.S. LEXIS 7155
United States Supreme Court, 1993

Facts: Teresa Harris was a manager at Forklift Systems; Charles Hardy was its president. Hardy frequently made inappropriate sexual comments to Harris and other women at the company. For example, he said to Harris, in the presence of others, "You're a woman, what do you know?" and "We need a man as the rental manager." He called her "a dumb-ass woman" and suggested that the two of them "go to the Holiday Inn to negotiate your raise." He also asked Harris and other female employees to get coins from his front pants pocket. He insisted that Harris and other women pick up objects he had thrown on the ground. When Harris complained to Hardy, he apologized and claimed he was only joking. A month later, while Harris was arranging a deal with one of Forklift's customers, he asked her, in front of other employees, "What did you do, promise the guy some sex Saturday night?"

Harris sued Forklift, claiming that Hardy had created an abusive work environment. The federal trial court ruled against Harris on the grounds that Hardy's comments might offend a reasonable woman, but they were not severe enough to have a serious impact on Harris's psychological well-being. The appeals court confirmed, and the Supreme Court granted *certiorari.*

Issue: *To be a violation of Title VII, must sexual harassment seriously affect the employee's psychological well-being?*

Excerpts from Justice O'Connor's Decision: Title VII of the Civil Rights Act of 1964 makes it "an unlawful employment practice for an employer to discriminate against any individual with respect to his compensation, terms, conditions, or privileges of employment, because of such individual's race, color, religion, sex, or national origin." [T]his language is not limited to economic or tangible discrimination. The phrase "terms, conditions, or privileges of employment" evinces a congressional intent to strike at the entire spectrum of disparate treatment of men and women in employment, which includes requiring people to work in a discriminatorily hostile or abusive environment. When the workplace is permeated with discriminatory intimidation, ridicule, and insult that is sufficiently severe or pervasive to alter the conditions of the victim's employment and create an abusive working environment, Title VII is violated.

This standard takes a middle path between making actionable any conduct that is merely offensive and requiring the conduct to cause a tangible psychological injury. [M]ere utterance of an epithet which engenders offensive feelings in an employee does not sufficiently affect the conditions of employment to implicate Title VII. Conduct that is not severe or pervasive enough to create an objectively hostile or abusive work environment—an environment that a reasonable person would find hostile or abusive—is beyond Title VII's purview. Likewise, if the victim does not subjectively perceive the environment to be abusive, the conduct has not actually altered the conditions of the victim's employment, and there is no Title VII violation.

But Title VII comes into play before the harassing conduct leads to a nervous breakdown. A discriminatorily abusive work environment, even one that does not seriously affect employees' psychological well-being, can and often will detract from employees' job performance, discourage employees from remaining on the job, or keep them from advancing in their careers. Moreover, even without regard to these tangible effects, the very fact that the discriminatory conduct was so severe or pervasive that it created a work environment abusive to employees because of their race, gender, religion, or national origin offends Title VII's broad rule of workplace equality.

We therefore believe the [trial court] erred in relying on whether the conduct "seriously affected plaintiff's psychological well-being" or led her to "suffer injury." So long as the environment would reasonably be perceived, and is perceived, as hostile or abusive, there is no need for it also to be psychologically injurious.

Same-Sex Harassment Suppose that one man makes unwelcome sexual overtures to another man in the workplace. The Supreme Court ruled that same-sex harassment is also a violation of Title VII.[6]

Employer Liability for Sexual Harassment Employees who commit sexual harassment are liable for their own misdeeds. But is their company also liable? The Supreme Court has held that:

- The company is liable if it knew or should have known about the conduct and failed to stop it.
- Even if the company was unaware of the misbehavior, it is nonetheless liable if the victimized employee suffered a "tangible employment action" such as firing, demotion, or reassignment.
- If the company was unaware of the behavior and the victimized employee did not suffer a tangible employment action, the company is still liable unless it can prove that (1) it used reasonable care to prevent and correct sexually harassing behavior, and (2) the employee unreasonably failed to take advantage of the complaint procedure or other preventive opportunities provided by the company.[7]

Corning Consumer Products Co. provides a set of practical guidelines for eliminating sexual harassment. It asks employees to apply four tests in determining whether their behavior violates Title VII:

- Would you say or do this in front of your spouse or parents?
- What about in front of a colleague of the opposite sex?
- Would you like your behavior reported in your local newspaper?
- Does it need to be said or done at all?

Hostile Environment Based on Race When African American Brenda Chaney worked at the Plainfield nursing home, one of its patients refused to allow people of color to enter her room. In addition, Chaney's coworkers called her racial slurs.

[6]*Oncale v. Sundowner Offshore Services, Inc.*, 523 US 75 (S. Ct. 1998).
[7]*Burlington Industries, Inc. v. Ellerth*, 524 U.S. 742, 118 S. Ct. 2257, 1998 U.S. LEXIS 4217 (1998); *Faragher v. Boca Raton*, 524 U.S. 775, 118 S. Ct. 2275, 1998 U.S. LEXIS 4216 (1998).

The court ruled that the nursing home had violated Title VII by permitting a hostile work environment.[8]

Hostile Environment Based on Color   Title VII prohibits discrimination based on both race and color. Although many people assume that they are essentially the same, that is not necessarily the case. For example, Dwight Burch alleged that his coworkers at an Applebee's restaurant created a hostile work environment when they called him hateful names because of his dark skin color. These colleagues were also African American but were lighter-skinned. While denying any wrongdoing, Applebee's settled the case by paying Burch $40,000 and agreeing to conduct antidiscrimination training.

Hostile Environment Based on National Origin   Title VII also prohibits a hostile environment based on national origin. While working at Steel Technologies, Inc., Tony Cerros was promoted several times. So what was the problem? Coworkers and supervisors called him "brown boy," "spic," "wetback," "Julio," and "Javier" (although those were not his names). They also told him that "if it ain't white, it ain't right," and "Go Back to Mexico" was written on the bathroom wall. Although the company removed the bathroom graffiti, it did not investigate Cerros's complaints until he filed suit. At that point, it determined that Cerros had not been discriminated against. The trial court agreed because Cerros had, after all, been promoted. However, the appeals court overturned the decision, finding for Cerros on the grounds that he had suffered a hostile work environment, which is in itself a violation of Title VII, even if there is no evidence of adverse employment actions.[9]

Retaliation

Title VII also prohibits employers from retaliating against workers who oppose discrimination, bring a claim under the statute, or take part in an investigation or hearing. Retaliation means that the employer has done something that would deter a reasonable worker from complaining about discrimination. For example, a company was found liable when it demoted a woman who complained about sexual harassment by her boss.[10] Research indicates that retaliation occurs in as many as 60 percent of discrimination cases.

Title VII prohibits disparate treatment, disparate impact, hostile environment, and retaliation when used against any of the categories protected by Title VII—race, color, religion, sex, and national origin. Now we look at particular rules that apply to only some of these categories.

Religion

Employers cannot discriminate against a worker because of his religious beliefs. In addition, employers must make reasonable accommodation for a worker's religious practices unless the request would cause undue hardship for the business. A common issue involves employees who cannot work on their Sabbath. This refusal might be an "undue hardship" if there are no other employees who could perform that work on those days. What would you do in the following cases if you were the boss?

1. A Christian says he cannot work at Walmart on Sundays—his Sabbath. It also happens to be one of the store's busiest days.

2. A Jewish police officer wants to wear a beard and yarmulke as part of his religious observance. Facial hair and headgear are banned by the force.

---

[8]*Chaney v. Plainfield Healthcare Ctr.*, 612 F.3d 908 (7th Cir. 2010).
[9]*Cerros v. Steel Techs., Inc.*, 288 F.3d 1040 (7th Cir. 2002).
[10]*Burlington Northern v. White*, 126 S.Ct. 2405 (S.Ct. 2006).

3. Muslim workers at a meat-packing plant want to pray at sundown, but specific break times were specified in the labor contract and sundown changes from day to day. The workers begin to take bathroom breaks at sundown, stopping work on the production line.

Disputes such as these are on the rise and are not easy to handle fairly. In the end, Walmart fired the Christian, but when he sued on the grounds of religious discrimination, the company settled the case. A judge ruled that the police officer could keep his beard because the force allowed other employees with medical conditions to wear facial hair, but the head covering had to go. The boss at the meat-packing plant fired the Muslim employees who left their posts to pray.

Sex

Title VII has had an enormous impact on the American workplace—half of all workers are now women. But women are still underrepresented at the top of the employment ladder, as CEOs, partners in law and consulting firms, or department heads in hospitals. On average, women working full time earn only 80 percent as much as male coworkers, even after accounting for occupation, industry, race, marital status, and job tenure. Although there are undoubtedly many reasons for this inequality, such as women taking time out of work to care for children, gender discrimination also seems to play a role. For example, male CFOs in public companies earn 16 percent ($215,000) more than female CFOs, even after controlling for age, time in the job, company size, and market capitalization.[11]

What does discrimination on the basis of sex mean? In a landmark case that defined this provision of Title VII, the Supreme Court ruled that "gender must be irrelevant to employment decisions."[12] In this case, the accounting firm Price Waterhouse had refused to promote Ann Hopkins to partner. Of the 88 people who came up for partner that year, she was the only woman. She was not only a high performer, she was also the most successful in bringing in business. The problem? She was "sometimes overly aggressive, unduly harsh, difficult to work with, and impatient with staff." Partners commented that she was macho, overcompensated for being a woman, and needed to take a course at charm school. They were opposed to her use of profanity because it was a "lady using foul language." A partner explicitly told her that she should "walk more femininely, talk more femininely, dress more femininely, wear makeup, have her hair styled, and wear jewelry." In ruling in her favor, the Supreme Court held that Title VII forbids sex stereotyping. The opinion said, "An employer who objects to aggressiveness in women but whose positions require this trait places women in an intolerable and impermissible catch-22: out of a job if they behave aggressively and out of a job if they do not. Title VII lifts women out of this bind."

Family Responsibility Discrimination

Suppose that you are in charge of hiring at your company. You receive applications from four people: a mother, a father, a childless woman, and a childless man. All have equivalent qualifications. Which one would you hire? In studies, participants repeatedly rank mothers as less qualified than other employees and fathers as most desirable, even when their credentials are exactly the same.

Is parenthood a protected category under Title VII? Increasingly, courts have held that it is. For example, after Dawn Gallina, an associate at the Mintz, Levin law firm, revealed to her boss that she had a young child, he began to treat her differently from her male colleagues and spoke to her "about the commitment differential between men and

---

[11]*http://www3.cfo.com/article/2012/4/compensation_gmi-gender-gap-governance-metrics.*
[12]*Price Waterhouse v. Hopkins*, 490 U.S. 228 (S. Ct. 1989).

women." The court ruled that her belief of illegal discrimination was reasonable.[13] The EEOC has issued guidelines indicating that stereotypes are not a legitimate basis for personnel decisions and may violate Title VII.

Sexual Orientation

Neither Title VII nor any other *federal* statute protects against discrimination based on sexual orientation (being gay). However, President Bill Clinton did sign an executive order prohibiting discrimination based on sexual orientation in federal training and education programs.[14] In addition, almost half the states and hundreds of cities have statutes that prohibit discrimination based on sexual orientation.

Gender Identity

David Schroer was in the Army for 25 years, including a stint tracking terrorists. The Library of Congress offered him a job as a specialist in terrorism. (Who knew that libraries needed terrorism specialists?) However, when he revealed that he was in the process of becoming *Diane* Schroer, the Library of Congress withdrew the offer. As you can guess, he sued under Title VII.

Traditionally, courts took the view that sex under Title VII applied only to how people were born, not what they chose to become. Employers could and did fire workers for changing sex. However, a federal court found the Library of Congress in violation of Title VII for withdrawing Schroer's offer.[15] And the EEOC recently ruled that discriminating against someone for being transgender is a violation of Title VII. In addition, almost one-quarter of the states and hundreds of cities prohibit gender identity discrimination.

Defenses to Charges of Discrimination

Under Title VII, the defendant has four possible defenses.

Merit

A defendant is not liable if he shows that the person he favored was the most qualified. Test results, education, or productivity can all be used to demonstrate merit, provided they relate to the job in question. Harry can show that he hired Bruce for a coaching job instead of Louisa because Bruce has a master's degree in physical education and seven years of coaching experience. On the other hand, the fact that Bruce scored higher on the National Latin Exam in the eighth grade is not a good reason to hire him over Louisa.

Seniority

Many companies use seniority as an important factor in determining everything from compensation to layoffs. While such systems offer many advantages—they encourage a commitment to the company, an incentive to learn job-specific skills, and a willingness to train other workers without fear of losing one's job—they also tend to perpetuate prior discriminatory practices. If historic trends result in black employees having less seniority, they will also be paid less and laid off more. However, a seniority system violates Title VII only if it was designed with the *intention* to discriminate. **A legitimate seniority system is legal even if it perpetuates past discrimination.** Suppose that Harry has always chosen the most senior assistant coach to take over as head coach when a vacancy occurs. Because the majority of the senior assistant coaches are male, most of the head coaches are, too. Such a system does not violate Title VII.

---

[13]*Gallina v. Mintz, Levin*, 2005 U.S. App. LEXIS 1710 (4th Cir. 2005).
[14]Executive Order 13,160.
[15]*Schroer v. Billington*, 577 F. Supp. 2d 293, 2008 U.S. Dist. LEXIS 71358, (U.S. Dt. Ct. 2008).

Bona Fide Occupational Qualification (BFOQ)

Bona fide occupational qualification (BFOQ)

An employer is permitted to establish discriminatory job requirements if they are essential to the position in question.

An employer is permitted to establish discriminatory job requirements if they are *essential* to the position in question. The business must show that it cannot fulfill its primary function unless it discriminates. Such a requirement is called a **bona fide occupational qualification (BFOQ)**. (Note that only religion, sex, or national origin can be a BFOQ—never race or color.)

Catholic schools may, if they choose, refuse to hire non-Catholic teachers; clothing companies may refuse to hire men to model women's attire. Generally, however, courts are not sympathetic to claims of BFOQ. They have almost always rejected BFOQ claims that are based on customer preference. For example, an employer violated the law when it refused to appoint a woman to a position as vice president of international operations because of its fear that men in other countries might not want to work with her.[16]

However, the courts recognize three situations in which employers may consider customer preference:

- Safety: The Supreme Court ruled that a maximum security men's prison could refuse to hire women correctional officers. If a woman wanted to risk her life, that was her choice, but the court feared that an attack on her would threaten the safety of both male guards and inmates.[17]

- Privacy: An employer may refuse to hire women to work in a men's bathroom, and vice versa.

- Authenticity: An employer may refuse to hire a man for a woman's role in a movie. In addition, a court ruled that Disney could fire an Asian man from the Norwegian exhibit at its Epcot international theme park, not because he was Asian, but because he was not culturally authentic. He did not have first-hand knowledge of Norwegian culture and did not speak Norwegian.[18]

Affirmative Action

The goal of affirmative action programs is to remedy the effects of past discrimination. How people feel about affirmative action tends to be a function of how they define the term. Most people are opposed to quotas, but at the same time, they support outreach and recruitment efforts aimed at women and disadvantaged minorities.

Affirmative action is not required by Title VII, nor is it prohibited. Affirmative action programs have three different sources.

Litigation   Courts have the power under Title VII to order affirmative action to remedy the effects of past discrimination.

Voluntary Action   Employers can *voluntarily* introduce an affirmative action plan to remedy the effects of past practices or to achieve (but not to maintain) equitable representation of minorities and women, provided that the plan is not too unfair to majority members.[19] For example, in the university and community college system in Nevada, only 1 percent of the faculty were black (and roughly 25 percent were female). In response, the university instituted a policy that permitted any department that hired a minority candidate to also hire an additional candidate of any race. Although Yvette Farmer was one of three finalists for a job in the sociology department, it hired a black African male without even granting her an interview. The Court ruled that the university's affirmative action plan was legal.[20]

---

[16]*Fernandez v. Wynn Oil Co.*, 653 F.2d 1273, (9th Cir. 1981).

[17]*Dothard v. Rawlinson*, 433 U.S. 321, (S.Ct. 1977).

[18]*Gupta v. Walt Disney World Co.*, 256 Fed. Appx.279 (11th Cir. 2007).

[19]*In United Steelworkers of America v. Weber*, 443 US 193 (S. Ct. 1979).

[20]*University and Community College System of Nevada v. Farmer*, 113 Nev. 90 (S. Ct. Nev. 1997).

Government Contracts   In 1965, President Lyndon Johnson signed Executive Order 11246, which prohibits discrimination by federal contractors. This order had a profound impact on the American workplace because one-third of all workers are employed by companies that do business with the federal government. If an employer found that women or minorities were underrepresented in its workplace, it was required to establish goals and timetables to correct the deficiency.

In 1995, however, the Supreme Court dramatically limited the extent to which the government can *require* contractors to establish affirmative action programs. The Court ruled that, under the Fourteenth Amendment to the Constitution, these programs are permissible only if they serve a "compelling governmental interest" and are "narrowly tailored" so that they minimize the harm to white males.[21] This case led to a sharp decrease in the number of federal contracts awarded to companies owned by women and minorities.

EQUAL PAY ACT OF 1963

Under the Equal Pay Act, an employee may not be paid at a lesser rate than employees of the opposite sex for equal work. "Equal work" means tasks that require equal skill, effort, and responsibility under similar working conditions. For example, Corning Glass Works paid the inspectors on its night shift, who were all male, significantly more than the day inspectors who performed the same tasks but were female. After it allowed women to work at night, it equalized wages on the two shifts but grandfathered in the men who had been on the night shift and continued to pay them higher wages. The Supreme Court ruled that this practice violated the Equal Pay Act, on the grounds that:

- The term "working conditions" meant physical surroundings, not time of day.

- Men were paid more not because they worked at night, but because they would not work at the low rates paid to women.

- Grandfathering in the men at higher wages perpetuated the discrimination.[22]

If the employee proves that she is not being paid equally, the employer will be found liable unless the pay difference is based on merit, productivity, seniority, or some factor other than sex. A "factor other than sex" includes prior wages, training, profitability, performance in an interview, and value to the company. For example, female agents sued Allstate Insurance Co. because its salary for new agents was based, in part, on prior salary. The women argued that this system was unfair because it perpetuated the historic wage differences between men and women. The court, however, held for Allstate.[23]

PREGNANCY DISCRIMINATION ACT

Lucasfilm Ltd. (owned by filmmaker George Lucas) offered Julie Veronese a job as a manager on his California estate, but then it withdrew the offer when she revealed she was pregnant. Is that a problem? Under the Pregnancy Discrimination Act, an employer may not fire, refuse to hire, or fail to promote a woman because she is pregnant. An employer also violates this statute if the work environment is so hostile towards a pregnant woman that it affects her ability to do her job. And an employer must treat pregnancy and childbirth as any other temporary disability. If, for example, employees are allowed time off from work for

[21]*Adarand Constructors, Inc. v. Pena*, 515 U.S. 200, 115 S. Ct. 2097, 1995 U.S. LEXIS 4037 (S. Ct. 1995).
[22]*Corning Glass Works v. Brennan*, 417 U.S. 188 (S. Ct. 1974).
[23]*Kouba v. Allstate Insurance Co.*, 691 F.2d 873, 1982 U.S. App. LEXIS 24479 (9th Cir. 1982).

other medical disabilities, women must also be allowed a maternity leave. A jury ordered Lucasfilm to pay Veronese $113,800.

The Pregnancy Discrimination Act also protects a woman's right to terminate a pregnancy. An employer cannot fire a woman for having an abortion.[24]

AGE DISCRIMINATION IN EMPLOYMENT ACT

During the last decade, the number of workers over the age of 65 has doubled and the number of age discrimination cases has also increased dramatically. Under the Age Discrimination in Employment Act (ADEA), an employer with 20 or more workers may not fire, refuse to hire, fail to promote, or otherwise reduce a person's employment opportunities because he is 40 or older. Nor may an employer require workers to retire at a certain age. (This retirement rule does not apply to police and top-level corporate executives.) The goal of the statute is to counteract stereotypes about the abilities of older workers. A plaintiff in an age discrimination case can show discrimination in three ways: disparate treatment, disparate impact, and hostile work environment.

Disparate Treatment

In a disparate treatment claim, the plaintiff must show that the employer intentionally discriminated against him because of his age, or enacted a policy that intentionally treated employees differently because of their age. Proof of intent involves obvious statements and behavior or more subtle circumstantial evidence.

Under the ADEA, a disparate treatment case requires three steps.

Step 1. The plaintiff must show that:

- He is 40 or older.
- He suffered an adverse employment action.
- He was qualified for the job for which he was fired or not hired.
- He was replaced by a younger person.

Step 2. The employer must present evidence that its decision was based on legitimate, nondiscriminatory reasons.

Step 3. The plaintiff must now show that the employer's reasons are a pretext and, in fact, the employer intentionally discriminated. Note that the standard of proof is tougher in an age discrimination case than in Title VII litigation. Under the ADEA, the plaintiff must show that *but for* his age, the employer would not have taken the action it did. In other words, to win a case, the plaintiff must show that age was not just one factor, it was the *deciding* factor. For example, when Jack Gross was 54 years old, his employer transferred most of his responsibilities to a younger woman and "reassigned" him to a different job. Whatever the terminology used, this move was effectively a demotion. Evidence at trial indicated that age may have been one factor in his employer's decision, but there were other reasons as well. The Supreme Court ruled for the employer, on the grounds that Gross had not shown that age was the "but-for" cause of the disputed decision.[25] This case makes the road steeper for ADEA plaintiffs.

What protection does the ADEA provide? In passing this statute, Congress was particularly concerned about employers who relied on unfavorable stereotypes rather than job performance. The following case illustrates this issue.

[24]*Doe v. C.A.R.S Protection Plus, Inc.*; 527 F.3d 358 (3rd Cir. 2008).
[25]*Gross v. FBL Financial Services, Inc.*, 129 S. Ct. 2343; 2009 U.S. LEXIS 4535 (S. Ct., 2009).

REID V. GOOGLE, INC.

50 Cal. 4th 512, 2010 Cal. LEXIS 7544
Supreme Court of California, 2010

Facts: Google's vice-president of engineering, Wayne Rosing (aged 55), hired Brian Reid (52) as director of operations and director of engineering. Reid had a Ph.D. in computer science and had been a professor of electrical engineering at Stanford University. At the time, the top executives at Google were CEO Eric Schmidt (47), vice-president of engineering operations Urs Hölzle (38), and founders Sergey Brin (28), and Larry Page (29).

During his two years at Google, Reid's only written performance review stated that he had consistently met expectations. The comments indicated that Reid was very intelligent and creative and was a terrific problem solver, with an excellent aptitude and attitude. He also dealt confidently with fast-changing situations. However, the review also commented that "Adapting to Google culture is the primary task. Right or wrong, Google is simply different: younger contributors, inexperienced first-line managers, and the super-fast pace are just a few examples of the environment."

According to Reid, even as he received a positive review, Hölzle and other employees made derogatory age-related remarks such as his ideas were "obsolete," "ancient," and "too old to matter," that he was "slow," "fuzzy," "sluggish," and "lethargic," an "old man," an "old guy," and an "old fuddy-duddy," and that he did not "display a sense of urgency" and "lacked energy."

Fifteen months after Reid joined Google, cofounder Brin emailed several executives about Google's payroll: "We should avoid the tendency towards bloat here, particularly with highly paid individuals." A month later, Reid's duties were assigned to two men who were 15 and 20 years younger. Google asked Reid to develop two in-house educational programs but did not give him a budget or a staff.

Three months later, Reid was fired. Google said it was because of his poor performance and the termination of the educational programs. Reid alleged he was told it was based on a lack of "cultural fit."

Reid sued Google for age discrimination. The trial court granted Google's motion for summary judgment on the grounds that Reid did not have enough evidence of discrimination. The Court of Appeal overruled the trial court. The California Supreme Court agreed to hear the case.

Issues: *Did Reid have enough evidence of age discrimination to warrant a trial? Should the summary judgment motion be granted?*

Excerpts from Justice Chin's Decision expressing the unanimous view of the court: Google contends that the Court of Appeal should have applied the stray remarks doctrine, i.e., should have categorized the alleged statements by Hölzle and Rosing as irrelevant stray remarks and disregarded them in reviewing the merits of the summary judgment motion.

[Justice O'Connor of the Supreme Court of the United States has] stated that "'stray remarks'—statements by non-decisionmakers, or statements by decisionmakers unrelated to the decisional process itself"—do not constitute direct evidence of decision makers' illegitimate criterion in reaching their decision." However, Justice O'Connor explained that stray remarks can be probative of discrimination.

Google contends that we should adopt the stray remarks doctrine so that California courts can disregard discriminatory comments by coworkers and nondecisionmakers, or comments unrelated to the employment decision to ensure that unmeritorious cases principally supported by such remarks are disposed of before trial.

[S]trict application of the stray remarks doctrine, as urged by Google, would result in a court's categorical exclusion of evidence even if the evidence was relevant. An age-based remark not made directly in the context of an employment decision or uttered by a non-decision-maker may be relevant, circumstantial evidence of discrimination. In a later decision authored by Justice O'Connor, the United States Supreme Court indicates that even if age-related comments can be considered stray remarks because they were not made in the direct context of the decisional process, a court should not categorically discount the evidence if relevant; it should be left to the factfinder to assess its probative value.

[T]he stray remarks cases merely demonstrate the common-sense proposition that a slur, in and of itself, does not prove actionable discrimination. A stray remark alone may not create a triable issue of age discrimination. But when combined with other evidence, an otherwise stray remark may create an ensemble [that] *is* sufficient to defeat summary judgment.

For the reasons stated above, we affirm the judgment of the Court of Appeal.

Disparate Impact

Disparate impact claims arise when an employer's actions do not explicitly discriminate, but nonetheless have an adverse impact on people aged 40 or over. Here, too, the standards are different under the ADEA than under Title VII. Under the ADEA:

Step 1. The plaintiffs must present a *prima facie* case that the employment practice in question excludes a disproportionate number of people 40 and older.

Step 2. The employer wins if it can show that the discriminatory decision was based on a "reasonable factor other than age."

One reasonable factor other than age is cost. As a general rule, people in their 60s earn 50 percent more than workers in their early 30s. The older folks are more efficient, but not 50 percent more. So sometimes companies fire older workers because they are paid more, receive higher pension benefits, or generally cost more (e.g., higher healthcare expenses). Courts have supported these decisions, holding that an employer is entitled to prefer *lower-paid* workers even if that preference results in the company also choosing *younger* workers. As the court put it in one case, "An action based on price differentials represents the very quintessence of a legitimate business decision."[26] Indeed, economists argue that the U.S. economy's strength is based at least in part on its flexibility—an American employer can hire workers without fear of being stuck with them until retirement. Thus, for example, Circuit City Stores fired 8 percent of its employees because they could be replaced with people who would work for less. The fired workers were more experienced—and older. This action was legal under the ADEA.

Hostile Work Environment

Diane Kassner (age 79) and Marsha Reiffe (61) worked for 2nd Avenue Delicatessen. They filed suit under the ADEA, alleging that their boss and coworkers made comments to them about their age, such as "Drop dead," "Retire early," "Take off all of that makeup," and "Take off your wig." In addition, their boss pressured the two women to retire and pointed to the front of the restaurant and said, "There's the door." But the two women were never fired.

The court ruled that the ADEA prohibits a hostile work environment based on age. A workplace is considered hostile if a reasonable person would find that intimidation, ridicule, and insult based on age are pervasive.[27] In short, this case, combined with the *Google* case, indicate that it is wise to avoid any comments about an employee's age.

Bona Fide Occupational Qualification

As is the case under Title VII, age is rarely a BFOQ. To set a maximum age, the employer must show that:

- The age limit is reasonably necessary to the essence of the business; and either
- Virtually everyone that age is unqualified for the job, or
- Age is the only way an employer can determine who is qualified.

Although some courts have held that age can be a BFOQ in cases where public safety is at issue, such as for pilots and bus drivers, the EEOC is not always in agreement. In short, the BFOQ defense is very limited in ADEA cases.

---

[26] *Marks v. Loral Corp.*, 57 Cal. App. 4th 30, 1997 Cal. App. LEXIS 611 (Cal. Ct. App., 1997).
[27] *Kassner v. 2nd Ave. Delicatessen, Inc.*, 496 F.3d 229, (2nd Cir. 2007).

EXAM Strategy

Question: Solapere ran a job ad on Monster.com, which said that the company would only consider hiring people who either had a job or had been unemployed for less than six months. The average length of unemployment in the United States at that time was nine months, which meant that such a policy eliminated millions of job applicants. Did this ad violate federal law?

Strategy: Solapere was not intentionally discriminating against anyone, thus no disparate treatment claim. What about a disparate impact claim? Did this policy exclude too many people in a protected category? The unemployed are not a protected category under Title VII, but this policy might have had an impact on groups that are protected.

Result: Older people and some minority groups have higher unemployment rates than other workers. Therefore, this practice could violate both Title VII and the ADEA unless Solapere could show that it was a job-related business necessity. Could it be a job-related business necessity?

DISCRIMINATION ON THE BASIS OF DISABILITY

The Rehabilitation Act of 1973

The Rehabilitation Act of 1973 prohibits discrimination on the basis of disability by the executive branch of the federal government, federal contractors, and entities that receive federal funds. It also requires these organizations to develop affirmative action plans for the hiring, placement, and promotion of the disabled. The same legal standards apply to both this statute and the Americans with Disabilities Act, discussed next. Cases interpreting one statute also apply to the other.

Americans with Disabilities Act

The Americans with Disabilities Act (ADA) prohibits employers with 15 or more workers from discriminating on the basis of disability.

Disability

A **disabled person** is:

- Someone with a physical or mental impairment that substantially limits a major life activity or the operation of a major bodily function, or

- Someone who is regarded as having such an impairment.

Disabled person
Someone with a physical or mental impairment that substantially limits a major life activity, or someone who is regarded as having such an impairment

Major life activities include the following tasks: caring for oneself, performing manual tasks, seeing, hearing, eating, sleeping, walking, standing, lifting, bending, speaking, breathing, learning, reading, concentrating, thinking, communicating, and working. Major bodily functions include functions of the immune system, normal cell growth, digestive, bowel, bladder, neurological, brain, respiratory, circulatory, endocrine, and reproductive functions. The ADA applies to *recovered* drug addicts but not to the *current* use of drugs, sexual disorders, pyromania, exhibitionism, or compulsive gambling. Although the ADA protects alcoholics who can meet the definition of disabled, employers can nonetheless fire alcoholics if their drinking adversely affects job performance.

Suppose an employee has a disabling illness, but one that can be successfully treated. The employee is still considered to be disabled, even if the illness is well controlled. Thus, someone with diabetes is disabled, even if the illness is managed so well that it does not interfere with major life activities. There is one important exception—someone whose vision is normal when wearing glasses or contact lenses is not disabled for purposes of the ADA.

This description of the ADA reflects changes Congress made to the statute in 2008. It expanded the definition of "disability" as the term had been interpreted by the Supreme Court. The following case is one of the first by a circuit court of appeals to interpret the amended ADA. As you can see, despite Congress's intent to expand the scope of the statute, the appeals court did not support the plaintiff's claim. Indeed, by upholding a grant of summary judgment, it prevented her from even presenting her case to a jury.

ALLEN v. SOUTHCREST HOSPITAL

2011 U.S. App. LEXIS 25488
United States Court of Appeals for the Tenth Circuit, 2011

Facts: After some years as a medical assistant at South-Crest Hospital, Alethia Allen requested a transfer to work for a different physician in the same hospital. Unfortunately, Allen found her new job to be much more stressful than the old one. Indeed, it was so stressful that she began suffering severe migraine headaches several times a week. Prior to this new job, she had only had one migraine headache in her life.

Ultimately, Allen resigned because of the migraines. The hospital asked that she stay on to cover for some assistants who were on vacation. Allen agreed to do so and then decided she did not want to quit after all. But before the hospital made a decision about whether she could stay, she left work one day to seek treatment for a migraine at the emergency room. That night, the doctors in her practice decided she could not continue in her job. After leaving SouthCrest, her migraines stopped.

Allen filed suit against SouthCrest for violating the ADA. During discovery, she testified that on most days, she could care for herself and go to work, but that on days on which she took the migraine medication, she would come home from work and immediately "crash and burn." In other words, she could not care for herself but instead would go straight to bed.

The trial court granted SouthCrest's motion for summary judgment. Allen appealed.

Issue: Did Allen have a disability that interfered with one or more major life activities?

Excerpts from Justice Matheson's Decision: [T]he evidence showed that Ms. Allen's migraines, when active and treated with medication, did not permit her to perform activities to care for herself in the evenings and compelled her to go to sleep instead. But it was her burden to make more than a conclusory showing that she was substantially limited in the major life activity of caring for herself as compared to the average person in the general population.

Ms. Allen presented no evidence concerning such factors as how much earlier she went to bed than usual, which specific activities of caring for herself she was forced to forego as the result of going to bed early, how long she slept after taking her medication, what time she woke up the next day, whether it was possible for her to complete the activities of caring for herself the next morning that she had neglected the previous evening, or how her difficulties in caring for herself on days she had a migraine compared to her usual routine of evening self-care.

She also made no attempt to show how the alleged limitations created by her need to "crash and burn" compared to the average person's ability to care for herself in evenings after work. The average person, presumably, does not have to go to bed immediately upon returning from work and/or to medicate herself with somniferous medications to escape migraine symptoms. But this fact alone does not meet Ms. Allen's burden, since the average person also sleeps each evening and cannot care for herself while asleep, and sometimes goes to bed early. In sum, Ms. Allen's claim of a substantial limitation in the major life activity of caring for herself was insufficiently developed and insufficiently supported by the evidence.

We next address the major life activity of working. Ms. Allen admitted that her condition only affected her work for Dr. Myers. [W]here an individual has a need to demonstrate that an impairment substantially limits him or her in working, the individual can do so by showing that the impairment substantially limits his or her ability to perform a class of jobs or broad range of jobs in various classes as compared to most people having comparable training, skills, and abilities. Demonstrating a substantial limitation in performing the unique aspects of a single specific job is not sufficient to establish that a person is substantially limited in the major life activity of working.

The district court therefore properly granted summary judgment to SouthCrest.

Accommodating the Disabled Worker

Once it is established that a worker is disabled, employers may not discriminate on the basis of disability so long as the worker can, with *reasonable accommodation*, perform the *essential functions* of the job. An accommodation is not reasonable if it would create *undue hardship* for the employer. Let's look at those terms more closely.

Reasonable Accommodation   To meet this standard, employers are expected to:

- Make facilities accessible,

- Permit part-time schedules,

- Acquire or modify equipment, and

- Assign a disabled person to an open position that he can perform. (Note that the employer is not required to create a new job or find a perfect position, just a reasonable one.)

Essential Functions of the Job   A juvenile corrections officer was hit by a baseball that fractured her wrist. Nine months after returning to her job, she was assigned to the night shift, where the only other officer was a newcomer. Concerned that her wrist was not strong enough for her to restrain some of the children in the facility on her own, she asked to be paired with an experienced officer. Her employer fired her on the grounds that she could not perform the essential functions of the job. But the court ruled that since she had been working successfully as an officer during the day, clearly she could perform the essential functions.[28]

Undue Hardship   What constitutes undue hardship is the subject of much litigation. Many courts hold that employers may use cost-benefit analysis—they are not required to make an expensive accommodation that provides little benefit. Nor are they required to provide identical working conditions for all employees. For example, a woman who was wheelchair-bound asked that her employer to lower the sink in the kitchenettes that were being built in her building. Otherwise, she would have to use the bathroom sink, which she felt segregated and stigmatized her. The cost to lower the kitchen sinks ranged from as much as $2,000 (to do all the sinks in the building) to as little as $150 (for just the sink on her floor). The court ruled that the employer had no obligation to provide identical conditions and that it had already made a reasonable accommodation by lowering the sink in the bathroom. Although the employer could, in theory, afford this request, it did not have an obligation to spend so much money for so little benefit.[29]

Medical Exams

Employers interact with workers at three key stages: applying, entering (after hiring but before the job starts), and working. The ADA sets different standards for medical exams at these three stages:

- **With applicants,** an employer generally may not require a medical exam or ask about disabilities, except that the interviewer may ask:

  - whether an applicant can perform the work (provided that the same question is asked of all applicants);

---

[28]*Leuzinger v. County of Lake*, 2007 U.S. Dist. LEXIS 35955 (N.D. CA 2007).
[29]*Vande Aande v. Wisconsin Department of Administration*, 44 F.3d 538 (7th Cir. 1995).

  - the applicant to demonstrate how he would perform the job; and
  - (in the event that a disability is obvious) what accommodation the applicant would need.
- **With entering employees,** the company may require a medical test and make it a condition of employment, but the test must be:
  - Required of all employees, whether or not they are disabled; and
  - Treated as a confidential medical record (except in the case of managers who need to know).
- **With existing employees,** an employer may require medical exams or discuss any suspected disability, but only to determine if a worker is still able to perform the existing functions of her job.

Relationship with a Disabled Person

An employer may not discriminate against someone because of his *relationship* with a disabled person. For example, an employer cannot refuse to hire an applicant because he has a disabled child or a spouse with cancer.

Mental Disabilities

Under EEOC rules, physical and mental disabilities are to be treated the same. Physical ailments such as diabetes and deafness may sometimes be easier to diagnose, but psychological disabilities are also covered by the ADA. Among other accommodations, the EEOC rules indicate that employers should be willing to put up barriers to isolate people who have difficulty concentrating, provide detailed day-to-day feedback to those who need greater structure in performing their jobs, or allow workers on antidepressants to come to work later if they are groggy in the morning.

Disparate Treatment and Disparate Impact

Both disparate treatment and disparate impact claims are valid under the ADA. The steps in a disparate *treatment* case are:

Step 1. The plaintiff must offer *prima facie* evidence that the employer discriminated because of his disability.

Step 2. The employer must then offer a legitimate, nondiscriminatory reason for its action.

Step 3. To win, the plaintiff must now prove that the employer intentionally discriminated. She may do so either by showing that (1) the reasons offered were simply a *pretext*, or (2) that a discriminatory intent is more likely than not.

To win a disparate *impact* case, the plaintiff must show that a policy that *looks* neutral falls more harshly on a protected group and cannot be justified by business necessity.

The following Exam Strategy illustrates how disparate treatment and disparate impact are applied in an ADA case and also demonstrates the importance of choosing the correct theory.

EXAM Strategy

Question: Hughes Missile Systems fired Joel Hernandez because he tested positive for cocaine, which, not surprisingly, was a violation of workplace rules. He, however, had no hard feelings, and two years later, he reapplied for a job at Hughes. At the time, he provided evidence that he was clean. However, the company rejected his application because it had a policy against hiring anyone who had been fired for cause. Did the company violate the ADA?

Strategy: Under the ADA, it is legal to discriminate against a drug user, but not against a recovered drug addict. To win a disparate *treatment* case, Hernandez had to show that Hughes's excuse for not rehiring him was just a pretext and its decision was really motivated by an intent to discriminate based on his disability. To win a disparate *impact* claim, Hernandez had to show that the no-rehire policy affected disabled people more than others and that it was not justified by business necessity. Could he prove either of these claims?

Result: The Supreme Court ruled that Hernandez could not prove his disparate treatment claim because its no-rehire rule was legitimate and not just a pretext for discrimination. And because Hernandez had not raised the issue of disparate impact in the lower courts, the Supreme Court refused to consider it. So he lost his case.[30]

Hostile Work Environment

An employee may bring a claim under the ADA if she is subjected to a hostile work environment because of her disability. For example, Sandra Flowers's boss fired her eight months after finding out that she was HIV-positive. During that eight months, Flowers's entire work environment changed. Before, Flowers and her boss had been friends who went out together for lunch, drinks, and the movies. Afterward, the socializing stopped, the boss began monitoring Flowers's phone calls, and then subjected her to four "random" drug tests in one week. A jury found that Flowers's termination was not based on her disability, but that her boss had nonetheless created a hostile work environment by unreasonably interfering with Flowers's ability to work.[31]

While lauding the ADA's objectives, many managers have been apprehensive about its impact on the workplace. Most acknowledge, however, that society is better off if every member has the opportunity to work. And as advocates for the disabled point out, we are all, at best, only temporarily able-bodied. Even with the ADA, only 35 percent of the disabled population who are of working age are employed, whereas 78 percent of able-bodied people have jobs.

GENETIC INFORMATION NONDISCRIMINATION ACT

Suppose you want to promote someone to CFO, but you know that his father and brothers both died young of prostate cancer. Is it legal to consider that information in making a decision? Not since Congress passed the Genetic Information Nondiscrimination Act (GINA). Under this statute, employers with 15 or more workers may not require genetic testing or discriminate against workers because of their genetic makeup. Nor may health insurers use such information to decide coverage or premiums. Thus, neither employers nor health insurers may require you to provide your family medical history—who has died of cancer or heart disease, for instance. And if they find this information out from another source (such as a newspaper obituary), they may not use it in making an employment decision.

ENFORCEMENT

Employment laws provide plaintiffs with different enforcement options.

---

[30]*Raytheon Co. v. Hernandez*, 540 U.S. 44 (S.Ct. 2003).

[31]*Flowers v. S. Reg'l Physician Servs.*, 247 F.3d 229 (5th Cir. 2001).

Constitutional Claims

People bringing a claim under the Constitution must file suit on their own.

The Civil Rights Act of 1866

For plaintiffs alleging racial discrimination, the Civil Rights Act of 1866 offers substantial advantages over Title VII:

- A four-year statute of limitations

- Unlimited compensatory and punitive damages (which, in one case, amounted to $7 million)[32]

- Applicability to all employers, not just those with 15 or more employees

However, this statute is not enforced by the EEOC, which means that the plaintiff is on his own when it comes to negotiating with or filing suit against an employer.

The Rehabilitation Act of 1973

This statute is enforced by the EEOC (for claims against the executive branch of the federal government), the Department of Labor (for claims against federal contractors), and the Department of Justice (for claims against entities that receive federal funds).

Other Statutory Claims

The EEOC is the federal agency responsible for enforcing Title VII, the Equal Pay Act, the Pregnancy Discrimination Act, the ADEA, the ADA, and GINA.

Before a plaintiff can bring suit under one of these statutes, she must first file a complaint with the EEOC. Generally the plaintiff must file within 180 days of the wrong-doing.[33] But if the plaintiff is alleging that she was paid less than she should have been, each paycheck she receives starts the statute of limitations all over again. After it receives a filing, the EEOC conducts an investigation and also attempts to mediate the dispute. If it determines that discrimination has occurred, it will typically file suit on behalf of the plaintiff. This arrangement is favorable for the plaintiff because the government pays the legal bill. If the EEOC decides *not* to bring the case, or does not make a decision within six months, it issues a right to sue letter, and the plaintiff may proceed on her own in court within 90 days. Under the ADEA, a plaintiff may bring suit 60 days after filing a charge with the EEOC. Many states also have their own version of the EEOC.

Remedies available to the successful plaintiff include hiring, reinstatement, retroactive seniority, back pay, front pay (to compensate for future lost wages), and reasonable attorney's fees. Under Title VII and the ADA, plaintiffs are also entitled to compensatory and punitive damages up to $300,000, but only in certain disparate treatment cases, not disparate impact suits. Compensatory damages include future monetary losses, mental anguish, loss of enjoyment of life, and damage to reputation. Punitive damages are available if the defendant acted with malice or reckless indifference to the plaintiff's rights. Under the ADEA, plaintiffs can recover compensatory damages but are eligible for punitive damages only in the case of "willful" violations; that is, knowing or reckless disregard of the law. In the case of willful violations, the damage award is typically doubled.

Two trends, however, have reduced employees' chances of taking home substantial damages. Concerned about a rise in discrimination lawsuits, employers now often require

---

[32]*Edwards v. MBTA.* After the verdict, the case settled.

[33]This is the case unless he resides in a state with an appropriate state agency, in which case he has 300 days.

new hires to agree in advance to arbitrate, not litigate, any future employment claims. The Supreme Court has upheld the enforceability of mandatory arbitration provisions.[34] Employees sometimes receive worse results in the arbitrator's office than in the courtroom, because some arbitrators seem to favor repeat customers (such as management) over one-time users (such as employees). In addition, discovery is more limited in arbitration than in court, which means that the plaintiff may not be able to make the strongest case. Also, arbitration awards are usually not disclosed publicly, so employers have less incentive to avoid misbehavior.

But even if a case does go to trial, plaintiffs in job discrimination cases have a much worse track record than other types of plaintiffs—they win less often at trial, and they lose more often on appeal. As a result, the number of discrimination cases in the federal courts has declined.[35]

Every applicant feels slightly apprehensive before a job interview, but interviewers are also nervous—fearing that every question is a potential land mine of liability. Most interviewers (and students who have read this chapter) would know better than Delta Airlines interviewers who allegedly asked applicants about their sexual preference, birth control methods, and abortion history. The following list provides guidelines for interviewers.

Don't Even Consider Asking	Go Ahead and Ask
Can you perform this function with or without reasonable accommodation?	Would you need reasonable accommodation in this job?
How many days were you sick last year?	How many days were you absent from work last year?
What medications are you currently taking?	Are you currently using drugs illegally?
Where were you born? Are you a United States citizen?	Are you authorized to work in the United States?
How old are you?	What work experience have you had?
How tall are you? How much do you weigh?	Could you carry a 100-pound weight, as required by this job?
When did you graduate from college?	Where did you go to college?
How did you learn this language?	What languages do you speak and write fluently?
Have you ever been arrested?	Have you ever been convicted of a crime that would affect the performance of this job?
Do you plan to have children? How old are your children? What method of birth control do you use?	Can you work weekends? Travel extensively? Would you be willing to relocate?
What is your corrected vision?	Do you have 20/20 corrected vision?
Are you a man or a woman? Are you single or married? What does your spouse do? What will happen if your spouse is transferred? What clubs, societies, or lodges do you belong to?	Talk about the weather instead!

[34]*Gilmer v. Interstate/Johnson Lane Corp.*, 500 U.S. 20, (S.Ct. 1991).
[35]Kevin M. Clermont and Stewart J. Schwab, *Employment Discrimination Plaintiffs in Federal Court: From Bad to Worse?* 3 Harv. l. & Pol'y Rev. 103 (2009).

The most common gaffe on the part of interviewers? Asking women about their child-care arrangements. That question assumes the woman is responsible for child care.

Chapter Conclusion

As adults, we spend more time working than in any other single activity. A job that we love can permeate our lives with satisfaction and even joy. Work that bores or bedevils us may shorten our lives. We have devoted two chapters to employment law precisely because work *is* so important in our lives. Now you know both your rights as a worker and your obligations as an employer. We hope that when you have other people's lives in your hands, you will treat them as you would wish to be treated.

EXAM REVIEW

1. **CONSTITUTION** The U.S. Constitution prohibits employment discrimination by federal, state, and local governments. (p. 455)

2. **THE CIVIL RIGHTS ACT OF 1866** The Civil Rights Act of 1866 prohibits racial discrimination in both private and public employment (except it does not apply to the federal government). (p. 455)

3. **TITLE VII** Under Title VII of the Civil Rights Act of 1964, it is illegal for employers with 15 or more workers to discriminate on the basis of race, color, religion, sex, or national origin. (p. 455)

4. **TYPES OF DISCRIMINATION** There are four types of prohibited activities under Title VII: disparate treatment, disparate impact, hostile environment, and retaliation. (p. 455)

5. **DISPARATE TREATMENT** To prove a disparate treatment case, the plaintiff must show that she was *treated* less favorably than others because of her sex, race, color, religion, or national origin. (p. 455)

6. **DISPARATE IMPACT** Disparate impact applies if the employer has a rule that, *on its face*, is not discriminatory, but *in practice* excludes too many people in a protected group and the test is not a job-related business necessity. (p. 457)

7. **HOSTILE WORK ENVIRONMENT** Employers violate Title VII if they permit a work environment that is so hostile towards people in a protected category that it affects their ability to work. (p. 458)

8. **RETALIATION** Title VII also prohibits employers from retaliating against workers who oppose discrimination, bring a claim under the statute, or take part in an investigation or hearing. (p. 461)

9. **RELIGION** Employers cannot discriminate against a worker because of his religious beliefs. In addition, employers must make reasonable accommodation for a worker's religious practices unless the request would cause undue hardship for the business. (pp. 461–462)

10. **DEFENSES** Under Title VII, the defendant has four possible defenses: merit, seniority, bona fide occupational qualification (BFOQ), and affirmative action. (pp. 463–464)

11. **BONA FIDE OCCUPATIONAL QUALIFICATION** Under the BFOQ standard, an employer is permitted to establish discriminatory job requirements if they are essential to the position in question. (p. 464)

EXAM Strategy

Question: When Southwest Airlines first started, it refused to hire male flight attendants because its strategy was to court its (mostly male) customers by promoting an image of "feminine spirit, fun, and sex appeal." Its ads featured women in provocative uniforms serving "love bites" (almonds) and "love potions" (cocktails). Its ticketing system featured a "quickie machine" to provide "instant gratification." Is this refusal to hire men a violation of Title VII?

Strategy: Southwest argued that its "Love" campaign was an essential marketing tool. Was being a woman a BFOQ? Remember that the courts have almost always rejected BFOQ claims that are based on customer preference. (See the "Result" at the end of this section.)

12. **EQUAL PAY ACT** Under the Equal Pay Act, an employee may not be paid at a lesser rate than employees of the opposite sex for equal work. (p. 465)

13. **PREGNANCY DISCRIMINATION ACT** Under the Pregnancy Discrimination Act, an employer may not fire, refuse to hire, or fail to promote a woman because she is pregnant or because she has had an abortion. An employer must also treat pregnancy as it would any other temporary disability. (pp. 465–466)

14. **AGE DISCRIMINATION IN EMPLOYMENT ACT** Under the ADEA, an employer with 20 or more workers may not fire, refuse to hire, fail to promote, or otherwise reduce a person's employment opportunities because he is 40 or older. (p. 466)

EXAM Strategy

Question: Kathy was over 40 when SFI refused to hire her as an insurance agent. It claimed that it had not hired her because she did not have sales experience, but the job ad had not specified that sales experience was required. It turned out that when SFI hired agents from outside the company, it was much more likely to hire people under 40. But when promoting from within, it was much more likely to promote people over 40. Did SFI violate the ADEA when it refused to hire Kathy?

Strategy: An ADEA case involves a three-step analysis. In Step 1, Kathy has shown that she is older than 40, suffered an adverse employment action, was qualified for the job, and a younger person actually got the job. In Step 2, SFI has to show that its decision was based on a legitimate reason. No sales experience is a good reason. In Step 3, Kathy must prove that her age was the deciding factor. (See the "Result" at the end of this section.)

15. **REHABILITATION ACT** The Rehabilitation Act of 1973 prohibits discrimination on the basis of disability by the federal government, federal contractors, and all entities that receive federal funds. (p. 469)

16. **AMERICANS WITH DISABILITIES ACT** The ADA prohibits employers with 15 or more workers from discriminating on the basis of disability. (p. 469)

17. **DISABILITY** A disabled person is:

- Someone with a physical or mental impairment that substantially limits a major life activity or the operation of a major bodily function, or

- Someone who is regarded as having such an impairment. (p. 469)

18. **TREATMENT OF DISABLED WORKERS** Once it is established that a worker is disabled, employers may not discriminate on the basis of disability so long as she can, with reasonable accommodation, perform the essential functions of the job. An accommodation is not reasonable if it would create undue hardship for the employer. (p. 471)

EXAM Strategy

Question: When Thomas Lussier filled out a Postal Service employment application, he did not admit that he had twice pleaded guilty to charges of disorderly conduct. Lussier suffered from Post-Traumatic Stress Disorder (PTSD) acquired during military service. Because of this disorder, he sometimes had panic attacks that required him to leave meetings. He was also a recovered alcoholic and drug user. During his stint with the Postal Service, he had some personality conflicts with other employees. Once, another employee hit him. He also had one episode of "erratic emotional behavior and verbal outburst." In the meantime, a postal employee in Ridgewood, New Jersey, killed four colleagues. The postmaster general encouraged all supervisors to identify workers who had dangerous propensities. Lussier's boss discovered that he had lied on his employment application about the disorderly conduct charges and fired him. Is the Postal Service in violation of the law?

Strategy: Was Lussier disabled under the ADA? He had a mental impairment (PTSD) that substantially limited a major life activity. Could Lussier, with reasonable accommodation, perform his job? Yes. Was his firing illegal? (See the "Result" at the end of this section.)

19. **GENETIC INFORMATION NONDISCRIMINATION ACT** Under GINA, employers with 15 or more workers may not require genetic testing or discriminate against workers because of their genetic makeup. (p. 473)

11. Result: Safety, privacy, and authenticity are three situations in which customer preference can be a BFOQ. None of these issues was a factor in this case. The court ruled against Southwest on the grounds that it was "not a business where vicarious sex entertainment is the primary service provided."[36]

---

[36]*Wilson v. Southwest Airlines*, 517 F. Supp 292 (N.D. Tex 1981).

14. Result: In the absence of specific comments about age, it is very difficult to show that age is the deciding factor. Kathy is likely to lose her case.

18. Result: The court held that the Postal Service was in violation of the law because Lussier had been dismissed solely as a result of his disability. Clearly, he could perform his job with reasonable accommodation.

MULTIPLE-CHOICE QUESTIONS

1. Gregg Young, the CEO of BJY Inc., insisted on calling Mamdouh El-Hakem "Manny" or "Hank" even when El-Hakem asked him not to. El-Hakem was of Arab heritage. Young argued that a "Western" name would increase El-Hakem's chances for success and would be more acceptable to BJY's clientele. Does this behavior violate the law?

   (a) Yes, Young violated Title VII by discriminating against El-Hakem on the basis of his national origin.

   (b) Yes, Young was creating a hostile work environment.

   (c) Both (a) and (b)

   (d) No, Manny is just a nickname. No harm was intended and, indeed, no harm resulted.

   (e) No, because customers did prefer a Western name.

2. The CEO of BankTwo realized that not one single officer of the bank was female or minority. He announced that henceforth, the bank would only hire people in these two groups until they made up at least 30 percent of the officers. Is this plan legal?

   (a) Yes, voluntary affirmative action plans are always legal.

   (b) Yes, because fewer than 20 percent of the officers are female or minority.

   (c) No, to be legal, the goal of an affirmative action plan cannot be greater than 20 percent female or minority.

   (d) No, the plan is too unfair to white men, who have no chance of being hired for a long time.

3. When Allain University was looking for a diversity officer, it decided it would only hire a person of color. Is this decision legal?

   (a) Yes, color is a BFOQ for this position.

   (b) No, color is never a BFOQ, but race could be.

   (c) No, neither race nor color can be a BFOQ.

   (d) No, race and color can be a BFOQ, but is not in this situation. A person does not have to be a member of a minority group to promote diversity.

4. Ralph has worked as a model builder at Snowdrop Architects for 30 years. The firm replaces him with Charlotte, who is 24 and willing to work for much less than Ralph's salary. The firm never offered to let him stay for less pay. When he left, one of the

partners told him, "Frankly, it's not a bad thing to have a cute young person working with the clients." Which of the following statements is true?

(a) Snowdrop is liable because it had an obligation to offer Ralph the lower salary before firing him.

(b) Snowdrop is liable because it is illegal to replace an older worker with a younger one just to save money.

(c) Snowdrop is liable because age was a factor in Ralph's firing.

(d) Snowdrop is liable under Title VII because it replaced an old man with a young woman.

(e) Snowdrop is not liable because age was not the deciding factor in Ralph's firing.

5. During chemotherapy for bone cancer, a delivery person is exhausted, nauseous, and weak. He has asked permission to come in later, work a shorter day, and limit his lifting to 10 pounds. Delivery people typically carry packages of up to 70 pounds. Does Vulcan, his employer, have the right to fire him?

(a) Vulcan must create a new position so that the employee can do something else.

(b) Vulcan must transfer the employee to another position, but only if one is vacant and he is able to perform it.

(c) Vulcan can fire the man because none of his major life activities has been affected.

(d) Vulcan can fire the man because he cannot perform the essential functions of his job.

(e) Vulcan can fire him because he is not disabled—once the chemotherapy treatments end, he will feel fine again.

ESSAY QUESTIONS

1. Disney World and Abercrombie & Fitch both fired female employees who insisted upon wearing a Muslim headscarf because such apparel violated the companies' appearance policies. Can these employers make reasonable accommodation for this religious practice? Abercrombie also fired a salesperson who converted to a Christian religion that forbade her from showing skin. When she showed up for work in an ankle-length skirt, her manager told her she had to either wear jeans or short skirts with leggings, but she refused. Did Abercrombie violate Title VII in this case?

2. In the 2008 recession, Roger lost his job as a comptroller. Desperate for work after a year of unemployment, he began to apply for any accounting job at any company. But no one would hire him because he was "over-qualified and over-experienced." He repeatedly explained that he was eager to fill the job that was available. Have these companies that refused to hire Roger violated the ADEA?

3. More than 90 percent of employers conduct criminal background checks, and many of these automatically exclude any job applicant with a criminal record. Is this practice a violation of the law?

4. The Lillie Rubin boutique in Phoenix would hire only women to work in sales because fittings and alterations took place in the dressing room or immediately

outside. The customers were buying expensive clothes and demanded a male-free dressing area. Has the Lillie Rubin store violated Title VII? What would its defense be?

5. FedEx refused to promote José Rodriguez to a supervisor's position because of his accent and "how he speaks." Is FedEx in violation of the law?

DISCUSSION QUESTIONS

1. In the *Griggs* disparate impact case, Duke Power based employment decisions on written tests. Why do employers use these types of tests? When are they appropriate in the hiring or promotion process?

2. In disparate *treatment* cases, the plaintiff must show that the defendant intentionally discriminated, but not in disparate *impact* cases. Is it fair to hold employers liable when they have not engaged in intentional wrongdoing?

3. Generally, the BFOQ defense does not apply to customer preference. But recently, some clients have been pressuring their law firms to staff their cases with female and minority lawyers. If a firm does so, would the BFOQ defense be valid? Should it be?

4. Pam Huber worked at Walmart as a grocery order filler, earning $13 an hour. While on the job, she suffered a permanent injury to her right arm and hand. Both she and Walmart agreed that she was disabled under the ADA. As a reasonable accommodation, she asked for a job as a router, which was then vacant. Although she was qualified for that job, she was not the most qualified. Walmart filled the job with the most qualified person. It offered Huber a position as a janitor at $6.20 per hour. Did Walmart violate the ADA?

5. **ETHICS** Mary Ann Singleton was the librarian at a maximum-security prison located in Tazewell County, Virginia. About four times a week, Gene Shinault, assistant warden for operations, persistently complimented Singleton and stared at her breasts when he spoke to her. On one occasion, he measured the length of her skirt to judge its compliance with the prison's dress code and told her that it looked "real good"; constantly told her how attractive he found her; made references to his physical fitness, considering his advanced age; asked Singleton if he made her nervous (she answered "yes"); and repeatedly remarked to Singleton that if he had a wife as attractive as Singleton, he would not permit her to work in a prison facility around so many inmates. Shinault told Singleton's supervisor in her presence, "Look at her. I bet you have to spank her every day." The supervisor then laughed and said, "No. I probably should, but I don't." Shinault replied, "Well, I know I would." Shinault also had a security camera installed in her office in a way that permitted him to observe her as she worked. Singleton reported this behavior to her supervisor, who simply responded, "Boys will be boys." Did Shinault sexually harass Singleton? Whether or not Shinault violated the law, what *ethical* obligation did Singleton's supervisor have to protect her from this type of behavior?

6. Ronald Lockhart, who was deaf, worked for FedEx as a package handler. Although fluent in American Sign Language, he could not read lips. After 9/11, the company held meetings to talk about security issues. Lockhart complained to the EEOC that he could not understand these discussions. FedEx fired him. Has FedEx violated the law?

Business Organizations

CHAPTER 19

STARTING A BUSINESS: LLCs AND OTHER OPTIONS

© Werner H. Kunz/Flickr/Getty Images

Poor Jeffrey Horning. If only he had understood business law. Horning owned a thriving construction company which operated as a corporation—Horning Construction Company, Inc. To lighten his crushing workload, he decided to bring in two partners to handle more day-to-day responsibility. It seemed a good idea at the time.

Horning transferred the business to Horning Construction, LLC and then gave one-third ownership each to two trusted employees, Klimowski and Holdsworth. But Horning did not pay enough attention to the legal formalities—the new LLC had no operating agreement.

> **Jeffrey Horning was stuck in purgatory, with two business partners he loathed and no way out.**

Nothing worked out as he had planned. The two men did not take on extra work. Horning's relationship with them went from bad to worse, with the parties bickering over every petty detail and each man trying to sabotage the others. It got to the point that Klimowski sent Horning a letter full of foul language. At his wit's end, Horning proposed that the LLC buy out his share of the business. Klimowski and Holdsworth refused. Really frustrated, Horning asked a court to dissolve the business on the grounds that Klimowski despised him, Holdsworth resented him, and neither of them trusted him. In his view, it was their goal "to make my remaining time with Horning, LLC so unbearable that I will relent and give them for a pittance the remainder of the company for which they have paid nothing to date."

Although the court was sympathetic, it refused to help. Because Horning, LLC did not have an operating agreement that provided for a buyout, it had to depend upon the LLC statute, which only permitted dissolution "whenever it is not reasonably practicable to carry on the business." Unfortunately, Horning, LLC was very successful, grossing over $25 million annually. Jeffrey Horning was stuck in purgatory, with two business partners he loathed and no way out.[1]

Every business, no matter how large, was at one point little more than a gleam in an entrepreneur's eye. The goal of the law is to balance the rights, duties, and liabilities of entrepreneurs, managers, investors, and customers. Time and again in these next chapters, we will see that legal issues can have as profound an impact on the success of a company as any business decision. The law affects virtually every aspect of business. Wise (and successful) entrepreneurs know how to use the law to their advantage. Think of the grief Jeffrey Horning could have saved himself if he had understood the implications of the LLC statute.

To begin, entrepreneurs must select a form of organization. The correct choice can reduce taxes, liability, and conflict while facilitating outside investment. If entrepreneurs do not make a choice for themselves, the law will automatically select a (potentially undesirable) default option.

Sole Proprietorships

Sole proprietorships are the most common form of business, so we begin there. A **sole proprietorship** is an unincorporated business owned by one person. For example, Linda runs ExSciTe (which stands for Excellence in Science Teaching), a company that helps teachers prepare hands-on science experiments in the classroom using such basic items as vinegar, lemon juice, and red cabbage.

Sole proprietorship
An unincorporated business owned by one person.

If an individual runs a business without taking any formal steps to create an organization, she automatically has a sole proprietorship. It is, if you will, the default option. She is not required to hire a lawyer or register with the government. The company is not even required to file a separate tax return—because the business is a *flow-through* tax entity. In other words, Linda must pay *personal* income tax on the profits, but the *business* itself does not pay income taxes. A very few states, and some cities and towns, require sole proprietors to obtain a business license. And states generally require sole proprietors to register their business name if it is different from their own. Linda, for example, would file a "d/b/a" or "doing business as" certificate for ExSciTe.

Sole proprietorships also have some serious disadvantages. First, the owner of the business is responsible for all of the business's debts. If ExSciTe cannot pay its suppliers or if a student is injured by an exploding cabbage, Linda is *personally* liable. She may have to sell her house and car to pay the debt. Second, the owner of a sole proprietorship has limited options for financing her business. Debt is generally her only source of working capital because she has no stock or memberships to sell. If someone else brings in capital and helps with the management of the business, then it is a partnership, not a sole proprietorship. For this reason, sole proprietorships work best for small businesses without large capital needs.

---

[1]*In the Matter of Jeffrey M. Horning*, 816 N.Y.S.2d 877; 2006 N.Y. Misc. LEXIS 555.

CORPORATIONS

Corporations are the dominant form of organization for a simple reason—they have been around for a long time and, as a result, they are numerous and the law that regulates them is well developed.

The concept of a corporation is very old indeed—it began with the Greeks and spread from them through the Romans into English law. At the beginning, however, corporations were viewed with deep suspicion. A British jurist commented that they had "neither bodies to be punished nor souls to be condemned." And what were shareholders doing that they needed limited liability? Why did they have to cower behind a corporate shield? For this reason, shareholders originally had to obtain special permission to form a corporation. In England, corporations could be created only by special charter from the monarch or, later, from Parliament. But with the advent of the Industrial Revolution, large-scale manufacturing enterprises needed huge amounts of capital from investors who were not involved in management and did not want to be personally liable for the debts of an organization that they were not managing. In 1811, New York became the first jurisdiction in the United States to permit routine incorporation.[2]

Despite the initial suspicion with which corporations were viewed, economists now suggest that this form of organization, combined with technological advances such as double-entry bookkeeping and stockmarkets, provided the West with an enormous economic advantage. In particular, corporations permitted the investment of outside capital and were more likely than partnerships to survive the death of their founders. In short, corporations permitted the development of large, enduring businesses.

Corporations in General

As is the case for all forms of organization, corporations have their advantages and disadvantages.

Limited Liability

If a business flops and cannot pay its bills, shareholders lose their investment in the company but not their other assets. Likewise, if an employee is in an accident while driving a company van, the business is liable for any harm to the other driver, but its shareholders are not personally liable. Be aware, however, that limited liability does not protect against all debts. Individuals are always responsible for their *own* acts. Suppose that the careless employee who caused the accident was also a company shareholder. Both he and the company would be liable. If the company did not pay the judgment, the employee would have to, from his personal assets. **A corporation protects managers and investors from personal liability for the debts of the corporation and the actions of others, but not against liability for their** *own negligence (or other torts and crimes).*

Transferability of Interests

Corporations provide flexibility for enterprises small (with one owner) and large (with thousands of shareholders). As we will see, partnership interests are not transferable without the permission of the other partners, whereas corporate stock can be bought and sold easily.

Duration

When a sole proprietor dies, legally so does the business. But corporations have perpetual existence: they can continue without their founders.

---

[2]An Act Relative to Incorporation for Manufacturing Purpose, 1811 N.Y. Laws, ch. 67, §111.

Logistics

Corporations require substantial expense and effort to create and operate. The cost of establishing a corporation includes legal and filing fees, not to mention the cost of the annual filings that states require. Corporations must also hold meetings for both shareholders and directors. Minutes of these meetings must be kept indefinitely in the company minute book.

Taxes

Because corporations are taxable entities, they must pay taxes and file returns. This is a simple sentence that requires a complex explanation. Originally, there were only three ways to do business: as a sole proprietorship, a partnership, or a corporation. The sole proprietor pays taxes on all the business's profits. A partnership is not, as we say, a taxable entity, which means it does not pay taxes itself. All income and losses are passed through to the partners and reported on their personal income tax returns. Corporations, by contrast, are taxable entities and pay income tax on their profits. Shareholders must then pay tax on dividends from the corporation. Thus a dollar is taxed only once before it ends up in a partner's bank account, but twice before it is deposited by a shareholder.

Exhibit 19.1 compares the single taxation of partnerships with the double taxation of corporations. Suppose, as shown in the exhibit, that a corporation and a partnership each receives $10,000 in additional income. The corporation pays tax at a top rate of 35 percent.[3]

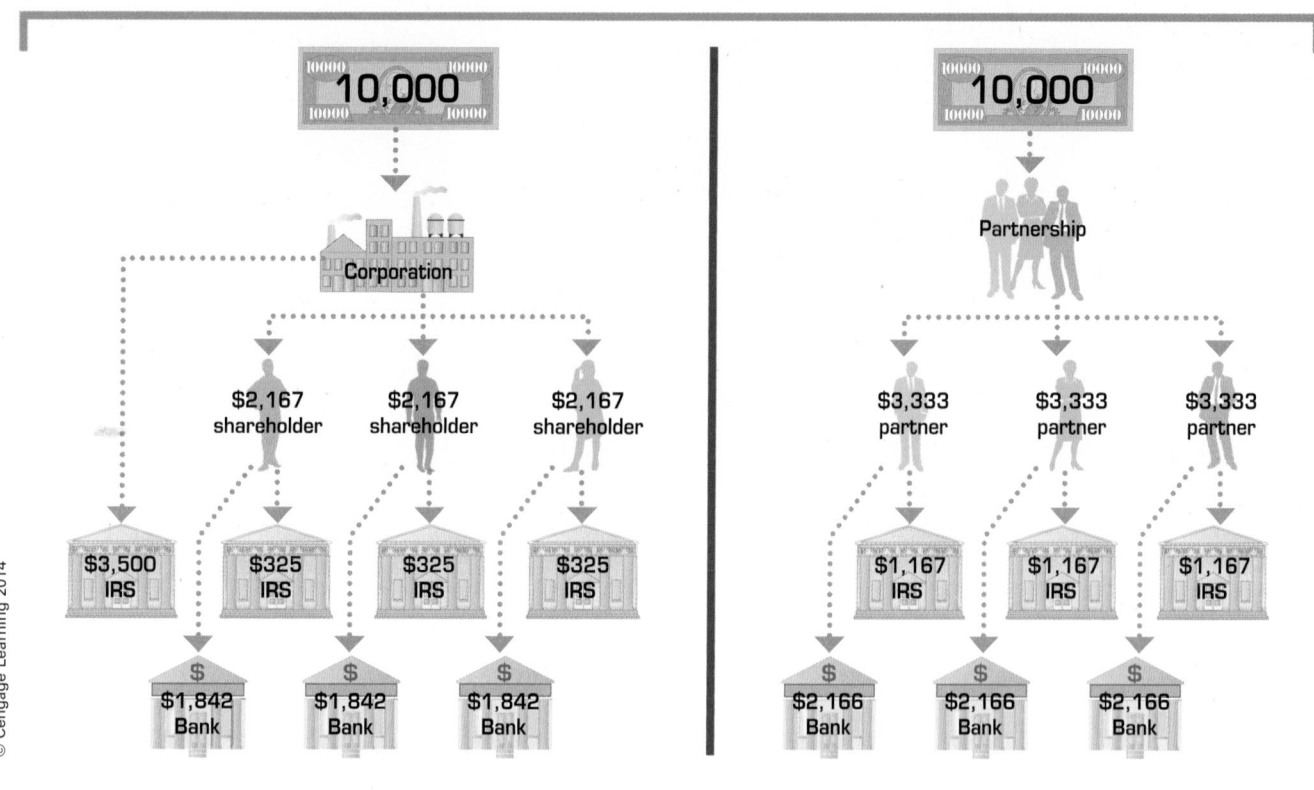

© Cengage Learning 2014

EXHIBIT 19.1   Partners pay lower taxes than shareholders.

---

[3]This is the federal tax rate; most states also levy a corporate tax.

Thus the corporation pays $3,500 of the $10,000 in tax. The corporation pays out the remaining $6,500 as a dividend of $2,167 to each of its three shareholders. Then the shareholders are taxed at the special dividend rate of 15 percent, which means they each pay a tax of $325. They are each left with $1,842. Of the initial $10,000, almost 45 percent ($4,475) has gone to the Internal Revenue Service (IRS).

Compare the corporation to a partnership. The partnership itself pays no taxes, so it can pass on $3,333 to each of its partners. At a 35 percent individual rate, each partner pays an income tax of $1,167. As partners, they pocket $2,166, which is $324 more than they could keep as shareholders. Of the partnership's initial $10,000, 35 percent ($3,501) has gone to the IRS, compared with the corporation's 45 percent.

One further tax issue. Corporations are created and regulated by state law but must pay both federal and state taxes. Federal law gives favorable tax treatment to some small corporations, which it calls "S corporations." Many states also treat small corporations differently but calls them "close corporations." Federal tax law and state corporation statutes are completely independent. Thus, an organization could be a close corporation under state law and not qualify as an S corporation or, conversely, could be an S corporation under federal law but may or may not be a close corporation for state purposes. Exhibit 19.2 illustrates the difference between state corporate law and federal taxation of corporations.

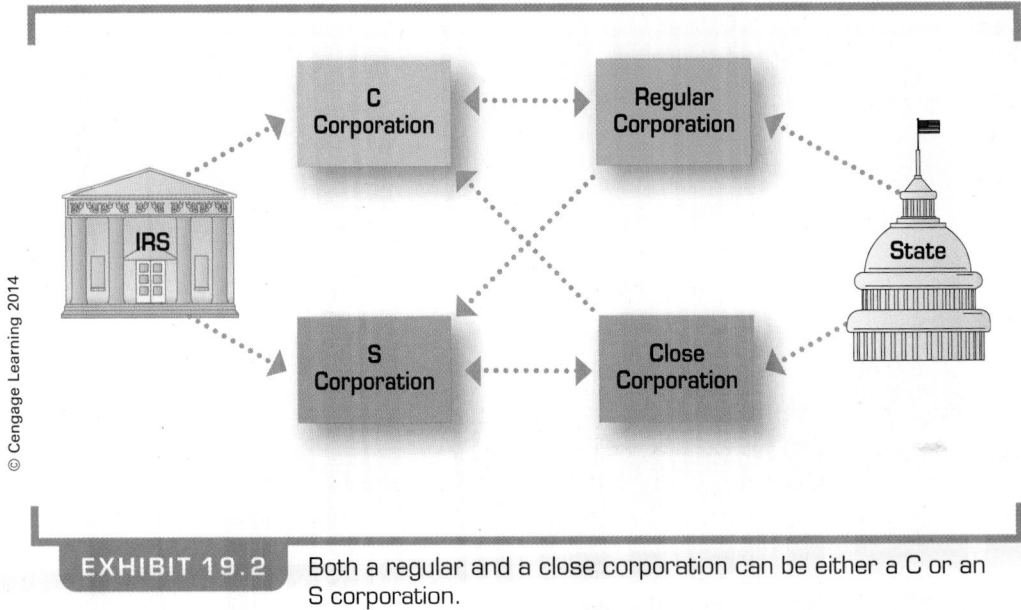

© Cengage Learning 2014

EXHIBIT 19.2   Both a regular and a close corporation can be either a C or an S corporation.

S Corporations

Although entrepreneurs are often optimistic about the likely success of their new enterprise, in truth, the majority of new businesses lose money in their early years. Congress created S corporations (aka "S corps") to encourage entrepreneurship by offering tax breaks. The name "S corporation" comes from the provision of the Internal Revenue Code that created this form of organization.[4] **Shareholders of S corps have both the limited**

---

[4] 26 U.S.C. §1361.

liability of a corporation and the tax status of a partnership. Like a partnership, an S corp is not a taxable entity—all the company's profits and losses pass through to the shareholders, who pay tax at their individual rates. It avoids the double taxation of a regular corporation (called a "C corporation"). If, as is often the case, the startup loses money, investors can deduct these losses against their other income.

S corps do face some major restrictions:

- There can be only one class of stock (although voting rights can vary within the class).

- There can be no more than 100 shareholders.

- Shareholders must be individuals, estates, charities, pension funds, or trusts, not partnerships or corporations.

- Shareholders must be citizens or residents of the United States, not nonresident aliens.

- All shareholders must agree that the company should be an S corporation.

Although *most* states follow the federal lead on S corporations, a small number require these companies to pay state corporate tax.

Close Corporations

Originally, the terms **close corporation** and **closely held corporation** referred simply to a company whose stock was not publicly traded (in other words, a "privately held" company). Most close corporations are small, although some privately held corporations, such as Hallmark Cards, Inc., and Mars, Inc. (maker of M&Ms and Snickers candy bars), are huge. Beginning in New York in 1948, some states amended their corporation statutes to make special provisions for entrepreneurs. In some cases, a corporation must affirmatively elect to be treated as a close corporation; in others, any corporation can take advantage of these special provisions. Now when lawyers refer to "close corporations," they usually mean not merely a privately held company, but one that has taken advantage of the close corporation provisions of its state code.

Although the provisions of close corporation statutes vary from state to state, they tend to have certain common themes:

- **Protection of minority shareholders.** As there is no public market for the stock of a close corporation, a minority shareholder who is being mistreated by the majority cannot simply sell his shares and depart. Therefore, close corporation statutes often provide some protection for minority shareholders. For example, the charter of a close corporation could require a unanimous vote of all shareholders to choose officers, set salaries, or pay dividends. It could grant each shareholder veto power over all important corporate decisions.

- **Transfer restrictions.** The shareholders of a close corporation often need to work closely together in the management of the company. Therefore, statutes typically permit the corporation to require that a shareholder first offer shares to the other owners before selling them to an outsider. In that way, the remaining shareholders have some control over who their new co-owners will be.

- **Flexibility.** Close corporations can typically operate without a board of directors, a formal set of bylaws, or annual shareholder meetings.

- **Dispute resolution.** The shareholders are allowed to agree in advance that any one of them can dissolve the corporation if some particular event occurs or, if they choose, for any reason at all. If the shareholders are in a stalemate, the problem can be solved

Close corporation
A company whose stock is not publicly traded. Also known as a *closely held corporation.*

by dissolving the corporation. Even without such an agreement, a shareholder can ask a court to dissolve a close corporation if the other owners behave "oppressively" or "unfairly."

EXAM Strategy

Question: Consider these two entrepreneurs: Judith formed a corporation to publish a newsletter that will not generate substantial revenues. Drexel operated his construction and remodeling business as a sole proprietorship. Were these forms of organization right for these businesses?

Strategy: Prepare a list of the advantages and disadvantages of each form of organization. Sole proprietorships are best for businesses without substantial capital needs. Corporations can raise capital but are expensive to operate.

Result: Judith would be better off with a sole proprietorship—her revenues will not support the expenses of a corporation. Also, her debts are likely to be small, so she will not need the limited liability of a corporation. And no matter what her form of organization, she would be personally liable for any negligent acts she commits, so a corporation would not provide any additional protection. But for Drexel, a sole proprietorship could be disastrous because his construction company will have substantial expenses and a large number of employees. If an employee causes an injury, Drexel might be personally liable. And if his business fails, the court would liquidate his personal assets. He would be better off with a form of organization that limits his liability, such as a corporation or a limited liability company.

LIMITED LIABILITY COMPANIES

An LLC offers the limited liability of a corporation and the tax status of a partnership.

Limited liability companies (LLCs) are a relatively new form of organization. Wyoming passed the first LLC statute in 1977, but most states did not follow suit until after 1991. An LLC is an extremely useful form of organization increasingly favored by entrepreneurs. It is not, however, as simple as it perhaps should be. Owing to a complex history that involves painful interaction between IRS regulations and state laws (the details of which we will spare you), the specific provisions of state laws vary greatly. An effort to remedy this confusion—the Uniform Limited Liability Company Act—has not at this point been widely accepted. Indeed, it was so heavily criticized that it was revised, but the revised statute has been adopted by only a handful of states. Thus, we can discuss only general trends in state laws. Before forming an LLC, you should review carefully the laws in your particular state.

Limited Liability

Members are not personally liable for the debts of the company. They risk only their investment, as if they were shareholders of a corporation. Are the members of the LLC liable in the following case? You be the judge.

You be the Judge

RIDGAWAY V. SILK
2004 Conn. Super. LEXIS 548
Superior Court of Connecticut, 2004

Facts: Norman Costello and Robert Giordano were members of Silk, LLC, which owned a bar and adult entertainment nightclub in Groton, Connecticut, called Silk Stockings. Anthony Sulls went drinking there one night—and drinking heavily. Although he was obviously drunk, employees at Silk Stockings continued to serve him. Costello and Giordano were working there that night. They both greeted customers (who numbered in the hundreds), supervised employees, and performed "other PR work." When Sulls left the nightclub at 1:45 a.m. with two friends, he drove off the highway at high speed, killing himself and one of his passengers, William Ridgaway, Jr.

Ridgaway's estate sued Costello and Giordano personally. The defendants filed a motion for summary judgment seeking dismissal of the complaint.

You Be the Judge: *Are Costello and Giordano personally liable to Ridgaway's estate?*

Argument for Costello and Giordano: The defendants did not own Silk Stockings; they were simply members of an LLC that owned the nightclub. The whole point of an LLC is to protect members against personal liability. The assets of Silk, LLC, are at risk, but not the personal assets of Costello and Giordano.

Argument for Ridgaway's Estate: The defendants are not liable for being members of Silk, LLC; they are liable for their own misdeeds as employees of the LLC. They were both present at Silk Stockings on the night in question, meeting and greeting customers and supervising employees. It is possible that they might actually have served drinks to Sulls, but in any event, they did not adequately supervise and train their employees to prevent them from serving alcohol to someone who was clearly drunk. The world would be an intolerable place to live if employees were free to be as careless as they wished, knowing that they were not liable because they were members of an LLC.

Tax Status

As in a partnership, income flows through the company to the individual members, avoiding the double taxation of a corporation.

Formation

To organize an LLC, you must have a charter and you should have an operating agreement. The charter is short, containing basic information such as name and address. It must be filed with the Secretary of State in the jurisdiction in which it is being formed. An operating agreement sets out the rights and obligations of the owners, who are called "members." If an LLC does not adopt its own operating agreement, LLC statutes provide a default option. However, these standardized provisions may not be what members would choose if they thought about it. Therefore, it is often better for an LLC to prepare its own personalized operating agreement. The Horning case that began this chapter illustrates one of the many things that can go wrong when an LLC does not have an operating agreement.

On this issue, corporations have an advantage over LLCs. Corporations are so familiar that the standard documents (such as a charter, bylaws, and shareholder agreement) are well established and widely available. Lawyers can form a corporation easily, and the Internet offers a host of free forms. This is not the case with LLCs. As yet, the law is so unsettled that standard forms may be dangerous, while customized forms can be expensive. The following case illustrates the importance of a well-drafted operating agreement.

WYOMING.COM, LLC V. LIEBERMAN

2005 WY 42; 109 P.3d 883; 2005 Wyo. LEXIS 48
Supreme Court of Wyoming, 2005

Facts: Lieberman was a member of an LLC called Wyoming.com. After he withdrew, he and the other members disagreed about what his membership was worth. Wyoming.com filed a lawsuit asking the court to determine the financial rights and obligations of the parties, if any, upon the withdrawal of a member.

The Supreme Court of Wyoming reached a decision that may have sounded logical but left Lieberman in a sad twilight zone—neither in nor out of the LLC. The court ruled that Lieberman still owned part of the business despite his withdrawal as a member. So far, so good. But neither the LLC statute nor the company's operating agreement required the LLC to pay a member the value of his share. Therefore, neither party had any further rights or obligations. In other words, Lieberman was still an owner, but he was not entitled to any payment. Not quite understanding the implications of this ruling, Lieberman filed a motion seeking financial information about the company. The original trial court denied the request on the theory that since Lieberman had no right to a payout, the company had no obligation to give him financial data.

Issue: *Does Lieberman have a right to any financial data about Wyoming.com?*

Excerpts from Justice Golden's Decision: [The prior Lieberman case] held that no provision exists either in Wyoming statutes or the operating agreements of Wyoming.com requiring any particular disposition of a member's equity interest upon his withdrawal as a member. Thus, Wyoming.com could not legally force Lieberman to sell his equity interest at any particular value, and Lieberman could not force Wyoming.com to buy his equity interest at any particular value.

This answered the question presented by Wyoming.com in its [lawsuit]. While not explicitly stated in the opinion, with the question answered, nothing remains but to dismiss the [case]. No further proceedings are required to resolve this action. As specifically applied to this case, Lieberman simply retains his equity interest and nothing further is required of either party as a direct result of Lieberman's withdrawal as a member.

Excerpts from Justice Kite's Concurring Decision: I concur with the result reached by the majority in this matter solely because it is mandated by [the prior Lieberman case]. I joined [the] dissenting opinion in that case because I found it more appropriate to allow a minority interest owner in an LLC a mechanism to realize the value of his equity interest. Given the majority's ruling that Mr. Lieberman owns an equity interest, but neither the operating agreement nor the statute provide a method for him to realize the value of that interest, there is nothing left for the district court to order Wyoming.com LLC to do. [The court should consider that] those rights and responsibilities in the context of other forms of business organizations are well developed and may provide guidance in the realm of the LLC.

Flexibility

Unlike S corporations, LLCs can have members that are corporations, partnerships, or nonresident aliens. LLCs can also have different classes of stock. Unlike corporations, LLCs are not required to hold annual meetings or maintain a minute book.

Transferability of Interests

Unless the operating agreement provides otherwise, the members of the LLC must obtain the unanimous permission of the remaining members before transferring their ownership rights. This is yet another reason to have an operating agreement.

LLCs cannot issue stock options, which is potentially a serious problem because options may be an essential lure in attracting and retaining top talent.

Duration

It used to be that LLCs automatically dissolved upon the withdrawal of a member (owing to, for example, death, resignation, or bankruptcy). The current trend in state laws, however, is to permit an LLC to continue in operation even after a member withdraws.

Going Public

Once an LLC goes public, it loses its favorable tax status and is taxed as a corporation, not a partnership.[5] Thus, there is no advantage to using the LLC form of organization for a publicly traded company. And there are some disadvantages: unlike corporations, publicly traded LLCs do not enjoy a well-established set of statutory and case law that is relatively consistent across the many states. For this reason, privately held companies that begin as LLCs usually change to corporations when they go public.

It is worth noting, too, that because of securities laws, it is important for an LLC to have an operating agreement that permits managers the right to convert the LLC into a corporation at the time of a public offering without the consent of the members.[6]

Changing Forms

Some companies that are now corporations might prefer to be LLCs. However, the IRS would consider this change to be a sale of the corporate assets and would levy a tax on the value of these assets. For this reason, few corporations have made the change. However, switching from a partnership to an LLC or from an LLC to a corporation is not considered a sale and does not have the same adverse tax impact.

Piercing the LLC Veil

It has long been the case that, if corporate shareholders do not comply with the technicalities of the law, they may be held personally liable for the debts of the corporation (an issue that will be discussed in more depth in Chapter 20). As the following case illustrates, members of an LLC can also be held liable under the same circumstances.

BLD PRODUCTS, LTD. v. TECHNICAL PLASTICS OF OREGON, LLC

2006 U.S. Dist. LEXIS 89874
United States District Court for the District of Oregon, 2006

Facts: Mark Hardie was the sole member of Technical Plastics of Oregon, LLC (TPO). He operated the business out of an office in his home. Hardie regularly used TPO's accounts to pay such expenses as landscaping and housecleaning. TPO also paid some of Hardie's personal credit card bills, loan payments on his Ford truck, the cost of constructing a deck on his house, his stepson's college bills, and the cost of family vacations to Disneyland, as well as miscellaneous bills from GI Joe's, Wrestler's World, K-Mart, and Mattress World. At the same time,

Hardie deposited cash advances from his personal credit cards into the TPO checking account. Hardie did not take a salary from TPO. When TPO filed for bankruptcy, it owed BLD Products approximately $120,000 for goods that it had purchased.

In some cases, a court will "pierce the veil" of a corporation and hold its shareholders personally liable for the debts of the business. BLD argued that the same doctrine should apply to LLCs and the court should hold Hardie personally liable for TPO's debts.

---

[5]26 U.S.C. §7704.
[6]In this way, under Rule 144 (which is discussed in Chapter 21 on securities regulation), members can include the time during which they owned interests in the LLC when calculating their holding period for stock.

BLD filed for summary judgment.

Issues: *Does the corporate doctrine of piercing the corporate veil apply to LLCs? Should Hardie be personally liable for TPO's debts?*

Excerpts from Judge King's Decision: I conclude that the piercing doctrine may be applied to LLCs under the same circumstances in which it is applied to corporations. We have characterized that formulation [for piercing a corporate veil] as a three-part test:

1. the defendant controlled the debtor corporation;

2. the defendant engaged in improper conduct; and

3. as a result of that improper conduct plaintiff was unable to collect on a debt against the insolvent corporation.

There is no issue that Hardie, as the sole member and manager of TPO, controlled the company. Turning to the second prong of the test, there is substantial evidence of improper conduct, particularly in the nature of commingling of assets and a general disregard of TPO's LLC form and status as a separate legal entity. Hardie frequently and in significant amounts paid his personal expenses from the TPO business account. The amounts are well beyond small dips into petty cash. There is inadequate documentation about how funds flowed between Hardie, as an individual, and TPO. I realize that Hardie elected to be paid in a manner other than by a regular salary, but that does not excuse the lack of documentation. Hardie treated TPO and its assets as his personal funds.

That leaves the third prong of the test, whether Hardie's improper conduct resulted in BLD being unable to collect on its approximately $120,000 debt. I cannot determine as a matter of law that the inability to pay the entire $120,000 debt was due to Hardie's improper conduct over the years. Consequently, I grant partial summary judgment that BLD is entitled to pierce the corporate veil, making Hardie personally liable, but that the amount for which Hardie is personally liable will have to be determined by the jury.

Legal Uncertainty

As we have observed, LLCs are a relatively new form of organization without a consistent and widely developed body of law. As a result, members of an LLC may find themselves in the unhappy position of litigating issues of law which, although well established for corporations, are not yet clear for LLCs. Win or lose, lawsuits are expensive in both time and money.

An important area of legal uncertainty involves managers' duties to the members of the organization. For example, it is not clear in many jurisdictions if managers of an LLC have a legal obligation to act in the best interest of members. Delaware courts have recently ruled that an LLC's managers do have a fiduciary duty to its members unless the operating agreement provides otherwise. (In that state, an operating agreement can limit any duty except the requirement of good faith and fair dealing.) However, this uncertainty means that, before becoming a member of an LLC, it is important to understand both state law and the terms of the operating agreement.

Furthermore, when managers of a corporation violate their duty to the organization by, say, approving a merger without sufficient investigation, shareholders are allowed to bring a so-called **derivative lawsuit** in the name of the corporation against the managers. This right was established by common law. It is unclear, however, if members of an LLC have the same right, especially in a state such as New York where the LLC statute does not explicitly authorize derivative lawsuits. The following case resolves this issue, but only for New York state.

Tzolis v. Wolff

884 N.E.2d 1005; 855 N.Y.S.2d 6; 2008 N.Y. LEXIS 226
Court of Appeals of New York, 2008

Facts: Soterios Tzolis owned 25 percent of Smith Pennington Property Co. LLC, which owned a Manhattan hotel. Herbert Wolff managed the LLC. Tzolis alleged that Wolff first leased and then sold the hotel to family and friends at a price below market value. Tzolis filed a derivative suit against Wolff on the grounds that the man had violated his duties to the LLC.

The trial court ruled that members of an LLC had no right to bring a derivative action because the statute had not explicitly permitted such suits. Tzolis appealed.

Issue: *Do members of an LLC have the right to bring a derivative suit against managers of the company?*

Excerpts from Justice Smith's Decision: The derivative suit has been part of the general corporate law of this state at least since 1832. It was not created by statute, but by case law. [The judge in a 1832 case said:]

"no injury the stockholders may sustain by a fraudulent breach of trust, can, upon the general principles of equity, be suffered to pass without a remedy. I will never determine that a court cannot lay hold of every such breach of trust. I will never determine that frauds of this kind are out of the reach of courts of law; for an intolerable grievance would follow from such a determination."

We now consider whether to recognize derivative actions on behalf of the LLC, as to which no statutory provision for such an action exists. In addressing the question, we continue to heed the realization: When fiduciaries are faithless to their trust, the victims must not be left wholly without a remedy. [T]o determine that frauds of this kind are out of the reach of courts of law would lead to "an intolerable grievance."

To hold that there is no remedy when corporate fiduciaries use corporate assets to enrich themselves was unacceptable in 1832, and it is still unacceptable today. Derivative suits are not the only possible remedy, but they are the one that has been recognized for most of two centuries, and to abolish them in the LLC context would be a radical step.

[C]ourts have repeatedly recognized derivative suits in the absence of express statutory authorization. In light of this, it could hardly be argued that the mere absence of authorizing language in the Limited Liability Company Law bars the courts from entertaining derivative suits by LLC members.

We therefore hold that members of LLCs may sue derivatively.

In its reasoning, this court relied on corporate law precedents. However, in a recent case also involving derivative actions, a Delaware court did not follow that approach. The Delaware LLC statute clearly provides that *members* can bring derivative actions. That bit of clarity is helpful. But what about *creditors* of an LLC? We know that creditors of a *corporation* have that right. Does the same rule apply to LLCs?

In the case in question, the board of JetDirect Aviation LLC approved four major acquisitions, all the while knowing that its financials were inaccurate. The company ultimately went bankrupt and, thus, was unable to repay a $34 million loan to CML. The lender filed a derivative action against JetDirect's careless board members. But, much to everyone's surprise, two Delaware courts ruled that CML could *not* bring a derivative action because the Delaware LLC statute had not explicitly authorized such lawsuits. CML was simply out of luck. The lower court observed, "[T]here is nothing absurd about different legal principles applying to corporations and LLCs."

CML would not necessarily agree. And the lower court itself acknowledged that commentators had all assumed that such suits were permitted. It turned out they were wrong. This result may make lenders less willing to finance LLCs and therefore render LLCs a less-desirable form of organization.[7] In short, many issues of law that are well established for corporations still reside in foggy territory when it comes to LLCs.

Choices: LLC v. Corporation

When starting a business, which form makes the most sense—LLC or corporation? The tax status of an LLC is a major advantage over a corporation. Although an S corporation has the same tax status as an LLC, it also has all the annoying rules about classes of stock and number of shareholders. Once an LLC is established, it does not have as many housekeeping rules as corporations—it does not, for example, have to make annual filings or hold annual meetings. However, the LLC is not right for everyone. If done properly, an LLC is more expensive to set up than a corporation because it needs to have a thoughtfully crafted

---

[7]*CML V, LLC v. Bax*, 2011 Del. LEXIS 480 (S. Ct. Del, 2011).

operating agreement. Also, venture capitalists almost always refuse to invest in LLCs, preferring C corporations instead. There are four reasons for this preference: (1) arcane tax issues, (2) C corporations are easier to merge, sell, or take public, (3) corporations can issue stock options, and (4) the general legal uncertainty involving LLCs.

EXAM Strategy

Question: Hortense and Gus are each starting a business. Hortense's business is an Internet startup. Gus will be opening a yarn store. Hortense needs millions of dollars in venture capital and expects to go public soon. Gus has borrowed $10,000 from his girlfriend, which he hopes to pay back soon. Should either of these businesses organize as an LLC?

Strategy: Sole proprietorships may be best for businesses without substantial capital needs and without significant liability issues. Corporations are best for businesses that will need substantial outside capital and expect to go public shortly.

Result: An LLC is not the best choice for either of these businesses. Venture capitalists will insist that Hortense's business be a corporation, especially if it is going public soon. A yarn store has few liability issues, and Gus does not expect to have any outside investors. Hence, a sole proprietorship would be more appropriate for Gus's business.

SOCIALLY CONSCIOUS ORGANIZATIONS

More than a dozen states now permit the formation of socially conscious business organizations. These hybrids are called **flexible-purpose organizations**, **benefit corporations** (B corporations), **low-profit limited liability companies** (L3Cs), and **community interest companies** (CICs). To form this type of organization, a business must pledge to behave in a socially responsible manner as it pursues profits. Note that these businesses are *not* nonprofits. Instead, they focus on the triple bottom line: "people, planet, and profits." Such businesses consider the interests of their stakeholders (employees, suppliers, customers, and creditors), the community, and the environment, in addition to investors. Company directors are not required to maximize shareholder returns but may instead trade off some profitability in the interests of social responsibility.

To become a socially conscious organization, typically two-thirds of the investors must first give their approval. Then, in the case of Benefit corporations, the company has to obtain certification from an independent third party, such as B Lab. Socially conscious organizations must also prepare regular reports that include an assessment of their societal and environmental impact. At the moment, these organizations do not receive favorable tax treatment, but some advocates are pushing Congress to change the tax code.

Businesses that have taken advantage of these new laws include King Arthur Flour Company, Patagonia, and Seventh Generation. Proponents praise this explicit opportunity to combine profitability and a social conscience. Critics caution, however, that much uncertainty remains. How will a board of directors make decisions? How will it decide, for example, what is more important—being kind to employees or to the environment? The rules are so vague that shareholders will have virtually no right to challenge board decisions because management can always say its goal was to promote the public benefit. Any new form of organization brings with it some legal uncertainty and, as a result, almost inevitable litigation.

GENERAL PARTNERSHIPS

A **partnership** is an unincorporated association of two or more co-owners who carry on a business for profit.[8] Each co-owner is called a *general partner*.

Traditionally, partnerships were regulated by common law, but a lack of consistency among the states became troublesome as interstate commerce grew. To solve this problem, the National Conference of Commissioners on Uniform State Laws proposed the Uniform Partnership Act (UPA) in 1914. Since then, there have been several revisions, the most recent coming in 1997. More than two-thirds of the states have now passed the latest revision, so we base our discussion on that version of the law.

Taxes

As we have seen above, partnerships are not a taxable entity, which means that profits flow through to the owners.

Liability

Each partner is personally liable for the debts of the enterprise, whether or not she caused them. Thus, a partner is liable for any injury that another partner or an employee causes while on partnership business as well as for any contract signed on behalf of the partnership. This form of organization can be particularly risky if the group of owners is large and the partners do not know each other.

Daniel Matter knows firsthand about the risks of a partnership. A former partner in the accounting firm Pannell Kerr Foster, he thought he had heard the last of the firm when he resigned his partnership. He was wrong. *Seven* years later, he and 260 other former partners of the California firm were served with a 78-page lawsuit seeking $24 million in damages. The lawsuit alleged that Pannell Kerr had been negligent in preparing financial reports for a bankrupt Tennessee savings and loan. Although Daniel Matter had never worked for that particular client, he was potentially liable because he had been a partner when the audit was done. At age 53, Matter feared losing everything he owned.

> ### At age 53, Matter feared losing everything he owned.

Management

The management of a partnership can be a significant challenge.

Management Rights   **Unless the partnership agrees otherwise, partners share both profits and losses equally, and each partner has an equal right to manage the business.**[9] In a large partnership, with hundreds of partners, too many cooks can definitely spoil the firm's profitability. That is why large partnerships are almost always run by one or a few partners who are designated as **managing partners** or **members of the executive committee.** Some firms are run almost dictatorially by the partner who brings in the most business (called a "rainmaker"). Nonetheless, even in relatively autocratic firms, the atmosphere tends to be less hierarchical than in a corporation, where employees are accustomed to the concept of having a boss. Whatever the reality, partners by and large like to think of themselves as being the equal of every other partner.

Partnership
An unincorporated association of two or more co-owners who operate a business for profit.

---

[8]Uniform Partnership Act §6(1).
[9]Partnerships have the right to change internal management rules, but they cannot alter the rules governing their relationship with outsiders (such as the rules on liability).

Management Duties   Partners have a *fiduciary duty* to the partnership. This duty means that:

- *Partners are liable to the partnership for gross negligence or intentional misconduct.*

- *Partners cannot compete with the partnership.* Each partner must turn over to the partnership all earnings from any activity that is related to the partnership's business. Thus, law firms would typically expect a partner to turn over any fees he earned as a director of a company, but he could keep the royalties he earned from his novel on scuba diving.

- *A partner may not take an opportunity away from the partnership unless the other partners consent.* If the partnership wants to buy a private plane and a partner hears of one for sale that she wants to buy herself, she must give the partnership an opportunity to buy it before she does.

- *If a partner engages in a conflict of interest, he must turn over to the partnership any profits he earned from that activity.* In the following case, one partner bought partnership property secretly. Is that a conflict of interest?

Marsh v. Gentry

642 S.W.2d 574, 1982 Ky. LEXIS 315
Supreme Court of Kentucky, 1982

Facts: Tom Gentry and John Marsh were partners in a business that bought and sold racehorses. The partnership paid $155,000 for Champagne Woman, who subsequently had a foal named Excitable Lady. The partners decided to sell Champagne Woman at the annual Keeneland auction, the world's premier thoroughbred horse auction. On the day of the auction, Gentry decided to bid on the horse personally, without telling Marsh. Gentry bought Champagne Woman for $135,000. Later, he told Marsh that someone from California had approached him about buying Excitable Lady. Marsh agreed to the sale. Although he repeatedly asked Gentry the name of the purchaser, Gentry refused to tell him. Not until 11 months later, when Excitable Lady won a race at Churchill Downs, did Marsh learn that Gentry had been the purchaser. Marsh became the Excitable Man.

Issue: *Did Gentry violate his fiduciary duty when he bought partnership property without telling his partner?*

Excerpts from Justice O'Hara's Decision: Admittedly, at an auction sale, the specific identity of a purchaser cannot be ascertained before the sale, but [Kentucky partnership law] required a full disclosure by Gentry to Marsh that he would be a prospective purchaser. As to the private sale of Excitable Lady, Marsh consented to a sale from the partnership, at a specified price, to the prospective purchaser in California. Even though Marsh obtained the stipulated purchase price, a partner has an absolute right to know when his partner is the purchaser. Partners scrutinize buyouts by their partners in an entirely different light than an ordinary third-party sale. This distinction is vividly made without contradiction when Marsh later indicated that he would not have consented to either sale had he known that Gentry was the purchaser. Under these facts, it is obvious that Gentry failed to disclose all that he knew concerning the sales, including his desire to purchase partnership property.

[P]artners, in their relations with other partners, [must] maintain a higher degree of good faith due to the partnership agreement. The requirement of full disclosure among partners as to partnership business cannot be escaped. Had Gentry made a full disclosure to his partner of his intentions to purchase the partnership property, Marsh would not later be heard to complain of the transaction.

Finally, Gentry maintains that it is an accepted practice at auction sales of thoroughbreds for one partner to secretly bid on partnership stock to accomplish a buyout. We would emphatically state, however, for the benefit of those engaged in such practices, that where an "accepted business practice" conflicts with existing law, the law, whether statutory or court ordered, is controlling. To hold otherwise would be chaotic.

Transfer of Ownership

Financing a partnership may be difficult because the firm cannot sell shares as a corporation does. The capital needs of the partnership must be provided by contributions from partners or by borrowing. Likewise, a partner only has the right to transfer the *value* of her partnership interest, not the interest itself. She cannot, for example, transfer the right to participate in firm management. Take the case of Evan and his mother. She is a partner in the immensely profitable McBain Consulting firm. She dies, leaving him an orphan with no siblings. He overcomes his grief as best he can and goes to her office on the next Monday to take over her job and her partnership. Imagine his surprise when her partners tell him that, as her sole heir, he can inherit the *value* of her partnership but he has no right to be a partner. He is out on the sidewalk within the hour. The partners have promised him a check in the mail.

Formation

Given the disadvantages, why does anyone do business as a partnership? A partnership has an important advantage over a sole proprietorship—partners. Sole proprietors are on their own; partners have colleagues to help them and, equally important, to supply capital for the business. Sole proprietorships sometimes turn into partnerships for exactly this reason.

In addition, partnerships are easy to form. Although a partnership *should* have a written agreement, it is perfectly legal without one. In fact, nothing is required in the way of forms or filings or agreements. **If two or more people do business together, sharing management, profits and losses, they have a partnership, whether they know it or not, and are subject to all the rules of partnership law.**

For example, Kevin and Brenda formed an electrical contracting business. The business did so well that Kevin's first wife, Cynthia, asked the court to increase his child support payments. Kevin argued that, because he and Brenda were partners, he was entitled to only half of the business's profits. Therefore, his child support should not be increased.

Cynthia claimed that Kevin and Brenda were not partners because Kevin had reported all the income from the business on his personal tax return, while Brenda had reported none. Kevin had even put "sole proprietorship" in bold letters on the top of his return. No written partnership agreement existed. Kevin and Brenda never informed their accountant that they were a partnership. When Kevin answered interrogatories for Cynthia's lawsuit, he stated that he was the sole owner and that Brenda worked for him. Nonetheless, the court held that Brenda and Kevin were partners because Brenda helped manage the business and shared in its profits.[10]

Partnership by Estoppel Brenda and Kevin wanted to be partners so that they could share the *profits* of their business. In *partnership by estoppel*, non-partners are treated as if they were actually partners and are forced to share *liability*. **A partnership by estoppel exists if:**

- Participants tell other people that they are partners (even though they are not), or they allow other people to say, without contradiction, that they are partners;

- A third party relies on this assertion; and

- The third party suffers harm.

For example, an obstetrician by the name of Dr. William Martin was held liable under a theory of partnership by estoppel because (1) he told a patient that he and Dr. John Maceluch were partners (although they were not); (2) in reliance on this statement, a patient made appointments to see Dr. Maceluch; and (3) she was harmed by Dr. Maceluch's

---

[10]*In Re Marriage of Cynthia Hassiepen*, 269 Ill. App. 3d 559, 646 N.E.2d 1348, 1995 Ill. App. LEXIS 101.

malpractice. He refused to come to the hospital when she was in labor and, as a result, her child was born with brain damage. Although Dr. Martin was out of the country at the time, he was as liable as if he had committed the malpractice himself.[11]

Termination

When a partner quits, that event is called a **dissociation**. A dissociation is a fork in the road: the partnership can either buy out the departing partner(s) and continue in business, or wind up the business and terminate the partnership. Most large firms provide in their partnership agreement that, upon dissociation, the business continues.

LIMITED LIABILITY PARTNERSHIPS

A limited liability partnership (LLP) is a type of general partnership that most states now permit. There is a very important distinction, however, between LLPs and general partnerships: **in an LLP, the partners are not liable for the debts of the partnership.**[12] They are, naturally, liable for their own misdeeds, just as if they were a member of an LLC or a shareholder of a corporation.

To form an LLP, the partners must file a statement of qualification with state officials. LLPs must also file annual reports. The other attributes of a partnership remain the same. Thus, an LLP is not a taxable entity, and it has the right to choose its duration (that is, it can, but does not have to, survive the dissociation of a member).

Although an LLP can be much more advantageous for partners than a general partnership, it is absolutely crucial to comply with all the technicalities of the LLP statute. Otherwise, partners lose protection against personal liability. Note the sad result for Michael Gaus and John West, who formed a Texas LLP. Unfortunately, they did not renew the LLP registration each year, as the statute required. Four years after its initial registration, the partnership entered into a lease. When the partners ultimately stopped paying rent and abandoned the premises, they were both were held personally liable for the rent because the LLP registration had expired. As the court pointed out, the statute did not contain a "substantial compliance" section, nor did it contain a grace period for filing a renewal application. In short, close only counts in horseshoes and hand grenades, not in LLPs.

LIMITED PARTNERSHIPS AND LIMITED LIABILITY LIMITED PARTNERSHIPS

Although limited partnerships and limited liability limited partnerships sound confusingly similar to limited liability partnerships and general partnerships, like many siblings, they operate very differently. And truth to tell, limited partnerships and limited liability limited partnerships are relatively rare—they are generally used only for estate planning purposes (usually, to reduce estate taxes) and for highly sophisticated investment vehicles. You should be aware of their existence, but you may not see them very often in your business life. Here are the major features:

Structure

Limited partnerships must have at least one *limited* partner and one *general* partner.

[11]*Haught v. Maceluch*, 681 F.2d 290, 1982 U.S. App. LEXIS 17123 (5th Cir. 1982).
[12]UPA §306(c).

Liability

Limited partners are not *personally* liable, but general partners are. Like corporate share-holders, limited partners risk only their investment in the partnership (which is called their "capital contribution"). In contrast, general partners of a limited partnership are personally liable for the debts of the organization.

However, the revised version of the Uniform Limited Partnership Act permits a limited partnership, in its certificate of formation and partnership agreement, simply to declare itself a *limited liability* limited partnership.[13] **In a limited liability limited partnership, the general partner is not personally liable for the debts of the partnership.** This provision effectively removes the major disadvantage of limited partnerships. Although, at this writing, fewer than half the states have actually passed the revised version of the Uniform Limited Partnership Act, this revision would seem to indicate the trend for the future.

Taxes

Limited partnerships are not taxable entities. Income is taxed only once before landing in a partner's pocket.

Formation

The general partners must file a **certificate of limited partnership** with their Secretary of State. Although most limited partnerships do have a partnership agreement, it is not required.

Management

General partners have the right to manage a limited partnership. Limited partners are essentially passive investors with few management rights beyond the right to be informed about the partnership business. Limited partnership agreements can, however, expand the rights of limited partners.

Transfer of Ownership

Limited partners have the right to transfer the *value* of their partnership interest, but they can sell or give away the interest itself only if the partnership agreement permits.

Duration

Unless the partnership agreement provides otherwise, limited partnerships enjoy perpetual existence—they continue even as partners come and go.

EXAM Strategy

Question: In which one or more of the following forms of organization is it true that none of the partners are liable for the debts of the partnership?

1. General partnership
2. Limited liability partnership
3. Limited partnership
4. Limited liability limited partnership

---

[13]ULPA §102(9).

> **Strategy:** All these partnerships sound similar, but they are in fact very different, so it is important to keep them straight!
>
> **Result:** In a general partnership, all the partners are liable. In a limited liability partnership, none are liable. In a limited partnership, the general partners are liable. In a limited liability limited partnership, none of the partners are liable. The correct answers are 2 and 4.

PROFESSIONAL CORPORATIONS

Traditionally, most professionals (such as lawyers and doctors) were not permitted to incorporate their businesses, so they organized as partnerships. Now professionals are allowed to incorporate, but in a special way. These organizations are called "professional corporations" or "PCs." **PCs provide more liability protection than a general partnership.** If a member of a PC commits malpractice, the corporation's assets are at risk, but not the personal assets of the innocent members. If Drs. Sharp, Payne, and Graves form a *partnership*, all the partners will be personally liable when Dr. Payne accidentally leaves her scalpel inside a patient. If the three doctors have formed a *PC* instead, Dr. Payne's Aspen condo and the assets of the PC will be at risk, but not the personal assets of the two other doctors.

Generally, the shareholders of a PC are not personally liable for the contract debts of the organization, such as leases or bank loans. Thus, if Sharp, Payne, & Graves, P.C. is unable to pay its rent, the landlord cannot recover from the personal assets of any of the doctors. As partners, the doctors would be personally liable.

PCs have some limitations. First, all shareholders of the corporation must be members of the same profession. For Sharp, Payne, & Graves, P.C., that means all shareholders must be licensed physicians. Other valued employees cannot own stock. Second, like other corporations, the required legal technicalities for forming and maintaining a PC are expensive and time-consuming. Third, tax issues can be complicated. A PC is a separate taxable entity, like any other corporation. It must pay tax on its profits, and then its shareholders pay tax on any dividends they receive. *Salaries,* however, are deductible from firm profits. Thus, the PC can avoid paying taxes on its profits by paying out all the profits as salary. But any profits remaining in firm coffers *at the end of the year* are taxable. To avoid tax, PCs must be careful to calculate their profits accurately and pay them out before year's end. This chore can be time-consuming, and any error may cause unnecessary tax liability.

JOINT VENTURES

Joint venture
A partnership for a limited purpose.

Imax Corp. decided that it would like to partner with cinema operators—it would supply its big screens to the cinemas in return for a share of the box office revenue. The arrangement that Imax is describing is not like the other partnerships we have discussed in this chapter—it is a joint venture. A **joint venture** is a partnership for a limited purpose. Imax and the cinema operators would not merge; they would simply work together. Each organization retains its own identity. Imax would be liable to an electrician whom the cinema operator had hired to install an Imax screen, but not to the cinema's popcorn supplier.

FRANCHISES

This chapter has presented an overview of the various forms of organization. Franchises are not, strictly speaking, a separate form of organization. They are included here because they represent an important option for entrepreneurs. The United States has nearly half a million franchised businesses, which employ almost 8 million people. Total sales are $1.3 trillion a year. Well-known franchises include Hampton Hotels, McDonald's, and Supercuts. Most franchisors and franchisees are corporations, although they could legally choose to be any of the forms discussed in this chapter.

Buying a franchise is a compromise between starting one's own business as an entrepreneur and working for someone else as an employee. Franchisees are free to choose which franchise to buy, where to locate it, and how to staff it. But they are not completely on their own. They are buying an established business with the kinks worked out. In case the owner has never boiled water before, the McDonald's operations manual explains everything from how to set the temperature controls on the stove, to the number of seconds that fries must cook, to the length of time they can be held in the rack before being discarded. And a well-known name like McDonald's or Subway ought, by itself, to bring customers through the door.

There is, however, a fine line between being helpful and being oppressive. Franchisees sometimes complain that franchisor control is too tight—tips on cooking fries might be appreciated, but rules on how often to sweep the floor are not. Sometimes franchisors, in their zeal to maintain standards, prohibit innovation that appeals to regional tastes. Just because spicy biscuits are not popular in New England does not mean they should be banned in the South.

Franchises can be very costly to acquire, anywhere from several thousand dollars to many millions. That fee is usually payable up front, whether or not a sandwich or burger is ever sold. On top of the up-front fee, franchisees also typically pay an annual fee that is a percentage of *gross sales revenues*, not *profit*. Sometimes the fee seems to eat up all the profits. Franchisees also complain when they are forced to buy supplies from headquarters. In theory, the franchisors can purchase hamburger meat and paper plates more cheaply in bulk and also maintain quality controls. On the other hand, the franchisees are a captive audience, and they sometimes allege that headquarters has little incentive to keep prices low. Indeed, some franchisors make most of their profit from the products they sell to their store owners. Often, the franchise agreement permits the company to change the terms of the agreement by raising fees or expenses. Franchisees also grumble when they are forced to contribute to expensive "co-op advertising" that benefits all the outlets in the region. The sandwich franchise Quiznos recently spent $100 million to settle litigation with potential franchisees, who claimed that the company took their fees without finding a store location for them, and some existing store owners, who complained that the company forced them to buy *everything* (including soap in the bathrooms and the piped-in music) from the company at inflated prices.

All franchisors must comply with the Federal Trade Commission's (FTC) Franchise Rule. In addition, some states also impose their own franchise requirements. Under FTC rules, a franchisor must deliver to a potential purchaser a so-called Franchise Disclosure Document (FDD) at least 14 calendar days before any contract is signed or money is paid. The FDD must provide information on:

- The history of the franchisor and its key executives
- Litigation with franchisees
- Bankruptcy filings by the company and its officers and directors
- Costs to buy and operate a franchise

- Restrictions, if any, on suppliers, products, and customers

- Territory—any limitations (in either the real or virtual worlds) on where the franchisee can sell or any restrictions on other franchisees selling in the same territory

- Business continuity—under what circumstances can the franchisor fire the franchisee, and the franchisee's rights to renew or sell the franchise

- Franchisor's training program

- Required advertising expenses

- A list of current franchisees and those that have left in the prior three years (a lot of either may be a bad sign)

- A report on prior owners of stores that the franchisor has reaquired

- Earnings information is not required; but if disclosed, the franchisor must reveal the basis for this information

- Audited financials for the franchisor

- A sample set of the contracts that a franchisee is expected to sign

The purpose of the FDD is to ensure that the franchisor discloses all relevant facts. It is not a guarantee of quality because the FTC does not investigate to make sure that the information is accurate. After the fact, if the FTC discovers the franchisor has violated the rules, it may sue on the franchisee's behalf. (The franchisee does not have the right to bring suit personally against someone who violates FTC franchise rules, but it may be able to sue under state law.)

Suppose you obtain an FDD for "Shrinking Cats," a franchise that offers psychiatric services for neurotic felines. The company has lost money on all the outlets it operates itself; it has sold only three franchises, two of which have gone out of business; and all the required contracts are ridiculously favorable to the franchisor. Nevertheless, the FTC will still permit sales as long as the franchisor discloses all the information required in the FDD.

As the following case illustrates, the franchisor has much of the power in a franchise relationship.

NATIONAL FRANCHISEE ASSOCIATION v. BURGER KING CORPORATION

2010 U.S. Dist. LEXIS 123065
United States District Court for the Southern District of Florida, 2010

Facts: The Burger King Corporation (BKC) would not allow franchisees to have it their way. Instead, BKC forced them to sell the double-cheeseburger (DCB) and, later, the Buck Double (the DCB minus one slice of cheese) for no more than $1.00. Franchisees alleged that, because this price was below their cost, they were losing money on every double cheeseburger they sold. The National Franchisee Association (NFA), to which 75 percent of BKC's individual franchisees belonged, filed suit alleging

that (1) BKC did not have the right to set maximum prices; and (2) that even if BKC had such a right, it had violated its obligation under the franchise agreement to act in good faith.

The court dismissed the first claim because the franchise agreement unambiguously permitted BKC to set whatever prices it wanted. But the court allowed the NFA to proceed with the second claim. BKC filed a motion to dismiss.

Issue: *Was BKC acting in good faith when it forced franchisees to sell items below cost?*

Excerpts from Judge Moore's Decision: The motive of BKC in exercising its discretion to set prices under the contract is key. [B]ad faith involves a subterfuge or evasion of contractual duties. [T]here are at least two ways a plaintiff can go about raising a claim of bad faith. Plaintiffs can allege facts identifying defendant's improper ulterior motive(s). For example, if a franchisee had evidence that a franchisor had a secret agenda to take over the franchise and operate it as a company-owned business, and was deliberately setting prices to weaken the targeted franchisee, such a plaintiff could raise a claim of bad faith by alleging the existence of that plan.

It is more likely, however, that plaintiffs will lack direct evidence of dishonesty. In these cases, plaintiffs must allege some facts tending to show that no reasonable person could have thought that the steps taken by the defendant were a reasonable means of carrying out the contract's defined purposes. If no reasonable person would have exercised discretion as defendant had, the natural inference is that defendant must have had some hidden improper motive.

[T]he magnitude of the injury claimed by plaintiff is of central importance. [A]n inference of bad faith may arise when the defendant exercises discretion in such a manner as to effectively destroy whatever benefits the plaintiff could have reasonably expected under the contract. The logic is that the measure with such severe results could not have been within the contemplation of the parties.

[N]one of the facts alleged by plaintiffs are sufficient to support a claim of bad faith. Plaintiffs rely principally on their allegation that franchisees could not produce and sell DCB or Buck Doubles at a cost less than $1.00, and therefore that franchisees suffer a loss on each of these items sold. There are a variety of legitimate reasons why a firm selling multiple products may choose to set the price of a single product below cost. Among other things, such a strategy might help build goodwill and customer loyalty, hold or shift customer traffic away from competitors, or serve as loss leaders to generate increased sales on other higher margin products.

The issue is not whether such a strategy was wise or ultimately successful or mistaken. In the absence of some other evidence of improper motive, the question is whether it was so irrational and capricious that no reasonable person would have made such a decision. There is nothing about the pricing decision that suggests BKC was doing anything other than seeking to promote the performance of its franchisees. Nothing about this action suggests bad faith.

[T]o the extent plaintiffs seek to raise a claim of bad faith by pointing to the injuries allegedly caused them by BKC's decision, plaintiffs must allege that the damage to their overall business was so severe as to deprive them of their reasonable expectations under the contract. Plaintiffs come nowhere close to alleging such an impact. Significantly, nowhere do plaintiffs claim that their overall business has been appreciably impaired. Nor do they allege that their overall businesses are no longer profitable or that their competitive positions or economic viability going forward are threatened.

For the foregoing reasons, it is ORDERED AND ADJUDGED that Defendant's Motion to Dismiss is GRANTED.

Chapter Conclusion

The process of starting a business is immensely time-consuming. Eighteen-hour days are the norm. Not surprisingly, entrepreneurs are sometimes reluctant to spend their valuable time on legal issues that, after all, do not contribute directly to the bottom line. No customer buys more fried chicken because the franchise is a limited liability company instead of a corporation. Wise entrepreneurs know, however, that careful attention to legal issues is an essential component of success. The form of organization affects everything from taxes to liability to management control. The idea for the business may come first, but legal considerations occupy a close second place.

EXAM REVIEW

	Separate Taxable Entity	Personal Liability for Owners	Ease of Formation	Transferable Interests (Easily Bought and Sold)	Perpetual Existence	Other Features
Sole Proprietorship	No	Yes	Very easy	No, can only sell entire business	No	
Corporation	Yes	No	Difficult	Yes	Yes	
Close Corporation	Yes, for C corporation No, for S corporation	No	Difficult	Transfer restrictions	Yes	Protection of minority shareholders. No board of directors required
S Corporation	No	No	Difficult	Transfer restrictions	Yes	Only 100 shareholders. Only one class of stock. Shareholders must be individuals, estates, trusts, charities, or pension funds and be citizens or residents of the United States. All shareholders must agree to S status
Limited Liability Company	No	No	Difficult	Yes, if the operating agreement permits	Varies by state, but generally, yes	No limit on the number of shareholders, the number of classes of stock, or the type of shareholder
General Partnership	No	Yes	Easy	No	Depends on the partnership agreement	Management can be difficult
Limited Liability Partnership	No	No	Difficult	No	Depends on the partnership agreement	
Limited Partnership	No	Yes, for general partner No, for limited partners	Difficult	Yes (for limited partners), if partnership agreement permits	Yes	
Limited Liability Limited Partnership	No	No	Difficult	Yes (for limited partners), if partnership agreement permits	Yes	
Professional Corporation	Yes	No	Difficult	Shareholders must all be members of same profession	Yes, as long as it has shareholders	Complex tax issues
Joint Venture	No	Yes	Easy	No	No	Partnership for a limited purpose
Franchise	All these issues depend on the form of organization chosen by participants.					Established business. Name recognition. Management assistance. Loss of control. Fees may be high

MULTIPLE-CHOICE QUESTIONS

1. A sole proprietorship:
   (a) must file a tax return.
   (b) requires no formal steps for its creation.
   (c) must register with the Secretary of State.
   (d) may sell stock.
   (e) provides limited liability to the owner.

EXAM Strategy

2. **CPA QUESTION** Assuming all other requirements are met, a corporation may elect to be treated as an S corporation under the Internal Revenue Code if it has:

   a. both common and preferred stockholders.

   b. a partnership as a stockholder.

   c. 100 or fewer stockholders.

   d. the consent of a majority of the stockholders.

   Strategy: Review the list of requirements for an S corporation. (See the "Result" at the end of this section.)

3. A limited liability company:
   (a) is regulated by a well-established body of law.
   (b) pays taxes on its income.
   (c) may issue stock options.
   (d) must register with state authorities.
   (e) protects the owners from personal liability for their own misdeeds.

4. **CPA QUESTION** A joint venture is a(n):
   (a) association limited to no more than two persons in business for profit.
   (b) enterprise of numerous co-owners in a nonprofit undertaking.
   (c) corporate enterprise for a single undertaking of limited duration.
   (d) association of persons engaged as co-owners in a single undertaking for profit.

5. A limited liability partnership:
   (a) has ownership interests that cannot be transferred.
   (b) protects the partners from liability for the debts of the partnership.
   (c) must pay taxes on its income.
   (d) requires no formal steps for its creation.
   (e) permits a limited number of partners.

6. **CPA QUESTION** Cobb, Inc., a partner in TLC Partnership, assigns its partnership interest to Bean, who is not made a partner. After the assignment, Bean asserts the right to (1) participate in the management of TLC and (2) take Cobb's share of TLC's partnership profits. Bean is correct as to which of these rights?

(a) 1 only

(b) 2 only

(c) 1 and 2

(d) Neither 1 nor 2

> **2. Result:** An S corporation can have only one class of stock. A partnership cannot be a stockholder, and all the shareholders must consent to S corporation status. C is the correct answer.

ESSAY QUESTIONS

EXAM Strategy

1. Question: Alan Dershowitz, a law professor famous for his wealthy clients (O. J. Simpson, among others), joined with other lawyers to open a kosher delicatessen, Maven's Court. Dershowitz met with greater success at the bar than in the kitchen—the deli failed after barely a year in business. One supplier sued for overdue bills. What form of organization would have been the best choice for Maven's Court?

Strategy: A sole proprietorship would not have worked because there was more than one owner. A partnership would have been a disaster because of unlimited liability. They could have met all the requirements of an S corporation or an LLC. (See the "Result" at the end of this section.)

EXAM Strategy

2. Question: Mrs. Meadows opened a biscuit shop called The Biscuit Bakery. The business was not incorporated. Whenever she ordered supplies, she was careful to sign the contract in the name of the business, not personally: The Biscuit Bakery by Daisy Meadows. Unfortunately, she had no money to pay her flour bill. When the vendor threatened to sue her, Mrs. Meadows told him that he could only sue the business because all the contracts were in the business's name. Will Mrs. Meadows lose her dough?

Strategy: The first step is to figure out what type of organization her business is. Then recall what liability protection that organization offers. (See the "Result" at the end of this section.)

3. **YOU BE THE JUDGE WRITING PROBLEM** Cellwave was a limited partnership that applied to the Federal Communications Commission (FCC) for a license to operate cellular telephone systems. After the FCC awarded the license, it discovered that, although all the limited partners had signed the limited partnership agreement, Cellwave had never filed its limited partnership certificate with the Secretary of State in Delaware. The FCC dismissed Cellwave's application on the grounds that the partnership did not exist when the application was filed. Did the FCC have the right to dismiss Cellwave's application? **Argument for Cellwave:** The limited partnership was effectively in existence as soon as the limited partners signed the agreement. The Secretary of State could not refuse to accept the certificate for filing; that was a mere formality. **Argument for the FCC:** When Cellwave applied for a license, it did not exist legally. Formalities matter.

4. Kristine bought a Rocky Mountain Chocolate Factory franchise. Her franchise agreement required her to purchase a cash register that cost $3,000, with an annual maintenance fee of $773. The agreement also provided that Rocky Mountain could change to a more expensive system. Within a few months after signing the agreement, Kristine learned that she would have to buy a new cash register that cost $20,000, with annual maintenance fees of $2,000. Does Kristine have to buy this new cash register? Did Rocky Mountain act in bad faith?

5. What is the difference between close corporations and S corporations?

6. Pedro and Juan have a business selling ties with fraternity insignia. Pedro finds out that an online shirt business is for sale. It sounds like a great idea—customers send in their measurements and get back a custom-made shirt at a price no higher than off-the-rack shirts at the local department store. Does Pedro have to let Juan in on the great opportunity?

---

1. Result: Maven's Court would have chosen an LLC or an S corporation.

2. Result: The Biscuit Bakery was a sole proprietorship. No matter how Mrs. Meadows signed the contracts, she is still personally liable for the debts of the business.

DISCUSSION QUESTIONS

1. **ETHICS** Lee McNeely told Hardee's officials that he was interested in purchasing multiple restaurants in Arkansas. A Hardee's officer assured him that any of the company-owned stores in Arkansas would be available for purchase. However, the company urged him to open a new store in Maumelle and sent him a letter estimating first-year sales at around $800,000. McNeely built the Maumelle restaurant, but gross sales the first year were only $508,000. When McNeely asked to buy an existing restaurant, a Hardee's officer refused, informing him that Hardee's rarely sold company-owned restaurants. The disclosure document contained no misstatements, but McNeely brought suit alleging fraud in the sale of the Maumelle franchise. Does McNeely have a valid claim against Hardee's? Apart from the legal issues, did Hardee's officers behave ethically? What Life Principles were they applying?

2. Leonard, an attorney, was negligent in his representation of Anthony. In settlement of Anthony's claim against him, Leonard signed a promissory note for $10,400 on behalf of his law firm, an LLC. When the law firm did not pay, Anthony filed suit against Leonard personally for payment of the note. Is a member personally liable for the debt of an LLC that was caused by his own negligence?

3. Think of a business concept that would be appropriate for each of the following: a sole proprietorship, a corporation, and a limited liability company.

4. As you will see in Chapter 20, Facebook began life as a corporation, not an LLC. Why did the founder, Mark Zuckerberg, make that decision?

5. Corporations developed to encourage investors to contribute the capital needed to create large-scale manufacturing enterprises. But LLCs are often start-ups or other small businesses. Why do their members deserve limited liability? And is it fair that LLCs do not have to pay income taxes?

CHAPTER 20

© Werner H. Kunz/Flickr/Getty Images

CORPORATIONS

On July 26, 2004, Mark Zuckerberg signed a Certificate of Incorporation for his company, which he called TheFacebook, Inc. At 11:34 a.m. on July 29, 2004, that Certificate was filed with the Secretary of State for Delaware, and TheFacebook began its life as a corporation. Zuckerberg had started this social networking Internet site the previous February in his dorm room at Harvard. By December of 2004, TheFacebook had almost 1 million users. Less than two years later, the company was estimated to be worth between $750 million and $2 billion. Since then, TheFacebook has been valued at more than $100 billion. As Zuckerberg built his company, what did he need to know about the law?

Most of the country's largest businesses, and many of its small ones, are corporations. In this chapter, you will learn how to form a corporation. You will also learn about the rights and responsibilities of corporate managers and shareholders.

Zuckerberg started TheFacebook in his dorm room at Harvard. Within 10 months, it had almost 1 million users.

PROMOTER'S LIABILITY

Someone who organizes a corporation is called a **promoter.** It is his idea; he raises the capital, hires the lawyers, calls the shots. Mark Zuckerberg was TheFacebook's promoter.

Adopt

Agree to be bound by the terms of a contract.

Novation

A new contract with different parties.

This role can carry some risk. **A promoter is personally liable on any contract he signs before the corporation is formed.** After formation, the corporation can **adopt** the contract, in which case, both it and the promoter are liable. The promoter can get off the hook personally only if the other party agrees to a **novation**—that is, a new contract with the corporation alone.

EXAM Strategy

Question: Dr. Warfield hired Wolfe, a young carpenter, to build his house. A week or so after they signed the contract, Wolfe filed Articles of Incorporation for Wolfe Construction, Inc. Warfield wrote checks to the corporation, which it cashed. Unfortunately, the work on the house was shoddy. The architect said he did not know whether to try to salvage the house or just blow it up. Warfield sued Wolfe and Wolfe Construction, Inc. for damages. Wolfe argued that if he was liable as a promoter, then the corporation must be absolved and that, conversely, if the corporation was held liable, he, as an individual, must not be. Who is liable to Warfield?

Strategy: Wolfe's argument is wrong—Warfield does not have to choose between suing him individually or suing the corporation. He can sue both.

Result: Wolfe is personally liable on any contract he signed before the corporation is filed, no matter whose name is on the contract. The corporation is liable only if it adopts the contract. Did it do so here? The fact that the corporation cashed checks that were made out to it means that the corporation is also liable. So Warfield can sue both Wolfe and the corporation.

INCORPORATION PROCESS

There is no federal corporation code, which means that a company can incorporate only under state, not federal, law. No matter where a company actually does business, it may incorporate in any state. This decision is important because the organization must live by the laws of whichever state it chooses for incorporation. To encourage similarity among state corporation statutes, the American Bar Association drafted the Model Business Corporation Act (the Model Act) as a guide. Many states do use the Model Act as a guide, although Delaware does not. Therefore, in this chapter we will give examples from both the Model Act and Delaware. Why Delaware? Despite its small size, it has a disproportionate influence on corporate law. More than half of all public companies have incorporated there, including 60 percent of Fortune 500 companies.

Domestic corporation

A corporation is a domestic corporation in the state in which it was formed.

Foreign corporation

A corporation formed in another state.

Where to Incorporate?

A company is called a **domestic corporation** in the state where it incorporates and a **foreign corporation** everywhere else. Companies generally incorporate either in the state where they do most of their business or in Delaware. They typically must pay filing fees and franchise taxes in their state of incorporation, plus in any state in which they do business. To avoid this double set of fees, a business that will be operating primarily in one state would probably select that state for incorporation rather than Delaware. But if a company is going to do business in several states, it might consider choosing Delaware, which offers several advantages:

- **Laws that Favor Management.** For example, if the shareholders want to take a vote in writing instead of holding a meeting, many other states require the vote to be unanimous; Delaware requires only a majority to agree. The Delaware legislature also tries to keep up-to-date by changing its code to reflect new developments in corporate law.

- **An Efficient Court System.** Delaware has a special court (called "Chancery Court") that hears nothing but business cases and has judges who are experts in corporate law.

- **An Established Body of Precedent.** Because so many businesses incorporate in the state, its courts hear a vast number of corporate cases, creating a large body of precedent. Thus, lawyers feel they can more easily predict the outcome of a case in Delaware than in a state where few corporate disputes are tried.

The Charter

Once a company has decided *where* to incorporate, the next step is to prepare and file the charter. The mechanics are easy: simply download the form and mail or fax it to the Secretary of State. (Some jurisdictions also require that it be filed in a county office.) But do not let this easy process fool you; the incorporation document needs to be completed with some care. The corporate charter defines the corporation, including everything from the company's name to the number of shares it will issue.

States use different terms to refer to a charter; some call it the "articles of incorporation," others use "articles of organization," and still others say "certificate" instead of "articles." All these terms mean the same thing. Similarly, some states use the term "shareholders," and others use "stockholders"; they are both the same.

Name

The Model Act imposes two requirements in selecting a name. First, all corporations must use one of the following words in their name: "corporation," "incorporated," "company," or "limited." Delaware also accepts some additional terms, such as "association" or "institute." Second, under both the Model Act and Delaware law, a new corporate name must be different from that of any corporation, limited liability company, or limited partnership that already exists in that state. If your name is Freddy DuPont, you cannot name your corporation "Freddy DuPont, Inc.," because Delaware already has a company named E. I. DuPont de Nemours & Company. It does not matter that Freddy DuPont is your real name or that the existing company is a large chemical business, whereas you want to open a game arcade. The names are too similar. Zuckerberg chose "TheFacebook" because that was what Harvard students called their freshman directory.

Address and Registered Agent

A company must have an official address in the state in which it is incorporated so that the Secretary of State knows where to contact it and so that anyone who wants to sue the corporation can serve the complaint in-state. Because most companies incorporated in Delaware do not actually have an office there, they hire a registered agent to serve as their official presence in the state.

Incorporator

The incorporator signs the charter and delivers it to the Secretary of State. Incorporators are not required to buy stock, nor do they necessarily have any future relationship with the company. Oftentimes, the lawyer who forms the corporation serves as its incorporator. If no lawyer is involved, typically the promoter is also the incorporator. That is what happened with TheFacebook—Mark Zuckerberg served as incorporator.

Purpose

The corporation is required to give its purpose for existence. Most companies use a very broad purpose clause such as TheFacebook's:

> The purpose of the Corporation is to engage in any lawful act or activity for which corporations may be organized under the General Corporation Law of Delaware.

Stock

The charter must provide three items of information about the company's stock.

Par Value   The concept of par value was designed to protect investors. Originally, par value was supposed to be close to market price. A company could not *issue* stock at a price less than par, which meant that it could not sell to insiders at a sweetheart price well below market value. (Once the stock was issued, it could be traded at any price.) In modern times, par value does not relate to market value; it is usually some nominal figure such as 1¢ or $1 per share. Companies may also issue stock with no par value. TheFacebook stock has a par value of $0.0001 per share.

Number of Shares   Before stock can be sold, it must first be authorized in the charter. The corporation can authorize as many shares as the incorporators choose, but the more shares, the higher the filing fee. After incorporation, a company can add authorized shares by simply amending its charter and paying the additional fee. TheFacebook charter authorizes the creation of 10,000,000 shares.

Stock that has been authorized but not yet sold is called **authorized and unissued**. Stock that has been sold is termed **authorized and issued** or **outstanding**. Stock that the company has sold but later bought back is **treasury stock**.

Authorized and unissued
Stock that has been authorized, but not yet sold.

Authorized and issued
Stock that has been authorized and sold; another word for it is *outstanding*.

Treasury stock
Stock that a company has sold, but later bought back.

Classes and Series   Different shareholders often make different contributions to a company. Some may be involved in management, whereas others may simply contribute financially. Early investors may feel that they are entitled to more control than those who come along later (and who perhaps take less risk). Corporate structure can be infinitely flexible in defining the rights of these various shareholders. Stock can be divided into categories called **classes,** and these classes can be further divided into subcategories called **series.** All stock in a series has the same rights, and all series in a class are fundamentally the same, except for minor distinctions. For example, in a class of preferred stock, all shareholders may be entitled to a dividend, but the amount of the dividend may vary by series. Different classes of stock, however, may have very different rights—a class of preferred stock is different from a class of common stock. Exhibit 20.1 illustrates the concept of class and series.

Defining the rights of a class or series of stock is like baking a cake—the stock can contain virtually any combination of the following ingredients (although the result may not be to everyone's taste):

- **Dividend Rights.** The charter establishes whether the shareholder is entitled to dividends and, if so, in what amount.

- **Voting Rights.** Shareholders are usually entitled to elect directors and vote on charter amendments, among other issues, but these rights can vary among different series and classes of stock. When Ford Motor Co. went public in 1956, it issued Class B

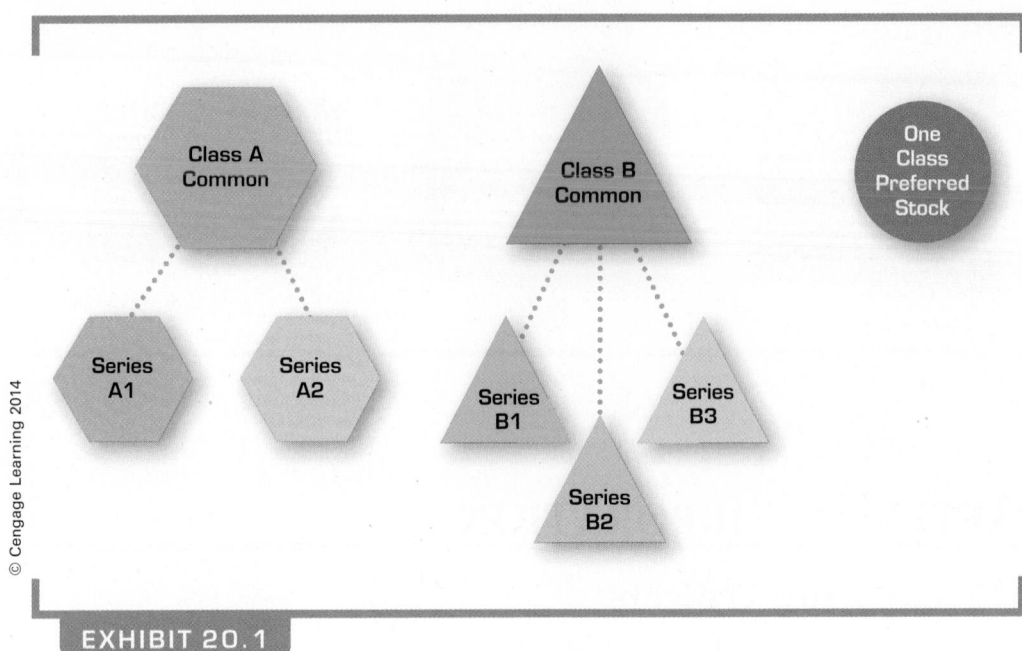

EXHIBIT 20.1

common stock to members of the Ford family. This class of stock holds about 40 percent of the voting power and, thereby, effectively controls the company. Not surprisingly, the chairman of the company has often been named "Ford." TheFacebook amended its charter to create two classes of stock with different voting rights, presumably so that Zuckerberg could maintain control when the company went public.

- **Liquidation Rights.** The charter specifies the order in which classes of stockholders will be paid upon dissolution of the company.

These are the ingredients for any class or series of stock. Some stock comes prepackaged like a cake mix. "Preferred" and "common" stock are two classic types. The Model Act does not use these terms, but many states still do.

Owners of *preferred stock* have preference on dividends and also, typically, in liquidation. If a class of preferred stock is entitled to dividends, then it must receive its dividends before common stockholders are paid theirs. If holders of **cumulative preferred stock** miss their dividend one year, common shareholders cannot receive a dividend until the cumulative preferred shareholders have been paid all that they are owed, no matter how long that takes. Alternatively, holders of ***non*-cumulative preferred stock** lose an annual dividend for good if the company cannot afford it in the year it is due. When a company dissolves, preferred stockholders typically have the right to receive their share of corporate assets before common shareholders.

***Common* stock is last in line for any corporate payouts, including dividends and liquidation payments.** If the company is liquidated, creditors of the company and preferred shareholders are paid before common shareholders. Exhibit 20.2 illustrates the order of payment for dividends.

Venture capitalists (professional investors who are in the business of financing companies) often choose a type of stock called **participating preferred stock**, which permits them to have their cake and eat it too. Upon liquidation of the company, these shareholders are paid first, receiving whatever they paid for the stock plus accrued dividends. Then they are treated as if they had converted their preferred shares into common stock, so they also share the rest of the proceeds with common shareholders.

Preferred stock

The owners of preferred stock have preference on dividends and also, typically, in liquidation.

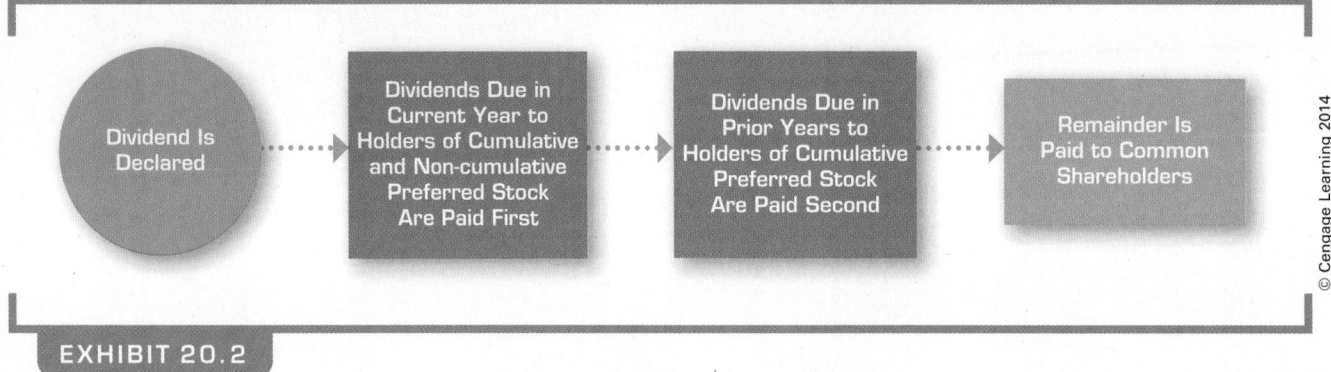

EXHIBIT 20.2

AFTER INCORPORATION

Directors and Officers

Once the corporation is organized, the incorporators elect the first set of directors. There-after, shareholders elect directors. Under the Model Act, a corporation is required to have at least one director, unless (1) all the shareholders sign an agreement that eliminates the board, or (2) the corporation has 50 or fewer shareholders. To elect directors, the share-holders may hold a meeting, or, in the more typical case for a small company, they elect directors by **written consent.** A typical written consent looks like this:

Classic American Novels, Inc.
Written Consent

The undersigned shareholders of Classic American Novels, Inc., a corporation organized and existing under the General Corporation Law of the State of Wherever, hereby agree that the following action shall be taken with full force and effect as if voted at a validly called and held meeting of the shareholders of the corporation:

 Agreed: That the following people are elected to serve as directors for one year, or until
    their successors have been duly elected and qualified:

  Herman Melville
  Louisa May Alcott
  Mark Twain

Dated: _____ Signed: _____

               Willa Cather

Dated: _____ Signed: _____

               Nathaniel Hawthorne

Dated: _____ Signed: _____

               Harriet Beecher Stowe

Once the incorporators or shareholders have chosen the directors, the directors must elect the officers of the corporation. They can use a consent form if they wish. The Model Act is flexible. It simply requires a corporation to have whatever officers are described in the

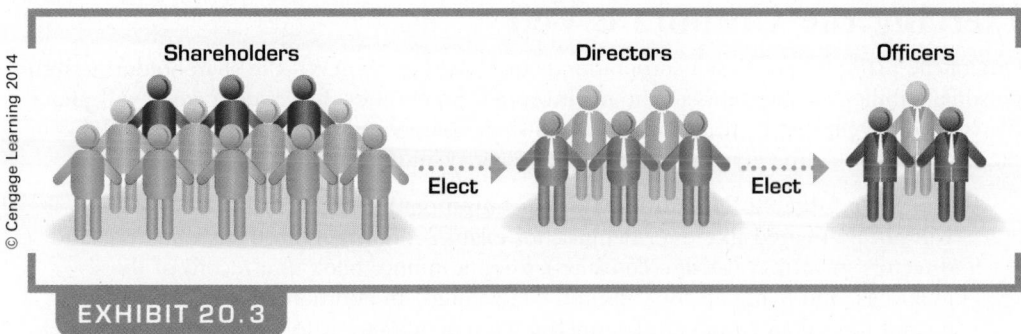

Shareholders **Directors** **Officers**

Elect → Elect →

EXHIBIT 20.3

bylaws. The same person can hold more than one office. Exhibit 20.3 illustrates the election process in corporations.

The written consents and any records of actual meetings are kept in a **minute book**, which is the official record of the corporation. Entrepreneurs sometimes feel they are too busy to bother with all these details, but if a corporation is ever sold, the lawyers for the buyers will *insist* on a well-organized and complete minute book. In one case, a company that was seeking a $100,000 bank loan could not find all its minutes. The company had to merge itself into a newly created corporation so it could start fresh with a new set of corporate records. The company spent $10,000 on this task, a large chunk out of the $100,000 loan.

Minute book
The official record of a corporation.

Bylaws

The **bylaws** list all the "housekeeping" details for the corporation. For example, bylaws set the date of the annual shareholders' meeting, define what a **quorum** is (i.e., what percentage of stock must be represented for a meeting to count), indicate how many directors there will be, give titles to officers, and establish the fiscal (i.e., tax) year of the corporation.

Bylaws
A document that specifies the organizational rules of a corporation or other organization, such as the date of the annual meeting and the required number of directors.

Issuing Debt

Most startup companies begin with some combination of equity and debt. Equity (i.e., stock) is described in the charter; debt is not. Authorizing debt is often one of the first steps a new company takes. There are several types of debt:

- **Bonds** are long-term debt secured by company assets. If the company is unable to pay the debt, creditors have a right to specific assets, such as accounts receivable or inventory.

- **Debentures** are long-term *unsecured* debt. If the company cannot meet its obligations, the debenture holders are paid after bondholders but before stockholders.

- **Notes** are short-term debt, typically payable within five years. They may be either secured or unsecured.

Quorum
The percentage of stock that must be represented for a meeting to count.

Bonds
Long-term secured debt.

Debentures
Long-term unsecured debt.

Notes
When issued by a company, short-term debt, typically payable within five years.

DEATH OF THE CORPORATION

Sometimes, business ideas are not successful and the corporation fails. This death can be voluntary (the shareholders elect to terminate the corporation) or forced (by court order). Sometimes, a court takes a step that is much more damaging to shareholders than simply dissolving the corporation—it removes the shareholders' limited liability.

Piercing the Corporate Veil

One of the major purposes of a corporation is to protect its owners—the shareholders—from personal liability for the debts of the organization. Sometimes, however, a court will **pierce the corporate veil**; that is, the court will hold shareholders personally liable for the debts of the corporation. Courts generally pierce a corporate veil in four circumstances:

- **Failure to Observe Formalities.** If an organization does not act like a corporation, it will not be treated like one. It must, for example, hold required shareholders' and directors' meetings (or sign consents), keep a minute book as a record of these meetings, and make all the required state filings. In addition, officers must be careful to sign all corporate documents with a corporate title, not as an individual. An officer should sign like this:

Classic American Novels, Inc.

By: *Stephen Crane*

Stephen Crane, President

- **Commingling of Assets.** Nothing makes a court more willing to pierce a corporate veil than evidence that shareholders have mixed their assets with those of the corporation. Sometimes, for example, shareholders may use corporate assets to pay their personal debts. If shareholders commingle assets, it is genuinely difficult for creditors to determine which assets belong to whom. This confusion is generally resolved in favor of the creditors—all assets are deemed to belong to the corporation.

- **Inadequate Capitalization.** If the founders of a corporation do not raise enough capital (either through debt or equity) to give the business a fighting chance of paying its debts, courts may require shareholders to pay corporate obligations. Therefore, if the corporation does not have sufficient capital, it needs to buy insurance, particularly to protect against tort liability. Judges are likelier to hold shareholders liable if the alternative is to send an injured tort victim away empty-handed. For example, Oriental Fireworks Co. had hundreds of thousands of dollars in annual sales, but only $13,000 in assets. The company did not bother to obtain any liability insurance, keep a minute book, or defend lawsuits. There was no need because the company had no money. But then a court pierced the corporate veil and found the owner of the company personally liable.[1]

- **Fraud.** If fraud is committed in the name of a corporation, victims can make a claim against the personal assets of the shareholders who profited from the fraud.

The following case is a good example of when a court should pierce the corporate veil.

BROOKS v. BECKER

2005 Va. Cir. LEXIS 13
Circuit Court of Fairfax County, Virginia, 2005

Facts: Ronald Becker was the sole shareholder, officer, and director of Becker Interiors. Becker and his partner, Robert LaPointe, used approximately $300,000 of Becker Interiors' funds to renovate their residence, pay their personal credit card bills, and invest in another company of which Becker was president. Becker sold a corporate car for $73,700 and deposited those funds into his personal account, along with the corporation's income tax refund check of $12,850.

Becker Interiors supervised the major renovation of a house in McLean, Virginia. The company hired Stephen

---

[1]*Rice v. Oriental Fireworks Co.*, 75 Or. App. 627, 707 P.2d 1250, 1985 Ore. App. LEXIS 3928.

Brooks as a subcontractor on the project. When the company refused to pay Brooks, he filed suit, winning a judgment against the company for $54,597.09. But it turned out that Becker Interiors had no assets.

Brooks then sued Ronald Becker in an attempt to pierce the corporate veil and hold Becker personally liable for the debts of the corporation.

Issues: *Can Brooks pierce the corporate veil? Is Becker personally liable for the debts of the corporation?*

Excerpts from Judge Roush's Decision: The decision to ignore the separate existence of a corporate entity and impose personal liability upon shareholders for debts of the corporation is an extraordinary act to be taken only when necessary to promote justice. Disregarding the corporate entity is usually warranted only under the extraordinary circumstances where: the shareholder has controlled or used the corporation to evade a personal obligation, to perpetrate fraud or a crime, to commit an injustice, or to gain an unfair advantage. Piercing the corporate veil is justified when the unity of interest and ownership is such that the separate personalities of the corporation and the individual no longer exist and to adhere to that separateness would work an injustice.

In this case, the evidence convinces the court that the extraordinary remedy of piercing the corporate veil should be granted. Becker knowingly violated his duties as an officer, director, and shareholder of Becker Interiors and treated the corporation's funds as his personal piggy bank. His testimony that the corporate expenditures on his personal residence were a legitimate business expense because he wanted to use the residence as a showcase of his work was simply not credible. Nor did the court believe Becker's testimony that he commingled his personal funds with the corporation's funds on the advice of his accountant. The court found more credible Becker's later testimony that his accountant was "mystified" by his commingling of funds between his personal and corporate accounts.

Accordingly, the court will enter judgment against Becker in the amount of $54,597.09.

Termination

Terminating a corporation is a three-step process:

- **Vote.** The directors recommend to the shareholders that the corporation be dissolved, and a majority of the shareholders agree.

- **Filing.** The corporation files "Articles of Dissolution" with the Secretary of State.

- **Winding Up.** The officers of the corporation pay its debts and distribute the remaining property to shareholders. When the winding up is completed, the corporation ceases to exist.

The Secretary of State may dissolve a corporation that violates state law by, for example, failing to pay the required annual fees. Indeed, many corporations, particularly small ones, do not bother with the formal dissolution process. They simply cease paying their annual fees and let the Secretary of State act. A court may dissolve a corporation if it is insolvent or if its directors and shareholders cannot resolve conflict over how the corporation should be managed.

THE ROLE OF CORPORATE MANAGEMENT

As business grows, entrepreneurs face new challenges. One of the most important is attracting outside investors—people with money but without the knowledge or desire to manage the enterprise. How can shareholders protect their interests in an organization without being involved in management themselves? They elect directors to manage for them. Directors set policy and then appoint officers to implement corporate goals. The Model Act describes the directors' role thus: "All corporate powers shall be exercised by or under the authority of, and the business and affairs of the corporation managed by or under the direction of, its board of directors...."

As managers of the corporation, directors have important responsibilities to shareholders and also to **stakeholders,** such as employees, customers, creditors, suppliers, and neighbors. However, the interests of these various groups often conflict. In the first decade of the twenty-first century, the world faced two financial crises that were caused, in part, by corporate executives who engaged in high-risk activities that left them wealthy, but their shareholders with nothing. Because of abuses by managers that, in some cases, included outright fraud, Congress and other regulators tried to rebalance the power among managers and shareholders. Part of their goal has been to enhance shareholder oversight of the companies they own. The rest of this chapter is about this balance of rights and responsibilities.

Managers have a fiduciary duty to act in the best interests of the corporation's shareholders. Because shareholders are primarily concerned about their return on investment, managers must *maximize shareholder value,* which means providing shareholders with the highest possible financial return from dividends and stock price. However, reality is more complicated than this simple rule indicates. It is often difficult to determine which strategy will best maximize shareholder value. And what about stakeholders? A number of states have adopted statutes that permit directors to take into account the interests of stakeholders as well as stockholders. The Indiana Code, for example, permits directors to consider "both the short term and long term best interests of the corporation, taking into account, and weighing as the directors deem appropriate, the effects thereof on the corporation's shareholders and the other corporate constituent groups...."[2] The next section looks more closely at directors' responsibilities to their various constituencies.

Stakeholder

Anyone who is affected by the activities of a corporation, such as a shareholder, employee, customer, creditor, supplier, or neighbor.

THE BUSINESS JUDGMENT RULE

Officers and directors have a fiduciary duty to act in the best interests of their stockholders, but under the **business judgment rule,** the courts allow managers great leeway in carrying out this responsibility. The business judgment rule is a common law concept that has achieved national acceptance. It is a fundamental principle of corporate law. To be protected by the business judgment rule, managers must act in good faith:

Duty of Loyalty	1. Without a conflict of interest
Duty of Care	2. With the care that an ordinarily prudent person would take in a similar situation and 3. In a manner they reasonably believe to be in the best interests of the corporation

© Cengage Learning 2014

The business judgment rule is two shields in one: it protects both the manager and her decisions. **If managers comply with the business judgment rule, a court will not hold them personally liable for any harm their decisions cause the company, nor will the court rescind their decisions.**

---

[2]Indiana Code §23-1-35-1.

The business judgment rule accomplishes three goals:

- **It permits directors to do their job.** If directors were afraid they would be liable for every decision that led to a loss, they would never make a decision, or at least not a risky one.

- **It keeps judges out of corporate management.** Without the business judgment rule, judges would be tempted, if not required, to second-guess managers' decisions.

- **It encourages directors to serve.** No one in his right mind would serve as a director if he knew that every decision was open to attack in the courtroom.

Analysis of the business judgment rule is divided into two parts. The obligation of a manager to act without a conflict of interest is called the **duty of loyalty.** The requirements that a manager act with care and in the best interests of the corporation are referred to as the **duty of care.**

Duty of Loyalty

The duty of loyalty prohibits managers from making a decision that benefits them at the expense of the corporation.

Self-Dealing

Self-dealing means that a manager makes a decision benefiting either himself or another company with which he has a relationship. While working at the Blue Moon restaurant, Zeke signs a contract on behalf of the restaurant to purchase bread from Rising Sun Bakery. Unbeknownst to anyone at Blue Moon, he is a part owner of Rising Sun. Zeke has engaged in self-dealing, which is a violation of the duty of loyalty.

Once a manager engages in self-dealing, the business judgment rule no longer applies. This does not mean the manager is automatically liable to the corporation or that his decision is automatically void. All it means is that the court will no longer presume that the transaction was acceptable. Instead, the court will scrutinize the deal more carefully. A self-dealing transaction is valid in any one of the following situations:

- **The disinterested members of the board of directors approve the transaction.** Disinterested directors are those who do not themselves benefit from the transaction.

- **The disinterested shareholders approve it.** The transaction is valid if the shareholders who do not benefit from it are willing to approve it.

- **The transaction was entirely fair to the corporation.** In determining fairness, the courts will consider the impact of the transaction on the corporation and whether the price was reasonable.

Although the business judgment rule did not protect Zeke, he would still not be liable if he sought permission first, or if a court found that he was buying great bread at an excellent price. Exhibit 20.4 illustrates the rules on self-dealing.

Corporate Opportunity

The self-dealing rules prevent managers from forcing their companies into unfair deals. The corporate opportunity doctrine is the reverse—it prohibits managers from excluding their company from favorable deals. **Managers are in violation of the corporate opportunity doctrine if they compete against the corporation without its consent.**

Long ago, Charles Guth was president of Loft, Inc., which operated a chain of candy stores. These stores sold Coca-Cola. Guth purchased the Pepsi-Cola Company personally, without

Duty of loyalty
The obligation of a manager to act without a conflict of interest.

Duty of care
The requirement that a manager act with care and in the best interests of the corporation.

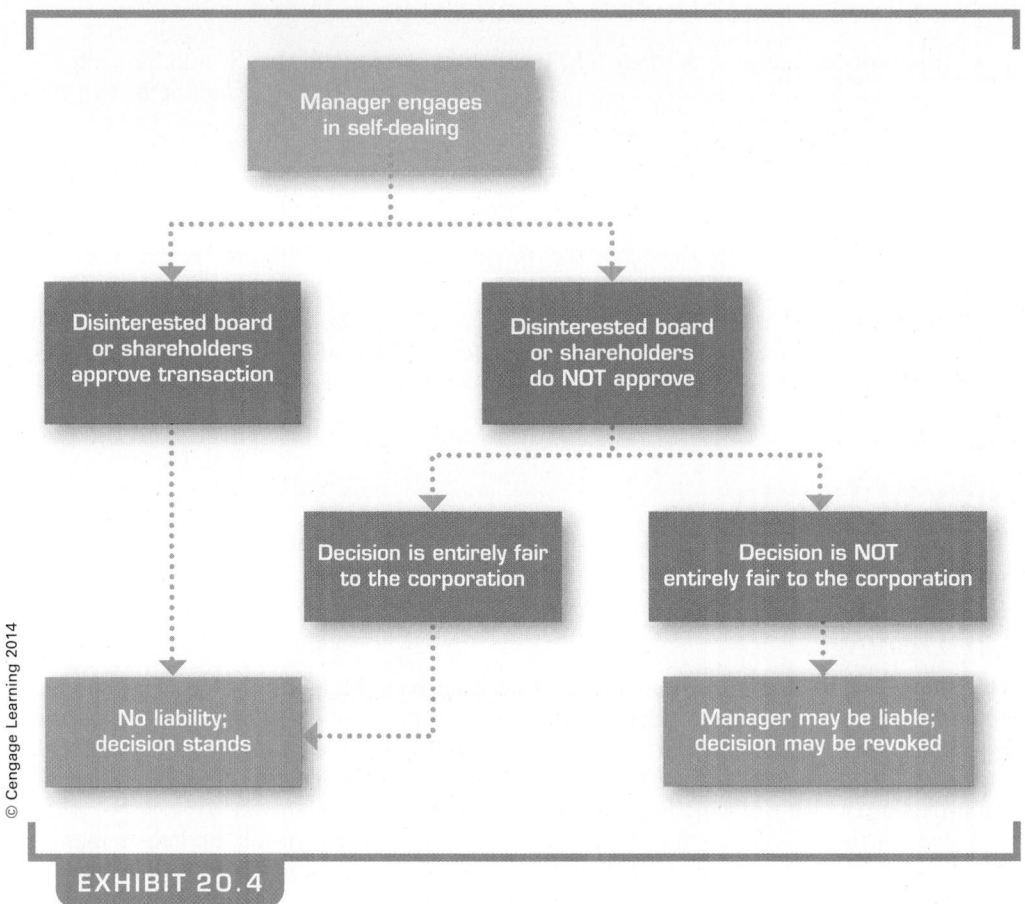

© Cengage Learning 2014

EXHIBIT 20.4

offering the opportunity to Loft. A Delaware court found that Guth had violated the corporate opportunity doctrine and ordered him to transfer all his shares in Pepsi to Loft.[3] That was in 1939, and Pepsi-Cola was bankrupt; today, PepsiCo, Inc. is worth more than $100 billion.

In the following case, the manager felt that he had a good reason for taking a corporate opportunity. Unfortunately, the court disagreed.

ANDERSON V. BELLINO

265 Neb. 577, 658 N.W.2d 645, 2003 LEXIS 49
Supreme Court of Nebraska, 2003

Facts: Richard Bellino and Robert Anderson formed LaVista Lottery, Inc. (Lottery) to operate a restaurant, lounge, and keno game in LaVista, Nevada.[4] They each owned 50 percent of the stock of Lottery, and both were officers and directors. During the next nine years, Lottery grossed more than $100 million. Bellino and Anderson each received over $4 million in salary and dividends. Although Bellino and Anderson were both involved in Lottery,

---

[3]*Guth v. Loft*, 5 A.2d 503, 23 Del. Ch. 255, 1939 Del. LEXIS 13 (Del. 1939).
[4]Keno is a game of chance similar to bingo except that in keno the players choose the numbers on their ticket.

Bellino spent more time, in part because of his personal relationship with Lottery's lounge manager. During this period, Bellino did not complain to Anderson about his lack of involvement in Lottery, and Anderson never refused to do anything that Bellino asked him to do.

Resentful of Anderson's work ethic, Bellino convinced LaVista's city council to put the keno contract up for competitive bid. Bellino incorporated LaVista Keno, Inc. (Keno), to bid on the contract.

Bellino wrote to Anderson complaining that because he (Bellino) was doing too much work for Lottery at too little pay, he intended to resign from Lottery and bid on the city contract himself. (Evidently, $4 million is not as much as it used to be.) Anderson offered to do more work or whatever Bellino wanted, but Bellino refused any effort at reconciliation. He then submitted a bid on behalf of Keno. At the time he submitted the bid, he was still an officer of Lottery, as well as a director and a 50 percent shareholder. Anderson also bid on the contract on behalf of Lottery. The city awarded the new contract to Keno.

Anderson and Lottery filed suit against Bellino and Keno, alleging that they had usurped a corporate opportunity. The lower court found for Anderson and Lottery. It ordered Bellino to pay $644,992.63 but provided that Bellino could receive a credit of $172,514.63 against the judgment, if Bellino transferred the stock of Keno to Lottery and persuaded the city to relicense the keno contract from Keno to Lottery.

Issues: *Did Bellino usurp a corporate opportunity? Is he liable to Lottery?*

Excerpts from Justice Miller-Lerman's Decision: Bellino and Keno claim that if a corporate opportunity existed, it was limited to the opportunity to bid for the keno contract, that Bellino did nothing to impede Lottery from bidding for the keno contract by merely submitting a competing bid, and that, therefore, Bellino did not usurp a corporate opportunity.

Contrary to the arguments asserted by Bellino and Keno, the corporate opportunity was not the right to bid; the bidding process was merely the "preliminary step" by which Lottery sought to acquire the opportunity embodied in the award of the keno contract. The facts thus establish that the keno contract was a corporate opportunity for Lottery.

> Although an officer or a director of a corporation is not necessarily precluded from entering into a separate business because it is in competition with the corporation, his fiduciary relationship to the corporation and its stockholders is such that if he does so he must prove that he did so in good faith and did not act in such a manner as to cause or contribute to the injury or damage of the corporation, or deprive it of business; if he fails in this proof, there has been a breach of that fiduciary trust or relationship.

The evidence is uncontroverted that Bellino's successful bid for the LaVista keno contract deprived Lottery of its only source of business. Bellino, through Keno, should not have competed with Lottery for the LaVista keno contract.

We affirm the district court's order.

EXAM Strategy

Question: Otto signed a lease with Landlord on a storefront in Georgetown, D.C. He convinced his nephew Nick to start a furniture store in the space. Otto and Nick formed a corporation to operate the store. Otto owned 51 percent and Nick 49 percent of the company's stock. Otto signed a lease between himself and the store at a price that was 20 percent higher than the rent Otto was paying Landlord. Otto purchased a warehouse and then rented it to the corporation at a fair-market rent. Nick sued, alleging that the two leases were not valid. Were they?

Strategy: If the business judgment rule applies, the court will not second-guess a corporate action. But here, the manager engaged in self-dealing, so the business judgment rule is not applicable.

Result: Otto violated the duty of loyalty twice. The lease for the storefront was self-dealing—it directly benefited him. When he purchased the warehouse, he took a corporate opportunity that he should have offered first to the company. He is personally liable for any damages to the corporation. The company also has the right to cancel both leases and to purchase the warehouse from him.

Duty of Care

In addition to the *duty of loyalty*, managers also owe a *duty of care*. **The duty of care requires officers and directors to act in the best interests of the corporation and to use the same care that an ordinarily prudent person would take in a similar situation.**

Rational Business Purpose

Courts generally agree in principle that directors and officers are liable for decisions that have no rational business purpose. In practice, however, these same courts have been extremely supportive of managerial decisions, looking hard to find some justification. For years, the Chicago Cubs baseball team was the only major American professional sports team to play in a stadium without lights. A shareholder sued on the grounds that the Cubs' revenues were peanuts and crackerjack compared with those generated by teams that played at night. In their defense, the Cubs argued that a large night crowd would cause the neighborhood to deteriorate, depressing the value of Wrigley Field (which the Cubs did not own). The court rooted for the home team and found that the Cubs' excuse was a "rational purpose" and a legitimate exercise of the business judgment rule.[5]

Legality

Courts are generally unsympathetic to managers who engage in illegal behavior, even if their goal is to help the company. For example, the managing director of an amusement park in New York State used corporate funds to purchase the silence of people who threatened to complain that the park was illegally operating on Sunday. The court ordered the director to repay the money he had spent on bribes, even though the company had earned large profits on Sundays.[6]

Informed Decision

Generally, courts will protect managers who make an *informed* decision, even if the decision ultimately harms the company. Making an informed decision means carefully investigating the facts. However, even if the decision is uninformed, the directors will not be held liable if the decision was entirely fair to the shareholders.

Exhibit 20.5 provides an overview of the duty of care.

EXAM Strategy

Question: You are the CEO of a software company. You will allow your engineers to create software only for Apple computers, not for PCs, because you think Apple is cooler. Some of your shareholders disagree with this policy. Is your decision protected by the business judgment rule?

Strategy: Remember that you owe a duty of care to the corporation. This means that you must have a rational business purpose for your decision.

Result: The courts are very generous in defining a rational business purpose. They would probably uphold your decision so long as it was not in some way personally benefiting you—e.g., so long as you were not a major shareholder of Apple.

---

[5] *Shlensky v. Wrigley*, 95 Ill. App. 2d 173, 237 N.E.2d 776, 1968 Ill. App. LEXIS 1107 (Ill. App. Ct. 1968).
[6] *Roth v. Robertson*, 64 Misc. 343, 118 N.Y.S. 351, 1909 N.Y. Misc. LEXIS 279 (N.Y. 1909).

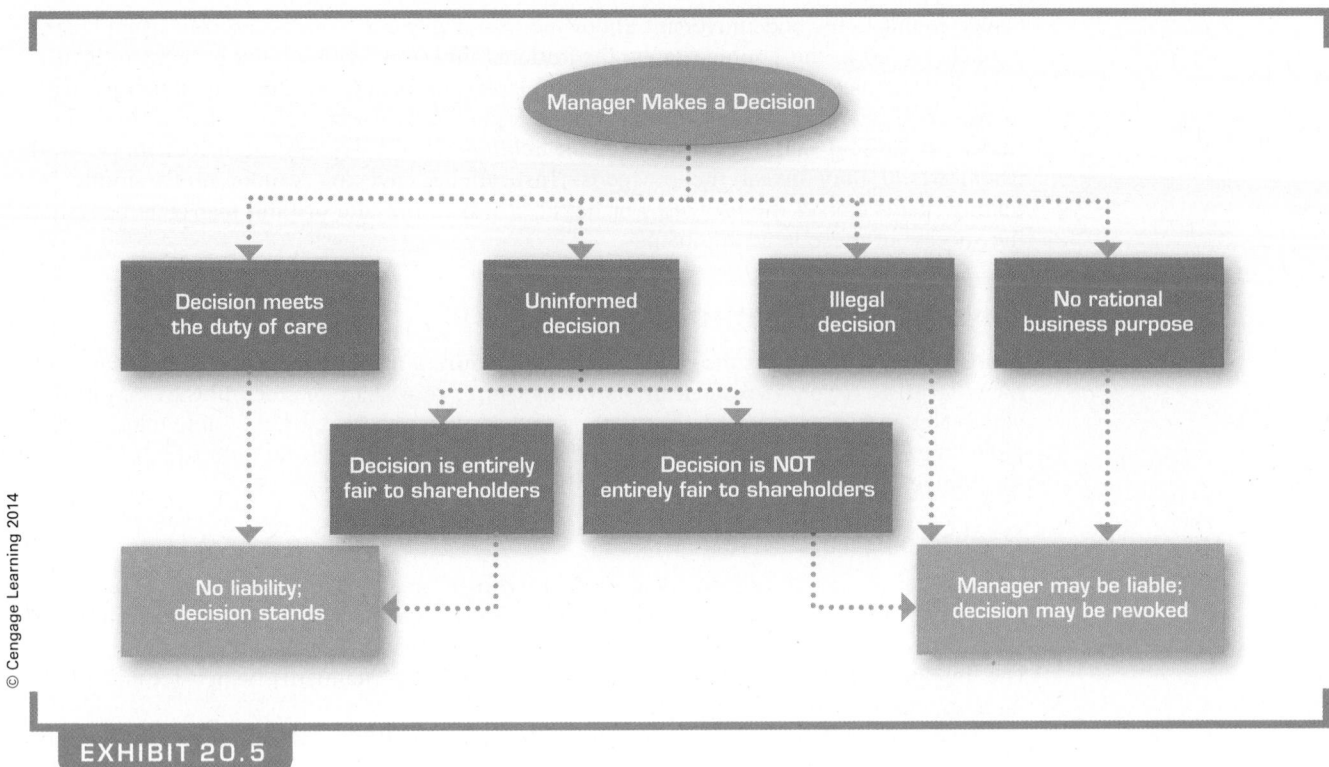

EXHIBIT 20.5

THE ROLE OF SHAREHOLDERS

We have explored the duties and responsibilities of directors and managers. In this section, we look at shareholders' rights—what control do they exercise over the enterprises they own?

The topic of shareholder rights is contentious. As pointed out earlier, in this century, we have already experienced two financial meltdowns—one at the beginning of the 2000s and one at the end—that starkly revealed the different incentives faced by shareholders and managers. Too often, managers earned exorbitant compensation from highly risky short-term decisions that in the longer run left shareholders holding an empty bag. If CEOs made a risky decision that paid off, they profited enormously. If the decision failed, they might be fired, but they would still get to keep all the generous compensation they had received. On the way out the door, many also got severance payments that left them wealthy beyond most people's dreams. For example, in the two years before the investment banks Bear Stearns Companies, Inc., and Lehman Brothers Holdings, Inc., failed, their top five executives took home $1.4 billion and $1 billion, respectively, even as their shareholders were left with nothing.

Even worse, investigations after the fact revealed that too many managers had gamed compensation plans, stacked their boards with friends, and ignored shareholder interests. Compliant boards had been little more than rubber stamps, approving whatever the officers wanted. In anger and frustration, shareholders, Congress, the Securities and Exchange Commission (SEC), and stock exchanges undertook an unprecedented effort to rebalance corporate power. Yet these changes are little more than a shot in the dark, without compelling evidence that they will enhance financial stability or improve shareholder results.

A note before we begin: at one time, corporate stock was primarily owned by individuals. But now institutional investors—pension plans, mutual funds, insurance companies, banks, foundations, and university endowments—own more than 50 percent of all shares publicly traded in the United States. Institutional investors, with enormous sums to invest, have little choice but to buy the stock of large companies. If they are unhappy with management, it is difficult for them to do the "Wall Street walk"—that is, sell their shares—because a sale of their large stock holdings would depress the market price. And where would they invest the proceeds? Institutional investors cannot profit simply by trading shares among themselves. For better or worse, the fate of fund managers hangs on the success of these large companies.

Rights of Shareholders

Shareholders have neither the right nor the obligation to manage the day-to-day business of the enterprise. If you own stock in Starbucks Corp., your share of stock plus $7.62 entitles you to a cup of Grande Vanilla Latte, the same as everyone else. By the same token, if the pipes freeze and the local Starbucks store floods, the manager has no right to call you, as a shareholder, to help clean up the mess. What rights do shareholders have?

Right to Information

Shareholders have the right to obtain certain information about the company they own, but the extent of this right depends on whether the organization is publicly or privately held. (A private corporation's stock is not publicly traded.) All corporations are regulated by state law, but publicly traded enterprises must also meet SEC standards, which require much more extensive information.

Under the Model Act, shareholders acting in good faith and with a proper purpose have the right to inspect and copy the corporation's minute book, accounting records, and shareholder lists. A proper purpose is one that aids the shareholder in managing and protecting her investment. If, for example, Celeste is convinced that the directors of Devil Desserts, Inc., are mismanaging the company, she might demand a list of other shareholders so that she can ask them to join her in a lawsuit. This purpose is proper—although the company may not like it—and the company is required to give her the list. If, however, Celeste wants to use the shareholder list as a potential source for her new online business selling exercise equipment, the company could legitimately turn her down.

Right to Vote

A corporation must have at least one class of stock with voting rights.

Shareholder Meetings   Although not all states require public companies to hold an annual meeting of shareholders, the New York Stock Exchange (NYSE) and NASDAQ require companies listed with them to do so. Thus, **annual shareholder meetings are the norm for publicly traded companies.**

Companies whose stock is not publicly traded can either hold an annual meeting or use written consents from their shareholders. In addition, under the Model Act, shareholders owning at least 10 percent of the company's stock and the board of directors each have the right to call a *special* meeting to vote on an emergency issue that cannot wait until the next annual meeting—for example, to conclude a merger or sell off substantial assets.

Everyone who owns stock on the **record date** must be sent notice of a meeting, whether it is an annual or special meeting. The record date can be any day that is no more than 70 days before the meeting. The votes taken at a shareholder meeting are not valid unless a quorum is present, meaning that shareholders owning a certain percentage of the shares are represented, either in person or by proxy.

Companies are permitted to hold shareholder meetings online rather than in person. Many companies do both—conducting a live meeting with virtual access. In 2010, Symantec

Corporation became the first Fortune 500 company to eliminate the in-person meeting and hold a virtual-only version. Unfortunately, the company used this opportunity to limit rather than expand access. It broadcast only in audio, not video, which meant that participants had no opportunity to read body language or even realize that three directors were absent. In the question-and-answer period, management read and answered only two questions from shareholders and provided no opportunity for follow-up questions. Nor did they reveal who had asked the questions, or even what questions they had chosen not to answer.

Ethics Symantec's actions in holding a virtual shareholder meeting were legal. If you had been a shareholder and had attended the meeting in cyberspace, would you have been satisfied with the company's virtual format? Did Symantec do the right thing?

Proxies   Shareholders who do not wish to attend a shareholders' meeting may appoint someone else to vote for them. Confusingly, both this person and the document the shareholder signs to appoint the substitute voter are called a **proxy.** Under SEC rules, companies are not required to solicit proxies, but virtually all of them do because the NYSE and NASDAQ require it, and in addition, that is the only practical way to obtain a quorum. Along with the proxy, the company must also give shareholders a **proxy statement** and an **annual report.** The proxy statement provides information on everything from management compensation to a list of directors who miss too many meetings. The annual report contains detailed financial data.

Shareholder Proposals   Shareholders who oppose a particular company policy may use the proxy process to challenge that policy. **Under SEC rules, any shareholder who has continuously owned for one year at least 1 percent of the company or $2,000 of stock can require that one proposal be placed in the company's proxy statement to be voted on at the shareholder meeting.** Most of these proposals involve issues of corporate governance (e.g., permitting secret ballots), executive compensation (e.g., "say on pay"), social issues (e.g., healthcare reform) or environmental policy (e.g., greenhouse gases). Prior to 1985, only two proposals had been approved—ever. Recently, 37 percent of the corporate governance proposals passed, but less than 5 percent of the others.

Note, however, that even if shareholders approve a proposal, the company may not implement it. Resolutions are binding on a company only if they are within the narrow realm of shareholder power. For example, because shareholders have the right to amend company bylaws, such proposals are binding. But, a shareholder vote that requires the board to take a specific action is not binding because shareholders have no legal right to manage the company. Thus, even though the SEC requires companies to allow a vote on proposals about succession planning, the board still does not have to develop a succession plan, even if a majority of shareholders vote in favor. Most proposals are nonbinding, and companies implement less than half of those that their shareholders approve.

Frustrated at this unresponsive behavior by boards, shareholders have begun to withhold their vote from any director who fails to support a successful shareholder proposal. However, even this threat has not yet had a significant impact on board responsiveness to shareholder proposals.

Ironically, companies sometimes implement shareholder proposals that have not received support from a majority of the shareholders. The pressure of shareholder proposals is credited with inducing many American companies to withdraw from South Africa in protest against its apartheid regime. Other companies implement shareholder proposals

---

Proxy

The person whom a shareholder appoints to vote for her at a meeting of the corporation. Also, the document a shareholder signs appointing this substitute voter.

Proxy Statement

Before its annual meeting, a public company provides a document to shareholders that contains information about the corporation.

Annual report

A document that the SEC requires public companies to provide to their shareholders each year. It contains financial data.

without even putting them up for a vote. Indeed, a substantial number of shareholder proposals are now withdrawn before a vote because the company is willing to negotiate and accommodate. For instance, Colgate-Palmolive Co. agreed to a proposal by institutional investors to permit secret ballots at shareholder meetings.

Election and Removal of Directors

The process of electing directors to the board of a publicly traded company is different from what most people think. Shareholders do *not* have the right to use the company's proxy statement to propose nominees for director. Instead, the nominating committee of the board of directors produces a slate of directors, with one name per opening. Typically, the names are approved by the CEO. This slate is then placed in the proxy statement and sent to shareholders, whose only choice is to vote in favor of a nominee or to withhold their vote (i.e., not vote at all). If shareholders want to vote for someone who was not selected by the company, they have to nominate their own slate, prepare and distribute a proxy statement to other shareholders, and then communicate why their slate is superior, all the while fighting against the company's almost unlimited financial resources. This process is complex, expensive, and disruptive to the company. Not surprisingly, only a few shareholder groups undertake this effort each year. Recent research does indicate, however, that companies with a director elected through proxy contests outperform their peers over both the short and long term.[7]

Plurality voting

To be elected, a candidate only needs to receive more votes than her opponent, not a majority of the votes cast.

This traditional corporate voting method is called **plurality voting**. A successful candidate does not need to receive a majority vote—he must simply receive more than any competitor. Since typically there are no competitors, one vote is sufficient (and that vote could be his own). Even if a large number of shareholders withhold their votes, the nominee may be embarrassed, but so long as he receives that one vote, he is elected. Thus, for example, in the waning years of Michael Eisner's rule at Disney Enterprises Inc., shareholders withheld 43 percent of their votes from him. But that vote of no confidence did not cause the board to fire him, nor did he immediately resign. Congress, other regulators, and major shareholders are now reforming corporate democracy in an effort to rebalance the relationship between managers and shareholders.

Majority Voting Systems   Because of pressure from shareholder activists, 79 percent of the S&P 500 (which consists of large companies) now refuse to seat a director if fewer than half of the shares that vote tick off her name on the ballot. However, of smaller companies—those in the Russell 3000 index—three-quarters still permit plurality voting, where one vote is often sufficient to insure election.[8]

Independent Directors   Congress began its reform effort by passing the Sarbanes-Oxley Act (SOX), which applies to all publicly traded corporations in the United States, as well as to all foreign companies listed on a U.S. stock exchange. Among other provisions, SOX stipulates that **all members of a board's audit committee must be independent, and at least one of these members must be a financial expert.** Independent directors are those who are *not employees of the company* and, therefore, presumably not in the pocket of the CEO.

Likewise, **the NYSE and NASDAQ require that, for companies listed on these exchanges,**

- Independent directors must comprise a majority of the board;

- They must meet regularly on their own, without inside directors;

---

[7]The Investor Responsibility Research Center Institute. See *http://www.irrcinstitute.org/pdf/PR_5_25_09.pdf*.
[8]The S&P 500 is composed of 500 leading companies in the most important U.S. industries, while the Russell 3000 is made up of the largest 3,000 companies in the United States, representing 98 percent of the investable U.S. equity market.

- Only independent directors can serve on audit, compensation, or nominating committees;

- Audit committees must have at least three directors who are financially literate.

The effectiveness of these reforms is uncertain. One study found that 45 percent of directors who are technically "independent" have friendship ties to the CEO. And even independent directors are often financially beholden to the CEO. At a minimum, the CEO is more likely to fire them from their lucrative directorship than shareholders are, so their incentives are often more aligned with the CEO. Some commentators even argue that because independent directors do not work full time for the company, they know *less* about what is really going on and have to rely *more* on company executives.

What happens to independent directors who fail to carry out their watchdog responsibilities? Unless they personally committed fraud, the answer is: not much. After all, if the SEC were aggressive about going after independent directors, few people would be willing to serve in that role. Even if they are sued, the corporation or its insurance company usually pays the damages.

Shareholder Activists Proxy advisors, such as Institutional Shareholder Services, Inc. (ISS), are a new development in corporate democracy. They advise institutional investors on how to vote their shares. Proxy advisors and hedge funds (who often have substantial stock holdings) wield significant power. ISS alone can affect up to 20 to 40 percent of the vote at a company. Corporate managers argue that it is too much power because (1) activists may well have an agenda that is contrary to that of other shareholders, and (2) they tend to support corporate governance initiatives without proof of effectiveness.

In any event, boards have become more responsive to the demands of shareholder activists and, as a result, are more likely to replace executives who perform badly, either in their corporate or personal lives. For example, the board of Hewlett-Packard fired CEO Mark Hurd for a combination of reasons that included his fudging of expense reports to hide his relationship with someone who accused him of sexual harassment, and, perhaps worst of all, bad press.

Proxy Access By a 3–2 vote of the commissioners, the SEC approved proxy access rules that required companies to include in their proxy material the names of board nominees selected by large shareholders (that is, those who had owned 3 percent of the company for three years). But when business groups sued the SEC to prevent implementation, a federal appeals court invalidated the proxy access rule on the grounds that the SEC had not followed required procedures in adopting it. The SEC elected not to appeal this decision.[9] However, proxy access survives in a weakened form: the SEC permits shareholders to make proposals that, if approved, would change company bylaws to require proxy access. This two-step process is more complicated, and less likely to succeed, than the one-step version the SEC originally proposed. Also, such proposals are binding on the company only if state law permits. Such a proposal could be binding in Delaware.

The effectiveness of this rule change is uncertain. At this stage, it has not altered the reality that for most companies, shareholders have little say on board nominations.

Compensation for Officers and Directors—The Problem

As we have seen, a CEO has significant influence over the selection process for the company's board of directors. So directors have an incentive to keep the CEO happy. As a result, between 2001 and 2003, public companies spent 9.8 percent of their net income on compensation for top executives. In 1975, the top 100 CEOs earned 39 times as much as the average worker. By 2005, that ratio was over 300. See Exhibit 20.6 for an illustration of this trend. Here are some examples of executive compensation that particularly agitated shareholders:

[9]*Business Roundtable v. SEC*, 2011 Y,S, Aoo, kexus 14988 (D.C. Cir. 2011).

- Michael Eisner was the head of Walt Disney Corporation for 20 years. At the beginning of his tenure, the company did very well and few complained when he was exceedingly well paid. But for the final *13 years*, he earned $800 million while the stock performed worse than government bonds (a low-risk, low-return investment).

- The CEO of Fannie Mae earned $90 million during a time when the company's accounting system was so flawed that it overstated its earnings by $11 billion.

- Executives whose companies survived the 2008 financial crisis only because of taxpayer bailouts still received enormous bonuses. For example, taxpayers spent $180 billion to save American International Group (AIG), Inc., even as the company awarded bonuses of $165 million.

© Cengage Learning 2014

EXHIBIT 20.6   CEOs' pay as a multiple of the average worker's pay, 1960-2007
Source: *Executive Excess* 2008, the 15th Annual CEO Compensation Survey from the Institute for Policy Studies and United for a Fair Economy.[10]

To many investors, sky-high executive salaries have become the symbol of all that is wrong with corporate governance. In many companies, salaries are the least of the compensation. Executives also received:

Stock Options   Concerned about escalating executive salaries, shareholder activists began advocating "pay-for-performance" plans. The theory was that if executives received stock options instead of cash salaries, their incentives would be more closely aligned with those of shareholders. It was a good theory, but in practice, it did not work as intended.

Stock options became a "heads, I win; tails, you lose" game. When stock prices soared in a bull market, options became unexpectedly valuable. In some cases, managers were richly rewarded even when their company had underperformed the (rising) market. However, when stock prices fell, boards lowered the price of the options.

---

[10]Prepared by Professor G. William Miller, University of California at Santa Cruz, *http://sociology.ucsc.edu/whorulesamerica/power/wealth.html.*

Also, companies played games with options. After the 9/11 terrorist attack, the stock market was closed for four days. When it reopened, stocks took a bigger plunge than they had in any week since Nazi Germany invaded France at the beginning of World War II. In what appeared to be an unseemly exploitation of a national tragedy, 186 companies granted stock options to 511 executives during those few weeks. That is more than twice the number of companies that usually issued stock options in September.[11] These grants were legal, at least; not so the backdated options that more than 2,000 companies appear to have issued their executives. In granting these options, companies claimed that they had been issued on an earlier date when the stock price was lower. This practice is fraud.

Termination, Retirement Plans, and Death Benefits Most public companies provide their top executives with generous termination payments, no matter how they leave their jobs. Indeed, many CEO employment contracts provide that the employee is entitled to severance pay unless fired for committing a particular type of felony. Dying also pays. For example, Nabor Industries Ltd. agreed to pay its 78-year-old CEO $263 million when he dies. The CEO of the Shaw Group was entitled to $17 million if he does not compete with the company after he dies. (Yes, you read that right—he was paid not to compete after his death.)

Lavish Perks Executives had long received perks such as country club memberships and cars, but the roster of options expanded. One of the most popular perks is use of the corporate jet. One study found a high correlation between the use of the company plane and membership in far-flung golf clubs. Unfortunately, the correlation is inverse: the more companies spend on private jets, the worse their stock performs.

Why has executive pay become so lavish?

Directors, not Shareholders, Set Executive Compensation Directors set the CEO's compensation, but shareholders are the ones who pay the money. People tend to spend someone else's money more generously than their own. Also, directors and the CEO are often friends. Imagine if you got to decide how much your friend could spend dining out, knowing that someone else, whom you had never met, would have to pay the bill. It would be easy to be generous.

Shareholders Bear the Risk Once again, executive compensation is a "Heads I win, tails you lose" game. As we discussed earlier in the chapter, if CEOs make a risky decision that pays off, they typically profit enormously. But even if the decision turns out badly, they are often well paid anyway. For example, Randall Stephenson, the CEO of AT&T, proposed that his company buy T-Mobile USA. A clever idea, except that the purchase violated the antitrust guidelines of the Justice Department. The risk that the government would not approve the deal was well known. Nonetheless, Stephenson promised that AT&T would pay T-Mobile $4.2 *billion* if the deal fell apart. The government did indeed object, the deal was scuttled, and AT&T had to make the enormous payment to T-Mobile. In response, the AT&T board imposed a punishment on Stephenson that was so harsh it made headlines: his compensation was reduced by $2.08 million to *only* $18.7 million. That was the penalty for losing $4.2 billion of shareholder money.

Benchmarking Games Compensation is rarely linked closely to individual performance, but instead to overall industry or stock market performance, which is defined in a way to favor executives. Two-thirds of the largest 1,000 U.S. companies report that they performed better than their peers.[12] That is, in part, because benchmarks can be manipulated. For example, Tootsie Roll Industries Inc., with $500 million in sales, benchmarked

[11]Charles Forelle, James Bandler, and Mark Maremont, "Executive Pay: The 9/11 Factor," *The Wall Street Journal,* July, 15, 2006, p. A1.
[12]Kevin J. Murphy, "Politics, Economics and Executive Compensation," reported in Lucian Bebchuk and Jesse Fried, *Pay Without Performance,* Harvard University Press, 2004, p. 71.

against Kraft Foods Inc., with $42.2 billion in earnings. Indeed, every company Tootsie Roll benchmarked against had higher revenues.

Campbell Soup used one set of benchmark companies to determine executive compensation, but another set to evaluate its total shareholder return. In all fairness, it seems that Campbell's ought to be consistent—presumably only one set of companies is the right comparison group.

The CEO Gets All the Credit   Compensation committees sometimes act as if the CEO (and maybe a few other top executives) are solely responsible for a company's success. Although there is much talk about "pay for performance," the reality is that luck can be as important a determinant of executive compensation as good performance.[13] After James Kilts became CEO of Gillette Co., the stock price went up 61 percent. He had added $20 billion in shareholder value, and therefore, to many it seemed only fair when he was rewarded with a $153 million payout when Procter & Gamble bought the company. Or was it? About half the increase in Gillette revenues during the time that Kilts was running the show were attributable to currency fluctuations. A cheaper dollar increased revenue overseas. If the dollar had moved in the opposite direction, there might not have been any increase in revenue.

The Busier the Directors, the Higher the Executive Pay   Generally, executives are more likely to be overpaid if directors serve on many boards. These directors may be too busy to pay attention to such details. Also, trophy directors may be afraid that if they offend a chief executive at one company, word will get around, jeopardizing their position on other boards.

Most Executives Are Above Average   Of course, not everyone can be above average, but most directors believe that their executives are. No one wants to admit to hiring incompetents. Suppose that you are on a company's compensation committee and have data about industry averages. If your executives are above average in performance, you should pay them above-average salaries. If they are not above average, you should fire them, which few boards want to do, except in the face of disaster. If *you* raise salaries, the industry average also rises. The next company that sets compensation has an even higher bar to jump. For example, Colgate-Palmolive awarded 2 million stock options to its CEO on the understanding that he would receive no further grants for five years. Three years later, however, when consultants found that the CEO's compensation had fallen below the median, the company immediately awarded him an additional 2.6 million options.

Compensation Consultants Often Have Conflicts of Interest   Many companies hire compensation consultants to offer advice on executive pay. These same consultants may also provide other services to the company—such as human resource management—for which the fees can be substantial. The consultants have every incentive to suggest generous packages. In any event, it is not their money.

To make matters even worse for shareholders, lavish compensation does not appear to improve a business's success. A study of the 58 companies that were most generous to their CEOs found that, on average, these companies significantly underperformed both the market generally and their industry in particular.[14]

Corporate executives are not the only people to earn fabulous salaries. Some athletes earn more even than CEOs. What is the difference between athletes and executives (besides a hook shot)? Athletes' salaries are negotiated at arm's length with the team owner who will actually be paying the bill. This negotiation process means that (1) athletes' pay is not camouflaged; (2) they do not receive enormous severance packages on their way out the

---

[13]See, for example, Marianne Bertrand and Sendhil Mullainathan, "Are CEOs Rewarded for Luck? The Ones Without Principals Are," *The Quarterly Journal of Economics*, August 2001.
[14]Reed Abelson, "Who Profits If the Boss Is Overfed?" *New York Times*, June 20, 1999, Business Section, p. 9.

door; and (3) their retirement pay is modest.[15] Also, an athlete's performance is transparent and easy to measure.

Compensation for Officers and Directors—A Solution?

The federal government has begun to respond to these compensation issues.

Proxy Rules   The SEC began this process by amending its proxy rules to require more information about executive compensation. A proxy statement must now include a summary table setting out the full amount of compensation for the five highest-earning executives. The company must explain, for example, why option grants were approved and how much retirement benefits are worth. Companies must also disclose if the pay package increases the risk of large losses. The goal of this provision is to discourage companies from offering pay plans that reward executives for taking excessive risks.

SOX   Under SOX:

- A company cannot make personal loans to its directors or officers.

- If a company has to restate its earnings, its CEO and CFO must reimburse the company for any bonus or profits they received from selling company stock within a year of the release of the flawed financials. This is a so-called claw-back provision.

Dodd-Frank   In 2010, Congress passed the Dodd-Frank Wall Street Reform and Consumer Protection Act. Dodd-Frank:

- Requires that compensation committees for all companies listed on a stock exchange must be composed solely of independent directors.

- Strengthens the claw-back provisions of SOX and extends it to three years.

- Requires "say on pay." At least once every three years, companies must take a *nonbinding* shareholder vote on executive compensation (that is, for executive officers, but not for directors). In 2010, for the first time ever, shareholders voted against an executive pay plan—54 percent of Motorola's shareholders opposed CEO Sanjay Jha's compensation. The board had promised him 3 percent of the company if the plan to split Motorola in two succeeded, or a guaranteed payment if it did not. This vote was nonbinding, and the company made no concrete promises to respond.

- At least once every six years, companies must take a *nonbinding* shareholder vote on how often to hold the say-on-pay vote—once a year, every two years, or every three years.

- In the event of a merger or sale of all company assets, shareholders have the right to a *nonbinding* vote on so-called golden parachutes—special payments to executives that result from the transaction.

- Companies must disclose the relationship between financial performance and the executive compensation they actually paid.

- Companies must disclose the CEO's compensation and the median compensation of all other company employees, as well as the ratio of these two numbers.

Even with these new protections in place, shareholder influence over executive compensation is far from guaranteed. Note that the shareholder resolutions are nonbinding. And

[15]Some of the material in this section on executive compensation is drawn from Lucian Bebchuk and Jesse Fried, *Pay Without Performance*, Harvard University Press, 2004.

there is little shareholders can do to challenge executive compensation in the courts. To be successful, shareholders must prove that the board violated the business judgment rule, either by making a decision that was *grossly uninformed* or by setting an amount so high that it had *no relation* to the value of the services performed and was really a gift. As the following case indicates, courts tend to be unsympathetic to this line of argument.

BREHM V. EISNER (IN RE WALT DISNEY CO. DERIVATIVE LITIG.)

2006 Del. LEXIS 307
Supreme Court of Delaware, 2006

Facts: Michael Ovitz founded Creative Artists Agency (CAA), the premier talent agency in Hollywood. As a partner at this agency, he earned between $20 and $25 million per year. He was also a longtime friend of Michael Eisner, chairman and CEO of the Walt Disney Company. Ovitz lacked experience managing a diversified public company, but Disney hired him to be its president with the hope that he could improve the company's relationships with talent and increase foreign revenues. Upon the advice of Graef Crystal, a compensation consultant, the board approved Ovitz's contract.

After 14 months, all parties agreed that the experiment had failed, so Ovitz left Disney—but not empty-handed. Under his contract, he was entitled to $130 million in severance pay.[16]

Shareholders of Disney sued the board, alleging that it had violated the business judgment rule and that such a large payout was a waste of corporate assets. The trial court held for Disney, and the shareholders appealed.

Issues: *Did Disney directors have the right to pay $130 million to an employee who had worked unsuccessfully at the company for only 14 months?*

Excerpts from Justice Jacobs's Decision: [T]he compensation committee [of the Board of Directors] was informed of the material facts relating to the payout. If measured in terms of the documentation that would have been generated if "best practices" had been followed, that record leaves much to be desired. [But, the] committee reasonably believed that the analysis of the terms of the [contract] was within Crystal's professional or expert competence, and the committee relied on the information, opinions, reports, and statements made by Crystal. Furthermore, Crystal appears to have been selected with reasonable care, especially in light of his previous engagements with the company.

[The purpose of the business judgment rule] is to protect directors who rely in good faith upon information presented to them from various sources, including any other person as to matters the member reasonably believes are within such person's professional or expert competence and who has been selected with reasonable care by and on behalf of the corporation. For these reasons, we uphold the Chancellor's [that is, the trial court's] determination that the compensation committee members did not breach their fiduciary duty of care.

The shareholders claim the payment of the severance amount to Ovitz constituted waste. A claim of waste will arise only in the rare, unconscionable case where directors irrationally squander or give away corporate assets.

[The shareholders] claim that provisions of the [contract] were wasteful because they incentivized Ovitz to perform poorly in order to obtain payment. The approval of the [contract] had a rational business purpose: to induce Ovitz to leave CAA, at what would otherwise be a considerable cost to him, in order to join Disney. To suggest that at the time he entered into the [contract,] Ovitz would engineer an early departure at the cost of his extraordinary reputation in the entertainment industry and his historical friendship with Eisner is not only fanciful but also without proof in the record.

For the reasons stated above, the judgment of the Chancellor is affirmed.

---

[16]As songwriter Ira Gershwin put it, "Nice work if you can get it, and if you get it—won't you tell me how?"

Emerging Growth Companies   In an effort to encourage investment in growth companies, Congress passed the Jumpstart Our Business Startups Act (the JOBS Act) in 2012. Under this statute, the Dodd-Frank rules about say-on-pay and the disclosure of executive compensation do not apply to emerging growth companies (EGCs). An EGC is one for which all the following statements are true:

- It has annual gross revenues of less than $1 billion (indexed for inflation).

- Its stock has been publicly traded for less than five years.

- It has issued less than $700 million in publicly traded stock.

- It has issued less than $1 billion in convertible debt in a three-year period.

Fundamental Corporate Changes

A corporation must seek shareholder approval before undergoing any of the following fundamental changes: a merger, a sale of major assets, dissolution of the corporation, or an amendment to the charter.

Right to Dissent

Because a private corporation does not have publicly traded stock, its shareholders may not have an easy way to sell their holdings. Therefore, if a private corporation decides to undertake a fundamental change, the Model Act and many state laws require the company to buy back the stock of any shareholders who object. This process is referred to as dissenters' rights, and the company must pay "fair value" for the stock. Fundamental changes include a merger or a sale of most of the company's assets.

Right to Protection from Other Shareholders

Anyone who owns enough stock to control a corporation has a fiduciary duty to minority shareholders. (Minority shareholders are those with less than a controlling interest.) The courts have long recognized that minority shareholders are entitled to extra protection because it is easy (perhaps even natural) for controlling shareholders to take advantage of them.

Although craigslist and eBay are both Internet companies, they have little in common (other than a lowercase first letter). What obligations do they owe each other? You be the judge.

You be the Judge

Facts: craigslist, Inc., owned the most popular website in the country for classified ads. It had just two shareholders—Craig Newmark and Jim Buckmaster—and only 34 employees. Rather than trying to maximize its profits or expand its business, craigslist focused instead on enhancing its user community (by, for example, offering free ads). eBay, Inc. was a publicly traded company that operated online auction sites worldwide. It employed over 16,000 people. Its primary focus was increasing profitability and market share.

EBAY DOMESTIC HOLDINGS, INC. V. NEWMARK

2010 Del. Ch. LEXIS 187
Court of Chancery of Delaware, 2010

eBay decided to buy 28.4 percent of craigslist's shares, with the goal of ultimately acquiring the company or, failing that, learning the "secret sauce" of craigslist's success. Under the explicit terms of the deal, it had the right to compete with craigslist. Newmark and Buckmaster said that if eBay was able to offer customers a better experience, then it should be allowed to do so.

When eBay realized that the two men would never sell craigslist to them, at least in this lifetime, it launched a competing classifieds website at **www.Kijiji.com**. In this process, it used nonpublic information about craigslist that it garnered from its relationship with the company. When the two men found out about this "betrayal," they demanded that eBay sell back its craigslist stock. eBay refused.

Newmark and Buckmaster, in their role as directors of craigslist, responded by prohibiting eBay from buying more shares of craigslist or selling its existing shares to anyone other than themselves. In response, eBay filed suit, alleging that the two men had violated the company's fiduciary rights to eBay as a minority shareholder.

You Be the Judge: *Did Newmark and Buckmaster violate their fiduciary duty to the minority shareholder?*

Argument for Newmark and Buckmaster: eBay has deliberately harmed craigslist by competing against it. And it used confidential information to do so! eBay does not deserve minority protection.

eBay has never grasped that craigslist's success is largely due to its unique corporate culture. The best way to protect shareholders is to prevent eBay (or any other shareholder, for that matter) from undermining all that makes craigslist exceptional. The only way to achieve this goal is to prohibit eBay from buying more stock or selling what they already own to someone who could be even worse.

Argument for eBay: Controlling stockholders are fiduciaries of the minority stockholders and must maximize the value of their investment. Instead, Newmark and Buckmaster have deliberately resisted making a profit. They talk a lot about culture. Offering free ads may be an essential component of a successful online classifieds venture, but it is a sales tactic, not a culture.

Also, Newmark and Buckmaster are majority shareholders. They can keep the company the way it is for their entire lives, if they so desire, as long as they hold onto their own shares. But their goal now is to keep craigslist the same forever, even after their deaths. Essentially, Newmark and Buckmaster regret the deal they made with eBay, and have decided that craigslist should be an eternal testament to their greatness, unchanging forever. That may be their personal preference, but it is not a legitimate corporate purpose.

ENFORCING SHAREHOLDER RIGHTS

Shareholders in serious conflict with management have two different mechanisms for enforcing their rights: a derivative lawsuit or a direct lawsuit.

Derivative Lawsuits

A derivative lawsuit is brought by *shareholders* to remedy a wrong that has been committed against the *corporation*. The suit is brought in the name of the corporation, and all proceeds of the litigation go to the corporation because it was the *company* that was harmed. Any injury to the shareholders was indirect, affecting only the value of their stock. Thus, only the corporation can bring suit in this situation.

Often in a derivative suit, the alleged wrong was committed by a corporate insider – either an officer or director. But the board has to approve the litigation. How can shareholders force the board to sue itself or some other insider? They have to make demand on the board, meaning they have to ask the board to bring suit. Boards have the right to turn down such a demand, and that is exactly what they generally do.

There is only one hope for shareholders: they have the right to file suit on behalf of the corporation without first seeking the approval of the board if *demand would be futile.* **Demand is considered to be futile if the directors violated the duty of care or the duty of loyalty that are required by the business judgment rule.** Showing a violation of the business judgment rule is, in essence, the only successful way to bring a derivative action.

In the *Brehm v. Eisner* case earlier in this chapter, shareholders of Disney wanted to sue the board of directors over Michael Ovitz's severance pay. But the shareholders had no right to sue *on their own behalf* because it was the corporation that had been damaged. Any harm to the shareholders was indirect, through the value of their shares in the company. As a result, shareholders had to bring a derivative action, *on behalf of the corporation*. They made demand on the board. But, of course, the board did not want to sue itself. And as you have seen, the court decided that the decision to pay Michael Ovitz $130 million did not violate the business judgment rule. Thus, the shareholders were denied their attempt to bring a derivative lawsuit.

To take another example, shareholders wanted to sue directors of eBay, Inc. who had personally received millions of dollars of stock options from investment bank Goldman Sachs even as they were hiring Goldman to do work for eBay. The court held that the directors had had a conflict of interest that violated the business judgment rule. Therefore, the shareholders could bring suit against them in the name of the corporation without their permission.[17]

If shareholders are permitted to proceed with their derivative action, all damages go to the corporation; the individual shareholders benefit only to the extent that the settlement causes their stock to rise in value. Litigation is tremendously expensive. How can shareholders afford to sue if they do not receive the damages? A corporation that loses a derivative suit must pay the legal fees of the victorious shareholders. (Losing shareholders are generally not required to pay the corporation's legal fees.) Most derivative lawsuits are brought by lawyers who seek out shareholders, persuade them to sue, and then collect a good part of any settlement. Without this incentive, few shareholders would bring derivative suits, and much corporate wrongdoing would go unchallenged. But this incentive system also means that some meritless suits are brought.

Direct Lawsuits

Shareholders are permitted to sue the corporation directly only if their own rights have been harmed. If, for example, the corporation denies shareholders the right to inspect its books and records or to hold a shareholder meeting, they may sue in their own names and keep any damages awarded. The corporation is not required to pay the shareholders' legal fees; winning shareholders can use part of any damage award for this purpose.

Chapter Conclusion

In corporations, shareholders without management skills complement managers without capital. Although this separation between management and owners makes great economic sense and has contributed significantly to the rise of the American economy, it also creates complex legal issues. How can shareholders ensure that the corporation will operate in their best interest? How can managers make tough decisions without being second-guessed by shareholders? Balancing the interests of managers and shareholders is a complex problem the law has struggled to resolve, without completely satisfying either side.

Exam Review

1. **PROMOTERS** Promoters are personally liable for contracts they sign before the corporation is formed unless the corporation and the third party agree to a novation. (p. 512)

---

[17] *In re eBay, Inc. Shareholder Litigation*, 2004 Del. Ch. LEXIS 4, (Del. 2004).

EXAM Strategy

Question: Ajouelo signed an employment contract with Wilkerson. The contract stated: "Whatever company, partnership, or corporation that Wilkerson may form for the purpose of manufacturing shall succeed Wilkerson and exercise the rights and assume all of Wilkerson's obligations as fixed by this contract." Two months later, Wilkerson formed Auto-Soler Co. Ajouelo entered into a new contract with Auto-Soler providing that the company was liable for Wilkerson's obligations under the old contract. Neither Wilkerson nor the company ever paid Ajouelo. He sued Wilkerson personally. Does Wilkerson have any obligations to Ajouelo?

Strategy: A promoter is not liable for a contract he signed on behalf of a yet-to-be-formed corporation if the third party (in this case, Wilkinson) agrees to a novation. (See the "Result" at the end of this section.)

2. **STATE OF INCORPORATION** Companies generally incorporate in the state in which they will be doing business. However, if they intend to operate in several states, they may choose to incorporate in a jurisdiction known for its favorable corporate laws, such as Delaware. (pp. 512–513)

3. **THE CHARTER** A corporate charter must generally include the company's name, address, registered agent, purpose, and a description of its stock. (pp. 513–515)

4. **PIERCING THE CORPORATE VEIL** A court may, under certain circumstances, pierce the corporate veil and hold shareholders personally liable for the debts of the corporation. (p. 518)

5. **TERMINATION** Termination of a corporation is a three-step process requiring a shareholder vote, the filing of "Articles of Dissolution," and the winding up of the enterprise's business. (p. 519)

6. **FIDUCIARY DUTY** Officers and directors have a fiduciary duty to act in the best interests of the shareholders of the corporation. Therefore, managers must maximize shareholder value. (p. 520)

7. **BUSINESS JUDGMENT RULE** If managers comply with the business judgment rule, a court will not hold them personally liable for any harm their decisions cause the company, nor will the court rescind their decisions. The business judgment rule has two parts: the duty of care and the duty of loyalty. (pp. 520–521)

8. **DUTY OF LOYALTY** Under the duty of loyalty, managers may not enter into an agreement on behalf of their corporation that benefits them personally, unless the disinterested directors or shareholders have first approved it. If the manager does not seek the necessary approval, the business judgment rule no longer applies, and the manager will be liable unless the transaction was entirely fair to the corporation. (p. 521)

9. **CORPORATE OPPORTUNITY** Under the duty of loyalty, managers may not take advantage of an opportunity that rightfully belongs to the corporation. (pp. 521–522)

Question: Vern owned 32 percent of Coast Oyster Co. and served as president and director. Coast was struggling to pay its debts, so Vern suggested that the company sell some of its oyster beds to Keypoint Co. After the sale, officers at Coast discovered that Vern owned 50 percent of Keypoint. They demanded that he give the Keypoint stock to Coast. Did Vern violate his duty to Coast?

Strategy: Here, Vern has violated the duty of loyalty not once, but twice. (See the "Result" at the end of this section.)

10. **DUTY OF CARE** Under the duty of care, managers must make honest, informed decisions that have a rational business purpose. (p. 524)

11. **PROXIES** Virtually all publicly held companies solicit proxies from their shareholders. A proxy authorizes someone else to vote in place of the shareholder at a company meeting. (p. 527)

12. **SHAREHOLDER PROPOSALS** Under certain circumstances, public companies must include shareholder proposals in the proxy statement. (p. 527)

13. **INDEPENDENT DIRECTORS** Under SOX, all members of a board's audit committee must be independent. For companies listed on the NYSE or NASDAQ, independent directors must comprise a majority of the board, and only independent directors can serve on audit, compensation, or nominating committees. (pp. 528–529)

14. **EXECUTIVE COMPENSATION**

    • Under SOX, a company cannot make personal loans to its directors or officers. If a company has to restate its earnings, its CEO and CFO must reimburse the company for any bonus or profits they received from selling company stock within a year of the release of the flawed financials.

    • Dodd-Frank requires shareholder "say on pay." In addition, companies must disclose the CEO's compensation and the median compensation of all other company employees, as well as the ratio of these two numbers.

    • Under the JOBS Act of 2012, the Dodd-Frank rules about say-on-pay and disclosure of executive compensation do not apply to emerging growth companies. (pp. 533–534)

15. **DISSENTERS' RIGHTS** A shareholder of a privately held company who objects to a fundamental change in the corporation can insist that her shares be bought out at fair value. (p. 535)

16. **MINORITY SHAREHOLDERS** Controlling shareholders have a fiduciary duty to minority shareholders. (p. 535)

17. **DERIVATIVE LAWSUITS** A derivative lawsuit is brought by shareholders to remedy a wrong to the corporation. The suit is brought in the name of the corporation, and all proceeds of the litigation go to the corporation. (pp. 536–537)

18. **DIRECT LAWSUITS** Shareholders are permitted to sue the corporation directly only if their own rights have been harmed. (p. 537)

EXAM Strategy

Question: Daniel Cowin was a minority shareholder of a public company that developed real estate in Washington, D.C. He alleged numerous instances of corporate mismanagement, fraud, self-dealing, and breach of fiduciary duty by the board of directors. He sought damages for the diminished value of his stock. Could Cowin bring this suit as a direct action, or must it be a derivative suit?

Strategy: If the wrong was to the corporation, then Cowin must bring a derivative lawsuit. He can only bring a direct action if the harm was to him personally. (See the "Result" at the end of this section.)

1. Result: Wilkerson may have had an ethical obligation to Ajouelo, but not a legal one. The court held that the second contract was a novation, which ended Wilkerson's obligations under the first contract.

9. Result: If the shareholders and directors did not know of Vern's interest in Keypoint, they could not evaluate the contract properly. Vern should have told them. Also, by purchasing stock in Keypoint, Vern took a corporate opportunity. He had to turn over any profits he had earned on the transaction, as well as his stock in Keypoint.

18. Result: The court ruled that the injury had fallen equally on all the shareholders, and therefore Cowin could only bring a derivative suit.

MULTIPLE-CHOICE QUESTIONS

1. **CPA QUESTION** Generally, a corporation's articles of incorporation must include all of the following except:
   (a) the name of the corporation's registered agent.
   (b) the name of each incorporator.
   (c) the number of authorized shares.
   (d) the quorum requirements.

2. **CPA QUESTION** A corporate stockholder is entitled to which of the following rights?
   (a) Elect officers.
   (b) Receive annual dividends.
   (c) Approve dissolution.
   (d) Prevent corporate borrowing.

3. Participating preferred stockholders:

    (a) only receive payment after other preferred shareholders have been paid.

    (b) only receive payment after common shareholders have been paid.

    (c) are treated like both a preferred shareholder and a common shareholder.

    (d) receive all their payments before all other shareholders.

4. If a manager engages in self-dealing, which of the following answers will *NOT* protect him from a finding that he violated the business judgment rule?

    (a) The disinterested members of the board approved the transaction.

    (b) The transaction was of minor importance to the company.

    (c) The disinterested shareholders approved the transaction.

    (d) The transaction was entirely fair to the corporation.

5. The duty of care:

    (a) is not a requirement of the business judgment rule.

    (b) protects directors who make an uninformed decision if it was entirely fair to the company.

    (c) protects a decision that has a rational business purpose, even if the activity was illegal.

    (d) will not protect directors who make a decision that harms the company.

6. The president of R. Hoe & Co., Inc., refused to call a special meeting of the shareholders although 55 percent of them requested it. One purpose of the meeting was to reinstate the former president. Do shareholders have the right to make these two requests?

    (a) Yes to both.

    (b) No to both.

    (c) The shareholders have the right to call a meeting, but not to reinstate the president.

    (d) The shareholders have the right to reinstate the president, but not to call a meeting.

7. Under SOX and Dodd-Frank:

    (a) companies are prohibited from making personal loans to directors and officers.

    (b) if a company restates its earnings, the five top executives must reimburse the company for any income they have received during that period.

    (c) all directors must be independent.

    (d) shareholders have the right to strike down golden parachutes.

ESSAY QUESTIONS

1. Michael incorporated Erin Homes, Inc., to manufacture mobile homes. He issued himself a stock certificate for 100 shares for which he made no payment. He and his wife served as officers and directors of the organization, but, during the eight years of its existence, the corporation held only one meeting. Erin always had its own checking account, and all proceeds from the sales of mobile homes were deposited

there. It filed federal income tax returns each year, using its own federal identification number. John and Thelma paid $17,500 to purchase a mobile home from Erin, but the company never delivered it to them. John and Thelma sued Erin Homes and Michael, individually. Should the court "pierce the corporate veil" and hold Michael personally liable?

2. ***YOU BE THE JUDGE* WRITING PROBLEM** Asher Hyman and Stephen Stahl formed a corporation named Ampersand to produce plays. Both men were employed by the corporation. After producing one play, Stahl decided to write *Phillys Beat,* focusing on the history of rock and roll in Philadelphia. As the play went into production, however, the two men quarreled over Hyman's repeated absences from work and the company's serious financial difficulties. Stahl resigned from Ampersand and formed another corporation to produce the play. Did the opportunity to produce *Phillys Beat* belong to Ampersand? **Argument for Stahl:** Ampersand was formed for the purpose of producing plays, not writing them. When Stahl wrote *Phillys Beat,* he was not competing against Ampersand. **Argument for Hyman:** Ampersand was in the business of producing plays, and it wanted *Phillys Beat.*

3. Angelica is planning to start a home security business in McGehee, Arkansas. She plans to start modestly but hopes to expand her business within 5 years to neighboring towns and, perhaps, within 10 years to neighboring states. Her inclination is to incorporate her business in Delaware. Is her inclination correct?

4. Eve bought defective ball bearings from Saginaw Corp. Alfred was the sole shareholder of the company and also its landlord. After Alfred sold all of Saginaw's assets, he withheld enough money to cover the rent that Saginaw owed him. As a result, Saginaw had no money to pay Eve. Does Eve have a claim against Alfred?

5. Congressional Airlines was highly profitable operating flights between Washington, D.C., and New York City. The directors approved a plan to offer flights from Washington to Boston. This decision turned out to be a major mistake and the airline ultimately went bankrupt. Under what circumstances would shareholders be successful in bringing suit against the directors?

Discussion Questions

1. States compete for lucrative corporate filing fees by passing statutes that favor management. One proposed solution to this problem would be a federal system of corporate registration. Is this a good idea? What are the impediments to such as system?

2. Ford Motor Co. and Facebook have both created dual classes of stock so that the founders can continue to control their company even after it goes public. Should corporate laws permit this? Should some shareholders be more equal than others? If the founders want to control a company, why shouldn't they buy enough regular stock to do so? It is one thing for Mark Zuckerberg to maintain control of Facebook, but should his *grandchildren* also have the right to control the company?

3. **ETHICS** Edgar Bronfman, Jr., dropped out of high school to go to Hollywood and write songs and produce movies. Eventually, he left Hollywood to work in the family business—the Bronfmans owned 36 percent of Seagram Co., a liquor and beverage

conglomerate. Promoted to president of the company at the age of 32, Bronfman seized a second chance to live his dream. Seagram received 70 percent of its earnings from its 24 percent ownership of DuPont Co. Bronfman sold this stock at less than market value to purchase (at an inflated price) 80 percent of MCA, a movie and music company that had been a financial disaster for its prior owners. Some observers thought Bronfman had gone Hollywood; others that he had gone crazy. After the deal was announced, the price of Seagram shares fell 18 percent. Was there anything Seagram shareholders could have done to prevent what to them was not a dream but a nightmare? Apart from legal issues, was Bronfman's decision ethical? What ethical obligations did he owe Seagram's shareholders?

4. Pfizer Inc. paid $2.3 billion to settle civil and criminal charges alleging that it had illegally marketed 13 of its most important drugs. This settlement made history, but not in a good way. It was both the largest criminal fine and the largest settlement of civil health care fraud charges *ever* paid. Shareholders filed a derivative suit against the Pfizer board and top executives. Defendants responded with a motion to dismiss on the grounds that shareholders had not made demand on the board. Is demand necessary?

5. **ETHICS** After a recent annual meeting, Cisco Systems reported the results of the votes on both management and shareholder proposals. The company reported the results of its own proposals as a simple ratio of those in favor divided by the total number of votes cast. But for shareholder proposals, it reported the percentage as a ratio of those in favor divided by all outstanding shares. As a result, it reported the favorable vote for one shareholder proposal as 19 percent when, in fact, 34 percent of the votes cast supported this proposal. Is Cisco behaving ethically?

CHAPTER 21

SECURITIES REGULATION

© Werner H. Kunz/Flickr/Getty Images

In 1926, America was gripped by a fever of stock market speculation. "Playing the market" became a national mania. The most engrossing news on any day's front page was the market. Up and up it soared. The cause of this psychological virus is uncertain, but the focus of the infection was the New York Stock Exchange (NYSE). Between 1926 and 1929, annual volume more than doubled.

Much of this feverish trading was done on margin. Customers put down only 10 or 20 percent of a stock's purchase price and then borrowed the rest from their broker. This easy-payment plan excited the gambling instinct of unwary amateurs and professional speculators alike. By September 1929, the volume of these margin loans was equal to about half the entire public debt of the United States.

On September 4, 1929, stock prices began to soften, and for the next month, they slid gently. Over the weekend of October 19, brokers sent out thousands of margin calls, asking customers to pay down loans that now exceeded the value of their stock. If customers failed to pay, brokers dumped their stock on the market, causing prices to fall further and brokers to make more margin calls. Soon there was a mad scramble of selling as prices plunged in wild disorder. Tens of thousands of investors across the country were wiped out as the value of their stock fell below what they had borrowed to buy it. On Tuesday, October 29, 1929, the speculative boom completely collapsed. That day, 4 million shares were traded, a record that stood for 30 years. From the peak of the bull market in September to the debacle of October 29, over $32 billion of equity value simply vanished from the earth.

The stock market crash spawned the Great Depression—the most pervasive, persistent, and destructive economic crisis the nation has ever faced. Retail trade fell by one-half, automobile production by two-thirds, steel by three-quarters. In 1933, more businesses

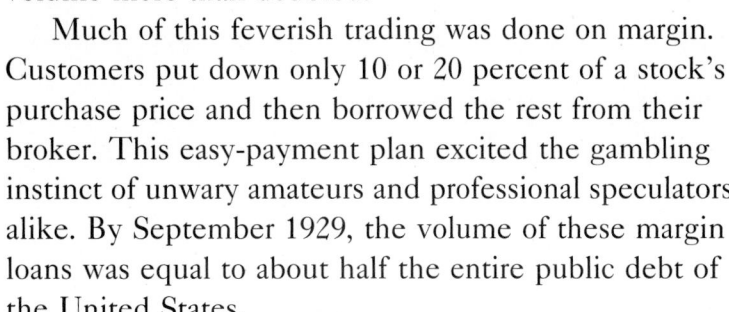

> Soon there was a mad scramble of selling as prices plunged in wild disorder.

failed than in any other year in history. Surviving businesses responded to the crisis by cutting dividends, reducing inventories, laying off workers, slashing wages, and canceling capital investments.

Unemployment statistics were the most poignant of all. In 1932, one in every five people in the labor force was out of a job, more than twice the highest level reached in the most recent U.S. recession. And this was at a time before widespread unemployment benefits. Millions of others were underemployed, working only two or three days a week for wages that could not support a family. Distress cut across all economic and social classes. Bankers, insurance agents, architects, and lawyers joined the throng of unemployed. Articles such as the following were common in newspapers across the land:

New York, Jan. 6, 1933 (AP)—After vainly trying to get a stay of dispossession until Jan. 15 from his apartment in Brooklyn, yesterday, Peter J. Cornell, 48 years old, a former roofing contractor out of work and penniless, fell dead in the arms of his wife. A doctor gave the cause of his death as heart disease, and the police said it had at least partly been caused by the bitter disappointment of a long day's fruitless attempt to prevent himself and his family being put out on the streets.[1]

INTRODUCTION

At the time of the great stock market crash, only state, not federal law, regulated securities (such as stocks and bonds). Congress recognized that the country needed a national securities system if it was to avoid another such catastrophe. In 1933, Congress passed the Securities Act of 1933 (1933 Act) to regulate the issuance of new securities. The next year, it passed the Securities Exchange Act of 1934 (1934 Act) to regulate companies with publicly traded securities. The 1934 Act also established the Securities and Exchange Commission (SEC), the regulatory agency that oversees the securities industry.

The Securities and Exchange Commission

The SEC creates law in three different ways:

- **Rules.** The securities statutes are often little more than general guides. Through its rules, the SEC fills in the crucial details.

- **Releases.** These are informal pronouncements from the SEC on current issues. Releases often operate as two-way communications. When the SEC issues a release to announce a proposed change in the rules, it also asks for comments on the proposal.

- **No-action Letters.** Anyone who is in doubt about whether a particular transaction complies with the securities laws can ask the SEC directly. The response is called a no-action letter because it states that "the staff will recommend that the Commission take no action" if the transaction is done in a specified manner.

In addition to creating laws, the SEC has the power to enforce them. It can bring **cease and desist orders** against those who violate the securities laws, and it can also levy fines or

[1]The material in this section is adapted from Cabell Phillips, *From the Crash to the Blitz* (Toronto: Macmillan, 1969).

confiscate profits from illegal transactions. Those accused of wrongdoing can appeal these sanctions to the courts. The SEC does not have the authority to bring a criminal action; it refers criminal cases to the Justice Department.

What Is a Security?

Both the 1933 and the 1934 Acts regulate securities. The official definition of a security includes stock, bonds, treasury stock, notes, debentures, evidence of indebtedness, certificates of interest or participation in any profit-sharing agreement, and 17 other equivalents. Courts have interpreted this definition to mean that a **security** is any transaction in which the buyer (1) invests money in a common enterprise and (2) expects to earn a profit predominantly from the efforts of others.

Security

Any transaction in which the buyer invests money in a common enterprise and expects to earn a profit predominantly from the efforts of others.

This definition covers investments that are not necessarily *called* securities. For example, they may be called orange trees. W. J. Howey Co. owned large citrus groves in Florida. It sold these trees to investors, most of whom were from out of state and knew nothing about farming. Purchasers were expected to hire someone to take care of their trees—someone like Howey-in the-Hills, Inc., a related company that just happened to be in the service business. Customers were free to hire any service company, but 85 percent of the acreage was covered by service contracts with Howey-in-the-Hills. The court held that Howey was selling a security (no matter how orange or tart), because the purchaser was investing in a common enterprise (the orange grove) expecting to earn a profit from Howey's farm work.

Other courts have interpreted the term "security" to include animal breeding arrangements (chinchillas, silver foxes, or beavers, take your pick); condominium purchases in which the developer promises the owner a certain level of income from rentals; and even investments in whiskey.

SECURITIES ACT OF 1933

The 1933 Act requires that before offering or selling securities, the issuer must register the securities with the SEC unless the securities qualify for an exemption. An **issuer** is the company that sells the stock initially. Registering securities with the SEC in a public offering is a major undertaking, but the 1933 Act exempts some securities and also some particular types of securities transactions from the full-blown registration requirements of a public offering.

Issuer

A company that sells its own stock.

It is also important to remember that **when an issuer registers securities, the SEC does not investigate the quality of the offering.** Permission from the SEC to sell securities does not mean that the company has a good product or will be successful. SEC approval simply means that, on the surface, the company has provided all required information about itself and its major products. The guiding principle of the federal securities laws is that investors can make a reasoned decision on whether to buy or sell securities if they have full and accurate information about a company and the security it is selling. For example, the Green Bay Packers football team sold an offering of stock to finance stadium improvements. The prospectus admitted:

> IT IS VIRTUALLY IMPOSSIBLE that any investor will ever make a profit on the stock purchase. The company will pay no dividends, and the shares cannot be sold.

This does not sound like a stock you want in your retirement fund; on the other hand, the SEC will not prevent Green Bay from selling it, or you from buying it, so long as you understand what the risks are.

Companies must deliver certain documents to investors and also file them with the SEC. Almost all filings with the SEC must be made electronically, using the Electronic Data Gathering, Analysis, and Retrieval (EDGAR) system. Once filed with the SEC, this information is available online (at **http://www.sec.gov**).

General Exemption

Before offering securities for sale, the issuer must determine whether they are exempt from registration under the 1933 Act. Typically, exemptions are based on two factors: the type of security and the type of transaction.

Exempt Securities

The 1933 Act exempts some types of securities from registration because they (1) are inherently low-risk, (2) are regulated by other statutes, or (3) are not really investments. The following securities are exempt from registration:

- **Government securities,** which include any security issued or guaranteed by federal or state government;

- **Bank securities,** which include any security issued or guaranteed by a bank;

- **Short-term notes,** which are high-quality negotiable notes or drafts that are due within nine months of issuance and are not sold to the general public;

- **Nonprofit issues,** which include any security issued by a nonprofit religious, educational, or charitable organization; and

- **Insurance policies and annuity contracts,** which are governed by insurance regulations.

Exempt Transactions

Section 4(2) of the 1933 Act exempts from registration "transactions by an issuer not involving any public offering." These are simple words to define a complex problem. In effect, this language means that an issuer is not required to register securities that are sold in a private offering; that is, an offering with only a few investors or a relatively small amount of money involved. In private offerings, the full-blown disclosure of a public offering is neither necessary nor appropriate. For instance, a group of sophisticated investors who know an industry well do not need full disclosure. Or, if the amount at stake is relatively small, it would not make economic sense for the issuer to incur the heavy expense of a public offering.

There is an important distinction between exempt *securities* and exempt *transactions*. Exempt *securities* are always exempt, throughout their lives, no matter how many times they are sold. Stock sold in an exempt *transaction* is exempt only that one time, not necessarily in any subsequent sale. Suppose that County Bank sells stock to the public. Under the 1933 Act, the bank is never required to register these securities, no matter how many times they are sold. On the other hand, suppose that Tumbleweed, Inc., a quilt maker, sells $5 million worth of stock in a private offering that is exempt from registration. Shamika buys 100 shares of this stock. Seven years later, the company decides to sell stock in a public offering that must be registered. As part of this public offering, Shamika sells her 100 shares. This time, the shares must be registered because they are being sold in a *public offering*.

Most small companies use private, not public, offerings to raise capital. There are four different types of private offerings—intrastate, Regulation D, Regulation A, and Crowd-funding—each with its own set of rules.

Intrastate Offering Exemption

Under SEC Rule 147, an issuer is not required to register securities that are *offered* and *sold* only to residents of the state in which the issuer is incorporated and does business. This exemption was designed to provide local financing for local businesses. To qualify under Rule 147, 80 percent of the issuer's revenues and assets must be in-state, and it must also intend to spend 80 percent of the offering's proceeds in-state. Neither the issuer nor any purchaser can sell the securities outside the state for nine months after the offering.

Safe harbor

A set of requirements that, if met, indicate *automatic* compliance with a law.

Rule 147 is a **safe harbor**—if an issuer totally complies with it, the offering definitely qualifies as intrastate. But even if the issuer does not comply absolutely with the rule, the SEC or the courts may still consider the offering to be intrastate; however, the issuer cannot be sure in advance how the decision will come out. Sonic was a Utah corporation that sold stock to Utah residents. *Seven* months later, the company sold stock to an Illinois company. Although Sonic violated Rule 147 by making the second sale too early, the court held that the company had nonetheless qualified for an intrastate offering because it had not intended, at the time of the original offering, to sell stock outside Utah.[2] A safe harbor is less dangerous, but a voyage outside its boundaries does not necessarily end in disaster.

Regulation D

Regulation D is far and away the most popular route for private offerings. Tens of thousands of these offerings take place each year. Three different types of private offerings can be made under Regulation D (often referred to as Reg D) using Rules 504, 505, and 506. To understand Reg D, there are several important definitions you need to know:

Accredited investors

Institutions (such as banks and insurance companies) or wealthy individuals. To qualify, individuals must have a net worth (not counting their home) of more than $1 million or an annual income of more than $200,000).

- **Accredited investors** are institutions (such as banks and insurance companies) or wealthy individuals. To qualify, individuals must have a net worth (not counting their home) of more than $1 million or an annual income of more than $200,000.

- **Sophisticated investors** Are *unsophisticated* investors people who do not care for opera? No, they are investors who are unable to assess the risks of an offering themselves.

Sophisticated investor

Someone who is able to assess the risk of an offering.

Restricted stock

Securities purchased strictly for investment purposes.

- **Restricted stock** means the securities must be purchased for investment purposes. As a general rule, the buyer cannot resell, either publicly or privately, for one year.

Rule 504   Under this rule (known as the "seed capital" rule), a company may either:

- Sell up to $1 million in restricted stock privately to anyone during each 12-month period; or

- Sell up to $1 million in non-restricted stock with public advertising if the transaction is registered under a state law with appropriate disclosure requirements; or

- Sell up to $1 million in non-restricted stock with public advertising if the transaction is exempted under a state law and sales are limited to accredited investors.

Rule 505   A company may sell up to $5 million of stock during each 12-month period, subject to the following restrictions:

- It may sell to an unlimited number of accredited investors, but to only 35 unaccredited investors.

- It may not advertise the stock publicly.

- It need not provide information to accredited investors but must make disclosure to unaccredited investors, including a certified balance sheet. This requirement is a high hurdle because the disclosure requirements, although less demanding than for a public offering, are nonetheless burdensome.

- Stock purchased under this rule is restricted.

---

[2]*Busch v. Carpenter*, 827 F.2d 653, 1987 U.S. App. LEXIS 11034 (10th Cir. 1987).

Rule 506 A company may sell an unlimited amount of stock, subject to the following restrictions:

- It may sell to an unlimited number of accredited investors, but to only 35 unaccredited investors.

- If it sells to unaccredited investors, it may not advertise the stock publicly. But if it limits sales to accredited investors, it may advertise publicly.

- It need not provide information to accredited investors but must make disclosure to unaccredited investors, including a certified balance sheet.

- Stock purchased under this rule is restricted.

- One further wrinkle: if an unaccredited purchaser is unsophisticated, he must have a **purchaser representative** to help him evaluate the investment.

The following table sets out the menu of choices under Reg D:

	Maximum Value of Securities Sold in a 12-Month Period	Maximum Number of Investors	Disclosure Required:	Is Public Advertising Permitted?	Are Securities Restricted?
Rule 504 Option 1:	$1 million	Unlimited	None	No	Yes
Option 2:	$1 million	Unlimited	Appropriate state disclosure	Yes	No
Option 3:	$1 million, provided offering is exempt under state law	Unlimited accredited investors	None	Yes	No
Rule 505	$5 million	No limit on accredited investors; no more than 35 unaccredited investors	Only for unaccredited investors	No	Yes
Rule 506	No limit	No limit on accredited investors; no more than 35 unaccredited investors, who must either be sophisticated or have a purchaser representative	Only for unaccredited investors	No, if sold to unaccredited investors; yes, if sales are limited to accredited investors	Yes

Regulation A

Although an offering under Regulation A (Reg A) is *called* a private offering, it really is a small public offering. **Reg A permits an issuer to sell up to $50 million of securities *publicly* in any 12-month period.** The issuer must give each purchaser an offering circular that provides the same disclosure required for unaccredited investors under Reg D. Stock sold in a Reg A offering is not restricted.

Crowdfunding

Congress recently passed the **Jumpstart Our Business Startups (JOBS) Act, which permits privately held companies to sell up to $1 million in securities in any 12-month period, provided that they do all of the following:**

- Make a filing with the SEC and provide appropriate disclosure to the purchaser at the time of purchase, and then annually;
- Limit investments as follows:
  - Investors with income or net worth that is less than $100,000 can invest no more than the maximum of $2,000 or 5 percent of their income or net worth.
  - Investors with income or net worth that is equal to or greater than $100,000 can invest no more than the maximum of $100,000 or 10 percent of their income or net worth.[3]
- Sell the securities through an **approved intermediary**, i.e., a broker or a so-called funding portal (e.g., a website) that is registered with the SEC;
- Do not advertise the offering (except to tell investors about the approved intermediary);
- Do not offer investment advice or pay anyone to sell their securities;
- Take steps (as determined by the SEC) to reduce the risk of fraud; and
- Do not resell the stock for one year (except to accredited investors or family members).

The following table compares a public offering, Reg A, Reg D, and Crowdfunding:

	Initial Public Offering	Regulation A	Regulation D	Crowdfunding
Maximum Value of Securities Sold	No limit	$5 million	$1 million, $5 million, or no limit, depending on the rule	$1 million
Public Solicitation of Purchasers	Permitted	Permitted	Permitted under Rule 504 Also permitted under Rule 506 if sales are limited to accredited investors	No
Suitability Requirements for Purchasers	No requirements	No requirements	Must determine if investors are accredited or sophisticated	Investors can only buy stock worth up to a certain percentage of their annual income or net worth
Disclosure Requirements	Elaborate registration statement, audited financials	Offering circular that is less detailed than a registration statement, unaudited financials	Rule 504: may require disclosure under state law Rules 505 and 506: none for accredited investors, the same requirements as Reg A for unaccredited investors	Disclosure is required at time of purchase and annually
Resale of Securities	Permitted	Permitted	Sometimes permitted under Rule 504, otherwise not permitted for one year	Prohibited within one year except to accredited investors and family members

© Cengage Learning 2014

[3]Note that these provisions are inconsistent. An investor whose income is $50,000 but whose net worth is $150,000 falls into both categories.

Direct Public Offerings

Traditionally, a small company either sold stock to people it knew well or hired an investment banker to place the securities with a wider public. But now, instead of going through Wall Street, many companies trying to raise capital for the first time sell stock to the public themselves through a direct public offering (DPO). In a DPO, the issuer typically sells shares to its stakeholders: customers, employees, suppliers, or the community. The issuer makes a DPO offering under Rule 147, Reg D, or Reg A.

Selling stock to the public without the help of an investment bank can be challenging. Thanksgiving Coffee Co. used both modern technology and old-fashioned methods. It advertised on its website but also placed ads on bags of coffee beans, in its catalogs, and in notices to suppliers. The company raised $1.25 million.

The advantages of a DPO are:

- It is much cheaper and faster than a regular public offering done through an underwriter.

- It can be an effective marketing tool—shareholders tend to become even more loyal customers.

- The Internet provides an easy and inexpensive mechanism for reaching potential investors.

The downsides of a DPO are:

- There is a limit to how much a company can raise in this way.

- Company officers typically do not have as much expertise about the securities markets as securities lawyers, investment bankers, and other professionals do.

- Each investor must receive written information about the company. The cost of this disclosure can be prohibitive when dealing with many small investors. Mailing a $10 disclosure document to hundreds of investors who only want to buy $50 worth of stock each may not be an efficient means of raising money.

- Although shareholders are warned that they should view their purchases as long-term investments, some will inevitably want to sell their shares. Setting up a system to permit these trades can be tricky and time-consuming.

EXAM Strategy

Question: As a pitcher for the Cleveland Indians farm team, Randy Newsom had dreams of glory but a paycheck that was a nightmare—$8,000 for the season. Newsom came up with a clever solution: he set up a website that offered fans the opportunity to buy a share of his future. For only $20, the buyer was entitled to .002 percent of his career pay. Any problems with this plan?

Strategy: Remember that even orange trees can be securities.

Result: Newsom was selling securities: buyers were investing in him, hoping that they could earn a profit from his efforts. He had neither registered the securities nor qualified for an exemption, so his plan was illegal.

Public Offerings

When a company wishes to raise significant amounts of capital from a large number of people, it has to do a public offering. A company's first public sale of securities is called an **initial public offering** or an **IPO**. Because companies are now more successful in raising money privately, the number of IPOs has declined from an annual average of around 500 in the 1990s to a current average of about 130. Any public sale of securities after the IPO is called a **secondary offering**. This is the process an issuer follows for either type of sale:

1. **Underwriting.** For a public offering, companies hire an investment bank to serve as underwriter. In a **firm commitment underwriting**, the underwriter buys the stock from the issuer and resells it to the public. The underwriter bears the risk that the stock may sell at a lower price than expected. In a **best efforts underwriting**, the underwriter does not buy the stock but instead acts as the company's agent in selling it. If the stock sells at a low price, the company, not the underwriter, is the loser.

2. **Registration Statement.** The **registration statement** has two purposes: to notify the SEC that a sale of securities is pending and to disclose information to prospective purchasers. The registration statement typically must include detailed information about the issuer and its business, a description of the stock, the proposed use of the proceeds from the offering, and two years of audited balance sheets and income statements. Preparing a registration statement is neither quick nor inexpensive— a typical IPO recently cost $8 million.

3. **Prospectus.** Typically, buyers never see the entire registration statement; they are given the **prospectus** instead. (The prospectus is included in the registration statement that is sent to the SEC.) The prospectus includes the important disclosures about the company, while the registration statement includes additional information that is of interest to the SEC but not to the typical investor, such as the names and addresses of the lawyers for the issuer and underwriter. All investors must receive a copy of the prospectus before purchasing the stock.

4. **Sales Effort.** Even before the final registration statement and prospectus are completed, the investment bank begins its sales effort. It cannot actually make sales during this period, but it can solicit offers. The SEC closely regulates an issuer's sales effort to make sure that no one is unduly hyping the stock. For example, the SEC delayed an offering of stock by Google Inc. after *Playboy* magazine published an interview with its founders.

5. **Going Effective.** Once its review of the preliminary registration statement is complete, the SEC sends the issuer a **comment letter**, listing changes that must be made to the registration statement. An issuer almost always amends the registration statement at least once, and sometimes more than once. Remember that the SEC does not assess the value of the stock or the merit of the investment. Its role is to ensure that the company has disclosed enough to enable investors to make an informed decision. After the SEC has approved a final registration statement (which includes, of course, the final prospectus), the issuer and underwriter agree on a price for the stock and the date to **go effective;** that is, to begin the sale.

In the following case, eToys sued its underwriter, Goldman Sachs, for underpricing its stock offering. Should Goldman be liable? You be the judge.

Initial public offering (IPO)
A company's first public sale of securities.

Secondary offering
Any public sale of securities by a company after the initial public offering.

Firm commitment underwriting
The underwriter buys stock from the issuer and sells it to the public.

Best efforts underwriting
The underwriter does not buy the stock from the issuer but instead acts as the issuer's agent in selling the securities.

You be the Judge

Facts: Goldman Sachs was the lead underwriter for eToys' initial public offering. In the IPO, eToys agreed to sell 8,320,000 shares of its stock to Goldman at a price of $18.65 per share, for resale to the public at $20. (Goldman had the option to buy an additional 1,248,000 shares at the same price.) The bank's potential profit was $1.35 per share, for a maximum of $12,916,800.

On the first day of the offering, the price of eToys' stock rose as high as $85 and closed at $76.56. Within a year, however, the price had fallen below $20. eToys ultimately filed for bankruptcy protection.

In its lawsuit, eToys alleged that Goldman made side deals with other clients, allowing them to purchase shares in eToys' offering in exchange for kickbacks to Goldman of a portion of their profits on the stock. This arrangement would have created an incentive for Goldman to underprice the stock. eToys also alleged that Goldman had a fiduciary duty to eToys that it violated by not disclosing this conflict of interest.

Goldman filed a motion to dismiss, denying that it had a fiduciary relationship to eToys.

You Be the Judge: *Did Goldman have a fiduciary duty to eToys? Did it violate this duty?*

Argument for eToys: A fiduciary relationship exists between two parties if one of them is under a duty to act for or to give advice for the benefit of the other. eToys hired Goldman for its expertise and paid handsomely for its advice about many aspects of going public. The company would

EBC I, INC. V. GOLDMAN SACHS & CO.
2005 N.Y. LEXIS 1178
Court of Appeals of New York, 2005

never have relied on this advice had it known about the side deals with other clients—deals that could harm eToys.

eToys trusted Goldman, the bank betrayed that trust, and eToys suffered an enormous financial penalty as a result.

Argument for Goldman Sachs: This is a simple case: eToys sold stock, Goldman bought it. Goldman negotiated the best price it could. If eToys was unhappy with this deal, it had no one to blame but itself.

If eToys expected Goldman to act as a fiduciary, the agreement should have said so explicitly. The company always knew that its interests were different from Goldman's. eToys sought the highest price; Goldman had to ensure that it could resell the shares at a profit. The lower the price to eToys, the lower the risk to Goldman. Goldman took a substantial risk buying this stock, and in this case, the risk paid off. That does not always happen.

eToys was a sophisticated company with sophisticated advisors. Its stockholders included well-known venture-capital firms. Its largest single stockholder, Idealab, was an incubator for successful technology companies. eToys' law firm—the Venture Law Group, P.C.—specialized in representing high-tech companies. During one year, this law firm was fourth on the list of firms that handled the most initial public offerings for technology companies.

In short, the offering price was not "set" by Goldman; it was negotiated by two sophisticated parties.

Sales of Restricted Securities

The SEC wants to ensure that the public sale of stock takes place in an orderly manner. Therefore, it imposes some restrictions on the sale of stock even after a company has gone public. **Rule 144 limits the resale of two types of securities issued by public companies:** *control securities* and *restricted securities*.

Any stock purchased from the issuer in a private offering (such as Reg D) is a **restricted security**. If the issuer is private (that is, not subject to the reporting requirements of the 1934 Act), these restricted securities cannot be sold for one year. But, once the company goes public, the holding period on restricted securities shrinks to six months from the date of purchase. After six months, these restricted securities can be sold freely unless they are also control securities, in which case those restrictions still apply.

A **control security** is stock held by any shareholder who owns more than 10 percent of a class of stock or by any officer or director of the company. In any three-month period, such an insider can sell only an amount of stock equal to the average weekly trading volume for

Restricted Security
Stock purchased in a private offering.

Control security
Stock held by any shareholder who owns more than 10 percent of a class of stock or by any officer or director of the company.

the prior four weeks or 1 percent of the number of shares outstanding, whichever is greater. The purpose of this rule is to protect other investors from precipitous declines in stock price. If company insiders sold all of their stock in one day, the price would plunge, causing losses to the other shareholders.

EXAM Strategy

Question: You are the CEO of Calmm.com, Inc. The company's board has decided to sell $2 million in stock. You have 40 wealthy friends who would like to invest a total of $1 million. What would be the best way to raise these funds? Would a public offering work?

Strategy: Review the options for both private and public offerings.

Result: A public offering is not a good idea—it would cost millions. Rule 504 is not suitable because it would limit you to raising only $1 million. Under Rule 505, you could sell to all your wealthy friends (if they are accredited investors), and as many as 35 unaccredited investors. Rule 506 is more complicated (and therefore more expensive), so Rule 505 would be a better choice.

Liability under the 1933 Act
Liability for Selling Unregistered Securities

Section 12(a)(1) of the 1933 Act imposes liability on anyone who sells a security that is neither registered nor exempt. The purchaser of the security can demand rescission—a return of his money (plus interest) in exchange for the stock—or, if he no longer owns the stock, he can ask for damages.

Fraud

Under Section 12(a)(2) of the 1933 Act, **the seller of a security is liable for making any material misstatement or omission, either oral or written, in connection with the offer or sale of a security.** This provision applies to offerings that are *public* or *private* and *registered* or *unregistered* if there is some use of interstate commerce, such as mail, telephone (even for an *intra*state call), or check (that clears). It is difficult to imagine a securities transaction that does not involve interstate commerce. Both the SEC and any purchasers of the stock can sue the issuer.

Criminal Liability

Under Section 24 of the 1933 Act, the Justice Department can prosecute anyone who willfully violates the Act.

Liability for the Registration Statement

Section 11 of the 1933 Act establishes the penalties for any errors in a registration statement. **If a final registration statement contains a material misstatement or omission, the purchaser of the security can recover from everyone who signed the registration statement.** This list of signatories includes the issuer, its directors, and chief officers; experts (such as auditors, engineers, or lawyers); and the underwriters. Everyone who signed the registration statement is jointly and severally liable for any error, except the experts, who are liable only for misstatements in the part of the registration statement for which they were responsible.[4] Thus, an auditor is liable for misstatements in the financials but not, say, for omissions about the CEO's criminal past.

Damages   To prevail under Section 11, the plaintiff need only prove that there was a material misstatement or omission and that she lost money. **Material** means important enough to affect an investor's decision. The plaintiff does not have to prove that she relied on (or even *read*) the registration statement, that she bought the stock from the issuer, or that the defendant was negligent. The plaintiff can recover the difference between what she paid for the stock and its value on the date of the lawsuit.

Suppose that Pet Detective, Inc., does an IPO at $10 per share. A week later, Ace Investora buys 1,000 shares at $10 each. He knows nothing about the company, but he likes the name. This stock turns out to be a dog—Pet Detective has only 2 agencies, not the 200 stated in the registration statement. After Investora sells the stock at 10 cents a share, he can sue under Section 11 for $9,900.

Due Diligence   All is not hopeless, however, for those who have signed the registration statement. If the statement contains a material misstatement or omission, the company is liable and has no defense. But everyone else who signed the registration statement can avoid liability by showing that he investigated the registration statement as thoroughly as a "prudent person in the management of his own property." This investigation is called **due diligence**. Its importance cannot be overstated. The SEC does not conduct its own investigation to ensure that the registration statement is accurate. It can only ensure that, on the surface, the issuer has supplied all relevant information. If an issuer chooses to lie, the SEC has no way of knowing. It is the job of the underwriters to check the accuracy of the filing. Thus, underwriters typically spend weeks visiting the company, reading all its corporate documents (including minutes back to the beginning), and calling its bankers, customers, suppliers, and competitors to ensure that the registration statement is accurate and no skeletons have been overlooked.

When Section 11 was first passed, investment bankers were outraged. Some predicted that this liability provision would cause capital in America to dry up, that grass would grow on Wall Street. In fact, the first case under Section 11 arose 35 years and 27,000 registration statements later. In this case—*Escott v. Barchris Construction Corp.*—the registration statement was profoundly flawed.[5] The underwriter failed to read the minutes of the executive committee meetings that revealed the company to be in serious financial condition. Much of the company's alleged backlog of orders was from nonexistent corporations. Proceeds of the offering were earmarked to pay off debt, not to buy new plant and equipment as the registration statement had indicated. The company's directors, underwriters, and underwriters' counsel were held liable.

SECURITIES EXCHANGE ACT OF 1934

Most buyers do not purchase new securities from the issuer in an initial public offering. Rather they buy stock that is publicly traded in the open market. This stock is, in a sense, *secondhand* because others, perhaps many others, have already owned it. The purpose of the 1934 Act is to maintain the integrity of this secondary market.

Material
Important enough to affect an investor's decision.

Due diligence
An investigation of the registration statement by someone who signs it.

---

[4]Joint and several liability means that all members of a group are liable. The plaintiff can sue them as a group or anyone of them individually for the full amount owing. The plaintiff cannot recover more than the total amount of the damages owing, however.
[5]283 F. Supp. 643, 1968 U.S. Dist. LEXIS 3853 (S.D.N.Y. 1968).

General Provisions of the 1934 Act
Registration Requirements

As we have seen, the 1933 Act requires an issuer to register securities before selling them. That is a onetime effort for the company. The 1933 Act does not require the issuer to provide shareholders with any additional information in later years. Suppose that an automobile company registered and sold securities for the first time in 1946. Purchasers of those securities knew a lot about the firm—in 1946. But how can current investors assess the company? The 1934 Act plugs this hole. It requires issuers with publicly traded stock to continue to make information available to the public so that current—and potential—shareholders can evaluate the company. It is often said that the 1933 Act registers securities and the 1934 Act registers companies.

Under the 1934 Act, an issuer must register with the SEC if (1) it completes a public offering under the 1933 Act, or (2) its securities are traded on a national exchange (such as the NYSE), or (3) it has at least 2,000 shareholders (with a maximum of 500 unaccredited investors) *and* total assets that exceed $10 million. Note, however, that shareholders who acquire stock through an employee compensation plan or through the crowdfunding exemption do not count toward these limits. A company can *de*register if its number of shareholders falls below 300 or if it has fewer than 500 shareholders and assets of less than $10 million.

Disclosure Requirements—Section 13

Reporting company
A company registered under the 1934 Act.

Like the 1933 Act, the 1934 Act focuses on disclosure. The difference is that the 1933 Act requires onetime disclosure when a company sells stock to the public. The 1934 Act requires *ongoing*, regular disclosure for any company with a class of stock that is publicly traded. Companies that register under the 1934 Act are called **reporting companies**. **Section 13 requires reporting companies to file the following documents:**

- An initial, detailed information statement when the company first registers (similar to the filing required under the 1933 Act);

- Annual reports on Form 10-K, containing audited financial statements, a detailed analysis of the company's performance, and information about officers and directors;

- Quarterly reports on Form 10-Q, which are less detailed than 10-Ks and contain unaudited financials; and

- Form 8-K to report any significant developments, such as bankruptcy, a change in control, a purchase or sale of significant assets, the resignation of a director as a result of a policy dispute, a change in fiscal year, or a change in auditing firms.

In response to corporate scandals, Congress passed the Sarbanes-Oxley Act of 2002 (SOX). It requires each company's CEO and CFO to certify that:

- The information in the quarterly and annual reports is true;

- The company has effective internal controls; and

- The officers have informed the company's audit committee and its auditors of any concerns that they have about the internal control system.

A reporting company must send its annual report to shareholders. All annual reports and other 1934 Act filings are available on the SEC website.

Proxy Requirements—Section 14

Most shareholders of public corporations do not attend annual shareholder meetings. Instead, the company solicits their proxies, permitting them to vote by mail rather than in person. If a company solicits proxies, it is required to supply shareholders with a proxy statement that is intended to give them enough information to make informed decisions about the company. The proxy statement contains detailed information about officers and directors, including their experience, relationship with the company, and compensation. (The annual report provides financial information.) Proxy statements must also be filed with the SEC. Proxy contests and shareholder proposals are discussed in Chapter 20.

Under SEC rules, a company is not *required* to solicit proxies from shareholders, but if it does not, it is unlikely to obtain the quorum needed for the meeting to be held. In any event, a company cannot avoid its responsibility to inform shareholders. Whether or not it solicits proxies, it is still required to furnish shareholders with an information statement that contains essentially the same material as a proxy statement.

Short-Swing Trading—Section 16

During congressional hearings after the 1929 stock market crash, witnesses testified that insiders had manipulated the stock market. For example, insiders would buy a large block of stock, announce a substantial dividend, and then divest before the dividend was reduced. Section 16 was designed to prevent corporate insiders—officers, directors, and shareholders who own more than 10 percent of the company—from taking unfair advantage of privileged information to manipulate the market.

Section 16 takes a two-pronged approach:

- First, insiders must *report* their trades within two business days. This report must also reveal their total stock holdings in the company. The filings must be made to the SEC electronically, and both the SEC and the company are required to post them on their respective websites within one business day after the report is made.

- Second, insiders must *turn over to the corporation* any profits they make from the purchase and sale or sale and purchase of company securities in a six-month period. Section 16 is a strict liability provision. It applies even if the insider did not actually take advantage of secret information or try to manipulate the market; if she bought and sold or sold and bought stock in a six-month period, she is liable.

Suppose that Manuela buys 20,000 shares of her company's stock in June at $10 a share. In September, her (uninsured) winter house in Florida is destroyed by a hurricane. To raise money for rebuilding, she sells the stock at $12 per share, making a profit of $40,000. But she has violated Section 16 and must turn over the profit to her company.

Liability under the 1934 Act
Section 18

Under Section 18, anyone who makes a false or misleading statement in a filing under the 1934 Act is liable to buyers or sellers who (1) acted in reliance on the statement and (2) can prove that the price at which they bought or sold was affected by the false filing. Section 18 applies to all filings under the 1934 Act, including proxy statements and annual reports. For example, a court ruled that plaintiffs could bring suit against the directors and officers of a pharmaceutical company that manufactured a contraceptive device called the Dalkon Shield. In its annual report filed with the SEC, the company emphasized the safety, reliability, and efficiency of the Dalkon Shield, failing to reveal that in fact, there was substantial evidence that the device was less effective and more harmful than it had disclosed. Indeed, seven women had died from using the Dalkon Shield, and many others were rendered infertile.[6]

Section 10(b)

Section 18 applies only to *filings* under the 1934 Act. What happens if a company executive makes a false public *statement* about the company, or writes an untrue statement somewhere other than in a filing? In one case, a corporate officer bought up shares of his company's

---

[6]*Ross v. A. H. Robins Co.*, 607 F.2d 545, (2d Cir, 1979).

stock even as he made pessimistic public statements about the company. That is the type of behavior that Section 10(b) is designed to prevent. **Section 10(b) prohibits fraud in connection with the purchase and sale of any security, whether or not the security is registered under the 1934 Act.**

The SEC adopted Rule 10b-5 to clarify Section 10(b), but the rule is still a relatively vague, catch-all provision designed to fill any holes left by other sections of the securities laws.[7] Interpretation has largely been left to the courts, which generally have interpreted Rule 10b-5 as follows:

- **A misstatement or omission of a material fact.** Anyone who fails to disclose material information, or makes incomplete or inaccurate disclosure, is liable.

- **Material.** This term has the same meaning as under the 1933 Act: important enough to affect an investor's decision. For example, a company repeatedly and falsely denied that it was involved in merger negotiations. It was liable even though the negotiations had only been in a preliminary stage.[8]

- **Scienter.** This is a legal term meaning *willfully, knowingly, or recklessly*. To be liable under Rule 10b-5, the defendant must have (1) known (or been reckless in not knowing) that the statement was inaccurate and (2) intended for the plaintiff to rely on the statement. Negligence is not enough. A group of shareholders sued the accounting firm Ernst & Ernst because it had failed to discover, during the course of an audit, that a company's chief executive was stealing funds. According to the shareholders, the auditors should have discovered that the executive refused to allow anyone else to open his mail and, therefore, should have been suspicious of wrongdoing. The court found Ernst & Ernst not liable. Although it may have been negligent, it had not *intentionally* or even *recklessly* facilitated fraud.[9]

- **Purchase or sale.** Rule 10b-5 covers both buyers and sellers. It does not include, however, someone who failed to purchase stock because of a material misstatement. In the case of the company executive who spread negative rumors about his company while he bought stock, those who sold because of his false rumors could sue under Rule 10b-5, but not those who simply failed to buy.

- **Reliance.** To bring suit, a plaintiff must show that she relied on the misstatement or omission. In the case of open-market trades, reliance is difficult to prove, so the courts are willing to assume it.

- **Economic loss.** The plaintiffs must suffer a loss in the value of their investment. For example, a couple sold their pharmaceutical business to another company in exchange for stock of the purchaser. Some time later, they discovered that the purchaser had lied about its financial condition. However, the court held that the couple could not recover because by the time they sold their stock in the purchaser, it was worth substantially more than when they acquired it. Thus, they had not suffered an economic loss.

- **Loss causation.** The economic loss must have been caused by the misstatement of a material fact. For example, a group of investors bought stock in Dura Pharmaceuticals. They alleged that, when making the purchase, they had relied on

---

[7]Rule 10b-5 prohibits any person, in connection with a purchase or sale of any security, from (1) employing any device, scheme, or artifice to defraud; (2) making any untrue statement of a material fact or omitting to state a material fact necessary in order to make the statements made, in light of the circumstances under which they were made, not misleading; or (3) engaging in any act, practice, or course of business that operates or would operate as a fraud or deceit upon any person.
[8]*Basic Inc. v. Levinson*, 485 U.S. 224, 108 S. Ct. 978, 1988 U.S. LEXIS 1197 (1988).
[9]*Ernst & Ernst v. Hochfelder*, 425 U.S. 185, 96 S. Ct. 1375, 1976 U.S. LEXIS 2 (1976).

statements by company executives that (1) its drug sales would be profitable and (2) the Food and Drug Administration would approve its new asthma spray device. Neither of these statements turned out to be true, and the company's stock price fell. Plaintiffs argued that, if it had not been for the misrepresentations, the stock price would have been lower when they purchased stock and then would not have fallen as far (or at all) when the truth came out.

The Supreme Court ruled, however, that the plaintiffs could not recover because there was no proof that the misstatements had *caused* the decline in stock price. The price drop could have been the result of other factors, such as changes in the industry or in the economy as a whole.[10]

Both the 1933 Act and the 1934 Act specify that misstatements and omissions create liability only if they are material. In the following case, a unanimous Supreme Court provided guidance on what "material" means.

MATRIXX INITIATIVES, INC. v. SIRACUSANO

2011 U.S. LEXIS 2416
Supreme Court of the United States, 2011

Facts: Zicam Cold Remedy was a nasal spray (or gel) that accounted for 70 percent of Matrixx's sales revenue. Its active ingredient was zinc gluconate. Matrixx began receiving reports that some Zicam users had developed anosmia (that is, they had lost their sense of smell). The company learned for the first time that some studies had linked the use of zinc sulfate to the loss of smell.

Matrixx then found out that two doctors were planning to make a presentation at a conference about patients who had developed anosmia after Zicam use. Matrixx sent them a letter warning them that they did not have permission to use the name of Matrixx or its products. The doctors deleted references to Zicam.

Nine people filed suit against Matrixx, alleging that Zicam had damaged their sense of smell. Matrixx then issued statements that Zicam was poised for growth and that revenues would increase by more than 80 percent. In its 10-Q filing with the SEC, Matrixx warned of the potential "material adverse effect" that could result from product liability claims, "whether or not proven to be valid." It did not disclose, however, that plaintiffs had already sued Matrixx.

After the Food and Drug Administration (FDA) announced that it was investigating Zicam, Matrixx's stock price fell. Matrixx issued a press release stating:

Matrixx believes statements alleging that Zicam products caused anosmia (loss of smell) are completely unfounded and misleading. In no clinical trial of zinc gluconate gel products has there been a single report of lost or diminished olfactory function (sense of smell). A multitude of environmental and biologic influences are known to affect the sense of smell. Chief among them is the common cold. As a result, the population most likely to use cold remedy products is already at increased risk of developing anosmia.

The day after this press release, Matrixx stock price bounced back. Shortly thereafter, however, the TV show *Good Morning America* reported that more than a dozen patients had suffered from anosmia after using Zicam and that some had filed lawsuits against Matrixx. The company's stock price plummeted.

A group of shareholders filed suit, alleging that Matrixx had violated Section 10(b) and Rule 10b-5. The trial court granted Matrixx's motion to dismiss on the grounds that, without a statistical correlation between the use of Zicam and anosmia, the reported incidents were not material. The Court of Appeals reversed. The Supreme Court granted *certiorari*.

Issues: *Was Matrixx required to disclose allegations of harm for which there was not statistical correlation? Did Matrixx violate §10(b) and Rule 10b-5?*

Excerpts from Justice Sotomayor's Decision, writing for a unanimous court: To prevail on a §10(b) claim, a plaintiff must show that the defendant made a statement

---

[10]*Dura Pharmaceuticals, Inc. v. Broudo*, 125 S. Ct. 1627, 2005 U.S. LEXIS 3478 (2005).

that was *misleading* as to a *material* fact. [T]his materiality requirement is satisfied when there is a substantial likelihood that the disclosure of the omitted fact would have been viewed by the reasonable investor as having significantly altered the "total mix" of information made available.

[M]edical researchers consider multiple factors in assessing causation. A lack of statistically significant data does not mean that medical experts have no reliable basis for inferring a causal link between a drug and adverse events. Not only does the FDA rely on a wide range of evidence of causation, it sometimes acts on the basis of evidence that suggests, but does not prove, causation. For example, the FDA requires manufacturers of over-the-counter drugs to revise their labeling to include a warning as soon as there is reasonable evidence of an association of a serious hazard with a drug; a causal relationship need not have been proved.

Given that medical professionals and regulators act on the basis of evidence of causation that is not statistically significant, it stands to reason that in certain cases, reasonable investors would as well. As a result, assessing the materiality of adverse event reports is a fact-specific inquiry that requires consideration of the source, content, and context of the reports.

Application of [the] "total mix" standard does not mean that pharmaceutical manufacturers must disclose all reports of adverse events. Adverse event reports are daily events in the pharmaceutical industry. The fact that a user of a drug has suffered an adverse event, standing alone, does not mean that the drug caused that event. Something more is needed, but that something more is not limited to statistical significance.

Moreover, it bears emphasis that §10(b) and Rule 10b-5(b) do not create an affirmative duty to disclose any and all material information. Disclosure is required under these provisions only when necessary to make statements made, in the light of the circumstances under which they were made, not misleading. Even with respect to information that a reasonable investor might consider material, companies can control what they have to disclose under these provisions by controlling what they say to the market.

[W]e conclude that respondents have adequately pleaded materiality. Matrixx received information that plausibly indicated a reliable causal link between Zicam and anosmia. Importantly, Zicam Cold Remedy accounted for 70 percent of Matrixx's sales.

It is substantially likely that a reasonable investor would have viewed this information as having significantly altered the "total mix" of information made available. Matrixx told the market that revenues were going to rise 50 and then 80 percent. [H]owever, Matrixx had information indicating a significant risk to its leading revenue-generating product.

For the reasons stated, the judgment of the Court of Appeals for the Ninth Circuit is

Affirmed.

Ethics Matrixx learned that its products were potentially causing a loss of smell, which is no minor matter. People with anosmia cannot properly taste food, so they often lose interest in eating, which can lead to malnutrition and depression. Was it ethical for the company to prohibit doctors from presenting information about Zicam at a conference? Did the company have an ethical obligation to alert the public to this issue? What about its obligation to its shareholders?

In the case of large frauds, where many people lose lots of money, the company at the heart of the wrongdoing is often bankrupt, so plaintiffs scramble to find other deep pockets from which to recover their losses. One approach they have tried is to go after those who did not commit the fraud themselves, but who aided and abetted it. Section 10 (b) is often their weapon of choice. Generally, however, the Supreme Court is unsympathetic to this approach. Although in the following case, the Supreme Court was divided 5-3, with one justice not taking part.

STONERIDGE INVESTMENT PARTNERS, LLC V. SCIENTIFIC-ATLANTA, INC.

28 S. Ct. 761; 2008 U.S. LEXIS 1091
Supreme Court of the United States, 2008

Facts: Charter Communications, Inc., a cable operator, engaged in a variety of fraudulent practices to pump up its financial statements so they would meet Wall Street expectations. When these efforts fell short, Charter approached two of its suppliers—Scientific-Atlanta and Motorola—for help in furthering the fraud. These two companies supplied Charter with the digital cable converter (set-top) boxes that Charter furnished its customers. Charter arranged to overpay the suppliers $20 for each set-top box it purchased, with the understanding that they would return the overpayment by purchasing advertising from Charter. These transactions had no economic purpose other than inflating Charter's revenue and operating cash flow numbers by $17 million. They violated generally accepted accounting principles. The plan was successful—Charter did manage to fool its auditors.

The inflated numbers were included in financial statements filed with the SEC and reported to the public. Purchasers of Charter stock sued the two suppliers, alleging that they had violated Section 10(b) and Rule 10b-5. The District Court granted defendants' motion to dismiss. The U.S. Court of Appeals for the Eighth Circuit affirmed. The Supreme Court granted *certiorari*.

Issue: *Is someone who aids and abets a violation of Section 10(b) liable under the statute?*

Excerpts from Justice Kennedy's Decision: Reliance by the plaintiff upon the defendant's deceptive acts is an essential element of the §10(b) cause of action. [In this case, no] member of the investing public had knowledge, either actual or presumed, of [defendants'] deceptive acts during the relevant times. Petitioner, as a result, cannot show reliance upon any of [defendants'] actions except in an indirect chain that we find too remote for liability.

It is true that a dynamic, free economy presupposes a high degree of integrity in all of its parts. Were the implied cause of action to be extended to the practices described here, however, there would be a risk that the federal power would be used to invite litigation beyond the immediate sphere of securities litigation and in areas already governed by functioning and effective state-law guarantees. Section 10(b) does not incorporate common-law fraud into federal law.

[E]xtensive discovery and the potential for uncertainty and disruption in a lawsuit allow plaintiffs with weak claims to extort settlements from innocent companies. Adoption of petitioner's approach would expose a new class of defendants to these risks. [C]ontracting parties might find it necessary to protect against these threats, raising the costs of doing business. Overseas firms with no other exposure to our securities laws could be deterred from doing business here. This, in turn, may raise the cost of being a publicly traded company under our law and shift securities offerings away from domestic capital markets.

Here respondents were acting in concert with Charter in the ordinary course as suppliers, not in the investment sphere. Charter was free to do as it chose in preparing its books, conferring with its auditor, and preparing and then issuing its financial statements. In these circumstances, the investors cannot be said to have relied upon any of [defendants'] deceptive acts in the decision to purchase or sell securities; and as the requisite reliance cannot be shown, respondents have no liability to petitioner. The judgment of the Court of Appeals is affirmed.

Devil's Advocate If the suppliers had not taken part in Charter's scheme, the company would not have been able to release fake numbers or fool its auditors. The suppliers knew exactly what they were doing and what the result would be. The court argues that holding the suppliers liable would harm domestic capital markets. But rampant fraud would also harm capital markets. The Court refers to this scheme as "unconventional." That is a nice word for deliberate, intentional fraud.

The Private Securities Litigation Reform Act of 1995

The Private Securities Litigation Reform Act modifies many existing laws, including the 1934 Act. Its amendment to the 1934 Act was intended to discourage fraud suits by shareholders. Under this amendment, companies are liable to shareholders for so-called forward-looking statements (that is, financial projections or statements about future plans) *only if* (1) the company fails to include a warning that the predictions may not come to pass, *and* (2) the shareholders can show that company executives knew the predictions were false. Suppose a pharmaceutical company predicts that a new drug will generate billions in sales, but two years later, the drug is a total failure. Before this statute, shareholders would have had a strong case, but now the company would not be liable as long as it had disclosed, at the time of making the prediction, reasons why the drug might not be a success. Even if the company failed to mention these reasons, it would be liable only if executives knew the prediction to be false when they made it.

> **The SEC has dramatically increased its number of insider trading prosecutions.**

Insider Trading

The case began with a text message buried deep in a set of documents that had been provided to the SEC as part of another investigation: Don't buy Polycom's stock "till I get guidance; want to make sure guidance OK," wrote Roomy Khan. Using wiretaps, informants, recordings, and other investigative techniques more commonly associated with organized crime and narcotics cases than Wall Street, the SEC went after Khan, convincing her to provide evidence against her network of contacts. The SEC ended up bringing charges against more than 20 people, including employees of Intel, IBM, and McKinsey. Many of them went to prison. Its biggest catch was Raj Rajaratnam, the billionaire head of a hedge fund. He was sentenced to 11 years in prison and ordered to turn over $63.8 million to the government.

The SEC has dramatically increased its number of insider trading prosecutions. Regulators in other large financial markets, such as London and Hong Kong, are also taking insider trading more seriously.

Insider trading is a crime punishable by fines and imprisonment. So now you know that insider trading is dangerous, but exactly what is it? The courts include insider trading as a category of securities fraud under the general provisions of Section 10(b) and Rule 10b-5. Although the courts are nominally *interpreting* the rule, in fact, they are more or less fashioning this crime out of whole cloth. Insider trading has been described as "the judicial oak that has grown from little more than a legislative acorn."

The SEC has argued many times that anyone in possession of nonpublic material information must disclose it or refrain from trading. But the Supreme Court has consistently rejected that view. Instead of the SEC's simple proposal, the courts have instead provided a much more complex set of rules:

Fiduciary Duty

Any corporate insider who trades while in possession of nonpublic material information in violation of his fiduciary duty to his company is liable under Rule 10b-5. Corporate insiders include board members, major shareholders, employees, and so-called temporary insiders, such as lawyers and investment bankers who are doing deals for the company. Examples:

- If the director of research for MediSearch, Inc. knows that the company will shortly announce a major breakthrough in the treatment of AIDS and then buys stock in the company before the information is public, she has violated Rule 10b-5. So has a lawyer who works at the firm that is patenting MediSearch's new discovery if he buys stock before the information is public.

- Suppose, however, that while looking in a dumpster, Harry finds correspondence that reveals MediSearch's new discovery. He then buys MediSearch stock that promptly quadruples in value. Harry will be dining at the Ritz, not in federal prison, because he has no fiduciary duty to MediSearch.

Misappropriation

The basic insider trading rule involves people with a *direct* relationship to the company whose stock was traded. But some people with a more remote connection can also be liable. **Anyone (1) with material, non-public information, (2) who breaches a fiduciary duty to the *source of the information* (3) by revealing or trading on it, is liable for insider trading.** A violation occurs even if the source was not the company whose stock was traded. In short, if you trade on material, secret information that you have obtained from your workplace, you have violated Rule 10b-5. Example:

- James O'Hagan was a lawyer in a firm that represented a company attempting to take over Pillsbury Co. Although O'Hagan did not work on the case, he heard about it and then bought stock in Pillsbury. After the takeover attempt was publicly announced, O'Hagan sold his stock in Pillsbury at profit of more than $4.3 million.[11] The Supreme Court ruled that O'Hagan had violated insider trading laws. While it was true that he had no fiduciary duty to Pillsbury, he did owe one to his law firm, which was the source of the information. According to the court, what he had done was the same thing as embezzlement.[12]

Tippers

Sometimes people do not trade themselves, but instead pass on information to others (such as friends and family). **Anyone who reveals material nonpublic information in violation of his fiduciary duty is liable if (1) he knows the information was confidential and (2) he expected some personal gain.** Essentially, any gift to a friend counts as personal gain. Examples:

- W. Paul Thayer was a corporate director, deputy secretary of defense, and former fighter pilot ace who gave stock tips to his girlfriend in lieu of paying her rent. That counted as personal gain, and he spent a year and a half in prison.

- Patrick cold-calls Jane to see if her company would like to buy his product. She tells him that her company is not undertaking any new initiatives at the moment because it may be taken over. Patrick buys stock in Jane's company. In this case, Jane has not violated Rule 10b-5 because she really did not expect any personal gain.

Tippees

Even without a fiduciary relationship to the company, those who receive tips are liable for trading on this inside information, if (1) they know the information is confidential, (2) they know that it came from an insider who was violating his fiduciary duty, and (3) the insider expected some personal gain. Examples:

- Barry Switzer, then head football coach at the University of Oklahoma, went to a track meet to see his son compete. While sunbathing on the bleachers, he overheard someone talking about a company that was going to be acquired. Switzer bought the stock but was acquitted of insider trading charges because the insider had not breached his fiduciary duty. He had not tipped anyone on purpose—he had simply been careless. Also, Switzer did not know that the insider was breaching a fiduciary duty, and the insider expected no personal gain.[13]

- In the case of Jane and Patrick, if Jane is not liable, neither is he.

---

[11]O'Hagan used the profits that he gained through this trading to conceal his previous embezzlement of client funds. There is a moral here.

[12]*United States v. O'Hagan*, 521 U.S. 642, 117 S. Ct. 2199, 1997 U.S. LEXIS 4033 (S Ct. 1997).

[13]*SEC v. Switzer*, 590 F. Supp. 756, 1984 U.S. Dist. LEXIS 15303 (W.D. Okla. 1984).

Takeovers

Rule 14e-3 prohibits trading on inside information during a tender offer if the trader knows the information was obtained from either the bidder or the target company. The trader or tipper need not have violated a fiduciary duty. Patrick would be liable under this rule.

Advanced Planning

Under Rule 10b5-1, an insider can avoid insider trading charges if she commits in advance to a plan to sell securities. Thus, if an insider knows that she will want to sell stock to pay a child's college tuition, she can establish such a sales plan in advance. She will then not be liable for the sales, no matter what inside information she knows. But, she *must* sell according to the plan, despite any change in circumstances.

In the following case, two employees are not *told* specific information, but they make an educated guess. Have they violated insider trading rules?

SECURITIES AND EXCHANGE COMMISSION V. STEFFES

2011 U.S. Dist. LEXIS 85496
United States District Court for the Northern District of Illinois

Facts: Florida East Coast Industries, Inc. (FECI), was a publicly traded company that operated a freight railroad between Jacksonville and Miami. Gary Griffiths was a vice president at FECI, whose job it was to oversee maintenance of the railcars. He was married to the sister of his high school friend, Rex Steffes. He had helped Rex's son Cliff obtain a job driving trains for FECI.

The CFO of FECI asked Griffiths to prepare an inventory of all the rolling stock the company owned and to arrange trips among its rail yards in a special railroad car reserved for visitors. Griffiths also heard that a large number of men in suits had been touring the company's rail yards. Yard employees began asking Griffiths whether FECI would be sold and whether they would lose their jobs. Indeed, it turned out that FECI's Board of Directors had secretly hired an investment bank to sell the company.

A day after Griffiths visited Rex in Chicago, Rex and Cliff spoke on the phone. Two days later, Rex bought $397,508 worth of FECI stock. He made this purchase over the objection of his broker, who thought his portfolio was then too undiversified. A similar pattern continued for a month: phone calls among Rex, Cliff, and Griffiths, followed by Rex buying more stock. In total, Rex purchased $1.14 million of FECI stock. During this same period, Cliff purchased the first call options of his life, spending $15,015 on FECI.[14] After the company was sold, both Rex and Cliff made substantial profits.

The SEC filed suit, alleging that Griffiths, Rex, and Cliff misappropriated information in violation of Section 10(b) and Rule 10b-5. The men filed a motion to dismiss.

Issue: *Did the defendants engage in illegal insider trading by misappropriating information from their employer?*

Excerpts from Judge Dow's Opinion: Unlike the typical insider trading case, Griffiths is not alleged to have been part of the confidential merger negotiations, or even directly informed of their existence. Instead, Griffiths is alleged to have pieced together for himself what was occurring based on information that was available to him as an employee. [A] defendant can be held liable for insider trading when he or she obtains and acts on pieces of information, which, pieced together, constitute material nonpublic information. Direct evidence of insider trading is, indeed, rare; and the SEC is entitled to prove its case through circumstantial evidence.

Defendants argue that the information allegedly possessed by Griffiths and Cliff—such as the fact that visitors were touring rail yards and taking trips in railway cars—cannot reasonably be considered material in the context of securities trading. But the SEC does not contend that each of these underlying facts on its own is a material non-public fact. Rather, the SEC alleges that Defendants' trades were based on the ultimate conclusion—deduced from the totality of the information available to Griffiths and Cliff—that FECI was in the process of being sold before the sale was announced.

The Court agrees with Griffiths' assertion that "mere telephone calls between family members, without more, do not plausibly support a conclusion that Griffiths misappropriated inside information." However, the SEC's

---

[14]Call options are the right to purchase stock of a company at a specific price for a specific period of time. A buyer purchases a call option in the expectation that the stock price will go up.

complaint contains more than just the fact that phone calls occurred—Griffiths overlooks the allegations that Rex engaged in suspicious trading shortly after his calls with Griffiths. Evidence of phone calls followed by such trading is sufficient to support a reasonable inference that Griffiths tipped [Rex] in each of the phone calls that preceded the suspicious trades. The larger and more profitable the trades, and the closer in time the trader's exposure to the insider, the stronger the inference that the trader was acting on the basis of inside information.

Griffiths argues that the complaint "fails to allege the way in which Griffiths may have benefitted directly or indirectly from the disclosure." Griffiths himself did not trade in FECI stock. And Griffiths points out that the complaint does not specifically allege that Griffiths knew that his family members would trade on the information that he provided. Nevertheless, the complaint adequately alleges a breach of fiduciary duty by Griffiths. It is well established that an insider who provides material nonpublic information to another may be found liable for insider trading, even if he or she did not personally buy or sell securities.

[T]he test is whether the insider personally will benefit, directly or indirectly, from his disclosure. [T]he concept of gain is a broad one, which can include a gift of confidential information to a relative or friend. Accordingly, it is reasonable to conclude that Griffiths received a personal benefit from making those tips.

Defendants' motions to dismiss are respectfully denied.

EXAM Strategy

Question: Paul was an investment banker who sometimes bragged about deals he was working on. One night he told a bartender, Ryanne, about an upcoming deal, without revealing his connection to it. Ryanne bought stock in the company Paul had mentioned. Both were prosecuted for insider trading. Ryanne was acquitted but Paul was convicted, even though Ryanne was the one who made money. How is that possible?

Strategy: Note that there are different standards for tippers and tippees.

Result: Paul is liable if he knew the information was confidential and he expected some personal gain. A gift counts as personal gain. (The courts have an expansive definition of "gift"—practically anything counts. Here, the information could be interpreted as a tip to the bartender.) Ryanne was not liable because she did not know the information was confidential and that it came from an insider who was violating his fiduciary duty.

Why is insider trading a crime? Who is harmed? After all, if you buy or sell stock in a company, presumably you are reasonably content with the price or you would not have traded. Insider trading is illegal because:

- It offends our fundamental sense of fairness. No one wants to be in a poker game with marked cards.

- Investors will lose confidence in the market if they feel that insiders have an unfair advantage.

- Investment banks typically "make a market" in stocks, meaning that they hold extra shares so that orders can be filled smoothly. If an insider buys stock because she knows the company is about to sign an important contract, she earns the profit on that information at the expense of the market maker who sold her the stock. These market makers expect to earn a certain profit. If they do not earn it from normal stock appreciation, they simply raise the commission they charge for being a market maker. As a result, everyone who buys and sells stock pays a slightly higher price because insider trading skims off some of the profits.

Sarbanes-Oxley

The Sarbanes-Oxley Act (SOX) is an amendment to the 1934 Act that applies to all U.S companies reporting under the 1934 Act, as well as to all foreign companies listed on a U.S. stock exchange. In addition to the provisions we discussed earlier, SOX:

- Requires companies to disclose if they have an ethics code and, if they do not, why not.

- Imposes fines and imprisonment on anyone who interferes with a federal investigation into fraud.

- Permits an employee who blows the whistle on a securities law violation to sue the company if it retaliates against the employee. SOX also makes it a crime to retaliate against someone who blows the whistle on any federal offense.

- Establishes a new Public Company Accounting Oversight Board to oversee the auditing of reporting companies.

Dodd-Frank

The Dodd-Frank Wall Street Reform and Consumer Protection Act amends the 1934 Act to provide a reward system for whistleblowers. Dodd-Frank also establishes a requirement that reporting companies tell the SEC and post on their websites information about their use of "conflict minerals" (such as tin, tungsten, and gold). A conflict mineral is one that is being used to finance the war in the Democratic Republic of the Congo or a neighboring country.

In addition, energy mining companies must disclose payments they make to other governments for oil, gas, and mineral rights. The goal of this provision is to provide information to the citizens of foreign countries about how much revenue their governments are receiving so that they can hold officials responsible for misspending.

BLUE SKY LAWS

At the end of the nineteenth century, years before the great stock market crash, states had already begun to regulate the sale of securities. These statutes are called **blue sky laws** (because crooks were willing to sell naive investors a "piece of the great blue sky"). Currently, all states and the District of Columbia have blue sky laws.

Exemption from State Regulation

To make life easier for issuers of stock, Congress passed the **National Securities Markets Improvement Act (NSMIA) of 1996.** Essentially, states may no longer regulate offerings of securities that are:

- Traded on a national exchange,
- Exempt under Rule 506, or
- Sold to a qualified purchaser.[15]

---

[15]The SEC was supposed to define this term in 1996, but has not yet done so.

State Regulation

Any securities offerings not covered by the NSMIA must comply with state securities laws. Easier said than done. The 50 states have exhibited great creativity in crafting their securities laws and, as a result, have caused many headaches for issuers of securities. To begin, the 1933 Act is primarily concerned with disclosure, but many state statutes focus on the quality of the investment and require a so-called *merit review*. For example, in 1981, the Massachusetts securities commissioner refused to allow Apple Computer Co. to sell its initial public offering in Massachusetts because he believed the stock, selling at 92 times earnings, was too risky. He "protected" Massachusetts residents from this investment.

Typically, states take one of the following approaches to securities offerings:

- **Registration by Notification.** Some states permit issuers with an established track record simply to file a notice before offering their securities.

- **Registration by Coordination.** Some states permit issuers that have registered with the SEC simply to file copies of the federal registration statement (and perhaps some additional documents) with the state.

- **Registration by Qualification**. Some states require issuers to undergo a full-blown registration, complete with a merit review.

Facilitating State Regulation

All is not bleak, however. There are three options that ease the process of complying with state securities requirements.

Coordinated Equity Review (CER)

For offerings over $5 million that are registered with the SEC, the issuer might be able to take advantage of the **Coordinated Equity Review (CER)** program. Under this program, the issuer files in every state in which it wants to sell securities, but it only has to deal with Pennsylvania, which takes responsibility for coordinating the comments from all other states. The process is simpler, but state officials still have the right to conduct a merit review.

Small Company Offering Registration (SCOR)

Most states permit a so-called **small company offering registration (SCOR)** for use in offerings of up to $1 million over any 12-month period. The issuer has the right to advertise publicly (even on the Internet) and can sell any amount of securities to any number of investors (as long as the total offering does not exceed $1 million). The relatively simple form (U-7) is in a question-and-answer format. It is designed to be filled out by company executives without the assistance of lawyers or accountants who are securities experts. Any company using a SCOR form can request a coordinated review from the states in which it has filed. Under this system, a designated lead state takes responsibility for coordinating the process with all other states. The result is a faster, simpler process. States do have the right to conduct a merit review, although it tends to be less burdensome than the usual merit examination. SCOR registration is designed to be used with Rule 147, Rule 504, and Reg A.

Uniform Limited Offering Exemption

Under the **Uniform Limited Offering Exemption,** most states largely exempt from registration any offerings under Rule 505.

The moral of the story? Securities offerings are exceedingly complex and require professional supervision. Do not attempt this at home!

Chapter Conclusion

The 1929 stock market crash and the Great Depression that followed were an economic catastrophe for the United States. The Securities Act of 1933 and the Securities Exchange Act of 1934 were designed to prevent such disasters from ever occurring again. Whether or not they achieve that goal, they undoubtedly enhance the reliability and stability of the securities markets.

EXAM REVIEW

1. **SECURITY** A security is any transaction in which the buyer invests money in a common enterprise and expects to earn a profit predominantly from the efforts of others. (p. 546)

EXAM Strategy

Question: Jonah bought 12 paintings from Theo's Art Gallery at a total cost of $1 million. Theo told Jonah that the paintings were a safe investment that could only go up in value. The gallery permitted any purchaser to trade in a painting in return for any other artwork the gallery owned. In the trade-in, the purchaser would get credit for the amount of the original painting and then pay the difference if the new painting was worth more. When Jonah's paintings did not increase in value, he sued Theo for a violation of the securities laws. Were these paintings securities?

Strategy: Are all three elements of a security present here? (See the "Result" at the end of this section.)

2. **REGISTRATION** Before any offer or sale, an issuer must register securities with the SEC unless the securities qualify for an exemption. (p. 546)

3. **EXEMPTIONS** These securities are exempt from the registration requirement: government securities, bank securities, short-term notes, nonprofit issues, insurance policies, and annuity contracts. (p. 547)

4. **SECURITIES OFFERINGS** The following table compares the different types of securities offerings: (pp. 547–550)

	Public Offering	Intrastate Offering	Regulation A	Regulation D: Rule 504	Regulation D: Rule 505	Regulation D: Rule 506	Crowdfunding
Maximum Value of Securities Sold	Unlimited	Unlimited	$5 million	$1 million	$5 million	Unlimited	$1 million
Public Solicitation of Purchasers	Permitted	Permitted	Permitted	Sometimes permitted	Not permitted	Yes, if sales are limited to accredited investors, otherwise, not permitted	No
Suitability Requirements for Purchasers	No requirements	Must reside in issuer's state	No requirements	May be limited to accredited investors	No limit on accredited investors; no more than 35 unaccredited investors	No limit on accredited investors; no more than 35 unaccredited investors who, if unsophisticated, must have a purchaser representative	Investors can only buy stock worth up to a certain percentage of their annual income or net worth
Disclosure Requirements	Elaborate registration statement; audited financials	None	Offering circular that is less detailed than a registration statement	May be required under state law	Same requirements as Reg A for unaccredited investors; no disclosure to accredited investors	Same requirements as Reg A for unaccredited investors; no disclosure to accredited investors	Disclosure is required at time of purchase and annually
Resale of Securities	Permitted	Permitted, but may not be made out of state for nine months	Permitted	Sometimes permitted	Not permitted for one year	Not permitted for one year	Prohibited within one year except to accredited investors and family members

© Cengage Learning 2014

CPA Question: Hamilton Corp. makes a $4.5 million securities offering under Rule 505 of Regulation D of the Securities Act of 1933. Under this regulation, Hamilton is:

a. Required to provide full financial information to accredited investors only

b. Allowed to make the offering through a general solicitation

c. Limited to selling to no more than 35 nonaccredited investors

d. Allowed to sell to an unlimited number of investors, both accredited and nonaccredited

Strategy: The answer is not (a) because accredited investors are never entitled to *more* disclosure than other investors. The answer is not (b) because Rule 505 does not permit a general solicitation. The answer is not (d) because Rule 505 is limited to only 35 unaccredited investors. (See the "Result" at the end of this section.)

5. **LIABILITY UNDER THE 1933 ACT** If a final registration statement contains a material misstatement or omission, the purchaser of a security offered under that statement can recover from everyone who signed it. (pp. 554–555)

6. **THE 1934 ACT** The 1934 Act requires public companies to make regular filings with the SEC. (pp. 555–557)

7. **SECTION 16** Under Section 16, insiders who buy and sell or sell and buy company stock within a six-month period must turn over to the corporation any profits from the trades. They must also disclose any trades they make in company stock. (p. 557)

EXAM Strategy

Question: You are the president of Turbocharge, Inc., a publicly traded company. You have been buying stock recently because you think the company's product—a more efficient hybrid engine—is very promising. One day, you show up at work and find your desk in the hallway. The CEO has fired you. In a huff, you sell all your company stock. The only silver lining to your cloud is that you make a large profit. Or is this a silver lining?

Strategy: You can be in violation of Section 16 even if you did not have any inside information when you trade. (See the "Result" at the end of this section.)

8. **SECTION 10(B)** Section 10(b) prohibits fraud in connection with the purchase and sale of any security, whether or not the issuer is registered under the 1934 Act. (pp. 557–561)

9. **INSIDER TRADING** Section 10(b) also prohibits insider trading. (pp. 562–566)

10. **SOX** Sarbanes Oxley:
    - imposes fines and imprisonment on anyone who interferes with a federal investigation into fraud.
    - permits an employee who blows the whistle on a securities law violation to sue the company if it retaliates against the employee. SOX also makes it a crime to retaliate against someone who blows the whistle on any federal offense. (p. 566)

11. **DODD-FRANK** The Dodd-Frank Act
    - provides a reward system for whistleblowers, and
    - requires that reporting companies tell the SEC and post on their websites information about their use of conflict minerals. (p. 566)

12. **THE NSMIA** The National Securities Markets Improvement Act prohibits states from regulating securities offerings that are:
    - traded on a national exchange,
    - exempt under Rule 506, or
    - sold to "qualified purchasers." (p. 566)

13. **BLUE SKY LAWS** Any securities offerings not covered by the NSMIA must comply with state securities laws, which are varied and complex. (pp. 566–568)

> **1. Result:** The paintings were not securities because there was no "common enterprise." The investors did not pool funds or share profits with other investors.
>
> **4. Result:** The answer is (c).
>
> **7. Result:** You are in violation of Section 16. Even though you acted without any bad intent, you must turn over all your profits to the company.

MULTIPLE-CHOICE QUESTIONS

1. **CPA QUESTION** When a common stock offering requires registration under the Securities Act of 1933:
   (a) the registration statement is automatically effective when filed with the SEC.
   (b) the issuer would act unlawfully if it were to sell the common stock without providing the investor with a prospectus.
   (c) the SEC will determine the investment value of the common stock before approving the offering.
   (d) the issuer may make sales 10 days after filing the registration statement.

2. **CPA QUESTION** Pace Corp. previously issued 300,000 shares of its common stock. The shares are now actively traded on a national securities exchange. The original offering was exempt from registration under the Securities Act of 1933. Pace has $2.5 million in assets and 425 unaccredited shareholders. With regard to the Securities Exchange Act of 1934, Pace is:
   (a) required to file a registration statement because its assets exceed $2 million in value.
   (b) required to file a registration statement even though it has fewer than unaccredited 500 shareholders.
   (c) not required to file a registration statement because the original offering of its stock was exempt from registration.
   (d) not required to file a registration statement unless insiders own at least 5 percent of its outstanding shares of stock.

3. Lily would like to raise money for her video game start-up by advertising the shares on her website, but without making substantial financial disclosure. What should she do?
   (a) Nothing. If she is going to solicit purchasers publicly, she must undertake an IPO.
   (b) Use Rule 504 to sell up to $1 million in stock to accredited investors, and make sure the offering is exempt under state law.
   (c) Use Rule 504 to sell up to $1 million in stock to any purchasers and register the stock under a state law.
   (d) Use Rule 505 sell up to $5 million in stock to an unlimited number of accredited investors and no more than 35 unaccredited investors.

4. If a publicly traded company wishes to issue more stock, it will undertake a(n)_____. If the underwriter buys the stock and resells it to the public, that is a _____ underwriting. Before buying the stock, investors must receive a copy of the _____.

   (a) IPO, best efforts, registration statement
   (b) IPO, firm commitment, registration statement
   (c) secondary offering, best efforts, prospectus
   (d) secondary offering, firm commitment, prospectus

5. Three months ago, Noah bought stock under Rule 506 in TreesNFlowers, Inc. He has lost interest in the company and would like to sell the stock. Which of the following statements is true?

   (a) He can sell the stock now, so long as he sells it to an accredited investor.
   (b) He can sell the stock now, so long as the company grants permission.
   (c) He must hold on to the stock for at least nine months.
   (d) He could sell the stock in three months, but only if the company goes public in the meantime.

ESSAY QUESTIONS

1. Refco Inc. failed to disclose in SEC filings that millions of dollars of its accounts receivables were uncollectible. Two months after its IPO, the company went bankrupt. Shareholders filed suit against the company's law firm, alleging that it was liable under Section 10(b) for drafting Refco's SEC filings that contained these material omissions. Is the law firm liable? Should it be? Is this a stronger or weaker case than *Stoneridge*?

2. Fluor, an engineering and construction company, was awarded a $1 billion project to build a coal gasification plant in South Africa. Fluor signed an agreement with a South African client that prohibited them both from announcing the agreement until March 10. Accordingly, Fluor denied all rumors that a major transaction was pending. Between March 3 and March 6, the State Teachers Retirement Board pension fund sold 288,257 shares of Fluor stock. After the contract was announced, the stock price went up. Did Fluor violate Rule 10b-5?

3. Do you love ice cream? Here is an opportunity for you! For only $800, you can buy a cow from Berkshire Ice Cream. The company gets milk from the cow, and you get to share in the profits from the sale of ice cream. Just last month, Berkshire mailed $32,000 worth of checks to investors, who are expecting a 20 percent annual rate of return. Are there any problems with this plan?

4. **ETHICS** ETS Payphones, Inc., sold pay phones to the public. The company then leased back the pay phones from the purchaser, promising a guaranteed 14 percent annual return on their investment. Although ETS's marketing materials trumpeted the "incomparable pay phone" as "an exciting business opportunity," the pay phones did not generate enough revenue for ETS to make the required payments. The SEC sued, alleging that ETS had been selling unregistered securities. Were the pay phone

contracts securities under the 1933 Act? These allegedly "guaranteed" investments are particularly attractive to older and less-sophisticated investors. Was it ethical to pitch a high-risk investment to vulnerable investors who were unable to assess the risks accurately? As a saleperson, what would your standards be?

5. Suppose that, while waiting in line at the grocery store, you overhear a stranger saying that the FDA is going to approve a new drug tomorrow—one that will be a huge success for Alpha Pharmaceuticals. Is it legal for you to buy stock in Alpha?

DISCUSSION QUESTIONS

1. Federal security laws are based on the assumption that investors are knowledgeable enough to assess the quality of a stock, so long as the issuer provides adequate disclosure. Many states take a different approach—they refuse to permit the sale of securities that they deem to be of poor quality. Should securities laws protect investors in this way?

2. **ETHICS** David Sokol worked at Berkshire Hathaway for legendary investor Warren Buffett, who is renowned not only for his investment skills but also his ethics. Bankers suggested to both Sokol and the CEO of Lubrizol that the company might be a good buy for Berkshire. Sokol then found out that the CEO of Lubrizol planned to ask his board for permission to approach Berkshire about a possible acquisition. Sokol purchased $10 million worth of Lubrizol stock before recommending Lubrizol to Buffett. Sokol mentioned to Buffett "in passing" that he owned shares of Lubrizol. Buffett did not ask any questions about the timing or amount of Sokol's purchases. Sokol made a $3 million profit when Berkshire acquired Lubrizol. Did Sokol violate insider trading laws? Did he behave ethically? What about Buffett?

3. Twitter is valued at close to $10 billion, and yet, because it is still privately held, it is not required to make any disclosure about its finances. Once the number of its shareholders reaches 2,000 (or it has 500 unaccredited shareholders) it will be deemed a public company and will be required to make significant (and expensive) financial disclosure. Should the SEC change its rules so that these reporting requirements are not triggered until companies have more than 2,000 shareholders? Which is more important—to minimize the disclosure burden on companies or to protect investors who are willing to buy stock even without financial disclosure?

4. Do you agree with the court's decision in the *Stoneridge* case?

5. Mark Cuban, the owner of the Dallas Mavericks basketball team, also owned stock in Mamma.com. At the request of the company's Board of Directors, the CEO called Cuban to tell him that the company was about to sell stock, which Cuban could buy if he wished. But before revealing this information, the CEO told Cuban that he had to keep the information confidential. After learning about the sale, Cuban responded, "Well, now I'm screwed. I can't sell." Afterward, he spoke with the investment

banker handling the deal to learn more about the company's financials. He then sold his entire holding of Momma.com shares before the stock sale was announced. Has Cuban violated Rule 10b-5?

6. The SEC believes that anyone in possession of material nonpublic information about a company should be required to disclose it before trading on the stock of that enterprise. Instead, the courts have developed a more complex set of rules. Do you agree with the SEC or the courts on this issue?

Government Regulation and Property

CHAPTER 22

ANTITRUST

On his way into Sleepy Time to buy a mattress for his new king-size bed, Sean noticed that Girl Scout Troop 1474 was selling cookies. There was nothing he liked more than Thin Mint cookies mixed into vanilla ice cream, and $3 a box seemed like a reasonable price. But he decided to focus on the task at hand and buy the mattress first. After much lying down on pocketed coils, pillowtops, and memory foam, he ultimately decided on a Tempur-Pedic made out of visco-elastic, temperature-sensitive material. Wouldn't that be bliss?

But Sean was no fool. He knew that the country was in the midst of a raging recession (or was it a depression?) and that retail stores were desperate for customers. He figured he could negotiate a handsome discount from the list price of $2,399. But when he asked Gavin, the sales guy, what his best price was, Gavin just shrugged, a hangdog expression on his face. "I'm on commission and would love to sell you a mattress, but Tempur-Pedic won't let us offer any discounts. If they found out I'd reduced the price, they'd yank those mattresses out of my store so fast, even the dust mites couldn't keep up. The price is $2,399 or nothing." He lowered his voice. "In the old days, manufacturers couldn't do that, but our company lawyer made this big deal about how the Supreme Court has changed antitrust law and made this kind of price fixing legal. They call it 'resale price maintenance' or something like that. Anyway, our hands are tied."

That was a stiff price for a soft mattress, so Sean decided he would shop around. By now he was hungry, and it was cold and dark outside, so he was eager at the thought of Girl Scout cookies. But Troop 1474 had gone home. It seemed as if this was just not his day.

His mood lifted, though, when he stopped at Video Horizons and noticed a different Girl Scout troop selling cookies. That was until he noticed the price was $4 a box. "Why the price gouging?" he demanded grouchily. One of the girls spoke up reluctantly, "When I was studying for my Law and Order badge, I found out that it's a violation of antitrust law for Girl Scout councils to get together and agree on the prices their troops will charge. Each

> "If they found out I'd reduced the price, they'd yank those mattresses out of my store so fast, even the dust mites couldn't keep up."

© picsbyst/Shutterstock.com

council has to decide its own price. We hear that Cambridge is charging $3, but in Winchester, it's $4."

Gavin the sales guy says that manufacturers can set the price for mattresses, but the Girl Scouts claim their councils do not have the right to agree on the cost of a box of cookies. Who is right? Are there different laws for cookies and mattresses?

Both the Girl Scouts and Gavin are correct in their interpretation of the law. They are each talking about a different type of price fixing. The sale of these mattresses involves *vertical price fixing*, so called because the manufacturer and the store are at different stages of the production process. Thus, they do not compete against each other, and that type of price fixing is generally legal. No matter how hard Sean looks, he is not likely to find a cheaper price on the mattress he wants. But *horizontal price fixing*—which involves agreements among competitors—is *automatically* illegal. The Girl Scout councils are competitors, so they are prohibited from agreeing among themselves what price they all will charge. If the consumer wants to save $1 a box on cookies, all he has to do is drive from Winchester to Cambridge.

Competition is an essential element of the American economic system. Antitrust laws are the rules that govern that competition. As this chapter opening illustrates, these laws affect many aspects of our lives—both as consumers and as businesspeople.

IN THE BEGINNING

Throughout much of the nineteenth century, competition in America was largely a local affair. The country was so big and transportation so poor that companies primarily competed in small local markets. It was too costly to transport goods great distances. State laws, rather than national statutes, regulated competition.

By the second half of the nineteenth century, four railroad lines crossed the continent from coast to coast. For the first time, national markets were a real possibility. John D. Rockefeller saw the potential. In 1859, Edwin L. Drake, a retired railroad conductor, drilled the first commercially successful oil well in the United States. Three years later, when the 23-year-old Rockefeller entered the scene, the oil industry was full of producers too small to benefit from economies of scale. Production was inefficient, and prices varied dramatically in different parts of the country.

Rockefeller set out to reorganize the industry. He began by buying refineries, first in Cleveland and then in other cities. He and his partners spread into all segments of the oil industry—buying oil fields, building pipelines, and establishing an efficient marketing system. To unify the management of these companies, they transferred their stock to the Standard Oil Trust. By 1870, Rockefeller had achieved his goal—the Standard Oil Trust controlled virtually all the oil in the country, from producer to consumer. At age 31, Rockefeller was the wealthiest person in the *world*.

Some of Rockefeller's tactics were controversial. When a competitor tried to build an oil pipeline, Rockefeller used every weapon short of violence to stop it. He planted stories in the press suggesting the pipes would leak and ruin nearby fields. He flooded local builders with orders for tank cars so no workers would be available to build the pipeline. When the pipeline was finished, he refused to allow his oil to flow through it. These tactics were frightening, especially in an industry as important as oil. What if Rockefeller decided to raise prices unfairly? Or cut off oil altogether? Newspapers began to attack him ferociously.

Antitrust Legislation

With the coming of the railroads, it became clear that large companies might be able to control other industries as well. To prevent extreme concentrations of economic power, Congress passed the **Sherman Act** in 1890. It was one of the first national laws designed to regulate competition. Because this statute was aimed at the Standard Oil Trust and other similar organizations, it was termed **antitrust** legislation. In 1892, the Ohio Supreme Court dissolved the Standard Oil Trust, which was replaced by the Standard Oil Co. But the government was not satisfied until a spring day in 1911, when Supreme Court Chief Justice Edward White quietly read aloud his dramatic 20,000-word opinion ordering the breakup of Standard Oil.[1] The 33 companies that made up Standard Oil were forced to compete as separate businesses. Today, descendants of Standard Oil include Atlantic Richfield, Chevron, Exxon-Mobil, Pennzoil, and parts of British Petroleum (BP). Imagine what kind of giant they would be if still united.

For the first 70 or so years after the passage of the Sherman Act, most scholars and judges took the view that large concentrations of economic power were suspect, even if they had no obvious impact on competition itself. Big was bad—it meant too much economic and political power. As Sen. John Sherman, sponsor of the Sherman Act, put it, a nation that "would not submit to an emperor should not submit to an autocrat of trade." Fragmented, competitive markets were desirable in and of themselves. Standard Oil should not control the oil markets even if the company was very efficient and had gained control by completely acceptable methods.

Chicago School

Beginning in the 1960s and 1970s, however, a group of influential economists and lawyers at the University of Chicago began to argue that the goal of antitrust enforcement should be *efficiency*. Let a company grow as large as it likes, provided that this growth is based on a superior product or lower costs, not ruthless tactics. Insist on a clean fight, but do not handicap large successful companies to help weaker competitors. Some companies will thrive, others will die, but in either case, the consumer will come out ahead. Adherents of the **Chicago School** argued further that the *market* should decide the most efficient size for each industry. In some cases, such as automobiles or aircrafts, the most efficient size might be very large indeed. Under traditional antitrust analysis, courts often asked, "Has a *competitor* been harmed?" The Chicago School suggests that courts should ask instead, "Has *competition* been harmed?"

At the turn of the twentieth century, President Theodore Roosevelt personally plotted the breakup of Standard Oil. (As one of Rockefeller's compatriots said of Roosevelt, "We bought the son of a bitch, and then he didn't stay bought.") At the turn of the twenty-first century, two descendants of Standard Oil—Exxon and Mobil—announced their intention to merge. This time, not one politician so much as grabbed a microphone to object to the recombination. Where once size alone was cause for concern, now regulators believe that a certain bulk may be necessary if American companies are to compete in the intense global economy.

Antitrust policy, however, continues to evolve. Adherents of the so-called **Post Chicago School** are beginning to recognize that competition alone may not be enough to protect consumers. For example, an industry with a large number of competitors may foster collusion, not competition. Or, activities that appear consumer-friendly, such as giving a product away for free, may in the long run harm consumers. (Take, for example, Microsoft's decision to give away its Internet browser. Although consumers benefited in the short

---

[1] *Standard Oil Company of New Jersey v. United States*, 221 U.S. 1, 31 S. Ct. 502, 1911 U.S. LEXIS 1725 (1911).

run, the Justice Department alleged that this giveaway harmed consumers by driving competitors out of business.) Now, when deciding whether to take action, federal trust-busters are beginning to focus directly on consumers, asking two questions:

- Will this action cause consumers to pay higher prices?

- Are the higher prices sustainable in the face of existing competition?

As you read the cases in this chapter, think about which factors the court considers important: size, competition, or the impact on consumers.

OVERVIEW OF ANTITRUST LAWS

The major provisions of the antitrust laws:

- Section 1 of the Sherman Act prohibits all agreements "in restraint of trade."

- Section 2 of the Sherman Act bans "monopolization"—the wrongful acquisition of a monopoly.

- The Clayton Act prohibits anticompetitive mergers, tying arrangements, and exclusive dealing agreements.

- The Robinson-Patman Act bans price discrimination that reduces competition.

In 1914, Congress passed the **Clayton Act** in part because the courts were not enforcing the Sherman Act as strictly as it had intended. The purpose of the Clayton Act was to clarify the earlier statute. As a result, the two laws overlap significantly. The **Robinson-Patman Act** (passed in 1936) is an amendment to the Clayton Act. Rather than systematically reviewing the terms of each statute in order, this chapter focuses instead on the *kinds of behavior* that the antitrust laws regulate.

Violations of the antitrust laws are divided into two categories: ***per se*** and **rule of reason.** As the name implies, *per se* violations are *automatic*. Defendants charged with this type of violation cannot defend themselves by saying, "But the impact wasn't so bad" or "No one was hurt." The court will not listen to excuses, and the defendants are subject to both *criminal* and *civil* penalties. Typically, the Justice Department has sought criminal sanctions only against *per se* violators.

Rule of reason violations, on the other hand, are illegal only if they have an *anticompetitive impact*. To determine if an activity is an unreasonable restraint of trade, the courts consider its circumstances, intent, and impact. For example, if competitors join together and agree that they will not deal with a particular supplier, their action is illegal only if it harms competition. Although rule of reason violators may be subject to civil penalties or private lawsuits, traditionally the Justice Department has not sought criminal penalties against them.

Both the Justice Department and the Federal Trade Commission (FTC) have authority to enforce the antitrust laws. However, only the Justice Department can bring criminal proceedings; the FTC is limited to civil injunctions and other administrative remedies. In addition to the government, anyone injured by an antitrust violation has the right to sue for damages. The United States is unusual in this regard—in most other countries, only the government is able to sue antitrust violators. A successful plaintiff can recover treble (that is, triple) damages from the defendant.

Another important point before we begin our discussion of particular antitrust provisions: **any conduct *overseas* that has an anticompetitive impact in the United States is a violation of U.S. law** provided that (1) the foreign actor *intended* to affect the U.S. market, and (2) the foreign conduct has a *direct and substantial effect* on the U.S. market. For example,

Per se violation

An automatic breach of antitrust laws.

Rule of reason violation

An action that breaches antitrust laws only if it has an anticompetitive impact.

the Justice Department indicted two Japanese businessmen because they met in Japan to fix the price of fax paper sold to an American company.

In developing a competitive strategy, managers typically consider two different approaches:

- Cooperative strategies that allow companies to work together to their mutual advantage

- Aggressive strategies, designed to create an advantage over competitors

COOPERATIVE STRATEGIES

Three types of cooperative strategies are potentially illegal:

- **Horizontal agreements** among competitors. An agreement between Levi Strauss and Wrangler—both manufacturers of denim jeans—would be a horizontal agreement. So would the agreement among the Girl Scout councils in the opening scenario.

- **Vertical agreements** among participants at different stages of the production process. An agreement between Levi Strauss and Macy's—one company makes jeans, the other sells them—would be a vertical agreement. So would an agreement between a mattress manufacturer and Sleepy Time.

- **Mergers and joint ventures** among competitors. Here, companies go beyond simple agreements to combine forces more permanently.

The following table lists the cooperative strategies that will be discussed in this chapter:

Horizontal agreement
An agreement among competitors.

Vertical agreement
An agreement among participants operating at different stages of the production process.

Horizontal Strategies	Vertical Strategies	Mergers
Market division	Reciprocal dealing	Horizontal mergers
Price fixing	Price discrimination	Vertical mergers
Bid rigging		Joint ventures
Refusal to deal		

© Cengage Learning 2014

Horizontal Cooperative Strategies

Although the term "cooperative strategies" *sounds* benign, these tactics can be harmful to competition. Indeed, many horizontal cooperative strategies are *per se* violations of the law and can lead to prison terms, heavy fines, and expensive lawsuits with customers and competitors.

Market Division

Any effort by a group of competitors to divide its market is a *per se* violation of Section 1 of the Sherman Act. Illegal arrangements include agreements to allocate customers, territory, or products. For example, these business schools would be in violation if:

- Georgetown agreed to accept only men and, in return, George Washington would take only women;[2]

- Stanford agreed to accept only students from west of the Mississippi, leaving the east to Yale; or

- Northwestern agreed not to provide courses in entrepreneurship, while the University of Chicago eliminated its international offerings.

Price Fixing and Bid Rigging

When competitors agree on the prices at which they will buy or sell products or services, their price fixing is a *per se* violation of Section 1 of the Sherman Act. Bid rigging is also a *per se* violation. In bid rigging, competitors eliminate price competition by agreeing on who will submit the lowest bid.

In the following Landmark Case, the defendants argued that price fixing was wrong only if the prices were *unfair*. Did the Supreme Court agree?

Landmark Case

UNITED STATES V. TRENTON POTTERIES COMPANY

273 U.S. 392; 1927 U.S. LEXIS 975
Supreme Court of the United States, 1927

Facts: This case involved dirty behavior in the bathroom fixture business. The federal government alleged 23 of the corporations that manufactured these fixtures had agreed on the prices they would charge their customers. The defendants argued that they had not violated the law because their prices had been reasonable.

They were found guilty at trial, but the appeals court overturned their convictions. The Supreme Court granted *certiorari*.

Issue: *Is price fixing a violation of the law if the prices are reasonable?*

Excerpts from Justice Stone's Decision: The trial court refused various requests to charge [the jury] that the agreement[s] to fix prices, if found, did not in themselves constitute violations of law unless it was also found that they unreasonably restrained interstate commerce.

Our view of what is a reasonable restraint of commerce is controlled by the recognized purpose of the Sherman Law itself. Whether this type of restraint is reasonable or not must be judged in part at least in the light of its effect on competition, for whatever difference of opinion there may be among economists as to the social and economic desirability of an unrestrained competitive system, it cannot be doubted that the Sherman Law and the judicial decisions interpreting it are based upon the assumption that the public interest is best protected from the evils of monopoly and price control by the maintenance of competition. The aim and result of every price-fixing agreement, if effective, is the elimination of one form of competition.

The power to fix prices, whether reasonably exercised or not, involves power to control the market and to fix arbitrary and unreasonable prices. The reasonable price fixed today may through economic and business changes become the unreasonable price of tomorrow. Once established, it may be maintained unchanged

---

[2]This, of course, does not mean that all single-sex schools are violating the antitrust laws. They are in violation only if their admissions policy results from an agreement with competitors.

because of the absence of competition secured by the agreement for a price reasonable when fixed. Agreements which create such potential power may well be held to be in themselves unreasonable or unlawful restraints, without the necessity of minute inquiry whether a particular price is reasonable or unreasonable as fixed and without placing on the government in enforcing the Sherman Law the burden of ascertaining from day to day whether it has become unreasonable through the mere variation of economic conditions.

Moreover, in the absence of express legislation requiring it, we should hesitate to adopt a construction making the difference between legal and illegal conduct in the field of business relations depend upon so uncertain a test as whether prices are reasonable—a determination which can be satisfactorily made only after a complete survey of our economic organization and a choice between rival philosophies. Thus viewed, the Sherman law is not only a prohibition against the infliction of a particular type of public injury. It is a limitation of rights which may be pushed to evil consequences and therefore restrained.

It follows that the judgment of the circuit court of appeals must be reversed and the judgment of the district court reinstated.

Reversed.

The Supreme Court has referred to this type of collusion as "the supreme evil of antitrust," and it has been illegal for the better part of a century.[3] But it never seems to go away. Here are some examples:

- Using a computer to analyze the bids that schools received on their milk contracts, the Florida attorney-general uncovered a pervasive price-fixing scheme. Forty-three companies were convicted or pleaded guilty; two dozen individuals went to prison. Companies paid fines in excess of $90 million.

- Colleges were concerned about the cost of their athletic programs. In particular, the cost of the coaching staffs seemed out of control. In response, NCAA schools (that is, members of the National Collegiate Athletic Association) agreed to cap the salaries of assistant coaches. But a court blew the whistle, finding that the NCAA had engaged in illegal price fixing. A jury awarded the coaches $66 million.

- Samsung Electronics Co. paid a $300 million fine for having conspired to fix the prices of computer chips. Other companies engaged in the conspiracy have paid $346 million in fines. These fines were topped by that paid by pharmaceutical company F. Hoffmann–La Roche—$500 million for conspiring to fix the prices of vitamins. Executives went to prison for their roles in these conspiracies.

In these cases, the Justice Department found hard evidence of an illegal agreement. But what if there is only *circumstantial* evidence? Suppose competitors just happen to charge the same prices. If competitors act in concert but without an explicit agreement, their behavior is called **conscious parallelism**. As the following case illustrates, **conscious parallelism is illegal only if plus factors are present**. Plus factors include:

- A motive to conspire

- A high level of communication among firms

conscious parallelism
When competitors who do not have an explicit agreement nonetheless all make the same competitive decisions.

[3]*Verizon Communs., Inc. v. Trinko, LLP*, 540 U.S. 398 (S.Ct. 2004).

FEARS V. WILHELMINA MODEL AGENCY, INC.

2004 U.S. DIST. LEXIS 4502
United States District Court for the Southern District of New York, 2004

Facts: A group of models sued some of the top agencies in New York, alleging that these firms had violated §1 of the Sherman Act by conspiring to fix the commissions that they charged the models for placing them. The agencies were all members of the International Model Managers Association, Inc. (IMMA).

Under New York law, *employment* agencies could not charge a commission of more than 10 percent, but *management* agencies could. All agencies that were members of IMMA changed their state registration from employment agency to management agency and then raised their standard commission to 20 percent. Several of the agencies used identical language in their contracts, specifying that they were personal managers, not employment agencies. At IMMA meetings, executives at various agencies announced that they were raising their commissions to 20 percent. One executive stated, "We are all committing suicide, if we do not stick together ..."

Executives at the agencies admitted that they knew instantly every time an agency raised prices. One executive stated, "The more uniformity in the prices, the more I think it was—it was something that you could then compete on the quality of your models on the service, and not just on—on rates, you know. So we were always favorable to letting everyone know as much as possible about—about our pricing policies."

The models also presented memoranda from the agencies, stating:

- "IMMA should send out a letter stating that we plan on pursuing a 1-1/2 percent finance charge on clients who pay after 30 days in lieu of increasing our service charge."

- The commission would increase from 15 to 20 percent, and "all other agencies will go along with this increase. Please inform your clients accordingly so that there is no misunderstanding."

- "Pauline's agreed with me but as usual, Bill Weinberg cautioned me about price fixing ... Ha! Ha! Ha! ... the usual bulls–t! I warned him that by not sticking together, we would have to make 40 percent more volume in order to make the same figures as last year, but you know Bill, he always thinks he can get more if he acts that way."

IMMA minutes reported that members had adopted uniform schedules for the Christmas holiday. In addition, the agencies agreed to operate "ethically," by which they meant that they would not try to hire models from other agencies. A letter to all members of IMMA reported that one agency had broken this rule by hiring model Michele Weweje.

The agencies admitted that they had engaged in parallel behavior, but they argued that these activities were not sufficient to support a charge of illegal price fixing. The agencies moved for summary judgment.

Issues: *Did the modeling agencies engage in illegal price fixing? Is parallel behavior illegal?*

Excerpts from Judge Baer's Decision: To be sure, business behavior is admissible circumstantial evidence from which the factfinder may infer agreement. But this Court has never held that proof of parallel business behavior conclusively establishes agreement or, phrased differently, that such behavior itself constitutes a Sherman Act offense. Because parallel activity may be equally suggestive of independent conduct, plaintiffs offering parallel conduct as evidence of an antitrust conspiracy must demonstrate additional circumstances, often referred to as "plus factors," which provide a supplemental basis to infer a conspiracy. Among recognized plus factors, two in particular have received significant exposure in case law, both of which have a strong presence in this case—a motive to conspire and a high level of inter-firm communication.

With regard to the first plus factor, there is no question that defendants possessed a common rational motive to conspire—the ability to raise models' commissions without suffering loss of business.

[As for the second plus factor,] I find that the extensive evidence of agreements between IMMA members, on various components of their businesses, such as client service fees, holiday closing schedules, cancellation policies, and penalties borne by management companies who attract models from competitors, may reasonably be inferred to demonstrate an industry inundated with collusion.

Plaintiffs have established that all defendants who were members of IMMA, and therefore participated in or were privy to the conversations and agreements discussed above, had a unity of purpose or a common design and understanding, or a meeting of minds in an unlawful arrangement. [Therefore, the court denies the agencies' motion for summary judgment.]

Refusals to Deal

Every company generally has the right to decide with whom it will or will not do business. However, a refusal to deal is a rule of reason violation of the Sherman Act, and illegal if it harms competition. In a refusal to deal, a group of competitors boycotts a buyer, supplier, or even another competitor. For example, a group of clothing manufacturers agreed that they would not sell apparel to retailers who also bought from style pirates—companies that copied the manufacturers' designs. The Supreme Court held that this was an illegal refusal to deal because it was harming competition.[4]

EXAM Strategy

Question: Lawyers who were paid by the district to represent poor clients in Washington, D.C., agreed among themselves not to accept any new cases until their fees were raised to the level they had agreed upon. Have the lawyers violated the Sherman Act? If so, what kind of violation is it?

Strategy: This is a trick question because the lawyers committed not one, but two violations of the Sherman Act. Remember, too, that there are two types of Sherman Act violations—rule of reason and *per se*.

Result: First, the attorneys were fixing prices—they agreed together on their fees. Price fixing is a *per se* violation and therefore automatically illegal. In addition, they engaged in a refusal to deal. This is a rule of reason violation, which is illegal only if it harms competition.

Vertical Cooperative Strategies

Vertical cooperative strategies are agreements among participants at different stages of the production process.

Reciprocal Dealing Agreements

Under a reciprocal dealing agreement, a buyer refuses to purchase goods from a supplier unless the supplier also purchases items from the buyer. Imagine that you are in the business of processing beets into sugar. During this process, it is easy to separate the seeds, which can then be used to grow more beets. Why not suggest to your beet suppliers that they buy their seeds from you? Why not further suggest that if *they* are not willing, you will find other suppliers who are?[5]

You are proposing a reciprocal dealing agreement. In the past, such arrangements were common. Many major corporations even kept records of purchases, sales, and "balance of trade" with other companies. Although these arrangements might have made *business* sense, the government took the view that they were also *rule of reason* violations of the Sherman Act; that is, they were illegal if they had an anticompetitive

[4]*Fashion Originators' Guild of America, Inc. v. Federal Trade Commission*, 312 U.S. 457, 1941 U.S. LEXIS 1318 (1941).
[5]See *Betaseed, Inc. v. U & I, Inc.*, 681 F.2d 1203, 1982 U.S. App. LEXIS 17190 (9th Cir. 1982).

effect. The government brought suit against several companies, including a beet processor. It also halted a number of mergers that might have resulted in internal reciprocal arrangements. In recent years, however, the government has brought few of these cases. Reciprocal dealing agreements today are likely to be a problem only if they foreclose a *significant share* of the market and if the participants *agree* not to buy from others.

Price Discrimination

Under the Robinson-Patman Act, it is illegal to charge different prices to different purchasers if:

- The items are the same, and
- The price discrimination lessens competition.

However, it is legal to charge a lower price to a particular buyer if:

- The costs of serving this buyer are lower, or
- The seller is simply meeting competition.

Congress passed the Robinson-Patman Act (RPA) in 1936 to prevent large chains from driving small, local stores out of business. Owners of these "Ma and Pa stores" complained that the large chains could sell goods cheaper because suppliers charged them lower prices. As a result of the RPA, managers who would otherwise like to develop different pricing strategies for specific customers or regions may hesitate to do so for fear of violating this statute. In reality, however, they have little to fear.

Under the RPA, a plaintiff must prove that price discrimination occurred and that it lessened competition. It is now perfectly permissible, for example, for a supplier to sell at a different price to its Texas and California distributors, or to its health care and educational distributors, so long as the distributors are not in competition with each other.

The RPA also expressly permits price variations that are based on differences in cost. Thus Kosmo's Kitchen would be perfectly within its legal rights to sell its frozen cheese enchiladas to Giant at a lower price than to Corner Grocery if Kosmo's costs are lower to do so. Giant often buys shipments the size of railroad containers that cost less to deliver than smaller boxes.

The federal government seems to have little interest in enforcing the RPA. Some federal officials have even urged that the RPA be repealed to prevent it from interfering with the smooth operation of the market. This fade-out of government action has left enforcement in the hands of individual plaintiffs, but these cases are receiving little encouragement from the courts.

The Supreme Court has, for instance, made it much more difficult for plaintiffs to win damages in price discrimination cases. Chrysler Motors charged higher prices to the J. Truett Payne dealership than to other car dealers in Birmingham, Alabama. Unable to compete, Payne went out of business. The accepted formula for determining damages in an RPA case *had been* the difference between the two prices multiplied by the number of units purchased. These numbers were easy to calculate. However, in *Payne*, the Supreme Court held that it is not enough to prove that competitors are able to buy at a lower cost. The plaintiff must also show that these competitors passed their savings on to customers and, as a result, the plaintiff lost profits.[6] These are difficult facts to prove. As a result of cases such as

---

[6] *J. Truett Payne Co., Inc. v. Chrysler Motors Corp.*, 451 U.S. 557, 1981 U.S. LEXIS 49 (1981).

this, antitrust lawyers sometimes advise their clients not to worry too much about price discrimination suits because dissatisfied customers will usually not seek damages in court but will instead try to negotiate a better price.

In the following case, a food fight broke out. Will the court intervene?

You be the Judge

FEESERS, INC. V. MICHAEL FOODS, INC.

591 F.3d 191, 2010 U.S. App. Lexis 337
United States Court of Appeals for
the Third Circuit, 2010

Facts: This case is about food that is served in institutions such as schools, hospitals, and nursing homes, likely including institutions in which you have eaten. Michael Foods was the nation's largest producer of a product unappetizingly referred to as "liquid eggs." It sold its egg products and potatoes to (1) distributors who simply resold the food to "self-ops" (who prepared it themselves in-house) and (2) food service management companies that bought, prepared, and served food in institutions. Feesers, Inc. distributed food to self-ops within a 200-mile radius of Harrisburg, Pennsylvania, while Sodexo, Inc. was a food service management company that served institutions worldwide. (Sodexo was the largest private purchaser of food in the world.) Both Feesers and Sodexo bought products from Michael's.

Institutions sometimes switched back and forth between preparing food themselves and hiring a food service management company to do it. Feesers and Sodexo competed against each other when a customer considered switching from self-op to food service management, or vice versa.

Michael's sold its products to Feesers at prices that were as much as 59 percent higher than those it charged Sodexo. Indeed, when courting customers, Sodexo touted its access to discounted food. However, when customers made a decision to hire Sodexo, they did not know the exact prices of food because they were buying the whole service package.

Feesers alleged that Michael's discounts to Sodexo violated the RPA. The trial court found for Feesers. Michael's appealed.

You Be the Judge: *Did Michael's engage in illegal price discrimination?*

Argument for Feesers: The behavior in this case is exactly why Congress passed the RPA. Because a multinational company is able to buy its products cheaper, it obtains a huge competitive advantage over a smaller, local distributor. This unfair advantage enables Sodexo to take customers away from Feesers.

In marketing its product, Sodexo brags that its food prices are lower. Although our customers may not know the exact cost of eggs and potatoes, they do know that Sodexo's prices are lower. That gives Sodexo an unfair competitive advantage.

Argument for Michael's: Although Feesers and Sodexo both buy food from Michael's, they are not competitors. Sodexo handles all dining services for its customers; supplying food is only a small part. Feesers just distributes food. No one would choose the full service option because of lower prices on eggs and potatoes.

The competition between Feesers and Sodexo occurs *before* they buy any food from Michael's. When customers consider switching from self-op to food service management, or vice versa, their decision is not based on the price of a limited number of food items. Indeed, they have no idea what they would be paying for eggs or potatoes at Sodexo. If an institution chooses to self-operate, Sodexo is eliminated from the competition, and if an institution chooses the full food service route, then Feesers cannot compete. Only after the winner of that competition is chosen does the customer actually pay, directly or indirectly, for any food from Michael's.

Even if Feesers and Sodexo did compete, there is no evidence that *competition* has been harmed. As we saw in the *Truett Payne* case, to win here, Feesers must show a connection between lower prices and injury to competition. That evidence is missing.

Mergers and Joint Ventures

The Clayton Act prohibits mergers that are anticompetitive. Companies with substantial assets must notify the FTC *before* consummating a merger.[7] This notification gives the government an opportunity to prevent a merger ahead of time rather than trying to untangle one after the fact.

Horizontal Mergers

A horizontal merger involves companies that compete in the same market. Traditionally, the government has aggressively sought to prevent horizontal mergers that could lead to a monopoly or even a highly concentrated industry. In the *Von's Grocery* case, decided in 1966, the Supreme Court upheld the Justice Department in its suit to prevent the merger of two grocery chains that represented only 7.5 percent of the grocery market in Los Angeles.[8] Compare that decision with the following landmark case, decided almost 20 years later.

Landmark Case

UNITED STATES V. WASTE MANAGEMENT, INC.

743 F.2d 976, 1984 U.S. App. LEXIS 18843
United States Court of Appeals for the Second Circuit, 1984

Facts: Waste Management, Inc. (WMI) acquired Texas Industrial Disposal, Inc. (TIDI). Both companies were in the trash collection business. In Dallas, their combined market share was 48.8 percent. The trial court held that the merger was illegal and ordered WMI to divest itself of TIDI.

Issue: *Did WMI violate the Clayton Act by acquiring TIDI?*

Excerpts from Judge Winter's Decision: A post-merger market share of 48.8 percent is sufficient to establish *prima facie* illegality under *United States v. Philadelphia National Bank* and its progeny. That decision held that large market shares are a convenient proxy for appraising the danger of monopoly power resulting from a horizontal merger. Under its rationale, a merger resulting in a large market share is presumptively illegal, rebuttable only by a demonstration that the merger will not have anticompetitive effects.

[In the present case, the *Philadelphia National Bank*] presumption is rebuted by the fact that competitors can enter the Dallas waste hauling market with such ease. WMI argues that it is unable to raise prices over the competitive level because new firms would quickly enter the market and undercut them. A person wanting to start in the trash collection business can acquire a truck, a few containers, drive the truck himself, and operate out of his home. A great deal depends on the individual's personal initiative, and whether he has the desire and energy to perform a high quality of service. If he measures up well by these standards, he can compete successfully with any other company for a portion of the trade, even though a small portion. Over the last 10 years or so, a number of companies have started in the commercial trash collection business.

We conclude that the 48.8 percent market share attributed to WMI does not accurately reflect future market power. Since that power is in fact insubstantial, the merger does not, therefore, substantially lessen competition in the relevant market and does not violate the [Clayton Act].

---

[7]Under a statutory amendment called Hart-Scott-Rodino, a transaction must be reported if it involves assets of $68.2 million or higher, or if one party has assets or net revenues of $136.4 million or higher and the other party has at least $13.6 million in assets or net revenues. The FTC adjusts these figures annually for inflation.

[8]*United States v. Von's Grocery Co.*, 384 U.S. 270, 1966 U.S. LEXIS 2823 (1966).

Traditionally, market share was the most important factor in evaluating mergers. As *Waste Management* indicates, however, market share is no longer the major issue in merger cases. The government and the courts now also consider how the merger will affect competition and consumers. Thus the government cleared a merger between aircraft giants Boeing and McDonnell Douglas, which together had a virtual monopoly on the American aircraft business. But the aircraft market is global, and American companies faced severe competition from Europe's Airbus consortium. Therefore, the government believed that the merger would not harm competition.

Conversely, the FTC blocked the merger of office supply giants Staples, Inc., and Office Depot. Nationally, these two retailers controlled only 4 percent of the market for office supplies. Was the FTC harking back to the days of *Von's Grocery*? Not exactly. The office superstores' *national* market share was relatively low because they had no stores at all in many areas of the country. Rather than national market share, the FTC focused instead on their ability to control prices *locally*. The agency found that, when both stores operated in the same market, prices were significantly lower than when only one store was present. Thus, a box of file folders cost $1.72 in Orlando, Florida (where both stores competed), and $4.17 in nearby Leesburg (where Office Depot had a monopoly). In the FTC's view, if the two stores combined, they would have had enough power in local markets to raise prices and harm consumers.

Vertical Mergers

A vertical merger involves companies at different stages of the production process—for example, when a producer of a final good acquires a supplier, or vice versa. If Staples bought a paper manufacturer, that would be a vertical merger. This type of merger can also be anticompetitive, especially if it reduces entry into a market by locking up an important supplier or a top distributor. However, the Justice Department's guidelines provide that it will challenge vertical mergers only if they are likely to increase entry barriers in a concentrated market.

Joint Ventures

A joint venture is a partnership for a limited purpose—the companies do not combine permanently, they simply work together on a specific project. The government will usually permit a joint venture, even between competitors with significant market power. The FTC approved, over strenuous objections from competitors, a joint venture between General Motors and Toyota to produce cars.

AGGRESSIVE STRATEGIES

The goal of an aggressive strategy is to gain an unfair advantage over competitors.

Monopolization

Aggressive competition is beneficial for consumers—up until the moment a company develops enough power to control a market. One purpose of the Sherman Act is to prevent this type of control. **Under Section 2 of the act, it is illegal to monopolize or attempt to monopolize a market.** To monopolize means to acquire a monopoly in the wrong way. *Having* a monopoly is legal unless it is *gained* or *maintained* by using wrongful tactics.

To determine if a defendant has illegally monopolized, we must ask three questions:

- **What is the market?** Without knowing the market, it is impossible to determine if someone is controlling it.

- **Does the company control the market?** Without control, there is no monopoly.

- **How did the company acquire or maintain its control?** Monopolization is illegal only if gained or kept in the wrong way.

What Is the Market?

This question is not as easy to answer as it sounds. **The short answer is that if buyers view two products as close substitutes, then the items are in the same market.** The longer answer is that every product actually has two markets. The **product market** consists of other *items* that a purchaser could buy; the **geographic market** is other *areas* where a purchase could be made.

Imagine that your company sells soft drinks in Smallville. These drinks have unusual food flavors—steak and cheese, among others. For some reason, you are the only company in that area that sells food-flavored soft drinks, so, by definition, you control 100 percent of the market. But is that the *relevant* market? Perhaps the relevant market is flavored drinks or soft drinks or all beverages. The question economists ask is: **How high can your prices rise before your buyers will switch to a different product?** (This concept is called *cross-elasticity of demand*.) If a price increase from $1 to $1.05 a bottle causes many of your customers to buy Coke instead, it is clear you are part of a larger market. Moreover, if changes in the prices of other drinks affect *your* sales, your products and theirs are probably close competitors. However, if you could raise your price to $5 per bottle and still hold on to many of your customers, then you might well be in your own market. **Likewise, the relevant geographic market is the area where buyers will go to buy your drink.** Thus, if you raise your prices in Smallville and then many of your customers begin buying your drinks at a lower price in Metropolis, both cities are in the same geographic market.

EXAM Strategy

Question: Ticketmaster sells tickets online to sports and entertainment events. RMG sued Ticketmaster, alleging that it was engaged in an illegal effort to monopolize national ticket sales. What was the relevant market?

Strategy: RMG had to define both a product market and a geographic market.

Result: If Ticketmaster raises the prices for NFL tickets in Miami, FL customers will probably not choose instead to buy seats to a Taylor Swift concert in Oakland, CA. Therefore, national ticket sales are not the relevant market. Rather, the markets are small and focused. The court dismissed RMG's monopolization claim because the company had defined the wrong market.

Does the Company Control the Market?

You have 100 percent of the food-flavored soft drink market (although only 1 percent of the overall soft drink market and an infinitesimal percentage of the total beverage market). Traditionally, courts considered a monopoly to be a share anywhere between 70 and 90 percent. However, under modern antitrust law, market share is not important if other competitors can enter the market anytime they want (or anytime you raise your prices or lower your quality). **No matter what your market share, you do not have a monopoly unless you can exclude competitors or control prices.** For example, the Justice Department sued a movie theater chain that possessed a 93 percent share of the box office in Las Vegas. But the court ruled against the Justice Department because the chain's market share decreased to 75 percent within three years. This decline indicated that the company did not control the market and that barriers to entry were low.[9]

How Did the Company Acquire or Maintain Its Control?

> Possessing a monopoly is not necessarily illegal; using *"bad acts"* to acquire or maintain one is.

Possessing a monopoly is not necessarily illegal; using *"bad acts"* to acquire or maintain one is. If the law prohibited the mere possession of a monopoly, it might discourage companies from producing excellent products or offering low prices. Anyone who can produce a better product cheaper is entitled to a monopoly. In your case, you have very cleverly developed a secret method for adding flavors to carbonated water. You also have an efficient factory and highly trained workers, so you can sell your drinks for 5¢ a bottle less than your competitors. If, in fact, you do have a monopoly, it is for all the right reasons. You have demonstrated exactly the kind of innovative, efficient behavior that benefits consumers. If you were sued for a violation of the antitrust laws, you would win.

Some companies use ruthless tactics to acquire or maintain a monopoly. It is these "bad acts" that render a monopoly illegal. In the past, the definition of bad acts was broad, and any company with a monopoly could be in violation unless it showed that, despite its best efforts to duck, a monopoly had been *thrust upon* it. In 1945, a famous judge, with the appropriate name of Learned Hand, found that Alcoa's monopoly in the aluminum industry was illegal because the company had repeatedly expanded capacity to anticipate demand.[10] In his view, the company should have waited to expand until demand actually existed. Alcoa was in violation because it could have easily *avoided* a monopoly—the monopoly had not been thrust upon it.

Everyone makes mistakes. Although Learned Hand is generally considered one of the greatest judges of his era, most commentators now believe that *Alcoa* was wrongly decided. *Berkey Photo* is a more typical modern case.[11] Berkey accused Eastman Kodak Co. of repeatedly and unnecessarily changing the size of its cameras to confound competitors who manufactured film to fit them. Although Learned Hand most likely would have found such actions to be illegal, the *Berkey* court rejected the view that monopolies are acceptable only if *thrust upon* the defendant and instead held that aggressive competitive strategies are legal even if they have the effect of hindering competitors. In finding Kodak not liable, the court reasoned that the company would not have repeatedly changed camera and film specifications if consumers had objected. The success or failure of Kodak's strategy ought to be determined in the market and not by the courts.

Today, a typical bad act is sham litigation in which a competitor files baseless lawsuits for the sole purpose of harming competition. For example, to prevent Glitzy Restaurant from opening its doors, Family Eatery files a suit against Glitzy alleging that this potential competitor has violated Family's trademark, even though Family knows the allegation is not true. That lawsuit would be a bad act.

[9]*United States v. Syufy Enterprises*, 903 F.2d 659, 1990 U.S. App. LEXIS 7396 (9th Cir. 1990).
[10]*United States v. Aluminum Co. of America*, 148 F.2d 416, 1945 U.S. App. LEXIS 4091 (2d Cir. 1945). *Note:* Judge Hand's parents did not necessarily foresee his illustrious career when naming him. "Learned" was his mother's maiden name, and it was the tradition in his family to give the mother's name to one of the children.
[11]*Berkey Photo, Inc. v. Eastman Kodak Co.*, 603 F.2d 263, 1979 U.S. App. LEXIS 13692 (2d Cir. 1979).

Predatory Pricing

Predatory pricing occurs when a company lowers its prices below cost to drive competitors out of business. Once the predator has the market to itself, it raises prices to make up lost profits—and more besides.

Recall that, under Section 2 of the Sherman Act, it is illegal "to monopolize" and also to "attempt to monopolize." Typically, the goal of a predatory pricing scheme is either to win control of a market or to maintain it. A ban on these schemes prevents monopolization and attempts to monopolize. To win a predatory pricing case, the plaintiff must prove three elements:

- The defendant is selling its products *below cost*.

- The defendant *intends* that the plaintiff go out of business.

- If the plaintiff does go out of business, the defendant will be able to earn sufficient profits to *recoup* its prior losses.

The classic example of predatory pricing is a large grocery store that comes into a small town offering exceptionally low prices subsidized by profits from its other branches. Once all the "Ma and Pa" corner groceries go out of business, MegaGrocery raises its prices to much higher levels.

Predatory pricing offers a good example of how attitudes toward antitrust laws have changed. Formerly, courts took predatory pricing very seriously. The term certainly *sounds* bad. But despite its name, courts generally are not as concerned about predatory pricing now as they used to be. For one thing, consumers benefit from price wars, at least in the short run. For another, the cases are hard to prove. Here is why:

- **The defendant is selling its products below cost.** This rule sounds sensible, but what does "cost" mean? As you know from your economics courses, there are many different kinds of costs—total, average variable, marginal, to name a few. Under current law, any price below *average variable cost* is generally presumed to be predatory.[12] The rule may be easy to state, but, in real life, average variable cost is difficult to calculate. First, plaintiffs must obtain most of the data from the defendant. Even if a defendant has a good idea of what its average variable costs are, it will not willingly tell all in court. Moreover, many of the economic decisions about what items fit into which cost category are subjective. It is difficult for the plaintiff to prove that its subjective view is closer to the truth than the defendant's.

- **The defendant intends that the plaintiff go out of business.** Even if Ma and Pa can calculate MegaGrocery's average variable cost to the satisfaction of a court, they will not necessarily win their case. They must prove that MegaGrocery intended to put them out of business. That is a pretty tall order, short of finding some smoking gun like a strategic plan that explicitly says MegaGrocery wants Ma and Pa gone.

- **If the plaintiff does go out of business, the defendant will be able to earn sufficient profits to recoup its prior losses.** Until Ma and Pa go out of business, MegaGrocery will lose money—after all, it is selling food below cost. To win their case, Ma and Pa must show that MegaGrocery will be able to make up all its lost profits once the corner grocery is out of the way. They need to prove, for example, that no other grocery chain will come to town. It is difficult to prove a negative proposition like that, especially in the grocery business where barriers to entry are low.

In recent times, plaintiffs have not had much success with predatory pricing suits. For example, Liggett began selling generic cigarettes 30 percent below the price of branded

---

[12]To calculate average variable cost, add all the firm's costs except its fixed costs and then divide by the total quantity of output.

cigarettes. Brown & Williamson retaliated by introducing its own generics at an even lower price. Liggett sued, claiming that Brown's prices were below cost. The Supreme Court agreed that Brown was not only selling below cost, but also intended to harm Liggett. Brown still won the case, however, because there was no evidence that it would be able to recover its losses from the below-cost pricing. If Brown raised its prices, other competitors would come back into the market.[13]

Tying Arrangements

A **tying arrangement** is an agreement to sell a product on the condition that the buyer also purchases a different (or tied) product. A tying arrangement is illegal under Section 3 of the Clayton Act and §1 of the Sherman Act if:

- The two products are clearly separate,
- The seller requires the buyer to purchase the two products together,
- The seller has significant power in the market for the tying product, and
- The seller is shutting out a significant part of the market for the tied product.

Six movie distributors refused to sell individual films to television stations. Instead, they insisted that a station buy an entire package of movies. To obtain classics such as *Treasure of the Sierra Madre* and *Casablanca* (the **tying product**), the station also had to purchase such forgettable films as *Nancy Drew Troubleshooter*, *Gorilla Man*, and *Tugboat Annie Sails Again* (the **tied product**).[14] The distributors engaged in an illegal tying arrangement. These are the questions that the court asked:

- **Are the two products clearly separate?** A left and right shoe are not separate products, and a seller can legally require that they be purchased together. *Gorilla Man*, on the other hand, is a separate product from *Casablanca*.

- **Is the seller requiring the buyer to purchase the two products together?** Yes, that is the whole point of these "package deals."

- **Does the seller have significant power in the market for the tying product?** In this case, the tying products are the classic movies. Since they are copyrighted, no one else can show them without the distributor's permission. The six distributors controlled a great many classic movies. So, yes, they do have significant market power.

- **Is the seller shutting out a significant part of the market for the tied product?** In this case, the tied products are the undesirable films like *Tugboat Annie Sails Again*. Television stations forced to take the unwanted films did not buy "B" movies from other distributors. These other distributors were effectively foreclosed from a substantial part of the market.

EXAM Strategy

Question: A group of cemeteries required everyone who purchased a burial plot to also buy the gravestone from the cemetery. Is this an illegal tying arrangement?

---

[13]*Brooke Group Ltd. v. Brown & Williamson Tobacco Corp.*, 509 U.S. 209, 1993 U.S. EXIS 4245 (1993).
[14]*United States v. Loew's Inc.*, 371 U.S. 38, 1962 U.S. LEXIS 2332 (1962).

Strategy: To answer this question, you need to determine if the seller has significant market power. To do that, you must first know what the relevant market is.

Result: The plaintiffs in this case argued that each cemetery was its own market and therefore, controlled the market. But if you look at the section above called "What Is the Market?" you will see that the relevant question is: if a cemetery raises its prices, what will consumers do? The answer is that they will choose another cemetery nearby, of which there are plenty. Thus, the tying arrangement was not illegal because the cemeteries did not have significant market power.[15]

Controlling Distributors and Retailers

The goal of an aggressive strategy is to force competitors out of a market—by undercutting their prices or tying products together, for example. Controlling distributors and retailers is another method for excluding competitors. It is difficult to compete in a market if you are foreclosed from the best distribution channels.

Allocating Customers and Territory

As we saw earlier in this chapter, a *horizontal* agreement by *competitors* to allocate customers and territories is a *per se* violation of Section 1 of the Sherman Act. **However, a vertical allocation of customers or territory is illegal only if it adversely affects competition in the market as a whole.** It is a rule of reason, not a *per se*, violation.

Suppose that Hot Sound, Inc. produces expensive, high-quality speakers. It grants its distributors the exclusive right to sell in a particular territory or the exclusive right over a particular type of customer (consumers, corporate, automobiles). In return for these exclusive rights, Hot Sound requires the distributors to stock a wide range of inventory, hire highly trained (expensive) sales help, and advertise widely. Such requirements not only increase sales, but also enhance distributor loyalty. The distributors have such a large investment in Hot Sound's products that they are reluctant to switch to another manufacturer. A change would mean unloading a large inventory, developing new advertisements, and retraining or laying off some of the sales force.

Hot Sound clearly has good business reasons for adopting such a plan. It is reducing intrabrand competition (among its dealers) but enhancing interbrand competition (between brands). With its committed dealer network, Hot Sound can compete more fiercely against other brands. Vertical allocation is a rule of reason violation, which means that the law will intervene only if Hot Sound's activities have an anticompetitive impact on the market as a whole. But because Hot Sound's plan increases interbrand competition, it is unlikely to have an anticompetitive impact.

Exclusive Dealing Agreements

An **exclusive dealing contract** is one in which a distributor or retailer agrees with a supplier not to carry the products of any other supplier. **Under Section 1 of the Sherman Act and Section 3 of the Clayton Act, exclusive dealing contracts are subject to a rule of reason and are illegal only if they have an anticompetitive effect.**

Consider the case of Ben & Jerry's. With more than $100 million in sales, it was a major player in the ice cream market. And some of its competitors alleged that it was playing hardball. Just ask Amy Miller. She started Amy's Ice Creams in a small storefront in Austin, Texas. Her ice cream was so popular that she decided to begin producing pints for sale in

Exclusive dealing contract
A contract in which a distributor or retailer agrees with a supplier not to carry the products of any other supplier.

[15]*Monument Builders v. Michigan Cemetery Association*, 2008 U.S. App. LEXIS 9381 (6th Cir. 2008).

grocery stores. But when she tried to enter the Houston market, Sunbelt, the dominant distributor in the area, refused to carry her desserts. She thinks Sunbelt turned her down because Ben & Jerry's had forbidden it to carry other premium brands.

Ironically, the ice cream was once in the other bowl, so to speak. When Ben and Jerry were the new boys on the block, they discovered that Pillsbury (owner of Häagen-Dazs) included provisions in its contracts that prohibited distributors from carrying Ben & Jerry's products. When Ben & Jerry's produced written contracts containing these exclusory clauses, Pillsbury backed down immediately. Thereafter, no one in the industry used written distribution contracts.

Amy Miller threatened to sue Ben & Jerry's for violating the antitrust laws with exclusive dealing contracts. In determining if these agreements had an anticompetitive impact on the market, a court would consider the following factors:

- **The number of other distributors available.** Amy said that no one but Sunbelt would do because only the best distributors were able to preserve her ice cream's quality.

- **The portion of the market foreclosed by the exclusive dealing agreements.** Without Sunbelt, Amy's Ice Creams could not penetrate the Houston market, so it had to shut down its pint production line.

- **The ease with which new distributors could enter the market.** Sunbelt had few, if any, competitors. Presumably, the market was a difficult one to enter.

- **The possibility that Amy could distribute the products herself.** Not likely. As we have seen, it was a tough market to enter.

- **The legitimate business reasons that might have led the distributor to accept an exclusive contract.** Here is what Sunbelt's vice-president had to say: "We already had our table full with super premium pints. We felt Amy's was an underfinanced product and we would have had to replace a high-volume product to give it a shot. And we personally did not think the product was very good."[16] (Although, in the authors' opinion, her ice cream is very fine indeed.)

Would an exclusive dealing agreement between Ben & Jerry's and Sunbelt be anticompetitive? If so, would their business reasons justify the contract?

Resale Price Maintenance

Resale price maintenance (RPM), also called *vertical price fixing,* means the manufacturer sets *minimum* prices that retailers may charge. In other words, it prevents retailers from discounting. Why does the manufacturer care? After all, once the retailer purchases the item, the manufacturer has made its profit. The only way the manufacturer makes more money is to raise its *wholesale* price, not the *retail* price. RPM guarantees a profit margin for the *retailer.*

Manufacturers care about retail prices because pricing affects the product's image with consumers. Armani men's suits sell for around $2,000. What conclusion do you draw about the quality of those suits? Would your opinion change if you saw Armani suits being sold at discounted prices? You can understand that Armani might want to prohibit retailers from lowering the prices on its suits. Consumer advocates contend, however, that manufacturers such as Armani are simply protecting dealers from competition. Discounting may or may not harm products, but, they insist, RPM certainly hurts consumers. As you saw in the opening scenario, Tempur-Pedic's RPM prevented Sean from negotiating a lower price for his mattress.

[16]Rickie Windle, "Ben & Jerry's Creams Amy's," *Austin Business Journal,* Oct. 4, 1993, vol. 13, no. 33, §1, p. 1.

In 1911, the Supreme Court ruled that RPM was a *per se* violation of Section 1 of the Sherman Act.[17] However, what the Supreme Court giveth, it can also taketh away. In 2007, the Supreme Court overruled itself and held that **RPM is a rule of reason violation**. The following case explains why.

LEEGIN CREATIVE LEATHER PRODUCTS, INC. v. PSKS, INC.

127 S. Ct. 2705, 2007 U.S. LEXIS 8668
Supreme Court of the United States, 2007

Facts: Leegin manufactured belts and other women's fashion accessories under the brand name "Brighton." It sold these products only to small boutiques and specialty stores. Sales of the Brighton brand accounted for about half the profits at Kay's Kloset, a boutique in Lewisville, Texas.

Leegin decided it would no longer sell to retailers who discounted Brighton prices. It wanted to ensure that stores could afford to offer excellent service. It was also concerned that discounting harmed Brighton's image. Despite warnings from Leegin, Kay's Kloset persisted in marking down Brighton products by 20 percent. So Leegin cut the store off.

Kay's sued Leegin, alleging that the manufacturer had violated the *per se* rule against RPM. The trial court found for Kay's and entered judgment against Leegin for almost $4 million. The Court of Appeals affirmed. The Supreme Court granted *certiorari*. On appeal, Leegin did not dispute that it had entered into RPM agreements with retailers. Rather, it contended that the rule of reason should apply to those agreements.

Issue: *Is resale price maintenance a* **per se** *or rule of reason violation of the Sherman Act?*

Excerpts from Justice Kennedy's Decision:[18] To justify a *per se* prohibition, a restraint must have manifestly anticompetitive effects and lack any redeeming virtue. The few recent studies documenting the competitive effects of resale price maintenance cast doubt on the conclusion that the practice meets the criteria for a *per se* rule.

Minimum resale price maintenance can stimulate inter-brand competition—the competition among manufacturers selling different brands of the same type of product—by reducing intrabrand competition—the competition among retailers selling the same brand. A single manufacturer's use of vertical price restraints tends to eliminate intrabrand price competition; this in turn encourages retailers to invest in tangible or intangible services or promotional efforts that aid the manufacturer's position as against rival manufacturers. Resale price maintenance also has the potential to give consumers more options so that they can choose among low-price, low-service brands; high-price, high-service brands; and brands that fall in between.

Absent vertical price restraints, the retail services that enhance interbrand competition might be underprovided. This is because discounting retailers can free-ride on retailers who furnish services and then capture some of the increased demand those services generate. Consumers might learn, for example, about the benefits of a manufacturer's product from a retailer that invests in fine showrooms, offers product demonstrations, or hires and trains knowledgeable employees. Or consumers might decide to buy the product because they see it in a retail establishment that has a reputation for selling high-quality merchandise. If the consumer can then buy the product from a retailer that discounts because it has not spent capital providing services or developing a quality reputation, the high-service retailer will lose sales to the discounter, forcing it to cut back its services to a level lower than consumers would otherwise prefer.

While vertical agreements setting minimum resale prices can have procompetitive justifications, they may have anticompetitive effects in other cases. A manufacturer with market power might use resale price maintenance to give retailers an incentive not to sell the products of smaller rivals or new entrants. If the rule of reason were to apply to vertical price restraints, courts would have to be diligent in eliminating their anticompetitive uses from the market.

Vertical price restraints are to be judged according to the rule of reason.

---

[17]*Dr. Miles Medical Co. v. John D. Park & Sons*, 220 U.S. 373 (1911).

[18]As an indication of how controversial this issue is, the court split 5-4.

Vertical Maximum Price Fixing

In the case of resale price maintenance, the manufacturer sets the *minimum* prices its distributors can charge. **Vertical maximum price fixing (when a manufacturer sets maximum prices), is also a rule of reason violation of the Sherman Act.** The defendant is liable only if the price fixing harms competition. (You remember, from earlier in this chapter, that all *horizontal* price fixing is a *per se* violation.)

When State Oil Co. leased a gas station to Barkat Khan, it set a maximum price that Khan could charge for gas. Khan sued State Oil, but the Supreme Court ruled in favor of the oil company on the grounds that cutting prices to increase business is the very essence of competition and, furthermore, low prices benefit consumers.[19]

Chapter Conclusion

The purpose of the antitrust laws in the United States is to keep businesses on a narrow road. On the one hand, they may not swerve to one side and work too closely with competitors. Nor may they swerve to the other side and attack competitors too aggressively. Although managers sometimes resent the constraints imposed on them by antitrust laws, it is these laws that ensure the fair and open competition necessary for a healthy economy. In the end, the antitrust laws benefit us all.

EXAM REVIEW

1. ***PER SE* V. RULE OF REASON** *Per se* violations are automatic; courts do not consider mitigating circumstances. Rule of reason violations, on the other hand, are illegal only if they have an anticompetitive effect. (p. 579)

2. **MARKET DIVISION** Any effort by a group of competitors to divide their market is a *per se* violation of the Sherman Act. Illegal arrangements include agreements to allocate customers, territory, or products. (pp. 580–581)

EXAM Strategy

Question: Harcourt Brace Jovanovich (HBJ) granted BRG an exclusive license to market HBJ's bar review materials for law students in Georgia. HBJ agreed not to compete with BRG in Georgia, and BRG agreed not to compete with HBJ outside the state. HBJ was entitled to receive $100 per student enrolled by BRG and 40 percent of revenues over $350 per student. Did this agreement violate the antitrust laws?

Strategy: These two competitors have agreed to allocate territory. (See the "Result" at the end of this section.)

---

[19]*State Oil Co. v. Khan*, 522 U.S. 3, 1997 U.S. LEXIS 6705 (1997).

3. **HORIZONTAL PRICE FIXING AND BID RIGGING** Horizontal price fixing and bid rigging are *per se* violations of the Sherman Act. (pp. 581–582)

4. **REFUSALS TO DEAL** The Sherman Act prohibits competitors from joining together in an agreement to exclude a particular supplier, buyer, or even another competitor, if the agreement would have an anticompetitive effect. (pp. 584)

5. **RECIPROCAL DEALING AGREEMENT** Under a reciprocal dealing agreement, a buyer refuses to purchase goods from a supplier unless the supplier also purchases items from the buyer. Reciprocal dealing agreements violate the Sherman Act if they foreclose competitors from a significant part of the market. (pp. 584–585)

6. **ROBINSON-PATMAN ACT** The Robinson-Patman Act prohibits companies from selling the same item at different prices if the sale lessens competition. However, a seller may charge different prices if these prices reflect different costs or if the seller is just meeting competition. (pp. 585–586)

7. **MERGERS AND JOINT VENTURES** Under the Clayton Act, the federal government has the authority to prohibit anticompetitive mergers and joint ventures. (pp. 587–588)

8. **MONOPOLIZATION** Possessing a monopoly need not be illegal; acquiring or maintaining it through "bad acts" is. To determine if a company is guilty of monopolization, ask three questions:

   - What is the market?

   - Does the company control the market?

   - How did the company acquire or maintain its control? (pp. 588–590)

EXAM Strategy

Question: Another example of a bar review company behaving badly—this industry is highly competitive because the product is relatively indistinguishable. BAR/BRI was the largest bar review company in the country, with branches in 45 states. Barpassers was a much smaller company located only in Arizona and California. BAR/ BRI distributed pamphlets on campuses falsely suggesting that Barpassers was near bankruptcy. Enrollments in Barpassers' courses dropped, and the company was forced to postpone plans for expansion. Did Barpassers have an antitrust claim against BAR/BRI?

Strategy: It does not matter if BAR/BRI *had* a monopoly. These "bad acts" could have helped the company *acquire* one. (See the "Result" at the end of this section.)

9. **PREDATORY PRICING** To win a predatory pricing case, a plaintiff must prove three elements:

   - The defendant is selling its products below cost.

   - The defendant intends that the plaintiff go out of business.

   - If the plaintiff does go out of business, the defendant will be able to earn sufficient profit to recoup its prior losses. (pp. 591–592)

10. **TYING ARRANGEMENT** A tying arrangement is illegal if:

- The two products are clearly separate,
- The seller requires that the buyer purchase the two products together,
- The seller has significant power in the market for the tying product, and
- The seller is shutting out a significant part of the market for the tied product. (pp. 592–593)

EXAM Strategy

Question: Barber publishes the most successful college textbooks on the market. Students love them! But the company has just told college bookstores that it will no longer sell its textbooks to them unless the stores also buy its backpacks, which are specially designed to hold the texts. Would this arrangement create an antitrust problem?

Strategy: Does the seller have significant power in the market for the tying product (textbooks)? Is it shutting out a significant part of the market for the tied product (backpacks)? (See the "Result" at the end of this section.)

11. **CONTROLLING DISTRIBUTION** Efforts by a manufacturer to allocate customers or territory among its distributors are subject to a rule of reason. These allocations are illegal only if they have an anticompetitive effect. (pp. 593–594)

12. **EXCLUSIVE DEALING** An exclusive dealing contract is one in which a distributor or retailer agrees with a supplier not to carry the products of any other supplier. These contracts are subject to a rule of reason and are illegal only if they have an anticompetitive effect. (pp. 593–594)

13. **RESALE PRICE MAINTENANCE** If a manufacturer enters into an agreement with distributors or retailers to fix minimum prices, this arrangement is subject to the rule of reason standard—illegal only if it has an anticompetitive effect. (pp. 594–595)

14. **VERTICAL MAXIMUM PRICE FIXING** An arrangement whereby a manufacturer sets maximum prices is a rule of reason violation and, therefore, illegal only if it has an anticompetitive effect. (p. 596)

2. Result: Agreements between competitors to allocate territories are illegal under Section 1 of the Sherman Act.

8. Result: A jury found that BAR/BRI had violated Section 2 of the Sherman Act by attempting to create an illegal monopoly. The jury ordered BAR/BRI to pay Barpassers more than $3 million plus attorneys' fees.

10. Result: This arrangement would be an illegal tying arrangement if Barber is cutting out a significant portion of the backpack market. Presumably, college bookstores are a significant market segment. It does not matter that the backpacks are specially designed— it is up to the customers to determine if they prefer them.

MULTIPLE-CHOICE QUESTIONS

1. Are horizontal price fixing and vertical price fixing *per se* violations of the Sherman Act?

    (a) Yes, Yes

    (b) Yes, No

    (c) No, Yes

    (d) No, No

2. If Sterling Steel (SS) refused to buy concrete from Carat Concrete (CC) unless CC bought steel from SS, would that refusal to deal be a violation of antitrust laws?

    (a) Yes, a *per se* violation.

    (b) It used to be a violation but is no longer.

    (c) Yes, if the competitive impact is highly significant.

    (d) Yes, if SS has a monopoly.

3. Reserve Supply Corp., a cooperative of 379 lumber dealers, charged that Owens-Corning Fiberglass Corp. violated the Robinson-Patman Act by selling at lower prices to Reserve's competitors. It presented proof that these prices had harmed competition. Owens-Corning admitted that it had granted lower prices to a number of Reserve's competitors to meet, but not beat, the prices of other insulation manufacturers. Is Owens-Corning in violation of the RPA?

    (a) Yes, because the RPA requires that manufacturers charge all competitors the same price.

    (b) Yes, because any difference in price is a *per se* violation of the RPA.

    (c) Yes, because these price variations harmed competition.

    (d) No, because a manufacturer is not liable under the RPA if it charges lower prices to meet competition.

4. Oftentimes, if one airline lowers its prices on a particular route, so will all of the others. What is this type of activity called, and is it a violation of the antitrust laws?

    (a) Refusal to deal; it is a rule of reason violation.

    (b) Conscious parallelism; it is not a violation in itself.

    (c) Price discrimination; it is a *per se* violation.

    (d) Resale price maintenance; it is a rule of reason violation.

5. A horizontal merger is illegal if:

    (a) the resulting company controls at least 90 percent of the market.

    (b) the resulting company controls at least 50 percent of the market.

    (c) the resulting company has the ability to exclude competitors.

    (d) the resulting company has assets of $136.4 million or higher.

ESSAY QUESTIONS

1. Samantha manufactures 60 percent of the titanium screws sold in the United States. Does she have a monopoly on this product? What would you need to know to answer this question?

2. Texaco sold gasoline in Spokane, Washington, to independent retailers and also to Gulf Oil, which operated its own filling stations and also sold to retailers. Texaco charged a substantially lower price to Gulf than to the independent retailers. These retailers sued Texaco, alleging that this price structure violated the RPA. At trial, the retailers presented evidence that they could not compete against Gulf. Texaco did not present evidence that the different prices it charged reflected the costs of serving these two sets of customers. Did Texaco violate the RPA?

3. In New York City, 50 bakeries formed an association. They developed a system of distribution under which stores were allowed to buy only from a single baker. A store that wanted to shift to another baker had to consult the association and pay cash to the former baker. The association also decided to raise the retail price of bread. All the association's members printed the new price on their bread sleeves. Are the bakeries in violation of the antitrust laws?

4. **YOU BE THE JUDGE WRITING PROBLEM** American Academic Suppliers (AAS) and Beckley-Cardy (B-C) both sold educational supplies to schools. When B-C's sales began to plummet, it responded by reducing its catalog prices. It also offered an additional discount in states in which AAS was making substantial gains. What claim might AAS make against B-C? Is it likely to prevail in court? **Argument for AAS:** B-C has committed predatory pricing. The company is selling below cost for the purpose of driving us out of business. **Argument for B-C:** Even if we were to drive AAS out of business, we do not have enough market power to recoup our losses.

5. Suppose that Disney insists that retailers cannot sell DVDs of *Brave* for less than $16.99. The company threatens to cut off any retailers who discount that price. But stores would like to use these movies as a loss leader—selling them at a very low price to lure customers. Is it legal for Disney to cut off retailers who discount prices?

DISCUSSION QUESTIONS

1. Proponents of the Post Chicago School argue that federal antitrust regulators should undertake enforcement actions that will lead to lower consumer prices. Look at the five cases in this chapter. Are the courts' decisions likely to cause consumer prices to go up or down? Do you agree with the courts' decisions?

2. Is it appropriate for U. S. antitrust laws to apply overseas? Should businesspeople who never set foot in the United States be liable for activities they conducted in their own countries?

3. Pricegrabber.com is a website that helps online shoppers find the lowest-priced goods on the Internet. But it cannot always find the cheapest items because some online sellers are afraid to list their prices. If you go to Amazon.com, for example, you will see some items for which there is no price, just the legend, "To see our price, add this item to your cart." Amazon does that for fear that, after the *Leegin* case, manufacturers will refuse to supply items that it sells below the established retail price. Manufacturers worry that if they do not set some floor to their prices, other retailers will drop the products altogether. eBay and Amazon argue that the consumer is best served by a free market that permits them to set whatever prices they want. What is your view on RPM?

4. In Boston, 50 restaurants threatened to stop accepting the American Express card if the company refused to reduce the commission it charged on each purchase. Visa International, one of American Express's rivals, offered to pay the group's legal expenses. American Express then lowered its commission for all restaurants except for those with a volume lower than $1 million a year. Have either the restaurants, Visa or American Express, potentially violated the antitrust laws?

5. After acquiring the Schick brand name and electric shaver assets, North American Phillips controlled 55 percent of the electric shaver industry in the United States. Remington, a competitor, claimed that the acquisition of such a large market share was a violation of the law because the increased competition from Phillips would decrease Remington's profits. Does Remington have a valid claim?

6. **ETHICS** Clarice, a young woman with a mental disability, brought a malpractice suit against a doctor at the Medical Center. As a result, the Medical Center refused to treat her on a nonemergency basis. Clarice then went to another local clinic, which was later acquired by the Medical Center. Because the new clinic also refused to treat her, Clarice had to seek medical treatment in another town 40 miles away. Has the Medical Center violated the antitrust laws? Was it ethical to deny treatment to a patient?

CHAPTER 23

CYBERLAW

Garrett always said that his computer was his best friend. He was online all the time, g-chatting with his friends, listening to music, doing research for his courses, and, okay, maybe playing a few games now and again. Occasionally, the computer could be annoying. It would crash once in a while, trashing part of a paper before he saved it. And there was the time that a copy of an email he sent Lizzie complaining about Caroline somehow ended up in Caroline's inbox. He was pretty irritated when the White Sox tickets he bought in an online auction turned out to be for a Little League team. And he was tired of all the spam advertising pornographic websites. But these things happen and, despite the petty annoyances, his computer was an important part of his life.

Then one day, Garrett received a panicked text message from a teammate on his college wrestling squad telling him to click on a certain website pronto to see someone they knew. Garrett eagerly clicked on the website and discovered, to his horror, that *he* was featured—in the nude. The website was selling DVDs showing him and other members of the wrestling team in the locker room in various states of undress. Other DVDs, from other locker and shower rooms, were for sale, too, showing football players and wrestlers from dozens of universities. The DVDs had titles like "Straight Off the Mat" and "Voyeur Time." No longer trusting technology, Garrett pulled on his running shoes and dashed over to the office of his business law professor for help figuring out what his rights were.

> **Garrett eagerly clicked on the website and discovered, to his horror, that *he* was featured—in the nude.**

Computers and the Internet—cyberspace—together comprise one of the great technological developments of modern times.[1] And its importance and impact continue to grow. Beginning in December 2010, the world watched the "Arab Spring"—popular uprisings throughout the Middle East that brought down governments in Tunisia, Egypt, and Libya, and challenged leaders throughout the area. These movements were organized and fueled by the Internet. In response, threatened governments fought back by trying to limit access to the Internet generally and social media sites in particular. In Syria, police demanded the Facebook passwords of suspected protest organizers. Meanwhile, in England, a different type of protest challenged a court ruling. A married soccer player obtained an injunction prohibiting newspapers from revealing his alleged affair, or even the existence of the injunction. Within days, Ryan Giggs and his affair was one of the top topics on Twitter.

Cyberspace is a disruptive technology which can both fight repression and undermine legitimate laws. It has brought change to every aspect of our lives—how we make friends, buy things, obtain news, campaign for election, start revolutions, challenge the status quo.

Inevitably, new technologies create the need for new law. In the thirteenth century, England was one of the first countries to develop passable roads. Like the Internet, these roadways greatly enhanced communication, creating social and business opportunities, but also enabled new crimes. Good roads meant that bad guys could sneak out of town without paying their bills. Parliament responded with laws to facilitate the collection of out-of-town debts. Similarly, while the Internet has opened up enormous opportunities in both our business and personal lives, it has also created the need for new laws, both to pave the way for these opportunities and to limit their dangers.

The process of lawmaking never stops. Judges sit and legislatures meet—all in an effort to create better rules and a better society. However, in an established area of law, such as contracts, the basic structure changes little. Cyberlaw is different because it is still very much in its infancy. Not only are new laws being created almost daily, but whole areas of regulation are, as yet, unpaved roads. Although the process of rule making has progressed well, much debate still surrounds cyberspace law and much work remains to be done. This chapter focuses on the existing rules and also discusses the areas of regulation that are still incomplete and being debated.

Cyberlaw affects many areas of our lives. This chapter, however, deals with issues that are unique to the cyberworld, such as online privacy, spam, and cybercrimes.

Before beginning the chapter in earnest, let's return briefly to Garrett, the wrestler. What recourse does Garrett have for his Internet injuries? The nude video incident happened at Illinois State University and seven other colleges. Approximately 30 athletes filed suit against GTE and PSINet for selling the films online, but the two web hosts were found not to be liable under the Communications Decency Act because they had not produced the films themselves—they had simply permitted the sale of someone else's content. What about Garrett's other computer injuries? Lizzie was not being a good friend, but it was perfectly legal for her to forward Garrett's email to Caroline. The seller of the White Sox tickets violated both federal and state fraud statutes. The federal CAN-SPAM Act regulates spam—unsolicited commercial email—but a lawsuit is a slow and awkward tool for killing such a flourishing weed.

---

[1]The term "Internet" means "the international computer network of both Federal and non-Federal interoperable packet switched data networks," according to 47 U.S. Section 230 (f)(1). It began in the 1960s as a project to link military contractors and universities. Now, it is a giant network that connects smaller groups of linked computer networks. The World Wide Web was created in 1991 by Tim Berners-Lee as a subnetwork of the Internet. It is a decentralized collection of documents containing text, pictures, and sound. Users can move from document to document using links that form a "web" of information.

PRIVACY

The Internet has vastly increased our ability to communicate quickly and widely. In the pre-Internet era, setting up a meeting required days of phone tag. Intraoffice memos were typed, photocopied, and then hand-delivered by messengers. Catalog orders were sent via regular mail, a slow, inefficient, and costly method. As wonderful as cybercommunication can be, though, it is not without its dangers.

Tracking Tools

Consumers enter the most personal data—credit card numbers, bank account information lists of friends, medical data, product preferences—on the Internet. Because our interactions with a computer often take place in isolation (sitting alone at home, at work, or in a cafe), the experience *feels* private. It is anything but. In effect, the Internet provides a very large window through which the government, employers, businesses, and criminals can find out more than they should about you and your money, habits, beliefs, and health. Even email has its dangers: who has not been embarrassed by an email that ended up in the wrong mailbox?

The most troubling aspect of these Internet privacy issues is that consumers are often unaware of who has access to what personal information, how it is being used, and with what consequences. As a result, a privacy discussion seems abstract. But the reality is that the Internet provides many opportunities for good guys and bad to secretly gather information for their own purposes, both good and bad.

It used to be that marketers geared their ads to specific websites, but now they target individual consumers. The 50 most popular websites in America (which account for 40 percent of all page views) install thousands of tracking tools on the computers of people who visit their sites. Called "behavioral targeting," these tools not only collect data on *all* the websites someone visits, they also record keystrokes to keep track of whatever information the consumer has entered online. These tools are placed on computers without notice or warning to the consumer. In a recent report, Dictionary.com was the worst offender, placing over 200 tools on the computers of unaware visitors. On the other hand, Wikipedia.org is one highly popular site that installs none.[2] To take another example of privacy issues, as part of its Street View program that provides photographs of streets around the world, Google (accidentally, it says) captured data from home Wi-Fi networks.

Once the trackers have gathered financial, health, and other personal information, they sell it to data-gathering companies that build profiles which, while technically anonymous, can include so much personal information that it is possible to identify individuals. How many times have you revealed your ZIP code, birth date, and gender on the Internet? Those three pieces of information are usually enough to identify an individual's name and address. The profiles are then sold to advertisers on stock market-like exchanges. Now that cell phones have GPS tracking devices and readers use electronic books, where you have been and what you are reading is also available. In a recent Dilbert cartoon, the boss refers to a smart phone as an "employee locator device."

Suppose, for example, that you look online at puppies in shelters. You may find that the next time you go to your gmail account, there will be dog ads. One company markets a databank with the names of 150 million registered voters. Anyone can buy a list of voters that is sliced and diced however they want (say, Republicans between the ages of 45 and 60 with Hispanic surnames and incomes greater than $50,000 who live in Kansas City). Puppy ads seem harmless, or even beneficial, but if marketers can put together a databank of

---

[2]Julia Angwin and Tom McGinty, "Sites Feed Personal Details to New Tracking Industry," *The Wall Street Journal*, July 30, 2010.

Hispanic Republican voters, they can also find out who has visited a website for recovering alcoholics or unrecovered gamblers or Nazi sympathizers. Or who uses antidepressants or reads socialist writings. Do you want all this information available to anyone who is willing to pay for it? What if employers buy information about job candidates so that they can refuse to hire someone with health issues?

In short, Internet users are inadvertently providing intensely personal data to unknown people for unknown uses. The problem is likely to grow. The newest web language, HTML5, permits tracking software to store larger amounts of data. Also, software developers have created tracking tools that are harder to delete. Every browser uses a different deletion system, which makes life even more complicated for the concerned consumer.

Many commentators argue that without significant changes in the law, our privacy will be obliterated. But, so far, consumers have been relatively unconcerned. They tend to be unaware of the dangers, and they appreciate the benefits—for example, this tracking software can be used to store passwords so that when you log on to Amazon.com, the site recognizes you and lets you in without your having to enter your email address and password. Consumers can also benefit from targeted advertisements—long-distance runners may like seeing ads for running shoes, not cigarettes. Industry representatives argue that without the revenue from ads, many Internet sites would not be free to consumers. As a result, privacy on the Internet is very much like the weather—everyone talks about it, but (so far) no one has done much about it. But this you should believe: highly personal information about *you* has been collected without your knowledge or approval.

Regulation of Online Privacy

There is a wide range of possible sources of laws and regulations to protect online privacy, but they are in an early, and relatively ineffective, stage of development.

Self-Regulation

In an effort to forestall government regulation, several marketing trade groups issued their own report, "Self-Regulatory Principles for Online Behavioral Advertising." These principles require websites that use tracking tools to provide notice of data collection that is "clear, prominent, and conveniently located." In addition, the websites must permit consumers to opt out of tracking with only a few clicks. However, we have been unable to find a single website that complies with these principles, even among the companies that sponsored the report.

Members of Congress have filed many bills to regulate online privacy. So intense, however, is the debate between industry and consumer advocates that no consensus—and little law—has emerged. There is, however, some applicable government regulation.

The First Amendment

How would you like to be called a cockroach, mega-scumbag, and crook in front of thousands of people? Or be accused of having a fake medical degree, fat thighs, and poor feminine hygiene? What would you think if your ex-wife told 55,000 people that your insensitivity made her so sick she was throwing up every day? **The First Amendment to the Constitution protects free speech,** and that includes these postings—and worse—which have appeared on Internet message boards and blogs. As upsetting as they may be, they are protected as free speech under the First Amendment so long as the poster is not violating some other law. In these cases, the plaintiffs argued that the statements were defamatory but the courts disagreed, ruling that they were simply opinions.

Explaining its ruling in one of the cases, the court said:

Users [of the Internet] are able to engage freely in informal debate and criticism, leading many to substitute gossip for accurate reporting and often to adopt a provocative, even combative tone. Hyperbole and exaggeration are common, and "venting" is at least as common as careful and considered argumentation. Some commentators have likened cyberspace to a frontier society free from the conventions and constraints that limit discourse in the real world.

It hardly need be said that this [court does not] condone [these] rude and childish posts; indeed, [the] intemperate, insulting, and often disgusting remarks understandably offended plaintiff and possibly many other readers. Nevertheless, the fact that society may find speech offensive is not a sufficient reason for suppressing it. Indeed, if it is the speaker's opinion that gives offense, that consequence is a reason for according it constitutional protection.[3]

In the following case, a teacher received hostile emails. Should the First Amendment protect the anonymous person who sent them?

[3]*Krinsky v. Doe*, 6159 Cal. App. 4th 1154, 2008 Cal. App. LEXIS 180.

You be the Judge

JUZWIAK V. JOHN/JANE DOE
**415 N.J. Super. 442; 2 A.3d 428;
2010 N.J. Super. LEXIS 154
Superior Court of New Jersey, Appellate Division, 2010**

Facts: Juzwiak was a tenured teacher at Hightstown High School in New Jersey. He received three emails from someone who signed himself "Josh," with the address, "Josh Hartnett jharthat@yahoo.com." The teacher did not know anyone of that name. These emails said:

1. Subject line: "Hopefully you will be gone permanently"

   Text: "We are all praying for that. Josh"

2. Subject line: "I hear Friday is 'D' day for you"

   Text: "I certainly hope so. You don't deserve to be allowed to teach anymore. Not just in Hightstown but anywhere. If Hightstown bids you farewell I will make it my lifes [sic] work to ensure that wherever you look for work they know what you have done."

3. Subject line: "Mr. Juzwiak in the Hightstown/East Windsor School System."

   Text: It has been brought to my attention and I am sure many of you know that Mr. J is reapplying for his position as a teacher in this town. It has further been pointed out that certain people are soliciting supporters for him. This is tantamount to supporting the devil himself. I am not asking anyone to speak out against Mr. J but I urge you to then be silent as we can not continue to allow the children of this school system nor the parents to be subjected to his evil ways. Thank you. Josh

It seems that this third email was sent to other people, but it was not clear to whom.

Because Juzwiak did not know who "Josh" was, he filed a complaint against "John/Jane Doe," seeking damages for intentional infliction of emotional distress. As part of the lawsuit, he served a subpoena on Yahoo!, asking it to reveal "Josh's" identity. When Yahoo! notified "Josh" of the lawsuit, he asked the court to quash the subpoena.

In a court hearing, Juzwiak testified that the threatening emails had severely disrupted his life, causing deep anger and depression, as well as insomnia that had impaired his ability to concentrate and function effectively. In addition, this emotional stress had exacerbated his back problems and caused him to lose 20 pounds. Although he had already been taking antidepressants, a psychiatrist prescribed four additional drugs for depression, anxiety, and insomnia, which were not effective in reducing his symptoms. Juzwiak also stated that he had thoughts of hurting himself and the entire episode had consumed his life for several months.

When the trial court refused to issue the subpoena against Yahoo!, Juzwiak appealed.

You Be the Judge: *Should the trial court have issued the subpoena? Which interest is more important: "Josh's" First Amendment right to free speech or Juzwiak's protection from harassing emails?*

Argument for "Josh": Free speech is the first, and most important, right in the Bill of Rights. To ensure a vibrant marketplace of ideas, the First Amendment protects not only open but also anonymous speech. Sometimes speakers must be allowed to withhold their identities to protect themselves from harassment and persecution.

Nothing in these messages was a realistic threat to the teacher's safety. "Hopefully you will be gone permanently" could easily mean "Hope you will move out of town." Juzwiak reported these emails to the police, but they took no action. Presumably they would have done so if there had been any real threat.

Nor did these emails constitute an intentional infliction of emotional distress. They were not so extreme and outrageous as to be utterly intolerable in a civilized community. "Josh" did not accuse Juzwiak of vile or criminal acts. The language was not obscene or profane. In short, if Juzwiak is going to teach high school, he needs to develop a thicker skin and a better sense of humor.

Argument for Juzwiak: The right to speak anonymously is not absolute. "*Josh*" requires protection from harassment? That is an absurd argument.

These emails contained death threats: "Hopefully you will be gone permanently" and "I hear Friday is 'D' day for you." Juzwiak was frightened enough to go to the police. He suffered serious physical and emotional harm. These emails are not entitled to the protection of the First Amendment.

Furthermore, the emails constituted intentional infliction of emotional distress. They were extreme and outrageous conduct designed to cause harm. They achieved their goal.

In balancing the rights in this case, why would the court protect "Josh," who has set out to cause harm, over the innocent teacher?

The Fourth Amendment

The Fourth Amendment to the Constitution prohibits unreasonable searches and seizures by the government. In enforcing this provision of the Constitution, the courts ask: did the person being searched have a legitimate expectation of privacy in the place searched or the item seized? If yes, then the government must obtain a warrant from a court before conducting the search. (For more on this topic, investigate Chapter 7, on crime.) The Fourth Amendment applies to computers.

The architecture professor in the following case would have benefited from a course in business law, and perhaps in computer science, too.

UNITED STATES OF AMERICA V. ANGEVINE

281 F.3d 1130, 2002 U.S. App. LEXIS 2746
United States Court of Appeals for the Tenth Circuit, 2002

Facts: Professor Eric Angevine taught architecture at Oklahoma State University. The university provided him with a computer that was linked to the university network, and through it to the Internet. Professor Angevine used this computer to download more than 3,000 pornographic images of young boys. After viewing the images and printing some of them, he deleted the files. Tipped off by Professor Angevine's wife, police officers seized the computer without first obtaining a search warrant. They then turned the machine over to a police computer expert, who retrieved the pornographic files that the professor had deleted.

The Oklahoma State University computer policy stated that:

• The contents of all storage media owned or stored on university computing facilities are the property of the university.

• Employees cannot use university computers to access obscene material.

• The university reserves the right to view or scan any file or software stored on a computer or passing through the network and will do so periodically to audit the use of university resources. The university cannot guarantee confidentiality of stored data.

• System administrators keep logs of file names that may indicate why a particular data file is being erased, when it was erased, and what user identification has erased it.

The trial court held that federal agents did not need a warrant to search Professor Angevine's office computer because he had no expectation of privacy. He was sentenced to 51 months in prison for "knowing possession of child pornography." The professor appealed.

Issue: *Did Professor Angevine have a reasonable expectation of privacy in his office computer?*

Excerpts from Judge Brorby's Decision: Oklahoma State University policies and procedures prevent its employees from reasonably expecting privacy in data downloaded from the Internet onto University computers. The University computer-use policy reserved the right to randomly audit Internet use and to monitor specific individuals suspected of misusing University computers. The policy explicitly cautions computer users that information flowing through the University network is not confidential either in transit or in storage on a University computer. These office practices and procedures should have warned reasonable employees not to access child pornography with University computers.

While Professor Angevine did attempt to erase the child pornography, the University computer policy warned system administrators kept file logs recording when and by whom files were deleted. Moreover, given his transmission of the pornographic data through a monitored University network, deleting the files alone was not sufficient to establish a reasonable expectation of privacy.

We hold Professor Angevine could not have an objectively reasonable expectation of privacy.

This case involved someone who transmitted information through an electronic system owned by his employer. What happens if a suspect in a crime sends emails through a system that he personally pays for? Does he have a reasonable expectation of privacy? The following case answers these questions.

UNITED STATES OF AMERICA v. WARSHAK

631 F.3d 266; 2010 U.S. App. LEXIS 25415
United States Court of Appeals for the Sixth Circuit, 2010

Facts: Steven Warshak owned Berkeley Premium Nutraceuticals, Inc., a company that sold herbal supplements. The company had only been modestly successful until it began to market Enzyte, a supplement that promised to increase masculine endowment. At its peak, Berkeley had annual sales of around $250 million.

As is the case with all such products, Enzyte was a fraud. Advertisements quoted surveys that had never been conducted and doctors who did not exist. As a result, customers typically did not buy the product a second time. Warshak had a solution to this problem—an auto-ship program. A man would order a free sample, providing his credit card to pay for the shipping. Berkeley would then automatically send him more product, and, of course, charge his credit card.

Without obtaining a search warrant first, a federal prosecutor asked Warshak's Internet service provider (ISP) for copies of his emails. Based on the evidence contained in these 25,000 emails, Warshak was convicted of mail, wire, and bank fraud and sentenced to 25 years in prison. He appealed on the grounds that the government had violated the Fourth Amendment by obtaining emails without a search warrant. He argued that he had had a reasonable expectation of privacy.

Issue: *Did Warshak have a reasonable expectation of privacy in his emails?*

Excerpts from Justice Boggs's Decision: Warshak plainly manifested an expectation that his emails would be shielded from outside scrutiny. [H]is entire business and personal life was contained within the emails seized. Given the often sensitive and sometimes damning substance of his emails, we think it highly unlikely that Warshak expected them to be made public, for people seldom unfurl their dirty laundry in plain view. Therefore, we conclude that Warshak had a subjective expectation of privacy in the contents of his emails.

The next question is whether society is prepared to recognize that expectation as reasonable. This question is one of grave import and enduring consequence, given the prominent role that email has assumed in modern communication. Since the advent of email, the telephone call and the letter have waned in importance, and an explosion of Internet-based communication has taken place. People are now able to send sensitive and intimate information, instantaneously, to friends, family, and colleagues half a world away. Lovers exchange sweet nothings, and businessmen swap ambitious plans, all with the click of a mouse button. Commerce has also taken hold in email. Online purchases are often documented in email accounts, and email is frequently used to remind patients and clients of imminent appointments.

In short, "account" is an apt word for the conglomeration of stored messages that comprises an email account, as it provides an account of its owner's life. By obtaining access to someone's email, government agents gain the ability to peer deeply into his activities.

[T]he Fourth Amendment must keep pace with the inexorable march of technological progress, or its guarantees will wither and perish. While a letter is in the mail, the police may not intercept it and examine its contents unless they first obtain a warrant based on probable cause. If we accept that an email is analogous to a letter or a phone call, it is manifest that agents of the government cannot compel a commercial ISP to turn over the contents of an email without triggering the Fourth Amendment.

Emails must pass through an ISP's servers to reach their intended recipient. Thus, the ISP is the functional equivalent of a post office or a telephone company. [T]he police may not storm the post office and intercept a letter, and they are likewise forbidden from using the phone system to make a clandestine recording of a telephone call—unless they get a warrant, that is. It only stands to reason that, if government agents compel an ISP to surrender the contents of a subscriber's emails, those agents have thereby conducted a Fourth Amendment search, which necessitates compliance with the warrant requirement.

Accordingly, we hold that a subscriber enjoys a reasonable expectation of privacy in the contents of emails that are stored with, or sent or received through, a commercial ISP. The government may not compel a commercial ISP to turn over the contents of a subscriber's emails without first obtaining a warrant based on probable cause.

As the *Warshak* court observes, electronic communications—email, text messages, instant messaging—have for many people taken the place of letters and telephone calls. So it is important to know your privacy rights. **Although the courts are feeling their way in this new territory, at this writing, for criminal cases:**

1. If your employer has a reasonably articulated policy notifying you that it has the right to access and read electronic communications on a system that it provides, then you do not have a reasonable expectation of privacy when using that system. The police need not obtain a search warrant before reading your messages.

2. You do have a reasonable right to privacy on a system that you provide for yourself, so the police must obtain a search warrant before accessing these messages.

Note that both of these Fourth Amendment cases involve criminal defendants. However, Fourth Amendment protections also apply to *government* workers in civil cases. For example, when a police officer persistently exceeded his monthly quota of text messages, his superior accessed these communications to determine if they were work-related. It turned out that they were mostly sexually suggestive texts sent to the married officer's mistress. After the officer was disciplined, he filed suit alleging that the department had violated his Fourth Amendment rights. The Supreme Court held that a government employer has the right to review its employee's electronic communications for a work-related purpose, if the search was "justified at its inception" and if "the measures adopted are reasonably related to the objectives of the search and not excessively intrusive in light of the circumstances giving rise to the search."[4]

The FTC

Section 5 of the FTC Act prohibits unfair and deceptive acts or practices. The Federal Trade Commission (FTC) applies this statute to online privacy policies. It does not require websites to have a privacy policy, but if they do have one, they must comply with it, and it cannot be deceptive. For example, Sears paid consumers who visited sears.com and kmart.com websites $10 to become members of the "My SHC Community" and participate in "exciting, engaging, and on-going interactions–always on your terms and always by your

[4]*City of Ontario v. Quon*, 130 S. Ct. 2619; 2010 U.S. LEXIS 4972 (S.Ct. 2010).

choice." As part of this process, consumers downloaded "research" software that tracked their online browsing. Only at the end of a lengthy user agreement did Sears reveal the full extent of the data collected, that it could include the contents of shopping carts, online bank statements, drug prescription records, DVD rental records, and some personal email information. In a consent decree with the FTC, Sears agreed to stop collecting data from consumers who downloaded the software and to destroy all data it had previously collected.

The FTC also brought action against Twitter after hackers gained access through its administrative system to Twitter accounts. Twitter had allowed any employee access to the administrative system, which was protected by an easy-to-guess password. The hackers reset passwords and sent fake tweets. For example, an unauthorized person sent a tweet from President-elect Barack Obama's Twitter account offering free gasoline to users who took an Internet poll (which seems benign compared with what the hacker could have said, but still not a good situation). The FTC found that Twitter had engaged in deceptive acts because its (lack of) security practices had violated the company's promise to users that it would protect their information from unauthorized access. As part of the settlement, Twitter agreed to strengthen its security practices.

In addition to cases the FTC has brought against individual companies, it also issued a report entitled "Self-Regulatory Principles for Online Behavioral Advertising." As the name implies, these rules are voluntary. They provide that companies should clearly disclose the information that they collect and also offer consumers an easy-to-use, easy-to-find method for opting out. However, we have not found a website that complies with this policy. The FTC has been working on a binding privacy policy for years, with no result yet.

One more cyberlaw issue: imagine that you are reading a blog that favorably reviews a new Microsoft product. Before clicking on the Buy button, would you want to know that Microsoft had given the blogger a free computer? The FTC thinks you should. Under FTC rules, bloggers face fines as high as $1,000 if they do not disclose all compensation they receive (either in cash or free products) for writing product reviews. Moreover, celebrities must disclose their relationships with advertisers when making endorsements outside of traditional ads, such as on talk shows or in social media.

Electronic Communications Privacy Act of 1986

The Electronic Communications Privacy Act of 1986 (ECPA) is a federal statute that prohibits unauthorized interception of, access to, or disclosure of wire and electronic communications. The definition of electronic communication includes email and transmissions from pagers and cell phones. Violators are subject to both criminal and civil penalties. An action does not violate the ECPA if it is unintentional or if either party consents. Also, the USA Patriot Act, passed after the September 11 attacks, has broadened the *government's* right to monitor electronic communications.

Under the ECPA:

1. **Any intended recipient of an electronic communication has the right to disclose it.** Thus, if you sound off in an email to a friend about your boss, the (erstwhile) friend may legally forward that email to the boss or anyone else.

2. **Internet service providers (ISPs) are generally prohibited from disclosing electronic messages to anyone other than the addressee,** unless this disclosure is necessary for the performance of their service or for the protection of their own rights or property.

3. **An employer has the right to monitor workers' electronic communications if (1) the employee consents, (2) the monitoring occurs in the ordinary course of business, or (3) in the case of email, if the employer provides the computer system.**[5] Note that an employer has the right to monitor electronic communication even if it does not relate to work activities.

---

[5]The ECPA provides that, under certain circumstances, the police can access email without a warrant, but the *Warshak* court declared that provision unconstitutional.

One lesson from the ECPA: email is not private, and it is dangerous. Although the *Warshak* court ruled that defendants have an expectation of privacy in emails they have sent over a system that they provide for themselves, that simply means the police must first obtain a search warrant before accessing emails, which is not that difficult. To get a search warrant, the police just need probable cause that they will find evidence of a crime in the place to be searched.

The majority of employers monitor their employees' email. In the event of litigation, the opposing party can access all emails—even messages that have in theory been deleted. Many people who should have known better have been caught in the email trap. Merrill Lynch stock analyst Henry Blodget praised stocks to the public even as he was referring to them in emails as a "piece of s***." He has been banned for life from the securities industry. Then there was Harry Stonecipher, the CEO of Boeing, who sent explicit emails to the employee with whom he was having an extramarital affair. When copies of the emails were sent to the board of directors, he was fired. In the following case, two important principles are at stake. Which one should win?

You be the Judge

Facts: Beth Israel Medical Center (BI)'s email policy stated:

> All information and documents created, received, saved, or sent on the Medical Center's computer or communications systems are the property of the Medical Center. Employees have no personal privacy right in any material created, received, saved, or sent using Medical Center communication or computer systems. The Medical Center reserves the right to access and disclose such material at any time without prior notice.

Dr. Norman Scott was head of the orthopedics department at BI. His contract with the hospital provided for $14 million in severance pay if he was fired without cause. BI did fire him, and the question was whether it was for cause or not. In preparation for a lawsuit against BI, Scott used the hospital's computer system to send emails to his lawyer. Each of these emails included the following notice:

> This message is intended only for the use of the Addressee and may contain information that is privileged and confidential. If you are not the intended recipient, you are hereby notified that any dissemination of this communication is strictly prohibited. If you have received this communication in error, please erase all copies of the message and its attachments and notify us immediately.

SCOTT V. BETH ISRAEL MEDICAL CENTER INC.

847 N.Y.S.2d 436; 2007 N.Y. Misc. LEXIS 7114
Supreme Court of New York, 2007

BI obtained copies of all of Scott's emails. It notified him that it had copies of the emails to his lawyer. No one at BI had read the emails yet, but they intended to do so. Communications between a client and lawyer are generally protected, but a client waives this privilege if he publicly discloses the information. When Scott requested that the emails be returned to him unread, BI refused. Scott filed a motion seeking the return of the documents.

You Be the Judge: *Did Scott have a right to privacy in emails he sent to his lawyer using the BI system?*

Argument for Scott: Despite BI's policy, all the emails Scott sent asserted that they were confidential. That should be enough to protect them. The attorney-client privilege is a foundation of our legal system. It is absolutely crucial for justice that clients be able to communicate with their lawyers in confidence. In a test between a core principle such as attorney-client privilege and a private entity's email policy, the privilege must win. The hospital should not be allowed to read Scott's emails.

Argument for BI: Scott was aware of BI's policy and knew that emails were the property of the hospital. Therefore, when he sent the emails, he was disclosing them publicly. If the communications were that important, he should have made a greater effort to protect them. BI has the right to read them.

Children's Online Privacy Protection Act of 1998

The Children's Online Privacy Protection Act of 1998 (COPPA) prohibits Internet operators from collecting information from children under 13 without parental permission. It also requires sites to disclose how they will use any information they acquire. Enforcement is in the hands of the FTC. The website for Mrs. Fields cookies offered birthday coupons for free cookies to children under 13. Although the company did not share information with outsiders, it did collect personal information without parental consent from 84,000 children. This information included names, home addresses, and birth dates. Mrs. Fields paid a penalty of $100,000 and agreed not to violate the law again.

State Regulation

Some states have passed their own online privacy laws. To take some examples, the California Online Privacy Act of 2003 requires any website that collects personal information from California residents to post a privacy policy conspicuously and then abide by its terms. (Further, the California state constitution confers the right to privacy.) Connecticut, Nebraska, and Pennsylvania also regulate online privacy policies.

Two states, Minnesota and Nevada, require ISPs to obtain their customers' consent before providing information about them. Connecticut and Delaware require employers to notify their workers before monitoring emails or Internet usage.

European Law

The European Convention on Human Rights declares, "Everyone has the right to respect for his private and family life, his home, and his correspondence." The European Union's e-Privacy Directive requires an opt-in system, under which tracking tools cannot be used unless the consumer is told how the tools will be used and then specifically grants permission for their use. However, this directive may be interpreted to mean that consumers have granted permission for tracking tools if they fail to change the default privacy settings on their web browsers. At this writing, European nations are just beginning to implement the e-Privacy Directive, so it may be some time before the impact of these rules is clear.

In theory, even companies outside Europe will have to comply with European rules if they interact with European customers. Recently, European agencies insisted that Google, Microsoft, and Yahoo! enhance their protection of users' search histories; and a court in Italy held that Google had violated that country's privacy laws by posting a video of students bullying an autistic boy. Stay tuned.

Spyware

Spyware
A computer program that enters a user's computer without permission and monitors and reports the user's activities.

Is your computer running sluggishly? Does it crash frequently? Has the home page on your web browser suddenly changed without your consent? Is there a program in your systems tray that you do not recognize? You might have **spyware** on your computer. Spyware is a computer program that enters a user's computer without permission and monitors and reports the user's activities.

Congress has considered legislation to control spyware but has not taken final action. California has enacted the Consumer Protection Against Computer Spyware Act, which makes spyware illegal.

SPAM

Spam is officially known as *unsolicited commercial email (UCE)* or *unsolicited bulk email (UBE)*. Whatever it is called, it is one of the most annoying aspects of email. It has been estimated that 90 percent of email is spam. And roughly half of these messages were fraudulent—either in content (promoting a scam) or in packaging (the headers or return address are false). Aside from the annoyance factor, bulk email adds to the cost of connecting to the Internet as ISPs increase server capacity to handle the millions of spam emails.

The Controlling the Assault of Non-Solicited Pornography and Marketing Act (CAN-SPAM) is a federal statute that does not prohibit spam but instead regulates it. This statute applies to virtually all promotional emails, whether or not the sender has a preexisting relationship with the recipient. Under this statute, commercial email:

- May not have deceptive headings (From, To, Reply To, Subject),

- Must offer an opt-out system permitting the recipient to unsubscribe (and must honor those requests promptly),

- Must clearly indicate that the email is an advertisement,

- Must provide a valid physical return address (not a post office box), and

- Must clearly indicate the nature of pornographic messages.

A company can avoid these requirements by obtaining advance permission from the recipients.

CAN-SPAM seems to have had little impact on the quantity of spam (although it has made opt-out provisions more common in legitimate commercial emails). More effective have been the tools developed by online security firms and governments that prevent as much as 98 percent of spam from reaching your email inbox.

But spammers have found other outlets. They post messages in the comment sections of websites and on social media sites such as Facebook and Twitter. Their goal is to entice you to click on a link that may take you to a website that sells foolproof "investments" or that simply steals bank information from your computer. If that link seems to come from a Facebook friend or someone whom you follow on Twitter, it seems more reliable. A recent study found that 8 percent of links sent via Twitter are fraudulent, but they are 20 times more likely to be clicked than those in spam email.[6]

EXAM Strategy

Question: Cruise.com operated a website selling cruise vacations. It sent unsolicited email advertisements—dubbed "E-deals"—to prospective customers. Eleven of these "E-deals" went to inbox@webguy.net. Each message offered the recipient an opportunity to be removed from the mailing list by clicking on a line of text or by writing to a specific postal address. Has Cruise.com violated the CAN-SPAM Act?

Strategy: Remember that this Act does not prohibit all unsolicited emails.

Result: Cruise.com was not in violation because it offered the recipients a way to unsubscribe. Also, it provided a valid physical return address.

---

[6]"Long life spam," *The Economist*, November 20, 2010, p. 67.

INTERNET SERVICE PROVIDERS AND WEB HOSTS: COMMUNICATIONS DECENCY ACT OF 1996

ISPs are companies, such as Earthlink, that provide connection to the Internet. Web hosts post web pages on the Internet. Both play important roles in cyberspace. As the legal structure that supports the Internet develops, so have legal issues involving these players.

The Internet is an enormously powerful tool for disseminating information. But what if some of this information happens to be false or in violation of our privacy rights? Is an ISP liable for transmitting it to the world? In 1995, a trial judge in New York held that an ISP, Prodigy Services Company, was potentially liable for defamatory statements that an unidentified person posted on one of its bulletin boards.[7] The message alleged that the president of an investment bank had committed "criminal and fraudulent acts." It was not only a false statement—it was posted on the most widely read financial online bulletin board in the country. Although one can only feel sympathy for the target of this slur, the decision nonetheless alarmed many observers who argued that there was no way ISPs could review every piece of information that hurtles through their portals. The next year, Congress overruled the Prodigy case by passing the Communications Decency Act of 1996 (CDA).[8] **Under the CDA, ISPs and web hosts are not liable for information that is provided by someone else. Only content providers are liable.** The following case lays out the arguments in favor of the CDA, but also illustrates some of the costs of the statute (and of the Internet).

CARAFANO V. METROSPLASH.COM, INC.[9]

339 F.3d 1119, 2003 U.S. App. LEXIS 16548
United States Court of Appeals for the Ninth Circuit, 2003

Facts: Matchmaker.com is an Internet dating service that permits members to post profiles of themselves and to view the profiles of other members. Matchmaker reviews photos for impropriety before posting them but does not examine the profiles.

Christianne Carafano is an actor who uses the stage name Chase Masterson. She has appeared in numerous films and television shows, such as *Star Trek: Deep Space Nine* and *General Hospital*. Without her knowledge, someone in Berlin posted a profile of her in the Los Angeles section of Matchmaker. In answer to the question "Main source of current events?" the person posting the profile put "*Playboy Playgirl*" and for "Why did you call?" responded "Looking for a one-night stand." In addition, the essays indicated that she was looking for a "hard and dominant" man with "a strong sexual appetite" and that she "liked sort of being controlled by a man, in and out of bed." Pictures of the actor taken off the Internet were included with the profile. The profile also provided her home address and an email address, which, when contacted, produced an automatic email reply stating, "You think you are the right one? Proof it!!" [sic], and providing Carafano's home address and telephone number.

Unaware of the improper posting, Carafano began receiving sexually explicit messages on her home voice mail, as well as a sexually explicit fax that threatened her and her son. She received numerous phone calls, letters, and email from male fans, expressing concern that she had given out her address and phone number (but simultaneously indicating an interest in meeting her). Feeling

---

[7]*Stratton Oakmont, Inc. v. Prodigy Services Company*, 1995 N.Y. Misc. LEXIS 229.
[8]47 U.S.C. 230.
[9]Matchmaker.com, Inc. changed its legal name to Metrosplash.com, Inc. but continued to do business as Matchmaker.com.

unsafe, Carafano and her son moved out of their home for several months.

One Saturday a week or two after the profile was first posted, Carafano's assistant, Siouxzan Perry, learned of the false profile through a message from "Jeff." Acting on Carafano's instructions, Perry contacted Matchmaker, demanding that the profile be removed immediately. The Matchmaker employee did not remove it then because Perry herself had not posted it, but on Monday morning, the company blocked the profile from public view and then deleted it the following day.

Carafano filed suit against Matchmaker alleging invasion of privacy, misappropriation of the right of publicity, defamation, and negligence. The district court rejected Matchmaker's argument for immunity under the CDA on the grounds that the company provided part of the profile content.

Issue: *Does the CDA protect Matchmaker from liability?*

Excerpts from Judge Thomas's Decision: Through [the CDA], Congress granted most Internet services immunity from liability for publishing false or defamatory material so long as the information was provided by another party. As a result, Internet publishers are treated differently from corresponding publishers in print, television, and radio. Congress enacted this provision for two basic policy reasons: to promote the free exchange of information and ideas over the Internet and to encourage voluntary monitoring for offensive or obscene material.

Interactive computer services have millions of users. It would be impossible for service providers to screen each of their millions of postings for possible problems. Faced with potential liability for each message republished by their services, interactive computer service providers might choose to severely restrict the number and type of messages posted. Congress considered the weight of the speech interests implicated and chose to immunize service providers to avoid any such restrictive effect. Under [the CDA], therefore, so long as a third party willingly provides the essential published content, the interactive service provider receives full immunity regardless of the specific editing or selection process.

The fact that some of the content [in Carafano's fake profile] was formulated in response to Matchmaker's questionnaire does not [make Matchmaker liable]. Doubtless, the questionnaire facilitated the expression of information by individual users. However, the selection of the content was left exclusively to the user. Matchmaker cannot be considered an "information content provider" under the statute because no profile has any content until a user actively creates it.

Further, even assuming Matchmaker could be considered an information content provider, the statute would still bar Carafano's claims unless Matchmaker created or developed the particular information at issue. In this case, critical information about Carafano's home address and the email address that revealed her phone number were transmitted unaltered to profile viewers. Thus, Matchmaker did not play a significant role in creating, developing, or "transforming" the relevant information.

Thus, despite the serious and utterly deplorable consequences that occurred in this case, we conclude that Congress intended that service providers such as Matchmaker be afforded immunity from suit.

Note that the CDA does not protect web hosts or ISPs that engage in wrongdoing. For example, Bright Builders, Inc, hosted copycatclubs.com, a website that, as you might guess, sold counterfeit golf clubs. The court held that Bright Builders was liable despite the CDA because it participated in the design, building, marketing, and support of copycatclubs.com. It even helped locate the counterfeit clubs that the website sold.[10] Ultimately, a jury returned a verdict of $770,750 against Bright Builders.

Also, the CDA does not protect web hosts and ISPs from contract liability. For example, after Cynthia Barnes broke up with her boyfriend, he created a profile of her on a Yahoo! website. He then spitefully posted nude photos of the two of them taken without her knowledge, together with her addresses and phone numbers at home and at work. He also suggested that she was interested in sex with random strangers. Many men were willing to oblige. For months, Yahoo! did not even respond to Barnes's request to remove the profile. Not until a TV show prepared to run a story about the incident did the company's director of communications contact Barnes to promise that the profile would be removed immediately.

[10] *Roger Cleveland Golf Co. v. Price*, 2010 U.S. Dist. LEXIS 128044.

Still Yahoo! took no action until two months later, when Barnes sued. The appeals court ruled that Barnes could bring a contract claim against Yahoo! under a theory of promissory estoppel–that she had relied on the company's promise. [11]

EXAM Strategy

Question: Someone posted an anonymous review on TripAdvisor.com alleging that the owner of a restaurant had entertained a prostitute there. The allegation was false. TripAdvisor refused to investigate or remove the review. Does the restaurant owner have a valid claim against the website?

Strategy: Remember that web hosts are liable only if they have engaged in wrongdoing.

Result: As a web host, TripAdvisor is not liable for content. It would be liable only if it promised to take down the review and then did not.

CRIME ON THE INTERNET

Despite its great benefits, the Internet has also opened new frontiers in crime for the dishonest and unscrupulous.

Hacking

During the 2008 presidential campaign, college student David Kernell guessed Sarah Palin's email password, accessed her personal Yahoo! account, and published the content of some of her emails. To many, his actions seemed like an amusing prank. The joke turned out not to be so funny when Kernell was sentenced to one year in prison.

Hacking
Gaining unauthorized access to a computer system.

Gaining unauthorized access to a computer system is called **hacking**. It is a major crime. The Federal Bureau of Investigation ranks cybercrime as its third-highest priority, right behind terrorism and spying. The Pentagon reports that hackers make more than 250,000 attempts annually on its computers. The goal of hackers is varied; some do it for little more than the thrill of the challenge. The objective for other hackers may be espionage, extortion, theft of credit card information, or revenge for perceived slights. Kernell hoped to prevent Palin from being elected vice president.

> The FBI ranks cybercrime as its third-highest priority, right behind terrorism and spying.

Hacking is a crime under the federal Computer Fraud and Abuse Act of 1986 (CFAA).[12] This statute applies to any computer, cell phone, iPod, iPad, or other gadget attached to the Internet. **The CFAA prohibits:**

---

[11]*Barnes v. Yahoo!, Inc.*, 570 F.3d 1096 (9th Cir., 2008). Promissory estoppel is discussed at greater length in Chapter 9
[12]18 U.S.C. Section 1030.

- Accessing a computer without authorization and obtaining information from it,

- Computer espionage,

- Theft of financial information,

- Theft of information from the U.S. government,

- Theft from a computer,

- Computer fraud,

- Intentional, reckless, and negligent damage to a computer,

- Trafficking in computer passwords, and

- Computer extortion.

The CFAA also provides for civil remedies so that someone who has been harmed by a hacker can personally recover damages from the wrongdoer. Employers have begun to use the CFAA to bring civil cases against former employees who take company information with them when they go to work for a competitor. At this writing, the courts are inconsistent on the issue of whether such an activity constitutes "unauthorized access" and is, therefore, a violation of the CFAA. Also, database owners sometimes claim that an unauthorized user who "shares" the login credentials of a legitimate purchaser has violated the CFAA. Because the courts have split on these issues, the outcome of such a case depends on geography.[13]

There are two problems with the CFAA. First, while the statute prohibits the use of a virus to harm a computer, it does not ban the creation of viruses that someone else could use for hacking. Thus, it is legal for websites to sell source code for viruses—codes that even beginners can use destructively.

Second, the CFAA applies only to U.S. criminals. Because the Internet is truly international, cybercriminals do not always fall within the jurisdiction of American laws. For example, a computer virus called ILOVEYOU caused an estimated $7 billion worth of damage worldwide. Although the perpetrator would have been subject to prosecution under the CFAA in the United States, he lived in the Philippines, which did not have laws prohibiting cybercrime. Nor could the suspect be extradited automatically to the United States because the extradition treaty only applied if both nations had the same law. The Philippines ultimately dropped all charges against the suspect.

Fraud

Fraud is a growth business on the Internet. The Internet's anonymity and speed facilitate fraud, and computers help criminals identify and contact victims. Common scams include advance fee scams,[14] the sale of merchandise that is either defective or nonexistent, the so-called Nigerian letter scam,[15] billing for services that are touted as "free," fake scholarship

---

[13]See, for example, *Int'l Airport Centers LLC v. Citrin*, 440 F 3d 418 (7th Cir., 2006); *Lasco Foods, Inc. v. Hall & Shaw Sales*, 600 F. Supp. 2d 1045 (E. Dist. Mo, 2009); *Orbit One Communications Inc. v. Numerex Corp*, 692 F. Supp. 2d 373 (S.D.N.Y. 2010); *State Analysis Inc. v. American Financial Services Assoc*, 621 F. Supp. 2d 309 (E.D. Va., 2009); and *AtPac Inc. v. Aptitude Solutions Inc.*, 730 F. Supp. 2d 1174, (E.D. CA, 2010).
[14]As in, "If you are willing to pay a fee in advance, then you will have access to (pick your choice) favorable financing, lottery winnings from overseas, attractive investment opportunities that will make you rich."
[15]Victims receive an email from someone alleging to be a Nigerian government official who has stolen money from the government. He needs some place safe to park the money for a short time. The official promises that, if the victim will permit her account to be used for this purpose, she will be allowed to keep a percentage of the stolen money. Instead, of course, once the "official" has the victim's bank information, he cleans out the account.

search services, romance fraud (you meet someone online who wants to visit you but needs money for travel expenses), and credit card scams (for a fee, you can get a credit card, even with a poor credit rating). One of the new scams involves *over*payment. You are renting out a house, selling a pet, or accepting a job, and "by accident," you are sent too much money. You wire the excess back, only to find out that the initial check or funds transfer was no good.

Fraud is the deception of another person for the purpose of obtaining money or property from him. It can be prosecuted under state law or the Computer Fraud and Abuse Act. In addition, federal mail and wire fraud statutes prohibit the use of mail or wire communication in furtherance of a fraudulent scheme.[16] The FTC can bring civil cases under Section 5 of the FTC Act. (Chapter 7, on crime, discusses fraud.)

Auctions

Internet auctions are the number one source of consumer complaints about online fraud. Wrongdoers either sell goods they do not own, provide defective goods, or offer fakes. In a recent case (which will not reduce the amount of auction fraud) a court held that eBay, the Internet auction site, was not liable to Tiffany & Company for the counterfeit Tiffany products sold on the site. The jewelry company had sued after discovering that most items advertised on eBay as Tiffany products were, in fact, fakes. The court held that eBay's only legal obligation was to remove products once told that they were counterfeit.[17]

Shilling

When a seller at auction either bids on his own goods or agrees to cross-bid with a group of other sellers.

Shilling is an increasingly popular online auction fraud. **Shilling means that a seller either bids on his own goods or agrees to cross-bid with a group of other sellers.** Shilling is prohibited because the owner drives up the price of his own item by bidding on it. Thus, for example, Kenneth Walton, a San Francisco lawyer, put up for auction on eBay an abstract painting purportedly by famous artist Richard Diebenkorn. A bidder offered $135,805 before eBay withdrew the item in response to charges that Walton had placed a bid on the painting himself and had also engaged in cross-bidding with a group of other eBay users. Although Walton claimed that he had placed the bids for friends, he ultimately pleaded guilty to charges of federal wire and mail fraud. He was sentenced to almost four years in prison and paid nearly $100,000 in restitution to those who overpaid for the items he bid on.

To date, eBay has generally responded to shillers by suspending them. Shillers are also subject to suit under general anti-fraud statutes. In addition, some states explicitly prohibit shilling.[18]

Identity Theft

Identity theft is one of the scariest crimes against property. Thieves steal the victim's social security number and other personal information such as bank account numbers and mother's maiden name, which they use to obtain loans and credit cards. The money owed is never repaid, leaving victims to prove that they were not responsible for the debts. The thieves may even commit (additional) crimes under their new identities. Meanwhile, the victim may find himself unable to obtain a credit card, loan, or job. One victim spent several nights in jail after he was arrested for a crime that his alter ego had committed.

Although identity fraud existed before computers, the Internet has made it much easier. For example, consumer activists were able to purchase the social security numbers of the

[16]U.S.C. Sections 1341–1346.
[17]*Tiffany Inc. v. eBay, Inc.*, 600 F.3d 93, 2010 U.S. App. LEXIS 6735 (2nd Cir., 2010) and, on remand, 2010 U.S. Dist. LEXIS 96596 (S.D.N.Y, 2010).
[18]For example, New Mexico law provides that "It shall be unlawful to employ shills or puffers at any such auction sale or to offer or to make or to procure to be offered or made any false bid or offer any false bid to buy or pretend to buy any article sold or offered for sale." N.M. Stat. Section 61-16-14.

director of the CIA, the Attorney General of the United States, and other top administration officials. The cost? Only $26 each. No surprise, then, that 8 million Americans are victims of this crime each year.

A number of federal statutes deal with identity theft or its consequences. **The Identity Theft and Assumption Deterrence Act of 1998 prohibits the use of false identification to commit fraud or other crimes, and it also permits the victim to seek restitution in court.**[19] The Truth in Lending Act limits liability on a stolen credit card to $50. The Social Security Protection Act of 2010 prohibits government agencies from printing social security numbers on checks.

A number of states have also passed identity theft statutes. Almost every state now requires companies to notify consumers when their personal information has been stolen. Many states also restrict the use and disclosure of social security numbers.

What can you do to prevent the theft of your identity?

1. Check your credit reports at least once a year. (Consumers are entitled by law to one free credit report every year from each of the three major reporting agencies. You can order these reports at **https://www.annualcreditreport.com.**)

2. Place a freeze on your credit report so that anyone who is about to issue a loan or credit card will double-check with you first.

3. If you suspect that your identity has been stolen, contact the FTC at 877-IDTHEFT, 877-438-4338, or google "ftc identity theft" to get to the FTC's identity theft site. Also, file a police report immediately and keep a copy to show creditors. Notify the three credit agencies.

Phishing

Have you ever received an instant message from a Facebook friend saying, "Hey, what's up?" with a link to an IQ test? This instant message is not from a friend, but rather from a fraudster hoping to lure you into revealing your personal information. In this case, people who clicked on the link were told that they had to provide their cell phone number to get the test results. Next thing they knew, they had been signed up for some expensive cell phone service. This scam is part of one of the most rapidly growing areas of Internet fraud: **phishing. In this crime, a fraudster sends a message directing the recipient to enter personal information on a website that is an illegal imitation of a legitimate site.**

In a traditional phishing scam, large numbers of generic emails are sprayed over the Internet asking millions of people to log on to, say, a fake bank site. But the latest development—called **spear phishing**—involves personalized messages sent from someone the victim knows. For example, your sister asks for your social security number so she can add you as a beneficiary to her life insurance policy. In reality, this email has come from a fraudster who hacked into her Facebook account to gain access to her lists of friends and family.[20] Even "Like" buttons can be "clickjacked" to take unwary users to bogus sites.

Prosecutors can bring criminal charges against phishers for fraud. The companies whose websites have been copied can sue these criminals for fraud, trademark infringement, false advertising, and cybersquatting (discussed further in Chapter 24, on intellectual property).

Phishing

A fraudster sends a message directing the recipient to enter personal information on a website that is an illegal imitation of a legitimate site.

---

[19]18 U.S. Section 1028.

[20]To prevent your Facebook account from being hijacked, be careful when accessing it over a public network (such as in a hotel or airport), where fraudsters might be able to capture your password. If you text "otp" to 32665, you will receive a password that can be used only once (a "one-time password"). Fraudsters thus cannot use this password to access your account.

No reputable company will ask customers to respond to an email with personal information. When in doubt, close the suspicious email, relaunch your web browser, and then go to the company's main website. If the legitimate company needs information from you, it will so indicate on the site.

EXAM Strategy

Question: TruePrint sent emails to thousands of consumers, advertising its business card service. The subject line said, "FREE GIFT!" Consumers who opened the email, were then asked to click on a link, which led to a web page that asked for personal information. After filling in the information and clicking a "Continue" button, they landed on a second web page. In the fine print at the bottom of this page was the following statement: "Printing is free. Pay only for shipping and processing. Please see our Free Offer Details for more information." Finally, at the end of the process on the next web page, consumers learned that shipping the free gift would cost $5.67, payable by credit card or check. The email did not make any reference to TruePrint. Has TruePrint violated the law?

Strategy: Indeed, TruePrint has violated two laws.

Result: First, it has advertised a "free gift" when, in fact, the gift costs $5.67. That is fraud. Second, it has violated the CAN-SPAM act because the subject line of the email is untrue—the gift is not free. It has further violated CAN-SPAM by its failure to provide TruePrint's valid physical return address.

Chapter Conclusion

The Internet has changed our lives in ways that were inconceivable a generation ago, and the law is rushing to catch up. Courts will apply some old laws in new ways and, as legislators, regulators and courts learn from experience, new laws will be enacted.

Inevitably, the law of cyberspace will become increasingly international. What does Europe accomplish by regulating Internet privacy if its citizens spend a good portion of their time on American websites? What will the FTC do if scam artists or spammers operate offshore? Effective regulation of cyberspace will require cooperation among nations and between government and industry.

EXAM REVIEW

1. **THE FIRST AMENDMENT** The First Amendment to the Constitution protects speech on the Internet so long as the speech does not violate some other law. (pp. 605–606)

2. **THE FOURTH AMENDMENT** The Fourth Amendment to the Constitution prohibits unreasonable searches and seizures by the government. This provision applies to computers. (pp. 607–609)

3. **REASONABLE EXPECTATION OF PRIVACY** Under criminal law, if your employer has a reasonably articulated policy notifying you that it has the right to access and read electronic communications on a system that it provides, then you do not have a reasonable expectation of privacy when using that system. You do have a reasonable right to privacy on a system that you provide for yourself. (pp. 607–609)

Question: Three travel agents use fictitious accounts to steal millions of frequent flyer miles. Must the police obtain a warrant before searching their email accounts?

Strategy: The answer depends on what type of email account the agents used.

4. **THE FTC ACT** Section 5 of the FTC Act prohibits unfair and deceptive practices. The FTC does not require websites to have a privacy policy, but if they do have one, it cannot be deceptive and they must comply with it. (pp. 609–610)

5. **THE ECPA** The Electronic Communications Privacy Act of 1986 is a federal statute that prohibits unauthorized interception or disclosure of wire and electronic communications. However, it permits an employer to monitor workers' electronic communications if (1) the employee consents, (2) the monitoring occurs in the ordinary course of business, or (3) the employer provides the computer system (in the case of email). (pp. 610–611)

6. **COPPA** The Children's Online Privacy Protection Act of 1998 prohibits Internet operators from collecting information from children under 13 without parental permission. It also requires sites to disclose how they will use any information they acquire. (p. 612)

7. **E-PRIVACY DIRECTIVE** The European Union's e-Privacy Directive requires an opt-in system under which tracking tools cannot be used unless the consumer is told how the tools will be used and then specifically grants permission for their use. (p. 612)

8. **CAN-SPAM** The Controlling the Assault of Non-Solicited Pornography and Marketing Act (CAN-SPAM) is a federal statute that does not prohibit spam but instead regulates it. Under this statute, commercial email:

   - May not have deceptive headings (From, To, Reply To, Subject),

   - Must offer an opt-out system permitting the recipient to unsubscribe (and must honor those requests promptly),

   - Must clearly indicate that the email is an advertisement,

   - Must provide a valid physical return address (not a post office box), and

   - Must clearly indicate the nature of pornographic messages. (p. 613)

9. **THE CDA** Under the Communications Decency Act of 1996, ISPs and web hosts are not liable for information that is provided by someone else. (pp. 614–616)

EXAM Strategy

Question: Ton Cremers was the director of security at Amsterdam's famous Rijksmuseum and the operator of the Museum Security Network (the Network) website. Robert Smith, a handyman working for Ellen Batzel in North Carolina, sent an email to the Network alleging that Batzel was the granddaughter of Heinrich Himmler (one of Hitler's henchmen) and that she had art that Himmler had stolen. These allegations were completely untrue. Cremers posted Smith's email on the Network's website and sent it to the Network's subscribers. Cremers exercised some editorial discretion in choosing which emails to send to subscribers, generally omitting any that were unrelated to stolen art. Is Cremers liable to Batzel for the harm that this inaccurate information caused?

Strategy: Cremers is liable only if he is a content provider. (See the "Result" at the end of this section.)

10. **THE CFAA** Hacking is a crime under the federal Computer Fraud and Abuse Act of 1986. The CFAA prohibits:

- Accessing a computer without authorization and obtaining information from it,
- Computer espionage,
- Theft of financial information,
- Theft of information from the U.S. government,
- Theft from a computer,
- Computer fraud,
- Intentional, reckless, and negligent damage to a computer,
- Trafficking in computer passwords, and
- Computer extortion. (pp. 616–617)

EXAM Strategy

Question: To demonstrate the inadequacies of existing computer security systems, Cornell student Robert Morris created a computer virus. His plan, however, went awry, as plans sometimes do. He thought his virus would be relatively harmless, but it ran amok, crashing scores of computers at universities, military sites, and medical research sites. Has he committed a crime, or is he liable only for civil penalties? Does it matter that he did not intend to cause damage?

Strategy: Review the provisions of the CFAA. (See the "Result" at the end of this section.)

11. **FRAUD** Fraud is the deception of another person for the purpose of obtaining money or property from him. (pp. 617–618)

12. **IDENTITY THEFT** The Identity Theft and Assumption Deterrence Act of 1998 prohibits the use of false identification to commit fraud or other crimes. (pp. 618–619)

> **3. Result:** If their employer owns the email system, the agents have no expectation of privacy and the police do not need a search warrant. If, however, they are sending emails over a system they are paying for themselves, then the police do need a warrant.
>
> **9. Result:** The court found that Cremers was not liable under the CDA.
>
> **10. Result:** Morris was convicted of a crime under the CFAA. He intended to trespass on a computer, so it did not matter that he had no intent to cause harm.

MULTIPLE-CHOICE QUESTIONS

1. Beth sent fraudulent emails through both her account at work and her personal account. Although Beth had never read her employer's handbook, it said the company had the right to access work emails. The police _____ obtain a search warrant before reading her work emails. They _____ obtain a search warrant before reading the emails from her personal account.

   (a) need to, need to
   (b) need not, need not
   (c) need to, need not
   (d) need not, need to

2. Because Blaine Blogger reviews movies on his blog, cinemas allow him in for free. Nellie Newspaper Reporter also gets free admission to movies. Blaine _____ disclose on his blog that he receives free tickets. Nellie _____ disclose in her articles that she receives free tickets.

   (a) must, must
   (b) need not, need not
   (c) must, need not
   (d) need not, must

3. An employer has the right to monitor workers' electronic communications if:
   (a) the employee consents.
   (b) the monitoring occurs in the ordinary course of business.
   (c) the employer provides the computer system.
   (d) all of the above
   (e) none of the above

4. Spiro Spammer sends millions of emails a day asking people to donate to his college tuition fund. Oddly enough, many people do. Everything in the emails is accurate (including his 1.9 GPA). Which of the following statements is true?

    (a) Spiro has violated the CAN-SPAM Act because he has sent unsolicited commercial emails.

    (b) Spiro has violated the CAN-SPAM Act if he has not offered recipients an opportunity to unsubscribe.

    (c) Spiro has violated the CAN-SPAM Act because he is asking for money.

    (d) Spiro has violated the CAN-SPAM Act unless the recipients have granted permission to him to send these emails.

5. Sushila suspects that her boyfriend is being unfaithful. While he is asleep, she takes his iPod out from under his pillow and goes through all his playlists. Then she finds what she has been looking for: Plum's Playlist. It is full of romantic songs. Sushila sends Plum an email that says, "You are the most evil person in the universe!" Which law has Sushila violated?

    (a) The First Amendment

    (b) The CDA

    (c) The ECPA

    (d) The CFAA

    (e) None

ESSAY QUESTIONS

1. **ETHICS** Chitika, Inc., provided online tracking tools on websites. When consumers clicked the "opt-out" button, indicating that they did not want to be tracked, they were not—for 10 days. After that, the software would resume tracking. Is there a legal problem with Chitika's system? An ethical problem? What Life Principles were operating here?

2. **YOU BE THE JUDGE WRITING PROBLEM** Jerome Schneider wrote several books on how to avoid taxes. These books were sold on Amazon.com. Amazon permits visitors to post comments about items for sale. Amazon's policy suggests that these comments should be civil (e.g., no profanity or spiteful remarks). The comments about Schneider's books were not so kind. One person alleged Schneider was a felon. When Schneider complained, an Amazon representative agreed that some of the postings violated its guidelines and promised that they would be removed within one to two business days. Two days later, the posting had not been removed. Schneider filed suit. **Argument for Schneider:** Amazon has editorial discretion over the posted comments. It both establishes guidelines and then monitors the comments to ensure that they comply with the guidelines. These activities make Amazon an information content provider, not protected by the Communications Decency Act. Also, Amazon violated its promise to take down the content. **Argument for Amazon:** The right to edit material is not the same thing as creating the material in the first place.

3. Over the course of 10 months, Joseph Melle sent more than 60 million unsolicited email advertisements to AOL members. What charges could be brought against him? Would you need more information before deciding?

4. What can you do to protect your privacy online? Draw up a concrete list of steps that you might reasonably consider. Are there some actions that you would not be willing to take because they are not worth it to you?

5. Craig Hare offered computers and related equipment for sale on various Internet auction websites. He accepted payment but not responsibility—he never shipped the goods. Which government agencies might bring charges against him?

DISCUSSION QUESTIONS

1. Marina Stengart used her company laptop to communicate with her lawyer via her personal, password-protected, web-based email account. The company's policy stated:

   > E-mail and voice mail messages, internet use and communication, and computer files are considered part of the company's business and client records. Such communications are not to be considered private or personal to any individual employee. Occasional personal use is permitted; however, the system should not be used to solicit for outside business ventures, charitable organizations, or for any political or religious purpose, unless authorized by the Director of Human Resources.

   After she filed an employment lawsuit against her employer, the company hired an expert to access her emails that had been automatically stored on the laptop. Are these emails protected by the attorney-client privilege? How does this case differ from *Scott v. Beth Israel* earlier in the chapter?

2. Roommates.com operated a website designed to match people renting spare rooms with those looking for a place to live. Before subscribers could search listings or post housing opportunities on Roommate's website, they had to create profiles, a process that required them to answer a series of questions that included the subscriber's sex, sexual orientation, and whether he would bring children to a household. The site also encouraged subscribers to provide "Additional Comments," describing themselves and their desired roommate in an open-ended essay. Here are some typical ads:

   - "I am not looking for Muslims."

   - "Not acceptable: freaks, geeks, prostitutes (male or female), druggies, pet cobras, drama queens, or mortgage brokers."

   - "Must be a black gay male!"

   - We are 3 Christian females who Love our Lord Jesus Christ…. We have weekly bible studies and bi-weekly times of fellowship."

   Many of the ads violated the Fair Housing Act. Is Roommates.com liable?

3. **ETHICS** Matt Drudge published a report on his website **(http://www.drudgereport.com)** that White House aide Sidney Blumenthal "has a spousal abuse past that has been effectively covered up....There are court records of Blumenthal's violence against his wife." The *Drudge Report* is an electronic publication focusing on Hollywood and Washington gossip. AOL paid Drudge $3,000 a month to make the *Drudge Report* available to AOL subscribers. Drudge emailed his reports to AOL, which then posted them. Before posting, however, AOL had the right to edit content. Drudge ultimately retracted his allegations against Blumenthal, who sued AOL. He alleged that under the Communications Decency Act of 1996, AOL was a "content provider" because it paid Drudge and edited what he wrote. Do you agree? Putting liability aside, what moral obligation did AOL have to its members? To Blumenthal? Should AOL be liable for content it bought and provided to its members?

4. Lori Drew created a fake MySpace profile, pretending to be a teenage boy. Through that boy's identity, she bullied 13-year-old Megan Meier. The girl killed herself shortly after receiving a message saying, "The world would be a better place without you." MySpace requires all users to agree to its terms of service which require "truthful and accurate" information. Has Drew violated the CFAA?

5. Tracking tools provide benefits to consumers but they also carry risks. Should Congress regulate them? If so, what should the law provide?

INTELLECTUAL PROPERTY

Cooper is a producer at a small indie film company in Los Angeles. He puts together packages that have a script, a director, and actors. He then finds investors who pay to make the movie and distributors who purchase the right to release it in cinemas, on TV, and on DVD. (Although most people think that box office results are what count, the reality is that, historically, over half of most movies' revenue came from home entertainment options such as DVD rentals and sales.)

Cooper is pretty excited about two packages he has put together: one stars established actor Robert de Niro, and the other features an up-and-coming director working with movie star Clive Owen. But his excitement has turned to disappointment—shockingly, he cannot find anyone willing to invest in either movie. Cooper hears the same thing from everyone: "DVD sales are way down, so we know we won't get the payback we used to. We can't afford to invest in as many movies."

> On a flight to New York in search of investors, Cooper finds himself sitting next to a man who is watching a movie on his computer…. Clearly, the man has downloaded it from an illegal website.

On a flight to New York in search of investors, Cooper finds himself sitting next to a man who is watching a movie on his computer. Cooper knows this movie has not even been released to DVD yet. Clearly, the man has downloaded it from an illegal website. Cooper slowly crushes the plastic cup in his hand. What's wrong with that guy? Doesn't he know that movies cost money to make? Doesn't he realize people like him are killing an industry?

INTRODUCTION

For much of history, land was the most valuable form of property. It was the primary source of wealth and social status. Today, intellectual property is a major source of wealth. New ideas—for manufacturing processes, software, apps, medicines, books—bring both affluence and influence.

Although both can be valuable assets, land and intellectual property are fundamentally different. The value of land lies in the owner's right to exclude, to prevent others from entering it. Intellectual property, however, has little economic value unless others use it. This ability to share intellectual property is both good news and bad. On the one hand, the owner can produce and sell unlimited copies of, say, software, but on the other hand, the owner has no easy way to determine if someone is using the program for free. The high cost of developing intellectual property, combined with the low cost of reproducing it, makes it particularly vulnerable to theft.

Because intellectual property is nonexclusive, many people see no problem with using it for free. But when consumers take intellectual property—movies, songs, and books—without paying for it, they ensure that fewer of these items will be produced.

Some commentators suggest that the United States has been a technological leader partly because its laws have always provided strong protection for intellectual property. The Constitution provided for patent protection early in the country's history.

The conflict between those who have intellectual property and those who want to use it has taken on a global dimension. Developing countries argue that American intellectual property laws increase the price of medicines, such as AIDS drugs and vaccines, that could save more lives if only they were cheaper and, therefore, more readily available. "Patents kill" is their slogan. The United States responds that without patent protection, there would be no innovation, no miracle drugs.

But even U.S. drug companies admit that patents can sometimes stifle innovation. The pharmaceutical company Bristol-Meyers Squibb says that it cannot conduct research on many cancer-fighting drugs because of patents held by its competitors. Information technology firms make a similar complaint. In a study of the American semiconductor business, researchers found that more patents did not necessarily mean more innovation. Instead, some companies were simply more aggressive about patenting every possible aspect of their research. Nor was there any evidence that innovation increased as patent rights were enhanced.

The role of intellectual property law is to balance the rights of those who create intellectual property and those who use it. And as this chapter reveals, such a balancing act is no easy feat.

PATENTS

Patent

A grant by the government permitting the inventor exclusive use of an invention for a specified period.

A **patent** is a grant by the government permitting the inventor exclusive use of an invention for 20 years from the date of filing (or 14 years from the date of issuance in the case of design patents). During this period, no one may make, use, or sell the invention without permission. In return, the inventor publicly discloses information about the invention that anyone can use upon expiration of the patent.

Types of Patents

There are three types of patents: utility patents, design patents, and plant patents.

Utility Patent

Whenever people use the word "patent" by itself, they are referring to a utility patent. This type of patent is available to those who invent (or significantly improve) any of the following:

Type of Invention	Example
Mechanical invention	A hydraulic jack used to lift heavy aircraft
Electrical invention	A prewired, portable wall panel for use in large, open-plan offices
Chemical invention	The chemical 2-chloroethylphosphonic acid used as a plant growth regulator
Process	A method for applying a chemical compound to an established plant such as rice in order to inhibit the growth of weeds selectively; the application can be patented separately from the actual chemical
Machine	A device that enables a helicopter pilot to control all flight functions (pitch, roll, and heave) with one hand
Composition of matter	A sludge used as an explosive at construction sites; the patent specifies the water content, the density, and the types of solids contained in the mixture

What about an electronic signal—is that patentable? An inventor filed a patent application for a method of encoding additional information on electronic signals emitted from digital audio files. The process was very useful, but the court ruled that it was not patentable because the signal is not a mechanical, electrical, or chemical invention, a process, a machine, or the composition of matter.[1]

A patent is not available solely for an idea, but only for its tangible application. Thus patents are not available for laws of nature, scientific principles, mathematical algorithms, mental processes, intellectual concepts, or formulas such as $a^2 + b^2 = c^2$.

Business Method Patents   In recent years, so-called "business method patents" have been controversial. These patents involve a particular way of doing business that often includes data processing or mathematical calculations. Business method patents have been particularly common in e-commerce. For example, Amazon.com patented its One-Click method of instant ordering. The company then obtained an injunction to prevent barnesandnoble.com from using its Express Lane service that was similar to One-Click. The judge directed barnesandnoble.com to add another step to its ordering process. The Patent and Trademark Office (PTO) affirmed the Amazon patent, which will expire in 2017.

Facebook has been granted a patent on a process that "dynamically provides a news feed about a user of a social network." Most social media sites, such as LinkedIn, Twitter, and Flickr, use some version of this technology. Two important issues are unknown: the exact scope of the patent and how aggressive Facebook will be in enforcing it.

It would be very helpful if the courts provided more clarity—and certainty—about the scope and enforceability of business method patents. In a recent case, *Bilski v. Kappos*, the Supreme Court ruled that business methods are *generally* patentable, even as it held that the *particular* patent in the case (a method for hedging risk in commodities trading) was too abstract to be acceptable.[2] In the same case, the Supreme Court encouraged lower courts

---

[1]*In re Nuijten*, 500 F.3d 1346; 2007 U.S. App. LEXIS 22426.
[2]2010 U.S. LEXIS 5521 (S.Ct. 2010).

to narrow the scope of business method patents, but did not offer guidance as to what these limits should be. As a result, inventors continue to apply for business method patents while waiting for lower courts to develop standards that meet the approval of the Supreme Court.

As a first step in this direction, a federal appeals court recently struck down a patent that covered a process for verifying credit card information over the Internet. This process determined which credit card numbers were linked with Internet Protocol (IP) or email addresses that had a high incidence of fraud. The court ruled that the patent simply covered a mental process and was, therefore, invalid.[3]

Congress also passed the America Invents Act (AIA). Under this statute, anyone who has been charged with infringement of certain *financial service* business method patents has the right (from 2012 to 2020) to challenge the validity of that patent.

Patents on Living Organisms   In 1980, the Supreme Court ruled that living organisms could be patented.[4] That case involved genetically engineered bacteria that was used to treat oil spills. The bacteria could be patented because it was different from anything found in nature and was also useful.

As a result of this ruling, the PTO began issuing patents on human genetic material. A total of 20 percent of all genes were patented, and the companies that owned these patents were valued at billions of dollars. Then, in 2010, a federal district court ruled that genes could not be patented. The patent at issue in this case allowed laboratories to isolate DNA that contained certain genes and then test them for mutations associated with breast and ovarian cancer. However, a federal appeals court overruled the district court, holding that the genes could be patented (but, in this case, not the process by which the genes were compared).[5] It seems likely that the Supreme Court will weigh in on this dispute.

Design Patent

A design patent protects the appearance, not the function, of an item. It is granted to anyone who invents a new, original, and ornamental design for an article. For example, Braun, Inc., patented the look of its handheld electric blenders. Design patents last 14 years from the date of issuance, not 20 years from the date of filing.

Plant Patent

Anyone who creates a new type of plant can patent it, provided that the inventor is able to reproduce it asexually—through grafting, for instance, rather than by planting its seeds. For example, one company patented its unique heather plant.

Requirements for a Patent

To receive a patent, an invention must be:

- **Novel**. An invention is not patentable if it has already been (1) patented, (2) described in a printed publication, (3) in public use, (4) on sale, or (5) otherwise available to the public anywhere in the world. For example, an inventor discovered a new use for existing chemical compounds but was not permitted to patent it because the compounds had already been described in prior publications, though the new uses had not.[6] Note, however, that a disclosure does not count under this provision if it was made by the inventor in the year prior to filing the application.

---

[3]*CyberSource Corp. v. Retail Decisions, Inc.*, 654 F.3d 1366 (Fed. Cir., 2011).
[4]*Diamond v. Chakrabarty*, 447 U.S. 303 (S. Ct. 1980).
[5]*Ass'n for Molecular Pathology v. United States PTO*, 2011 U.S. App. LEXIS 15649, 99 U.S.P.Q.2D (BNA) 1398. (Fed Cir., 2011).
[6]*In re Schoenwald*, 964 F.2d 1122, 1992 U.S. App. LEXIS 10181 (Fed. Cir. 1992).

- **Nonobvious**. An invention is not patentable if it is obvious to a person with ordinary skill in that particular area. An inventor was not allowed to patent a waterflush system designed to remove cow manure from the floor of a barn because it was obvious.[7]

- **Useful**. To be patented, an invention must be useful. It need not necessarily be commercially valuable, but it must have some current use. Being merely of scientific interest is not enough. Thus, a company was denied a patent for a novel process for making steroids because they had no therapeutic value.[8]

EXAM Strategy

Question: In 1572, during the reign of Queen Elizabeth I of England, a patent application was filed for a knife with a bone handle rather than a wooden one. Would this patent be granted under current U.S. law?

Strategy: Was a bone handle novel, nonobvious, and useful?

Result: It was useful—no splinters from a bone handle. It was novel—no one had ever done it before. But the patent was denied because it was obvious.

Patent Application and Issuance

To obtain a patent, the inventor must file a complex application with the PTO. If a patent examiner determines that the application meets all legal requirements, the PTO will issue the patent. If an examiner denies a patent application for any reason, the inventor can appeal that decision to the Patent Trial and Appeal Board in the PTO and from there to the Court of Appeals for the Federal Circuit in Washington.[9]

During the patent application process, third parties have the right to submit evidence that the invention is not novel. For the nine months after a patent has been granted, third parties have a broad right to challenge its validity in the PTO (without having to go to court). Thereafter, a patent may still be challenged, but the grounds are limited to evidence of a prior patent or publication.

Priority between Two Inventors

When two people invent the same product, who is entitled to a patent—the first to invent or the first to file an application? Until 2013, the person who invented and put the invention into practice had priority over the first filer. But the AIA changed the law so that, beginning in 2013, the first person to *file* a patent application has priority. The AIA brought the United States into conformity with most of the rest of the world.

Prior Sale

An inventor must apply for a patent within one year of selling the product commercially anywhere in the world. The purpose of this rule is to encourage prompt disclosure of inventions. It prevents someone from inventing a product, selling it for years, and then obtaining a 20-year monopoly with a patent.

---

[7]*Sakraida v. Ag Pro, Inc.*, 425 U.S. 273, 96 S. Ct. 1532, 1976 U.S. LEXIS 146 (1976).
[8]*Brenner v. Manson*, 383 U.S. 519, 86 S. Ct. 1033, 1966 U.S. LEXIS 2907 (1966).
[9]Recall from Chapter 3 that the Court of Appeals for the Federal Circuit is the 13th United States Court of Appeals. It hears appeals from specialized trial courts.

Provisional Patent Application

Inventors who are unable to assess the market value of their ideas sometimes hesitate to file a patent application because the process is expensive and cumbersome. A successful application can cost tens of thousands of dollars because the PTO charges a separate fee for each step of the process. Thus, for example, an inventor must pay a fee each time a patent examiner raises a legitimate question that requires an amendment to the application. Even if the examiner is wrong, the applicant may have to pay a fee even to file a disagreement. Thus, an inventor may struggle to raise sufficient funds to pay for the patent process. However, the AIA now permits the PTO to charge lower fees to individuals or small entities.

In addition, the PTO permits inventors to make a simpler, shorter filing called a **provisional patent application (PPA)**. This application provides a provable date of filing. Once filed, the application sits dormant for a year, giving the inventors an opportunity to show their ideas to potential investors without incurring the full expense of a patent application. PPA protection lasts only one year. To maintain protection after that time, the inventor must file a nonprovisional patent application.

Duration of a Patent

Patents are valid for 20 years from the date of *filing* the application (except design patents, which are valid for 14 years from date of *issuance*). In the last 15 years, the number of patent applications has increased from 950 a *day* to 2,000. And the typical patent application is longer and more complicated. As a result, more than 1 million applications are now pending. Approval of a patent can take anywhere from 3 to 6 years from the date of filing. These delays mean that patent holders effectively receive much less than 20 years of protection (although in the case of exceptional delays, it is possible to request an extension). They also threaten the ability of American inventors to attract investors, monetize their inventions, and compete with foreign businesses.

As permitted under the AIA, the PTO has set up a Track One system that permits inventors to buy their way to the head of the line by paying an additional fee of $4,800 (for large companies) and $2,400 (for small). Track One applications are supposed to be decided within one year. Only 10,000 Track One applications will be accepted in any given year.

Infringement

A patent holder has the exclusive right to use the invention during the term of the patent. A holder can prohibit others from using any product that is substantially the same, license the product to others for a fee, and recover damages from anyone who uses the product without permission.

Patent Trolls

As we have seen, the patent office must deal with a growing caseload. As a result, the examiners typically spend less than 25 hours reviewing each application. Applicants are not required to demonstrate that the invention is novel, and often the examiner neither knows nor has the time to research the issue. Thus, patents are sometimes issued for inventions that are not really new.

Traditionally, this issue was not that important because companies with overlapping patents did not litigate who the real inventor was. They were too busy developing products to sell. But then came **patent trolls**. They do not make or market products—they simply buy portfolios of patents for the purpose of bringing patent infringement claims against companies already using the technology. Typically, patent trolls request an injunction to prevent the use of the technology during litigation, potentially harming a multimillion-dollar product over a patent worth much less. Because the trolls are not

Patent troll
Someone who buys a portfolio of patents for the purpose of making patent infringement claims.

using the technology themselves, they do not have to worry about a cross-injunction preventing them from using it. Oftentimes, patent trolls are simply hoping that even legitimate users will pay them to go away. In a recent report, the FTC found that these practices "can deter innovation by raising costs and risks without making a technological contribution."[10] In response to criticism, patent trolls argue that they are encouraging innovation by making patents more valuable.

Some hedge funds have entered the patent troll business. In addition, a company owned by Paul Allen, one of Microsoft's founders, recently began filing suit against companies that are using technology that his research lab allegedly invented prior to 2005. These suits have been filed against most of the major players in Silicon Valley—Apple, eBay, Facebook, Google, and Netflix—for their use of technology that improves users' online experience. (Such as suggestions for related reading and pop-up ads or stock quotes.) The technology at issue is key to these companies.

> **Ethics** Is the patent troll business ethical? Under what circumstances would you be willing to engage in this practice? Paul Allen is wealthy beyond most people's dreams. Why would he be involved in this litigation? What is your Life Principle in this case?

International Patent Treaties

About half of all patent applications are filed in more than one country. This process used to be a logistical nightmare because almost every country had its own unique filing procedures and standards. Companies were reluctant to develop products based on technology that they were not sure they actually owned. Several treaties now facilitate this process, although it is still not the one-stop (or one-click) effort that inventors desire. These treaties were drafted by the World Intellectual Property Organization (WIPO) of the United Nations.

The Paris Convention for the Protection of Industrial Property (Paris Convention) requires each member country to grant to citizens of other member countries the same rights under patent law as its own citizens enjoy. Thus, the patent office in each member country must accept and recognize all patent and trademark applications filed with it by anyone who lives in any member country. For example, the French patent office cannot refuse to accept an application from an American, so long as the American has complied with French law. Under this treaty, inventors who file in one country have up to one year to file elsewhere and still maintain patent protection.

The Patent Law Treaty requires that countries use the same standards for the form and content of patent applications (whether submitted on paper or electronically). This treaty reduces the procedural conflicts over issues such as translations and fees.

The **Patent Cooperation Treaty** (PCT) is a step toward providing more coordinated patent review across many countries. Inventors who pay a fee and file a so-called PCT patent application are granted patent protection in the 143 PCT countries for up to 30 months. During this time, they can decide how many countries they actually want to file in. (Inventors have one year of protection under the Paris Convention; this treaty grants an additional 18 months.)

---

[10]U.S. Fed. Trade Comm'n, *The Evolving IP Marketplace: Aligning Patent Notice and Remedies with Competition* (March 7, 2011).

Once a PCT application is filed, one of the major patent offices prepares an "international search report" and issues a nonbinding opinion on whether the invention is patentable. This report, while nonbinding, helps applicants assess the patentability of their inventions and provides persuasive evidence to national patent offices. Inventors who wish to proceed internationally must then have the report translated and file it with applications and fees in whichever countries they want a patent.

The United States PTO has bilateral agreements with 16 other patent offices under a so-called **Patent Prosecution Highway**. Under this system, once a patent is approved by one country, it goes to the head of the line for patent examination in the other country.

In addition to these treaties, any country that joins the World Trade Organization (WTO) must agree to trade-related aspects of intellectual property rights (TRIPS). This agreement does not create an international patent system, but it does require all participants to meet minimum standards for the protection of intellectual property. How individual countries achieve that goal is left to them.

Finally, the European Union is in the process of developing a single European patent that would require only one application.

COPYRIGHTS

The holder of a copyright owns the *particular tangible expression* **of an idea, but not the underlying idea or method of operation**. Abner Doubleday could have copyrighted a book setting out his particular version of the rules of baseball, but he could not have copyrighted the rules themselves, nor could he have required players to pay him a royalty. Similarly, the inventor of double-entry bookkeeping could copyright a pamphlet explaining his system, but not the system itself.

Unlike patents, the ideas underlying copyrighted material need not be novel. For example, three movies—*Like Father Like Son, Vice Versa, and Freaky Friday*—are about a parent and child who switch bodies. The movies all have the same plot, but there is no copyright violation because their *expressions* of the basic idea are different.

The Copyright Act protects literature, music, drama, choreography, pictures, sculpture, movies, recordings, architectural works, and computer databases, and computer programs "to the extent that they incorporate authorship in the programmer's expression of original ideas, as distinguished from the ideas themselves."

A work is copyrighted *automatically* once it is in tangible form. For example, once a songwriter puts notes on paper, the work is copyrighted without further ado. But if she whistles a happy tune without writing it down, the song is not copyrighted, and anyone else can use it without permission. Registration with the Copyright Office of the Library of Congress is necessary only if the holder wishes to bring suit to enforce the copyright. Although authors still routinely place the copyright symbol (©) on their works, such a precaution is not necessary in the United States. However, some lawyers still recommend using the copyright symbol because other countries recognize it. Also, the penalties for intentional copyright infringement are heavier than for unintentional violations, and the presence of a copyright notice is evidence that the infringer's actions were intentional.

In the following case, you can imagine the author's frustration when a celebrity stole her thunder and her sales by writing a book on the very same topic. But did the celebrity violate copyright law? This case also anticipates our discussion of trademarks.

LAPINE V. SEINFELD

375 Fed. Appx. 81; 2010 U.S. App. Lexis 8778
United States Court of Appeals for the Second Circuit, 2010

Facts: Missy Chase Lapine wrote a book called *The Sneaky Chef: Simple Strategies for Hiding Healthy Foods in Kids' Favorite Meals*, which was about how to disguise vegetables so that children would eat them. Her strategy was to add pureed vegetables to food that children like, such as macaroni and cheese. (We are not making this up.) Four months later, Jessica Seinfeld, wife of comedian Jerry Seinfeld, published a book entitled *Deceptively Delicious: Simple Secrets To Get Your Kids Eating Good Food*, which featured recipes involving pureed vegetables in (guess what?) macaroni and cheese and other kid-friendly foods.

Lapine filed suit against Seinfeld, alleging violation of her copyright in the content of the book, as well as her trademark in the name and cover design. The district court granted Seinfeld's motion for summary judgment, and Lapine appealed.

Issue: *Did Seinfeld violate Lapine's copyright and trademark in* The Sneaky Chef?

Excerpts from the Decision of the Court:

1. Copyright Infringement
   Plaintiffs assert that the two works are substantially similar in their unique and innovative expression of the idea of sneaking vegetables into children's food by means of a cookbook containing comprehensive instructions for making and storing a variety of vegetable purees in advance, and then using the purees in specially created recipes for children's favorite foods. We are not persuaded.

   Stockpiling vegetable purees for covert use in children's food is an idea that cannot be copyrighted. In no case does copyright protection for an original work of authorship extend to any idea, procedure, process, system, method of operation, concept, principle, or discovery, regardless of the form in which it is described, explained, illustrated, or embodied in such work. It is a fundamental principle of our copyright doctrine that ideas, concepts, and processes are not protected from copying.

   Further, to the extent the two works have general and abstract similarities—including their vaguely similar titles and inclusion of illustrations of prepared dishes, health advice, personal narrative, descriptions of how to make purees, instructions for preparing dishes, and language about children's healthy eating—the district court correctly concluded that these elements do not raise a fact issue for trial because they are "scenes a faire," or unprotectible elements that follow naturally from the work's theme rather than from the author's creativity.

   Our independent comparison of the two cookbooks confirms that the total concept and feel of *Deceptively Delicious* is very different from that of *The Sneaky Chef*. *Deceptively Delicious* lacks the extensive discussion of child behavior, food philosophy, and parenting that pervades *The Sneaky Chef*. Unlike *The Sneaky Chef*, which uses primarily black, gray, and shades of brownish orange, *Deceptively Delicious* employs bright colors and more photographs. While *The Sneaky Chef* assumes greater familiarity with cooking, recommends thirteen methods for hiding healthy foods, and provides recipes for multiple-ingredient purees, *Deceptively Delicious* instructs readers about only single-ingredient purees and contains more basic instructions.

   Plaintiffs correctly note that no plagiarist can excuse the wrong by showing how much of her work she did not pirate. Like the district court, we nevertheless conclude as a matter of law that the two cookbooks lack the substantial similarity required to support an inference of copyright infringement.

2. Trademark Infringement
   Having considered the overall impression on a consumer and the context in which the competing marks are displayed, we reach the same conclusion as the district court: the marks are not confusingly similar. Defendants' depictions of a winking woman holding brownies near carrots or simply "shushing" are very different from plaintiffs' considerably less detailed and less colorful image of a female chef winking and "shushing" while holding carrots behind her back. Further, defendants' use of the famous "Seinfeld" name reduces any likelihood of confusion regarding the marks. In sum, like the district court, we conclude that dissimilarity of the marks is dispositive.

Copyright Term

More than 300 years ago, on April 10, 1710, Queen Anne of England approved the first copyright statute. Called the Statute of Anne, it provided copyright protection for 14 years, which could be extended by another 14 years if the copyright owner was still alive when the first term expired. Many credit the Statute of Anne with greatly expanding the burst of intellectual activity that we now refer to as the Enlightenment.

American law adopted these same time limits, which stayed in effect until the twentieth century. Since then, copyright holders have fought aggressively to lengthen the copyright period. These efforts have been led by the Walt Disney Company, which wants to protect its rights in Mickey Mouse. Today, a copyright is valid until 70 years after the death of the work's only or last living author, or, in the case of works owned by a corporation, the copyright lasts 95 years from publication or 120 years from creation, whichever is shorter. Once a copyright expires, anyone may use the material. Mark Twain died in 1910, so anyone may now publish *Tom Sawyer* without permission and without paying a copyright fee.

Infringement

Anyone who uses copyrighted material without permission is violating the Copyright Act. **To prove a violation, the plaintiff must present evidence that the work was original** and that either:

- The infringer actually copied the work, or

- The infringer had access to the original and the two works are substantially similar.

A court may (1) prohibit the infringer from committing further violations, (2) order destruction of the infringing material, and (3) require the infringer to pay damages, profits earned, and attorney's fees. Damages can be substantial. In a recent case, a jury ordered SAP to pay Oracle $1.3 *billion* for copyright infringement of Oracle's software.

First Sale Doctrine

Suppose you buy a CD that, in the end, you do not like. Under the **first sale doctrine,** you have the legal right to sell that CD. **The first sale doctrine permits a person who owns a lawfully made copy of a copyrighted work to sell or otherwise dispose of the copy**. Note, however, that the first sale doctrine does not permit the owner to *make a copy and sell it*. If you listen to a CD and then decide to sell it, that is legal. But it is not legal to copy the CD onto your iPod and then sell the original or any copy of it.

Fair Use

Fair use doctrine

Permits limited use of copyrighted material without permission of the author for purposes such as criticism, comment, news reporting, scholarship, or research.

Because the period of copyright protection is so long, it has become even more important to uphold the exceptions to the law. Bear in mind that the point of copyright laws is to encourage creative work. A writer who can control, and profit from, artistic work will be inclined to produce more. If enforced oppressively, however, the copyright laws could stifle creativity by denying access to copyrighted work. The **fair use doctrine** permits limited use of copyrighted material without permission of the author for purposes such as criticism, comment, news reporting, scholarship, or research. Courts generally do not permit a use that will decrease revenues from the original work by, say, competing with it. A reviewer is permitted, for example, to quote from a book without the author's permission, but could not reproduce so much that the review was competing with the book itself.

Fair use has become a highly controversial issue in this age of the Internet. For example, Universal Music demanded that YouTube remove a home video of a toddler dancing to a Prince song. A director making a documentary on torture was denied permission to use a short clip showing torture on the TV show *24*. Then J. K. Rowling, the author of the *Harry Potter* series of books, sued to prevent the publication of the *Harry Potter Lexicon*, an unauthorized reference guide to the books that contained direct quotations, paraphrases, and plot summaries. The court ruled that although such a guide can be fair use, this one was not because the author had copied too much of Rowling's distinctive original language.[11]

Also under the fair use doctrine, faculty members are permitted to distribute copyrighted materials to students, so long as the materials are brief and the teacher's action is spontaneous. If, over his breakfast coffee one morning, Professor Learned spots a terrific article in *Mad Magazine* that perfectly illustrates a point he intends to make in class that day, the fair use doctrine permits him to distribute it to his class. However, under a misinterpretation of the fair use doctrine, some faculty had been in the habit of routinely preparing lengthy course packets of copyrighted material without permission of the authors. In *Basic Books, Inc. v. Kinkos Graphic Corp.*,[12] a federal court held that this practice violated the copyright laws because the material was more than one short passage and because it was sold to students. Now, when professors put together course packets, they (or the copy shop) must obtain permission and pay a royalty for the use of copyrighted material. Likewise, it is illegal for students to make photocopies of a classmate's course packet or textbook.

Parody

Parody has a long history in the United States—some of our most cherished songs have been based on parodies. Before Francis Scott Key wrote the words to "The Star-Spangled Banner," other lyrics that mocked colonial governors had been set to the same music. (The tune was well known as a drinking song.)

Because of the political and social commentary that is inherent in many parodies, courts have long granted them special respect. In a case involving a 2 Live Crew parody of the song "Pretty Woman," the Supreme Court decided in favor of 2 Live Crew, holding that **parody is a fair use of copyrighted material so long as the use of the original is not excessive.**[13] The parody may copy enough to remind the audience of the original work, but not so much that the parody harms the market for the original.

The following email exchange between Richard Saperstein, a movie producer, and Tom Strickler, a talent agent, which zapped around Hollywood, illustrates the importance of the 2 Live Crew case (to which Strickler refers).

> I wish you good luck on your journey to deny our First Amendment rights.

---

[11] *Warner Bros. Entertainment Inc. v. RDR Books*, 575 F. Supp. 2d 513; 2008 U.S. Dist. LEXIS 67771, (S. D.N.Y., 2008).

[12] 758 F. Supp. 1522, 1991 U.S. Dist. LEXIS 3804 (S.D.N.Y. 1991). A federal appeals court reached the same result in *Princeton University Press v. Michigan Document Services, Inc.*, 99 F.3d 1381, 1996 U.S. App. LEXIS 29132 (6th Cir. 1996).

[13] *Campbell v. Acuff-Rose Music, Inc.*, 510 U.S. 569, 114 S. Ct. 1164, 1994 U.S. LEXIS 2052 (1994).

[From Saperstein to Strickler:]
Tom—
Please give me a call about a spec script Elia Infascelli-Smith has gone out with called $40,000
MAN. As you know, along with Universal, we control the rights to SIX MILLION DOLLAR
MAN. My understanding is this spec includes characters we own.
Best—Richard

[Strickler's response:]
Richard:
Good news. As you may know, The United States Supreme Court has affirmed the right of Parody
as an unassailable First Amendment Right. This has enabled you to make movies like *Scream* and
Scary Movie, in which you parody many films which Dimension does not own or control.

The script is a parody, and if you have any problems, I suggest you hire a Constitutional
lawyer and file a brief with the US Supreme Court. This will be an uphill battle—the court voted
9 to 0 when this last hit the docket and those stubborn justices all believe in Stare Decisis.

And if you succeed at the Supreme Court—you will have to stop making *Scream* and *Scary Movie*.

This will take about 5 to 7 years ... and lawyers are an expensive breed, but I wish you good
luck on your journey to deny our First Amendment rights.
All the best,
Tom

Digital Music and Movies

One of the major challenges for legal institutions in regulating copyrights is simply that
modern intellectual property is so easy to copy. Many consumers are in the habit of
violating the law by downloading copyrighted material—music, movies and books—for
free. They seem to believe that if it is easy to steal something, then the theft is
somehow acceptable. In one survey of adolescents aged 12 to 17, 75 percent agreed
with the statement, "file-sharing is so easy to do, it's unrealistic to expect people not to
do it."[14]

The entertainment world used to turn a blind eye, but illegal downloading is
threatening the viability of recording companies, movie studios, and publishers. The
statistics are compelling: in 2008, 40 *billion* songs were downloaded illegally, which is as
much as 95 percent of all downloaded music! In the first decade of this century, music
sales at American record labels declined by 58 percent. Without profitable record labels,
who will find and promote new stars? As we saw in the opening scenario, which is a true
story, this type of theft is having a profound effect on entertainment and publishing. But
it is not just "big companies" that suffer—it is also the artists, musicians, actors, and
writers, most of whom are not wealthy rock stars.

Government and industry are striking back. The Prioritizing Resources and Organization for Intellectual Property Act (Pro-IP) permits law enforcement officials to
confiscate any equipment used to steal copyrighted material. In addition, the Recording
Industry Association of America (RIAA) developed a strategy of aggressively suing those
who download music illegally. Then a coalition of entertainment businesses sued two
companies that distributed the software used by many consumers to violate copyright
law. So important was this issue that the Supreme Court waded into these murky
waters.

[14]*http://pewinternet.org/Reports/2009/9-The-State-of-Music-Online-Ten-Years-After-Napster/The-State-of-
Music-Online-Ten-Years-After-Napster.aspx?view=all#footnote25* or google *"pew 10 years after napster"*.

METRO-GOLDWYN-MAYER STUDIOS, INC. v. GROKSTER, LTD.

125 S. Ct. 2764, 2005 U.S. Lexis 5212
Supreme Court of the United States, 2005

Facts: Grokster, Ltd., and StreamCast Networks, Inc., distributed free software that allowed computer users to share electronic files through peer-to-peer networks, so called because users' computers communicated directly with each other, not through central servers. The Grokster and StreamCast software could be used for legal purposes. Indeed, peer-to-peer networks were utilized by universities, government agencies, corporations, libraries, and individuals, among others. Even the briefs in this very case could be downloaded legally with the StreamCast software.

Nonetheless, nearly 90 percent of the files available for download through Grokster or StreamCast were copyrighted. Billions of files were shared each month—the probable scope of copyright infringement was staggering. The two companies encouraged the illegal uses of their software. For example, the chief technology officer of StreamCast said that "the goal is to get in trouble with the law and get sued. It's the best way to get in the news."

A group of copyright holders (MGM and others) sued Grokster and StreamCast, alleging that they were violating the copyright law by knowingly and intentionally distributing their software to users who would reproduce and distribute copyrighted works illegally. Both parties moved for summary judgment. The trial court held for Grokster and StreamCast; the appeals court affirmed. The Supreme Court granted *certiorari*.

Issue: *Were Grokster and StreamCast violating copyright law?*

Excerpts from Justice Souter's Decision: The more artistic protection is favored, the more technological innovation may be discouraged; the administration of copyright law is an exercise in managing the trade-off. [T]he indications are that the ease of copying songs or movies using software like Grokster's is fostering disdain for copyright protection. When a widely shared service or product is used to commit infringement, it may be impossible to enforce rights in the protected work effectively against all direct infringers, the only practical alternative being to go against the distributor of the copying device. We hold that one who distributes a device with the object of promoting its use to infringe copyright, as shown by clear expression or other affirmative steps taken to foster infringement, is liable for the resulting acts of infringement by third parties.

We are, of course, mindful of the need to keep from trenching on regular commerce or discouraging the development of technologies with lawful and unlawful potential. Accordingly, mere knowledge of infringing potential or of actual infringing uses would not be enough here to subject a distributor to liability. The inducement rule, instead, premises liability on purposeful, culpable expression and conduct, and thus does nothing to compromise legitimate commerce or discourage innovation having a lawful promise.

Grokster distributed an electronic newsletter containing links to articles promoting its software's ability to access popular copyrighted music. And both companies communicated a clear message by responding affirmatively to requests for help in locating and playing copyrighted materials. [N]either company attempted to develop filtering tools or other mechanisms to diminish the infringing activity using their software. It is useful to recall that StreamCast and Grokster make money by selling advertising space, by directing ads to the screens of computers employing their software. As the record shows, the more the software is used, the more ads are sent out and the greater the advertising revenue becomes. Since the extent of the software's use determines the gain to the distributors, the commercial sense of their enterprise turns on high-volume use, which the record shows is infringing. The unlawful objective is unmistakable.

In addition to intent to bring about infringement and distribution of a device suitable for infringing use, [MGM must show] evidence of actual infringement by recipients of the software. As the account of the facts indicates, there is evidence of infringement on a gigantic scale.

On remand, reconsideration of MGM's motion for summary judgment will be in order.

The No Electronic Theft Act

Enacted in 1997, the **No Electronic Theft Act** is intended to deter the downloading of copyrighted material. It provides for criminal penalties for the reproduction or distribution of copyrighted material that has a retail value greater than $1,000, even if the offender has no profit motive. Thus, for instance, if a student photocopied for 10 of her friends a textbook that is worth $150, she could be subject to criminal penalties, including a prison term of one year. Originally, the Justice Department did not enforce this statute, but it has now begun to do so, particularly against those who set up networks to trade games, movies, and music.

The Family Entertainment and Copyright Act

Under the **Family Entertainment and Copyright Act,** it is a criminal offense to use a camcorder to film a movie in the theater. This statute also establishes criminal penalties for willful copyright infringement that involves distributing software, music, or film on a computer network.

The Digital Millennium Copyright Act

The good news is that Mary Schmich wrote an influential article in the *Chicago Tribune*. The bad news is that people deleted her name, attributed the article to Kurt Vonnegut, and sent it around the world via email. Tom Tomorrow's cartoon was syndicated to 100 newspapers, but by the time the last papers received it, the cartoon had already gone zapping around cyberspace. Because his name had been deleted from the original, some editors thought he had plagiarized it.

In response to such incidents, Congress passed the **Digital Millennium Copyright Act** (DMCA), which provides that:

- **It is illegal to delete copyright information, such as the name of the author or the title of the article**. It is also illegal to distribute false copyright information. Thus, anyone who emailed Schmich's article without her name on it, or who claimed it was his own work, would be violating the law.

- **It is illegal to circumvent encryption or scrambling devices that protect copyrighted works**. For example, some software programs are designed so that they can only be copied once. Anyone who overrides this protective device to make another copy is violating the law. (The statute does permit purchasers of copyrighted software to make one backup copy.) If you buy a Disney DVD that prevents you from fast-forwarding through commercials, you are violating the DMCA if you figure out how to do it anyway.

- **It is illegal to distribute tools and technologies used to circumvent encryption devices.** If you tell others how to fast-forward through the Disney commercials, you have violated the statute.

- **Online service providers (OSPs) are not liable for posting copyrighted material so long as they are unaware that the material is illegal and they remove it promptly after receiving notice that it violates copyright law.** This type of provision is called a *safe harbor*.

EXAM Strategy

Question: Many of the videos posted on YouTube are copyrighted material, including thousands of hours of shows owned by Viacom, such as *The Colbert Report* and *The Daily Show*. Viacom sued YouTube for violating its copyrights. Among the evidence Viacom presented was an email from one YouTube founder to another, saying, "… please stop putting stolen videos on the site. We're going to have a tough time defending the fact that we're not liable for the copyrighted material on the site because we didn't put it up when one of the co-founders is blatantly stealing content from other sites and trying to get everyone to see it."[15] YouTube presented evidence that it had responded within one day to Viacom's "takedown notice." Is YouTube liable?

Strategy: Viacom argued that YouTube was well aware that much of its content was illegal. YouTube responded that it met the requirements of the safe harbor provision.

Result: The court found for YouTube. General awareness that many postings infringed copyrights did not impose a duty for YouTube to monitor its videos. Its only requirement was to respond when notified of infringement. YouTube did just that in this case.[16]

International Copyright Treaties

The Berne Convention requires member countries to provide automatic copyright protection to any works created in another member country. The protection does not expire until 50 years after the death of the author.[17] The WIPO Copyright Treaty and the WIPO Performances and Phonograms Treaty add computer programs, movies, and music to the list of copyrightable materials.

In 2004, Congress enacted a law that permits the president to appoint a copyright law enforcement officer charged with the responsibility for stopping copyright infringement overseas. Also, for the first time, Congress funded the National Intellectual Property Law Enforcement Coordination Council, which was established to protect American intellectual property internationally.

TRADEMARKS

A **trademark** is any combination of words and symbols that a business uses to identify its products or services and distinguish them from others. Trademarks are important to both consumers and businesses. Consumers use trademarks to distinguish between competing products. People who feel that Nike shoes fit their feet best can rely on the Nike trademark to know they are buying the shoe they want. A business with a high-quality product can use a trademark to develop a loyal base of customers who are able to distinguish its product from another.

Trademark
Any combination of words and symbols that a business uses to identify its products or services and distinguish them from others.

[15]Quoted in "Federal Judge Hands Google Victory in Viacom's $1 Billion Suit Over YouTube Content" by Michael Liedtke on Law.com, June 24, 2010.
[16]*Viacom Int'l, Inc. v. YouTube, Inc.*, 718 F. Supp. 2d 514 (S.D.N.Y., 2010).
[17]Under U.S. law, copyrights last 70 years. The United States must grant works created in other signatory countries a copyright that lasts either 50 years or the length of time granted in that country, whichever is longer, but in no case longer than 70 years.

Types of Marks

There are four different types of marks:

- **Trademarks** are affixed to *goods* in interstate commerce.

- **Service marks** are used to identify *services*, not products. Fitness First, Burger King, and Weight Watchers are service marks. In this chapter, the terms "trademark" and "mark" are used to refer to both trademarks and service marks.

- **Certification marks** are words or symbols used by a person or organization to attest that products and services produced by others meet certain standards. The Good Housekeeping Seal of Approval means that the Good Housekeeping organization has determined that a product meets its standards.

- **Collective marks** are used to identify members of an organization. The Lions Club, the Girl Scouts of America, and the Masons are examples of collective marks.

Ownership and Registration

Under common law, the first person to use a mark in trade owns it. Registration with the federal government is not necessary. However, under the federal Lanham Act, the owner of a mark may register it on the Lanham Act Principal Register. A trademark owner may use the symbol ™ at any time, even before registering it, but not until the mark is registered can the symbol ® be placed next to it. Registration has several advantages:

- Even if a mark has been used in only one or two states, registration makes it valid nationally.

- Registration notifies the public that a mark is in use because anyone who applies for registration first searches the Public Register to ensure that no one else has rights to the mark.

- Five years after registration, a mark becomes virtually incontestable because most challenges are barred.

- The damages available under the Lanham Act are higher than under common law.

- The holder of a registered trademark generally has the right to use it as an Internet domain name.

Under the Lanham Act, the owner files an application with the PTO. The PTO will accept an application only if the owner has already used the mark attached to a product in interstate commerce or promises to use the mark within six months after the filing. In addition, the applicant must be the *first* to use the mark in interstate commerce. Initially, the trademark is valid for 10 years, but the owner can renew it for an unlimited number of 10-year terms as long as the mark is still in use.

Valid Trademarks

Words (Reebok), symbols (Microsoft's flying window logo), phrases (Nike's "Just do it"), shapes (Apple's iPod), sounds (NBC's three chimes), colors (Owens Corning's pink insulation), and even scents (plumeria blossoms on sewing thread) can be trademarked. **To be valid, a trademark must be distinctive**—that is, the mark must clearly distinguish one product from another. There are five basic categories of distinctive marks:

- **Fanciful marks** are made-up words such as Kodak or Saucony.

- **Arbitrary marks** use existing words that do *not* describe the product—Prince tennis racquets, for example. No one really thinks that these racquets are designed by or for royalty.

- **Suggestive marks** *indirectly* describe the product's function. "Greyhound" implies that the bus line is swift, and "Coppertone" suggests what customers will look like after applying the product.

- Marks with **secondary meaning** cannot, by themselves, be trademarked unless they have been used for so long that they are now associated with the product in the public's mind. When a film company released a movie called *Ape*, it used as an illustration a picture that looked like a scene from *King Kong*—a gigantic gorilla astride the World Trade Center in New York City. The court held that the movie posters of *King Kong* had acquired a secondary meaning in the mind of the public, so the *Ape* producers were forced to change their poster.[18]

- **Trade dress** is the image and overall appearance of a business or product. It may include size, shape, color, or texture. The Supreme Court held that a Mexican restaurant was entitled to protection under the Lanham Act for the shape and general appearance of the exterior of its building as well as the decor, menu, servers' uniforms, and other features reflecting the total image of the restaurant.[19]

The following categories *cannot* be trademarked:

- **Similar to an existing mark**. To avoid confusion, the PTO will not grant a trademark that is similar to one already in existence on a similar product. Once the PTO had granted a trademark for "Pledge" furniture polish, it refused to trademark "Promise" for the same product. "Chat noir" and "black cat" were also too similar because one is simply a translation of the other. Houghton-Mifflin Co. successfully sued to prevent a punk rock band from calling itself Furious George because the name is too similar to Curious George, the star of a series of children's books.

- **Generic trademarks**. No one is permitted to trademark an item's ordinary name— "shoe" or "book," for example. Sometimes, however, a word begins as a trademark and later becomes a generic name. Zipper, escalator, aspirin, linoleum, thermos, yo-yo, band-aid, ping-pong, and nylon all started out as trademarks but became generic. Once a name is generic, the owner loses the trademark because the name can no longer be used to distinguish one product from another—all products are called the same thing. That is why Xerox Corp. encourages people to say, "I'll photocopy this document," rather than "I'll xerox it." Jeep, Rollerblade, and TiVo are names that began as trademarks and may now be generic. What about "app store"? Microsoft has sued Apple, disputing its right to trademark this term. Meanwhile, Facebook has trademarked, "face," "book," "like," "wall," and "poke." The goal is not to prevent consumers from using these terms but rather to warn off other companies.

- **Descriptive marks**. Words cannot be trademarked if they simply describe the product— such as "low-fat," "green," or "crunchy." Descriptive words can, however, be trademarked if they do *not* describe that particular product because

[18]*Paramount Pictures Corp. v. Worldwide Entertainment Corp.*, 2 Media L. Rep. 1311, 195 U.S.P.Q. (BNA) 539, 1977 U.S. Dist. LEXIS 17931 (S.D.N.Y. 1977).
[19]*Two Pesos, Inc. v. Taco Cabana, Inc.*, 505 U.S. 763, 112 S. Ct. 2753, 1992 U.S. LEXIS 4533 (1992).

they then become distinctive rather than descriptive. "Blue Diamond" is an acceptable trademark for nuts so long as the nuts are neither blue nor diamond-shaped.

- **Names.** The PTO generally will not grant a trademark in a surname because other people are already using it and have the right to continue. No one could register "Jefferson" as a trademark. However, a surname can be used as part of a longer title— "Jefferson Home Tours," for instance. Similarly, no one can register a geographical name such as "Boston" unless it is also associated with another word, such as "Boston Ale."

- **Deceptive marks**. The PTO will not register a mark that is deceptive. It refused to register a trademark with the words "National Collection and Credit Control" and an eagle superimposed on a map of the United States because this trademark gave the false impression that the organization was an official government agency.

- **Scandalous or immoral trademarks**. The PTO refused to register a mark that featured a nude man and woman embracing. In upholding the PTO's decision, the court was unsympathetic to arguments that this was the perfect trademark for a newsletter on sex.[20] This author once had a client who wanted to apply for a trademark for marijuana: "Sweet Mary Jane, she never lets you down." However, the client was unwilling to admit to affixing the name to his product and shipping it in interstate commerce. Now, medical marijuana is legal in 16 states but the PTO refuses to register marijuana trademarks.

Infringement

To win an infringement suit, the trademark owner must show that the defendant's trademark is likely to deceive customers about who has made the goods or provided the services. As we saw in the *Seinfeld* case, the court ruled there was no trademark infringement because consumers would not be confused by the names or covers of the two books.

In the event of infringement, the rightful owner is entitled to (1) an injunction prohibiting further violations, (2) destruction of the infringing material, (3) up to three times actual damages, (4) any profits the infringer earned on the product, and (5) attorney's fees.

What about a perfume for dogs? Would a reasonable consumer confuse Pucci with Gucci, Bono Sports with Ralph Lauren Polo Sports, or Miss Claybone for Liz Claiborne? None of these companies challenged the parody use of their names for a dog perfume. But Tommy Hilfiger Licensing, Inc. did not see the humor in the name Timmy Holedigger. The court, however, advised Hilfiger "to chill," pointing out that there was no evidence of actual confusion.[21] On the other hand, auction website eBay did prevent a seller of perfumes from using the name Perfumebay. The court ruled that the use of "ebay" confused consumers.[22]

The following case raises an issue of confusion in cyberspace. Once again, the Internet is challenging intellectual property laws that were not conceived with this technology in mind.

---

[20]*In re McGinley*, 660 F.2d 481, 211 U.S.P.Q. (BNA) 668, 1981 CCPA LEXIS 177 (C.C.P.A. 1981).

[21]*Tommy Hilfiger Licensing, Inc. v. Nature Labs, LLC*, 221 F. Supp. 2d 410; 2002 U.S. Dist. LEXIS 14841 (2002).

[22]*Perfumebay.com Inc. v. eBay Inc.*, 506 F.3d 1165, 2007 U.S. App. LEXIS 25726.

You be the Judge

NETWORK AUTOMATION, INC. V. ADVANCED SYSTEMS CONCEPTS, INC.

2011 U.S. App. Lexis 4488
United States Court of Appeals for the
Ninth Circuit, 2011

Facts: Network Automation and Advanced Systems Concepts both sold job scheduling and management software, and both advertised on the Internet. Network sold its software under the trademarked name Auto-Mate, while Systems used the trademark ActiveBatch. Customers paid between $995 and $10,995 to use these software programs.

Google AdWords is a program that sells "keywords," which are search terms that trigger the display of a sponsor's advertisement. When a user enters a keyword, Google displays the links generated by its own algorithm in the main part of the page, along with advertisements in a separate "Sponsored Links" section next to or above the objective results. Multiple advertisers can purchase the same keyword.

Although ActiveBatch was Systems's trademark, Network purchased it as a keyword. This purchase meant that anyone who googled "ActiveBatch" would see a web page where the top results were links to Systems' own website and various articles about the product. But in the "Sponsored Sites" section of the page, users would see the following ad:

Job Scheduler

Windows Job Scheduling + Much More. Easy to Deploy, Scalable. D/L Trial **www.NetworkAutomation.com**

Sometimes, they would also see an equivalent ad for Systems' software—the real ActiveBatch.

Systems alleged that this use of ActiveBatch was a violation of its trademark on the word. The trial court issued an injunction prohibiting Network's purchase of the Google keyword. Network appealed.

You Be the Judge: *Has Network violated Systems's trademark by purchasing it as a Google keyword?*

Argument for Systems: Network and Systems are direct competitors. Their two products—AutoMate and ActiveBatch—perform the same functions and are both advertised on the Internet. Network is deliberately confusing customers about whose product ActiveBatch really is.

When consumers use the Internet, they tend not to read carefully—they just click away. Few customers analyze the web address of an ad to make sure they are going to the right website. Indeed, customers may not even be aware of who owns ActiveBatch. The Network ad certainly does not reveal that Systems owns this software. Customers could easily assume that whatever web address comes up belongs to the rightful owner.

When customers search for a generic term, they know that they will encounter links from a variety of sources, but when they look for a trade name, their expectation is that they will only be linked to that specific product. For this reason, the use of another company's trade name can create tremendous confusion.

Network has bought the right to use Systems's trademark as a ruse to fool potential customers. This subterfuge is exactly the sort of behavior that trademark laws are designed to prevent.

Argument for Network: Today, most consumers are sophisticated about the Internet. They skip from site to site, ready to hit the Back button whenever they are not satisfied with a site's contents. They fully expect to find some sites that are not what they imagine based on a glance at the domain name or search engine summary. Consumers do not form any firm expectations about the sponsorship of a website until they have seen the landing page—if then.

Even if Systems's arguments were true for consumer purchases, the typical customer for this software is a sophisticated businessperson buying an expensive product. These purchasers are likely to be very careful and will not be confused by Google ads. Also, they will probably understand the mechanics of Internet search engines and the nature of sponsored links.

In the end, Network's intent was not to confuse consumers but rather to allow them to compare its product to ActiveBatch. That goal is a completely appropriate use of a trademark.

Federal Trademark Dilution Act of 1995

Before Congress passed the Federal Trademark Dilution Act of 1995 (FTDA), a trademark owner could win an infringement lawsuit only by proving that consumers would be deceived about who had really made the product. **This statute prevents others from using a trademark in a way that (1) dilutes its value, even though consumers are not confused about the origin of the product; or (2) tarnishes it by association with unwholesome goods or services.** For example, Barbie's Playhouse was a website with a font and colors similar to those used by Mattel for its copyrighted Barbie doll. Also, the doll at the bottom of the website looked like a Barbie doll. The court found that Barbie's Playhouse had violated the FTDA.[23]

Domain Names

Over 130 million Internet addresses, known as *domain names*, are currently active, so it is often difficult to find a distinctive name for a new business. Domain names can be immensely valuable as they are an important component of doing business. Suppose you want to buy a new pair of jeans. Without thinking twice, you type in **http://www.jcrew.com** and there you are, ready to order. What if that address took you to a different site altogether, say, the personal site of one Jackie Crew? The store might lose out on a sale. Companies not only want to own their own domain name, they want to prevent complaint sites such as **http://www.untied.com** (about United Airlines), **http://www.ihatestarbucks.com**, or the always popular variation on the "sucks" theme, such as **http://macdonaldssucks.com**. Generic domain names can be valuable, too. Shopping.com paid $750,000 to acquire its domain name from the previous (lucky) owner.

Cybersquatting

Who has the right to a domain name? In the beginning, the National Science Foundation, which maintained the Internet, granted Network Solutions, Inc. (NSI), a private company, the right to allocate domain names. NSI charged no fee for domain names and the rule was "first come, first served." Then so-called cybersquatters began to register domain names, not to use, but to sell to others. Someone, for example, tried to sell the name "Bill Gates" for $1 million.

In response to complaints, NSI began suspending any domain name that was challenged by the holder of a registered trademark. For instance, NSI would not allow Princeton Review to keep kaplan.com, which Princeton had acquired simply to inconvenience its arch rival in the test preparation business. Congress then passed the **Anticybersquatting Consumer Protection Act (ACPA), which permits both trademark owners and famous people to sue anyone who registers their name as a domain name in "bad faith."** The rightful owner of a trademark is entitled to damages of up to $100,000. Verizon was awarded damages of $33.15 million against OnlineNIC Inc., which had registered 663 domain names that were confusingly similar to Verizon trademarks.

ICANN

As both the value and the number of domain names soared, the U.S. government transferred management of the Internet, including the allocation of names, to a private, nonprofit, international organization, the Internet Corporation for Assigned Names and Numbers (ICANN). Disputes over domain names can be decided by arbitration under ICANN's Uniform Domain Name Dispute Resolution Policy (UDRP) rather than by litigation under the ACPA. For example, Jay Leno used the ICANN process to win a

---

[23]*Mattel, Inc. v. Jcom, Inc.*, 1998 U.S. Dist. LEXIS 16195.

cybersquatting case against someone who was using thejaylenoshow.com to attract viewers to his own real estate website.

To bring a UDRP case, the complainant (i.e., the plaintiff) must allege that:

- The domain name creates confusion because it is similar to a registered trademark.

- The respondent (i.e., the defendant) has no legitimate reason to use the domain name.

- The respondent registered the domain name in bad faith. If the respondent is a competitor of the complainant and has acquired the domain name to disrupt the complainant's business (à la Princeton Review), that is evidence of bad faith. So is an attempt by the respondent to sell the name to the complainant.

If the complainant wins, it is entitled either to take over the domain name or to cancel it. For example, in a dispute over wal-martsucks.com, the WIPO arbitrator ordered that the name be transferred to Walmart. The respondent had demonstrated his bad faith by attempting to sell the name for $530,000. In a similar case, however, the WIPO arbitrator found for a respondent who had registered Wallmartcanadasucks.com. In this case, the respondent had not tried to sell the name and was using the website to criticize Walmart. As the arbitrator stated in his opinion: "Posting defamatory material on a website would not justify revocation of a domain name. The Policy should not be used to shut down robust debate and criticism." Either party has the option before or after an ICANN arbitration to litigate the issue in court.

At this writing, the courts have also held that criticism sites do not violate the ACPA so long as they do not have a bad faith intent to make a profit. The sites do not violate trademark law unless they create consumer confusion.[24]

Theft of Domain Name

In this crowded world, few people are the first to do anything. David Goncalves achieved this distinction in an unfortunate way—he became the first person in the United States to be convicted of stealing a domain name. After hacking into the files of a domain name registrar, he transferred to himself ownership of P2P.com. He then sold this name for $111,211 to professional basketball player Mark Madsen, who was running a business that bought and sold domain names. P2P could be a valuable name for someone who wanted to operate a peer-to-peer network. Goncalves was convicted under a state fraud statute as well as the Computer Fraud and Abuse Act (which we discussed in Chapter 23, on cyberlaw).

Trademarking a Domain Name

Our discussion thus far has been about registering a trademark as a domain name. Sometimes businesses want to do the opposite—trademark a domain name. The PTO will issue such a trademark only for services offered via the Internet. Thus, it trademarked "eBay" for "on-line trading services in which seller posts items to be auctioned and bidding is done electronically." The PTO will not trademark a domain name that is merely an address and does not identify the service provided.

International Trademark Treaties

Under the **Paris Convention**, if someone registers a trademark in one country, then he has a grace period of six months, during which he can file in any other country using the same original filing date. Under the **Madrid Agreement**, any trademark registered with the international registry is valid in all signatory countries. (The United States is a signatory.) The **Trademark Law Treaty** simplifies and harmonizes the process of applying

---

[24]See, for example, *Career Agents Network, Inc. v. careeragentsnetwork.biz*, 2010 U.S. Dist. LEXIS 17263 (E.D.MI, 2010).

for trademarks around the world. Now, a U.S. firm seeking international trademark protection need only file one application, in English, with the PTO, which sends the application to the WIPO, which transmits it to each country in which the applicant would like trademark protection.

EXAM Strategy

Question: Jerry Falwell was a nationally known Baptist minister. You can read about him on falwell.com. You can also read about him at fallwell.com—a site critical of his views on homosexuality. This site has a disclaimer indicating that it is not affiliated with Reverend Falwell. The minister sued fallwell.com, alleging a violation of trademark law and the anti-cybersquatting statute. Was there a violation?

Strategy: To win a trademark claim, the reverend had to show that there was some confusion between the two sites. To win the cybersquatting claim, he had to show bad faith on the part of fallwell.com.

Result: The reverend lost on both counts. The court ruled that there was no confusion— fallwell.com had a clear disclaimer. Also, there was no indication of bad faith. The court was reluctant to censor political commentary.

TRADE SECRETS

Trade secret
A formula, device, process, method, or compilation of information that, when used in business, gives the owner an advantage over competitors.

What do the formulas for Coke and motor oil have in common with computer circuitry, a machine for making adhesive tape, and a procedure for applying hair dye? They are all trade secrets. **A trade secret is a formula, device, process, method, or compilation of information that, when used in business, gives the owner an advantage over competitors who do not know it**. In determining if information is a trade secret, courts consider:

- How difficult (and expensive) was the information to obtain? Was it readily available from other sources?

- Does the information create an important competitive advantage?

- Did the company make a reasonable effort to protect it?

It has been estimated that the theft of trade secrets costs U.S. businesses $100 billion a year. In response, most states have now adopted the **Uniform Trade Secrets Act (UTSA)**. Anyone who misappropriates a trade secret is liable to the owner for (1) actual damages, (2) unjust enrichment, or (3) a reasonable royalty. If the misappropriation was willful or malicious, the court may award attorney's fees and double damages. A jury awarded Avery Dennison Corp. $40 million in damages from a competitor that had misappropriated secret information about the adhesives used in self-stick stamps.

Although a company can patent some types of trade secrets, it may be reluctant to do so because patent registration requires that the formula be disclosed publicly. In addition, patent protection expires after 20 years. Some types of trade secrets cannot be patented— such as customer lists, business plans, and marketing strategies.

The following case deals with a typical issue: how much information can employees take with them when they start their own, competing business?

POLLACK V. SKINSMART DERMATOLOGY AND AESTHETIC CENTER P.C.

2004 Pa. Dist. & Cnty. Dec. Lexis 214
Common Pleas Court of Philadelphia County, Pennsylvania, 2004

Facts: Dr. Andrew Pollack owned the Philadelphia Institute of Dermatology (PID), a dermatology practice. Drs. Toby Shawe and Samy Badawy worked for PID as independent contractors, receiving a certain percentage of the revenues from each patient they treated. Natalie Wilson was Dr. Pollack's medical assistant.

Pollack tentatively agreed to sell the practice to Shawe and Badawy. But instead of buying his practice, the two doctors decided to start their own, which they called Skinsmart. They executed a lease for the Skinsmart office space, offered Wilson a job, and instructed PID staff members to make copies of their appointment books and printouts of the patient list. Then they abruptly resigned from PID. Wilson called PID patients to reschedule procedures at Skinsmart. The two doctors also called patients and sent out a mailing to patients and referring physicians to tell them about Skinsmart.

Pollack filed suit, alleging that the two doctors had misappropriated trade secrets.

Issue: *Did Shawe and Badawy misappropriate trade secrets from PID?*

Excerpts from Judge Cohen's Decision: The right of a business person to be protected against unfair competition stemming from the usurpation of his or her trade secrets must be balanced against the right of an individual to the unhampered pursuit of the occupations and livelihoods for which he or she is best suited. For this reason, to qualify for protection, the information must be the particular secrets of the complaining employer, not general secrets of the trade in which he is engaged.

Against this backdrop, it is clear the patient list is a trade secret, worthy of protection. As conceded by defendants, the confidentiality of patient information ensures that it remain unknown to those outside the practice and makes the patient list valuable. Through the substantial efforts of plaintiff, the patient list was compiled over numerous years, and contained 20,000 names with related information. PID spent money for computers, software, and employees to keep and maintain the patient list. Within the offices of PID, the information was not universally known or accessible. Not every staff member, including the practicing physicians, could pull the records. Wilson did not have access to them and the doctors relied on other PID employees to access the patient list. These same factors demonstrate that plaintiff sought to protect the secrecy of the information.

The plaintiff must demonstrate that the trade secret has value and importance to him and his business. As noted above, defendants acknowledge the value of the patient list to PID's practice. In addition, plaintiff relied upon the patient list as the core component of his practice.

To have the rights to the use of the trade secret, the plaintiff needs to show he either discovered or owned the trade secret. Plaintiff compiled the patient list over numerous years. The patient list was maintained on PID's computers by PID's employees. Plaintiff's tax returns show that PID was owned solely by plaintiff. These facts establish plaintiff's ownership of the patient list.

Summary judgment is granted on the issue of liability against defendants Shawe, Badawy, and Wilson.

Only civil penalties are available under the Uniform Trade Secrets Act. To safeguard national security and maintain the nation's industrial and economic edge, Congress passed the **Economic Espionage Act of 1996, which makes it a *criminal* offense to steal (or attempt to steal) trade secrets for the benefit of someone other than the owner, including for the benefit of any foreign government.** Xiaodong Sheldon Meng was convicted of violating this statute after he was caught stealing computer code used in military weapons. He had committed the theft on behalf of the government of China. Meng was sentenced to 24 months in prison. Timothy Kissane received the same sentence for stealing computer source code from an employer. He planned to sell it to the company's competitors.

Chapter Conclusion

Intellectual property takes many different forms. It can be an Internet domain name, a software program, a cartoon character, a formula for motor oil, or a process for making drugs. Because of its great variety, intellectual property can be difficult to protect. Yet, for many individuals and companies, intellectual property is the most valuable asset they will ever own. As its economic value increases, so does the need to understand the rules of intellectual property law.

EXAM REVIEW

	Patent	Copyright	Trademark	Trade Secrets
Protects:	Mechanical, electrical, chemical inventions; processes; machines; composition of matter; designs; plants	The tangible expression of an idea, but not the idea itself	Words and symbols that a business uses to identify its products or services	A formula, device, process, method, or compilation of information that, when used in business, gives the owner an advantage over competitors who do not know it
Requirements for Legal Protection:	Application approved by PTO	An item is automatically copyrighted once it is in tangible form	Use is the only requirement; registration is not necessary but does offer some benefits	Must be kept confidential
Duration:	20 years after the application is filed (14 years from date of issuance for a design patent)	70 years after the death of the work's only or last living author or, for a corporation, 95 years from publication or 120 years from creation	Valid for 10 years but the owner can renew for an unlimited number of terms as long as the mark is still being used	As long as it is kept confidential

MULTIPLE-CHOICE QUESTIONS

1. Thomas's English muffins wanted to protect the method by which it makes muffins with air pockets—what it calls "nooks and crannies." What would be the best way to achieve this goal?

   (a) Patent

   (b) Copyright

   (c) Trademark

   (d) Trade secret

   (e) This method cannot be protected.

2. VitaminWater has become such a success that other companies are also now selling similar (but not identical) flavored colored water. Some competitors bottle their drinks in a similar bell-shaped bottle with a two-toned label that has a horizontal color band. What is the best infringement claim for VitaminWater to make against these competitors?

   (a) Patent

   (b) Copyright

   (c) Trademark

   (d) Trade secret

   (e) There is no good claim.

3. Faber-Castell began manufacturing pencils in 1761. Although pencils and erasers had both existed for some time, the company did not begin putting erasers on the ends of its pencils until the 1870s. The company was sued by an inventor who had previously patented this idea. The case went to the Supreme Court. Who won the case?

   (a) The patent holder, because no one had ever put an eraser on a pencil before.

   (b) The patent holder, because the PTO had approved his patent.

   (c) Faber-Castell, because the pencil with an eraser was not novel.

   (d) Faber-Castell, because the pencil with an eraser was not useful.

4. If you buy a DVD, you have the legal right to:

   (a) watch it as many times as you want and then give it away.

   (b) copy it to your computer and then give it to a friend.

   (c) copy it to your computer and sell it on eBay.

   (d) all of the above.

   (e) a and b only.

5. A couple thought of a clever name for an automobile. They wanted to protect this name so that they could ultimately sell it to a car manufacturer. What would be the best method to obtain this goal?

   (a) Patent

   (b) Copyright

   (c) Trademark

   (d) Trade secret

   (e) This name cannot be protected.

ESSAY QUESTIONS

1. In the documentary movie *Expelled: No Intelligence Allowed*, there was a 15-second clip of "Imagine," a song by John Lennon. The purpose of the scene was to criticize the song's message. His wife and sons, who held the copyright, sued to block this use of the song. Under what theory did the movie makers argue that they had the right to use this music? Did they win?

2. **ETHICS** After Edward Miller left his job as a salesperson at the New England Insurance Agency, Inc., he took some of his New England customers to his new employer. At New England, the customer lists had been kept in file cabinets. Although the company did not restrict access to these files, it claimed there was a "You do not peruse my files and I do not peruse yours" understanding. The lists were not marked "confidential" or "not to be disclosed." Did Miller steal New England's trade secrets? Whether or not he violated the law, was it ethical for him to use this information at his new job? What is your Life Principle?

3. Rebecca Reyher wrote (and copyrighted) a children's book entitled *My Mother Is the Most Beautiful Woman in the World*. The story was based on a Russian folk tale told to her by her own mother. Years later, the children's TV show *Sesame Street* televised a skit entitled "The Most Beautiful Woman in the World." The *Sesame Street* version took place in a different locale and had fewer frills, but the sequence of events in both stories was identical. Has *Sesame Street* infringed Reyher's copyright?

4. Roger Schlafly applied for a patent for two prime numbers. (A prime number cannot be evenly divided by any number other than itself and 1. Examples of primes are 2, 3, 5, 7, 11, and 13.) Schlafly's numbers are a bit longer—one is 150 digits, the other is 300. His numbers, when used together, can help perform the type of mathematical operation necessary for exchanging coded messages by computer. Should the PTO issue this patent?

5. Frank B. McMahon wrote one of the first psychology textbooks to feature a light, easily readable style. He also included many colloquialisms and examples that appealed to a youthful student market. Charles G. Morris wrote a psychology textbook that copied McMahon's style. Has Morris infringed McMahon's copyright?

6. Victoria's Secret, a well-known lingerie company, found out that a man named Victor Moseley was running a small store in Kentucky named "Victor's Little Secret." Moseley's shop sold clocks, patches, temporary tattoos, stuffed animals, coffee mugs, leather biker wallets, Zippo lighters, diet formula, jigsaw puzzles, handcuffs, hosiery, greeting cards, incense burners, car air fresheners, sunglasses, jewelry, candles, and adult novelties. Women's lingerie represented about 5 percent of its sales. Does Victoria's Secret have a valid intellectual property claim?

EXAM Strategy

7. **Question:** DatagraphiX manufactured and sold computer graphics equipment that allowed users to transfer large volumes of information directly from computers to microfilm. Customers were required to keep maintenance documentation on site for the DatagraphiX service personnel. The service manual carried this legend: "No other use, direct or indirect, of this document or of any information derived there from is authorized. No copies of any part of this document shall be

made without written approval by DatagraphiX." In addition, on every page of the maintenance manual, the company placed warnings that the information was proprietary and not to be duplicated. Frederick J. Lennen left DatagraphiX to start his own company that serviced DatagraphiX equipment. Can DatagraphiX prevent Lennen from using its manuals?

Strategy: With trade secrets, the key is that the owner has made a reasonable effort to protect them. (See the "Result" at the end of this section.)

EXAM Strategy

8. Question: "Hey, Paula," a pop hit that spent months on the music charts, was back on the radio 30 years later, but in a form the song's author never intended. Talk-show host Rush Limbaugh played a version with the same music as the original but with lyrics that made fun of President Bill Clinton's alleged sexual misconduct with Paula Jones. Has Limbaugh violated the author's copyright?

Strategy: Although this example may look like a copyright violation, it falls under an exception. (See the "Result" at the end of this section.)

EXAM Strategy

9. Question: Research Corp. applied for a patent for a so-called halftoning technique that uses a mathematical formula to enable monitors and printers with limited color options to simulate a wider range of colors. Is this technique patentable?

Strategy: Are these inventors attempting to patent a mathematical algorithm or formula? (See the "Result" at the end of this section.)

7. Result: The court held that these manuals were DatagraphiX's trade secrets.

8. Result: Parody (especially about politics!) is a fair use of copyrighted material so long as use of the original is not excessive.

9. Result: The trial court ruled that this patent application was invalid because it was too abstract. But the appellate court overruled, holding that, although the patent used mathematical algorithms, the inventors were patenting the process not the algorithms. It upheld the patent.[25]

---

[25]*Research Corporation Technologies, Inc., v. Microsoft Corporation*, 627 F.3d 859; 2010 U.S. App. LEXIS 24984; 97 U.S.P.Q.2D (BNA) 1274, (Fed. Cir., 2010).

DISCUSSION QUESTIONS

1. **ETHICS** Virtually any TV show, movie, or song can be downloaded for free on the Internet. Most of this material is copyrighted and was very expensive to produce. Most of it is also available for a fee through such legitimate sites as iTunes. What is your ethical obligation? Should you pay $1.99 to download an episode of *American Idol* from iTunes or take it for free from an illegal site? What is your Life Principle?

2. For much of history, the copyright term was limited to 28 years. Now it is as long as 120 years. What is a fair copyright term? Some commentators argue that because so much intellectual property is stolen, owners need longer protection. Do you agree with this argument?

3. Do you agree with the court that the band Furious George violated the copyright of Curious George?

4. Should Amazon be able to patent the One-Click method of ordering? What about Facebook's patent on a process that "dynamically provides a news feed about a user of a social network"? Were these inventions really novel and nonobvious? What should the standard be for business method patents?

5. Fredrik Colting wrote a book entitled *60 Years Later: Coming Through the Rye*, a riff on J. D. Salinger's famous *Catcher in the Rye*. Colting's book imagined how Salinger's protagonist, Holden Caulfield, would view life as a 76-year old. Alice Randall wrote a novel entitled *The Wind Done Gone*, which retells the Civil War novel *Gone with the Wind* from the perspective of Scarlett O'Hara's (imagined) black half-sister. Both Colting and Randall were sued and both alleged fair use. Should they win?

6. The Susan G. Komen breast cancer charity trademarked the term "for the cure." It has brought suit against other charities that use the term, as in "run for the cure" or "kites for the cure." It also sues charities that use the same shade of pink that it has long used on its ribbons. Should Komen be able to trademark "for the cure" and the color pink?

7. Should a wildflower garden be eligible for intellectual property protection?

CHAPTER 25

PROPERTY

© picsbyst/Shutterstock.com

"My only child is a no-good thief," Riley murmurs sadly to his visitors. "He has always treated me contemptuously. Now he's been sentenced to five years for stealing from a children's charity. He is my only heir, but why should I leave him everything?"

Riley continues talking to his three guests: a bishop, a rabbi, and Earnest, a Boy Scout leader. "I have $500,000 in stocks and bonds in my bank deposit box. Tomorrow morning, I'm going to go down to the bank, take out all the papers, and hand them over to the Boy Scouts so that other kids won't turn out so bad." Everyone applauds his generosity, and they photograph Riley and Earnest shaking hands. But the following morning, on his way to the bank, Riley is struck by an ambulance and killed. A dispute arises over the money. The three witnesses assure the court that Riley was on his way to give the money to the Boy Scouts. From prison, the ne'er-do-well son demands the money as Riley's sole heir. Who wins? Property law holds the answer.

> My only child is a no-good thief. He is my only heir, but why should I leave him everything?

In this chapter, we will examine personal property. In the section on gifts, we learn that Riley's no-good son gets the money. Riley intended to give the stocks and bonds to the Boy Scouts the following day, but he never completed a valid gift because he failed to *deliver* the papers.

But first, we will take a look at real property and landlord-tenant law.

NATURE OF REAL PROPERTY

Property falls into three categories: real, personal, and intellectual. Real property consists of the following:

- **Land.** Land is the most common and important form of real property. In England, land was historically the greatest source of wealth and social status, far more important than industrial or commercial enterprises. As a result, the law of real property has been of paramount importance for nearly 1,000 years, developing very gradually to reflect changing conditions. Some real property terms sound medieval for the simple reason that they *are* medieval. By contrast, the common law of torts and contracts is comparatively new.

  Real property usually also includes anything underground (subsurface right), and some amount of airspace above land (air rights).

- **Buildings.** Buildings are real property. Houses, office buildings, apartment complexes, and factories all fall in this category.

- **Plant life.** Plant life growing on land is real property whether the plants are naturally occurring, such as trees, or cultivated crops. When a landowner sells his property, plant life is automatically included in the sale unless the parties agree otherwise. A landowner may also sell the plant life separately if he wishes. A sale of the plant life alone, without the land, is a sale of goods. (Goods, as you may recall, are movable things.) If Douglas agrees to sell all of the fir trees on his property, this sale of goods will be governed by the Uniform Commercial Code (UCC), regardless of whether Douglas or the buyer is obligated to cut the trees.[1]

- **Fixtures.** Fixtures are goods that have become attached to real property. A house (which is real property) contains many fixtures. The furnace and heating ducts were goods when they were manufactured and when they were sold to the builder because they were movable. But when the builder attached them to the house, the items became fixtures. By contrast, neither the refrigerator nor the grand piano is a fixture.

When an owner sells real property, the buyer normally obtains the fixtures unless the parties specify otherwise. Sometimes it is difficult to determine whether something is a fixture. The general rule is this: **an object is a fixture if a reasonable person would consider the item to be a permanent part of the property.**

For many, beef is a dietary fixture. But is the cattle scale in the following case a fixture?

---

[1] UCC §2-107(2).

FREEMAN V. BARRS

237 S.W.3d 285
Missouri Court of Appeals, 2007

Facts: Mary Ann Barrs paid $3.5 million to Francis Freeman for 4,000 acres of ranch land, including a covered "pole-barn," which had open sides, a large cattle scale, and an enclosed veterinarian's office. The parties used a form contract, which stated that all fixtures were included with the sale. The document offered space for the parties to specify items that were included or excluded with the sale, but neither party listed the cattle scale as either in or out of the deal. After the agreement went through, Barrs and Freeman got into a beef over who owned the scale. The trial judge grilled numerous witnesses and ultimately weighed in on the side of Barrs, declaring the scale a fixture that belonged to the real estate. Broiling, Freeman appealed.

Issue: *Was the cattle scale a fixture?*

Excerpts from Judge Parrish's Decision: Steve McFadden, the president of Sooner Scale, Inc., the maker of the scale, testified that he had designed the present scale. The scale was designed to be portable, and 70% of the scales he sold were installed in the present manner. He further stated that he could move the present scales by cutting away a welded metal fence and lifting the scale with heavy machinery, [a] process he often performs. McFadden further stated that the removal of the fence would take approximately one hour with use of a cutting torch, and thereafter the scale could be moved within fifteen minutes.

Characterization of an item as a fixture depends upon the finding of three elements: annexation to the realty, adaptation to the use to which the realty is devoted, and intent of the annexor that the object become a permanent accession to the freehold. The latter two elements, adaptation and intent, are more important in determining whether a chattel became a fixture than the method by which the chattel is affixed to a freehold.

Annexation. The scale was purchased by plaintiff to "start selling cattle from the ranch and not sending them to

the sale barn to keep the price up a little." The scale weighs approximately 6,500 pounds. A fence and gates within the structure had to be cut off in order to install the scale. A concrete slab was poured in the structure for placement of the scale. The scale was placed on pipes on the ground and pushed with a tractor across the pipes onto the slab. Concrete ramps were installed on two sides of the scale and fencing was constructed to direct cattle onto the scale. The metal posts for the fence were set in the concrete. The scale has remained in place since its installation.

Adaptation. Ray Stone had been ranch manager for plaintiff. At the time of trial he had an agreement with defendant that permitted him to run cattle on the property. He "just kind of saw after the place" for her. He told the court that the scale was integral to a cattle-working facility. The scale was used to weigh cattle for sale and to determine required dosages of medicine administered to cattle.

Intent. The manufacturer sold peripheral items that permitted the scale to be moved. This included a trailer and an inverter. Plaintiff did not buy that equipment. Ray Stone told the court that the scale was purchased "to be stationary whether it was portable or not."

This court concludes that the scale was a fixture; that, therefore, the sale of the real estate on which it was situate included the sale of the scale. A 6,500-pound scale placed on a specially sized concrete pad and surrounded by metal pole fencing set in the concrete is annexed to the real estate on which the concrete pad is poured. The permanency of the installation is emphasized by the fact the facility is covered and has a veterinary office in which the printer for the scale may be operated. The scale was put in place to facilitate the cattle operation on the premises. It had been used for that purpose since its purchase. Its adaptation for that purpose enhanced the operation of the cattle ranch.

Affirmed.

ESTATES IN REAL PROPERTY

Use and ownership of real estate can take many different legal forms. A person may own property outright, having the unrestricted use of the land and an unlimited right to sell it. Such a person owns a **fee simple absolute**. However, someone may also own a lesser interest

Fee simple absolute
Full ownership privileges in a property.

in real property. The different rights that someone can hold in real property are known as **estates** or **interests.** Both terms simply indicate specified rights in property.

Concurrent Estates

Concurrent estate
Two or more people owning property at the same time.

When two or more people own real property at the same time, they have **concurrent estates**. The most common forms of concurrent estates are tenancy in common, joint tenancy, and tenancy by the entirety.

Tenancy in Common

Tenancy in common
Two or more people holding equal interest in a property, but with no right of survivorship.

The most common form of concurrent estate is **tenancy in common**. Suppose Patricia owns a house. Patricia agrees to sell her house to Quincy and Rebecca. When she **conveys** the deed (that is, transfers the deed) "to Quincy and Rebecca," those two now have a tenancy in common. This kind of estate can also be created in a will. If Patricia had died still owning the house, and left it in her will to "Sam and Tracy," then Sam and Tracy would have a tenancy in common. Tenancy in common is the "default setting" when multiple people acquire property. Co-owners are automatically considered tenants in common unless another type of interest (joint tenancy, tenancy by the entirety) is specified.

A tenancy in common might have 2 owners, or 22, or any number. The tenants in common do not own a particular section of the property; they own an equal interest in the entire property. Quincy and Rebecca each own a 50 percent interest in the entire house.

Any co-tenant may convey her interest in the property to another person. Thus, if Rebecca moves 1,000 miles away, she may sell her 50 percent interest in the house to Sidney. Further, when a co-tenant dies, her interest in the property passes to her heirs, along with all of her other assets.

Partition   Since any tenant in common has the power to convey her interest, some people may find themselves sharing ownership with others they do not know or, worse, dislike. What to do? Partition, or division of the property among the co-tenants. Any co-tenant is entitled to demand partition of the property. If the various co-tenants cannot agree on a fair division, a co-tenant may request a court to do it. **All co-tenants have an absolute right to partition.**

A court will normally attempt a **partition by kind,** meaning that it actually divides the land equally among the co-tenants. If three co-tenants own a 300-acre farm and the court can divide the land so that the three sections are of roughly equal value, it will perform a partition in kind, even if one or two of the co-tenants oppose partition. If partition by kind is impossible because there is no fair way to divide the property, the court will order the real estate sold and the proceeds divided equally.

Joint Tenancy

Joint tenancy
Two or more people holding equal interest in a property, with the right of survivorship.

Joint tenancy is similar to tenancy in common but is used less frequently. The parties, called joint tenants, again own a percentage of the entire property and also have the absolute right of partition. The primary difference is that a **joint tenancy** includes the right of survivorship. This means that when one joint tenant dies, his interest in the property passes to *the surviving joint tenants.* Recall that a tenant in common, by contrast, has the power to leave his interest in the real estate to his heirs. Because a joint tenant cannot leave the property to his heirs, courts do not favor this form of ownership. The law presumes that a concurrent estate is a tenancy in common; a court will interpret an estate as a joint tenancy only if the parties creating it clearly intended that result.

Joint tenancy has one other curious feature. Although joint tenants may not convey their interest by will, they may do so during their lifetime. If Frank and George own vacation property as joint tenants, Frank has the power to sell his interest to Harry. But as soon as he does so, the joint tenancy is **severed;** that is, broken. Harry and George are now tenants in common, and the right of survivorship is destroyed.

But when does a severance officially take place? The answer was of critical importance in the following case.

JACKSON V. ESTATE OF GREEN

771 N.W.2d 675
Supreme Court of Michigan, 2009

Facts: Green and Jackson owned land as joint tenants. Green filed a petition asking a court to partition the parcels, but he died while the partition was still pending.

The lower courts found that because the partition was not complete at the time of Green's death, the land reverted to Jackson.

Green's estate appealed.

Issue: *Does filing for the partition of a joint tenancy terminate survivorship rights?*

Excerpts from Justice Corrigan's Decision: We agree with the Court of Appeals that defendant's interest in the parcel of land automatically reverted to plaintiff when defendant died. Thus, defendant's estate has no interest in the property, and even if defendant's partition action survived his death under Michigan's survival statute, nothing remains to partition.

The principal characteristic of the joint tenancy is the right of survivorship. Upon the death of one joint tenant, the surviving tenant or tenants take the whole estate. An ordinary joint tenancy may be severed, and the right of survivorship thereby destroyed, by an act of the parties, conveyance by either party, or levy and sale on an execution against one of the parties.

A party can sever a joint tenancy by compelling a partition. Until an order of partition has been entered, however, a partition has not been compelled and, thus, the joint tenancy has not been severed. It is not the filing of the partition action which terminates the joint tenancy, but only the judgment in such action which has that effect.

This rule is based on two related concepts: First, the theory of survivorship—that at the moment of death, ownership vests exclusively in the surviving joint tenant or tenants—and second, the doctrine that severance of the joint tenancy does not occur until the partition suit reaches final judgment.

Accordingly, we would hold that the filing of the partition action did not sever the joint tenancy because an order effectuating a partition had not entered at the time of defendant's death. Therefore, regardless whether defendant's partition action survived his death under the survival statute, his interest in the parcel of land did not.

Affirmed.

EXAM Strategy

Question: Thomas, aged 80, has spent a lifetime accumulating unspoiled land in Oregon. He owns 16,000 acres, which he plans to leave to his five children. He is not so crazy about his grandchildren. Thomas cringes at the problems the grandchildren would cause if some of them inherited an interest in the land and became part-owners along with Thomas's own children. Should Thomas leave his land to his children as tenants in common or joint tenants?

Strategy: When a co-tenant dies, her interest in property passes to her heirs. When a joint tenant dies, his interest in the property passes to the surviving joint tenants.

Result: Thomas is better off leaving the land to his children as joint tenants. That way, when one of his children dies, that child's interest in the land will go to Thomas's surviving children, not to his grandchildren.

Exhibit 25.1 illustrates tenancy in common and joint tenancy.

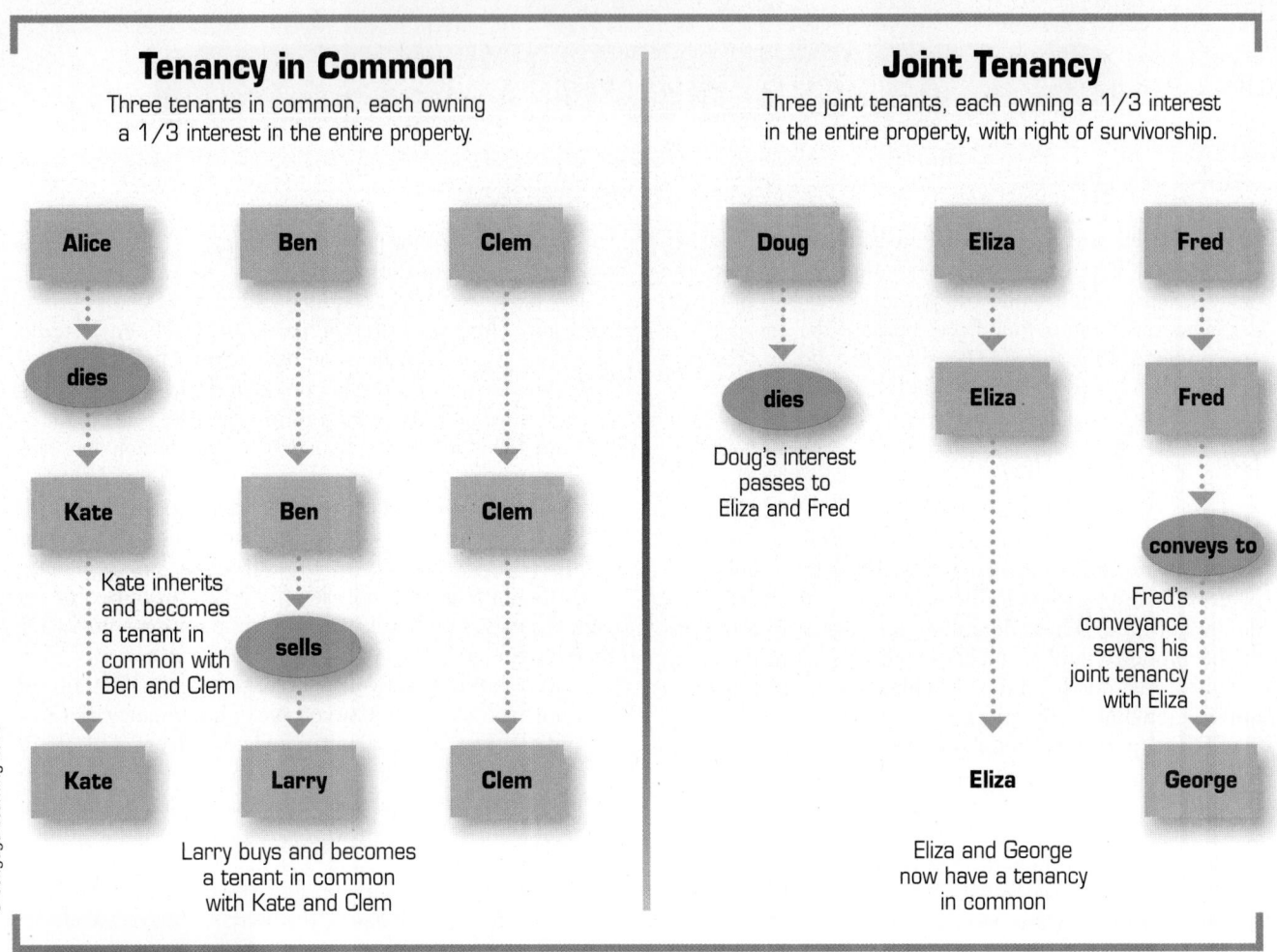

Tenancy in Common

Three tenants in common, each owning a 1/3 interest in the entire property.

Alice
↓
dies
↓
Kate

Kate inherits and becomes a tenant in common with Ben and Clem
↓
Kate

Ben
↓
Ben
↓
sells
↓
Larry

Larry buys and becomes a tenant in common with Kate and Clem

Clem
↓
Clem
↓
Clem

Joint Tenancy

Three joint tenants, each owning a 1/3 interest in the entire property, with right of survivorship.

Doug
↓
dies

Doug's interest passes to Eliza and Fred

Eliza
↓
Eliza
↓
Eliza

Fred
↓
Fred
↓
conveys to

Fred's conveyance severs his joint tenancy with Eliza
↓
George

Eliza and George now have a tenancy in common

EXHIBIT 25.1

Tenancy by the Entirety

This form of ownership exists in slightly over half of the states. **The husband and wife each own the entire property, and they both have a right of survivorship.** So when the husband dies, his one-half interest in the property automatically passes to his wife. Neither party has a right to convey his or her interest. If the parties wish to sell their interests, they must do so together. An advantage of this is that no creditor may seize the property based on a debt incurred by only one spouse. If a husband goes bankrupt, creditors may not take his house if he and his wife own it as tenants by the entirety. Divorce terminates a tenancy by the entirety and leaves the two parties as tenants in common.

NONPOSSESSORY INTERESTS

All of the estates and interests that we have examined thus far focused on one thing: possession of the land. Now we look at interests that *never* involve possession. These interests may be very valuable, even though the holder never lives on the land.

Easements

The Alabama Power Co. drove a flatbed truck over land owned by Thomas Burgess, damaging the property. The power company did this to reach its power lines and wooden transmission poles. Burgess had never given Alabama Power permission to enter his land, and he sued for the damage that the heavy trucks caused. He recovered—nothing. Alabama Power had an *easement* to use Burgess's land.

An **easement** gives one person the right to enter land belonging to another and make a limited use of it, without taking anything away. Burgess had bought his land from a man named Denton, who years earlier had sold an easement to Alabama Power. The easement gave the power company the right to construct several transmission poles on one section of Denton's land and to use reasonable means to reach the poles. Alabama Power owned that easement forever, and when Burgess bought the land, he took it subject to the easement. Alabama Power drove its trucks across a section of land where the power company had never gone before, and the easement did not explicitly give the company this right. But the court found that the company had no other way to reach its poles, and therefore, the easement allowed this use. Burgess is stuck with his uninvited guest as long as he owns the land.[2]

Easement
The right to enter land belonging to another and make limited use of it.

Profit

A **profit** gives one person the right to enter land belonging to another and take something away. You own 100 acres of vacation property, and suddenly a mining company informs you that the land contains valuable nickel deposits. You may choose to sell a profit to the mining company, allowing it to enter your land and take away the nickel. You receive cash up front, and the company earns money from the sale of the mineral. The rules about creating and transferring easements apply to profits as well.

Profit
The right to enter land belonging to another and take something from it.

License

A **license** gives the holder temporary permission to enter another's property. Unlike an easement or profit, a license is a *temporary* right. When you attend a basketball game by buying a ticket, the basketball team that sells you the ticket is the licensor and you are the licensee. You are entitled to enter the licensor's premises, namely the basketball arena, and to remain during the game, though the club can revoke the license if you behave unacceptably, and you must leave when the game is over.

License
The right to enter land belonging to another temporarily.

Mortgage

Generally, in order to buy a house, a prospective owner must borrow money. The bank or other lender will require security before it hands over its money, and the most common form of security for a real estate loan is a mortgage. A **mortgage** is a security interest in real property. The homeowner who borrows money is the **mortgagor** because she is *giving* the mortgage to the lender. The lender, in turn, is the **mortgagee**, the party acquiring a security interest. The mortgagee in most cases obtains a **lien** on the house, meaning the right to foreclose on the property if the mortgagor fails to pay back the money borrowed. A mortgagee forecloses by taking legal possession of the property, auctioning it to the highest bidder, and using the proceeds to pay off the loan.

Mortgage
A security interest in real property.

Mortgagor
An owner who gives a security interest in property in order to obtain a loan.

Mortgagee
The party acquiring a security interest in property.

---

[2]*Burgess v. Alabama Power Co.*, 658 So. 2d 435, 1995 Ala. LEXIS 119 (Ala. 1995).

LAND USE REGULATION

Nuisance Law

A **nuisance** is an unprivileged interference with a person's use and enjoyment of her property. Offensive noise, odors, or smoke often give rise to nuisance claims. Courts typically balance the utility of the act that is causing the problem against the harm done to neighboring property owners. If a suburban homeowner begins to raise pigs in her backyard, the neighbors may find the bouquet offensive; a court will probably issue an **abatement;** that is, an order requiring the homeowner to eliminate the nuisance.

Community members can use the old doctrine of nuisance for more serious problems than pigs. An apartment building in Berkeley, California, became widely known as a drug house, and the neighbors suffered. Here is how two of the neighbors described their lives:

> I have been confronted by the drug dealers, drug customers, and prostitutes that frequent and work around and from 1615–1617 Russell Street. Weekly I have lost many hours of sleep from the cars that burn rubber after each drug buy in the middle of the night.
>
> Because of this illegal activity, my child is unable to use our front yard, and I even have to check the back yard since it has been intruded upon from time to time by people running from the police. He is learning to count by how many gunshots he hears and can't understand why he can't even enjoy our rose garden.

These were but two of the affidavits written by neighbors of a 36-unit building owned by Albert Lew. Month after month neighbors complained to Lew that his tenants were destroying the neighborhood. But Lew refused to evict the drug dealers or take any serious steps to limit the crime. So the neighbors used the law of nuisance to restore their community.

Sixty-six neighbors of the drug house each filed a small claims case against Lew, claiming that he was permitting a nuisance to exist on his property. The neighbors won their small claims cases, but Lew appealed, as he had a right to, for a new trial in Superior Court. A sergeant testified that he had been to the building over 250 times during two years. Residents testified about how frightening life had become. The Superior Court awarded damages of $218,325 to the neighbors, and the court of appeals affirmed the award, holding that neighbors injured by a nuisance may seek an abatement and damages. As Lew discovered, the law of nuisance can be a powerful weapon for creating a better neighborhood.[3]

Zoning

Zoning statutes are state laws that permit local communities to regulate building and land use. The local communities, whether cities, towns, or counties, then pass zoning ordinances that control many aspects of land development. For example, a town's zoning ordinance may divide the community into an industrial zone where factories may be built, a commercial zone in which stores of a certain size are allowed, and several residential zones in which only houses may be constructed. Within the residential zones, there may be further divisions, for example, permitting two-family houses in certain areas and requiring larger lots in others.

An owner prohibited by an ordinance from erecting a certain kind of building, or adding on to his present building, may seek a **variance** from the zoning board, meaning an exception granted for special reasons unique to the property. Whether a board will grant a variance generally depends upon the type of the proposed building, the nature of the community, the reason the owner claims he is harmed by the ordinance, and the reaction of neighbors.

---

[3]*Lew v. Superior Court,* 20 Cal. App. 4th 866, 1993 Cal. App. LEXIS 1198 (Cal. Ct. App. 1993).

Ethics Many people abhor "adult" businesses, such as strip clubs and pornography shops. Urban experts agree that a large number of these concerns in a neighborhood often causes crime to increase and property values to drop. Nonetheless, many people patronize such businesses, which can earn a good profit. Should a city have the right to restrict adult businesses? New York City officials determined that the number of sex shops had grown steadily for two decades and that their presence harmed various neighborhoods. With the support of community groups, the city passed a zoning ordinance that prohibited adult businesses from all residential neighborhoods, from some commercial districts, *and* from being within 500 feet of schools, houses of worship, day-care centers, or other sex shops (to avoid clustering). Owners and patrons of these shops protested, claiming that the city was unfairly denying the public access to a form of entertainment that it obviously desired. Is the New York City zoning ordinance reasonable?

Eminent Domain

Eminent domain is the power of the government to take private property for public use. A government may need land to construct a highway, airport, university, or public housing. All levels of government—federal, state, and local—have this power. But the Fifth Amendment of the United States Constitution states: "… nor shall private property be taken for public use, without just compensation." The Supreme Court has held that this clause, the Takings Clause, applies not only to the federal government but also to state and local governments. So, although all levels of government have the power to take property, they must pay the owner a fair price.

A "fair price" generally means the reasonable market value of the land. Generally, if the property owner refuses the government's offer, the government will file suit seeking **condemnation** of the land; that is, a court order specifying what compensation is just and awarding title to the government.

A related issue concerns local governments requiring property owners to *dedicate* some of their land to public use in exchange for zoning permission to build or expand on their own property. For example, if a store owner wishes to expand his store, a town might grant zoning permission only if the owner dedicates a different part of his property for use as a public bike path. The Supreme Court has recently diminished the power of local governments to require such dedication.[4]

Eminent domain
The power of the government to take private property for public use.

LANDLORD-TENANT LAW

Apartments are certainly a type of real property, and many students are keenly interested in renters' rights. We now turn our attention to landlord-tenant law.

A freehold estate is the right to possess real property and use it in any lawful manner. What we think of as "owning" land is in fact a freehold estate. **When an owner of a freehold estate allows another person temporary, exclusive possession of the property, the parties have created a landlord-tenant relationship.** The freehold owner is the **landlord**, and the person allowed to possess the property is the **tenant**. The landlord has conveyed a **leasehold** interest to the tenant, meaning the right to temporary possession. Courts also use the word *tenancy* to describe the tenant's right to possession.

Landlord
The owner of a freehold estate who allows another person temporarily to live on his property.

Tenant
A person given temporary possession of the landlord's property.

---

[4]The Supreme Court's ruling came in *Dolan v. City of Tigard*, 512 U.S. 374, 114 S. Ct. 2309, 1994 U.S. LEXIS 4836 (1994).

A leasehold may be commercial or residential. In a commercial tenancy, the owner of a building may rent retail space to a merchant, offices to a business, or industrial space to a manufacturer. When someone rents an apartment or house, he has a residential leasehold.

Three Legal Areas Combined

Reversion
The right of an owner (or her heirs) to property upon the death of a life tenant.

Property law influences landlord-tenant cases because the landlord is conveying rights in real property to the tenant. She is also keeping a **reversionary interest** in the property, meaning the right to possess the property when the lease ends. Contract law plays a role because the basic agreement between the landlord and tenant is a contract. A **lease** is a contract that creates a landlord-tenant relationship. And negligence law increasingly determines the liability of landlord and tenant when there is an injury to a person or property. Many states have combined these three legal issues into landlord-tenant statutes.

Lease
An agreement in which an owner gives a tenant the right to use property.

Lease

The statute of frauds generally requires that a lease be in writing. Some states will enforce an oral lease if it is for a short term, such as one year or less, but even when an oral lease is permitted, it is wiser for the parties to put their agreement in writing because a written lease avoids many misunderstandings. At a minimum, a lease must state the names of the parties, the premises being leased, the duration of the agreement, and the rent. But a well-drafted lease generally includes many provisions, called *covenants* and *conditions*. A **covenant** is simply a promise by either the landlord or the tenant to do something or refrain from doing something. For example, most leases include a covenant concerning the tenant's payment of a security deposit and the landlord's return of the deposit, a covenant describing how the tenant may use the premises, and several covenants about who must maintain and repair the property. Generally, tenants may be fined but not evicted for violating lease covenants. A **condition** is similar to a covenant, but it allows for a landlord to evict a tenant if there is a violation. In many states, conditions in leases must be clearly labeled as "conditions" or "evictable offenses."

TYPES OF TENANCY

There are four types of tenancy: a tenancy for years, a periodic tenancy, a tenancy at will, and a tenancy at sufferance. The most important feature distinguishing one from the other is how each tenancy terminates. In some cases, a tenancy terminates automatically, while in others, one party must take certain steps to end the agreement.

Tenancy for Years

Tenancy for years
A lease for a stated, fixed period.

Any lease for a stated, fixed period is a **tenancy for years**. If a landlord rents a summer apartment for the months of June, July, and August of next year, that is a tenancy for years. A company that rents retail space in a mall beginning January 1, 2012, and ending December 31, 2015, also has a tenancy for years. A tenancy for years terminates automatically when the agreed period ends.

Periodic Tenancy

Periodic tenancy
A lease for a fixed period, automatically renewable unless terminated.

A **periodic tenancy** is created for a fixed period and then automatically continues for additional periods until either party notifies the other of termination. This is probably the most common variety of tenancy, and the parties may create one in either of two ways. Suppose a landlord agrees to rent you an apartment "from month to month, rent payable on the first." That is a periodic tenancy. The tenancy automatically renews itself every month unless either party gives adequate notice to the other that she wishes to terminate. A periodic tenancy could also be for one-year periods—in which case it automatically renews for an additional year if neither party terminates—or for any other period.

Tenancy at Will

A **tenancy at will** has no fixed duration and may be terminated by either party at any time. Tenancies at will are unusual tenancies.[5] Typically, the agreement is vague, with no specified rental period and with payment, perhaps, to be made in kind. The parties might agree, for example, that a tenant farmer could use a portion of his crop as rent. Since either party can end the agreement at any time, it provides no security for either landlord or tenant.

Tenancy at Sufferance

A **tenancy at sufferance** occurs when a tenant remains on the premises, against the wishes of the landlord, after the expiration of a true tenancy. Thus, a tenancy at sufferance is not a true tenancy because the tenant is staying without the landlord's agreement. The landlord has the option of seeking to evict the tenant or of forcing the tenant to pay a *use and occupancy fee* for as long as she stays.

LANDLORD'S DUTIES

Duty to Deliver Possession

The landlord's first important duty is to deliver possession of the premises at the beginning of the tenancy; that is, to make the rented space available to the tenant. In most cases, this presents no problems and the new tenant moves in. But what happens if the previous tenant has refused to leave when the new tenancy begins? In most states, the landlord is legally required to remove the previous tenant. In some states, it is up to the new tenant either to evict the existing occupant or begin charging him rent.

Quiet Enjoyment

All tenants are entitled to quiet enjoyment of the premises, meaning the right to use the property without the interference of the landlord. Most leases expressly state this covenant of quiet enjoyment. And if a lease includes no such covenant, the law implies the right of quiet enjoyment anyway, so all tenants are protected. If a landlord interferes with the tenant's quiet enjoyment, he has breached the lease, entitling the tenant to damages.

The most common interference with quiet enjoyment is an **eviction**, meaning some act that forces the tenant to abandon the premises. Of course, some evictions are legal, as when a tenant fails to pay the rent. But some evictions are illegal. There are two types of eviction: actual and constructive.

Actual Eviction

If a landlord prevents the tenant from possessing the premises, he has actually evicted her. Suppose a landlord decides that a group of students are "troublemakers." Without going through lawful eviction procedures in court, the landlord simply waits until the students are

---

Tenancy at will
A tenancy with no fixed duration, which may be terminated by either party at any time.

Tenancy at sufferance
A tenancy that exists without the permission of the landlord, after the expiration of a true tenancy.

Eviction
An act that forces a tenant to abandon the property.

---

[5]The courts of some states, annoyingly, use the term "tenancy at will" for what are, in reality, periodic tenancies. They do this to bewilder law students and even lawyers, a goal at which they are quite successful. This text uses tenancy at will in its more widely known sense, meaning a tenancy terminable at any time.

out of the apartment and changes all the locks. By denying the students access to the premises, the landlord has actually evicted them and has breached their right of quiet enjoyment. He is liable for all expenses they suffer, such as retrieving their possessions, the cost of alternate housing, and moving expenses. In some states, he may be liable for punitive damages for failing to go through proper eviction procedures.

Even a partial eviction is an interference with quiet enjoyment. Suppose Louise rents an apartment with a storage room. If the landlord places his own goods in the storage room, he has partially evicted Louise because a tenant is entitled to the *exclusive* possession of the premises. In all states, Louise would be allowed to deduct from her rent the value of the storage space, and in many states, she would not be obligated to pay any rent for the apartment so long as the landlord continued the partial eviction.

Constructive Eviction

If a landlord substantially interferes with the tenant's use and enjoyment of the premises, he has constructively evicted her. Courts construe certain behavior as the equivalent of an eviction. In these cases, the landlord has not actually prevented the tenant from *possessing* the premises but has instead interfered so greatly with her *use and enjoyment* that the law regards the landlord's actions as equivalent to an eviction. Suppose the heating system in an apartment house in Juneau, Alaska, fails during January. The landlord, an avid sled dog racer, tells the tenants he is too busy to fix the problem. If the tenants move out, the landlord has constructively evicted them and is liable for all expenses they suffer.

To claim a constructive eviction, the tenant must vacate the premises. The tenant must also prove that the interference was sufficiently serious and lasted long enough that she was forced to move out. A lack of hot water for two days is not fatal, but lack of any water for two weeks creates a constructive eviction.

Duty to Maintain Premises

Historically, the common law placed no burden on the landlord to repair and maintain the premises. This made sense because rental property had traditionally been farmland. Buildings, such as a house or barn, were far less important than the land itself, and no one expected the landlord to fix a leaking roof. Today, the vast majority of rental property is used for housing or business purposes. Space in a building is frequently all that a tenant is renting, and the condition of the building is of paramount importance. Most states have changed the common law rule and placed various obligations on the landlord to maintain the property.

In most states, a landlord has a duty to deliver the premises in a habitable condition and a continuing duty to maintain the habitable condition. This duty overlaps with the quiet enjoyment obligation, but it is not identical. The tenant's right to quiet enjoyment focuses primarily on the tenant's *ability to use* the rented property. The landlord's duty to maintain the property focuses on whether the property *meets a particular legal standard*. The required standard may be stated in the lease, created by a state statute, or implied by law.

Lease

The lease itself generally obligates the landlord to maintain the exterior of any buildings and the common areas. If a lease does not do so, state law may imply the obligation.

Building Codes

Many state and local governments have passed building codes, which mandate minimum standards for commercial and/or residential property. The codes are likely to be stricter for residential property and may demand such things as minimum room size, sufficient hot water, secure locks, proper working kitchens and bathrooms, absence of insects and rodents, and other basics of decent housing. Generally, all rental property must comply with the building code, whether the lease mentions the code or not.

Implied Warranty of Habitability

Students Maria Ivanow, Thomas Tecza, and Kenneth Gearin rented a house from Les and Martha Vanlandingham. The monthly rent was $900. But the roommates failed to pay any rent for the final five months of the tenancy. After they moved out, the Vanlandinghams sued. How much did the landlords recover? Nothing. The landlords had breached the implied warranty of habitability.

The implied warranty of habitability requires that a landlord meet all standards set by the local building code, or that the premises be fit for human habitation. Most states, though not all, *imply* this warranty of habitability, meaning that the landlord must meet this standard whether the lease includes it or not. In some states, the implied warranty means that the premises must at least satisfy the local building code. Other states require property that is "fit for human habitation," which means that a landlord might comply with the building code, yet still fail the implied warranty of habitability if the rental property is unfit to live in.

The Vanlandinghams breached the implied warranty. The students had complained repeatedly about a variety of problems. The washer and dryer, which were included in the lease, frequently failed. A severe roof leak caused water damage in one of the bedrooms. Defective pipes flooded the bathroom. The refrigerator frequently malfunctioned, and the roommates repaired it several times. The basement often flooded, and when it was dry, rats and opossums lived in it. The heat sometimes failed.

In warranty of habitability cases, a court normally considers the severity of the problems and their duration. If the defective conditions seriously interfere with the tenancy, the court declares the implied warranty breached and orders a **rent abatement;** that is, a reduction in the rent owed. The longer the defects continued and the greater their severity, the more the rent is abated. In the case of Maria Ivanow and friends, the court abated the rent 50 percent. The students had already paid more than the abated rent to the landlord, so they owed nothing for the last five months.[6]

Duty to Return Security Deposit

Most landlords require tenants to pay a security deposit, in case the tenant damages the premises. In many states, a landlord must either return the security deposit soon after the tenant has moved out or notify the tenant of the damage and the cost of the repairs. In addition, landlords are often obligated to credit tenants with interest earned on the deposit. In many states, a landlord who fails to return the deposit in a timely fashion can be forced to pay double or even triple damages to the tenant, a question raised in the following dispute.

MISHKIN V. YOUNG

107 P.3d 393, 2005 WL 452168
Supreme Court of Colorado, 2005

Facts: A Colorado statute required a landlord either to return a security deposit or provide an accounting of why money was being withheld. The landlord had to do this within one month of the tenant's surrender of the property, or up to 60 days if the lease permitted. If the landlord failed to refund the money, the tenant, after giving seven days'

notice, could sue for treble damages. The landlord could avoid the treble damages by refunding the deposit within those seven days.

Marc Mishkin leased an apartment from Dean Young, paying a security deposit of $1,625. The lease stated that the deposit would be returned no later than 45 days after

---

[6]*Vanlandingham v. Ivanow*, 246 Ill. App. 3d 348, 615 N.E.2d 1361, 1993 Ill. App. LEXIS 985 (Ill. Ct. App. 1993).

the tenant moved out. After Mishkin left, Young did not return the money. Forty-eight days after leaving, Mishkin sent a demand for the deposit, notifying Young that in seven days, he would sue for treble damages. Six days later, Young gave Mishkin a statement detailing $1,574.60 worth of property damage, along with a check for $50.40.

Mishkin sued. The trial court ruled that Young was entitled to withhold the money because of the damages. Mishkin appealed. The appellate court ruled that the Colorado statute required the landlord to return the full security deposit within the seven-day period. Young appealed.

Issue: *May a landlord avoid the treble damages by accounting for the security deposit within seven days of the tenant's notice to sue?*

Excerpts from Justice Kourlis's Decision: [Earlier] cases implicitly indicate that a landlord's failure to account for a security deposit as required by subsection (1) [of the statute] constitutes a forfeiture of all rights to withhold any portion of the deposit and subjects the landlord to treble damages. A landlord may avoid treble damages only by returning the entire security deposit during the seven days following a tenant's demand notice. An accounting during this seven-day period does not protect a landlord from treble damages because this period is beyond the statutory deadline of subsection (1) and the landlord has already forfeited all rights to retain the deposit. The purpose of the seven-day notice provision is to give landlords one last week to avoid treble damages by returning the security deposit. It does not give landlords a second chance to account for the deposit. The money actually belongs to the tenant; it was only security for the landlord, who has by unilateral action forfeited all right to retain any of it. Therefore, we now make explicit what has been implicit in our prior rulings: We hold that a landlord may not avoid treble damages by accounting for a security deposit during the seven-day period following a tenant's demand notice.

Contrary to the landlord's contention, our interpretation does not render the remaining provisions of the Act meaningless. Subsection (2) [which states that the landlord forfeits the entire deposit if he fails to return the money or account for it within the statutory period] performs a critical function by encouraging most landlords to expeditiously account for their tenants' security deposits. Yet the case may arise where a landlord finds forfeiture an insufficient inducement to account for the withholding of a tenant's security deposit. In such situations, the prospect of treble damages provided for by subsection (3) proves instrumental. Not only do treble damages act as a formidable deterrent to landlords who might otherwise wrongfully withhold a tenant's security deposit, but they also give tenants an enticing legal remedy where the alternative is to forgo a relatively small but often vital sum of money.

[Affirmed.]

Final Word on Security Deposits   The discussion and case both concerned residential leases, where security deposits are almost inevitable. Note that, in a commercial lease, the tenant may have less statutory protection but more bargaining power. A financially sound company might negotiate a lease with no security deposit or perhaps offer a letter of credit for security instead of cash. The interest saved over several years could be substantial.

TENANT'S DUTIES

Duty to Pay Rent

Rent
Compensation paid by a tenant to a landlord.

Rent is the compensation the tenant pays the landlord for use of the premises, and paying the rent is the tenant's foremost obligation. The lease normally specifies the amount of rent and when it must be paid. Typically, the landlord requires that rent be paid at the beginning of each rental period, whether that is monthly, annually, or otherwise.

Both parties must be certain they understand whether the rent includes utilities such as heat and hot water. Some states mandate that the landlord pay certain utilities, such as water. Many leases include an **escalator clause**, permitting the landlord to raise the rent during the course of the lease if his expenses increase for specified reasons. For example, a tax escalator clause allows the landlord to raise the rent if his real estate taxes go up. Any escalator clause should state the percentage of the increase that the landlord may pass on to the tenant.

Escalator clause
A clause in a lease allowing the landlord to raise the rent for specified reasons

Landlord's Remedies for Nonpayment of Rent

If the tenant fails to pay rent on time, the landlord has several remedies. She is entitled to apply the security deposit to the unpaid rent. She may also sue the tenant for nonpayment of rent, demanding the unpaid sums, cost of collection, and interest. Finally, the landlord may evict a tenant who has failed to pay rent.

State statutes prescribe the steps a landlord must take to evict a tenant for nonpayment. Typically, the landlord must serve a termination notice on the tenant and wait for a court hearing. At the hearing, the landlord must prove that the tenant has failed to pay rent on time. If the tenant has no excuse for the nonpayment, the court grants an order evicting him. The order authorizes a sheriff to remove the tenant's goods and place them in storage, at the tenant's expense. However, if the tenant was withholding rent because of unlivable conditions, the court may refuse to evict.

EXAM Strategy

Question: Leo rents an apartment from Donna for $900 per month, both parties signing a lease. After six months, Leo complains about defects, including bugs, inadequate heat, and window leaks. He asks Donna to fix the problems, but she responds that the heat is fine and that Leo caused the insects and leaks. Leo begins to send in only $700 for the monthly rent. Donna repeatedly phones Leo, asking for the remaining rent. When he refuses to pay, she waits until he leaves for the day, then has a moving company place his belongings in storage. She changes the locks, making it impossible for him to re-enter. Leo sues. What is the likely outcome?

Strategy: A landlord is entitled to begin proper eviction proceedings against a tenant who has not paid rent. However, the landlord must follow specified steps, including a termination notice and a court hearing. Review the consequences for actual eviction, described in the section "Quiet Enjoyment."

Result: Donna has ignored the legal procedures for evicting a tenant. Instead, she engaged in *actual eviction*, which is quick, and in the short term, effective. However, by breaking the law, Donna has ensured that Leo will win his lawsuit. He is entitled to possession of the apartment, as well as damages for rent he may have been forced to pay elsewhere, injury to his possessions, and the cost of retrieving them. He may receive punitive damages as well. Bad strategy, Donna.

Duty to Mitigate

Pickwick & Perkins, Ltd., was a store in the Burlington Square Mall in Burlington, Vermont. Pickwick had a five-year lease but abandoned the space almost two years early and ceased paying rent. The landlord waited approximately eight months before renting the space to a new tenant and then sued, seeking the unpaid rent. Pickwick defended on the grounds that Burlington had failed to **mitigate damages;** that is, to keep its losses to a minimum by promptly seeking another tenant. Burlington argued that it had no legal obligation to mitigate. Burlington's position accurately reflected the common law rule, which permitted the landlord to let the property lie vacant and allow the damages to add up. But the common law evolves over time, and this time, the Vermont Supreme Court changed the rule. The judges pointed out that, historically, a lease was a conveyance of an estate, and property law had never required mitigation. However, the court asserted, a lease is now regarded as both a contract and a conveyance. Under contract law, the nonbreaching party must make a reasonable effort to minimize losses, and that same rule applies, said the court, to a landlord. Burlington lost. The Vermont ruling is typical of current decisions, although some courts still do not require mitigation.[7]

Duty to Use Premises for Proper Purpose

A lease normally lists what a tenant may do in the premises and prohibits other activities. For example, a residential lease allows the tenant to use the property for normal living purposes, but not for any retail, commercial, or industrial purpose. A commercial lease might allow a tenant to operate a retail clothing store, but not a restaurant. A landlord may evict a tenant who violates the lease by using the premises for prohibited purposes.

A tenant may not use the premises for any illegal activity, such as gambling or selling drugs. The law itself implies this condition in every lease, so a tenant who engages in illegal acts on the leased property is subject to eviction, regardless of whether the lease mentions such conduct.

Duty Not to Damage Premises

A tenant is liable to the landlord for any significant damage he causes to the property. The tenant is not liable for normal wear and tear. If, however, he knocks a hole in a wall or damages the plumbing, the landlord may collect the cost of repairs, either by using the security deposit or by suing, if necessary. A landlord may also seek to evict a tenant for serious damage to the property.

A tenant is permitted to make reasonable changes in the leased property so that he can use it as intended. Someone leasing an apartment is permitted to hang pictures on the wall. But a tenant leasing commercial space should make certain that the lease specifies the alterations he can make and whether he is obligated to return the premises to their original condition at the end of the lease.

Duty Not to Disturb Other Tenants

Most leases, commercial and residential, include a covenant that the tenant will not disturb other tenants in the building. A landlord may evict a tenant who unreasonably disturbs others. The test is *reasonableness*. A landlord does not have the right to evict a residential tenant for giving one loud party but may evict a tenant who repeatedly plays loud music late at night and disturbs the quiet enjoyment of other tenants.

INJURIES

You invite a friend to dinner in your rented home, but after the meal, she slips and falls, seriously injuring her back. Are you liable? Is the landlord?

Tenant's Liability

A tenant is generally liable for injuries occurring within the premises she is leasing, whether that is an apartment, a store, or otherwise. If a tenant permits grease to accumulate on a kitchen floor and a guest slips and falls, the tenant is liable. If a merchant negligently installs display shelving that tips onto a customer, the merchant pays for the harm. Generally, a tenant is not liable for injuries occurring in common areas over which she has no control,

[7]*O'Brien v. Black*, 162 Vt. 448, 648 A.2d 1374, 1994 Vt. LEXIS 89 (1994).

such as exterior walkways. If a tenant's dinner guest falls because the building's common stairway has loose steps, the landlord is probably liable.

Landlord's Liability
Common Law Rules

Historically, the common law held a landlord responsible for injuries on the premises only in a limited number of circumstances, which we will describe. In reading these common law rules, be aware that many states have changed them, dramatically increasing the landlord's liability.

Latent Defects   If the landlord knows of a dangerous condition on the property and realizes the tenant will not notice it, the landlord is liable for any injuries. For example, if a landlord knows that a porch railing is weak and fails to inform the tenant, the landlord is responsible if the tenant plunges off the porch. But notice that, under the common law, if the landlord notifies the tenant of the latent defect, he is no longer liable.

Common Areas   The landlord is usually responsible for maintaining the common areas, and along with this obligation may go liability for torts. As we saw above, if your guest falls downstairs in a common hallway because the stairs were defective, the landlord is probably liable.

Negligent Repairs   Even in areas where the landlord has no duty to make repairs, if he volunteers to do so and does the work badly, he is responsible for any resulting harm.

Public Use   If the premises are to be used for a public purpose, such as a store or office, the landlord is generally obligated to repair any dangerous defects, although the tenant is probably liable as well. The purpose of this stricter rule is to ensure that the general public can safely visit commercial establishments. If a landlord realizes that the plate glass in a store's door is loose, he must promptly repair it or suffer liability for any injuries.

Modern Trend

Increasingly, state legislatures and courts are discarding the common law classifications described above and holding landlords liable under the normal rules of negligence law. **In many states, a landlord must use reasonable care to maintain safe premises and is liable for foreseeable harm.** For example, the common law rule merely required a landlord to notify a tenant of a latent defect, such as a defective porch railing. Most states now have building codes that require a landlord to maintain structural elements such as railings in safe condition. States further imply a warranty of habitability, which mandates reasonably safe living conditions. So, in many states, a landlord is no longer saved from negligence suits merely by giving notice of defects—he has to fix them.

PERSONAL PROPERTY

Personal property is all property other than real property. In this section, we look at two important aspects of personal property: gifts and bailments.

GIFTS

A gift is a voluntary transfer of property from one person to another without any consideration. Recall from Chapter 9 that, for consideration to exist, parties must normally make an exchange. But a gift is a one-way transaction, without anything given in return. The person who gives property away is the *donor*, and the one who receives it is the *donee*.

A gift involves three elements:

- The donor *intends to transfer* ownership of the property to the donee immediately.
- The donor *delivers* the property to the donee.
- The donee *accepts* the property.

If all three elements are met, the donee becomes the legal owner of the property. If the donor later says, "I've changed my mind, give that back!" the donee is free to refuse.

Intention to Transfer Ownership

The donor must intend to transfer ownership to the property right away, immediately giving up all control of the item. Notice the two important parts of this element. First, the donor's intention must be to *transfer ownership;* that is, to give title to the donee. Merely proving that the owner handed you property does not guarantee that you have received a gift; if the owner only intended that you *use* the item, there is no gift, and she can demand it back.

Second, the donor must also intend the property to transfer *immediately*. A promise to make a gift in the future is unenforceable. Promises about future behavior are governed by contract law, and a contract is unenforceable without consideration. If Sarah hands Lenny the keys to a $600,000 yacht and says, "Lenny, it's yours," then it *is* his, since Sarah intends to transfer ownership right away. But if Sarah says to Max, "Next week, I'm going to give you my yacht," Max has not received a gift because Sarah did not intend an immediate transfer. Neither does Max have an enforceable contract since there is no consideration for Sarah's promise.

A *revocable gift* is governed by a special rule, and it is actually not a gift at all. Suppose Harold tells his daughter Faith, "The mule is yours from now on, but if you start acting stupid again, I'm taking her back." Harold has retained some control over the animal, which means he has not intended to transfer ownership. There is no gift, and no transfer of ownership. Harold still owns the mule.

When Dominic Tenaglia's automobile broke down, his brother Nick generously offered to give him a replacement car. Nick delivered a Chevrolet to Dominic, and both brothers understood that the car was a gift. Nick wrote "gift" on the car's certificate of title, but he did not immediately give the certificate to Dominic. A week later, while Dominic was driving the Chevrolet, he was involved in an accident. Both brothers had insurance, through different insurers, for cars they owned. The two companies disputed which one was liable for Dominic's accident. The court determined that Nick's company was still liable for any damage caused by the Chevrolet. Nick had presented the car to Dominic but had not relinquished *all* control over it. Ownership of a car is unlike ownership of a computer or a sweater because it requires possession of a certificate of title. Because Nick still had the certificate at the time of the accident, he had the power to take back the Chevrolet whenever he wanted. He had not made a valid gift of the automobile, and Dominic's insurer won the case.[8]

Delivery
Physical Delivery

The donor must deliver the property to the donee. Generally, this involves physical delivery—a handoff, if you will. If Anna hands Eddie a Rembrandt drawing, saying "I want you to have this forever," she has satisfied the delivery requirement. In the chapter opening, Riley promised to give half a million dollars to the Boy Scouts the following day. But he never delivered the stocks and bonds, so there was no gift. The Boy Scouts received nothing, and all the money became part of Riley's estate, to be inherited by his unworthy son.

---

[8]*Motorists Mutual Insurance Co. v. State Farm Mutual Automobile Insurance Co.*, 1990 Ohio App. LEXIS 3027 (Ohio Ct. App. 1990).

Constructive Delivery

Physical delivery is the most common and the surest way to make a gift, but it is not always necessary. **A donor makes constructive delivery by transferring ownership without a physical delivery.** Most courts permit constructive delivery only when physical delivery is impossible or extremely inconvenient. Suppose that Anna wants to give her niece Jen a blimp, which is parked in a hangar at the airport. The blimp will not fit through the doorway of Jen's dorm. Instead of flying the aircraft to the university, Anna may simply deliver to Jen the certificate of title and the keys to the blimp. When she has done that, Jen owns the aircraft.

Delivery to an Agent

A donor might deliver the property to an agent, either someone working for him or for the donee. Assume that Randolph says to Mortimer, "Old boy, I should like for you to have my Rolls Royce." If Randolph gives the keys and the title to his own butler, there is no gift. By definition, the agent works for the donor, and thus the donor still has control and ownership of the property. But if the donor delivers the property to the donee's agent, the gift is made. So, if Randolph delivers the car to Mortimer's butler, then Mortimer owns the car.

Property Already in Donee's Possession

Sometimes a donor decides to give property to a donee who already has possession of it. In that case, no delivery is required, and the donee need only demonstrate that the donor intended to transfer present *ownership*. Larry lends a grand piano to Leslie for the summer. At the end of the summer, Larry announces that she can keep the instrument. So long as Larry clearly intends that Leslie gets ownership of the piano, the gift is completed.

Inter Vivos Gifts and Gifts *Causa Mortis*

A gift can be either *inter vivos* or *causa mortis*. An *inter vivos* gift means a gift made "during life"; that is, when the donor is not under any fear of impending death. The vast majority of gifts are *inter vivos*, involving a healthy donor and donee. Shirley, age 30 and in good health, gives Terry an eraser for his birthday. This is an *inter vivos* gift, which is absolute. The gift becomes final upon delivery, and the donor may *not* revoke it. If Shirley and Terry have a fight the next day, Shirley has no power to erase her eraser gift.

A gift *causa mortis* is one made in contemplation of approaching death. The gift is valid if the donor dies as expected, but it is revoked if he recovers. Suppose that Lenny's doctors have told him he will probably die of a liver ailment within a month. Lenny calls Jane to his bedside and hands her a fistful of cash, saying, "I'm dying, this money is yours." Jane sheds a tear, then sprints to the bank. If Lenny dies of the liver ailment within a few weeks, Jane gets to keep the money. The law permits the gift *causa mortis* to act as a kind of substitute for a will since the donor's delivery of the property clearly indicates his intentions. But note that this kind of gift is revocable. Since a gift *causa mortis* is conditional (upon the donor's death), the donor has the right to revoke it at any time before he dies. If Lenny telephones Jane the next day and says that he has changed his mind, he gets the money back. Further, if the donor recovers and does not die as expected, the gift is automatically revoked.

EXAM Strategy

Question: Julie does good deeds for countless people, and many are deeply grateful. On Monday, Wilson tells Julie, "You are a wonderful person, and I have a present for you. I am giving you this baseball, which was the 500th home run hit by one of the great players of all time." He hands her the ball, which is worth nearly half a million dollars.

Julie's good fortune continues on Tuesday, when another friend, Cassandra, tells Julie, "I only have a few weeks to live. I want you to have this signed first edition of *Ulysses*. It is priceless, and it is yours." The book is worth about $200,000. On Wednesday, Wilson and Cassandra decide they have been foolhardy, and both demand that Julie return the items. Must she do so?

Strategy: Both of these donors are attempting to revoke their gifts. An *inter vivos* gift cannot be revoked, but a gift *causa mortis* can be. To answer the question, you must know what kind of gifts these were.

Result: A gift *causa mortis* is one made in fear of approaching death, and this rule applies to Cassandra. Such a gift is revocable any time before the donor dies, so Cassandra gets her book back. A gift *inter vivos* is one made without any such fear of death. Most gifts fall in this category, and they are irrevocable. Wilson was not anticipating his demise, so his was a gift *inter vivos*. Julie keeps the baseball.

Acceptance

The donee must accept the gift. This rarely leads to disputes, but if a donee should refuse a gift and then change her mind, she is out of luck. Her repudiation of the donor's offer means there is no gift, and she has no rights in the property.

The following case offers a combination of love, alcohol, and diamonds—always a volatile mix.

You be the Judge

ALBINGER V. HARRIS
2002 Mont. 118, 2002 WL 1226858
Montana Supreme Court, 2002

Facts: Michelle Harris and Michael Albinger lived together, on and off, for three years. Their roller-coaster relationship was marred by alcohol abuse and violence. When they announced their engagement, Albinger gave Harris a $29,000 diamond ring, but the couple broke off their wedding plans because of emotional and physical turmoil. Harris returned the ring. Later, they reconciled and resumed their marriage plans, and Albinger gave his fiancée the ring again. This cycle repeated several times over the three years. Each time they broke off their relationship, Harris returned the ring to Albinger, and each time they made up, he gave it back to her.

On one occasion, Albinger held a knife over Harris as she lay in bed, threatening to chop off her finger if she didn't remove the ring. He beat her and forcibly removed the ring. Criminal charges were brought but then dropped when, inevitably, the couple reconciled. Another time,

Albinger told her to "take the car, the horse, the dog, and the ring and get the hell out." Finally, mercifully, they ended their stormy affair, and Harris moved to Kentucky—keeping the ring.

Albinger sued for the value of the ring. The trial court found that the ring was a conditional gift, made in contemplation of marriage, and ordered Harris to pay its full value. She appealed. The Montana Supreme Court had to decide, in a case of first impression, whether an engagement ring was given in contemplation of marriage. (In Montana, and many states, neither party to a broken engagement may sue for breach of contract.)

You Be the Judge: *Who owns the ring?*

Argument for Harris: The main problem with calling the ring a "conditional gift" is that there is no such thing. The elements of a gift are intent, delivery, and acceptance, and Harris has proved all three. A gift is not a contract, nor is it a loan. Once a gift has been accepted, the donor has no more rights in the property and may not demand its return. Hundreds of years of litigation have resulted in only one exception to this rule—a gift *causa mortis*—and despite some cynical claims to the contrary, marriage is not death. If this court carves a new exception to the longstanding rule, other unhappy donors will dream up more "conditions" that supposedly entitle them to their property. What is more, to create a special rule for engagement rings would be blatant gender bias because the exception would only benefit men. This court should stick to settled law and permit the recipient of a gift to keep it.

Argument for Albinger: The symbolism of an engagement ring is not exactly news. For decades, Americans have given rings—frequently diamond—in contemplation of marriage. All parties understand why the gift is made and what is expected if the engagement is called off: the ring must be returned. Albinger's *intent*, to focus on one element, was conditional—and Michelle Harris understood that. Each time the couple separated, she gave the ring back. She knew that she could wear this beautiful ring in anticipation of their marriage, but that custom and decency required its return if the wedding was off. She knew it, that is, until greed got the better of her and she fled to Kentucky, attempting to profit at the expense of Albinger's generosity. We are not asking for new law, but for confirmation of what everyone has known for generations: there is no wedding ring when there is no wedding.

The following table distinguishes between a contract and a gift:

A Contract and a Gift Distinguished

A Contract:

Lou: I will pay you $2,000 to paint the house, if you promise to finish by July 3.	Abby: I agree to paint the house by July 3, for $2,000.

Lou and Abby have a contract. Each promise is consideration in support of the other promise. Lou and Abby can each enforce the other's promise.

A Gift:

Lou hands Phil two opera tickets, saying: I want you to have these two tickets to *Rigoletto.*"	Phil says, "Hey, thanks."

This is a valid *inter vivos* gift. Lou intended to transfer ownership immediately and delivered the property to Phil, who now owns the tickets.

Neither Contract nor Gift:

Lou: You're a great guy. Next week, I'm going to give you two tickets to *Rigoletto*.	Jason: Hey, thanks.

There is no gift because Lou did not intend to transfer ownership immediately, and he did not deliver the tickets. There is no contract because Jason has given no consideration to support Lou's promise.

© Cengage Learning 2014

BAILMENT

A **bailment** is the rightful possession of goods by someone who is not the owner. The one who delivers the goods is the *bailor* and the one in possession is the *bailee*. Bailments are common. Suppose that you are going out of town for the weekend and lend your motorcycle to Stan. You are the bailor, and your friend is the bailee. When you check your suitcase with

Bailment

The rightful possession of goods by someone who is not the owner, usually by mutual agreement between the bailor and bailee.

the airline, you are again the bailor and the airline is the bailee. If you rent a car at your destination, you become the bailee, while the rental agency is the bailor. In each case, someone other than the true owner has rightful, temporary possession of personal property.

Parties generally create a bailment by agreement. In each of the examples above, the parties agreed to the bailment. In two cases, the agreement included payment, which is common but not essential. When you buy your airline ticket, you pay for your ticket, and the price includes the airline's agreement, as bailee, to transport your suitcase. When you rent a car, you pay the bailor for the privilege of using it. By lending your motorcycle, you engage in a bailment without either party paying compensation.

A bailment without any agreement is called a *constructive,* or *involuntary,* **bailment.** Suppose that you find a wristwatch in your house that you know belongs to a friend. You are obligated to return the watch to the true owner, and until you do so, you are the bailee, liable for harm to the property. This is called a constructive bailment because, with no agreement between the parties, the law is *construing* a bailment.

Involuntary bailment
A bailment that occurs without an agreement between the bailor and bailee.

Control

To create a bailment, the bailee must assume physical control of an item with intent to possess. A bailee may be liable for loss or damage to the property, so it is not fair to hold him liable unless he has taken physical control of the goods, intending to possess them.

Disputes about whether someone has taken control often arise in parking lot cases. When a car is damaged or stolen, the lot's owner may try to avoid liability by claiming it lacked control of the parked auto and therefore was not a bailee. If the lot is a "park and lock" facility, where the car's owner retains the key and the lot owner exercises *no control at all*, there is probably no bailment and no liability for damage.

By contrast, when a driver leaves her keys with a parking attendant, the lot clearly is exercising control of the auto, and the parties have created a bailment. The lot is probably liable for loss or damage in that case.

Rights of the Bailee

The bailee's primary right is possession of the property. **Anyone who interferes with the bailee's rightful possession is liable to her.** Suppose that, after you lend your motorcycle to Stan, Mel sees Stan park the bike, realizes Stan isn't the owner, rides the motorcycle away, and locks it up until you return. Mel is liable to Stan for any damages Stan suffered while deprived of transportation.

Even a bailor is liable if he wrongfully takes back property from a bailee. If a car agency rents Francine a car for a three-day weekend but then repossesses it for use elsewhere, it is liable to her for any damages, even though it owns the car. The bailor must abide by the agreement.

The bailee is typically, though not always, permitted to use the property. Obviously, a customer is permitted to drive a car rented from an agency. When a farmer lends his tractor to a neighbor, the bailee is entitled to use the machine for normal farm purposes. But some bailees have no authority to use the goods. If you store your furniture in a warehouse, the storage company is your bailee, but it has no right to curl up in your bed. The bailee may be entitled to compensation. This depends upon the agreement. If Owner leaves a power boat at the boatyard for repairs, the boatyard, a bailee, is entitled to payment for the work it does. As with any contract, the exact compensation should be clearly agreed upon before any work

> **If you store your furniture in a warehouse, the storage company is your bailee, but it has no right to curl up in your bed.**

begins. If there is no agreement, the boatyard will probably receive the reasonable value of its services.

Duties of the Bailee

The bailee is strictly liable to redeliver the goods on time to the bailor, or to whomever the bailor designates. Strict liability means there are virtually no exceptions. Rudy stores his $6,000 drum set with Melissa's Warehouse while he is on vacation. Blake arrives at the warehouse and shows a forged letter, supposedly from Rudy, granting Blake permission to remove the drums. If Melissa permits Blake to take the drums, she will owe Rudy $6,000, even if the forgery was a high-quality job.

Due Care

The bailee is obligated to exercise due care. **The level of care required depends upon who receives the benefit of the bailment.** There are three possibilities:

- *Sole benefit of bailee.* If the bailment is for the sole benefit of the bailee, the bailee is required to use **extraordinary care** with the property. Generally, in these cases, the bailor lends something for free to the bailee. Since the bailee is paying nothing for the use of the goods, most courts consider her the only one to benefit from the bailment. If your neighbor lends you a power lawn mower, the bailment is probably for your sole benefit. You are liable if you are even slightly inattentive in handling the lawn mower and can expect to pay for virtually any harm done.

- *Mutual benefit.* When the bailment is for the mutual benefit of bailor and bailee, the bailee must use **ordinary care** with the property. Ordinary care is what a reasonably prudent person would use under the circumstances. When you rent a car, you benefit from the use of the car, and the agency profits from the fee you pay. When the airline hauls your suitcase to your destination, both parties benefit. Most bailments benefit both parties, and courts decide the majority of bailment disputes under this standard.

- *Sole benefit of bailor.* When the bailment benefits only the bailor, the bailee must use only **slight care.** This kind of bailment is called a **gratuitous bailment,** and the bailee is liable only for **gross negligence.** Sheila enters a pie-eating contest and asks you to hold her $14,000 diamond engagement ring while she competes. You put the ring in your pocket. Sheila wins the $20 first prize, but the ring has disappeared. This was a gratuitous bailment, and you are not liable to Sheila unless she can prove gross negligence on your part. If the ring dropped from your pocket or was stolen, you are not liable. If you used the ring to play catch with friends, you are liable.

Burden of Proof

In an ordinary negligence case, the plaintiff has the burden of proof to demonstrate that the defendant was negligent and caused the harm alleged. In bailment cases, the burden of proof is reversed. **Once the bailor has proven the existence of a bailment and loss or harm to the goods, a presumption of negligence arises, and the burden shifts to the bailee to prove adequate care.** This is a major change from ordinary negligence cases. Georgina's car is struck by another auto. If Georgina sues for negligence, it is her burden to prove that the defendant was driving unreasonably and caused the harm. By comparison, assume that Georgina rents Chance her sailboat for a month. At the end of the month, Chance announces that the boat is at the bottom of Lake Michigan. If Georgina sues Chance, she only needs to demonstrate that the parties had a bailment and that Chance failed to return the boat. The burden then shifts to Chance to prove that the boat was lost through no fault of his own. If Chance cannot meet that burden, Georgina recovers the full value of the boat.

The following case raises many of the issues in this section. Long before his time as president, Abraham Lincoln was a lawyer who argued more than 150 cases before the Supreme Court of Illinois. The case for Weedman is modeled after the arguments that a young Lincoln actually made.

You be the Judge

JOHNSON V. WEEDMAN
5 Ill. 495
Supreme Court of Illinois, 1843

Facts: Johnson left his horse with Weedman, paying him to board and feed the animal. Johnson did not grant Weedman permission to ride the horse. Nonetheless, Weedman took the horse for a 15-mile ride.

Later that day, the horse died. However, the trial court found that Weedman had not abused the animal and that the ride had not caused the horse's death. The court did not grant damages to Johnson, and Johnson appealed.

You Be the Judge: *Should Weedman pay for Johnson's dead horse?*

Argument for Johnson: Your honor, Weedman was in possession of my client's horse only to feed him and see to his basic needs. My client did not give him permission to take the horse out of the pasture. Weedman made personal use of my client's property when he took a 15-mile ride that was in no way necessary. The trial court's finding that Weedman did not abuse the horse during the ride is irrelevant. My client must be compensated for the loss of his animal.

Argument for Weedman: My client had a legal right to possession of the horse. Riding the horse was not a substantial abuse of his rights as bailee. The horse was returned to the pasture in good condition. It was not abandoned and was not devalued in any way by the ride. The plaintiff is therefore not entitled to any compensation. The coincidental death of the horse does not change that fact.

Rights and Duties of the Bailor

The bailor's rights and duties are the reverse of the bailee's. The bailor is entitled to the return of his property on the agreed-upon date. He is also entitled to receive the property in good condition and to recover damages for harm to the property if the bailee failed to use adequate care.

Chapter Conclusion

Real property law is ancient but forceful. Although real property today is not the dominant source of wealth that it was in medieval England, it is still the greatest asset that most people will ever possess—and it is worth understanding.

EXAM REVIEW

1. **REAL PROPERTY; FIXTURES** Real property includes land, buildings, air and subsurface rights, plant life, and fixtures. A fixture is any good that has become attached to other real property, such as land. (pp. 656–657)

EXAM Strategy

Question: Paul and Shelly Higgins had two wood stoves in their home. Each rested on, but was not attached to, a built-in brick platform. The downstairs wood stove was connected to the chimney flue and was used as part of the main heating system for the house. The upstairs stove, in the master bedroom, was purely decorative. It had no stovepipe connecting it to the chimney. The Higginses sold their house to Jack Everitt, and neither party said anything about the two stoves. Is Everitt entitled to either stove? Both stoves?

Strategy: An object is a fixture if a reasonable person would consider the item to be a permanent part of the property, taking into account attachment, adaptation, and other objective manifestations of permanence. (See the "Result" at the end of this section.)

2. **CONCURRENT ESTATES** When two or more people own real property at the same time, they have a concurrent estate. In both a tenancy in common and a joint tenancy, all owners have a share in the entire property. The primary difference is that joint tenants have the right of survivorship, meaning that when a joint tenant dies, his interest passes to the other joint tenants. A tenant in common has the power to leave her estate to her heirs. (pp. 658–660)

EXAM Strategy

Question: Howard Geib, Walker McKinney, and John D. McKinney owned two vacation properties as joint tenants with right of survivorship. The parties were not getting along well, and Geib petitioned the court to partition the properties. The trial court ruled that the fairest way to do this was to sell both properties and divide the proceeds. The two McKinneys appealed, claiming that a partition by sale was improper because it would destroy their right of survivorship. Comment.

Strategy: Do joint tenants have a right to partition? Are there any limits on that right? (See the "Result" at the end of this section.)

3. **NONPOSSESSORY INTERESTS** Some valuable interests in real property do not involve possession. Easements, profits, and licenses grant limited rights to use property owned by someone else. (pp. 660–661)

4. **GOVERNMENT REGULATION** Nuisance law, zoning ordinances, and eminent domain all permit a government to regulate property and, in some cases, to take it for public use. (pp. 662–663)

5. **LANDLORD-TENANT** When an owner of a freehold estate allows another person temporary, exclusive possession of the property, the parties have created a landlord-tenant relationship. (pp. 663–664)

6. **TENANCIES** Any lease for a stated, fixed period is a tenancy for years. A periodic tenancy is created for a fixed period and then automatically continues for additional periods until either party notifies the other of termination. A tenancy at will has no fixed duration and may be terminated by either party at any time. A tenancy at sufferance occurs when a tenant remains, against the wishes of the landlord, after the expiration of a true tenancy. (pp. 664–665)

7. **QUIET ENJOYMENT** All tenants are entitled to the quiet enjoyment of the premises, without the interference of the landlord. (pp. 665–666)

8. **SECURITY DEPOSITS**. Landlords may require tenants to post a deposit that can be used to pay for repairs if a tenant damages the property. But many landlords fail to promptly return security deposits to tenants who leave no damage behind. In those cases, tenants are often able to sue for as much as three times their security deposit. (pp. 667–668)

9. **RENT** The tenant is obligated to pay the rent, and the landlord may evict for nonpayment. The modern trend is to require a landlord to mitigate damages caused by a tenant who abandons the premises before the lease expires. (pp. 668–670)

EXAM Strategy

Question: Loren Andreo leased retail space in his shopping plaza to Tropical Isle Pet Shop for five years, at a monthly rent of $2,100. Tropical Isle vacated the premises 18 months early, turned in the key to Andreo, and acknowledged liability for the unpaid rent. Andreo placed a "for rent" sign in the store window and spoke to a commercial real estate broker about the space. But he did not enter into a formal listing agreement with the broker, or take any other steps to rent the space, for about nine months. With approximately nine months remaining on the unused part of Tropical's lease, Andreo hired a commercial broker to rent the space. He also sued Tropical for 18 months' rent. Comment.

Strategy: When a tenant abandons leased property early, the landlord is obligated to mitigate damages. Did Andreo? (See the "Result" at the end of this section.)

---

10. **TENANT'S LIABILITY** A tenant is liable to the landlord for any significant damage he causes to the property. A tenant is also generally liable for injuries occurring within the premises she is leasing. (pp. 670–671)

11. **PERSONAL INJURY** At common law, a landlord had very limited liability for injuries on the premises, but today, many courts require a landlord to use reasonable care and hold her liable for foreseeable harm. (pp. 670–671)

12. **GIFTS** A gift is a voluntary transfer of property from one person to another without consideration. The elements of a gift are intention to transfer ownership immediately, delivery, and acceptance. (pp. 671–674)

13. **BAILMENT** A bailment is the rightful possession of goods by one who is not the owner. The one who delivers the goods is the bailor, and the one in possession is the bailee. To create a bailment, the bailee must assume physical control with intent to possess. (pp. 675–676)

14. **BAILEE'S RIGHTS** The bailee is always entitled to possess the property, is frequently allowed to use it, and may be entitled to compensation. (pp. 676–677)

15. **BAILEE'S DUTY OF CARE** The bailee is obligated to exercise due care. The level of care required depends upon who receives the benefit of the bailment: if the bailee is the sole beneficiary, she must use extraordinary care; if the parties mutually benefit, the bailee must use ordinary care; and if the bailor is the sole beneficiary of the bailment, the bailee must use only slight care. (pp. 677–678)

---

1. Result: A buyer normally takes all fixtures. The downstairs stove was permanently attached to the house and used as part of the heating system. The owner who installed it *intended* that it remain, and it was a fixture; Everitt got it. The upstairs stove was not permanently attached and was not a fixture; the sellers could take it with them.

2. Result: The McKinneys lost. Any co-tenant (including a joint tenant) has an absolute right to partition. Difficulties in partitioning are irrelevant.

9. Result: For about nine months, Andreo made no serious effort to lease the store. The court rejected his rent claim for that period, permitting him to recover unpaid money only for the period he made a genuine effort to lease the space.

MULTIPLE-CHOICE QUESTIONS

1. Quick, Onyx, and Nash were deeded a piece of land as tenants in common. The deed provided that Quick owned one-half the property and Onyx and Nash owned one-quarter each. If Nash dies, the property will be owned as follows:

   (a) Quick 1/2, Onyx 1/2

   (b) Quick 5/8, Onyx 3/8

   (c) Quick 1/3, Onyx 1/3, Nash's heirs 1/3

   (d) Quick 1/2, Onyx 1/4, Nash's heirs 1/4

2. Which of the following forms of tenancy will be created if a tenant stays in possession of leased premises without the landlord's consent, after the tenant's one-year written lease expires?

   (a) Tenancy at will

   (b) Tenancy for years

   (c) Periodic tendency

   (d) Tenancy at sufferance

3. Consider the following:

   I.   A house (value: $150,000)
   II. A giant high-definition television in the house (value: $4,999)
   III. The land that the house sits upon (value: $30,000)
   IV. An old car in the house's garage (value: $5,001)

   How many of these items are personal property?

   (a) All four of them
   (b) Three of them
   (c) Two of them
   (d) One of them
   (e) None of them

4. Holding out an envelope, Alan says, "Ben, I'm giving you these opera tickets." Without taking the envelope, Ben replies, "Why would I want opera tickets? Loser." Alan leaves, crestfallen. Later that day, a girl whom Ben has liked for some time says, "I sure wish I were going to the opera tonight." Ben scrambles, calls Alan, and says, "Alan, old buddy, I accept your gift of the opera tickets. I'm on my way over to pick them up."

   Does Ben have a legal right to the tickets?

   (a) Yes, because Alan intended to transfer ownership.
   (b) Yes, because offers to give gifts cannot be revoked.
   (c) No, because no consideration was given.
   (d) No, because Ben did not accept the gift when offered.

5. A tenant renting an apartment under a three-year written lease that does not contain any specific restrictions may be evicted for:

   (a) counterfeiting money in the apartment.
   (b) keeping a dog in the apartment.
   (c) failing to maintain a liability insurance policy on the apartment.
   (d) making structural repairs to the apartment.

ESSAY QUESTIONS

1. **YOU BE THE JUDGE WRITING PROBLEM** Frank Deluca and his son David owned the Sportsman's Pub on Fountain Street in Providence, Rhode Island. The Delucas applied to the city for a license to employ topless dancers in the pub. Did the city have the power to deny the Delucas' request? **Argument for the Delucas:** Our pub is perfectly legal. Further, no law in Rhode Island prohibits topless dancing. We are morally and legally entitled to present this entertainment. The city should not use some phony moralizing to deny customers what they want. **Argument for Providence:** This section of Providence is zoned to prohibit topless dancing, just as it is zoned to bar manufacturing. There are other parts of town where the Delucas can open one of their sleazy clubs if they want to, but we are entitled to deny a permit in this area.

2. Kenmart Realty sued to evict Mr. and Ms. Alghalabio for nonpayment of rent and sought the unpaid monies, totaling several thousand dollars. In defense, the Alghalabios claimed that their apartment was infested with rats. They testified that there were numerous rat holes in the walls of the living room, bedroom, and kitchen, that there were rat droppings all over the apartment, and that on one occasion, they saw their toddler holding a live rat. They testified that the landlord had refused numerous requests to exterminate. Please rule on the landlord's suit.

3. Lisa Preece rented an apartment from Turman Realty, paying a $300 security deposit. Georgia law states: "Any landlord who fails to return any part of a security deposit which is required to be returned to a tenant pursuant to this article shall be liable to the tenant in the amount of three times the sum improperly withheld plus reasonable attorney's fees." When Preece moved out, Turman did not return her security deposit, and she sued for triple damages plus attorney's fees, totaling $1,800. Turman offered evidence that its failure to return the deposit was inadvertent and that it had procedures reasonably designed to avoid such errors. Is Preece entitled to triple damages? Attorney's fees?

4. Ronald Armstead worked for First American Bank as a courier. His duties included making deliveries between the bank's branches in Washington, D.C. Armstead parked the bank's station wagon near the entrance of one branch in violation of a sign saying: "No Parking—Rush Hour Zone." In the rear luggage section of the station wagon were four locked bank dispatch bags containing checks and other valuable documents. Armstead had received tickets for illegal parking at this spot on five occasions. Shortly after Armstead entered the bank, a tow truck arrived, and its operator prepared to tow the station wagon. Transportation Management, Inc., operated the towing service on behalf of the District of Columbia. Armstead ran out to the vehicle and told the tow truck operator that he was prepared to drive the vehicle away immediately. But the operator drove away with the station wagon in tow. One-and-a-half hours later, a bank employee paid for the car's release, but one dispatch bag, containing documents worth $107,000, was missing. First American sued Transportation Management and the District of Columbia. The defendants sought summary judgment, claiming they *could not* be liable. Were they correct?

5. **YOU BE THE JUDGE WRITING PROBLEM** Eileen Murphy often cared for her elderly neighbor, Thomas Kenney. He paid her $25 per day for her help and once gave her a bank certificate of deposit worth $25,000. She spent the money. Murphy alleged that shortly before his death, Kenney gave her a large block of shares in three corporations. He called his broker, intending to instruct him to transfer the shares to Murphy's name, but the broker was ill and unavailable. So Kenney told Murphy to write her name on the shares and keep them, which she did. Two weeks later, Kenney died. When Murphy presented the shares to Kenney's broker to transfer ownership to her, the broker refused because Kenney had never endorsed the shares as the law requires—that is, signed them over to Murphy. Was Murphy entitled to the $25,000? To the shares? **Argument for Murphy:** The purpose of the law is to do what a donor intended, and it is obvious that Kenney intended Murphy to have the $25,000 and the shares. Why else would he have given them to her? A greedy estate should not be allowed to interfere with the deceased's intentions. **Argument for the Estate:** Murphy is not entitled to the $25,000 because we have no way of knowing what Kenney's intentions were when he gave her the money. She is not entitled to the shares of stock because Kenney's failure to endorse them over to her meant he never *delivered* them, and that is an essential element of a gift.

DISCUSSION QUESTIONS

1. Is it sensible to distinguish between *inter vivos* gifts and gifts *causa mortis*? Should someone "on his deathbed" be able to change his mind so easily?

2. Donny Delt and Sammy Sigma are students and roommates. They lease a house in a neighborhood near campus. Few students live on the block. The students do not have large parties, but they often have friends over at night. The friends sometimes play high-volume music in their cars and sometimes speak loudly when going to and from their cars. Also, departing late-night guests often leave beer cans and fast-food wrappers in the street.

   Neighbors complain about being awakened in the wee hours of the morning. They are considering filing a nuisance lawsuit against Donny and Sammy. Would such an action be reasonable? Do you think Donny and Sammy are creating a nuisance? If so, why? If not, where is the line—what amount of late-night noise does amount to a nuisance?

3. Imagine that you sign a lease and that you are to move into your new apartment on August 15. When you arrive, the previous tenant has not moved out. In fact, he has no intention of moving out. Should the landlord be in charge of getting rid of the old tenant, or should you have the obligation to evict him?

4. When landlords wrongfully withhold security deposits, they can often be sued for three times the amount of the security deposit. Is this reasonable? Should a landlord have to pay $3,000 for a $1,000 debt? What if you fail to pay a rent on time? Should you have to pay three times the amount of your normal rent? If your answers to these two questions are different, why?

5. In the case of a gratuitous bailment, the bailee is liable only if he is grossly negligent. Is this good policy? If you agree to watch someone's property, shouldn't you be required to be careful even if you are not being paid?

© picsbyst/Shutterstock.com

CONSUMER LAW

Three women signed up for a lesson at the Arthur Murray dance studio in Washington, D.C. Expecting a session of quiet fun, they instead found themselves in a nightmare of humiliation and coercion:

- "First of all, I did not want the [additional] lesson, and I think it was unpleasant because I had three, maybe four, people, as I say, pressuring me to buy something by a certain time, and I do recall asking that I be let to think, let me think it over, and I was told that the contest would end at 6 o'clock or something to that effect and if I did not sign by a certain time, it would be too late. I think we got under the deadline by maybe a minute or two. If I had been given time to think, I would not have signed that contract."

- "I tried to say no and get out of it and I got very, very upset because I got frightened at paying out all that money and having nothing to fall back on. I remember I started crying and couldn't stop crying. All I thought of was getting out of there. So finally after I don't know how much time, Mr. Mara said, well, I could sign up for 250 hours, which was half the 500 Club, which would amount to $4,300. So I finally signed it. After that, I tried to raise the money from the bank and found I couldn't get a loan for that amount and I didn't have any savings and I had to get a bank loan to pay for it. That was when I went back and asked him to cancel that contract. But Mr. Mara said that he couldn't cancel it."

- "I did not wish to join the carnival, and while it was only an additional $55, I had no desire to join. [My instructor] asked everyone in the room to sit down in a circle around me and he stood me up in that circle, in the middle of the circle, and said, 'Everybody, I want you to look at this woman here who is too cheap to join the carnival. I just want you to look at a woman like that. Isn't it awful?'"

> I remember I started crying and couldn't stop crying. All I thought of was getting out of there.

Because of abuses such as these, the Federal Trade Commission (FTC) ordered the Arthur Murray dance studio to halt its high-pressure sales techniques, limit each contract to no more than $1,500 in dance lessons, and permit all contracts to be canceled within seven days.[1]

INTRODUCTION

Years ago, consumers typically dealt with merchants they knew well. A dance instructor in a small town would not stay in business long if he tormented his elderly, vulnerable clients. As the population grew and cities expanded, however, merchants became less and less subject to community pressure. The law has supplemented, if not replaced, these informal policing mechanisms. Both Congress and the states have passed statutes that protect consumers from the unscrupulous. But the legal system is generally too slow and expensive to handle small cases. The women who fell into the web of Arthur Murray had neither the wealth nor the energy to sue the studio themselves. To aid consumers such as these, Congress empowered federal agencies to enforce consumer laws.

Federal Trade Commission

Congress created the FTC in 1915 to regulate business. Although its original focus was on antitrust law, it now regulates a wide range of business activities that affect consumers— everything from advertising to consumer loans to warranties to debt collection practices. The FTC has several options for enforcing the law:

- **Voluntary Compliance.** When the FTC determines that a business has violated the law, it first asks the offender to sign a voluntary compliance affidavit promising to stop the prohibited activity.

- **Administrative Hearings and Appeals.** If the company refuses to stop voluntarily, the FTC takes the case to an administrative law judge (ALJ) within the agency. The violator may settle the case at this point by signing a **consent order.** If the case proceeds to a hearing, the ALJ has the right to issue a **cease and desist order,** commanding the violator to stop the offending activity. The FTC issued a cease and desist order against the Arthur Murray dance studio. A defendant can appeal such an order to the five Commissioners of the FTC, from there to a federal appeals court, and ultimately to the United States Supreme Court. Both the Commissioners and the Fifth Circuit Court of Appeals confirmed the cease and desist order against Arthur Murray. The case never reached the Supreme Court.

- **Penalties.** The FTC can impose a fine for each violation of a voluntary compliance affidavit, a consent order, a cease and desist order, an FTC rule, or a cease and desist order issued against *someone else.* For example, the Arthur Murray studio could be liable for violating an FTC cease and desist order prohibiting high-pressure sales by the Fred Astaire studio. In addition, the FTC can file suit in federal court asking for damages on behalf of an injured consumer if (1) the defendant has violated FTC rules and (2) a reasonable person would have known under the circumstances that the conduct was dishonest or fraudulent.

---

[1]*In re Arthur Murray Studio of Washington, Inc.,* 78 F.T.C. 401, 1971 FTC LEXIS 75 (1971).

Consumer Financial Protection Bureau

In 2010, Congress created the Consumer Financial Protection Bureau (CFPB) to regulate consumer financial products and services, including mortgages, credit cards, and private student loans. (It does not have the authority to regulate car loans.) Among its goals is to clarify and simplify the terms of credit cards, checking accounts, and mortgage disclosure forms.

Already, the CFPB has proposed rules that would require banks to clearly reveal overdraft fees on checking accounts, announced its intent to closely supervise credit reporting agencies, and obtained a $210 million settlement from Capital One for deceptive marketing of credit cards.

SALES

Section 5 of the Federal Trade Commission Act (FTC Act) prohibits "unfair and deceptive acts or practices."

Deceptive Acts or Practices

Many deceptive acts or practices involve advertisements. **Under the FTC Act, an advertisement is deceptive if it contains an important misrepresentation or omission that is likely to mislead a reasonable consumer.** A company advertised that a pain-relief ointment called "Aspercreme" provided "the strong relief of aspirin right where you hurt." From this ad and the name of the product, do you assume that the ointment contains aspirin? Are you a reasonable consumer? Consumers surveyed in a shopping mall believed the product contained aspirin. In fact, it does not. The FTC required the company to disclose that there is no aspirin in Aspercreme.[2]

In another example, Nestlé sold a drink called Boost Kid Essentials, which contained probiotics, good bacteria that aid digestion and fight bad germs. But Nestlé went further than that in its ads, claiming that Boost would prevent children from getting sick or missing school. How could any parent resist that drink? Only Nestlé had no evidence for these claims. In a settlement with the FTC, Nestlé agreed not to make any claims for which it did not have scientific evidence.

In the following case, the court discussed the type of scientific evidence required to support health claims.

FEDERAL TRADE COMMISSION v. DIRECT MARKETING CONCEPTS, INC.

624 F.3d 1; 2010 U.S. App. LEXIS 21743
United States Court of Appeals for the First Circuit, 2010

Facts: Direct Marketing Concepts, Inc., broadcast an infomercial for Coral Calcium that featured a spokesperson named Robert Barefoot. In the ad, his claims were as bare as his feet. He asserted that virtually all diseases—heart disease, cancer, lupus, multiple sclerosis, and Parkinson's, among others—are caused by a condition called acidosis. He further claimed that calcium derived from Okinawan coral cures these diseases by rendering the body more alkaline: "I've had 1,000 people tell me how they've cured their cancer. I've witnessed people get out of wheelchairs with multiple sclerosis just by getting on the coral."

---

[2]*In re Thompson Medical Co., Inc.,* 104 F.T.C. 648, 1984 FTC LEXIS 6 (1984).

To bolster his claims, Barefoot noted that unspecified articles from the *Journal of the American Medical Association* and the *New England Journal of Medicine* "said that calcium supplements reverse cancer…that's a quote." During an 18-month period, this infomercial generated $54 million in sales.

The FTC filed suit against the company and its owners, alleging that the infomercials were deceptive. The trial court granted the FTC's motion for summary judgment, ruling that the infomercials were misleading as a matter of law and, therefore, there was no need for a trial. The defendants appealed.

Issue: *Were these infomercials misleading as a matter of law?*

Excerpts from Judge Thompson's Decision: When the FTC brings an action based on the theory that advertising is deceptive because the advertisers lacked a reasonable basis for their claims, the FTC must: (1) demonstrate what evidence would in fact establish such a claim in the relevant scientific community; and (2) compare the advertisers' evidence to that required by the scientific community to see if the claims have been established.

On the first prong, the FTC produced four expert declarations which demonstrated that the claims could be substantiated by double-blind, placebo-controlled human studies. To be sure, there may be other scientific evidence that could be sufficient. But the government established that some scientific evidence is required for substantiation, and thus satisfied the first prong. Because the Defendants neither produced nor pointed to any evidence to raise even the tiniest of fact issues, summary judgment was appropriate on the first prong.

On the second prong, the FTC relied on the same four expert declarations, in which the experts compared the Defendants' evidence to the available literature and concluded in each case that the Defendants' evidence was woefully inadequate. The experts specifically opined that: (1) there was no evidence that calcium cures cancer; (2) there was some evidence that calcium might lower blood pressure but none that it cures heart disease; (3) there was no evidence whatsoever that calcium has any effect on autoimmune disorders; [and] (4) there has been no research published in the *Journal of the American Medical Association* or the *New England Journal of Medicine* indicating that calcium "reverses" cancer.

The record contains a slew of documents, including excerpts from Barefoot's books, excerpts from Barefoot's deposition testimony, a number of popular science and pseudoscientific articles, and one preliminary study. Barefoot's books present jumbles of quotes from scientists, scientific review articles, and scientific studies interspersed with references to *Reader's Digest* and other general-consumption reductions of these studies. However, none of these scientists or studies supports the panacean claims made in the Coral Calcium infomercial. The Defendants therefore engaged in deceptive advertising as a matter of law.

The Defendants attempt to head off the above analysis by asserting that their infomercials advanced no actual health claims but, instead, presented only puffery which was further attenuated by the presence of general disclaimers. However, specific and measurable claims are not puffery, and may be the subject of deceptive advertising claims. [T]he Defendants' infomercials presented specific and measurable health claims.

Disclaimers or qualifications in any particular ad are not adequate to avoid liability unless they are sufficiently prominent and unambiguous to change the apparent meaning of the claims and to leave an accurate impression. The disclaimers at issue here did nothing to affect the meaning of the infomercials' health claims. The infomercial transcripts reveal only disclaimers that the infomercials are paid advertising. In contrast, the health claims were bold and straightforward, presented by supposed experts as testable observations backed up by clinical trials and studies.

[W]e affirm the district court's grant of summary judgment.

Unfair Practices

The FTC Act also prohibits unfair acts or practices. **The Commission considers a practice to be *unfair* if it meets all of the following three tests:**

- *It causes a substantial consumer injury.* This can mean physical or financial injury. A furnace repair company that dismantled home furnaces for "inspection" and then refused to reassemble them until the consumers agreed to buy services or replacement parts had caused a substantial consumer injury.

- *The harm of the injury outweighs any countervailing benefit.* A pharmaceutical company sold a sunburn remedy without conducting adequate tests to ensure that it worked. The expense of these tests would have forced the company to raise the product's price. The company had demonstrated that the product was safe, and there was evidence in the medical literature that the ingredients when used in other products were effective. The FTC determined that, although the company was technically in violation of its rules, the benefit to consumers of a cheaper product more than outweighed the risk of injury to them.

- *The consumer could not reasonably avoid the injury.* The FTC is particularly vigilant in protecting susceptible consumers—such as the elderly or the ill—who are less able to avoid injury. For instance, the Commission looks especially carefully at those who offer a cure for cancer, as the defendants did in the *Direct Marketing* case.

In addition, the FTC may decide that a practice is unfair simply because it violates public policy, even if it does not meet these three tests. The Commission refused to allow a mail-order company to file collection suits in states far from where the defendants lived because the practice was unfair, whether or not it met the three tests.

Additional Sales Rules
Bait-and-Switch

FTC rules prohibit bait-and-switch advertisements: a merchant may not advertise a product and then disparage it to consumers in an effort to sell a different (more expensive) item.

Seven websites based in Brooklyn, New York, such as Best Price Photo and 86th Street Photo, engaged in a classic bait-and-switch operation. They advertised products at a much lower price than competitors. That was the **bait**—an alluring offer that sounds almost too good to be true. Of course, it is. Once a customer placed an order, the company tried to sell an upgraded product at a much higher price. That is the **switch**. The real purpose of the advertisement was simply to find customers who were interested in buying. If customers refused the new item, they would be told that the original product was backordered, and the sale was cancelled. If customers agreed to buy the more expensive product, it would turn out to be of poor quality. But the company would not allow returns—either the return fees would be high or the "customer service" department would refuse to answer the phone.

Bait-and-switch
A practice where sellers advertise products that are not generally available but are being used to draw interested parties in so that they will buy other products.

Merchandise Bought by Mail, by Telephone, or Online

Many consumers buy virtually everything—food, clothing, furnishings—online. **The FTC has established the following rules for this type of merchandise:**

- Sellers must ship an item within the time stated or, if no time is given, within 30 days after receipt of the order.

- If a company cannot ship the product when promised, it must send the customer a notice with the new shipping date and an opportunity to cancel. If the new shipping date is within 30 days of the one originally promised and the customer does not cancel, the order is still valid.

- If the company cannot ship by the second shipment date it must send the customer another notice. This time, however, the company must cancel the order unless the customer returns the notice, indicating that he still wants the item.

Staples, Inc. violated these FTC rules when it told customers that they were viewing "real-time" inventory and that products would be delivered in one day, even on weekends. In fact, the website was not updated in real time, one-day delivery only applied to customers who lived within 20 miles of a Staples store, and it never happened on weekends. The company paid a fine of $850,000 to settle these charges.

Telemarketing

It used to be that telemarketers would practically ruin dinner hour in the United States with their relentless phone calls. But now, FTC rules prohibit telemarketers from calling any telephone number listed on its do-not-call registry. You can register your home and cell phone numbers with the FTC online at **http://www.donotcall.gov** or by telephone at (888) 382-1222. FTC rules also prohibit telemarketers from blocking their names and telephone numbers on Caller ID systems.

What is even more annoying than telemarketing calls from a live person? Robocalls (pre-recorded commercial telemarketing calls) from a machine. Such calls are illegal unless the telemarketer obtains written permission from the person being called. You can file a complaint by calling (877) FTC-HELP or by going to the **ftc.gov** website. Exempted from this ban are informational calls (cancellations of a flight or a school day), debt collection calls (as long as they are not trying to sell anything), political messages, charitable outreach, and health care messages.

Unordered Merchandise

Under §5 of the FTC Act, anyone who receives unordered merchandise in the mail can treat it as a gift. She can use it, throw it away, or do whatever else she wants with it.

There you are, watching an infomercial for Anushka products, guaranteed to fight that scourge of modern life—cellulite! Rushing to your phone, you place an order. The Anushka cosmetics arrive, but for some odd reason, the cellulite remains. A month later, another bottle arrives, like magic, in the mail. The magic spell is broken, however, when you get your credit card bill and see that, without your authorization, the company has charged you for the new supply of Anushka. Is this a hot new marketing technique? Not exactly. The FTC ordered the company to cease and desist this unfair and deceptive practice. The company improperly billed its customers, said the FTC, and should have notified them that they were free to treat the unauthorized products as a gift, to use or throw out as they wished.[3]

Door-to-Door Sales

Consumers at home need special protection from unscrupulous salespeople. In a store, customers can simply walk out, but at home, they may feel trapped. Under the FTC door-to-door rules, **a salesperson is required to notify the buyer that she has the right to cancel the transaction prior to midnight of the third business day thereafter.** This notice must be given both orally and in writing; the actual cancellation must be in writing. The seller must return the buyer's money within 10 days.

EXAM Strategy

Question: Mantra Films sold "Girls Gone Wild" DVDs on the Internet. When customers ordered one DVD, the company would enroll them automatically in a "continuity program" and send them unordered DVDs each month on a "negative-option" basis, charging consumers' credit cards for each DVD until consumers took action to stop the shipments. Is Mantra's marketing plan legal?

Strategy: Review the various sales regulations—more than one is involved in this case.

Result: This marketing plan was deceptive because customers were not told that they would be enrolled in the continuity program. Also, Mantra could not legally bill for the unordered DVDs. Under the unordered merchandise rule, consumers had the right to treat them as gifts.

---

[3]*In the Matter of Synchronal Corp.*, 116 F.T.C. 1189, 1993 FTC LEXIS 280 (1993).

CONSUMER CREDIT

Historically, the practice of charging interest on loans was banned by most countries and by three of the most prominent religions—Christianity, Islam, and Judaism. As the European economy developed, however, moneylending became essential. To compromise, governments began to permit interest charges but limited the maximum rate.

Even in modern times, many states limit the maximum interest rate a lender may charge consumers. (Although, usury laws typically do not apply to credit card debt, mortgages, consumer leases, or commercial loans.) The penalty for violating usury statutes varies among the states. Depending upon the jurisdiction, the lender may forfeit (1) the interest above the usury limit, (2) all of the interest, or (3) all of the loan and the interest.

Truth in Lending Act—General Provisions

To avoid the penalties of usury laws, lenders found many creative methods to disguise the real interest rate from the authorities. In the process, they also hid it from borrowers. Many consumers had no idea what interest rate they were really paying. Congress passed the Truth in Lending Act (TILA) with the simple goal of ensuring that when consumers borrowed money, they understood the terms and costs of the loan. Note that TILA does *not* regulate the actual interest rates or the terms of a loan; that responsibility is left to the states. TILA simply requires lenders to *disclose* the terms of a loan in an understandable and complete manner.

Applicability

TILA applies to a transaction only if all of the following tests are met:

- *It is a consumer loan.* That means a loan to an individual for personal, family, or household purposes, not a loan to a business.

- *The loan has a finance charge or will be repaid in more than four installments.* Sometimes finance charges masquerade as installment plans. Boris can pay for his 3D TV in six monthly installments of $400 each, or he can pay $1,800 cash up front. If he chooses the installment plan, he is effectively paying a finance charge of $600. That is why TILA applies to loans with more than four installments.

- *The loan is for less than $51,800, is secured by a mortgage on real estate, or is a private education loan.*[4]

- *The loan is made by someone in the business of offering credit.* If Boris borrows from his friend to buy the TV, TILA does not apply.

Disclosure

In all loans regulated by TILA:

- *The disclosure must be clear and in meaningful sequence.* For example, a finance company made all the necessary disclosures, but it violated TILA nonetheless because it scattered the required terms throughout the loan document, intermixed with confusing provisions that were not required by TILA.[5] A loan document should not be a scavenger hunt.

---

[4]This amount adjusts every December 31, to reflect inflation.
[5]*Allen v. Beneficial Fin. Co. of Gary*, 531 F.2d 797, 1976 U.S. App. LEXIS 12935 (7th Cir. 1976).

- *The lender must disclose the finance charge.* The finance charge is the amount, in dollars, the consumer will pay in interest and fees over the life of the loan. It is important for consumers to know this amount because otherwise, they may not understand the real cost of the loan. Of course, the longer the loan, the higher the finance charge. Someone who borrows $5,000 for 10 years at 10 percent annual interest will pay $500 each year for 10 years, for a total finance charge of $5,000—equal to the principal borrowed. In 30-year mortgages, the finance charge will typically exceed the amount of the principal.

- *The creditor must also disclose the annual percentage rate (APR).* This number is the actual rate of interest the consumer pays on an annual basis. Without this disclosure, it would be easy in a short-term loan to disguise a very high APR because the finance charge is low. Boris borrows $5 for lunch from his employer's credit union. Under the terms of the loan, he must repay $6 the following week. His finance charge is only $1, but his APR is astronomical—20 percent per week—which is over 1,000 percent for a year.

All TILA loans must meet these three requirements. TILA requires additional disclosure for two types of loans: open-end credit (discussed later in the chapter) and closed-end credit.

Closed-end Credit   In a closed-end transaction, the loan is a fixed amount and the borrower knows the payment schedule in advance. Boris enters into a closed-end transaction when he buys a $30,000 car and agrees to make specified monthly payments over five years. Before a consumer enters into a closed-end transaction, the lender must disclose:

- The cash price;

- The total down payment;

- The amount financed;

- An itemized list of all other charges;

- The number, amount, and due dates of payments;

- The total amount of payments;

- Late payment charges;

- Penalties for prepaying the loan; and

- The lender's security interest in the item purchased.

Enforcement   The FTC generally has the right to enforce TILA. In addition, consumers who have been injured by any violation (except for the advertising provisions) have the right to file suit.

Home Loans
Mortgage Loans

TILA prohibits unfair, abusive, or deceptive home mortgage lending practices. In what seems like an exercise in stating the obvious, TILA (as amended by the Dodd-Frank Wall Street Reform and Consumer Protection Act):

- Requires lenders to make a good-faith effort to determine whether a borrower can afford to repay the loan,

- Prohibits lenders from coercing or bribing an appraiser into misstating a home's value, and

- Bans prepayment penalties on adjustable rate mortgages.

TILA also regulates so-called **subprime loans** (also known as **higher-priced mortgage loans**). These are loans that have an above-market interest rate because they involve high-risk borrowers.[6] For subprime loans, a lender:

- Must collect property taxes and homeowners insurance for all first mortgages.

- May not make loans that have balloon payments (very large payments at the end).

- May not charge excessive late fees.

Subprime loan

A loan that has an above-market interest rate because the borrower is high-risk.

Home Equity Loans

Scam artists sometimes prey upon the elderly, who are vulnerable to pressure, and upon the poor, who may not have access to conventional financing. These swindlers offer home equity loans, secured by a second mortgage, to finance fraudulent repairs. (There are, of course, many legitimate lenders in the home equity business.) The following news report shows scam artists at work:

> Mack and Jacqueline Moon of East Baltimore hired a home improvement contractor to install a dropped ceiling, paneling, and cabinets in the unfinished basement of their rowhouse. The couple was determined not to put a second mortgage on their house, anticipating they would need backup money to pay medical expenses for their 10-year-old daughter, who had lupus. They signed the contract a few days later after a second salesman assured them, "We were able to work it out, and you don't have to worry about a mortgage." The Moons were never given copies of the loan documents nor told of the 17 percent interest rate. A year later, when they tried to use their home's equity to pay medical bills for their daughter, who had since died, they discovered they had given a second mortgage to the lender without knowing it.[7]

In response to such scams, Congress amended TILA to provide additional consumer safeguards for certain home equity installment loans. If a home equity installment loan:

- Has an APR (interest rate) that is more than 10 percentage points higher than Treasury securities, or

- The consumer must pay fees and points at closing that are higher than 8 percent of the total loan amount, then,

- At least three business days before the loan closing, the lender must notify the consumer that (1) he does not have to go through with the loan (even if he has signed the loan agreement) and (2) he could lose his house if he fails to make payments, and

- Loans that are for less than five years may not contain balloon payments (that is, a payment at the end that is more than twice the regular monthly payment).

Rescission

This change in the law came too late to help the Moons, but they found relief in a different TILA provision. Under TILA, consumers have the right to rescind a mortgage for up to three business days after the signing (including Saturdays). However, if the lender does not comply with the disclosure provisions of TILA, the consumer can rescind for up to three *years* from the date of the mortgage.

---

[6]In the official definition, subprime loans (also referred to as higher-priced loans) are first mortgages that have an APR 1.5 percentage points or more above the average prime offer rate or second mortgages that have an APR 3.5 percentage points or more above that index.

[7]Lorraine Mirabella, "With Hopes of Improving Their Homes, Many Owners Fall Prey to Loan Scams." Copyright 1994 by Baltimore Sun Company. Reproduced by permission of Baltimore Sun Company via Copyright Clearance Center.

The Moons were able to rescind the loan because the lender had not made adequate disclosure. This right of rescission does *not* apply to a *first* mortgage used to finance a house purchase or to any refinancing with the consumer's existing lender. (Note that some states have passed, and others are considering, predatory lending laws that more strictly regulate loans with high fees or interest rates.)

The table below summarizes the major provisions of TILA that we have discussed so far.

TILA applies to a transaction only if:	It is a consumer loan.
	The loan has a finance charge or will be repaid in more than four installments.
	The loan is for less than $51,800, is secured by a mortgage on real estate, or is a private education loan.
	The loan is made by someone in the business of offering credit.
In all loans regulated by TILA:	The disclosure must be clear and in meaningful sequence.
	The lender must disclose the finance charge and the APR.
For regular mortgage loans:	Lenders must verify the borrowers' ability to repay the loan. Lenders may not coerce or bribe an appraiser into misstating a home's value. Lenders cannot charge prepayment penalties on adjustable rate mortgages.
For subprime mortgage loans:	Loans with balloon payments are prohibited.
	Late fees are limited.

© Cengage Learning 2014

Credit Cards

Credit and debit cards are extremely important to most consumers, so lately they have come under increased scrutiny from Congress and the regulatory agencies.

Disclosure

TILA establishes disclosure rules for credit cards, which it calls **open-end credit**. This is a credit transaction in which the lender makes a *series* of loans that the consumer can repay at once or in installments. These rules apply to all consumer credit cards, such as VISA or MasterCard, which permit installment payments, and even to those, such as American Express, that require the full balance to be paid each month.

In any advertisement or solicitation, the lender must disclose:

- Credit terms.

- In the case of a *teaser rate*, it must clearly disclose that the rate is introductory, when it expires, and the permanent rate that will replace it.

Before establishing an open-end credit account, the lender must disclose to the consumer:

- When a finance charge will be imposed, and

- How the finance charge will be calculated (for example, whether it will be based on the account balance at the beginning of the billing cycle, the end, or somewhere in between).

In each monthly statement, the lender must disclose:

- The amount owed at the beginning of the billing cycle (the previous balance);

- Amounts and dates of all purchases, credits, and payments;

- Finance charges and late fees;

- The date by which a bill must be paid to avoid these charges; and

- Either the consequences of making the monthly minimum payment or a toll-free number that can be used to obtain such information.

Regulation of Credit Card Debt

Credit Card Act of 2009   During the economic crisis that began in 2008, many consumers struggled to pay their credit card bills. In response, Congress increased oversight of credit card companies by passing the Credit Card Act of 2009. Under the new rules, these companies:

- Cannot increase the interest rate, fees, or charges on balances a consumer has already run up unless she is more than 60 days late in making the minimum payment.

- Must give 45 days' notice before increasing a card's annual percentage rate (APR) or making any other significant change in credit terms (which gives the consumer a chance to pay off the bill ahead of the increase).

- Must re-evaluate any rate increase every six months, and then, if a decrease is warranted, it must occur within 45 days after the evaluation.

- Must give notice of the consumer's right to cancel a card and pay off the debt once the APR is changed.

- Cannot charge interest on fees or on a bill that is paid on time or during a grace period.

- Cannot charge late payment fees of more than $25 (unless one of the consumer's last six payments was late, in which case the fee may be up to $35 or the company can show that its costs justify a higher fee).

- Cannot charge late fees that are greater than the minimum payment owed.

- Cannot charge more than one fee per event, such as a single late payment.

- Must mail the bill at least 21 days before the due date, disclose what the due date is, and set the same due date each month.

- Cannot set due dates on weekends or in the middle of the day. If the payment arrives by 5 p.m. on the day it is due, or if it arrives on the weekend after a Friday due date, it is on time.

- Must warn consumers about the impact of making minimum-only payments.

- Must apply any payments to whichever debt on the card has the highest interest rate (say, a cash advance rather than a new purchase).

- Must offer consumers the right to set a fixed credit limit. Consumers cannot be charged a fee if the company accepts charges above that limit unless the consumer has agreed to the fee.

- Cannot issue credit cards to people under 21 unless the young person has income or the application is co-signed by someone who can afford to pay the bills, such as a parent or spouse. The co-signer must also approve any increase in the credit limit.

Ethics   Each of the rules in the previous section was aimed at eliminating existing practices. Looking at this list, would you judge any of these practices to be unethical? Banks argue that they will have to replace this lost income by charging other fees for, say, maintaining a basic checking account. What Life Principles should bankers apply when they set fees?

Liability

Stolen Cards   Your wallet is missing, and with it your cash, your driver's license, a photo of your dog, a Groupon, and—oh, no!—all your credit cards! It is a disaster, to be sure. But it could have been worse. There was a time when you would have been responsible for every charge a thief rang up. **Now, under TILA, you are liable only for the first $50 in charges the thief makes before you notify the credit card company.** If you call the company before any charges are made, you have no liability at all. But if, by the time you contact the company, a speedy robber has completely furnished her apartment on your card, you are still liable only for $50. Of course, if you carry a wallet full of cards, $50 for each one can add up to a sizable total. If the thief steals just your credit card number, but not the card itself, you are not liable for any unauthorized charges.

Disputes with Merchants   You use your credit card to buy a new tablet computer at ShadyComputers, but when you take it out of the box, it will not even turn on. You have a major $600 problem. But all is not lost. **In the event of a dispute between a customer and a merchant, the credit card company cannot bill the customer if** (1) she makes a good faith effort to resolve the dispute, (2) the dispute is for more than $50, and (3) the merchant is in the same state where she lives or is within 100 miles of her house.

What happens if the merchant and the consumer cannot resolve their dispute, or if the merchant is not in the same state as the consumer? Clearly, credit card companies do not want to be caught in the middle between consumer and merchant. In practice, they now require all merchants to sign a contract specifying that, in the event of a dispute between the merchant and a customer, the credit card company has the right to charge back the merchant's account. If a customer seems to have a reasonable claim against a merchant, the credit card company will typically transfer the credit it has given the merchant back to the customer's account. Of course, the merchant can try to sue the customer for any money owed.

Disputes with the Credit Card Company   The Fair Credit Billing Act (FCBA) provides additional protection for credit card holders (and for holders of so-called **revolving charge accounts**—such as those from stores). Is there anyone in America who has not sometime or other discovered an error in a credit card bill? Before Congress passed the FCBA in 1975, a dispute with a credit card company often deteriorated into an avalanche of threatening form letters that ignored any response from the hapless cardholder.

Under the FCBA:

- If, within 60 days of receipt of a bill, a consumer writes to a credit card company to complain about the bill, the company must acknowledge receipt of the complaint within 30 days.

- Within two billing cycles (but no more than 90 days), the credit card company must investigate the complaint and respond:

- In the case of an error, by correcting the mistake and notifying the consumer

- If there is no error, by writing to the consumer with an explanation

- Whether or not there was a mistake, if the consumer requests it, the credit card company must supply documentary evidence to support its position—for example, copies of the bill signed by the consumer or evidence that the package actually arrived.

- The credit card company cannot try to collect the disputed debt or close or suspend the account until it has responded to the consumer complaint.

- The credit card company cannot report to credit agencies that the consumer has an unpaid bill until 10 days after the response. If the consumer still disputes the charge, the credit card company may report the amount to a credit agency but must disclose that it is disputed.

In the following case, American Express made a big mistake picking on a law professor. The court's opinion was written by Abner J. Mikva, a highly regarded judge on the federal appeals court. He was clearly exasperated by American Express's arguments and used strong language to reprimand the company—and the lower court. Since Judge Mikva had served in Congress, he could speak with some authority about Congress's approach to consumer legislation.

GRAY V. AMERICAN EXPRESS CO.

743 F.2d 10, 240 U.S. App. D.C. 10, 1984 U.S. App. LEXIS 19033
United States Court of Appeals for the District of Columbia Circuit, 1984

Facts: In December, Oscar Gray used his American Express credit card to buy airline tickets costing $9,312. American Express agreed that Gray could pay for the tickets in 12 monthly installments. In January, Gray paid $3,500 and then in February, an additional $1,156. In March, American Express billed Gray by mistake for the entire remaining balance, which he did not pay. In April, Gray and his wife went out for dinner to celebrate their wedding anniversary. When he tried to pay with his American Express card, the restaurant told him that the credit card company had not only refused to accept the charges for the meal but had instructed the restaurant to confiscate and destroy the card. While still at the restaurant, Gray spoke on the telephone to an American Express employee, who informed him, "Your account is canceled as of now."

Gray wrote to American Express, pointing out the error. For more than a year, the company failed to respond to Gray or to investigate his claim. It then turned the bill over to a collection agency. Gray sued American Express for violating the Fair Credit Billing Act. The trial court granted summary judgment to American Express and dis-

missed the complaint on the grounds that Gray had waived his rights under the Act.

Issue: *Is American Express liable to Gray for violating the FCBA?*

Excerpts from Judge Mikva's Decision: The contract between Gray and American Express provides: "We can revoke your right to use [the card] at any time. We can do this with or without cause and without giving you notice." American Express concludes from this language that the cancellation was not of the kind prohibited by the Act, even though the Act regulates other aspects of the relationship between the cardholder and the card issuer.

[T]he Act states that, during the pendency of a disputed billing, the card issuer shall not cause the cardholder's account to be restricted or closed because of the failure of the obligor to pay the amount in dispute. American Express seems to argue that, despite that provision, it can exercise its right to cancellation for cause unrelated to the disputed amount, or for no cause, thus bringing itself out from under the statute. At the very least, the argument is audacious. American Express would restrict the efficacy of the statute to those situations where the parties had not agreed to a "without cause, without notice" cancellation clause, or to those cases where the cardholder can prove that the sole reason for cancellation was the amount in dispute. We doubt that Congress painted with such a faint brush.

The effect of American Express's argument is to allow the equivalent of a "waiver" of coverage of the Act simply by allowing the parties to contract it away. Congress usually is not so tepid in its approach to consumer problems. The rationale of consumer protection legislation is to even out the inequalities that consumers normally bring to the bargain. To allow such protection to be waived by boiler plate language of the contract puts the legislative process to a foolish and unproductive task. A court ought not impute such nonsense to a Congress intent on correcting abuses in the market place.

The district court's order of summary judgment and dismissal is hereby *vacated*.

> Debit cards look and feel like credit cards, but legally they are a different plastic altogether.

Check card
Another name for a debit card.

Debit Cards
Liability

So your wallet is missing, and with it your *debit* card. No problem, right—it is just like a credit card? Wrong. Debit cards look and feel like credit cards, but legally they are a different plastic altogether. Debit cards work like checks (which is why they are also called **check cards**). When you use your debit card, the bank deducts money directly from your account, which means there is no bill to pay at the end of the month (and no interest charges on unpaid bills). That is the good news.

The bad news is that your liability for a stolen debit card is much greater. If you report the loss before anyone uses your card, you are not liable for any unauthorized withdrawals. If you report the theft within two days of discovering it, the bank will make good on all losses above $50. If you wait until after two days, your bank will only replace stolen funds above $500. After 60 days of receipt of your bank statement, all losses are yours: the bank will not repay any stolen funds. If an unauthorized transfer takes place using just your number, not your card, then you are not liable at all as long as you report the loss within 60 days of receiving the bank statement showing the loss. After 60 days, however, you are liable for the full amount.

Fees

Many people like to use debit cards to help keep track of their spending and to avoid paying the interest rates on credit cards. However, traditionally there was a large downside to debit cards: banks would charge a flat fee of $20 to $30 *each time* cardholders overdrew their bank account, no matter how small the overdraft. A customer could easily be charged $150 in overdraft fees on $50 worth of overdrafts. Suppose that someone makes a $20 overdraft that he repays in two weeks, but in the meantime, he incurs a $27 fee. In that case, he has paid an interest rate of 3,520 percent.

Under new rules, though, banks are not allowed to overdraw an account and charge the fee unless the consumer signs up for an overdraft plan. Of course, this rule means that consumers who do not "opt in" to the overdraft plan will not be allowed to overdraw their account, no matter how desperate they are. (The same rule applies to ATM withdrawals.)

Credit Reports
Accuracy of Credit Reports

Gossip and rumor can cause great harm. Bad enough when whispered behind one's back, worse yet when placed in files and distributed to potential creditors. Most adults rely on credit—to acquire a house, credit cards, overdraft privileges at the bank, or even obtain a job or rent an apartment. A sullied credit report makes life immensely more difficult. A number of statutes, including the Fair Credit Reporting Act (FCRA), the Fair and Accurate Credit Transactions Act (FACTA), and Dodd-Frank regulate credit reports.

Consumer reporting agencies are businesses that supply consumer reports to third parties. A **consumer report** is any communication about a consumer's creditworthiness, character, general reputation, or lifestyle that is considered as a factor in establishing credit, obtaining insurance, securing a job, acquiring a government license, or for any other *legitimate business* need.

Under the FCRA:

- A consumer reporting agency cannot report obsolete information. Ordinary credit information is obsolete after seven years, bankruptcies after 10 years. (But if a consumer is applying for more than $150,000 of credit or life insurance, or for a job that pays more than $75,000 a year, then there is no time limit.)

- **Investigative reports** that discuss character, reputation, or lifestyle become obsolete in three *months*. An investigative report cannot be ordered without first informing the consumer.

- A consumer reporting agency cannot report medical information without the consumer's permission.

- An employer cannot request a consumer report on any current or potential employee without the employee's permission. An employer cannot take action because of information in the consumer report without first giving the current or potential employee a copy of the report and a description of the employee's rights under this statute.

- Anyone who makes an adverse decision against a consumer because of a credit report must reveal the name and address of the reporting agency that supplied the information. An "adverse decision" includes denying credit or charging higher rates.

- Upon request from a consumer, a reporting agency must disclose all information in his file, the source of the information (except for investigative reports), the name of anyone to whom a report has been sent in the prior year (two years for employment purposes), and the name of anyone who has requested a report in the prior year.

- If a consumer tells an agency that some of the information in his file is incorrect, the agency must both investigate and forward the data to the information provider. The information provider must investigate and report the results to the agency. If the data are inaccurate, the information provider must so notify all national credit agencies. The consumer also has the right to give the agency a short report telling his side of the story. The agency must then include the consumer's statement with any credit reports it supplies and also, at the consumer's request, send the statement to anyone who has received a report within six months (or two years for employment purposes).

Investigative reports
Reports that discuss character, reputation or lifestyle. They become obsolete in three months.

EXAM Strategy

Question: Edo applied for insurance with Geico. In calculating his premium, Geico looked at his credit history and his financial circumstances. It did not offer him the best possible premium, but this was because of his current finances, not his credit history. Was this an "adverse decision" under the FCRA, and was Geico required to notify him?

Strategy: Review the requirements of the FCRA. An adverse decision means that Edo was worse off because of a bad credit report.

Result: Edo's premium was based on his *current* situation, not his credit history. Therefore, Geico did not have to notify Edo of an adverse decision because his premium would have been the same even if his credit report had been neutral.

Access to Credit Reports and Credit Scores

Under FACTA, consumers are entitled by law to one free credit report every year from each of the three major reporting agencies: Equifax, Experian, and TransUnion. You can order these reports at **https://www.annualcreditreport.com**. Consumer advocates recommend that you check your credit reports every year to make sure they are accurate and that no one else has been obtaining credit in your name. If you find any errors, notify the agency in writing and warn it that failing to make corrections is a violation of the law. (Note, though, that many websites with similar names *pretend* to offer a free credit report but instead enroll customers in paid programs to monitor their credit reports. Be sure to go to the right website.)

Although your credit report is valuable information, you do not know how creditors will evaluate it. For that, you need to know your credit score (usually called a FICO score).[8] This number (which ranges between 300 and 850) is based on your credit report and is supposed to predict your ability to pay your bills. However, it is not automatically included as part of your credit report. But now, under Dodd-Frank, anyone who penalizes you because of your score has to give it to you for free, as well as information about how your score compares with others.

Identity Theft

In identity theft, a fraudster steals the victim's personal information, such as social security number, credit card information, or mother's maiden name, and uses it to obtain credit or goods in the victim's name and otherwise wreak havoc in the victim's life. One goal of FACTA was to reduce identity theft. Therefore, in addition to your right to a free credit report each year, FACTA also created the National Fraud Alert System, which permits consumers who fear they may be the victim of identity theft to place an alert in their credit files, warning financial institutions to investigate carefully before issuing any new credit. It also requires credit bureaus to share information about identity theft.

A fraud alert does not prevent identity theft—culprits may still be able to open a new account or obtain a credit card. Therefore, many states permit a "security freeze," which prohibits any access to a consumer's credit report. Once an account is frozen, no one, including the consumer, can obtain a new line of credit. The downside is that to obtain new credit, the consumer must pay a fee to thaw the account.

Also, under the Gramm-Leach-Bliley Privacy Act of 1999, banks, other financial institutions, and consumer reporting agencies must notify a consumer (1) before disclosing any personal information to a third party or (2) if there has been unauthorized access to the

[8]It is called a FICO score because it was developed by the Fair Isaac Corporation.

consumer's sensitive personal information.[9] The company cannot disclose private information if the consumer *opts out* (that is, denies permission).

Debt Collection

Have you ever fallen behind on your car payments? That is hardly a crime—but in the past, debt collectors might have *treated* you as a criminal. They might have threatened to arrest you. Or they might have changed the password on your cell-phone account and obtained your cell-phone records so that they could pose as a police officer and call your friends, relatives, and past employers to tell them there was an arrest warrant out for you, even if this was not true.

It is bad enough to be hassled over a debt that one does, in fact, owe, but many times, consumers are threatened and harangued for debts that are not legitimate. Indeed, this author has had such an experience: a hospital billed the wrong insurance company and then notified her (at the wrong address) when the insurance company did not pay. When she failed to pay a bill she had never received and did not owe, the hospital turned it over to a collector who, in violation of state law, called her to yell, harangue, and threaten. In the end, all was resolved (she is, after all, a lawyer aware of her rights), but the experience was terribly unpleasant. Typically, companies sell their consumer debts for pennies on the dollar to collection agencies that are not overly scrupulous in ascertaining whether the debt is legitimate. Hoping for a little help from Washington? In a recent year, the FTC received 66,000 complaints about debt collectors, yet it brought enforcement action against only 10 companies.

The Fair Debt Collection Practices Act (FDCPA) is designed to protect consumers from abusive debt collection efforts. This statute provides that a collector must, within five days of contacting a debtor, send the debtor a written notice containing the amount of the debt, the name of the creditor to whom the debt is owed, and a statement that if the debtor disputes the debt (in writing), the collector will cease all collection efforts until it has sent evidence of the debt. **Also, under the FDCPA, collectors may not:**

- Call or write a debtor who has notified the collector in writing that he wishes no further contact,

- Call or write a debtor who is represented by an attorney,

- Call a debtor before 8:00 a.m. or after 9:00 p.m.,

- Threaten a debtor or use obscene or abusive language,

- Call or visit the debtor at work if the consumer's employer prohibits such contact,

- Imply that they are attorneys or government representatives when they are not, or use a false name,

- Threaten to arrest consumers who do not pay their debts,

- Make other false or deceptive threats—that is, threats that would be illegal if carried out or which the collector has no intention of doing—such as suing the debtor or seizing property,

- Contact acquaintances of the debtor for any reason other than to locate the debtor (and then only once), or

- Tell acquaintances that the consumer is in debt.

Of course, these rules do not prevent the collector from filing suit against the debtor.

In the event of a violation of the FDCPA, the debtor is entitled to damages, court costs, and attorney's fees. The FTC also has authority to enforce the Act.

---

[9] 15 U.S.C. §6801.

In the following case, a collection agency skates close to the edge. Does it go too far?

You be the Judge

BROWN V. CARD SERVICE CENTER

464 F.3d 450; 2006 U.S. App. LEXIS 24579
United States Court of Appeals for the Third Circuit, 2006

Facts: Card Service Center (CSC) sent Elizabeth Brown a collection letter demanding payment of a delinquent credit card balance of $1,874. The letter said:

> "You are requested to contact the Recovery Unit of the Card Service Center…to discuss your account. Refusal to cooperate could result in a legal suit being filed for collection of the account.
>
> You now have five (5) days to make arrangements for payment of this account. Failure on your part to cooperate could result in our forwarding this account to our attorney with directions to continue collection efforts."

Brown did not contact CSC within five days, and CSC did nothing other than send her more collection letters.

Brown filed suit, alleging that CSC had violated the FDCPA. She alleged that the letter was deceptive because the company never had any intention of carrying out its threats. The district court granted CSC's motion to dismiss. Brown appealed.

Issue: *Did CSC's letter violate the FDCPA?*

Argument for Brown: CSC's letter indicated that there were two options: a lawsuit or referral to an attorney. Neither happened, and CSC knew when it sent the letter that neither would happen. This letter was an empty threat, plain and simple— exactly the type of behavior the FDCPA prohibits. It is deceptive for CSC to assert that it *could* take an action that it had no intention of taking and has never or very rarely taken before.

It is possible that a sophisticated debtor would realize that CSC had no intention of filing suit against Brown, but the point of the FCDPA is to protect all consumers, even those who are unsophisticated. As Supreme Court Justice Hugo Black observed, our laws "are made to protect the trusting as well as the suspicious."

Argument for CSC: The letter said "could," not "will." It did not imply that legal action was imminent, only that it was possible. This was not a threat, it was a statement of fact— CSC could file suit if it wanted. That was an option available to CSC, whether or not the company elected to pursue it.

Equal Credit Opportunity Act

The Equal Credit Opportunity Act (ECOA) prohibits any creditor from discriminating against a borrower because of race, color, religion, national origin, sex, marital status, age (as long as the borrower is old enough to enter into a legal contract), or because the borrower is receiving welfare. A lender must respond to a credit application within 30 days. If a lender rejects an application, it must either tell the applicant why or notify him that he has the right to a written explanation of the reasons for this adverse action.

As an example of the types of abuses that the ECOA is designed to prevent, consider the plight of this African American couple. Florence and Joe made an offer to buy a new home at the Meadowood housing development near Tampa. The developer accepted their offer, contingent upon their obtaining a mortgage. When the couple filed an application with Rancho Mortgage and Investment Corp., they were surprised by the hostility of Rancho's loan processor. She requested information they had already supplied and repeatedly questioned them about whether they intended to occupy the house, which was about 80 miles from their jobs. Florence and Joe insisted they wanted to live near their son and daughter-in-law and escape city crime. Rancho turned down their mortgage, refusing to give either an oral or a written explanation. The house was sold to another buyer.

Joe and Florence didn't get mad, they got even. They sued under the ECOA. Rancho was ordered to pay damages to the couple.[10]

As the following case illustrates, the ECOA protects against a broad range of wrongdoing.

TREADWAY v. GATEWAY CHEVROLET OLDSMOBILE INC.

362 F.3d 971, 2004 U.S. App. LEXIS 6325
United States Court of Appeals for the Seventh Circuit, 2004

Facts: Gateway Chevrolet Oldsmobile, a car dealership, sent an unsolicited letter to Tonja Treadway notifying her that she was "pre-approved" for the financing to purchase a car. Gateway did not provide financing itself; instead, it arranged loans through banks or finance companies.

Treadway called the dealer to say that she was interested in purchasing a used car. She divulged her social security number so that Gateway could obtain her credit report. Based on this report, the dealer determined that Treadway was not eligible for financing. This was not surprising, given that Gateway had purchased Treadway's name from a list of people who had recently filed for bankruptcy.

Instead of applying for a loan on behalf of Treadway, Gateway called her and invited her to come to the dealership. There, she was told that Gateway had found a bank that would finance her transaction, but only if she purchased a new car and provided a co-signer. Treadway agreed to purchase a new car and came up with Pearlie Smith, her godmother, to serve as a co-signer.

Concerned as it was with customer convenience, Gateway had an agent deliver papers directly to Smith's house to be signed immediately. If Smith had read the papers before she signed them, she might have realized that she had committed herself to be the sole purchaser and owner of the car. But she had no idea that she was the owner until she began receiving bills on the car loan. After Treadway made the first payment on behalf of Smith, both women refused to pay more—Smith because she did not want a new car; Treadway because the car was not hers. The car was repossessed, but the financing company continued to demand payment.

On closer inspection, it appears that Gateway was running a scam. It would lure desperate prospects off the bankruptcy rolls and into the showroom with promises of financing for a used car, and then sell a new car to their

"co-signer" (who was, in fact, the sole signer). Instead of selling a used car to Tonja Treadway, Gateway sold a new car to Pearlie Smith.

Treadway filed suit against Gateway, alleging that it had violated the ECOA by not notifying her that it had taken an adverse action against her. The district court granted Gateway's motion for summary judgment on the grounds that Gateway had not committed an adverse action under the ECOA. An appeal followed.

Issue: *Did Gateway violate the ECOA?*

Excerpts from Judge Cudahy's Decision: The term "adverse action" is defined in relevant part by the ECOA as "a denial or revocation of credit." By unilaterally deciding not to send Treadway's application to *any* lender, Gateway effectively denied credit to Treadway. Whether it is the lender or the dealership that makes the decision, both the action and the outcome are the same. In both cases, the decision maker (1) reviews the applicant's credit report to determine whether she is creditworthy, (2) makes a determination adverse to the applicant (i.e., that she is not creditworthy), (3) decides not to proceed any further in arranging credit and (4) as a result the applicant is not granted credit. There is no logical reason why these same steps would be considered an "adverse action" when taken by a lender but not when taken by a dealership, given that the result is the same in either case.

If an automobile dealership that decides against referring a particular applicant to any lender need not provide notice of this decision to the applicant, then it becomes significantly easier for it to discriminate. [I]f an applicant never receives notice, it will be difficult for her to ever determine that she was the victim of discrimination. This is particularly true because, as was the case here, without proper notice, the applicant may assume that her application *was* sent to lenders, and it was the lenders who did

[10]Robert J. Bruss, "Home Buyers Sue Mortgage Lender for Racial Discrimination," *Tampa Tribune*, November 5, 1994, p. 3.

the rejecting. Car dealers could throw the credit report of every minority applicant in the "circular file" and none would be the wiser.

Therefore, based on the foregoing analysis, we find that Gateway's action constitutes an "adverse action" for purposes of the ECOA.

Consumer Leasing Act

If you, like many other consumers, lease a car rather than buy it, you are protected under the Consumer Leasing Act (CLA). The CLA does not apply to any lease for more than $50,000 or to the rental of real property—that is, to house or apartment leases. **Before a lease is signed, a lessor must disclose the following in writing:**

- All required payments, including deposits, down payments, taxes, and license fees,

- The number and amount of each monthly payment and how payments are calculated,

- Balloon payments (that is, payments due at the end of the lease),

- Required insurance payments,

- Annual mileage allowance,

- The total amount the consumer will have paid by the end of the lease,

- Available warranties,

- Maintenance requirements and a description of the lessor's wear and use standards,

- Penalties for late payments,

- The consumer's right to purchase the leased property, and at what price,

- The consumer's right to terminate a lease early, and

- Any penalties for early termination.

EXAM Strategy

Question: Clyde goes into a Tesla dealership to investigate buying an electric sports car. He does not look as if he can afford a six-figure purchase, so the sales staff orders a credit report on him. After all, no point in wasting their time. Do they have the right to order a report on Clyde? Which consumer statute applies?

Strategy: The FCRA regulates the issuance of consumer reports. These reports can be used only for a legitimate business need.

Result: A car dealership cannot obtain a consumer report on someone who simply asks general questions about prices and financing or who wants to test-drive a car; nor can the dealer order a report to use in negotiations. However, a dealer has the right to a report that is needed to arrange financing requested by the consumer or to verify a buyer's creditworthiness when he presents a personal check to pay for the vehicle.

MAGNUSON-MOSS WARRANTY ACT

When Senator Frank E. Moss sponsored the Magnuson-Moss Warranty Act, this is how he explained the need for such a statute:

> [W]arranties have for many years confused, misled, and frequently angered American consumers.... Consumer anger is expected when purchasers of consumer products discover that their warranty may cover a 25-cent part but not the $100 labor charge, or that there is full coverage on a piano so long as it is shipped at the purchaser's expense to the factory.... There is a growing need to generate consumer understanding by clearly and conspicuously disclosing the terms and conditions of the warranty and by telling the consumer what to do if his guaranteed product becomes defective or malfunctions.[11]

The Magnuson-Moss Warranty Act does not require manufacturers or sellers to provide a warranty on their products. **The Act does require any supplier that offers a written warranty on a consumer product that costs more than $15 to disclose the terms of the warranty in simple, understandable language** *before the sale*. This statute applies only to written warranties on goods (not services) sold to consumers. It does cover sales by catalog or on the Internet. Required disclosure includes the following:

- The name and address of the person the consumer should contact to obtain warranty service,
- The parts that are covered and those that are not,
- What services the warrantor will provide, at whose expense, and for what period of time, and
- A statement of what the consumer must do and what expenses he must pay.

Although suppliers are not required to offer a warranty, if they do offer one, they must indicate whether it is *full* or *limited*. Under a **full warranty,** the warrantor must promise to fix a defective product for a reasonable time without charge. If, after a reasonable number of efforts to fix the defective product, it still does not work, the consumer must have the right to a refund or a replacement without charge; but the warrantor is not required to cover damage caused by the consumer's unreasonable use.

CONSUMER PRODUCT SAFETY

In 1969, the federal government estimated that consumer products caused 30,000 deaths, 110,000 disabling injuries, and 20 million trips to the doctor. Toys were among the worst offenders, injuring 700,000 children a year. Children were cut by Etch-a-Sketch glass panels, choked by Zulu gun darts, and burned by Little Lady toy ovens. Although injured consumers had the right to seek damages under tort law, the goal of the Consumer Product Safety Act of 1972 (CPSA) was to prevent injuries in the first place. This act created the Consumer Product Safety Commission (CPSC) to evaluate consumer products and develop safety standards. Manufacturers must report all potentially hazardous product defects within 24 hours of discovery. The Commission can impose civil and criminal penalties on those who violate its standards. Individuals have the right to sue under the CPSA for damages, including attorney's fees, from anyone who knowingly violates a consumer product safety

---

[11]Quoted in David G. Epstein and Steve H. Nickles, *Consumer Law* (Eagan, Minn.: West, 1981).

rule. You can find out about product recalls or file a report on an unsafe product at the Commission's website (**http://www.cpsc.gov**) or at **saferproducts.gov**.

Ethics   Imagine that you are Robert Eckert, chairman and CEO of Mattel, Inc. Your company has sold millions of Jeep Wrangler Power Wheels. These toys are designed for children as young as two years old. You have just been notified that 150 of the cars have caught on fire, while thousands of others have overheated. In some cases, these toys have burned so fiercely that they have caught their garages on fire, endangering all of the home's occupants. You know that under CPSC rules, you are required to report toy defects within 24 hours. You also know that making the required report could have a significant impact on Mattel's profitability. What would you do?

Mattel decided to figure out what the problem was before reporting anything to the CPSC. In the end, it delayed months. Eckert was quoted as saying that the law was unreasonable and the company would not follow it.[12]

Is Mattel's stance ethical? What Life Principle is he applying?

Chapter Conclusion

Virtually no one will go through life without reading an advertisement, ordering online, borrowing money, acquiring a credit report, or using a consumer product. It is important to know your rights.

EXAM REVIEW

1. **UNFAIR PRACTICES** The Federal Trade Commission (FTC) prohibits "unfair and deceptive acts or practices." A practice is unfair if it violates public policy or if it meets the following three tests:

   • It causes a substantial consumer injury.

   • The harm of the injury outweighs any countervailing benefit.

   • The consumer could not reasonably avoid the injury. (pp. 687–689)

2. **DECEPTIVE ADVERTISEMENTS** The FTC considers an advertisement to be deceptive if it contains an important misrepresentation or omission that is likely to mislead a reasonable consumer. (pp. 687–688)

3. **BAIT-AND-SWITCH** FTC rules prohibit bait-and-switch advertisements. A merchant may not advertise a product and then disparage it to consumers in an effort to sell a different item. (p. 689)

---

[12]Based on an article by Nicholas Casey and Andy Pasztor, "Safety Agency, Mattel Clash Over Disclosures," *The Wall Street Journal*, September 4, 2007, p. A1.

4. **MERCHANDISE BOUGHT BY MAIL, BY TELEPHONE, OR ONLINE** Under FTC rules for this type of merchandise, sellers must ship an item within the time stated or, if no time is given, within 30 days after receipt of the order. (p. 689)

5. **DO-NOT-CALL REGISTRY** The FTC prohibits telemarketers from calling telephone numbers listed on its do-not-call registry. Telemarketers may not make robocalls unless without written permission from the person being called. (p. 690)

6. **UNORDERED MERCHANDISE** Consumers may keep as a gift any unordered merchandise that they receive in the mail. (p. 690)

7. **DOOR-TO-DOOR RULES** Under the FTC door-to-door rules, a salesperson is required to notify the buyer that she has the right to cancel the transaction prior to midnight of the third business day thereafter. (p. 690)

8. **TILA DISCLOSURE** In all loans regulated by the Truth in Lending Act, the disclosure must be clear and in meaningful sequence. The lender must disclose the finance charge and the annual percentage rate. (pp. 691–692)

9. **MORTGAGES** Lenders must make a good faith effort to determine whether a borrower can afford to repay the loan. They may not coerce or bribe an appraiser into misstating a home's value. Nor may they charge prepayment penalties on adjustable rate mortgages. (pp. 692–693)

10. **SUBPRIME LOANS** For subprime loans, a lender:

    - May not make loans with balloon payments.

    - Is limited in the late fees it may charge. (p. 693)

11. **HOME EQUITY LOANS** In the case of a high-rate home equity loan, the lender must notify the consumer at least three business days before the closing that (1) he does not have to go through with the loan (even if he has signed the loan agreement) and (2) he could lose his house if he fails to make payments. If the duration of a high-rate home equity loan is less than five years, it may not contain balloon payments. (p. 693)

12. **RESCINDING A MORTGAGE** Under TILA, consumers have the right to rescind a mortgage (other than a first mortgage) for three business days after the signing if the lender is not the same as for the first mortgage. If the lender does not comply with the disclosure provisions of TILA, the consumer may rescind for up to three years from the date of the mortgage. (pp. 693–694)

EXAM Strategy

Question: In August, Ethel went to First American Mortgage and Loan Association of Virginia (the Bank) to sign a second mortgage on her home. Her first mortgage was with a different bank. She left the closing without a copy of the required TILA disclosure forms. Ethel defaulted on her loan payments, and, the following May, the Bank began foreclosure proceedings on her house. In June, she notified the Bank that she wished to rescind the loan. Does Ethel have a right to rescind the loan 10 months after it was made?

> **Strategy:** In questions about mortgages, it is important to notice if the question involves a first or subsequent mortgage because the rules are different. Also, it matters whether the bank is the same for both mortgages. (See the "Result" at the end of this section.)

13. **CREDIT V. DEBIT CARDS** Under TILA, a *credit* card holder is liable only for the first $50 in unauthorized charges made before the credit card company is notified that the card was stolen. If, however, you wait more than two days to report the loss of a *debit* card, your bank will reimburse you only for losses in excess of $500. If you fail to report the lost debit card within 60 days of receipt of your bank statement, the bank is not liable at all. (pp. 694–698)

14. **CREDIT CARD DEBT** Credit card companies cannot increase the interest rate, fees, or charges on balances unless the consumer is more than 60 days late in making the minimum payment, nor can they charge interest or fees on a bill that is paid on time or during the grace period. Credit card companies must give 45 days' notice before increasing a card's APR. (pp. 695–696)

15. **CREDIT CARD DISPUTE** In the event of a dispute between a customer and a merchant, the credit card company cannot bill the customer if:

    * She makes a good faith effort to resolve the dispute,

    * The dispute is for more than $50, and

    * The merchant is in the same state where she lives or is within 100 miles of her house. (pp. 696–697)

16. **MORE CREDIT CARD DISPUTES** Under the Fair Credit Billing Act, a credit card company must promptly investigate and respond to any consumer complaints about a credit card bill. (pp. 696–697)

17. **DEBIT CARD FEES** Banks may not overdraw an account and charge an overdraft fee unless the consumer signs up for an overdraft plan. (p. 698)

18. **CREDIT REPORTS** Under the Fair Credit Reporting Act:

    * A consumer report can be used only for a legitimate business need,

    * A consumer reporting agency cannot report obsolete information,

    * An employer cannot request a consumer report on any current or potential employee without the employee's permission, and

    * Anyone who makes an adverse decision against a consumer because of a credit report must reveal the name and address of the reporting agency that supplied the negative information. (pp. 699–700)

19. **ACCESS TO CREDIT REPORTS AND CREDIT SCORES** The Fair and Accurate Credit Transactions Act permits consumers to obtain one free credit report every year from each of the three major reporting agencies. Also, anyone who penalizes a consumer because of her credit score must give it to her at no charge. (p. 700)

20. **DEBT COLLECTION** Under the Fair Debt Collection Practices Act, a debt collector may not harass or abuse debtors. (pp. 701–702)

21. **ECOA** The Equal Credit Opportunity Act prohibits any creditor from discriminating against a borrower on the basis of race, color, religion, national origin, sex, marital status, age, or because the borrower is receiving welfare. (pp. 702–703)

EXAM Strategy

Question: Kathleen, a single woman, applied for an Exxon credit card. Exxon rejected her application without giving any specific reason and without providing the name of the credit bureau it had used. When Kathleen asked for a reason for the rejection, she was told that the credit bureau did not have enough information about her to establish creditworthiness. In fact, Exxon had denied her credit application because she did not have a major credit card or a savings account, she had been employed for only one year, and she had no dependents. Did Exxon violate the law?

Strategy: Exxon violated two laws. Review the statutes in the "Consumer Credit" section of the chapter. (See the "Result" at the end of this section.)

22. **CONSUMER LEASING ACT** This statute applies to any lease up to $50,000 (except for real property). The lessor is required to make certain disclosures before the lease is signed. (p. 704)

23. **WARRANTIES** The Magnuson-Moss Warranty Act requires any supplier that offers a written warranty on a consumer product costing more than $15 to disclose the terms of the warranty in simple and readily understandable language before the sale. (p. 705)

24. **CONSUMER PRODUCT SAFETY** The Consumer Product Safety Commission evaluates consumer products and develops safety standards. (pp. 705–706)

EXAM Strategy

Question: Joel was two years old and his brother, Joshua, was three when their father left both children asleep in the rear seat of his automobile while visiting a friend. A cigarette lighter was on the dashboard of the car. After awaking, Joshua began playing with the lighter and set fire to Joel's diaper. Do the parents have a claim against the manufacturer of the lighter under the Consumer Product Safety Act?

Strategy: The CPSA regulates unsafe products. Was the cigarette lighter unsafe? (See the "Result" at the end of this section.)

> **12. Result:** Ethel entered into a second mortgage that was not from the same bank as her first mortgage. Therefore, under TILA, Ethel had an automatic right to rescind for three business days. However, because the lender did not give the required forms to her at the closing, she could rescind for up to three years.
>
> **21. Result:** The court held that Exxon violated both the Fair Credit Reporting Act (FCRA) and the Equal Credit Opportunity Act (ECOA). The FCRA requires Exxon to tell Kathleen the name of the credit bureau that it used. Under the ECOA, Exxon was required to tell Kathleen the real reasons for the credit denial.
>
> **24. Result:** The court held that the plaintiff did not have a claim because there was no evidence that the manufacturer had knowingly violated a consumer product safety rule.

MULTIPLE-CHOICE QUESTIONS

1. Dell advertised that a computer came with particular software. In fact, the software was not available for several months. Instead, Dell sent customers a coupon for the software "when available." What did Dell do wrong?

   I.   Failed to offer buyers the opportunity to cancel their orders
   II. Did not automatically cancel the orders
   III. Did not ship the software within 30 days

   (a) I and II
   (b) I, II, and III
   (c) I and III
   (d) II and III

2.
GET ENOUGH BROADLOOM TO CARPET ANY AREA OF YOUR HOME OR APARTMENT UP TO 150 SQUARE FEET CUT, MEASURED, AND READY FOR INSTALLATION FOR ONLY $77. GET 100% DUPONT CONTINUOUS FILAMENT NYLON PILE BROADLOOM. CALL COLLECT

   When customers called the number provided, New Rapids Carpet Center, Inc., sent salespeople to visit them at home to sell them carpet that was not as advertised—it was not continuous filament nylon pile broadloom, and the price was not $77. What set of rules has New Rapids violated?

   (a) Unordered merchandise
   (b) Consumer Product Safety Act
   (c) Bait-and-switch
   (d) Fair Credit Reporting Act

3. Which of the following laws set limits on interest rates?

   (a) State usury laws
   (b) TILA and state usury laws
   (c) TILA
   (d) None; there are no limits on interest rates.

4. Companies must obtain permission from a consumer before charging for overdrafts on:

   (a) debit cards.

   (b) credit cards.

   (c) neither

   (d) both

5. You notice a charge on your credit card bill of $149.99 for a kayak. This seems very strange to you because you have not purchased a kayak. What do you need to do to avoid having to pay this charge?

   (a) Call the store.

   (b) Call the credit card company.

   (c) Write the store.

   (d) Write the credit card company.

ESSAY QUESTIONS

1. **YOU BE THE JUDGE WRITING PROBLEM** Process cheese food slices must contain at least 51 percent natural cheese. Imitation cheese slices, by contrast, contain little or no natural cheese and consist primarily of water, vegetable oil, flavoring, and fortifying agents. Kraft, Inc., makes Kraft Singles, which are individually wrapped process cheese food slices. When Kraft began losing market share to imitation slices that were advertised as both less expensive and equally nutritious as Singles, Kraft responded with a series of advertisements informing consumers that Kraft Singles cost more than imitation slices because they are made from 5 ounces of milk. Kraft does use 5 ounces of milk in making each Kraft Single, but 30 percent of the calcium contained in the milk is lost during processing. Imitation slices contain the same amount of calcium as Kraft Singles. Are the Kraft advertisements deceptive? **Argument for Kraft:** This statement is completely true—Kraft does use 5 ounces of milk in each Kraft Single. The FTC is assuming that the only value of milk is the calcium. In fact, people might prefer having milk rather than vegetable oil, regardless of the calcium. **Argument for the FTC:** It is deceptive to advertise more milk if the calcium is the same after all the processing.

2. Josephine was a 60-year-old widow who suffered from high blood pressure and epilepsy. A bill collector from Collections Accounts Terminal, Inc., called her and demanded that she pay $56 she owed to Cabrini Hospital. She told him that Medicare was supposed to pay the bill. Shortly thereafter, Josephine received a letter from Collections that stated:

   > You have shown that you are unwilling to work out a friendly settlement with us to clear the above debt. Our field investigator has now been instructed to make an investigation in your neighborhood and to personally call on your employer. The immediate payment of the full amount, or a personal visit to this office, will spare you this embarrassment.

   Has Collections violated the law?

3. Thomas worked at a Sherwin-Williams paint store that James managed. Thomas and James had a falling out when, according to Thomas, "a relationship began to bloom between Thomas and one of the young female employees, the one James was obsessed with." After Thomas quit, James claimed that Thomas owed the store $121. Sherwin-Williams reported this information to the Chilton credit reporting agency. Thomas sent a letter to Chilton disputing the accuracy of the Sherwin-Williams charges. Chilton contacted James who confirmed that Thomas still owed the money. Chilton failed to note in Thomas's file that a dispute was pending. Thereafter, two of Thomas's requests for credit cards were denied. Have James and Chilton violated the Fair Credit Reporting Act?

4. In October, Renie Guimond discovered that her credit report at TransUnion incorrectly stated that she was married, used the name "Ruth Guimond," and had a credit card from Saks Fifth Avenue. After she reported the errors, TransUnion wrote her in November to say that it had removed this information. However, in March, TransUnion again published the erroneous information. The following October, TransUnion finally removed the incorrect information from her file. Guimond was never denied credit because of these mistakes. Is TransUnion liable for violating the Fair Credit Reporting Act?

5. Thomas Waldock purchased a used BMW 320i from Universal Motors, Inc. It was warranted "to be free of defects in materials or workmanship for a period of three years or 36,000 miles, whichever occurs first." Within the warranty period, the car's engine failed, and upon examination, it was found to be extensively damaged. Universal denied warranty coverage because it concluded that Waldock damaged the engine by over-revving it. Waldock vehemently disputed BMW's contention. He claimed that, while the car was being driven at a low speed, the engine emitted a gear-crunching noise, ceased operation, and would not restart. Is Universal in violation of the law?

6. **ETHICS** After TNT Motor Express hired Joseph Bruce Drury as a truck driver, it ordered a background check from Robert Arden & Associates. TNT provided Drury's social security number and date of birth, but not his middle name. Arden discovered that a Joseph *Thomas* Drury, who coincidentally had the same birth date as Joseph *Bruce* Drury, had served a prison sentence for drunk driving. Not knowing that it had the wrong Drury, Arden reported this information to TNT, which promptly fired Drury. When he asked why, the TNT executive refused to tell him. Did TNT violate the law? Whether or not TNT was in violation, did its executives behave ethically? Who would have been harmed or helped if TNT managers had informed Drury of the Arden report?

Discussion Questions

1. Should employers use credit checks as part of the hiring process? On one hand, each year employers suffer losses of $55 million because of workplace violence, while retailers lose $30 *billion* a year from employee theft. Those who commit fraud are often living above their means. On the other hand, there is no evidence that workers with poor credit reports are more likely to be violent, steal from their employers, or quit their jobs. And refusing to hire someone with a low credit score may simply be kicking him when he is down. What would you do if you were an employer?

2. The fee on a debit card overdraft can be as high or higher than the amount taken out. Instead of overdrawing their accounts, consumers would be much better off either not spending the money, using a credit card, or paying cash. Typically, the people most likely to sign up for overdraft "protection" are those who can least afford it—they have maxed out their credit cards and used up any home equity. Is it ethical for a bank to offer an overdraft plan?

3. Look at the section entitled "Credit Card Act of 2009" on page **695.** All of these activities used to be legal. Which ones were unethical?

4. Go to **youtube.com** and search for "free credit reports." Watch the advertisements for **freecreditreport.com**. Although the characters repeat the word, "free" over and over, in fact the reports are not free unless the consumer signs up for the paid credit monitoring service. At the end of the ad, a voice quickly says, "Offer applies with enrollment in Triple Advantage." Are these ads deceptive under FTC rules? Are they ethical according to your Life Principles?

5. Advertisements for Listerine mouthwash claimed that it was as effective as flossing in preventing tooth plaque and gum disease. This statement was true, but only if the flossing was done incorrectly. In fact, many consumers do floss incorrectly. However, if flossing is done right, it is more effective against plaque and gum disease than Listerine. Is this advertisement deceptive?

CHAPTER 27

ENVIRONMENTAL LAW

"When my mother was left a widow almost 50 years ago, she taught school to support her family. A few years after my father's death, she took her savings and bought a small commercial building on a downtown lot in our little town in Oregon. The building, she said, would offer what my father couldn't—a source of support in her old age. In one half of the building was a children's clothing store, in the other a dry cleaner. The two stores served Main Street shoppers for years."

© picsbyst/Shutterstock.com

"Now the building that once represented security has produced a menace with the potential to bankrupt my mother. The discovery of contamination in city park well water triggered groundwater tests in the area. Waste products discarded by dry cleaners were identified as a likely source of contamination. Although a dry cleaner hasn't operated for 20 years on my mother's property, chemicals remain in the soil. Mother knew nothing of this hazard until a letter came from the Oregon Department of Environmental Quality. It said she should decide if she would oversee further testing and cleanup herself or if she would let the government handle it. In either case, my mother would pay the costs."

> The building that once represented security has produced a menace with the potential to bankrupt my mother.

"The building is worth just under $70,000. Cleanup costs will be at least $200,000. At 84, my mother has enough savings to preserve her independence. She does not have enough money to bear the enormous costs of new community standards. The dry cleaner that operated in my mother's building disposed of chemicals the same way other dry cleaners did. None of these businesses was operated in a negligent fashion. They followed standards accepted by the community at the time. Now we are learning that we must live more carefully if we are to survive in a world that is safe and clean. My question is: Who will pay? Who will be responsible for cleaning up environmental messes made before we knew better?"[1]

---

[1]Excerpt from Carolyn Scott Kortge, "Taken to the Cleaners," *Newsweek*, October 23, 1995, p.16. Reprinted with permission of the author.

INTRODUCTION

The environmental movement in the United States began in 1962 with the publication of Rachel Carson's book *Silent Spring*. She was the first to expose the deadly—and lingering— impact of DDT and other pesticides. These chemicals spread a wide web, poisoning not only the targeted insects, but the entire food chain—fish, birds, and even humans. Since Carson first sounded the alarm, environmental issues have appeared regularly in the news—everything from acute disasters such as the 2010 explosion of BP's Deepwater Horizon drilling platform in the Gulf of Mexico to chronic concerns over pesticide residues in food.

The environmental movement began with the fervor of a moral crusade. How could anyone be against a clean environment? It has become clear, however, that the issue is more complex. It is not enough simply to say, "We are against pollution." As the opening vignette reveals, the question is: who will pay? Who will pay for past damage inflicted before anyone understood the harm that pollutants cause? Who will pay for current changes necessary to prevent damage now and in the future? Are car owners willing to spend $100 or $1,000 more per car to prevent air pollution? Are easterners ready to ban oil drilling in the Arctic National Wildlife Refuge in Alaska if that means higher prices for heating oil? Will loggers in the West give up their jobs to protect endangered species? Are all consumers willing to pay more to insulate their homes?

The first President George Bush, a Republican, said, "Beyond all the studies, the figures, and the debates, the environment is a moral issue." But Newt Gingrich, the Republican Speaker of the House of Representatives, called the Environmental Protection Agency "the biggest job-killing agency in inner-city America."[2]

The cost-benefit trade-off is particularly complex in environmental issues because those who pay the cost often do not receive the benefit. If a company dumps toxic wastes into a stream, its shareholders benefit by avoiding the expense of safe disposal. Those who fish or drink the waters pay the real cost without receiving any of the benefit. Economists use the term **externality** to describe the situation in which people do not bear the full cost of their decisions. Externalities prevent the market system from achieving a clean environment on its own. Most commonly, government involvement is required to realign costs and benefits.

Externality
When people do not bear the full cost of their decisions.

Environmental Protection Agency

Forty years ago, environmental abuses were (ineffectively) governed by tort law and a smattering of local ordinances. Now, environmental law is a mammoth structure of federal and state regulation. In 1970, Congress created the Environmental Protection Agency (EPA) to consolidate environmental regulation under one roof. When Congress passes a new environmental law, the EPA issues regulations to implement it. The agency can bring administrative enforcement action against those who violate its regulations.

Those who violate environmental laws are liable for civil damages. In addition, some statutes, such as the Clean Water Act, the Resource Conservation and Recovery Act, and the Endangered Species Act, provide for *criminal* penalties, including imprisonment. The EPA is not shy about seeking criminal prosecutions of those who knowingly violate these statutes and of those corporate officers who fail to prevent criminal negligence by their employees.

---

[2]Both men are quoted in Robert V. Percival, Alan S. Miller, Christopher H. Schroeder, and James P. Leape, *Environmental Regulation* (Boston: Little, Brown & Co., 1992), p. 1, and 1995 supp. p. 2.

AIR POLLUTION

On October 26, 1948, almost half of the 10,000 people in Donora, Pennsylvania, fell ill from air pollution. A weather inversion trapped industrial pollutants in the air, creating a lethal smog. Twenty residents ultimately died. Although air pollution rarely causes this type of acute illness, it can cause or increase the severity of diseases that are annoying, chronic, or even fatal—such as pneumonia, bronchitis, emphysema, cancer, and heart disease. Exposure before birth is linked to lower IQ scores in children.

There are three major sources of air pollution: coal-burning utility plants, factories, and motor vehicles. Residential furnaces, farm operations, forest fires, and dust from mines and construction sites also contribute. Local regulation is ineffective in controlling air pollution. For instance, when cities limited pollution from factory smokestacks, plants simply built taller stacks that sent the pollution hundreds, or even thousands, of miles away. Local governments had little incentive to prevent this long-distance migration. Recognizing the national nature of the problem, Congress passed the Clean Air Act of 1963.

Clean Air Act

The Clean Air Act has four major provisions:

NAAQS

National ambient air quality standards.

- **Primary standards.** Congress directed the EPA to establish national ambient air quality standards (**NAAQS**) for primary pollution, that is, pollution that harms the public health. The EPA has created NAAQS for carbon monoxide, ozone, mercury, nitrogen dioxide, and many other substances. The EPA's mandate was to set standards that protected public health and provided an adequate margin of safety *without regard to cost*. Pollution may not exceed these limits anyplace in the country. The EPA must regularly update the rules to reflect the latest scientific evidence.

- **Secondary standards.** Congress also directed the EPA to establish NAAQS for pollution that may not be a threat to health but has other unpleasant effects, such as obstructing visibility and harming plants or other materials.

- **State implementation plans (SIPs).** The Clean Air Act envisioned a partnership between the EPA and the states. After the EPA set primary and secondary standards, states would produce SIPs to meet the primary standards within three years and the secondary standards within a reasonable time. If a SIP was not acceptable, the EPA would produce its own plan for that state. In formulating their SIPs, states were required to identify the major sources of pollution. Each polluter would then be given a pollution limit to bring the area into compliance with national standards. The worse the pollution in a particular area, the tougher the regulations. Sanctions for unsatisfactory SIPs include withholding of federal highway funding.

- **Citizen suits.** The Clean Air Act (and many other environmental statutes) permits anyone who is or might be adversely affected by any violation to file suit against a polluter or against the EPA for failing to enforce the statute. Citizens have often been more assertive than the EPA in enforcing environmental statutes. For instance, the Arizona Center for Law in the Public Interest has sued the EPA many times for failing to impose sufficiently strict air quality standards on Phoenix and Tucson.

In the following case, a power plant argued that the EPA had imposed a solution whose cost far outweighed its benefit. There is only one Grand Canyon. Should visibility there be preserved at any cost?

You be the Judge

CENTRAL ARIZONA WATER CONSERVATION DISTRICT V. EPA

990 F.2d 1531, 1993 U.S. App. LEXIS 5881
United States Court of Appeals for
the Ninth Circuit, 1993

Facts: In the Clean Air Act, Congress directed the EPA to issue regulations that would protect visibility at national landmarks. The Navaho Generating Station (NGS) is a power plant 12 miles from the Grand Canyon. In response to a citizen suit filed by the Environmental Defense Fund under the Clean Air Act, the EPA ordered NGS to reduce its sulfur dioxide emissions by 90 percent. To do so would cost NGS $430 million initially in capital expenditures and then $89.6 million annually. Average winter visibility in the Grand Canyon would be improved by at most 7 percent, but perhaps less. NGS sued to prevent implementation of the EPA's order. A court may nullify an EPA order if it determines that the agency action was arbitrary and capricious.

You Be the Judge: *Did the EPA act arbitrarily and capriciously in requiring NGS to spend half a billion dollars to improve winter visibility at the Grand Canyon by at most 7 percent?*

Argument for NGS: This case is a perfect example of environmentalism run amok. Half a billion dollars for the *chance* of increasing winter visibility at the Grand Canyon by 7 percent? No rational person would choose to spend his own money that way, but the EPA is happy to spend NGS's. Winter visitors to the Grand Canyon would undoubtedly prefer that NGS provide them with a free lunch rather than a 7 percent improvement in visibility. The EPA order is simply a waste of money.

Argument for the EPA: Under the Clean Air Act, Congress instructed the EPA to protect visibility at national landmarks such as the Grand Canyon. How can NGS, or anyone else, measure the benefit of protecting a national treasure like the Grand Canyon? Even people who never have and never will visit it during the winter sleep better at night knowing that the canyon is protected. NGS has been causing harm to the Grand Canyon, and now it should remedy the damage.

Courts generally defer to federal agencies, whose experts deal with similar problems all the time. The EPA has greater expertise in these matters than either NGS or this court.

New Sources of Pollution

Some states had air so clean that they could have allowed air quality to decline and still have met EPA standards. However, the Clean Air Act declared that one of its purposes was to "protect and enhance" air quality. Using this phrase, the Sierra Club sued the EPA to prevent it from approving any SIPs that met EPA standards but nonetheless permitted a decline in air quality. As a result of this suit, the EPA developed a **prevention of significant deterioration (PSD) program. No one may undertake a building project that will cause a major increase in pollution without first obtaining a permit from the EPA.** The agency will grant permits only if an applicant can demonstrate that (1) its emissions will not cause an overall decline in air quality and (2) it has installed the **best available control technology** for every pollutant.

The PSD program prohibits any deterioration in current air quality, *regardless of health impact.* In essence, national policy values a clean environment for its own sake, apart from any health benefits.

Acid Rain

In some places, rain is now 10 times more acidic than it would naturally be. The results of acid rain are visible in the eastern United States and Canada—damaged forests, crops, and lakes. Acid is primarily created by sulfur dioxide emissions from large coal-burning utility plants in Pennsylvania and the Midwest. Many of these plants were built before the Clean Air Act, when the easiest way to meet state and local standards (while keeping electricity prices low) was to build tall stacks that would send the sulfur dioxide far away. Terrific for Ohio, not so wonderful for Maine.

The Clean Air Act required power plants to cut their sulfur dioxide emissions using one of four methods: **(1) installing scrubbers, (2) using low-sulfur coal, (3) switching to alternative fuels (such as natural gas), or (4) trading emissions allowances.** This last alternative (often referred to as **cap and trade**) requires some explanation. Each year, every utility receives an emissions allowance, meaning that it is allowed to emit a certain number of tons of pollutants. If a company does not need its entire allowance because it uses cleaner fuels or has installed pollution control devices, it can sell the leftover allowance to other companies or stockpile the allowance for future use. Plants with high levels of pollution either buy more allowances or reduce their own emissions, depending on which alternative is cheaper. In effect, the government establishes the maximum amount of pollution, and then the market sets the price for meeting the national standard.

The market for sulfur dioxide emissions had become reasonably efficient and effective because power plants had a financial incentive to reduce pollution through innovation. However, in 2008, a federal appeals court struck down parts of the cap and trade rules.[3] In response, the EPA issued new rules that rely more on changes in the power plants themselves than on cap and trade. The new program has its own set of allowances, rendering the old ones essentially worthless. At this writing, it is not clear if the cap and trade system will remain as effective under these new rules.

There is one additional problem in regulating sulfur dioxide emissions: **new source review**. Originally, Congress had exempted the oldest power plants and factories from the Clean Air Act on the theory that they would be very expensive to upgrade and would be replaced soon enough anyway. As it turned out, many companies discovered it was easier to patch up the old plants than it was to replace them with new, clean operations. Congress amended the Act to impose the new source review system: companies are required to upgrade pollution devices any time they renovate a plant (but not when they undertake routine maintenance). In the end, though, few plants have complied with the new source review requirements, at least in part because the EPA issued weak regulations to implement the law. For instance, the EPA defined routine maintenance as any activity that costs less than 20 percent of the value of the generating unit—which meant a company could spend hundreds of millions of dollars on so-called routine maintenance and not be required to upgrade pollution facilities. The American Lung Association termed these rules "the most harmful and unlawful air-pollution initiative ever undertaken by the federal government."[4]

Greenhouse Gases and Global Warming

During the last 100 years, the average temperature worldwide has increased between 0.5 degree and 1.1 °F. Thus far in this century, every year has been warmer than any year in the last century except 1998. If current trends continue, the world's average temperature during the next 100 years will rise another 2 to 6 °F, producing the warmest climate in the history of humankind. (By comparison, the planet is only 5 to 9 °F warmer than during the last Ice Age.)

The impact of this climate change is potentially catastrophic: a devastating decline in fishing stocks, the death of major forests, and a loss of farmland worldwide. Already, grain yields are down because of droughts. But even worse is the flooding that will result from a worldwide rise in sea levels. Hundreds of millions of people—including two-thirds of the world's megacities—are in coastal areas. To take one example, Bangladesh is slightly

Cap and trade
A market-based system for reducing emissions.

[3]*North Carolina v. EPA*, 531 F.3d 896 (D.C. Cir., 2008).
[4]Bruce Barcott, "Changing All the Rules," *New York Times*, April 4, 2004, §6, p. 38.

smaller than Iowa, but it has a population of 160 million people, with most living at sea level. Where will they go if their country floods? What will happen to that country's nearest neighbor, India, if 100 million people swarm its borders?

Scientific evidence underlying the theory of global warming has been debated for a long time, but today, scientists accept that the burning of fossil fuels produces gases—carbon dioxide, methane, and nitrous oxide—that create a greenhouse effect by trapping heat in the Earth's atmosphere. Because rays from the sun have a high frequency, they pass easily through these gases on their way to the Earth. But once sunlight is absorbed by the Earth, it is re-emitted as infrared radiation, which cannot pass through the gases as easily. In short, more energy enters the Earth's atmosphere than leaves it. The result is global warming.[5]

Identifying the problem, however, does not illuminate the solution. Global warming is the most complex environmental problem of the new millennium because any solution requires international political cooperation coupled with major behavioral changes.

International Treaties

The United States plays a particularly important role in finding a solution because even though it has only 5 percent of the world's population, it consumes 25 percent of the world's energy. However, it is the only leading industrialized nation that refused to ratify the 1997 Kyoto Protocol. This treaty required emissions of greenhouse gases (GHGs) in developed nations to be reduced by the year 2012 to a level 5.2 percent below 1990 amounts. It did so by setting emission levels for each country. From the perspective of the United States, there were two problems with the treaty: (1) developing countries such as China and India, which are important economic competitors of the United States, were not bound by the treaty; and (2) economists had estimated the cost of compliance at $5 trillion, with little benefit to the United States, at least in the short run.

In any event, the Kyoto Protocol had little impact on GHGs, and not just because the United States did not take part. Many countries were well over their treaty quotas. The same impasse continues over the second phase of the treaty (beginning in 2013)—the United States will not be bound by a treaty that excludes China and India, while those countries will not enter into an agreement when America has no real plan to cut its emissions. However, in Copenhagen in 2009, delegates of 193 countries, including both the United States and China, agreed to a "statement of intention" to reduce GHGs, to supply developing countries with green technology, and to help them adapt to climate change.

In short, while countries continue to meet and discuss solutions to climate change, they have been unable to reach an effective, binding agreement. Some commentators suggest that more effort should now focus on adapting to climate change rather than preventing it.

Domestic Regulation

The EPA had traditionally refused to regulate GHGs, arguing that it did not have statutory authority over issues of global climate change. However, in 2007, the Supreme Court ruled that the EPA must regulate these gases if they were found to endanger health or welfare.[6] Beginning in 2011, the EPA has required plants that produce at least 100,000 tons of GHGs a year (or that increase their production by 75,000 tons) to obtain a permit from the EPA. Under the permitting process, plants must use the best available technology to reduce emissions.

In addition, states are able to set their own standards, so long as they do not conflict with federal rules. Ten eastern states, including New York and New England, have adopted a cap and trade plan for GHGs produced by electric utilities. California instituted a broader cap and

[5]For an explanation of the physics, see Michio Kaku, *Physics of the Future* (New York: Doubleday Press, 2011).
[6]*Massachusetts v. Environmental Protection Agency*, 549 U.S. 497; 2007 U.S. LEXIS 3785.

trade program, which has been challenged in court. However, the appellate court allowed the program to continue, pending appeal. In any event, whether these limited plans can affect an international problem is uncertain.

Automobile Pollution

The Clean Air Act directed the EPA to reduce automobile pollution levels by 90 percent within six years. That goal was not achieved, although there has been significant progress. Thanks to catalytic converters and other innovations, new cars run 97 percent cleaner than 1970 models. Each car may be cleaner, but Americans are driving more—and bigger—cars more miles on more trips. As a result, motor vehicles are still a major source of air pollution, releasing more than 50 percent of the hazardous pollutants in the air.

Car manufacturers long fought federal emission standards, but after General Motors (GM) and Chrysler received a substantial government bailout in 2008, they became more cooperative with government regulators. In 2010, for the first time, the EPA issued regulations on car and light truck emissions of GHGs. By 2016, each manufacturer must produce vehicles that have an average fuel economy of 35.5 miles per gallon. These cars and trucks will be almost 40 percent more fuel efficient and cleaner than existing vehicles. The EPA predicts that these new rules will reduce climate changing gases by 30 percent between 2012 and 2016 and save owners $3,000 in fuel over a vehicle's life. But new cars will cost an average of $1,000 more.

These national standards are based on rules first issued by California. Generally, states are not permitted to adopt their own vehicle emission standards because automobile makers would struggle to meet 50 different sets of rules. But because California regulated automobile pollution before the Clean Air Act was passed, the Act grants it special permission to set even stricter pollution standards. Other states then have the right to adopt California standards instead of federal rules. California is already beginning to develop standards for 2017 so that car manufacturers will have time to comply.

Soot Particles

Produced primarily by power plants and diesel fuel, microscopic soot particles substantially increase the risk of premature death from lung cancer and other breathing and heart disorders. Because of these particles, residing in a city has the same impact on a person's lungs as living with a smoker. The life expectancy of residents in cities with the cleanest air is on average two years longer than those in the dirtiest cities. In 1997, the EPA issued regulations limiting soot. However, a lawsuit by power plant operators and automobile manufacturers delayed the rules until 2001, when the Supreme Court ruled that the EPA had the right to impose these new regulations without conducting a cost-benefit analysis.[7] In 2005, the EPA set standards for soot emissions from buses and power plants that were weaker than its own Scientific Advisory Committee had recommended. In 2009, a federal appeals court ruled that the EPA's rules did not adequately protect public health and had to be revised.[8] In 2011, an EPA report agreed that its standards were inadequate. The agency has now issued preliminary rules but they have not yet been finalized.

Air Toxics

Some pollutants are so potent that even tiny amounts cause harm. For instance, the EPA has never been able to identify a safe level of exposure to asbestos. Each year, 2.7 billion pounds of toxics spew into the air in the United States, causing an estimated annual increase of 3,000 cancer deaths. Two-thirds of Americans face an increased cancer risk from exposure

---

[7]*Whitman v. American Trucking Associations*, 531 U.S. 457; 2001 U.S. LEXIS 1952.
[8]*Am. Farm Bureau Fedn v. EPA*, 559 F.3d 512 (D.C. Cir., 2009).

to toxic chemicals in the air. The Clean Air Act directed the EPA to set so-called National Emission Standards for Hazardous Air Pollutants (NESHAPS), which are safety standards for toxics that provide an adequate margin of safety without regard to cost.

The Environmental Defense Fund sued the EPA to force compliance with the law. Nevertheless, by 1990, the agency had proposed standards for only seven substances. Although these standards do not eliminate health risks, they are set at the lowest feasible level given existing technology, and the courts have upheld them.

In 1990 amendments to the Clean Air Act, Congress directed the EPA to set standards for each of 189 specific pollutants and any other toxics the EPA wanted to include. The EPA was permitted to base these standards initially on the maximum achievable control technology (MACT).

However, it was not until 2011, more than 20 years later, that the EPA issued regulations on air toxics. For example, it has ruled that power plants must reduce these pollutants by 91 percent within five years. The EPA blames congressional budget cuts for its tardiness.

EXAM Strategy

Question: Suppose that the legislature of the state of Kentucky was unhappy with the national automobile emissions standards set by the EPA. Under the Clean Air Act, could it pass a statute setting a different standard? What if it wanted its standards for air toxics to be different from those set by the EPA?

Strategy: There are different rules for automobile emissions and other air pollutants. Why is that?

Result: Kentucky does not have the right to create its own standards for auto pollution, but it does have the right to adopt California's rules. States can set tighter, but not looser, standards for other air pollutants. It is important to have national standards for auto emissions because car manufacturers cannot produce different vehicles for each state. For the other pollutants, uniformity does not matter.

WATER POLLUTION

One day in 1993, thousands of Milwaukeeans began to suffer nausea, cramps, and diarrhea. The suspected culprit? *Cryptosporidium*, a tiny protozoan that usually resides in the intestines of cattle and other animals. Ironically, the parasite may have entered Milwaukee's water supply at a purification plant on Lake Michigan. Officials suspect that infected runoff from dairy farms spilled into Lake Michigan near the plant's intake pipe. Doctors advised those with a damaged immune system (such as AIDS patients) to avoid drinking municipal water. Most Milwaukeeans were taking no chances—more than 800,000 switched to boiled or bottled water.

Polluted water can cause a number of loathsome diseases, such as typhus and dysentery. But by 1930, most American cities had dramatically reduced outbreaks of waterborne diseases by chlorinating their water. (The parasite that caused the Milwaukee outbreak is relatively immune to chlorine.) However, industrial discharges into the water supply have increased rapidly, with a significant impact on water quality. These industrial wastes may not induce acute illnesses like typhus, but they can cause serious diseases such as cancer. There is more at stake than health; clean water is valued for esthetics, recreation, and fishing.

Clean Water Act

In 1972, Congress passed a statute, now called the Clean Water Act (CWA), with two ambitious goals: (1) to make all navigable water suitable for swimming and fishing by 1983, and (2) to eliminate the discharge of pollutants into navigable water by 1985. Like the Clean Air Act, the CWA leaves enforcement primarily to the states, with oversight by the EPA, and permits citizen suits. Also, like the Clean Air Act, the CWA's goals have not been met.

Traditionally, the courts had interpreted the term "navigable water" very broadly to include wetlands, intermittent streams (those that do not flow all the time), and ponds that might affect other bodies of water. This definition gave the EPA the right to regulate virtually all water polluters. But the Supreme Court changed the interpretation of navigable water to *exclude* (1) intermittent streams or wetlands, (2) ponds or lakes that are not connected to open bodies of water, and (3) waterways that are all within one state, even though pollutants can leak from them into drinking water.[9] The EPA estimates that almost one-third of the nation's population drinks water fed by waterways that are no longer covered by the CWA.

The uncertainty created by these rulings has led the EPA to cut its water pollution investigations dramatically. Almost half of the largest polluters are not being investigated, simply because proving jurisdiction would be too difficult. EPA lawsuits against water polluters have fallen by almost half since the Supreme Court decided these cases.

In the case about the Grand Canyon that you read earlier, the court dealt with the issue of cost-benefit analysis under the Clean Air Act. In the following case, the Supreme Court takes up the same issue under the CWA. Until this case, the CWA had been interpreted to prevent the EPA from using cost-benefit analysis (except in a situation in which the cost of technology was so high as to make it not "available"). The EPA was required to prevent pollution at any cost. The Supreme Court has now changed that interpretation of the CWA.

ENTERGY CORPORATION V. RIVERKEEPER, INC.

129 S. Ct. 1498; 2009 U.S. Lexis 2498
Supreme Court of the United States, 2009

Facts: Power plants generate lots of heat. To cool down, they flush vast amounts of water through a cooling system (called "cooling water intake structures"). In the process, aquatic organisms (fish, shellfish, and plants) that live in this water get squashed against the screens ("impingement") or in the cooling system itself ("entrainment"). Under the Clean Water Act, these cooling systems must use the "best technology available for minimizing adverse environmental impact."

It took the EPA three decades to issue regulations for these structures. For new power plants, the EPA required the best technology available, which would reduce fish mortality by 98 percent. But for existing plants, the EPA permitted technology that reduced impingement by 80 to 95 percent and entrainment by 60 to 90 percent. The agency made this choice because the cost of converting existing plants to the better system would be $3.5 billion per year, which was nine times the cost of the cheaper version. In

addition, the EPA reserved the right to reduce standards for specific plants if they demonstrated that the costs of compliance would be significantly greater than the benefits.

Riverkeeper, Inc., an environmental organization, challenged these regulations. The appeals court ruled that the EPA could only consider costs in two circumstances: (1) determining if they could be "reasonably borne" by the industry, or (2) if there were two ways to achieve the same goal, the EPA could mandate the cheaper option. The court said, however, that the EPA could not compare the costs and benefits of various methods and choose the technology with the best net benefits. Nor could the EPA alter standards for specific sites based on cost-benefit analysis. The Supreme Court granted *certiorari*.

Issue: *Is the EPA permitted to use cost-benefit analysis when issuing regulations?*

---

[9]*Solid Waste Agency v. United States Army Corps of Eng'Rs*, 531 U.S. 159 (S.Ct. 2001); *Rapanos v. United States*, 547 U.S. 715 (S.Ct. 2006).

Excerpts from Justice Scalia's Decision: [The CWA] instructs the EPA to set standards for cooling water intake structures that reflect "the best technology available for minimizing adverse environmental impact." The Second Circuit took that language to mean the technology that achieves the greatest reduction in adverse environmental impacts at a cost that can reasonably be borne by the industry. That is certainly a plausible interpretation of the statute. But "best technology" may also describe the technology that *most efficiently* produces some good. In common parlance, one could certainly use the phrase "best technology" to refer to that which produces a good at the lowest per-unit cost, even if it produces a lesser quantity of that good than other available technologies.

[Plaintiffs] contend that this latter reading is precluded by the statute's use of the phrase "for minimizing adverse environmental impact." Minimizing, they argue, means reducing to the smallest amount possible, and the "best technology available for minimizing adverse environmental impacts" must be the economically feasible technology that achieves the greatest possible reduction in environmental harm. But "minimize" is a term that admits of degree and is not necessarily used to refer exclusively to the "greatest possible reduction." It seems to us, therefore, that the phrase "best technology available," even with the added specification "for minimizing adverse environmental impact," does not unambiguously preclude cost-benefit analysis.

[I]t was well within the bounds of reasonable interpretation for the EPA to conclude that cost-benefit analysis is not categorically forbidden. In the requirements challenged here, the EPA sought only to avoid extreme disparities between costs and benefits. The agency limited variances from the national performance standards to circumstances where the costs are significantly greater than the benefits of compliance. And finally, the EPA's assessment of the relatively meager financial benefits of the regulations that it adopted—reduced impingement and entrainment of 1.4 billion aquatic organisms, with annualized benefits of $83 million, when compared to annual costs of $389 million, demonstrates quite clearly that the agency did not select the regulatory requirements because their benefits equaled their costs.

While not conclusive, it surely tends to show that the EPA's current practice is a reasonable and hence legitimate exercise of its discretion to weigh benefits against costs. In the last analysis, even [plaintiffs] ultimately recognize that some form of cost-benefit analysis is permissible. They acknowledge that the statute's language is "plainly not so constricted as to require EPA to require industry petitioners to spend billions to save one more fish or plankton." This concedes the principle—the permissibility of at least some cost-benefit analysis—and we see no statutory basis for limiting its use to situations where the benefits are *de minimis* rather than significantly disproportionate.

The judgment of the Court of Appeals is reversed.

Industrial Discharges

The CWA prohibits any single producer from discharging pollution into water without a permit from the EPA. Before granting a permit, the EPA must set limits, by industry, on the amount of each type of pollution any single producer (called a **point source**) can discharge. These limits must be based on the best available technology. The EPA faces a gargantuan task in determining the best available technology that *each* industry can use to reduce pollution. Furthermore, standards become obsolete quickly as technology changes.

Point source
A single producer of pollution.

The CWA also requires the EPA to measure water quality broadly to determine if the permit system is working. Until clean water standards are met, every point source is held to the same standard, whether it is discharging into a clean ocean that can handle more pollution or a stagnant lake that cannot. Since determining the impact of a particular discharge may not be possible, especially when it is mingled with others, it is easier for the EPA to set the same standards for everyone. Easier and fairer—Congress did not want states to lure industry with promises of laxer pollution rules.

The EPA faces a major challenge regulating water discharges from power plants. To meet EPA air quality standards, many plants installed scrubbers that pull pollutants out of the air and into wastewater. This water is then discharged into rivers and lakes, where it can pollute drinking water supplies. An EPA report indicates that some people living near power plant discharges face a cancer risk that is 2,000 times normal. Although these discharges may violate the CWA, the EPA does not have enough resources to impose meaningful sanctions. In 2009, the EPA announced its intention to set new standards for discharges from power plants, but it has not done so yet.

Water Quality Standards

The CWA requires states to set EPA-approved water quality standards and develop plans to achieve them. The first step in developing a plan is to determine how each body of water is used. Standards may vary depending upon the designated use—higher for recreational lakes than for a river used to irrigate farmland. No matter what the water's designated use, standards may not be set at a level lower than its current condition. Congress is not in the business of permitting *more* pollution.

Non-point source

When pollutants have no single source, such as water run-off from city streets.

States are supposed to pay special attention to so-called **non-point sources;** that is, pollutants with no single source, such as water runoff from agricultural land or city streets. This runoff may contain gasoline, pesticides, or bacteria. Congress left non-point source pollution to the states because it is so difficult to regulate. This regulation also involves complex issues such as land use planning that are, in theory, better handled at the local level than by national fiat. However optimistic Congress may have been, to date the states have not successfully implemented this section of the CWA. They appear to lack both the political will and the technical know-how, for which they are not totally to blame. Determining the impact of individual pollutants on the overall quality of a body of water used for many different purposes is a complex problem. Land use planning requires a delicate and volatile mix of consensus and control.

As the ambitious goals set by the CWA have not been met, Congress has granted numerous extensions. At the same time, environmental advocates have filed citizen suits to force the EPA to toughen its enforcement.

Wetlands

Wetlands are the transition areas between land and open water. They may look like swamps, they may even *be* swamps, but their unattractive appearance should not disguise their vital role in the aquatic world. They are natural habitats for many fish and wildlife. They also serve as a filter for neighboring bodies of water, trapping chemicals and sediments. Moreover, they are an important aid in flood control because they can absorb a high level of water and then release it slowly after the emergency is past.

The CWA prohibits any discharge of dredge and fill material into wetlands without a permit. Although filling in wetlands requires a permit, many other activities that harm wetlands, such as draining them, originally did not. (However, many states require permits for draining wetlands.) After some particularly egregious abuses, the EPA issued regulations to limit the destruction of wetlands. These new regulations were, however, successfully challenged in the courts.[10] The EPA then rewrote the regulations to accomplish the same goal within the parameters set out by the courts.

Although, in theory, the government's official policy is no net loss of wetlands, the reality has been different. Since the country was settled, about half of the original 230 million acres of wetlands in the continental United States have been destroyed. In 2002, the Bush administration amended the "no net loss" rule so that it could issue waivers in some cases.

Sewage

Plumbing drains must be attached to either a septic system or a sewer line. A septic system is, in effect, a freestanding waste treatment plant. A sewer line, on the other hand, feeds into a publicly owned wastewater treatment plant, also known as a municipal sewage plant. **Under the CWA, a municipality must obtain a permit for any discharge from a wastewater treatment plant.** To obtain a permit, the municipality must first treat the waste to reduce its toxicity. However, taxpayers have resisted the large increases in taxes or fees necessary to

---

[10]*National Mining Ass'n v. U.S. Army Corps of Engineers*, 145 F.3d 1399 (D.C. Cir. 1998).

fund required treatments. Since the fines imposed by the EPA are almost always less than the cost of treatment, some cities have been slow to comply.

Between 2006 and 2009, more than a third of the sewage systems in this country admitted to violating the law by dumping incompletely treated human waste and harmful chemicals into waterways. Fewer than 20 percent of those were penalized. There have, however, been some notable successes. For instance, the Charles River in Boston, which was the inspiration for the pop song, "Dirty Water," recently received a grade of B by the EPA—an impressive improvement over the D it received in 1995. The river is now almost always safe for boating and is swimmable 54 percent of the time.

Other Water Pollution Statutes

The Safe Drinking Water Act of 1974:

- Requires the EPA to set national standards for contaminants potentially harmful to human health that are found in drinking water,

- Assigns enforcement responsibility to the states but permits the EPA to take enforcement action against states that do not adhere to the standards,

- Prohibits the use of lead in any pipes through which drinking water flows, and

- Requires community water systems to send every customer an annual consumer confidence report disclosing the level of contaminants in the drinking water. (We can only hope that consumers will remain confident after receiving the report.)

Between 2004 and 2009, 15 percent of the U.S. population had drinking water that contained hazardous chemicals and bacteria from human waste. Violations of the Safe Drinking Water Act have occurred in every state. The EPA is reluctant to sanction local governments because they are often short of money.

This 15 percent calculation is probably low, because it only includes 91 chemicals out of the 80,000 currently sold in the United States. The EPA does not regulate the others. It has not added any chemicals to the regulatory list since 2000.

The **Ocean Dumping Act of 1972** prohibits the dumping of wastes in ocean water without a permit from the EPA.

Congress passed the **Oil Pollution Act of 1990** in response to the mammoth 1989 *Exxon Valdez* tanker oil spill in Prince William Sound, Alaska. To prevent defective boats from leaking oil, this statute sets design standards for ships operating in U.S. waters. It also requires shipowners to pay for damage caused by oil discharged from their ships.

EXAM Strategy

Question: Edward lives on a ranch near Wind River. He uses water from the river for irrigation. To divert more water to his ranch, he builds a dike in the river using scrap metal, cottonwood trees, car bodies, and a washing machine. This material does not harm downstream water. Has Edward violated the CWA?

Strategy: The CWA prohibits the discharge of pollution. Was this pollution?

Result: Yes, the court ruled that the material Edward placed in the water was pollution. It was irrelevant that the material did not flow downstream.

WASTE DISPOSAL

The time is 1978. The place is 96th Street in Niagara Falls, New York. Six women are afflicted with breast cancer, one man has bladder cancer, another suffers from throat cancer. A seven-year-old boy suddenly goes into convulsions and dies of kidney failure. Other residents have chromosomal abnormalities, epilepsy, respiratory problems, and skin diseases. This street is three blocks away from Love Canal.

In 1945, Hooker Chemical Co. disposed of 21,800 tons of 82 different chemicals by dumping them into Love Canal or burying them nearby. An internal memorandum warned that this decision would lead to "potential future hazard" and be a "potential source of lawsuits." A year later, the company's lawyer wrote that "children in the neighborhood use portions of the water for swimming and, as a matter of fact, just before we left the site, we saw several young children walking down the path with what appeared to be bathing costumes in hand." He suggested that Hooker build a fence around the canal, but the company never did. Instead, it sold the land to the local school board to build an elementary school. When the company's executive vice president recommended against the sale, the company inserted a clause in the deed to eliminate the company's liability.

> **Schoolchildren tripped over drums of chemicals that worked their way up to the surface.**

Schoolchildren tripped over drums of chemicals that worked their way up to the surface. Some children were burned playing with hot balls of chemical residue—what they called "fire stones"—that popped up through the ground. Homeowners noticed foul odors in their basements after heavy rains. Finally, a national health emergency was declared at Love Canal, and a joint federal-state program relocated 800 families. In 1994, Occidental Chemical Corp. (which had since bought Hooker) agreed to pay the state of New York $98 million to settle a lawsuit over Love Canal.[11] Two years later, the EPA settled its lawsuit with Occidental for $129 million. In the end, the cleanup cost almost $400 million and took 21 years to complete.

In its time, what Hooker did was not unusual. Companies historically dumped waste in waterways, landfills, or open dumps. Out of sight was out of mind. Waste disposal continues to be a major problem in the United States. It has been estimated that the cost of cleaning up existing waste products will exceed $1 *trillion*. At the same time, the country continues to produce more than 6 billion tons of agricultural, commercial, industrial, and domestic waste each year.

Two major statutes regulate wastes. The Resource Conservation and Recovery Act (RCRA) focuses on *preventing* future Love Canals by regulating the production, transportation and disposal of solid wastes, both toxic and otherwise. It also regulates spills at RCRA regulated facilities. The Comprehensive Environmental Response, Compensation, and Liability Act (CERCLA), often referred to as **Superfund**, focuses on *cleaning up* inactive or abandoned hazardous waste sites.

Resource Conservation and Recovery Act

The RCRA establishes rules for treating both hazardous wastes and other forms of solid waste (such as ordinary garbage).

---

[11]William Glaberson, "Love Canal: Suit Focuses on Records from 1940s," *New York Times*, October 22, 1990, p. B1. Copyright © 1990 by The New York Times Co.

Solid Waste

Before 1895, the city of New York did not collect garbage. Residents simply piled it up in the streets, causing the streets to rise 5 feet in height over the century. At present, each American generates 4.3 pounds of solid waste a *day*, an increase of 60 percent since 1960 and more waste per capita than any other country.

But most Americans never gave much thought to their waste until the infamous case of the garbage barge. The trouble arose in 1983, when the New York legislature banned new landfills (garbage dumps) on Long Island. Three years later, the landfill began to fill up in Islip, a bedroom community outside New York City. Lowell Herrelson, an Alabama businessman, offered to put the Islip garbage on a barge and ship it to another state. But once he filled the barge, no other state would take the garbage. Loaded with 3,186 tons of waste, the barge traveled over 6,000 miles in five months and was turned away by six states and three countries before returning to New York and anchoring near the Statue of Liberty. Its movements were reported daily in the newspapers and even became the subject of the *Tonight Show* monologue: "The only town to send its garbage on a 6,000-mile cruise." The garbage was ultimately burned in a Brooklyn incinerator. Islip introduced recycling and built a $38 million garbage incinerator.

The disposal of nonhazardous solid waste has generally been left to the states, but they must follow guidelines set by the RCRA. **The RCRA:**

- Bans new open dumps,
- Requires that garbage be sent to sanitary landfills,
- Sets minimum standards for landfills,
- Requires landfills to monitor nearby groundwater,
- Requires states to develop a permit program for landfills, and
- Provides some financial assistance to aid states in waste management.

Ethics   Computers and other consumer electronic devices have created the most rapidly growing waste problem in the world. Containing chemicals such as lead and mercury, these products produce not only large volume, but also dangerous toxicity. Industrialized nations have found a simple solution—between 50 and 80 percent of the "e-waste" collected for recycling is sent to countries such as China, India, and Pakistan.

Once the e-waste is in Asia, adults and children, working without any protective clothing or equipment, burn the plastic casings in the open air, dismantle toner cartridges by hand, and melt circuit boards. The ground, air, and water are polluted with the residue of these toxic components. Because this disposal method is so easy and cheap (for the industrialized nations), manufacturers have not attempted to reduce toxic components in electronic products and governments have not forced them to take responsibility for safe disposal at the end of the product's life.[12]

What is the ethical obligation of developed nations to dispose of toxic e-waste?

What will you do with your old computer when you buy a new one? Staples will safely recycle e-waste, whether or not it was bought at the store, for a fee of $10. Would you pay that sum?

[12]The Basel Action Networks, "Exporting Harm: The Techno-Trashing of Asia," February 25, 2002, available at **http://www.ban.org**.

Underground Storage Tanks

Concerned that underground gasoline storage tanks were leaking into water supplies, Congress required the EPA to issue regulations for detecting and correcting leaks in existing tanks and establishing specifications for new receptacles. Anyone who owns property with an underground storage tank must notify the EPA and comply with regulations that require installation of leak detectors, periodic testing, and, in some cases, removal of old tanks.

Identifying Hazardous Wastes

The EPA must establish criteria for determining what is, and is not, hazardous waste. It must then prepare a list of wastes that qualify as hazardous.

Tracking Hazardous Wastes

Anyone who creates, transports, stores, treats, or disposes of more than a certain quantity of hazardous wastes must apply for an EPA permit. All hazardous wastes must be tracked from creation to final disposal. They must be disposed of at a certified facility. Any company that generates more than 100 kilograms of hazardous waste in any month must obtain an identification number for its wastes. When it ships this waste to a disposal facility, it must send along a manifest that identifies the waste, the transporter, and the destination. The company must notify the EPA if it does not receive a receipt from the disposal site indicating that the waste has been received.

Superfund

In the vignette that opened this chapter, an elderly woman faced financial ruin from the cost of cleaning up pollutants that her dry cleaner tenants had left. The RCRA was designed to ensure safe disposal of current hazardous wastes. In contrast, the goal of Superfund (also known as CERCLA) is to clean up hazardous wastes improperly dumped in the past.

The philosophy of Superfund is "the polluter pays." **Therefore, anyone who has *ever owned or operated* a site on which hazardous wastes are found, or who has transported wastes to the site, or who has arranged for the disposal of wastes that were released at the site, is liable for (1) the cost of cleaning up the site, (2) any damage done to natural resources, and (3) any required health assessments.** All polluters at a site are jointly and severally liable unless they can show that they were only responsible for a portion of the damages. In practical terms, this means that the EPA seeks full recovery from whichever polluters are financially sound. These defendants then seek to reduce their liability by showing that they were only responsible for part of the damage at the site.

In a "shovels first, lawyers later" approach, Congress established a revolving trust fund for the EPA to use in cleaning up sites even before obtaining reimbursement from those responsible for the damage. The trust fund was initially financed by a tax on the oil and chemical industries, which produce the bulk of hazardous waste. In 1995, however, the taxes expired, and Congress refused to renew them. Since then, the EPA has had to rely on reimbursements from polluters and congressional appropriations of about $1.2 billion a year. That sounds like a lot of money, but according to the EPA, there could be as many as 355,000 hazardous waste sites that would require up to $250 billion to restore. Currently, the EPA has a list of about 1,300 sites that represent a "'significant risk to human health or the environment."

Property owners have complained, and litigated, bitterly because:

- Current and former owners are liable even though they did nothing illegal at the time, and indeed even if they did nothing more than own property where someone else dumped hazardous wastes. In addition, officers or controlling shareholders in closely held corporations can be personally liable for operations of the company.

- Joint and several liability means that a small amount of pollution can lead to a very large damage claim.

- The expense of a Superfund cleanup can be devastating—higher than $100 million on some sites. Property owners have often viewed litigation as a better investment.

- Congress requires that land be returned to pristine condition. Owners point to scientific evidence indicating that this goal is often impossible to achieve, given existing knowledge. Once again, cost-benefit analysis enters the picture, as property owners argue that the cost of perfection is higher than the benefit. To encourage redevelopment of contaminated land, the EPA has implemented a "Brownfields" program that bases the cleanup levels for some property on potential risk to human health. However, Superfund proponents counter that, to be safe, all hazardous wastes should be removed. They offer as Exhibit A the Forrest Glen real estate development in upstate New York. The developers knew they could buy the land cheap because it had been used as a hazardous waste dump. Instead of cleaning it up, they slapped on a bucolic name. Then chemicals oozed up on lawns.

EXAM Strategy

Question: Leo was an auto mechanic who owned his own business. One morning, after a heavy rainstorm, he noticed the edge of what turned out to be an underground storage tank sticking out of the ground. He dug it up and, without looking to see what was inside it, sent the tank to an auto salvage site. Has Leo violated the law?

Strategy: Review the requirements on waste disposal.

Result: Leo did violate the law. To start, he should have notified the EPA of the underground tank. Second, he needed to determine if the tank contained any hazardous wastes. If it did, then he needed an EPA permit to dispose of the waste. He also should have sent the tank to a certified facility, not to an auto salvage site.

CHEMICALS

More than 70,000 chemicals are used in food, drugs, cosmetics, pesticides, and other products. Some of these chemicals are known to accumulate in human tissue and cause, among other harm, cancer, birth defects, and neurological damage. However, only 2 percent of these 70,000 chemicals have been adequately tested to determine their total health impact. Almost 70 percent have not been tested at all. Moreover, scientists know virtually nothing about their impact on the health of wildlife.

Several federal agencies share responsibility for regulating chemicals. The Food and Drug Administration (FDA) has control over foods, drugs, and cosmetics. The Occupational Safety and Health Administration (OSHA) is responsible for protecting workers from exposure to toxic chemicals. The Nuclear Regulatory Commission (NRC) regulates radioactive substances. The EPA regulates pesticides and other toxic chemicals.

Federal Insecticide, Fungicide, and Rodenticide Act

The Federal Insecticide, Fungicide, and Rodenticide Act (FIFRA) requires manufacturers to register all pesticides with the EPA. Before registering a pesticide, the EPA must ensure that its benefits exceed its (then-known) risks. However, many of the 50,000 pesticides currently registered with the EPA were approved at a time when little was known about their risks. In 1972, Congress directed the EPA to reevaluate all registered pesticides and cancel those whose risks exceed their benefits. This process has been very slow. Before the EPA cancels a registration, the manufacturer is entitled to a formal hearing, which may take several years. In the event of an emergency, the EPA may order an immediate suspension; otherwise, the chemical stays on the market until the hearing. If a pesticide is banned, the EPA must reimburse end users of the chemicals for their useless inventory.

Federal Food, Drug, and Cosmetic Act

The Federal Food, Drug, and Cosmetic Act requires the EPA to set maximum levels for pesticide residue in raw or processed food. The FDA can confiscate food with pesticide levels that exceed the EPA standards.

Food Quality Protection Act of 1996

The Food Quality Protection Act requires the EPA to set pesticide standards at levels that are safe for children. If the data for children are unclear, the EPA must reduce levels to one-tenth the amount then permitted in food. The EPA must also consider all sources of exposure. Thus, for example, in setting limits for pesticides on grapes, the EPA must factor in other sources of pesticides, such as drinking water.

   This statute is highly controversial. The pesticide industry argues that the EPA could effectively ban many valuable chemicals for years while careful research into their impact on children is conducted. Environmental advocates, on the other hand, are dismayed that the EPA has not demanded more thorough research before setting standards for some pesticides.

Toxic Substances Control Act

The Toxic Substances Control Act (TSCA) regulates chemicals other than pesticides, foods, drugs, and cosmetics. For example, it regulates lead in gasoline and paints. **Before selling a new chemical (or an old chemical being used for a new purpose), the manufacturer must register it with the EPA.** However, *registering* a chemical under the TSCA does not require *testing* it. Under the TSCA, the EPA can require testing of a chemical only if there is evidence that it is dangerous. Since this statute was passed in 1976, the EPA has required testing of only 200 of the more than 80,000 chemicals currently sold in the United States. Thus, for example, many manufacturers have elected to remove Bisphenol A (BPA) from their products because of concern that it is dangerous, particularly for children. But they have replaced BPA with untested chemicals, such as Polyethersulfone (PES) plastic, which have some of the same characteristics as BPA—not a reassuring choice for parents trying to buy a safe bottle for their children.

NATURAL RESOURCES

Thus far, this chapter has focused on the regulation of pollution. Congress has also passed statutes whose purpose is to preserve the country's natural resources.

National Environmental Policy Act

The National Environmental Policy Act of 1969 (NEPA) requires all *federal agencies* to prepare an *environmental impact statement* (EIS) for every major federal action significantly affecting the quality of the human environment. An agency need not prepare an EIS for a particular proposal if it finds, on the basis of a shorter environmental assessment (EA), that the action will not have a significant impact on the environment. An EIS is a major undertaking—often hundreds, if not thousands, of pages long. It must discuss (1) environmental consequences of the proposed action, (2) available alternatives, (3) direct and indirect effects, (4) energy requirements, (5) impact on urban quality, historic, and cultural resources, and (6) the means to mitigate adverse environmental impacts. Once a draft report is ready, the federal agency must hold a hearing to allow for outside comments.

The EIS requirement applies not only to actions *undertaken* by the federal government, but also to activities *regulated* or *approved* by the government. For instance, the following projects required an EIS:

- Expanding the Snowmass ski area in Aspen, Colorado, because approval was required by the Forest Service;

- Killing a herd of wild goats that was causing damage at the Olympic National Park (outside Seattle);

- Closing a road to create a beachside pavilion in Redondo Beach, California; and

- Creating a golf course outside Los Angeles, because the project required a government permit to build in wetlands.

The EIS process is controversial. If a project is likely to have an important impact, environmentalists almost always litigate the adequacy of the EIS. Industry advocates argue that environmentalists are simply using the EIS process to delay—or halt—any projects they oppose. In 1976, seven years after NEPA was passed, a dam on the Teton River in Idaho burst, killing 17 people and causing $1 billion in property damage. The Department of the Interior had built the dam in the face of allegations that its EIS was incomplete; it did not, for example, confirm that a large, earth-filled dam resting on a riverbed was safe. To environmentalists, this tragedy graphically illustrated the need for a thorough EIS.

Researchers have found that the EIS process generally has a beneficial impact on the environment. The mere prospect of preparing an EIS tends to eliminate the worst projects. Litigation over the EIS eliminates the next weakest group. If an agency does a good faith EIS, honestly looking at the available alternatives, projects tend to be kinder to the environment, at little extra cost.

In the following case, the Navy argues that it should be exempt from EIS requirements. Do you agree?

You be the Judge

Facts: The Navy wanted to conduct training exercises off the coast of California for sonar submarines. Scientists were concerned that the sounds emitted by the sonar would harm marine mammals, such as whales, dolphins, and sea lions. The Navy's EA determined that the sonar training would not adversely affect the animals or the environment, and therefore, it did not have to prepare an EIS.

Environmental groups filed suit, asking that the Navy be required to prepare an EIS and also requesting an injunction to prevent it from conducting the training exercises

WINTER V. NATURAL RESOURCES DEFENSE COUNCIL, INC.
555 U.S. 7; 2008 U.S. Lexis 8343
Supreme Court of the United States, 2008

until the EIS was complete. The trial court ruled that the Navy had to prepare an EIS, but could nonetheless proceed with the exercises beforehand, if it took certain steps to mitigate harm to the marine mammals. The Navy appealed, but the appellate court affirmed this decision. The Supreme Court granted *certiorari*.

You Be the Judge: *Must the Navy prepare an EIS before it can conduct sonar training exercises?*

Argument for the Environmental Groups: Even the Navy admits that the training exercises would cause hundreds of physical injuries to marine mammals, as well as 170,000 disturbances of marine mammals' behavior. But the sonar can cause much more serious injuries than the Navy acknowledges, including permanent hearing loss, decompression sickness, and major behavioral disruptions. Moreover, in the past, sonar has been associated with mass strandings of marine mammals. Certain species—such as beaked whales—are uniquely susceptible to injury from sonar. These injuries would not necessarily be detected by the Navy because these whales are very deep divers that spend little time at the surface.

The trial court found that there was a "near certainty" of irreparable injury to the environment and that this injury outweighed any possible harm to the Navy. The appeals court ruled that the Navy report was cursory, unsupported by evidence, and unconvincing.

The trial court did not ban all sonar exercises—it simply established rules to protect the marine mammals. Since the Navy has never tried operating under these rules, it cannot say that they are harmful. Once it prepares an EIS, it may well be able to go ahead with the sonar exercises without any limitation. But in the meantime, it is important, and required by law, to protect the animals from irreparable harm.

Argument for the Navy: Antisubmarine warfare is currently the Pacific fleet's top priority. With all due respect to the lower courts, the Navy is in the best position to determine how much harm this ban on sonar will cause to its training process. Moreover, the president—the commander in chief—determined that training with sonar is essential to national security. As the Supreme Court said last term, "Neither members of this Court nor most federal judges begin the day with briefings that may describe new and serious threats to our Nation and its people." The courts are not the best judges of national security issues.

Moreover, an EIS is only required if an action affects the quality of the *human* environment. Plaintiffs argue that they like to go on whale watching trips, observe marine mammals underwater, conduct scientific research, and photograph these animals in their natural habitats. But these pursuits are minor compared with the Navy's interest in protecting the safety of our nation.

Also, the Navy conducted an EA which revealed that these training exercises would not have a significant environmental impact. Indeed, the Navy has been conducting sonar training exercises for 40 years without a single documented sonar-related injury to any marine mammal. At most, sonar may cause temporary hearing loss or brief disruptions of marine mammals' behavioral patterns.

While it is true that, even without an EIS, the lower court would permit some use of sonar in the exercises, Navy officers testified that these restrictions would greatly undermine the value of the training. Essentially, the trial court would require submarines to turn off the sonar any time a marine animal was within 2,200 yards. The sailors would have to spend all of their time looking for animals and turning equipment on and off. The training would be virtually useless.

We do not discount the importance of plaintiffs' ecological, scientific, and recreational interests in marine mammals. Those interests, however, are plainly outweighed by the Navy's need to conduct realistic training exercises. The tradeoff in this case is simple: on the one hand is possible harm to an unknown number of marine mammals. On the other is the safety of the U.S. fleet. Any delay—and certainly the delay required to prepare an EIS—jeopardizes the safety of all of us. It is clear where the public interest lies.

Endangered Species Act

Worldwide, 25 percent of mammals, 22 percent of reptiles, and 13 percent of birds are threatened with extinction. This threat is largely caused by humans. **The Endangered Species Act (ESA):**

- Requires the Department of the Interior's Fish and Wildlife Service (FWS) to prepare a list of species that are in danger of becoming extinct;

- Requires the government to develop plans to revive these species;

- Requires all federal agencies to ensure that their actions will not jeopardize an endangered species;

- Prohibits any sale or transport of these species;

- Makes any taking of an endangered animal species unlawful (taking is defined as harassing, harming, killing, or capturing any endangered species or modifying its habitat in such a way that its population is likely to decline); and

- Prohibits the taking of any endangered plant species on federal property.

No environmental statute has been more controversial than the ESA. In theory, everyone is in favor of saving endangered species. To quote the House of Representatives Report on the ESA:

> As we homogenize the habitats in which these plants and animals evolved … we threaten their—and our own—genetic heritage… . Who knows, or can say, what potential cures for cancer or other scourges, present or future, may lie locked up in the structures of plants which may yet be undiscovered, much less analyzed?

In practice, however, the cost of saving a species can be astronomical. One of the earliest ESA battles involved the snail darter—a 3-inch fish that lived in the Little Tennessee River. The Supreme Court upheld a decision under the ESA to halt work on a dam that would have blocked the river, flooding 16,500 acres of farmland and destroying the snail darter's habitat. To the dam's supporters, this decision was ludicrous: stopping a dam (on which $100 million in taxpayer money had already been spent) to save a little fish that no one had ever even thought of before the dam (or damn) controversy. The real agenda, they argued, was simply to halt development. Environmental advocates argued, however, that the wanton destruction of whole species will ultimately and inevitably lead to disaster for humankind. In the end, Congress overruled the Supreme Court and authorized completion of the dam. It turned out that the snail darter survived in other rivers.

The snail darter was the first in a long line of ESA controversies that have included charismatic animals such as bald eagles, grizzly bears, bighorn sheep, and rockhopper penguins, but also more obscure fauna such as the Banbury Springs limpet and the triple-ribbed milkvetch. In 2007, a federal court moved to protect the delta smelt by ordering officials to shut down temporarily pumps that supplied as much as one-third of southern California's water.[13] Opponents argue that too much time and money have been spent to save too few species of too little importance.

The FWS is having an enormous battle with environmental organizations, who complain that it is too slow in listing endangered species. In the four decades since Congress passed the ESA, species have been listed at a rate of about 35 a year. Nearly 100 species have become extinct while on the list or waiting to be listed. Over the past few years, these environmental groups have asked that 1,200 species be listed as endangered. Under the statute, once the FWS receives a petition requesting endangered status for a species, it must make a ruling within 12 months. But it often misses that statutory deadline, and then environmental groups sue, which uses up agency resources in responding to the suits.

The following case discusses the advantages of protecting endangered species.

GIBBS V. BABBITT

214 F.3D 483, 2000 U.S. App. Lexis 12280
United States Court of Appeals for the Fourth Circuit, 2000

Facts: The red wolf used to roam throughout the southeastern United States. Owing to wetlands drainage, dam construction, and hunting, this wolf is now on the endangered species list. The Fish and Wildlife Service (FWS) trapped the remaining red wolves, placed them in a captive breeding program, and then reintroduced them into the wild. Ultimately, the FWS reintroduced 75 wolves into the 120,000-acre Alligator River National Wildlife Refuge in eastern North Carolina and the Pocosin Lakes National Wildlife Refuge in Tennessee.

After reintroduction, about 41 red wolves wandered from federal refuges onto private property. Richard Mann shot a red wolf that he feared might attack his cattle. Mann pled guilty to violating a provision of the ESA that prohibits the taking of any endangered species without a permit.

---

[13]*Natural Resources Defense Council v. Kempthorne*, 2007 U.S. Dist. LEXIS 91968.

Two individuals and two counties in North Carolina filed suit against the U.S. government, alleging that the anti-taking regulation as applied to the red wolves on private land exceeded Congress's power under the interstate Commerce Clause of the U.S. Constitution.

Issue: *Is the anti-taking provision of the ESA constitutional?*

Excerpts from Justice Wilkinson's Decision: Congress' commerce authority includes the power to regulate those activities having a substantial relation to interstate commerce. Although the connection to economic or commercial activity plays a central role in whether a regulation will be upheld under the Commerce Clause, economic activity must be understood in broad terms.

The red wolves are part of a $29.2 billion national wildlife-related recreational industry that involves tourism and interstate travel. Many tourists travel to North Carolina from throughout the country for "howling events"— evenings of listening to wolf howls accompanied by educational programs. According to a study conducted by Dr. William E. Rosen of Cornell University, the recovery of the red wolf and increased visitor activities could result in a significant regional economic impact. Rosen estimates that northeastern North Carolina could see an increase of between $39.61 and $183.65 million per year in tourism-related activities, and that the Great Smoky Mountains National Park could see an increase of between $132.09 and $354.50 million per year. This is hardly a trivial impact on interstate commerce.

The regulation of red wolf takings is also closely connected to a second interstate market—scientific research. Scientific research generates jobs. It also deepens our knowledge of the world in which we live. The red wolf reintroduction program has already generated numerous scientific studies. Scientific research can also reveal other uses for animals—for instance, approximately 50 percent of all modern medicines are derived from wild plants or animals.

The anti-taking regulation is also connected to a third market—the possibility of a renewed trade in fur pelts. Wolves have historically been hunted for their pelts. In such a case, businessmen may profit from the trading and marketing of that species for an indefinite number of years, where otherwise it would have been completely eliminated from commercial channels. The American alligator is a case in point. In 1975, the American alligator was nearing extinction and listed as endangered, but by 1987 conservation efforts restored the species. Now there is a vigorous trade in alligator hides.

Finally, the taking of red wolves is connected to interstate markets for agricultural products and livestock. For instance, appellant landowners find red wolves a menace because they threaten livestock and other animals of economic and commercial value. This effect on commerce, however, still qualifies as a legitimate subject for regulation.

It is well-settled under Commerce Clause cases that a regulation can involve the promotion or the restriction of commercial enterprises and development.

It is anything but clear that red wolves harm farming enterprises. They may in fact help them, and in so doing confer additional benefits on commerce. For instance, red wolves prey on animals like raccoons, deer, and rabbits—helping farmers by killing the animals that destroy their crops.

[I]t is reasonable for Congress to decide that conservation of species will one day produce a substantial commercial benefit to this country and that failure to preserve a species will result in permanent, though unascertainable, commercial loss. If a species becomes extinct, we are left to speculate forever on what we might have learned or what we may have realized. If we conserve the species, it will be available for the study and benefit of future generations. We therefore hold that the anti-taking provision at issue here involves regulable economic and commercial activity as understood by current Commerce Clause jurisprudence.

The government has introduced the Habitat Conservation Plan (HCP) as a blueprint for compromise over the ESA. In an HCP, developers agree to conserve some land in return for developing other property as they want. These deals contain a "no surprises" clause, meaning that the government has no right to retrieve land once it has been approved for development, even if scientists later determine that a particular species needs that habitat for survival. Unfortunately, the natural world is full of surprises, and environmentalists worry about the ultimate impact of these HCPs. In the short run, however, the success has been striking. For example, to save the gnatcatcher, a songbird found near San Diego, federal and local governments agreed to set aside 82,000 acres that they owned. They bought an additional 27,000 acres and developers donated 63,000 acres more. In return, the developers earned the right to build on their remaining land without limitation. More than 16 million acres, including 10 percent of timberland in the Pacific Northwest, are now designated HCPs.

Chapter Conclusion

Environmental laws have a pervasive impact on our lives. The cost has been great, whether it is higher prices for fuel-efficient cars or the time spent filling out environmental impact statements. Some argue that cost is irrelevant—that a clean environment has incalculable value for its own sake. Others insist on a more pragmatic approach and want to know if the benefits outweigh the costs. They worry that environmental regulations hurt employment.

What benefits has the country gained from environmental regulation? Since 1970, when Congress created the EPA, the record on common air pollutants, such as lead, has been extraordinarily successful. Total emissions of lead nationwide have declined by 96 percent. Before 1970, emissions of sulfur dioxide had been increasing rapidly. Since then, in spite of strong economic growth and an increase in population, these emissions have dropped. Despite this progress, however, many Americans live in areas that still do not meet EPA quality standards.

As for water, wetland acreage continues to decline at a rapid rate. However, the number of Americans whose sewage goes to wastewater treatment facilities has more than doubled. Two-thirds of the nation's waters are safe for fishing and swimming, up from only one-third when the Clean Water Act was passed.

Despite this progress, as a nation we still face many intractable problems. We have not developed a political consensus on global warming. The health effects of pesticides in our food supply are uncertain. Superfund and the Endangered Species Act are mired in a thornbush of litigation. The EPA is overwhelmed by its obligations, sometimes taking decades to issue regulations. Yet, Congress has reduced its budget.

Although many people, including many politicians, readily acknowledge the importance of the environment to both present and future generations, when the time comes to allocate funds, change lifestyles, and make tough choices, the consensus too often breaks down, with the result that resources are spent on litigation instead of the environment.

EXAM REVIEW

1. **ENVIRONMENTAL STATUTES** The following table provides a list of environmental statutes:

Air Pollution	Water Pollution	Waste Disposal	Chemicals	Natural Resources
Clean Air Act	Clean Water Act	Resource Conservation and Recovery Act	Federal Insecticide, Fungicide, and Rodenticide Act	National Environmental Policy Act
	Safe Drinking Water Act			
	Ocean Dumping Act	Comprehensive Environmental Response, Compensation, and Liability Act (Superfund or CERCLA)	Federal Food, Drug, Cosmetic Act	Endangered Species Act
	Oil Pollution Act		Food Quality Protection Act	
			Toxic Substances Control Act	

© Cengage Learning 2014

2. **AIR** Under the Clean Air Act, the EPA must establish national ambient air quality standards for both primary and secondary pollution. States must produce implementation plans to meet the EPA standards. The EPA must also regulate greenhouse gases. (pp. 716–721)

3. **WATER** The Clean Water Act (CWA) prohibits the discharge of pollution into navigable water without a permit from the EPA. States must set EPA-approved water quality standards and develop plans to achieve them. The Clean Water Act also prohibits any discharge of dredge and fill material into a wetland without a permit. (pp. 722–725)

EXAM Strategy

Question: In theory, Astro Circuit Corp. in Lowell, Massachusetts, pretreated its industrial waste to remove toxic metals. In practice, however, the factory was producing twice as much wastewater as the treatment facility could handle, and therefore, it was dumping the surplus directly into the city sewer. It was David Boldt's job to keep the production line moving. Has Boldt violated the law by dumping polluted water into the city sewer? What penalties might he face?

Strategy: Whenever water is involved, look at the provisions of the CWA. (See the "Result" at the end of this section.)

4. **DRINKING WATER** The Safe Drinking Water Act requires the EPA to set national standards for every contaminant potentially harmful to human health that is found in drinking water. (p. 725)

5. **OCEANS** The Ocean Dumping Act prohibits the dumping of wastes in ocean water without a permit from the EPA. (p. 725)

6. **SHIPS** The Oil Pollution Act of 1990 sets design standards for ships operating in U.S. waters and requires shipowners to pay for damage caused by oil discharged from their ships. (p. 725)

7. **RCRA** The Resource Conservation and Recovery Act establishes rules for treating hazardous wastes and other forms of solid waste. (pp. 726–728)

8. **SUPERFUND** Under Superfund (CERCLA), anyone who has ever owned or operated a site on which hazardous wastes are found, who has transported wastes to the site, or who has arranged for the disposal of wastes that were released at the site is liable for (1) the cost of cleaning up the site, (2) any damage done to natural resources, and (3) any required health assessments. (pp. 728–729)

EXAM Strategy

Question: In 1963, FMC Corp. purchased a manufacturing plant in Virginia from American Viscose Corp., the owner of the plant since 1937. During World War II, the government's War Production Board had commissioned American Viscose to make rayon for airplanes and truck tires. In 1982, inspections revealed carbon disulfide, a chemical used to manufacture this rayon, in groundwater near the plant. American Viscose was out of business. Who is responsible for cleaning up the carbon disulfide? Under what statute?

Strategy: Look at the statutes that govern waste disposal. (See the "Result" at the end of this section.)

9. PESTICIDES

- The Federal Insecticide, Fungicide, and Rodenticide Act (FIFRA) requires manufacturers to register all pesticides with the EPA.

- The Federal Food, Drug, and Cosmetic Act requires the EPA to set maximum levels for pesticide residue in raw or processed food.

- The Food Quality Protection Act (FQPA) requires the EPA to set pesticide standards at levels that are safe for children. (pp. 729–730)

10. CHEMICALS Under the Toxic Substances Control Act, manufacturers must register new chemicals with the EPA. (p. 730)

11. NEPA The National Environmental Policy Act requires all federal agencies to prepare an environmental impact statement (EIS) for every major federal action significantly affecting the quality of the environment. (pp. 730–731)

EXAM Strategy

Question: The U.S. Forest Service planned to build a road in the Nez Perce National Forest in Idaho to provide access to loggers. Is the Forest Service governed by any environmental statutes? Must it seek permission before building the road?

Strategy: Does a road significantly affect the quality of the environment? Is an EIS required? (See the "Result" at the end of this section.)

12. ESA The Endangered Species Act requires the FWS to list endangered species and then prohibits activities that harm them. (pp. 732–734)

3. Result: Although Boldt was in an unfortunate situation—he could have lost his job if he had not been willing to dump the industrial waste—he was found guilty of a criminal violation of the CWA. There are worse things than being fired—such as being fired *and* sent to prison.

8. Result: Both FMC and the U.S. government were liable for cleanup under CERCLA.

11. Result: As an agency of the federal government, the Forest Service must prepare an EIS (under the National Environmental Policy Act) for every action that significantly affects the quality of the environment. Although the road itself may not have been significant enough to require an impact statement, its purpose was to provide access for logging, which did require an EIS.

MULTIPLE-CHOICE QUESTIONS

1. Suppose that you are the manager of a General Motors plant that is about to start producing Hummers. The Hummer requires special protective paint that, as it turns out, reacts with other chemicals during the application process to create a pollutant. What does the Clean Air Act require of you?

   (a) Reduce other emissions from the plant so that the total quantity of pollutants is the same.

   (b) Provide an analysis showing that the benefits outweigh the costs.

   (c) Provide the EPA with evidence that your plant meets the national ambient air quality standards.

   (d) Obtain a PSD certificate from the EPA.

2. The EPA _____ have authority to regulate greenhouse gases. The states _____ impose their own standards for these gases.

   (a) does, can

   (b) does, cannot

   (c) does not, cannot

   (d) does not, can

3. For purposes of the Clean Water Act, Farmer Brown's fields _____ a point source. A canal that collects rainwater and discharges it into the Everglades _____ a point source.

   (a) are, is

   (b) are, is not

   (c) are not, is

   (d) are not, is not

4. You own property on which hazardous wastes are found. You know the identity of three former owners. You are:

   (a) liable for all the costs of the cleanup because you are the current owner.

   (b) liable for one-quarter of the costs of the cleanup.

   (c) liable for the percentage of the harm that you are able to show that you actually caused.

   (d) not liable for any of the costs of the cleanup because the damage occurred before you bought the land.

5. The Toxic Substances Control Act:

   (a) requires manufacturers to test for safety all chemicals before they can be used in products.

   (b) requires the EPA to test for safety all chemicals before they can be used in products.

   (c) requires the EPA to test all chemicals, even if they are already being used in products.

   (d) permits the EPA to require testing of a chemical only if there is evidence that it is dangerous.

ESSAY QUESTIONS

1. Tariq Ahmad decided to dispose of some of his laboratory's hazardous chemicals by shipping them to his home in Pakistan. He sent the chemicals to Castelazo (a company in the United States) to prepare the materials for shipment. Ahmad did not tell the driver who picked up the chemicals that they were hazardous, nor did he give the driver any written documentation. Has Ahmad violated U.S. law? What penalties might he face?

2. The marbled murrelet is a seabird on the list of endangered species. Pacific Lumber Co. received permission to harvest trees from land on which the murrelet nested, on the condition that it would cooperate with regulators to protect the murrelet. But the company went in one weekend and cut down trees before it met the condition. Caught in the act, it promised no more logging until it had a plan to protect the birds. It waited until the long weekend over Thanksgiving to take down some more trees. A federal court then ordered a permanent halt to any further logging. There was no evidence that the company had harmed the murrelet. Had it violated the law?

3. **YOU BE THE JUDGE WRITING PROBLEM** The Lordship Point Gun Club operated a trap and skeet shooting club in Stratford, Connecticut, for 70 years. During this time, customers deposited millions of pounds of lead shot and clay target fragments on land around the club and in the Long Island Sound. Forty-five percent of sediment samples taken from the Sound exceeded the established limits for lead. Was the Gun Club in violation of the RCRA? **Argument for the Gun Club**: The Gun Club does not *dispose* of hazardous wastes, within the meaning of the RCRA. Congress meant the statute to apply only to companies in the business of manufacturing articles that produce hazardous waste. If the Gun Club happens to produce wastes, that is only *incidental* to the normal use of a product. **Argument for the Plaintiff**: Under the RCRA, lead shot is hazardous waste. The law applies to anyone who produces hazardous waste, no matter how.

4. Shell Oil sold pesticides to B&B, which allowed these chemicals to leak into the ground. Shell was aware that the leaks were occurring. B&B ultimately went bankrupt. Is Shell liable for the costs of cleaning up this site? Under what law?

5. Before the Department of Agriculture issued regulations on genetically modified beets, what steps did it need to take under the environmental statutes?

DISCUSSION QUESTIONS

1. Life is about choices—and never more so than with the environment. Being completely honest, which of the following are you willing to do?

   - Drive a smaller, lighter, more fuel-efficient car.

   - Take public transportation or ride your bike to work.

   - Vote for political candidates who are willing to impose higher taxes on pollutants.

   - Insulate your home.

- Unplug appliances when not in use.
- Recycle your wastes.
- Pay higher taxes to clean up Superfund sites.
- Buy (more expensive) pesticide-free produce.

2. Externalities pose an enormous problem for the environment. Often, the people making decisions do not bear the full cost of their choices. Thus, the owners of a power plant that emits tons of greenhouse gases are shifting some of these costs to the rest of the world, and even to future generations. Businesses tend to fight efforts to make them pay these externalities. For example, CropLife America lobbied against a bill that would support research on the effects of chemicals on children. On the other hand, Nike recently announced that it had resigned its seat on the board of the United States Chamber of Commerce in response to the Chamber's active lobbying against legislation that would regulate greenhouse gases. But Nike will remain a member of this group. What ethical obligation do American companies have to support environmental legislation that may impose higher costs? Do they have an obligation to look out for the greater good, or should they focus on maximizing their shareholder returns? What Life Principles would you apply?

3. Is cost-benefit analysis an effective tool in environmental disputes? How do we measure the costs and benefits? How do we know what benefits we might gain from saving endangered species, or improving visibility at the Grand Canyon? In the *Entergy* case, how does the EPA calculate the benefits of not squashing fish against intake screens? Should you survey people to ask them how much it is worth? Or just think in terms of lives saved or sick days avoided? Or should we protect the environment regardless of cost?

4. Many of the environmental statutes permit citizen suits. As a result, environmental groups bring many lawsuits against both the EPA and polluters, alleging violations of these statutes. Are these suits a good idea? The Fish and Wildlife Service says that it spends so much of its resources responding to litigation over why it has not listed endangered species that it has no resources left to actually to do the listing. Businesses argue that it is unfair for every citizen to be a cop on the beat. On the other hand, environmental groups often supplement the limited resources of the EPA.

5. The *Winter* case deals with the balance between national security and the environment. Consider these additional issues: what if the president felt it was important to national security to store reserves of oil in a manner that could harm groundwater? Or permit oil drilling in areas that are environmentally fragile, such as Alaska or the Gulf Coast? Would you support such decisions? Should there be a review process for these decisions?

THE CONSTITUTION OF THE UNITED STATES

Preamble

We the People of the United States, in Order to form a more perfect Union, establish Justice, insure domestic Tranquility, provide for the common defense, promote the general Welfare, and secure the Blessings of Liberty to ourselves and our Posterity, do ordain and establish this Constitution for the United States of America.

ARTICLE I

Section 1.

All legislative Powers herein granted shall be vested in a Congress of the United States, which shall consist of a Senate and House of Representatives.

Section 2.

The House of Representatives shall be composed of Members chosen every second Year by the People of the several States, and the Electors in each State shall have the Qualifications requisite for Electors of the most numerous Branch of the State Legislature.

No Person shall be a Representative who shall not have attained to the Age of twenty five Years, and been seven Years a Citizen of the United States, and who shall not, when elected, be an Inhabitant of that State in which he shall be chosen.

Representatives and direct Taxes shall be apportioned among the several States which may be included within this Union, according to their respective Numbers, which shall be determined by adding to the whole Number of free Persons, including those bound to Service for a Term of Years, and excluding Indians not taxed, three fifths of all other Persons. The actual Enumeration shall be made within three Years after the first Meeting of the Congress of the United States, and within every subsequent Term of ten Years, in such Manner as they shall by Law direct. The number of Representatives shall not exceed one for every thirty Thousand, but each State shall have at Least one Representative; and until such enumeration shall be made, the State of New Hampshire shall be entitled to chuse three, Massachusetts eight, Rhode Island and Providence Plantations one, Connecticut five, New-York six, New Jersey four, Pennsylvania eight, Delaware one, Maryland six, Virginia ten, North Carolina five, South Carolina five, and Georgia three.

When vacancies happen in the Representation from any State, the Executive Authority thereof shall issue Writs of Election to fill such vacancies.

The House of Representatives shall chuse their Speaker and other Officers; and shall have the sole Power of Impeachment.

Section 3.

The Senate of the United States shall be composed of two Senators from each State, chosen by the Legislature thereof, for six Years; and each Senator shall have one Vote.

Immediately after they shall be assembled in Consequence of the first Election, they shall be divided as equally as may be into three Classes. The Seats of the Senators of the first Class shall be vacated at the Expiration of the second Year, of the second Class at the Expiration of the fourth Year, and of the third Class at the Expiration of the sixth Year, so that one third may be chosen every second Year; and if Vacancies happen by Resignation or otherwise, during the Recess of the Legislature of any State, the Executive thereof may make temporary Appointments until the next Meeting of the Legislature, which shall then fill such Vacancies.

No Person shall be a Senator who shall not have attained to the Age of thirty Years, and been nine Years a Citizen of the United States, and who shall not, when elected, be an Inhabitant of that State for which he shall be chosen.

The Vice President of the United States shall be President of the Senate, but shall have no Vote, unless they be equally divided.

The Senate shall chuse their other Officers, and also a President pro tempore, in the Absence of the Vice President, or when he shall exercise the Office of President of the United States.

The Senate shall have the sole power to try all Impeachments. When sitting for that Purpose, they shall be an Oath or Affirmation. When the President of the United States is tried, the Chief Justice shall preside: And no Person shall be convicted without the Concurrence of two thirds of the Members present.

Judgment in Cases of Impeachment shall not extend further than to removal from Office, and disqualification to hold and enjoy any Office of honor, Trust or Profit under the United States: but the Party convicted shall nevertheless be liable and subject to Indictment, Trial, Judgment and Punishment, according to Law.

Section 4.

The Times, Places and Manner of holding Elections for Senators and Representatives, shall be prescribed in each State by the Legislature thereof: but the Congress may at any time by Law make or alter such Regulations, except as to the Places of chusing Senators.

The Congress shall assemble at least once in every Year, and such Meeting shall be on the first Monday in December, unless they shall by Law appoint a different Day.

Section 5.

Each House shall be the Judge of the Elections, Returns and Qualifications of its own Members, and a Majority of each shall constitute a Quorum to do Business; but a smaller Number may adjourn from day to day, and may be authorized to compel the Attendance of absent Members, in such Manner, and under such Penalties as each House may provide.

Each House may determine the Rules of its Proceedings, punish its Members for disorderly Behaviour, and, with the Concurrence of two thirds, expel a Member.

Each House shall keep a Journal of its Proceedings, and from time to time publish the same, excepting such Parts as may in their Judgment require Secrecy; and the Yeas and Nays of the Members of either House on any question shall, at the Desire of one fifth of those Present, be entered on the Journal.

Neither House, during the Session of Congress, shall, without the Consent of the other, adjourn for more than three days, nor to any other Place than that in which the two Houses shall be sitting.

Section 6.

The Senators and Representatives shall receive a Compensation for their Services, to be ascertained by Law, and paid out of the Treasury of the United States. They shall in all Cases, except Treason, Felony and Breach of the Peace, be privileged from Arrest during their Attendance at the Session of their respective Houses, and in going to and returning from the same; and for any Speech or Debate in either House, they shall not be questioned in any other Place.

No Senator or Representative shall, during the Time for which he was elected, be appointed to any civil Office under the Authority of the United States, which shall have been created, or the Emoluments whereof shall have been encreased during such time; and no Person holding any Office under the United States, shall be a Member of either House during his Continuance in Office.

Section 7.

All Bills for raising Revenue shall originate in the House of Representatives; but the Senate may propose or concur with Amendments as on other Bills.

Every Bill which shall have passed the House of Representatives and the Senate, shall, before it become a Law, be presented to the President of the United States; If he approve he shall sign it, but if not he shall return it, with his Objections to that House in which it shall have originated, who shall enter the Objections at large on their Journal, and proceed to reconsider it. If after such Reconsideration two thirds of that House shall agree to pass the Bill, it shall be sent, together with the Objections, to the other House, by which it shall likewise be reconsidered, and if approved by two thirds of that House, it shall become a Law. But in all such Cases the Votes of both Houses shall be determined by Yeas and Nays, and the Names of the Persons voting for and against the Bill shall be entered on the Journal of each House respectively. If any Bill shall not be returned by the President within ten Days (Sundays excepted) after it shall have been presented to him, the Same shall be a Law, in like Manner as if he had signed it, unless the Congress by their Adjournment prevent its Return, in which Case it shall not be a Law.

Every Order, Resolution, or Vote to which the Concurrence of the Senate and House of Representatives may be necessary (except on a question of Adjournment) shall be presented to the President of the United States; and before the Same shall take Effect, shall be approved by him, or being disapproved by him, shall be repassed by two thirds of the Senate and House of Representatives, according to the Rules and Limitations prescribed in the Case of a Bill.

Section 8.

The Congress shall have Power to lay and collect Taxes, Duties, Imposts and Excises, to pay the Debts and provide for the common Defence and general Welfare of the United States; but all Duties, Imposts and Excises shall be uniform throughout the United States;

To borrow Money on the credit of the United States;

To regulate Commerce with foreign Nations, and among the several States, and with the Indian Tribes;

To establish an uniform Rule of Naturalization, and uniform Laws on the subject of Bankruptcies throughout the United States;

To coin Money, regulate the Value thereof, and of foreign Coin, and fix the Standard of Weights and Measures;

To provide for the Punishment of counterfeiting the Securities and current Coin of the United States;

To establish Post Offices and post Roads;

To promote the Progress of Science and useful Arts, by securing for limited Times to Authors and Inventors the exclusive Right to their respective Writings and Discoveries;

To constitute Tribunals inferior to the Supreme Court;

To define and punish Piracies and Felonies committed on the high Seas, and Offenses against the Law of Nations;

To declare War, grant Letters of Marque and Reprisal, and make Rules concerning Captures on Land and Water;

To raise and support Armies, but no Appropriation of Money to that Use shall be for a longer Term than two Years;

To provide and maintain a Navy;

To make Rules for the Government and Regulation of the land and naval Forces;

To provide for calling forth the Militia to execute the Laws of the Union, suppress Insurrections and repel Invasions;

To provide for organizing, arming, and disciplining, the Militia, and for governing such Part of them as may be employed in the Service of the United States, reserving to the States respectively, the Appointment of the Officers, and the Authority of training the Militia according to the discipline described by Congress;

To exercise exclusive Legislation in all Cases whatsoever, over such District (not exceeding ten Miles square) as may, by Cession of particular States, and the Acceptance of Congress, become the Seat of the Government of the United States, and to exercise like Authority over all Places purchased by the Consent of the Legislature of the State in which the Same shall be, for the Erection of Forts, Magazines, Arsenals, dock-Yards, and other needful Buildings;—And

To make all Laws which shall be necessary and proper for carrying into Execution the foregoing Powers, and all other Powers vested by this Constitution in the Government of the United States, or in any Department or Officer thereof.

Section 9.

The Migration or Importation of such Persons as any of the States now existing shall think proper to admit, shall not be prohibited by the Congress prior to the Year one thousand eight hundred and eight, but a Tax or Duty may be imposed on such Importation, not exceeding ten dollars for each Person.

The Privilege of the Writ of Habeas Corpus shall not be suspended, unless when in Cases of Rebellion or Invasion the public Safety may require it.

No Bill of Attainder or ex post facto Law shall be passed.

No Capitation, or other direct, Tax shall be laid, unless in Proportion to the Census or Enumeration herein before directed to be taken.

No Tax or Duty shall be laid on Articles exported from any State.

No Preference shall be given by any Regulation of Commerce or Revenue to the Ports of one State over those of another; nor shall Vessels bound to, or from, one State, be obliged to enter, clear, or pay Duties in another.

No Money shall be drawn from the Treasury, but in Consequence of Appropriations made by Laws; and a regular Statement and Account of the Receipts and Expenditures of all public Money shall be published from time to time.

No Title of Nobility shall be granted by the United States: And no Person holding any Office of Profit or Trust under them, shall, without the Consent of the Congress, accept of any present, Emolument, Office, or Title, of any kind whatever, from any King, Prince, or foreign State.

Section 10.

No State shall enter into any Treaty, Alliance, or Confederation; grant Letters of Marque and Reprisal; coin Money; emit Bills of Credit; make any Thing but gold and silver Coin a Tender in Payment of Debts; pass any Bill of Attainder, ex post facto Law, or Law impairing the Obligation of Contracts, or grant any Title of Nobility.

No State shall, without the Consent of the Congress, lay any Imposts or Duties on Imports or Exports, except what may be absolutely necessary for executing its inspection Laws: and the net Produce of all Duties and Imposts, laid by any State on Imports or Exports, shall be for the Use of the Treasury of the United States; and all such Laws shall be subject to the Revision and Controul of the Congress.

No State shall, without the Consent of Congress, lay any Duty of Tonnage, keep Troops, or Ships of War in time of Peace, enter into any Agreement or Compact with another State, or with a foreign Power, or engage in War, unless actually invaded, or in such imminent Danger as will not admit of delay.

ARTICLE II

Section 1.

The executive Power shall be vested in a President of the United States of America. He shall hold his Office during the Term of four Years, and, together with the Vice President, chosen for the same Term, be elected, as follows:

Each State shall appoint, in such Manner as the Legislature thereof may direct, a Number of Electors, equal to the whole Number of Senators and Representatives to which the State may be entitled in the Congress: but no Senator or Representative, or Person holding an Office of Trust or Profit under the United States, shall be appointed an Elector.

The Electors shall meet in their respective States, and vote by Ballot for two Persons, of whom one at least shall not be an Inhabitant of the same State with themselves. And they shall make a list of all the Persons voted for, and of the Number of Votes for each; which List they shall sign and certify, and transmit sealed to the Seat of the Government of the United States, directed to the President of the Senate. The President of the Senate shall, in the presence of the Senate and House of Representatives, open all the Certificates, and the Votes shall be counted. The Person having the greatest Number of Votes shall be the President, if such Number be a Majority of the whole Number of Electors appointed; and if there be more than one who have such Majority, and have an equal Number of Votes, then the House of Representatives shall immediately chuse by Ballot one of them for President; and if no Person have a Majority, then from the five highest on the List the said House shall in like Manner chuse the President. But in chusing the President, the Votes shall be taken by States, the Representation from each State having one Vote; A quorum for this Purpose shall consist of a Member or Members from two thirds of the States, and a Majority of all the States shall be necessary to a Choice. In every Case, after the Choice of the President, the Person having the greatest Number of Votes of the Electors shall be the Vice President. But if there should remain two or more who have equal Votes, the Senate shall chuse from them by Ballot the Vice President.

The Congress may determine the Time of Chusing the Electors, and the Day on which they shall give their Votes; which Day shall be the same throughout the United States.

No Person except a natural born Citizen, or a Citizen of the United States, at the time of the Adoption of this Constitution, shall be eligible to the Office of President; neither shall any Person be eligible to that Office who shall not have attained to the Age of thirty five Years, and been fourteen Years a Resident within the United States.

In Case of the Removal of the President from Office, or of his Death, Resignation, or Inability to discharge the Powers and Duties of the said Office, the Same shall devolve on the Vice President, and the Congress may by Law provide for the Case of Removal, Death, Resignation or Inability, both of the President and Vice President, declaring what Officer shall then act as President, and such Officer shall act accordingly, until the Disability be removed, or a President shall be elected.

The President shall, at stated Times, receive for his Services, a Compensation, which shall neither be encreased nor diminished during the Period for which he shall have been elected, and he shall not receive within that Period any other Emolument from the United States, or any of them.

Before he enter on the Execution of his Office, he shall take the following Oath or Affirmation:—"I do solemnly swear (or affirm) that I will faithfully execute the Office of President of the United States, and will to the best of my Ability, preserve, protect and defend the Constitution of the United States."

Section 2.

The President shall be Commander in Chief of the Army and Navy of the United States, and of the Militia of the several States, when called into the actual Service of the United States; he may require the Opinion, in writing, of the principal Officer in each of the executive Departments, upon any Subject relating to the Duties of their respective Offices, and he shall have Power to grant Reprieves and Pardons for Offenses against the United States, except in Cases of Impeachment.

He shall have Power, by and with the Advice and Consent of the Senate, to make Treaties, providing two thirds of the Senators present concur; and he shall nominate, and by and with the Advice and Consent of the Senate, shall appoint Ambassadors, other public Ministers and Consuls, Judges of the supreme Court, and all other Officers of the United States, whose Appointments are not herein otherwise provided for, and which shall be established by Law: but the Congress may by Law vest the Appointment of such inferior Officers, as they think proper, in the President alone, in the Courts of Law, or in the Heads of Departments.

The President shall have Power to fill up all Vacancies that may happen during the Recess of the Senate, by granting Commissions which shall expire at the End of their next Session.

Section 3.   He shall from time to time give to the Congress Information of the State of the Union, and recommend to their Consideration such Measures as he shall judge necessary and expedient; he may, on extraordinary Occasions, convene both Houses, or either of them, and in Case of Disagreement between them, with Respect to the Time of Adjournment, he may adjourn them to such Time as he shall think proper, he shall receive Ambassadors and other public Ministers; he shall take Care that the Laws be faithfully executed, and shall Commission all the Offices of the United States.

Section 4.   The President, Vice President and all civil Officers of the United States, shall be removed from Office on Impeachment for, and Conviction of, Treason, Bribery, or other high Crimes and Misdemeanors.

ARTICLE III

Section 1.   The judicial Power of the United States, shall be vested in one supreme Court, and in such inferior Courts as the Congress may from time to time ordain and establish. The Judges, both of the supreme and inferior Courts, shall hold their Offices during good Behaviour, and shall, at Times, receive for their Services, a Compensation, which shall not be diminished during their Continuance in Office.

Section 2.   The judicial Power shall extend to all Cases, in Law and Equity, arising under this Constitution, the Laws of the United States, and Treaties made, or which shall be made, under their Authority;—to all Cases affecting Ambassadors, other public Ministers and Consuls;—to all Cases of admiralty and maritime Jurisdiction;—to Controversies to which the United States shall be a Party;—to controversies between two or more States;—between a State and Citizens of another State;—between Citizens of different States;—between Citizens of the same State claiming Lands under Grants of different States; and between a State, or the Citizens thereof, and foreign States, Citizens or Subjects.

In all Cases affecting Ambassadors, other public Ministers and Consuls, and those in which a State shall be Party, the supreme Court shall have original Jurisdiction. In all the other Cases before mentioned, the supreme Court shall have appellate Jurisdiction, both as to Law and Fact, with such Exceptions, and under such Regulations as the Congress shall make.

The Trial of all Crimes, except in Cases of Impeachment, shall be by Jury; and such Trial shall be held in the State where the said Crimes shall have been committed; but when not committed within any State, the Trial shall be at such Place or Places as the Congress may by Law have directed.

Section 3.

Treason against the United States, shall consist only in levying War against them, or in adhering to their Enemies, giving them Aid and Comfort. No Person shall be convicted of Treason unless on the Testimony of two Witnesses to the same overt Act, or on Confession in open Court.

The Congress shall have Power to declare the Punishment of Treason, but no Attainder of Treason shall work Corruption of Blood, or Forfeiture except during the Life of the Person attainted.

ARTICLE IV

Section 1.

Full Faith and Credit shall be given in each State to the public Acts, Records, and judicial Proceedings of every other State. And the Congress may by general Laws prescribe the Manner in which such Acts, Records and Proceedings shall be proved, and the Effect thereof.

Section 2.

The Citizens of each State shall be entitled to all Privileges and Immunities of Citizens in the several States.

A Person charged in any State with Treason, Felony, or other Crime, who shall flee from Justice, and be found in another State, shall on Demand of the executive Authority of the State from which he fled, be delivered up, to be removed to the State having Jurisdiction of the Crime.

No Person held to Service or Labour in one State, under the Laws thereof, escaping into another, shall, in Consequence of any Law or Regulation therein, be discharged from such Service or Labour, but shall be delivered up on Claim of the Party to whom such Service or Labour may be due.

Section 3.

New States may be admitted by the Congress into this Union; but no new State shall be formed or erected within the Jurisdiction of any other State; nor any State be formed by the Junction of two or more States, or Parts of States, without the Consent of the Legislatures of the States concerned as well as the Congress.

The Congress shall have Power to dispose of and make all needful Rules and Regulations respecting the Territory or other Property belonging to the United States; and nothing in this Constitution shall be so construed as to Prejudice any Claims of the United States, or of any particular State.

Section 4.

The United States shall guarantee to every State in this Union a Republican Form of Government, and shall protect each of them against Invasion; and on Application of the Legislature, or of the Executive (when the Legislature cannot be convened) against domestic Violence.

ARTICLE V

The Congress, whenever two thirds of both Houses shall deem it necessary, shall propose Amendments to this Constitution, or, on the Application of the Legislatures of two thirds of the several States, shall call a Convention for proposing Amendments, which, in either Case, shall be valid to all Intents and Purposes, as Part of this Constitution, when ratified by the Legislatures of three fourths of the several States, or by Conventions in three fourths thereof, as the one or the other Mode of Ratification may be proposed by the Congress; Provided that no Amendment which may be made prior to the Year One thousand eight hundred and eight shall in any Manner affect the first and fourth Clauses in the Ninth Section of the first Article; and that no State, without its Consent, shall be deprived of its equal Suffrage in the Senate.

ARTICLE VI

All Debts contracted and Engagements entered into, before the Adoption of this Constitution, shall be as valid against the United States under this Constitution, as under the Confederation.

This Constitution, and the Laws of the United States which shall be made in Pursuance thereof; and all Treaties made, or which shall be made, under the Authority of the United States, shall be the supreme Law of the Land; and the Judges in every State shall be bound thereby, any Thing in the Constitution or Laws of any State to the Contrary notwithstanding.

The Senators and Representatives before mentioned, and the Members of the several State Legislatures, and all executive and judicial Officers, both of the United States and of the Several States, shall be bound by Oath or Affirmation, to support this Constitution; but no religious Test shall ever be required as a Qualification to any Office or public Trust under the United States.

ARTICLE VII

The Ratification of the Conventions of nine States, shall be sufficient for the Establishment of this Constitution between the States so ratifying the Same.

Amendment I [1791].

Congress shall make no law respecting an establishment of religion, or prohibiting the free exercise thereof; or abridging the freedom of speech, or the press; or the right of the people peaceably to assemble, and to petition the Government for a redress of grievances.

Amendment II [1791].

A well regulated Militia, being necessary to the security for a free State, the right of the people to keep and bear Arms, shall not be infringed.

Amendment III [1791].

No Soldier shall, in time of peace be quartered in any house, without the consent of the Owner, nor in time of war, but in a manner to be prescribed by law.

Amendment IV [1791].

The right of the people to be secure in their persons, houses, papers, and effects, against unreasonable searches and seizures, shall not be violated, and no Warrants shall issue, but upon probable cause, supported by Oath or Affirmation, and particularly describing the place to be searched, and the persons or things to be seized.

Amendment V [1791].

No person shall be held to answer for a capital, or otherwise infamous crime, unless on a presentment or indictment of a Grand Jury, except in cases arising in the land or naval forces, or in the Militia, when in actual service in time of War or public danger;

nor shall any person be subject for the same offense to be twice put in jeopardy of life or limb; nor shall be compelled in any criminal case to be a witness against himself, nor be deprived of life, liberty, or property, without due process of law; nor shall private property be taken for public use, without just compensation.

Amendment VI [1791].

In all criminal prosecutions, the accused shall enjoy the right to a speedy and public trial, by an impartial jury of the State and district wherein the crime shall have been committed, which district shall have been previously ascertained by law, and to be informed of the nature and cause of the accusation; to be confronted with the Witnesses against him; to have compulsory process for obtaining witnesses in his favor, and to have the Assistance of counsel for his defence.

Amendment VII [1791].

In suits at common law, where the value in controversy shall exceed twenty dollars, the right of trial by jury shall be preserved, and no fact tried by a jury, shall be otherwise re-examined in any Court of the United States, than according to the rules of the common law.

Amendment VIII [1791].

Excessive bail shall not be required, no excessive fines imposed, nor cruel and unusual punishments inflicted.

Amendment IX [1791].

The enumeration in the Constitution, of certain rights, shall not be construed to deny or disparage others retained by the people.

Amendment X [1791].

The powers not delegated to the United States by the Constitution, nor prohibited by it to the States, are reserved to the States respectively, or to the people.

Amendment XI [1798].

The judicial power of the United States shall not be construed to extend to any suit in law or equity, commenced or prosecuted against one of the United States by Citizens of another State, or by Citizens or Subjects of any Foreign State.

Amendment XII [1804].

The Electors shall meet in their respective states and vote by ballot for President and Vice-President, one of whom, at least, shall not be an inhabitant of the same state with themselves; they shall name in their ballots the person voted for as President, and in distinct ballots the person voted for as Vice-President, and they shall make distinct lists of all persons voted for as President, and of all persons voted for as Vice-President, and of the number of votes for each, which lists they shall sign and certify, and transmit sealed to the seat of the government of the United States, directed to the President of the Senate;—The President of the Senate shall, in the presence of the Senate and House of Representatives, open all the certificates and the votes shall then be counted;—The person having the greatest number of votes for President, shall be the President, if such number be a majority of the whole number of Electors appointed; and if no person have such majority, then from the persons having the highest numbers not exceeding three on the list of those voted for as President, the House of Representatives shall choose immediately, by ballot, the President. But in choosing the President, the votes shall be taken by states, the representation from each state having one vote; a quorum for this purpose shall consist of a member or members from two-thirds of the states, and a majority of all the states shall be necessary to a choice. And if the House of Representatives shall not choose a President when-ever the right of choice shall devolve upon them, before the fourth day of March next following, then the Vice-President shall act as President, as in the case of the death or other constitutional disability of the President. The person having the greatest number of votes as Vice-President, shall be the Vice-President, if such number be a majority of the whole number of Electors appointed, and if no person have a majority, then from the two highest numbers on the list, the Senate shall choose the Vice-President; a quorum for the purpose shall consist of two-thirds of the whole number of Senators, and a majority of the whole number shall be necessary to a choice. But no person constitutionally ineligible to the office of President shall be eligible to that of the Vice-President of the United States.

Amendment XIII [1865].

Section 1. Neither slavery nor involuntary servitude, except as a punishment for crime whereof the party shall have been duly convicted, shall exist within the United States, or any place subject to their jurisdiction.

Section 2. Congress shall have power to enforce this article by appropriate legislation.

Amendment XIV [1868].

Section 1. All persons born or naturalized in the United States, and subject to the jurisdiction thereof, are citizens of the United States and of the State wherein they reside. No State shall make or enforce any law which shall abridge the privileges or immunities of citizens of the United States; nor shall any State deprive any person of life, liberty, or property, without due process of law; nor deny to any person within its jurisdiction the equal protection of the laws.

Section 2. Representatives shall be appointed among the several States according to their respective numbers, counting the whole number of persons in each State, excluding Indians not taxed. But when the right to vote at any election for the choice of electors for President and Vice President of the United States, Representatives in Congress, the Executive and Judicial officers of a State, or the members of the Legislature thereof, is denied to any of the male inhabitants of such State, being twenty-one years of age, and citizens of the United States, or in any way abridged, except for participation in rebellion, or other crime, the basis of representation therein shall be reduced in the proportion which the number of such male citizens shall bear the whole number of male citizens twenty-one years of age in such State.

Section 3. No person shall be a Senator or Representative in Congress, or elector of President and Vice President, or hold any office, civil or military, under the United States, or under any State, who, having previously taken an oath, as a member of Congress, or as an officer of the United States, or as a member of any State legislature, or as an executive or judicial officer of any State, to support the Constitution of the United States, shall have engaged in insurrection or rebellion against the same, or given aid or comfort to the enemies thereof. But Congress may by a vote of two-thirds of each House, remove such disability.

Section 4. The validity of the public debt of the United States, authorized by law, including debts incurred for payment of pensions and bounties for services in suppressing insurrection or rebellion, shall not be questioned. But neither the United States nor any State shall assume or pay any debt or obligation incurred in aid of insurrection of rebellion against the United States, or any claim for the loss or emancipation of any slave; but all such debts, obligations and claims shall be held illegal and void.

Section 5. The Congress shall have power to enforce, by appropriate legislation, the provisions of this article.

Amendment XV [1870].

Section 1. The right of citizens of the United States to vote shall not be denied or abridged by the United States or by any State on account of race, color, or previous condition of servitude.

Section 2. The Congress shall have power to enforce this article by appropriate legislation.

Amendment XVI [1913].

The Congress shall have power to lay and collect taxes on incomes, from whatever source derived, without apportionment among the several States, and without regard to any census or enumeration.

Amendment XVII [1913].

The Senate of the United States shall be composed of two Senators from each State, elected by the people thereof, for six years; and each Senator shall have one vote. The electors in each State shall have the qualifications requisite for electors of the most numerous branch of the State legislatures.

When vacancies happen in the representation of any State in the Senate, the executive authority of each State shall issue writs of election to fill such vacancies; *Provided*, That the legislature of any State may empower the executive thereof to make temporary appointments until the people fill the vacancies by election as the legislature may direct.

This amendment shall not be construed as to affect the election or term of any Senator chosen before it becomes valid as part of the Constitution.

Amendment XVIII [1919].

Section 1. After one year from the ratification of this article the manufacture, sale, or transportation of intoxicating liquors within, the importation thereof into, or the exportation thereof from the United States and all territory subject to the jurisdiction thereof for beverage purposes is hereby prohibited.

Section 2. The Congress and the several States shall have concurrent power to enforce this article by appropriate legislation.

Section 3. This article shall be inoperative unless it shall have been ratified as an amendment to the Constitution by the legislatures of the several States, as provided in the Constitution, within seven years from the date of the submission hereof to the States by the Congress.

Amendment XIX [1920].

The right of citizens of the United States to vote shall not be denied or abridged by the United States or by any State on account of sex.

Congress shall have power to enforce this article by appropriate legislation.

Amendment XX [1933].

Section 1. The terms of the President and Vice President shall end at noon on the 20th day of January, and the terms of Senators and Representatives at noon on the 3d day of January, of the years in which such terms would have ended if this article had not been ratified; and the terms of their successors shall then begin.

Section 2. The Congress shall assemble at least once in every year, and such meeting shall begin at noon on the 3d day of January, unless they shall by law appoint a different day.

Section 3. If, at the time fixed for the beginning of the term of the President, the President elect shall have died, the Vice President elect shall become President. If a President shall not have been chosen before the time fixed for the beginning of his term, or if the President elect shall have failed to qualify, then the Vice President elect shall act as President until a President shall have qualified; and the Congress may by law provide for the case wherein neither a President elect nor a Vice President elect shall have qualified, declaring who shall then act as President, or the manner in which one who is to act shall be selected, and such person shall act accordingly until a President or Vice President shall have qualified.

Section 4. The Congress may by law provide for the case of the death of any of the persons from whom the House of Representatives may choose a President whenever the right of choice shall have devolved upon them, and for the case of the death of any of the persons from whom the Senate may choose a Vice President whenever the right of choice shall have devolved upon them.

Section 5. Sections 1 and 2 shall take effect on the 15th day of October following the ratification of this article.

Section 6. This article shall be inoperative unless it shall have been ratified as an amendment to the Constitution by the legislatures of three-fourths of the several States within seven years from the date of its submission.

Amendment XXI [1933].

Section 1. The eighteenth article of amendment to the Constitution of the United States is hereby repealed.

Section 2. The transportation or importation into any State, Territory, or possession of the United States for delivery or use therein of intoxicating liquors, in violation of the laws thereof, is hereby prohibited.

Section 3. This article shall be inoperative unless it shall have been ratified as an amendment to the Constitution by conventions in the several States, as provided in the Constitution, within seven years from the date of the submission hereof to the States by the Congress.

Amendment XXII [1951].

Section 1. No person shall be elected to the office of the President more than twice, and no person who has held the office of President, or acted as President, for more than two years of a term to which some other person was elected President shall be elected to the office of the President more than once. But this Article shall not apply to any person holding the office of President when this Article was proposed by the Congress, and shall not prevent any person who may be holding the office of President, or acting as President, during the term within which this Article becomes operative from holding the office of President, or acting as President during the remainder of such term.

Section 2. This article shall be inoperative unless it shall have been ratified as an amendment to the Constitution by the legislatures of three-fourths of the several States within seven years from the date of its submission to the States by the Congress.

Amendment XXIII [1961].

Section 1. The District constituting the seat of Government of the United States shall appoint in such manner as the Congress may direct:

A number of electors of President and Vice President equal to the whole number of Senators and Representatives in Congress to which the District would be entitled if it were a State, but in no event more than the least populous State; they shall be in addition to those appointed by the States, but they shall be considered, for the purposes of the election of President and Vice President, to be electors appointed by a State; and they shall meet in the District and perform such duties as provided by the twelfth article of amendment.

Section 2. The Congress shall have power to enforce this article by appropriate legislation.

Amendment XXIV [1964].

Section 1. The right of citizens of the United States to vote in any primary or other election for President or Vice President, for electors for President or Vice President, or for Senator or Representative in Congress, shall not be denied or abridged by the United States or any State by reason of failure to pay any poll tax or other tax.

Section 2. The Congress shall have power to enforce this article by appropriate legislation.

Amendment XXV [1967].

Section 1. In case of the removal of the President from office or of his death or resignation, the Vice President shall become President.

Section 2. Whenever there is a vacancy in the office of the Vice President, the President shall nominate a Vice President who shall take office upon confirmation by a majority vote of both Houses of Congress.

Section 3. Whenever the President transmits to the President pro tempore of the Senate and the Speaker of the House of Representatives his written declaration that he is unable to discharge the powers and duties of his office, and until he transmits to them a written declaration to the contrary, such powers and duties shall be discharged by the Vice President as Acting President.

Section 4. Whenever the Vice President and a majority of either the principal officers of the executive departments or of such other body as Congress may by law provide, transmit to the President pro tempore of the Senate and the Speaker of the House of Representatives their written declaration that the President is unable to discharge the powers and duties of his office, the Vice President shall immediately assume the powers and duties of the office as Acting President.

Thereafter, when the President transmits to the President pro tempore of the Senate and the Speaker of the House of Representatives his written declaration that no inability exists, he shall resume the powers and duties of his office unless the Vice President and a majority of either the principal officers of the executive department or of such other body as Congress may by law provide, transmit within four days to the President pro tempore of the Senate and the Speaker of the House of Representatives their written declaration that the President is unable to discharge the powers and duties of his office. Thereupon Congress shall decide the issue, assembling within forty-eight hours for that purpose if not in session. If the Congress, within twenty-one days after receipt of the latter written declaration, or, if Congress is not in session, within twenty-one days after Congress is required to assemble, determines by two-thirds vote of both Houses that the President is unable to discharge the powers and duties of his office, the Vice President shall continue to discharge the same as Acting President; otherwise, the President shall resume the powers and duties of his office.

Amendment XXVI [1971].

Section 1. The right of citizens of the United States, who are eighteen years of age or older, to vote shall not be denied or abridged by the United States or by any State on account of age.

Section 2. The Congress shall have power to enforce this article by appropriate legislation.

Amendment XXVII [1992].

No law, varying the compensation for the services of the Senators and Representatives, shall take effect, until an election of Representatives shall have intervened.

UNIFORM COMMERCIAL CODE (SELECTED PROVISIONS)

The code consists of the following articles:

Art.

1. General provisions
2. Sales
2A. Leases
3. Negotiable instruments
4. Bank deposits and collections
4A. Fund transfers
5. Letters of credit
6. Repealer of Article 6—Bulk Transfers and [Revised] Article 6—Bulk sales
7. Warehouse Receipts, Bills of Lading and Other Documents of Title
8. Investment Securities
9. Secured Transactions
10. Effective Date and Repealer
11. Effective Date and Transmission provisions

ARTICLE I
GENERAL PROVISIONS

PART 1   Short Title, Construction, Application and Subject Matter of the Act

§ 1–101.   Short Title.

This Act shall be known and may be cited as Uniform Commercial Code.

§ 1–102.   Purposes; Rules of Construction; Variation by Agreement.

(1) This Act shall be liberally construed and applied to promote its underlying purposes and policies.

(2) Underlying purposes and policies of this Act are

(a) to simplify, clarify and modernize the law governing commercial transactions;

(b) to permit the continued expansion of commercial practices through custom, usage and agreement of the parties;

(c) to make uniform the law among the various jurisdictions.

(3) The effect of provisions of this Act may be varied by agreement, except as otherwise provided in this Act and except that the obligations of good faith, diligence, reasonableness and care prescribed by this Act may not be disclaimed by agreement but the parties may by agreement determine the standards by which the performance of such obligations is to be measured if such standards are not manifestly unreasonable.

(4) The presence in certain provisions of this Act of the words "unless otherwise agreed" or words of similar import does not imply that the effect of other provisions may not be varied by agreement under subsection (3).

(5) In this Act unless the context otherwise requires

(a) words in the singular number include the plural, and in the plural include the singular;

(b) words of the masculine gender include the feminine and the neuter, and when the sense so indicates words of the neuter gender may refer to any gender.

§ 1–103.   Supplementary General Principles of Law Applicable.

Unless displaced by the particular provisions of this Act, the principles of law and equity, including the law merchant and the law relative to capacity to contract, principal and agent, estoppel, fraud, misrepresentation, duress, coercion, mistake, bankruptcy, or other validating or invalidating cause shall supplement its provisions.

§ 1–104.   Construction Against Implicit Repeal.

This Act being a general act intended as a unified coverage of its subject matter, no part of it shall be deemed to be impliedly repealed by subsequent legislation if such construction can reasonably be avoided.

§ 1–105.   Territorial Application of the Act; Parties' Power to Choose Applicable Law.

(1) Except as provided hereafter in this section, when a transaction bears a reasonable relation to this state and also to

another state or nation the parties may agree that the law either of this state or of such other state or nation shall govern their rights and duties. Failing such agreement this Act applies to transactions bearing an appropriate relation to this state.

(2) Where one of the following provisions of this Act specifies the applicable law, that provision governs and a contrary agreement is effective only to the extent permitted by the law (including the conflict of laws rules) so specified:

> Rights of creditors against sold goods. Section 2–402.
>
> Applicability of the Article on Leases. Sections 2A–105 and 2A–106.
>
> Applicability of the Article on Bank Deposits and Collections. Section 4–102.
>
> Governing law in the Article on Funds Transfers. Section 4A–507.
>
> Letters of Credit, Section 5–116.
>
> Bulk sales subject to the Article on Bulk Sales. Section 6–103.
>
> Applicability of the Article on Investment Securities. Section 8–106.
>
> Law governing perfection, the effect of perfection or nonperfection, and the priority of security interests and agricultural liens. Sections 9–301 through 9–307.
>
> As amended in 1972, 1987, 1988, 1989, 1994, 1995, and 1999.

§ 1–106.   Remedies to Be Liberally Administered.

(1) The remedies provided by this Act shall be liberally administered to the end that the aggrieved party may be put in as good a position as if the other party had fully performed but neither consequential or special nor penal damages may be had except as specifically provided in this Act or by other rule of law.

(2) Any right or obligation declared by this Act is enforceable by action unless the provision declaring it specifies a different and limited effect.

§ 1–107.   Waiver or Renunciation of Claim or Right After Breach.

Any claim or right arising out of an alleged breach can be discharged in whole or in part without consideration by a written waiver or renunciation signed and delivered by the aggrieved party.

§ 1–108.   Severability.

If any provision or clause of this Act or application thereof to any person or circumstances is held invalid, such invalidity shall not affect other provisions or applications of the Act which can be given effect without the invalid provision or application, and to this end the provisions of this Act are declared to be severable.

§ 1–109.   Section Captions.

Section captions are parts of this Act.

PART 2   General Definitions and Principles of Interpretation

§ 1–201.   General Definitions.

Subject to additional definitions contained in the subsequent Articles of this Act which are applicable to specific Articles or Parts thereof, and unless the context otherwise requires, in this Act:

(1) "Action" in the sense of a judicial proceeding includes recoupment, counterclaim, set-off, suit in equity and any other proceedings in which rights are determined.

(2) "Aggrieved party" means a party entitled to resort to a remedy.

(3) "Agreement" means the bargain of the parties in fact as found in their language or by implication from other circumstances including course of dealing or usage of trade or course of performance as provided in this Act (Sections 1–205 and 2–208). Whether an agreement has legal consequences is determined by the provisions of this Act, if applicable; otherwise by the law of contracts (Section 1–103). (Compare "Contract".)

(4) "Bank" means any person engaged in the business of banking.

(5) "Bearer" means the person in possession of an instrument, document of title, or certificated security payable to bearer or indorsed in blank.

(6) "Bill of lading" means a document evidencing the receipt of goods for shipment issued by a person engaged in the business of transporting or forwarding goods, and includes an airbill. "Airbill" means a document serving for air transportation as a bill of lading does for marine or rail transportation, and includes an air consignment note or air waybill.

(7) "Branch" includes a separately incorporated foreign branch of a bank.

(8) "Burden of establishing" a fact means the burden of persuading the triers of fact that the existence of the fact is more probable than its non-existence.

(9) "Buyer in ordinary course of business" means a person that buys goods in good faith, without knowledge that the sale violates the rights of another person in the goods, and in the ordinary course from a person, other than a pawnbroker, in the business of selling goods of that kind. A person buys goods in the ordinary course if the sale to the person comports with the usual or customary practices in the kind of business in which the seller is engaged or with the seller's own usual or customary practices. A person that sells oil, gas, or other minerals at the wellhead or minehead is a person in the business of selling goods of that kind. A buyer in ordinary course of business may buy for cash, by exchange of other property, or on secured or unsecured credit, and may acquire goods or documents of title

under a pre-existing contract for sale. Only a buyer that takes possession of the goods or has a right to recover the goods from the seller under Article 2 may be a buyer in ordinary course of business. A person that acquires goods in a transfer in bulk or as security for or in total or partial satisfaction of a money debt is not a buyer in ordinary course of business.

(10) "Conspicuous": A term or clause is conspicuous when it is so written that a reasonable person against whom it is to operate ought to have noticed it. A printed heading in capitals (as: NON-NEGOTIABLE BILL OF LADING) is conspicuous. Language in the body of a form is "conspicuous" if it is in larger or other contrasting type or color. But in a telegram any stated term is "conspicuous". Whether a term or clause is "conspicuous" or not is for decision by the court.

(11) "Contract" means the total legal obligation which results from the parties' agreement as affected by this Act and any other applicable rules of law. (Compare "Agreement".)

(12) "Creditor" includes a general creditor, a secured creditor, a lien creditor and any representative of creditors, including an assignee for the benefit of creditors, a trustee in bankruptcy, a receiver in equity and an executor or administrator of an insolvent debtor's or assignor's estate.

(13) "Defendant" includes a person in the position of defendant in a cross-action or counterclaim.

(14) "Delivery" with respect to instruments, documents of title, chattel paper, or certificated securities means voluntary transfer of possession.

(15) "Document of title" includes bill of lading, dock warrant, dock receipt, warehouse receipt or order for the delivery of goods, and also any other document which in the regular course of business or financing is treated as adequately evidencing that the person in possession of it is entitled to receive, hold and dispose of the document and the goods it covers. To be a document of title a document must purport to be issued by or addressed to a bailee and purport to cover goods in the bailee's possession which are either identified or are fungible portions of an identified mass.

(16) "Fault" means wrongful act, omission or breach.

(17) "Fungible" with respect to goods or securities means goods or securities of which any unit is, by nature or usage of trade, the equivalent of any other like unit. Goods which are not fungible shall be deemed fungible for the purposes of this Act to the extent that under a particular agreement or document unlike units are treated as equivalents.

(18) "Genuine" means free of forgery or counterfeiting.

(19) "Good faith" means honesty in fact in the conduct or transaction concerned.

(20) "Holder" with respect to a negotiable instrument, means the person in possession if the instrument is payable to bearer or, in the cases of an instrument payable to an identified person, if the identified person is in possession. "Holder" with respect to a document of title means the person in possession if the goods are deliverable to bearer or to the order of the person in possession.

(21) To "honor" is to pay or to accept and pay, or where a credit so engages to purchase or discount a draft complying with the terms of the credit.

(22) "Insolvency proceedings" includes any assignment for the benefit of creditors or other proceedings intended to liquidate or rehabilitate the estate of the person involved.

(23) A person is "insolvent" who either has ceased to pay his debts in the ordinary course of business or cannot pay his debts as they become due or is insolvent within the meaning of the federal bankruptcy law.

(24) "Money" means a medium of exchange authorized or adopted by a domestic or foreign government and includes a monetary unit of account established by an intergovernmental organization or by agreement between two or more nations.

(25) A person has "notice" of a fact when

(a) he has actual knowledge of it; or

(b) he has received a notice or notification of it; or

(c) from all the facts and circumstances known to him at the time in question he has reason to know that it exists.

A person "knows" or has "knowledge" of a fact when he has actual knowledge of it. "Discover" or "learn" or a word or phrase of similar import refers to knowledge rather than to reason to know. The time and circumstances under which a notice or notification may cease to be effective are not determined by this Act.

(26) A person "notifies" or "gives" a notice or notification to another by taking such steps as may be reasonably required to inform the other in ordinary course whether or not such other actually comes to know of it. A person "receives" a notice or notification when

(a) it comes to his attention; or

(b) it is duly delivered at the place of business through which the contract was made or at any other place held out by him as the place for receipt of such communications.

(27) Notice, knowledge or a notice or notification received by an organization is effective for a particular transaction from the time when it is brought to the attention of the individual conducting that transaction, and in any event from the time when it would have been brought to his attention if the organization had exercised due diligence. An organization exercises due diligence if it maintains reasonable routines for communicating significant information to the person conducting the transaction and there is reasonable compliance with the routines. Due diligence does not require an individual acting for the organization to communicate information unless such communication is part of his regular duties or unless he has reason to know of the transaction and that the transaction would be materially affected by the information.

(28) "Organization" includes a corporation, government or governmental subdivision or agency, business trust, estate, trust, partnership or association, two or more persons having a joint or common interest, or any other legal or commercial entity.

(29) "Party", as distinct from "third party", means a person who has engaged in a transaction or made an agreement within this Act.

(30) "Person" includes an individual or an organization (See Section 1–102).

(31) "Presumption" or "presumed" means that the trier of fact must find the existence of the fact presumed unless and until evidence is introduced which would support a finding of its non-existence.

(32) "Purchase" includes taking by sale, discount, negotiation, mortgage, pledge, lien, issue or re-issue, gift or any other voluntary transaction creating an interest in property.

(33) "Purchaser" means a person who takes by purchase.

(34) "Remedy" means any remedial right to which an aggrieved party is entitled with or without resort to a tribunal.

(35) "Representative" includes an agent, an officer of a corporation or association, and a trustee, executor or administrator of an estate, or any other person empowered to act for another.

(36) "Rights" includes remedies.

(37) "Security interest" means an interest in personal property or fixtures which secures payment or performance of an obligation. The term also includes any interest of a consignor and a buyer of accounts, chattel paper, a payment intangible, or a promissory note in a transaction that is subject to Article 9. The special property interest of a buyer of goods on identification of those goods to a contract for sale under Section 2–401 is not a "security interest", but a buyer may also acquire a "security interest" by complying with Article 9. Except as otherwise provided in Section 2–505, the right of a seller or lessor of goods under Article 2 or 2A to retain or acquire possession of the goods is not a "security interest", but a seller or lessor may also acquire a "security interest" by complying with Article 9. The retention or reservation of title by a seller of goods notwithstanding shipment or delivery to the buyer (Section 2–401) is limited in effect to a reservation of a "security interest".

Whether a transaction creates a lease or security interest is determined by the facts of each case; however, a transaction creates a security interest if the consideration the lessee is to pay the lessor for the right to possession and use of the goods is an obligation for the term of the lease not subject to termination by the lessee, and

(a) the original term of the lease is equal to or greater than the remaining economic life of the goods,

(b) the lessee is bound to renew the lease for the remaining economic life of the goods or is bound to become the owner of the goods,

(c) the lessee has an option to renew the lease for the remaining economic life of the goods for no additional consideration or nominal additional consideration upon compliance with the lease agreement, or

(d) the lessee has an option to become the owner of the goods for no additional consideration or nominal additional consideration upon compliance with the lease agreement.

A transaction does not create a security interest merely because it provides that

(a) the present value of the consideration the lessee is obligated to pay the lessor for the right to possession and use of the goods is substantially equal to or is greater than the fair market value of the goods at the time the lease is entered into,

(b) the lessee assumes risk of loss of the goods, or agrees to pay taxes, insurance, filing, recording, or registration fees, or service or maintenance costs with respect to the goods,

(c) the lessee has an option to renew the lease or to become the owner of the goods,

(d) the lessee has an option to renew the lease for a fixed rent that is equal to or greater than the reasonably predictable fair market rent for the use of the goods for the term of the renewal at the time the option is to be performed, or

(e) the lessee has an option to become the owner of the goods for a fixed price that is equal to or greater than the reasonably predictable fair market value of the goods at the time the option is to be performed.

For purposes of this subsection (37):

(x) Additional consideration is not nominal if (i) when the option to renew the lease is granted to the lessee the rent is stated to be the fair market rent for the use of the goods for the term of the renewal determined at the time the option is to be performed, or (ii) when the option to become the owner of the goods is granted to the lessee the price is stated to be the fair market value of the goods determined at the time the option is to be performed. Additional consideration is nominal if it is less than the lessee's reasonably predictable cost of performing under the lease agreement if the option is not exercised;

(y) "Reasonably predictable" and "remaining economic life of the goods" are to be determined with reference to the facts and circumstances at the time the transaction is entered into; and

(z) "Present value" means the amount as of a date certain of one or more sums payable in the future, discounted to the date certain. The discount is determined by the interest rate specified by the parties if the rate is not manifestly unreasonable at the time the transaction is entered into; otherwise, the discount is determined by a commercially reasonable rate that takes into account the facts and circumstances of each case at the time the transaction was entered into.

(38) "Send" in connection with any writing or notice means to deposit in the mail or deliver for transmission by any other usual means of communication with postage or cost of transmission provided for and properly addressed and in the case of an instrument to an address specified thereon or otherwise agreed, or if there be none to any address reasonable under the circumstances. The receipt of any writing or notice within the time at which it would have arrived if properly sent has the effect of a proper sending.

(39) "Signed" includes any symbol executed or adopted by a party with present intention to authenticate a writing.

(40) "Surety" includes guarantor.

(41) "Telegram" includes a message transmitted by radio, teletype, cable, any mechanical method of transmission, or the like.

(42) "Term" means that portion of an agreement which relates to a particular matter.

(43) "Unauthorized" signature means one made without actual, implied or apparent authority and includes a forgery.

(44) "Value". Except as otherwise provided with respect to negotiable instruments and bank collections (Sections 3–303, 4–210 and 4–211) a person gives "value" for rights if he acquires them

(a) in return for a binding commitment to extend credit or for the extension of immediately available credit whether or not drawn upon and whether or not a chargeback is provided for in the event of difficulties in collection; or

(b) as security for or in total or partial satisfaction of a pre-existing claim; or

(c) by accepting delivery pursuant to a preexisting contract for purchase; or

(d) generally, in return for any consideration sufficient to support a simple contract.

(45) "Warehouse receipt" means a receipt issued by a person engaged in the business of storing goods for hire.

(46) "Written" or "writing" includes printing, typewriting or any other intentional reduction to tangible form.

§ 1–202. Prima Facie Evidence by Third Party Documents.

A document in due form purporting to be a bill of lading, policy or certificate of insurance, official weigher's or inspector's certificate, consular invoice, or any other document authorized or required by the contract to be issued by a third party shall be prima facie evidence of its own authenticity and genuineness and of the facts stated in the document by the third party.

§ 1–203. Obligation of Good Faith.

Every contract or duty within this Act imposes an obligation of good faith in its performance or enforcement.

§ 1–204. Time; Reasonable Time; "Seasonably".

(1) Whenever this Act requires any action to be taken within a reasonable time, any time which is not manifestly unreasonable may be fixed by agreement.

(2) What is a reasonable time for taking any action depends on the nature, purpose and circumstances of such action.

(3) An action is taken "seasonably" when it is taken at or within the time agreed or if no time is agreed at or within a reasonable time.

§ 1–205. Course of Dealing and Usage of Trade.

(1) A course of dealing is a sequence of previous conduct between the parties to a particular transaction which is fairly to be regarded as establishing a common basis of understanding for interpreting their expressions and other conduct.

(2) A usage of trade is any practice or method of dealing having such regularity of observance in a place, vocation or trade as to

justify an expectation that it will be observed with respect to the transaction in question. The existence and scope of such a usage are to be proved as facts. If it is established that such a usage is embodied in a written trade code or similar writing the interpretation of the writing is for the court.

(3) A course of dealing between parties and any usage of trade in the vocation or trade in which they are engaged or of which they are or should be aware give particular meaning to and supplement or qualify terms of an agreement.

(4) The express terms of an agreement and an applicable course of dealing or usage of trade shall be construed wherever reasonable as consistent with each other; but when such construction is unreasonable express terms control both course of dealing and usage of trade and course of dealing controls usage trade.

(5) An applicable usage of trade in the place where any part of performance is to occur shall be used in interpreting the agreement as to that part of the performance.

(6) Evidence of a relevant usage of trade offered by one party is not admissible unless and until he has given the other party such notice as the court finds sufficient to prevent unfair surprise to the latter.

§ 1–206. Statute of Frauds for Kinds of Personal Property Not Otherwise Covered.

(1) Except in the cases described in subsection (2) of this section a contract for the sale of personal property is not enforceable by way of action or defense beyond five thousand dollars in amount or value of remedy unless there is some writing which indicates that a contract for sale has been made between the parties at a defined or stated price, reasonably identifies the subject matter, and is signed by the party against whom enforcement is sought or by his authorized agent.

(2) Subsection (1) of this section does not apply to contracts for the sale of goods (Section 2–201) nor of securities (Section 8–113) nor to security agreements (Section 9–203).

As amended in 1994.

§ 1–207. Performance or Acceptance Under Reservation of Rights.

(1) A party who with explicit reservation of rights performs or promises performance or assents to performance in a manner demanded or offered by the other party does not thereby prejudice the rights reserved. Such words as "without prejudice", "under protest" or the like are sufficient.

(2) Subsection (1) does not apply to an accord and satisfaction.

As amended in 1990.

§ 1–208. Option to Accelerate at Will.

A term providing that one party or his successor in interest may accelerate payment or performance or require collateral or additional collateral "at will" or "when he deems himself insecure" or in words of similar import shall be construed to mean that he shall have power to do so only if he in good faith believes that the prospect of payment or performance is impaired. The burden of establishing lack of good faith is on the party against whom the power has been exercised.

§ 1–209.   Subordinated Obligations.

An obligation may be issued as subordinated to payment of another obligation of the person obligated, or a creditor may subordinate his right to payment of an obligation by agreement with either the person obligated or another creditor of the person obligated. Such a subordination does not create a security interest as against either the common debtor or a subordinated creditor. This section shall be construed as declaring the law as it existed prior to the enactment of this section and not as modifying it. Added 1966.

Note: *This new section is proposed as an optional provision to make it clear that a subordination agreement does not create a security interest unless so intended.*

ARTICLE II
SALES

PART 1   Short Title, General Construction and Subject Matter

§ 2–101.   Short Title.

This Article shall be known and may be cited as Uniform Commercial Code—Sales.

§ 2–102.   Scope; Certain Security and Other Transactions Excluded From This Article.

Unless the context otherwise requires, this Article applies to transactions in goods; it does not apply to any transaction which although in the form of an unconditional contract to sell or present sale is intended to operate only as a security transaction nor does this Article impair or repeal any statute regulating sales to consumers, farmers or other specified classes of buyers.

§ 2–103.   Definitions and Index of Definitions.

(1) In this Article unless the context otherwise requires

(a) "Buyer" means a person who buys or contracts to buy goods.

(b) "Good faith" in the case of a merchant means honesty in fact and the observance of reasonable commercial standards of fair dealing in the trade.

(c) "Receipt" of goods means taking physical possession of them.

(d) "Seller" means a person who sells or contracts to sell goods.

(2) Other definitions applying to this Article or to specified Parts thereof, and the sections in which they appear are:

"Acceptance". Section 2–606.
"Banker's credit". Section 2–325.
"Between merchants". Section 2–104.
"Cancellation". Section 2–106(4).
"Commercial unit". Section 2–105.
"Confirmed credit". Section 2–325.
"Conforming to contract". Section 2–106.
"Contract for sale". Section 2–106.
"Cover". Section 2–712.
"Entrusting". Section 2–403.
"Financing agency". Section 2–104.
"Future goods". Section 2–105.
"Goods". Section 2–105.
"Identification". Section 2–501.
"Installment contract". Section 2–612.
"Letter of Credit". Section 2–325.
"Lot". Section 2–105
"Merchant". Section 2–104.
"Overseas". Section 2–323.
"Person in position of seller". Section 2–707.
"Present sale". Section 2–106.
"Sale". Section 2–106.
"Sale on approval". Section 2–326.
"Sale or return". Section 2–326.
"Termination". Section 2–106.

(3) The following definitions in other Articles apply to this Article:

"Check". Section 3–104.
"Consignee". Section 7–102.
"Consignor". Section 7–102.
"Consumer goods". Section 9–109.
"Dishonor". Section 3–507.
"Draft". Section 3–104.

(4) In addition Article 1 contains general definitions and principles of construction and interpretation applicable throughout this Article.

As amended in 1994 and 1999.

§ 2–104.   Definitions: "Merchant"; "Between Merchants"; "Financing Agency".

(1) "Merchant" means a person who deals in goods of the kind or otherwise by his occupation holds himself out as having knowledge or skill peculiar to the practices or goods involved in the transaction or to whom such knowledge or skill may be attributed by his employment of an agent or broker or other intermediary who by his occupation holds himself out as having such knowledge or skill.

(2) "Financing agency" means a bank, finance company or other person who in the ordinary course of business makes advances against goods or documents of title or who by arrangement with either the seller or the buyer intervenes in ordinary course to

make or collect payment due or claimed under the contract for sale, as by purchasing or paying the seller's draft or making advances against it or by merely taking it for collection whether or not documents of title accompany the draft. "Financing agency" includes also a bank or other person who similarly intervenes between persons who are in the position of seller and buyer in respect to the goods (Section 2–707).

(3) "Between merchants" means in any transaction with respect to which both parties are chargeable with the knowledge or skill of merchants.

§ 2–105.   Definitions: Transferability; "Goods"; "Future" Goods; "Lot"; "Commercial Unit".

(1) "Goods" means all things (including specially manufactured goods) which are movable at the time of identification to the contract for sale other than the money in which the price is to be paid, investment securities (Article 8) and things in action. "Goods" also includes the unborn young of animals and growing crops and other identified things attached to realty as described in the section on goods to be severed from realty (Section 2–107).

(2) Goods must be both existing and identified before any interest in them can pass. Goods which are not both existing and identified are "future" goods. A purported present sale of future goods or of any interest therein operates as a contract to sell.

(3) There may be a sale of a part interest in existing identified goods.

(4) An undivided share in an identified bulk of fungible goods is sufficiently identified to be sold although the quantity of the bulk is not determined. Any agreed proportion of such a bulk or any quantity thereof agreed upon by number, weight or other measure may to the extent of the seller's interest in the bulk be sold to the buyer who then becomes an owner in common.

(5) "Lot" means a parcel or a single article which is the subject matter of a separate sale or delivery, whether or not it is sufficient to perform the contract.

(6) "Commercial unit" means such a unit of goods as by commercial usage is a single whole for purposes of sale and division of which materially impairs its character or value on the market or in use. A commercial unit may be a single article (as a machine) or a set of articles (as a suite of furniture or an assortment of sizes) or a quantity (as a bale, gross, or carload) or any other unit treated in use or in the relevant market as a single whole.

§ 2–106.   Definitions: "Contract"; "Agreement"; "Contract for Sale"; "Sale"; "Present Sale"; "Conforming" to Contract; "Termination"; "Cancellation".

(1) In this Article unless the context otherwise requires "contract" and "agreement" are limited to those relating to the present or future sale of goods. "Contract for sale" includes both a present sale of goods and a contract to sell goods at a future time. A "sale" consists in the passing of title from the seller to the buyer for a price (Section 2–401). A "present sale" means a sale which is accomplished by the making of the contract.

(2) Goods or conduct including any part of a performance are "conforming" or conform to the contract when they are in accordance with the obligations under the contract.

(3) "Termination" occurs when either party pursuant to a power created by agreement or law puts an end to the contract otherwise than for its breach. On "termination" all obligations which are still executory on both sides are discharged but any right based on prior breach or performance survives.

(4) "Cancellation" occurs when either party puts an end to the contract for breach by the other and its effect is the same as that of "termination" except that the cancelling party also retains any remedy for breach of the whole contract or any unperformed balance.

§ 2–107.   Goods to Be Severed From Realty: Recording.

(1) A contract for the sale of minerals or the like (including oil and gas) or a structure or its materials to be removed from realty is a contract for the sale of goods within this Article if they are to be severed by the seller but until severance a purported present sale thereof which is not effective as a transfer of an interest in land is effective only as a contract to sell.

(2) A contract for the sale apart from the land of growing crops or other things attached to realty and capable of severance without material harm thereto but not described in subsection (1) or of timber to be cut is a contract for the sale of goods within this Article whether the subject matter is to be severed by the buyer or by the seller even though it forms part of the realty at the time of contracting, and the parties can by identification effect a present sale before severance.

(3) The provisions of this section are subject to any third party rights provided by the law relating to realty records, and the contract for sale may be executed and recorded as a document transferring an interest in land and shall then constitute notice to third parties of the buyer's rights under the contract for sale.

As amended in 1972.

PART 2   Form, Formation and Readjustment of Contract

§ 2–201.   Formal Requirements; Statute of Frauds.

(1) Except as otherwise provided in this section a contract for the sale of goods for the price of $500 or more is not enforceable by way of action or defense unless there is some writing sufficient to indicate that a contract for sale has been made between the parties and signed by the party against whom enforcement is sought or by his authorized agent or broker. A writing is not insufficient because it omits or incorrectly states a term agreed upon but the contract is not enforceable under this paragraph beyond the quantity of goods shown in such writing.

(2) Between merchants if within a reasonable time a writing in confirmation of the contract and sufficient against the sender is received and the party receiving it has reason to know its contents, it satisfies the requirements of subsection (1) against such party unless written notice of objection to its contents is given within ten days after it is received.

(3) A contract which does not satisfy the requirements of subsection (1) but which is valid in other respects is enforceable

(a) if the goods are to be specially manufactured for the buyer and are not suitable for sale to others in the ordinary course of the seller's business and the seller, before notice of repudiation is received and under circumstances which reasonably indicate that the goods are for the buyer, has made either a substantial beginning of their manufacture or commitments for their procurement; or

(b) if the party against whom enforcement is sought admits in his pleading, testimony or otherwise in court that a contract for sale was made, but the contract is not enforceable under this provision beyond the quantity of goods admitted; or

(c) with respect to goods for which payment has been made and accepted or which have been received and accepted (Sec. 2–606).

§ 2–202. Final Written Expression: Parol or Extrinsic Evidence.

Terms with respect to which the confirmatory memoranda of the parties agree or which are otherwise set forth in a writing intended by the parties as a final expression of their agreement with respect to such terms as are included therein may not be contradicted by evidence of any prior agreement or of a contemporaneous oral agreement but may be explained or supplemented

(a) by course of dealing or usage of trade (Section 1–205) or by course of performance (Section 2–208); and

(b) by evidence of consistent additional terms unless the court finds the writing to have been intended also as a complete and exclusive statement of the terms of the agreement.

§ 2–203. Seals Inoperative.

The affixing of a seal to a writing evidencing a contract for sale or an offer to buy or sell goods does not constitute the writing a sealed instrument and the law with respect to sealed instruments does not apply to such a contract or offer.

§ 2–204. Formation in General.

(1) A contract for sale of goods may be made in any manner sufficient to show agreement, including conduct by both parties which recognizes the existence of such a contract.

(2) An agreement sufficient to constitute a contract for sale may be found even though the moment of its making is undetermined.

(3) Even though one or more terms are left open a contract for sale does not fail for indefiniteness if the parties have intended

to make a contract and there is a reasonably certain basis for giving an appropriate remedy.

§ 2–205. Firm Offers.

An offer by a merchant to buy or sell goods in a signed writing which by its terms gives assurance that it will be held open is not revocable, for lack of consideration, during the time stated or if no time is stated for a reasonable time, but in no event may such period of irrevocability exceed three months; but any such term of assurance on a form supplied by the offeree must be separately signed by the offeror.

§ 2–206. Offer and Acceptance in Formation of Contract.

(1) Unless other unambiguously indicated by the language or circumstances

(a) an offer to make a contract shall be construed as inviting acceptance in any manner and by any medium reasonable in the circumstances;

(b) an order or other offer to buy goods for prompt or current shipment shall be construed as inviting acceptance either by a prompt promise to ship or by the prompt or current shipment of conforming or nonconforming goods, but such a shipment of non-conforming goods does not constitute an acceptance if the seller seasonably notifies the buyer that the shipment is offered only as an accommodation to the buyer.

(2) Where the beginning of a requested performance is a reasonable mode of acceptance an offeror who is not notified of acceptance within a reasonable time may treat the offer as having lapsed before acceptance.

§ 2–207. Additional Terms in Acceptance or Confirmation.

(1) A definite and seasonable expression of acceptance or a written confirmation which is sent within a reasonable time operates as an acceptance even though it states terms additional to or different from those offered or agreed upon, unless acceptance is expressly made conditional on assent to the additional or different terms.

(2) The additional terms are to be construed as proposals for addition to the contract. Between merchants such terms become part of the contract unless:

(a) the offer expressly limits acceptance to the terms of the offer;

(b) they materially alter it; or

(c) notification of objection to them has already been given or is given within a reasonable time after notice of them is received.

(3) Conduct by both parties which recognizes the existence of a contract is sufficient to establish a contract for sale although the writings of the parties do not otherwise establish a contract. In such case the terms of the particular contract consist of those

terms on which the writings of the parties agree, together with any supplementary terms incorporated under any other provisions of this Act.

§ 2–208.   Course of Performance or Practical Construction.

(1) Where the contract for sale involves repeated occasions for performance by either party with knowledge of the nature of the performance and opportunity for objection to it by the other, any course of performance accepted or acquiesced in without objection shall be relevant to determine the meaning of the agreement.

(2) The express terms of the agreement and any such course of performance, as well as any course of dealing and usage of trade, shall be construed whenever reasonable as consistent with each other; but when such construction is unreasonable, express terms shall control course of performance and course of performance shall control both course of dealing and usage of trade (Section 1–205).

(3) Subject to the provisions of the next section on modification and waiver, such course of performance shall be relevant to show a waiver or modification of any term inconsistent with such course of performance.

§ 2–209.   Modification, Rescission and Waiver.

(1) An agreement modifying a contract within this Article needs no consideration to be binding.

(2) A signed agreement which excludes modification or rescission except by a signed writing cannot be otherwise modified or rescinded, but except as between merchants such a requirement on a form supplied by the merchant must be separately signed by the other party.

(3) The requirements of the statute of frauds section of this Article (Section 2–201) must be satisfied if the contract as modified is within its provisions.

(4) Although an attempt at modification or rescission does not satisfy the requirements of subsection (2) or (3) it can operate as a waiver.

(5) A party who has made a waiver affecting an executory portion of the contract may retract the waiver by reasonable notification received by the other party that strict performance will be required of any term waived, unless the retraction would be unjust in view of a material change of position in reliance on the waiver.

§ 2–210.   Delegation of Performance; Assignment of Rights.

(1) A party may perform his duty through a delegate unless otherwise agreed or unless the other party has a substantial interest in having his original promisor perform or control the acts required by the contract. No delegation of performance relieves the party delegating of any duty to perform or any liability for breach.

(2) Except as otherwise provided in Section 9–406, unless otherwise agreed, all rights of either seller or buyer can be assigned except where the assignment would materially change the duty of the other party, or increase materially the burden or risk imposed on him by his contract, or impair materially his chance of obtaining return performance. A right to damages for breach of the whole contract or a right arising out of the assignor's due performance of his entire obligation can be assigned despite agreement otherwise.

(3) The creation, attachment, perfection, or enforcement of a security interest in the seller's interest under a contract is not a transfer that materially changes the duty of or increases materially the burden or risk imposed on the buyer or impairs materially the buyer's chance of obtaining return performance within the purview of subsection (2) unless, and then only to the extent that, enforcement actually results in a delegation of material performance of the seller. Even in that event, the creation, attachment, perfection, and enforcement of the security interest remain effective, but (i) the seller is liable to the buyer for damages caused by the delegation to the extent that the damages could not reasonably by prevented by the buyer, and (ii) a court having jurisdiction may grant other appropriate relief, including cancellation of the contract for sale or an injunction against enforcement of the security interest or consummation of the enforcement.

(4) Unless the circumstances indicate the contrary a prohibition of assignment of "the contract" is to be construed as barring only the delegation to the assignee of the assignor's performance.

(5) An assignment of "the contract" or of "all my rights under the contract" or an assignment in similar general terms is an assignment of rights and unless the language or the circumstances (as in an assignment for security) indicate the contrary, it is a delegation of performance of the duties of the assignor and its acceptance by the assignee constitutes a promise by him to perform those duties. This promise is enforceable by either the assignor or the other party to the original contract.

(6) The other party may treat any assignment which delegates performance as creating reasonable grounds for insecurity and may without prejudice to his rights against the assignor demand assurances from the assignee (Section 2–609).

As amended in 1999.

PART 3   General Obligation and Construction of Contract

§ 2–301.   General Obligations of Parties.

The obligation of the seller is to transfer and deliver and that of the buyer is to accept and pay in accordance with the contract.

§ 2–302.   Unconscionable Contract or Clause.

(1) If the court as a matter of law finds the contract or any clause of the contract to have been unconscionable at the time it was made the court may refuse to enforce the contract, or it may enforce the remainder of the contract without the

unconscionable clause, or it may so limit the application of any unconscionable clause as to avoid any unconscionable result.

(2) When it is claimed or appears to the court that the contract or any clause thereof may be unconscionable the parties shall be afforded a reasonable opportunity to present evidence as to its commercial setting, purpose and effect to aid the court in making the determination.

§ 2–303.   Allocations or Division of Risks.

Where this Article allocates a risk or a burden as between the parties "unless otherwise agreed", the agreement may not only shift the allocation but may also divide the risk or burden.

§ 2–304.   Price Payable in Money, Goods, Realty, or Otherwise.

(1) The price can be made payable in money or otherwise. If it is payable in whole or in part in goods each party is a seller of the goods which he is to transfer.

(2) Even though all or part of the price is payable in an interest in realty the transfer of the goods and the seller's obligations with reference to them are subject to this Article, but not the transfer of the interest in realty or the transferor's obligations in connection therewith.

§ 2–305.   Open Price Term.

(1) The parties if they so intend can conclude a contract for sale even though the price is not settled. In such a case the price is a reasonable price at the time for delivery if

    (a) nothing is said as to price; or

    (b) the price is left to be agreed by the parties and they fail to agree; or

    (c) the price is to be fixed in terms of some agreed market or other standard as set or recorded by a third person or agency and it is not so set or recorded.

(2) A price to be fixed by the seller or by the buyer means a price for him to fix in good faith.

(3) When a price left to be fixed otherwise than by agreement of the parties fails to be fixed through fault of one party the other may at his option treat the contract as cancelled or himself fix a reasonable price.

(4) Where, however, the parties intend not to be bound unless the price be fixed or agreed and it is not fixed or agreed there is no contract. In such a case the buyer must return any goods already received or if unable so to do must pay their reasonable value at the time of delivery and the seller must return any portion of the price paid on account.

§ 2–306.   Output, Requirements and Exclusive Dealings.

(1) A term which measures the quantity by the output of the seller or the requirements of the buyer means such actual output or requirements as may occur in good faith, except that no quantity unreasonably disproportionate to any stated estimate or in the absence of a stated estimate to any normal or otherwise comparable prior output or requirements may be tendered or demanded.

(2) A lawful agreement by either the seller or the buyer for exclusive dealing in the kind of goods concerned imposes unless otherwise agreed an obligation by the seller to use best efforts to supply the goods and by the buyer to use best efforts to promote their sale.

§ 2–307.   Delivery in Single Lot or Several Lots.

Unless otherwise agreed all goods called for by a contract for sale must be tendered in a single delivery and payment is due only on such tender but where the circumstances give either party the right to make or demand delivery in lots the price if it can be apportioned may be demanded for each lot.

§ 2–308.   Absence of Specified Place for Delivery.

Unless otherwise agreed

    (a) the place for delivery of goods is the seller's place of business or if he has none his residence; but

    (b) in a contract for sale of identified goods which to the knowledge of the parties at the time of contracting are in some other place, that place is the place for their delivery; and

    (c) documents of title may be delivered through customary banking channels.

§ 2–309.   Absence of Specific Time Provisions; Notice of Termination.

(1) The time for shipment or delivery or any other action under a contract if not provided in this Article or agreed upon shall be a reasonable time.

(2) Where the contract provides for successive performances but is indefinite in duration it is valid for a reasonable time but unless otherwise agreed may be terminated at any time by either party.

(3) Termination of a contract by one party except on the happening of an agreed event requires that reasonable notification be received by the other party and an agreement dispensing with notification is invalid if its operation would be unconscionable.

§ 2–310.   Open Time for Payment or Running of Credit; Authority to Ship Under Reservation.

Unless otherwise agreed

    (a) payment is due at the time and place at which the buyer is to receive the goods even though the place of shipment is the place of delivery; and

(b) if the seller is authorized to send the goods he may ship them under reservation, and may tender the documents of title, but the buyer may inspect the goods after their arrival before payment is due unless such inspection is inconsistent with the terms of the contract (Section 2–513); and

(c) if delivery is authorized and made by way of documents of title otherwise than by subsection (b) then payment is due at the time and place at which the buyer is to receive the documents regardless of where the goods are to be received; and

(d) where the seller is required or authorized to ship the goods on credit the credit period runs from the time of shipment but post-dating the invoice or delaying its dispatch will correspondingly delay the starting of the credit period.

§ 2–311.   Options and Cooperation Respecting Performance.

(1) An agreement for sale which is otherwise sufficiently definite (subsection (3) of Section 2–204) to be a contract is not made invalid by the fact that it leaves particulars of performance to be specified by one of the parties. Any such specification must be made in good faith and within limits set by commercial reasonableness.

(2) Unless otherwise agreed specifications relating to assortment of the goods are at the buyer's option and except as otherwise provided in subsections (1)(c) and (3) of Section 2–319 specifications or arrangements relating to shipment are at the seller's option.

(3) Where such specification would materially affect the other party's performance but is not seasonably made or where one party's cooperation is necessary to the agreed performance of the other but is not seasonably forthcoming, the other party in addition to all other remedies

(a) is excused for any resulting delay in his own performance; and

(b) may also either proceed to perform in any reasonable manner or after the time for a material part of his own performance treat the failure to specify or to cooperate as a breach by failure to deliver or accept the goods.

§ 2–312.   Warranty of Title and Against Infringement; Buyer's Obligation Against Infringement.

(1) Subject to subsection (2) there is in a contract for sale a warranty by the seller that

(a) the title conveyed shall be good, and its transfer rightful; and

(b) the goods shall be delivered free from any security interest or other lien or encumbrance of which the buyer at the time of contracting has no knowledge.

(2) A warranty under subsection (1) will be excluded or modified only by specific language or by circumstances which give the buyer reason to know that the person selling does not claim title

in himself or that he is purporting to sell only such right or title as he or a third person may have.

(3) Unless otherwise agreed a seller who is a merchant regularly dealing in goods of the kind warrants that the goods shall be delivered free of the rightful claim of any third person by way of infringement or the like but a buyer who furnishes specifications to the seller must hold the seller harmless against any such claim which arises out of compliance with the specifications.

§ 2–313.   Express Warranties by Affirmation, Promise, Description, Sample.

(1) Express warranties by the seller are created as follows:

(a) Any affirmation of fact or promise made by the seller to the buyer which relates to the goods and becomes part of the basis of the bargain creates an express warranty that the goods shall conform to the affirmation or promise.

(b) Any description of the goods which is made part of the basis of the bargain creates an express warranty that the goods shall conform to the description.

(c) Any sample or model which is made part of the basis of the bargain creates an express warranty that the whole of the goods shall conform to the sample or model.

(2) It is not necessary to the creation of an express warranty that the seller use formal words such as "warrant" or "guarantee" or that he have a specific intention to make a warranty, but an affirmation merely of the value of the goods or a statement purporting to be merely the seller's opinion or commendation of the goods does not create a warranty.

§ 2–314.   Implied Warranty: Merchantability; Usage of Trade.

(1) Unless excluded or modified (Section 2–316), a warranty that the goods shall be merchantable is implied in a contract for their sale if the seller is a merchant with respect to goods of that kind. Under this section the serving for value of food or drink to be consumed either on the premises or elsewhere is a sale.

(2) Goods to be merchantable must be at least such as

(a) pass without objection in the trade under the contract description; and

(b) in the case of fungible goods, are of fair average quality within the description; and

(c) are fit for the ordinary purposes for which such goods are used; and

(d) run, within the variations permitted by the agreement, of even kind, quality and quantity within each unit and among all units involved; and

(e) are adequately contained, packaged, and labeled as the agreement may require; and

(f) conform to the promises or affirmations of fact made on the container or label if any.

(3) Unless excluded or modified (Section 2–316) other implied warranties may arise from course of dealing or usage of trade.

§ 2-315. Implied Warranty: Fitness for Particular Purpose.

Where the seller at the time of contracting has reason to know any particular purpose for which the goods are required and that the buyer is relying on the seller's skill or judgment to select or furnish suitable goods, there is unless excluded or modified under the next section an implied warranty that the goods shall be fit for such purpose.

§ 2-316. Exclusion or Modification of Warranties.

(1) Words or conduct relevant to the creation of an express warranty and words or conduct tending to negate or limit warranty shall be construed wherever reasonable as consistent with each other; but subject to the provisions of this Article on parol or extrinsic evidence (Section 2–202) negation or limitation is inoperative to the extent that such construction is unreasonable.

(2) Subject to subsection (3), to exclude or modify the implied warranty of merchantability or any part of it the language must mention merchantability and in case of a writing must be conspicuous, and to exclude or modify any implied warranty of fitness the exclusion must be by a writing and conspicuous. Language to exclude all implied warranties of fitness is sufficient if it states, for example, that "There are no warranties which extend beyond the description on the face hereof."

(3) Notwithstanding subsection (2)

(a) unless the circumstances indicate otherwise, all implied warranties are excluded by expressions like "as is", "with all faults" or other language which in common understanding calls the buyer's attention to the exclusion of warranties and makes plain that there is no implied warranty; and

(b) when the buyer before entering into the contract has examined the goods or the sample or model as fully as he desired or has refused to examine the goods there is no implied warranty with regard to defects which an examination ought in the circumstances to have revealed to him; and

(c) an implied warranty can also be excluded or modified by course of dealing or course of performance or usage of trade.

(4) Remedies for breach of warranty can be limited in accordance with the provisions of this Article on liquidation or limitation of damages and on contractual modification of remedy (Sections 2–718 and 2–719).

§ 2-317. Cumulation and Conflict of Warranties Express or Implied.

Warranties whether express or implied shall be construed as consistent with each other and as cumulative, but if such construction is unreasonable the intention of the parties shall determine which warranty is dominant. In ascertaining that intention the following rules apply:

(a) Exact or technical specifications displace an inconsistent sample or model or general language of description.

(b) A sample from an existing bulk displaces inconsistent general language of description.

(c) Express warranties displace inconsistent implied warranties other than an implied warranty of fitness for a particular purpose.

§ 2-318. Third Party Beneficiaries of Warranties Express or Implied.

Note: If this Act is introduced in the Congress of the United States this section should be omitted. (States to select one alternative.)

Alternative A A seller's warranty whether express or implied extends to any natural person who is in the family or household of his buyer or who is a guest in his home if it is reasonable to expect that such person may use, consume or be affected by the goods and who is injured in person by breach of the warranty. A seller may not exclude or limit the operation of this section.

Alternative B A seller's warranty whether express or implied extends to any natural person who may reasonably be expected to use, consume or be affected by the goods and who is injured in person by breach of the warranty. A seller may not exclude or limit the operation of this section.

Alternative C A seller's warranty whether express or implied extends to any person who may reasonably be expected to use, consume or be affected by the goods and who is injured by breach of the warranty. A seller may not exclude or limit the operation of this section with respect to injury to the person of an individual to whom the warranty extends.

As amended 1966.

§ 2-319. F.O.B. and F.A.S. Terms.

(1) Unless otherwise agreed the term F.O.B. (which means "free on board") at a named place, even though used only in connection with the stated price, is a delivery term under which

(a) when the term is F.O.B. the place of shipment, the seller must at that place ship the goods in the manner provided in this Article (Section 2–504) and bear the expense and risk of putting them into the possession of the carrier; or

(b) when the term is F.O.B. the place of destination, the seller must at his own expense and risk transport the goods to that place and there tender delivery of them in the manner provided in this Article (Section 2–503);

(c) when under either (a) or (b) the term is also F.O.B. vessel, car or other vehicle, the seller must in addition at his own expense and risk load the goods on board. If the term is F.O.B. vessel the buyer must name the vessel and in an appropriate case the seller must comply with the provisions of this Article on the form of bill of lading (Section 2–323).

(2) Unless otherwise agreed the term F.A.S. vessel (which means "free alongside") at a named port, even though used only in connection with the stated price, is a delivery term under which the seller must

(a) at his own expense and risk deliver the goods alongside the vessel in the manner usual in that port or on a dock designated and provided by the buyer; and

(b) obtain and tender a receipt for the goods in exchange for which the carrier is under a duty to issue a bill of lading.

(3) Unless otherwise agreed in any case falling within subsection (1)(a) or (c) or subsection (2) the buyer must seasonably give any needed instructions for making delivery, including when the term is F.A.S. or F.O.B. the loading berth of the vessel and in an appropriate case its name and sailing date. The seller may treat the failure of needed instructions as a failure of cooperation under this Article (Section 2–311). He may also at his option move the goods in any reasonable manner preparatory to delivery or shipment.

(4) Under the term F.O.B. vessel or F.A.S. unless otherwise agreed the buyer must make payment against tender of the required documents and the seller may not tender nor the buyer demand delivery of the goods in substitution for the documents.

§ 2–320.   C.I.F. and C. & F. Terms.

(1) The term C.I.F. means that the price includes in a lump sum the cost of the goods and the insurance and freight to the named destination. The term C. & F. or C.F. means that the price so includes cost and freight to the named destination.

(2) Unless otherwise agreed and even though used only in connection with the stated price and destination, the term C.I.F. destination or its equivalent requires the seller at his own expense and risk to

(a) put the goods into the possession of a carrier at the port for shipment and obtain a negotiable bill or bills of lading covering the entire transportation to the named destination; and

(b) load the goods and obtain a receipt from the carrier (which may be contained in the bill of lading) showing that the freight has been paid or provided for; and

(c) obtain a policy or certificate of insurance, including any war risk insurance, of a kind and on terms then current at the port of shipment in the usual amount, in the currency of the contract, shown to cover the same goods covered by the bill of lading and providing for payment of loss to the order of the buyer or for the account of whom it may concern; but the seller may add to the price the amount of the premium for any such war risk insurance; and

(d) prepare an invoice of the goods and procure any other documents required to effect shipment or to comply with the contract; and

(e) forward and tender with commercial promptness all the documents in due form and with any indorsement necessary to perfect the buyer's rights.

(3) Unless otherwise agreed the term C. & F. or its equivalent has the same effect and imposes upon the seller the same obligations and risks as a C.I.F. term except the obligation as to insurance.

(4) Under the term C.I.F. or C. & F. unless otherwise agreed the buyer must make payment against tender of the required documents and the seller may not tender nor the buyer demand delivery of the goods in substitution for the documents.

§ 2–321.   C.I.F. or C. & F.: "Net Landed Weights"; "Payment on Arrival"; Warranty of Condition on Arrival.

Under a contract containing a term C.I.F. or C. & F.

(1) Where the price is based on or is to be adjusted according to "net landed weights", "delivered weights", "out turn" quantity or quality or the like, unless otherwise agreed the seller must reasonably estimate the price. The payment due on tender of the documents called for by the contract is the amount so estimated, but after final adjustment of the price a settlement must be made with commercial promptness.

(2) An agreement described in subsection (1) or any warranty of quality or condition of the goods on arrival places upon the seller the risk of ordinary deterioration, shrinkage and the like in transportation but has no effect on the place or time of identification to the contract for sale or delivery or on the passing of the risk of loss.

(3) Unless otherwise agreed where the contract provides for payment on or after arrival of the goods the seller must before payment allow such preliminary inspection as is feasible; but if the goods are lost delivery of the documents and payment are due when the goods should have arrived.

§ 2–322.   Delivery "Ex-Ship".

(1) Unless otherwise agreed a term for delivery of goods "ex-ship" (which means from the carrying vessel) or in equivalent language is not restricted to a particular ship and requires delivery from a ship which has reached a place at the named port of destination where goods of the kind are usually discharged.

(2) Under such a term unless otherwise agreed

(a) the seller must discharge all liens arising out of the carriage and furnish the buyer with a direction which puts the carrier under a duty to deliver the goods; and

(b) the risk of loss does not pass to the buyer until the goods leave the ship's tackle or are otherwise properly unloaded.

§ 2–323.   Form of Bill of Lading Required in Overseas Shipment; "Overseas".

(1) Where the contract contemplates overseas shipment and contains a term C.I.F. or C. & F. or F.O.B. vessel, the seller unless otherwise agreed must obtain a negotiable bill of lading stating that the goods have been loaded on board or, in the case of a term C.I.F. or C. & F., received for shipment.

(2) Where in a case within subsection (1) a bill of lading has been issued in a set of parts, unless otherwise agreed if the documents are not to be sent from abroad the buyer may demand tender of

the full set; otherwise only one part of the bill of lading need be tendered. Even if the agreement expressly requires a full set

(a) due tender of a single part is acceptable within the provisions of this Article on cure of improper delivery (subsection (1) of Section 2–508); and

(b) even though the full set is demanded, if the documents are sent from abroad the person tendering an incomplete set may nevertheless require payment upon furnishing an indemnity which the buyer in good faith deems adequate.

(3) A shipment by water or by air or a contract contemplating such shipment is "overseas" insofar as by usage of trade or agreement it is subject to the commercial, financing or shipping practices characteristic of international deep water commerce.

§ 2–324.   "No Arrival, No Sale" Term.

Under a term "no arrival, no sale" or terms of like meaning, unless otherwise agreed,

(a) the seller must properly ship conforming goods and if they arrive by any means he must tender them on arrival but he assumes no obligation that the goods will arrive unless he has caused the non-arrival; and

(b) where without fault of the seller the goods are in part lost or have so deteriorated as no longer to conform to the contract or arrive after the contract time, the buyer may proceed as if there had been casualty to identified goods (Section 2–613).

§ 2–325.   "Letter of Credit" Term; "Confirmed Credit".

(1) Failure of the buyer seasonably to furnish an agreed letter of credit is a breach of the contract for sale.

(2) The delivery to seller of a proper letter of credit suspends the buyer's obligation to pay. If the letter of credit is dishonored, the seller may on seasonable notification to the buyer require payment directly from him.

(3) Unless otherwise agreed the term "letter of credit" or "banker's credit" in a contract for sale means an irrevocable credit issued by a financing agency of good repute and, where the shipment is overseas, of good international repute. The term "confirmed credit" means that the credit must also carry the direct obligation of such an agency which does business in the seller's financial market.

§ 2–326.   Sale on Approval and Sale or Return; Rights of Creditors.

(1) Unless otherwise agreed, if delivered goods may be returned by the buyer even though they conform to the contract, the transaction is

(a) a "sale on approval" if the goods are delivered primarily for use, and

(b) a "sale or return" if the goods are delivered primarily for resale.

(2) Goods held on approval are not subject to the claims of the buyer's creditors until acceptance; goods held on sale or return are subject to such claims while in the buyer's possession.

(3) Any "or return" term of a contract for sale is to be treated as a separate contract for sale within the statute of frauds section of this Article (Section 2–201) and as contradicting the sale aspect of the contract within the provisions of this Article or on parol or extrinsic evidence (Section 2–202).

As amended in 1999.

§ 2–327.   Special Incidents of Sale on Approval and Sale or Return.

(1) Under a sale on approval unless otherwise agreed

(a) although the goods are identified to the contract the risk of loss and the title do not pass to the buyer until acceptance; and

(b) use of the goods consistent with the purpose of trial is not acceptance but failure seasonably to notify the seller of election to return the goods is acceptance, and if the goods conform to the contract acceptance of any part is acceptance of the whole; and

(c) after due notification of election to return, the return is at the seller's risk and expense but a merchant buyer must follow any reasonable instructions.

(2) Under a sale or return unless otherwise agreed

(a) the option to return extends to the whole or any commercial unit of the goods while in substantially their original condition, but must be exercised seasonably; and

(b) the return is at the buyer's risk and expense.

§ 2–328.   Sale by Auction.

(1) In a sale by auction if goods are put up in lots each lot is the subject of a separate sale.

(2) A sale by auction is complete when the auctioneer so announces by the fall of the hammer or in other customary manner. Where a bid is made while the hammer is falling in acceptance of a prior bid the auctioneer may in his discretion reopen the bidding or declare the goods sold under the bid on which the hammer was falling.

(3) Such a sale is with reserve unless the goods are in explicit terms put up without reserve. In an auction with reserve the auctioneer may withdraw the goods at any time until he announces completion of the sale. In an auction without reserve, after the auctioneer calls for bids on an article or lot, that article or lot cannot be withdrawn unless no bid is made within a reasonable time. In either case a bidder may retract his bid until the auctioneer's announcement of completion of the sale, but a bidder's retraction does not revive any previous bid.

(4) If the auctioneer knowingly receives a bid on the seller's behalf or the seller makes or procures such as bid, and notice has not been given that liberty for such bidding is reserved, the buyer may at his option avoid the sale or take the goods at the price of the last good faith bid prior to the completion of the sale. This subsection shall not apply to any bid at a forced sale.

PART 4   Title, Creditors and Good Faith Purchasers

§ 2–401.   Passing of Title; Reservation for Security; Limited Application of This Section.

Each provision of this Article with regard to the rights, obligations and remedies of the seller, the buyer, purchasers or other third parties applies irrespective of title to the goods except where the provision refers to such title. Insofar as situations are not covered by the other provisions of this Article and matters concerning title became material the following rules apply:

(1) Title to goods cannot pass under a contract for sale prior to their identification to the contract (Section 2–501), and unless otherwise explicitly agreed the buyer acquires by their identification a special property as limited by this Act. Any retention or reservation by the seller of the title (property) in goods shipped or delivered to the buyer is limited in effect to a reservation of a security interest. Subject to these provisions and to the provisions of the Article on Secured Transactions (Article 9), title to goods passes from the seller to the buyer in any manner and on any conditions explicitly agreed on by the parties.

(2) Unless otherwise explicitly agreed title passes to the buyer at the time and place at which the seller completes his performance with reference to the physical delivery of the goods, despite any reservation of a security interest and even though a document of title is to be delivered at a different time or place; and in particular and despite any reservation of a security interest by the bill of lading

(a) if the contract requires or authorizes the seller to send the goods to the buyer but does not require him to deliver them at destination, title passes to the buyer at the time and place of shipment; but

(b) if the contract requires delivery at destination, title passes on tender there.

(3) Unless otherwise explicitly agreed where delivery is to be made without moving the goods,

(a) if the seller is to deliver a document of title, title passes at the time when and the place where he delivers such documents; or

(b) if the goods are at the time of contracting already identified and no documents are to be delivered, title passes at the time and place of contracting.

(4) A rejection or other refusal by the buyer to receive or retain the goods, whether or not justified, or a justified revocation of acceptance revests title to the goods in the seller. Such revesting occurs by operation of law and is not a "sale".

§ 2–402.   Rights of Seller's Creditors Against Sold Goods.

(1) Except as provided in subsections (2) and (3), rights of unsecured creditors of the seller with respect to goods which have been identified to a contract for sale are subject to the buyer's rights to recover the goods under this Article (Sections 2–502 and 2–716).

(2) A creditor of the seller may treat a sale or an identification of goods to a contract for sale as void if as against him a retention of possession by the seller is fraudulent under any rule of law of the state where the goods are situated, except that retention of possession in good faith and current course of trade by a merchant-seller for a commercially reasonable time after a sale or identification is not fraudulent.

(3) Nothing in this Article shall be deemed to impair the rights of creditors of the seller

(a) under the provisions of the Article on Secured Transactions (Article 9); or

(b) where identification to the contract or delivery is made not in current course of trade but in satisfaction of or as security for a pre-existing claim for money, security or the like and is made under circumstances which under any rule of law of the state where the goods are situated would apart from this Article constitute the transaction a fraudulent transfer or voidable preference.

§ 2–403.   Power to Transfer; Good Faith Purchase of Goods; "Entrusting".

(1) A purchaser of goods acquires all title which his transferor had or had power to transfer except that a purchaser of a limited interest acquires rights only to the extent of the interest purchased. A person with voidable title has power to transfer a good title to a good faith purchaser for value. When goods have been delivered under a transaction of purchase the purchaser has such power even though

(a) the transferor was deceived as to the identity of the purchaser, or

(b) the delivery was in exchange for a check which is later dishonored, or

(c) it was agreed that the transaction was to be a "cash sale", or

(d) the delivery was procured through fraud punishable as larcenous under the criminal law.

(2) Any entrusting of possession of goods to a merchant who deals in goods of that kind gives him power to transfer all rights of the entruster to a buyer in ordinary course of business.

(3) "Entrusting" includes any delivery and any acquiescence in retention of possession regardless of any condition expressed between the parties to the delivery or acquiescence and regardless of whether the procurement of the entrusting or the possessor's disposition of the goods have been such as to be larcenous under the criminal law.

(4) The rights of other purchasers of goods and of lien creditors are governed by the Articles on Secured Transactions (Article 9), Bulk Transfers (Article 6) and Documents of Title (Article 7).

As amended in 1988.

PART 5   Performance

§ 2–501.   Insurable Interest in Goods; Manner of Identification of Goods.

(1) The buyer obtains a special property and an insurable interest in goods by identification of existing goods as goods to which the contract refers even though the goods so identified are non-conforming and he has an option to return or reject them. Such identification can be made at any time and in any manner explicitly agreed to by the parties. In the absence of explicit agreement identification occurs

(a) when the contract is made if it is for the sale of goods already existing and identified;

(b) if the contract is for the sale of future goods other than those described in paragraph (c), when goods are shipped, marked or otherwise designated by the seller as goods to which the contract refers;

(c) when the crops are planted or otherwise become growing crops or the young are conceived if the contract is for the sale of unborn young to be born within twelve months after contracting or for the sale of crops to be harvested within twelve months or the next normal harvest season after contracting whichever is longer.

(2) The seller retains an insurable interest in goods so long as title to or any security interest in the goods remains in him and where the identification is by the seller alone he may until default or insolvency or notification to the buyer that the identification is final substitute other goods for those identified.

(3) Nothing in this section impairs any insurable interest recognized under any other statute or rule of law.

§ 2–502.   Buyer's Right to Goods on Seller's Insolvency.

(1) Subject to subsections (2) and (3) and even though the goods have not been shipped a buyer who has paid a part or all of the price of goods in which he has a special property under the provisions of the immediately preceding section may on making and keeping good a tender of any unpaid portion of their price recover them from the seller if:

(a) in the case of goods bought for personal, family, or household purposes, the seller repudiates or fails to deliver as required by the contract; or

(b) in all cases, the seller becomes insolvent within ten days after receipt of the first installment on their price.

(2) The buyer's right to recover the goods under subsection (1) (a) vests upon acquisition of a special property, even if the seller had not then repudiated or failed to deliver.

(3) If the identification creating his special property has been made by the buyer he acquires the right to recover the goods only if they conform to the contract for sale.

As amended in 1999.

§ 2–503.   Manner of Seller's Tender of Delivery.

(1) Tender of delivery requires that the seller put and hold conforming goods at the buyer's disposition and give the buyer any notification reasonably necessary to enable him to take delivery. The manner, time and place for tender are determined by the agreement and this Article, and in particular

(a) tender must be at a reasonable hour, and if it is of goods they must be kept available for the period reasonably necessary to enable the buyer to take possession; but

(b) unless otherwise agreed the buyer must furnish facilities reasonably suited to the receipt of the goods.

(2) Where the case is within the next section respecting shipment tender requires that the seller comply with its provisions.

(3) Where the seller is required to deliver at a particular destination tender requires that he comply with subsection (1) and also in any appropriate case tender documents as described in subsections (4) and (5) of this section.

(4) Where goods are in the possession of a bailee and are to be delivered without being moved

(a) tender requires that the seller either tender a negotiable document of title covering such goods or procure acknowledgment by the bailee of the buyer's right to possession of the goods; but

(b) tender to the buyer of a non-negotiable document of title or of a written direction to the bailee to deliver is sufficient tender unless the buyer seasonably objects, and receipt by the bailee of notification of the buyer's rights fixes those rights as against the bailee and all third persons; but risk of loss of the goods and of any failure by the bailee to honor the non-negotiable document of title or to obey the direction remains on the seller until the buyer has had a reasonable time to present the document or direction, and a refusal by the bailee to honor the document or to obey the direction defeats the tender.

(5) Where the contract requires the seller to deliver documents

(a) he must tender all such documents in correct form, except as provided in this Article with respect to bills of lading in a set (subsection (2) of Section 2–323); and

(b) tender through customary banking channels is sufficient and dishonor of a draft accompanying the documents constitutes non-acceptance or rejection.

§ 2–504.   Shipment by Seller.

Where the seller is required or authorized to send the goods to the buyer and the contract does not require him to deliver them at a particular destination, then unless otherwise agreed he must

(a) put the goods in the possession of such a carrier and make such a contract for their transportation as may be reasonable having regard to the nature of the goods and other circumstances of the case; and

(b) obtain and promptly deliver or tender in due form any document necessary to enable the buyer to obtain possession of the goods or otherwise required by the agreement or by usage of trade; and

(c) promptly notify the buyer of the shipment.

Failure to notify the buyer under paragraph (c) or to make a proper contract under paragraph (a) is a ground for rejection only if material delay or loss ensues.

§ 2–505. Seller's Shipment under Reservation.

(1) Where the seller has identified goods to the contract by or before shipment:

(a) his procurement of a negotiable bill of lading to his own order or otherwise reserves in him a security interest in the goods. His procurement of the bill to the order of a financing agency or of the buyer indicates in addition only the seller's expectation of transferring that interest to the person named.

(b) a non-negotiable bill of lading to himself or his nominee reserves possession of the goods as security but except in a case of conditional delivery (subsection (2) of Section 2–507) a non-negotiable bill of lading naming the buyer as consignee reserves no security interest even though the seller retains possession of the bill of lading.

(2) When shipment by the seller with reservation of a security interest is in violation of the contract for sale it constitutes an improper contract for transportation within the preceding section but impairs neither the rights given to the buyer by shipment and identification of the goods to the contract nor the seller's powers as a holder of a negotiable document.

§ 2–506. Rights of Financing Agency.

(1) A financing agency by paying or purchasing for value a draft which relates to a shipment of goods acquires to the extent of the payment or purchase and in addition to its own rights under the draft and any document of title securing it any rights of the shipper in the goods including the right to stop delivery and the shipper's right to have the draft honored by the buyer.

(2) The right to reimbursement of a financing agency which has in good faith honored or purchased the draft under commitment to or authority from the buyer is not impaired by subsequent discovery of defects with reference to any relevant document which was apparently regular on its face.

§ 2–507. Effect of Seller's Tender; Delivery on Condition.

(1) Tender of delivery is a condition to the buyer's duty to accept the goods and, unless otherwise agreed, to his duty to pay for them. Tender entitles the seller to acceptance of the goods and to payment according to the contract.

(2) Where payment is due and demanded on the delivery to the buyer of goods or documents of title, his right as against the seller to retain or dispose of them is conditional upon his making the payment due.

§ 2–508. Cure by Seller of Improper Tender or Delivery; Replacement.

(1) Where any tender or delivery by the seller is rejected because non-conforming and the time for performance has not yet expired, the seller may seasonably notify the buyer of his intention to cure and may then within the contract time make a conforming delivery.

(2) Where the buyer rejects a non-conforming tender which the seller had reasonable grounds to believe would be acceptable with or without money allowance the seller may if he seasonably notifies the buyer have a further reasonable time to substitute a conforming tender.

§ 2–509. Risk of Loss in the Absence of Breach.

(1) Where the contract requires or authorizes the seller to ship the goods by carrier

(a) if it does not require him to deliver them at a particular destination, the risk of loss passes to the buyer when the goods are duly delivered to the carrier even though the shipment is under reservation (Section 2–505); but

(b) if it does require him to deliver them at a particular destination and the goods are there duly tendered while in the possession of the carrier, the risk of loss passes to the buyer when the goods are there duly so tendered as to enable the buyer to take delivery.

(2) Where the goods are held by a bailee to be delivered without being moved, the risk of loss passes to the buyer

(a) on his receipt of a negotiable document of title covering the goods; or

(b) on acknowledgment by the bailee of the buyer's right to possession of the goods; or

(c) after his receipt of a non-negotiable document of title or other written direction to deliver, as provided in subsection (4)(b) of Section 2–503.

(3) In any case not within subsection (1) or (2), the risk of loss passes to the buyer on his receipt of the goods if the seller is a merchant; otherwise the risk passes to the buyer on tender of delivery.

(4) The provisions of this section are subject to contrary agreement of the parties and to the provisions of this Article on sale on approval (Section 2–327) and on effect of breach on risk of loss (Section 2–510).

§ 2–510. Effect of Breach on Risk of Loss.

(1) Where a tender or delivery of goods so fails to conform to the contract as to give a right of rejection the risk of their loss remains on the seller until cure or acceptance.

(2) Where the buyer rightfully revokes acceptance he may to the extent of any deficiency in his effective insurance

coverage treat the risk of loss as having rested on the seller from the beginning.

(3) Where the buyer as to conforming goods already identified to the contract for sale repudiates or is otherwise in breach before risk of their loss has passed to him, the seller may to the extent of any deficiency in his effective insurance coverage treat the risk of loss as resting on the buyer for a commercially reasonable time.

§ 2–511.   Tender of Payment by Buyer; Payment by Check.

(1) Unless otherwise agreed tender of payment is a condition to the seller's duty to tender and complete any delivery.

(2) Tender of payment is sufficient when made by any means or in any manner current in the ordinary course of business unless the seller demands payment in legal tender and gives any extension of time reasonably necessary to procure it.

(3) Subject to the provisions of this Act on the effect of an instrument on an obligation (Section 3–310), payment by check is conditional and is defeated as between the parties by dishonor of the check on due presentment.

As amended in 1994.

§ 2–512.   Payment by Buyer Before Inspection.

(1) Where the contract requires payment before inspection non-conformity of the goods does not excuse the buyer from so making payment unless

(a) the non-conformity appears without inspection; or

(b) despite tender of the required documents the circumstances would justify injunction against honor under this Act (Section 5–109(b)).

(2) Payment pursuant to subsection (1) does not constitute an acceptance of goods or impair the buyer's right to inspect or any of his remedies.

As amended in 1995.

§ 2–513.   Buyer's Right to Inspection of Goods.

(1) Unless otherwise agreed and subject to subsection (3), where goods are tendered or delivered or identified to the contract for sale, the buyer has a right before payment or acceptance to inspect them at any reasonable place and time and in any reasonable manner. When the seller is required or authorized to send the goods to the buyer, the inspection may be after their arrival.

(2) Expenses of inspection must be borne by the buyer but may be recovered from the seller if the goods do not conform and are rejected.

(3) Unless otherwise agreed and subject to the provisions of this Article on C.I.F. contracts (subsection (3) of Section 2–321), the buyer is not entitled to inspect the goods before payment of the price when the contract provides

(a) for delivery "C.O.D." or on other like terms; or

(b) for payment against documents of title, except where such payment is due only after the goods are to become available for inspection.

(4) A place or method of inspection fixed by the parties is presumed to be exclusive but unless otherwise expressly agreed it does not postpone identification or shift the place for delivery or for passing the risk of loss. If compliance becomes impossible, inspection shall be as provided in this section unless the place or method fixed was clearly intended as an indispensable condition failure of which avoids the contract.

§ 2–514.   When Documents Deliverable on Acceptance; When on Payment.

Unless otherwise agreed documents against which a draft is drawn are to be delivered to the drawee on acceptance of the draft if it is payable more than three days after presentment; otherwise, only on payment.

§ 2–515.   Preserving Evidence of Goods in Dispute.

In furtherance of the adjustment of any claim or dispute

(a) either party on reasonable notification to the other and for the purpose of ascertaining the facts and preserving evidence has the right to inspect, test and sample the goods including such of them as may be in the possession or control of the other; and

(b) the parties may agree to a third party inspection or survey to determine the conformity or condition of the goods and may agree that the findings shall be binding upon them in any subsequent litigation or adjustment.

PART 6   Breach, Repudiation and Excuse

§ 2–601.   Buyer's Rights on Improper Delivery.

Subject to the provisions of this Article on breach in installment contracts (Section 2–612) and unless otherwise agreed under the sections on contractual limitations of remedy (Sections 2–718 and 2–719), if the goods or the tender of delivery fail in any respect to conform to the contract, the buyer may

(a) reject the whole; or

(b) accept the whole; or

(c) accept any commercial unit or units and reject the rest.

§ 2–602.   Manner and Effect of Rightful Rejection.

(1) Rejection of goods must be within a reasonable time after their delivery or tender. It is ineffective unless the buyer seasonably notifies the seller.

(2) Subject to the provisions of the two following sections on rejected goods (Sections 2–603 and 2–604),

(a) after rejection any exercise of ownership by the buyer with respect to any commercial unit is wrongful as against the seller; and

(b) if the buyer has before rejection taken physical possession of goods in which he does not have a security interest under the provisions of this Article (subsection (3) of Section 2–711), he is under a duty after rejection to hold them with reasonable care at the seller's disposition for a time sufficient to permit the seller to remove them; but

(c) the buyer has no further obligations with regard to goods rightfully rejected.

(3) The seller's rights with respect to goods wrongfully rejected are governed by the provisions of this Article on Seller's remedies in general (Section 2–703).

§ 2–603. Merchant Buyer's Duties as to Rightfully Rejected Goods.

(1) Subject to any security interest in the buyer (subsection (3) of Section 2–711), when the seller has no agent or place of business at the market of rejection a merchant buyer is under a duty after rejection of goods in his possession or control to follow any reasonable instructions received from the seller with respect to the goods and in the absence of such instructions to make reasonable efforts to sell them for the seller's account if they are perishable or threaten to decline in value speedily. Instructions are not reasonable if on demand indemnity for expenses is not forthcoming.

(2) When the buyer sells goods under subsection (1), he is entitled to reimbursement from the seller or out of the proceeds for reasonable expenses of caring for and selling them, and if the expenses include no selling commission then to such commission as is usual in the trade or if there is none to a reasonable sum not exceeding ten per cent on the gross proceeds.

(3) In complying with this section the buyer is held only to good faith and good faith conduct hereunder is neither acceptance nor conversion nor the basis of an action for damages.

§ 2–604. Buyer's Options as to Salvage of Rightfully Rejected Goods.

Subject to the provisions of the immediately preceding section on perishables if the seller gives no instructions within a reasonable time after notification of rejection the buyer may store the rejected goods for the seller's account or reship them to him or resell them for the seller's account with reimbursement as provided in the preceding section. Such action is not acceptance or conversion.

§ 2–605. Waiver of Buyer's Objections by Failure to Particularize.

(1) The buyer's failure to state in connection with rejection a particular defect which is ascertainable by reasonable inspection precludes him from relying on the unstated defect to justify rejection or to establish breach

(a) where the seller could have cured it if stated seasonally; or

(b) between merchants when the seller has after rejection made a request in writing for a full and final written statement of all defects on which the buyer proposes to rely.

(2) Payment against documents made without reservation of rights precludes recovery of the payment for defects apparent on the face of the documents.

§ 2–606. What Constitutes Acceptance of Goods.

(1) Acceptance of goods occurs when the buyer

(a) after a reasonable opportunity to inspect the goods signifies to the seller that the goods are conforming or that he will take or retain them in spite of their nonconformity; or

(b) fails to make an effective rejection (subsection (1) of Section 2–602), but such acceptance does not occur until the buyer has had a reasonable opportunity to inspect them; or

(c) does any act inconsistent with the seller's ownership; but if such act is wrongful as against the seller it is an acceptance only if ratified by him.

(2) Acceptance of a part of any commercial unit is acceptance of that entire unit.

§ 2–607. Effect of Acceptance; Notice of Breach; Burden of Establishing Breach After Acceptance; Notice of Claim or Litigation to Person Answerable Over.

(1) The buyer must pay at the contract rate for any goods accepted.

(2) Acceptance of goods by the buyer precludes rejection of the goods accepted and if made with knowledge of a non-conformity cannot be revoked because of it unless the acceptance was on the reasonable assumption that the non-conformity would be seasonably cured but acceptance does not of itself impair any other remedy provided by this Article for non-conformity.

(3) Where a tender has been accepted

(a) the buyer must within a reasonable time after he discovers or should have discovered any breach notify the seller of breach or be barred from any remedy; and

(b) if the claim is one for infringement or the like (subsection (3) of Section 2–312) and the buyer is sued as a result of such a breach he must so notify the seller within a reasonable time after he receives notice of the litigation or be barred from any remedy over for liability established by the litigation.

(4) The burden is on the buyer to establish any breach with respect to the goods accepted.

(5) Where the buyer is sued for breach of a warranty or other obligation for which his seller is answerable over

(a) he may give his seller written notice of the litigation. If the notice states that the seller may come in and defend and that if the seller does not do so he will be bound in any action against him by his buyer by any determination of fact common to the two litigations, then unless the seller after seasonable receipt of the notice does come in and defend he is so bound.

(b) if the claim is one for infringement or the like (subsection (3) of Section 2–312) the original seller may demand in writing that his buyer turn over to him control of the litigation including settlement or else be barred from any remedy over and if he also agrees to bear all expense and to satisfy any adverse judgment, then unless the buyer after seasonable receipt of the demand does turn over control the buyer is so barred.

(6) The provisions of subsections (3), (4) and (5) apply to any obligation of a buyer to hold the seller harmless against infringement or the like (subsection (3) of Section 2–312).

§ 2–608.   Revocation of Acceptance in Whole or in Part.

(1) The buyer may revoke his acceptance of a lot or commercial unit whose non-conformity substantially impairs its value to him if he has accepted it

(a) on the reasonable assumption that its nonconformity would be cured and it has not been seasonably cured; or

(b) without discovery of such non-conformity if his acceptance was reasonably induced either by the difficulty of discovery before acceptance or by the seller's assurances.

(2) Revocation of acceptance must occur within a reasonable time after the buyer discovers or should have discovered the ground for it and before any substantial change in condition of the goods which is not caused by their own defects. It is not effective until the buyer notifies the seller of it.

(3) A buyer who so revokes has the same rights and duties with regard to the goods involved as if he had rejected them.

§ 2–609.   Right to Adequate Assurance of Performance.

(1) A contract for sale imposes an obligation on each party that the other's expectation of receiving due performance will not be impaired. When reasonable grounds for insecurity arise with respect to the performance of either party the other may in writing demand adequate assurance of due performance and until he receives such assurance may if commercially reasonable suspend any performance for which he has not already received the agreed return.

(2) Between merchants the reasonableness of grounds for insecurity and the adequacy of any assurance offered shall be determined according to commercial standards.

(3) Acceptance of any improper delivery or payment does not prejudice the party's right to demand adequate assurance of future performance.

(4) After receipt of a justified demand failure to provide within a reasonable time not exceeding thirty days such assurance of due performance as is adequate under the circumstances of the particular case is a repudiation of the contract.

§ 2–610.   Anticipatory Repudiation.

When either party repudiates the contract with respect to a performance not yet due the loss of which will substantially impair the value of the contract to the other, the aggrieved party may

(a) for a commercially reasonable time await performance by the repudiating party; or

(b) resort to any remedy for breach (Section 2–703 or Section 2–711), even though he has notified the repudiating party that he would await the latter's performance and has urged retraction; and

(c) in either case suspend his own performance or proceed in accordance with the provisions of this Article on the seller's right to identify goods to the contract notwithstanding breach or to salvage unfinished goods (Section 2–704).

§ 2–611.   Retraction of Anticipatory Repudiation.

(1) Until the repudiating party's next performance is due he can retract his repudiation unless the aggrieved party has since the repudiation cancelled or materially changed his position or otherwise indicated that he considers the repudiation final.

(2) Retraction may be by any method which clearly indicates to the aggrieved party that the repudiating party intends to perform, but must include any assurance justifiably demanded under the provisions of this Article (Section 2–609).

(3) Retraction reinstates the repudiating party's rights under the contract with due excuse and allowance to the aggrieved party for any delay occasioned by the repudiation.

§ 2–612.   "Installment Contract"; Breach.

(1) An "installment contract" is one which requires or authorizes the delivery of goods in separate lots to be separately accepted, even though the contract contains a clause "each delivery is a separate contract" or its equivalent.

(2) The buyer may reject any installment which is non-conforming if the non-conformity substantially impairs the value of that installment and cannot be cured or if the non-conformity is a defect in the required documents; but if the non-conformity does not fall within subsection (3) and the seller gives adequate assurance of its cure the buyer must accept that installment.

(3) Whenever non-conformity or default with respect to one or more installments substantially impairs the value of the whole contract there is a breach of the whole. But the aggrieved party reinstates the contract if he accepts a non-conforming installment without seasonably notifying of cancellation or if he brings an action with respect only to past installments or demands performance as to future installments.

§ 2-613.   Casualty to Identified Goods.

Where the contract requires for its performance goods identified when the contract is made, and the goods suffer casualty without fault of either party before the risk of loss passes to the buyer, or in a proper case under a "no arrival, no sale" term (Section 2–324) then

(a) if the loss is total the contract is avoided; and

(b) if the loss is partial or the goods have so deteriorated as no longer to conform to the contract the buyer may nevertheless demand inspection and at his option either treat the contract as voided or accept the goods with due allowance from the contract price for the deterioration or the deficiency in quantity but without further right against the seller.

§ 2-614.   Substituted Performance.

(1) Where without fault of either party the agreed berthing, loading, or unloading facilities fail or an agreed type of carrier becomes unavailable or the agreed manner of delivery otherwise becomes commercially impracticable but a commercially reasonable substitute is available, such substitute performance must be tendered and accepted.

(2) If the agreed means or manner of payment fails because of domestic or foreign governmental regulation, the seller may withhold or stop delivery unless the buyer provides a means or manner of payment which is commercially a substantial equivalent. If delivery has already been taken, payment by the means or in the manner provided by the regulation discharges the buyer's obligation unless the regulation is discriminatory, oppressive or predatory.

§ 2-615.   Excuse by Failure of Presupposed Conditions.

Except so far as a seller may have assumed a greater obligation and subject to the preceding section on substituted performance:

(a) Delay in delivery or non-delivery in whole or in part by a seller who complies with paragraphs (b) and (c) is not a breach of his duty under a contract for sale if performance as agreed has been made impracticable by the occurrence of a contingency the nonoccurrence of which was a basic assumption on which the contract was made or by compliance in good faith with any applicable foreign or domestic governmental regulation or order whether or not it later proves to be invalid.

(b) Where the causes mentioned in paragraph (a) affect only a part of the seller's capacity to perform, he must allocate production and deliveries among his customers but may at his option include regular customers not then under contract as well as his own requirements for further manufacture. He may so allocate in any manner which is fair and reasonable.

(c) The seller must notify the buyer seasonably that there will be delay or non-delivery and, when allocation is required under paragraph (b), of the estimated quota thus made available for the buyer.

§ 2-616.   Procedure on Notice Claiming Excuse.

(1) Where the buyer receives notification of a material or indefinite delay or an allocation justified under the preceding section he may by written notification to the seller as to any delivery concerned, and where the prospective deficiency substantially impairs the value of the whole contract under the provisions of this Article relating to breach of installment contracts (Section 2–612), then also as to the whole,

(a) terminate and thereby discharge any unexecuted portion of the contract; or

(b) modify the contract by agreeing to take his available quota in substitution.

(2) If after receipt of such notification from the seller the buyer fails so to modify the contract within a reasonable time not exceeding thirty days the contract lapses with respect to any deliveries affected.

(3) The provisions of this section may not be negated by agreement except in so far as the seller has assumed a greater obligation under the preceding section.

PART 7   Remedies

§ 2-701.   Remedies for Breach of Collateral Contracts Not Impaired.

Remedies for breach of any obligation or promise collateral or ancillary to a contract for sale are not impaired by the provisions of this Article.

§ 2-702.   Seller's Remedies on Discovery of Buyer's Insolvency.

(1) Where the seller discovers the buyer to be insolvent he may refuse delivery except for cash including payment for all goods theretofore delivered under the contract, and stop delivery under this Article (Section 2–705).

(2) Where the seller discovers that the buyer has received goods on credit while insolvent he may reclaim the goods upon demand made within ten days after the receipt, but if misrepresentation of solvency has been made to the particular seller in writing within three months before delivery the ten day limitation does not apply. Except as provided in this subsection the seller may not base a right to reclaim goods on the buyer's fraudulent or innocent misrepresentation of solvency or of intent to pay.

(3) The seller's right to reclaim under subsection (2) is subject to the rights of a buyer in ordinary course or other good faith purchaser under this Article (Section 2–403). Successful reclamation of goods excludes all other remedies with respect to them.

§ 2-703.   Seller's Remedies in General.

Where the buyer wrongfully rejects or revokes acceptance of goods or fails to make a payment due on or before delivery or repudiates with respect to a part or the whole, then with respect to any goods directly affected and, if the breach is of the whole contract (Section 2–612), then also with respect to the whole undelivered balance, the aggrieved seller may

(a) withhold delivery of such goods;

(b) stop delivery by any bailee as hereafter provided (Section 2–705);

(c) proceed under the next section respecting goods still unidentified to the contract;

(d) resell and recover damages as hereafter provided (Section 2–706);

(e) recover damages for non-acceptance (Section 2–708) or in a proper case the price (Section 2–709);

(f) cancel.

§ 2–704. Seller's Right to Identify Goods to the Contract Notwithstanding Breach or to Salvage Unfinished Goods.

(1) An aggrieved seller under the preceding section may

(a) identify to the contract conforming goods not already identified if at the time he learned of the breach they are in his possession or control;

(b) treat as the subject of resale goods which have demonstrably been intended for the particular contract even though those goods are unfinished.

(2) Where the goods are unfinished an aggrieved seller may in the exercise of reasonable commercial judgment for the purposes of avoiding loss and of effective realization either complete the manufacture and wholly identify the goods to the contract or cease manufacture and resell for scrap or salvage value or proceed in any other reasonable manner.

§ 2–705. Seller's Stoppage of Delivery in Transit or Otherwise.

(1) The seller may stop delivery of goods in the possession of a carrier or other bailee when he discovers the buyer to be insolvent (Section 2–702) and may stop delivery of carload, truckload, planeload or larger shipments of express or freight when the buyer repudiates or fails to make a payment due before delivery or if for any other reason the seller has a right to withhold or reclaim the goods.

(2) As against such buyer the seller may stop delivery until

(a) receipt of the goods by the buyer; or

(b) acknowledgment to the buyer by any bailee of the goods except a carrier that the bailee holds the goods for the buyer; or

(c) such acknowledgment to the buyer by a carrier by reshipment or as warehouseman; or

(d) negotiation to the buyer of any negotiable document of title covering the goods.

(3) (a) To stop delivery the seller must so notify as to enable the bailee by reasonable diligence to prevent delivery of the goods.

(b) After such notification the bailee must hold and deliver the goods according to the directions of the seller but the seller is liable to the bailee for any ensuing charges or damages.

(c) If a negotiable document of title has been issued for goods the bailee is not obliged to obey a notification to stop until surrender of the document.

(d) A carrier who has issued a non-negotiable bill of lading is not obliged to obey a notification to stop received from a person other than the consignor.

§ 2–706. Seller's Resale Including Contract for Resale.

(1) Under the conditions stated in Section 2–703 on seller's remedies, the seller may resell the goods concerned or the undelivered balance thereof. Where the resale is made in good faith and in a commercially reasonable manner the seller may recover the difference between the resale price and the contract price together with any incidental damages allowed under the provisions of this Article (Section 2–710), but less expenses saved in consequence of the buyer's breach.

(2) Except as otherwise provided in subsection (3) or unless otherwise agreed resale may be at public or private sale including sale by way of one or more contracts to sell or of identification to an existing contract of the seller. Sale may be as a unit or in parcels and at any time and place and on any terms but every aspect of the sale including the method, manner, time, place and terms must be commercially reasonable. The resale must be reasonably identified as referring to the broken contract, but it is not necessary that the goods be in existence or that any or all of them have been identified to the contract before the breach.

(3) Where the resale is at private sale the seller must give the buyer reasonable notification of his intention to resell.

(4) Where the resale is at public sale

(a) only identified goods can be sold except where there is a recognized market for a public sale of futures in goods of the kind; and

(b) it must be made at a usual place or market for public sale if one is reasonably available and except in the case of goods which are perishable or threaten to decline in value speedily the seller must give the buyer reasonable notice of the time and place of the resale; and

(c) if the goods are not to be within the view of those attending the sale the notification of sale must state the place where the goods are located and provide for their reasonable inspection by prospective bidders; and

(d) the seller may buy.

(5) A purchaser who buys in good faith at a resale takes the goods free of any rights of the original buyer even though the seller fails to comply with one or more of the requirements of this section.

(6) The seller is not accountable to the buyer for any profit made on any resale. A person in the position of a seller (Section 2–707) or a buyer who has rightfully rejected or justifiably revoked acceptance must account for any excess over the amount of his security interest, as hereinafter defined (subsection (3) of Section 2–711).

§ 2–707.   "Person in the Position of a Seller".

(1) A "person in the position of a seller" includes as against a principal an agent who has paid or become responsible for the price of goods on behalf of his principal or anyone who otherwise holds a security interest or other right in goods similar to that of a seller.

(2) A person in the position of a seller may as provided in this Article withhold or stop delivery (Section 2–705) and resell (Section 2–706) and recover incidental damages (Section 2–710).

§ 2–708.   Seller's Damages for Non-Acceptance or Repudiation.

(1) Subject to subsection (2) and to the provisions of this Article with respect to proof of market price (Section 2–723), the measure of damages for non-acceptance or repudiation by the buyer is the difference between the market price at the time and place for tender and the unpaid contract price together with any incidental damages provided in this Article (Section 2–710), but less expenses saved in consequence of the buyer's breach.

(2) If the measure of damages provided in subsection (1) is inadequate to put the seller in as good a position as performance would have done then the measure of damages is the profit (including reasonable overhead) which the seller would have made from full performance by the buyer, together with any incidental damages provided in this Article (Section 2–710), due allowance for costs reasonably incurred and due credit for payments or proceeds of resale.

§ 2–709.   Action for the Price.

(1) When the buyer fails to pay the price as it becomes due the seller may recover, together with any incidental damages under the next section, the price

(a) of goods accepted or of conforming goods lost or damaged within a commercially reasonable time after risk of their loss has passed to the buyer; and

(b) of goods identified to the contract if the seller is unable after reasonable effort to resell them at a reasonable price or the circumstances reasonably indicate that such effort will be unavailing.

(2) Where the seller sues for the price he must hold for the buyer any goods which have been identified to the contract and are still in his control except that if resale becomes possible he may resell them at any time prior to the collection of the judgment. The net proceeds of any such resale must be credited to the buyer and payment of the judgment entitles him to any goods not resold.

(3) After the buyer has wrongfully rejected or revoked acceptance of the goods or has failed to make a payment due or has repudiated (Section 2–610), a seller who is held not entitled to the price under this section shall nevertheless be awarded damages for non-acceptance under the preceding section.

§ 2–710.   Seller's Incidental Damages.

Incidental damages to an aggrieved seller include any commercially reasonable charges, expenses or commissions incurred in stopping delivery, in the transportation, care and custody of goods after the buyer's breach, in connection with return or resale of the goods or otherwise resulting from the breach.

§ 2–711.   Buyer's Remedies in General; Buyer's Security Interest in Rejected Goods.

(1) Where the seller fails to make delivery or repudiates or the buyer rightfully rejects or justifiably revokes acceptance then with respect to any goods involved, and with respect to the whole if the breach goes to the whole contract (Section 2–612), the buyer may cancel and whether or not he has done so may in addition to recovering so much of the price as has been paid

(a) "cover" and have damages under the next section as to all the goods affected whether or not they have been identified to the contract; or

(b) recover damages for non-delivery as provided in this Article (Section 2–713).

(2) Where the seller fails to deliver or repudiates the buyer may also

(a) if the goods have been identified recover them as provided in this Article (Section 2–502); or

(b) in a proper case obtain specific performance or replevy the goods as provided in this Article (Section 2–716).

(3) On rightful rejection or justifiable revocation of acceptance a buyer has a security interest in goods in his possession or control for any payments made on their price and any expenses reasonably incurred in their inspection, receipt, transportation, care and custody and may hold such goods and resell them in like manner as an aggrieved seller (Section 2–706).

§ 2–712.   "Cover"; Buyer's Procurement of Substitute Goods.

(1) After a breach within the preceding section the buyer may "cover" by making in good faith and without unreasonable delay any reasonable purchase of or contract to purchase goods in substitution for those due from the seller.

(2) The buyer may recover from the seller as damages the difference between the cost of cover and the contract price together with any incidental or consequential damages as hereinafter defined (Section 2–715), but less expenses saved in consequence of the seller's breach.

(3) Failure of the buyer to effect cover within this section does not bar him from any other remedy.

§ 2-713. Buyer's Damages for Non-Delivery or Repudiation.

(1) Subject to the provisions of this Article with respect to proof of market price (Section 2–723), the measure of damages for non-delivery or repudiation by the seller is the difference between the market price at the time when the buyer learned of the breach and the contract price together with any incidental and consequential damages provided in this Article (Section 2–715), but less expenses saved in consequence of the seller's breach.

(2) Market price is to be determined as of the place for tender or, in cases of rejection after arrival or revocation of acceptance, as of the place of arrival.

§ 2-714. Buyer's Damages for Breach in Regard to Accepted Goods.

(1) Where the buyer has accepted goods and given notification (subsection (3) of Section 2–607) he may recover as damages for any non-conformity of tender the loss resulting in the ordinary course of events from the seller's breach as determined in any manner which is reasonable.

(2) The measure of damages for breach of warranty is the difference at the time and place of acceptance between the value of the goods accepted and the value they would have had if they had been as warranted, unless special circumstances show proximate damages of a different amount.

(3) In a proper case any incidental and consequential damages under the next section may also be recovered.

§ 2-715. Buyer's Incidental and Consequential Damages.

(1) Incidental damages resulting from the seller's breach include expenses reasonably incurred in inspection, receipt, transportation and care and custody of goods rightfully rejected, any commercially reasonable charges, expenses or commissions in connection with effecting cover and any other reasonable expense incident to the delay or other breach.

(2) Consequential damages resulting from the seller's breach include

(a) any loss resulting from general or particular requirements and needs of which the seller at the time of contracting had reason to know and which could not reasonably be prevented by cover or otherwise; and

(b) injury to person or property proximately resulting from any breach of warranty.

§ 2-716. Buyer's Right to Specific Performance or Replevin.

(1) Specific performance may be decreed where the goods are unique or in other proper circumstances.

(2) The decree for specific performance may include such terms and conditions as to payment of the price, damages, or other relief as the court may deem just.

(3) The buyer has a right of replevin for goods identified to the contract if after reasonable effort he is unable to effect cover for such goods or the circumstances reasonably indicate that such effort will be unavailing or if the goods have been shipped under reservation and satisfaction of the security interest in them has been made or tendered. In the case of goods bought for personal, family, or household purposes, the buyer's right of replevin vests upon acquisition of a special property, even if the seller had not then repudiated or failed to deliver.

As amended in 1999.

§ 2-717. Deduction of Damages From the Price.

The buyer on notifying the seller of his intention to do so may deduct all or any part of the damages resulting from any breach of the contract from any part of the price still due under the same contract.

§ 2-718. Liquidation or Limitation of Damages; Deposits.

(1) Damages for breach by either party may be liquidated in the agreement but only at an amount which is reasonable in the light of the anticipated or actual harm caused by the breach, the difficulties of proof of loss, and the inconvenience or nonfeasibility of otherwise obtaining an adequate remedy. A term fixing unreasonably large liquidated damages is void as a penalty.

(2) Where the seller justifiably withholds delivery of goods because of the buyer's breach, the buyer is entitled to restitution of any amount by which the sum of his payments exceeds

(a) the amount to which the seller is entitled by virtue of terms liquidating the seller's damages in accordance with subsection (1), or

(b) in the absence of such terms, twenty per cent of the value of the total performance for which the buyer is obligated under the contract or $500, whichever is smaller.

(3) The buyer's right to restitution under subsection (2) is subject to offset to the extent that the seller establishes

(a) a right to recover damages under the provisions of this Article other than subsection (1), and

(b) the amount or value of any benefits received by the buyer directly or indirectly by reason of the contract.

(4) Where a seller has received payment in goods their reasonable value or the proceeds of their resale shall be treated as payments for the purposes of subsection (2); but if the seller has notice of the buyer's breach before reselling goods received in part performance, his resale is subject to the conditions laid down in this Article on resale by an aggrieved seller (Section 2–706).

§ 2-719. Contractual Modification or Limitation of Remedy.

(1) Subject to the provisions of subsections (2) and (3) of this section and of the preceding section on liquidation and limitation of damages,

(a) the agreement may provide for remedies in addition to or in substitution for those provided in this Article and may limit or alter the measure of damages recoverable under this Article, as by limiting the buyer's remedies to return of the goods and repayment of the price or to repair and replacement of nonconforming goods or parts; and

(b) resort to a remedy as provided is optional unless the remedy is expressly agreed to be exclusive, in which case it is the sole remedy.

(2) Where circumstances cause an exclusive or limited remedy to fail of its essential purpose, remedy may be had as provided in this Act.

(3) Consequential damages may be limited or excluded unless the limitation or exclusion is unconscionable. Limitation of consequential damages for injury to the person in the case of consumer goods is prima facie unconscionable but limitation of damages where the loss is commercial is not.

§ 2–720. Effect of "Cancellation" or "Rescission" on Claims for Antecedent Breach.

Unless the contrary intention clearly appears, expressions of "cancellation" or "rescission" of the contract or the like shall not be construed as a renunciation or discharge of any claim in damages for an antecedent breach.

§ 2–721. Remedies for Fraud.

Remedies for material misrepresentation or fraud include all remedies available under this Article for non-fraudulent breach. Neither rescission or a claim for rescission of the contract for sale nor rejection or return of the goods shall bar or be deemed inconsistent with a claim for damages or other remedy.

§ 2–722. Who Can Sue Third Parties for Injury to Goods.

Where a third party so deals with goods which have been identified to a contract for sale as to cause actionable injury to a party to that contract

(a) a right of action against the third party is in either party to the contract for sale who has title to or a security interest or a special property or an insurable interest in the goods; and if the goods have been destroyed or converted a right of action is also in the party who either bore the risk of loss under the contract for sale or has since the injury assumed that risk as against the other;

(b) if at the time of the injury the party plaintiff did not bear the risk of loss as against the other party to the contract for sale and there is no arrangement between them for disposition of the recovery, his suit or settlement is, subject to his own interest, as a fiduciary for the other party to the contract;

(c) either party may with the consent of the other sue for the benefit of whom it may concern.

§ 2–723. Proof of Market Price: Time and Place.

(1) If an action based on anticipatory repudiation comes to trial before the time for performance with respect to some or all of the goods, any damages based on market price (Section 2–708 or Section 2–713) shall be determined according to the price of such goods prevailing at the time when the aggrieved party learned of the repudiation.

(2) If evidence of a price prevailing at the times or places described in this Article is not readily available the price prevailing within any reasonable time before or after the time described or at any other place which in commercial judgment or under usage of trade would serve as a reasonable substitute for the one described may be used, making any proper allowance for the cost of transporting the goods to or from such other place.

(3) Evidence of a relevant price prevailing at a time or place other than the one described in this Article offered by one party is not admissible unless and until he has given the other party such notice as the court finds sufficient to prevent unfair surprise.

§ 2–724. Admissibility of Market Quotations.

Whenever the prevailing price or value of any goods regularly bought and sold in any established commodity market is in issue, reports in official publications or trade journals or in newspapers or periodicals of general circulation published as the reports of such market shall be admissible in evidence. The circumstances of the preparation of such a report may be shown to affect its weight but not its admissibility.

§ 2–725. Statute of Limitations in Contracts for Sale.

(1) An action for breach of any contract for sale must be commenced within four years after the cause of action has accrued. By the original agreement the parties may reduce the period of limitation to not less than one year but may not extend it.

(2) A cause of action accrues when the breach occurs, regardless of the aggrieved party's lack of knowledge of the breach. A breach of warranty occurs when tender of delivery is made, except that where a warranty explicitly extends to future performance of the goods and discovery of the breach must await the time of such performance the cause of action accrues when the breach is or should have been discovered.

(3) Where an action commenced within the time limited by subsection (1) is so terminated as to leave available a remedy by another action for the same breach such other action may be commenced after the expiration of the time limited and within six months after the termination of the first action unless the termination resulted from voluntary discontinuance or from dismissal for failure or neglect to prosecute.

(4) This section does not alter the law on tolling of the statute of limitations nor does it apply to causes of action which have accrued before this Act becomes effective.

ARTICLE II
AMENDMENTS (EXCERPTS)[1]

PART 1   Short Title, General Construction and Subject Matter

§ 2-103.   Definitions and Index of Definitions.
* * * *

(1) In this article unless the context otherwise requires
* * * *

(b) "Conspicuous", with reference to a term, means so written, displayed, or presented that a reasonable person against which it is to operate ought to have noticed it. A term in an electronic record intended to evoke a response by an electronic agent is conspicuous if it is presented in a form that would enable a reasonably configured electronic agent to take it into account or react to it without review of the record by an individual. Whether a term is "conspicuous" or not is a decision for the court. Conspicuous terms include the following:

(i) for a person:

(A) a heading in capitals equal to or greater in size than the surrounding text, or in contrasting type, font, or color to the surrounding text of the same or lesser size;

(B) language in the body of a record or display in larger type than the surrounding text, or in contrasting type, font, or color to the surrounding text of the same size, or set off from surrounding text of the same size by symbols or other marks that call attention to the language; and

(ii) for a person or an electronic agent, a term that is so placed in a record or display that the person or electronic agent cannot proceed without taking action with respect to the particular term.

(c) "Consumer" means an individual who buys or contracts to buy goods that, at the time of contracting, are intended by the individual to be used primarily for personal, family, or household purposes.

(d) "Consumer contract" means a contract between a merchant seller and a consumer.
* * * *

(j) "Good faith" means honesty in fact and the observance of reasonable commercial standards of fair dealing.

(k) "Goods" means all things that are movable at the time of identification to a contract for sale. The term includes future goods, specially manufactured goods, the unborn young of animals, growing crops, and other identified things attached to realty as described in Section 2-107. The term does not include information, the money in which the price is to be paid, investment securities under Article 8, the subject matter of foreign exchange transactions, and choses in action.
* * * *

(m) "Record" means information that is inscribed on a tangible medium or that is stored in an electronic or other medium and is retrievable in perceivable form.

(n) "Remedial promise" means a promise by the seller to repair or replace the goods or to refund all or part of the price upon the happening of a specified event.
* * * *

(p) "Sign" means, with present intent to authenticate or adopt a record,

(i) to execute or adopt a tangible symbol; or

(ii) to attach to or logically associate with the record an electronic sound, symbol, or process.
* * * *

PART 2   Form, Formation, Terms and Readjustment of Contract; Electronic Contracting

§ 2-201.   Formal Requirements; Statute of Frauds.

(1) A contract for the sale of goods for the price of $5,000 or more is not enforceable by way of action or defense unless there is some record sufficient to indicate that a contract for sale has been made between the parties and signed by the party against whom which enforcement is sought or by the party's authorized agent or broker. A record is not insufficient because it omits or incorrectly states a term agreed upon but the contract is not enforceable under this subsection beyond the quantity of goods shown in the record.

(2) Between merchants if within a reasonable time a record in confirmation of the contract and sufficient against the sender is received and the party receiving it has reason to know its contents, it satisfies the requirements of subsection (1) against such party the recipient unless notice of objection to its contents is given in a record within 10 days after it is received.

(3) A contract which does not satisfy the requirements of subsection (1) but which is valid in other respects is enforceable

(a) if the goods are to be specially manufactured for the buyer and are not suitable for sale to others in the ordinary course of the seller's business and the seller, before notice of repudiation is received and under circumstances which reasonably indicate that the goods are for the buyer, has made either a substantial beginning of their manufacture or commitments for their procurement; or

(b) if the party against whom which enforcement is sought admits in the party's pleading, or in the party's testimony or otherwise under oath that a contract for sale was made, but the contract is not enforceable under this paragraph beyond the quantity of goods admitted; or

(c) with respect to goods for which payment has been made and accepted or which have been received and accepted (Sec. 2–606).

(4) A contract that is enforceable under this section is not rendered unenforceable merely because it is not capable of being performed within one year or any other applicable period after its making.

* * * *

§ 2-207. Terms of Contract; Effect of Confirmation.

If (i) conduct by both parties recognizes the existence of a contract although their records do not otherwise establish a contract, (ii) a contract is formed by an offer and acceptance, or (iii) a contract formed in any manner is confirmed by a record that contains terms additional to or different from those in the contract being confirmed, the terms of the contract, subject to Section 2–202, are:

(a) terms that appear in the records of both parties;

(b) terms, whether in a record or not, to which both parties agree; and

(c) terms supplied or incorporated under any provision of this Act.

* * * *

PART 3 General Obligation and Construction of Contract

* * * *

§ 2-312. Warranty of Title and Against Infringement; Buyer's Obligation Against Infringement.

(1) Subject to subsection (2) there is in a contract for sale a warranty by the seller that

(a) the title conveyed shall be good, good and its transfer rightful and shall not, because of any colorable claim to or interest in the goods, unreasonably expose the buyer to litigation; and

(b) the goods shall be delivered free from any security interest or other lien or encumbrance of which the buyer at the time of contracting has no knowledge.

(2) Unless otherwise agreed a seller that is a merchant regularly dealing in goods of the kind warrants that the goods shall be delivered free of the rightful claim of any third person by way of infringement or the like but a buyer that furnishes specifications to the seller must hold the seller harmless against any such claim that arises out of compliance with the specifications.

(3) A warranty under this section may be disclaimed or modified only by specific language or by circumstances that give the buyer reason to know that the seller does not claim title, that the seller is purporting to sell only the right or title as the seller or a third person may have, or that the seller is selling subject to any claims of infringement or the like.

§ 2-313. Express Warranties by Affirmation, Promise, Description, Sample; Remedial Promise.

(1) In this section, "immediate buyer" means a buyer that enters into a contract with the seller.

* * * *

(4) Any remedial promise made by the seller to the immediate buyer creates an obligation that the promise will be performed upon the happening of the specified event.

§ 2-313A. Obligation to Remote Purchaser Created by Record Packaged with or Accompanying Goods.

(1) This section applies only to new goods and goods sold or leased as new goods in a transaction of purchase in the normal chain of distribution. In this section:

(a) "Immediate buyer" means a buyer that enters into a contract with the seller.

(b) "Remote purchaser" means a person that buys or leases goods from an immediate buyer or other person in the normal chain of distribution.

(2) If a seller in a record packaged with or accompanying the goods makes an affirmation of fact or promise that relates to the goods, provides a description that relates to the goods, or makes a remedial promise, and the seller reasonably expects the record to be, and the record is, furnished to the remote purchaser, the seller has an obligation to the remote purchaser that:

(a) the goods will conform to the affirmation of fact, promise or description unless a reasonable person in the position of the remote purchaser would not believe that the affirmation of fact, promise or description created an obligation; and

(b) the seller will perform the remedial promise.

(3) It is not necessary to the creation of an obligation under this section that the seller use formal words such as "warrant" or "guarantee" or that the seller have a specific intention to undertake an obligation, but an affirmation merely of the value of the goods or a statement purporting to be merely the seller's opinion or commendation of the goods does not create an obligation.

(4) The following rules apply to the remedies for breach of an obligation created under this section:

(a) The seller may modify or limit the remedies available to the remote purchaser if the modification or limitation is furnished to the remote purchaser no later than the time of purchase or if the modification or limitation is contained in the record that contains the affirmation of fact, promise or description.

(b) Subject to a modification or limitation of remedy, a seller in breach is liable for incidental or consequential damages under Section 2–715, but the seller is not liable for lost profits.

(c) The remote purchaser may recover as damages for breach of a seller's obligation arising under subsection (2) the loss resulting in the ordinary course of events as determined in any manner that is reasonable.

(5) An obligation that is not a remedial promise is breached if the goods did not conform to the affirmation of fact, promise or description creating the obligation when the goods left the seller's control.

§ 2–313B. Obligation to Remote Purchaser Created by Communication to the Public.

(1) This section applies only to new goods and goods sold or leased as new goods in a transaction of purchase in the normal chain of distribution. In this section:

(a) "Immediate buyer" means a buyer that enters into a contract with the seller.

(b) "Remote purchaser" means a person that buys or leases goods from an immediate buyer or other person in the normal chain of distribution.

(2) If a seller in advertising or a similar communication to the public makes an affirmation of fact or promise that relates to the goods, provides a description that relates to the goods, or makes a remedial promise, and the remote purchaser enters into a transaction of purchase with knowledge of and with the expectation that the goods will conform to the affirmation of fact, promise, or description, or that the seller will perform the remedial promise, the seller has an obligation to the remote purchaser that:

(a) the goods will conform to the affirmation of fact, promise or description unless a reasonable person in the position of the remote purchaser would not believe that the affirmation of fact, promise or description created an obligation; and

(b) the seller will perform the remedial promise.

(3) It is not necessary to the creation of an obligation under this section that the seller use formal words such as "warrant" or "guarantee" or that the seller have a specific intention to undertake an obligation, but an affirmation merely of the value of the goods or a statement purporting to be merely the seller's opinion or commendation of the goods does not create an obligation.

(4) The following rules apply to the remedies for breach of an obligation created under this section:

(a) The seller may modify or limit the remedies available to the remote purchaser if the modification or limitation is furnished to the remote purchaser no later than the time of purchase. The modification or limitation may be furnished as part of the communication that contains the affirmation of fact, promise or description.

(b) Subject to a modification or limitation of remedy, a seller in breach is liable for incidental or consequential damages under Section 2–715, but the seller is not liable for lost profits.

(c) The remote purchaser may recover as damages for breach of a seller's obligation arising under subsection (2) the loss resulting in the ordinary course of events as determined in any manner that is reasonable.

(5) An obligation that is not a remedial promise is breached if the goods did not conform to the affirmation of fact, promise or description creating the obligation when the goods left the seller's control.

* * * *

§ 2–316. Exclusion or Modification of Warranties.

* * * *

(2) Subject to subsection (3), to exclude or modify the implied warranty of merchantability or any part of it in a consumer contract the language must be in a record, be conspicuous and state "The seller undertakes no responsibility for the quality of the goods except as otherwise provided in this contract," and in any other contract the language must mention merchantability and in case of a record must be conspicuous. Subject to subsection (3), to exclude or modify the implied warranty of fitness the exclusion must be in a record and be conspicuous. Language to exclude all implied warranties of fitness in a consumer contract must state "The seller assumes no responsibility that the goods will be fit for any particular purpose for which you may be buying these goods, except as otherwise provided in the contract," and in any other contract the language is sufficient if it states, for example, that "There are no warranties which extend beyond the description on the face hereof." Language that satisfies the requirements of this subsection for the exclusion and modification of a warranty in a consumer contract also satisfies the requirements for any other contract.

(3) Notwithstanding subsection (2):

(a) unless the circumstances indicate otherwise, all implied warranties are excluded by expressions like "as is", "with all faults" or other language which in common understanding calls the buyer's attention to the exclusion of warranties, makes plain that there is no implied warranty, and in a consumer contract evidenced by a record is set forth conspicuously in the record; and

(b) when the buyer before entering into the contract has examined the goods or the sample or model as fully as desired or has refused to examine the goods after a demand by the seller there is no implied warranty with regard to defects which an examination ought in the circumstances to have revealed to the buyer; and

(c) an implied warranty can also be excluded or modified by course of dealing or course of performance or usage of trade.

* * * *

§ 2–318. Third Party Beneficiaries of Warranties Express or Implied.

(1) In this section:

(a) "Immediate buyer" means a buyer that enters into a contract with the seller.

(b) "Remote purchaser" means a person that buys or leases goods from an immediate buyer or other person in the normal chain of distribution.

Alternative A to subsection (2)   (2) A seller's warranty whether express or implied to an immediate buyer, a seller's remedial promise to an immediate buyer, or a seller's obligation to a remote purchaser under Section 2–313A or 2–313B extends to any natural person who is in the family or household of the immediate buyer or the remote purchaser or who is a guest in the home of either if it is reasonable to expect that the person may use, consume or be affected by the goods and who is injured in person by breach of the warranty, remedial promise or obligation. A seller may not exclude or limit the operation of this section.

Alternative B to subsection (2)   (2) A seller's warranty whether express or implied to an immediate buyer, a seller's remedial promise to an immediate buyer, or a seller's obligation to a remote purchaser under Section 2–313A or 2–313B extends to any natural person who may reasonably be expected to use, consume or be affected by the goods and who is injured in person by breach of the warranty, remedial promise or obligation. A seller may not exclude or limit the operation of this section.

Alternative C to subsection (2)   (2) A seller's warranty whether express or implied to an immediate buyer, a seller's remedial promise to an immediate buyer, or a seller's obligation to a remote purchaser under Section 2–313A or 2–313B extends to any person that may reasonably be expected to use, consume or be affected by the goods and that is injured by breach of the warranty, remedial promise or obligation. A seller may not exclude or limit the operation of this section with respect to injury to the person of an individual to whom the warranty, remedial promise or obligation extends.

* * * *

PART 5   Performance
* * * *

§ 2–502.   Buyer's Right to Goods on Seller's Insolvency.

(1) Subject to subsections (2) and (3) and even though the goods have not been shipped a buyer who that has paid a part or all of the price of goods in which the buyer has a special property under the provisions of the immediately preceding section may on making and keeping good a tender of any unpaid portion of their price recover them from the seller if:

(a) in the case of goods bought by a consumer, the seller repudiates or fails to deliver as required by the contract; or

(b) in all cases, the seller becomes insolvent within ten days after receipt of the first installment on their price.

(2) The buyer's right to recover the goods under subsection (1) vests upon acquisition of a special property, even if the seller had not then repudiated or failed to deliver.

(3) If the identification creating the special property has been made by the buyer, the buyer acquires the right to recover the goods only if they conform to the contract for sale.

* * * *

§ 2–508.   Cure by Seller of Improper Tender or Delivery; Replacement.

(1) Where the buyer rejects goods or a tender of delivery under Section 2–601 or 2–612 or except in a consumer contract justifiably revokes acceptance under Section 2–608(1)(b) and the agreed time for performance has not expired, a seller that has performed in good faith, upon seasonable notice to the buyer and at the seller's own expense, may cure the breach of contract by making a conforming tender of delivery within the agreed time. The seller shall compensate the buyer for all of the buyer's reasonable expenses caused by the seller's breach of contract and subsequent cure.

(2) Where the buyer rejects goods or a tender of delivery under Section 2–601 or 2–612 or except in a consumer contract justifiably revokes acceptance under Section 2–608(1)(b) and the agreed time for performance has expired, a seller that has performed in good faith, upon seasonable notice to the buyer and at the seller's own expense, may cure the breach of contract, if the cure is appropriate and timely under the circumstances, by making a tender of conforming goods. The seller shall compensate the buyer for all of the buyer's reasonable expenses caused by the seller's breach of contract and subsequent cure.

§ 2–509.   Risk of Loss in the Absence of Breach.

(1) Where the contract requires or authorizes the seller to ship the goods by carrier

(a) if it does not require the seller to deliver them at a particular destination, the risk of loss passes to the buyer when the goods are delivered to the carrier even though the shipment is under reservation (Section 2–505); but

(b) if it does require the seller to deliver them at a particular destination and the goods are there tendered while in the possession of the carrier, the risk of loss passes to the buyer when the goods are there so tendered as to enable the buyer to take delivery.

(2) Where the goods are held by a bailee to be delivered without being moved, the risk of loss passes to the buyer

(a) on the buyer's receipt of a negotiable document of title covering the goods; or

(b) on acknowledgment by the bailee to the buyer of the buyer's right to possession of the goods; or

(c) after the buyer's receipt of a non-negotiable document of title or other direction to deliver in a record, as provided in subsection (4)(b) of Section 2–503.

(3) In any case not within subsection (1) or (2), the risk of loss passes to the buyer on the buyer's receipt of the goods.

* * * *

§ 2–513.   Buyer's Right to Inspection of Goods.

* * * *

(3) Unless otherwise agreed, the buyer is not entitled to inspect the goods before payment of the price when the contract provides

(a) for delivery on terms that under applicable course of performance, course of dealing, or usage of trade are interpreted to preclude inspection before payment; or

(b) for payment against documents of title, except where such payment is due only after the goods are to become available for inspection.

* * * *

PART 6   Breach, Repudiation and Excuse

* * * *

§ 2–605.   Waiver of Buyer's Objections by Failure to Particularize.

(1) The buyer's failure to state in connection with rejection a particular defect or in connection with revocation of acceptance a defect that justifies revocation precludes the buyer from relying on the unstated defect to justify rejection or revocation of acceptance if the defect is ascertainable by reasonable inspection

(a) where the seller had a right to cure the defect and could have cured it if stated seasonably; or

(b) between merchants when the seller has after rejection made a request in a record for a full and final statement in record form of all defects on which the buyer proposes to rely.

(2) A buyer's payment against documents tendered to the buyer made without reservation of rights precludes recovery of the payment for defects apparent on the face of the documents.

* * * *

§ 2–607.   Effect of Acceptance; Notice of Breach; Burden of Establishing Breach After Acceptance; Notice of Claim or Litigation to Person Answerable Over.

(3) Where a tender has been accepted

(a) the buyer must within a reasonable time after the buyer discovers or should have discovered any breach notify the seller; however, failure to give timely notice bars the buyer from a remedy only to the extent that the seller is prejudiced by the failure and

(b) if the claim is one for infringement or the like (subsection (3) of Section 2–312) and the buyer is sued as a result of such a breach the buyer must so notify the seller within a reasonable time after the buyer receives notice of the litigation or be barred from any remedy over for liability established by the litigation.

* * * *

§ 2–608.   Revocation of Acceptance in Whole or in Part.

* * * *

(4) If a buyer uses the goods after a rightful rejection or justifiable revocation of acceptance, the following rules apply:

(a) Any use by the buyer that is unreasonable under the circumstances is wrongful as against the seller and is an acceptance only if ratified by the seller.

(b) Any use of the goods that is reasonable under the circumstances is not wrongful as against the seller and is not an acceptance, but in an appropriate case the buyer shall be obligated to the seller for the value of the use to the buyer.

* * * *

§ 2–612.   "Installment Contract"; Breach.

* * * *

(2) The buyer may reject any installment which is -non-conforming if the non-conformity substantially impairs the value of that installment to the buyer or if the non-conformity is a defect in the required documents; but if the non-conformity does not fall within subsection (3) and the seller gives adequate assurance of its cure the buyer must accept that installment.

(3) Whenever non-conformity or default with respect to one or more installments substantially impairs the value of the whole contract there is a breach of the whole. But the aggrieved party reinstates the contract if the party accepts a non-conforming installment without seasonably notifying of cancellation or if the party brings an action with respect only to past installments or demands performance as to future installments.

* * * *

PART 7   Remedies

§ 2–702.   Seller's Remedies on Discovery of Buyer's Insolvency.

* * * *

(2) Where the seller discovers that the buyer has received goods on credit while insolvent the seller may reclaim the goods upon demand made within a reasonable time after the buyer's receipt of the goods. Except as provided in this subsection the seller may not base a right to reclaim goods on the buyer's fraudulent or innocent misrepresentation of solvency or of intent to pay.

* * * *

§ 2–705.   Seller's Stoppage of Delivery in Transit or Otherwise.

(1) The seller may stop delivery of goods in the possession of a carrier or other bailee when the seller discovers the buyer to be insolvent (Section 2–702) or when the buyer repudiates or fails to make a payment due before delivery or if for any other reason the seller has a right to withhold or reclaim the goods.

* * * *

§ 2–706.   Seller's Resale Including Contract for Resale.

(1) In an appropriate case involving breach by the buyer, the seller may resell the goods concerned or the undelivered balance thereof. Where the resale is made in good faith and in a commercially reasonable manner the seller may recover the difference between the contract price and the resale price together with any incidental or consequential damages allowed under the provisions of this Article (Section 2–710), but less expenses saved in consequence of the buyer's breach.

* * * *

§ 2–708.   Seller's Damages for Non-Acceptance or Repudiation.

(1) Subject to subsection (2) and to the provisions of this Article with respect to proof of market price (Section 2–723)

(a) the measure of damages for non-acceptance by the buyer is the difference between the contract price and the market price at the time and place for tender together with any incidental or consequential damages provided in this Article (Section 2–710), but less expenses saved in consequence of the buyer's breach; and

(b) the measure of damages for repudiation by the buyer is the difference between the contract price and the market price at the place for tender at the expiration of a commercially reasonable time after the seller learned of the repudiation, but no later than the time stated in paragraph (a), together with any incidental or consequential damages provided in this Article (Section 2–710), but less expenses saved in consequence of the buyer's breach.

(2) If the measure of damages provided in subsection (1) or in Section 2–706 is inadequate to put the seller in as good a position as performance would have done then the measure of damages is the profit (including reasonable overhead) which the seller would have made from full performance by the buyer, together with any incidental or consequential damages provided in this Article (Section 2–710).

§ 2–709.   Action for the Price.

(1) When the buyer fails to pay the price as it becomes due the seller may recover, together with any incidental or consequential damages under the next section, the price

(a) of goods accepted or of conforming goods lost or damaged within a commercially reasonable time after risk of their loss has passed to the buyer; and

(b) of goods identified to the contract if the seller is unable after reasonable effort to resell them at a reasonable price or the circumstances reasonably indicate that such effort will be unavailing.

* * * *

* * * *

* * * *

§ 2–710.   Seller's Incidental and Consequential Damages.

(1) Incidental damages to an aggrieved seller include any commercially reasonable charges, expenses or commissions incurred in stopping delivery, in the transportation, care and custody of goods after the buyer's breach, in connection with return or resale of the goods or otherwise resulting from the breach.

(2) Consequential damages resulting from the buyer's breach include any loss resulting from general or particular requirements and needs of which the buyer at the time of contracting had reason to know and which could not reasonably be prevented by resale or otherwise.

(3) In a consumer contract, a seller may not recover consequential damages from a consumer.

* * * *

§ 2–713.   Buyer's Damages for Non-Delivery or Repudiation.

(1) Subject to the provisions of this Article with respect to proof of market price (Section 2–723), if the seller wrongfully fails to deliver or repudiates or the buyer rightfully rejects or justifiably revokes acceptance

(a) the measure of damages in the case of wrongful failure to deliver by the seller or rightful rejection or justifiable revocation of acceptance by the buyer is the difference between the market price at the time for tender under the contract and the contract price together with any incidental or consequential damages provided in this Article (Section 2–715), but less expenses saved in consequence of the seller's breach; and

(b) the measure of damages for repudiation by the seller is the difference between the market price at the expiration of a commercially reasonable time after the buyer learned of the repudiation, but no later than the time stated in paragraph (a), and the contract price together with any incidental or consequential damages provided in this Article (Section 2–715), but less expenses saved in consequence of the seller's breach.

* * * *

§ 2–725.   Statute of Limitations in Contracts for Sale.

(1) Except as otherwise provided in this section, an action for breach of any contract for sale must be commenced within the later of four years after the right of action has accrued under subsection (2) or (3) or one year after the breach was or should have been discovered, but no longer than five years after the right of action accrued. By the original agreement the parties may reduce the period of limitation to not less than one year but may not extend it; however, in a consumer contract, the period of limitation may not be reduced.

(2) Except as otherwise provided in subsection (3), the following rules apply:

(a) Except as otherwise provided in this subsection, a right of action for breach of a contract accrues when the breach occurs, even if the aggrieved party did not have knowledge of the breach.

(b) For breach of a contract by repudiation, a right of action accrues at the earlier of when the aggrieved party elects to treat the repudiation as a breach or when a commercially reasonable time for awaiting performance has expired.

(c) For breach of a remedial promise, a right of action accrues when the remedial promise is not performed when due.

(d) In an action by a buyer against a person that is answerable over to the buyer for a claim asserted against the buyer, the buyer's right of action against the person answerable over accrues at the time the claim was originally asserted against the buyer.

(3) If a breach of a warranty arising under Section 2–312, 2–313 (2), 2–314, or 2–315, or a breach of an obligation other than a remedial promise arising under Section 2–313A or 2–313B, is claimed the following rules apply:

(a) Except as otherwise provided in paragraph (c), a right of action for breach of a warranty arising under Section 2–313(2), 2–314 or 2–315 accrues when the seller has tendered delivery to the immediate buyer, as defined in Section 2–313, and has completed performance of any agreed installation or assembly of the goods.

(b) Except as otherwise provided in paragraph (c), a right of action for breach of an obligation other than a remedial promise arising under Section 2–313A or 2–313B accrues when the remote purchaser, as defined in sections 2–313A and 2–313B, receives the goods.

(c) Where a warranty arising under Section 2–313(2) or an obligation other than a remedial promise arising under 2–313A or 2–313B explicitly extends to future performance of the goods and discovery of the breach must await the time for performance the right of action accrues when the immediate buyer as defined in Section 2–313 or the remote purchaser as defined in Sections 2–313A and 2–313B discovers or should have discovered the breach.

(d) A right of action for breach of warranty arising under Section 2–312 accrues when the aggrieved party discovers or should have discovered the breach. However, an action for breach of the warranty of non-infringement may not be commenced more than six years after tender of delivery of the goods to the aggrieved party.

* * * *

ARTICLE IIA
LEASES

PART 1   General Provisions

§ 2A–101. Short Title.

This Article shall be known and may be cited as the Uniform Commercial Code—Leases.

§ 2A–102. Scope.

This Article applies to any transaction, regardless of form, that creates a lease.

§ 2A–103. Definitions and Index of Definitions.

(1) In this Article unless the context otherwise requires:

(a) "Buyer in ordinary course of business" means a person who in good faith and without knowledge that the sale to him [or her] is in violation of the ownership rights or security interest or leasehold interest of a third party in the goods buys in ordinary course from a person in the business of selling goods of that kind but does not include a pawnbroker. "Buying" may be for cash or by exchange of other property or on secured or unsecured credit and includes receiving goods or documents of title under a pre-existing contract for sale but does not include a transfer in bulk or as security for or in total or partial satisfaction of a money debt.

(b) "Cancellation" occurs when either party puts an end to the lease contract for default by the other party.

(c) "Commercial unit" means such a unit of goods as by commercial usage is a single whole for purposes of lease and division of which materially impairs its character or value on the market or in use. A commercial unit may be a single article, as a machine, or a set of articles, as a suite of furniture or a line of machinery, or a quantity, as a gross or carload, or any other unit treated in use or in the relevant market as a single whole.

(d) "Conforming" goods or performance under a lease contract means goods or performance that are in accordance with the obligations under the lease contract.

(e) "Consumer lease" means a lease that a lessor regularly engaged in the business of leasing or selling makes to a lessee who is an individual and who takes under the lease primarily for a personal, family, or household purpose [, if the total payments to be made under the lease contract, excluding payments for options to renew or buy, do not exceed $_____].

(f) "Fault" means wrongful act, omission, breach, or default.

(g) "Finance lease" means a lease with respect to which:

(i) the lessor does not select, manufacture or supply the goods;

(ii) the lessor acquires the goods or the right to possession and use of the goods in connection with the lease; and

(iii) one of the following occurs:

(A) the lessee receives a copy of the contract by which the lessor acquired the goods or the right to possession and use of the goods before signing the lease contract;

(B) the lessee's approval of the contract by which the lessor acquired the goods or the right to possession and use of the goods is a condition to effectiveness of the lease contract;

(C) the lessee, before signing the lease contract, receives an accurate and complete statement designating the promises and warranties, and any disclaimers of warranties, limitations or modifications of remedies, or liquidated damages, including those of a third party, such as the manufacturer of the goods, provided to the lessor by the person supplying the goods in connection with or as part of the contract by which the lessor acquired the goods or the right to possession and use of the goods; or

(D) if the lease is not a consumer lease, the lessor, before the lessee signs the lease contract, informs the lessee in writing (a) of the identity of the person supplying the goods to the lessor, unless the lessee has selected that person and directed the lessor to acquire the goods or the right to possession and use of the goods from that person, (b) that the lessee is entitled under this Article to any promises and warranties, including those of any third party, provided to the lessor by the person supplying the goods in connection with or as part of the contract by which the lessor acquired the goods or the right to possession and use of the goods, and (c) that the lessee may communicate with the person supplying the goods to the lessor and receive an accurate and complete statement of those promises and warranties, including any disclaimers and limitations of them or of remedies.

(h) "Goods" means all things that are movable at the time of identification to the lease contract, or are fixtures (Section 2A–309), but the term does not include money, documents, instruments, accounts, chattel paper, general intangibles, or minerals or the like, including oil and gas, before extraction. The term also includes the unborn young of animals.

(i) "Installment lease contract" means a lease contract that authorizes or requires the delivery of goods in separate lots to be separately accepted, even though the lease contract contains a clause "each delivery is a separate lease" or its equivalent.

(j) "Lease" means a transfer of the right to possession and use of goods for a term in return for consideration, but a sale, including a sale on approval or a sale or return, or retention or creation of a security interest is not a lease. Unless the context clearly indicates otherwise, the term includes a sublease.

(k) "Lease agreement" means the bargain, with respect to the lease, of the lessor and the lessee in fact as found in their language or by implication from other circumstances including course of dealing or usage of trade or course of performance as provided in this Article. Unless the context clearly indicates otherwise, the term includes a sublease agreement.

(l) "Lease contract" means the total legal obligation that results from the lease agreement as affected by this Article and any other applicable rules of law. Unless the context clearly indicates -otherwise, the term includes a sublease contract.

(m) "Leasehold interest" means the interest of the lessor or the lessee under a lease contract.

(n) "Lessee" means a person who acquires the right to possession and use of goods under a lease. Unless the context clearly indicates otherwise, the term includes a sublessee.

(o) "Lessee in ordinary course of business" means a person who in good faith and without knowledge that the lease to him [or her] is in violation of the ownership rights or security interest or leasehold interest of a third party in the goods, leases in ordinary course from a person in the business of selling or leasing goods of that kind but does not include a pawnbroker. "Leasing" may be for cash or by exchange of other property or on secured or unsecured credit and includes receiving goods or documents of title under a pre-existing lease contract but does not include a transfer in bulk or as security for or in total or partial satisfaction of a money debt.

(p) "Lessor" means a person who transfers the right to possession and use of goods under a lease. Unless the context clearly indicates otherwise, the term includes a sublessor.

(q) "Lessor's residual interest" means the lessor's interest in the goods after expiration, termination, or cancellation of the lease contract.

(r) "Lien" means a charge against or interest in goods to secure payment of a debt or performance of an obligation, but the term does not include a security interest.

(s) "Lot" means a parcel or a single article that is the subject matter of a separate lease or delivery, whether or not it is sufficient to perform the lease contract.

(t) "Merchant lessee" means a lessee that is a merchant with respect to goods of the kind subject to the lease.

(u) "Present value" means the amount as of a date certain of one or more sums payable in the future, discounted to the date certain. The discount is determined by the interest rate specified by the parties if the rate was not manifestly unreasonable at the time the transaction was entered into; otherwise, the discount is determined by a commercially reasonable rate that takes into account the facts and circumstances of each case at the time the transaction was entered into.

(v) "Purchase" includes taking by sale, lease, mortgage, security interest, pledge, gift, or any other voluntary transaction creating an interest in goods.

(w) "Sublease" means a lease of goods the right to possession and use of which was acquired by the lessor as a lessee under an existing lease.

(x) "Supplier" means a person from whom a lessor buys or leases goods to be leased under a finance lease.

(y) "Supply contract" means a contract under which a lessor buys or leases goods to be leased.

(z) "Termination" occurs when either party pursuant to a power created by agreement or law puts an end to the lease contract otherwise than for default.

(2) Other definitions applying to this Article and the sections in which they appear are:

"Accessions". Section 2A–310(1).
"Construction mortgage". Section 2A–309(1)(d).
"Encumbrance". Section 2A–309(1)(e).
"Fixtures". Section 2A–309(1)(a).
"Fixture filing". Section 2A–309(1)(b).
"Purchase money lease". Section 2A–309(1)(c).

(3) The following definitions in other Articles apply to this Article:

"Accounts". Section 9–106.
"Between merchants". Section 2–104(3).
"Buyer". Section 2–103(1)(a).
"Chattel paper". Section 9–105(1)(b).
"Consumer goods". Section 9–109(1).
"Document". Section 9–105(1)(f).
"Entrusting". Section 2–403(3).
"General intangibles". Section 9–106.
"Good faith". Section 2–103(1)(b).
"Instrument". Section 9–105(1)(i).
"Merchant". Section 2–104(1).
"Mortgage". Section 9–105(1)(j).
"Pursuant to commitment". Section 9–105(1)(k).
"Receipt". Section 2–103(1)(c).
"Sale". Section 2–106(1).
"Sale on approval". Section 2–326.
"Sale or return". Section 2–326.
"Seller". Section 2–103(1)(d).

(4) In addition Article 1 contains general definitions and principles of construction and interpretation applicable throughout this Article.

As amended in 1990 and 1999.

§ 2A–104. Leases Subject to Other Law.

(1) A lease, although subject to this Article, is also subject to any applicable:

(a) certificate of title statute of this State: (list any certificate of title statutes covering automobiles, trailers, mobile homes, boats, farm tractors, and the like);

(b) certificate of title statute of another jurisdiction (Section 2A–105); or

(c) consumer protection statute of this State, or final consumer protection decision of a court of this State existing on the effective date of this Article.

(2) In case of conflict between this Article, other than Sections 2A–105, 2A–304(3), and 2A–305(3), and a statute or decision referred to in subsection (1), the statute or decision controls.

(3) Failure to comply with an applicable law has only the effect specified therein.

As amended in 1990.

§ 2A–105. Territorial Application of Article to Goods Covered by Certificate of Title.

Subject to the provisions of Sections 2A–304(3) and 2A–305(3), with respect to goods covered by a certificate of title issued under a statute of this State or of another jurisdiction, compliance and the effect of compliance or noncompliance with a certificate of title statute are governed by the law (including the conflict of laws rules) of the jurisdiction issuing the certificate until the earlier of (a) surrender of the certificate, or (b) four months after the goods are removed from that jurisdiction and thereafter until a new certificate of title is issued by another jurisdiction.

§ 2A–106. Limitation on Power of Parties to Consumer Lease to Choose Applicable Law and Judicial Forum.

(1) If the law chosen by the parties to a consumer lease is that of a jurisdiction other than a jurisdiction in which the lessee resides at the time the lease agreement becomes enforceable or within 30 days thereafter or in which the goods are to be used, the choice is not enforceable.

(2) If the judicial forum chosen by the parties to a consumer lease is a forum that would not otherwise have jurisdiction over the lessee, the choice is not enforceable.

§ 2A–107. Waiver or Renunciation of Claim or Right After Default.

Any claim or right arising out of an alleged default or breach of warranty may be discharged in whole or in part without consideration by a written waiver or renunciation signed and delivered by the aggrieved party.

§ 2A–108. Unconscionability.

(1) If the court as a matter of law finds a lease contract or any clause of a lease contract to have been unconscionable at the time it was made the court may refuse to enforce the lease contract, or it may enforce the remainder of the lease contract without the unconscionable clause, or it may so limit the application of any unconscionable clause as to avoid any unconscionable result.

(2) With respect to a consumer lease, if the court as a matter of law finds that a lease contract or any clause of a lease contract has been induced by unconscionable conduct or that unconscionable conduct has occurred in the collection of a claim arising from a lease contract, the court may grant appropriate relief.

(3) Before making a finding of unconscionability under subsection (1) or (2), the court, on its own motion or that of a party, shall afford the parties a reasonable opportunity to present evidence as to the setting, purpose, and effect of the lease contract or clause thereof, or of the conduct.

(4) In an action in which the lessee claims unconscionability with respect to a consumer lease:

(a) If the court finds unconscionability under subsection (1) or (2), the court shall award reasonable attorney's fees to the lessee.

(b) If the court does not find unconscionability and the lessee claiming unconscionability has brought or maintained an action he [or she] knew to be groundless, the court shall award reasonable attorney's fees to the party against whom the claim is made.

(c) In determining attorney's fees, the amount of the recovery on behalf of the claimant under subsections (1) and (2) is not controlling.

§ 2A–109. Option to Accelerate at Will.

(1) A term providing that one party or his [or her] successor in interest may accelerate payment or performance or require collateral or additional collateral "at will" or "when he [or she] deems himself [or herself] insecure" or in words of similar import must be construed to mean that he [or she] has power to do so only if he [or she] in good faith believes that the prospect of payment or performance is impaired.

(2) With respect to a consumer lease, the burden of establishing good faith under subsection (1) is on the party who exercised the power; otherwise the burden of establishing lack of good faith is on the party against whom the power has been exercised.

PART 2   Formation and Construction of Lease Contract

§ 2A–201. Statute of Frauds.

(1) A lease contract is not enforceable by way of action or defense unless:

(a) the total payments to be made under the lease contract, excluding payments for options to renew or buy, are less than $1,000; or

(b) there is a writing, signed by the party against whom enforcement is sought or by that party's authorized agent, sufficient to indicate that a lease contract has been made between the parties and to describe the goods leased and the lease term.

(2) Any description of leased goods or of the lease term is sufficient and satisfies subsection (1)(b), whether or not it is specific, if it reasonably identifies what is described.

(3) A writing is not insufficient because it omits or incorrectly states a term agreed upon, but the lease contract is not enforceable under subsection (1)(b) beyond the lease term and the quantity of goods shown in the writing.

(4) A lease contract that does not satisfy the requirements of subsection (1), but which is valid in other respects, is enforceable:

(a) if the goods are to be specially manufactured or obtained for the lessee and are not suitable for lease or sale to others in the ordinary course of the lessor's business, and the lessor, before notice of repudiation is received and under circumstances that reasonably indicate that the goods are for the lessee, has made either a substantial beginning of their manufacture or commitments for their procurement;

(b) if the party against whom enforcement is sought admits in that party's pleading, testimony or otherwise in court that a lease contract was made, but the lease contract is not enforceable under this provision beyond the quantity of goods admitted; or

(c) with respect to goods that have been received and accepted by the lessee.

(5) The lease term under a lease contract referred to in subsection (4) is:

(a) if there is a writing signed by the party against whom enforcement is sought or by that party's authorized agent specifying the lease term, the term so specified;

(b) if the party against whom enforcement is sought admits in that party's pleading, testimony, or otherwise in court a lease term, the term so admitted; or

(c) a reasonable lease term.

§ 2A–202. Final Written Expression: Parol or Extrinsic Evidence.

Terms with respect to which the confirmatory memoranda of the parties agree or which are otherwise set forth in a writing intended by the parties as a final expression of their agreement with respect to such terms as are included therein may not be contradicted by evidence of any prior agreement or of a contemporaneous oral agreement but may be explained or supplemented:

(a) by course of dealing or usage of trade or by course of performance; and

(b) by evidence of consistent additional terms unless the court finds the writing to have been intended also as a complete and exclusive statement of the terms of the agreement.

§ 2A–203. Seals Inoperative.

The affixing of a seal to a writing evidencing a lease contract or an offer to enter into a lease contract does not render the writing a sealed instrument and the law with respect to sealed instruments does not apply to the lease contract or offer.

§ 2A–204. Formation in General.

(1) A lease contract may be made in any manner sufficient to show agreement, including conduct by both parties which recognizes the existence of a lease contract.

(2) An agreement sufficient to constitute a lease contract may be found although the moment of its making is undetermined.

(3) Although one or more terms are left open, a lease contract does not fail for indefiniteness if the parties have intended to make a lease contract and there is a reasonably certain basis for giving an appropriate remedy.

§ 2A–205. Firm Offers.

An offer by a merchant to lease goods to or from another person in a signed writing that by its terms gives assurance it will be held open is not revocable, for lack of consideration, during the time stated or, if no time is stated, for a reasonable time, but in no event may the period of irrevocability exceed 3 months. Any such term of assurance on a form supplied by the offeree must be separately signed by the offeror.

§ 2A–206. Offer and Acceptance in Formation of Lease Contract.

(1) Unless otherwise unambiguously indicated by the language or circumstances, an offer to make a lease contract must be construed as inviting acceptance in any manner and by any medium reasonable in the circumstances.

(2) If the beginning of a requested performance is a reasonable mode of acceptance, an offeror who is not notified of acceptance within a reasonable time may treat the offer as having lapsed before acceptance.

§ 2A–207. Course of Performance or Practical Construction.

(1) If a lease contract involves repeated occasions for performance by either party with knowledge of the nature of the performance and opportunity for objection to it by the other, any course of performance accepted or acquiesced in without objection is relevant to determine the meaning of the lease agreement.

(2) The express terms of a lease agreement and any course of performance, as well as any course of dealing and usage of trade, must be construed whenever reasonable as consistent with each other; but if that construction is unreasonable, express terms control course of performance, course of performance controls both course of dealing and usage of trade, and course of dealing - controls usage of trade.

(3) Subject to the provisions of Section 2A–208 on modification and waiver, course of performance is relevant to show a waiver or modification of any term inconsistent with the course of performance.

§ 2A–208. Modification, Rescission and Waiver.

(1) An agreement modifying a lease contract needs no consideration to be binding.

(2) A signed lease agreement that excludes modification or rescission except by a signed writing may not be otherwise modified or rescinded, but, except as between merchants, such a requirement on a form supplied by a merchant must be separately signed by the other party.

(3) Although an attempt at modification or rescission does not satisfy the requirements of subsection (2), it may operate as a waiver.

(4) A party who has made a waiver affecting an executory portion of a lease contract may retract the waiver by reasonable notification received by the other party that strict performance will be required of any term waived, unless the retraction would be unjust in view of a material change of position in reliance on the waiver.

§ 2A–209. Lessee under Finance Lease as Beneficiary of Supply Contract.

(1) The benefit of the supplier's promises to the lessor under the supply contract and of all warranties, whether express or implied, including those of any third party provided in connection with or as part of the supply contract, extends to the lessee to the extent of the lessee's leasehold interest under a finance lease related to the supply contract, but is subject to the terms warranty and of the supply contract and all defenses or claims arising therefrom.

(2) The extension of the benefit of supplier's promises and of warranties to the lessee (Section 2A–209(1)) does not: (i) modify the rights and obligations of the parties to the supply contract, whether arising therefrom or otherwise, or (ii) impose any duty or liability under the supply contract on the lessee.

(3) Any modification or rescission of the supply contract by the supplier and the lessor is effective between the supplier and the lessee unless, before the modification or rescission, the supplier has received notice that the lessee has entered into a finance lease related to the supply contract. If the modification or rescission is effective between the supplier and the lessee, the lessor is deemed to have assumed, in addition to the obligations of the lessor to the lessee under the lease contract, promises of the supplier to the lessor and warranties that were so modified or rescinded as they existed and were available to the lessee before modification or rescission.

(4) In addition to the extension of the benefit of the supplier's promises and of warranties to the lessee under subsection (1), the lessee retains all rights that the lessee may have against the supplier which arise from an agreement between the lessee and the supplier or under other law.

As amended in 1990.

§ 2A–210. Express Warranties.

(1) Express warranties by the lessor are created as follows:

(a) Any affirmation of fact or promise made by the lessor to the lessee which relates to the goods and becomes part of the basis of the bargain creates an express warranty that the goods will conform to the affirmation or promise.

(b) Any description of the goods which is made part of the basis of the bargain creates an express warranty that the goods will conform to the description.

(c) Any sample or model that is made part of the basis of the bargain creates an express warranty that the whole of the goods will conform to the sample or model.

(2) It is not necessary to the creation of an express warranty that the lessor use formal words, such as "warrant" or "guarantee," or that the lessor have a specific intention to make a warranty, but an affirmation merely of the value of the goods or a statement purporting to be merely the lessor's opinion or commendation of the goods does not create a warranty.

§ 2A–211. Warranties Against Interference and Against Infringement; Lessee's Obligation Against Infringement.

(1) There is in a lease contract a warranty that for the lease term no person holds a claim to or interest in the goods that arose from an act or omission of the lessor, other than a claim by way of infringement or the like, which will interfere with the lessee's enjoyment of its leasehold interest.

(2) Except in a finance lease there is in a lease contract by a lessor who is a merchant regularly dealing in goods of the kind a warranty that the goods are delivered free of the rightful claim of any person by way of infringement or the like.

(3) A lessee who furnishes specifications to a lessor or a supplier shall hold the lessor and the supplier harmless against any claim by way of infringement or the like that arises out of compliance with the specifications.

§ 2A–212. Implied Warranty of Merchantability.

(1) Except in a finance lease, a warranty that the goods will be merchantable is implied in a lease contract if the lessor is a merchant with respect to goods of that kind.

(2) Goods to be merchantable must be at least such as

(a) pass without objection in the trade under the description in the lease agreement;

(b) in the case of fungible goods, are of fair average quality within the description;

(c) are fit for the ordinary purposes for which goods of that type are used;

(d) run, within the variation permitted by the lease agreement, of even kind, quality, and quantity within each unit and among all units involved;

(e) are adequately contained, packaged, and labeled as the lease agreement may require; and

(f) conform to any promises or affirmations of fact made on the container or label.

(3) Other implied warranties may arise from course of dealing or usage of trade.

§ 2A–213. Implied Warranty of Fitness for Particular Purpose.

Except in a finance of lease, if the lessor at the time the lease contract is made has reason to know of any particular purpose for which the goods are required and that the lessee is relying on the lessor's skill or judgment to select or furnish suitable goods, there is in the lease contract an implied warranty that the goods will be fit for that purpose.

§ 2A–214. Exclusion or Modification of Warranties.

(1) Words or conduct relevant to the creation of an express warranty and words or conduct tending to negate or limit a warranty must be construed wherever reasonable as consistent with each other; but, subject to the provisions of Section 2A–202 on parol or extrinsic evidence, negation or limitation is inoperative to the extent that the construction is unreasonable.

(2) Subject to subsection (3), to exclude or modify the implied warranty of merchantability or any part of it the language must mention "merchantability", be by a writing, and be conspicuous. Subject to subsection (3), to exclude or modify any implied warranty of fitness the exclusion must be by a writing and be conspicuous. Language to exclude all implied warranties of

fitness is sufficient if it is in writing, is conspicuous and states, for example, "There is no warranty that the goods will be fit for a particular purpose".

(3) Notwithstanding subsection (2), but subject to subsection (4),

(a) unless the circumstances indicate otherwise, all implied warranties are excluded by expressions like "as is" or "with all faults" or by other language that in common understanding calls the lessee's attention to the exclusion of warranties and makes plain that there is no implied warranty, if in writing and conspicuous;

(b) if the lessee before entering into the lease contract has examined the goods or the sample or model as fully as desired or has refused to examine the goods, there is no implied warranty with regard to defects that an examination ought in the circumstances to have revealed; and

(c) an implied warranty may also be excluded or modified by course of dealing, course of performance, or usage of trade.

(4) To exclude or modify a warranty against interference or against infringement (Section 2A–211) or any part of it, the language must be specific, be by a writing, and be conspicuous, unless the circumstances, including course of performance, course of dealing, or usage of trade, give the lessee reason to know that the goods are being leased subject to a claim or interest of any person.

§ 2A–215. Cumulation and Conflict of Warranties Express or Implied.

Warranties, whether express or implied, must be construed as consistent with each other and as cumulative, but if that construction is unreasonable, the intention of the parties determines which warranty is dominant. In ascertaining that intention the following rules apply:

(a) Exact or technical specifications displace an inconsistent sample or model or general language of description.

(b) A sample from an existing bulk displaces inconsistent general language of description.

(c) Express warranties displace inconsistent implied warranties other than an implied warranty of fitness for a particular purpose.

§ 2A–216. Third-Party Beneficiaries of Express and Implied Warranties.

Alternative A A warranty to or for the benefit of a lessee under this Article, whether express or implied, extends to any natural person who is in the family or household of the lessee or who is a guest in the lessee's home if it is reasonable to expect that such person may use, consume, or be affected by the goods and who is injured in person by breach of the warranty. This section does not displace principles of law and equity that extend a warranty to or for the benefit of a lessee to other persons. The operation of this section may not be excluded, modified, or limited, but an exclusion, modification, or limitation of the warranty, including any with respect to rights and remedies, effective against the lessee is also effective against any beneficiary designated under this section.

Alternative B   A warranty to or for the benefit of a lessee under this Article, whether express or implied, extends to any natural person who may reasonably be expected to use, consume, or be affected by the goods and who is injured in person by breach of the warranty. This section does not displace principles of law and equity that extend a warranty to or for the benefit of a lessee to other persons. The operation of this section may not be excluded, modified, or limited, but an exclusion, modification, or limitation of the warranty, including any with respect to rights and remedies, effective against the lessee is also effective against the beneficiary designated under this section.

Alternative C   A warranty to or for the benefit of a lessee under this Article, whether express or implied, extends to any person who may reasonably be expected to use, consume, or be affected by the goods and who is injured by breach of the warranty. The operation of this section may not be excluded, modified, or limited with respect to injury to the person of an individual to whom the warranty extends, but an exclusion, modification, or limitation of the warranty, including any with respect to rights and remedies, effective against the lessee is also effective against the beneficiary designated under this section.

§ 2A–217. Identification.

Identification of goods as goods to which a lease contract refers may be made at any time and in any manner explicitly agreed to by the parties. In the absence of explicit agreement, identification occurs:

(a) when the lease contract is made if the lease contract is for a lease of goods that are existing and identified;

(b) when the goods are shipped, marked, or otherwise designated by the lessor as goods to which the lease contract refers, if the lease contract is for a lease of goods that are not existing and identified; or

(c) when the young are conceived, if the lease contract is for a lease of unborn young of animals.

§ 2A–218. Insurance and Proceeds.

(1) A lessee obtains an insurable interest when existing goods are identified to the lease contract even though the goods identified are nonconforming and the lessee has an option to reject them.

(2) If a lessee has an insurable interest only by reason of the lessor's identification of the goods, the lessor, until default or insolvency or notification to the lessee that identification is final, may substitute other goods for those identified.

(3) Notwithstanding a lessee's insurable interest under subsections (1) and (2), the lessor retains an insurable interest until an option to buy has been exercised by the lessee and risk of loss has passed to the lessee.

(4) Nothing in this section impairs any insurable interest recognized under any other statute or rule of law.

(5) The parties by agreement may determine that one or more parties have an obligation to obtain and pay for insurance covering the goods and by agreement may determine the beneficiary of the proceeds of the insurance.

§ 2A–219. Risk of Loss.

(1) Except in the case of a finance lease, risk of loss is retained by the lessor and does not pass to the lessee. In the case of a finance lease, risk of loss passes to the lessee.

(2) Subject to the provisions of this Article on the effect of default on risk of loss (Section 2A–220), if risk of loss is to pass to the lessee and the time of passage is not stated, the following rules apply:

(a) If the lease contract requires or authorizes the goods to be shipped by carrier

(i) and it does not require delivery at a particular destination, the risk of loss passes to the lessee when the goods are duly delivered to the carrier; but

(ii) if it does require delivery at a particular destination and the goods are there duly tendered while in the possession of the carrier, the risk of loss passes to the lessee when the goods are there duly so tendered as to enable the lessee to take delivery.

(b) If the goods are held by a bailee to be delivered without being moved, the risk of loss passes to the lessee on acknowledgment by the bailee of the lessee's right to possession of the goods.

(c) In any case not within subsection (a) or (b), the risk of loss passes to the lessee on the lessee's receipt of the goods if the lessor, or, in the case of a finance lease, the supplier, is a merchant; otherwise the risk passes to the lessee on tender of delivery.

§ 2A–220. Effect of Default on Risk of Loss.

(1) Where risk of loss is to pass to the lessee and the time of passage is not stated:

(a) If a tender or delivery of goods so fails to conform to the lease contract as to give a right of rejection, the risk of their loss remains with the lessor, or, in the case of a finance lease, the supplier, until cure or acceptance.

(b) If the lessee rightfully revokes acceptance, he [or she], to the extent of any deficiency in his [or her] effective insurance coverage, may treat the risk of loss as having remained with the lessor from the beginning.

(2) Whether or not risk of loss is to pass to the lessee, if the lessee as to conforming goods already identified to a lease contract repudiates or is otherwise in default under the lease contract, the lessor, or, in the case of a finance lease, the supplier, to the extent of any deficiency in his [or her] effective insurance coverage may treat the risk of loss as resting on the lessee for a commercially reasonable time.

§ 2A–221. Casualty to Identified Goods.

If a lease contract requires goods identified when the lease contract is made, and the goods suffer casualty without fault of the lessee, the lessor or the supplier before delivery, or the goods suffer casualty before risk of loss passes to the lessee pursuant to the lease agreement or Section 2A–219, then:

(a) if the loss is total, the lease contract is avoided; and

(b) if the loss is partial or the goods have so deteriorated as to no longer conform to the lease contract, the lessee may nevertheless demand inspection and at his [or her] option either treat the lease contract as avoided or, except in a finance lease that is not a consumer lease, accept the goods with due allowance from the rent payable for the balance of the lease term for the deterioration or the deficiency in quantity but without further right against the lessor.

PART 3   Effect of Lease Contract

§ 2A–301. Enforceability of Lease Contract.

Except as otherwise provided in this Article, a lease contract is effective and enforceable according to its terms between the parties, against purchasers of the goods and against creditors of the parties.

§ 2A–302. Title to and Possession of Goods.

Except as otherwise provided in this Article, each provision of this Article applies whether the lessor or a third party has title to the goods, and whether the lessor, the lessee, or a third party has possession of the goods, notwithstanding any statute or rule of law that possession or the absence of possession is fraudulent.

§ 2A–303. Alienability of Party's Interest Under Lease Contract or of Lessor's Residual Interest in Goods; Delegation of Performance; Transfer of Rights.

(1) As used in this section, "creation of a security interest" includes the sale of a lease contract that is subject to Article 9, Secured Transactions, by reason of Section 9–109(a)(3).

(2) Except as provided in subsections (3) and Section 9–407, a provision in a lease agreement which (i) prohibits the voluntary or involuntary transfer, including a transfer by sale, sublease, creation or enforcement of a security interest, or attachment, levy, or other judicial process, of an interest of a party under the lease contract or of the lessor's residual interest in the goods, or (ii) makes such a transfer an event of default, gives rise to the rights and remedies provided in subsection (4), but a transfer that is prohibited or is an event of default under the lease agreement is otherwise effective.

(3) A provision in a lease agreement which (i) prohibits a transfer of a right to damages for default with respect to the whole lease contract or of a right to payment arising out of the transferor's due performance of the transferor's entire obligation, or (ii) makes such a transfer an event of default, is not enforceable, and such a transfer is not a transfer that materially impairs the propsect of obtaining return performance by, materially changes the duty of, or materially increases the burden or risk imposed on, the other party to the lease contract within the purview of subsection (4).

(4) Subject to subsection (3) and Section 9–407:

(a) if a transfer is made which is made an event of default under a lease agreement, the party to the lease contract not making the transfer, unless that party waives the default or otherwise agrees, has the rights and remedies described in Section 2A–501(2);

(b) if paragraph (a) is not applicable and if a transfer is made that (i) is prohibited under a lease agreement or (ii) materially impairs the prospect of obtaining return performance by, materially changes the duty of, or materially increases the burden or risk imposed on, the other party to the lease contract, unless the party not making the transfer agrees at any time to the transfer in the lease contract or otherwise, then, except as limited by contract, (i) the transferor is liable to the party not making the transfer for damages caused by the transfer to the extent that the damages could not reasonably be prevented by the party not making the transfer and (ii) a court having jurisdiction may grant other appropriate relief, including cancellation of the lease contract or an injunction against the transfer.

(5) A transfer of "the lease" or of "all my rights under the lease", or a transfer in similar general terms, is a transfer of rights and, unless the language or the circumstances, as in a transfer for security, indicate the contrary, the transfer is a delegation of duties by the transferor to the transferee. Acceptance by the transferee constitutes a promise by the transferee to perform those duties. The promise is enforceable by either the transferor or the other party to the lease contract.

(6) Unless otherwise agreed by the lessor and the lessee, a delegation of performance does not relieve the transferor as against the other party of any duty to perform or of any liability for default.

(7) In a consumer lease, to prohibit the transfer of an interest of a party under the lease contract or to make a transfer an event of default, the language must be specific, by a writing, and conspicuous.

As amended in 1990 and 1999.

§ 2A–304. Subsequent Lease of Goods by Lessor.

(1) Subject to Section 2A–303, a subsequent lessee from a lessor of goods under an existing lease contract obtains, to the extent of the leasehold interest transferred, the leasehold interest in the goods that the lessor had or had power to transfer, and except as provided in subsection (2) and Section 2A–527(4), takes subject to the existing lease contract. A lessor with voidable title has power to transfer a good leasehold interest to a good faith subsequent lessee for value, but only to the extent set forth in the preceding sentence. If goods have been delivered under a transaction of purchase the lessor has that power even though:

(a) the lessor's transferor was deceived as to the identity of the lessor;

(b) the delivery was in exchange for a check which is later dishonored;

(c) it was agreed that the transaction was to be a "cash sale"; or

(d) the delivery was procured through fraud punishable as larcenous under the criminal law.

(2) A subsequent lessee in the ordinary course of business from a lessor who is a merchant dealing in goods of that kind to whom the goods were entrusted by the existing lessee of that lessor before the interest of the subsequent lessee became enforceable against that lessor obtains, to the extent of the leasehold interest transferred, all of that lessor's and the existing lessee's rights to the goods, and takes free of the existing lease contract.

(3) A subsequent lessee from the lessor of goods that are subject to an existing lease contract and are covered by a certificate of title issued under a statute of this State or of another jurisdiction takes no greater rights than those provided both by this section and by the certificate of title statute.

As amended in 1990.

§ 2A-305. Sale or Sublease of Goods by Lessee.

(1) Subject to the provisions of Section 2A–303, a buyer or sublessee from the lessee of goods under an existing lease contract obtains, to the extent of the interest transferred, the leasehold interest in the goods that the lessee had or had power to transfer, and except as provided in subsection (2) and Section 2A–511(4), takes subject to the existing lease contract. A lessee with a voidable leasehold interest has power to transfer a good leasehold interest to a good faith buyer for value or a good faith sublessee for value, but only to the extent set forth in the preceding sentence. When goods have been delivered under a transaction of lease the lessee has that power even though:

(a) the lessor was deceived as to the identity of the lessee;

(b) the delivery was in exchange for a check which is later dishonored; or

(c) the delivery was procured through fraud punishable as larcenous under the criminal law.

(2) A buyer in the ordinary course of business or a sublessee in the ordinary course of business from a lessee who is a merchant dealing in goods of that kind to whom the goods were entrusted by the lessor obtains, to the extent of the interest transferred, all of the lessor's and lessee's rights to the goods, and takes free of the existing lease contract.

(3) A buyer or sublessee from the lessee of goods that are subject to an existing lease contract and are covered by a certificate of title issued under a statute of this State or of another jurisdiction takes no greater rights than those provided both by this section and by the certificate of title statute.

§ 2A-306. Priority of Certain Liens Arising by Operation of Law.

If a person in the ordinary course of his [or her] business furnishes services or materials with respect to goods subject to a lease contract, a lien upon those goods in the possession of that person given by statute or rule of law for those materials or services takes priority over any interest of the lessor or lessee

under the lease contract or this Article unless the lien is created by statute and the statute provides otherwise or unless the lien is created by rule of law and the rule of law provides otherwise.

§ 2A-307. Priority of Liens Arising by Attachment or Levy on, Security Interests in, and Other Claims to Goods.

(1) Except as otherwise provided in Section 2A–306, a creditor of a lessee takes subject to the lease contract.

(2) Except as otherwise provided in subsection (3) and in Sections 2A–306 and 2A–308, a creditor of a lessor takes subject to the lease contract unless the creditor holds a lien that attached to the goods before the lease contract became enforceable.

(3) Except as otherwise provided in Sections 9–317, 9–321, and 9–323, a lessee takes a leasehold interest subject to a security interest held by a creditor of the lessor.

As amended in 1990 and 1999.

§ 2A-308. Special Rights of Creditors.

(1) A creditor of a lessor in possession of goods subject to a lease contract may treat the lease contract as void if as against the creditor retention of possession by the lessor is fraudulent under any statute or rule of law, but retention of possession in good faith and current course of trade by the lessor for a commercially reasonable time after the lease contract becomes enforceable is not fraudulent.

(2) Nothing in this Article impairs the rights of creditors of a lessor if the lease contract (a) becomes enforceable, not in current course of trade but in satisfaction of or as security for a pre-existing claim for money, security, or the like, and (b) is made under circumstances which under any statute or rule of law apart from this Article would constitute the transaction a fraudulent transfer or voidable preference.

(3) A creditor of a seller may treat a sale or an identification of goods to a contract for sale as void if as against the creditor retention of possession by the seller is fraudulent under any statute or rule of law, but retention of possession of the goods pursuant to a lease contract entered into by the seller as lessee and the buyer as lessor in connection with the sale or identification of the goods is not fraudulent if the buyer bought for value and in good faith.

§ 2A-309. Lessor's and Lessee's Rights When Goods Become Fixtures.

(1) In this section:

(a) goods are "fixtures" when they become so related to particular real estate that an interest in them arises under real estate law;

(b) a "fixture filing" is the filing, in the office where a mortgage on the real estate would be filed or recorded, of a financing statement covering goods that are or are to become fixtures and conforming to the requirements of Section 9–502(a) and (b);

(c) a lease is a "purchase money lease" unless the lessee has possession or use of the goods or the right to possession or use of the goods before the lease agreement is enforceable;

(d) a mortgage is a "construction mortgage" to the extent it secures an obligation incurred for the construction of an improvement on land including the acquisition cost of the land, if the recorded writing so indicates; and

(e) "encumbrance" includes real estate mortgages and other liens on real estate and all other rights in real estate that are not ownership interests.

(2) Under this Article a lease may be of goods that are fixtures or may continue in goods that become fixtures, but no lease exists under this Article of ordinary building materials incorporated into an improvement on land.

(3) This Article does not prevent creation of a lease of fixtures pursuant to real estate law.

(4) The perfected interest of a lessor of fixtures has priority over a conflicting interest of an encumbrancer or owner of the real estate if:

(a) the lease is a purchase money lease, the conflicting interest of the encumbrancer or owner arises before the goods become fixtures, the interest of the lessor is perfected by a fixture filing before the goods become fixtures or within ten days thereafter, and the lessee has an interest of record in the real estate or is in possession of the real estate; or

(b) the interest of the lessor is perfected by a fixture filing before the interest of the encumbrancer or owner is of record, the lessor's interest has priority over any conflicting interest of a predecessor in title of the encumbrancer or owner, and the lessee has an interest of record in the real estate or is in possession of the real estate.

(5) The interest of a lessor of fixtures, whether or not perfected, has priority over the conflicting interest of an encumbrancer or owner of the real estate if:

(a) the fixtures are readily removable factory or office machines, readily removable equipment that is not primarily used or leased for use in the operation of the real estate, or readily removable replacements of domestic appliances that are goods subject to a consumer lease, and before the goods become fixtures the lease contract is enforceable; or

(b) the conflicting interest is a lien on the real estate obtained by legal or equitable proceedings after the lease contract is enforceable; or

(c) the encumbrancer or owner has consented in writing to the lease or has disclaimed an interest in the goods as fixtures; or

(d) the lessee has a right to remove the goods as against the encumbrancer or owner. If the lessee's right to remove terminates, the priority of the interest of the lessor continues for a reasonable time.

(6) Notwithstanding paragraph (4)(a) but otherwise subject to subsections (4) and (5), the interest of a lessor of fixtures, including the lessor's residual interest, is subordinate to the conflicting interest of an encumbrancer of the real estate under a construction mortgage recorded before the goods become fixtures if the goods become fixtures before the completion of the construction. To the extent given to refinance a construction mortgage, the conflicting interest of an encumbrancer of the real estate under a mortgage has this priority to the same extent as the encumbrancer of the real estate under the construction mortgage.

(7) In cases not within the preceding subsections, priority between the interest of a lessor of fixtures, including the lessor's residual interest, and the conflicting interest of an encumbrancer or owner of the real estate who is not the lessee is determined by the priority rules governing conflicting interests in real estate.

(8) If the interest of a lessor of fixtures, including the lessor's residual interest, has priority over all conflicting interests of all owners and encumbrancers of the real estate, the lessor or the lessee may (i) on default, expiration, termination, or cancellation of the lease agreement but subject to the agreement and this Article, or (ii) if necessary to enforce other rights and remedies of the lessor or lessee under this Article, remove the goods from the real estate, free and clear of all conflicting interests of all owners and encumbrancers of the real estate, but the lessor or lessee must reimburse any encumbrancer or owner of the real estate who is not the lessee and who has not otherwise agreed for the cost of repair of any physical injury, but not for any diminution in value of the real estate caused by the absence of the goods removed or by any necessity of replacing them. A person entitled to reimbursement may refuse permission to remove until the party seeking removal gives adequate security for the performance of this obligation.

(9) Even though the lease agreement does not create a security interest, the interest of a lessor of fixtures, including the lessor's residual interest, is perfected by filing a financing statement as a fixture filing for leased goods that are or are to become fixtures in accordance with the relevant provisions of the Article on Secured Transactions (Article 9).

As amended in 1990 and 1999.

§ 2A–310.   Lessor's and Lessee's Rights When Goods Become Accessions.

(1) Goods are "accessions" when they are installed in or affixed to other goods.

(2) The interest of a lessor or a lessee under a lease contract entered into before the goods became accessions is superior to all interests in the whole except as stated in subsection (4).

(3) The interest of a lessor or a lessee under a lease contract entered into at the time or after the goods became accessions is superior to all subsequently acquired interests in the whole except as stated in subsection (4) but is subordinate to interests in the whole existing at the time the lease contract was made unless the holders of such interests in the whole have in writing consented to the lease or disclaimed an interest in the goods as part of the whole.

(4) The interest of a lessor or a lessee under a lease contract described in subsection (2) or (3) is subordinate to the interest of

(a) a buyer in the ordinary course of business or a lessee in the ordinary course of business of any interest in the whole acquired after the goods became accessions; or

(b) a creditor with a security interest in the whole perfected before the lease contract was made to the extent that the creditor makes subsequent advances without knowledge of the lease contract.

(5) When under subsections (2) or (3) and (4) a lessor or a lessee of accessions holds an interest that is superior to all interests in the whole, the lessor or the lessee may (a) on default, expiration, termination, or cancellation of the lease contract by the other party but subject to the provisions of the lease contract and this Article, or (b) if necessary to enforce his [or her] other rights and remedies under this Article, remove the goods from the whole, free and clear of all interests in the whole, but he [or she] must reimburse any holder of an interest in the whole who is not the lessee and who has not otherwise agreed for the cost of repair of any physical injury but not for any diminution in value of the whole caused by the absence of the goods removed or by any necessity for replacing them. A person entitled to reimbursement may refuse permission to remove until the party seeking removal gives adequate security for the performance of this obligation.

§ 2A–311. Priority Subject to Subordination.

Nothing in this Article prevents subordination by agreement by any person entitled to priority.

As added in 1990.

PART 4   Performance of Lease Contract: Repudiated, Substituted and Excused

§ 2A–401. Insecurity: Adequate Assurance of Performance.

(1) A lease contract imposes an obligation on each party that the other's expectation of receiving due performance will not be impaired.

(2) If reasonable grounds for insecurity arise with respect to the performance of either party, the insecure party may demand in writing adequate assurance of due performance. Until the insecure party receives that assurance, if commercially reasonable the insecure party may suspend any performance for which he [or she] has not already received the agreed return.

(3) A repudiation of the lease contract occurs if assurance of due performance adequate under the circumstances of the particular case is not provided to the insecure party within a reasonable time, not to exceed 30 days after receipt of a demand by the other party.

(4) Between merchants, the reasonableness of grounds for insecurity and the adequacy of any assurance offered must be determined according to commercial standards.

(5) Acceptance of any nonconforming delivery or payment does not prejudice the aggrieved party's right to demand adequate assurance of future performance.

§ 2A–402. Anticipatory Repudiation.

If either party repudiates a lease contract with respect to a performance not yet due under the lease contract, the loss of which performance will substantially impair the value of the lease contract to the other, the aggrieved party may:

(a) for a commercially reasonable time, await retraction of repudiation and performance by the repudiating party;

(b) make demand pursuant to Section 2A–401 and await assurance of future performance adequate under the circumstances of the particular case; or

(c) resort to any right or remedy upon default under the lease contract or this Article, even though the aggrieved party has notified the repudiating party that the aggrieved party would await the repudiating party's performance and assurance and has urged retraction. In addition, whether or not the aggrieved party is pursuing one of the foregoing remedies, the aggrieved party may suspend performance or, if the aggrieved party is the lessor, proceed in accordance with the provisions of this Article on the lessor's right to identify goods to the lease contract notwithstanding default or to salvage unfinished goods (Section 2A–524).

§ 2A–403. Retraction of Anticipatory Repudiation.

(1) Until the repudiating party's next performance is due, the repudiating party can retract the repudiation unless, since the repudiation, the aggrieved party has cancelled the lease contract or materially changed the aggrieved party's position or otherwise indicated that the aggrieved party considers the repudiation final.

(2) Retraction may be by any method that clearly indicates to the aggrieved party that the repudiating party intends to perform under the lease contract and includes any assurance demanded under Section 2A–401.

(3) Retraction reinstates a repudiating party's rights under a lease contract with due excuse and allowance to the aggrieved party for any delay occasioned by the repudiation.

§ 2A–404. Substituted Performance.

(1) If without fault of the lessee, the lessor and the supplier, the agreed berthing, loading, or unloading facilities fail or the agreed type of carrier becomes unavailable or the agreed manner of delivery otherwise becomes commercially impracticable, but a commercially reasonable substitute is available, the substitute performance must be tendered and accepted.

(2) If the agreed means or manner of payment fails because of domestic or foreign governmental regulation:

(a) the lessor may withhold or stop delivery or cause the supplier to withhold or stop delivery unless the lessee provides a means or manner of payment that is commercially a substantial equivalent; and

(b) if delivery has already been taken, payment by the means or in the manner provided by the regulation discharges the lessee's obligation unless the regulation is discriminatory, oppressive, or predatory.

§ 2A–405. Excused Performance.

Subject to Section 2A–404 on substituted performance, the following rules apply:

(a) Delay in delivery or nondelivery in whole or in part by a lessor or a supplier who complies with paragraphs (b) and (c) is not a default under the lease contract if performance as agreed has been made impracticable by the occurrence of a contingency the nonoccurrence of which was a basic assumption on which the lease contract was made or by compliance in good faith with any applicable foreign or domestic governmental regulation or order, whether or not the regulation or order later proves to be invalid.

(b) If the causes mentioned in paragraph (a) affect only part of the lessor's or the supplier's capacity to perform, he [or she] shall allocate production and deliveries among his [or her] customers but at his [or her] option may include regular customers not then under contract for sale or lease as well as his [or her] own requirements for further manufacture. He [or she] may so allocate in any manner that is fair and reasonable.

(c) The lessor seasonably shall notify the lessee and in the case of a finance lease the supplier seasonably shall notify the lessor and the lessee, if known, that there will be delay or nondelivery and, if allocation is required under paragraph (b), of the estimated quota thus made available for the lessee.

§ 2A–406. Procedure on Excused Performance.

(1) If the lessee receives notification of a material or indefinite delay or an allocation justified under Section 2A–405, the lessee may by written notification to the lessor as to any goods involved, and with respect to all of the goods if under an installment lease contract the value of the whole lease contract is substantially impaired (Section 2A–510):

(a) terminate the lease contract (Section 2A–505(2)); or

(b) except in a finance lease that is not a consumer lease, modify the lease contract by accepting the available quota in substitution, with due allowance from the rent payable for the balance of the lease term for the deficiency but without further right against the lessor.

(2) If, after receipt of a notification from the lessor under Section 2A–405, the lessee fails so to modify the lease agreement within a reasonable time not exceeding 30 days, the lease contract lapses with respect to any deliveries affected.

§ 2A–407. Irrevocable Promises: Finance Leases.

(1) In the case of a finance lease that is not a consumer lease the lessee's promises under the lease contract become irrevocable and independent upon the lessee's acceptance of the goods.

(2) A promise that has become irrevocable and independent under subsection (1):

(a) is effective and enforceable between the parties, and by or against third parties including assignees of the parties, and

(b) is not subject to cancellation, termination, modification, repudiation, excuse, or substitution without the consent of the party to whom the promise runs.

(3) This section does not affect the validity under any other law of a covenant in any lease contract making the lessee's promises irrevocable and independent upon the lessee's acceptance of the goods.

As amended in 1990.

PART 5   Default

A. In General

§ 2A–501. Default: Procedure.

(1) Whether the lessor or the lessee is in default under a lease contract is determined by the lease agreement and this Article.

(2) If the lessor or the lessee is in default under the lease contract, the party seeking enforcement has rights and remedies as provided in this Article and, except as limited by this Article, as provided in the lease agreement.

(3) If the lessor or the lessee is in default under the lease contract, the party seeking enforcement may reduce the party's claim to judgment, or otherwise enforce the lease contract by self-help or any available judicial procedure or nonjudicial procedure, including administrative proceeding, arbitration, or the like, in accordance with this Article.

(4) Except as otherwise provided in Section 1–106(1) or this Article or the lease agreement, the rights and remedies referred to in subsections (2) and (3) are cumulative.

(5) If the lease agreement covers both real property and goods, the party seeking enforcement may proceed under this Part as to the goods, or under other applicable law as to both the real property and the goods in accordance with that party's rights and remedies in respect of the real property, in which case this Part does not apply.

As amended in 1990.

§ 2A–502. Notice After Default.

Except as otherwise provided in this Article or the lease agreement, the lessor or lessee in default under the lease contract is not entitled to notice of default or notice of enforcement from the other party to the lease agreement.

§ 2A–503. Modification or Impairment of Rights and Remedies.

(1) Except as otherwise provided in this Article, the lease agreement may include rights and remedies for default in

addition to or in substitution for those provided in this Article and may limit or alter the measure of damages recoverable under this Article.

(2) Resort to a remedy provided under this Article or in the lease agreement is optional unless the remedy is expressly agreed to be exclusive. If circumstances cause an exclusive or limited remedy to fail of its essential purpose, or provision for an exclusive remedy is unconscionable, remedy may be had as provided in this Article.

(3) Consequential damages may be liquidated under Section 2A–504, or may otherwise be limited, altered, or excluded unless the limitation, alteration, or exclusion is unconscionable. Limitation, alteration, or exclusion of consequential damages for injury to the person in the case of consumer goods is prima facie unconscionable but limitation, alteration, or exclusion of damages where the loss is commercial is not prima facie unconscionable.

(4) Rights and remedies on default by the lessor or the lessee with respect to any obligation or promise collateral or ancillary to the lease contract are not impaired by this Article.

As amended in 1990.

§ 2A–504. Liquidation of Damages.

(1) Damages payable by either party for default, or any other act or omission, including indemnity for loss or diminution of anticipated tax benefits or loss or damage to lessor's residual interest, may be liquidated in the lease agreement but only at an amount or by a formula that is reasonable in light of the then anticipated harm caused by the default or other act or omission.

(2) If the lease agreement provides for liquidation of damages, and such provision does not comply with subsection (1), or such provision is an exclusive or limited remedy that circumstances cause to fail of its essential purpose, remedy may be had as provided in this Article.

(3) If the lessor justifiably withholds or stops delivery of goods because of the lessee's default or insolvency (Section 2A–525 or 2A–526), the lessee is entitled to restitution of any amount by which the sum of his [or her] payments exceeds:

(a) the amount to which the lessor is entitled by virtue of terms liquidating the lessor's damages in accordance with subsection (1); or

(b) in the absence of those terms, 20 percent of the then present value of the total rent the lessee was obligated to pay for the balance of the lease term, or, in the case of a consumer lease, the lesser of such amount or $500.

(4) A lessee's right to restitution under subsection (3) is subject to offset to the extent the lessor establishes:

(a) a right to recover damages under the provisions of this Article other than subsection (1); and

(b) the amount or value of any benefits received by the lessee directly or indirectly by reason of the lease contract.

§ 2A–505. Cancellation and Termination and Effect of Cancellation, Termination, Rescission, or Fraud on Rights and Remedies.

(1) On cancellation of the lease contract, all obligations that are still executory on both sides are discharged, but any right based on prior default or performance survives, and the cancelling party also retains any remedy for default of the whole lease contract or any unperformed balance.

(2) On termination of the lease contract, all obligations that are still executory on both sides are discharged but any right based on prior default or performance survives.

(3) Unless the contrary intention clearly appears, expressions of "cancellation," "rescission," or the like of the lease contract may not be construed as a renunciation or discharge of any claim in damages for an antecedent default.

(4) Rights and remedies for material misrepresentation or fraud include all rights and remedies available under this Article for default.

(5) Neither rescission nor a claim for rescission of the lease contract nor rejection or return of the goods may bar or be deemed inconsistent with a claim for damages or other right or remedy.

§ 2A–506. Statute of Limitations.

(1) An action for default under a lease contract, including breach of warranty or indemnity, must be commenced within 4 years after the cause of action accrued. By the original lease contract the parties may reduce the period of limitation to not less than one year.

(2) A cause of action for default accrues when the act or omission on which the default or breach of warranty is based is or should have been discovered by the aggrieved party, or when the default occurs, whichever is later. A cause of action for indemnity accrues when the act or omission on which the claim for indemnity is based is or should have been discovered by the indemnified party, whichever is later.

(3) If an action commenced within the time limited by subsection (1) is so terminated as to leave available a remedy by another action for the same default or breach of warranty or indemnity, the other action may be commenced after the expiration of the time limited and within 6 months after the termination of the first action unless the termination resulted from voluntary discontinuance or from dismissal for failure or neglect to prosecute.

(4) This section does not alter the law on tolling of the statute of limitations nor does it apply to causes of action that have accrued before this Article becomes effective.

§ 2A–507. Proof of Market Rent: Time and Place.

(1) Damages based on market rent (Section 2A–519 or 2A–528) are determined according to the rent for the use of the goods concerned for a lease term identical to the remaining lease term of the original lease agreement and prevailing at the times specified in Sections 2A–519 and 2A–528.

(2) If evidence of rent for the use of the goods concerned for a lease term identical to the remaining lease term of the original lease agreement and prevailing at the times or places described in this Article is not readily available, the rent prevailing within any reasonable time before or after the time described or at any other place or for a different lease term which in commercial judgment or under usage of trade would serve as a reasonable substitute for the one described may be used, making any proper allowance for the difference, including the cost of transporting the goods to or from the other place.

(3) Evidence of a relevant rent prevailing at a time or place or for a lease term other than the one described in this Article offered by one party is not admissible unless and until he [or she] has given the other party notice the court finds sufficient to prevent unfair surprise.

(4) If the prevailing rent or value of any goods regularly leased in any established market is in issue, reports in official publications or trade journals or in newspapers or periodicals of general circulation published as the reports of that market are admissible in evidence. The circumstances of the preparation of the report may be shown to affect its weight but not its admissibility.

As amended in 1990.

B. Default by Lessor

§ 2A–508. Lessee's Remedies.

(1) If a lessor fails to deliver the goods in conformity to the lease contract (Section 2A–509) or repudiates the lease contract (Section 2A–402), or a lessee rightfully rejects the goods (Section 2A–509) or justifiably revokes acceptance of the goods (Section 2A–517), then with respect to any goods involved, and with respect to all of the goods if under an installment lease contract the value of the whole lease contract is substantially impaired (Section 2A–510), the lessor is in default under the lease contract and the lessee may:

   (a) cancel the lease contract (Section 2A–505(1));

   (b) recover so much of the rent and security as has been paid and is just under the circumstances;

   (c) cover and recover damages as to all goods affected whether or not they have been identified to the lease contract (Sections 2A–518 and 2A–520), or recover damages for nondelivery (Sections 2A–519 and 2A–520);

   (d) exercise any other rights or pursue any other remedies provided in the lease contract.

(2) If a lessor fails to deliver the goods in conformity to the lease contract or repudiates the lease contract, the lessee may also:

   (a) if the goods have been identified, recover them (Section 2A–522); or

   (b) in a proper case, obtain specific performance or replevy the goods (Section 2A–521).

(3) If a lessor is otherwise in default under a lease contract, the lessee may exercise the rights and pursue the remedies provided

in the lease contract, which may include a right to cancel the lease, and in Section 2A–519(3).

(4) If a lessor has breached a warranty, whether express or implied, the lessee may recover damages (Section 2A–519(4)).

(5) On rightful rejection or justifiable revocation of acceptance, a lessee has a security interest in goods in the lessee's possession or control for any rent and security that has been paid and any expenses reasonably incurred in their inspection, receipt, transportation, and care and custody and may hold those goods and dispose of them in good faith and in a commercially reasonable manner, subject to Section 2A–527(5).

(6) Subject to the provisions of Section 2A–407, a lessee, on notifying the lessor of the lessee's intention to do so, may deduct all or any part of the damages resulting from any default under the lease contract from any part of the rent still due under the same lease contract.

As amended in 1990.

§ 2A–509. Lessee's Rights on Improper Delivery; Rightful Rejection.

(1) Subject to the provisions of Section 2A–510 on default in installment lease contracts, if the goods or the tender or delivery fail in any respect to conform to the lease contract, the lessee may reject or accept the goods or accept any commercial unit or units and reject the rest of the goods.

(2) Rejection of goods is ineffective unless it is within a reasonable time after tender or delivery of the goods and the lessee seasonably notifies the lessor.

§ 2A–510. Installment Lease Contracts: Rejection and Default.

(1) Under an installment lease contract a lessee may reject any delivery that is nonconforming if the nonconformity substantially impairs the value of that delivery and cannot be cured or the nonconformity is a defect in the required documents; but if the nonconformity does not fall within subsection (2) and the lessor or the supplier gives adequate assurance of its cure, the lessee must accept that delivery.

(2) Whenever nonconformity or default with respect to one or more deliveries substantially impairs the value of the installment lease contract as a whole there is a default with respect to the whole. But, the aggrieved party reinstates the installment lease contract as a whole if the aggrieved party accepts a nonconforming delivery without seasonably notifying of cancellation or brings an action with respect only to past deliveries or demands performance as to future deliveries.

§ 2A–511. Merchant Lessee's Duties as to Rightfully Rejected Goods.

(1) Subject to any security interest of a lessee (Section 2A–508(5)), if a lessor or a supplier has no agent or place of business at the market of rejection, a merchant lessee, after rejection of goods in his [or her] possession or control, shall follow any

reasonable instructions received from the lessor or the supplier with respect to the goods. In the absence of those instructions, a merchant lessee shall make reasonable efforts to sell, lease, or otherwise dispose of the goods for the lessor's account if they threaten to decline in value speedily. Instructions are not reasonable if on demand indemnity for expenses is not forthcoming.

(2) If a merchant lessee (subsection (1)) or any other lessee (Section 2A–512) disposes of goods, he [or she] is entitled to reimbursement either from the lessor or the supplier or out of the proceeds for reasonable expenses of caring for and disposing of the goods and, if the expenses include no disposition commission, to such commission as is usual in the trade, or if there is none, to a reasonable sum not exceeding 10 percent of the gross proceeds.

(3) In complying with this section or Section 2A–512, the lessee is held only to good faith. Good faith conduct hereunder is neither acceptance or conversion nor the basis of an action for damages.

(4) A purchaser who purchases in good faith from a lessee pursuant to this section or Section 2A–512 takes the goods free of any rights of the lessor and the supplier even though the lessee fails to comply with one or more of the requirements of this Article.

§ 2A–512. Lessee's Duties as to Rightfully Rejected Goods.

(1) Except as otherwise provided with respect to goods that threaten to decline in value speedily (Section 2A–511) and subject to any security interest of a lessee (Section 2A–508(5)):

(a) the lessee, after rejection of goods in the lessee's possession, shall hold them with reasonable care at the lessor's or the supplier's disposition for a reasonable time after the lessee's seasonable notification of rejection;

(b) if the lessor or the supplier gives no instructions within a reasonable time after notification of rejection, the lessee may store the rejected goods for the lessor's or the supplier's account or ship them to the lessor or the supplier or dispose of them for the lessor's or the supplier's account with reimbursement in the manner provided in Section 2A–511; but

(c) the lessee has no further obligations with regard to goods rightfully rejected.

(2) Action by the lessee pursuant to subsection (1) is not acceptance or conversion.

§ 2A–513. Cure by Lessor of Improper Tender or Delivery; Replacement.

(1) If any tender or delivery by the lessor or the supplier is rejected because nonconforming and the time for performance has not yet expired, the lessor or the supplier may seasonably notify the lessee of the lessor's or the supplier's intention to cure and may then make a conforming delivery within the time provided in the lease contract.

(2) If the lessee rejects a nonconforming tender that the lessor or the supplier had reasonable grounds to believe would be acceptable with or without money allowance, the lessor or the supplier may have a further reasonable time to substitute a conforming tender if he [or she] seasonably notifies the lessee.

§ 2A–514. Waiver of Lessee's Objections.

(1) In rejecting goods, a lessee's failure to state a particular defect that is ascertainable by reasonable inspection precludes the lessee from relying on the defect to justify rejection or to establish default:

(a) if, stated seasonably, the lessor or the supplier could have cured it (Section 2A–513); or

(b) between merchants if the lessor or the supplier after rejection has made a request in writing for a full and final written statement of all defects on which the lessee proposes to rely.

(2) A lessee's failure to reserve rights when paying rent or other consideration against documents precludes recovery of the payment for defects apparent on the face of the documents.

§ 2A–515. Acceptance of Goods.

(1) Acceptance of goods occurs after the lessee has had a reasonable opportunity to inspect the goods and

(a) the lessee signifies or acts with respect to the goods in a manner that signifies to the lessor or the supplier that the goods are conforming or that the lessee will take or retain them in spite of their nonconformity; or

(b) the lessee fails to make an effective rejection of the goods (Section 2A–509(2)).

(2) Acceptance of a part of any commercial unit is acceptance of that entire unit.

§ 2A–516. Effect of Acceptance of Goods; Notice of Default; Burden of Establishing Default after Acceptance; Notice of Claim or Litigation to Person Answerable Over.

(1) A lessee must pay rent for any goods accepted in accordance with the lease contract, with due allowance for goods rightfully rejected or not delivered.

(2) A lessee's acceptance of goods precludes rejection of the goods accepted. In the case of a finance lease, if made with knowledge of a nonconformity, acceptance cannot be revoked because of it. In any other case, if made with knowledge of a nonconformity, acceptance cannot be revoked because of it unless the acceptance was on the reasonable assumption that the nonconformity would be seasonably cured. Acceptance does not of itself impair any other remedy provided by this Article or the lease agreement for nonconformity.

(3) If a tender has been accepted:

(a) within a reasonable time after the lessee discovers or should have discovered any default, the lessee shall notify the lessor and the supplier, if any, or be barred from any remedy against the party notified;

(b) except in the case of a consumer lease, within a reasonable time after the lessee receives notice of litigation for infringement or the like (Section 2A–211) the lessee shall notify the lessor or be barred from any remedy over for liability established by the litigation; and

(c) the burden is on the lessee to establish any default.

(4) If a lessee is sued for breach of a warranty or other obligation for which a lessor or a supplier is answerable over the following apply:

(a) The lessee may give the lessor or the supplier, or both, written notice of the litigation. If the notice states that the person notified may come in and defend and that if the person notified does not do so that person will be bound in any action against that person by the lessee by any determination of fact common to the two litigations, then unless the person notified after seasonable receipt of the notice does come in and defend that person is so bound.

(b) The lessor or the supplier may demand in writing that the lessee turn over control of the litigation including settlement if the claim is one for infringement or the like (Section 2A–211) or else be barred from any remedy over. If the demand states that the lessor or the supplier agrees to bear all expense and to satisfy any adverse judgment, then unless the lessee after seasonable receipt of the demand does turn over control the lessee is so barred.

(5) Subsections (3) and (4) apply to any obligation of a lessee to hold the lessor or the supplier harmless against infringement or the like (Section 2A–211).

As amended in 1990.

§ 2A–517. Revocation of Acceptance of Goods.

(1) A lessee may revoke acceptance of a lot or commercial unit whose nonconformity substantially impairs its value to the lessee if the lessee has accepted it:

(a) except in the case of a finance lease, on the reasonable assumption that its nonconformity would be cured and it has not been seasonably cured; or

(b) without discovery of the nonconformity if the lessee's acceptance was reasonably induced either by the lessor's assurances or, except in the case of a finance lease, by the difficulty of discovery before acceptance.

(2) Except in the case of a finance lease that is not a consumer lease, a lessee may revoke acceptance of a lot or commercial unit if the lessor defaults under the lease contract and the default substantially impairs the value of that lot or commercial unit to the lessee.

(3) If the lease agreement so provides, the lessee may revoke acceptance of a lot or commercial unit because of other defaults by the lessor.

(4) Revocation of acceptance must occur within a reasonable time after the lessee discovers or should have discovered the ground for it and before any substantial change in condition of the goods which is not caused by the nonconformity. Revocation is not effective until the lessee notifies the lessor.

(5) A lessee who so revokes has the same rights and duties with regard to the goods involved as if the lessee had rejected them.

As amended in 1990.

§ 2A–518. Cover; Substitute Goods.

(1) After a default by a lessor under the lease contract of the type described in Section 2A–508(1), or, if agreed, after other default by the lessor, the lessee may cover by making any purchase or lease of or contract to purchase or lease goods in substitution for those due from the lessor.

(2) Except as otherwise provided with respect to damages liquidated in the lease agreement (Section 2A–504) or otherwise determined pursuant to agreement of the parties (Sections 1–102(3) and 2A–503), if a lessee's cover is by lease agreement substantially similar to the original lease agreement and the new lease agreement is made in good faith and in a commercially reasonable manner, the lessee may recover from the lessor as damages (i) the present value, as of the date of the commencement of the term of the new lease agreement, of the rent under the new lease agreement applicable to that period of the new lease term which is comparable to the then remaining term of the original lease agreement minus the present value as of the same date of the total rent for the then remaining lease term of the original lease agreement, and (ii) any incidental or consequential damages, less expenses saved in consequence of the lessor's default.

(3) If a lessee's cover is by lease agreement that for any reason does not qualify for treatment under subsection (2), or is by purchase or otherwise, the lessee may recover from the lessor as if the lessee had elected not to cover and Section 2A–519 governs.

As amended in 1990.

§ 2A–519. Lessee's Damages for Non-Delivery, Repudiation, Default, and Breach of Warranty in Regard to Accepted Goods.

(1) Except as otherwise provided with respect to damages liquidated in the lease agreement (Section 2A–504) or otherwise determined pursuant to agreement of the parties (Sections 1–102(3) and 2A–503), if a lessee elects not to cover or a lessee elects to cover and the cover is by lease agreement that for any reason does not qualify for treatment under Section 2A–518(2), or is by purchase or otherwise, the measure of damages for non-delivery or repudiation by the lessor or for rejection or revocation of acceptance by the lessee is the present value, as of the date of the default, of the then market rent minus the present value as of the same date of the original rent, computed for the remaining lease term of the original lease

agreement, together with incidental and consequential damages, less expenses saved in consequence of the lessor's default.

(2) Market rent is to be determined as of the place for tender or, in cases of rejection after arrival or revocation of acceptance, as of the place of arrival.

(3) Except as otherwise agreed, if the lessee has accepted goods and given notification (Section 2A–516(3)), the measure of damages for non-conforming tender or delivery or other default by a lessor is the loss resulting in the ordinary course of events from the lessor's default as determined in any manner that is reasonable together with incidental and consequential damages, less expenses saved in consequence of the lessor's default.

(4) Except as otherwise agreed, the measure of damages for breach of warranty is the present value at the time and place of acceptance of the difference between the value of the use of the goods accepted and the value if they had been as warranted for the lease term, unless special circumstances show proximate damages of a different amount, together with incidental and consequential damages, less expenses saved in consequence of the lessor's default or breach of warranty.

As amended in 1990.

§ 2A–520. Lessee's Incidental and Consequential Damages.

(1) Incidental damages resulting from a lessor's default include expenses reasonably incurred in inspection, receipt, transportation, and care and custody of goods rightfully rejected or goods the acceptance of which is justifiably revoked, any commercially reasonable charges, expenses or commissions in connection with effecting cover, and any other reasonable expense incident to the default.

(2) Consequential damages resulting from a lessor's default include:

(a) any loss resulting from general or particular requirements and needs of which the lessor at the time of contracting had reason to know and which could not reasonably be prevented by cover or otherwise; and

(b) injury to person or property proximately resulting from any breach of warranty.

§ 2A–521. Lessee's Right to Specific Performance or Replevin.

(1) Specific performance may be decreed if the goods are unique or in other proper circumstances.

(2) A decree for specific performance may include any terms and conditions as to payment of the rent, damages, or other relief that the court deems just.

(3) A lessee has a right of replevin, detinue, sequestration, claim and delivery, or the like for goods identified to the lease contract if after reasonable effort the lessee is unable to effect cover for those goods or the circumstances reasonably indicate that the effort will be unavailing.

§ 2A–522. Lessee's Right to Goods on Lessor's Insolvency.

(1) Subject to subsection (2) and even though the goods have not been shipped, a lessee who has paid a part or all of the rent and security for goods identified to a lease contract (Section 2A–217) on making and keeping good a tender of any unpaid portion of the rent and security due under the lease contract may recover the goods identified from the lessor if the lessor becomes insolvent within 10 days after receipt of the first installment of rent and security.

(2) A lessee acquires the right to recover goods identified to a lease contract only if they conform to the lease contract.

C. Default by Lessee

§ 2A–523. Lessor's Remedies.

(1) If a lessee wrongfully rejects or revokes acceptance of goods or fails to make a payment when due or repudiates with respect to a part or the whole, then, with respect to any goods involved, and with respect to all of the goods if under an installment lease contract the value of the whole lease contract is substantially impaired (Section 2A–510), the lessee is in default under the lease contract and the lessor may:

(a) cancel the lease contract (Section 2A–505(1));

(b) proceed respecting goods not identified to the lease contract (Section 2A–524);

(c) withhold delivery of the goods and take possession of goods previously delivered (Section 2A–525);

(d) stop delivery of the goods by any bailee (Section 2A–526);

(e) dispose of the goods and recover damages (Section 2A–527), or retain the goods and recover damages (Section 2A–528), or in a proper case recover rent (Section 2A–529)

(f) exercise any other rights or pursue any other remedies provided in the lease contract.

(2) If a lessor does not fully exercise a right or obtain a remedy to which the lessor is entitled under subsection (1), the lessor may recover the loss resulting in the ordinary course of events from the lessee's default as determined in any reasonable manner, together with incidental damages, less expenses saved in consequence of the lessee's default.

(3) If a lessee is otherwise in default under a lease contract, the lessor may exercise the rights and pursue the remedies provided in the lease contract, which may include a right to cancel the lease. In addition, unless otherwise provided in the lease contract:

(a) if the default substantially impairs the value of the lease contract to the lessor, the lessor may exercise the rights and pursue the remedies provided in subsections (1) or (2); or

(b) if the default does not substantially impair the value of the lease contract to the lessor, the lessor may recover as provided in subsection (2).

As amended in 1990.

§ 2A–524. Lessor's Right to Identify Goods to Lease Contract.

(1) After default by the lessee under the lease contract of the type described in Section 2A–523(1) or 2A–523(3)(a) or, if agreed, after other default by the lessee, the lessor may:

(a) identify to the lease contract conforming goods not already identified if at the time the lessor learned of the default they were in the lessor's or the supplier's possession or control; and

(b) dispose of goods (Section 2A–527(1)) that demonstrably have been intended for the particular lease contract even though those goods are unfinished.

(2) If the goods are unfinished, in the exercise of reasonable commercial judgment for the purposes of avoiding loss and of effective realization, an aggrieved lessor or the supplier may either complete manufacture and wholly identify the goods to the lease contract or cease manufacture and lease, sell, or otherwise dispose of the goods for scrap or salvage value or proceed in any other reasonable manner.

As amended in 1990.

§ 2A–525. Lessor's Right to Possession of Goods.

(1) If a lessor discovers the lessee to be insolvent, the lessor may refuse to deliver the goods.

(2) After a default by the lessee under the lease contract of the type described in Section 2A–523(1) or 2A–523(3)(a) or, if agreed, after other default by the lessee, the lessor has the right to take possession of the goods. If the lease contract so provides, the lessor may require the lessee to assemble the goods and make them available to the lessor at a place to be designated by the lessor which is reasonably convenient to both parties. Without removal, the lessor may render unusable any goods employed in trade or business, and may dispose of goods on the lessee's premises (Section 2A–527).

(3) The lessor may proceed under subsection (2) without judicial process if that can be done without breach of the peace or the lessor may proceed by action.

As amended in 1990.

§ 2A–526. Lessor's Stoppage of Delivery in Transit or Otherwise.

(1) A lessor may stop delivery of goods in the possession of a carrier or other bailee if the lessor discovers the lessee to be insolvent and may stop delivery of carload, truckload, planeload, or larger shipments of express or freight if the lessee repudiates or fails to make a payment due before delivery, whether for rent, security or otherwise under the lease contract, or for any other reason the lessor has a right to withhold or take possession of the goods.

(2) In pursuing its remedies under subsection (1), the lessor may stop delivery until

(a) receipt of the goods by the lessee;

(b) acknowledgment to the lessee by any bailee of the goods, except a carrier, that the bailee holds the goods for the lessee; or

(c) such an acknowledgment to the lessee by a carrier via reshipment or as warehouseman.

(3) (a) To stop delivery, a lessor shall so notify as to enable the bailee by reasonable diligence to prevent delivery of the goods.

(b) After notification, the bailee shall hold and deliver the goods according to the directions of the lessor, but the lessor is liable to the bailee for any ensuing charges or damages.

(c) A carrier who has issued a nonnegotiable bill of lading is not obliged to obey a notification to stop received from a person other than the consignor.

§ 2A–527. Lessor's Rights to Dispose of Goods.

(1) After a default by a lessee under the lease contract of the type described in Section 2A–523(1) or 2A–523(3)(a) or after the lessor refuses to deliver or takes possession of goods (Section 2A–525 or 2A–526), or, if agreed, after other default by a lessee, the lessor may dispose of the goods concerned or the undelivered balance thereof by lease, sale, or otherwise.

(2) Except as otherwise provided with respect to damages liquidated in the lease agreement (Section 2A–504) or otherwise determined pursuant to agreement of the parties (Sections 1–102(3) and 2A–503), if the disposition is by lease agreement substantially similar to the original lease agreement and the new lease agreement is made in good faith and in a commercially reasonable manner, the lessor may recover from the lessee as damages (i) accrued and unpaid rent as of the date of the commencement of the term of the new lease agreement, (ii) the present value, as of the same date, of the total rent for the then remaining lease term of the original lease agreement minus the present value, as of the same date, of the rent under the new lease agreement applicable to that period of the new lease term which is comparable to the then remaining term of the original lease agreement, and (iii) any incidental damages allowed under Section 2A–530, less expenses saved in consequence of the lessee's default.

(3) If the lessor's disposition is by lease agreement that for any reason does not qualify for treatment under subsection (2), or is by sale or otherwise, the lessor may recover from the lessee as if the lessor had elected not to dispose of the goods and Section 2A–528 governs.

(4) A subsequent buyer or lessee who buys or leases from the lessor in good faith for value as a result of a disposition under this section takes the goods free of the original lease contract and any rights of the original lessee even though the lessor fails to comply with one or more of the requirements of this Article.

(5) The lessor is not accountable to the lessee for any profit made on any disposition. A lessee who has rightfully rejected or justifiably revoked acceptance shall account to the lessor for any excess over the amount of the lessee's security interest (Section 2A–508(5)).

As amended in 1990.

§ 2A–528. Lessor's Damages for Non-acceptance, Failure to Pay, Repudiation, or Other Default.

(1) Except as otherwise provided with respect to damages liquidated in the lease agreement (Section 2A–504) or otherwise determined pursuant to agreement of the parties (Section 1–102(3) and 2A–503), if a lessor elects to retain the goods or a lessor elects to dispose of the goods and the disposition is by lease agreement that for any reason does not qualify for treatment under Section 2A–527(2), or is by sale or otherwise, the lessor may recover from the lessee as damages for a default of the type described in Section 2A–523(1) or 2A–523(3)(a), or if agreed, for other default of the lessee, (i) accrued and unpaid rent as of the date of the default if the lessee has never taken possession of the goods, or, if the lessee has taken possession of the goods, as of the date the lessor repossesses the goods or an earlier date on which the lessee makes a tender of the goods to the lessor, (ii) the present value as of the date determined under clause (i) of the total rent for the then remaining lease term of the original lease agreement minus the present value as of the same date of the market rent as the place where the goods are located computed for the same lease term, and (iii) any incidental damages allowed under Section 2A–530, less expenses saved in consequence of the lessee's default.

(2) If the measure of damages provided in subsection (1) is inadequate to put a lessor in as good a position as performance would have, the measure of damages is the present value of the profit, including reasonable overhead, the lessor would have made from full performance by the lessee, together with any incidental damages allowed under Section 2A–530, due allowance for costs reasonably incurred and due credit for payments or proceeds of disposition.

As amended in 1990.

§ 2A–529. Lessor's Action for the Rent.

(1) After default by the lessee under the lease contract of the type described in Section 2A–523(1) or 2A–523(3)(a) or, if agreed, after other default by the lessee, if the lessor complies with subsection (2), the lessor may recover from the lessee as damages:

(a) for goods accepted by the lessee and not repossessed by or tendered to the lessor, and for conforming goods lost or damaged within a commercially reasonable time after risk of loss passes to the lessee (Section 2A–219), (i) accrued and unpaid rent as of the date of entry of judgment in favor of the lessor (ii) the present value as of the same date of the rent for the then remaining lease term of the lease agreement, and (iii) any incidental damages allowed under Section 2A–530, less expenses saved in consequence of the lessee's default; and

(b) for goods identified to the lease contract if the lessor is unable after reasonable effort to dispose of them at a reasonable price or the circumstances reasonably indicate that effort will be unavailing, (i) accrued and unpaid rent as of the date of entry of judgment in favor of the lessor, (ii) the present value as of the

same date of the rent for the then remaining lease term of the lease agreement, and (iii) any incidental damages allowed under Section 2A–530, less expenses saved in consequence of the lessee's default.

(2) Except as provided in subsection (3), the lessor shall hold for the lessee for the remaining lease term of the lease agreement any goods that have been identified to the lease contract and are in the lessor's control.

(3) The lessor may dispose of the goods at any time before collection of the judgment for damages obtained pursuant to subsection (1). If the disposition is before the end of the remaining lease term of the lease agreement, the lessor's recovery against the lessee for damages is governed by Section 2A–527 or Section 2A–528, and the lessor will cause an appropriate credit to be provided against a judgment for damages to the extent that the amount of the judgment exceeds the recovery available pursuant to Section 2A–527 or 2A–528.

(4) Payment of the judgment for damages obtained pursuant to subsection (1) entitles the lessee to the use and possession of the goods not then disposed of for the remaining lease term of and in accordance with the lease agreement.

(5) After default by the lessee under the lease contract of the type described in Section 2A–523(1) or Section 2A–523(3)(a) or, if agreed, after other default by the lessee, a lessor who is held not entitled to rent under this section must nevertheless be awarded damages for non-acceptance under Sections 2A–527 and 2A–528.

As amended in 1990.

§ 2A–530. Lessor's Incidental Damages.

Incidental damages to an aggrieved lessor include any commercially reasonable charges, expenses, or commissions incurred in stopping delivery, in the transportation, care and custody of goods after the lessee's default, in connection with return or disposition of the goods, or otherwise resulting from the default.

§ 2A–531. Standing to Sue Third Parties for Injury to Goods.

(1) If a third party so deals with goods that have been identified to a lease contract as to cause actionable injury to a party to the lease contract (a) the lessor has a right of action against the third party, and (b) the lessee also has a right of action against the third party if the lessee:

(i) has a security interest in the goods;

(ii) has an insurable interest in the goods; or

(iii) bears the risk of loss under the lease contract or has since the injury assumed that risk as against the lessor and the goods have been converted or destroyed.

(2) If at the time of the injury the party plaintiff did not bear the risk of loss as against the other party to the lease contract and there is no arrangement between them for disposition of the recovery,

his [or her] suit or settlement, subject to his [or her] own interest, is as a fiduciary for the other party to the lease contract.

(3) Either party with the consent of the other may sue for the benefit of whom it may concern.

§ 2A–532. Lessor's Rights to Residual Interest.

In addition to any other recovery permitted by this Article or other law, the lessor may recover from the lessee an amount that will fully compensate the lessor for any loss of or damage to the lessor's residual interest in the goods caused by the default of the lessee.

As added in 1990.

REVISED ARTICLE III
NEGOTIABLE INSTRUMENTS

PART 1   General Provisions and Definitions

§ 3–101.   Short Title.

This Article may be cited as Uniform Commercial Code–Negotiable Instruments.

§ 3–102.   Subject Matter.

(a) This Article applies to negotiable instruments. It does not apply to money, to payment orders governed by Article 4A, or to securities governed by Article 8.

(b) If there is conflict between this Article and Article 4 or 9, Articles 4 and 9 govern.

(c) Regulations of the Board of Governors of the Federal Reserve System and operating circulars of the Federal Reserve Banks supersede any inconsistent provision of this Article to the extent of the inconsistency.

§ 3–103.   Definitions.

(a) In this Article:

(1) "Acceptor" means a drawee who has accepted a draft.

(2) "Drawee" means a person ordered in a draft to make payment.

(3) "Drawer" means a person who signs or is identified in a draft as a person ordering payment.

(4) "Good faith" means honesty in fact and the observance of reasonable commercial standards of fair dealing.

(5) "Maker" means a person who signs or is identified in a note as a person undertaking to pay.

(6) "Order" means a written instruction to pay money signed by the person giving the instruction. The instruction may be addressed to any person, including the person giving the instruction, or to one or more persons jointly or in the alternative

but not in succession. An authorization to pay is not an order unless the person authorized to pay is also instructed to pay.

(7) "Ordinary care" in the case of a person engaged in business means observance of reasonable commercial standards, prevailing in the area in which the person is located, with respect to the business in which the person is engaged. In the case of a bank that takes an instrument for processing for collection or payment by automated means, reasonable commercial standards do not require the bank to examine the instrument if the failure to examine does not violate the bank's prescribed procedures and the bank's procedures do not vary unreasonably from general banking usage not disapproved by this Article or Article 4.

(8) "Party" means a party to an instrument.

(9) "Promise" means a written undertaking to pay money signed by the person undertaking to pay. An acknowledgment of an obligation by the obligor is not a promise unless the obligor also undertakes to pay the obligation.

(10) "Prove" with respect to a fact means to meet the burden of establishing the fact (Section 1–201(8)).

(11) "Remitter" means a person who purchases an instrument from its issuer if the instrument is payable to an identified person other than the purchaser.

(b) [Other definitions' section references deleted.]

(c) [Other definitions' section references deleted.]

(d) In addition, Article 1 contains general definitions and principles of construction and interpretation applicable throughout this Article.

§ 3–104.   Negotiable Instrument.

(a) Except as provided in subsections (c)and (d), "negotiable instrument" means an unconditional promise or order to pay a fixed amount of money, with or without interest or other charges described in the promise or order, if it:

(1) is payable to bearer or to order at the time it is issued or first comes into possession of a holder;

(2) is payable on demand or at a definite time; and

(3) does not state any other undertaking or instruction by the person promising or ordering payment to do any act in addition to the payment of money, but the promise or order may contain (i) an undertaking or power to give, maintain, or protect collateral to secure payment, (ii) an authorization or power to the holder to confess judgment or realize on or dispose of collateral, or (iii) a waiver of the benefit of any law intended for the advantage or protection of an obligor.

(b) "Instrument" means a negotiable instrument.

(c) An order that meets all of the requirements of subsection (a), except paragraph (1), and otherwise falls within the definition of "check" in subsection (f) is a negotiable instrument and a check.

(d) A promise or order other than a check is not an instrument if, at the time it is issued or first comes into possession of a holder, it contains a conspicuous statement, however expressed, to the effect that the promise or order is not negotiable or is not an instrument governed by this Article.

(e) An instrument is a "note" if it is a promise and is a "draft" if it is an order. If an instrument falls within the definition of both "note" and "draft," a person entitled to enforce the instrument may treat it as either.

(f) "Check" means (i) a draft, other than a documentary draft, payable on demand and drawn on a bank or (ii) a cashier's check or teller's check. An instrument may be a check even though it is described on its face by another term, such as "money order."

(g) "Cashier's check" means a draft with respect to which the drawer and drawee are the same bank or branches of the same bank.

(h) "Teller's check" means a draft drawn by a bank (i) on anoth- er bank, or (ii) payable at or through a bank.

(i) "Traveler's check" means an instrument that (i) is payable on demand, (ii) is drawn on or payable at or through a bank, (iii) is designated by the term "traveler's check" or by a substantially similar term, and (iv) requires, as a condition to payment, a countersignature by a person whose specimen signature appears on the instrument.

(j) "Certificate of deposit" means an instrument containing an acknowledgment by a bank that a sum of money has been received by the bank and a promise by the bank to repay the sum of money. A certificate of deposit is a note of the bank.

§ 3–105.   Issue of Instrument.

(a) "Issue" means the first delivery of an instrument by the maker or drawer, whether to a holder or nonholder, for the purpose of giving rights on the instrument to any person.

(b) An unissued instrument, or an unissued incomplete instrument that is completed, is binding on the maker or drawer, but nonissuance is a defense. An instrument that is conditionally issued or is issued for a special purpose is binding on the maker or drawer, but failure of the condition or special purpose to be fulfilled is a defense.

(c) "Issuer" applies to issued and unissued instruments and means a maker or drawer of an instrument.

§ 3–106.   Unconditional Promise or Order.

(a) Except as provided in this section, for the purposes of Section 3–104(a), a promise or order is unconditional unless it states (i) an express condition to payment, (ii) that the promise or order is subject to or governed by another writing, or (iii) that rights or obligations with respect to the promise or order are stated in another writing. A reference to another writing does not of itself make the promise or order conditional.

(b) A promise or order is not made conditional (i) by a reference to another writing for a statement of rights with respect to collateral, prepayment, or acceleration, or (ii) because payment is limited to resort to a particular fund or source.

(c) If a promise or order requires, as a condition to payment, a countersignature by a person whose specimen signature

appears on the promise or order, the condition does not make the promise or order conditional for the purposes of Section 3–104(a). If the person whose specimen signature appears on an instrument fails to countersign the instrument, the failure to countersign is a defense to the obligation of the issuer, but the failure does not prevent a transferee of the instrument from becoming a holder of the instrument.

(d) If a promise or order at the time it is issued or first comes into possession of a holder contains a statement, required by applicable statutory or administrative law, to the effect that the rights of a holder or transferee are subject to claims or defenses that the issuer could assert against the original payee, the promise or order is not thereby made conditional for the purposes of Section 3–104(a); but if the promise or order is an instrument, there cannot be a holder in due course of the instrument.

§ 3–107.   Instrument Payable in Foreign Money.

Unless the instrument otherwise provides, an instrument that states the amount payable in foreign money may be paid in the foreign money or in an equivalent amount in dollars calculated by using the current bank-offered spot rate at the place of payment for the purchase of dollars on the day on which the instrument is paid.

§ 3–108.   Payable on Demand or at Definite Time.

(a) A promise or order is "payable on demand" if it (i) states that it is payable on demand or at sight, or otherwise indicates that it is payable at the will of the holder, or (ii) does not state any time of payment.

(b) A promise or order is "payable at a definite time" if it is payable on elapse of a definite period of time after sight or acceptance or at a fixed date or dates or at a time or times readily ascertainable at the time the promise or order is issued, subject to rights of (i) prepayment, (ii) acceleration, (iii) extension at the option of the holder, or (iv) extension to a further definite time at the option of the maker or acceptor or automatically upon or after a specified act or event.

(c) If an instrument, payable at a fixed date, is also payable upon demand made before the fixed date, the instrument is payable on demand until the fixed date and, if demand for payment is not made before that date, becomes payable at a definite time on the fixed date.

§ 3–109.   Payable to Bearer or to Order.

(a) A promise or order is payable to bearer if it:

(1) states that it is payable to bearer or to the order of bearer or otherwise indicates that the person in possession of the promise or order is entitled to payment;

(2) does not state a payee; or

(3) states that it is payable to or to the order of cash or otherwise indicates that it is not payable to an identified person.

(b) A promise or order that is not payable to bearer is payable to order if it is payable (i) to the order of an identified person or (ii) to an identified person or order. A promise or order that is payable to order is payable to the identified person.

(c) An instrument payable to bearer may become payable to an identified person if it is specially indorsed pursuant to Section 3–205(a). An instrument payable to an identified person may become payable to bearer if it is indorsed in blank pursuant to Section 3–205(b).

§ 3–110.   Identification of Person to Whom Instrument Is Payable.

(a) The person to whom an instrument is initially payable is determined by the intent of the person, whether or not authorized, signing as, or in the name or behalf of, the issuer of the instrument. The instrument is payable to the person intended by the signer even if that person is identified in the instrument by a name or other identification that is not that of the intended person. If more than one person signs in the name or behalf of the issuer of an instrument and all the signers do not intend the same person as payee, the instrument is payable to any person intended by one or more of the signers.

(b) If the signature of the issuer of an instrument is made by automated means, such as a check-writing machine, the payee of the instrument is determined by the intent of the person who supplied the name or identification of the payee, whether or not authorized to do so.

(c) A person to whom an instrument is payable may be identified in any way, including by name, identifying number, office, or account number. For the purpose of determining the holder of an instrument, the following rules apply:

(1) If an instrument is payable to an account and the account is identified only by number, the instrument is payable to the person to whom the account is payable. If an instrument is payable to an account identified by number and by the name of a person, the instrument is payable to the named person, whether or not that person is the owner of the account identified by number.

(2) If an instrument is payable to:

(i) a trust, an estate, or a person described as trustee or representative of a trust or estate, the instrument is payable to the trustee, the representative, or a successor of either, whether or not the beneficiary or estate is also named;

(ii) a person described as agent or similar representative of a named or identified person, the instrument is payable to the represented person, the representative, or a successor of the representative;

(iii) a fund or organization that is not a legal entity, the instrument is payable to a representative of the members of the fund or organization; or

(iv) an office or to a person described as holding an office, the instrument is payable to the named person, the incumbent of the office, or a successor to the incumbent.

(d) If an instrument is payable to two or more persons alternatively, it is payable to any of them and may be negotiated, discharged, or enforced by any or all of them in possession of the instrument. If an instrument is payable to two or more persons not alternatively, it is payable to all of them and may be negotiated, discharged, or enforced only by all of them. If an instrument payable to two or more persons is ambiguous as to whether it is payable to the persons alternatively, the instrument is payable to the persons alternatively.

§ 3–111.   Place of Payment.

Except as otherwise provided for items in Article 4, an instrument is payable at the place of payment stated in the instrument. If no place of payment is stated, an instrument is payable at the address of the drawee or maker stated in the instrument. If no address is stated, the place of payment is the place of business of the drawee or maker. If a drawee or maker has more than one place of business, the place of payment is any place of business of the drawee or maker chosen by the person entitled to enforce the instrument. If the drawee or maker has no place of business, the place of payment is the residence of the drawee or maker.

§ 3–112.   Interest.

(a) Unless otherwise provided in the instrument, (i) an instrument is not payable with interest, and (ii) interest on an interest-bearing instrument is payable from the date of the instrument.

(b) Interest may be stated in an instrument as a fixed or variable amount of money or it may be expressed as a fixed or variable rate or rates. The amount or rate of interest may be stated or described in the instrument in any manner and may require reference to information not contained in the instrument. If an instrument provides for interest, but the amount of interest payable cannot be ascertained from the description, interest is payable at the judgment rate in effect at the place of payment of the instrument and at the time interest first accrues.

§ 3–113.   Date of Instrument.

(a) An instrument may be antedated or postdated. The date stated determines the time of payment if the instrument is payable at a fixed period after date. Except as provided in Section 4–401(c), an instrument payable on demand is not payable before the date of the instrument.

(b) If an instrument is undated, its date is the date of its issue or, in the case of an unissued instrument, the date it first comes into possession of a holder.

§ 3–114.   Contradictory Terms of Instrument.

If an instrument contains contradictory terms, typewritten terms prevail over printed terms, handwritten terms prevail over both, and words prevail over numbers.

§ 3–115.   Incomplete Instrument.

(a) "Incomplete instrument" means a signed writing, whether or not issued by the signer, the contents of which show at the time of signing that it is incomplete but that the signer intended it to be completed by the addition of words or numbers.

(b) Subject to subsection (c), if an incomplete instrument is an instrument under Section 3–104, it may be enforced according to its terms if it is not completed, or according to its terms as augmented by completion. If an incomplete instrument is not an instrument under Section 3–104, but, after completion, the requirements of Section 3–104 are met, the instrument may be enforced according to its terms as augmented by completion.

(c) If words or numbers are added to an incomplete instrument without authority of the signer, there is an alteration of the incomplete instrument under Section 3–407.

(d) The burden of establishing that words or numbers were added to an incomplete instrument without authority of the signer is on the person asserting the lack of authority.

§ 3–116.   Joint and Several Liability; Contribution.

(a) Except as otherwise provided in the instrument, two or more persons who have the same liability on an instrument as makers, drawers, acceptors, indorsers who indorse as joint payees, or anomalous indorsers are jointly and severally liable in the capacity in which they sign.

(b) Except as provided in Section 3–419(e) or by agreement of the affected parties, a party having joint and several liability who pays the instrument is entitled to receive from any party having the same joint and several liability contribution in accordance with applicable law.

(c) Discharge of one party having joint and several liability by a person entitled to enforce the instrument does not affect the right under subsection (b) of a party having the same joint and several liability to receive contribution from the party discharged.

§ 3–117.   Other Agreements Affecting Instrument.

Subject to applicable law regarding exclusion of proof of contemporaneous or previous agreements, the obligation of a party to an instrument to pay the instrument may be modified, supplemented, or nullified by a separate agreement of the obligor and a person entitled to enforce the instrument, if the instrument is issued or the obligation is incurred in reliance on the agreement or as part of the same transaction giving rise to the agreement. To the extent an obligation is modified, supplemented, or nullified by an agreement under this section, the agreement is a defense to the obligation.

§ 3–118.   Statute of Limitations.

(a) Except as provided in subsection (e), an action to enforce the obligation of a party to pay a note payable at a definite time must be commenced within six years after the due date or dates stated in the note or, if a due date is accelerated, within six years after the accelerated due date.

(b) Except as provided in subsection (d) or (e), if demand for payment is made to the maker of a note payable on demand, an action to enforce the obligation of a party to pay the note must be commenced within six years after the demand. If no demand for payment is made to the maker, an action to enforce the note is barred if neither principal nor interest on the note has been paid for a continuous period of 10 years.

(c) Except as provided in subsection (d), an action to enforce the obligation of a party to an unaccepted draft to pay the draft must be commenced within three years after dishonor of the draft or 10 years after the date of the draft, whichever period expires first.

(d) An action to enforce the obligation of the acceptor of a certified check or the issuer of a teller's check, cashier's check, or traveler's check must be commenced within three years after demand for payment is made to the acceptor or issuer, as the case may be.

(e) An action to enforce the obligation of a party to a certificate of deposit to pay the instrument must be commenced within six years after demand for payment is made to the maker, but if the instrument states a due date and the maker is not required to pay before that date, the six-year period begins when a demand for payment is in effect and the due date has passed.

(f) An action to enforce the obligation of a party to pay an accepted draft, other than a certified check, must be commenced (i) within six years after the due date or dates stated in the draft or acceptance if the obligation of the acceptor is payable at a definite time, or (ii) within six years after the date of the acceptance if the obligation of the acceptor is payable on demand.

(g) Unless governed by other law regarding claims for indemnity or contribution, an action (i) for conversion of an instrument, for money had and received, or like action based on conversion, (ii) for breach of warranty, or (iii) to enforce an obligation, duty, or right arising under this Article and not governed by this section must be commenced within three years after the [cause of action] accrues.

§ 3–119.   Notice of Right to Defend Action.

In an action for breach of an obligation for which a third person is answerable over pursuant to this Article or Article 4, the defendant may give the third person written notice of the litigation, and the person notified may then give similar notice to any other person who is answerable over. If the notice states (i) that the person notified may come in and defend and (ii) that failure to do so will bind the person notified in an action later brought by the person giving the notice as to any determination of fact common to the two litigations, the person notified is so bound unless after seasonable receipt of the notice the person notified does come in and defend.

PART 2   Negotiation, Transfer, and Indorsement

§ 3–201.   Negotiation.

(a) "Negotiation" means a transfer of possession, whether voluntary or involuntary, of an instrument by a person other than the issuer to a person who thereby becomes its holder.

(b) Except for negotiation by a remitter, if an instrument is payable to an identified person, negotiation requires transfer of possession of the instrument and its indorsement by the holder. If an instrument is payable to bearer, it may be negotiated by transfer of possession alone.

§ 3–202.   Negotiation Subject to Rescission.

(a) Negotiation is effective even if obtained (i) from an infant, a corporation exceeding its powers, or a person without capacity, (ii) by fraud, duress, or mistake, or (iii) in breach of duty or as part of an illegal transaction.

(b) To the extent permitted by other law, negotiation may be rescinded or may be subject to other remedies, but those remedies may not be asserted against a subsequent holder in due course or a person paying the instrument in good faith and without knowledge of facts that are a basis for rescission or other remedy.

§ 3–203.   Transfer of Instrument; Rights Acquired by Transfer.

(a) An instrument is transferred when it is delivered by a person other than its issuer for the purpose of giving to the person receiving delivery the right to enforce the instrument.

(b) Transfer of an instrument, whether or not the transfer is a negotiation, vests in the transferee any right of the transferor to enforce the instrument, including any right as a holder in due course, but the transferee cannot acquire rights of a holder in due course by a transfer, directly or indirectly, from a holder in due course if the transferee engaged in fraud or illegality affecting the instrument.

(c) Unless otherwise agreed, if an instrument is transferred for value and the transferee does not become a holder because of lack of indorsement by the transferor, the transferee has a specifically enforceable right to the unqualified indorsement of the transferor, but negotiation of the instrument does not occur until the indorsement is made.

(d) If a transferor purports to transfer less than the entire instrument, negotiation of the instrument does not occur. The transferee obtains no rights under this Article and has only the rights of a partial assignee.

§ 3–204.   Indorsement.

(a) "Indorsement" means a signature, other than that of a signer as maker, drawer, or acceptor, that alone or accompanied by other words is made on an instrument for the purpose of (i) negotiating the instrument, (ii) restricting payment of the instrument, or (iii) incurring indorser's liability on the instrument, but regardless of the intent of the signer, a signature and its accompanying words is an indorsement unless the accompanying words, terms of the instrument, place of the signature, or other circumstances unambiguously indicate that the signature was made for a purpose other than indorsement. For the purpose of determining whether a signature is made on an instrument, a paper affixed to the instrument is a part of the instrument.

(b) "Indorser" means a person who makes an indorsement.

(c) For the purpose of determining whether the transferee of an instrument is a holder, an indorsement that transfers a security interest in the instrument is effective as an unqualified indorsement of the instrument.

(d) If an instrument is payable to a holder under a name that is not the name of the holder, indorsement may be made by the holder in the name stated in the instrument or in the holder's name or both, but signature in both names may be required by a person paying or taking the instrument for value or collection.

§ 3–205.   Special Indorsement; Blank Indorsement; Anomalous Indorsement.

(a) If an indorsement is made by the holder of an instrument, whether payable to an identified person or payable to bearer, and the indorsement identifies a person to whom it makes the instrument payable, it is a "special indorsement." When specially indorsed, an instrument becomes payable to the identified person and may be negotiated only by the indorsement of that person. The principles stated in Section 3–110 apply to special indorsements.

(b) If an indorsement is made by the holder of an instrument and it is not a special indorsement, it is a "blank indorsement." When indorsed in blank, an instrument becomes payable to bearer and may be negotiated by transfer of possession alone until specially indorsed.

(c) The holder may convert a blank indorsement that consists only of a signature into a special indorsement by writing, above the signature of the indorser, words identifying the person to whom the instrument is made payable.

(d) "Anomalous indorsement" means an indorsement made by a person who is not the holder of the instrument. An anomalous indorsement does not affect the manner in which the instrument may be negotiated.

§ 3–206.   Restrictive Indorsement.

(a) An indorsement limiting payment to a particular person or otherwise prohibiting further transfer or negotiation of the instrument is not effective to prevent further transfer or negotiation of the instrument.

(b) An indorsement stating a condition to the right of the indorsee to receive payment does not affect the right of the indorsee to enforce the instrument. A person paying the instrument or taking it for value or collection may disregard the condition, and the rights and liabilities of that person are not affected by whether the condition has been fulfilled.

(c) If an instrument bears an indorsement (i) described in Section 4–201(b), or (ii) in blank or to a particular bank using the words "for deposit," "for collection," or other words indicating a purpose of having the instrument collected by a bank for the indorser or for a particular account, the following rules apply:

(1) A person, other than a bank, who purchases the instrument when so indorsed converts the instrument unless the amount paid for the instrument is received by the indorser or applied consistently with the indorsement.

(2) A depositary bank that purchases the instrument or takes it for collection when so indorsed converts the instrument unless the amount paid by the bank with respect to the instrument is received by the indorser or applied consistently with the indorsement.

(3) A payor bank that is also the depositary bank or that takes the instrument for immediate payment over the counter from a person other than a collecting bank converts the instrument unless the proceeds of the instrument are received by the indorser or applied consistently with the indorsement.

(4) Except as otherwise provided in paragraph (3), a payor bank or intermediary bank may disregard the indorsement and is not liable if the proceeds of the instrument are not received by the indorser or applied consistently with the indorsement.

(d) Except for an indorsement covered by subsection (c), if an instrument bears an indorsement using words to the effect that payment is to be made to the indorsee as agent, trustee, or other fiduciary for the benefit of the indorser or another person, the following rules apply:

(1) Unless there is notice of breach of fiduciary duty as provided in Section 3–307, a person who purchases the instrument from the indorsee or takes the instrument from the indorsee for collection or payment may pay the proceeds of payment or the value given for the instrument to the indorsee without regard to whether the indorsee violates a fiduciary duty to the indorser.

(2) A subsequent transferee of the instrument or person who pays the instrument is neither given notice nor otherwise affected by the restriction in the indorsement unless the transferee or payor knows that the fiduciary dealt with the instrument or its proceeds in breach of fiduciary duty.

(e) The presence on an instrument of an indorsement to which this section applies does not prevent a purchaser of the instrument from becoming a holder in due course of the instrument unless the purchaser is a converter under subsection (c) or has notice or knowledge of breach of fiduciary duty as stated in subsection (d).

(f) In an action to enforce the obligation of a party to pay the instrument, the obligor has a defense if payment would violate an indorsement to which this section applies and the payment is not permitted by this section.

§ 3–207.   Reacquisition.

Reacquisition of an instrument occurs if it is transferred to a former holder, by negotiation or otherwise. A former holder who reacquires the instrument may cancel indorsements made after the reacquirer first became a holder of the instrument. If the cancellation causes the instrument to be payable to the reacquirer or to bearer, the reacquirer may negotiate the instrument. An indorser whose indorsement is canceled is discharged, and the discharge is effective against any subsequent holder.

PART 3   Enforcement of Instruments

§ 3–301.   Person Entitled to Enforce Instrument.

"Person entitled to enforce" an instrument means (i) the holder of the instrument, (ii) a nonholder in possession of the instrument who has the rights of a holder, or (iii) a person not in possession of the instrument who is entitled to enforce the instrument pursuant to Section 3–309 or 3–418(d). A person may be a person entitled to enforce the instrument even though the person is not the owner of the instrument or is in wrongful possession of the instrument.

§ 3–302.   Holder in Due Course.

(a) Subject to subsection (c) and Section 3–106(d), "holder in due course" means the holder of an instrument if:

(1) the instrument when issued or negotiated to the holder does not bear such apparent evidence of forgery or alteration or is not otherwise so irregular or incomplete as to call into question its authenticity; and

(2) the holder took the instrument (i) for value, (ii) in good faith, (iii) without notice that the instrument is overdue or has been dishonored or that there is an uncured default with respect to payment of another instrument issued as part of the same series, (iv) without notice that the instrument contains an unauthorized signature or has been altered, (v) without notice of any claim to the instrument described in Section 3–306, and (vi) without notice that any party has a defense or claim in recoupment described in Section 3–305(a).

(b) Notice of discharge of a party, other than discharge in an insolvency proceeding, is not notice of a defense under subsection (a), but discharge is effective against a person who became a holder in due course with notice of the discharge. Public filing or recording of a document does not of itself constitute notice of a defense, claim in recoupment, or claim to the instrument.

(c) Except to the extent a transferor or predecessor in interest has rights as a holder in due course, a person does not acquire rights of a holder in due course of an instrument taken (i) by legal process or by purchase in an execution, bankruptcy, or creditor's sale or similar proceeding, (ii) by purchase as part of a bulk transaction not in ordinary course of business of the transferor, or (iii) as the successor in interest to an estate or other organization.

(d) If, under Section 3–303(a)(1), the promise of performance that is the consideration for an instrument has been partially performed, the holder may assert rights as a holder in due course of the instrument only to the fraction of the amount payable under the instrument equal to the value of the partial performance divided by the value of the promised performance.

(e) If (i) the person entitled to enforce an instrument has only a security interest in the instrument and (ii) the person obliged to pay the instrument has a defense, claim in recoupment, or claim to the instrument that may be asserted against the person who granted the security interest, the person entitled to enforce the instrument may assert rights as a holder in due course only to an amount payable under the instrument which, at the time of enforcement of the instrument, does not exceed the amount of the unpaid obligation secured.

(f) To be effective, notice must be received at a time and in a manner that gives a reasonable opportunity to act on it.

(g) This section is subject to any law limiting status as a holder in due course in particular classes of transactions.

§ 3–303.   Value and Consideration.

(a) An instrument is issued or transferred for value if:

(1) the instrument is issued or transferred for a promise of performance, to the extent the promise has been performed;

(2) the transferee acquires a security interest or other lien in the instrument other than a lien obtained by judicial proceeding;

(3) the instrument is issued or transferred as payment of, or as security for, an antecedent claim against any person, whether or not the claim is due;

(4) the instrument is issued or transferred in exchange for a negotiable instrument; or

(5) the instrument is issued or transferred in exchange for the incurring of an irrevocable obligation to a third party by the person taking the instrument.

(b) "Consideration" means any consideration sufficient to support a simple contract. The drawer or maker of an instrument has a defense if the instrument is issued without consideration. If an instrument is issued for a promise of performance, the issuer has a defense to the extent performance of the promise is due and the promise has not been performed. If an instrument is issued for value as stated in subsection (a), the instrument is also issued for consideration.

§ 3–304.   Overdue Instrument.

(a) An instrument payable on demand becomes overdue at the earliest of the following times:

(1) on the day after the day demand for payment is duly made;

(2) if the instrument is a check, 90 days after its date; or

(3) if the instrument is not a check, when the instrument has been outstanding for a period of time after its date which is unreasonably long under the circumstances of the particular case in light of the nature of the instrument and usage of the trade.

(b) With respect to an instrument payable at a definite time the following rules apply:

(1) If the principal is payable in installments and a due date has not been accelerated, the instrument becomes overdue upon default under the instrument for nonpayment of an installment, and the instrument remains overdue until the default is cured.

(2) If the principal is not payable in installments and the due date has not been accelerated, the instrument becomes overdue on the day after the due date.

(3) If a due date with respect to principal has been accelerated, the instrument becomes overdue on the day after the accelerated due date.

(c) Unless the due date of principal has been accelerated, an instrument does not become overdue if there is default in payment of interest but no default in payment of principal.

§ 3–305.   Defenses and Claims in Recoupment.

(a) Except as stated in subsection (b), the right to enforce the obligation of a party to pay an instrument is subject to the following:

(1) a defense of the obligor based on (i) infancy of the obligor to the extent it is a defense to a simple contract, (ii) duress, lack of legal capacity, or illegality of the transaction which, under other law, nullifies the obligation of the obligor, (iii) fraud that induced the obligor to sign the instrument with neither knowledge nor reasonable opportunity to learn of its character or its essential terms, or (iv) discharge of the obligor in insolvency proceedings;

(2) a defense of the obligor stated in another section of this Article or a defense of the obligor that would be available if the person entitled to enforce the instrument were enforcing a right to payment under a simple contract; and

(3) a claim in recoupment of the obligor against the original payee of the instrument if the claim arose from the transaction that gave rise to the instrument; but the claim of the obligor may be asserted against a transferee of the instrument only to reduce the amount owing on the instrument at the time the action is brought.

(b) The right of a holder in due course to enforce the obligation of a party to pay the instrument is subject to defenses of the obligor stated in subsection (a)(1), but is not subject to defenses of the obligor stated in subsection (a)(2) or claims in recoupment stated in subsection (a)(3) against a person other than the holder.

(c) Except as stated in subsection (d), in an action to enforce the obligation of a party to pay the instrument, the obligor may not assert against the person entitled to enforce the instrument a defense, claim in recoupment, or claim to the instrument (Section 3–306) of another person, but the other person's claim to the instrument may be asserted by the obligor if the other person is joined in the action and personally asserts the claim against the person entitled to enforce the instrument. An obligor is not obliged to pay the instrument if the person seeking enforcement of the instrument does not have rights of a holder in due course and the obligor proves that the instrument is a lost or stolen instrument.

(d) In an action to enforce the obligation of an accommodation party to pay an instrument, the accommodation party may assert against the person entitled to enforce the instrument any defense or claim in recoupment under subsection (a) that the accommodated party could assert against the person entitled to enforce the instrument, except the defenses of discharge in insolvency proceedings, infancy, and lack of legal capacity.

§ 3–306.   Claims to an Instrument.

A person taking an instrument, other than a person having rights of a holder in due course, is subject to a claim of a property or possessory right in the instrument or its proceeds, including a claim to rescind a negotiation and to recover the instrument or its proceeds. A person having rights of a holder in due course takes free of the claim to the instrument.

§ 3–307.   Notice of Breach of Fiduciary Duty.

(a) In this section:

(1) "Fiduciary" means an agent, trustee, partner, corporate officer or director, or other representative owing a fiduciary duty with respect to an instrument.

(2) "Represented person" means the principal, beneficiary, partnership, corporation, or other person to whom the duty stated in paragraph (1) is owed.

(b) If (i) an instrument is taken from a fiduciary for payment or collection or for value, (ii) the taker has knowledge of the fiduciary status of the fiduciary, and (iii) the represented person makes a claim to the instrument or its proceeds on the basis that the transaction of the fiduciary is a breach of fiduciary duty, the following rules apply:

(1) Notice of breach of fiduciary duty by the fiduciary is notice of the claim of the represented person.

(2) In the case of an instrument payable to the represented person or the fiduciary as such, the taker has notice of the breach of fiduciary duty if the instrument is (i) taken in payment of or as security for a debt known by the taker to be the personal debt of the fiduciary, (ii) taken in a transaction known by the taker to be for the personal benefit of the fiduciary, or (iii) deposited to an account other than an account of the fiduciary, as such, or an account of the represented person.

(3) If an instrument is issued by the represented person or the fiduciary as such, and made payable to the fiduciary personally, the taker does not have notice of the breach of fiduciary duty unless the taker knows of the breach of fiduciary duty.

(4) If an instrument is issued by the represented person or the fiduciary as such, to the taker as payee, the taker has notice of the breach of fiduciary duty if the instrument is (i) taken in payment of or as security for a debt known by the taker to be the personal debt of the fiduciary, (ii) taken in a transaction known by the taker to be for the personal benefit of the fiduciary, or (iii) deposited to an account other than an account of the fiduciary, as such, or an account of the represented person.

§ 3–308.   Proof of Signatures and Status as Holder in Due Course.

(a) In an action with respect to an instrument, the authenticity of, and authority to make, each signature on the instrument is admitted unless specifically denied in the pleadings. If the validity of a signature is denied in the pleadings, the burden of establishing validity is on the person claiming validity, but the signature is presumed to be authentic and authorized unless the action is to enforce the liability of the purported signer and the signer is dead or incompetent at the time of trial of the issue of validity of the signature. If an action to enforce the instrument is brought against a person as the undisclosed principal of a person who signed the instrument as a party to the instrument, the plaintiff has the burden of establishing that the defendant is liable on the instrument as a represented person under Section 3–402(a).

(b) If the validity of signatures is admitted or proved and there is compliance with subsection (a), a plaintiff producing the instrument is entitled to payment if the plaintiff proves entitlement to enforce the instrument under Section 3–301, unless the defendant proves a defense or claim in recoupment. If a defense or claim in recoupment is proved, the right to payment of the plaintiff is subject to the defense or claim, except to the extent the plaintiff proves that the plaintiff has rights of a holder in due course which are not subject to the defense or claim.

§ 3–309.   Enforcement of Lost, Destroyed, or Stolen Instrument.

(a) A person not in possession of an instrument is entitled to enforce the instrument if (i) the person was in possession of the instrument and entitled to enforce it when loss of possession occurred, (ii) the loss of possession was not the result of a transfer by the person or a lawful seizure, and (iii) the person cannot reasonably obtain possession of the instrument because the instrument was destroyed, its whereabouts cannot be determined, or it is in the wrongful possession of an unknown person or a person that cannot be found or is not amenable to service of process.

(b) A person seeking enforcement of an instrument under subsection (a) must prove the terms of the instrument and the person's right to enforce the instrument. If that proof is made, Section 3–308 applies to the case as if the person seeking enforcement had produced the instrument. The court may not enter judgment in favor of the person seeking enforcement unless it finds that the person required to pay the instrument is adequately protected against loss that might occur by reason of a claim by another person to enforce the instrument. Adequate protection may be provided by any reasonable means.

§ 3–310.   Effect of Instrument on Obligation for Which Taken.

(a) Unless otherwise agreed, if a certified check, cashier's check, or teller's check is taken for an obligation, the obligation is discharged to the same extent discharge would result if an amount of money equal to the amount of the instrument were taken in payment of the obligation. Discharge of the obligation does not affect any liability that the obligor may have as an indorser of the instrument.

(b) Unless otherwise agreed and except as provided in subsection (a), if a note or an uncertified check is taken for an obligation, the obligation is suspended to the same extent the obligation would be discharged if an amount of money equal to the amount of the instrument were taken, and the following rules apply:

(1) In the case of an uncertified check, suspension of the obligation continues until dishonor of the check or until it is paid or certified. Payment or certification of the check results in discharge of the obligation to the extent of the amount of the check.

(2) In the case of a note, suspension of the obligation continues until dishonor of the note or until it is paid. Payment of the note results in discharge of the obligation to the extent of the payment.

(3) Except as provided in paragraph (4), if the check or note is dishonored and the obligee of the obligation for which the instrument was taken is the person entitled to enforce the instrument, the obligee may enforce either the instrument or the obligation. In the case of an instrument of a third person which is negotiated to the obligee by the obligor, discharge of the obligor on the instrument also discharges the obligation.

(4) If the person entitled to enforce the instrument taken for an obligation is a person other than the obligee, the obligee may not enforce the obligation to the extent the obligation is suspended. If the obligee is the person entitled to enforce the instrument but no longer has possession of it because it was lost, stolen, or destroyed, the obligation may not be enforced to the extent of the amount payable on the instrument, and to that extent the obligee's rights against the obligor are limited to enforcement of the instrument.

(c) If an instrument other than one described in subsection (a) or (b) is taken for an obligation, the effect is (i) that stated in subsection (a) if the instrument is one on which a bank is liable as maker or acceptor, or (ii) that stated in subsection (b) in any other case.

§ 3–311.   Accord and Satisfaction by Use of Instrument.

(a) If a person against whom a claim is asserted proves that (i) that person in good faith tendered an instrument to the claimant as full satisfaction of the claim, (ii) the amount of the claim was unliquidated or subject to a bona fide dispute, and (iii) the claimant obtained payment of the instrument, the following subsections apply.

(b) Unless subsection (c) applies, the claim is discharged if the person against whom the claim is asserted proves that the instrument or an accompanying written communication contained a conspicuous statement to the effect that the instrument was tendered as full satisfaction of the claim.

(c) Subject to subsection (d), a claim is not discharged under subsection (b) if either of the following applies:

(1) The claimant, if an organization, proves that (i) within a reasonable time before the tender, the claimant sent a conspicuous statement to the person against whom the claim is asserted that communications concerning disputed debts, including an instrument tendered as full satisfaction of a debt, are to be sent to a designated person, office, or place, and (ii) the instrument or accompanying communication was not received by that designated person, office, or place.

(2) The claimant, whether or not an organization, proves that within 90 days after payment of the instrument, the claimant tendered repayment of the amount of the instrument to the person against whom the claim is asserted. This paragraph does not apply if the claimant is an organization that sent a statement complying with paragraph (1)(i).

(d) A claim is discharged if the person against whom the claim is asserted proves that within a reasonable time before collection of the instrument was initiated, the claimant, or an agent of the claimant having direct responsibility with respect to the disputed obligation, knew that the instrument was tendered in full satisfaction of the claim.

§ 3–312.   Lost, Destroyed, or Stolen Cashier's Check, Teller's Check, or Certified Check. *

(a) In this section:

(1) "Check" means a cashier's check, teller's check, or certified check.

(2) "Claimant" means a person who claims the right to receive the amount of a cashier's check, teller's check, or certified check that was lost, destroyed, or stolen.

(3) "Declaration of loss" means a written statement, made under penalty of perjury, to the effect that (i) the declarer lost possession of a check, (ii) the declarer is the drawer or payee of the check, in the case of a certified check, or the remitter or payee of the check, in the case of a cashier's check or teller's check, (iii) the loss of possession was not the result of a transfer by the declarer or a lawful seizure, and (iv) the declarer cannot reasonably obtain possession of the check because the check was destroyed, its whereabouts cannot be determined, or it is in the wrongful possession of an unknown person or a person that cannot be found or is not amenable to service of process.

(4) "Obligated bank" means the issuer of a cashier's check or teller's check or the acceptor of a certified check.

(b) A claimant may assert a claim to the amount of a check by a communication to the obligated bank describing the check with reasonable certainty and requesting payment of the amount of the check, if (i) the claimant is the drawer or payee of a certified check or the remitter or payee of a cashier's check or teller's check, (ii) the communication contains or is accompanied by a declaration of loss of the claimant with respect to the check, (iii) the communication is received at a time and in a manner affording the bank a reasonable time to act on it before the check is paid, and (iv) the claimant provides reasonable identification if requested by the obligated bank. Delivery of a declaration of loss is a warranty of the truth of the statements made in the declaration. If a claim is asserted in compliance with this subsection, the following rules apply:

(1) The claim becomes enforceable at the later of (i) the time the claim is asserted, or (ii) the 90th day following the date of the check, in the case of a cashier's check or teller's check, or the 90th day following the date of the acceptance, in the case of a certified check.

(2) Until the claim becomes enforceable, it has no legal effect and the obligated bank may pay the check or, in the case of a teller's check, may permit the drawee to pay the check. Payment to a person entitled to enforce the check discharges all liability of the obligated bank with respect to the check.

(3) If the claim becomes enforceable before the check is presented for payment, the obligated bank is not obliged to pay the check.

(4) When the claim becomes enforceable, the obligated bank becomes obliged to pay the amount of the check to the claimant if payment of the check has not been made to a person entitled to enforce the check. Subject to Section 4–302(a)(1), payment to the claimant discharges all liability of the obligated bank with respect to the check.

(c) If the obligated bank pays the amount of a check to a claimant under subsection (b)(4) and the check is presented for payment by a person having rights of a holder in due course, the claimant is obliged to (i) refund the payment to the obligated bank if the check is paid, or (ii) pay the amount of the check to the person having rights of a holder in due course if the check is dishonored.

(d) If a claimant has the right to assert a claim under subsection (b) and is also a person entitled to enforce a cashier's check, teller's check, or certified check which is lost, destroyed, or stolen, the claimant may assert rights with respect to the check either under this section or Section 3–309.

Added in 1991.

PART 4   Liability of Parties

§ 3–401.   Signature.

(a) A person is not liable on an instrument unless (i) the person signed the instrument, or (ii) the person is represented by an agent or representative who signed the instrument and the signature is binding on the represented person under Section 3–402.

(b) A signature may be made (i) manually or by means of a device or machine, and (ii) by the use of any name, including a trade or assumed name, or by a word, mark, or symbol executed or adopted by a person with present intention to authenticate a writing.

§ 3–402.   Signature by Representative.

(a) If a person acting, or purporting to act, as a representative signs an instrument by signing either the name of the represented person or the name of the signer, the

represented person is bound by the signature to the same extent the represented person would be bound if the signature were on a simple contract. If the represented person is bound, the signature of the representative is the "authorized signature of the represented person" and the represented person is liable on the instrument, whether or not identified in the instrument.

(b) If a representative signs the name of the representative to an instrument and the signature is an authorized signature of the represented person, the following rules apply:

(1) If the form of the signature shows unambiguously that the signature is made on behalf of the represented person who is identified in the instrument, the representative is not liable on the instrument.

(2) Subject to subsection (c), if (i) the form of the signature does not show unambiguously that the signature is made in a representative capacity or (ii) the represented person is not identified in the instrument, the representative is liable on the instrument to a holder in due course that took the instrument without notice that the representative was not intended to be liable on the instrument. With respect to any other person, the representative is liable on the instrument unless the representative proves that the original parties did not intend the representative to be liable on the instrument.

(c) If a representative signs the name of the representative as drawer of a check without indication of the representative status and the check is payable from an account of the represented person who is identified on the check, the signer is not liable on the check if the signature is an authorized signature of the represented person.

§ 3–403.   Unauthorized Signature.

(a) Unless otherwise provided in this Article or Article 4, an unauthorized signature is ineffective except as the signature of the unauthorized signer in favor of a person who in good faith pays the instrument or takes it for value. An unauthorized signature may be ratified for all purposes of this Article.

(b) If the signature of more than one person is required to constitute the authorized signature of an organization, the signature of the organization is unauthorized if one of the required signatures is lacking.

(c) The civil or criminal liability of a person who makes an unauthorized signature is not affected by any provision of this Article which makes the unauthorized signature effective for the purposes of this Article.

§ 3–404.   Impostors; Fictitious Payees.

(a) If an impostor, by use of the mails or otherwise, induces the issuer of an instrument to issue the instrument to the impostor, or to a person acting in concert with the impostor, by impersonating the payee of the instrument or a person authorized to act for the payee, an indorsement of the instrument by any person in the name of the payee is effective as the indorsement of the payee in favor of a person who, in good faith, pays the instrument or takes it for value or for collection.

(b) If (i) a person whose intent determines to whom an instrument is payable (Section 3–110(a) or (b)) does not intend the person identified as payee to have any interest in the instrument, or (ii) the person identified as payee of an instrument is a fictitious person, the following rules apply until the instrument is negotiated by special indorsement:

(1) Any person in possession of the instrument is its holder.
(2) An indorsement by any person in the name of the payee stated in the instrument is effective as the indorsement of the payee in favor of a person who, in good faith, pays the instrument or takes it for value or for collection.

(c) Under subsection (a) or (b), an indorsement is made in the name of a payee if (i) it is made in a name substantially similar to that of the payee or (ii) the instrument, whether or not indorsed, is deposited in a depositary bank to an account in a name substantially similar to that of the payee.

(d) With respect to an instrument to which subsection (a) or (b) applies, if a person paying the instrument or taking it for value or for collection fails to exercise ordinary care in paying or taking the instrument and that failure substantially contributes to loss resulting from payment of the instrument, the person bearing the loss may recover from the person failing to exercise ordinary care to the extent the failure to exercise ordinary care contributed to the loss.

§ 3–405. Employer's Responsibility for Fraudulent Indorsement by Employee.

(a) In this section:

(1) "Employee" includes an independent contractor and employee of an independent contractor retained by the employer.
(2) "Fraudulent indorsement" means (i) in the case of an instrument payable to the employer, a forged indorsement purporting to be that of the employer, or (ii) in the case of an instrument with respect to which the employer is the issuer, a forged indorsement purporting to be that of the person identified as payee.
(3) "Responsibility" with respect to instruments means authority (i) to sign or indorse instruments on behalf of the employer, (ii) to process instruments received by the employer for bookkeeping purposes, for deposit to an account, or for other disposition, (iii) to prepare or process instruments for issue in the name of the employer, (iv) to supply information determining the names or addresses of payees of instruments to be issued in the name of the employer, (v) to control the disposition of instruments to be issued in the name of the employer, or (vi) to act otherwise with respect to instruments in a responsible capacity. "Responsibility" does not include authority that merely allows an employee to have access to instruments or blank or incomplete instrument forms that are being stored or transported or are part of incoming or outgoing mail, or similar access.

(b) For the purpose of determining the rights and liabilities of a person who, in good faith, pays an instrument or takes it for value or for collection, if an employer entrusted an employee with responsibility with respect to the instrument and the employee or a person acting in concert with the employee makes a fraudulent indorsement of the instrument, the indorsement is effective as the indorsement of the person to whom the instrument is payable if it is made in the name of that person. If the person paying the instrument or taking it for value or for collection fails to exercise ordinary care in paying or taking the instrument and that failure substantially contributes to loss resulting from the fraud, the person bearing the loss may recover from the person failing to exercise ordinary care to the extent the failure to exercise ordinary care contributed to the loss.

(c) Under subsection (b), an indorsement is made in the name of the person to whom an instrument is payable if (i) it is made in a name substantially similar to the name of that person or (ii) the instrument, whether or not indorsed, is deposited in a depositary bank to an account in a name substantially similar to the name of that person.

§ 3–406. Negligence Contributing to Forged Signature or Alteration of Instrument.

(a) A person whose failure to exercise ordinary care substantially contributes to an alteration of an instrument or to the making of a forged signature on an instrument is precluded from asserting the alteration or the forgery against a person who, in good faith, pays the instrument or takes it for value or for collection.

(b) Under subsection (a), if the person asserting the preclusion fails to exercise ordinary care in paying or taking the instrument and that failure substantially contributes to loss, the loss is allocated between the person precluded and the person asserting the preclusion according to the extent to which the failure of each to exercise ordinary care contributed to the loss.

(c) Under subsection (a), the burden of proving failure to exercise ordinary care is on the person asserting the preclusion. Under subsection (b), the burden of proving failure to exercise ordinary care is on the person precluded.

§ 3–407. Alteration.

(a) "Alteration" means (i) an unauthorized change in an instrument that purports to modify in any respect the obligation of a party, or (ii) an unauthorized addition of words or numbers or other change to an incomplete instrument relating to the obligation of a party.

(b) Except as provided in subsection (c), an alteration fraudulently made discharges a party whose obligation is affected by the alteration unless that party assents or is precluded from asserting the alteration. No other alteration discharges a party, and the instrument may be enforced according to its original terms.

(c) A payor bank or drawee paying a fraudulently altered instrument or a person taking it for value, in good faith and without notice of the alteration, may enforce rights with respect to the instrument (i) according to its original terms, or (ii) in the case of an incomplete instrument altered by unauthorized completion, according to its terms as completed.

§ 3–408.   Drawee Not Liable on Unaccepted Draft.

A check or other draft does not of itself operate as an assignment of funds in the hands of the drawee available for its payment, and the drawee is not liable on the instrument until the drawee accepts it.

§ 3–409.   Acceptance of Draft; Certified Check.

(a) "Acceptance" means the drawee's signed agreement to pay a draft as presented. It must be written on the draft and may consist of the drawee's signature alone. Acceptance may be made at any time and becomes effective when notification pursuant to instructions is given or the accepted draft is delivered for the purpose of giving rights on the acceptance to any person.

(b) A draft may be accepted although it has not been signed by the drawer, is otherwise incomplete, is overdue, or has been dishonored.

(c) If a draft is payable at a fixed period after sight and the acceptor fails to date the acceptance, the holder may complete the acceptance by supplying a date in good faith.

(d) "Certified check" means a check accepted by the bank on which it is drawn. Acceptance may be made as stated in subsection (a) or by a writing on the check which indicates that the check is certified. The drawee of a check has no obligation to certify the check, and refusal to certify is not dishonor of the check.

§ 3–410.   Acceptance Varying Draft.

(a) If the terms of a drawee's acceptance vary from the terms of the draft as presented, the holder may refuse the acceptance and treat the draft as dishonored. In that case, the drawee may cancel the acceptance.

(b) The terms of a draft are not varied by an acceptance to pay at a particular bank or place in the United States, unless the acceptance states that the draft is to be paid only at that bank or place.

(c) If the holder assents to an acceptance varying the terms of a draft, the obligation of each drawer and indorser that does not expressly assent to the acceptance is discharged.

§ 3–411.   Refusal to Pay Cashier's Checks, Teller's Checks, and Certified Checks.

(a) In this section, "obligated bank" means the acceptor of a certified check or the issuer of a cashier's check or teller's check bought from the issuer.

(b) If the obligated bank wrongfully (i) refuses to pay a cashier's check or certified check, (ii) stops payment of a teller's check, or (iii) refuses to pay a dishonored teller's check, the person asserting the right to enforce the check is entitled to compensation for expenses and loss of interest resulting from the nonpayment and may recover consequential damages if the obligated bank refuses to pay after receiving notice of particular circumstances giving rise to the damages.

(c) Expenses or consequential damages under subsection (b) are not recoverable if the refusal of the obligated bank to pay occurs because (i) the bank suspends payments, (ii) the obligated bank asserts a claim or defense of the bank that it has reasonable grounds to believe is available against the person entitled to enforce the instrument, (iii) the obligated bank has a reasonable doubt whether the person demanding payment is the person entitled to enforce the instrument, or (iv) payment is prohibited by law.

§ 3–412.   Obligation of Issuer of Note or Cashier's Check.

The issuer of a note or cashier's check or other draft drawn on the drawer is obliged to pay the instrument (i) according to its terms at the time it was issued or, if not issued, at the time it first came into possession of a holder, or (ii) if the issuer signed an incomplete instrument, according to its terms when completed, to the extent stated in Sections 3–115 and 3–407. The obligation is owed to a person entitled to enforce the instrument or to an indorser who paid the instrument under Section 3–415.

§ 3–413.   Obligation of Acceptor.

(a) The acceptor of a draft is obliged to pay the draft (i) according to its terms at the time it was accepted, even though the acceptance states that the draft is payable "as originally drawn" or equivalent terms, (ii) if the acceptance varies the terms of the draft, according to the terms of the draft as varied, or (iii) if the acceptance is of a draft that is an incomplete instrument, according to its terms when completed, to the extent stated in Sections 3–115 and 3–407. The obligation is owed to a person entitled to enforce the draft or to the drawer or an indorser who paid the draft under Section 3–414 or 3–415.

(b) If the certification of a check or other acceptance of a draft states the amount certified or accepted, the obligation of the acceptor is that amount. If (i) the certification or acceptance does not state an amount, (ii) the amount of the instrument is subsequently raised, and (iii) the instrument is then negotiated to a holder in due course, the obligation of the acceptor is the amount of the instrument at the time it was taken by the holder in due course.

§ 3–414.   Obligation of Drawer.

(a) This section does not apply to cashier's checks or other drafts drawn on the drawer.

(b) If an unaccepted draft is dishonored, the drawer is obliged to pay the draft (i) according to its terms at the time it was issued or, if not issued, at the time it first came into possession of a holder, or (ii) if the drawer signed an incomplete instrument, according to its terms when completed, to the extent stated in Sections 3–115 and 3–407. The obligation is owed to a person entitled to enforce the draft or to an indorser who paid the draft under Section 3–415.

(c) If a draft is accepted by a bank, the drawer is discharged, regardless of when or by whom acceptance was obtained.

(d) If a draft is accepted and the acceptor is not a bank, the obligation of the drawer to pay the draft if the draft is dishonored by the acceptor is the same as the obligation of an indorser under Section 3–415(a) and (c).

(e) If a draft states that it is drawn "without recourse" or otherwise disclaims liability of the drawer to pay the draft, the drawer is not liable under subsection (b) to pay the draft if the draft is not a check. A disclaimer of the liability stated in subsection (b) is not effective if the draft is a check.

(f) If (i) a check is not presented for payment or given to a depositary bank for collection within 30 days after its date, (ii) the drawee suspends payments after expiration of the 30-day period without paying the check, and (iii) because of the suspension of payments, the drawer is deprived of funds maintained with the drawee to cover payment of the check, the drawer to the extent deprived of funds may discharge its obligation to pay the check by assigning to the person entitled to enforce the check the rights of the drawer against the drawee with respect to the funds.

§ 3–415. Obligation of Indorser.

(a) Subject to subsections (b), (c), and (d) and to Section 3–419(d), if an instrument is dishonored, an indorser is obliged to pay the amount due on the instrument (i) according to the terms of the instrument at the time it was indorsed, or (ii) if the indorser indorsed an incomplete instrument, according to its terms when completed, to the extent stated in Sections 3–115 and 3–407. The obligation of the indorser is owed to a person entitled to enforce the instrument or to a subsequent indorser who paid the instrument under this section.

(b) If an indorsement states that it is made "without recourse" or otherwise disclaims liability of the indorser, the indorser is not liable under subsection (a) to pay the instrument.

(c) If notice of dishonor of an instrument is required by Section 3–503 and notice of dishonor complying with that section is not given to an indorser, the liability of the indorser under subsection (a) is discharged.

(d) If a draft is accepted by a bank after an indorsement is made, the liability of the indorser under subsection (a) is discharged.

(e) If an indorser of a check is liable under subsection (a) and the check is not presented for payment, or given to a depositary bank for collection, within 30 days after the day the indorsement was made, the liability of the indorser under subsection (a) is discharged.

As amended in 1993.

§ 3–416. Transfer Warranties.

(a) A person who transfers an instrument for consideration warrants to the transferee and, if the transfer is by indorsement, to any subsequent transferee that:

(1) the warrantor is a person entitled to enforce the instrument;
(2) all signatures on the instrument are authentic and authorized;
(3) the instrument has not been altered;
(4) the instrument is not subject to a defense or claim in recoupment of any party which can be asserted against the warrantor; and
(5) the warrantor has no knowledge of any insolvency proceeding commenced with respect to the maker or acceptor or, in the case of an unaccepted draft, the drawer.

(b) A person to whom the warranties under subsection (a) are made and who took the instrument in good faith may recover from the warrantor as damages for breach of warranty an amount equal to the loss suffered as a result of the breach, but not more than the amount of the instrument plus expenses and loss of interest incurred as a result of the breach.

(c) The warranties stated in subsection (a) cannot be disclaimed with respect to checks. Unless notice of a claim for breach of warranty is given to the warrantor within 30 days after the claimant has reason to know of the breach and the identity of the warrantor, the liability of the warrantor under subsection (b) is discharged to the extent of any loss caused by the delay in giving notice of the claim.

(d) A [cause of action] for breach of warranty under this section accrues when the claimant has reason to know of the breach.

§ 3–417. Presentment Warranties.

(a) If an unaccepted draft is presented to the drawee for payment or acceptance and the drawee pays or accepts the draft, (i) the person obtaining payment or acceptance, at the time of presentment, and (ii) a previous transferor of the draft, at the time of transfer, warrant to the drawee making payment or accepting the draft in good faith that:

(1) the warrantor is, or was, at the time the warrantor transferred the draft, a person entitled to enforce the draft or authorized to obtain payment or acceptance of the draft on behalf of a person entitled to enforce the draft;
(2) the draft has not been altered; and
(3) the warrantor has no knowledge that the signature of the drawer of the draft is unauthorized.

(b) A drawee making payment may recover from any warrantor damages for breach of warranty equal to the amount paid by the drawee less the amount the drawee received or is entitled to receive from the drawer because of the payment. In addition, the drawee is entitled to compensation for expenses and loss of interest resulting from the breach. The right of the drawee to recover damages under this subsection is not affected by any failure of the drawee to exercise ordinary care in making payment. If the drawee accepts the draft, breach of warranty is a defense to the obligation of the acceptor. If the acceptor makes payment with respect to the draft, the acceptor is entitled to recover from any warrantor for breach of warranty the amounts stated in this subsection.

(c) If a drawee asserts a claim for breach of warranty under subsection (a) based on an unauthorized indorsement of the draft or an alteration of the draft, the warrantor may defend by proving that the indorsement is effective under Section 3–404 or 3–405 or the drawer is precluded under Section 3–406 or 4–406 from asserting against the drawee the unauthorized indorsement or alteration.

(d) If (i) a dishonored draft is presented for payment to the drawer or an indorser or (ii) any other instrument is presented for payment to a party obliged to pay the instrument, and (iii) payment is received, the following rules apply:

(1) The person obtaining payment and a prior transferor of the instrument warrant to the person making payment in good faith that the warrantor is, or was, at the time the warrantor transferred the instrument, a person entitled to enforce the instrument or authorized to obtain payment on behalf of a person entitled to enforce the instrument.
(2) The person making payment may recover from any warrantor for breach of warranty an amount equal to the amount paid plus expenses and loss of interest resulting from the breach.

(e) The warranties stated in subsections (a) and (d) cannot be disclaimed with respect to checks. Unless notice of a claim for breach of warranty is given to the warrantor within 30 days after the claimant has reason to know of the breach and the identity of the warrantor, the liability of the warrantor under subsection (b) or (d) is discharged to the extent of any loss caused by the delay in giving notice of the claim.

(f) A [cause of action] for breach of warranty under this section accrues when the claimant has reason to know of the breach.

§ 3–418.   Payment or Acceptance by Mistake.

(a) Except as provided in subsection (c), if the drawee of a draft pays or accepts the draft and the drawee acted on the mistaken belief that (i) payment of the draft had not been stopped pursuant to Section 4–403 or (ii) the signature of the drawer of the draft was authorized, the drawee may recover the amount of the draft from the person to whom or for whose benefit payment was made or, in the case of acceptance, may revoke the acceptance. Rights of the drawee under this subsection are not affected by failure of the drawee to exercise ordinary care in paying or accepting the draft.

(b) Except as provided in subsection (c), if an instrument has been paid or accepted by mistake and the case is not covered by subsection (a), the person paying or accepting may, to the extent permitted by the law governing mistake and restitution, (i) recover the payment from the person to whom or for whose benefit payment was made or (ii) in the case of acceptance, may revoke the acceptance.

(c) The remedies provided by subsection (a) or (b) may not be asserted against a person who took the instrument in good

faith and for value or who in good faith changed position in reliance on the payment or acceptance. This subsection does not limit remedies provided by Section 3–417 or 4–407.

(d) Notwithstanding Section 4–215, if an instrument is paid or accepted by mistake and the payor or acceptor recovers payment or revokes acceptance under subsection (a) or (b), the instrument is deemed not to have been paid or accepted and is treated as dishonored, and the person from whom payment is recovered has rights as a person entitled to enforce the dishonored instrument.

§ 3–419.   Instruments Signed for Accommodation.

(a) If an instrument is issued for value given for the benefit of a party to the instrument ("accommodated party") and another party to the instrument ("accommodation party") signs the instrument for the purpose of incurring liability on the instrument without being a direct beneficiary of the value given for the instrument, the instrument is signed by the accommodation party "for accommodation."

(b) An accommodation party may sign the instrument as maker, drawer, acceptor, or indorser and, subject to subsection (d), is obliged to pay the instrument in the capacity in which the accommodation party signs. The obligation of an accommodation party may be enforced notwithstanding any statute of frauds and whether or not the accommodation party receives consideration for the accommodation.

(c) A person signing an instrument is presumed to be an accommodation party and there is notice that the instrument is signed for accommodation if the signature is an anomalous indorsement or is accompanied by words indicating that the signer is acting as surety or guarantor with respect to the obligation of another party to the instrument. Except as provided in Section 3–605, the obligation of an accommodation party to pay the instrument is not affected by the fact that the person enforcing the obligation had notice when the instrument was taken by that person that the accommodation party signed the instrument for accommodation.

(d) If the signature of a party to an instrument is accompanied by words indicating unambiguously that the party is guaranteeing collection rather than payment of the obligation of another party to the instrument, the signer is obliged to pay the amount due on the instrument to a person entitled to enforce the instrument only if (i) execution of judgment against the other party has been returned unsatisfied, (ii) the other party is insolvent or in an insolvency proceeding, (iii) the other party cannot be served with process, or (iv) it is otherwise apparent that payment cannot be obtained from the other party.

(e) An accommodation party who pays the instrument is entitled to reimbursement from the accommodated party and is entitled to enforce the instrument against the accommodated party. An accommodated party who pays the instrument has no right of recourse against, and is not entitled to contribution from, an accommodation party.

§ 3–420. Conversion of Instrument.

(a) The law applicable to conversion of personal property applies to instruments. An instrument is also converted if it is taken by transfer, other than a negotiation, from a person not entitled to enforce the instrument or a bank makes or obtains payment with respect to the instrument for a person not entitled to enforce the instrument or receive payment. An action for conversion of an instrument may not be brought by (i) the issuer or acceptor of the instrument or (ii) a payee or indorsee who did not receive delivery of the instrument either directly or through delivery to an agent or a co-payee.

(b) In an action under subsection (a), the measure of liability is presumed to be the amount payable on the instrument, but recovery may not exceed the amount of the plaintiff's interest in the instrument.

(c) A representative, other than a depositary bank, who has in good faith dealt with an instrument or its proceeds on behalf of one who was not the person entitled to enforce the instrument is not liable in conversion to that person beyond the amount of any proceeds that it has not paid out.

PART 5 Dishonor

§ 3–501. Presentment.

(a) "Presentment" means a demand made by or on behalf of a person entitled to enforce an instrument (i) to pay the instrument made to the drawee or a party obliged to pay the instrument or, in the case of a note or accepted draft payable at a bank, to the bank, or (ii) to accept a draft made to the drawee.

(b) The following rules are subject to Article 4, agreement of the parties, and clearing-house rules and the like:

(1) Presentment may be made at the place of payment of the instrument and must be made at the place of payment if the instrument is payable at a bank in the United States; may be made by any commercially reasonable means, including an oral, written, or electronic communication; is effective when the demand for payment or acceptance is received by the person to whom presentment is made; and is effective if made to any one of two or more makers, acceptors, drawees, or other payors.

(2) Upon demand of the person to whom presentment is made, the person making presentment must (i) exhibit the instrument, (ii) give reasonable identification and, if presentment is made on behalf of another person, reasonable evidence of authority to do so, and (…) sign a receipt on the instrument for any payment made or surrender the instrument if full payment is made.

(3) Without dishonoring the instrument, the party to whom presentment is made may (i) return the instrument for lack of a necessary indorsement, or (ii) refuse payment or acceptance for failure of the presentment to comply with the terms of the instrument, an agreement of the parties, or other applicable law or rule.

(4) The party to whom presentment is made may treat presentment as occurring on the next business day after the day of presentment if the party to whom presentment is made has established a cut-off hour not earlier than 2 P.M. for the receipt and processing of instruments presented for payment or acceptance and presentment is made after the cut-off hour.

§ 3–502. Dishonor.

(a) Dishonor of a note is governed by the following rules:

(1) If the note is payable on demand, the note is dishonored if presentment is duly made to the maker and the note is not paid on the day of presentment.

(2) If the note is not payable on demand and is payable at or through a bank or the terms of the note require presentment, the note is dishonored if presentment is duly made and the note is not paid on the day it becomes payable or the day of presentment, whichever is later.

(3) If the note is not payable on demand and paragraph (2) does not apply, the note is dishonored if it is not paid on the day it becomes payable.

(b) Dishonor of an unaccepted draft other than a documentary draft is governed by the following rules:

(1) If a check is duly presented for payment to the payor bank otherwise than for immediate payment over the counter, the check is dishonored if the payor bank makes timely return of the check or sends timely notice of dishonor or nonpayment under Section 4–301 or 4–302, or becomes accountable for the amount of the check under Section 4–302.

(2) If a draft is payable on demand and paragraph (1) does not apply, the draft is dishonored if presentment for payment is duly made to the drawee and the draft is not paid on the day of presentment.

(3) If a draft is payable on a date stated in the draft, the draft is dishonored if (i) presentment for payment is duly made to the drawee and payment is not made on the day the draft becomes payable or the day of presentment, whichever is later, or (ii) presentment for acceptance is duly made before the day the draft becomes payable and the draft is not accepted on the day of presentment.

(4) If a draft is payable on elapse of a period of time after sight or acceptance, the draft is dishonored if presentment for acceptance is duly made and the draft is not accepted on the day of presentment.

(c) Dishonor of an unaccepted documentary draft occurs according to the rules stated in subsection (b)(2), (3), and (4), except that payment or acceptance may be delayed without dishonor until no later than the close of the third business day of the drawee following the day on which payment or acceptance is required by those paragraphs.

(d) Dishonor of an accepted draft is governed by the following rules:

(1) If the draft is payable on demand, the draft is dishonored if presentment for payment is duly made to the acceptor and the draft is not paid on the day of presentment.

(2) If the draft is not payable on demand, the draft is dishonored if presentment for payment is duly made to the acceptor and

payment is not made on the day it becomes payable or the day of presentment, whichever is later.

(e) In any case in which presentment is otherwise required for dishonor under this section and presentment is excused under Section 3–504, dishonor occurs without presentment if the instrument is not duly accepted or paid.

(f) If a draft is dishonored because timely acceptance of the draft was not made and the person entitled to demand acceptance consents to a late acceptance, from the time of acceptance the draft is treated as never having been dishonored.

§ 3–503. Notice of Dishonor.

(a) The obligation of an indorser stated in Section 3–415(a) and the obligation of a drawer stated in Section 3–414(d) may not be enforced unless (i) the indorser or drawer is given notice of dishonor of the instrument complying with this section or (ii) notice of dishonor is excused under Section 3–504(b).

(b) Notice of dishonor may be given by any person; may be given by any commercially reasonable means, including an oral, written, or electronic communication; and is sufficient if it reasonably identifies the instrument and indicates that the instrument has been dishonored or has not been paid or accepted. Return of an instrument given to a bank for collection is sufficient notice of dishonor.

(c) Subject to Section 3–504(c), with respect to an instrument taken for collection by a collecting bank, notice of dishonor must be given (i) by the bank before midnight of the next banking day following the banking day on which the bank receives notice of dishonor of the instrument, or (ii) by any other person within 30 days following the day on which the person receives notice of dishonor. With respect to any other instrument, notice of dishonor must be given within 30 days following the day on which dishonor occurs.

§ 3–504. Excused Presentment and Notice of Dishonor.

(a) Presentment for payment or acceptance of an instrument is excused if (i) the person entitled to present the instrument cannot with reasonable diligence make presentment, (ii) the maker or acceptor has repudiated an obligation to pay the instrument or is dead or in insolvency proceedings, (iii) by the terms of the instrument presentment is not necessary to enforce the obligation of indorsers or the drawer, (iv) the drawer or indorser whose obligation is being enforced has waived presentment or otherwise has no reason to expect or right to require that the instrument be paid or accepted, or (v) the drawer instructed the drawee not to pay or accept the draft or the drawee was not obligated to the drawer to pay the draft.

(b) Notice of dishonor is excused if (i) by the terms of the instrument notice of dishonor is not necessary to enforce the obligation of a party to pay the instrument, or (ii) the party whose obligation is being enforced waived notice of dishonor. A waiver of presentment is also a waiver of notice of dishonor.

(c) Delay in giving notice of dishonor is excused if the delay was caused by circumstances beyond the control of the person giving the notice and the person giving the notice exercised reasonable diligence after the cause of the delay ceased to operate.

§ 3–505. Evidence of Dishonor.

(a) The following are admissible as evidence and create a presumption of dishonor and of any notice of dishonor stated:

(1) a document regular in form as provided in subsection (b) which purports to be a protest;

(2) a purported stamp or writing of the drawee, payor bank, or presenting bank on or accompanying the instrument stating that acceptance or payment has been refused unless reasons for the refusal are stated and the reasons are not consistent with dishonor;

(3) a book or record of the drawee, payor bank, or collecting bank, kept in the usual course of business which shows dishonor, even if there is no evidence of who made the entry.

(b) A protest is a certificate of dishonor made by a United States consul or vice consul, or a notary public or other person authorized to administer oaths by the law of the place where dishonor occurs. It may be made upon information satisfactory to that person. The protest must identify the instrument and certify either that presentment has been made or, if not made, the reason why it was not made, and that the instrument has been dishonored by nonacceptance or nonpayment. The protest may also certify that notice of dishonor has been given to some or all parties.

PART 6   Discharge and Payment

§ 3–601. Discharge and Effect of Discharge.

(a) The obligation of a party to pay the instrument is discharged as stated in this Article or by an act or agreement with the party which would discharge an obligation to pay money under a simple contract.

(b) Discharge of the obligation of a party is not effective against a person acquiring rights of a holder in due course of the instrument without notice of the discharge.

§ 3–602. Payment.

(a) Subject to subsection (b), an instrument is paid to the extent payment is made (i) by or on behalf of a party obliged to pay the instrument, and (ii) to a person entitled to enforce the instrument. To the extent of the payment, the obligation of the party obliged to pay the instrument is discharged even though payment is made with knowledge of a claim to the instrument under Section 3–306 by another person.

(b) The obligation of a party to pay the instrument is not discharged under subsection (a) if:

(1) a claim to the instrument under Section 3–306 is enforceable against the party receiving payment and (i) payment is made

with knowledge by the payor that payment is prohibited by injunction or similar process of a court of competent jurisdiction, or (ii) in the case of an instrument other than a cashier's check, teller's check, or certified check, the party making payment accepted, from the person having a claim to the instrument, indemnity against loss resulting from refusal to pay the person entitled to enforce the instrument; or

(2) the person making payment knows that the instrument is a stolen instrument and pays a person it knows is in wrongful possession of the instrument.

§ 3–603.   Tender of Payment.

(a) If tender of payment of an obligation to pay an instrument is made to a person entitled to enforce the instrument, the effect of tender is governed by principles of law applicable to tender of payment under a simple contract.

(b) If tender of payment of an obligation to pay an instrument is made to a person entitled to enforce the instrument and the tender is refused, there is discharge, to the extent of the amount of the tender, of the obligation of an indorser or accommodation party having a right of recourse with respect to the obligation to which the tender relates.

(c) If tender of payment of an amount due on an instrument is made to a person entitled to enforce the instrument, the obligation of the obligor to pay interest after the due date on the amount tendered is discharged. If presentment is required with respect to an instrument and the obligor is able and ready to pay on the due date at every place of payment stated in the instrument, the obligor is deemed to have made tender of payment on the due date to the person entitled to enforce the instrument.

§ 3–604.   Discharge by Cancellation or Renunciation.

(a) A person entitled to enforce an instrument, with or without consideration, may discharge the obligation of a party to pay the instrument (i) by an intentional voluntary act, such as surrender of the instrument to the party, destruction, mutilation, or cancellation of the instrument, cancellation or striking out of the party's signature, or the addition of words to the instrument indicating discharge, or (ii) by agreeing not to sue or otherwise renouncing rights against the party by a signed writing.

(b) Cancellation or striking out of an indorsement pursuant to subsection (a) does not affect the status and rights of a party derived from the indorsement.

§ 3–605.   Discharge of Indorsers and Accommodation Parties.

(a) In this section, the term "indorser" includes a drawer having the obligation described in Section 3–414(d).

(b) Discharge, under Section 3–604, of the obligation of a party to pay an instrument does not discharge the obligation of an indorser or accommodation party having a right of recourse against the discharged party.

(c) If a person entitled to enforce an instrument agrees, with or without consideration, to an extension of the due date of the obligation of a party to pay the instrument, the extension discharges an indorser or accommodation party having a right of recourse against the party whose obligation is extended to the extent the indorser or accommodation party proves that the extension caused loss to the indorser or accommodation party with respect to the right of recourse.

(d) If a person entitled to enforce an instrument agrees, with or without consideration, to a material modification of the obligation of a party other than an extension of the due date, the modification discharges the obligation of an indorser or accommodation party having a right of recourse against the person whose obligation is modified to the extent the modification causes loss to the indorser or accommodation party with respect to the right of recourse. The loss suffered by the indorser or accommodation party as a result of the modification is equal to the amount of the right of recourse unless the person enforcing the instrument proves that no loss was caused by the modification or that the loss caused by the modification was an amount less than the amount of the right of recourse.

(e) If the obligation of a party to pay an instrument is secured by an interest in collateral and a person entitled to enforce the instrument impairs the value of the interest in collateral, the obligation of an indorser or accommodation party having a right of recourse against the obligor is discharged to the extent of the impairment. The value of an interest in collateral is impaired to the extent (i) the value of the interest is reduced to an amount less than the amount of the right of recourse of the party asserting discharge, or (ii) the reduction in value of the interest causes an increase in the amount by which the amount of the right of recourse exceeds the value of the interest. The burden of proving impairment is on the party asserting discharge.

(f) If the obligation of a party is secured by an interest in collateral not provided by an accommodation party and a person entitled to enforce the instrument impairs the value of the interest in collateral, the obligation of any party who is jointly and severally liable with respect to the secured obligation is discharged to the extent the impairment causes the party asserting discharge to pay more than that party would have been obliged to pay, taking into account rights of contribution, if impairment had not occurred. If the party asserting discharge is an accommodation party not entitled to discharge under subsection (e), the party is deemed to have a right to contribution based on joint and several liability rather than a right to reimbursement. The burden of proving impairment is on the party asserting discharge.

(g) Under subsection (e) or (f), impairing value of an interest in collateral includes (i) failure to obtain or maintain perfection or recordation of the interest in collateral, (ii) release of collateral without substitution of collateral of equal value, (iii) failure to perform a duty to preserve the value of collateral owed, under Article 9 or other law, to a debtor or surety or other person secondarily liable, or (iv) failure to comply with applicable law in disposing of collateral.

(h) An accommodation party is not discharged under subsection (c), (d), or (e) unless the person entitled to enforce the instrument knows of the accommodation or has notice under Section 3–419(c) that the instrument was signed for accommodation.

(i) A party is not discharged under this section if (i) the party asserting discharge consents to the event or conduct that is the basis of the discharge, or (ii) the instrument or a separate agreement of the party provides for waiver of discharge under this section either specifically or by general language indicating that parties waive defenses based on suretyship or impairment of collateral.

ADDENDUM TO REVISED ARTICLE III

Notes to Legislative Counsel

1. If revised Article 3 is adopted in your state, the reference in Section 2–511 to Section 3–802 should be changed to Section 3–310.

2. If revised Article 3 is adopted in your state and the Uniform Fiduciaries Act is also in effect in your state, you may want to consider amending Uniform Fiduciaries Act § 9 to conform to Section 3–307(b)(2)(iii) and (4)(iii). See Official Comment 3 to Section 3–307.

REVISED ARTICLE IV BANK DEPOSITS AND COLLECTIONS

PART 1   General Provisions and Definitions

§ 4–101.   Short Title.

This Article may be cited as Uniform Commercial Code—Bank Deposits and Collections.

As amended in 1990.

§ 4–102.   Applicability.

(a) To the extent that items within this Article are also within Articles 3 and 8, they are subject to those Articles. If there is conflict, this Article governs Article 3, but Article 8 governs this Article.

(b) The liability of a bank for action or non-action with respect to an item handled by it for purposes of presentment, payment, or collection is governed by the law of the place where the bank is located. In the case of action or non-action by or at a branch or separate office of a bank, its liability is governed by the law of the place where the branch or separate office is located.

§ 4–103.   Variation by Agreement; Measure of Damages; Action Constituting Ordinary Care.

(a) The effect of the provisions of this Article may be varied by agreement, but the parties to the agreement cannot disclaim a bank's responsibility for its lack of good faith or failure to exercise ordinary care or limit the measure of damages for the lack or failure. However, the parties may determine by agreement the standards by which the bank's responsibility is to be measured if those standards are not manifestly unreasonable.

(b) Federal Reserve regulations and operating circulars, clearing-house rules, and the like have the effect of agreements under subsection (a), whether or not specifically assented to by all parties interested in items handled.

(c) Action or non-action approved by this Article or pursuant to Federal Reserve regulations or operating circulars is the exercise of ordinary care and, in the absence of special instructions, action or non-action consistent with clearing-house rules and the like or with a general banking usage not disapproved by this Article, is prima facie the exercise of ordinary care.

(d) The specification or approval of certain procedures by this Article is not disapproval of other procedures that may be reasonable under the circumstances.

(e) The measure of damages for failure to exercise ordinary care in handling an item is the amount of the item reduced by an amount that could not have been realized by the exercise of ordinary care. If there is also bad faith it includes any other damages the party suffered as a proximate consequence.

As amended in 1990.

§ 4–104.   Definitions and Index of Definitions.

(a) In this Article, unless the context otherwise requires:

(1) "Account" means any deposit or credit account with a bank, including a demand, time, savings, passbook, share draft, or like account, other than an account evidenced by a certificate of deposit;

(2) "Afternoon" means the period of a day between noon and midnight;

(3) "Banking day" means the part of a day on which a bank is open to the public for carrying on substantially all of its banking functions;

(4) "Clearing house" means an association of banks or other payors regularly clearing items;

(5) "Customer" means a person having an account with a bank or for whom a bank has agreed to collect items, including a bank that maintains an account at another bank;

(6) "Documentary draft" means a draft to be presented for acceptance or payment if specified documents, certificated securities (Section 8–102) or instructions for uncertificated securities (Section 8–102), or other certificates, statements, or the like are to be received by the drawee or other payor before acceptance or payment of the draft;

(7) "Draft" means a draft as defined in Section 3–104 or an item, other than an instrument, that is an order;

(8) "Drawee" means a person ordered in a draft to make payment;

(9) "Item" means an instrument or a promise or order to pay money handled by a bank for collection or payment. The term does not include a payment order governed by Article 4A or a credit or debit card slip;

(10) "Midnight deadline" with respect to a bank is midnight on its next banking day following the banking day on which it receives the relevant item or notice or from which the time for taking action commences to run, whichever is later;

(11) "Settle" means to pay in cash, by clearing-house settlement, in a charge or credit or by remittance, or otherwise as agreed. A settlement may be either provisional or final;

(12) "Suspends payments" with respect to a bank means that it has been closed by order of the supervisory authorities, that a public officer has been appointed to take it over, or that it ceases or refuses to make payments in the ordinary course of business.

    (b) [Other definitions' section references deleted.]

    (c) [Other definitions' section references deleted.]

    (d) In addition, Article 1 contains general definitions and principles of construction and interpretation applicable throughout this Article.

§ 4–105. "Bank"; "Depositary Bank"; "Payor Bank"; "Intermediary Bank"; "Collecting Bank"; "Presenting Bank".

In this Article:

(1) "Bank" means a person engaged in the business of banking, including a savings bank, savings and loan association, credit union, or trust company;

(2) "Depositary bank" means the first bank to take an item even though it is also the payor bank, unless the item is presented for immediate payment over the counter;

(3) "Payor bank" means a bank that is the drawee of a draft;

(4) "Intermediary bank" means a bank to which an item is transferred in course of collection except the depositary or payor bank;

(5) "Collecting bank" means a bank handling an item for collection except the payor bank;

(6) "Presenting bank" means a bank presenting an item except a payor bank.

§ 4–106. Payable Through or Payable at Bank: Collecting Bank.

(a) If an item states that it is "payable through" a bank identified in the item, (i) the item designates the bank as a collecting bank and does not by itself authorize the bank to pay the item, and (ii) the item may be presented for payment only by or through the bank.

Alternative A   (b) If an item states that it is "payable at" a bank identified in the item, the item is equivalent to a draft drawn on the bank.

Alternative B   (b) If an item states that it is "payable at" a bank identified in the item, (i) the item designates the bank as a collecting bank and does not by itself authorize the bank to pay the item, and (ii) the item may be presented for payment only by or through the bank.

(c) If a draft names a nonbank drawee and it is unclear whether a bank named in the draft is a co-drawee or a collecting bank, the bank is a collecting bank.

As added in 1990.

§ 4–107. Separate Office of Bank.

A branch or separate office of a bank is a separate bank for the purpose of computing the time within which and determining the place at or to which action may be taken or notices or orders shall be given under this Article and under Article 3.

As amended in 1962 and 1990.

§ 4–108. Time of Receipt of Items.

    (a) For the purpose of allowing time to process items, prove balances, and make the necessary entries on its books to determine its position for the day, a bank may fix an afternoon hour of 2 P.M. or later as a cutoff hour for the handling of money and items and the making of entries on its books.

    (b) An item or deposit of money received on any day after a cutoff hour so fixed or after the close of the banking day may be treated as being received at the opening of the next banking day.

As amended in 1990.

§ 4–109. Delays.

    (a) Unless otherwise instructed, a collecting bank in a good faith effort to secure payment of a specific item drawn on a payor other than a bank, and with or without the approval of any person involved, may waive, modify, or extend time limits imposed or permitted by this [act] for a period not exceeding two additional banking days without discharge of drawers or indorsers or liability to its transferor or a prior party.

    (b) Delay by a collecting bank or payor bank beyond time limits prescribed or permitted by this [act] or by instructions is excused if (i) the delay is caused by interruption of communication or computer facilities, suspension of payments by another bank, war, emergency conditions, failure of equipment, or other circumstances beyond the control of the bank, and (ii) the bank exercises such diligence as the circumstances require.

§ 4–110.   Electronic Presentment.

(a) "Agreement for electronic presentment" means an agreement, clearing-house rule, or Federal Reserve regulation or operating circular, providing that presentment of an item may be made by transmission of an image of an item or information describing the item ("presentment notice") rather than delivery of the item itself. The agreement may provide for procedures governing retention, presentment, payment, dishonor, and other matters concerning items subject to the agreement.

(b) Presentment of an item pursuant to an agreement for presentment is made when the presentment notice is received.

(c) If presentment is made by presentment notice, a reference to "item" or "check" in this Article means the presentment notice unless the context otherwise indicates.

As added in 1990.

§ 4–111.   Statute of Limitations.

An action to enforce an obligation, duty, or right arising under this Article must be commenced within three years after the [cause of action] accrues.

As added in 1990.

PART 2   Collection of Items: Depositary and Collecting Banks

§ 4–201.   Status of Collecting Bank as Agent and Provisional Status of Credits; Applicability of Article; Item Indorsed "Pay Any Bank".

(a) Unless a contrary intent clearly appears and before the time that a settlement given by a collecting bank for an item is or becomes final, the bank, with respect to an item, is an agent or sub-agent of the owner of the item and any settlement given for the item is provisional. This provision applies regardless of the form of indorsement or lack of indorsement and even though credit given for the item is subject to immediate withdrawal as of right or is in fact withdrawn; but the continuance of ownership of an item by its owner and any rights of the owner to proceeds of the item are subject to rights of a collecting bank, such as those resulting from outstanding advances on the item and rights of recoupment or setoff. If an item is handled by banks for purposes of presentment, payment, collection, or return, the relevant provisions of this Article apply even though action of the parties clearly establishes that a particular bank has purchased the item and is the owner of it.

(b) After an item has been indorsed with the words "pay any bank" or the like, only a bank may acquire the rights of a holder until the item has been:

(1) returned to the customer initiating collection; or

(2) specially indorsed by a bank to a person who is not a bank.

As amended in 1990.

§ 4–202.   Responsibility for Collection or Return; When Action Timely.

(a) A collecting bank must exercise ordinary care in:

(1) presenting an item or sending it for presentment;

(2) sending notice of dishonor or nonpayment or returning an item other than a documentary draft to the bank's transferor after learning that the item has not been paid or accepted, as the case may be;

(3) settling for an item when the bank receives final settlement; and

(4) notifying its transferor of any loss or delay in transit within a reasonable time after discovery thereof.

(b) A collecting bank exercises ordinary care under subsection (a) by taking proper action before its midnight deadline following receipt of an item, notice, or settlement. Taking proper action within a reasonably longer time may constitute the exercise of ordinary care, but the bank has the burden of establishing timeliness.

(c) Subject to subsection (a)(1), a bank is not liable for the insolvency, neglect, misconduct, mistake, or default of another bank or person or for loss or destruction of an item in the possession of others or in transit.

As amended in 1990.

§ 4–203.   Effect of Instructions.

Subject to Article 3 concerning conversion of instruments (Section 3–420) and restrictive indorsements (Section 3–206), only a collecting bank's transferor can give instructions that affect the bank or constitute notice to it, and a collecting bank is not liable to prior parties for any action taken pursuant to the instructions or in accordance with any agreement with its transferor.

§ 4–204.   Methods of Sending and Presenting; Sending Directly to Payor Bank.

(a) A collecting bank shall send items by a reasonably prompt method, taking into consideration relevant instructions, the nature of the item, the number of those items on hand, the cost of collection involved, and the method generally used by it or others to present those items.

(b) A collecting bank may send:

(1) an item directly to the payor bank;

(2) an item to a nonbank payor if authorized by its transferor; and

(3) an item other than documentary drafts to a nonbank payor, if authorized by Federal Reserve regulation or operating circular, clearing-house rule, or the like.

(c) Presentment may be made by a presenting bank at a place where the payor bank or other payor has requested that presentment be made.

As amended in 1990.

§ 4–205.   Depository Bank Holder of Unindorsed Item.

If a customer delivers an item to a depository bank for collection:

(1) the depository bank becomes a holder of the item at the time it receives the item for collection if the customer at the time of delivery was a holder of the item, whether or not the customer indorses the item, and, if the bank satisfies the other requirements of Section 3–302, it is a holder in due course; and

(2) the depository bank warrants to collecting banks, the payor bank or other payor, and the drawer that the amount of the item was paid to the customer or deposited to the customer's account.

As amended in 1990.

§ 4–206.   Transfer Between Banks.

Any agreed method that identifies the transferor bank is sufficient for the item's further transfer to another bank.

As amended in 1990.

§ 4–207.   Transfer Warranties.

(a) A customer or collecting bank that transfers an item and receives a settlement or other consideration warrants to the transferee and to any subsequent collecting bank that:

(1) the warrantor is a person entitled to enforce the item;

(2) all signatures on the item are authentic and authorized;

(3) the item has not been altered;

(4) the item is not subject to a defense or claim in recoupment (Section 3–305(a)) of any party that can be asserted against the warrantor; and

(5) the warrantor has no knowledge of any insolvency proceeding commenced with respect to the maker or acceptor or, in the case of an unaccepted draft, the drawer.

(b) If an item is dishonored, a customer or collecting bank transferring the item and receiving settlement or other consideration is obliged to pay the amount due on the item (i) according to the terms of the item at the time it was transferred, or (ii) if the transfer was of an incomplete item, according to its terms when completed as stated in Sections 3–115 and 3–407. The obligation of a transferor is owed to the transferee and to any subsequent collecting bank that takes the item in good faith. A transferor cannot disclaim its obligation under this subsection by an indorsement stating that it is made "without recourse" or otherwise disclaiming liability.

(c) A person to whom the warranties under subsection (a) are made and who took the item in good faith may recover from the warrantor as damages for breach of warranty an amount equal to the loss suffered as a result of the breach, but not more than the amount of the item plus expenses and loss of interest incurred as a result of the breach.

(d) The warranties stated in subsection (a) cannot be disclaimed with respect to checks. Unless notice of a claim for breach of warranty is given to the warrantor within 30 days after the claimant has reason to know of the breach and the identity of the warrantor, the warrantor is discharged to the extent of any loss caused by the delay in giving notice of the claim.

(e) A cause of action for breach of warranty under this section accrues when the claimant has reason to know of the breach.

As amended in 1990.

§ 4–208.   Presentment Warranties.

(a) If an unaccepted draft is presented to the drawee for payment or acceptance and the drawee pays or accepts the draft, (i) the person obtaining payment or acceptance, at the time of presentment, and (ii) a previous transferor of the draft, at the time of transfer, warrant to the drawee that pays or accepts the draft in good faith that:

(1) the warrantor is, or was, at the time the warrantor transferred the draft, a person entitled to enforce the draft or authorized to obtain payment or acceptance of the draft on behalf of a person entitled to enforce the draft;

(2) the draft has not been altered; and

(3) the warrantor has no knowledge that the signature of the purported drawer of the draft is unauthorized.

(b) A drawee making payment may recover from a warrantor damages for breach of warranty equal to the amount paid by the drawee less the amount the drawee received or is entitled to receive from the drawer because of the payment. In addition, the drawee is entitled to compensation for expenses and loss of interest resulting from the breach. The right of the drawee to recover damages under this subsection is not affected by any failure of the drawee to exercise ordinary care in making payment. If the drawee accepts the draft (i) breach of warranty is a defense to the obligation of the acceptor, and (ii) if the acceptor makes payment with respect to the draft, the acceptor is entitled to recover from a warrantor for breach of warranty the amounts stated in this subsection.

(c) If a drawee asserts a claim for breach of warranty under subsection (a) based on an unauthorized indorsement of the draft or an alteration of the draft, the warrantor may defend by proving that the indorsement is effective under Section 3–404 or 3–405 or the drawer is precluded under Section 3–406 or 4–406 from asserting against the drawee the unauthorized indorsement or alteration.

(d) If (i) a dishonored draft is presented for payment to the drawer or an indorser or (ii) any other item is presented for payment to a party obliged to pay the item, and the item is paid, the person obtaining payment and a prior transferor of the item warrant to the person making payment in good faith that the warrantor is, or was, at the time the warrantor transferred the item, a person entitled to enforce the item or authorized to obtain payment on behalf of a person entitled to enforce the item. The person making payment may recover from any warrantor for breach of warranty an amount equal to the amount paid plus expenses and loss of interest resulting from the breach.

(e) The warranties stated in subsections (a) and (d) cannot be disclaimed with respect to checks. Unless notice of a claim for breach of warranty is given to the warrantor within 30 days after the claimant has reason to know of the breach and the identity of the warrantor, the warrantor is discharged to the extent of any loss caused by the delay in giving notice of the claim.

(f) A cause of action for breach of warranty under this section accrues when the claimant has reason to know of the breach.

As amended in 1990.

§ 4–209.   Encoding and Retention Warranties.

(a) A person who encodes information on or with respect to an item after issue warrants to any subsequent collecting bank and to the payor bank or other payor that the information is correctly encoded. If the customer of a depositary bank encodes, that bank also makes the warranty.

(b) A person who undertakes to retain an item pursuant to an agreement for electronic presentment warrants to any subsequent collecting bank and to the payor bank or other payor that retention and presentment of the item comply with the agreement. If a customer of a depositary bank undertakes to retain an item, that bank also makes this warranty.

(c) A person to whom warranties are made under this section and who took the item in good faith may recover from the warrantor as damages for breach of warranty an amount equal to the loss suffered as a result of the breach, plus expenses and loss of interest incurred as a result of the breach.

As added in 1990.

§ 4–210.   Security Interest of Collecting Bank in Items, Accompanying Documents and Proceeds.

(a) A collecting bank has a security interest in an item and any accompanying documents or the proceeds of either:

(1) in case of an item deposited in an account, to the extent to which credit given for the item has been withdrawn or applied;

(2) in case of an item for which it has given credit available for withdrawal as of right, to the extent of the credit given, whether or not the credit is drawn upon or there is a right of charge-back; or

(3) if it makes an advance on or against the item.

(b) If credit given for several items received at one time or pursuant to a single agreement is withdrawn or applied in part,

the security interest remains upon all the items, any accompanying documents or the proceeds of either. For the purpose of this section, credits first given are first withdrawn.

(c) Receipt by a collecting bank of a final settlement for an item is a realization on its security interest in the item, accompanying documents, and proceeds. So long as the bank does not receive final settlement for the item or give up possession of the item or accompanying documents for purposes other than collection, the security interest continues to that extent and is subject to Article 9, but:

(1) no security agreement is necessary to make the security interest enforceable (Section 9–203(1)(a));

(2) no filing is required to perfect the security interest; and

(3) the security interest has priority over conflicting perfected security interests in the item, accompanying documents, or proceeds.

As amended in 1990 and 1999.

§ 4–211.   When Bank Gives Value for Purposes of Holder in Due Course.

For purposes of determining its status as a holder in due course, a bank has given value to the extent it has a security interest in an item, if the bank otherwise complies with the requirements of Section 3–302 on what constitutes a holder in due course.

As amended in 1990.

§ 4–212.   Presentment by Notice of Item Not Payable by, Through, or at Bank; Liability of Drawer or Indorser.

(a) Unless otherwise instructed, a collecting bank may present an item not payable by, through, or at a bank by sending to the party to accept or pay a written notice that the bank holds the item for acceptance or payment. The notice must be sent in time to be received on or before the day when presentment is due and the bank must meet any requirement of the party to accept or pay under Section 3–501 by the close of the bank's next banking day after it knows of the requirement.

(b) If presentment is made by notice and payment, acceptance, or request for compliance with a requirement under Section 3–501 is not received by the close of business on the day after maturity or, in the case of demand items, by the close of business on the third banking day after notice was sent, the presenting bank may treat the item as dishonored and charge any drawer or indorser by sending it notice of the facts.

As amended in 1990.

§ 4–213.   Medium and Time of Settlement by Bank.

(a) With respect to settlement by a bank, the medium and time of settlement may be prescribed by Federal Reserve regulations or circulars, clearing-house rules, and the like, or agreement. In the absence of such prescription:

(1) the medium of settlement is cash or credit to an account in a Federal Reserve bank of or specified by the person to receive settlement; and

(2) the time of settlement is:

(i) with respect to tender of settlement by cash, a cashier's check, or teller's check, when the cash or check is sent or delivered;

(ii) with respect to tender of settlement by credit in an account in a Federal Reserve Bank, when the credit is made;

(iii) with respect to tender of settlement by a credit or debit to an account in a bank, when the credit or debit is made or, in the case of tender of settlement by authority to charge an account, when the authority is sent or delivered; or

(iv) with respect to tender of settlement by a funds transfer, when payment is made pursuant to Section 4A–406(a) to the person receiving settlement.

(b) If the tender of settlement is not by a medium authorized by subsection (a) or the time of settlement is not fixed by subsection (a), no settlement occurs until the tender of settlement is accepted by the person receiving settlement.

(c) If settlement for an item is made by cashier's check or teller's check and the person receiving settlement, before its midnight deadline:

(1) presents or forwards the check for collection, settlement is final when the check is finally paid; or

(2) fails to present or forward the check for collection, settlement is final at the midnight deadline of the person receiving settlement.

(d) If settlement for an item is made by giving authority to charge the account of the bank giving settlement in the bank receiving settlement, settlement is final when the charge is made by the bank receiving settlement if there are funds available in the account for the amount of the item.

As amended in 1990.

§ 4–214.   Right of Charge-Back or Refund; Liability of Collecting Bank: Return of Item.

(a) If a collecting bank has made provisional settlement with its customer for an item and fails by reason of dishonor, suspension of payments by a bank, or otherwise to receive settlement for the item which is or becomes final, the bank may revoke the settlement given by it, charge back the amount of any credit given for the item to its customer's account, or obtain refund from its customer, whether or not it is able to return the item, if by its midnight deadline or within a longer reasonable time after it learns the facts it returns the item or sends notification of the facts. If the return or notice is delayed beyond the bank's midnight deadline or a longer reasonable time after it learns the facts, the bank may revoke the settlement, charge back the credit, or obtain refund from its customer, but it is liable for any loss resulting from the delay. These rights to revoke, charge back,

and obtain refund terminate if and when a settlement for the item received by the bank is or becomes final.

(b) A collecting bank returns an item when it is sent or delivered to the bank's customer or transferor or pursuant to its instructions.

(c) A depositary bank that is also the payor may charge back the amount of an item to its customer's account or obtain refund in accordance with the section governing return of an item received by a payor bank for credit on its books (Section 4–301).

(d) The right to charge back is not affected by:

(1) previous use of a credit given for the item; or

(2) failure by any bank to exercise ordinary care with respect to the item, but a bank so failing remains liable.

(e) A failure to charge back or claim refund does not affect other rights of the bank against the customer or any other party.

(f) If credit is given in dollars as the equivalent of the value of an item payable in foreign money, the dollar amount of any charge-back or refund must be calculated on the basis of the bank-offered spot rate for the foreign money prevailing on the day when the person entitled to the charge-back or refund learns that it will not receive payment in ordinary course.

As amended in 1990.

§ 4–215.   Final Payment of Item by Payor Bank; When Provisional Debits and Credits Become Final; When Certain Credits Become Available for Withdrawal.

(a) An item is finally paid by a payor bank when the bank has first done any of the following:

(1) paid the item in cash;

(2) settled for the item without having a right to revoke the settlement under statute, clearing-house rule, or agreement; or

(3) made a provisional settlement for the item and failed to revoke the settlement in the time and manner permitted by statute, clearing-house rule, or agreement.

(b) If provisional settlement for an item does not become final, the item is not finally paid.

(c) If provisional settlement for an item between the presenting and payor banks is made through a clearing house or by debits or credits in an account between them, then to the extent that provisional debits or credits for the item are entered in accounts between the presenting and payor banks or between the presenting and successive prior collecting banks seriatim, they become final upon final payment of the item by the payor bank.

(d) If a collecting bank receives a settlement for an item which is or becomes final, the bank is accountable to its customer for the amount of the item and any provisional credit given for the item in an account with its customer becomes final.

(e) Subject to (i) applicable law stating a time for availability of funds and (ii) any right of the bank to apply the credit to an obligation of the customer, credit given by a bank for an item in a customer's account becomes available for withdrawal as of right:

(1) if the bank has received a provisional settlement for the item, when the settlement becomes final and the bank has had a reasonable time to receive return of the item and the item has not been received within that time;

(2) if the bank is both the depositary bank and the payor bank, and the item is finally paid, at the opening of the bank's second banking day following receipt of the item.

(f) Subject to applicable law stating a time for availability of funds and any right of a bank to apply a deposit to an obligation of the depositor, a deposit of money becomes available for withdrawal as of right at the opening of the bank's next banking day after receipt of the deposit.

As amended in 1990.

§ 4–216.   Insolvency and Preference.

(a) If an item is in or comes into the possession of a payor or collecting bank that suspends payment and the item has not been finally paid, the item must be returned by the receiver, trustee, or agent in charge of the closed bank to the presenting bank or the closed bank's customer.

(b) If a payor bank finally pays an item and suspends payments without making a settlement for the item with its customer or the presenting bank which settlement is or becomes final, the owner of the item has a preferred claim against the payor bank.

(c) If a payor bank gives or a collecting bank gives or receives a provisional settlement for an item and thereafter suspends payments, the suspension does not prevent or interfere with the settlement's becoming final if the finality occurs automatically upon the lapse of certain time or the happening of certain events.

(d) If a collecting bank receives from subsequent parties settlement for an item, which settlement is or becomes final and the bank suspends payments without making a settlement for the item with its customer which settlement is or becomes final, the owner of the item has a preferred claim against the collecting bank.

As amended in 1990.

PART 3   Collection of Items: Payor Banks

§ 4–301.   Deferred Posting; Recovery of Payment by Return of Items; Time of Dishonor; Return of Items by Payor Bank.

(a) If a payor bank settles for a demand item other than a documentary draft presented otherwise than for immediate payment over the counter before midnight of the banking day

of receipt, the payor bank may revoke the settlement and recover the settlement if, before it has made final payment and before its midnight deadline, it

(1) returns the item; or

(2) sends written notice of dishonor or nonpayment if the item is unavailable for return.

(b) If a demand item is received by a payor bank for credit on its books, it may return the item or send notice of dishonor and may revoke any credit given or recover the amount thereof withdrawn by its customer, if it acts within the time limit and in the manner specified in subsection (a).

(c) Unless previous notice of dishonor has been sent, an item is dishonored at the time when for purposes of dishonor it is returned or notice sent in accordance with this section.

(d) An item is returned:

(1) as to an item presented through a clearing house, when it is delivered to the presenting or last collecting bank or to the clearing house or is sent or delivered in accordance with clearing-house rules; or

(2) in all other cases, when it is sent or delivered to the bank's customer or transferor or pursuant to instructions.

As amended in 1990.

§ 4–302.   Payor Bank's Responsibility for Late Return of Item.

(a) If an item is presented to and received by a payor bank, the bank is accountable for the amount of:

(1) a demand item, other than a documentary draft, whether properly payable or not, if the bank, in any case in which it is not also the depositary bank, retains the item beyond midnight of the banking day of receipt without settling for it or, whether or not it is also the depositary bank, does not pay or return the item or send notice of dishonor until after its midnight deadline; or

(2) any other properly payable item unless, within the time allowed for acceptance or payment of that item, the bank either accepts or pays the item or returns it and accompanying documents.

(b) The liability of a payor bank to pay an item pursuant to subsection (a) is subject to defenses based on breach of a presentment warranty (Section 4–208) or proof that the person seeking enforcement of the liability presented or transferred the item for the purpose of defrauding the payor bank.

As amended in 1990.

§ 4–303.   When Items Subject to Notice, Stop-Payment Order, Legal Process, or Setoff; Order in Which Items May Be Charged or Certified.

(a) Any knowledge, notice, or stop-payment order received by, legal process served upon, or setoff exercised by a payor bank comes too late to terminate, suspend, or modify the bank's right or duty to pay an item or to charge its customer's account for the item if the knowledge, notice, stop-payment order, or legal process is received or served and a reasonable time for the bank to act thereon expires or the setoff is exercised after the earliest of the following:

(1) the bank accepts or certifies the item;

(2) the bank pays the item in cash;

(3) the bank settles for the item without having a right to revoke the settlement under statute, clearing-house rule, or agreement;

(4) the bank becomes accountable for the amount of the item under Section 4–302 dealing with the payor bank's responsibility for late return of items; or

(5) with respect to checks, a cutoff hour no earlier than one hour after the opening of the next banking day after the banking day on which the bank received the check and no later than the close of that next banking day or, if no cutoff hour is fixed, the close of the next banking day after the banking day on which the bank received the check.

(b) Subject to subsection (a), items may be accepted, paid, certified, or charged to the indicated account of its customer in any order.

As amended in 1990.

PART 4   Relationship Between Payor Bank and Its Customer

§ 4–401.   When Bank May Charge Customer's Account.

(a) A bank may charge against the account of a customer an item that is properly payable from the account even though the charge creates an overdraft. An item is properly payable if it is authorized by the customer and is in accordance with any agreement between the customer and bank.

(b) A customer is not liable for the amount of an overdraft if the customer neither signed the item nor benefited from the proceeds of the item.

(c) A bank may charge against the account of a customer a check that is otherwise properly payable from the account, even though payment was made before the date of the check, unless the customer has given notice to the bank of the postdating describing the check with reasonable certainty. The notice is effective for the period stated in Section 4–403(b) for stop-payment orders, and must be received at such time and in such manner as to afford the bank a reasonable opportunity to act on it before the bank takes any action with respect to the check described in Section 4–303. If a bank charges against the account of a customer a check before the date stated in the notice of postdating, the bank is liable for damages for the loss resulting from its act. The loss may include damages for dishonor of subsequent items under Section 4–402.

(d) A bank that in good faith makes payment to a holder may charge the indicated account of its customer according to:

(1) the original terms of the altered item; or

(2) the terms of the completed item, even though the bank knows the item has been completed unless the bank has notice that the completion was improper.

As amended in 1990.

§ 4–402.   Bank's Liability to Customer for Wrongful Dishonor; Time of Determining Insufficiency of Account.

(a) Except as otherwise provided in this Article, a payor bank wrongfully dishonors an item if it dishonors an item that is properly payable, but a bank may dishonor an item that would create an overdraft unless it has agreed to pay the overdraft.

(b) A payor bank is liable to its customer for damages proximately caused by the wrongful dishonor of an item. Liability is limited to actual damages proved and may include damages for an arrest or prosecution of the customer or other consequential damages. Whether any consequential damages are proximately caused by the wrongful dishonor is a question of fact to be determined in each case.

(c) A payor bank's determination of the customer's account balance on which a decision to dishonor for insufficiency of available funds is based may be made at any time between the time the item is received by the payor bank and the time that the payor bank returns the item or gives notice in lieu of return, and no more than one determination need be made. If, at the election of the payor bank, a subsequent balance determination is made for the purpose of reevaluating the bank's decision to dishonor the item, the account balance at that time is determinative of whether a dishonor for insufficiency of available funds is wrongful.

As amended in 1990.

§ 4–403.   Customer's Right to Stop Payment; Burden of Proof of Loss.

(a) A customer or any person authorized to draw on the account if there is more than one person may stop payment of any item drawn on the customer's account or close the account by an order to the bank describing the item or account with reasonable certainty received at a time and in a manner that affords the bank a reasonable opportunity to act on it before any action by the bank with respect to the item described in Section 4–303. If the signature of more than one person is required to draw on an account, any of these persons may stop payment or close the account.

(b) A stop-payment order is effective for six months, but it lapses after 14 calendar days if the original order was oral and was not confirmed in writing within that period. A stop-payment order may be renewed for additional six-month periods by a writing given to the bank within a period during which the stop-payment order is effective.

(c) The burden of establishing the fact and amount of loss resulting from the payment of an item contrary to a stop-payment order or order to close an account is on the customer.

The loss from payment of an item contrary to a stop-payment order may include damages for dishonor of subsequent items under Section 4–402.

As amended in 1990.

§ 4–404. Bank Not Obliged to Pay Check More Than Six Months Old.

A bank is under no obligation to a customer having a checking account to pay a check, other than a certified check, which is presented more than six months after its date, but it may charge its customer's account for a payment made thereafter in good faith.

§ 4–405. Death or Incompetence of Customer.

(a) A payor or collecting bank's authority to accept, pay, or collect an item or to account for proceeds of its collection, if otherwise effective, is not rendered ineffective by incompetence of a customer of either bank existing at the time the item is issued or its collection is undertaken if the bank does not know of an adjudication of incompetence. Neither death nor incompetence of a customer revokes the authority to accept, pay, collect, or account until the bank knows of the fact of death or of an adjudication of incompetence and has reasonable opportunity to act on it.

(b) Even with knowledge, a bank may for 10 days after the date of death pay or certify checks drawn on or before the date unless ordered to stop payment by a person claiming an interest in the account.

As amended in 1990.

§ 4–406. Customer's Duty to Discover and Report Unauthorized Signature or Alteration.

(a) A bank that sends or makes available to a customer a statement of account showing payment of items for the account shall either return or make available to the customer the items paid or provide information in the statement of account sufficient to allow the customer reasonably to identify the items paid. The statement of account provides sufficient information if the item is described by item number, amount, and date of payment.

(b) If the items are not returned to the customer, the person retaining the items shall either retain the items or, if the items are destroyed, maintain the capacity to furnish legible copies of the items until the expiration of seven years after receipt of the items. A customer may request an item from the bank that paid the item, and that bank must provide in a reasonable time either the item or, if the item has been destroyed or is not otherwise obtainable, a legible copy of the item.

(c) If a bank sends or makes available a statement of account or items pursuant to subsection (a), the customer must exercise reasonable promptness in examining the statement or the items to determine whether any payment was not authorized because of an alteration of an item or because a purported signature by or on behalf of the customer was not authorized. If, based on the statement or items provided, the customer should reasonably have discovered the unauthorized payment, the customer must promptly notify the bank of the relevant facts.

(d) If the bank proves that the customer failed, with respect to an item, to comply with the duties imposed on the customer by subsection (c), the customer is precluded from asserting against the bank:

(1) the customer's unauthorized signature or any alteration on the item, if the bank also proves that it suffered a loss by reason of the failure; and

(2) the customer's unauthorized signature or alteration by the same wrongdoer on any other item paid in good faith by the bank if the payment was made before the bank received notice from the customer of the unauthorized signature or alteration and after the customer had been afforded a reasonable period of time, not exceeding 30 days, in which to examine the item or statement of account and notify the bank.

(e) If subsection (d) applies and the customer proves that the bank failed to exercise ordinary care in paying the item and that the failure substantially contributed to loss, the loss is allocated between the customer precluded and the bank asserting the preclusion according to the extent to which the failure of the customer to comply with subsection (c) and the failure of the bank to exercise ordinary care contributed to the loss. If the customer proves that the bank did not pay the item in good faith, the preclusion under subsection (d) does not apply.

(f) Without regard to care or lack of care of either the customer or the bank, a customer who does not within one year after the statement or items are made available to the customer (subsection (a)) discover and report the customer's unauthorized signature on or any alteration on the item is precluded from asserting against the bank the unauthorized signature or alteration. If there is a preclusion under this subsection, the payor bank may not recover for breach or warranty under Section 4–208 with respect to the unauthorized signature or alteration to which the preclusion applies.

As amended in 1990.

§ 4–407. Payor Bank's Right to Subrogation on Improper Payment.

If a payor has paid an item over the order of the drawer or maker to stop payment, or after an account has been closed, or otherwise under circumstances giving a basis for objection by the drawer or maker, to prevent unjust enrichment and only to the extent necessary to prevent loss to the bank by reason of its payment of the item, the payor bank is subrogated to the rights

(1) of any holder in due course on the item against the drawer or maker;

(2) of the payee or any other holder of the item against the drawer or maker either on the item or under the transaction out of which the item arose; and

(3) of the drawer or maker against the payee or any other holder of the item with respect to the transaction out of which the item arose.

As amended in 1990.

PART 5   Collection of Documentary Drafts

§ 4–501.   Handling of Documentary Drafts; Duty to Send for Presentment and to Notify Customer of Dishonor.

A bank that takes a documentary draft for collection shall present or send the draft and accompanying documents for presentment and, upon learning that the draft has not been paid or accepted in due course, shall seasonably notify its customer of the fact even though it may have discounted or bought the draft or extended credit available for withdrawal as of right.

As amended in 1990.

§ 4–502.   Presentment of "On Arrival" Drafts.

If a draft or the relevant instructions require presentment "on arrival", "when goods arrive" or the like, the collecting bank need not present until in its judgment a reasonable time for arrival of the goods has expired. Refusal to pay or accept because the goods have not arrived is not dishonor; the bank must notify its transferor of the refusal but need not present the draft again until it is instructed to do so or learns of the arrival of the goods.

§ 4–503.   Responsibility of Presenting Bank for Documents and Goods; Report of Reasons for Dishonor; Referee in Case of Need.

Unless otherwise instructed and except as provided in Article 5, a bank presenting a documentary draft:

(1) must deliver the documents to the drawee on acceptance of the draft if it is payable more than three days after presentment, otherwise, only on payment; and

(2) upon dishonor, either in the case of presentment for acceptance or presentment for payment, may seek and follow instructions from any referee in case of need designated in the draft or, if the presenting bank does not choose to utilize the referee's services, it must use diligence and good faith to ascertain the reason for dishonor, must notify its transferor of the dishonor and of the results of its effort to ascertain the reasons therefor, and must request instructions.

However, the presenting bank is under no obligation with respect to goods represented by the documents except to follow any reasonable instructions seasonably received; it has a right to reimbursement for any expense incurred in following instructions and to prepayment of or indemnity for those expenses.

As amended in 1990.

§ 4–504.   Privilege of Presenting Bank to Deal With Goods; Security Interest for Expenses.

(a) A presenting bank that, following the dishonor of a documentary draft, has seasonably requested instructions but does not receive them within a reasonable time may store, sell, or otherwise deal with the goods in any reasonable manner.

(b) For its reasonable expenses incurred by action under subsection (a) the presenting bank has a lien upon the goods or their proceeds, which may be foreclosed in the same manner as an unpaid seller's lien.

As amended in 1990.

REVISED ARTICLE IX
SECURED TRANSACTIONS

PART 1   General Provisions

[Subpart 1. Short Title, Definitions, and General Concepts]

§ 9–101.   Short Title.

This article may be cited as Uniform Commercial Code—Secured Transactions.

§ 9–102.   Definitions and Index of Definitions.

(a) In this article:

(1) "Accession" means goods that are physically united with other goods in such a manner that the identity of the original goods is not lost.

(2) "Account", except as used in "account for", means a right to payment of a monetary obligation, whether or not earned by performance, (i) for property that has been or is to be sold, leased, licensed, assigned, or otherwise disposed of, (ii) for services rendered or to be rendered, (iii) for a policy of insurance issued or to be issued, (iv) for a secondary obligation incurred or to be incurred, (v) for energy provided or to be provided, (vi) for the use or hire of a vessel under a charter or other contract, (vii) arising out of the use of a credit or charge card or information contained on or for use with the card, or (viii) as winnings in a lottery or other game of chance operated or sponsored by a State, governmental unit of a State, or person licensed or authorized to operate the game by a State or governmental unit of a State. The term includes health-care insurance receivables. The term does not include (i) rights to payment evidenced by chattel paper or an instrument, (ii) commercial tort claims, (iii) deposit accounts, (iv) investment property, (v) letter-of-credit rights or letters of credit, or (vi) rights to payment for money or funds advanced or

sold, other than rights arising out of the use of a credit or charge card or information contained on or for use with the card.

(3) "Account debtor" means a person obligated on an account, chattel paper, or general intangible. The term does not include persons obligated to pay a negotiable instrument, even if the instrument constitutes part of chattel paper.

(4) "Accounting", except as used in "accounting for", means a record:

(A) authenticated by a secured party;

(B) indicating the aggregate unpaid secured obligations as of a date not more than 35 days earlier or 35 days later than the date of the record; and

(C) identifying the components of the obligations in reasonable detail.

(5) "Agricultural lien" means an interest, other than a security interest, in farm products:

(A) which secures payment or performance of an obligation for:

(i) goods or services furnished in connection with a debtor's farming operation; or

(ii) rent on real property leased by a debtor in connection with its farming operation;

(B) which is created by statute in favor of a person that:

(i) in the ordinary course of its business furnished goods or services to a debtor in connection with a debtor's farming operation; or

(ii) leased real property to a debtor in connection with the debtor's farming operation; and

(C) whose effectiveness does not depend on the person's possession of the personal property.

(6) "As-extracted collateral" means:

(A) oil, gas, or other minerals that are subject to a security interest that:

(i) is created by a debtor having an interest in the minerals before extraction; and

(ii) attaches to the minerals as extracted; or

(B) accounts arising out of the sale at the wellhead or minehead of oil, gas, or other minerals in which the debtor had an interest before extraction.

(7) "Authenticate" means:

(A) to sign; or

(B) to execute or otherwise adopt a symbol, or encrypt or similarly process a record in whole or in part, with the present intent of the authenticating person to identify the person and adopt or accept a record.

(8) "Bank" means an organization that is engaged in the business of banking. The term includes savings banks, savings and loan associations, credit unions, and trust companies.

(9) "Cash proceeds" means proceeds that are money, checks, deposit accounts, or the like.

(10) "Certificate of title" means a certificate of title with respect to which a statute provides for the security interest in question to be indicated on the certificate as a condition or result of the security interest's obtaining priority over the rights of a lien creditor with respect to the collateral.

(11) "Chattel paper" means a record or records that evidence both a monetary obligation and a security interest in specific goods, a security interest in specific goods and software used in the goods, a security interest in specific goods and license of software used in the goods, a lease of specific goods, or a lease of specific goods and license of software used in the goods. In this paragraph, "monetary obligation" means a monetary obligation secured by the goods or owed under a lease of the goods and includes a monetary obligation with respect to software used in the goods. The term does not include (i) charters or other contracts involving the use or hire of a vessel or (ii) records that evidence a right to payment arising out of the use of a credit or charge card or information contained on or for use with the card. If a transaction is evidenced by records that include an instrument or series of instruments, the group of records taken together constitutes chattel paper.

(12) "Collateral" means the property subject to a security interest or agricultural lien. The term includes:

(A) proceeds to which a security interest attaches;

(B) accounts, chattel paper, payment intangibles, and promissory notes that have been sold; and

(C) goods that are the subject of a consignment.

(13) "Commercial tort claim" means a claim arising in tort with respect to which:

(A) the claimant is an organization; or

(B) the claimant is an individual and the claim:

(i) arose in the course of the claimant's business or profession; and

(ii) does not include damages arising out of personal injury to or the death of an individual.

(14) "Commodity account" means an account maintained by a commodity intermediary in which a commodity contract is carried for a commodity customer.

(15) "Commodity contract" means a commodity futures contract, an option on a commodity futures contract, a commodity option, or another contract if the contract or option is:

(A) traded on or subject to the rules of a board of trade that has been designated as a contract market for such a contract pursuant to federal commodities laws; or

(B) traded on a foreign commodity board of trade, exchange, or market, and is carried on the books of a commodity intermediary for a commodity customer.

(16) "Commodity customer" means a person for which a commodity intermediary carries a commodity contract on its books.

(17) "Commodity intermediary" means a person that:

(A) is registered as a futures commission merchant under federal commodities law; or

(B) in the ordinary course of its business provides clearance or settlement services for a board of trade that has been designated as a contract market pursuant to federal commodities law.

(18) "Communicate" means:

(A) to send a written or other tangible record;

(B) to transmit a record by any means agreed upon by the persons sending and receiving the record; or

(C) in the case of transmission of a record to or by a filing office, to transmit a record by any means prescribed by filing-office rule.

(19) "Consignee" means a merchant to which goods are delivered in a consignment.

(20) "Consignment" means a transaction, regardless of its form, in which a person delivers goods to a merchant for the purpose of sale and:

(A) the merchant:

(i) deals in goods of that kind under a name other than the name of the person making delivery;

(ii) is not an auctioneer; and

(iii) is not generally known by its creditors to be substantially engaged in selling the goods of others;

(B) with respect to each delivery, the aggregate value of the goods is $1,000 or more at the time of delivery;

(C) the goods are not consumer goods immediately before delivery; and

(D) the transaction does not create a security interest that secures an obligation.

(21) "Consignor" means a person that delivers goods to a consignee in a consignment.

(22) "Consumer debtor" means a debtor in a consumer transaction.

(23) "Consumer goods" means goods that are used or bought for use primarily for personal, family, or household purposes.

(24) "Consumer goods transaction" means a consumer transaction in which:

(A) an individual incurs an obligation primarily for personal, family, or household purposes; and

(B) a security interest in consumer goods secures the obligation.

(25) "Consumer obligor" means an obligor who is an individual and who incurred the obligation as part of a transaction entered into primarily for personal, family, or household purposes.

(26) "Consumer transaction" means a transaction in which (i) an individual incurs an obligation primarily for personal, family, or household purposes, (ii) a security interest secures the obligation, and (iii) the collateral is held or acquired primarily for personal, family, or household purposes. The term includes consumer-goods transactions.

(27) "Continuation statement" means an amendment of a financing statement which:

(A) identifies, by its file number, the initial financing statement to which it relates; and

(B) indicates that it is a continuation statement for, or that it is filed to continue the effectiveness of, the identified financing statement.

(28) "Debtor" means:

(A) a person having an interest, other than a security interest or other lien, in the collateral, whether or not the person is an obligor;

(B) a seller of accounts, chattel paper, payment intangibles, or promissory notes; or

(C) a consignee.

(29) "Deposit account" means a demand, time, savings, passbook, or similar account maintained with a bank. The term does not include investment property or accounts evidenced by an instrument.

(30) "Document" means a document of title or a receipt of the type described in Section 7–201(2).

(31) "Electronic chattel paper" means chattel paper evidenced by a record or records consisting of information stored in an electronic medium.

(32) "Encumbrance" means a right, other than an ownership interest, in real property. The term includes mortgages and other liens on real property.

(33) "Equipment" means goods other than inventory, farm products, or consumer goods.

(34) "Farm products" means goods, other than standing timber, with respect to which the debtor is engaged in a farming operation and which are:

(A) crops grown, growing, or to be grown, including:

(i) crops produced on trees, vines, and bushes; and

(ii) aquatic goods produced in aquacultural operations;

(B) livestock, born or unborn, including aquatic goods produced in aquacultural operations;

(C) supplies used or produced in a farming operation; or

(D) products of crops or livestock in their unmanufactured states.

(35) "Farming operation" means raising, cultivating, propagating, fattening, grazing, or any other farming, livestock, or aquacultural operation.

(36) "File number" means the number assigned to an initial financing statement pursuant to Section 9–519(a).

(37) "Filing office" means an office designated in Section 9–501 as the place to file a financing statement.

(38) "Filing-office rule" means a rule adopted pursuant to Section 9–526.

(39) "Financing statement" means a record or records composed of an initial financing statement and any filed record relating to the initial financing statement.

(40) "Fixture filing" means the filing of a financing statement covering goods that are or are to become fixtures and satisfying Section 9–502(a) and (b). The term includes the filing of a

financing statement covering goods of a transmitting utility which are or are to become fixtures.

(41) "Fixtures" means goods that have become so related to particular real property that an interest in them arises under real property law.

(42) "General intangible" means any personal property, including things in action, other than accounts, chattel paper, commercial tort claims, deposit accounts, documents, goods, instruments, investment property, letter-of-credit rights, letters of credit, money, and oil, gas, or other minerals before extraction. The term includes payment intangibles and software.

(43) "Good faith" means honesty in fact and the observance of reasonable commercial standards of fair dealing.

(44) "Goods" means all things that are movable when a security interest attaches. The term includes (i) fixtures, (ii) standing timber that is to be cut and removed under a conveyance or contract for sale, (iii) the unborn young of animals, (iv) crops grown, growing, or to be grown, even if the crops are produced on trees, vines, or bushes, and (v) manufactured homes. The term also includes a computer program embedded in goods and any supporting information provided in connection with a transaction relating to the program if (i) the program is associated with the goods in such a manner that it customarily is considered part of the goods, or (ii) by becoming the owner of the goods, a person acquires a right to use the program in connection with the goods. The term does not include a computer program embedded in goods that consist solely of the medium in which the program is embedded. The term also does not include accounts, chattel paper, commercial tort claims, deposit accounts, documents, general intangibles, instruments, investment property, letter-of-credit rights, letters of credit, money, or oil, gas, or other minerals before extraction.

(45) "Governmental unit" means a subdivision, agency, department, county, parish, municipality, or other unit of the government of the United States, a State, or a foreign country. The term includes an organization having a separate corporate existence if the organization is eligible to issue debt on which interest is exempt from income taxation under the laws of the United States.

(46) "Health-care-insurance receivable" means an interest in or claim under a policy of insurance which is a right to payment of a monetary obligation for health-care goods or servies provided.

(47) "Instrument" means a negotiable instrument or any other writing that evidences a right to the payment of a monetary obligation, is not itself a security agreement or lease, and is of a type that in ordinary course of business is transferred by delivery with any necessary indorsement or assignment. The term does not include (i) investment property, (ii) letters of credit, or (iii) writings that evidence a right to payment arising out of the use of a credit or charge card or information contained on or for use with the card.

(48) "Inventory" means goods, other than farm products, which:

(A) are leased by a person as lessor;

(B) are held by a person for sale or lease or to be furnished under a contract of service;

(C) are furnished by a person under a contract of service; or

(D) consist of raw materials, work in process, or materials used or consumed in a business.

(49) "Investment property" means a security, whether certificated or uncertificated, security entitlement, securities account, commodity contract, or commodity account.

(50) "Jurisdiction of organization", with respect to a registered organization, means the jurisdiction under whose law the organization is organized.

(51) "Letter-of-credit right" means a right to payment or performance under a letter of credit, whether or not the beneficiary has demanded or is at the time entitled to demand payment or performance. The term does not include the right of a beneficiary to demand payment or performance under a letter of credit.

(52) "Lien creditor" means:

(A) a creditor that has acquired a lien on the property involved by attachment, levy, or the like;

(B) an assignee for benefit of creditors from the time of assignment;

(C) a trustee in bankruptcy from the date of the filing of the petition; or

(D) a receiver in equity from the time of appointment.

(53) "Manufactured home" means a structure, transportable in one or more sections, which, in the traveling mode, is eight body feet or more in width or 40 body feet or more in length, or, when erected on site, is 320 or more square feet, and which is built on a permanent chassis and designed to be used as a dwelling with or without a permanent foundation when connected to the required utilities, and includes the plumbing, heating, air-conditioning, and electrical systems contained therein. The term includes any structure that meets all of the requirements of this paragraph except the size requirements and with respect to which the manufacturer voluntarily files a certification required by the United States Secretary of Housing and Urban Development and complies with the standards established under Title 42 of the United States Code.

(54) "Manufactured-home transaction" means a secured transaction:

(A) that creates a purchase-money security interest in a manufactured home, other than a manufactured home held as inventory; or

(B) in which a manufactured home, other than a manufactured home held as inventory, is the primary collateral.

(55) "Mortgage" means a consensal interest in real property, including fixtures, which secures payment or performance of an obligation.

(56) "New debtor" means a person that becomes bound as debtor under Section 9–203(d) by a security agreement previously entered into by another person.

(57) "New value" means (i) money, (ii) money's worth in property, services, or new credit, or (iii) release by a transferee of an interest in property previously transferred to the transferee.

The term does not include an obligation substituted for another obligation.

(58) "Noncash proceeds" means proceeds other than cash proceeds.

(59) "Obligor" means a person that, with respect to an obligation secured by a security interest in or an agricultural lien on the collateral, (i) owes payment or other performance of the obligation, (ii) has provided property other than the collateral to secure payment or other performance of the obligation, or (iii) is otherwise accountable in whole or in part for payment or other performance of the obligation. The term does not include issuers or nominated persons under a letter of credit.

(60) "Original debtor", except as used in Section 9–310(c), means a person that, as debtor, entered into a security agreement to which a new debtor has become bound under Section 9–203(d).

(61) "Payment intangible" means a general intangible under which the account debtor's principal obligation is a monetary obligation.

(62) "Person related to", with respect to an individual, means:

(A) the spouse of the individual;

(B) a brother, brother-in-law, sister, or sister-in-law of the individual;

(C) an ancestor or lineal descendant of the individual or the individual's spouse; or

(D) any other relative, by blood or marriage, of the individual or the individual's spouse who shares the same home with the individual.

(63) "Person related to", with respect to an organization, means:

(A) a person directly or indirectly controlling, controlled by, or under common control with the organization;

(B) an officer or director of, or a person performing similar functions with respect to, the organization;

(C) an officer or director of, or a person performing similar functions with respect to, a person described in subparagraph (A);

(D) the spouse of an individual described in subparagraph (A), (B), or (C); or

(E) an individual who is related by blood or marriage to an individual described in subparagraph (A), (B), (C), or (D) and shares the same home with the individual.

(64) "Proceeds", except as used in Section 9–609(b), means the following property:

(A) whatever is acquired upon the sale, lease, license, exchange, or other disposition of collateral;

(B) whatever is collected on, or distributed on account of, collateral;

(C) rights arising out of collateral;

(D) to the extent of the value of collateral, claims arising out of the loss, nonconformity, or interference with the use of, defects or infringement of rights in, or damage to, the collateral; or (E) to the extent of the value of collateral and to the extent payable to the debtor or the secured party, insurance payable by reason of the loss or nonconformity of, defects or infringement of rights in, or damage to, the collateral.

(65) "Promissory note" means an instrument that evidences a promise to pay a monetary obligation, does not evidence an order to pay, and does not contain an acknowledgment by a bank that the bank has received for deposit a sum of money or funds.

(66) "Proposal" means a record authenticated by a secured party which includes the terms on which the secured party is willing to accept collateral in full or partial satisfaction of the obligation it secures pursuant to Sections 9–620, 9–621, and 9–622.

(67) "Public-finance transaction" means a secured transaction in connection with which:

(A) debt securities are issued;

(B) all or a portion of the securities issued have an initial stated maturity of at least 20 years; and

(C) the debtor, obligor, secured party, account debtor or other person obligated on collateral, assignor or assignee of a secured obligation, or assignor or assignee of a security interest is a State or a governmental unit of a State.

(68) "Pursuant to commitment", with respect to an advance made or other value given by a secured party, means pursuant to the secured party's obligation, whether or not a subsequent event of default or other event not within the secured party's control has relieved or may relieve the secured party from its obligation.

(69) "Record", except as used in "for record", "of record", "record or legal title", and "record owner", means information that is inscribed on a tangible medium or which is stored in an electronic or other medium and is retrievable in perceivable form.

(70) "Registered organization" means an organization organized solely under the law of a single State or the United States and as to which the State or the United States must maintain a public record showing the organization to have been organized.

(71) "Secondary obligor" means an obligor to the extent that:

(A) the obligor's obligation is secondary; or

(B) the obligor has a right of recourse with respect to an obligation secured by collateral against the debtor, another obligor, or property of either.

(72) "Secured party" means:

(A) a person in whose favor a security interest is created or provided for under a security agreement, whether or not any obligation to be secured is outstanding;

(B) a person that holds an agricultural lien;

(C) a consignor;

(D) a person to which accounts, chattel paper, payment intangibles, or promissory notes have been sold;

(E) a trustee, indenture trustee, agent, collateral agent, or other representative in whose favor a security interest or agricultural lien is created or provided for; or

(F) a person that holds a security interest arising under Section 2–401, 2–505, 2–711(3), 2A–508(5), 4–210, or 5–118.

(73) "Security agreement" means an agreement that creates or provides for a security interest.

(74) "Send", in connection with a record or notification, means:

(A) to deposit in the mail, deliver for transmission, or transmit by any other usual means of communication, with postage or cost of transmission provided for, addressed to any address reasonable under the circumstances; or

(B) to cause the record or notification to be received within the timce that it would have been received if properly sent under subparagraph (A).

(75) "Software" means a computer program and any supporting information provided in connection with a transaction relating to the program. The term does not include a computer program that is included in the definition of goods.

(76) "State" means a State of the United States, the District of Columbia, Puerto Rico, the United States Virgin Islands, or any territory or insular possession subject to the jurisdiction of the United States.

(77) "Supporting obligation" means a letter-of-credit right or secondary obligation that supports the payment or performance of an account, chattel paper, a document, a general intangible, an instrument, or investment property.

(78) "Tangible chattel paper" means chattel paper evidenced by a record or records consisting of information that is inscribed on a tangible medium.

(79) "Termination statement" means an amendment of a financing statement which:

(A) identifies, by its file number, the initial financing statement to which it relates; and

(B) indicates either that it is a termination statement or that the identified financing statement is no longer effective.

(80) "Transmitting utility" means a person primarily engaged in the business of:

(A) operating a railroad, subway, street railway, or trolley bus;

(B) transmitting communications electrically, electromagnetically, or by light;

(C) transmitting goods by pipeline or sewer; or

(D) transmitting or producing and transmitting electricity, steam, gas, or water.

(b) The following definitions in other articles apply to this article:

"Applicant." Section 5–102

"Beneficiary." Section 5–102

"Broker." Section 8–102

"Certificated security." Section 8–102

"Check." Section 3–104

"Clearing corporation." Section 8–102

"Contract for sale." Section 2–106

"Customer." Section 4–104

"Entitlement holder." Section 8–102

"Financial asset." Section 8–102

"Holder in due course." Section 3–302

"Issuer" (with respect to a letter of credit or letter-of-credit right). Section 5–102

"Issuer" (with respect to a security). Section 8–201

"Lease." Section 2A–103

"Lease agreement." Section 2A–103

"Lease contract." Section 2A–103

"Leasehold interest." Section 2A–103

"Lessee." Section 2A–103

"Lessee in ordinary course of business." Section 2A–103

"Lessor." Section 2A–103

"Lessor's residual interest." Section 2A–103

"Letter of credit." Section 5–102

"Merchant." Section 2–104

"Negotiable instrument." Section 3–104

"Nominated person." Section 5–102

"Note." Section 3–104

"Proceeds of a letter of credit." Section 5–114

"Prove." Section 3–103

"Sale." Section 2–106

"Securities account." Section 8–501

"Securities intermediary." Section 8–102

"Security." Section 8–102

"Security certificate." Section 8–102

"Security entitlement." Section 8–102

"Uncertificated security." Section 8–102

(c) Article 1 contains general definitions and principles of construction and interpretation applicable throughout this article.

Amended in 1999 and 2000.

§ 9–103.   Purchase-Money Security Interest; Application of Payments; Burden of Establishing.

(a) In this section:

(1) "purchase-money collateral" means goods or software that secures a purchase-money obligation incurred with respect to that collateral; and

(2) "purchase-money obligation" means an obligation of an obligor incurred as all or part of the price of the collateral or for value given to enable the debtor to acquire rights in or the use of the collateral if the value is in fact so used.

(b) A security interest in goods is a purchase-money security interest:

(1) to the extent that the goods are purchase-money collateral with respect to that security interest;

(2) if the security interest is in inventory that is or was purchase-money collateral, also to the extent that the security interest secures a purchase-money obligation incurred with respect to other inventory in which the secured party holds or held a purchase-money security interest; and

(3) also to the extent that the security interest secures a purchase-money obligation incurred with respect to software in which the secured party holds or held a purchase-money security interest.

(c) A security interest in software is a purchase-money security interest to the extent that the security interest also secures a purchase-money obligation incurred with respect to goods in which the secured party holds or held a purchase-money security interest if:

(1) the debtor acquired its interest in the software in an integrated transaction in which it acquired an interest in the goods; and

(2) the debtor acquired its interest in the software for the principal purpose of using the software in the goods.

(d) The security interest of a consignor in goods that are the subject of a consignment is a purchase-money security interest in inventory.

(e) In a transaction other than a consumer-goods transaction, if the extent to which a security interest is a purchase-money security interest depends on the application of a payment to a particular obligation, the payment must be applied:

(1) in accordance with any reasonable method of application to which the parties agree;

(2) in the absence of the parties' agreement to a reasonable method, in accordance with any intention of the obligor manifested at or before the time of payment; or

(3) in the absence of an agreement to a reasonable method and a timely manifestation of the obligor's intention, in the following order:

(A) to obligations that are not secured; and

(B) if more than one obligation is secured, to obligations secured by purchase-money security interests in the order in which those obligations were incurred.

(f) In a transaction other than a consumer-goods transaction, a purchase-money security interest does not lose its status as such, even if:

(1) the purchase-money collateral also secures an obligation that is not a purchase-money obligation;

(2) collateral that is not purchase-money collateral also secures the purchase-money obligation; or

(3) the purchase-money obligation has been renewed, refinanced, consolidated, or restructured.

(g) In a transaction other than a consumer-goods transaction, a secured party claiming a purchase-money security interest has the burden of establishing the extent to which the security interest is a purchase-money security interest.

(h) The limitation of the rules in subsections (e), (f), and (g) to transactions other than consumer-goods transactions is intended to leave to the court the determination of the proper rules in consumer-goods transactions. The court may not infer from that limitation the nature of the proper rule in consumer-goods transactions and may continue to apply established approaches.

§ 9–104.   Control of Deposit Account.

(a) A secured party has control of a deposit account if:

(1) the secured party is the bank with which the deposit account is maintained;

(2) the debtor, secured party, and bank have agreed in an authenticated record that the bank will comply with instructions originated by the secured party directing disposition of the funds in the deposit account without further consent by the debtor; or

(3) the secured party becomes the bank's customer with respect to the deposit account.

(b) A secured party that has satisfied subsection (a) has control, even if the debtor retains the right to direct the disposition of funds from the deposit account.

§ 9–105.   Control of Electronic Chattel Paper.

A secured party has control of electronic chattel paper if the record or records comprising the chattel paper are created, stored, and assigned in such a manner that:

(1) a single authoritative copy of the record or records exists which is unique, identifiable and, except as otherwise provided in paragraphs (4), (5), and (6), unalterable;

(2) the authoritative copy identifies the secured party as the assignee of the record or records;

(3) the authoritative copy is communicated to and maintained by the secured party or its designated custodian;

(4) copies or revisions that add or change an identified assignee of the authoritative copy can be made only with the participation of the secured party;

(5) each copy of the authoritative copy and any copy of a copy is readily identifiable as a copy that is not the authoritative copy; and

(6) any revision of the authoritative copy is readily identifiable as an authorized or unauthorized revision.

§ 9–106.   Control of Investment Property.

(a) A person has control of a certificated security, uncertificated security, or security entitlement as provided in Section 8–106.

(b) A secured party has control of a commodity contract if:

(1) the secured party is the commodity intermediary with which the commodity contract is carried; or

(2) the commodity customer, secured party, and commodity intermediary have agreed that the commodity intermediary will apply any value distributed on account of the commodity contract as directed by the secured party without further consent by the commodity customer.

(c) A secured party having control of all security entitlements or commodity contracts carried in a securities account or commodity account has control over the securities account or commodity account.

§ 9–107.   Control of Letter-of-Credit Right.

A secured party has control of a letter-of-credit right to the extent of any right to payment or performance by the issuer or any nominated person if the issuer or nominated person has consented to an assignment of proceeds of the letter of credit under Section 5–114(c) or otherwise applicable law or practice.

§ 9–108.   Sufficiency of Description.

(a) Except as otherwise provided in subsections (c), (d), and (e), a description of personal or real property is sufficient, whether or not it is specific, if it reasonably identifies what is described.

(b) Except as otherwise provided in subsection (d), a description of collateral reasonably identifies the collateral if it identifies the collateral by:

(1) specific listing;

(2) category;

(3) except as otherwise provided in subsection (e), a type of collateral defined in [the Uniform Commercial Code];

(4) quantity;

(5) computational or allocational formula or procedure; or

(6) except as otherwise provided in subsection (c), any other method, if the identity of the collateral is objectively determinable.

(c) A description of collateral as "all the debtor's assets" or "all the debtor's personal property" or using words of similar import does not reasonably identify the collateral.

(d) Except as otherwise provided in subsection (e), a description of a security entitlement, securities account, or commodity account is sufficient if it describes:

(1) the collateral by those terms or as investment property; or

(2) the underlying financial asset or commodity contract.

(e) A description only by type of collateral defined in [the Uniform Commercial Code] is an insufficient description of:

(1) a commercial tort claim; or

(2) in a consumer transaction, consumer goods, a security entitlement, a securities account, or a commodity account.

[Subpart 2. Applicability of Article]

§ 9–109.   Scope.

(a) Except as otherwise provided in subsections (c) and (d), this article applies to:

(1) a transaction, regardless of its form, that creates a security interest in personal property or fixtures by contract;

(2) an agricultural lien;

(3) a sale of accounts, chattel paper, payment intangibles, or promissory notes;

(4) a consignment;

(5) a security interest arising under Section 2–401, 2–505, 2–711 (3), or 2A–508(5), as provided in Section 9–110; and

(6) a security interest arising under Section 4–210 or 5–118.

(b) The application of this article to a security interest in a secured obligation is not affected by the fact that the obligation is itself secured by a transaction or interest to which this article does not apply.

(c) This article does not apply to the extent that:

(1) a statute, regulation, or treaty of the United States preempts this article;

(2) another statute of this State expressly governs the creation, perfection, priority, or enforcement of a security interest created by this State or a governmental unit of this State;

(3) a statute of another State, a foreign country, or a governmental unit of another State or a foreign country, other than a statute generally applicable to security interests, expressly governs creation, perfection, priority, or enforcement of a security interest created by the State, country, or governmental unit; or

(4) the rights of a transferee beneficiary or nominated person under a letter of credit are independent and superior under Section 5–114.

(d) This article does not apply to:

(1) a landlord's lien, other than an agricultural lien;

(2) a lien, other than an agricultural lien, given by statute or other rule of law for services or materials, but Section 9–333 applies with respect to priority of the lien;

(3) an assignment of a claim for wages, salary, or other compensation of an employee;

(4) a sale of accounts, chattel paper, payment intangibles, or promissory notes as part of a sale of the business out of which they arose;

(5) an assignment of accounts, chattel paper, payment intangibles, or promissory notes which is for the purpose of collection only;

(6) an assignment of a right to payment under a contract to an assignee that is also obligated to perform under the contract;

(7) an assignment of a single account, payment intangible, or promissory note to an assignee in full or partial satisfaction of a preexisting indebtedness;

(8) a transfer of an interest in or an assignment of a claim under a policy of insurance, other than an assignment by or to a health-care provider of a health-care-insurance receivable and any subsequent assignment of the right to payment, but Sections 9–315 and 9–322 apply with respect to proceeds and priorities in proceeds;

(9) an assignment of a right represented by a judgment, other than a judgment taken on a right to payment that was collateral;

(10) a right of recoupment or set-off, but:

(A) Section 9–340 applies with respect to the effectiveness of rights of recoupment or set-off against deposit accounts; and

(B) Section 9–404 applies with respect to defenses or claims of an account debtor;

(11) the creation or transfer of an interest in or lien on real property, including a lease or rents thereunder, except to the extent that provision is made for:

(A) liens on real property in Sections 9–203 and 9–308;

(B) fixtures in Section 9–334;

(C) fixture filings in Sections 9–501, 9–502, 9–512, 9–516, and 9–519; and

(D) security agreements covering personal and real property in Section 9–604;

(12) an assignment of a claim arising in tort, other than a commercial tort claim, but Sections 9–315 and 9–322 apply with respect to proceeds and priorities in proceeds; or

(13) an assignment of a deposit account in a consumer transaction, but Sections 9–315 and 9–322 apply with respect to proceeds and priorities in proceeds.

§ 9–110.   Security Interests Arising under Article 2 or 2A.

A security interest arising under Section 2–401, 2–505, 2–711(3), or 2A–508(5) is subject to this article. However, until the debtor obtains possession of the goods:

(1) the security interest is enforceable, even if Section 9–203(b) (3) has not been satisfied;

(2) filing is not required to perfect the security interest;

(3) the rights of the secured party after default by the debtor are governed by Article 2 or 2A; and

(4) the security interest has priority over a conflicting security interest created by the debtor.

PART 2   Effectiveness of Security Agreement; Attachment of Security Interest; Rights of Parties to Security Agreement

[Subpart 1. Effectiveness and Attachment]

§ 9–201.   General Effectiveness of Security Agreement.

(a) Except as otherwise provided in [the Uniform Commercial Code], a security agreement is effective according to its terms between the parties, against purchasers of the collateral, and against creditors.

(b) A transaction subject to this article is subject to any applicable rule of law which establishes a different rule for consumers and [insert reference to (i) any other statute or regulation that regulates the rates, charges, agreements, and practices for loans, credit sales, or other extensions of credit and (ii) any consumer-protection statute or regulation].

(c) In case of conflict between this article and a rule of law, statute, or regulation described in subsection (b), the rule of law, statute, or regulation controls. Failure to comply with a statute or regulation described in subsection (b) has only the effect the statute or regulation specifies.

(d) This article does not:

(1) validate any rate, charge, agreement, or practice that violates a rule of law, statute, or regulation described in subsection (b); or

(2) extend the application of the rule of law, statute, or regulation to a transaction not otherwise subject to it.

§ 9–202.   Title to Collateral Immaterial.

Except as otherwise provided with respect to consignments or sales of accounts, chattel paper, payment intangibles, or promissory notes, the provisions of this article with regard to rights and obligations apply whether title to collateral is in the secured party or the debtor.

§ 9–203.   Attachment and Enforceability of Security Interest; Proceeds; Supporting Obligations; Formal Requisites.

(a) A security interest attaches to collateral when it becomes enforceable against the debtor with respect to the collateral, unless an agreement expressly postpones the time of attachment.

(b) Except as otherwise provided in subsections (c) through (i), a security interest is enforceable against the debtor and third parties with respect to the collateral only if:

(1) value has been given;

(2) the debtor has rights in the collateral or the power to transfer rights in the collateral to a secured party; and

(3) one of the following conditions is met:

(A) the debtor has authenticated a security agreement that provides a description of the collateral and, if the security interest covers timber to be cut, a description of the land concerned;

(B) the collateral is not a certificated security and is in the possession of the secured party under Section 9–313 pursuant to the debtor's security agreement;

(C) the collateral is a certificated security in registered form and the security certificate has been delivered to the secured party under Section 8–301 pursuant to the debtor's security agreement; or

(D) the collateral is deposit accounts, electronic chattel paper, investment property, or letter-of-credit rights, and the secured party has control under Section 9–104, 9–105, 9–106, or 9–107 pursuant to the debtor's security agreement.

(c) Subsection (b) is subject to Section 4–210 on the security interest of a collecting bank, Section 5–118 on the security interest of a letter-of-credit issuer or nominated person, Section 9–110 on a security interest arising under Article 2 or 2A, and Section 9–206 on security interests in investment property.

(d) A person becomes bound as debtor by a security agreement entered into by another person if, by operation of law other than this article or by contract:

(1) the security agreement becomes effective to create a security interest in the person's property; or

(2) the person becomes generally obligated for the obligations of the other person, including the obligation secured under the security agreement, and acquires or succeeds to all or substantially all of the assets of the other person.

(e) If a new debtor becomes bound as debtor by a security agreement entered into by another person:

(1) the agreement satisfies subsection (b)(3) with respect to existing or after-acquired property of the new debtor to the extent the property is described in the agreement; and

(2) another agreement is not necessary to make a security interest in the property enforceable.

(f) The attachment of a security interest in collateral gives the secured party the rights to proceeds provided by Section 9–315 and is also attachment of a security interest in a supporting obligation for the collateral.

(g) The attachment of a security interest in a right to payment or performance secured by a security interest or other lien on personal or real property is also attachment of a security interest in the security interest, mortgage, or other lien.

(h) The attachment of a security interest in a securities account is also attachment of a security interest in the security entitlements carried in the securities account.

(i) The attachment of a security interest in a commodity account is also attachment of a security interest in the commodity contracts carried in the commodity account.

§ 9–204. After-Acquired Property; Future Advances.

(a) Except as otherwise provided in subsection (b), a security agreement may create or provide for a security interest in after-acquired collateral.

(b) A security interest does not attach under a term constituting an after-acquired property clause to:

(1) consumer goods, other than an accession when given as additional security, unless the debtor acquires rights in them within 10 days after the secured party gives value; or

(2) a commercial tort claim.

(c) A security agreement may provide that collateral secures, or that accounts, chattel paper, payment intangibles, or promissory notes are sold in connection with, future advances or other value, whether or not the advances or value are given pursuant to commitment.

§ 9–205. Use or Disposition of Collateral Permissible.

(a) A security interest is not invalid or fraudulent against creditors solely because:

(1) the debtor has the right or ability to:

(A) use, commingle, or dispose of all or part of the collateral, including returned or repossessed goods;

(B) collect, compromise, enforce, or otherwise deal with collateral;

(C) accept the return of collateral or make repossessions; or

(D) use, commingle, or dispose of proceeds; or

(2) the secured party fails to require the debtor to account for proceeds or replace collateral.

(b) This section does not relax the requirements of possession if attachment, perfection, or enforcement of a security interest depends upon possession of the collateral by the secured party.

§ 9–206. Security Interest Arising in Purchase or Delivery of Financial Asset.

(a) A security interest in favor of a securities intermediary attaches to a person's security entitlement if:

(1) the person buys a financial asset through the securities intermediary in a transaction in which the person is obligated to

pay the purchase price to the securities intermediary at the time of the purchase; and

(2) the securities intermediary credits the financial asset to the buyer's securities account before the buyer pays the securities intermediary.

(b) The security interest described in subsection (a) secures the person's obligation to pay for the financial asset.

(c) A security interest in favor of a person that delivers a certificated security or other financial asset represented by a writing attaches to the security or other financial asset if:

(1) the security or other financial asset:

(A) in the ordinary course of business is transferred by delivery with any necessary indorsement or assignment; and

(B) is delivered under an agreement between persons in the business of dealing with such securities or financial assets; and

(2) the agreement calls for delivery against payment.

(d) The security interest described in subsection (c) secures the obligation to make payment for the delivery.

[Subpart 2. Rights and Duties]

§ 9–207. Rights and Duties of Secured Party Having Possession or Control of Collateral.

(a) Except as otherwise provided in subsection (d), a secured party shall use reasonable care in the custody and preservation of collateral in the secured party's possession. In the case of chattel paper or an instrument, reasonable care includes taking necessary steps to preserve rights against prior parties unless otherwise agreed.

(b) Except as otherwise provided in subsection (d), if a secured party has possession of collateral:

(1) reasonable expenses, including the cost of insurance and payment of taxes or other charges, incurred in the custody, preservation, use, or operation of the collateral are chargeable to the debtor and are secured by the collateral;

(2) the risk of accidental loss or damage is on the debtor to the extent of a deficiency in any effective insurance coverage;

(3) the secured party shall keep the collateral identifiable, but fungible collateral may be commingled; and

(4) the secured party may use or operate the collateral:

(A) for the purpose of preserving the collateral or its value;

(B) as permitted by an order of a court having competent jurisdiction; or

(C) except in the case of consumer goods, in the manner and to the extent agreed by the debtor.

(c) Except as otherwise provided in subsection (d), a secured party having possession of collateral or control of collateral under Section 9–104, 9–105, 9–106, or 9–107:

(1) may hold as additional security any proceeds, except money or funds, received from the collateral;

(2) shall apply money or funds received from the collateral to reduce the secured obligation, unless remitted to the debtor; and

(3) may create a security interest in the collateral.

(d) If the secured party is a buyer of accounts, chattel paper, payment intangibles, or promissory notes or a consignor:

(1) subsection (a) does not apply unless the secured party is entitled under an agreement:

(A) to charge back uncollected collateral; or

(B) otherwise to full or limited recourse against the debtor or a secondary obligor based on the nonpayment or other default of an account debtor or other obligor on the collateral; and

(2) subsections (b) and (c) do not apply.

§ 9–208. Additional Duties of Secured Party Having Control of Collateral.

(a) This section applies to cases in which there is no outstanding secured obligation and the secured party is not committed to make advances, incur obligations, or otherwise give value.

(b) Within 10 days after receiving an authenticated demand by the debtor:

(1) a secured party having control of a deposit account under Section 9–104(a)(2) shall send to the bank with which the deposit account is maintained an authenticated statement that releases the bank from any further obligation to comply with instructions originated by the secured party;

(2) a secured party having control of a deposit account under Section 9–104(a)(3) shall:

(A) pay the debtor the balance on deposit in the deposit account; or

(B) transfer the balance on deposit into a deposit account in the debtor's name;

(3) a secured party, other than a buyer, having control of electronic chattel paper under Section 9–105 shall:

(A) communicate the authoritative copy of the electronic chattel paper to the debtor or its designated custodian;

(B) if the debtor designates a custodian that is the designated custodian with which the authoritative copy of the electronic chattel paper is maintained for the secured party, communicate to the custodian an authenticated record releasing the designated custodian from any further obligation to comply with instructions originated by the secured party and instructing the custodian to comply with instructions originated by the debtor; and

(C) take appropriate action to enable the debtor or its designated custodian to make copies of or revisions to the authoritative copy which add or change an identified assignee of the authoritative copy without the consent of the secured party;

(4) a secured party having control of investment property under Section 8–106(d)(2) or 9–106(b) shall send to the securities intermediary or commodity intermediary with which the security entitlement or commodity contract is maintained an authenticated record that releases the securities intermediary or commodity intermediary from any further obligation to comply with entitlement orders or directions originated by the secured party; and

(5) a secured party having control of a letter-of-credit right under Section 9–107 shall send to each person having an unfulfilled obligation to pay or deliver proceeds of the letter of credit to the secured party an authenticated release from any further obligation to pay or deliver proceeds of the letter of credit to the secured party.

§ 9–209.   Duties of Secured Party If Account Debtor Has Been Notified of Assignment.

(a) Except as otherwise provided in subsection (c), this section applies if:

(1) there is no outstanding secured obligation; and

(2) the secured party is not committed to make advances, incur obligations, or otherwise give value.

(b) Within 10 days after receiving an authenticated demand by the debtor, a secured party shall send to an account debtor that has received notification of an assignment to the secured party as assignee under Section 9–406(a) an authenticated record that releases the account debtor from any further obligation to the secured party.

(c) This section does not apply to an assignment constituting the sale of an account, chattel paper, or payment intangible.

§ 9–210.   Request for Accounting; Request Regarding List of Collateral or Statement of Account.

(a) In this section:

(1) "Request" means a record of a type described in paragraph (2), (3), or (4).

(2) "Request for an accounting" means a record authenticated by a debtor requesting that the recipient provide an accounting of the unpaid obligations secured by collateral and reasonably identifying the transaction or relationship that is the subject of the request.

(3) "Request regarding a list of collateral" means a record authenticated by a debtor requesting that the recipient approve or correct a list of what the debtor believes to be the collateral securing an obligation and reasonably identifying the transaction or relationship that is the subject of the request.

(4) "Request regarding a statement of account" means a record authenticated by a debtor requesting that the recipient approve or correct a statement indicating what the debtor believes to be the aggregate amount of unpaid obligations secured by collateral as of a specified date and reasonably identifying the transaction or relationship that is the subject of the request.

(b) Subject to subsections (c), (d), (e), and (f), a secured party, other than a buyer of accounts, chattel paper, payment intangibles, or promissory notes or a consignor, shall comply with a request within 14 days after receipt:

(1) in the case of a request for an accounting, by authenticating and sending to the debtor an accounting; and

(2) in the case of a request regarding a list of collateral or a request regarding a statement of account, by authenticating and sending to the debtor an approval or correction.

(c) A secured party that claims a security interest in all of a particular type of collateral owned by the debtor may comply with a request regarding a list of collateral by sending to the debtor an authenticated record including a statement to that effect within 14 days after receipt.

(d) A person that receives a request regarding a list of collateral, claims no interest in the collateral when it receives the request, and claimed an interest in the collateral at an earlier time shall comply with the request within 14 days after receipt by sending to the debtor an authenticated record:

(1) disclaiming any interest in the collateral; and

(2) if known to the recipient, providing the name and mailing address of any assignee of or successor to the recipient's interest in the collateral.

(e) A person that receives a request for an accounting or a request regarding a statement of account, claims no interest in the obligations when it receives the request, and claimed an interest in the obligations at an earlier time shall comply with the request within 14 days after receipt by sending to the debtor an authenticated record:

(1) disclaiming any interest in the obligations; and

(2) if known to the recipient, providing the name and mailing address of any assignee of or successor to the recipient's interest in the obligations.

(f) A debtor is entitled without charge to one response to a request under this section during any six-month period. The secured party may require payment of a charge not exceeding $25 for each additional response.

As amended in 1999.

PART 3   Perfection and Priority

[Subpart 1. Law Governing Perfection and Priority]

§ 9–301.   Law Governing Perfection and Priority of Security Interests.

Except as otherwise provided in Sections 9–303 through 9–306, the following rules determine the law governing perfection, the effect of perfection or nonperfection, and the priority of a security interest in collateral:

(1) Except as otherwise provided in this section, while a debtor is located in a jurisdiction, the local law of that jurisdiction governs perfection, the effect of perfection or nonperfection, and the priority of a security interest in collateral.

(2) While collateral is located in a jurisdiction, the local law of that jurisdiction governs perfection, the effect of perfection or nonperfection, and the priority of a possessory security interest in that collateral.

(3) Except as otherwise provided in paragraph (4), while negotiable documents, goods, instruments, money, or tangible chattel paper is located in a jurisdiction, the local law of that jurisdiction governs:

(A) perfection of a security interest in the goods by filing a fixture filing;

(B) perfection of a security interest in timber to be cut; and

(C) the effect of perfection or nonperfection and the priority of a nonpossessory security interest in the collateral.

(4) The local law of the jurisdiction in which the wellhead or minehead is located governs perfection, the effect of perfection or nonperfection, and the priority of a security interest in as-extracted collateral.

§ 9–302.   Law Governing Perfection and Priority of Agricultural Liens.

While farm products are located in a jurisdiction, the local law of that jurisdiction governs perfection, the effect of perfection or nonperfection, and the priority of an agricultural lien on the farm products.

§ 9–303.   Law Governing Perfection and Priority of Security Interests in Goods Covered by a Certificate of Title.

(a) This section applies to goods covered by a certificate of title, even if there is no other relationship between the jurisdiction under whose certificate of title the goods are covered and the goods or the debtor.

(b) Goods become covered by a certificate of title when a valid application for the certificate of title and the applicable fee are delivered to the appropriate authority. Goods cease to be covered by a certificate of title at the earlier of the time the certificate of title ceases to be effective under the law of the issuing jurisdiction or the time the goods become covered subsequently by a certificate of title issued by another jurisdiction.

(c) The local law of the jurisdiction under whose certificate of title the goods are covered governs perfection, the effect of perfection or nonperfection, and the priority of a security interest in goods covered by a certificate of title from the time the goods become covered by the certificate of title until the goods cease to be covered by the certificate of title.

§ 9–304.   Law Governing Perfection and Priority of Security Interests in Deposit Accounts.

(a) The local law of a bank's jurisdiction governs perfection, the effect of perfection or nonperfection, and the priority of a security interest in a deposit account maintained with that bank.

(b) The following rules determine a bank's jurisdiction for purposes of this part:

(1) If an agreement between the bank and the debtor governing the deposit account expressly provides that a particular jurisdiction is the bank's jurisdiction for purposes of this part, this article, or [the Uniform Commercial Code], that jurisdiction is the bank's jurisdiction.

(2) If paragraph (1) does not apply and an agreement between the bank and its customer governing the deposit account expressly provides that the agreement is governed by the law of a particular jurisdiction, that jurisdiction is the bank's jurisdiction.

(3) If neither paragraph (1) nor paragraph (2) applies and an agreement between the bank and its customer governing the deposit account expressly provides that the deposit account is maintained at an office in a particular jurisdiction, that jurisdiction is the bank's jurisdiction.

(4) If none of the preceding paragraphs applies, the bank's jurisdiction is the jurisdiction in which the office identified in an account statement as the office serving the customer's account is located.

(5) If none of the preceding paragraphs applies, the bank's jurisdiction is the jurisdiction in which the chief executive office of the bank is located.

§ 9–305.   Law Governing Perfection and Priority of Security Interests in Investment Property.

(a) Except as otherwise provided in subsection (c), the following rules apply:

(1) While a security certificate is located in a jurisdiction, the local law of that jurisdiction governs perfection, the

effect of perfection or nonperfection, and the priority of a security interest in the certificated security represented thereby.

(2) The local law of the issuer's jurisdiction as specified in Section 8–110(d) governs perfection, the effect of perfection or nonperfection, and the priority of a security interest in an uncertificated security.

(3) The local law of the securities intermediary's jurisdiction as specified in Section 8–110(e) governs perfection, the effect of perfection or nonperfection, and the priority of a security interest in a security entitlement or securities account.

(4) The local law of the commodity intermediary's jurisdiction governs perfection, the effect of perfection or nonperfection, and the priority of a security interest in a commodity contract or commodity account.

(b) The following rules determine a commodity intermediary's jurisdiction for purposes of this part:

(1) If an agreement between the commodity intermediary and commodity customer governing the commodity account expressly provides that a particular jurisdiction is the commodity intermediary's jurisdiction for purposes of this part, this article, or [the Uniform Commercial Code], that jurisdiction is the commodity intermediary's jurisdiction.

(2) If paragraph (1) does not apply and an agreement between the commodity intermediary and commodity customer governing the commodity account expressly provides that the agreement is governed by the law of a particular jurisdiction, that jurisdiction is the commodity intermediary's jurisdiction.

(3) If neither paragraph (1) nor paragraph (2) applies and an agreement between the commodity intermediary and commodity customer governing the commodity account expressly provides that the commodity account is maintained at an office in a particular jurisdiction, that jurisdiction is the commodity intermediary's jurisdiction.

(4) If none of the preceding paragraphs applies, the commodity intermediary's jurisdiction is the jurisdiction in which the office identified in an account statement as the office serving the commodity customer's account is located.

(5) If none of the preceding paragraphs applies, the commodity intermediary's jurisdiction is the jurisdiction in which the chief executive office of the commodity intermediary is located.

(c) The local law of the jurisdiction in which the debtor is located governs:

(1) perfection of a security interest in investment property by filing;

(2) automatic perfection of a security interest in investment property created by a broker or securities intermediary; and

(3) automatic perfection of a security interest in a commodity contract or commodity account created by a commodity intermediary.

§ 9–306. Law Governing Perfection and Priority of Security Interests in Letter-of-Credit Rights.

(a) Subject to subsection (c), the local law of the issuer's jurisdiction or a nominated person's jurisdiction governs perfection, the effect of perfection or nonperfection, and the priority of a security interest in a letter-of-credit right if the issuer's jurisdiction or nominated person's jurisdiction is a State.

(b) For purposes of this part, an issuer's jurisdiction or nominated person's jurisdiction is the jurisdiction whose law governs the liability of the issuer or nominated person with respect to the letter-of-credit right as provided in Section 5–116.

(c) This section does not apply to a security interest that is perfected only under Section 9–308(d).

§ 9–307. Location of Debtor.

(a) In this section, "place of business" means a place where a debtor conducts its affairs.

(b) Except as otherwise provided in this section, the following rules determine a debtor's location:

(1) A debtor who is an individual is located at the individual's principal residence.

(2) A debtor that is an organization and has only one place of business is located at its place of business.

(3) A debtor that is an organization and has more than one place of business is located at its chief executive office.

(c) Subsection (b) applies only if a debtor's residence, place of business, or chief executive office, as applicable, is located in a jurisdiction whose law generally requires information concerning the existence of a nonpossessory security interest to be made generally available in a filing, recording, or registration system as a condition or result of the security interest's obtaining priority over the rights of a lien creditor with respect to the collateral. If subsection (b) does not apply, the debtor is located in the District of Columbia.

(d) A person that ceases to exist, have a residence, or have a place of business continues to be located in the jurisdiction specified by subsections (b) and (c).

(e) A registered organization that is organized under the law of a State is located in that State.

(f) Except as otherwise provided in subsection (i), a registered organization that is organized under the law of the United Statesand a branch or agency of a bank that is not organized under the law of the United States or a State are located:

(1) in the State that the law of the United States designates, if the law designates a State of location;

(2) in the State that the registered organization, branch, or agency designates, if the law of the United States authorizes the

registered organization, branch, or agency to designate its State of location; or

(3) in the District of Columbia, if neither paragraph (1) nor paragraph (2) applies.

(g) A registered organization continues to be located in the jurisdiction specified by subsection (e) or (f) notwithstanding:

(1) the suspension, revocation, forfeiture, or lapse of the registered organization's status as such in its jurisdiction of organization; or

(2) the dissolution, winding up, or cancellation of the existence of the registered organization.

(h) The United States is located in the District of Columbia.

(i) A branch or agency of a bank that is not organized under the law of the United States or a State is located in the State in which the branch or agency is licensed, if all branches and agencies of the bank are licensed in only one State.

(j) A foreign air carrier under the Federal Aviation Act of 1958, as amended, is located at the designated office of the agent upon which service of process may be made on behalf of the carrier.

(k) This section applies only for purposes of this part.

[Subpart 2. Perfection]

§ 9–308.   When Security Interest or Agricultural Lien Is Perfected; Continuity of Perfection.

(a) Except as otherwise provided in this section and Section 9–309, a security interest is perfected if it has attached and all of the applicable requirements for perfection in Sections 9–310 through 9–316 have been satisfied. A security interest is perfected when it attaches if the applicable requirements are satisfied before the security interest attaches.

(b) An agricultural lien is perfected if it has become effective and all of the applicable requirements for perfection in Section 9–310 have been satisfied. An agricultural lien is perfected when it becomes effective if the applicable requirements are satisfied before the agricultural lien becomes effective.

(c) A security interest or agricultural lien is perfected continuously if it is originally perfected by one method under this article and is later perfected by another method under this article, without an intermediate period when it was unperfected.

(d) Perfection of a security interest in collateral also perfects a security interest in a supporting obligation for the collateral.

(e) Perfection of a security interest in a right to payment or performance also perfects a security interest in a security interest, mortgage, or other lien on personal or real property securing the right.

(f) Perfection of a security interest in a securities account also perfects a security interest in the security entitlements carried in the securities account.

(g) Perfection of a security interest in a commodity account also perfects a security interest in the commodity contracts carried in the commodity account.

Legislative Note: Any statute conflicting with subsection (e) must be made expressly subject to that subsection.

§ 9–309.   Security Interest Perfected upon Attachment.

The following security interests are perfected when they attach:

(1) a purchase-money security interest in consumer goods, except as otherwise provided in Section 9–311(b) with respect to consumer goods that are subject to a statute or treaty described in Section 9–311(a);

(2) an assignment of accounts or payment intangibles which does not by itself or in conjunction with other assignments to the same assignee transfer a significant part of the assignor's outstanding accounts or payment intangibles;

(3) a sale of a payment intangible;

(4) a sale of a promissory note;

(5) a security interest created by the assignment of a health-care-insurance receivable to the provider of the health-care goods or services;

(6) a security interest arising under Section 2–401, 2–505, 2–711 (3), or 2A–508(5), until the debtor obtains possession of the collateral;

(7) a security interest of a collecting bank arising under Section 4–210;

(8) a security interest of an issuer or nominated person arising under Section 5–118;

(9) a security interest arising in the delivery of a financial asset under Section 9–206(c);

(10) a security interest in investment property created by a broker or securities intermediary;

(11) a security interest in a commodity contract or a commodity account created by a commodity intermediary;

(12) an assignment for the benefit of all creditors of the transferor and subsequent transfers by the assignee thereunder; and

(13) a security interest created by an assignment of a beneficial interest in a decedent's estate; and

(14) a sale by an individual of an account that is a right to payment of winnings in a lottery or other game of chance.

§ 9–310. When Filing Required to Perfect Security Interest or Agricultural Lien; Security Interests and Agricultural Liens to Which Filing Provisions Do Not Apply.

(a) Except as otherwise provided in subsection (b) and Section 9–312(b), a financing statement must be filed to perfect all security interests and agricultural liens.

(b) The filing of a financing statement is not necessary to perfect a security interest:

(1) that is perfected under Section 9–308(d), (e), (f), or (g);

(2) that is perfected under Section 9–309 when it attaches;

(3) in property subject to a statute, regulation, or treaty described in Section 9–311(a);

(4) in goods in possession of a bailee which is perfected under Section 9–312(d)(1) or (2);

(5) in certificated securities, documents, goods, or instruments which is perfected without filing or possession under Section 9–312(e), (f), or (g);

(6) in collateral in the secured party's possession under Section 9–313;

(7) in a certificated security which is perfected by delivery of the security certificate to the secured party under Section 9–313;

(8) in deposit accounts, electronic chattel paper, investment property, or letter-of-credit rights which is perfected by control under Section 9–314;

(9) in proceeds which is perfected under Section 9–315; or

(10) that is perfected under Section 9–316.

(c) If a secured party assigns a perfected security interest or agricultural lien, a filing under this article is not required to continue the perfected status of the security interest against creditors of and transferees from the original debtor.

§ 9–311. Perfection of Security Interests in Property Subject to Certain Statutes, Regulations, and Treaties.

(a) Except as otherwise provided in subsection (d), the filing of a financing statement is not necessary or effective to perfect a security interest in property subject to:

(1) a statute, regulation, or treaty of the United States whose requirements for a security interest's obtaining priority over the rights of a lien creditor with respect to the property preempt Section 9–310(a);

(2) [list any certificate-of-title statute covering automobiles, trailers, mobile homes, boats, farm tractors, or the like, which provides for a security interest to be indicated on the certificate as a condition or result of perfection, and any non-Uniform Commercial Code central filing statute]; or

(3) a certificate-of-title statute of another jurisdiction which provides for a security interest to be indicated on the certificate as a condition or result of the security interest's obtaining priority over the rights of a lien creditor with respect to the property.

(b) Compliance with the requirements of a statute, regulation, or treaty described in subsection (a) for obtaining priority over the rights of a lien creditor is equivalent to the filing of a financing statement under this article. Except as otherwise provided in subsection (d) and Sections 9–313 and 9–316(d) and (e) for goods covered by a certificate of title, a security interest in property subject to a statute, regulation, or treaty described in subsection (a) may be perfected only by compliance with those requirements, and a security interest so perfected remains perfected notwithstanding a change in the use or transfer of possession of the collateral.

(c) Except as otherwise provided in subsection (d) and Section 9–316(d) and (e), duration and renewal of perfection of a security interest perfected by compliance with the requirements prescribed by a statute, regulation, or treaty described in subsection (a) are governed by the statute, regulation, or treaty. In other respects, the security interest is subject to this article.

(d) During any period in which collateral subject to a statute specified in subsection (a)(2) is inventory held for sale or lease by a person or leased by that person as lessor and that person is in the business of selling goods of that kind, this section does not apply to a security interest in that collateral created by that person.

Legislative Note: This Article contemplates that perfection of a security interest in goods covered by a certificate of title occurs upon receipt by appropriate State officials of a properly tendered application for a certificate of title on which the security interest is to be indicated, without a relation back to an earlier time. States whose certificate-of-title statutes provide for perfection at a different time or contain a relation-back provision should amend the statutes accordingly.

§ 9–312. Perfection of Security Interests in Chattel Paper, Deposit Accounts, Documents, Goods Covered by Documents, Instruments, Investment Property, Letter-of-Credit Rights, and Money; Perfection by Permissive Filing; Temporary Perfection without Filing or Transfer of Possession.

(a) A security interest in chattel paper, negotiable documents, instruments, or investment property may be perfected by filing.

(b) Except as otherwise provided in Section 9–315(c) and (d) for proceeds:

(1) a security interest in a deposit account may be perfected only by control under Section 9–314;

(2) and except as otherwise provided in Section 9–308(d), a security interest in a letter-of-credit right may be perfected only by control under Section 9–314; and

(3) a security interest in money may be perfected only by the secured party's taking possession under Section 9–313.

(c) While goods are in the possession of a bailee that has issued a negotiable document covering the goods:

(1) a security interest in the goods may be perfected by perfecting a security interest in the document; and

(2) a security interest perfected in the document has priority over any security interest that becomes perfected in the goods by another method during that time.

(d) While goods are in the possession of a bailee that has issued a nonnegotiable document covering the goods, a security interest in the goods may be perfected by:

(1) issuance of a document in the name of the secured party;

(2) the bailee's receipt of notification of the secured party's interest; or

(3) filing as to the goods.

(e) A security interest in certificated securities, negotiable documents, or instruments is perfected without filing or the taking of possession for a period of 20 days from the time it attaches to the extent that it arises for new value given under an authenticated security agreement.

(f) A perfected security interest in a negotiable document or goods in possession of a bailee, other than one that has issued a negotiable document for the goods, remains perfected for 20 days without filing if the secured party makes available to the debtor the goods or documents representing the goods for the purpose of:

(1) ultimate sale or exchange; or

(2) loading, unloading, storing, shipping, transshipping, manufacturing, processing, or otherwise dealing with them in a manner preliminary to their sale or exchange.

(g) A perfected security interest in a certificated security or instrument remains perfected for 20 days without filing if the secured party delivers the security certificate or instrument to the debtor for the purpose of:

(1) ultimate sale or exchange; or

(2) presentation, collection, enforcement, renewal, or registration of transfer.

(h) After the 20-day period specified in subsection (e), (f), or (g) expires, perfection depends upon compliance with this article.

§ 9–313. When Possession by or Delivery to Secured Party Perfects Security Interest without Filing.

(a) Except as otherwise provided in subsection (b), a secured party may perfect a security interest in negotiable documents, goods, instruments, money, or tangible chattel paper by taking possession of the collateral. A secured party may perfect a security interest in certificated securities by taking delivery of the certificated securities under Section 8–301.

(b) With respect to goods covered by a certificate of title issued by this State, a secured party may perfect a security interest in the goods by taking possession of the goods only in the circumstances described in Section 9–316(d).

(c) With respect to collateral other than certificated securities and goods covered by a document, a secured party takes possession of collateral in the possession of a person other than the debtor, the secured party, or a lessee of the collateral from the debtor in the ordinary course of the debtor's business, when:

(1) the person in possession authenticates a record acknowledging that it holds possession of the collateral for the secured party's benefit; or

(2) the person takes possession of the collateral after having authenticated a record acknowledging that it will hold possession of collateral for the secured party's benefit.

(d) If perfection of a security interest depends upon possession of the collateral by a secured party, perfection occurs no earlier than the time the secured party takes possession and continues only while the secured party retains possession.

(e) A security interest in a certificated security in registered form is perfected by delivery when delivery of the certificated security occurs under Section 8–301 and remains perfected by delivery until the debtor obtains possession of the security certificate.

(f) A person in possession of collateral is not required to acknowledge that it holds possession for a secured party's benefit.

(g) If a person acknowledges that it holds possession for the secured party's benefit:

(1) the acknowledgment is effective under subsection (c) or Section 8–301(a), even if the acknowledgment violates the rights of a debtor; and

(2) unless the person otherwise agrees or law other than this article otherwise provides, the person does not owe any duty to the secured party and is not required to confirm the acknowledgment to another person.

(h) A secured party having possession of collateral does not relinquish possession by delivering the collateral to a person other than the debtor or a lessee of the collateral from the debtor in the ordinary course of the debtor's business if the person was instructed before the delivery or is instructed contemporaneously with the delivery:

(1) to hold possession of the collateral for the secured party's benefit; or

(2) to redeliver the collateral to the secured party.

(i) A secured party does not relinquish possession, even if a delivery under subsection (h) violates the rights of a debtor. A person to which collateral is delivered under subsection (h) does not owe any duty to the secured party and is not required to confirm the delivery to another person unless the person otherwise agrees or law other than this article otherwise provides.

§ 9–314.   Perfection by Control.

(a) A security interest in investment property, deposit accounts, letter-of-credit rights, or electronic chattel paper may be perfected by control of the collateral under Section 9–104, 9–105, 9–106, or 9–107.

(b) A security interest in deposit accounts, electronic chattel paper, or letter-of-credit rights is perfected by control under Section 9–104, 9–105, or 9–107 when the secured party obtains control and remains perfected by control only while the secured party retains control.

(c) A security interest in investment property is perfected by control under Section 9–106 from the time the secured party obtains control and remains perfected by control until:

(1) the secured party does not have control; and

(2) one of the following occurs:

(A) if the collateral is a certificated security, the debtor has or acquires possession of the security certificate;

(B) if the collateral is an uncertificated security, the issuer has registered or registers the debtor as the registered owner; or

(C) if the collateral is a security entitlement, the debtor is or becomes the entitlement holder.

(2) if the proceeds are not goods, to the extent that the secured party identifies the proceeds by a method of tracing, including application of equitable principles, that is permitted under law other than this article with respect to commingled property of the type involved.

(c) A security interest in proceeds is a perfected security interest if the security interest in the original collateral was perfected.

(d) A perfected security interest in proceeds becomes unperfected on the 21st day after the security interest attaches to the proceeds unless:

(1) the following conditions are satisfied:

(A) a filed financing statement covers the original collateral;

(B) the proceeds are collateral in which a security interest may be perfected by filing in the office in which the financing statement has been filed; and

(C) the proceeds are not acquired with cash proceeds;

(2) the proceeds are identifiable cash proceeds; or

(3) the security interest in the proceeds is perfected other than under subsection (c) when the security interest attaches to the proceeds or within 20 days thereafter.

(e) If a filed financing statement covers the original collateral, a security interest in proceeds which remains perfected under subsection (d)(1) becomes unperfected at the later of:

(1) when the effectiveness of the filed financing statement lapses under Section 9–515 or is terminated under Section 9–513; or

(2) the 21st day after the security interest attaches to the proceeds.

§ 9–315.   Secured Party's Rights on Disposition of Collateral and in Proceeds.

(a) Except as otherwise provided in this article and in Section 2–403(2):

(1) a security interest or agricultural lien continues in collateral notwithstanding sale, lease, license, exchange, or other disposition thereof unless the secured party authorized the disposition free of the security interest or agricultural lien; and

(2) a security interest attaches to any identifiable proceeds of collateral.

(b) Proceeds that are commingled with other property are identifiable proceeds:

(1) if the proceeds are goods, to the extent provided by Section 9–336; and

§ 9–316.   Continued Perfection of Security Interest Following Change in Governing Law.

(a) A security interest perfected pursuant to the law of the jurisdiction designated in Section 9–301(1) or 9–305(c) remains perfected until the earliest of:

(1) the time perfection would have ceased under the law of that jurisdiction;

(2) the expiration of four months after a change of the debtor's location to another jurisdiction; or

(3) the expiration of one year after a transfer of collateral to a person that thereby becomes a debtor and is located in another jurisdiction.

(b) If a security interest described in subsection (a) becomes perfected under the law of the other jurisdiction before the earliest time or event described in that subsection, it remains perfected thereafter. If the security interest does not become perfected under the law of the other jurisdiction before the earliest time or event, it becomes unperfected and is deemed never to have been perfected as against a purchaser of the collateral for value.

(c) A possessory security interest in collateral, other than goods covered by a certificate of title and as-extracted collateral consisting of goods, remains continuously perfected if:

(1) the collateral is located in one jurisdiction and subject to a security interest perfected under the law of that jurisdiction;

(2) thereafter the collateral is brought into another jurisdiction; and

(3) upon entry into the other jurisdiction, the security interest is perfected under the law of the other jurisdiction.

(d) Except as otherwise provided in subsection (e), a security interest in goods covered by a certificate of title which is perfected by any method under the law of another jurisdiction when the goods become covered by a certificate of title from this State remains perfected until the security interest would have become unperfected under the law of the other jurisdiction had the goods not become so covered.

(e) A security interest described in subsection (d) becomes unperfected as against a purchaser of the goods for value and is deemed never to have been perfected as against a purchaser of the goods for value if the applicable requirements for perfection under Section 9–311(b) or 9–313 are not satisfied before the earlier of:

(1) the time the security interest would have become unperfected under the law of the other jurisdiction had the goods not become covered by a certificate of title from this State; or

(2) the expiration of four months after the goods had become so covered.

(f) A security interest in deposit accounts, letter-of-credit rights, or investment property which is perfected under the law of the bank's jurisdiction, the issuer's jurisdiction, a nominated person's jurisdiction, the securities intermediary's jurisdiction, or the commodity intermediary's jurisdiction, as applicable, remains perfected until the earlier of:

(1) the time the security interest would have become unperfected under the law of that jurisdiction; or

(2) the expiration of four months after a change of the applicable jurisdiction to another jurisdiction.

(g) If a security interest described in subsection (f) becomes perfected under the law of the other jurisdiction before the earlier of the time or the end of the period described in that subsection, it remains perfected thereafter. If the security interest does not become perfected under the law of the other jurisdiction before the earlier of that time or the end of that period, it becomes unperfected and is deemed never to have been perfected as against a purchaser of the collateral for value.

[Subpart 3. Priority]

§ 9–317.   Interests That Take Priority over or Take Free of Security Interest or Agricultural Lien.

(a) A security interest or agricultural lien is subordinate to the rights of:

(1) a person entitled to priority under Section 9–322; and

(2) except as otherwise provided in subsection (e), a person that becomes a lien creditor before the earlier of the time:

(A) the security interest or agricultural lien is perfected; or

(B) one of the conditions specified in Section 9–203(b)(3) is met and a financing statement covering the collateral is filed.

(b) Except as otherwise provided in subsection (e), a buyer, other than a secured party, of tangible chattel paper, documents, goods, instruments, or a security certificate takes free of a security interest or agricultural lien if the buyer gives value and receives delivery of the collateral without knowledge of the security interest or agricultural lien and before it is perfected.

(c) Except as otherwise provided in subsection (e), a lessee of goods takes free of a security interest or agricultural lien if the lessee gives value and receives delivery of the collateral without knowledge of the security interest or agricultural lien and before it is perfected.

(d) A licensee of a general intangible or a buyer, other than a secured party, of accounts, electronic chattel paper, general intangibles, or investment property other than a certificated security takes free of a security interest if the licensee or buyer gives value without knowledge of the security interest and before it is perfected.

(e) Except as otherwise provided in Sections 9–320 and 9–321, if a person files a financing statement with respect to a purchase-money security interest before or within 20 days after the debtor receives delivery of the collateral, the security interest takes priority over the rights of a buyer, lessee, or lien creditor which arise between the time the security interest attaches and the time of filing.

As amended in 2000.

§ 9–318.   No Interest Retained in Right to Payment That Is Sold; Rights and Title of Seller of Account or Chattel Paper with Respect to Creditors and Purchasers.

(a) A debtor that has sold an account, chattel paper, payment intangible, or promissory note does not retain a legal or equitable interest in the collateral sold.

(b) For purposes of determining the rights of creditors of, and purchasers for value of an account or chattel paper from, a debtor that has sold an account or chattel paper, while the buyer's security interest is unperfected, the debtor is deemed to have rights and title to the account or chattel paper identical to those the debtor sold.

§ 9–319. Rights and Title of Consignee with Respect to Creditors and Purchasers.

(a) Except as otherwise provided in subsection (b), for purposes of determining the rights of creditors of, and purchasers for value of goods from, a consignee, while the goods are in the possession of the consignee, the consignee is deemed to have rights and title to the goods identical to those the consignor had or had power to transfer.

(b) For purposes of determining the rights of a creditor of a consignee, law other than this article determines the rights and title of a consignee while goods are in the consignee's possession if, under this part, a perfected security interest held by the consignor would have priority over the rights of the creditor.

§ 9–320. Buyer of Goods.

(a) Except as otherwise provided in subsection (e), a buyer in ordinary course of business, other than a person buying farm products from a person engaged in farming operations, takes free of a security interest created by the buyer's seller, even if the security interest is perfected and the buyer knows of its existence.

(b) Except as otherwise provided in subsection (e), a buyer of goods from a person who used or bought the goods for use primarily for personal, family, or household purposes takes free of a security interest, even if perfected, if the buyer buys:

(1) without knowledge of the security interest;

(2) for value;

(3) primarily for the buyer's personal, family, or household purposes; and

(4) before the filing of a financing statement covering the goods.

(c) To the extent that it affects the priority of a security interest over a buyer of goods under subsection (b), the period of effectiveness of a filing made in the jurisdiction in which the seller is located is governed by Section 9–316(a) and (b).

(d) A buyer in ordinary course of business buying oil, gas, or other minerals at the wellhead or minehead or after extraction takes free of an interest arising out of an encumbrance.

(e) Subsections (a) and (b) do not affect a security interest in goods in the possession of the secured party under Section 9–313.

§ 9–321. Licensee of General Intangible and Lessee of Goods in Ordinary Course of Business.

(a) In this section, "licensee in ordinary course of business" means a person that becomes a licensee of a general intangible in good faith, without knowledge that the license violates the rights of another person in the general intangible, and in the ordinary course from a person in the business of licensing general intangibles of that kind. A person becomes a licensee in the ordinary course if the license to the person comports with the usual or customary practices in the kind of business in which the licensor is engaged or with the licensor's own usual or customary practices.

(b) A licensee in ordinary course of business takes its rights under a nonexclusive license free of a security interest in the general intangible created by the licensor, even if the security interest is perfected and the licensee knows of its existence.

(c) A lessee in ordinary course of business takes its leasehold interest free of a security interest in the goods created by the lessor, even if the security interest is perfected and the lessee knows of its existence.

§ 9–322. Priorities among Conflicting Security Interests in and Agricultural Liens on Same Collateral.

(a) Except as otherwise provided in this section, priority among conflicting security interests and agricultural liens in the same collateral is determined according to the following rules:

(1) Conflicting perfected security interests and agricultural liens rank according to priority in time of filing or perfection. Priority dates from the earlier of the time a filing covering the collateral is first made or the security interest or agricultural lien is first perfected, if there is no period thereafter when there is neither filing nor perfection.

(2) A perfected security interest or agricultural lien has priority over a conflicting unperfected security interest or agricultural lien.

(3) The first security interest or agricultural lien to attach or become effective has priority if conflicting security interests and agricultural liens are unperfected.

(b) For the purposes of subsection (a)(1):

(1) the time of filing or perfection as to a security interest in collateral is also the time of filing or perfection as to a security interest in proceeds; and

(2) the time of filing or perfection as to a security interest in collateral supported by a supporting obligation is also the time of filing or perfection as to a security interest in the supporting obligation.

(c) Except as otherwise provided in subsection (f), a security interest in collateral which qualifies for priority over a conflicting security interest under Section 9–327, 9–328, 9–329, 9–330, or 9–331 also has priority over a conflicting security interest in:

(1) any supporting obligation for the collateral; and

(2) proceeds of the collateral if:

(A) the security interest in proceeds is perfected;

(B) the proceeds are cash proceeds or of the same type as the collateral; and

(C) in the case of proceeds that are proceeds of proceeds, all intervening proceeds are cash proceeds, proceeds of the same type as the collateral, or an account relating to the collateral.

(d) Subject to subsection (e) and except as otherwise provided in subsection (f), if a security interest in chattel paper, deposit accounts, negotiable documents, instruments, investment property, or letter-of-credit rights is perfected by a method other than filing, conflicting perfected security interests in proceeds of the collateral rank according to priority in time of filing.

(e) Subsection (d) applies only if the proceeds of the collateral are not cash proceeds, chattel paper, negotiable documents, instruments, investment property, or letter-of-credit rights.

(f) Subsections (a) through (e) are subject to:

(1) subsection (g) and the other provisions of this part;

(2) Section 4–210 with respect to a security interest of a collecting bank;

(3) Section 5–118 with respect to a security interest of an issuer or nominated person; and

(4) Section 9–110 with respect to a security interest arising under Article 2 or 2A.

(g) A perfected agricultural lien on collateral has priority over a conflicting security interest in or agricultural lien on the same collateral if the statute creating the agricultural lien so provides.

§ 9–323.   Future Advances.

(a) Except as otherwise provided in subsection (c), for purposes of determining the priority of a perfected security interest under Section 9–322(a)(1), perfection of the security interest dates from the time an advance is made to the extent that the security interest secures an advance that:

(1) is made while the security interest is perfected only:

(A) under Section 9–309 when it attaches; or

(B) temporarily under Section 9–312(e), (f), or (g); and

(2) is not made pursuant to a commitment entered into before or while the security interest is perfected by a method other than under Section 9–309 or 9–312(e), (f), or (g).

(b) Except as otherwise provided in subsection (c), a security interest is subordinate to the rights of a person that becomes a lien creditor to the extent that the security interest secures an advance made more than 45 days after the person becomes a lien creditor unless the advance is made:

(1) without knowledge of the lien; or

(2) pursuant to a commitment entered into without knowledge of the lien.

(c) Subsections (a) and (b) do not apply to a security interest held by a secured party that is a buyer of accounts, chattel paper, payment intangibles, or promissory notes or a consignor.

(d) Except as otherwise provided in subsection (e), a buyer of goods other than a buyer in ordinary course of business takes free of a security interest to the extent that it secures advances made after the earlier of:

(1) the time the secured party acquires knowledge of the buyer's purchase; or

(2) 45 days after the purchase.

(e) Subsection (d) does not apply if the advance is made pursuant to a commitment entered into without knowledge of the buyer's purchase and before the expiration of the 45-day period.

(f) Except as otherwise provided in subsection (g), a lessee of goods, other than a lessee in ordinary course of business, takes the leasehold interest free of a security interest to the extent that it secures advances made after the earlier of:

(1) the time the secured party acquires knowledge of the lease; or

(2) 45 days after the lease contract becomes enforceable.

(g) Subsection (f) does not apply if the advance is made pursuant to a commitment entered into without knowledge of the lease and before the expiration of the 45-day period.

As amended in 1999.

§ 9–324.   Priority of Purchase-Money Security Interests.

(a) Except as otherwise provided in subsection (g), a perfected purchase-money security interest in goods other than inventory or livestock has priority over a conflicting security interest in the same goods, and, except as otherwise provided in Section 9–327, a perfected security interest in its identifiable proceeds also has priority, if the purchase-money security interest is perfected when the debtor receives possession of the collateral or within 20 days thereafter.

(b) Subject to subsection (c) and except as otherwise provided in subsection (g), a perfected purchase-money security interest in inventory has priority over a conflicting security interest in the same inventory, has priority over a conflicting security interest in chattel paper or an instrument constituting proceeds of the inventory and in proceeds of the chattel paper, if so provided in Section 9–330, and, except as otherwise provided in Section 9–327, also has priority in identifiable cash proceeds of the inventory to the extent the identifiable cash proceeds are received on or before the delivery of the inventory to a buyer, if:

(1) the purchase-money security interest is perfected when the debtor receives possession of the inventory;

(2) the purchase-money secured party sends an authenticated notification to the holder of the conflicting security interest;

(3) the holder of the conflicting security interest receives the notification within five years before the debtor receives possession of the inventory; and

(4) the notification states that the person sending the notification has or expects to acquire a purchase-money security interest in inventory of the debtor and describes the inventory.

(c) Subsections (b)(2) through (4) apply only if the holder of the conflicting security interest had filed a financing statement covering the same types of inventory:

(1) if the purchase-money security interest is perfected by filing, before the date of the filing; or

(2) if the purchase-money security interest is temporarily perfected without filing or possession under Section 9–312(f), before the beginning of the 20-day period thereunder.

(d) Subject to subsection (e) and except as otherwise provided in subsection (g), a perfected purchase-money security interest in livestock that are farm products has priority over a conflicting security interest in the same livestock, and, except as otherwise provided in Section 9–327, a perfected security interest in their identifiable proceeds and identifiable products in their unmanufactured states also has priority, if:

(1) the purchase-money security interest is perfected when the debtor receives possession of the livestock;

(2) the purchase-money secured party sends an authenticated notification to the holder of the conflicting security interest;

(3) the holder of the conflicting security interest receives the notification within six months before the debtor receives possession of the livestock; and

(4) the notification states that the person sending the notification has or expects to acquire a purchase-money security interest in livestock of the debtor and describes the livestock.

(e) Subsections (d)(2) through (4) apply only if the holder of the conflicting security interest had filed a financing statement covering the same types of livestock:

(1) if the purchase-money security interest is perfected by filing, before the date of the filing; or

(2) if the purchase-money security interest is temporarily perfected without filing or possession under Section 9–312(f), before the beginning of the 20-day period thereunder.

(f) Except as otherwise provided in subsection (g), a perfected purchase-money security interest in software has

priority over a conflicting security interest in the same collateral, and, except as otherwise provided in Section 9–327, a perfected security interest in its identifiable proceeds also has priority, to the extent that the purchase-money security interest in the goods in which the software was acquired for use has priority in the goods and proceeds of the goods under this section.

(g) If more than one security interest qualifies for priority in the same collateral under subsection (a), (b), (d), or (f):

(1) a security interest securing an obligation incurred as all or part of the price of the collateral has priority over a security interest securing an obligation incurred for value given to enable the debtor to acquire rights in or the use of collateral; and

(2) in all other cases, Section 9–322(a) applies to the qualifying security interests.

§ 9–325.   Priority of Security Interests in Transferred Collateral.

(a) Except as otherwise provided in subsection (b), a security interest created by a debtor is subordinate to a security interest in the same collateral created by another person if:

(1) the debtor acquired the collateral subject to the security interest created by the other person;

(2) the security interest created by the other person was perfected when the debtor acquired the collateral; and

(3) there is no period thereafter when the security interest is unperfected.

(b) Subsection (a) subordinates a security interest only if the security interest:

(1) otherwise would have priority solely under Section 9–322(a) or 9–324; or

(2) arose solely under Section 2–711(3) or 2A–508(5).

§ 9–326.   Priority of Security Interests Created by New Debtor.

(a) Subject to subsection (b), a security interest created by a new debtor which is perfected by a filed financing statement that is effective solely under Section 9–508 in collateral in which a new debtor has or acquires rights is subordinate to a security interest in the same collateral which is perfected other than by a filed financing statement that is effective solely under Section 9–508.

(b) The other provisions of this part determine the priority among conflicting security interests in the same collateral perfected by filed financing statements that are effective solely under Section 9–508. However, if the security agreements to which a new debtor became bound as debtor were not entered into by the same original debtor, the conflicting security interests rank according to priority in time of the new debtor's having become bound.

§ 9–327. Priority of Security Interests in Deposit Account.

The following rules govern priority among conflicting security interests in the same deposit account:

(1) A security interest held by a secured party having control of the deposit account under Section 9–104 has priority over a conflicting security interest held by a secured party that does not have control.

(2) Except as otherwise provided in paragraphs (3) and (4), security interests perfected by control under Section 9–314 rank according to priority in time of obtaining control.

(3) Except as otherwise provided in paragraph (4), a security interest held by the bank with which the deposit account is maintained has priority over a conflicting security interest held by another secured party.

(4) A security interest perfected by control under Section 9–104 (a)(3) has priority over a security interest held by the bank with which the deposit account is maintained.

§ 9–328. Priority of Security Interests in Investment Property.

The following rules govern priority among conflicting security interests in the same investment property:

(1) A security interest held by a secured party having control of investment property under Section 9–106 has priority over a security interest held by a secured party that does not have control of the investment property.

(2) Except as otherwise provided in paragraphs (3) and (4), conflicting security interests held by secured parties each of which has control under Section 9–106 rank according to priority in time of:

(A) if the collateral is a security, obtaining control;

(B) if the collateral is a security entitlement carried in a securities account and:

(i) if the secured party obtained control under Section 8–106(d)(1), the secured party's becoming the person for which the securities account is maintained;

(ii) if the secured party obtained control under Section 8–106(d)(2), the securities intermediary's agreement to comply with the secured party's entitlement orders with respect to security entitlements carried or to be carried in the securities account; or

(iii) if the secured party obtained control through another person under Section 8–106(d)(3), the time on which priority would

be based under this paragraph if the other person were the secured party; or

(C) if the collateral is a commodity contract carried with a commodity intermediary, the satisfaction of the requirement for control specified in Section 9–106(b)(2) with respect to commodity contracts carried or to be carried with the commodity intermediary.

(3) A security interest held by a securities intermediary in a security entitlement or a securities account maintained with the securities intermediary has priority over a conflicting security interest held by another secured party.

(4) A security interest held by a commodity intermediary in a commodity contract or a commodity account maintained with the commodity intermediary has priority over a conflicting security interest held by another secured party.

(5) A security interest in a certificated security in registered form which is perfected by taking delivery under Section 9–313(a) and not by control under Section 9–314 has priority over a conflicting security interest perfected by a method other than control.

(6) Conflicting security interests created by a broker, securities intermediary, or commodity intermediary which are perfected without control under Section 9–106 rank equally.

(7) In all other cases, priority among conflicting security interests in investment property is governed by Sections 9–322 and 9–323.

§ 9–329. Priority of Security Interests in Letter-of-Credit Right.

The following rules govern priority among conflicting security interests in the same letter-of-credit right:

(1) A security interest held by a secured party having control of the letter-of-credit right under Section 9–107 has priority to the extent of its control over a conflicting security interest held by a secured party that does not have control.

(2) Security interests perfected by control under Section 9–314 rank according to priority in time of obtaining control.

§ 9–330. Priority of Purchaser of Chattel Paper or Instrument.

(a) A purchaser of chattel paper has priority over a security interest in the chattel paper which is claimed merely as proceeds of inventory subject to a security interest if:

(1) in good faith and in the ordinary course of the purchaser's business, the purchaser gives new value and takes possession of the chattel paper or obtains control of the chattel paper under Section 9–105; and

(2) the chattel paper does not indicate that it has been assigned to an identified assignee other than the purchaser.

(b) A purchaser of chattel paper has priority over a security interest in the chattel paper which is claimed other than merely as proceeds of inventory subject to a security interest if the purchaser gives new value and takes possession of the chattel paper or obtains control of the chattel paper under Section 9–105 in good faith, in the ordinary course of the purchaser's business, and without knowledge that the purchase violates the rights of the secured party.

(c) Except as otherwise provided in Section 9–327, a purchaser having priority in chattel paper under subsection (a) or (b) also has priority in proceeds of the chattel paper to the extent that:

(1) Section 9–322 provides for priority in the proceeds; or

(2) the proceeds consist of the specific goods covered by the chattel paper or cash proceeds of the specific goods, even if the purchaser's security interest in the proceeds is unperfected.

(d) Except as otherwise provided in Section 9–331(a), a purchaser of an instrument has priority over a security interest in the instrument perfected by a method other than possession if the purchaser gives value and takes possession of the instrument in good faith and without knowledge that the purchase violates the rights of the secured party.

(e) For purposes of subsections (a) and (b), the holder of a purchase-money security interest in inventory gives new value for chattel paper constituting proceeds of the inventory.

(f) For purposes of subsections (b) and (d), if chattel paper or an instrument indicates that it has been assigned to an identified secured party other than the purchaser, a purchaser of the chattel paper or instrument has knowledge that the purchase violates the rights of the secured party.

§ 9–331. Priority of Rights of Purchasers of Instruments, Documents, and Securities under Other Articles; Priority of Interests in Financial Assets and Security Entitlements under Article 8.

(a) This article does not limit the rights of a holder in due course of a negotiable instrument, a holder to which a negotiable document of title has been duly negotiated, or a protected purchaser of a security. These holders or purchasers take priority over an earlier security interest, even if perfected, to the extent provided in Articles 3, 7, and 8.

(b) This article does not limit the rights of or impose liability on a person to the extent that the person is protected against the assertion of a claim under Article 8.

(c) Filing under this article does not constitute notice of a claim or defense to the holders, or purchasers, or persons described in subsections (a) and (b).

§ 9–332. Transfer of Money; Transfer of Funds from Deposit Account.

(a) A transferee of money takes the money free of a security interest unless the transferee acts in collusion with the debtor in violating the rights of the secured party.

(b) A transferee of funds from a deposit account takes the funds free of a security interest in the deposit account unless the transferee acts in collusion with the debtor in violating the rights of the secured party.

§ 9–333. Priority of Certain Liens Arising by Operation of Law.

(a) In this section, "possessory lien" means an interest, other than a security interest or an agricultural lien:

(1) which secures payment or performance of an obligation for services or materials furnished with respect to goods by a person in the ordinary course of the person's business;

(2) which is created by statute or rule of law in favor of the person; and

(3) whose effectiveness depends on the person's possession of the goods.

(b) A possessory lien on goods has priority over a security interest in the goods unless the lien is created by a statute that expressly provides otherwise.

§ 9–334. Priority of Security Interests in Fixtures and Crops.

(a) A security interest under this article may be created in goods that are fixtures or may continue in goods that become fixtures. A security interest does not exist under this article in ordinary building materials incorporated into an improvement on land.

(b) This article does not prevent creation of an encumbrance upon fixtures under real property law.

(c) In cases not governed by subsections (d) through (h), a security interest in fixtures is subordinate to a conflicting interest of an encumbrancer or owner of the related real property other than the debtor.

(d) Except as otherwise provided in subsection (h), a perfected security interest in fixtures has priority over a conflicting interest of an encumbrancer or owner of the real property if the debtor has an interest of record in or is in possession of the real property and:

(1) the security interest is a purchase-money security interest;

(2) the interest of the encumbrancer or owner arises before the goods become fixtures; and

(3) the security interest is perfected by a fixture filing before the goods become fixtures or within 20 days thereafter.

(e) A perfected security interest in fixtures has priority over a conflicting interest of an encumbrancer or owner of the real property if:

(1) the debtor has an interest of record in the real property or is in possession of the real property and the security interest:

(A) is perfected by a fixture filing before the interest of the encumbrancer or owner is of record; and

(B) has priority over any conflicting interest of a predecessor in title of the encumbrancer or owner;

(2) before the goods become fixtures, the security interest is perfected by any method permitted by this article and the fixtures are readily removable:

(A) factory or office machines;

(B) equipment that is not primarily used or leased for use in the operation of the real property; or

(C) replacements of domestic appliances that are consumer goods;

(3) the conflicting interest is a lien on the real property obtained by legal or equitable proceedings after the security interest was perfected by any method permitted by this article; or

(4) the security interest is:

(A) created in a manufactured home in a manufactured-home transaction; and

(B) perfected pursuant to a statute described in Section 9–311(a)(2).

(f) A security interest in fixtures, whether or not perfected, has priority over a conflicting interest of an encumbrancer or owner of the real property if:

(1) the encumbrancer or owner has, in an authenticated record, consented to the security interest or disclaimed an interest in the goods as fixtures; or

(2) the debtor has a right to remove the goods as against the encumbrancer or owner.

(g) The priority of the security interest under paragraph (f)(2) continues for a reasonable time if the debtor's right to remove the goods as against the encumbrancer or owner terminates.

(h) A mortgage is a construction mortgage to the extent that it secures an obligation incurred for the construction of an improvement on land, including the acquisition cost of the land, if a recorded record of the mortgage so indicates. Except as otherwise provided in subsections (e) and (f), a security interest in fixtures is subordinate to a construction mortgage if a record of the mortgage is recorded before the goods become fixtures and the goods become fixtures before the completion of the construction. A mortgage has this priority to the same extent as a construction mortgage to the extent that it is given to refinance a construction mortgage.

(i) A perfected security interest in crops growing on real property has priority over a conflicting interest of an encumbrancer or owner of the real property if the debtor has an interest of record in or is in possession of the real property.

(j) Subsection (i) prevails over any inconsistent provisions of the following statutes:

[List here any statutes containing provisions inconsistent with subsection (i).]

Legislative Note: States that amend statutes to remove provisions inconsistent with subsection (i) need not enact subsection (j).

§ 9–335. Accessions.

(a) A security interest may be created in an accession and continues in collateral that becomes an accession.

(b) If a security interest is perfected when the collateral becomes an accession, the security interest remains perfected in the collateral.

(c) Except as otherwise provided in subsection (d), the other provisions of this part determine the priority of a security interest in an accession.

(d) A security interest in an accession is subordinate to a security interest in the whole which is perfected by compliance with the requirements of a certificate-of-title statute under Section 9–311(b).

(e) After default, subject to Part 6, a secured party may remove an accession from other goods if the security interest in the accession has priority over the claims of every person having an interest in the whole.

(f) A secured party that removes an accession from other goods under subsection (e) shall promptly reimburse any holder of a security interest or other lien on, or owner of, the whole or of the other goods, other than the debtor, for the cost of repair of any physical injury to the whole or the other goods. The secured party need not reimburse the holder or owner for any diminution in value of the whole or the other goods caused by the absence of the accession removed or by any necessity for replacing it. A person entitled to reimbursement may refuse permission to remove until the secured party gives adequate assurance for the performance of the obligation to reimburse.

§ 9–336. Commingled Goods.

(a) In this section, "commingled goods" means goods that are physically united with other goods in such a manner that their identity is lost in a product or mass.

(b) A security interest does not exist in commingled goods as such. However, a security interest may attach to a product or mass that results when goods become commingled goods.

(c) If collateral becomes commingled goods, a security interest attaches to the product or mass.

(d) If a security interest in collateral is perfected before the collateral becomes commingled goods, the security interest that attaches to the product or mass under subsection (c) is perfected.

(e) Except as otherwise provided in subsection (f), the other provisions of this part determine the priority of a security interest that attaches to the product or mass under subsection (c).

(f) If more than one security interest attaches to the product or mass under subsection (c), the following rules determine priority:

(1) A security interest that is perfected under subsection (d) has priority over a security interest that is unperfected at the time the collateral becomes commingled goods.

(2) If more than one security interest is perfected under subsection (d), the security interests rank equally in proportion to the value of the collateral at the time it became commingled goods.

§ 9–337.   Priority of Security Interests in Goods Covered by Certificate of Title.

If, while a security interest in goods is perfected by any method under the law of another jurisdiction, this State issues a certificate of title that does not show that the goods are subject to the security interest or contain a statement that they may be subject to security interests not shown on the certificate:

(1) a buyer of the goods, other than a person in the business of selling goods of that kind, takes free of the security interest if the buyer gives value and receives delivery of the goods after issuance of the certificate and without knowledge of the security interest; and

(2) the security interest is subordinate to a conflicting security interest in the goods that attaches, and is perfected under Section 9–311(b), after issuance of the certificate and without the conflicting secured party's knowledge of the security interest.

§ 9–338.   Priority of Security Interest or Agricultural Lien Perfected by Filed Financing Statement Providing Certain Incorrect Information.

If a security interest or agricultural lien is perfected by a filed financing statement providing information described in Section 9–516(b)(5) which is incorrect at the time the financing statement is filed:

(1) the security interest or agricultural lien is subordinate to a conflicting perfected security interest in the collateral to the extent that the holder of the conflicting security interest gives value in reasonable reliance upon the incorrect information; and

(2) a purchaser, other than a secured party, of the collateral takes free of the security interest or agricultural lien to the extent that, in reasonable reliance upon the incorrect information, the purchaser gives value and, in the case of chattel paper, documents, goods, instruments, or a security certificate, receives delivery of the collateral.

§ 9–339.   Priority Subject to Subordination.

This article does not preclude subordination by agreement by a person entitled to priority.

[Subpart 4. Rights of Bank]

§ 9–340.   Effectiveness of Right of Recoupment or Set-Off against Deposit Account.

(a) Except as otherwise provided in subsection (c), a bank with which a deposit account is maintained may exercise any right of recoupment or set-off against a secured party that holds a security interest in the deposit account.

(b) Except as otherwise provided in subsection (c), the application of this article to a security interest in a deposit account does not affect a right of recoupment or set-off of the secured party as to a deposit account maintained with the secured party.

(c) The exercise by a bank of a set-off against a deposit account is ineffective against a secured party that holds a security interest in the deposit account which is perfected by control under Section 9–104(a)(3), if the set-off is based on a claim against the debtor.

§ 9–341.   Bank's Rights and Duties with Respect to Deposit Account.

Except as otherwise provided in Section 9–340(c), and unless the bank otherwise agrees in an authenticated record, a bank's rights and duties with respect to a deposit account maintained with the bank are not terminated, suspended, or modified by:

(1) the creation, attachment, or perfection of a security interest in the deposit account;

(2) the bank's knowledge of the security interest; or

(3) the bank's receipt of instructions from the secured party.

§ 9–342.   Bank's Right to Refuse to Enter into or Disclose Existence of Control Agreement.

This article does not require a bank to enter into an agreement of the kind described in Section 9–104(a)(2), even if its customer so requests or directs. A bank that has entered into such an agreement is not required to confirm the existence of the agreement to another person unless requested to do so by its customer.

PART 4   Rights of Third Parties

§ 9–401.   Alienability of Debtor's Rights.

(a) Except as otherwise provided in subsection (b) and Sections 9–406, 9–407, 9–408, and 9–409, whether a debtor's rights in collateral may be voluntarily or involuntarily transferred is governed by law other than this article.

(b) An agreement between the debtor and secured party which prohibits a transfer of the debtor's rights in collateral or makes the transfer a default does not prevent the transfer from taking effect.

§ 9–402.   Secured Party Not Obligated on Contract of Debtor or in Tort.

The existence of a security interest, agricultural lien, or authority given to a debtor to dispose of or use collateral, without more, does not subject a secured party to liability in contract or tort for the debtor's acts or omissions.

§ 9–403.   Agreement Not to Assert Defenses against Assignee.

(a) In this section, "value" has the meaning provided in Section 3–303(a).

(b) Except as otherwise provided in this section, an agreement between an account debtor and an assignor not to assert against an assignee any claim or defense that the account debtor may have against the assignor is enforceable by an assignee that takes an assignment:

(1) for value;

(2) in good faith;

(3) without notice of a claim of a property or possessory right to the property assigned; and

(4) without notice of a defense or claim in recoupment of the type that may be asserted against a person entitled to enforce a negotiable instrument under Section 3–305(a).

(c) Subsection (b) does not apply to defenses of a type that may be asserted against a holder in due course of a negotiable instrument under Section 3–305(b).

(d) In a consumer transaction, if a record evidences the account debtor's obligation, law other than this article requires that the record include a statement to the effect that the rights of an assignee are subject to claims or defenses that the account debtor could assert against the original obligee, and the record does not include such a statement:

(1) the record has the same effect as if the record included such a statement; and

(2) the account debtor may assert against an assignee those claims and defenses that would have been available if the record included such a statement.

(e) This section is subject to law other than this article which establishes a different rule for an account debtor who is an individual and who incurred the obligation primarily for personal, family, or household purposes.

(f) Except as otherwise provided in subsection (d), this section does not displace law other than this article which gives effect to an agreement by an account debtor not to assert a claim or defense against an assignee.

§ 9–404.   Rights Acquired by Assignee; Claims and Defenses against Assignee.

(a) Unless an account debtor has made an enforceable agreement not to assert defenses or claims, and subject to subsections (b) through (e), the rights of an assignee are subject to:

(1) all terms of the agreement between the account debtor and assignor and any defense or claim in recoupment arising from the transaction that gave rise to the contract; and

(2) any other defense or claim of the account debtor against the assignor which accrues before the account debtor receives a notification of the assignment authenticated by the assignor or the assignee.

(b) Subject to subsection (c) and except as otherwise provided in subsection (d), the claim of an account debtor against an assignor may be asserted against an assignee under subsection (a) only to reduce the amount the account debtor owes.

(c) This section is subject to law other than this article which establishes a different rule for an account debtor who is an individual and who incurred the obligation primarily for personal, family, or household purposes.

(d) In a consumer transaction, if a record evidences the account debtor's obligation, law other than this article requires that the record include a statement to the effect that the account debtor's recovery against an assignee with respect to claims and defenses against the assignor may not exceed amounts paid by the account debtor under the record, and the record does not include such a statement, the extent to which a claim of an account debtor against the assignor may be asserted against an assignee is determined as if the record included such a statement.

(e) This section does not apply to an assignment of a health-care-insurance receivable.

§ 9–405.   Modification of Assigned Contract.

(a) A modification of or substitution for an assigned contract is effective against an assignee if made in good faith. The assignee acquires corresponding rights under the modified or substituted contract. The assignment may provide that the modification or substitution is a breach of contract by the assignor. This subsection is subject to subsections (b) through (d).

(b) Subsection (a) applies to the extent that:

(1) the right to payment or a part thereof under an assigned contract has not been fully earned by performance; or

(2) the right to payment or a part thereof has been fully earned by performance and the account debtor has not received notification of the assignment under Section 9–406(a).

(c) This section is subject to law other than this article which establishes a different rule for an account debtor who is an individual and who incurred the obligation primarily for personal, family, or household purposes.

(d) This section does not apply to an assignment of a health-care-insurance receivable.

§ 9–406.   Discharge of Account Debtor; Notification of Assignment; Identification and Proof of Assignment; Restrictions on Assignment of Accounts, Chattel Paper, Payment Intangibles, and Promissory Notes Ineffective.

(a) Subject to subsections (b) through (i), an account debtor on an account, chattel paper, or a payment intangible may discharge its obligation by paying the assignor until, but not after, the account debtor receives a notification, authenticated by the assignor or the assignee, that the amount due or to become due has been assigned and that payment is to be made to the assignee. After receipt of the notification, the account debtor may discharge its obligation by paying the assignee and may not discharge the obligation by paying the assignor.

(b) Subject to subsection (h), notification is ineffective under subsection (a):

(1) if it does not reasonably identify the rights assigned;

(2) to the extent that an agreement between an account debtor and a seller of a payment intangible limits the account debtor's duty to pay a person other than the seller and the limitation is effective under law other than this article; or

(3) at the option of an account debtor, if the notification notifies the account debtor to make less than the full amount of any installment or other periodic payment to the assignee, even if:

(A) only a portion of the account, chattel paper, or payment intangible has been assigned to that assignee;

(B) a portion has been assigned to another assignee; or

(C) the account debtor knows that the assignment to that assignee is limited.

(c) Subject to subsection (h), if requested by the account debtor, an assignee shall seasonably furnish reasonable proof that the assignment has been made. Unless the assignee complies, the account debtor may discharge its obligation by paying the assignor, even if the account debtor has received a notification under subsection (a).

(d) Except as otherwise provided in subsection (e) and Sections 2A–303 and 9–407, and subject to subsection (h), a term in an agreement between an account debtor and an assignor or in a promissory note is ineffective to the extent that it:

(1) prohibits, restricts, or requires the consent of the account debtor or person obligated on the promissory note to the assignment or transfer of, or the creation, attachment, perfection, or enforcement of a security interest in, the account, chattel paper, payment intangible, or promissory note; or

(2) provides that the assignment or transfer or the creation, attachment, perfection, or enforcement of the security interest may give rise to a default, breach, right of recoupment, claim, defense, termination, right of termination, or remedy under the account, chattel paper, payment intangible, or promissory note.

(e) Subsection (d) does not apply to the sale of a payment intangible or promissory note.

(f) Except as otherwise provided in Sections 2A–303 and 9–407 and subject to subsections (h) and (i), a rule of law, statute, or regulation that prohibits, restricts, or requires the consent of a government, governmental body or official, or account debtor to the assignment or transfer of, or creation of a security interest in, an account or chattel paper is ineffective to the extent that the rule of law, statute, or regulation:

(1) prohibits, restricts, or requires the consent of the government, governmental body or official, or account debtor to the assignment or transfer of, or the creation, attachment, perfection, or enforcement of a security interest in the account or chattel paper; or

(2) provides that the assignment or transfer or the creation, attachment, perfection, or enforcement of the security interest

may give rise to a default, breach, right of recoupment, claim, defense, termination, right of termination, or remedy under the account or chattel paper.

(g) Subject to subsection (h), an account debtor may not waive or vary its option under subsection (b)(3).

(h) This section is subject to law other than this article which establishes a different rule for an account debtor who is an individual and who incurred the obligation primarily for personal, family, or household purposes.

(i) This section does not apply to an assignment of a health-care-insurance receivable.

(j) This section prevails over any inconsistent provisions of the following statutes, rules, and regulations:

[List here any statutes, rules, and regulations containing provisions inconsistent with this section.]

Legislative Note: States that amend statutes, rules, and regulations to remove provisions inconsistent with this section need not enact subsection (j).

As amended in 1999 and 2000.

§ 9–407.   Restrictions on Creation or Enforcement of Security Interest in Leasehold Interest or in Lessor's Residual Interest.

(a) Except as otherwise provided in subsection (b), a term in a lease agreement is ineffective to the extent that it:

(1) prohibits, restricts, or requires the consent of a party to the lease to the assignment or transfer of, or the creation, attachment, perfection, or enforcement of a security interest in an interest of a party under the lease contract or in the lessor's residual interest in the goods; or

(2) provides that the assignment or transfer or the creation, attachment, perfection, or enforcement of the security interest may give rise to a default, breach, right of recoupment, claim, defense, termination, right of termination, or remedy under the lease.

(b) Except as otherwise provided in Section 2A–303(7), a term described in subsection (a)(2) is effective to the extent that there is:

(1) a transfer by the lessee of the lessee's right of possession or use of the goods in violation of the term; or

(2) a delegation of a material performance of either party to the lease contract in violation of the term.

(c) The creation, attachment, perfection, or enforcement of a security interest in the lessor's interest under the lease contract or the lessor's residual interest in the goods is not a transfer that materially impairs the lessee's prospect of obtaining return performance or materially changes the duty of or materially increases the burden or risk imposed on the lessee

within the purview of Section 2A–303(4) unless, and then only to the extent that, enforcement actually results in a delegation of material performance of the lessor.

As amended in 1999.

§ 9–408.   Restrictions on Assignment of Promissory Notes, Health-Care-Insurance Receivables, and Certain General Intangibles Ineffective.

(a) Except as otherwise provided in subsection (b), a term in a promissory note or in an agreement between an account debtor and a debtor which relates to a health-care-insurance receivable or a general intangible, including a contract, permit, license, or franchise, and which term prohibits, restricts, or requires the consent of the person obligated on the promissory note or the account debtor to, the assignment or transfer of, or creation, attachment, or perfection of a security interest in, the promissory note, health-care-insurance receivable, or general intangible, is ineffective to the extent that the term:

(1) would impair the creation, attachment, or perfection of a security interest; or

(2) provides that the assignment or transfer or the creation, attachment, or perfection of the security interest may give rise to a default, breach, right of recoupment, claim, defense, termination, right of termination, or remedy under the promissory note, health-care-insurance receivable, or general intangible.

(b) Subsection (a) applies to a security interest in a payment intangible or promissory note only if the security interest arises out of a sale of the payment intangible or promissory note.

(c) A rule of law, statute, or regulation that prohibits, restricts, or requires the consent of a government, governmental body or official, person obligated on a promissory note, or account debtor to the assignment or transfer of, or creation of a security interest in, a promissory note, health-care-insurance receivable, or general intangible, including a contract, permit, license, or franchise between an account debtor and a debtor, is ineffective to the extent that the rule of law, statute, or regulation:

(1) would impair the creation, attachment, or perfection of a security interest; or

(2) provides that the assignment or transfer or the creation, attachment, or perfection of the security interest may give rise to a default, breach, right of recoupment, claim, defense, termination, right of termination, or remedy under the promissory note, health-care-insurance receivable, or general intangible.

(d) To the extent that a term in a promissory note or in an agreement between an account debtor and a debtor which relates to a health-care-insurance receivable or general intangible or a rule of law, statute, or regulation described in subsection (c) would be effective under law other than this article but is ineffective under subsection (a) or (c), the creation, attachment, or perfection of a security interest in the promissory note, health-care-insurance receivable, or general intangible:

(1) is not enforceable against the person obligated on the promissory note or the account debtor;

(2) does not impose a duty or obligation on the person obligated on the promissory note or the account debtor;

(3) does not require the person obligated on the promissory note or the account debtor to recognize the security interest, pay or render performance to the secured party, or accept payment or performance from the secured party;

(4) does not entitle the secured party to use or assign the debtor's rights under the promissory note, health-care-insurance receivable, or general intangible, including any related information or materials furnished to the debtor in the transaction giving rise to the promissory note, health-care-insurance receivable, or general intangible;

(5) does not entitle the secured party to use, assign, possess, or have access to any trade secrets or confidential information of the person obligated on the promissory note or the account debtor; and

(6) does not entitle the secured party to enforce the security interest in the promissory note, health-care-insurance receivable, or general intangible.

(e) This section prevails over any inconsistent provisions of the following statutes, rules, and regulations:

[List here any statutes, rules, and regulations containing provisions inconsistent with this section.]

Legislative Note: States that amend statutes, rules, and regulations to remove provisions inconsistent with this section need not enact subsection (e).

As amended in 1999.

§ 9–409. Restrictions on Assignment of Letter-of-Credit Rights Ineffective.

(a) A term in a letter of credit or a rule of law, statute, regulation, custom, or practice applicable to the letter of credit which prohibits, restricts, or requires the consent of an applicant, issuer, or nominated person to a beneficiary's assignment of or creation of a security interest in a letter-of-credit right is ineffective to the extent that the term or rule of law, statute, regulation, custom, or practice:

(1) would impair the creation, attachment, or perfection of a security interest in the letter-of-credit right; or

(2) provides that the assignment or the creation, attachment, or perfection of the security interest may give rise to a

default, breach, right of recoupment, claim, defense, termination, right of termination, or remedy under the letter-of-credit right.

(b) To the extent that a term in a letter of credit is ineffective under subsection (a) but would be effective under law other than this article or a custom or practice applicable to the letter of credit, to the transfer of a right to draw or otherwise demand performance under the letter of credit, or to the assignment of a right to proceeds of the letter of credit, the creation, attachment, or perfection of a security interest in the letter-of-credit right:

(1) is not enforceable against the applicant, issuer, nominated person, or transferee beneficiary;

(2) imposes no duties or obligations on the applicant, issuer, nominated person, or transferee beneficiary; and

(3) does not require the applicant, issuer, nominated person, or transferee beneficiary to recognize the security interest, pay or render performance to the secured party, or accept payment or other performance from the secured party.

As amended in 1999.

PART 5   Filing

[Subpart 1. Filing Office; Contents and Effectiveness of Financing Statement]

§ 9–501.   Filing Office.

(a) Except as otherwise provided in subsection (b), if the local law of this State governs perfection of a security interest or agricultural lien, the office in which to file a financing statement to perfect the security interest or agricultural lien is:

(1) the office designated for the filing or recording of a record of a mortgage on the related real property, if:

(A) the collateral is as-extracted collateral or timber to be cut; or

(B) the financing statement is filed as a fixture filing and the collateral is goods that are or are to become fixtures; or

(2) the office of [ ] [or any office duly authorized by [ ]], in all other cases, including a case in which the collateral is goods that are or are to become fixtures and the financing statement is not filed as a fixture filing.

(b) The office in which to file a financing statement to perfect a security interest in collateral, including fixtures, of a transmitting utility is the office of [ ]. The financing statement also constitutes a fixture filing as to the collateral indicated in the financing statement which is or is to become fixtures.

Legislative Note: The State should designate the filing office where the brackets appear. The filing office may be that of a governmental official (e.g., the Secretary of State) or a private party that maintains the State's filing system.

§ 9–502.   Contents of Financing Statement; Record of Mortgage as Financing Statement; Time of Filing Financing Statement.

(a) Subject to subsection (b), a financing statement is sufficient only if it:

(1) provides the name of the debtor;

(2) provides the name of the secured party or a representative of the secured party; and

(3) indicates the collateral covered by the financing statement.

(b) Except as otherwise provided in Section 9–501(b), to be sufficient, a financing statement that covers as-extracted collateral or timber to be cut, or which is filed as a fixture filing and covers goods that are or are to become fixtures, must satisfy subsection (a) and also:

(1) indicate that it covers this type of collateral;

(2) indicate that it is to be filed [for record] in the real property records;

(3) provide a description of the real property to which the collateral is related [sufficient to give constructive notice of a mortgage under the law of this State if the description were contained in a record of the mortgage of the real property]; and

(4) if the debtor does not have an interest of record in the real property, provide the name of a record owner.

(c) A record of a mortgage is effective, from the date of recording, as a financing statement filed as a fixture filing or as a financing statement covering as-extracted collateral or timber to be cut only if:

(1) the record indicates the goods or accounts that it covers;

(2) the goods are or are to become fixtures related to the real property described in the record or the collateral is related to the real property described in the record and is as-extracted collateral or timber to be cut;

(3) the record satisfies the requirements for a financing statement in this section other than an indication that it is to be filed in the real property records; and

(4) the record is [duly] recorded.

(d) A financing statement may be filed before a security agreement is made or a security interest otherwise attaches.

Legislative Note: Language in brackets is optional. Where the State has any special recording system for real property other than the usual grantor-grantee index (as, for instance, a tract system or a title registration or Torrens system) local adaptations of subsection (b) and Section

9–519(d) and (e) may be necessary. See, e.g., Mass. Gen. Laws Chapter 106, Section 9–410.

§ 9–503.   Name of Debtor and Secured Party.

(a) A financing statement sufficiently provides the name of the debtor:

(1) if the debtor is a registered organization, only if the financing statement provides the name of the debtor indicated on the public record of the debtor's jurisdiction of organization which shows the debtor to have been organized;

(2) if the debtor is a decedent's estate, only if the financing statement provides the name of the decedent and indicates that the debtor is an estate;

(3) if the debtor is a trust or a trustee acting with respect to property held in trust, only if the financing statement:

(A) provides the name specified for the trust in its organic documents or, if no name is specified, provides the name of the settlor and additional information sufficient to distinguish the debtor from other trusts having one or more of the same settlors; and

(B) indicates, in the debtor's name or otherwise, that the debtor is a trust or is a trustee acting with respect to property held in trust; and

(4) in other cases:

(A) if the debtor has a name, only if it provides the individual or organizational name of the debtor; and

(B) if the debtor does not have a name, only if it provides the names of the partners, members, associates, or other persons comprising the debtor.

(b) A financing statement that provides the name of the debtor in accordance with subsection (a) is not rendered ineffective by the absence of:

(1) a trade name or other name of the debtor; or

(2) unless required under subsection (a)(4)(B), names of partners, members, associates, or other persons comprising the debtor.

(c) A financing statement that provides only the debtor's trade name does not sufficiently provide the name of the debtor.

(d) Failure to indicate the representative capacity of a secured party or representative of a secured party does not affect the sufficiency of a financing statement.

(e) A financing statement may provide the name of more than one debtor and the name of more than one secured party.

§ 9–504.   Indication of Collateral.

A financing statement sufficiently indicates the collateral that it covers if the financing statement provides:

(1) a description of the collateral pursuant to Section 9–108; or

(2) an indication that the financing statement covers all assets or all personal property.

As amended in 1999.

§ 9–505.   Filing and Compliance with Other Statutes and Treaties for Consignments, Leases, Other Bailments, and Other Transactions.

(a) A consignor, lessor, or other bailor of goods, a licensor, or a buyer of a payment intangible or promissory note may file a financing statement, or may comply with a statute or treaty described in Section 9–311(a), using the terms "consignor", "consignee", "lessor", "lessee", "bailor", "bailee", "licensor", "licensee", "owner", "registered owner", "buyer", "seller", or words of similar import, instead of the terms "secured party" and "debtor".

(b) This part applies to the filing of a financing statement under subsection (a) and, as appropriate, to compliance that is equivalent to filing a financing statement under Section 9–311 (b), but the filing or compliance is not of itself a factor in determining whether the collateral secures an obligation. If it is determined for another reason that the collateral secures an obligation, a security interest held by the consignor, lessor, bailor, licensor, owner, or buyer which attaches to the collateral is perfected by the filing or compliance.

§ 9–506.   Effect of Errors or Omissions.

(a) A financing statement substantially satisfying the requirements of this part is effective, even if it has minor errors or omissions, unless the errors or omissions make the financing statement seriously misleading.

(b) Except as otherwise provided in subsection (c), a financing statement that fails sufficiently to provide the name of the debtor in accordance with Section 9–503(a) is seriously misleading.

(c) If a search of the records of the filing office under the debtor's correct name, using the filing office's standard search logic, if any, would disclose a financing statement that fails sufficiently to provide the name of the debtor in accordance with Section 9–503(a), the name provided does not make the financing statement seriously misleading.

(d) For purposes of Section 9–508(b), the "debtor's correct name" in subsection (c) means the correct name of the new debtor.

§ 9–507.   Effect of Certain Events on Effectiveness of Financing Statement.

(a) A filed financing statement remains effective with respect to collateral that is sold, exchanged, leased, licensed, or otherwise disposed of and in which a security interest or agricultural lien continues, even if the secured party knows of or consents to the disposition.

(b) Except as otherwise provided in subsection (c) and Section 9–508, a financing statement is not rendered ineffective if, after the financing statement is filed, the information provided in the financing statement becomes seriously misleading under Section 9–506.

(c) If a debtor so changes its name that a filed financing statement becomes seriously misleading under Section 9–506:

(1) the financing statement is effective to perfect a security interest in collateral acquired by the debtor before, or within four months after, the change; and

(2) the financing statement is not effective to perfect a security interest in collateral acquired by the debtor more than four months after the change, unless an amendment to the financing statement which renders the financing statement not seriously misleading is filed within four months after the change.

§ 9–508.   Effectiveness of Financing Statement If New Debtor Becomes Bound by Security Agreement.

(a) Except as otherwise provided in this section, a filed financing statement naming an original debtor is effective to perfect a security interest in collateral in which a new debtor has or acquires rights to the extent that the financing statement would have been effective had the original debtor acquired rights in the collateral.

(b) If the difference between the name of the original debtor and that of the new debtor causes a filed financing statement that is effective under subsection (a) to be seriously misleading under Section 9–506:

(1) the financing statement is effective to perfect a security interest in collateral acquired by the new debtor before, and within four months after, the new debtor becomes bound under Section 9B–203(d); and

(2) the financing statement is not effective to perfect a security interest in collateral acquired by the new debtor more than four months after the new debtor becomes bound under Section 9–203(d) unless an initial financing statement providing the name of the new debtor is filed before the expiration of that time.

(c) This section does not apply to collateral as to which a filed financing statement remains effective against the new debtor under Section 9–507(a).

§ 9–509.   Persons Entitled to File a Record.

(a) A person may file an initial financing statement, amendment that adds collateral covered by a financing statement, or amendment that adds a debtor to a financing statement only if:

(1) the debtor authorizes the filing in an authenticated record or pursuant to subsection (b) or (c); or

(2) the person holds an agricultural lien that has become effective at the time of filing and the financing statement covers only collateral in which the person holds an agricultural lien.

(b) By authenticating or becoming bound as debtor by a security agreement, a debtor or new debtor authorizes the filing of an initial financing statement, and an amendment, covering:

(1) the collateral described in the security agreement; and

(2) property that becomes collateral under Section 9–315(a)(2), whether or not the security agreement expressly covers proceeds.

(c) By acquiring collateral in which a security interest or agricultural lien continues under Section 9–315(a)(1), a debtor authorizes the filing of an initial financing statement, and an amendment, covering the collateral and property that becomes collateral under Section 9–315(a)(2).

(d) A person may file an amendment other than an amendment that adds collateral covered by a financing statement or an amendment that adds a debtor to a financing statement only if:

(1) the secured party of record authorizes the filing; or

(2) the amendment is a termination statement for a financing statement as to which the secured party of record has failed to file or send a termination statement as required by Section 9–513(a) or (c), the debtor authorizes the filing, and the termination statement indicates that the debtor authorized it to be filed.

(e) If there is more than one secured party of record for a financing statement, each secured party of record may authorize the filing of an amendment under subsection (d).

As amended in 2000.

§ 9–510.   Effectiveness of Filed Record.

(a) A filed record is effective only to the extent that it was filed by a person that may file it under Section 9–509.

(b) A record authorized by one secured party of record does not affect the financing statement with respect to another secured party of record.

(c) A continuation statement that is not filed within the six-month period prescribed by Section 9–515(d) is ineffective.

§ 9–511.   Secured Party of Record.

(a) A secured party of record with respect to a financing statement is a person whose name is provided as the name of the secured party or a representative of the secured party in an initial financing statement that has been filed. If an initial financing statement is filed under Section 9–514(a), the assignee named in the initial financing statement is the

secured party of record with respect to the financing statement.

(b) If an amendment of a financing statement which provides the name of a person as a secured party or a representative of a secured party is filed, the person named in the amendment is a secured party of record. If an amendment is filed under Section 9–514(b), the assignee named in the amendment is a secured party of record.

(c) A person remains a secured party of record until the filing of an amendment of the financing statement which deletes the person.

§ 9–512.   Amendment of Financing Statement.
[Alternative A]

(a) Subject to Section 9–509, a person may add or delete collateral covered by, continue or terminate the effectiveness of, or, subject to subsection (e), otherwise amend the information provided in, a financing statement by filing an amendment that:

(1) identifies, by its file number, the initial financing statement to which the amendment relates; and

(2) if the amendment relates to an initial financing statement filed [or recorded] in a filing office described in Section 9–501(a)(1), provides the information specified in Section 9–502(b).

[Alternative B]

(a) Subject to Section 9–509, a person may add or delete collateral covered by, continue or terminate the effectiveness of, or, subject to subsection (e), otherwise amend the information provided in, a financing statement by filing an amendment that:

(1) identifies, by its file number, the initial financing statement to which the amendment relates; and

(2) if the amendment relates to an initial financing statement filed [or recorded] in a filing office described in Section 9–501(a)(1), provides the date [and time] that the initial financing statement was filed [or recorded] and the information specified in Section 9–502(b).

[End of Alternatives]

(b) Except as otherwise provided in Section 9–515, the filing of an amendment does not extend the period of effectiveness of the financing statement.

(c) A financing statement that is amended by an amendment that adds collateral is effective as to the added collateral only from the date of the filing of the amendment.

(d) A financing statement that is amended by an amendment that adds a debtor is effective as to the added debtor only from the date of the filing of the amendment.

(e) An amendment is ineffective to the extent it:

(1) purports to delete all debtors and fails to provide the name of a debtor to be covered by the financing statement; or

(2) purports to delete all secured parties of record and fails to provide the name of a new secured party of record.

Legislative Note: States whose real-estate filing offices require additional information in amendments and cannot search their records by both the name of the debtor and the file number should enact Alternative B to Sections 9–512(a), 9–518(b), 9–519(f), and 9–522(a).

§ 9–513. Termination Statement.

(a) A secured party shall cause the secured party of record for a financing statement to file a termination statement for the financing statement if the financing statement covers consumer goods and:

(1) there is no obligation secured by the collateral covered by the financing statement and no commitment to make an advance, incur an obligation, or otherwise give value; or

(2) the debtor did not authorize the filing of the initial financing statement.

(b) To comply with subsection (a), a secured party shall cause the secured party of record to file the termination statement:

(1) within one month after there is no obligation secured by the collateral covered by the financing statement and no commitment to make an advance, incur an obligation, or otherwise give value; or

(2) if earlier, within 20 days after the secured party receives an authenticated demand from a debtor.

(c) In cases not governed by subsection (a), within 20 days after a secured party receives an authenticated demand from a debtor, the secured party shall cause the secured party of record for a financing statement to send to the debtor a termination statement for the financing statement or file the termination statement in the filing office if:

(1) except in the case of a financing statement covering accounts or chattel paper that has been sold or goods that are the subject of a consignment, there is no obligation secured by the collateral covered by the financing statement and no commitment to make an advance, incur an obligation, or otherwise give value;

(2) the financing statement covers accounts or chattel paper that has been sold but as to which the account debtor or other person obligated has discharged its obligation;

(3) the financing statement covers goods that were the subject of a consignment to the debtor but are not in the debtor's possession; or

(4) the debtor did not authorize the filing of the initial financing statement.

(d) Except as otherwise provided in Section 9–510, upon the filing of a termination statement with the filing office, the financing statement to which the termination statement relates ceases to be effective. Except as otherwise provided in Section 9–510, for purposes of Sections 9–519(g), 9–522(a), and 9–523 (c), the filing with the filing office of a termination statement relating to a financing statement that indicates that the debtor

is a transmitting utility also causes the effectiveness of the financing statement to lapse.

As amended in 2000.

§ 9–514. Assignment of Powers of Secured Party of Record.

(a) Except as otherwise provided in subsection (c), an initial financing statement may reflect an assignment of all of the secured party's power to authorize an amendment to the financing statement by providing the name and mailing address of the assignee as the name and address of the secured party.

(b) Except as otherwise provided in subsection (c), a secured party of record may assign of record all or part of its power to authorize an amendment to a financing statement by filing in the filing office an amendment of the financing statement which:

(1) identifies, by its file number, the initial financing statement to which it relates;

(2) provides the name of the assignor; and

(3) provides the name and mailing address of the assignee.

(c) An assignment of record of a security interest in a fixture covered by a record of a mortgage which is effective as a financing statement filed as a fixture filing under Section 9–502(c) may be made only by an assignment of record of the mortgage in the manner provided by law of this State other than [the Uniform Commercial Code].

§ 9–515. Duration and Effectiveness of Financing Statement; Effect of Lapsed Financing Statement.

(a) Except as otherwise provided in subsections (b), (e), (f), and (g), a filed financing statement is effective for a period of five years after the date of filing.

(b) Except as otherwise provided in subsections (e), (f), and (g), an initial financing statement filed in connection with a public-finance transaction or manufactured-home transaction is effective for a period of 30 years after the date of filing if it indicates that it is filed in connection with a public-finance transaction or manufactured-home transaction.

(c) The effectiveness of a filed financing statement lapses on the expiration of the period of its effectiveness unless before the lapse a continuation statement is filed pursuant to subsection (d). Upon lapse, a financing statement ceases to be effective and any security interest or agricultural lien that was perfected by the financing statement becomes unperfected, unless the security interest is perfected otherwise. If the security interest or agricultural lien becomes unperfected upon lapse, it is deemed never to have been perfected as against a purchaser of the collateral for value.

(d) A continuation statement may be filed only within six months before the expiration of the five-year period specified in subsection (a) or the 30-year period specified in subsection (b), whichever is applicable.

(e) Except as otherwise provided in Section 9–510, upon timely filing of a continuation statement, the effectiveness of the initial financing statement continues for a period of five years commencing on the day on which the financing statement would have become ineffective in the absence of the filing. Upon the expiration of the five-year period, the financing statement lapses in the same manner as provided in subsection (c), unless, before the lapse, another continuation statement is filed pursuant to subsection (d). Succeeding continuation statements may be filed in the same manner to continue the effectiveness of the initial financing statement.

(f) If a debtor is a transmitting utility and a filed financing statement so indicates, the financing statement is effective until a termination statement is filed.

(g) A record of a mortgage that is effective as a financing statement filed as a fixture filing under Section 9–502(c) remains effective as a financing statement filed as a fixture filing until the mortgage is released or satisfied of record or its effectiveness otherwise terminates as to the real property.

§ 9–516. What Constitutes Filing; Effectiveness of Filing.

(a) Except as otherwise provided in subsection (b), communication of a record to a filing office and tender of the filing fee or acceptance of the record by the filing office constitutes filing.

(b) Filing does not occur with respect to a record that a filing office refuses to accept because:

(1) the record is not communicated by a method or medium of communication authorized by the filing office;

(2) an amount equal to or greater than the applicable filing fee is not tendered;

(3) the filing office is unable to index the record because:

(A) in the case of an initial financing statement, the record does not provide a name for the debtor;

(B) in the case of an amendment or correction statement, the record:

(i) does not identify the initial financing statement as required by Section 9–512 or 9–518, as applicable; or

(ii) identifies an initial financing statement whose effectiveness has lapsed under Section 9–515;

(C) in the case of an initial financing statement that provides the name of a debtor identified as an individual or an amendment that provides a name of a debtor identified as an individual which was not previously provided in the financing statement to which the record relates, the record does not identify the debtor's last name; or

(D) in the case of a record filed [or recorded] in the filing office described in Section 9–501(a)(1), the record does not provide a sufficient description of the real property to which it relates;

(4) in the case of an initial financing statement or an amendment that adds a secured party of record, the record does not provide a name and mailing address for the secured party of record;

(5) in the case of an initial financing statement or an amendment that provides a name of a debtor which was not previously provided in the financing statement to which the amendment relates, the record does not:

(A) provide a mailing address for the debtor;

(B) indicate whether the debtor is an individual or an organization; or

(C) if the financing statement indicates that the debtor is an organization, provide:

(i) a type of organization for the debtor;

(ii) a jurisdiction of organization for the debtor; or

(iii) an organizational identification number for the debtor or indicate that the debtor has none;

(6) in the case of an assignment reflected in an initial financing statement under Section 9–514(a) or an amendment filed under Section 9–514(b), the record does not provide a name and mailing address for the assignee; or

(7) in the case of a continuation statement, the record is not filed within the six-month period prescribed by Section 9–515(d).

(c) For purposes of subsection (b):

(1) a record does not provide information if the filing office is unable to read or decipher the information; and

(2) a record that does not indicate that it is an amendment or identify an initial financing statement to which it relates, as required by Section 9–512, 9–514, or 9–518, is an initial financing statement.

(d) A record that is communicated to the filing office with tender of the filing fee, but which the filing office refuses to accept for a reason other than one set forth in subsection (b), is effective as a filed record except as against a purchaser of the collateral which gives value in reasonable reliance upon the absence of the record from the files.

§ 9–517. Effect of Indexing Errors.

The failure of the filing office to index a record correctly does not affect the effectiveness of the filed record.

§ 9–518. Claim Concerning Inaccurate or Wrongfully Filed Record.

(a) A person may file in the filing office a correction statement with respect to a record indexed there under the person's name if the person believes that the record is inaccurate or was wrongfully filed.

[Alternative A]

(b) A correction statement must:
(1) identify the record to which it relates by the file number assigned to the initial financing statement to which the record relates;

(2) indicate that it is a correction statement; and

(3) provide the basis for the person's belief that the record is inaccurate and indicate the manner in which the person believes the record should be amended to cure any inaccuracy or provide the basis for the person's belief that the record was wrongfully filed.

[Alternative B]

(b) A correction statement must:
(1) identify the record to which it relates by:

(A) the file number assigned to the initial financing statement to which the record relates; and

(B) if the correction statement relates to a record filed [or recorded] in a filing office described in Section 9–501(a)(1), the date [and time] that the initial financing statement was filed [or recorded] and the information specified in Section 9–502(b);

(2) indicate that it is a correction statement; and

(3) provide the basis for the person's belief that the record is inaccurate and indicate the manner in which the person believes the record should be amended to cure any inaccuracy or provide the basis for the person's belief that the record was wrongfully filed.

[End of Alternatives]

(c) The filing of a correction statement does not affect the effectiveness of an initial financing statement or other filed record. *Legislative Note: States whose real-estate filing offices require additional information in amendments and cannot search their records by both the name of the debtor and the file number should enact Alternative B to Sections 9–512(a), 9–518(b), 9–519(f), and 9–522(a).*

[Subpart 2. Duties and Operation of Filing Office]

§ 9–519. Numbering, Maintaining, and Indexing Records; Communicating Information Provided in Records.

(a) For each record filed in a filing office, the filing office shall:

(1) assign a unique number to the filed record;

(2) create a record that bears the number assigned to the filed record and the date and time of filing;

(3) maintain the filed record for public inspection; and

(4) index the filed record in accordance with subsections (c), (d), and (e).

(b) A file number [assigned after January 1, 2002,] must include a digit that:

(1) is mathematically derived from or related to the other digits of the file number; and

(2) aids the filing office in determining whether a number communicated as the file number includes a single-digit or transpositional error.

(c) Except as otherwise provided in subsections (d) and (e), the filing office shall:

(1) index an initial financing statement according to the name of the debtor and index all filed records relating to the initial financing statement in a manner that associates with one another an initial financing statement and all filed records relating to the initial financing statement; and

(2) index a record that provides a name of a debtor which was not previously provided in the financing statement to which the record relates also according to the name that was not previously provided.

(d) If a financing statement is filed as a fixture filing or covers as-extracted collateral or timber to be cut, [it must be filed for record and] the filing office shall index it:

(1) under the names of the debtor and of each owner of record shown on the financing statement as if they were the mortgagors under a mortgage of the real property described; and

(2) to the extent that the law of this State provides for indexing of records of mortgages under the name of the mortgagee, under the name of the secured party as if the secured party were the mortgagee thereunder, or, if indexing is by description, as if the financing statement were a record of a mortgage of the real property described.

(e) If a financing statement is filed as a fixture filing or covers as-extracted collateral or timber to be cut, the filing office shall index an assignment filed under Section 9–514(a) or an amendment filed under Section 9–514(b):

(1) under the name of the assignor as grantor; and

(2) to the extent that the law of this State provides for indexing a record of the assignment of a mortgage under the name of the assignee, under the name of the assignee.

[Alternative A]

(f) The filing office shall maintain a capability:
(1) to retrieve a record by the name of the debtor and by the file number assigned to the initial financing statement to which the record relates; and

(2) to associate and retrieve with one another an initial financing statement and each filed record relating to the initial financing statement.

[Alternative B]

(f) The filing office shall maintain a capability:
(1) to retrieve a record by the name of the debtor and:

(A) if the filing office is described in Section 9–501(a)(1), by the file number assigned to the initial financing statement to which the record relates and the date [and time] that the record was filed [or recorded]; or

(B) if the filing office is described in Section 9–501(a)(2), by the file number assigned to the initial financing statement to which the record relates; and

(2) to associate and retrieve with one another an initial financing statement and each filed record relating to the initial financing statement.

[End of Alternatives]

(g) The filing office may not remove a debtor's name from the index until one year after the effectiveness of a financing statement naming the debtor lapses under Section 9–515 with respect to all secured parties of record.

(h) The filing office shall perform the acts required by subsections (a) through (e) at the time and in the manner prescribed by filing-office rule, but not later than two business days after the filing office receives the record in question.

[(i) Subsection[s] [(b)] [and] [(h)] do[es] not apply to a filing office described in Section 9–501(a)(1).]

Legislative Notes:

1. States whose filing offices currently assign file numbers that include a verification number, commonly known as a "check digit," or can implement this requirement before the effective date of this Article should omit the bracketed language in subsection (b).

2. In States in which writings will not appear in the real property records and indices unless actually recorded the bracketed language in subsection (d) should be used.

3. States whose real-estate filing offices require additional information in amendments and cannot search their records by both the name of the debtor and the file number should enact Alternative B to Sections 9–512 (a), 9–518(b), 9–519(f), and 9–522(a).

4. A State that elects not to require real-estate filing offices to comply with either or both of subsections (b) and (h) may adopt an applicable variation of subsection (i) and add "Except as otherwise provided in subsection (i)," to the appropriate subsection or subsections.

§ 9–520.   Acceptance and Refusal to Accept Record.

(a) A filing office shall refuse to accept a record for filing for a reason set forth in Section 9–516(b) and may refuse to accept a record for filing only for a reason set forth in Section 9–516(b).

(b) If a filing office refuses to accept a record for filing, it shall communicate to the person that presented the record the fact of and reason for the refusal and the date and time the record would have been filed had the filing office accepted it. The communication must be made at the time and in the manner prescribed by filing-office rule but [, in the case of a filing office described in Section 9–501(a)(2),] in no event more than two business days after the filing office receives the record.

(c) A filed financing statement satisfying Section 9–502(a) and (b) is effective, even if the filing office is required to refuse to accept it for filing under subsection (a). However, Section 9–338 applies to a filed financing statement providing information described in Section 9–516(b)(5) which is incorrect at the time the financing statement is filed.

(d) If a record communicated to a filing office provides information that relates to more than one debtor, this part applies as to each debtor separately.

Legislative Note: A State that elects not to require real-property filing offices to comply with subsection (b) should include the bracketed language.

§ 9–521.   Uniform Form of Written Financing Statement and Amendment.

(a) A filing office that accepts written records may not refuse to accept a written initial financing statement in the following form and format except for a reason set forth in Section 9–516(b):

[NATIONAL UCC FINANCING STATEMENT (FORM UCC1)(REV. 7/29/98]

[NATIONAL UCC FINANCING STATEMENT ADDENDUM (FORM UCC1Ad)(REV. 07/29/98)]

(b) A filing office that accepts written records may not refuse to accept a written record in the following form and format except for a reason set forth in Section 9–516(b):

[NATIONAL UCC FINANCING STATEMENT AMENDMENT (FORM UCC3)(REV. 07/29/98)]

[NATIONAL UCC FINANCING STATEMENT AMENDMENT ADDENDUM (FORM UCC3Ad)(REV. 07/29/98)]

§ 9–522.   Maintenance and Destruction of Records.

[Alternative A]

(a) The filing office shall maintain a record of the information provided in a filed financing statement for at least one year after the effectiveness of the financing statement has lapsed under Section 9–515 with respect to all secured parties of record. The record must be retrievable by using the name of the debtor and by using the file number assigned to the initial financing statement to which the record relates.

[Alternative B]

(a) The filing office shall maintain a record of the information provided in a filed financing statement for at least one year after the effectiveness of the financing statement has lapsed under Section 9–515 with respect to all secured parties of record. The record must be retrievable by using the name of the debtor and:

(1) if the record was filed [or recorded] in the filing office described in Section 9–501(a)(1), by using the file number assigned to the initial financing statement to which the record relates and the date [and time] that the record was filed [or recorded]; or

(2) if the record was filed in the filing office described in Section 9–501(a)(2), by using the file number assigned to the initial financing statement to which the record relates.

[End of Alternatives]

(b) Except to the extent that a statute governing disposition of public records provides otherwise, the filing office immediately may destroy any written record evidencing a financing statement. However, if the filing office destroys a written record, it shall maintain another record of the financing statement which complies with subsection (a).

Legislative Note: States whose real-estate filing offices require additional information in amendments and cannot search their records by both the name of the debtor and the file number should enact Alternative B to Sections 9–512(a), 9–518(b), 9–519(f), and 9–522(a).

§ 9–523.   Information from Filing Office; Sale or License of Records.

(a) If a person that files a written record requests an acknowledgment of the filing, the filing office shall send to the person an image of the record showing the number assigned to the record pursuant to Section 9–519(a)(1) and the date and time of the filing of the record. However, if the person furnishes a copy of the record to the filing office, the filing office may instead:

(1) note upon the copy the number assigned to the record pursuant to Section 9–519(a)(1) and the date and time of the filing of the record; and

(2) send the copy to the person.

(b) If a person files a record other than a written record, the filing office shall communicate to the person an acknowledgment that provides:

(1) the information in the record;

(2) the number assigned to the record pursuant to Section 9–519(a)(1); and

(3) the date and time of the filing of the record.

(c) The filing office shall communicate or otherwise make available in a record the following information to any person that requests it:

(1) whether there is on file on a date and time specified by the filing office, but not a date earlier than three business days before the filing office receives the request, any financing statement that:

(A) designates a particular debtor [or, if the request so states, designates a particular debtor at the address specified in the request];

(B) has not lapsed under Section 9–515 with respect to all secured parties of record; and

(C) if the request so states, has lapsed under Section 9–515 and a record of which is maintained by the filing office under Section 9–522(a);

(2) the date and time of filing of each financing statement; and

(3) the information provided in each financing statement.

(d) In complying with its duty under subsection (c), the filing office may communicate information in any medium. However, if requested, the filing office shall communicate information by issuing [its written certificate] [a record that can be admitted into evidence in the courts of this State without extrinsic evidence of its authenticity].

(e) The filing office shall perform the acts required by subsections (a) through (d) at the time and in the manner prescribed by filing-office rule, but not later than two business days after the filing office receives the request.

(f) At least weekly, the [insert appropriate official or governmental agency] [filing office] shall offer to sell or license to the public on a nonexclusive basis, in bulk, copies of all records filed in it under this part, in every medium from time to time available to the filing office.

Legislative Notes:

1. States whose filing office does not offer the additional service of responding to search requests limited to a particular address should omit the bracketed language in subsection (c)(1)(A).

2. A State that elects not to require real-estate filing offices to comply with either or both of subsections (e) and (f) should specify in the appropriate subsection(s) only the filing office described in Section 9–501(a)(2).

§ 9–524.   Delay by Filing Office.

Delay by the filing office beyond a time limit prescribed by this part is excused if:

(1) the delay is caused by interruption of communication or computer facilities, war, emergency conditions, failure of equipment, or other circumstances beyond control of the filing office; and

(2) the filing office exercises reasonable diligence under the circumstances.

§ 9–525.   Fees.

(a) Except as otherwise provided in subsection (e), the fee for filing and indexing a record under this part, other than an initial financing statement of the kind described in subsection (b), is [the amount specified in subsection (c), if applicable, plus]:

(1) $[X] if the record is communicated in writing and consists of one or two pages;

(2) $[2X] if the record is communicated in writing and consists of more than two pages; and

(3) $[1/2X] if the record is communicated by another medium authorized by filing-office rule.

(b) Except as otherwise provided in subsection (e), the fee for filing and indexing an initial financing statement of the following kind is [the amount specified in subsection (c), if applicable, plus]:

(1) $——— if the financing statement indicates that it is filed in connection with a public-finance transaction;

(2) $——— if the financing statement indicates that it is filed in connection with a manufactured-home transaction.

[Alternative A]

(c) The number of names required to be indexed does not affect the amount of the fee in subsections (a) and (b).

[Alternative B]

(c) Except as otherwise provided in subsection (e), if a record is communicated in writing, the fee for each name more than two required to be indexed is $———.

[End of Alternatives]

(a) The fee for responding to a request for information from the filing office, including for [issuing a certificate showing] [communicating] whether there is on file any financing statement naming a particular debtor, is:

(1) $——— if the request is communicated in writing; and

(2) $——— if the request is communicated by another medium authorized by filing-office rule.

(e) This section does not require a fee with respect to a record of a mortgage which is effective as a financing statement filed as a fixture filing or as a financing statement covering as-extracted collateral or timber to be cut under Section 9–502(c). However, the recording and satisfaction fees that otherwise would be applicable to the record of the mortgage apply.

Legislative Notes:

1. To preserve uniformity, a State that places the provisions of this section together with statutes setting fees for other services should do so without modification.

2. A State should enact subsection (c), Alternative A, and omit the bracketed language in subsections (a) and (b) unless its indexing system entails a substantial additional cost when indexing additional names.

As amended in 2000.

§ 9–526.   Filing-Office Rules.

(a) The [insert appropriate governmental official or agency] shall adopt and publish rules to implement this article. The filing-office rules must be[:

(1) consistent with this article[; and

(2) adopted and published in accordance with the [insert any applicable state administrative procedure act]].

(b) To keep the filing-office rules and practices of the filing office in harmony with the rules and practices of filing offices in other jurisdictions that enact substantially this part, and to keep the technology used by the filing office compatible with the technology used by filing offices in other jurisdictions that enact

substantially this part, the [insert appropriate governmental official or agency], so far as is consistent with the purposes, policies, and provisions of this article, in adopting, amending, and repealing filing-office rules, shall:

(1) consult with filing offices in other jurisdictions that enact substantially this part; and

(2) consult the most recent version of the Model Rules promulgated by the International Association of Corporate Administrators or any successor organization; and

(3) take into consideration the rules and practices of, and the technology used by, filing offices in other jurisdictions that enact substantially this part.

§ 9–527.   Duty to Report.

The [insert appropriate governmental official or agency] shall report [annually on or before ———] to the [Governor and Legislature] on the operation of the filing office. The report must contain a statement of the extent to which:

(1) the filing-office rules are not in harmony with the rules of filing offices in other jurisdictions that enact substantially this part and the reasons for these variations; and

(2) the filing-office rules are not in harmony with the most recent version of the Model Rules promulgated by the International Association of Corporate Administrators, or any successor organization, and the reasons for these variations.

PART 6   Default

[Subpart 1. Default and Enforcement of Security Interest]

§ 9–601.   Rights after Default; Judicial Enforcement; Consignor or Buyer of Accounts, Chattel Paper, Payment Intangibles, or Promissory Notes.

(a) After default, a secured party has the rights provided in this part and, except as otherwise provided in Section 9–602, those provided by agreement of the parties. A secured party:

(1) may reduce a claim to judgment, foreclose, or otherwise enforce the claim, security interest, or agricultural lien by any available judicial procedure; and

(2) if the collateral is documents, may proceed either as to the documents or as to the goods they cover.

(b) A secured party in possession of collateral or control of collateral under Section 9–104, 9–105, 9–106, or 9–107 has the rights and duties provided in Section 9–207.

(c) The rights under subsections (a) and (b) are cumulative and may be exercised simultaneously.

(d) Except as otherwise provided in subsection (g) and Section 9–605, after default, a debtor and an obligor have the rights provided in this part and by agreement of the parties.

(e) If a secured party has reduced its claim to judgment, the lien of any levy that may be made upon the collateral by virtue of an execution based upon the judgment relates back to the earliest of:

(1) the date of perfection of the security interest or agricultural lien in the collateral;

(2) the date of filing a financing statement covering the collateral; or

(3) any date specified in a statute under which the agricultural lien was created.

(f) A sale pursuant to an execution is a foreclosure of the security interest or agricultural lien by judicial procedure within the meaning of this section. A secured party may purchase at the sale and thereafter hold the collateral free of any other requirements of this article.

(g) Except as otherwise provided in Section 9–607(c), this part imposes no duties upon a secured party that is a consignor or is a buyer of accounts, chattel paper, payment intangibles, or promissory notes.

§ 9–602.   Waiver and Variance of Rights and Duties.

Except as otherwise provided in Section 9–624, to the extent that they give rights to a debtor or obligor and impose duties on a secured party, the debtor or obligor may not waive or vary the rules stated in the following listed sections:

(1) Section 9–207(b)(4)(C), which deals with use and operation of the collateral by the secured party;

(2) Section 9–210, which deals with requests for an accounting and requests concerning a list of collateral and statement of account;

(3) Section 9–607(c), which deals with collection and enforcement of collateral;

(4) Sections 9–608(a) and 9–615(c) to the extent that they deal with application or payment of noncash proceeds of collection, enforcement, or disposition;

(5) Sections 9–608(a) and 9–615(d) to the extent that they require accounting for or payment of surplus proceeds of collateral;

(6) Section 9–609 to the extent that it imposes upon a secured party that takes possession of collateral without judicial process the duty to do so without breach of the peace;

(7) Sections 9–610(b), 9–611, 9–613, and 9–614, which deal with disposition of collateral;

(8) Section 9–615(f), which deals with calculation of a deficiency or surplus when a disposition is made to the secured

party, a person related to the secured party, or a secondary obligor;

(9) Section 9–616, which deals with explanation of the calculation of a surplus or deficiency;

(10) Sections 9–620, 9–621, and 9–622, which deal with acceptance of collateral in satisfaction of obligation;

(11) Section 9–623, which deals with redemption of collateral;

(12) Section 9–624, which deals with permissible waivers; and

(13) Sections 9–625 and 9–626, which deal with the secured party's liability for failure to comply with this article.

§ 9–603.   Agreement on Standards Concerning Rights and Duties.

(a) The parties may determine by agreement the standards measuring the fulfillment of the rights of a debtor or obligor and the duties of a secured party under a rule stated in Section 9–602 if the standards are not manifestly unreasonable.

(b) Subsection (a) does not apply to the duty under Section 9–609 to refrain from breaching the peace.

§ 9–604.   Procedure If Security Agreement Covers Real Property or Fixtures.

(a) If a security agreement covers both personal and real property, a secured party may proceed:

(1) under this part as to the personal property without prejudicing any rights with respect to the real property; or

(2) as to both the personal property and the real property in accordance with the rights with respect to the real property, in which case the other provisions of this part do not apply.

(b) Subject to subsection (c), if a security agreement covers goods that are or become fixtures, a secured party may proceed:

(1) under this part; or

(2) in accordance with the rights with respect to real property, in which case the other provisions of this part do not apply.

(c) Subject to the other provisions of this part, if a secured party holding a security interest in fixtures has priority over all owners and encumbrancers of the real property, the secured party, after default, may remove the collateral from the real property.

(d) A secured party that removes collateral shall promptly reimburse any encumbrancer or owner of the real property, other than the debtor, for the cost of repair of any physical injury caused by the removal. The secured party need not reimburse the encumbrancer or owner for any diminution in value of the real property caused by the absence of the goods removed or by any necessity of replacing them. A person entitled to reimbursement may refuse permission to remove until the secured party gives adequate assurance for the performance of the obligation to reimburse.

§ 9-605. Unknown Debtor or Secondary Obligor.

A secured party does not owe a duty based on its status as secured party:

(1) to a person that is a debtor or obligor, unless the secured party knows:

(A) that the person is a debtor or obligor;

(B) the identity of the person; and

(C) how to communicate with the person; or

(2) to a secured party or lienholder that has filed a financing statement against a person, unless the secured party knows:

(A) that the person is a debtor; and

(B) the identity of the person.

§ 9-606. Time of Default for Agricultural Lien.

For purposes of this part, a default occurs in connection with an agricultural lien at the time the secured party becomes entitled to enforce the lien in accordance with the statute under which it was created.

§ 9-607. Collection and Enforcement by Secured Party.

(a) If so agreed, and in any event after default, a secured party:

(1) may notify an account debtor or other person obligated on collateral to make payment or otherwise render performance to or for the benefit of the secured party;

(2) may take any proceeds to which the secured party is entitled under Section 9–315;

(3) may enforce the obligations of an account debtor or other person obligated on collateral and exercise the rights of the debtor with respect to the obligation of the account debtor or other person obligated on collateral to make payment or otherwise render performance to the debtor, and with respect to any property that secures the obligations of the account debtor or other person obligated on the collateral;

(4) if it holds a security interest in a deposit account perfected by control under Section 9–104(a)(1), may apply the balance of the deposit account to the obligation secured by the deposit account; and

(5) if it holds a security interest in a deposit account perfected by control under Section 9–104(a)(2) or (3), may instruct the bank to pay the balance of the deposit account to or for the benefit of the secured party.

(b) If necessary to enable a secured party to exercise under subsection (a)(3) the right of a debtor to enforce a mortgage nonjudicially, the secured party may record in the office in which a record of the mortgage is recorded:

(1) a copy of the security agreement that creates or provides for a security interest in the obligation secured by the mortgage; and

(2) the secured party's sworn affidavit in recordable form stating that:

(A) a default has occurred; and

(B) the secured party is entitled to enforce the mortgage nonjudicially.

(c) A secured party shall proceed in a commercially reasonable manner if the secured party:

(1) undertakes to collect from or enforce an obligation of an account debtor or other person obligated on collateral; and

(2) is entitled to charge back uncollected collateral or otherwise to full or limited recourse against the debtor or a secondary obligor.

(d) A secured party may deduct from the collections made pursuant to subsection (c) reasonable expenses of collection and enforcement, including reasonable attorney's fees and legal expenses incurred by the secured party.

(e) This section does not determine whether an account debtor, bank, or other person obligated on collateral owes a duty to a secured party.

As amended in 2000.

§ 9-608. Application of Proceeds of Collection or Enforcement; Liability for Deficiency and Right to Surplus.

(a) If a security interest or agricultural lien secures payment or performance of an obligation, the following rules apply:

(1) A secured party shall apply or pay over for application the cash proceeds of collection or enforcement under Section 9–607 in the following order to:

(A) the reasonable expenses of collection and enforcement and, to the extent provided for by agreement and not prohibited by law, reasonable attorney's fees and legal expenses incurred by the secured party;

(B) the satisfaction of obligations secured by the security interest or agricultural lien under which the collection or enforcement is made; and

(C) the satisfaction of obligations secured by any subordinate security interest in or other lien on the collateral subject to the security interest or agricultural lien under which the collection or enforcement is made if the secured party receives an authenticated demand for proceeds before distribution of the proceeds is completed.

(2) If requested by a secured party, a holder of a subordinate security interest or other lien shall furnish reasonable proof of the interest or lien within a reasonable time. Unless the holder complies, the secured party need not comply with the holder's demand under paragraph (1)(C).

(3) A secured party need not apply or pay over for application noncash proceeds of collection and enforcement under Section 9–607 unless the failure to do so would be commercially unreasonable. A secured party that applies or pays over for

application noncash proceeds shall do so in a commercially reasonable manner.

(4) A secured party shall account to and pay a debtor for any surplus, and the obligor is liable for any deficiency.

(b) If the underlying transaction is a sale of accounts, chattel paper, payment intangibles, or promissory notes, the debtor is not entitled to any surplus, and the obligor is not liable for any deficiency.

As amended in 2000.

§ 9–609.   Secured Party's Right to Take Possession after Default.

(a) After default, a secured party:

(1) may take possession of the collateral; and

(2) without removal, may render equipment unusable and dispose of collateral on a debtor's premises under Section 9–610.

(b) A secured party may proceed under subsection (a):

(1) pursuant to judicial process; or

(2) without judicial process, if it proceeds without breach of the peace.

(c) If so agreed, and in any event after default, a secured party may require the debtor to assemble the collateral and make it available to the secured party at a place to be designated by the secured party which is reasonably convenient to both parties.

§ 9–610.   Disposition of Collateral after Default.

(a) After default, a secured party may sell, lease, license, or otherwise dispose of any or all of the collateral in its present condition or following any commercially reasonable preparation or processing.

(b) Every aspect of a disposition of collateral, including the method, manner, time, place, and other terms, must be commercially reasonable. If commercially reasonable, a secured party may dispose of collateral by public or private proceedings, by one or more contracts, as a unit or in parcels, and at any time and place and on any terms.

(c) A secured party may purchase collateral:

(1) at a public disposition; or

(2) at a private disposition only if the collateral is of a kind that is customarily sold on a recognized market or the subject of widely distributed standard price quotations.

(d) A contract for sale, lease, license, or other disposition includes the warranties relating to title, possession, quiet enjoyment, and the like which by operation of law accompany a voluntary disposition of property of the kind subject to the contract.

(e) A secured party may disclaim or modify warranties under subsection (d):

(1) in a manner that would be effective to disclaim or modify the warranties in a voluntary disposition of property of the kind subject to the contract of disposition; or

(2) by communicating to the purchaser a record evidencing the contract for disposition and including an express disclaimer or modification of the warranties.

(f) A record is sufficient to disclaim warranties under subsection (e) if it indicates "There is no warranty relating to title, possession, quiet enjoyment, or the like in this disposition" or uses words of similar import.

§ 9–611.   Notification before Disposition of Collateral.

(a) In this section, "notification date" means the earlier of the date on which:

(1) a secured party sends to the debtor and any secondary obligor an authenticated notification of disposition; or

(2) the debtor and any secondary obligor waive the right to notification.

(b) Except as otherwise provided in subsection (d), a secured party that disposes of collateral under Section 9–610 shall send to the persons specified in subsection (c) a reasonable authenticated notification of disposition.

(c) To comply with subsection (b), the secured party shall send an authenticated notification of disposition to:

(1) the debtor;

(2) any secondary obligor; and

(3) if the collateral is other than consumer goods:

(A) any other person from which the secured party has received, before the notification date, an authenticated notification of a claim of an interest in the collateral;

(B) any other secured party or lienholder that, 10 days before the notification date, held a security interest in or other lien on the collateral perfected by the filing of a financing statement that:

(i) identified the collateral;

(ii) was indexed under the debtor's name as of that date; and

(iii) was filed in the office in which to file a financing statement against the debtor covering the collateral as of that date; and

(C) any other secured party that, 10 days before the notification date, held a security interest in the collateral perfected by compliance with a statute, regulation, or treaty described in Section 9–311(a).

(d) Subsection (b) does not apply if the collateral is perishable or threatens to decline speedily in value or is of a type customarily sold on a recognized market.

(e) A secured party complies with the requirement for notification prescribed by subsection (c)(3)(B) if:

(1) not later than 20 days or earlier than 30 days before the notification date, the secured party requests, in a commercially reasonable manner, information concerning financing statements indexed under the debtor's name in the office indicated in subsection (c)(3)(B); and

(2) before the notification date, the secured party:

(A) did not receive a response to the request for information; or

(B) received a response to the request for information and sent an authenticated notification of disposition to each secured party or other lienholder named in that response whose financing statement covered the collateral.

§ 9–612. Timeliness of Notification before Disposition of Collateral.

(a) Except as otherwise provided in subsection (b), whether a notification is sent within a reasonable time is a question of fact.

(b) In a transaction other than a consumer transaction, a notification of disposition sent after default and 10 days or more before the earliest time of disposition set forth in the notification is sent within a reasonable time before the disposition.

§ 9–613. Contents and Form of Notification before Disposition of Collateral: General.

Except in a consumer-goods transaction, the following rules apply:

(1) The contents of a notification of disposition are sufficient if the notification:

(A) describes the debtor and the secured party;

(B) describes the collateral that is the subject of the intended disposition;

(C) states the method of intended disposition;

(D) states that the debtor is entitled to an accounting of the unpaid indebtedness and states the charge, if any, for an accounting; and

(E) states the time and place of a public disposition or the time after which any other disposition is to be made.

(2) Whether the contents of a notification that lacks any of the information specified in paragraph (1) are nevertheless sufficient is a question of fact.

(3) The contents of a notification providing substantially the information specified in paragraph (1) are sufficient, even if the notification includes:

(A) information not specified by that paragraph; or

(b) minor errors that are not seriously misleading.

(4) A particular phrasing of the notification is not required.

(5) The following form of notification and the form appearing in Section 9–614(3), when completed, each provides sufficient information:

NOTIFICATION OF DISPOSITION OF COLLATERAL

To: [*Name of debtor, obligor, or other person to which the notification is sent*]

From: [*Name, address, and telephone number of secured party*]

Name of Debtor(s): [*Include only if debtor(s) are not an addressee*]

[*For a public disposition:*]

We will sell [or lease or license, *as applicable*] the [*describe collateral*] [to the highest qualified bidder] in public as follows:

Day and Date: _____

Time: _____

Place: _____

[*For a private disposition:*]

We will sell [or lease or license, *as applicable*] the [*describe collateral*] privately sometime after [*day and date*].

You are entitled to an accounting of the unpaid indebtedness secured by the property that we intend to sell [or lease or license as *applicable*] [for a charge of $_____]. You may request an accounting by calling us at [*telephone number*].

[End of Form]

As amended in 2000.

§ 9–614. Contents and Form of Notification before Disposition of Collateral: Consumer-Goods Transaction.

In a consumer-goods transaction, the following rules apply:

(1) A notification of disposition must provide the following information:

(A) the information specified in Section 9–613(1);

(B) a description of any liability for a deficiency of the person to which the notification is sent;

(C) a telephone number from which the amount that must be paid to the secured party to redeem the collateral under Section 9–623 is available; and

(D) a telephone number or mailing address from which additional information concerning the disposition and the obligation secured is available.

(2) A particular phrasing of the notification is not required.

(3) The following form of notification, when completed, provides sufficient information:

[*Name and address of secured party*]

[*Date*]

NOTICE OF OUR PLAN TO SELL PROPERTY

[*Name and address of any obligor who is also a debtor*]

Subject: [*Identification of Transaction*]

We have your [*describe collateral*], because you broke promises in our agreement.

[*For a public disposition:*]

We will sell [*describe collateral*] at public sale. A sale could include a lease or license. The sale will be held as follows:

Date: _____

Time: _____

Place: _____

You may attend the sale and bring bidders if you want.

[*For a private disposition:*]

We will sell [*describe collateral*] at private sale sometime after

[*date*]. A sale could include a lease or license.

The money that we get from the sale (after paying our costs) will reduce the amount you owe. If we get less money than you owe, you [*will or will not, as applicable*] still owe us the difference. If we get more money than you owe, you will get the extra money, unless we must pay it to someone else.

You can get the property back at any time before we sell it by paying us the full amount you owe (not just the past due payments), including our expenses. To learn the exact amount you must pay, call us at [*telephone number*].

If you want us to explain to you in writing how we have figured the amount that you owe us, you may call us at [*telephone number*] [or write us at [*secured party's address*]] and request a written explanation. [We will charge you $_____ for the explanation if we sent you another written explanation of the amount you owe us within the last six months.]

If you need more information about the sale call us at [*telephone number*] [or write us at [*secured party's address*]].

We are sending this notice to the following other people who have an interest in [*describe collateral*] or who owe money under your agreement:

[*Names of all other debtors and obligors, if any*]

[End of Form]

(4) A notification in the form of paragraph (3) is sufficient, even if additional information appears at the end of the form.

(5) A notification in the form of paragraph (3) is sufficient, even if it includes errors in information not required by paragraph (1), unless the error is misleading with respect to rights arising under this article.

(6) If a notification under this section is not in the form of paragraph (3), law other than this article determines the effect of including information not required by paragraph (1).

§ 9–615. Application of Proceeds of Disposition; Liability for Deficiency and Right to Surplus.

(a) A secured party shall apply or pay over for application the cash proceeds of disposition under Section 9–610 in the following order to:

(1) the reasonable expenses of retaking, holding, preparing for disposition, processing, and disposing, and, to the extent provided for by agreement and not prohibited by law, reasonable attorney's fees and legal expenses incurred by the secured party;

(2) the satisfaction of obligations secured by the security interest or agricultural lien under which the disposition is made;

(3) the satisfaction of obligations secured by any subordinate security interest in or other subordinate lien on the collateral if:

(A) the secured party receives from the holder of the subordinate security interest or other lien an authenticated demand for proceeds before distribution of the proceeds is completed; and

(B) in a case in which a consignor has an interest in the collateral, the subordinate security interest or other lien is senior to the interest of the consignor; and

(4) a secured party that is a consignor of the collateral if the secured party receives from the consignor an authenticated demand for proceeds before distribution of the proceeds is completed.

(b) If requested by a secured party, a holder of a subordinate security interest or other lien shall furnish reasonable proof of the interest or lien within a reasonable time. Unless the holder does so, the secured party need not comply with the holder's demand under subsection (a)(3).

(c) A secured party need not apply or pay over for application noncash proceeds of disposition under Section 9–610 unless the failure to do so would be commercially unreasonable. A secured party that applies or pays over for application noncash proceeds shall do so in a commercially reasonable manner.

(d) If the security interest under which a disposition is made secures payment or performance of an obligation, after making the payments and applications required by subsection (a) and permitted by subsection (c):

(1) unless subsection (a)(4) requires the secured party to apply or pay over cash proceeds to a consignor, the secured party shall account to and pay a debtor for any surplus; and

(2) the obligor is liable for any deficiency.

(e) If the underlying transaction is a sale of accounts, chattel paper, payment intangibles, or promissory notes:

(1) the debtor is not entitled to any surplus; and

(2) the obligor is not liable for any deficiency.

(f) The surplus or deficiency following a disposition is calculated based on the amount of proceeds that would have been realized in a disposition complying with this part to a transferee other than the secured party, a person related to the secured party, or a secondary obligor if:

(1) the transferee in the disposition is the secured party, a person related to the secured party, or a secondary obligor; and

(2) the amount of proceeds of the disposition is significantly below the range of proceeds that a complying disposition to a person other than the secured party, a person related to the secured party, or a secondary obligor would have brought.

(g) A secured party that receives cash proceeds of a disposition in good faith and without knowledge that the receipt violates the rights of the holder of a security interest or other lien that is not subordinate to the security interest or agricultural lien under which the disposition is made:

(1) takes the cash proceeds free of the security interest or other lien;

(2) is not obligated to apply the proceeds of the disposition to the satisfaction of obligations secured by the security interest or other lien; and

(3) is not obligated to account to or pay the holder of the security interest or other lien for any surplus.

As amended in 2000.

§ 9–616.   Explanation of Calculation of Surplus or Deficiency.

(a) In this section:

(1) "Explanation" means a writing that:

(A) states the amount of the surplus or deficiency;

(B) provides an explanation in accordance with subsection (c) of how the secured party calculated the surplus or deficiency;

(C) states, if applicable, that future debits, credits, charges, including additional credit service charges or interest, rebates, and expenses may affect the amount of the surplus or deficiency; and

(D) provides a telephone number or mailing address from which additional information concerning the transaction is available.

(2) "Request" means a record:

(A) authenticated by a debtor or consumer obligor;

(B) requesting that the recipient provide an explanation; and

(C) sent after disposition of the collateral under Section 9–610.

(b) In a consumer-goods transaction in which the debtor is entitled to a surplus or a consumer obligor is liable for a deficiency under Section 9–615, the secured party shall:

(1) send an explanation to the debtor or consumer obligor, as applicable, after the disposition and:

(A) before or when the secured party accounts to the debtor and pays any surplus or first makes written demand on the consumer obligor after the disposition for payment of the deficiency; and

(B) within 14 days after receipt of a request; or

(2) in the case of a consumer obligor who is liable for a deficiency, within 14 days after receipt of a request, send to the consumer obligor a record waiving the secured party's right to a deficiency.

(c) To comply with subsection (a)(1)(B), a writing must provide the following information in the following order:

(1) the aggregate amount of obligations secured by the security interest under which the disposition was made, and, if the amount reflects a rebate of unearned interest or credit service charge, an indication of that fact, calculated as of a specified date:

(A) if the secured party takes or receives possession of the collateral after default, not more than 35 days before the secured party takes or receives possession; or

(B) if the secured party takes or receives possession of the collateral before default or does not take possession of the collateral, not more than 35 days before the disposition;

(2) the amount of proceeds of the disposition;

(3) the aggregate amount of the obligations after deducting the amount of proceeds;

(4) the amount, in the aggregate or by type, and types of expenses, including expenses of retaking, holding, preparing for disposition, processing, and disposing of the collateral, and attorney's fees secured by the collateral which are known to the secured party and relate to the current disposition;

(5) the amount, in the aggregate or by type, and types of credits, including rebates of interest or credit service charges, to which the obligor is known to be entitled and which are not reflected in the amount in paragraph (1); and

(6) the amount of the surplus or deficiency.

(d) A particular phrasing of the explanation is not required. An explanation complying substantially with the requirements of subsection (a) is sufficient, even if it includes minor errors that are not seriously misleading.

(e) A debtor or consumer obligor is entitled without charge to one response to a request under this section during any six-month period in which the secured party did not send to the debtor or consumer obligor an explanation pursuant to subsection (b)(1). The secured party may require payment of a charge not exceeding $25 for each additional response.

§ 9–617.   Rights of Transferee of Collateral.

(a) A secured party's disposition of collateral after default:

(1) transfers to a transferee for value all of the debtor's rights in the collateral;

(2) discharges the security interest under which the disposition is made; and

(3) discharges any subordinate security interest or other subordinate lien [other than liens created under [cite acts or statutes providing for liens, if any, that are not to be discharged]].

(b) A transferee that acts in good faith takes free of the rights and interests described in subsection (a), even if the secured party fails to comply with this article or the requirements of any judicial proceeding.

(c) If a transferee does not take free of the rights and interests described in subsection (a), the transferee takes the collateral subject to:

(1) the debtor's rights in the collateral;

(2) the security interest or agricultural lien under which the disposition is made; and

(3) any other security interest or other lien.

§ 9–618.   Rights and Duties of Certain Secondary Obligors.

(a) A secondary obligor acquires the rights and becomes obligated to perform the duties of the secured party after the secondary obligor:

(1) receives an assignment of a secured obligation from the secured party;

(2) receives a transfer of collateral from the secured party and agrees to accept the rights and assume the duties of the secured party; or

(3) is subrogated to the rights of a secured party with respect to collateral.

(b) An assignment, transfer, or subrogation described in subsection (a):

(1) is not a disposition of collateral under Section 9–610; and

(2) relieves the secured party of further duties under this article.

§ 9–619.   Transfer of Record or Legal Title.

(a) In this section, "transfer statement" means a record authenticated by a secured party stating:

(1) that the debtor has defaulted in connection with an obligation secured by specified collateral;

(2) that the secured party has exercised its post-default remedies with respect to the collateral;

(3) that, by reason of the exercise, a transferee has acquired the rights of the debtor in the collateral; and

(4) the name and mailing address of the secured party, debtor, and transferee.

(b) A transfer statement entitles the transferee to the transfer of record of all rights of the debtor in the collateral specified in the statement in any official filing, recording, registration, or certificate-of-title system covering the collateral. If a transfer statement is presented with the applicable fee and request form to the official or office responsible for maintaining the system, the official or office shall:

(1) accept the transfer statement;

(2) promptly amend its records to reflect the transfer; and

(3) if applicable, issue a new appropriate certificate of title in the name of the transferee.

(c) A transfer of the record or legal title to collateral to a secured party under subsection (b) or otherwise is not of itself a disposition of collateral under this article and does not of itself relieve the secured party of its duties under this article.

§ 9–620.   Acceptance of Collateral in Full or Partial Satisfaction of Obligation; Compulsory Disposition of Collateral.

(a) Except as otherwise provided in subsection (g), a secured party may accept collateral in full or partial satisfaction of the obligation it secures only if:

(1) the debtor consents to the acceptance under subsection (c);

(2) the secured party does not receive, within the time set forth in subsection (d), a notification of objection to the proposal authenticated by:

(A) a person to which the secured party was required to send a proposal under Section 9–621; or

(B) any other person, other than the debtor, holding an interest in the collateral subordinate to the security interest that is the subject of the proposal;

(3) if the collateral is consumer goods, the collateral is not in the possession of the debtor when the debtor consents to the acceptance; and

(4) subsection (e) does not require the secured party to dispose of the collateral or the debtor waives the requirement pursuant to Section 9–624.

(b) A purported or apparent acceptance of collateral under this section is ineffective unless:

(1) the secured party consents to the acceptance in an authenticated record or sends a proposal to the debtor; and

(2) the conditions of subsection (a) are met.

(c) For purposes of this section:

(1) a debtor consents to an acceptance of collateral in partial satisfaction of the obligation it secures only if the debtor agrees to the terms of the acceptance in a record authenticated after default; and

(2) a debtor consents to an acceptance of collateral in full satisfaction of the obligation it secures only if the debtor agrees to the terms of the acceptance in a record authenticated after default or the secured party:

(A) sends to the debtor after default a proposal that is unconditional or subject only to a condition that collateral not in the possession of the secured party be preserved or maintained;

(B) in the proposal, proposes to accept collateral in full satisfaction of the obligation it secures; and

(C) does not receive a notification of objection authenticated by the debtor within 20 days after the proposal is sent.

(d) To be effective under subsection (a)(2), a notification of objection must be received by the secured party:

(1) in the case of a person to which the proposal was sent pursuant to Section 9–621, within 20 days after notification was sent to that person; and

(2) in other cases:

(A) within 20 days after the last notification was sent pursuant to Section 9–621; or

(B) if a notification was not sent, before the debtor consents to the acceptance under subsection (c).

(e) A secured party that has taken possession of collateral shall dispose of the collateral pursuant to Section 9–610 within the time specified in subsection (f) if:

(1) 60 percent of the cash price has been paid in the case of a purchase-money security interest in consumer goods; or

(2) 60 percent of the principal amount of the obligation secured has been paid in the case of a non-purchase-money security interest in consumer goods.

(f) To comply with subsection (e), the secured party shall dispose of the collateral:

(1) within 90 days after taking possession; or

(2) within any longer period to which the debtor and all secondary obligors have agreed in an agreement to that effect entered into and authenticated after default.

(g) In a consumer transaction, a secured party may not accept collateral in partial satisfaction of the obligation it secures.

§ 9–621.   Notification of Proposal to Accept Collateral.

(a) A secured party that desires to accept collateral in full or partial satisfaction of the obligation it secures shall send its proposal to:

(1) any person from which the secured party has received, before the debtor consented to the acceptance, an authenticated notification of a claim of an interest in the collateral;

(2) any other secured party or lienholder that, 10 days before the debtor consented to the acceptance, held a security interest in or other lien on the collateral perfected by the filing of a financing statement that:

(A) identified the collateral;

(B) was indexed under the debtor's name as of that date; and

(C) was filed in the office or offices in which to file a financing statement against the debtor covering the collateral as of that date; and

(3) any other secured party that, 10 days before the debtor consented to the acceptance, held a security interest in the collateral perfected by compliance with a statute, regulation, or treaty described in Section 9–311(a).

(b) A secured party that desires to accept collateral in partial satisfaction of the obligation it secures shall send its proposal to any secondary obligor in addition to the persons described in subsection (a).

§ 9–622.   Effect of Acceptance of Collateral.

(a) A secured party's acceptance of collateral in full or partial satisfaction of the obligation it secures:

(1) discharges the obligation to the extent consented to by the debtor;

(2) transfers to the secured party all of a debtor's rights in the collateral;

(3) discharges the security interest or agricultural lien that is the subject of the debtor's consent and any subordinate security interest or other subordinate lien; and

(4) terminates any other subordinate interest.

(b) A subordinate interest is discharged or terminated under subsection (a), even if the secured party fails to comply with this article.

§ 9–623.   Right to Redeem Collateral.

(a) A debtor, any secondary obligor, or any other secured party or lienholder may redeem collateral.

(b) To redeem collateral, a person shall tender:

(1) fulfillment of all obligations secured by the collateral; and

(2) the reasonable expenses and attorney's fees described in Section 9–615(a)(1).

(c) A redemption may occur at any time before a secured party:

(1) has collected collateral under Section 9–607;

(2) has disposed of collateral or entered into a contract for its disposition under Section 9–610; or

(3) has accepted collateral in full or partial satisfaction of the obligation it secures under Section 9–622.

§ 9–624.   Waiver.

(a) A debtor or secondary obligor may waive the right to notification of disposition of collateral under Section 9–611 only by an agreement to that effect entered into and authenticated after default.

(b) A debtor may waive the right to require disposition of collateral under Section 9–620(e) only by an agreement to that effect entered into and authenticated after default.

(c) Except in a consumer-goods transaction, a debtor or secondary obligor may waive the right to redeem collateral under Section 9–623 only by an agreement to that effect entered into and authenticated after default.

[Subpart 2. Noncompliance with Article]

§ 9-625.   Remedies for Secured Party's Failure to Comply with Article.

(a) If it is established that a secured party is not proceeding in accordance with this article, a court may order or restrain collection, enforcement, or disposition of collateral on appropriate terms and conditions.

(b) Subject to subsections (c), (d), and (f), a person is liable for damages in the amount of any loss caused by a failure to comply with this article. Loss caused by a failure to comply may include loss resulting from the debtor's inability to obtain, or increased costs of, alternative financing.

(c) Except as otherwise provided in Section 9-628:

(1) a person that, at the time of the failure, was a debtor, was an obligor, or held a security interest in or other lien on the collateral may recover damages under subsection (b) for its loss; and

(2) if the collateral is consumer goods, a person that was a debtor or a secondary obligor at the time a secured party failed to comply with this part may recover for that failure in any event an amount not less than the credit service charge plus 10 percent of the principal amount of the obligation or the time-price differential plus 10 percent of the cash price.

(d) A debtor whose deficiency is eliminated under Section 9-626 may recover damages for the loss of any surplus. However, a debtor or secondary obligor whose deficiency is eliminated or reduced under Section 9-626 may not otherwise recover under subsection (b) for noncompliance with the provisions of this part relating to collection, enforcement, disposition, or acceptance.

(e) In addition to any damages recoverable under subsection (b), the debtor, consumer obligor, or person named as a debtor in a filed record, as applicable, may recover $500 in each case from a person that:

(1) fails to comply with Section 9-208;

(2) fails to comply with Section 9-209;

(3) files a record that the person is not entitled to file under Section 9-509(a);

(4) fails to cause the secured party of record to file or send a termination statement as required by Section 9-513(a) or (c);

(5) fails to comply with Section 9-616(b)(1) and whose failure is part of a pattern, or consistent with a practice, of noncompliance; or

(6) fails to comply with Section 9-616(b)(2).

(f) A debtor or consumer obligor may recover damages under subsection (b) and, in addition, $500 in each case from a person that, without reasonable cause, fails to comply with a request under Section 9-210. A recipient of a request under Section 9-210 which never claimed an interest in the collateral or obligations that are the subject of a request under that section

has a reasonable excuse for failure to comply with the request within the meaning of this subsection.

(g) If a secured party fails to comply with a request regarding a list of collateral or a statement of account under Section 9-210, the secured party may claim a security interest only as shown in the list or statement included in the request as against a person that is reasonably misled by the failure.

As amended in 2000.

§ 9-626.   Action in Which Deficiency or Surplus Is in Issue.

(a) In an action arising from a transaction, other than a consumer transaction, in which the amount of a deficiency or surplus is in issue, the following rules apply:

(1) A secured party need not prove compliance with the provisions of this part relating to collection, enforcement, disposition, or acceptance unless the debtor or a secondary obligor places the secured party's compliance in issue.

(2) If the secured party's compliance is placed in issue, the secured party has the burden of establishing that the collection, enforcement, disposition, or acceptance was conducted in accordance with this part.

(3) Except as otherwise provided in Section 9-628, if a secured party fails to prove that the collection, enforcement, disposition, or acceptance was conducted in accordance with the provisions of this part relating to collection, enforcement, disposition, or acceptance, the liability of a debtor or a secondary obligor for a deficiency is limited to an amount by which the sum of the secured obligation, expenses, and attorney's fees exceeds the greater of:

(A) the proceeds of the collection, enforcement, disposition, or acceptance; or

(B) the amount of proceeds that would have been realized had the noncomplying secured party proceeded in accordance with the provisions of this part relating to collection, enforcement, disposition, or acceptance.

(4) For purposes of paragraph (3)(B), the amount of proceeds that would have been realized is equal to the sum of the secured obligation, expenses, and attorney's fees unless the secured party proves that the amount is less than that sum.

(5) If a deficiency or surplus is calculated under Section 9-615 (f), the debtor or obligor has the burden of establishing that the amount of proceeds of the disposition is significantly below the range of prices that a complying disposition to a person other than the secured party, a person related to the secured party, or a secondary obligor would have brought.

(b) The limitation of the rules in subsection (a) to transactions other than consumer transactions is intended to leave to the court the determination of the proper rules in consumer transactions. The court may not infer from that limitation the nature of the proper rule in consumer transactions and may continue to apply established approaches.

§ 9–627.   Determination of Whether Conduct Was Commercially Reasonable.

(a) The fact that a greater amount could have been obtained by a collection, enforcement, disposition, or acceptance at a different time or in a different method from that selected by the secured party is not of itself sufficient to preclude the secured party from establishing that the collection, enforcement, disposition, or acceptance was made in a commercially reasonable manner.

(b) A disposition of collateral is made in a commercially reasonable manner if the disposition is made:

(1) in the usual manner on any recognized market;

(2) at the price current in any recognized market at the time of the disposition; or

(3) otherwise in conformity with reasonable commercial practices among dealers in the type of property that was the subject of the disposition.

(c) A collection, enforcement, disposition, or acceptance is commercially reasonable if it has been approved:

(1) in a judicial proceeding;

(2) by a bona fide creditors' committee;

(3) by a representative of creditors; or

(4) by an assignee for the benefit of creditors.

(d) Approval under subsection (c) need not be obtained, and lack of approval does not mean that the collection, enforcement, disposition, or acceptance is not commercially reasonable.

§ 9–628.   Nonliability and Limitation on Liability of Secured Party; Liability of Secondary Obligor.

(a) Unless a secured party knows that a person is a debtor or obligor, knows the identity of the person, and knows how to communicate with the person:

(1) the secured party is not liable to the person, or to a secured party or lienholder that has filed a financing statement against the person, for failure to comply with this article; and

(2) the secured party's failure to comply with this article does not affect the liability of the person for a deficiency.

(b) A secured party is not liable because of its status as secured party:

(1) to a person that is a debtor or obligor, unless the secured party knows:

(A) that the person is a debtor or obligor;

(B) the identity of the person; and

(C) how to communicate with the person; or

(2) to a secured party or lienholder that has filed a financing statement against a person, unless the secured party knows:

(A) that the person is a debtor; and

(B) the identity of the person.

(c) A secured party is not liable to any person, and a person's liability for a deficiency is not affected, because of any act or omission arising out of the secured party's reasonable belief that a transaction is not a consumer-goods transaction or a consumer transaction or that goods are not consumer goods, if the secured party's belief is based on its reasonable reliance on:

(1) a debtor's representation concerning the purpose for which collateral was to be used, acquired, or held; or

(2) an obligor's representation concerning the purpose for which a secured obligation was incurred.

(d) A secured party is not liable to any person under Section 9–625(c)(2) for its failure to comply with Section 9–616.

(e) A secured party is not liable under Section 9–625(c)(2) more than once with respect to any one secured obligation.

PART 7   Transition

§ 9–701.   Effective Date.

This [Act] takes effect on July 1, 2001.

§ 9–702.   Savings Clause.

(a) Except as otherwise provided in this part, this [Act] applies to a transaction or lien within its scope, even if the transaction or lien was entered into or created before this [Act] takes effect.

(b) Except as otherwise provided in subsection (c) and Sections 9–703 through 9–709:

(1) transactions and liens that were not governed by [former Article 9], were validly entered into or created before this [Act] takes effect, and would be subject to this [Act] if they had been entered into or created after this [Act] takes effect, and the rights, duties, and interests flowing from those transactions and liens remain valid after this [Act] takes effect; and

(2) the transactions and liens may be terminated, completed, consummated, and enforced as required or permitted by this [Act] or by the law that otherwise would apply if this [Act] had not taken effect.

(c) This [Act] does not affect an action, case, or proceeding commenced before this [Act] takes effect.

As amended in 2000.

§ 9–703.   Security Interest Perfected before Effective Date.

(a) A security interest that is enforceable immediately before this [Act] takes effect and would have priority over the rights of a person that becomes a lien creditor at that time is a perfected security interest under this [Act] if, when this [Act] takes effect, the applicable requirements for enforceability and perfection under this [Act] are satisfied without further action.

(b) Except as otherwise provided in Section 9–705, if, immediately before this [Act] takes effect, a security interest is enforceable and would have priority over the rights of a person that becomes a lien creditor at that time, but the applicable requirements for enforceability or perfection under this [Act] are not satisfied when this [Act] takes effect, the security interest:

(1) is a perfected security interest for one year after this [Act] takes effect;

(2) remains enforceable thereafter only if the security interest becomes enforceable under Section 9–203 before the year expires; and

(3) remains perfected thereafter only if the applicable requirements for perfection under this [Act] are satisfied before the year expires.

§ 9–704.   Security Interest Unperfected before Effective Date.

A security interest that is enforceable immediately before this [Act] takes effect but which would be subordinate to the rights of a person that becomes a lien creditor at that time:

(1) remains an enforceable security interest for one year after this [Act] takes effect;

(2) remains enforceable thereafter if the security interest becomes enforceable under Section 9–203 when this [Act] takes effect or within one year thereafter; and

(3) becomes perfected:

(A) without further action, when this [Act] takes effect if the applicable requirements for perfection under this [Act] are satisfied before or at that time; or

(B) when the applicable requirements for perfection are satisfied if the requirements are satisfied after that time.

§ 9–705.   Effectiveness of Action Taken before Effective Date.

(a) If action, other than the filing of a financing statement, is taken before this [Act] takes effect and the action would have resulted in priority of a security interest over the rights of a person that becomes a lien creditor had the security interest become enforceable before this [Act] takes effect, the action is effective to perfect a security interest that attaches under this [Act] within one year after this [Act] takes effect. An attached security interest becomes unperfected one year after this [Act] takes effect unless the security interest becomes a perfected security interest under this [Act] before the expiration of that period.

(b) The filing of a financing statement before this [Act] takes effect is effective to perfect a security interest to the extent the filing would satisfy the applicable requirements for perfection under this [Act].

(c) This [Act] does not render ineffective an effective financing statement that, before this [Act] takes effect, is filed and satisfies the applicable requirements for perfection under the law of the jurisdiction governing perfection as provided in [former Section 9–103]. However, except as otherwise provided in subsections (d) and (e) and Section 9–706, the financing statement ceases to be effective at the earlier of:

(1) the time the financing statement would have ceased to be effective under the law of the jurisdiction in which it is filed; or

(2) June 30, 2006.

(d) The filing of a continuation statement after this [Act] takes effect does not continue the effectiveness of the financing statement filed before this [Act] takes effect. However, upon the timely filing of a continuation statement after this [Act] takes effect and in accordance with the law of the jurisdiction governing perfection as provided in Part 3, the effectiveness of a financing statement filed in the same office in that jurisdiction before this [Act] takes effect continues for the period provided by the law of that jurisdiction.

(e) Subsection (c)(2) applies to a financing statement that, before this [Act] takes effect, is filed against a transmitting utility and satisfies the applicable requirements for perfection under the law of the jurisdiction governing perfection as provided in [former Section 9–103] only to the extent that Part 3 provides that the law of a jurisdiction other than the jurisdiction in which the financing statement is filed governs perfection of a security interest in collateral covered by the financing statement.

(f) A financing statement that includes a financing statement filed before this [Act] takes effect and a continuation statement filed after this [Act] takes effect is effective only to the extent that it satisfies the requirements of Part 5 for an initial financing statement.

§ 9–706.   When Initial Financing Statement Suffices to Continue Effectiveness of Financing Statement.

(a) The filing of an initial financing statement in the office specified in Section 9–501 continues the effectiveness of a financing statement filed before this [Act] takes effect if:

(1) the filing of an initial financing statement in that office would be effective to perfect a security interest under this [Act];

(2) the pre-effective-date financing statement was filed in an office in another State or another office in this State; and

(3) the initial financing statement satisfies subsection (c).

(b) The filing of an initial financing statement under subsection (a) continues the effectiveness of the pre-effective-date financing statement:

(1) if the initial financing statement is filed before this [Act] takes effect, for the period provided in [former Section 9–403] with respect to a financing statement; and

(2) if the initial financing statement is filed after this [Act] takes effect, for the period provided in Section 9–515 with respect to an initial financing statement.

(c) To be effective for purposes of subsection (a), an initial financing statement must:

(1) satisfy the requirements of Part 5 for an initial financing statement;

(2) identify the pre-effective-date financing statement by indicating the office in which the financing statement was filed and providing the dates of filing and file numbers, if any, of the financing statement and of the most recent continuation statement filed with respect to the financing statement; and

(3) indicate that the pre-effective-date financing statement remains effective.

§ 9–707. Amendment of Pre-Effective-Date Financing Statement.

(a) In this section, "Pre-effective-date financing statement" means a financing statement filed before this [Act] takes effect.

(b) After this [Act] takes effect, a person may add or delete collateral covered by, continue or terminate the effectiveness of, or otherwise amend the information provided in, a pre-effective-date financing statement only in accordance with the law of the jurisdiction governing perfection as provided in Part 3. However, the effectiveness of a pre-effective-date financing statement also may be terminated in accordance with the law of the jurisdiction in which the financing statement is filed.

(c) Except as otherwise provided in subsection (d), if the law of this State governs perfection of a security interest, the information in a pre-effective-date financing statement may be amended after this [Act] takes effect only if:

(1) the pre-effective-date financing statement and an amendment are filed in the office specified in Section 9–501;

(2) an amendment is filed in the office specified in Section 9–501 concurrently with, or after the filing in that office of, an initial financing statement that satisfies Section 9–706(c); or

(3) an initial financing statement that provides the information as amended and satisfies Section 9–706(c) is filed in the office specified in Section 9–501.

(d) If the law of this State governs perfection of a security interest, the effectiveness of a pre-effective-date financing statement may be continued only under Section 9–705(d) and (f) or 9–706.

(e) Whether or not the law of this State governs perfection of a security interest, the effectiveness of a pre-effective-date financing statement filed in this State may be terminated after this [Act] takes effect by filing a termination statement in the office in which the pre-effective-date financing statement is filed, unless an initial financing statement that satisfies Section 9–706(c) has been filed in the office specified by the law of the jurisdiction governing perfection as provided in Part 3 as the office in which to file a financing statement.

As amended in 2000.

§ 9–708. Persons Entitled to File Initial Financing Statement or Continuation Statement.

A person may file an initial financing statement or a continuation statement under this part if:

(1) the secured party of record authorizes the filing; and

(2) the filing is necessary under this part:

(A) to continue the effectiveness of a financing statement filed before this [Act] takes effect; or

(B) to perfect or continue the perfection of a security interest.

As amended in 2000.

§ 9–709. Priority.

(a) This [Act] determines the priority of conflicting claims to collateral. However, if the relative priorities of the claims were established before this [Act] takes effect, [former Article 9] determines priority.

(b) For purposes of Section 9–322(a), the priority of a security interest that becomes enforceable under Section 9–203 of this [Act] dates from the time this [Act] takes effect if the security interest is perfected under this [Act] by the filing of a financing statement before this [Act] takes effect which would not have been effective to perfect the security interest under [former Article 9]. This subsection does not apply to conflicting security interests each of which is perfected by the filing of such a financing statement.

A

Absolute privilege Existing in courtrooms and legislative hearings, this is additional protection that allows anyone speaking there, such as a witness in a trial, to say anything at all and never be sued for defamation.

Acceptor A bank (or other drawee) that accepts a check (or other draft), thereby becoming primarily liable on it.

Accredited investor Under the Securities Act of 1933, an accredited investor is an institution (such as a bank or insurance company) or any individual with a net worth of more than $1 million or an annual income of more than $200,000.

Adopt Agree to be bound by the terms of a contract.

Ad valorem Customs officials impose duties "according to the value of the goods."

Additional terms Raise issues not covered in the offer.

Adjudicate To hold a formal hearing in a disputed matter and issue an official decision.

Administrative law judge (ALJ) In an adjudicate hearing, one who is employed by the agency but is expected to be impartial in his or her rulings.

Agent A person who acts for a principal.

Annual report Each year, public companies must send their shareholders an annual report that contains detailed financial data.

Arson Malicious use of fire or explosives to damage or destroy real estate or personal property.

Assault An intentional act that causes the plaintiff to fear an imminent battery.

Assignment of rights A transfer of benefits under a contract to another person.

Attachment A court order seizing property of a party to a civil action, so that there will be sufficient assets available to pay the judgment.

Authorized and issued Stock that has been authorized and sold; another word for it is *outstanding*.

Authorized and unissued Stock that has been authorized, but not yet sold.

Automatic stay Prohibits creditors from collecting debts that the bankrupt incurred before the petition was filed.

B

Bait and switch A practice where sellers advertise products that are not generally available but are being used to draw interested parties in so that they will buy other products.

Bankruptcy estate The new legal entity created when a debtor files a bankruptcy petition. All of the debtor's existing assets pass into the estate.

Battery The intentional touching of another person in a way that is unwanted or offensive.

Bearer paper A note is bearer paper if it is made out to "bearer" or it is not made out to any specific person. It can be redeemed by any holder in due course.

Best efforts underwriting The underwriter does not buy the stock but instead acts as the company's agent in selling it.

Beyond a reasonable doubt The very high burden of proof in a criminal trial, demanding much more evidence and certainty than required in a civil trial.

Bilateral contract A binding agreement in which each party has made a promise to the other.

Bilateral mistake Error occurring when both parties negotiate based on the same factual error.

Bill A proposed statute that has been submitted for consideration to Congress or a state legislature.

Bona fide occupational qualification (BFOQ) A job requirement that would otherwise be discriminatory is permitted in situations in which it is essential to the position in question.

Bonds Long-term debt secured by some of the issuing company's assets.

Buyer in ordinary course of business (BIOC) Someone who buys goods in good faith from a seller who routinely deals in such goods.

Bylaws A document that specifies the organizational rules of a corporation or other organization, such as the date of the annual meeting and the required number of directors.

C

Cap and trade A market-based system for reducing emissions.

Cashier's check A check drawn on the bank itself. It is a promise that the bank will pay out of its own funds.

Certified check A check the issuer's bank has signed, indicating its acceptance of the check.

Check An instrument in which the drawer orders the drawee bank to pay money to the payee.

Check card Another name for a debit card.

Choice of forum provisions Determine the state in which any litigation would take place.

Choice of law provisions Determine which state's laws will be used to interpret the contract.

Civil law The large body of law concerning the rights and duties between parties. It is distinguished from criminal law, which concerns behavior outlawed by a government.

Close corporation A corporation with a small number of shareholders. Its stock is not publicly traded.

Collateral The property subject to a security interest.

Commerce clause One of the powers granted by Article I, §8 of the Constitution, it gives Congress exclusive power to regulate international commerce and concurrent power with the states to regulate domestic commerce.

Commercial speech Communication, such as television advertisements, that has the dominant theme of proposing a commercial transaction.

Common law Judge-made law; that is, the body of all decisions made by appellate courts over the years.

Compensatory damages Those that flow directly from a contract.

Compliance program A plan to prevent and detect criminal conduct at all levels of a company.

Concurrent estates When two or more people own real property at the same time.

Conditional promises Promises that a party agrees to perform only if the other side has first done what it promised.

Conscious parallelism When competitors who do not have an explicit agreement nonetheless all make the same competitive decisions.

Consequential damages Those resulting from the unique circumstances of this injured party.

Consumer credit contract A contract in which a consumer borrows money from a lender to purchase goods and services from a seller who is affiliated with the lender.

Control security Stock owned by any officer or director of the issuer, or by any shareholder who holds more than 10 percent of a class of stock of the issuer.

Conversion Taking or using someone's personal property without consent.

Covenant A promise by either the landlord or the tenant to do something or refrain from doing something.

Criminal law Rules that permit a government to punish certain behavior by fine or imprisonment.

Criminal procedure The process of investigating, interrogating, and trying a criminal defendant.

D

Debentures Long-term, unsecured debt, typically issued by a corporation.

Debtor A person who owes money or some other obligation to another party.

Debtor in possession A debtor who acts as trustee in a Chapter 11 bankruptcy.

Default The failure to perform an obligation, such as the failure to pay money when due.

Defendant The person being sued.

Delegation of duties A transfer of obligations in a contract.

Deontological From the Greek word for *obligatory*, the duty to do the right thing, regardless of the result.

Difference principle The philosopher John Rawls's suggestion that society should reward behavior that provides the most benefit to the community as a whole.

Direct damages Are those that flow directly from the contract.

Disabled person Someone with a physical or mental impairment that substantially limits a major life activity, or someone who is regarded as having such an impairment.

Disaffirm To give notice of refusal to be bound by an agreement.

Discharge A party to an instrument is released from liability.

Dissociation Occurs when a partner leaves a partnership.

Double jeopardy The principle that a criminal defendant may be prosecuted only once for a particular criminal offense.

Draft The drawer of this instrument orders someone else to pay money. Checks are the most common form of draft. The drawer of a check orders a bank to pay money.

Drawee The person who pays a draft. In the case of a check, the bank is the drawee.

Drawer The person who issues a draft.

Due diligence An investigation of the registration statement by someone who signs it.

Due process Requires fundamental fairness at all stages of the case.

Dumping Selling merchandise at one price in the domestic market and at a cheaper, unfair price in an international market.

Duress An improper threat made to force another party to enter into a contract.

Duty of care Requires officers and directors to act in the best interests of the corporation and to use the same care that an ordinarily prudent person would in the management of her own assets.

Duty of loyalty Prohibits managers from making a decision that benefits them at the expense of the corporation.

E

Easement The right to enter land belonging to another and make a limited use of it, without taking anything away.

Embezzlement Fraudulent conversion of property already in the defendant's possession.

Eminent domain The power of the government to take private property for public use.

Equal dignities rule If an agent is empowered to enter into a contract that must be in writing, then the appointment of the agent must also be written.

Equal Protection Clause Part of the Fourteenth Amendment, it generally requires the government to treat equally situated people the same.

Escalator clause A clause in a lease allowing the landlord to raise the rent for specified reasons.

Eviction An act that forces a tenant to abandon the property.

Exclusive dealing contract A contract in which a distributor or retailer agrees with a supplier not to carry the products of any other supplier.

Exculpatory clause A contract provision that attempts to release one party from liability in the event the other party is injured.

Executed contract A binding agreement in which all parties have fulfilled all obligations.

Executory contract A binding agreement in which one or more of the parties has not fulfilled its obligations.

Exporting Shipping goods or services out of a country.

Express contract A binding agreement in which the parties explicitly state all important terms.

Externality An economics term used to describe the situation in which people do not bear the full cost of their decisions.

F

Fair use doctrine Permits limited use of copyrighted material without permission of the author for purposes such as criticism, comment, news reporting, scholarship, or research.

False imprisonment The intentional restraint of another person without reasonable cause and without her consent.

Federal Sentencing Guidelines The detailed rules that judges must follow when sentencing defendants convicted of crimes in federal court.

Fee simple absolute The greatest possible ownership right in real property, including the right to possess, use, and dispose of the property in any lawful manner.

Felony The most serious crimes, typically those for which the defendant could be imprisoned for more than a year.

Financing statement A document that a secured party files to give the general public notice that the secured party has a secured interest in the collateral.

Firm commitment underwriting The underwriter buys stock from the issuer and sells it to the public.

Fixtures Goods that are attached to real estate.

Forbearance Refraining from doing something that one has a legal right to do.

Force majeure event A disruptive, unexpected occurrence for which neither party is to blame that prevents one or both parties from complying with a contract.

Foreign Sovereign Immunities Act (FSIA) A federal statute that protects other nations from suit in courts of the United States, except under specified circumstances.

Fraud Deception of another person to obtain money or property from her.

Fresh start After the termination of a bankruptcy case, creditors cannot make a claim against the debtor for money owed before the initial bankruptcy petition was filed.

Fundamental rights In constitutional law, those rights that are so basic that any governmental interference with them is suspect and likely to be unconstitutional.

G

GATT The General Agreement on Tariffs and Trade (GATT) is a treaty designed to reduce tariffs and trade barriers among countries.

Gap period The period between the time that a creditor files an involuntary petition and the court issues the order for relief.

Good faith An honest effort to meet both the spirit and letter of a contract.

Goods Anything movable, except for money, securities, and certain legal rights.

Grand jury A group of ordinary citizens that decides whether there is probable cause the defendant committed the crime and should be tried.

Guilty A court's finding that a defendant has committed a crime.

H

Hacking Gaining unauthorized access to a computer system.

Holder For order paper, anyone in possession of the instrument if it is payable to or indorsed to her. For bearer paper, anyone in possession.

Holder in due course Someone who has given value for an instrument, in good faith, without notice of outstanding claims or other defenses.

Horizontal agreement An agreement among competitors.

Hostile takeover An outsider buys a company in the face of opposition from the target company's board of directors.

I

Importing Shipping goods or services into a country.

Incidental damages The relatively minor costs, such as storage and advertising, that the injured party suffered when responding to a contract breach.

Indictment The government's formal charge that a defendant has committed a crime.

Indorsement The signature of the payee.

Initial public offering (IPO) A company's first public sale of securities.

Insider Family members of an individual debtor, officers and directors of a corporation, or partners of a partnership.

Integrated contract A writing that the parties intend as the complete and final expression of their agreement.

Intentional infliction of emotional distress Results from extreme and outrageous conduct that causes serious emotional harm.

Intentional tort An act deliberately performed that violates a legally imposed duty and injures someone.

Interest A legal right in something, such as ownership or a mortgage or a tenancy.

Intrusion A tort if a reasonable person would find the invasion of her private life offensive.

Investigative reports Reports that discuss character, reputation, or lifestyle. They become obsolete in three months.

Invitee A person who has a right to enter another's property because it is a public place or a business open to the public.

Involuntary petition Filed by creditors to initiate a bankruptcy case.

Issuer The maker of a promissory note or the drawer of a draft.

J

Joint tenancy Upon the death of one joint tenant (owner), his interest passes to the surviving joint tenants, not to his heirs.

Joint venture A partnership for a limited purpose.

Judicial activism The willingness shown by certain courts (and not by others) to decide issues of public policy, such as constitutional questions (free speech, equal protection, etc.) and matters of contract fairness (promissory estoppel, unconscionability, etc.).

Judicial restraint A court's preference to abstain from adjudicating major social issues and to leave such matters to legislatures.

Jurisprudence The study of the purposes and philosophies of the law, as opposed to particular provisions of the law.

K

Kant's Categorical Imperative An act is ethical only if it would be acceptable for everyone to do the same thing.

L

Landlord The owner of a freehold estate who allows another person temporarily to live on his property.

Lease A contract creating a landlord-tenant relationship.

Letter of credit A commercial device used to guarantee payment in international trade, usually between parties that have not previously worked together.

Letter of intent A letter that summarizes negotiating progress.

License To grant permission to another person to enter property.

Licensee A person on another's land for her own purposes but with the owner's permission.

Liquidated damages A contract clause specifying how much a party must pay upon breach.

M

Maker The issuer of a promissory note.

Material Important or significant. Information that would affect a person's decision if he knew it.

Material breach A violation of a contract that defeats an essential purpose of the agreement.

Merchant One who routinely deals in the particular goods involved, or who appears to have special knowledge or skill in those goods, or who uses agents with special knowledge or skill in those goods.

Minute book Records of shareholder meetings and directors' meetings are kept in the corporation's minute book.

Mirror image rule Requires that acceptance be on precisely the same terms as the offer.

Misdemeanor A less serious crime than a felony, typically one for which the maximum penalty is incarceration for less than a year, often in a jail, as opposed to a prison.

Mitigate To keep damages as low as is reasonable.

Money laundering Taking the proceeds of certain criminal acts and either (1) using the money to promote crime, or (2) attempting to conceal the source of the money.

Mortgage A security interest in real property.

Mortgagee A creditor who obtains a security interest in real property, typically in exchange for money given to the mortgagor to buy the property.

Mortgagor A debtor who gives a mortgage (security interest) in real property to a creditor, typically in exchange for money used to buy the property.

N

Nationalize The government assumes ownership of a business or industry.

Negotiation An instrument that has been transferred to the holder by someone other than the issuer.

Non-point source When pollutants are released simultaneously from more than one source.

Note An unconditional, written promise that the maker of the instrument will pay a specific amount of money on demand or at a definite time. When issued by a corporation, a note refers to short-term debt, typically payable within five years.

Novation If there is an existing contract between A and B, a novation occurs when A agrees to release B from all liability on the contract in return for C's willingness to accept B's liability.

O

Obligor The party to a contract who is required to do something for the benefit of the other party.

Offer An act or statement that proposes definite terms and permits the other party to create a contract by accepting those terms.

Offeree The party in contract negotiations who receives the first offer.

Offeror The party in contract negotiations who makes the first offer.

Oppression When one party uses its superior power to force a contract on the weaker party.

Order for relief An official acknowledgment that a debtor is under the jurisdiction of the bankruptcy court.

Order paper An instrument that includes the words "pay to the order of" or their equivalent.

P

Partnership An association of two or more persons to carry on as co-owners of a business for profit.

Patent The right to the exclusive use of an invention for 20 years.

Patent troll Someone who buys a portfolio of patents for the purpose of making patent infringement claims.

Payee Someone who is owed money under the terms of an instrument.

Perfection A series of steps a secured party must take to protect its rights in collateral against people other than the debtor.

Periodic tenancy A lease for a fixed period, automatically renewable unless terminated.

***Per* se violation of an antitrust law** An automatic breach. Courts will generally not consider mitigating factors.

Phishing Type of fraud in which an individual sends an email directing the recipient to enter personal information on a website that is an illegal imitation of a legitimate site.

Pierce the corporate veil A court holds shareholders personally liable for the debts of the corporation.

Plaintiff The person who is suing.

Plea bargain An agreement between prosecution and defense that the defendant will plead guilty to a reduced charge, and the prosecution will recommend to the judge a relatively lenient sentence.

Plurality voting To be elected, a candidate only needs to receive more votes than her opponent, not a majority of the votes cast.

Point source A single producer of pollution.

Precedent An earlier case that decided the same legal issue as that presently in dispute, and which therefore will control the outcome of the current case.

Preference When a debtor unfairly pays creditors immediately before filing a bankruptcy petition.

Preferred stock Owners of preferred stock have a right to receive dividends and liquidation proceeds of the company before common shareholders.

Prima facie "At first sight." A fact or conclusion that is presumed to be true unless someone presents evidence to disprove it.

Principal In an agency relationship, the principal is the person for whom the agent is acting.

Probable cause In a search and seizure case, it means that the information available indicates it is more likely than not that a search will uncover particular criminal evidence.

Profit The right to enter land belonging to another and take something away, such as minerals or timber.

Promissory estoppel A doctrine in which a court may enforce a promise made by the defendant even when there is no contract, if the defendant knew that the plaintiff was likely to rely on the promise, the plaintiff did in fact rely, and enforcement of it is the only way to avoid injustice.

Proof of claim A simple form stating the name of the creditor and the amount of the claim.

Punitive damages Intended to punish the defendant for conduct that is extreme and outrageous.

Q

Quantum meruit "As much as she deserves." The damages awarded in a quasi-contract case.

Quasi-contract A legal fiction in which, to avoid injustice, the court awards damages as if a contract had existed, although one did not.

Quid pro quo "This for that." A type of sexual harassment that occurs if any aspect of a job is made contingent upon sexual activity.

Quorum The number of voters that must be present for a meeting to count.

R

Racketeer Influenced and Corrupt Organizations Act (RICO) A law passed by Congress to prevent gangsters from taking money they earned illegally and investing it in legitimate businesses.

Racketeering act Any of a long list of specialized crimes, including embezzlement, arson, mail fraud, and wire fraud.

Reaffirm To promise to pay a debt even after it is discharged.

Reasonable Ordinary or usual under the circumstances.

Reciprocal promises Promises that are each enforceable independently.

Reformation The process by which a court rewrites a contract to ensure its accuracy or viability.

Reliance interest A remedy in a contract case that puts the injured party in the position he would have been in had the parties never entered into a contract.

Rent Compensation the tenant pays the landlord for use of the premises.

Reporting company A company registered under the Securities Exchange Act of 1934.

Repossess A secured party takes collateral because the debtor has defaulted on payments.

Representations and warranties Statements of fact about the past or present.

Rescind To cancel a contract.

Res ipsa loquitur A doctrine of tort law holding that the facts may imply negligence when the defendant had exclusive control of the thing that caused the harm, the accident would not normally have occurred without negligence, and the plaintiff played no role in causing the injury.

Restitution Restoring an injured party to its original position.

Restitution interest A remedy in a contract case that returns to the injured party a benefit that he has conferred on the other party, which it would be unjust to leave with that person.

Restricted stock Securities purchased strictly for investment purposes.

Reversion The right of an owner (or her heirs) to property upon the death of a life tenant.

Rider An amendment or addition to a contract.

Rule of reason violation An action that breaches the antitrust laws only if it has an anticompetitive impact.

S

Safe harbor A set of requirements that, if met, indicate *automatic* compliance with a law.

Scrivener's error A typo.

Secondary offering Any public sale of securities by a company after the initial public offering (IPO).

Secured party The person or company that holds a security interest.

Security Any transaction in which the buyer (1) invests money in a common enterprise and (2) expects to earn a profit predominantly from the efforts of others.

Security agreement A contract in which the debtor gives a security interest to the secured party.

Security interest An interest in personal property or fixtures that secures the performance of some obligation.

Shilling When a seller at auction either bids on his own goods or agrees to cross-bid with a group of other sellers.

Signatory A person, company, or nation that has signed a legal document, such as a contract, agreement, or treaty.

Single recovery principle Requires a court to settle the matter once and for all by awarding a lump sum for past and future expenses.

Sole discretion When a party to a contract has the absolute right to make a decision on an issue.

Sole proprietorship An unincorporated business owned by a single person.

Sophisticated investor Someone who is able to assess the risk of an offering.

Sovereign Refers to the recognized political power whom citizens obey. In the United States, the federal and all of the state governments are sovereigns.

Spyware A computer program that slips onto your computer without your permission, through emails, Internet downloads, or software installations.

Stakeholders Anyone who is affected by the activities of a corporation, such as employees, customers, creditors, suppliers, shareholders, and neighbors.

Stare decisis "Let the decision stand." A basic principle of the common law, it means that precedent is usually binding.

Statute A law passed by a legislative body, such as Congress.

Statute of limitations A statute that determines the period within which a particular kind of lawsuit must be filed.

Straight bankruptcy Also known as *liquidation*, this form of bankruptcy mandates that the bankrupt's assets be sold to pay creditors, but the creditor has no obligation to share future earnings.

Strict liability A tort doctrine holding to a very high standard all those who engage in ultrahazardous activity (e.g., using explosives) or who manufacture certain products.

Strict performance Requires one party to perform its obligations precisely, with no deviation from the contract terms.

Subpoena An order to appear, issued by a court or government body.

Subprime loan A loan that has an above-market interest rate because the borrower is high-risk.

Substantial performance Occurs when one party fulfills enough of its contract obligations to warrant payment.

Supremacy Clause From Article VI of the Constitution, it declares that federal statutes and treaties take priority over any state law, if there is a conflict between the two or, even absent a conflict, if Congress manifests an intent to preempt the field.

T

Takings Clause Part of the Fifth Amendment, it ensures that when any governmental unit takes private property for public use, it must compensate the owner.

Tariff A duty imposed on imported goods by the government of the importing nation.

Tenancy at sufferance A tenancy that exists without the permission of the landlord, after the expiration of a true tenancy.

Tenancy at will A tenancy with no fixed duration, which may be terminated by either party at any time.

Tenancy for years A lease for a stated, fixed period.

Tenancy in common Occurs when the owners have an equal interest in the entire property.

Tenant A person given temporary possession of the landlord's property.

Tied product In a tying arrangement, the product that a buyer must purchase as the condition for being allowed to buy another product.

Time of the essence clause Generally makes contract dates strictly enforceable.

Tort A civil wrong, committed in violation of a duty that the law imposes.

Tortious interference with a contract The defendant improperly induced a third party to breach a contract with the plaintiff.

Tortious interference with a prospective advantage Malicious interference with a developing economic relationship between two other parties.

Trademark Any combination of words and symbols that a business uses to identify its products or services and that federal law will protect.

Trade secret A formula, device, process, method, or compilation of information that, when used in business, gives the owner an advantage over competitors who do not know it.

Treasury stock Stock that has been bought back by its issuing corporation.

Trespass Intentionally entering land that belongs to someone else, or remaining on the land after being asked to leave.

Trespasser A person on another's property without consent.

Tying arrangement A violation of the Sherman and Clayton Acts in which a seller requires that two distinct products be purchased together. The seller uses its significant power in the market for the tying product to shut out a substantial part of the market for the tied product.

Tying product In a tying arrangement, the product offered for sale on the condition that another product be purchased as well.

U

Unilateral mistake When only one party enters a contract under a mistaken assumption.

U.S. Trustee Oversees the administration of bankruptcy law in a region.

V

Value The holder has *already* done something in exchange for the instrument.

Veil of Ignorance We set up a societal system without knowing whether we would personally be one of its winners or losers.

Vertical agreement An agreement or merger between two companies at different stages of the production process, such as when a company acquires one of its suppliers or distributors.

Veto When the president opposes a bill that has passed through both houses; a veto means that the bill will not become law.

Voidable contract An agreement that, because of some defect, may be terminated by one party, such as a minor, but not by both parties.

Void agreement An agreement that neither party may legally enforce, usually because the purpose of the bargain was illegal or because one of the parties lacked capacity to make it.

Voluntary petition Filed by a debtor to initiate a bankruptcy case.

W

World Trade Organization (WTO) Created by the General Agreement on Tariffs and Trade (GATT) to stimulate international commerce and resolve trade disputes.